80025 75540

ENCYCLOPEDIA OF
WATER POLITICS AND POLICY
IN THE UNITED STATES

ENCYCLOPEDIA OF WATER POLITICS AND POLICY IN THE UNITED STATES

Steven L. Danver

John R. Burch Jr.

Editors

Los Angeles | London | New Delhi
Singapore | Washington DC

CQ Press
2300 N Street, NW, Suite 800
Washington, DC 20037

Phone: 202-729-1900; toll-free, 1-866-4CQ-PRESS (1-866-427-7737)

Web: www.cqpress.com

Cover design: Anne C. Kerns, Anne Likes Red, Inc.
Cover photograph: Jon Brenneis; TIME & LIFE Images
Typesetting: C&M Digitals (P) Ltd.

♾ The paper used in this publication exceeds the requirements of the American National Standard for Information Sciences—Permanence of Paper for Printed Library Materials, ANSI Z39.48-1992.

Printed and bound in the United States of America

15 14 13 12 11   1 2 3 4 5

Library of Congress Cataloging-in-Publication Data

Encyclopedia of water politics and policy in the United States / Steven L. Danver, John R. Burch, Jr. editors.
    p. cm.
  Includes bibliographical references and index.
    ISBN 978-1-60426-614-6 (hardcover : alk. paper) 1. Water resources development—Government policy—United States—Encyclopedia. 2. Water-supply—Government policy—United States—Encyclopedia. I. Danver, Steven Laurence. II. Burch, John R.
    HD1694.A5E265 2011
    333.9100973′03—dc22

                                                                                            2011006718

About the Editors

STEVEN L. DANVER, born and raised in the American West, has spent his entire academic life studying the region, its peoples, and its resources. He is a member of the Core Faculty in Social Sciences at the Center for Undergraduate Studies at Walden University. He received his doctorate in American history, with a focus on the history of water in the American West and American Indian history, from the University of Utah. He currently serves as managing editor of *Journal of the West* and has edited and written many historical reference works, journal articles, and book chapters on subjects covering the broad spectrum of American and world history. His current work explores an issue that has modern relevance to the American Indian peoples of the Southwest and to many other Americans as well: the scarce waters of the West, their histories, and how to equitably distribute them.

JOHN R. BURCH JR. is presently serving as Dean of Distance Learning and Library Services at Campbellsville University in Kentucky. He received his doctorate in history, focusing primarily on American Indian history during the Colonial era and Appalachian studies, from the University of Kentucky. His professional activities include serving as a book reviewer for *Library Journal, CHOICE: Current Reviews for Academic Libraries*, and *American Reference Books Annual (ARBA)*. In addition to writing numerous journal and encyclopedia articles, he is the author or coauthor of four books, including *Owsley County, Kentucky, and the Perpetuation of Poverty* (2007).

Contents

Alphabetical Table of Contents

Thematic Table of Contents

Features

Contributors

Rolando Avila
University of Texas–Pan American

John H. Barnhill
Independent Scholar

Walter F. Bell
Aurora University

Margaret A. Bickers
Independent Scholar

Stephen Bogener
West Texas A&M University

Kevin Brady
Texas Christian University

Lorri Brown
Independent Scholar

John R. Burch Jr.
Campbellsville University

David Carle
Independent Scholar

Justin Corfield
Geelong Grammar School

Jeff Crane
Sam Houston State University

Mary Varson Cromer
Appalachian Citizens' Law Center

Denise Holladay Damico
Saint Francis University

Steven L. Danver
Walden University

Michael B. Dougan
Arkansas State University

Mary Durfee
Michigan Technological University

Adam Eastman
University of Oklahoma

Julia Fallon
University of Wales Institute, Cardiff, UK

Meigan M. Fields
Fort Valley State University

Jeffrey B. Flagg
Siena College

Denise Fort
University of New Mexico Law School

Philip Garone
California State University, Stanislaus

Roger D. Hansen
Federal Resource Agency

Skylar Harris
SUNY–University at Buffalo

Ralph Hartsock
University of North Texas

Theresa Hefner-Babb
Lamar University

Kevin Hillstrom
Independent Scholar

Chuck Howlett
Molloy College

Mark S. Joy
Jamestown College

Daniel Karalus
Northern Arizona University

Sya Buryn Kedzior
Humboldt State University

Stephanie M. Lang
University of Kentucky

Shevon J. Letang
Montclair State University

A. M. Mannion
University of Reading, UK

Eliza L. Martin
University of California, Santa Cruz

Daniel McCool
University of Utah

Isaac Moriwake
EarthJustice

Stephen P. Mumme
Colorado State University

Jerry Murtagh
Fort Valley State University

Caryn Neumann
Miami University

James Newman
Idaho State University

Kevin Olsen
Montclair State University

Jedediah Rogers
Arizona State University

Charles Rosenberg
Independent Scholar

Gregory Rosenthal
SUNY Stony Brook

Paul C. Rosier
Villanova University

Cameron L. Saffell
New Mexico Farm & Ranch Heritage Museum

Adam M. Sowards
University of Idaho

Thomas E. Sowers II
Lamar University

Mark G. Spencer
Brock University

Samuel Stalcup
Natural Resources Conservation Service
*   U.S. Department of Agriculture*

Arthur Steinberg, PhD, JD
Independent Scholar

Brit Allan Storey
United States Bureau of
*   Reclamation*

April Summitt
Arizona State University

Randy Taylor
Howard Payne University

Landon S. Utterback
Northern Michigan University

Laura Woodworth-Ney
Idaho State University

David Zetland
Aguanomics

Introduction

Water, in all its forms, has had an immeasurable impact on the development of North America. During the ice ages, it shaped the physiography of the continent. Following the melting of the glaciers, many of the great rivers and lakes that we recognize today emerged in their free-flowing forms. These waters helped shape the cultures of many diverse Native American groups. In the Southwest, the Anasazi thrived when water was plentiful, but their civilization declined rapidly as the land grew more arid. Centuries later, near the site of present-day Saint Louis, Missouri, the Mississippian community known as Cahokia became the largest city in North America. The agriculturally rich bottomlands fed by the waters of the Mississippi River supplied many of the foodstuffs required by the city's approximately 15,000 inhabitants. The settlement declined when extended periods of drought made it impossible to sustain such a large population.

Natural cycles dictated that the availability of water varied greatly, even within a specific locale. At times there was too much water, and flooding occurred. At other times, water was merely plentiful. Inevitably there were also times of drought, resulting in great suffering. Recognizing that they required a more dependable source of water, some Native American groups built extensive irrigation systems, which were later adopted and modified by Europeans.

European Settlement and Water Use

When European explorers began arriving in the land that would one day comprise the United States, they used rivers to investigate the landscape. Many were drawn to the rivers leading west, as explorers searched for the fabled trade route to the Pacific known as the Northwest Passage. Although unsuccessful in their search for a water route through North America, the explorers did establish trade routes that enabled them to trade with Native Americans for much of the continent's natural wealth. Towns such as New Amsterdam, later New York, were subsequently founded along the rivers to facilitate trade between the New and Old Worlds. The desire to dominate trade in North America would eventually lead to clashes among the European powers. Conflicts such as the French and Indian War, also known as the Seven Years' War, were often centered around controlling waterways such as the Hudson River, Lake Champlain, and the Three Rivers region, where the Monongahela and Allegheny Rivers come together to create the Ohio.

Since the American Revolution, the development of the United States has been marked by the waters both within and along its geographical borders. When the country was newly founded, trade was facilitated by its waterways. The physical limitations of these waterways led politicians, such as DeWitt Clinton, to advocate for the construction of canals that linked previously separate water networks. Clinton's Ditch, as the Erie Canal was derisively called, was emblematic of the future role that government investment would play in the development of large-scale water projects. Artificially created bodies of water not only fueled the economic development of the new country but also the movement of its people westward. Not surprisingly, competition among those looking to prosper economically from the water created conflicts. Early disagreements over the water rights of businesses on streams and rivers, such as mills, guided the development of legal statutes that varied widely by locale. The resulting legal morass has continued to confound the nation's legal system to the present day.

Legal Foundations

Often, legal disputes over water have been the harbingers of water policy and law in the United States, as the courts have played a very active and central role in defining the doctrines of water rights law. Water law in the United States first descended (like much of our legal system) from English common law. The courts' role has been to codify that law and make any adjustments required by the particular circumstances in which people live. The riparian system of water rights was in use from the start, but it became legally enshrined with the U.S. Circuit Court for Rhode Island's decision in *Tyler v. Wilkinson* in 1827.

Although the federal courts have been involved in water-related questions, both due to the interstate nature of many river systems and the trust relationship between the federal government and American Indian tribes, much of American water law has been determined by state courts. As Americans moved west, the system of riparian rights proved less feasible, and state courts made new policies based on the situations people found there. Most influential was the case of *Coffin v. Left Hand Ditch Co.*, decided in 1882 by the Colorado Supreme Court. This decision established the water rights law known as prior appropriation, where the first party to make beneficial use of a water source has the right to all the water needed to fulfill his or her purposes. Most western states adopted a version of prior appropriation, with their courts determining the extent to which that doctrine would be blended with the more traditional riparian system. The federal courts became involved once again, with the U.S. Supreme Court's 1908 decision in *Winters v. United States*, which accepted the paramount right of Native Americans to the waters that ran through and along their reservations.

Westward Movement and Urban Water Demands

During the nineteenth century, the growth of trade along waterways was accompanied by urbanization and industrialization. Combined with the agricultural practices of the day, these severely damaged waterways and their watersheds. Pollution rendered the water undrinkable. The befouled water contributed to numerous outbreaks of disease, especially cholera and typhoid fever. Cities responded to the crisis by trying to create clean water supplies through the construction of reservoirs. In addition, cities also began building sewer systems to disperse pollutants.

As the pulse of Manifest Destiny enticed Americans to move west, and settlers attempted to turn prairies into fertile land suitable for agriculture through irrigation, the waters of that region began to undergo significant changes. The West had its own particular set of water-related issues, as much of the land west of the 100th meridian is characterized by a dearth of rainfall. Although explorer and founder of the U.S. Geological Survey John Wesley Powell warned against untrammeled growth in the arid and semiarid regions of the West, Americans still came in droves. With little guidance of irrigation project management by any governmental entity, it is not surprising that a small number of individuals managed to acquire more than their fair share of the region's waters. Small farmers were often left to fend for themselves, casting their fates on the drought cycles endemic to the region, but they were not the only ones to lose out on the West's scarce waters. Hispanics living in areas such as New Mexico and California when the United States gained title

to the Southwest in 1848 were overrun by American miners and farmers. Despite theoretically huge water rights, upheld by the Supreme Court in the 1908 case of *Winters v. United States*, American Indians, as had already occurred with their lands, were deprived of their water rights as a matter of course as the tidal wave of non-Indian development continued. The federal government began installing a regulatory system through the Carey Act of 1894. It would be followed by further legislation regarding irrigation, including the Reclamation Act of 1902, which created the Reclamation Service, later renamed the Bureau of Reclamation.

At the dawn of the twentieth century, the water needs of growing cities, such as San Francisco, California, created the environmental conservation movement that would impact water development projects from then on. In order to secure itself a dependable supply of water, San Francisco had the Hetch Hetchy Valley in Yosemite National Park dammed. The dam was bitterly, but unsuccessfully, contested by John Muir and the newly created Sierra Club. This event echoed in later conflicts over dam construction, most notably when the Dinosaur National Monument was threatened by the proposed construction of the Echo Park Dam during the 1950s and 1960s.

The Politics of Water

Water has long been a political issue for numerous reasons. First, and especially in the western states, water is a zero-sum game because of its scarcity. Granting water rights to one constituency necessarily results in diminishing the rights claimed by another. An example of this is the course of the political arguments that have flowed from the largest river in the Southwest, the Colorado. An attempt to equitably divide the waters of the Colorado was made in 1922, when the seven states having claims to the Colorado signed the Colorado River Compact. However, uneven growth in the West, specifically the migration of millions to California, has kept the Colorado a political issue. Also, the 1922 compact did not take Native American claims to the Colorado into account at all. These shortcomings meant that the compact did nothing to cool the anger of western states toward one another, nor did it quell increasingly strident Native American voices that demanded their fair share. Urbanization pitted the water needs of city dwellers in places like Los Angeles; Las Vegas, Nevada; Phoenix, Arizona; and Albuquerque, New Mexico, against agricultural interests. Reclamation interests were pitted against the political goals of the nascent environmental movement in the 1960s. So many competing interests meant that the U.S. Supreme Court would have to step in, which it did in the numerous decisions in the case of *Arizona v. California*, the two most important being in 1963 and 1984. The existence of so many interest groups with often opposing goals has kept water a politically charged issue ever since the first American settlers came west.

Flood Control

The country's attention, especially that of politicians, was drawn to flood control during the 1920s due to massive flooding, for example, of the Mississippi River in 1927. Numerous flood control projects would subsequently be proposed and funded for construction by the U.S. Army Corps of Engineers. Not to be outdone, the Bureau of Reclamation also began clamoring for flood control projects. Legislators from western states were happy to oblige. They were aided by the New Deal, which provided significant amounts of cheap labor to construct water infrastructure at a scale that had not been witnessed before. This era saw many dams constructed, including two of the largest dams in the world at the time, Hoover Dam on the Colorado River at the Nevada-Arizona border and Grand Coulee Dam on the Columbia River in Washington State. These engineering feats only encouraged the Corps of Engineers and the Bureau of Reclamation to continue to propose even grander projects, which politicians continued to embrace enthusiastically for approximately half of the century.

Pollution and Restoration

Following World War II, it became increasingly apparent that pollution was becoming a critical problem in the United States. Agricultural dependence on fertilizers resulted in large amounts of nitrogen and phosphorous finding its way into rivers and streams. These chemicals helped lead to eutrophication, whereby the presence of large quantities of fertilizers in the watershed causes excessive plant growth in rivers and lakes. Industrial pollution also rendered many waterways lifeless. The Cuyahoga River in Cleveland, Ohio, was so polluted during the 1960s that it actually caught fire on two occasions.

In 1962, Rachel Carson published *Silent Spring*, which detailed how toxic chemicals, such as the widely used insecticide DDT (dichloro-diphenyl-tricholoro-ethane),

were destroying ecosystems. These chemicals posed a threat to humans, who ate many of the plants and animals that had been exposed to the toxic substances. Public outrage over the threat posed by the pollutants provided environmental groups with a rapidly growing constituency, which drew the attention of politicians. Significant legislation soon followed, including the National Environmental Policy Act of 1969, the Clean Water Act of 1972, and the Safe Drinking Water Act of 1974. The vast amount of legislation that began to sprout during the 1960s and 1970s required the Army Corps of Engineers and the Bureau of Reclamation to assess the environmental impact of their projects. Increased scrutiny of the environmental consequences of their work has succeeded in limiting the scale of the projects they undertake. Recent decades have seen the benefits of environmental regulations come to the fore, as many waterways have begun to significantly recover from their polluted states. Unfortunately, very few run free, as they have been tamed by the construction of dams along their entire respective courses. In many cases, this has led to the destruction of various species that depended on free-flowing rivers, such as the cui-ui and Lahontan cutthroat trout that inhabit Pyramid Lake in Nevada. Dam building has also resulted in increased silting and salination. In recent years, many environmentalists have turned their efforts toward the removal of some of the most environmentally destructive dams in recognition that waterways can become even healthier by being allowed to flow freely.

Future Challenges

The nation's waterways are vital to not only its economic activity but to the very survival of the population. Recent decades have seen shortages of water arise due to drought around the country. For instance, one recent drought threatened Atlanta, Georgia, as Lake Lanier's water level dropped precipitously. Water issues that were once primarily problems of western states now plague states around the country. This is not going to change as the country's population continues to grow, inevitably placing more demands on water, a finite resource. Hopefully, attention to our waterways and how they are managed will enable our society to develop ways to preserve the ecological necessity of free waterways and wetlands, while equitably distributing the water bounty for the maximum benefit of all.

Note on Legal References and Citations

Law is the end result of politics, and political debate often begins with "There oughta be a law . . ." Water politics inevitably leads to law concerning use of water. Many articles in this encyclopedia contain legal citations, which are helpful to those who want to do further reading. Like any technical shorthand, they can also be confusing to those not trained in the meaning of the abbreviations and the method by which law is organized.

Almost all legal citation consists of two numbers separated by a group of letters. The letters in the middle refer to the body of law, such as U.S. Supreme Court decisions (U.S., S.Ct., or L.Ed.), *Code of Federal Regulations* (CFR), *Statutes of the United States* (Stat.), or Wisconsin-published appellate court decisions (Wis). The number to the left is generally a volume or code number, while the number on the right is a more specific page or section number.

One of the simplest examples is the numbering of official published reports of U.S. Supreme Court rulings. One of the cases cited in this book is *Arizona v. California* (1963). The complete citation for this case in the Court's official published reports is ***Arizona v. California*, 373 U.S. 546 (1963)**. The name of the case provides the two parties who have a dispute before the Court. The numeral 373 means the case is found in the 373rd volume, the initials *U.S.* identify that this would be a volume of *United States Reports*, and the numeral 546 means the case begins on page 546 of the 373rd volume. The year the case was decided, 1963, follows in parentheses.

There are in fact fourteen separate Supreme Court rulings concerning disputes between the states of Arizona and California, from 1931 to 2000, appearing in different volumes from 283 to 531. All of these cases relate to disputes over water rights to the Colorado River; many issue supplemental orders that refer to earlier cases.

Similar systems of citation are used for judicial rulings, legislation, and administrative codes. **Legislation** is law enacted by vote of the U.S. Congress or by a state legislature. Courts often have to *interpret* how a law applies to a set of facts, but in general, courts must *follow* the law set forth in legislation. An exception is when courts find the legislation to be in conflict with the federal constitution or a state constitution. **Administrative codes** are written by administrative agencies to exercise powers granted by legislation. For example, the Environmental Protection Agency is authorized by Congress to exercise certain powers, and it writes more specific regulations governing how it will exercise those powers.

Federal legislation is recorded using three different systems, each with a distinct purpose. That can be very confusing to someone who simply wants to know "What does the law say about _____?" When Congress passes a law and the president signs it, it becomes a Public Law of the United States. When first published, it is called a "slip law." Generally it has a name, such as "**Water Pollution Control Act Amendments of 1972**." That law was passed by the 92nd Congress and was the 500th law passed in that Congress to be approved. So it is **P.L. 92-500**. (Note that this does *not* follow the common format of number, letter, number—the numbers are all to the right of the letter abbreviation.) Then, the laws are assembled into bound volumes called *United States Statutes at Large*. The 1972 water pollution control amendments appear in volume 86 from page 816 to page 905. So the citation is **86 Stat. 816–905**. In common usage, the page on which the law begins may be adequate citation.

A public law, or a statute, may add to existing law, but it may also repeal or rewrite previous law. This can make it extremely confusing to track down what the law is *now*. One might have to read through scattered portions of several different laws, contained in many different volumes. There is always the possibility of missing something essential. So, federal laws are republished in the *United States Code*. The latest edition of the *Code* provides the law currently in force; repealed and expired laws are omitted, and the latest amendments are included. There are forty-nine titles to the *United States Code*, each concerning a specific subject area of the law. Title 18 is the criminal code. The federal Water Pollution Control Act, with all amendments, some of which established the title **Clean Water Act**, is found in Title 33, Sections 1251–1387. So the code citation is **33 U.S.C. 1251–1387**.

Administrative law, the regulations written by federal agencies to guide employees of the agency and to inform the public of specific standards for administering a law, are published in two forms. When a rule is first proposed, it must be published in the *Federal Register*. Publication of a rule can be cited in the usual format. For example, **40 Fed.Reg. 31320** is a rule published by the U.S. Army Corps of Engineers that includes freshwater wetlands among the "waters of the United States" protected by the Clean Water Act. Once a rule is formally adopted, it is included in the *Code of Federal Regulations,* organized into titles covering different areas of the law. The Corps of Engineers' definition of "waters of the United States" is cited as **33 CFR 328.2(a),** in other words, Title 33 (which may be more than one physical volume), part 328, subsection 2, paragraph (a).

State laws and court rulings follow similar systems. Almost all judicial rulings follow a format similar to that of the U.S. Supreme Court. For example, the Wisconsin case *Coleman v. Percy* is cited as **96 Wis. 2d 578**. One would find this case in volume 96 of the second series of *Callaghan's Wisconsin Reports* at page 578. Some states codify legislation a little differently than does the *United States Code.* For example, Wisconsin does not use titles for its code of laws but a numbered series of chapters, so a citation would read **Wis. Stat. 304.06.** Judicial rulings may be published by the court system, or they may be published by a commercial legal reporter that has its own citation system.

Two commercial companies publish decisions of the U.S. Supreme Court. Decisions published in *Supreme Court Reports,* abbreviated S.Ct., are cited with different volume and page numbers than in the official *United States Reports.* Another system, *U.S. Supreme Court Reports, Lawyer's Edition* (L.Ed.), not only has to be cited by different volume and page numbers but has one series of volumes for the years 1754–1956 and a second series for cases decided from 1956 to the present. The abbreviation for the second series is L.Ed.2. All three publishers can be, and have been, cited in Supreme Court decisions and those of lower federal courts.

Decisions by federal courts of appeal are reported by a commercial publisher that is universally relied upon by courts and attorneys. *Federal Reporter* has a first, second, and third series, cited as F., F.2d, and F.3d, respectively. The volume numbers start over at 1 for each new series, so it is important to get the series correct in citing a case. Otherwise, they are similar to all three systems of citation for Supreme Court decisions. For example, one decision of the U.S. Court of Appeals for the Sixth Circuit in *United States v. Rapanos* is **235 F.3d 256 (6th Cir. 2000)**. That citation refers to the third series of *Federal Reporter*, volume 235, page 256. The case came back to the court of appeals in 2003, and that decision is **339 F.3d 447**. State appellate decisions can be reported in the state's own reporter or by a commercial regional reporter, and they often appear in both. For example, *Atlantic Reporter,* abbreviated A. or A.2d, covers several states on the mid-Atlantic coast, while *Northwest Reporter,* abbreviated N.W. or N.W.2d, reports on several states in the upper Midwest.

Most rulings by trial courts are not published and are not authority for future court decisions. Published judicial decisions generally come from courts of appeal, also known as appellate courts. All decisions of the U.S. Supreme Court are published. State supreme court rulings generally are also—although not all states title their highest court of appeal "Supreme Court." In New York, trial courts have the name Supreme Court, while the highest court is the New York Court of Appeals. Some federal district court cases are published in a series called *Federal Supplement,* abbreviated F. Supp. For example, the first decision in the *Rapanos* case by a federal district court is cited as **895 F.Supp. 165**, but a later case, after the case was sent back (remanded) from the Supreme Court and the Sixth Circuit appeals court, is **190 F.Supp.2d 1011**. Note that between the two hearings, the publisher started a second series and already was up to 190 volumes in the new sequence when the later decision was published.

—Charles Rosenberg

Part I Regional Water Politics and Policy

Intermountain West

The feature most commonly associated with the western environment, aridity, is perhaps at its most dominant in the Intermountain West—the area spanning the eastern slopes of the Sierra Nevada, through the Great Basin of Nevada and Utah, through the Wasatch Mountains of northern Utah and southern Idaho, into Montana and Wyoming, and ending with the Rocky Mountains of Colorado. Aridity has done much to shape the social and cultural life of the region, both before and after the onset of Euro-American settlement. Since the onset of Americanization, the importance of water has only increased, and the role of water, and of governmental control of water resources, has been the formative factor in the development of the region (Hardesty 1991). Although other factors have motivated the settlement and development of the Intermountain West (most notably religion), profit has been a primary motivating factor in the expansion of agriculture in the region.

The arrival of the Mormons in the Salt Lake Valley in 1847 brought a new type of what Donald Worster called "hydraulic societies" to the Intermountain West. Water resources in the Utah Territory were not, for practical purposes, under the control of the federal government. Instead, the area's few rivers were under the complete control of the territorial government and, thus, under the control of the Church of Jesus Christ of Latter-day Saints and its president, Brigham Young. Not until 1880 did Utah change its laws to allow for the private ownership of water resources (Worster 1985).

Water Allocation and Western Settlement

With the beginning of large-scale immigration to the West after the Civil War, the American system of water allotment was in a state of flux. In the eastern United States, the states had regulated the use of water by a system of riparian rights, which came down from English law. In this system, all who own land along a water source have the right to the use of the water from that source. However, this system only works well in places with average to heavy rainfall, where the utilization of water by upstream users does not have a detrimental effect on downstream users.

In the arid lands of the Intermountain West, water rights were governed by state laws, most of which were founded on the principle of prior appropriation. Prior appropriation can be best summed up by the phrase "first in time, first in right." In practical terms, this means that the oldest water right must be satisfied in full before later users can have any access to the water supply. In other words, the first user to make beneficial use of the water has the right to all of the water originally used. Whatever is left after the first claimant's use of the water is the property of the second claimant, and so on down the line. This worked well in the nineteenth-century West, as the institutions necessary to govern and determine rights in a riparian system were lacking. In a system of prior appropriation, the users themselves were able to determine the first in right, at least initially.

In addition, the Supreme Court has long recognized that both federal and Indian water rights exist outside of the state-regulated water rights systems. Rights under these competing systems must be satisfied as well (Wilkinson 1992). Such a competing system was created in the Intermountain West by a Supreme Court decision, *Winters v. United States* (1908), which formed the most generous basis for Indian water rights, the reserved rights doctrine, and thus caused the most contention with non-Indian water claimants. The roots of the case lie in a series of treaties signed by Montana Indian tribes, including the 1851 Treaty of Fort Laramie, in which they ceded much of their ancestral lands to the U.S. government. The treaties fixed the boundaries of the Fort Belknap reservation, with its northern boundary as the "middle of the main channel of Milk River." After the Indians began to settle on the reservation, however, it became clear that government efforts to turn the Indians into farmers were failing because they preferred to raise livestock on the reservation and maintain their cultural traditions.

After 1888, non-Indian homesteaders began settling lands around the reservation and drawing off water for irrigation and stock watering. Reservation agents facilitated the opening of the reservation to non-Indian ownership and leasing agreements so that by 1920, non-Indians controlled over 58 percent of the tribe's irrigated lands. The year 1905 saw a severe drought strike the region, and upstream irrigation bled the river all but dry, leaving little water for reservation and other downstream users. Ironically, when off-reservation ranchers blocked the flow of the Milk River onto the reservation, agent William R. Logan worked for the restoration of Indian water rights mainly to aid the large white population on the reservation.

The federal government sued on behalf of the Fort Belknap tribes to protect their rights to Milk River water. The case was filed to adjudicate the water rights of the tribes of the Fort Belknap Reservation as well as those of local,

Bitter disputes can break out over allocations of water resources in the Intermountain West. Such a dispute broke out on Montana's Flathead Indian Reservation (seen above) when a state agency granted a water permit to a non–tribe member to open a bottled water company. The case was taken to the Montana Supreme Court in 2001.

AP Photo/*Daily Inter Lake*, Dave Reese

white farmers who owned lands along the northern border of the Fort Belknap Reservation in Montana. Both Indians and non-Indians needed the waters of the Milk, as it was the only reliable source of water in the region. Further, the Bureau of Indian Affairs (BIA) had promised to develop irrigation for the reservation from the river, while at the same time the non-Indian settlers had been promised a federal reclamation project to irrigate their lands from the Milk. The Indians claimed that when they ceded aboriginal lands surrounding the reservation, they retained for themselves the rest of the reservation land and enough water to make it useful. In 1908 the Supreme Court for the first time acknowledged the existence of Indian water rights, holding that when Indian reservations were established, the tribes and the United States implicitly reserved, along with the land, sufficient water to fulfill the purposes of the reservations (Hundley 1982).

So in theory, Indian water rights are defined and governed by a body of federal law that recognizes that Indian tribes have sovereignty rights to the water on their reservations. The Supreme Court has held that tribal governments have jurisdiction over both tribal members and activities on the Indian reservations, and this position has affected the ways in which Indians can use the water that flows through or adjacent to their reservations. However, by handing down its 1908 decision without providing any way of reconciling it with the prior appropriation system already in use, the Court did more to provoke further conflicts over water between Indian and non-Indian populations than it did to settle them. *Winters* neither indicated the scope of its

application, nor did it set any parameters for determining the amount of water Indian tribes could claim (Hundley 1978). Almost from the time the decision was handed down in 1908, and especially during the 1980s and 1990s, many tribes have gone to the courts in an effort to quantify their federal water rights, even though judicial decisions have often meant a serious diminution of the possible extent of those rights.

Consequently, water policy has been determined by the implementation of two apparently contradictory methods of water allocation: the "prior-appropriation" doctrine and the "reserved rights" (or "Winters") Doctrine. When the doctrine of prior appropriation is taken to include Indian tribal use, the courts necessarily enter the picture to allocate the amount of water that the tribe would have the rights to as determined by their use of a given water source. Because Indian reservations were established before most other water uses began in the Intermountain West, tribes often hold the oldest and, thus, the most valuable water rights. State water laws, by and large, place a priority on the idea of "beneficial use," which, more often than not, has to do with agriculture. However, many of the area's tribes, such as the Utes, have a mixed subsistence tradition; the realities of modern reservation life do not always mean that the tribes will use the water in the ways that state or federal laws would prefer.

As Indian tribes are theoretically not subject to state laws in these matters, conflicts have continually risen over which water rights doctrine is applicable to the adjudication of rivers that flow through both Indian and non-Indian lands. The Winters Doctrine would seem to support the view that Indians have the right to enough water to irrigate reservation agricultural lands. The doctrine of prior appropriation, on the other hand, supports the idea that, if the Indians did not historically irrigate their lands, then the rights of non-Indian water claimants would be substantiated. The courts then have to examine what water was reserved for use on the Indian reservations, how tribal water rights are quantified and used, and how these water rights are regulated and enforced. Because of the great value of the water that could be claimed by Indian tribes under the Winters Doctrine, especially in the American West where water has become increasingly scarce, Indian water rights have constantly been under attack in both the federal and state courts and in other political arenas.

As clearly contradictory as these two dominant systems of water-rights allocation, *Winters* and prior appropriation, may seem, the actual situation in practice has been both less contradictory and more confusing than the various federal decisions would make it seem. The two contradictory theories of water allotment created a conflict of interest within the Justice Department. Because the Justice Department was to be the legal representative for all federal interests, its official position in favor of prior appropriation in the West was in conflict with the Winters Doctrine, which was supposed to determine Indian water rights (McCool 1987). The Winters Doctrine theoretically makes the prior-appropriation doctrine irrelevant. In practice, however, federal irrigation and reclamation programs were rarely undertaken in the interests of Indian peoples, even when they were constructed adjacent to Indian lands.

Although most Americans were unaware of the inherent issues of water scarcity as they came west, either to establish Zion during the Antebellum era or to "grow with the country" in the late nineteenth century, a few voices began to raise a note of caution. One of the earliest American explorers of the Southwest, John Wesley Powell, expressed a very different vision for western settlement, acknowledging the problems endemic to that enterprise due to the aridity of the Intermountain West. Powell's prophetic vision of the problems of untrammeled western settlement and his accurate views on what would happen were his plan not implemented brought the issue of western water to the consciousness of many historians. His 1877 *Report on the Lands of the Arid Region of the United States* summed up many of his views about the Southwest, concluding that without the aid of large-scale irrigation (which was always going to be problematic in such an arid area), agriculture on the same model as that used in the eastern United States would not be possible. Furthermore, he stated that large-scale irrigation would not be possible without the federal government being involved in a large way.

The Bureau of Reclamation (BOR), which was dedicated to the doctrine of prior appropriation and the promotion of non-Indian irrigated agriculture in the Southwest, exercised great power and acted decisively in the interests of its constituents when allocating the waters that its own infrastructure construction projects had made useful. Historian Donald Worster (1985) has noted that "neither the courts nor Congress managed to settle the issue," and "white appropriators had an uneasy but clear edge: they were already in possession" (298). *Winters* might have given the tribes a theoretically large claim to the waters of the West, but battles over access to those waters would occupy the tribes; the federal and state courts; the Department of the Interior (DOI), as both the promoter of non-Indian development through the BOR and as the defender of Indian rights through the BIA; and Congress throughout the twentieth century.

Management and Development of the West

The beginnings of federal management of the environment stem from the Progressive reforms of the late nineteenth and early twentieth centuries. However, a possible blueprint for the rational development of the West had been in place for at least twenty-five years. Explorer, bureaucrat, and iconoclast John Wesley Powell had issued his *Arid Lands* report in 1877, which noted that aridity was the common feature of the land west of the 100th meridian and that only through irrigation and limited, rational settlement along the sources of scarce water could the West be made to prosper. However, the push to settle and develop the lands of the Intermountain West was too great and the ideology that "rain follows the plow," promoted by the boosters of western settlement and land speculators (who were often the same people), were too persuasive for Powell's report to counter. Powell's expertise on the matter of the West was pushed aside because it did not fit with Americans' views of themselves. Manifest Destiny meant that Americans could and would conquer the West.

With the advent of the Progressive Era and the realization of the harsh difficulties of settlement in the Intermountain West, Americans sought to harness the power of the federal government to accomplish what individual settlers could not. The Reclamation (or Newlands) Act of 1902 was one of the most decisive laws in shaping the region for the rest of the twentieth century. The Act established the Bureau of Reclamation (BOR) and established a system whereby irrigation in the West would be accomplished in a way that would benefit small, family farms. The BOR was to be continually funded by the payments of those small, family farms that reaped the benefits of the reclamation projects. The first project to make use of the new Act was the Truckee-Carson Project (completed in 1915 and later renamed the Newlands Project) in west-central Nevada. This project followed Worster's (1985) model of the "hydraulic society," and its system of dams, reservoirs, and canals introduced an administrative hierarchy, the Truckee-Carson Irrigation District. New towns, such as Fallon, Nevada, were created, and areas that had once been only arid desert were transformed (at least for a time) into

Bernard Augustine DeVoto

Bernard DeVoto was a novelist, journalist, and historian whose work reflected his belief that the western frontier had positively shaped the American character. As a conservationist, he worked to ensure that the West did not have its natural resources exploited by individuals residing outside the region.

DeVoto was born January 11, 1897, in Ogden, Utah. His undergraduate education began at the University of Utah, but he transferred to Harvard University and graduated in 1922. After failing to gain acclaim as a novelist, DeVoto began writing a column in 1935 entitled "The Easy Chair" for *Harper's Magazine*. Whether he was writing about the oil, cattle, or timber industries of the West, his constant theme was that business interests in the East were "raping" the West. His views changed during a 1946 trip to his beloved West when he observed the denuded land left in the wake of the timber industry. He bitterly realized that the inhabitants of the West were not victims of exploitation but were actually complicit in destroying the region's natural habitat. He put his faith in the U.S. government to protect the West, and he thus promoted the creation and maintenance of national parks and supported the construction of many dams. He died on November 13, 1955.

—John R. Burch Jr.

See also: *Conservation Movement; Dam Building; National Parks and Water*

BIBLIOGRAPHY
Brummer, Ross. "DeVoto, Bernard Augustine." In *Modern American Environmentalists: A Biographical Encyclopedia*, edited by G. Cevasco and R. Harmond, 126–129. Baltimore: The Johns Hopkins University Press, 2009.

DeVoto, Bernard Augustine. *DeVoto's West: History, Conservation, and the Public Good.* Edited by E. Muller. Athens: Ohio University Press, 2005.

productive agricultural lands (Hardesty 1991). Of course, at the time the BOR and the region's farmers did not know of the nightmare of soil salination with which later generations would contend.

However, not until the 1930s would the BOR be able to fulfill its promise to develop the West. Even then, the character of that development would be quite different from what the framers of the Newlands Act had envisioned. In the aftermath of the Newlands Act, the two agencies that have had the greatest impact on the management of western lands are the U.S. Army Corps of Engineers (Corps) and the BOR. These two bureaucracies have both been able to procure needed federal funding because they both have established expertise in the fields of dam building and water manipulation, they both have enjoyed a close relationship with congressional committees, and they both have produced projects that benefited specific segments of the population that supported the two organizations.

The Corps's projects have been chosen specifically for the reasons of distributing political rewards for political gain. The BOR has had ups and downs throughout its history, largely dependent on funding and political climate. Its geographical limitation to the West and its mandate to develop projects for small farms originally limited the amount of "pork" that it could procure for powerful eastern members of Congress (McCool 1987). However, that changed with the advent of the New Deal and the growth in power of the BOR during the 1950s. During the 1950s and 1960s, the federal government's role in increasing the utilization of water resources in the Intermountain West expanded, and the BOR's mandate expanded accordingly. Rather than producing small projects to benefit small farms, the BOR began to concentrate on larger projects such as Flaming Gorge Dam and Glen Canyon Dam, which turned the free-flowing rivers of the region into a series of large reservoirs and benefited large landowners. Later the BOR, under the direction of charismatic leader Floyd Dominy, would fund such projects as the Central Utah Project, which sought to develop large-scale agriculture in arid regions of the Intermountain West.

The seeds of the end of large-scale development of reclamation projects in the Intermountain West were sown with the passage of the National Environmental Policy Act of 1970 (NEPA), which requires environmental impact statements before any federal project can be implemented. This brought a new cadre of engineers and administrators to the BOR, ones who had a very different vision of water in the West. Additionally, the Federal Land Policy and Management Act of 1976 (FLPMA) consolidated and modernized hundreds of public land laws and articulated the specific mission of the Bureau of Land Management (BLM). In addition, the economic crisis that the nation as a whole faced during the 1970s caused President Jimmy Carter and his administration to rethink the wisdom of untrammeled development of western water resources. In 1977, the

Carter administration released its infamous "hit list" of thirty-three BOR and Corps water projects that they wanted to eliminate from the budget. The states of the Intermountain West, and the West as a whole, rose up almost unanimously against Carter's list, with Colorado governor Richard Lamm being one of the most vocal opponents. That the projects were both economically and environmentally unsound was less important than the flow of federal dollars that they brought into the region. The cuts in funding along with enforcement of the new environmental laws like NEPA and FLPMA met with intense western resistance in what became known as the "Sagebrush Rebellion" of the early 1980s (Getches 2003).

It appeared that the Sagebrush rebels might win a considerable victory with the election of Ronald Reagan and his appointment of one of the rebels' own, James Watt, as secretary of the interior. The administration might have succeeded in selling off much of the BLM-managed western lands, but Congress was not as enthusiastic about the idea as Reagan and Watt were. The varying federal bureaucracies now had their actions dictated by a need to diffuse the costs of their projects and concentrate the distribution of benefits; in this way, the agencies would gain powerful allies who would approve whatever they wanted to do.

Of course, the development of environmental resources in the Intermountain West by this means has had unintended effects on the landscape. The damming of western rivers has resulted in the increased salination of the water, making parts of the region unusable for agriculture. Furthermore, in many cases, the growing urbanization of the Intermountain West has meant that water that was intended to irrigate western fields has flowed into cities instead. The building of dams in the West has had dramatic effects on the ecosystems of the region. Species that rely on free-flowing rivers have been made extinct. Weather patterns and the ecological makeup of entire regions have been changed. These factors have led to the call for a new

Sagebrush Rebellion

The Sagebrush Rebellion, also known as the Rocky Mountain West Movement, began in the mid-1970s, when the livestock industry began protesting federal environmental legislation that limited its use of federal lands. The so-called Sagebrush rebels called for transferring the jurisdiction of federal lands, especially those managed by the Bureau of Land Management (BLM), to individual states. They believed that individual state legislatures would be more sympathetic to their economic needs than the federal government.

The movement's zenith came in 1979, when Nevada's legislative bodies claimed state jurisdiction over lands within the state's borders that were managed by the BLM. The states of Arizona, New Mexico, Utah, and Wyoming soon followed Nevada's example. Their efforts were undercut by President Ronald Reagan's administration, most notably Interior Secretary James Watt, who offered an alternative to state management of public lands, namely privatization. Many Sagebrush rebels opposed privatization because selling formerly public lands to private interests would negatively impact their economic interests. The Reagan administration's ploy robbed the movement of its momentum, leading to its end by the mid-1980s.

—John R. Burch Jr.

See also: *Evolution of Environmental Law; Privatization of Water Services*

BIBLIOGRAPHY
Cawley, R. McGreggor. *Federal Land, Western Anger: The Sagebrush Rebellion and Environmental Politics.* Lawrence: University Press of Kansas, 1993.
Davis, Charles, ed. *Western Public Lands and Environmental Politics.* 2nd ed. Boulder, CO: Westview Press, 2001.
Lehmann, Scott. *Privatizing Public Lands.* New York: Oxford University Press, 1995.

paradigm for determining environmental policy in the Intermountain West.

This new paradigm may be closer than many think. Many of the nine "signals" indicating changes in how western water resources are developed and managed are coming to pass, as noted by historian Patricia Nelson Limerick in her 2003 essay "Western Water Resources and 'Climate of Opinion' Variables." Specifically, Limerick addresses how the "enthusiasm for the reversal of time and progress may grow in power" (276–77), and this certainly appears to be the case in the current move to decommission many of the dams and irrigation projects built during the second half of the twentieth century. A new call for a more realistic water policy in the Intermountain West, one that realizes that infinite growth is not possible, that dams are destructive to the western environment, that low-value crops are not a wise use of limited water resources, and that polluters (agriculture being one of the foremost) must clean up their messes, is necessary in order to create a sustainable water future for this region (McCool 2010).

—Steven L. Danver

See also: *Agriculture; American Indian Water Rights; Government Water Decision Making; Privatization of Water Services; Riparian Ecosystems*

BIBLIOGRAPHY

Getches, David H. "Constraints of Law and Policy on the Management of Western Water." In *Water and Climate in the Western United States*, edited by William M. Lewis Jr., 183–234. Boulder: University Press of Colorado, 2003.

Hardesty, Donald L. "Toward an Historical Archaeology of the Intermountain West." *Historical Archaeology* 25, no. 3 (1991): 29–35.

Hundley, Norris, Jr. "The Dark and Bloody Ground of Indian Water Rights: Confusion Elevated to Principle." *The Western Historical Quarterly* 9, no. 4 (1978): 454–82.

Hundley, Norris, Jr. *Water and the West: The Colorado River Compact and the Politics of Water in the American West*. Berkeley: University of California Press, 1975.

Hundley, Norris, Jr. "The Winters Decision and Indian Water Rights: A Mystery Reexamined." *The Western Historical Quarterly* 13, no. 1 (1982): 17–42.

Jackson, Donald C. *Building the Ultimate Dam: John S. Eastwood and the Control of Water in the West*. Lawrence: University Press of Kansas, 1995.

Limerick, Patricia Nelson. "Western Water Resources and 'Climate of Opinion' Variables." In *Water and Climate in the Western United States*, edited by William M. Lewis Jr., 273–81. Boulder: University Press of Colorado, 2003.

McCool, Daniel. *Command of the Waters: Iron Triangles, Federal Water Development, and Indian Water*. Tucson: University of Arizona Press, 1987.

McCool, Daniel. "Warning: Water Policy Faces an Age of Limits." *High Country News*, April 22, 2010.

Pisani, Donald J. *To Reclaim a Divided West: Water, Law, and Public Policy, 1848–1902*. Albuquerque: University of New Mexico Press, 1992.

Powell, James Lawrence. *Dead Pool: Lake Powell, Global Warming, and the Future of Water in the West*. Berkeley: University of California Press, 2009.

Powell, John Wesley. *The Arid Lands*. Edited by Wallace Stegner. Lincoln: University of Nebraska Press, 2004.

Rowley, William D. *Reclaiming the Arid West: The Career of Francis G. Newlands*. Bloomington: Indiana University Press, 1996.

Stegner, Wallace. *Beyond the Hundredth Meridian: John Wesley Powell and the Second Opening of the West*. New York: Penguin, 1954.

Wilkinson, Charles. *Crossing the Next Meridian: Land, Water, and the Future of the American West*. Washington, DC: Island Press, 1992.

Worster, Donald. *Rivers of Empire: Water, Aridity, and the Growth of the American West*. New York: Oxford University Press, 1985.

Midwest

The Midwestern region of the United States of America encompasses three major drainage basins and a small part of a fourth. It includes the southern shores of three of the Great Lakes (Superior, Huron, and Erie) and the entirety of Lake Michigan. The five Great Lakes are estimated to hold 64 quadrillion gallons, 21 percent of the world's freshwater supply and 84 percent of the North American continent's. The lakes and surrounding shores drain into the Saint Lawrence River. Most of the northern Mississippi River drainage basin lies in the Midwest, as does the northern side of the Ohio River valley. A portion of northern Minnesota drains via the Red River into Hudson Bay. Waterways in this region were traveled for centuries by Native American nations; served as entry to the interior of the continent for French exploration, fur trade, and isolated settlements; and provided convenient transportation for later Anglo-American and other immigrant settlement. Many canal systems have been developed to connect different drainage basins, and a few remain in use. Development of the Midwest established large urban industrial concentrations along the lakeshores and major rivers, as well as intensive agriculture on medium-sized family farms. Copper and lead mines in Michigan, Wisconsin, and Illinois are now largely abandoned. Iron ore in Minnesota, Wisconsin, and Michigan is mostly exhausted, but some mining continues. Coal mining continues in Ohio, Indiana, and Illinois as it has for nearly two centuries.

Exactly which states are considered "Midwestern" varies. One definition includes the Old Northwest Territory states—Ohio, Michigan, Indiana, Illinois, and Wisconsin—plus Iowa and Minnesota. Some sources add Missouri, which lies at the juncture of the southeastern, Great Plains, and Midwestern regions. North and South Dakota and Nebraska are sometimes referenced as Midwestern, but these lie in the more arid Great Plains region while most of the Midwest was originally temperate forest. A wedge of prairie across southern Iowa and northern Illinois, Indiana and Ohio reflects lower rainfall in those areas, where summer drought is more common. A thick layer of black to brown soil, with abundant humus, overlies glacial deposits, except in the upper Great Lakes areas. Some of the most productive soils in the world, in the Farm Belt, contrast with those of the northern parts of Minnesota, Wisconsin, and Michigan, which are of lower fertility and poor drainage. Recent rainfall shortages may be attributable to rising global temperatures, which have moderated winters in the Midwest.

Rivers and Aquifers

Midwestern tributaries of the Ohio include the Muskingum, Big Sandy, Scioto, Little and Great Miami, Green, and Wabash Rivers. The upper Mississippi River is fed from the

Midwest by the Wisconsin, Illinois, Kaskaskia, Black, Saint Croix, Minnesota, Des Moines, Iowa, and many smaller rivers, while the Missouri, flowing in from the Great Plains, joins the Mississippi at the southwestern extremity of the Midwest. Major rivers flowing into the Great Lakes include the Cuyahoga, Maumee, Fox, Milwaukee, Menomonee, Clinton, Saginaw, and Grand Rivers. The North Central Research Station of the U.S. Forest Service estimates that 8 to 13 percent of Midwestern land is riparian, varying according to a somewhat-arbitrary choice of buffer width from the stream bank. Of this riparian land, 77 percent is in the states of Minnesota, Wisconsin, and Michigan; much less is in the Farm Belt states further south. Only 2 percent of land in Iowa and 4 percent each in Illinois and Missouri is considered riparian. Almost three-fourths of riparian land is forested, a little over one-fourth is in agricultural use, and less than 2 percent is urban.

Of the twenty-five regional aquifers in the United States that are identified by the U.S. Geological Survey, four are defined as northern Midwest, central Midwest, Michigan, and Midwestern basins and arches. Most of the Midwest—particularly Wisconsin, Michigan, Illinois, Indiana, and to some extent Minnesota and Iowa—lies over sand and gravel aquifers of alluvial and glacial origin. Silurian-Devonian aquifers have been mapped under Illinois, Michigan, Indiana, Ohio, Wisconsin, and Iowa, and an upper carbonate aquifer lies under Minnesota and Iowa. A Cambrian-Ordovician aquifer system underlies the states of Illinois, Indiana, Iowa, Wisconsin, Minnesota, and Missouri. It consists of three major aquifers composed of sandstone and dolomite and two formations of sandstone and shale. Water has been pumped from this system since 1860. By 1976–1980, 781 million gallons per day were being pumped from the system, with the largest amounts of water use occurring in the Twin Cities area of Minnesota and the Chicago/Milwaukee area.

Water Power, Industry, and Canals

The availability of river and lake transport made the region a cost-effective exporter of agricultural produce by the mid-nineteenth century. Produce and meat from areas possessing navigable waterways feeding into the Ohio and Mississippi were able to ship through the port of New Orleans. Farms with access to waters feeding into the Great Lakes could export to the east coast of the United States or for international trade via the Erie Canal. Industries making extensive use of water for manufacturing flourished everywhere. The Ohio River hosted iron works and glass and pottery works

while becoming an early meatpacking center. Water-powered gristmills, sawmills, carding mills, and other nineteenth-century industries lined many rivers.

Canals were dug or attempted wherever waterfalls and rapids blocked shipping or overland barriers between rivers offered a possible point for connection. The Erie Canal, completed in 1825, has its western terminus on Lake Erie, where it drew upon commerce from the entire upper Midwest. Between 1853 and 1855, a canal was constructed at Sault Saint Marie, Michigan, bypassing the rapids between Lake Superior and Lake Huron; this canal remains in use by lake- and ocean-going cargo vessels. Sault Saint Marie, like most canals, required legislation, subsidies, and generous land donations by both federal and state governments, in addition to private capital investment, to enable the privately incorporated St. Mary's Falls Ship Canal Company to finance the necessary locks and other construction. Both the northern Michigan copper mines and the Minnesota iron mines provided impetus to complete it.

The nearly 1,000 miles of canals that were built in Ohio between 1825 and 1847 reached their peak revenue in 1855, then fell out of use as commerce and passenger travel shifted to railroads. Some of the most important canals connected the Ohio River basin, to the south, with the Lake Erie basin at the north end of the state. The Ohio and Erie Canal, from Cleveland to Portsmouth, connected the Scioto watershed to that of the Cuyahoga. The Miami and Erie Canal ran further west, from Toledo to Cincinnati, connecting the Maumee basin to the Miami. With a land grant from Congress, Indiana began construction in 1827 on the Wabash and Erie Canal, which ran from the Maumee River in Ohio through Fort Wayne to Terre Haute, then to Evansville on the Ohio River. By 1876, all portions of the 468-mile canal had fallen into disuse, and remaining property was auctioned off. Efforts to build a canal at Portage, Wisconsin, a transfer point between the Fox River and the Wisconsin River—a well-established juncture of the Great Lakes and the Mississippi drainage basins—was also abandoned due to the expense of getting around rapids on the Fox and the growing dominance of railroads.

The Ohio River itself became fully useable for commercial shipping only after construction of a series of 51 wooden wicket dams that were bypassed by 600-by-110-foot locks and the dredging of some parts of the river to deepen channels. This process was more or less completed by 1929, when President Herbert Hoover observed the opening of the system. The system has also moderated

Designed and constructed between 1823 and 1848, the 96-mile-long Illinois and Michigan Canal connected Lake Michigan and the Mississippi River, greatly facilitating the shipment of goods from the East to the Midwest.
Library of Congress

flooding on the river, which has been beneficial for industrial and residential uses, but in so doing it eliminated a natural process that had previously replenished the fertility of the soil for agriculture in wide areas bordering the river. The 1929 dams were replaced in the 1950s with twenty-one modernized dams that were bypassed by a larger lock system. Four of the dams also produce hydroelectricity.

Chicago Sanitary and Ship Canal

One of the most controversial cases of water engineering in the region remains the Chicago Sanitary and Ship Canal. In 1822, Congress authorized the State of Illinois to open the Illinois and Michigan Canal from Lake Michigan to the Illinois River, connecting the Great Lakes drainage basin to the Mississippi drainage basin. Between 1865 and 1872, the city devised a plan to relieve the Chicago River of untreated sewage by lowering the level of the canal, in hopes of generating a permanent flow of lake water to dilute and flush away the sewage. Proposals noted the navigable waterway that would also be created in the process. A new drainage canal opened in 1900, reversing the flow of the Chicago

River into the Des Plaines and Illinois Rivers.

Twenty-eight years later, this resulted in the case of *Wisconsin v. Illinois*, 278 U.S. 367 (1929). The U.S. Supreme Court ruled that Chicago's permit from the secretary of war (who was responsible for the U.S. Army Corps of Engineers) exceeded the secretary's legal authority, and that diversions of water from Lake Michigan must be curtailed. Arguments on the side of Wisconsin were joined by Minnesota, Ohio, Pennsylvania, Michigan, and New York to protect water levels in the Great Lakes generally. Missouri, Kentucky, Tennessee, Louisiana, Mississippi, and Arkansas filed arguments on the side of Illinois, asserting that the additional water flow benefited navigation on the Mississippi. More detailed decrees from the Supreme Court limited diversion of water from the Great Lakes/Saint Lawrence watershed through the canal to 6,500 cubic feet per second after July 1, 1930, to 5,000 cubic feet per second after December 31, 1935, and to 1,500 cubic feet per second after December 31, 1938 (281 U.S. 696). The court had to issue another decree in 1933 (289 U.S. 395) to enforce compliance by a most-reluctant sanitary district. The previous decrees came back before the court as recently as 1967 (388 U.S. 426), with many Chicago suburbs included in a revised injunction against diverting Lake Michigan water into the canal in amounts greater than 3,200 feet per second total, from all the municipalities combined. The court's decree was amended yet again in 1980 (449 U.S. 48).

In the late twentieth and early twenty-first century, this canal remained a matter of public concern as the Asian silver carp, an invasive species that had escaped from containment ponds into the Mississippi River in the 1960s, entered the Illinois River. Weighing up to fifty pounds, the carp overwhelm native fish by eating most of the available food supply, and they also pose a hazard to recreational boaters by jumping out of the water. The canal provides a path by which the silver carp could enter the entire Great Lakes system. By 2009, the fish was believed to be in the Des Plaines River, poised to enter the Great Lakes. An electric barrier is the final measure intended to prevent the carp from reaching Lake Michigan.

Wetlands and River Ecosystems

Draining wetlands in Midwestern prairies during the nineteenth century greatly improved public health and reduced mortality by eliminating stagnant water that had bred mosquitoes and other insects, which at one time had made malaria a common disease in the region. Extensive marshes around Lake Erie were drained starting as early as 1836. The Black Swamp in northern Ohio, an elm- and ash-forested wetland perhaps 40 by 120 miles, had been totally drained and turned to other uses by the dawn of the twentieth century. Tallgrass prairie included seasonal wetlands, inundated with water from early spring to midsummer, covering a fifth of Illinois (about 5 million acres). By the mid-1900s, approximately 85 percent of these wetlands had been drained. Wisconsin's Horicon Marsh was dammed in 1846, creating a lake four miles wide by fourteen miles long, to flood the area for water transportation and commercial fishing. The dam was removed in 1869, and an unsuccessful attempt was made to drain the marsh for farming in 1904. The Horicon Marsh Wildlife Refuge was established in 1927. As wetlands have disappeared, the beneficial purposes of wetlands have been highlighted by their absence; they not only supported wildlife habitat but prevented erosion, mitigated flooding, trapped non–point source pollutants, and replenished soil fertility.

Soil erosion and the resulting non–point source water pollution is a hazard across most of the Midwest. Excess nutrients increase algae blooms in the Great Lakes and at the mouth of the Mississippi, creating dead zones where animal life cannot obtain sufficient oxygen. The Water Resources Development Act of 1996 (Pub. L. 104-303, 110 Stat. 3658) included creation of the Great Lakes Tributary Modeling Program—in Section 516(e) of the Act—authorizing the U.S. Army Corps of Engineers to develop sediment transport models for each tributary to the Great Lakes to support soil conservation and pollution prevention.

Metal Mining and Water

Industrial development of copper mines on upper Michigan's Keweenaw Peninsula began in 1843. The industry constructed stamping mills to extract copper from mined ore, using large quantities of water and releasing poisoned wastes, both tailings and dissolved metals, into Lake Superior and tributary waterways. By the 1890s, stamp machines crushed 225 to 700 tons of ore per day, requiring as much as 30 tons of water for each ton of rock. Mine tailings were remined using more advanced technologies in the 1920s and 1930s, but to this day beaches of coarse, gray-black tailings lie along the lake shore. Within the lake, among other signs of degradation, fish develop unusual cancers. Two commercially viable deposits of copper and other metals have been exploited in the last decades of the twentieth century: the Flambeau copper and gold deposit and the Crandon copper and zinc deposit in northern Wisconsin. Although studies prepared in cooperation with mining companies stated that

Dust Bowl

The Dust Bowl was an area on the High Plains during the 1930s that encompassed portions of Oklahoma, Texas, New Mexico, Colorado, and Kansas. The region was continuously ravaged by dust storms that picked up the dry topsoil and carried it eastward, sometimes for hundreds of miles.

Controversy rages over the cause of the environmental calamity. Some researchers posit that the farmers residing within the Dust Bowl were merely victims of a severe drought. Others blame the agricultural methods used for destroying the grasslands that secured the topsoil to the ground.

The Dust Bowl was not only an agro-ecological catastrophe but also a humanitarian disaster. The farmers and their families, many of whom were suffering from health problems related to the dust storms, were forced to migrate from the region after having lost everything.

—John R. Burch Jr.

See also: Drought; Southwest

BIBLIOGRAPHY

Hurt, R. Douglas. The Dust Bowl: An Agricultural and Social History. Chicago: Nelson-Hall, 1981.
Worster, Donald. Dust Bowl: The Southern Plains in the 1930s. New York: Oxford University Press, 1979.

modern water treatment produced mine discharge that was safe for aquatic life, the Wisconsin Resources Protective Council reported in 1997 that water flowing into the Flambeau River system contained copper seven times the Wisconsin standard and manganese four times the concentration provided for by permit.

Lead mining in the Midwest centered on the upper Mississippi River, especially in Galena, Illinois; southwestern Wisconsin; and eastern Iowa. Surface deposits were exhausted by 1840. Up to 7,000 Cornish immigrant miners pioneered deep mining methods. Production peaked in the 1850s, but lead production was estimated at 50,000 pigs (2,000 tons) per year in the 1880s, and industrial mining continued into the twentieth century. Most mines in the area were abandoned without any formal reclamation process. In 2003, nearly two-thirds of lead used in the United States came from recycling, rather than new mining. Although polluted areas from lead mining in Missouri have been designated Superfund cleanup sites supervised by the Environmental Protection Agency, sites in Illinois and Wisconsin have received little attention.

Coal and Steel

Three Midwestern states are significant coal producers: Ohio, Illinois, and Indiana. Minerals exposed by either surface or underground mining dissolve in runoff water, infiltrating the soil or groundwater aquifers, as well as entering surface streams. Unreclaimed spoil from surface mining generally contains pyrite, which produces sulfuric acid when it is exposed to oxygen and water, particularly in the presence of *Bacillus feroxidans,* a bacterium that oxidizes pyrite. In Illinois, approximately 103,000 acres were mined before the state's first mine reclamation law was adopted in 1962. Another 152,000 acres have been mined since 1962, under increasingly strict regulations. Ohio is estimated to have 23.7 billion tons of coal reserves, the seventh largest of any state. Coal mined in Ohio since 1800 totals 3.6 billion tons, including 1.4 billion tons from surface mining (mostly since 1948) and 2.2 billion tons from underground mines. Ohio's first surface coal-mining regulatory law was adopted in 1947, and it was strengthened in 1972. Since 1978, permits have been granted for the surface mining of 102,752 acres, with a mandate to restore original contours and establish vegetation to sustain a functioning ecosystem. In Indiana, approximately 180,000 acres have been disturbed by surface mining. Reclamation of surface-mined land is regulated by the Surface Mining Control and Reclamation Act of 1977

(Pub. L. 95-87, 91 Stat. 445, 30 U.S.C. 1201–1328), which has been amended by the Abandoned Mine Reclamation Act of 1990 and the Energy Policy Act of 1992, as well as by state laws.

Of U.S. iron ore reserves, 80 percent have been found in the Lake Superior region in the states of Minnesota, Wisconsin, and Michigan. Between 1855 and 1960, 3.3 billion tons of ore were shipped. Minnesota's Mesabi Range accounted for two-thirds of these shipments, having by far the richest ores, much of them with 50 to 55 percent iron content. The concentration of the American steel industry in the Great Lakes states and Pennsylvania was built on this iron, which was brought by Great Lakes freighters to manufacturing centers in Chicago, Gary, Toledo, Cleveland, Akron, and Youngstown. It was then taken by rail to Pittsburgh, where coal mined in Pennsylvania, Ohio, Illinois, and Indiana provided the second crucial ingredient. Limestone, a third requirement, is also plentiful in the region. Most of the iron was mined by open-pit methods.

In the past fifty years, as higher-quality hematite ores have been exhausted, mining operations have sought taconite, a lower-grade ore requiring considerable processing that uses large amounts of water. Taconite tailings do not contain acid-forming sulfides, but they do bear fibers that can cause asbestosis; mesothelioma; and cancers of the lung, gastrointestinal tract, and larynx. They have dispersed throughout large areas of Lake Superior and entered the drinking water supply of Duluth and other areas. Disposal of tailings in Lake Superior ended after 1980 in compliance with a federal court order issued in 1974 that was repeatedly appealed (*United States et al. v. Reserve Mining company et al.,* 380 F. Supp. 11, 498 F. 2d 1073, 419 U.S. 802). A slurry of tailings is now pumped inland into a reservoir.

A large part of the Midwestern steel industry shut down in the 1970s and 1980s. This was largely due to competition from imports, as reduced ocean transport costs allowed plants on the Atlantic, Pacific, and Gulf coasts to import iron and bulk steel from overseas at just 5 to 10 percent of the cost to ship these products domestically by rail. Production of raw steel in the United States peaked in 1973 at 150.8 million tons and by 1985 had fallen to 88.3 million. A new mini mill steel industry has grown up, melting scrap in smaller-scale electric furnaces for reuse. Northwest Steel and Wire in Chicago is one of the few mini mill operators located in the Midwest. Sources of scrap iron are widely distributed, as are markets for finished product. From 1970 to 1985, mini mills expanded from 7 million tons to 18 million tons of production. Because these mills operate on a relatively small scale, technology can be updated every four or five years, and more efficient methods reduce energy used per ton of steel produced and waste product from production. Moreover, producers use discarded metal, which would otherwise generate pollution of groundwater and surface water. Because the source of raw material is not newly mined, the toxic impact of mining operations on water supply is eliminated.

Rise and Decline of the Paper Industry

Another declining industry in the Midwest is papermaking, which has left behind long-term degradation of many waterways. In 1947, Wisconsin and Michigan were the second- and third-largest paper-producing states in the nation, with Minnesota fifteenth (New York was first). States bordering on the Great Lakes accounted for 18 percent of total value added in the U.S. paper industry. When the first mill was built in the region in 1834, paper mills produced for a local or small regional market. Soon, however, a plentiful supply of wood and water made the region a major paper producer for export. Water power attracted industry for much of the nineteenth century, but by 1890 most industries turned to steam power. Papermaking requires tremendous quantities of fresh, clean water, as much as 40,000 gallons for one ton of paper. Production keeps a dilute suspension of fiber continuously and evenly distributed over a horizontally moving screen while the water drains and then is further removed by suction and pressing. Pulped wood as a source of fiber for paper came into use in the 1890s, replacing rags and straw as primary sources. The upper Midwest had land from which virgin forest had been logged for timber but did not have suitable soils for agriculture. Therefore, a good deal of forest remained or had grown back. Paper mills became a dominant industry in Wisconsin along the Fox, Peshtigo, Oconto, Wolf, and Menominee Rivers, which drain into Lake Michigan via Green Bay, and the Wisconsin, Flambeau, and Chippewa Rivers, which drain into the Mississippi.

Hypochlorites of potassium, sodium, and calcium are used for bleaching paper, and wood is cooked under pressure in sodium hydroxide to prepare it for pulping. A large part of these chemicals are recovered for recycling, but not 100 percent. Effluent from paper mills includes suspended solids, dissolved organic compounds, dissolved inorganic compounds, and toxic substances including sulfur dioxide, chlorine, resin acids, and other sulfur compounds. Waste fiber and wood sugars that are dissolved in sulfite liquor discharge into rivers, forming a sludge. This sludge is subject to anaerobic fermentation, and the resulting high biological oxygen demand suffocates aquatic life.

Use of spruce and pine trees at a faster rate than reforestation programs could replace them left the industry without an adequate local supply of wood. Paper companies subsequently found new centers for production. Some higher-quality specialty papers are still manufactured in the Midwest.

Saint Lawrence Seaway: Commerce and Invasive Species

In 1959, the Saint Lawrence Seaway opened Great Lakes ports as far inland as Duluth, Minnesota, to oceangoing ships. The Seaway consists of three dams on the Saint Lawrence River and a series of seven locks between Montreal and Lake Ontario. From there, ships also must pass through the older Welland Canal around Niagara Falls, into Lake Erie, then through the Detroit River and Lake Saint Clair into Lake Huron and, to reach Lake Superior, the Sault Saint Marie locks on Michigan's Upper Peninsula. The seaway ended virtually all commerce on the Erie Canal through New York State. An estimated 2.5 billion metric tons of cargo moved through the seaway in its first fifty years, with a value in excess of $375 billion. Most oceangoing ships use the seaway to bring steel imports to North America and to export grain abroad. Along with this cargo, ships have brought 84 to 100 nonnative species of plants and fish. These include the lamprey eel, Eurasian ruffe, zebra mussel, quagga mussel, spiny water flea, and round goby.

A study released in 2008 by the Center for Aquatic Conservation at the University of Notre Dame estimated that invasive species caused damage to commercial and sport fishing and to the region's water supply costing $200 million a year in the United States alone, with comparable damage expected in Canada. Since 2006, saltwater ships have been required to flush their ballast tanks and take in new water before entering the Great Lakes. Enforcement of current policy is overseen by a Ballast Water Working Group (BWWG) with representatives from the U.S. Department of Commerce, the U.S. Coast Guard, Transport Canada, and the Canadian Saint Lawrence Seaway Management Corporation. Since the latest tightening of enforcement in 2006, no new invasive species have been reported. Proponents of the seaway cite this information to counter demands that

Trout Unlimited

Trout Unlimited is a nonprofit conservation group that has more than 152,000 members. It was founded on July 15, 1959, by anglers in Michigan dedicated to the conservation of trout and their cold-water habitats. The organization's conservation efforts gradually expanded to include all other salmonids found in North America, including char, steelheads, graylings, whitefish, and salmon. Members of the Salmonidae family are noted as being especially susceptible to changes in their respective ecosystems. Trout Unlimited endeavors to protect their ecosystems through the protection and restoration of watersheds and the rivers and streams that they sustain. The protection of individual watersheds is managed at the local level by one of this organization's 450 affiliated chapters. The chapters receive scientific and legal support from more than thirty offices scattered throughout the United States. The organization's national headquarters, located in Washington, D.C., helps lobby to protect the environment in general and, specifically, the cold-water habitats of trout and other salmonids. The organization's members stay abreast of Trout Unlimited's activities at all levels through the quarterly periodical entitled *Trout*.

—John R. Burch Jr.

See also: *Clean Water Act of 1972*

BIBLIOGRAPHY

Behnke, Robert J. *About Trout: The Best of Robert J. Behnke from* Trout *Magazine*. Guilford, CT: Lyons Press, 2007.
Ross, John. *Rivers of Restoration: Trout Unlimited's First 50 Years of Conservation*. New York: Skyhorse, 2008.

oceangoing ships be banned entirely. The U.S. Environmental Protection Agency announced in February 2009 that terms of a general license for cargo vessels entering the Great Lakes are being reviewed for the purpose of imposing more stringent conditions. Saltwater ships account for only 7 percent of total commerce on the lakes.

Cleaning and Monitoring the Waters

Midwestern waters provided many case studies for passage of the Water Pollution Control Act Amendments of 1972 (Pub. L. 92-500, 86 Stat. 816, 33 U.S.C. 1251–1387), also known as the Clean Water Act. One of the most famous was the Cuyahoga River fire of 1969, in which a slick of oil and debris on the river caught fire, doing $50,000 in property damage. The Federal Water Pollution Control Administration noted at the time that the lower Cuyahoga had "no visible signs of life." The Clean Water Act is often credited with having stemmed damage to the Great Lakes after 1972 and with beginning a recovery in water quality, although it has not delivered the goal of eliminating all water pollution. Similar impact has been observed on the major rivers of all four drainage basins. As major industries have closed, recreation and tourism have become more important economically, increasing the political constituency for continued improvement in water quality. The John Glenn Great Lakes Basin Program (42 U.S.C. 1962d-21) provides for comprehensive study and monitoring of the lakes, including in terms of navigation, recreation, environmental restoration, water levels, sediment transport, and flood damage.

Twenty-six areas of concern with severely degraded water quality, likely to cause impairment of beneficial use, have been identified in U.S. waters on the Great Lakes. These areas are governed by both the Great Lakes Water Quality Agreement between the United States and Canada and by the Great Lakes Legacy Act of 2002. Frequent flooding of lands drained for agriculture in the past eighty years has inspired increased attention to programs to restore wetlands and waterfowl habitat, such as the U.S. Department of Agriculture Wetlands Reserve Program and the Environmental Conservation Acreage Reserve Program. Non–point source pollution from agricultural runoff throughout the Ohio and upper Mississippi drainage basins remains a significant threat to water quality all the way to the Gulf of Mexico. A bill introduced in the last several sessions of Congress, the Upper Mississippi River Basin Protection Act, would provide for the study and management of sediment and nutrient loss. As of the 111th (2009–2010) Congress, the bill had yet to be approved.

—Charles Rosenberg

See also: *Acid Rain; Dredging; Great Lakes; Great Lakes Legacy Act of 2002; Illinois and Michigan Canal; International Joint Commission (United States and Canada); Mining and Water Resources; Mississippi River Basin; Nonindigenous Aquatic Nuisance Prevention and Control Act of 1990; Ohio River Basin; Rapanos v. United States (2006); Solid Waste Agency of Northern Cook County v. United States Army Corps of Engineers et al. (2001); Water Resources Development Act of 1996; Wetlands*

BIBLIOGRAPHY

Barnett, Donald F. and Robert W. Crandall. *Up from the Ashes: The Rise of the Steel Minimill in the United States.* Washington, DC: The Brookings Institution, 1986.

Bartlett, Robert V. *The Reserve Mining Controversy: Science, Technology, and Environmental Quality.* Bloomington: Indiana University Press, 1980.

Branch, Maurice Lloyd. "The Paper Industry in the Lakes States Region, 1834–1947." PhD thesis. University of Wisconsin, 1954.

Dempsey, Dave. *On the Brink: The Great Lakes in the 21st Century.* East Lansing: Michigan State University Press, 2004.

Fisher, Douglas Alan. *The Epic of Steel.* New York: Harper and Row, 1963.

Lankton, Larry. *Beyond the Boundaries: Life and Landscape at the Lake Superior Copper Mines, 1840–1875.* New York: Oxford University Press, 1997.

Lankton, Larry. *Cradle to Grave: Life, Work, and Death at the Lake Superior Copper Mines.* New York: Oxford University Press, 1991.

Lemley, Patricia, William Shanker, Dennis Sustare, and Royden Tull. *Students to Oppose Pollution (STOP) Report on Wisconsin Paper and Pulp Mills.* Madison: Wisconsin Department of Justice, 1971.

McIsaac, Gregory, and William R. Edwards. *Sustainable Agriculture in the American Midwest: Lessons from the Past, Prospects for the Future.* Urbana: University of Illinois Press, 1994.

National Research Council. *Mississippi River Water Quality and the Clean Water Act: Progress, Challenges, and Opportunities.* Washington, DC: National Academies Press, 2007.

National Research Council. *Surface Mining: Soil, Coal, and Society: A Report.* Washington, DC: National Academy Press, 1981.

Nesbit, Robert C. and William Fletcher Thompson. *Wisconsin: A History.* Madison: University of Wisconsin Press, 1989.

Prince, Hugh C. *Wetlands of the American Midwest: A Historical Geography of Changing Attitudes.* Chicago: University of Chicago Press, 1997.

Shaw, Ronald E. *Canals for a Nation: The Canal Era in the United States, 1790–1860.* Lexington: University Press of Kentucky, 1993.

Sisson, Richard, Christian Zacher, and Andrew Cayton, eds. *The American Midwest: An Interpretive Encyclopedia.* Bloomington: Indiana University Press, 2007.

Willoughby, William R. *The St. Lawrence Waterway: A Study in Politics and Diplomacy.* Madison: University of Wisconsin Press, 1961.

Northeast

In the United States, the waterways of the Northeast were the birthplace of the nation. Before the first Europeans arrived in present-day New England and New York, Native American tribes gathered along the rivers and seacoast. As European colonies were established and grew, the local waterways provided food, jobs, and transportation. While the waterways of the Northeast were a vital resource for both Native Americans and European colonists, they were also a cause of conflict between the two groups. The Industrial Revolution ushered in a new era for lakes, rivers, and streams. Textile mills and steel factories sprang up along the rivers throughout New England and New York. To keep up with the fast pace of manufacturing, many new waterway-engineering projects were put into place, including the Erie Canal and the Saint Lawrence Seaway along with many other dams, canals, and locks, all aimed at keeping the economy of the Northeast moving.

All this progress was not without problems. Pollution from industrial plants became a major problem during the twentieth century. With the help of environmental groups, many streams and rivers in the Northeast have been restored to safe waters once more. Problems like flooding have also been addressed in a variety of ways, from dams to wetland preservation. Today, the waterways throughout New England and the rest of the Northeast are protected by laws that balance the economy with the environment.

In terms of geography, the Northeast is distinct from the rest of the United States; jagged coastlines, shallow rivers, and mountains hemmed in early settlements. Unlike the southern states or the Midwest, the Northeast lacks large expanses of farmland or a mild climate. Despite these drawbacks, the Northeast played a dominate role in shaping the United States and remains an economic capital of the global economy. Bays and inlets offered food and, eventually, a thriving fishing industry. The many rivers that crisscross New England and New York, while not deep enough for navigation, could be harnessed to provide power for mills and factories at the start of the Industrial Revolution. The geography of the Northeast varies within the region from north to south and from east to west. While similar in climate and vegetation, New England differs from southern portions of the Northeast in that it is relatively isolated by the Atlantic Ocean to the east and the Appalachian Mountains to the west.

Early European Settlement

For thousands of years, the rivers, lakes, and streams of the Northeast remained unchanged, flowing from springs and creeks toward the Atlantic Ocean. The first Europeans to set eyes on the northeastern states were the Norse, as early as the eleventh century. Perhaps the jagged coastline and unfriendly-looking forests deterred the Vikings from setting up colonies. As early as the 1500s, Europeans sought the New World for its raw materials, like fur and lumber. Advisors of Elizabeth I encouraged her to sponsor expeditions to the Northeast in an effort to discover new forms of wealth. However, not until the early seventeenth century were the first European colonies established in

Allegany Senecas and the Cornplanter Grant

The 1794 Treaty of Canandaigua designated that approximately 10,000 acres of land, known as the Cornplanter Grant, was to be owned in perpetuity by the Allegany Senecas. Stipulations included a promise from the federal government that it would never disturb the property. The treaty terms were broken by the U.S. government in order to construct the Kinzua Dam.

The dam was constructed during the 1960s in northwestern Pennsylvania for the purposes of flood control and the generation of electricity. Its construction resulted in the forced relocation of most of the Allegany Senecas to New York State. Sacred locales, such as the Cold Spring Longhouse, were lost. Fewer than seventy acres of the Cornplanter Grant escaped being flooded by the Kinzua Dam's reservoir.

The Treaty of Canandaigua was the oldest treaty being honored by the federal government up until the time that its terms were broken. The federal government's willingness to break its treaty obligations was a signal to native peoples engaged in water disputes with government entities that previous agreements would not be honored.

—John R. Burch Jr.

See also: *Kinzua Dam*

BIBLIOGRAPHY

Bilharz, Joy A. *The Allegany Senecas and the Kinzua Dam: Forced Relocation Through Two Generations.* Lincoln: University of Nebraska Press, 1998.

the New World. The lives of the men and women who traveled thousands of miles from their homelands would be shaped almost wholly by the geography of this new land and their proximity to its waterways.

Early European explorers of the region, like Henry Hudson, found the area inhospitable, with rough rivers, dense forests, and a volatile climate. Though deeming the region too harsh for everyday life, Europeans saw many economic possibilities, especially in the fur trade. As religious persecution increased throughout Europe in the seventeenth and eighteenth centuries, some religious groups sought an escape in the New World, and many of their members settled in the Northeast. The early European colonists settled along rivers throughout New England and New York, first building crude wooden houses and forts; then small, bustling villages; and eventually thriving cities, such as Boston and New York City. Early explorers in the Northeast mapped rivers and other inland channels, citing some, like the Hudson River in New York, as inhospitable due to wild animals, poisonous snakes, and dense forests. Early settlers along waterways like the Hudson River or the Charles

River in Boston made a living from fishing and used the rivers as alternative transportation to rutted, muddy roads. Colonial populations grew steadily during the seventeenth century, with waterways continuing to play a vital role in facilitating both transportation and the rapidly expanding economy.

During the American Revolution, men ventured far from their homes and soon realized that abundant land, resources, and opportunities could be found farther afield. Following the Revolution and a postwar recession, the U.S. economy prospered, and as trade and manufacturing increased, the waterways provided power for textile mills, like the earliest ones in Lowell, Massachusetts. Goods were also shipped on barges downriver toward cities along the northeast coast. Rivers to the north, such as the Kennebec in Maine, were used to transport lumber from remote forests to seaports like Bath and Portland. The invention of the steamboat in 1807 meant that people now had an affordable and fast mode of transportation, rather than slow-moving coaches on poorly maintained roads. There were 150 steamboats along the Hudson River alone by 1850.

As traffic along the waterways in the Northeast grew, the government, along with local business leaders, took steps to maintain and encourage economic growth. Dams, locks, and canals were built throughout the Northeast, providing new routes and enlarging riverbeds. One of the biggest projects in the Northeast was the Erie Canal, finished in 1825. By connecting Lake Erie to the Hudson River, it made the Hudson River Valley a major economic hub. The Erie Canal provided a gateway to newly opened territory in the West. It cut travel time significantly, thereby reducing freight shipping costs by half and spurring canal building in rivers throughout the Northeast and beyond. Trade flowed both east and west, with finished goods from the Northeast being shipped west and raw materials coming back.

The earliest English settlers did not venture far from the Atlantic coastline, settling in thick pockets around bays and inlets and along portions of rivers that could be navigated by oceangoing vessels. Thanks to their location along the

P91664

Completed in 1825, the 363-mile Erie Canal was a major technological feat that greatly facilitated the movement of people and goods from New York City to the Great Lakes. The above print, from the 1830s, shows the locks on the canal at Lockport, New York, in the western part of the state.
Library of Congress

bays and inlets around New England, the Pilgrims soon established fishing and trading posts at Wessgusset and Merry Mount (today known as Quincy, Massachusetts) and at Naumkeag (Salem). A hundred years later, fish, lumber and farm produce were being shipped to Europe via ships built in Massachusetts and manned by local sailors.

The settlement patterns of coastal New England were in contrast to those of French settlers along the Saint Lawrence River, Hudson River, and Lake Champlain in upstate New York and western Vermont. Because of the depth and navigability of both the Saint Lawrence and Hudson Rivers, settlements in these areas were much more far-flung and sparse. Indeed, when Henry Hudson sailed up the Hudson River, he did so in the same vessel with which he had crossed the Atlantic. He was able to go as far upriver as Albany before the waters became too shallow for his ship.

Early settlements in the Northeast, such as the Pilgrims's colony at Plymouth in 1620, eventually became cities like Boston; New York; and Providence, Rhode Island. It is no coincidence that every major city in the Northeast lies on the coast or along a major river. The waterways of the

colonial era provided transportation of goods and people. They also provided a highway for communication in an otherwise isolated society. However, much of inland New England remained untouched due to a lack of transportation. There were only three narrow entrances into New England from the north: through waterways at the headwaters of the St. John River to a branch of the Chaudière, at the head of the Kennebec River in Maine to the Chaudière, and along a branch of the Connecticut River to a stream entering Lake Memephremagog to the Saint Francis River. These routes were impeded by falls, rapids, and dense forests along their banks.

The state of New Hampshire is an excellent example of how local waterways were carefully manipulated for the early growth of industry in the New World. Unlike other colonies, such as Massachusetts or Rhode Island, New Hampshire was not formed by persecuted religious groups. It was established by a group of merchants with the support of King James I and the English Parliament. King James I promised provisions and free land in return for unwavering loyalty to the crown. In 1623, fish merchants from London established a fishing colony at the mouth of the Piscataqua River. Two divisions were established for the fishing colony. In Rye, salt-drying fish racks and a factory, where fish were cured, were set up. The second division, headed by brothers Edward and Thomas Hilton, was at Dover. The prosperity of the New Hampshire fishing colony drew immigrants from England and Scotland, who had heard of the "silent streams of a calm sea," as described by Captain John Smith.

Maine, originally part of the Massachusetts Bay Colony, was the most remote region of the Northeast. Exploration from the coast was difficult because of Maine's hundreds of small islands and rocky coastline. The tides made it difficult for large vessels to navigate, which hindered the development of communities and isolated colonial settlements. Rivers and shores were dotted with crude wooden forts and stone structures, sometimes miles apart. Fort Western, situated along the Kennebec River in Maine, is the oldest existing wooden fort. Its location was chosen for economy, rather than defense, although it would have a minor role in the war for independence. Built by the Boston-based group Kennebec Proprietors, Old Fort Western was the center of navigation on the river. Goods were shipped upstream via sloop and schooner and then stored in the fort. They then made the arduous seventeen-mile trip north to Fort Halifax on flat-bottom boats. Because of the inconvenience of travel, goods were usually not shipped more than four times a year.

Once the fur trade was depleted in the Northeast, settlers were forced to look for other avenues of industry, leading to the development of lumber, shipbuilding, and fishing industries. Fishing in the Northeast is still an important industry. In colonial times, settlers turned to fishing out of necessity. The Appalachian Mountains and shallow rivers kept them from exploring inland, and the coast, with its poor soil, discouraged large-scale farming. The ocean, with its bays and inlets, offered limitless wealth for those daring enough to pursue it. Cod, herring, and other fish thrived in the cold waters of the Labrador Current, and thus the fishing industry became a cornerstone of prosperity in New England. Salted, dried fish was soon a staple of exchange with England. Cities like Providence and Newport in Rhode Island became among the busiest seaports in the world.

Shipbuilding was another natural industry for the Northeast, where forests grew right up to the edge of the bays. There were many shipyards in colonial times. But as lumber grew scarce near the coast and the tonnage of vessels increased, lowering demand, shipyards became fewer in number. In places such as Bath, Maine, however, shipyards are still in operation.

As the Industrial Revolution spread from Europe to the United States, waterways were harnessed as a natural source of power for mills and factories. America's textile industry began along the banks of the Blackstone River in Pawtucket, Rhode Island, with the Slater Mill. It was followed by mills in Woonsocket, Rhode Island, and Uxbridge and Lawrence in Massachusetts. By the early 1800s, Massachusetts, Connecticut, and Rhode Island were leading producers of textiles, as well as of guns and clocks.

Another industry born in the Northeast during the Industrial Revolution was that of papermaking. The first paper mill in the United States opened in 1690 at Wissahickon Creek, just outside of Philadelphia. In the 1730s, another papermaking mill opened along the Presumscot River in Westbrook, Maine. Because early papermaking techniques used rags rather than wood, it was not important to be near forests. It was important, however, to be near water for power. By the 1850s, an increased demand for paper and a short supply of cloth rags led to the use of wood pulp. More mills began opening in the Northeast, and the previously dense, unwelcoming forests of the interior were now seen as a valuable commodity. Places like western and northern Maine, which had been virtually uninhabited by whites prior to the 1850s, became papermaking boomtowns. Paper mills were established along the Penobscot River, at the Otis Falls in western Maine, and on the Kennebec River in Madison, Maine. By the 1890s, twenty-five pulp mills were operating in Maine alone. Soon this isolated territory would lead the nation in papermaking thanks to its swift-flowing rivers.

Water Projects and Transportation

Manmade changes to waterways began almost immediately with European settlement. The Charles River, which runs through the greater Boston area, is a prime example. In 1640, an engineered diversion of the Charles to the Neposet River was built to power early mills. As industry grew, engineering projects such as dams, locks, and canals changed the dynamics of the waterways. One of the most important rivers in the Northeast is the Connecticut River, which begins in the granite hills of northern New Hampshire and empties into the Atlantic at Hartford, Connecticut. The Connecticut River is called by some the "Mississippi of New England," because it is the source of five great streams within New England: the Pemigewasset River, the Merrimac River, the Piscataqua River, the Androscoggin River, and the Saco River. Although not a navigable river like the Hudson or Saint Lawrence Rivers, the Connecticut River was the first river in the United States to have a canal built along its banks, at South Hadley, Massachusetts. It became the prototype of water transportation during the first half of the nineteenth century.

The need for canals was noted early. The first U.S. president, George Washington, knew that if the United States were to expand, it needed to move inland. Up until the 1800s, only seacoast communities or those on rivers that could support oceangoing vessels could become major economic centers. River transportation was absolutely vital to the economy during the early 1800s, when roads were poorly maintained and slow to travel. Moving goods on land was prohibitively expensive, costing roughly ten times as much as transporting goods by water. Looking for ways to cut travel costs, a group of merchants, lawyers, and politicians raised funds for a canal at the Great Falls at South Hadley.

The Connecticut River was navigable by boat for roughly sixty miles from its mouth at Hartford to Enfield Rapids. From the rapids, smaller vessels could still navigate the river. However, the biggest obstacle along the river was the falls at South Hadley. Here, cargo had to be unloaded and taken two miles upstream (or downstream, depending on the route) and reloaded onto boats. The South Hadley Canal opened in 1792. It was two and a half miles long and was cut through shale rock. Passage through the canal took roughly fifteen minutes, versus several hours of overland travel. Over the next thirty years, four more canals were built in New England: the Middlesex-Union canal in Boston in 1803; the Farmington Canal in 1822, linking Hartford and Long Island; the Blackstone Valley Canal in 1815, linking Worcester and Providence; and the Cumberland-Oxford Canal in 1820, linking Sebago Lake with Portland, Maine. However, it was the most famous canal in the Northeast, the Erie Canal, that became the prototype for future canals.

Johnstown Flood

An earthen dam built between 1838 and 1853 across the Little Conemaugh River in Pennsylvania created Lake Conemaugh. In 1879, the lake, dam, and some surrounding acreage was purchased by the South Fork Fishing and Hunting Club for use as a summer resort by its members, which included luminaries such as Andrew Carnegie, Andrew Mellon, and Henry Clay Frick. Knowing that the dam was unstable, the South Fork Fishing and Hunting Club made some improvements to the structure. The work was not completed in a professional manner, as the club failed to employ an engineer to oversee the project.

On May 31, 1889, the South Fork Dam containing Lake Conemaugh failed, releasing more than 20 million tons of water onto the town of Johnstown, Pennsylvania. Much of the debris carried by the flood was caught by the Pennsylvania Railroad Company's bridge. The debris subsequently caught fire, compounding the community's problems. More than 2,200 people perished in a disaster that could have been avoided.

Spurred by fantastic accounts in the media, the incident became a national outrage. The disaster illuminated the need for the regulation of dam construction, because individuals could not be trusted to act responsibly on their own.

—John R. Burch Jr.

See also: *Dam Building; Dam Safety and Security Act of 2002*

BIBLIOGRAPHY
McCullough, David. *The Johnstown Flood*. New York: Simon & Schuster, 1968.

The Erie Canal, which connects Lake Erie with the Hudson River, was completed in 1825. The success of the Erie Canal spurred canal building from rivers all around the Great Lakes. Trade flowed both east and west between the Northeast and the Great Lakes region. Railroad lines, telegraphs, and eventually highways would build upon the economic success of the Erie Canal. The canal further established the Northeast as an economic hub of the United States.

Despite their benefits to transportation, canals still had several drawbacks. They were useless during a drought, and in the winter, they froze and became impassable. They only offered accessibility near rivers and did little to help expansion into the western portion of the Northeast, beyond the Appalachian Mountains. Beginning in the 1850s, railroads, which could pass through mountains and rough terrain, rapidly replaced canals and natural waterways as a means of transportation. However, water still played a vital role in local economies.

The Merrimac River in New Hampshire is not large, wide, or deep. But in the nineteenth century, this quiet

The Johnstown Flood of 1889 occurred in Johnstown, Pennsylvania. It was the result of several days of heavy rain, coupled with the catastrophic failure of the South Fork Dam. The flood caused millions of dollars in damage to Johnstown and the surrounding areas.
Library of Congress

New England river was the world's top producer of wooden spindles. Dams along the Merrimac harnessed its power to operate mills and factories throughout New Hampshire. This was true of nearly every other major river in the Northeast. The many falls and rapids within these rivers, coupled with regular rainfall and an abundance of lakes to serve as natural reservoirs, caused New England's river flows to be more constant than those of other rivers in the United States. The rapid growth of industry in the Northeast would not have been possible without the power of its rivers and streams, harnessed by dams.

The Saint Lawrence Seaway, situated between New York and Canada, was one of the Northeast's most ambitious waterways projects and cost $47.3 million. The seaway provides a vital link between the Atlantic Ocean and the Great Lakes. Opened to navigation in 1959, the Saint Lawrence Seaway stretches 189 miles between Montreal and Lake Ontario. Its system of seven locks lifts boats and other vessels 246 feet

above sea level. In 1993, the seaway was enlarged to accommodate bigger loads. It is estimated that 2 billion tons of cargo have passed through the seaway in the fifty years it has been open. This represents more than $300 billion in business.

As industrialization along rivers and waterways grew during the nineteenth and twentieth centuries, so did problems with pollution. Con Edison fought a seventeen-year battle with environmentalist groups in the Hudson River Valley, where the power company wanted to build a new plant. Concern over the safety of the river and surrounding lands led to the National Environmental Policy Act of 1969. Con Edison eventually donated the land it had purchased for its plant to the state, which made it into a park. Another threat to the Hudson River were the high levels of PCB (polychlorinated biphenyl) concentrated around two General Electric (GE) power plants at Hudson Falls and Fort Edward. GE was banned from dumping chemicals into the water, resulting in a steady growth of the fish population. In Massachusetts, the Charles River is the most densely populated river in New England. It is also one of the most protected. In 1974, the Charles River Natural Valley Storage Areas were established, protecting seventeen wetland areas within the middle and upper watersheds of the river. With a value of $830,000, these wetlands act as a natural storage area for floodwaters. This project mixes flood control with wildlife management as well as recreation.

Economic progress along the waterways of the Northeast did not come without a hefty price. As the Industrial Revolution continued throughout the nineteenth century and the human population exploded in the Northeast, rivers and waterways bore the brunt of the resulting waste and other environmental pollutants. The Charles River, in Boston, is a prime example. With twenty dams built along its length, the Charles was slowed down so much it could no longer clean itself. The dams also caused flooding of pastureland and cut off migratory fish from their breeding grounds. By-products from mills plus wastes from roads and homes killed entire fish populations. By 1875, the pollution from the forty-three mills along the Charles River was so bad that cleanup efforts were begun. Today the river is guarded in part by the Charles River Watershed Association (CRWA), whose goal is to leave the river's natural system healthy enough to withstand the effects of continuous withdrawal and discharges and to recover from unpredictable shocks like floods, droughts, and manmade spills.

Because of increased population as well as rapid industrial growth, pollution remained a problem in the Northeast throughout the twentieth century. Concentrated pesticides, herbicides, fertilizers, animal feces, grease, metals, salts, and other sediments are carried by rainwater through storm drains to discharge into rivers. In an effort to reduce pollutants in waterways, the government passed the Clean Water Act of 1972, which promoted the construction of

Hudson River Pollution

New York's Hudson River, which extends from Mount Marcy in the Adirondack Mountains to the New York Harbor, is approximately 315 miles long. During the eighteenth century, the waterway began to become polluted as commercial trade along the river led to industrial expansion and the creation of numerous communities. The river was often utilized to discard sewage and industrial waste. Centuries of pollution degraded the river and its watershed to a level where the water was toxic and unable to sustain many species of animal and plant life.

During the early 1960s, environmentalists began working to address the degradation of the river. The Scenic Hudson Preservation Conference was formed in 1963 to oppose Consolidated Edison's construction of a plant at Storm King Mountain to generate electricity. The seventeen-year legal and political battle over the plant led to the company abandoning its plans and signing the Hudson River Compact. That effort served as a model for action against other companies. General Electric, which had dumped more than 1 million pounds of toxic PCBs into the Hudson River over a thirty-year period, was also forced to help clean up the river. The efforts of the many environmental groups working to protect the Hudson River ultimately reversed the river's decline, although its recovery is moving at a glacial pace.

—John R. Burch Jr.

See also: Detergents; Erie Canal; Fertilizers; Phosphorus in Lakes and Rivers; Sewage

BIBLIOGRAPHY

Benke, Arthur C., and Colbert E. Cushing, eds. Rivers of North America. New York: Elsevier, 2005.
Levinton, Jeffrey S., and John R. Waldman, eds. The Hudson River Estuary. New York: Cambridge University Press, 2006.

modern wastewater plants and placed strict limitations on industrial discharge.

Not all manmade changes have been harmful, though. As with the Charles River, new stretches of shoreline and expanded water and land habitats have been created, such as the Lake District, which was a fashionable recreation area during the nineteenth century. The Moody Street Dam, built in 1814, created a 200-acre mill pond that became a popular summer destination for tourists. Today, the Charles River Basin, a manmade preserve, is home to yacht clubs and the world-class rowing regatta "Head of the Charles." A variety of environmental regulations protect rivers, streams, lakes, and shoreline, which have become destinations for tourists and outdoor enthusiasts.

A lack of inland navigation along rivers in the Northeast, particularly in New England, led to a concentration of settlements along the Atlantic coast and lower portions of rivers. This would in turn hasten the progress of railroads and turnpikes in New England, as government and businesses sought cheaper means of transportation, causing the northeastern portion of the United States to develop faster than anywhere else in the country. At the same time, thriving industries such as fishing, lumber, and shipbuilding were based on northeastern waterways. The need for labor brought thousands of immigrants from Europe and French Canada, increasing the population throughout New England and New York. Without the power that local waterways provided, the Northeast would not have developed as rapidly as it did, nor would it have become a cultural and economic center of the United States. But rapid progress exacted a heavy price. Pollution in rivers and bays killed entire fish populations and threatened the livelihood of many cities, whose freshwater supplies began to dwindle. Beginning as early as the nineteenth century, conservation efforts to clean up local rivers and other waterways helped to curb many problems. However, the waterways of the Northeast are an ongoing project, balancing economic needs with environmental concerns.

—Lorri Brown

See also: *Agriculture; American Indian Water Rights; American Indian Water Settlements; River Transportation; Urbanization; Urban Rivers*

BIBLIOGRAPHY

Barrett, Robert. *Proprietors of the Locks and Canals: A History of South Hadley.* 2nd ed. Holyoke, MA: Holyoke Water Power Company, 1985.

Charles River Watershed Association. "Charles River History." http://www.crwa.org/cr_history.html.

Clark, Victor S. *History of Manufactures in the United States, 1607–1860.* Washington, DC: Carnegie Institution of Washington, 1916.

Davis, William M. *The Physical Geography of Southern New England.* New York: American Book Company, 1896.

Fawcett, Charles B. *Frontiers: A Study in Political Geography.* Oxford, England: Clarendon Press, 1918.

Maine Pulp & Paper Association. "History of Papermaking." http://www.pulpandpaper.org/history.shtml.

Martin, Margaret. *Merchants and Trade of the Connecticut River Valley, 1750–1820.* Northampton, MA: The Department of History of Smith College, 1939.

New Hampshire State Library. "New Hampshire Almanac: A Brief History of New Hampshire." http://www.nh.gov/nhinfo/history.html.

Semple, Ellen C. *Influences of Geographic Environment.* New York: H. Holt, 1911.

State of Rhode Island. "Early Rhode Island." http://www.sos.ri.gov/library/history/natives/.

Pacific Coast

Among all of the regions covered in this work, perhaps no other has such a diversity of landscapes and water-use patterns as the Pacific coast. From the Mojave Desert to the Quinalult Rainforest, all extremes and every point in between are covered within the region. From rainy Seattle, where the fictional television psychologist Frasier Crane once quipped that the state flower was mold, to sunny Los Angeles, where the water necessary for the city's survival has to be brought in from far-flung locations across the arid West, the Pacific coast region defies generalities. However, for the majority of the Pacific coast, as historian Donald Worster has asserted, the scarcity of water has led to the fact that the control and manipulation of water is the main source of power in the region. The largest river in the region, the Colorado, is so vital that writer Marc Reisner astutely noted that much of the West is as dependent on the Colorado River as Cairo is on the Nile (Reisner 1986, 120).

The celebrated explorer and mountain man Jedediah Smith was among the first Americans to see the Pacific coast and experience both the bounty and the barrenness of the region. The Native populations of California had not significantly altered the waterways of the region, and the impact of the Spanish had been minimal, as water was viewed as a community resource not to be exploited (Sowards 2007). It was clear to Smith and many others who followed that the water-use patterns that had dominated east of the 100th meridian were not applicable in the staggering aridity that faced them in the West. Explorer and, later, bureaucrat John Wesley Powell was the first American to reconnoiter what would become the lifeline of southern California, not to mention much of the Southwest: the Colorado River. A true renaissance man, Powell wrote about the West as it really was and the potential that lay there for good and bad (Reisner 1986).

However, neither Smith nor Powell was able to gain the American public's imagination in the way that Charles Dana or William Gilpin did with their efforts to promote the settlement of the West. The California Gold Rush and then construction of the Transcontinental Railroad brought a flood of settlers to the region for which it was unprepared. Some might even argue that the Pacific coast has never been adequately prepared for the torrent of humanity that has ebbed and flowed but never stopped. For his part, Powell saw that the West was the future of a nation that was fixed upon its Manifest Destiny, and he proposed a new system of settlement for the West. Powell's ideas differed greatly from tradition, in that they would disrupt the normal square pattern of settlements in favor of settlements based on water access and establish irrigation districts capable of self-government. Powell recognized that more than individual initiative was needed to break the western wilderness (Stegner 1954). However, Powell's 1877 *Report on the Lands of the Arid Region of the United States* did not play well with westerners and politicians because it disputed the accepted ideas about the West. It challenged the idea that the West was a region that could be made fruitful if only Americans would go there and make it so, and it proposed limitations on the number of settlers based on how many people the region could realistically support.

By the 1890s, however, it was apparent that both private and state efforts to fund western irrigation were insufficient to meet the growing needs of farmers in the Pacific coast region and elsewhere. William Smythe's *The Conquest of Arid America* expressed a vision of federally funded western water development that would create an agrarian republic. This, along with the Homestead Act, would relieve eastern cities by giving people a chance to go back to the land. Land in the Pacific West, however, was only useful if the owner had access to water, which was incredibly scarce. That scarcity made the eastern "riparian rights" model of water allotment, in which stream-front landowners have unfettered access to the water, unfeasible in the West. On the other hand, the "prior appropriation" system favored in other western states like Colorado, which basically says that the first person to put the water to "beneficial use" (usually meaning agriculture) has first rights to it, did not work either. This was due to the fact that urban development drove much of the growth of the Pacific coast. In response, a "California doctrine" was created that blended riparian rights and prior appropriation yet still favored the irrigator on the stream front (Worster 1985).

Those rights were meaningless for most, however, unless massive water development was undertaken—so massive that only the federal government had the resources necessary to make it happen. By the 1890s, the West had gone as far as it could on its own. Partnerships, theocracies, and projects funded by foreign and local capital had accomplished much, but most rivers still ran freely to the sea. To conquer the large rivers, the West needed major capital investment from Washington, D.C. (Worster 1985). The Newlands Act in 1902 created a system by which the federal government would fund western water development, through the Bureau of Reclamation (BOR), and sell 160-acre tracts of irrigated land to settlers. The funds would, in theory, go back into the system to fund future water projects. However, the Newlands Act never achieved Smythe's vision. Instead, it created a West where state power, state expertise, state technology, and state bureaucracy benefited corporate farmers (White 1993). The aim of the Newlands Act had been to create homesteads with irrigation for small farmers. What actually happened was that the irrigated land was grabbed up by land speculators, such as those from the city of Los Angeles, who had ulterior motives. Much of the reclamation occurred on private rather than public land, leading to wealthy large landowners being able to control much of the water in the few free-running rivers of the southern Pacific coast region (Worster 1985).

Los Angeles and the Need for Water

Agricultural problems did not deter those who stood to make money from the development of the urban areas of the Pacific coast. The best-known part of the Pacific coast's water story is that of Los Angeles. Popularized in the film *Chinatown* and written about in Marc Reisner's widely read 1984 *Cadillac Desert: The American West and Its Disappearing Water*, the epic story of the growth of Los Angeles from a sleepy Mexican town to the second largest city in the United States was driven by prototypically western motivations. Historian Donald Worster stated that "in a dry country, unlike a wet one, rain can be grasped and held. The hands that do the grasping are also powerful shaping hands, capable of doling out life and death, wealth and status" (Worster 1985, 171). The two men at the head of the drive to develop Los Angeles, William Mulholland and Fred Eaton, knew this well. Los Angeles's drive for growth, and the water needed for that growth, is replete with motives of exploitation, duplicity, and greed. Both men wanted to see Los Angeles grow into a metropolis, and both men would stop at nothing to see that vision become reality.

Mulholland seemed to thrive on the challenge of creating a large city in a place where a large city had no business being—an area with no major water sources. The region's largest river, the Colorado, already had many claims on its waters, so a closer source that ran through a less-populated region was needed. Fred Eaton was born in Los Angeles, and his family had founded its first suburb, Pasadena. He saw the future of Los Angeles in terms of water—water that was available only a few hundred miles away, in eastern California's Owens Valley. To accomplish the importation of

The population growth of Los Angeles has placed incredible demands on the region's water supply. The city, developed in an area lacking an adequate source of freshwater, had to look to eastern California's Owens River Valley to satisfy its growing demands, not without serious environmental repercussions.

iStockphoto

water, Mulholland and Eaton purchased almost all of the riverfront property on the Owens River (along with the water rights that came with it), often using pseudonyms and shadow companies to hide the fact that the city of Los Angeles would be the new landowner. To justify the importation of hundreds of thousands of acre-feet of water to a city whose current population did not yet need it (but that, they hoped, would eventually grow to need it), Mulholland and Eaton engineered the expansion of the city limits of Los Angeles to include the San Fernando Valley. With the Owens Valley water, carried south by a new aqueduct, the San Fernando Valley would be filled with citrus orchards and other agricultural pursuits, at least until enough settlers came in to replace them. Once those settlers did come, starting in the 1920s and continuing through the rest of the

twentieth century, the water that had been imported for agriculture instead went to fill residents' washtubs and water their lawns. In essence, the entire venture turned the desert of southern California into a garden, and the garden of the Owens Valley back into a desert, with people like Mulholland and Eaton making a fortune in the process.

Although Los Angeles is a unique case, it does illustrate one important truth about the Pacific coast region as a whole: development was the overriding factor in determining how water would be handled, where dams would be built, and who would benefit from them. In northern California, the fight over the Hetch Hetchy Valley between environmentalists (led by John Muir and the Sierra Club) and conservationists (like U.S. Forest Service chief Gifford Pinchot), who favored development over pure scenic value, was indicative of the future direction of water development in the region (White 1993). The rise of cities along the west coast saw a shift in power away from the rural West. Powerlessness was unfamiliar to those who had come to the West as conquerors. Rural westerners exemplified western individualism and self-reliance. Rural areas were localistic and decentralized, lacking connections with each other or the sources of power. Those who prospered, on the other hand, cooperated with corporations and bureaucracies to develop the West. The case of Los Angeles illustrated this contrast, as it shows how the twentieth century saw the rural West become increasingly dependent on the urban seats of economic and political power but, at the same time, become powerless to control them (White 1993).

Other Pacific Coast Reclamation Projects

This is not to say that developing resources for agriculture was not a motive in California. The BOR's efforts in the Pacific coast region were largely considered failures through the 1920s, but the agency came into its own in the 1930s. It expanded beyond its original mandate to irrigate small farms and instead began to build large, multipurpose dams that controlled entire river systems, often in the service of agribusiness and industrial interests. Competition between the BOR and the U.S. Army Corps of Engineers (Corps) heated up during the 1930s, with the BOR building Boulder (later renamed Hoover) Dam, the Central Valley Project, and the Grand Coulee Dam and the Corps building Bonneville Dam and planning the Columbia River drainage (White 1993).

The 1940s through the 1960s was the golden age of reclamation, as the BOR and the Corps raced to dam the free-flowing rivers of the West. The BOR-produced and federally subsidized water sold for far less than it cost to produce. The BOR redefined its task as getting appropriations from Congress and building dams. It did not care who benefited from the dams. It chose not to fight for either acreage limitations or public power when such crusades brought powerful enemies into the field against it and could thus compromise its ability to build more dams. Arizona senator Carl Hayden became the BOR's congressional champion, but it was BOR director Floyd Dominy who pulled the strings. Under Dominy, the BOR perfected its technique of providing supporters with money for projects and denying their enemies (those who dared question the utility and made an issue of the environmental consequences of BOR projects). As its power grew, its projects grew more grandiose, while the actual benefits became more dubious (White 1993).

By the early twentieth century, the BOR had decided to concentrate less on the arid Great Basin and more on the profitable core of western agriculture: the California valleys, which were already populated. The product of this reclamation effort was the development of the Imperial Valley in inland southern California. The Imperial Irrigation District came into being in 1911 and was fought over between local farmers and the BOR. The district eventually came to be monopolized by hired administrators; largely immune to individual farmers' needs, it became a quasi-private agency run by a local elite. In 1919, the Imperial Irrigation District formed a partnership with the BOR to develop the Colorado River (via the All-American Canal). This led to the Colorado River Compact, which eventually led to the construction of Boulder Dam. It was coordinated group action like this that made California the main recipient of reclamation activity, but by the Great Depression of the 1930s, many saw that reclamation and agriculture in California did not lead to an egalitarian society but a pronounced system of class relations and exploitation (Worster 1985).

Much of the water in northern California was needed to help irrigate the state's Central Valley, which, like much of the West, is susceptible to cycles of deluge and drought.

Santa Barbara Oil Spill

On January 28, 1969, an oil-production well owned by the Union Oil Company suffered a blowout in the Santa Barbara Channel, approximately six miles off of the California coast. In the nearly two weeks that it took to stop the spill, more than 200,000 gallons of oil was released. The resulting oil slick fouled more than 150 miles of California's coastline and killed thousands of birds and marine mammals.

The environmental disaster drew national media coverage. Public outrage was fueled by video footage of suffering wildlife covered in oil. The event galvanized the environmental movement, which called for changes in the regulation of the oil industry's offshore drilling operations. The state of California responded to the demands by creating a Coastal Commission in 1972. On the national level, the Santa Barbara oil spill was partially credited with the passage of the National Environmental Policy Act of 1969. The event was also pivotal to the passage of the 1978 amendments to the Outer Continental Shelf Lands Act of 1953.

—John R. Burch Jr.

See also: *National Environmental Policy Act of 1969*

BIBLIOGRAPHY
Freudenburg, William R. *Oil in Troubled Waters: Perceptions, Politics, and the Battle over Offshore Drilling.* Albany: State University of New York Press, 1994.

Before the construction of projects like Hetch Hetchy, underground wells were seen as insufficient to allow the Central Valley to meet its agricultural potential. The need for and rise of technology behind underground well drilling in the Central Valley forced small farmers out and enhanced the position of larger landowners. However, in the 1930s, the BOR used federal money to create the Central Valley Project (CVP) and the Central Valley Authority (CVA) to manage water there, which saved agriculture in the Central Valley and created electricity through Shasta Dam. The Newlands Act allowed the BOR to get Congress to allocate the money, but the Act's provision on acreage limitation created problems for the Central Valley and the CVA, as they were already dominated by large landowners. However, the end of World War II and the end of the tenure of Franklin D. Roosevelt's interior secretary, Harold Ickes, opened the way for the acreage provisions to be ignored in the Central Valley. The success of the CVP gave the BOR new power in the region, which it would use to promote the development of large-scale farming for the next twenty years. By that the end of the period, though, the Westlands Project (the southern part of the CVP) had become a case study in what happens when arid western

Saint Francis Dam Failure

The Los Angeles Department of Water and Power constructed the Saint Francis Dam in San Francisquito Canyon, California, from 1924 to 1926. On March 12, 1928, the dam lifted off of its foundation and collapsed, releasing more than 38,000 acre-feet of water into the Santa Clara Valley. More than 400 people were killed or injured by the floodwaters.

In the aftermath of the disaster, William Mulholland accepted the blame. He had selected the site for the dam in a locale that was geologically unstable. He also designed the curved concrete gravity dam. Since Mulholland was a city employee, Los Angeles also took responsibility. It spent $13.5 million to repair the Santa Clara Valley's infrastructure and paid more than $5 million to compensate the injured and the families of the dead.

—John R. Burch Jr.

See also: *Mulholland, William*

BIBLIOGRAPHY

Hundley, Norris, Jr. *The Great Thirst: Californians and Water; A History.* Rev. ed. Berkeley: University of California Press, 2001.
Mulholland, Catherine. *William Mulholland and the Rise of Los Angeles.* Berkeley: University of California Press, 2000.
Nichols, John. *St. Francis Dam Disaster.* Chicago: Arcadia Publishing, 2002.

built since the turn of the twentieth century) have interfered with the spawning grounds of certain salmon species.

However, irrigation in the Pacific Northwest is largely a late twentieth-century phenomenon. Once agriculture had recovered from its post–World War I slump, the effort to irrigate the inland Pacific Northwest began in earnest. By the early 1920s, boosters were pushing for the construction of a Columbia Basin Project. The Herbert Hoover administration was on board with the construction of the Grand Coulee Dam by the late 1920s, although large-scale development would not start until the influx of federal money from the Depression-era programs of the 1930s. The project of irrigating the inland Pacific Northwest fit the Franklin D. Roosevelt administration's twin goals of providing jobs to large numbers of the unemployed and facilitating irrigated agriculture. The dam was completed in 1941, and irrigation began in 1948. From the time of its construction to 1990, the dam's other aim, hydroelectric power, had generated some $40 billion (Rowley 2006).

lands are overirrigated. Salination made much of the irrigated lands useless—a harbinger of things to come for many other western irrigation projects.

Further north, the largest river of the Pacific Northwest, the Columbia, was needed as much for power as it was for agriculture. Reclamation efforts aimed at fulfilling both goals would turn the Columbia River Basin, which dominates the region, from a free-flowing river in the 1920s into what historian Richard White called an "organic machine" (White 1996). Even though the water supply in the western half of the region is abundant, it still has been the recipient of large-scale BOR and Corps development efforts. The Grand Coulee Dam, the second largest BOR project of the twentieth century, was built to provide irrigation to farmers in the West, but it also generated electricity to help offset the cost of the water (Reisner 1986). East of the Cascades, irrigation is just as necessary for agriculture as it is in California. Even in western Washington State, irrigation is needed during the summer months. However, an additional concern related to damming the rivers of the Pacific Northwest is the success of salmon, a significant resource protected by numerous treaties with Indian tribes. Water shortages, along with extensive damming (over 300 dams

Although the Pacific Coast region has, possibly, the most diverse set of ecosystems in the United States, much less the American West, irrigation is a constant. Whether in the relatively wet Pacific Northwest or the semiarid Central Valley of California, the landscape has been transformed by the irrigation efforts of the twentieth century. Only in the late twentieth and early twenty-first century has the wisdom of those efforts been questioned on a large scale. The Pacific coast region is not immune to the effort to remove dams and restore free-flowing rivers. Perhaps if that happens, many of the salmon runs will be restored, and many of the treaties with Indian tribes that have long been ignored by the federal government will be honored.

—Steven L. Danver

See also: *Dam Building; Urbanization; Wells*

BIBLIOGRAPHY

Fernald, Gordon H., Jr. "Water Resources of the Pacific Northwest." *Journal (Water Pollution Control Federation)* 36, no. 10 (1964): 1225–28.
Hundley, Norris, Jr. *The Great Thirst: Californians and Water, 1770s–1990s.* Berkeley: University of California Press, 1992.

Hundley, Norris, Jr. *Water and the West: The Colorado River Compact and the Politics of Water in the American West.* Berkeley: University of California Press, 1975.

McCool, Daniel. *Command of the Waters: Iron Triangles, Federal Water Development, and Indian Water.* Tucson: University of Arizona Press, 1987.

Pisani, Donald J. *From the Family Farm to Agribusiness: The Irrigation Crusade in California and the West, 1850–1931.* Berkeley: University of California Press, 1984.

Pisani, Donald J. *To Reclaim a Divided West: Water, Law, and Public Policy, 1848–1902.* Albuquerque: University of New Mexico Press, 1992.

Pitzer, Paul C. "The World Commission on Dams: A Case Study on Grand Coulee Dam and the Columbia River Basin Project; Process and Lessons Learned." In *The Bureau of Reclamation: History Essays from the Centennial Symposium Volumes I and II,* edited by Brit Allan Storey, 801–24. Denver, CO: U.S. Bureau of Reclamation, 2008. Available at http://www.usbr.gov/history/Symposium_2008/Historical_Essays.pdf.

Powell, John Wesley. *The Arid Lands.* Edited by Wallace Stegner. Lincoln: University of Nebraska Press, 2004.

Reisner, Marc. *Cadillac Desert: The American West and Its Disappearing Water.* New York: Viking, 1986.

Rowley, William D. *The Bureau of Reclamation: Origins and Growth to 1945.* Denver, CO: U.S. Bureau of Reclamation, 2006.

Smyth, William Ellsworth. *The Conquest of Arid America.* Seattle: University of Washington Press, 1969.

Sowards, Adam. *United States West Coast: An Environmental History.* Santa Barbara, CA: ABC-CLIO, 2007.

Stegner, Wallace. *Beyond the Hundredth Meridian: John Wesley Powell and the Second Opening of the West.* New York: Penguin, 1954.

White, Richard. *It's Your Misfortune and None of My Own: A New History of the American West.* Norman: University of Oklahoma Press, 1993.

White, Richard. *The Organic Machine: The Remaking of the Columbia River.* New York: Hill and Wang, 1996.

Wilkinson, Charles. *Crossing the Next Meridian: Land, Water, and the Future of the American West.* Washington, DC: Island Press, 1992.

Worster, Donald. *Rivers of Empire: Water, Aridity, and the Growth of the American West.* New York: Oxford University Press, 1985.

South

The United States used 148 trillion gallons of water in 2000, half a million gallons per person. Average rainfall in the Southeast is 50 inches a year, and both the Atlantic Ocean and Gulf of Mexico are good storm generators. Most precipitation in the Southeast comes in spring and summer from rain. There is little winter precipitation and only a small amount of snow to run off and fill the reservoirs. A single tropical storm can replenish the water supply lost to a drought, but that lasts only until the next drought. Drought is expected to be the South's future. Climatologists predict that the Southeast will continue to experience recurring drought as part of its natural climate pattern, and droughts

should become more severe with the passing of time and global warming.

America has water. The problem is that the water is where the people are not. For half a century, Americans have moved away from the water and toward the desert. More went to the West, but the South attracted those following factory jobs coming from the North. Current patterns of growth and development, says Brian Fuchs of the National Drought Mitigation Center, may not be sustainable.

In November 2007, Orme, Tennessee, ran out of water. Each evening at 6:00, the mayor went to the town water tower and turned a valve that released water for three hours—three hours in which the 145 residents took care of all water-related chores. Previously, the hamlet in Tennessee's mountains had enjoyed abundant water from a waterfall and the town creek, but the drought ran both dry. Three days a week, in the wee hours, the volunteer fire chief and another driver hauled 20,000 gallons of water from a hydrant in New Hope, Alabama, to Orme. This water allowed the three hours for showers, bottling drinking water, washing clothes, cooking supper, and washing dishes. The hamlet spends $8,000 on water from an annual budget of only $13,000. A grant from the U.S. Department of Agriculture for $377,590 allowed the laying of a pipe two and a half miles to Bridgeport, Alabama, which had water.

Clean Water

Not all of the South is short on water, but water is a source of conflict nonetheless. In Tennessee, the state legislature and environmentalists were at odds in May 2009, with the environmentalists contending that pending legislation would weaken clean water laws and give too much to coal companies, developers, and road builders. One bill would change the method of measuring selenium levels. Selenium is common at coal mine and coal ash sites, and the U.S. Environmental Protection Agency (EPA) credits it with causing deformities and poisoning fish and other aquatic life. Mining interests argue that the more lenient standard rests on newer science and is necessary to save jobs. The Tennessee standard for selenium is the 1987 EPA guideline. The proposal is to use 2004 draft guidelines not yet recommended by the EPA. The 1987 standard measures content in the water, while the 2004 draft guidelines measure the amount in fish tissue. The Tennessee Mining Association likes the latter and maintains that technology is unavailable to clean the extremely low amount of selenium currently causing

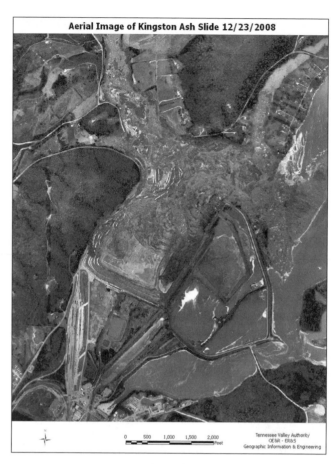

In December 2008, a dam holding back millions of cubic yards of coal ash, a by-product of coal-burning energy plants, broke at the Kingston Fossil Plant in Tennessee. Millions of gallons of coal ash sludge flooded the neighboring area, including the nearby Emory River. The Tennessee Valley Authority, owner of the power plant, expected that cleanup would cost approximately $1.2 billion.

Tennessee Valley Authority

a violation. The U.S. Fish and Wildlife Service, U.S. Geological Survey, and many scientists found that the 2004 draft had basic scientific flaws, with one Wake Forest University scientist claiming that the new standard would allow poisoning of up to 85 percent of fish and waterfowl.

A second bill before the Tennessee legislature, the Wet Weather Conveyance and Stream Determination Protocol Act of 2009, created a new definition of what is a stream in that state. Much of the language came from the Tennessee Responsible Water Coalition, which included the Home Builders Association of Tennessee, Tennessee Road Builders Association, Tennessee Mining Association, Farm Bureau, and Tennessee Chamber of Commerce and Industry.

Water in Appalachia is a mining resource, as well as an environmental disaster waiting to happen when it is mixed with coal ash to form sludge. In 2008, at Kingston, Tennessee, a wall at the Tennessee Valley Authority (TVA) power plant's

pond failed, and 500 million gallons of sludge poured from the 80-acre coal pond into the local area. The sludge, 6 feet deep in areas, damaged homes and over 400 acres of land, forced an evacuation, and threatened the Clinch River, a tributary of the Tennessee River. The spill was larger than the 1989 *Exxon Valdez* oil spill. The fly ash in the sludge contained benzene, arsenic, and mercury. In March 2009, the TVA was repairing roads and dredging rivers but had not yet decided where to relocate the 5.4 million cubic yards of coal ash that had spilled into the Emory and Clinch Rivers as well as onto 300 acres of eastern Tennessee.

Environmentalists were not impressed with the TVA commitment to give medical attention to those claiming to be affected by the contamination. The environmentalists noted that there were no federal regulations or inspections of such sites; if there had been, they believed, the accident probably would not have occurred. Environmentalists were also skeptical of TVA reports that samples of air and water showed compliance with standards and that heavy metals were below the standard for hazardous waste. United Mountain Defense indicated it would take its own samples and run its own tests. The TVA said that it was safe to engage in water sports away from the spill, but environmentalists contended that the entire Emory and Clinch Rivers were unsafe because of high levels of heavy metals. Eight years earlier, in eastern Kentucky, a sludge pond had failed when its bottom fell out, and 300 million gallons of waste had leaked into an abandoned underground mine and, eventually, into rivers and streams that provided the water supply for over 25,000 people. The Kingston spill was at least 50 percent larger.

Scarce Water

Atlanta's Coca-Cola advertises at its website that it will "REDUCE, RECYCLE, REPLENISH" and will use only a liter of water for each liter of product it makes. The goal is water neutrality. The company currently uses 1.77 liters of water per liter of product generated.

During the 2007 drought, 145 people in Orme were out of water; in Atlanta, the number was 4.5 million. The Intergovernmental Panel on Climate Change reported in 2007 that the Southeast should expect continuing water problems in the future. Water shortages will have a serious impact on the economy, and conflict will arise over who gets how much, how, and when. In 2003, a government report indicated that thirty-six states anticipated local or statewide shortages of water in the coming decade. In 2007, the government reiterated that thirty-six states or more would be short of water within five years. The drought raised the number to forty-six. The shortfall in water supplies was due to urban sprawl, rising temperatures, drought, population increase, extravagance, and waste. The solution, experts said, was planning, including conservation, recycling, desalination, and tighter controls on development. The cost of upgrading pipes to handle new demand was estimated at $300 billion over thirty years. Cheap water was a thing of the past.

Coastal states, including Florida, face greater loss of water to evaporation as temperatures rise, and higher seas might force saltwater into coastal underground supplies of freshwater. In May 2009, Miami-Dade County recorded the highest ever saltwater concentration in its monitoring wells. During the same period, marshy areas on the western edge of Miami-Dade, Palm Beach, and Broward counties became

totally dry; those areas could not turn to Lake Okeechobee for relief because its water level of 10.63 feet above sea level was too low for it to serve as a water source. Several areas—Lake Worth, Dania Beach, and Hallandale Beach—had already been limited to once-weekly irrigation for several years because of the salt risk. Wells in the Keys showed salt at thirty times normal concentrations.

The low water level meant that the freshwater buffer was a fourth of the desired level. Thus, well fields and Everglades marshes were at increasing risk from saltwater contamination from Biscayne Bay. Environmentalists and district scientists wanted pulse releases from Lake Okeechobee down the Caloosahatchee River to protect the sea grasses in the estuary, with a one-third-inch drop in the lake level. Others countered that the water, if the drought continued, would be needed to protect water wells in the Keys, Homestead, and Florida City.

For six months, the area was without rainfall, and farmers who used Okeechobee water had their supply halved. The sixteen counties from Orlando to Key West were all near record lows, but south Miami-Dade was hit the worst, with a limit of once-weekly sprinkling. Nonetheless, the water management district ordered no new suburban restrictions, continuing the limit on sprinkling of twice a week and hoping for rain to get the lake to an adequate level. Rescue by rainfall was projected to take into the next year unless rains hit record levels.

A century before, Florida had too much water, but over the decades it had built dikes and dams and canals and made swamps into urban areas. By the turn of the twenty-first century, it had paved over areas where, previously, absorption would have replenished the aquifers. Florida was short of places to store water during wet seasons, which forced it to discharge millions of gallons of freshwater into the ocean to reduce flooding. Hundreds of billions of gallons of treated wastewater went into the Atlantic annually, water that could have been used for irrigation. The state's environmental chief wanted a law requiring cities to reuse the wastewater they sent through pipes into the ocean, because doing so would be cheaper than building new water treatment plants. Florida reuses 240 billion gallons of water a year, the most of any state in the United States, but that is not enough. Floridians use 2.4 trillion gallons of freshwater a year and an unknown amount of treated or desalinated water. With a projected population increase of 34 percent, from 18 to 24 million people, annual freshwater demand will eventually near

New Orleans Levee Failure

Hurricane Katrina struck Louisiana and Mississippi as a Category 3 storm on August 29, 2005. New Orleans' flood-control system was compromised during the storm as a number of levees failed, allowing waters from Lake Pontchartrain to flood significant portions of the city.

The levee failures were largely blamed on shoddy construction by the U.S. Army Corps of Engineers. The levees were built on soil that was too soft to support the concrete levees when they were stressed by floodwaters. This design flaw was compounded by pilings that were too short.

In the aftermath of the disaster, the U.S. Army Corps of Engineers began repairing and upgrading New Orleans' flood-control system. Critics noted that the planned upgrades were not sufficient for the city to withstand a direct blow from a Category 3 hurricane. The levee failures also forced upgrades to flood control systems around the United States.

—John R. Burch Jr.

See also: *Army Corps of Engineers, United States; Levees*

BIBLIOGRAPHY

Brinkley, Douglas. *The Great Deluge: Hurricane Katrina, New Orleans, and the Mississippi Gulf Coast.* New York: HarperCollins, 2006.

Van Heerden, Ivor, and Mike Bryan. *The Storm: What Went Wrong and Why During Hurricane Katrina; The Inside Story from One Louisiana Scientist.* New York: Viking, 2006.

Competing Demands

Atlanta and other Sunbelt cities are made possible by the car, the air conditioner, and a former-Yankee aversion to cold and ice. Warmth and sunshine attracted consumers of water in large numbers, and the resulting water shortages have disturbed the environment. Personal and political resource competition has generated lawsuits, restrictions on water use, and rivers overstrained and damaged by the disruption of their natural cycles.

As of January 2008, Georgia was in its worst drought in 100 years. Lake Lanier, the source of Atlanta's water supply, was fifteen feet below normal and receding to nothingness. In response, the state limited lawn watering and car washing and turned off its outdoor fountains.

Lake Lanier was built by the U.S. Army Corps of Engineers in the 1950s to prevent flooding in Atlanta and points downstream, not to supply Atlanta's drinking water. Atlanta is on the Eastern Continental Divide, so water naturally flows away from it. Its watershed is the smallest of any major metropolitan area, insufficient to handle over 5 million people. Lanier's drainage basin is only 1,040 square miles. The Corps regulates flooding by controlled release into the Chattahoochee River, which runs through Atlanta, along the Georgia-Alabama state line, and then to the Florida panhandle, where it drains into the Gulf of Mexico.

Lake Lanier water supplies towns, farms, factories, recreational facilities, and power plants by the hundreds on its way to the Gulf. It has also become the chief source of water for the 5.4 million people of the Atlanta metropolitan area. Since the reservoir was built, the state's population has grown from 4 to 10 million, and metro Atlanta grew from 1 to over 5 million. When Atlanta went through a drought in the 1980s, it had a million fewer people than it does now. Thus, it had enough Lake Lanier water to get by. Georgia's population growth is presently 200,000 per year.

Georgia, Alabama, and Florida have been in court against the Corps for nearly twenty years. Atlanta, Florida, and Alabama share the same watershed, with Atlanta to the north and thus upstream on the Chattahoochee. Joining the Flint River, the Chattahoochee becomes the Apalachicola, a river flowing through the Florida panhandle. Water taken by

3.3 trillion gallons. Complicating the situation is the fact that more than half of the new population, approximately 3 million people, will be in the three-county area encompassing Miami, Palm Beach, and Fort Lauderdale. Consumption there is already 1.5 trillion gallons a year. The South Florida Water Management District director said that the area had exhausted its major water sources. Many of the 1,000 desalination plants in the United States are in the Sunbelt. The $158 million plant in Tampa Bay, the largest in North America, produces 25 million gallons of drinking water a day, but that is only 10 percent of demand.

The TVA did not stop the drought in its area, but it did ameliorate it significantly. Customarily awash in water thanks to dams built in the 1930s for electricity and flood control, the TVA area had adequate amounts during the drought. TVA customers take 12 billion gallons of river water daily. About 94 percent of water taken from the Tennessee River is returned for reuse. Eighty-four percent of water is used for cooling power plants, and 99 percent of this water is returned to the river. Industry takes 10 percent, public water 5 percent, and irrigation 1 percent.

Atlanta upstream is unavailable downstream in Alabama and Florida. The result is a water crisis involving three states. In 2003, Georgia got the Corps to increase Atlanta's share by 65 percent. The request of Atlanta and Georgia, while pending at the federal level, brought out attorneys, environmentalists, businesspeople, government, and others with a vested interest in the outcome. Alabama's governor labeled the deal a "massive water grab," and a federal court overturned the decision. The dispute continued, and Georgians blamed the delay on official foot dragging. The director of Upper Chattahoochee Riverkeepers contended that leaders were refusing to face the need for more efficient use.

For Floridians, the issue is not one of conflict between wildlife and people but between a wasteful, overgrown Atlanta and a rural lifestyle along the river. The Corps has to release water from Lake Lanier periodically to safeguard ecosystems in accord with the Endangered Species Act. In 2007, with only eighty-one days of water left and Georgia heading into its driest month, Georgians were already restricting their use of water (but only after decades of limited planning and unrestricted growth), and the legislature decided to act. Proposed laws would suspend compliance with the Endangered Species Act and halt water releases. The Corps opposed the legislation. Florida wanted more water, not less, to protect biodiversity, and Alabama wanted more as well to ease its shortage.

The Apalachicola is the source of a living for farmers and fishermen in the Florida panhandle. Without the annual river flood, the oyster beds are salty enough to attract saltwater predators, and young oysters in normally low-salinity beds are taken by stone crabs and German conches. Florida oyster harvesters whose families have harvested oysters for generations were displeased. They regarded Georgians as wastrels who had not even made token conservation efforts, instead building the Atlanta metro area as fast as possible and demanding more and more water.

In October 2007, the Corps wanted to release Lanier water into the Apalachicola to protect at-risk sturgeon and mussels. This proposal led Georgia governor Sonny Perdue to seek a court order, arguing that people were more valuable

Gulf of Mexico Oil Spill

The Deepwater Horizon, an oil rig being used by British Petroleum (BP) in the Gulf of Mexico to explore an oil field one mile under the surface of the ocean, exploded on April 20, 2010. The accident resulted in the death of eleven members of the 126-person crew and the fracturing of the pipes used by BP to extract oil, thereby spilling approximately 5 million barrels of crude oil into the Gulf of Mexico. Initial efforts to stem the flow of oil over the first five weeks of the disaster met with failure. Oil contaminated the shores of Louisiana, Mississippi, Alabama, and Florida. The fishing, shrimping, and tourism industries in affected areas will be negatively impacted for decades. There are also concerns about the environmental impact of the more than 1 million gallons of toxic chemical dispersants that have been used to fight the spread of oil. Oil erupted into the Gulf of Mexico until mid-July 2010, when a cap was finally developed to staunch virtually all of the flow. On August 5, 2010, a permanent solution known as the "static kill" was completed, which poured cement on top of drilling mud that had been inserted days earlier. As a precautionary measure, two relief wells were used to pump even more mud and cement into the well, and on September 19, five months after it had exploded, the well was declared truly "dead."

—John R. Burch Jr.

BIBLIOGRAPHY

British Petroleum. "Gulf of Mexico Response." http://www.bp.com/extendedsection genericarticle.do?categoryId=40&contentId=7061813.
CNN. "Gulf Coast Oil Disaster." http://www.cnn.com/SPECIALS/2010/gulf.coast.oil.spill/.
Deepwater Horizon Unified Command. RestoreTheGulf.gov. http://www.restorethe gulf.gov/.

than mussels and sturgeon. The Corps agreed to cut back the flow 16 percent, and the governor withdrew his request.

Atlantans countered that they had mandatory bans on lawn watering, outdoor fountains, and car washing. The water district also offered residents vouchers for the purchase of low-flow toilets. On the other hand, real estate pressure killed a bill that would have required retrofitting of older houses with modern plumbing prior to putting them on the market. Georgians blamed the Corps for both not storing enough water in the reservoirs and for releasing too much into the Apalachicola. When Governor Perdue ordered north Georgians to reduce water use by 10 percent, he also indicated that there would be no enforcement. Had he admitted that conservation was necessary, he would have been admitting that Atlanta had overgrown its resources. That would have been political suicide. The in-migration continues.

Planning—or Politics?

In the midst of the 2007 drought, in November, Georgia governor Sonny Perdue led 250 people on the capitol steps

The 2010 BP oil spill off the coast of the Gulf of Mexico was the worst American spill in history. In this May 2010 photo, oil has been corralled and is being burned off.

MC2 Justin Stumberg/Dept. of Defense

in a prayer for rain. The next day rain fell in the area, and rains were consistent for the next two months. With the return of rain to north Georgia and the Southeast, Birmingham, Alabama, reported its reservoir at near normal for the first time in nearly a year. Rainfall year to date was 12.09 inches, close to the average 12.78, and some Alabama farmers were reporting it was too wet to plant. North Carolina declared thirty-nine previously identified counties no longer in the most severe category of drought. The chief of the Atlanta Regional Commission's environmental planning arm declared the drought over, even though the reservoir was still five feet below normal. With the drought in the past, the next step was to settle the disputes over water, some old and some new, that had to be resolved if the regional economy and population were to continue growing.

The Southeast historically has had no concern about having enough water, so the drought and shortages are a new situation. Historically, southerners endured a drought, then reverted to their water-flush habits. Optimists were hoping that the most recent drought would cause an awareness of

water scarcity and a long-term commitment to wise use. The region needed an attitude adjustment.

At stake was development into one of the ten U.S. mega regions. To handle it, the area needed a regional water plan, a way of managing watersheds that cross state lines equitably. San Diego was finishing its driest summer ever, with fall wildfires complicating matters; calls were being made for San Diegans to replace grass with succulents and cacti. The western governors had signed a water-sharing compact. Probably the southeastern governors should do the same. Georgia, Florida, and Alabama were negotiating a potential agreement.

New Mexico's governor called for a national water policy, with the northern states sharing their abundant water with the water-shy Sunbelt. He also wanted state-to-state discussions on conservation, reuse, delivery, and production of water. In April 2009, the House of Representatives passed H.R. 1145, the National Water Research and Development Act of 2009, which sought better federal performance in research, development, data collection, and dissemination with the goal of changing national water use, supply, and demand. The bill to begin the rudiments of a national water policy went to the Senate. The Recovery Act of 2009 put $4 billion into the Clean Water State Revolving Fund Programs (CWSRF) and $2 billion into the Drinking Water State Revolving Fund Programs (DWSRF), while also authorizing 20 percent to go to green infrastructure, energy and water efficiency, and other environmentally creative programs. It required no state match, waiving the customary 20 percent.

The TVA in late 2007 had been changing its water transfer policies, but not to make it easier for non-TVA areas to get TVA water. The TVA claimed it was not acting in response to Atlanta's effort to get Tennessee River water piped south. Atlanta subsequently dropped the idea of appropriating waters from the TVA. Experts regarded interbasin transfers as a risk to the system, and one pointed out that taking water from one system and giving it to another just created two systems with water shortages during drought. The TVA, by federal rule, has to give priority to its seven-state region. The interbasin policy had been reviewed in 2005, but the drought occasioned a new review of all TVA policies. In 2005, the TVA water supply manager was leery of pipeline transfers because water diverted that way rarely came back to the system. Also in 2005, Alabama counties served by the TVA outlawed pipeline transfers from their territory. Water transfers to the south would have affected TVA users as far north as Virginia.

In March 2008, Lake Lanier was still ten feet below normal. The dispute over the cause of the drop continued, with Atlanta blaming the Corps for mismanaging the reservoir and the Corps countering that it was a lack of rainfall.

In South Carolina, the state was preparing to spend upwards of $3 million in legal fees over three years in its dispute with North Carolina over North Carolina's Concord and Kannapolis Rivers taking millions of gallons from the Catawba River each day.

Georgia's establishment of a commission to work on moving the border with Tennessee 1.1 miles north was an attempt to take part of the Tennessee River. Georgia claimed the current border was a surveyor's mistake in 1818. The Tennessee governor's office noted that both states had problems with water and drought and moving the border would solve nothing.

Meanwhile, despite forecasts for additional rain, the National Drought Mitigation Center reported that the drought was less intense but still in effect. Several months

more of rain would be necessary to end the drought. Perdue's gimmick and the rain were not enough. The Southeast was in its worst drought in a century, and water disputes among states and between cities and rural areas would continue in an area accustomed to abundant to excessive water.

In 2001, George W. Bush had tried to get Canadian water piped to Texas, but the effort failed. In 2008, when Rep. John Linder (R-GA) tried to get a national water use policy, two of Michigan's legislators read it as an attempt to grab northern water for the south. The 2005 Great Lakes–Saint Lawrence River Basin Water Resources Compact banned all large-scale transfers of water from the basin, but as of 2008, it had not been ratified by all eight affected legislatures, after which it still had to pass Congress. The goal was to get it ratified before 2012, when the Southwest was expected to gain eight more congressional seats as the Midwest lost eight. The last reapportionment had cost every Great Lakes state except Minnesota congressional seats, while water-poor states such as Georgia, Texas, and Arizona gained seats.

Local squabbles and overlapping jurisdictions hamstrung solutions to water shortages. In 2009, the Charlottesville-Albemarle, Virginia, fifty-year water plan was almost finished after local, state, and federal agencies had agreed to enlarge the Ragged Mountain Reservoir by raising the dam there. An opposing group called for dredging the South Fork Rivanna Reservoir instead. They contended that preliminary engineering studies at the site of the proposed dam expansion revealed fractured bedrock, a problem that would increase the cost of raising the dam significantly. The dredging advocates also alleged that official studies exaggerated the cost of their proposal. Dredgers claimed that the dam costs were enough to justify abandoning that approach in favor of dredging, but dam proponents claimed that even with higher costs, the dam was the more reliable long-term solution to water needs

Charlottesville was leaning toward dredging because several of the dredging advocates lived there. The city council joined the fray by endorsing the request for a dredging study. The Rivanna Water & Sewer Authority (RWSA) subsequently agreed to join too, but only if Charlottesville paid the bulk of the cost. The Albemarle County Service Authority (ACSA), the water and sewer provider for the county, committed to paying the portion of the study that dealt with general interest matters such as stream flow and other data that might justify building a forebay to block sedimentation of the reservoir. The ACSA was unwilling to pay for studies that might warrant undoing the dam-lifting agreement.

Even the multistate TVA had no water use policy. Each member state was responsible for making a policy; nonetheless, Alabama had no statewide plan in 2007. The dispute among Georgia, Florida, and Alabama over apportionment of the water of six rivers lasted eighteen years before the three states made a deal—which quickly fell apart. Since the states could not reach another agreement by a self-imposed deadline in 2008, the Corps inherited the job of allocating the water. The Corps opted to give the respective states another three years to come to an arrangement. Otherwise, a sharing plan would be imposed in 2011 for the Alabama, Coosa, Tallapoosa, Apalachicola, Chattahoochee, and Flint Rivers.

Hugh McDiarmid Jr., representing the Michigan Environmental Council, was unsympathetic to the plight of the southerners, saying that suffering Sunbelters could cure their woes by moving to Michigan. Cleveland, Ohio, and Syracuse, New York, are potential destinations too. All three cities share a common virtue—they are located next to 6 quadrillion gallons of water, nearly 20 percent of the earth's freshwater supply.

William Frey, an expert on U.S. migration, anticipates a reverse migration from the South to the Midwest and North because of southern water problems. Before that happens, the old cities would have to rework their economies and their waterfronts, which are built around rusted factories.

—John H. Barnhill

See also: *Climate Change; Drought; Urbanization; Wastewater Treatment*

BIBLIOGRAPHY

Associated Press. "Crisis Feared as U.S. Water Supplies Dry Up: Government Projects at Least 36 States Will Face Shortages within Five Years." *MSNBC.com,* October 27, 2007. Available at http://www.msnbc.msn.com/id/21494919/.

Associated Press. "Tennessee Town Runs Out of Water in Southeast Drought." *FoxNews.com,* November 1, 2007. Available at http://www.foxnews.com/story/0,2933,307437,00.html.

Barnett, Cynthia. *Mirage: Florida and the Vanishing Water of the Eastern U.S.* Ann Arbor: University of Michigan Press, 2008.

Copeland, Larry. "Drought Eases, Water Wars Persist." *USA Today,* March 18, 2008. Available at http://www.usatoday.com/news/nation/environment/2008-03-17-water-wars_N.htm.

Ellington, M. J. "TVA Plans Changes in Water Transfer Policy." *Decatur (TN) Daily,* December 5, 2007. Available at http://www.decaturdaily.com/stories/1104.html.

EPA (U.S. Environmental Protection Agency), Region 6. "Recovery Funding for Clean Water and Drinking Water Infrastructure: Putting People to Work for Clean, Safe Drinking Water and a Cleaner Environment." http://www.epa.gov/region6/eparecovery/cleanwater6.htm.

McClelland, Edward. "How to Solve America's Water Problems." *Salon.com,* January 7, 2008. Available at http://www.salon.com/news/feature/2008/01/07/water_problems/.

Miami Herald. "South Florida Suburbs, Not Farms, Spared New Water Restrictions." May 15, 2009. Available at http://riverofgrasscoalition.org/article.php?id=south-florida-suburbs-not-farms-spared-new-water-restrictions-2009-05-15.

Mid-South Farmer. "Water Research and Development Act Passes House: House Approves Legislation to Improve Water Research." April 28, 2009. Available at http://midsouthfarmer.com/story.aspx?s=23186&c=8.

Shelburne, Anita. "Water Politics Are Muddied" (editorial). *Daily Progress,* May 20, 2009. Available at http://www2.dailyprogress.com/news/cdp-news-editorial/2009/may/20/water_politics_are_muddied-ar-88297/.

Simone, Samira J. "Tennessee Sludge Spill Runs Over Homes, Water." *CNN.com,* December 24, 2008. Available at http://www.cnn.com/2008/US/12/23/tennessee.sludge.spill/.

Wigder, David. "Drought Can Spark a National Dialogue on Climate Change—Part II." *Marketing Green* (blog), October 20, 2007. Available at http://marketinggreen.wordpress.com/2007/10/20/drought-can-spark-a-national-dialogue-on-climate-change-part-ii/.

Southwest

Although much of the North American continent west of the 100th meridian is arid, the southwestern corner of the United States is by far the driest. Here, water is a lifeline in short supply and currently stretched to its limits. During the nineteenth and twentieth centuries, indigenous peoples were gradually removed and confined to reservations, and both agricultural and metropolitan areas developed and grew. What was once considered a "great American desert" soon supported a growing population through locally and federally funded water reclamation. In the early years of the twenty-first century, however, the American Southwest struggles with competing goals regarding water.

In recent decades, it has become obvious that most of the water resources in the Southwest are both completely developed and overallocated. Users of the Colorado River, for example, have argued and litigated over shares of its water for nearly a century. These arguments seem settled for now, as long as enough water runs in the river. Other major water sources in the region face similar challenges as Indian communities seek water rights to which they are legally entitled but are allocated to others. Population growth in major metropolitan areas of the Southwest has increased the need for water conservation; water users have responded, but more will have to occur. In short, the story of water in the Southwest is now one of reallocation, conservation, and innovation.

The region most often referred to as the Southwest generally consists of the states of California, Arizona, Nevada, Utah, Colorado, and New Mexico. The geography of these states varies from high mountains to deserts to coastal plains. This variation in topography means that the climate is also varied. In midsummer, high temperatures can range from 115-plus degrees (Fahrenheit) in the deserts to the low 70s or even cooler in the mountain ranges. January temperatures can reach below zero at the highest elevations or remain a pleasant 75 in the Valley of the Sun in Arizona.

Two distinct climate conditions dictate both temperature and precipitation in the Southwest. The first is a generally permanent, subtropical high-pressure system that keeps the region mostly dry and mild in temperature. When rain occurs in January or February, it mostly comes from large storms in the Pacific that generally make landfall on the coast of California. The second condition is the annual North American Monsoon. A monsoon is a cyclical change in wind direction of at least 120 degrees. When this change occurs, it often (but not always) brings precipitation. The North American Monsoon generally affects Mexico and the U.S. states of New Mexico and Arizona.

The major sources of water in the Southwest are from surface water (rivers and reservoirs) and groundwater in aquifers. There are generally three types of groundwater aquifers in the region: the sandstone aquifers of the Colorado Plateau, the volcanic rock aquifer in southern Nevada (and in northern California and central New Mexico), and the unconsolidated sand and gravel aquifers that underlie most of the Southwest. While most of these aquifers can be recharged with surface water, they have been overpumped and are still being drained. Surface water in the region is divided into seven watersheds: the San Joaquin, the Upper Colorado River Basin, the Lower Colorado Basin, the Arkansas-White-Red River, the Rio Grande, and the Great Basin. In these watershed areas, the few and relatively small-flow rivers and lakes provide the bulk of the Southwest water supply.

Two primary principles underpin water rights and water law in the United States: riparian and prior-appropriation water rights. In most of the United States east of the 100th meridian, riparian rights dominate water law. These rights are granted to landowners along the banks of a surface water source. In the West, however, prior appropriation is the basis of most water rights. This principle stipulates that the first to appropriate or use water has a right to it as long as the uses of this water are beneficial. Thus, "First in time, first in right," is often a phrase used to describe this water right. If a rights holder stops putting the water to beneficial use, then the water right is considered abandoned and can be appropriated by the next person with the earliest claim in time.

Early Water Use and Westward Expansion

Water history in the Southwest begins with indigenous peoples and their survival in an arid land. There were four major civilizations in the region prior to the arrival of the Spanish in the seventeenth century: the Hohokam, the Anasazi, the Mogollon, and the Patayan. All four groups practiced agriculture, mostly situating their fields along riverbanks or in floodplains. The Hohokam, however, began irrigating their fields using a system of canals in the Sonoran Desert between 300 and 500 CE. This large system of canals stretched hundreds of miles and used the water of the Gila and Salt Rivers in present-day Arizona. Sometime between 1350 and 1375, the Hohokam abandoned their canals and settlements, moving off to new places to be absorbed by other indigenous groups. While the cause of their disappearance is still debated, there are several plausible explanations. First, cataclysmic flooding could have destroyed canals and raised the riverbeds, requiring the extension of canals farther and farther upstream. Long-term, cyclical drought and soil damage from salinity are also real possibilities. Perhaps all of these causes, common to the Southwest, persuaded the Hohokam to migrate elsewhere.

The first nonindigenous people to see the Southwest were the Spanish conquistadors whom Coronado sent north to search for the fabled "seven cities of gold." The first written record of the Colorado River, for example, comes from Francisco de Ulloa, who explored part of the river's mouth at the Gulf of California in 1539. Sent by Hernán Cortés to explore the Pacific coast, he is credited with the drawings of the Baja Peninsula that made cartographers assume that California was an island.

A few other Spaniards explored the region just after Ulloa's expedition, including Melchior Díaz and García López de Cárdenas. The latter was the first nonindigenous person on record to view the Grand Canyon. After the 1540s, no other exploration of the region enters the records, but cartographers illustrated the region with various names

Mayordomo (Book)

Mayordomo recounts Stanley Crawford's experiences as the *mayordomo* (Spanish for "ditch boss") of one of New Mexico's more than 1,000 *acequias* from March 1985 to March 1986. The post was an elected position whose authority derived from traditions based on centuries-old Spanish law. Communities charged their *mayordomo* to oversee the maintenance and needed repairs of irrigation ditches, known locally as *acequias*. Crawford's responsibilities also required that he fairly distribute the waters of the Acequia de la Jara to a community split into two competing factions bent on controlling the water supply for agricultural purposes. Through the distrust and struggles evident within the otherwise closely knit Hispanic community, the author was able both to provide a detailed look at the day-to-day operations of an *acequia* and examine a community whose centuries-old culture and traditions were threatened by modern society and its natural resource requirements. Although the community had a water distribution system that had enabled generations of the community to subsist equitably, the passage of new water laws promised to end their way of life.

—John R. Burch Jr.

BIBLIOGRAPHY
Crawford, Stanley. *Mayordomo: Chronicle of an Acequia in Northern New Mexico.* Albuquerque: University of New Mexico Press, 1988.

and descriptions. In 1776, a Franciscan missionary named Silvestre Velez de Escalante recorded his trek across the Southwest and his encounter with the Grand Canyon and the Colorado River.

In the years that followed, the region remained largely unexplored and unmapped. Most maps of North America showed a large blank in the Southwest, with only a few notations and incorrect assumptions about California as being an island or a river that ran into a large, inland lake. Jesuit missionaries were sent by the Spanish government in Mexico to establish missions to the Indians in California, and during the seventeenth and eighteenth centuries, they built a string of these missions. While most of them were not self-sustaining, the Spanish used simple irrigation techniques along the major rivers and dug *acequias*, or aqueducts, throughout the region. Some of these canals are still evident today. The nonmissionary settlers on the *ranchos* of California and New Mexico mostly raised sheep and cattle and did not engage in much agriculture.

One of the first groups of Anglo-American settlers in the Southwest was the Mormons or Latter-day Saints. In 1830, Joseph Smith formally founded the Church of Jesus Christ of Latter-day Saints and soon encountered conflict with other Protestant groups. Moving first from upstate New York and then from Missouri, Smith and his successor, Brigham Young, decided the young church needed to separate itself from established society for its members to practice their religious beliefs freely. Thus in 1847, the Mormons began a migration to the Great Basin and established the present-day city of Salt Lake City, Utah. By the time the Transcontinental Railroad stretched across the country, more than 60,000 Mormons had settled in the desert.

To farm the dry land, the Mormons constructed a large network of irrigation ditches and canals. Tightly controlled by Brigham Young at the top, the Salt Lake community was organized according to wards, with each ward bishop in charge of water for his area. Using the basic principle of prior appropriation, the Mormons created what were essentially collective farms and water projects, with families assigned certain diversion dams and ditches to create and maintain. Each farmer cultivated and watered ten acres or less so that the community could use and share the water effectively. By 1865, the Mormons had created more than 1,000 miles of irrigation canals in the Great Basin. With firm control at the top and collective responsibility, the Mormons were able to make the desert bloom and dramatically increase their population to almost 300,000 by the turn of the twentieth century.

Elsewhere in the West, almost the same number of settlers made the difficult journey across the arid land via wagon train or ocean liner to California. This desirable paradise became part of the United States by the Treaty of Guadalupe-Hidalgo that ended the 1846–1848 war with Mexico. Forced to the peace table, Mexico agreed to cede its claim to the North American Southwest, including all of present-day California, Arizona, New Mexico, Utah, and Nevada. When gold was discovered in 1848 at Sutter's Mill, California rapidly filled with eager fortune hunters, propelling the territory to statehood in a little over one year. By the end of 1850, more than 100,000 people had migrated to California.

Although western migration and exploration were slowed by the outbreak of the American Civil War in 1861, the years that followed saw huge waves of migration westward across the Colorado River. A thirty-six-year-old Civil War veteran named John Wesley Powell became the next and perhaps last great explorer of the river. In 1869, he led an expedition down the Green River into the main body of the Colorado River, determined to explore the length of the Grand Canyon and complete the map of this great river. Against all odds, he and most of his men made it through alive to tell their stories. Powell led another expedition in 1871 and finally published detailed records and maps of the river after this journey.

In the years after his expeditions, Powell used his expertise as a geologist to work as director of the U.S. Geological Survey. In this position, he was responsible for further exploration, mapping, and planning for irrigation and land use. In 1878, Powell issued a report on the American West and his views of its needs and potentials. This landmark study was largely ignored at the time of its publication, but within it are the foundations of the reclamation projects of the twentieth century. Powell's main argument in this report was that the arid West would never succeed agriculturally without large-scale, government planning for the entire region. He asserted that individual farmers would seldom be able to construct the necessary irrigation infrastructure, nor could they afford its costs. He used the Mormons as an example of successful irrigation with a church organization to organize and fund irrigation projects. Powell believed that without this kind of structured planning, most of the western irrigable lands would never be utilized successfully.

Powell further argued that large water-storage reservoirs would have to be constructed in order to ensure adequate water supply year-round. In general, however, Powell's vision was one of yeoman farmers settling on homesteads and cooperating with others in creating water districts, which would conform to basic government laws for western water. Powell did not believe the arid West would support large-scale settlement. He warned against a lack of control and advocated strict laws on land allocations, land grants that were small enough to irrigate properly, and strong oversight of all water issues.

While few were interested in government support for western water projects when Powell wrote about his ideas, some were already beginning to see the potential for profit through irrigating the West. One such individual was Charles Rockwood, who saw enormous agricultural

potential in the region he later named Imperial Valley, if only it had water. In 1901, he and irrigation engineer George Chaffey dug a diversion canal to bring water from the Colorado River into a dry riverbed that ran into this valley. With rich soil and plenty of water, Imperial Valley soon filled with farmers eager to purchase land and participate in what would be a financial bonanza.

After only a year, the population in the valley boomed, and at least 120,000 acres were under cultivation with Colorado River water. After several canals were silted up, heavy flows breached a canal and its temporary gates, flooding the region known as the Salton Sink. After fifteen months of uncontrolled flooding, the U.S. Army Corps of Engineers managed to stop the flow of the Colorado River into this valley, but not before a new, inland lake (the Salton Sea) had been created. Farmers in the valley rebuilt their farms and continued to profit from Colorado River water.

Although John Wesley Powell did not see all of his ideas put into practice, the U.S. government soon took responsibility for developing water resources for the arid West. Several congressional acts had already paved the way for government responsibility for water reclamation, such as the Desert Land Act of 1877 and the Carey Act of 1894. From 1888 through 1891, the U.S. Geological Survey (USGS) conducted detailed studies for irrigating the West.

When Theodore Roosevelt became president in 1901, the West had a new champion. Roosevelt had spent time in the West and was interested in resource management, becoming both a friend to a growing national park system and, ironically, to dam-building projects. Under his leadership, Congress passed the Reclamation Act in 1902. Housed in the Department of the Interior, the U.S. Reclamation Service was created within the USGS. In 1907, the Reclamation Service was separated from the USGS to become an independent bureau and became known as the Bureau of Reclamation.

Bureau of Reclamation Work

In many ways, the story of twentieth-century western water is, in fact, the story of the Bureau of Reclamation. Although the U.S. Army Corps of Engineers would eventually involve itself in western water development, mostly it was the bailiwick of the new Bureau. The original purpose of all its water development was mainly to create irrigated farmland for small, independent farmers. Large dams were built to control flooding, improve

Employing some 21,000 people during its construction between 1931 and 1936, the Hoover Dam (formerly Boulder Dam) stands over 700 feet high. Its hydroelectric plant generates approximately 4 billion kilowatt-hours of electricity a year for residents of Arizona, California, and Nevada.

Bureau of Reclamation

transportation, but most importantly provide irrigation water to small farms of 160 acres or less (320 acres to married couples). Although the government did try to keep these acreage limitations in place, land developers found various ways to get around the limits and collect large, cheaply irrigated tracts of land.

To provide water for farmers in the fertile but dry soil of the West, the Bureau began an ambitious dam-building spree that would not stop until the early years of the Cold War. During the twentieth century, the Bureau created over 180 projects. Congress approved approximately seventy of these in the years before World War II. The first major project, and one that continued to define western water development for the next fifty years or so, was the 1928 Boulder Dam. Completed in 1936, this large and magnificent dam, renamed Hoover Dam, made it possible for cities like Los Angeles to obtain cheap

electricity and to construct aqueducts from the Colorado River to the city. Many dams and water projects followed, all making the irrigation of dry lands possible and affordable.

In the years following World War II, building dams continued to be the major focus of water development in the West. The last of these major dams was Glen Canyon Dam, begun in 1956 and finished in 1963. However, conflicts that had been brewing for many decades began to cause problems, particularly between Arizona and California. In one of the longest Supreme Court cases in U.S. history, these two arid states fought over shares of the Colorado River. When the case was finally settled in 1963 after eleven years, Arizona began what would be the last major water diversion project in the West, the Central Arizona Project Canal.

By the early 1960s, a growing environmentalist movement began fighting critical battles to prevent dam construction and wildlife habitat destruction. One of the major turning points that helped to spur the movement onward was a controversial proposal to build dams in parts of the Grand Canyon. David Brower of the Sierra Club fought these proposals in the wake of the closing of Glen Canyon Dam. He and others believed they had lost an important piece of American wilderness below the rising waters of Lake Powell, and allowed this "failure" to fuel later battles. These battles, along with the publication of Rachel Carson's Silent Spring in 1962, turned public attention toward issues of pollution of both air and water. By 1970, the establishment of the National Environmental Protection Agency launched a new era, and various clean air and water acts would follow. The Wildlife Protection Act of 1972 further changed the environment in which the Bureau of Reclamation had always operated. Now, environmental impact statements were required, and projects were scrutinized for adverse costs in ways they had never been before.

In the last two decades of the twentieth century and the first decade of the twenty-first, the Bureau has struggled to find its purpose. The story of western water is no longer one of big projects and dam building. It is, however, still one of conflict and struggle over water. Major western water issues include competing claims for a declining resource, drought management, urban versus agricultural water allocations, water salinity and quality, and water conservation and sustainability initiatives. While government bodies such as Congress or the Bureau of Reclamation still play vital roles in the story of southwestern water, the major players of the current decade seem to be metropolitan water districts and other citizen groups.

Current Issues

One of the most interesting issues is also a very old one: Indian water rights. In 1908, the Supreme Court ruled that federal Indian reservations contained original water rights to enable these lands to be productive. Known as the Winters Doctrine, it became the basis for western Indian water claims up to the present day. In the latter part of the twentieth century, various Southwestern indigenous groups have used the Winters Doctrine as a legal basis to acquire specific water rights. The first group to negotiate a share of the Colorado River was the Gila-Maricopa Indian Community near Phoenix, Arizona. After first filing for water rights in 1976, they reached a final settlement in 2004 with the Gila River Water Settlement Act. This act gave the community a very large title to approximately 47 percent of the water flow in the Central Arizona Project canal. Other southwestern Indian peoples are now seeking similar water rights. For example, the Taos Pueblo in New Mexico and the White Mountain Apache in Arizona both filed legal cases in 2009.

Directly connected to the issue of Indian water rights is the ongoing drought in the Southwest. For almost a decade, a severe drought has lowered water tables and river flows. Water levels in Lake Mead behind the Hoover Dam are at their lowest since 1965. The dual challenges of climate change and a burgeoning population will not be easy to solve. An example can be seen by looking at the Colorado River, one of the most important sources of water in the region. When the seven states served by that river divided up its flow in the 1922 Colorado River Compact, the division was based on an assumption that at least 16.6 million acre-feet (MAF) of water flowed annually down its long course. In 2002, one of the driest years of this decade, the actual flow was around 5.4 MAF. Growing demands for water now face a smaller and smaller supply.

To address water shortages, cities are increasingly looking at reallocation as the answer and buying water rights from farmers, who use perhaps 70 percent of the region's water resources. Cities like Los Angeles and San Diego already purchase water from farmers in the Imperial Valley. In

Yavapai Fight against the Orme Dam

The Orme Dam was authorized to be constructed by the Bureau of Reclamation in 1968 as part of the Central Arizona Project. The dam was trumpeted by Interior Secretary Stewart Udall as a recreational development project for the benefit of the Yavapai residing on the Fort McDowell Reservation. What was not stated was that the proposed dam and reservoir stood to flood half of the reservation, including the homes of most of the Yavapai, their sacred burial grounds, and the tribal farm.

Although tribal members opposed the Orme Dam from the beginning, the Yavapai did not begin to mobilize against the dam until 1972. Their opposition was aided by environmental groups such as the Audubon Society, who wanted to protect the streamside habitats favored by several hawk species and the bald eagle, and federal agencies, most notably the Fish and Wildlife Service and the Forest Service.

The Bureau of Reclamation offered to buy the lands required for construction of the dam for $33.5 million and 2,500 acres of other land, but the Yavapai rejected the offer. The Bureau of Reclamation then threatened to seize the land through condemnation, but the Yavapai and their allies refused to be cowed. The Yavapai raised money to travel to Washington, D.C., where they met with federal officials to voice their opposition to the project. Members of the tribe also staged a three-day march from the Fort McDowell Reservation to Phoenix, Arizona, to bring attention to their cause.

President Jimmy Carter stopped the funding of the Orme Dam in 1977 as part of his effort to balance the federal budget. Arizona officials began resuscitating the project in the early 1980s. The Yavapai responded by inviting Interior Secretary James Watt to their reservation to see firsthand the land proposed for flooding. Watt announced in November 1981 that the Orme Dam project had been cancelled. The Fort McDowell Yavapai commemorate the event every November with the Orme Dam Victory Days Celebration.

—John R. Burch Jr.

See also: *American Indian Water Rights; American Indian Water Settlements; Bureau of Reclamation; Central Arizona Project; Fish and Wildlife Service, United States; Orme Dam; Udall, Stewart; Watt, James G.*

BIBLIOGRAPHY
McCool, Daniel. *Command of the Waters: Iron Triangles, Federal Water Development, and Indian Water.* Tucson: University of Arizona Press, 1994.
Parker, Linda S. *Native American Estate: The Struggle over Indian and Hawaiian Lands.* Honolulu: University of Hawaii Press, 1989.

October 2009, the *Arizona Republic* published a series of stories discussing possible plans for Phoenix to do something similar. To many people, reducing water irrigation for farming and diverting it to urban centers is the best answer to water shortages. However, others argue that if a region produces less and less of its own food, it will contribute to climate change through transportation pollution, among other consequences.

While buying and selling water does seem to be one answer to water issues in the Southwest, a water market will only be as good as its product. Water quality is another problem facing the Southwest as salinity levels rise. Caused by large-scale irrigation and the cultivation of short-rooted grass and plants in residential landscaping, rising salt levels make it necessary to work harder to clean up what water is available. Damage to infrastructure and agricultural land is also rising; recent costs from salinity damage were estimated at nearly $750 million per year. In spite of all the challenges, water continues to flow in the Southwest, and to many experts it is flowing too fast and too cheap.

Others focus on rejuvenating overused rivers and streams in order to recover endangered river species of fish. One of the most comprehensive river restoration projects focused on Fossil Creek in Arizona. Flowing into the Verde River, Fossil Creek was tapped for hydropower as early as 1916. When the dam was scheduled for its fifty-year review for relicensing in the early 1990s, environmentalists urged that the Fossil Creek Dam be decommissioned and removed as part of a restoration plan for the creek. After several years of effort, all parties agreed to the decommissioning and an intense restoration project for the creek. By 2005, it became perhaps the best example of river restoration in the United States. While the future of water in the Southwest may look grim, the ongoing efforts to address the many challenges have produced some reason for hope.

—April Summitt

See also: *Dam Building; Ecosystem Management; Urbanization; Urban Rivers*

BIBLIOGRAPHY

Clark, Ira G. *Water in New Mexico: A History of Its Management and Use.* Albuquerque: University of New Mexico Press, 1987.

Coate, Charles. "'The Biggest Water Fight in American History': Stewart Udall and the Central Arizona Project." *Journal of the Southwest* 37, no. 1 (1995): 79–101.

Dean, Robert. "'Dam Building Still Had Some Magic Then': Steward Udall, the Central Arizona Project, and the Evolution of the Pacific Southwest Water Plan, 1963–1968." *Pacific Historical Review* 66, no. 1 (1997): 81–98.

Espeland, Wendy Nelson. *The Struggle for Water: Politics, Rationality, and Identity in the American Southwest.* Chicago: University of Chicago Press, 1998.

Hundley, Norris, Jr. *Water and the West: The Colorado River Compact and the Politics of Water in the American West.* Berkeley: University of California Press, 1975.

Hundley, Norris, Jr. "The 'Winters' Decision and Indian Water Rights: A Mystery Reexamined." *Western Historical Quarterly* 13, no. 1 (1982): 17–42.

Jackson, Donald C. *Building the Ultimate Dam: John S. Eastwood and the Control of Water in the West.* Lawrence: University Press of Kansas, 1995.

Lewis, William M., Jr., ed. *Water and Climate in the Western United States.* Boulder: University Press of Colorado, 2003.

McCool, Daniel. *Command of the Waters: Iron Triangles, Federal Water Development, and Indian Water.* Tucson: University of Arizona Press, 1987.

Meyer, Michael C. *Water in the Hispanic Southwest: A Social and Legal History.* Tucson: University of Arizona Press, 1984.

Pisani, Donald J. *To Reclaim a Divided West: Water, Law, and Public Policy, 1848–1902.* Albuquerque: University of New Mexico Press, 1992.

Powell, James Lawrence. *Dead Pool: Lake Powell, Global Warming, and the Future of Water in the West.* Berkeley: University of California Press, 2009.

Rivera, José A. *Acequia Culture: Water, Land, and Community in the Southwest.* Albuquerque: University of New Mexico Press, 1998.

Stegner, Wallace. *Beyond the Hundredth Meridian: John Wesley Powell and the Second Opening of the West.* New York: Penguin, 1954.

Wilkinson, Charles. *Crossing the Next Meridian: Land, Water, and the Future of the American West.* Washington, DC: Island Press, 1992.

Worster, Donald. *Rivers of Empire: Water, Aridity, and the Growth of the American West.* New York: Oxford University Press, 1985.

Part II Major Issues in Water Politics and Policy

42

Acid Mine Drainage

Acid mine drainage is acidic water that forms when pyrite, an iron sulfide, is exposed to oxygen and water. The pyrite forms white and yellow salts of sulfuric acid and iron sulfate as the oxidation process begins. This process includes various chemical and biological reactions that vary in speed depending on environmental conditions. Once formed, acid mine drainage can enter streams, rivers, or other waterways through either runoff or the contamination of groundwater.

Acid mine drainage can result from highway construction or other large excavation ventures, but it is most commonly a by-product of the mining process. In coal mining, the layers of rock located above the coal often contain traces of iron, aluminum, manganese, mercury, and other heavy

Mining has exposed thousands of minerals found in soil to water and oxygen, which can cause the formation of sulfuric acid as at Iron Mountain Mine in northern California. Furthermore, acid mine drainage has polluted nearby tributaries to the Colorado River, causing the death of many fish. Acid mine drainage frequently occurs at large excavation and mining sites.

National Oceanographic and Atmospheric Administration

metals (EPA 1997). Acid releases these metals and washes them into bodies of water. Low-pH (high-acidity) waters severely degrade ground and drinking water as well as ecosystems related to streams, rivers, and lakes. Once the pH falls below 3, a slimy red, orange, or yellow precipitate known as "yellow boy" accumulates in water. The presence of acid mine drainage in waterways not only disrupts the wildlife dependent upon these water sources but can also accelerate the corrosion of metal pipes used in homes and municipal facilities such as water treatment plants. These effects, if not treated, can last for decades.

Mining Influences

The acid mine drainage issue can be traced back over 200 years to early mining practices in the United States. Coal mining in the northern mountains of Appalachia, including in Maryland and Pennsylvania, began in the early nineteenth century and later spread south to West Virginia, Kentucky, Virginia, and Tennessee. In the western half of the United States, the 1840s and 1850s saw a sharp increase in mining due in large part to newly discovered gold and silver mines. Also around this time, but often overshadowed by the mining boom in the West, rich iron ore mines opened in the Great Lakes region near Lake Superior (Smith 1993). In these early underground mines, men hand-dug and loaded the excavated materials into horse-drawn carts. Mechanization, including the use of power drills, roof bolters, shuttle cars, and steam shovels, later increased the speed and overall volume of mineral extraction after the turn of the twentieth century. Entrance into underground mines could be vertical, horizontal, or sloped, depending upon the location of the mineral seam/deposit. In many old and abandoned mines, miles of tunnels might collect water that had passed through the overburden above. As air and water circulated in the maze of tunnels, they reacted with acid-producing materials released through the mining process to create acid mine drainage, which seeped out of the mines into local water supplies.

Mining, particularly coal production, increased during World War I, then declined sharply during the Great Depression. It peaked again during World War II, as the nation's appetite for energy resources grew. In order to meet this growing demand, mining operators utilized new technologies that allowed them to move larger amounts of earth. Although strip-mining techniques had been employed by mineral companies since the turn of the twentieth century, not until after World War II did the practice become widespread in areas such as Appalachia. Steam shovels and massive draglines were used to strip-mine coal seams located close to the surface. This practice employed a contour cut that followed the natural contour of the mountain, removing the overburden of soil, rocks, and trees to expose the seam of coal. Once removed, a highwall and flat bench large enough to accommodate extraction machinery were created. A vertical highwall was formed as the overburden was pushed away from the coal seam. As miners finished the section, the remaining overburden was pushed against the highwall and another section started, beginning the process again until the coal seam was depleted. If left near a drainage zone and exposed to water, the disturbed overburden could become a source of acid water runoff as pyrite and other materials began to oxidize.

Auger mining was used in conjunction with the contour cut. To access the remaining coal or minerals that were not removed by contour mining, coal operators lined up an auger drill at the base of the highwall at the level of the coal seam and drilled into the hillside. Auger holes could penetrate up to 200 feet into the mountain. Following the highwall, the auger drilled holes side by side for the length of the exposed seam, recovering a considerable percentage of the remaining coal. Once complete, the holes were often left unfilled, and the overburden was simply pushed up against the hillside to cover the outside of the holes. The drill holes caused small cracks in the surface, which allowed water to seep into the unfilled areas and contaminate groundwater supplies.

One growing source of acid mine drainage and environmental degradation is mountaintop removal, a mining method in which the uppermost top of a mountain is removed in order to expose a seam/deposit of coal, thus creating level land. Once the coal is extracted, the area is reclaimed but not to the approximate original contour, as is required with strip mining. Rather, it is reclaimed to flat or rolling contours, which can later be used for other developmental/industrial purposes. The overburden removed through this method is often used in valley fills, which directly impact the biological characteristics of headwater streams. Valley fills can either completely reduce the flow of water in these streams or become a source of acid mine drainage as contaminants leech out of the overburden directly into the body of water.

Legislative Initiatives

By the late twentieth century, many coal mining operators had turned toward alternate methods of coal extraction, including strip-mining and mountaintop removal. In addition, the legacy of abandoned mines and poor reclamation efforts had increased the occurrence of acid mine drainage from mining sites. As a result of new mining technologies, and in order to address growing environmental concerns, Congress enacted the Surface Mining Control and Reclamation Act (SMCRA) in August 1977. The Office of Surface Mining Reclamation and Enforcement was the agency charged with supervising the Act's provisions, but enforcement could be delegated to state governments if they passed laws and regulations that were more strict than the federal law. The Act also created the Abandoned Mine Reclamation Fund, which could be used to restore pre-1977 mining sites as well as poorly reclaimed lands. Individual states created their own abandoned-mine funds using grants from this larger federal fund, pursuant to an approved state program. Amended in 1992, the Act required coal operators to pay a reclamation fee of thirty-five cents per ton of coal produced by surface mining, fifteen cents per ton of coal produced by underground mining, or 10 percent of the determined value of the coal at the mine, whichever was less. In regard to acid mine drainage, money from the fund could be used specifically for the restoration of land and water resources adversely affected by mining as well as the "prevention, abatement, treatment, and control of water pollution created by coal mine drainage including restoration of stream beds, and construction and operation of water treatment plants" (SMCRA § 401[c][1]).

Another piece of legislation, passed in December 1977, was an amendment to the Clean Water Act of 1972. The goal of the amendment, known as the Clean Water Act of 1977, was to make navigable waters in the United States fishable and swimmable, as well as to control the discharge of pollutants into these waters. In order to achieve these goals, the Act worked in conjunction with a permit system known as the National Pollutant Discharge Elimination System (NPDES), which regulated companies that discharged water into streams, rivers, and lakes. Chemical, energy, mining, industrial, and manufacturing companies whose discharges went directly into bodies of water were required to obtain permits that held the company to a set of compliance standards. For those companies utilizing strip-mining or mountaintop-removal extraction methods, mining operators were required not only to obtain SMCRA permits but also NPDES permits.

In Appalachia, where approximately 95 percent of acid mine drainage issues in the eastern United States are found, the Office of Surface Mining Reclamation and Enforcement (OSM) began the Appalachian Clean Streams Initiative (ACSI) in late 1994. Working in conjunction with the Environmental Protection Agency (EPA), this initiative was undertaken by OSM in direct response to the acid mine drainage problems that had plagued the region for decades. It was intended to stimulate new projects by the states that administered abandoned-mine-fund tax receipts under SMCRA. The intentions of ACSI were not only to facilitate the spread of information to various groups to prevent the duplication of restoration projects, but also to raise the level of awareness about the environmental dangers associated with acid mine drainage.

In the western half of the country, the U.S. Geological Survey, in conjunction with the U.S. Department of the Interior and the U.S. Department of Agriculture, conducted the Abandoned Mine Land Initiative from 1997 through 2001 to address the pollution and acid mine drainage left behind by hard-rock metal mines (e.g., copper, gold, zinc). The initiative employed a variety of people from different academic backgrounds, and this interdisciplinary approach to acid mine drainage generated new ways to approach the issue of cleanup and reclamation.

Acid mine drainage treatment methods focus on isolating, neutralizing, and/or removing pollutants through chemical, physical, and biological processes. Active treatment systems use strong alkaline chemicals, including lime ammonia, caustic soda, or calcium oxide, to neutralize the acid so that metals found in the stream can be removed. Passive treatment systems include aerobic and anaerobic wetlands, limestone ponds, open limestone channels, and reverse alkalinity-producing systems. These systems treat pollutants by exposing them to air, limestone, wetlands, neutralization ditches, and vegetation in ponds. This helps to precipitate metals through the oxidation process, neutralize acid by adding alkalinity, or, in the case of wetland use, provide habitat bacteria that aid in the breakdown of sulfates. Under certain conditions, it is also possible to contain the source of the drainage. The capping of mine waste involves applying a layer of impermeable clay to prevent the seepage of water into the mine. If recoverable coal is still located near the mine site, coal operators can rework the site with modern equipment, if they obtain permits designed to adhere to environmental standards (EPA 1997). Federal initiatives such as ACSI, as well as a growing response from citizens' groups and agencies concerned about water quality, will continue to promote the protection of streams and rivers from this toxic environmental pollutant.

—Stephanie M. Lang

See also: *Clean Water Act of 1972; Mining and Water Resources; Valley Fill Litigation*

BIBLIOGRAPHY

Ashworth, William, and Charles E. Little. "Clean Water Act." In *Encyclopedia of Environmental Studies,* new ed., 88–89. New York: Facts on File, 2001.

EPA (U.S. Environmental Protection Agency). *A Citizen's Handbook to Address Contaminated Coal Mine Drainage* (EPA-903-K-97-003). Philadelphia: EPA, 1997. Available at http://www.techtransfer.osmre.gov/nttmainsite/Library/hbmanual/citizen/front.pdf.

Goode, James B. *The Cutting Edge: Mining in the 21st Century.* Ashland, KY: The Jesse Stuart Foundation, 2002.

Kendrick, P. J. "Acid Mine Drainage: An Old Problem with a New Dimension." *Water Pollution Control Federation Journal* 49, no. 7 (1977): 1576–77.

SMCRA (Surface Mining Control and Reclamation Act of 1977), Pub. L. 95-87 (30 U.S.C. 1201–1328). Available at http://www.osmre.gov/topic/smcra/smcra.shtm.

Smith, Duane. *Mining America: The Industry and the Environment, 1800–1980.* Niwot: University Press of Colorado, 1993.

Acid Rain

Acid rain is a mix of wet and dry material that contains unusually high amounts of nitric and sulfuric acid. It may come from volcanic activity, decay of vegetation, or man-made sources such as sulfur and nitrogen oxide emissions from the burning of fossil fuels. In the atmosphere, sulfur dioxide and nitrogen oxide, in gaseous or particulate form, contribute to smog, which reduces visibility and causes health problems.

Roughly two-thirds of the sulfur dioxide (SO_2) and a fourth of the nitrogen oxides (NO_x) in the United States come from the burning of fossil fuels in electric power generation. Electric utilities generate about 70 percent of SO_2 and 40 percent of NO_x, while transportation adds significant NO_x. Other generators of sulfur and nitrogen compounds, the key components of acid rain, include factories, power plants, and vehicles.

When SO_2 and NO_x react with water, oxygen, or other chemicals in the atmosphere, a number of acids form, most notably sulfuric and nitric acid. When the acids in the air encounter wet weather, they can fall as rain, snow, mist, or fog, otherwise known as wet deposition. Wet deposition affects plants and animals to a degree depending on the acidity of the wet deposition, the buffering capacity of the

Fraser fir and red spruce trees have been damaged by acid rain in Mt. Mitchell State Park in western North Carolina. Acid rain harms trees by inhibiting their ability to gather nutrients and by changing the pH level of the soil.

Rob and Ann Simpson/Getty Images

Effects and Efforts at Reduction

Acid rain alters an ecosystem extensively, often reducing the livable space to virtually nothing. Recovery is sometimes a multiyear process, particularly for streams, lakes, forests, and soils. If the damage is extreme, recovery may take centuries. Acid rain's effects on surface water are more severe when the type of underlying soil provides limited buffering capacity. A National Surface Water Survey of over 1,000 lakes and thousands of miles of streams revealed that acid rain was the cause of acidity in 75 percent of the lakes and about half of the streams. The most severely affected regions were the Adirondacks, the mid-Appalachian highlands, the higher elevations of the West, and the upper Midwest. In some cases, lakes and streams had no fish. In the Adirondacks, hundreds of surveyed lakes were unable to support a significant fish population. In eastern Canada, where soils are similar to those of the Adirondacks, 14,000 lakes were affected. Acidification can be episodic too, as characterized by occasional fish kills after storms and snowmelt. In the Adirondacks, episodic acidification affected seven times the number of streams that routine acidification did.

One way to reduce acidity is to add large amounts of lime to the water. Liming, used in Scandinavia, is not common in the United States because it is expensive and requires repeated applications. It is, thus, not regarded as a practical long-term solution. Besides, application of limestone or lime does not correct forest or soil chemistry, even if it does allow fish to remain in the lakes.

Title IV of the Clean Air Act Amendments of 1990 established the Acid Rain Program. The program endeavors to reduce sulfur dioxide and nitrogen oxides in order to improve public health and the environment. The goal of the Clean Air Act is to halve the total emissions of SO_2 and NO_x by cutting 10 million tons of SO_2. The program caps power plant SO_2 emissions at 8.95 million tons, starting in 2010, and allows plants to trade allowances. It also lowers NO_x emission rates, encourages the prevention of pollution, and calls for greater energy efficiencies.

The U.S. Geological Survey (USGS) is the lead agency for monitoring wet deposition. It leads the National Atmospheric Deposition Program (NADP) and National Trends Network (NTN) and also performs research and assessment of the impact of acid rain on aquatic and land ecosystems. The NADP includes over 250 NTN monitoring sites, and the USGS maintains seventy-four of them. The purpose of the NADP is to develop quality long-term

soil(s), and the types of living things the water affects. In dry weather, the acid chemicals may combine with dust or smoke and precipitate as dry deposition, which can adhere to trees, cars, buildings, and the ground. These gases and particles can become acidic runoff during rainstorms. Approximately half of the acids in the atmosphere return to earth as dry deposition. The prevailing winds above power plants and other sources sometimes blow atmospheric acids hundreds of miles across state and national borders.

Sulfur and nitrogen oxides in the air have increased since the advent of the Industrial Revolution, with industrialized China, Eastern Europe, and Russia all reporting atmospheric pH readings below that of vinegar. Comparably high-acidity readings occur downwind of these sulfur coal–burning regions.

data concerning atmospheric deposition's impacts on air, water, agriculture, forests, watersheds, ecosystems, and human beings.

Historical Background and Current Policy

The first to notice acid rain was Robert Angus Smith of Manchester, England. In 1852, he reported a connection between acid rain and atmospheric pollution. For a century, the phenomenon was ignored. Acid rain has become increasingly serious since the 1950s, especially in the northeastern United States, Canada, and Western Europe.

Swedish researchers began monitoring freshwater acidity in the 1940s and noticed significant increases in the 1950s and 1960s. In northern Europe and the United States, the pH level of lake water decreased in the 1970s, compared with the 1930s. The deposit of acids into lakes beyond those waters' buffering capacity led to a decline in fish populations and other environmental problems, including nutrient imbalance and acidic soil. The end result was dead lakes.

Scientific evidence grew in the 1960s and 1970s that SO_2 traveled long distances, from the United States to Canada and from continental Europe to Scandinavia, and acidified water sources, lakes, and streams. Svante Oden published a paper in 1968 arguing that Scandinavian precipitation was becoming increasingly acidic and, thus, causing damage to fish and lakes. He found the source of the pollution in Great Britain and Central Europe. Sweden and Norway subsequently led the campaign to make acid rain an international issue, but polluting nations ignored their call until the 1970s, when more convincing proof became available.

Sweden presented that evidence in 1972 to the international community at a United Nations meeting held in Stockholm. The Organization for Economic Cooperation and Development (OECD) began a long-range study of acid rain that same year, and the results, when published in 1977 and revised in 1979, supported the Scandinavian position that imported sulfur was acidifying Sweden's lakes.

In the late 1970s, Canadians began federal-province negotiations, which culminated in the 1985 Eastern Canada Acid Rain Program. This set caps on the amount of sulfates in precipitation. During the 1980s, Canada claimed that U.S. pollutants were damaging Canadian waters and forests. In response, countries in North America and Europe have since enacted controls on SO_2 emissions. In the United States, the Clean Air Act of 1972, reauthorized and amended

in 1990, is the applicable legislation. Thirty-four countries and the European Commission signed a convention on long-range pollution in 1979, agreeing to reduce SO_2 to 70 percent of 1980 levels by 1993. In addition, the Helsinki Protocol of 1985 obligated twenty-one European nations to reduce emissions by set amounts. The joint effort reduced acid rain in Europe and North America noticeably.

The problem of acid rain once again came forcibly to the fore in the 1990s after the *New York Times* reported on the environmental problems acid rain had caused in New Hampshire's Hubbard Brook Experimental Forest (see, e.g., Stevens 1996). In 1991, the United States and Canada signed the Canada-U.S. Air Quality Agreement, which required both countries to reduce emissions of SO_2 and NO_x, particularly from power plants. Canada tightened its standards in 1998, then began negotiations with members of the United Nations Economic Commission for Europe on reducing emissions of SO_2 and NO_x.

In 2002, the Environmental Protection Agency (EPA) attempted to ease pollution standards to enable an expansion in the construction of power plants and factories, while Congress considered amending the Clean Air Act. At the same time, a study was released that indicated that acid rain potentially caused trees to develop a problem analogous to a compromised immune system in a human. The report indicated that affected trees appeared to be healthy but that even routine stress or disease would cause exaggerated decline. The authors had previously shown how acid rain depleted calcium and made red spruce trees more vulnerable to disease from freezing. The new report indicated that similar problems applied to other species. Depleted calcium deteriorates a tree's stress response, making the tree more vulnerable to environmental problems. Furthermore, the calcium deficiency and its consequences passed through the food chain to herbivores such as birds, insects, and humans. The study was funded by the EPA with the backing of Senator Jeffords (I-VT), chair of the Environment and Public Works Committee and coauthor of the Clean Power Act first introduced in 2001 (Schaberg, Hawley, and DeHayes 2002).

The current approach is cap and trade. Advocates of cap and trade tout the virtue of market forces in achieving cost-effective environmental solutions. Businesses would have more flexibility and stronger financial incentives to limit emissions. Cap and trade was authorized by the 1990 Clean Air Act Amendments. The anticipated market price of an SO_2 allowance was $579 to $1,935 a ton, but in January 2003 it was only $150 a ton. In the 1990s, cap and trade achieved 100 percent compliance in reducing SO$_2$ emissions, with participating power plants reducing SO$_2$ by 22 percent or 7.3 tons below the requirement. The program was initially expected to cost between $3 and $25 billion a year, but after two years it had only cost about $0.8 billion a year, with long-range costs estimated at around $1.0 to $1.4 billion a year. Given the figures, advocates claimed there was no longer any conflict between the environment and the economy. Cap and trade made environmentalism economically smart.

Other measures that can reduce acid rain include changes in individual and societal behaviors. Individuals can use a catalytic converter to reduce automobile NO$_x$ emissions. Cleaner gasoline and tighter tailpipe restrictions are also helping to reduce NO$_x$ emissions. Alternatives to fossil fuels that reduce acid rain include nuclear, hydroelectric, wind, solar, and geothermal power, all of which are expensive because they are not yet used on a cost-effective scale.

—John H. Barnhill

See also: *Adirondack Park*

BIBLIOGRAPHY

Ellerman, A. Denny, Paul L. Joskow, Richard Schmalensee, Juan-Pablo Montero, and Elizabeth M. Bailey. *Markets for Clean Air: The U.S. Acid Rain Program.* New York: Cambridge University Press, 2000.

Environmental Defense Fund. "The Cap and Trade Success Story." http://www.edf.org/page.cfm?tagID=1085/.

Environmental Protection Agency. "What Is Acid Rain?" http://www.epa.gov/acidrain/what/index.html.

Freese, Barbara. *Coal: A Human History.* New York: Da Capo Press, 2003.

Jenkins, Jerry C., Karen Roy, Charles Driscoll, and Christopher Buerkett. *Acid Rain in the Adirondacks: An Environmental History.* Ithaca, NY: Cornell University Press, 2007.

Otoshi, Tsunehiko. Environmental Impact of Acid Rain and "Acid Deposition Monitoring Network in East Asia (EANET)." http://www.unu.edu/gs/files/2007/tohoku/TH07_Otoshi_ENabstract.pdf.

Schaberg, Paul G., Gary J. Hawley, and Donald H. DeHayes. "Forest Management Impacts on Genetic Diversity: A Case Study with Eastern Hemlock." Paper presented at a meeting of the International Society for Ecosystem Health in association with the Center for Applied Biodiversity Science, Washington, DC, June 2002.

Schmandt, Jurgen, Judith Clarkson, and Hilliard Roderick. *Acid Rain and Friendly Neighbors: The Policy Dispute between Canada and the United States.* Durham, NC: Duke University Press, 1988.

ScienceDaily. "Damage from Acid Rain Pollution Is Far Worse Than Previously Believed," July 18, 2002. Available at http://www.sciencedaily.com/releases/2002/07/020718075630.htm.

Stevens, William K. "The Forest That Stopped Growing: Trail Is Traced to Acid Rain." *New York Times,* April 16, 1996. Available at http://www.nytimes.com/1996/04/16/science/the-forest-that-stopped-growing-trail-is-traced-to-acid-rain.html.

U.S. Geological Survey. "Acid Rain, Atmospheric Deposition, and Precipitation Chemistry." http://bqs.usgs.gov/AcidRain/.

Agriculture

Federal water policy concerning agriculture focused on transportation of agricultural products and reclamation of wetlands until the late nineteenth century. At that point, the desire to irrigate federal lands so that they could be settled became paramount. Over the course of the twentieth century, federal agricultural water policy changed from one of promoting the full development of all water resources to one of balancing the needs of other water users against those of agricultural users.

Transportation and Obstructions

Federal water policy prior to 1862 dealt with agriculture by focusing on waterborne transportation of agricultural goods and on conversion of wetlands to other uses rather than on water and farming per se. Early federal government water policies were based on English common law and focused on riparian rights: the rights and duties of those living alongside a stream or river. Landowners could use the water for their livestock and for domestic needs and were entitled to the usufruct of the stream, but they could not do anything to harm downstream riparian property owners. The first people to build dams on streams for the purpose of running a mill were required to construct them in such a way as not to interfere with others' rights. As a result, many early court cases concerning water were based on claims of flooding or obstructions to navigation.

Early federal interest in water stemmed from transportation and questions regarding "internal improvements," meaning infrastructure such as canals and bridges. The Constitution, in Article I, Section 8, grants Congress the power to regulate commerce. Early on, this was taken to include maintaining harbors and waterways for the benefit of trade, including shipping agricultural products. The construction of the Erie Canal and other privately funded or state-funded water projects led to major debates in Congress over the role of the federal government in financing internal improvements; while constructing roads for the postal service is specified in the Constitution, federal funding of canals for transporting agricultural products and other goods is not.

The first law passed to encourage the draining and reclaiming of wetlands for agricultural purposes was the 1849 Swamp Land Act, which was expanded and amended in 1850 and 1860. As the U.S. Geological Survey (USGS) Northern Prairie Research Center's summary explains, this

Act first transferred wetlands (swamps) in Louisiana to the state and then did the same in other "public land" states, with the total land area affected being almost 65 million acres. The goals of this Act and its amendments were to reduce flooding, to promote settlement and reclamation by encouraging draining and channeling, and to improve public health by draining areas where mosquitoes bred. The law was successful in eliminating many wetlands and marshes in the Midwest and parts of the South, as well as in Oregon and Washington State.

Land, Water, and Reclamation

The expansion of U.S. settlement west of the 100th meridian and the need for irrigation to allow agriculture to take hold in the arid West led to the expansion of federal water policies. As settlement of North America flowed westward, it became apparent to many that water would be as important as free land in populating the West. Irrigation in some form was necessary to have reliable crops from year to year in the lands west of the twenty-inch rainfall line (roughly modern Oklahoma City— Pierre, South Dakota—Bismarck, North Dakota), and early settlers tried to secure water as well as land. However, the 160 acres specified in the Homestead Act were too many for a family to irrigate on their own and, at the same time, too few on which to raise livestock. At the same time, ranchers and speculators quickly filed both valid and illegal claims to areas along watercourses and near springs, effectively locking away most of the surrounding land from "genuine homesteaders." These problems led to several congressional investigations and some modifications of the original Homestead Act, including the Timber Culture Act (1873), the Desert Land Act (1877), and the Enlarged Homestead Act (1909).

During this time, from 1849 until 1902, federal water policy was delegated to some extent to the western states. Starting with California, each state and territory was allowed to organize its own code of water laws and to assign water rights if applicable. Navigable streams, such as the Rio Grande, the Sacramento, and the Colorado Rivers, came under federal jurisdiction when navigation might be affected or when international boundaries were in question. But the federal government did not have a policy per se related to water and agriculture aside from swamp draining. This situation began changing with the work of John Wesley Powell and the lobbying of western politicians and developers interested in irrigation.

The late 1800s was an era of populism, scientific confidence, and engineering optimism. Out of this mix came the ideas behind the Reclamation Agency (later the Bureau of Reclamation), a branch of the Department of the Interior that aimed at reclaiming farmland from the "desert wastes" and thus promoting farm ownership and rural settlement. One of the chief proponents of this goal was the geographer John Wesley Powell, who pointed out the critical flaw in the Homestead Act's acreage limitation in his 1878 *Report on Lands of the Arid Region of the United States*. Powell envisioned a West where every drop of water would be scientifically husbanded and managed by farmers and ranchers working together in watershed-based districts, using irrigation systems that they managed and paid for. To this end, with the backing of Senator William Stewart of Nevada, Powell proposed and was granted funds for an irrigation survey of the West that would locate every possible site for dams, canals, and fields. Eastern legislators, including Preston Plumber of Kansas, were not in favor of the government spending money on irrigation when there were already complaints about low commodity prices and federal land remained open to settlement farther east. The opposition eventually yielded, and the survey began in 1888. To stop speculators from filing on the designated areas, Congress halted entry on those sites and later halted entry on all western lands. Powell's groups moved too slowly for those interested in settling and profiting from the western lands, and the survey was eventually halted, but the first steps toward federal reclamation had been taken (Worster 2001).

Meanwhile, private attempts at reclamation were tried and found wanting. The Mormon pioneers in Utah, the Pueblo Indians of New Mexico and Arizona, and the Hispanic settlers of New Mexico and California had constructed local irrigation systems. Attempts by private individuals and by irrigation corporations to build and manage larger systems generally proved unsuccessful for a number of reasons. Farmers often were unable or unwilling to pay the costs of water and of upkeep on the systems, leaving the companies in debt. In other places, the engineering demands of dam, ditch, and flume construction proved too expensive for private investors. By the early twentieth century, several private irrigation systems had been taken over by the federal government because of bankruptcy, flooding, or interference with downstream navigation (Bogner 2003).

Out of this came the Bureau of Reclamation, tasked with building the systems that would reclaim the West. Created by the Newlands Act of 1902, the Bureau faced a number of challenges, including the fact that in most western states, the states themselves owned the water that the Bureau would need for its projects. Another challenge was that the U.S. Army Corps of Engineers was also in the dam-building business because of the needs of navigation and flood control. Despite these and other difficulties, the Bureau moved forward with a number of projects across the West, including one of the most famous, the Central Valley Project in California. The federal government now had an agricultural water policy, one aimed at promoting small, irrigated farms.

New Users and New Conflicts

Over the course of the twentieth century, conflicts arose between changing federal water policies and the needs and desires of agriculturalists, leading to confusion and anger among a large number of water users. The federal government led water development during the first half of the twentieth century, but other state and local entities were not far behind. Irrigation projects and flood control measures as well as hydropower dams sprang up along the nation's major rivers, including the Tennessee, Colorado, Columbia, Sacramento, Rio Grande, and others. Wetland drainage continued despite increasing concerns from hunters about the loss of waterfowl habitat. Municipalities, most famously Los Angeles, California, began developing their own water systems that put them in conflict with farmers and ranchers. The Reclamation Bureau, despite efforts to restrict the size of farms on its projects, found itself providing water to large corporate-owned tracts of farmland, especially in California.

After 1850, questions about environmental preservation and water quality became considerations in federal water policy. Once water pollution came under scrutiny and legislation, it became apparent that agricultural runoff contributed to the eutrophication (overfertilization) of lakes and the poor quality of some major rivers. Starting in 1899, federal law prohibited dumping things into rivers that would interfere with navigation. But not until passage of the Federal Water Pollution Control Amendments of 1972 (the Clean Water Act) did chemical and biological material in streams become a matter for federal attention. At the same time, conservationists began discussing the value of keeping certain amounts of water within streams ("in-stream flow") for the benefit of wildlife and recreation.

Concerns also arose about the costs and fees associated with the distribution of water from federal projects.

Corporations, including insurance companies, bought many of the Reclamation Project acres in California's Central Valley Project, turning them into large corporate holdings. Because of long-term water sales contracts, in 1988 water users paid $6.51 per acre-foot of water, which cost the Bureau $72.99 to deliver. As a result of the disparity between cost and repayment, only 5 percent of the previous forty years' spending, or $50 million, had been repaid to the Bureau from lands that should have been paid off ten years after the first water reached the fields (El-Ashry and Gibbons 1988). This in turn raised questions from other water users as to whether agriculture was the best use of this water or if the federal government should put it to a higher-paying use, such as for municipalities.

One of the most visible examples of this new era in federal water policy and the difficulties of trying to satisfy all stakeholders is the case of the Sacramento–San Joaquin River Delta, formed by the estuaries of the Sacramento and San Joaquin rivers. The delta is a vital wetland habitat and fish hatchery. It also serves as part of the water system for southern California through a series of flumes, canals, and pumps and as a diversion point for irrigation water for the western San Joaquin Valley. In 1993, the Delta smelt, a small fish, was placed on the Endangered Species list as threatened, along with several salmon species (Tarlock, Corbridge, and Getches 2009). Concerns voiced about the delta included "water quality, watershed protection, ecosystem restoration, water use efficiency, water transfers, instream flow maintenance, flood control, and managing water storage and conveyance facilities" (Getches 2001, 43). This led to meetings, investigations, lawsuits, the development of the CALFED Bay-Delta Program, and, in 2009, to a significant reduction in the amount of water drawn off for irrigation in part of the San Joaquin Valley in an effort to protect the smelt. The loss of water caused crop losses and high unemployment in the formerly irrigated area.

Federal water policy began with very limited efforts to secure waterways for transportation of agricultural products and to drain swamps. It developed into complicated and sometimes conflicting attempts to balance irrigation and farm preservation with habitat preservation, flood control, recreation, and water quality assurance.

—Margaret A. Bickers

See also: *Desertification; Drought; Erosion; Fertilizers*

BIBLIOGRAPHY

Bogner, Stephen. *Ditches Across the Desert: Irrigation in the Lower Pecos Valley*. Lubbock: Texas Tech University Press, 2003.

El-Ashry, Mohamed T., and Diana C. Gibbons, eds. *Water and Arid Lands of the Western United States*. New York: Cambridge University Press, 1988.

Getches, David H. "The Metamorphosis of Western Water Policy: Have Federal Laws and Local Decisions Eclipsed the States' Role?" *Stanford Environmental Law Journal* 20, no. 3 (2001): 4–72. Available at http://lawweb.colorado.edu/profiles/pubpdfs/getches/Getches SELJ.pdf.

Tarlock, A. Dan, James N. Corbridge Jr., David H. Getches, and Reed D. Benson. *Water Resource Management: A Casebook in Law and Public Policy*. 6th ed. New York: Foundation Press, 2009.

USGS Northern Prairie Wildlife Research Center. "Wetlands of the United States." Last modified August 3, 2006. http://www.npwrc.usgs.gov/resource/wetlands/uswetlan/century.htm.

Worster, Donald. *A River Running West: The Life of John Wesley Powell*. New York: Oxford University Press, 2001.

American Indian Water Rights

The beginnings of U.S. policy toward American Indians can be seen in the Northwest Ordinance of 1787, which placed responsibility for Indian relations in the territory with the federal government, stating: "The utmost good faith shall always be observed towards the Indians." Later, the Constitution placed the entire responsibility for Indian relations with the federal government. In theory, if not in practice, Indian tribes were treated as sovereign states, with the same rights as any European powers. What evolved thereafter is what is called the "trust relationship" between the tribes and the United States. This relationship, which places the federal government in a supervisory role over the interactions between Indians and non-Indians, has at its core the 1790 Trade and Intercourse Act, which not only placed under federal control Indian relations but also the "protection" of Indian lands and natural resources, including water.

Early Treaties and Rulings

Land and water rights were two of the most common points discussed in treaties, which were the primary mechanisms of Indian relations during the late eighteenth and nineteenth centuries. Usually designed to transfer land, and that land's accompanying water rights, to the federal government, the treaties proved to be useful tools for expanding the land base available to non-Indian settlers. For Indians, however, the treaties proved to be nothing other than a means of depriving them of their land and its spiritual, cultural, and physical resources. However unfair the terms, the treaties at least acknowledged Indian tribes as sovereign nations, able to make decisions regarding their own fate. That view of Indian tribes continued until a series of three U.S. Supreme Court decisions rendered under Chief Justice John Marshall, the so-called Marshall Trilogy: *Johnson v. McIntosh* (1823), *Cherokee Nation v. Georgia* (1831), and *Worcester v. Georgia* (1832). Not only did these cases redefine the status of Indian tribes, turning them into "domestic dependent nations," but they also transformed the sovereignty of Indian lands, making

During the nineteenth century, American Indian tribes lost much of their land and water rights in the government's push westward. Here, Hopi women collect water.
Library of Congress

it possible for the federal government to move Indian tribes away from their ancestral lands and resources, such as water, at will. Title to Indian lands, as well as their attached resources, was now under federal, not Indian, control. Sometimes for good, but mostly for ill, this has been the case ever since.

For most of the rest of the nineteenth century, the hallmark of U.S. Indian policy was to move Indians out of the way of the onrushing flood of non-Indian immigrants and onto small reservations, where they would go about practicing agriculture (on lands that were seldom productive) and learning the "arts of civilization" (often by force). What this meant for Indian water rights and policy was that the trust relationship was implemented to benefit non-Indian settlers rather than to protect Indian resources. In 1849, the federal responsibility for Indian policy was transferred from the Department of War to the Department of the Interior, which was the same department charged with opening up western lands to non-Indian settlers. What was a conflict of interest from many Indian perspectives was an efficient means of transferring lands to settlers from the government's perspective.

That said, some halting efforts were made toward helping Indians to use their scant water resources. Those efforts, beginning in the late nineteenth century and continuing into the early twentieth century, paled in comparison to the reclamation efforts aimed at providing water to non-Indian farmers and the region's growing cities. With the establishment of what would become the Bureau of Reclamation (BOR) in 1902, the rush to make the best use of the West's scarce water was on, and Indians would be left in its wake. Many Indian water projects would be approved over the course of the twentieth century, but when it came time for Congress to vote for appropriations to fund the projects, the Bureau of Indian Affairs (BIA) always came a distant second to the BOR. The solution often was to sell Indian lands in order to pay for water development projects, leading to a further reduction of the Indian land base and making their water rights less meaningful.

Winters v. United States

Even where they were able to build dams, canals, and other infrastructure, the Indian claims on the West's water often went unfilled. Using the prior-appropriation system, most of the West's rivers were already overappropriated, and the state courts (which had a long track record of antipathy toward Indians) had jurisdiction over the rivers. Most Indian tribes during the early twentieth century have had to base their hopes for justice in water rights on federal court decisions,

as Congress had not passed any definitive, all-encompassing water rights bills supporting or even defining Indian rights. The court decision that formed the most generous basis for Indian water rights, therefore causing the most contention with non-Indian water claimants, is the Supreme Court opinion in *Winters v. United States* (1908). The roots of the case lie in a series of treaties signed by Montana Indian tribes, including the 1851 Treaty of Fort Laramie and four later treaties in 1855, 1874, 1888, and 1896. The Indians who signed these treaties ceded much of their ancestral lands to the U.S. government. The last two treaties fixed the current boundaries of the Fort Belknap reservation, with its northern boundary being the "middle of the main channel of Milk River."

After the Indians began to settle on the reservation, however, it became clear that government efforts to turn the Indians into farmers were failing because they preferred to raise livestock on the reservation and maintain their cultural traditions. After 1888, non-Indian homesteaders began settling lands around the reservation and drawing off water for irrigation and stock watering. Reservation agents facilitated the opening of the reservation to non-Indian ownership and leasing agreements so that by 1920, non-Indians controlled over 58 percent of the tribe's irrigated lands. The year 1905 saw a severe drought strike the region, and upstream irrigation bled the river all but dry, leaving little water for reservation and other downstream users. Ironically, when off-reservation ranchers blocked the flow of the Milk River onto the reservation, agent William R. Logan worked for restoration of Indian water rights mainly to aid the large white population on the reservation (Massie 1987).

The federal government sued on behalf of the Fort Belknap Reservation tribes to adjudicate their water rights and those of the local, white-owned farms that existed along the northern border of the reservation. Both Indians and non-Indians needed the waters of the Milk River, as it was the only reliable source of water in the region. Furthermore, the BIA had promised to develop irrigation for the reservation from the river, while at the same time the non-Indian settlers had been promised a federal reclamation project to irrigate their lands from the Milk. The Indians claimed that when they had ceded aboriginal lands surrounding the reservation, they had retained for themselves the rest of the reservation land and enough water to make it useful. For the first time, in 1908 the Supreme Court acknowledged the existence of Indian water rights. In *Winters,* the Supreme Court held in an eight-to-one decision that when Indian reservations were established, the tribes and the United States implicitly reserved, along with the land, sufficient water to fulfill the purposes of the reservations (Hundley 1982, 17).

The efforts of the federal government to defend the water rights of the tribes residing on the Fort Belknap Reservation met with the approval of the Supreme Court when it decided that Indians' "command of the lands and the waters" before non-Indian occupation overrode the claims of the non-Indian settlers. The case is significant not only because its decision restored water to the tribes but even more so for the reasoning that led to the decision. Justice Joseph McKenna, speaking for the majority, reasoned:

> The lands ceded, were, it is true, also arid; and some argument may be urged, and is urged, that with their cession there was the cession of the waters, without which they would be valueless, and "civilized communities could not be established thereon." And this, it is further contended, the Indians knew, and yet made no reservation of the waters. We realize that there is a conflict of implications, but that which makes for the retention of the waters is of greater force than that which makes for their cession. The Indians had command of the lands and the waters— command of all their beneficial use, whether kept for hunting, "and grazing roving herds of stock," or turned to agriculture and the arts of civilization. Did they give up all this? Did they reduce the area of their occupation and give up the waters which made it valuable or adequate?
>
> —*Winters v. United States,* 207 U.S. 564 (1908)

McKenna based his reasoning on the section of the 1888 agreement that said: "Whereas the said Indians are desirous of disposing of so much [land] as they do not require, in order to obtain the means to enable them to become self-supporting, as a pastoral and agricultural people, and to educate their children in the paths of civilization." Even though no treaty or written agreement between the Fort Belknap tribes and the government specified water rights for the tribe, rights to enough water to make the land productive were implied in order to fulfill provisions of the treaty. The treaty stated that reservation lands were set aside so that tribal people could become self-supporting through an agricultural existence. The court then drew the inference that land without water is useless for the purposes of

farming and ranching. Therefore, when the federal government set up the reservations, they also, the theory went, reserved enough water for the Indians to turn the terrain into productive farmland.

Winters (or reserved) rights, if implemented to their maximum effect, would be extensive, as American Indians in many cases could claim the earliest priority dates in a system of prior appropriation. Unfortunately for Indian nations, there has been an immense chasm between the theory of Indian water rights (as expressed in *Winters*) and the reality. A case in point is the Colorado River. For most of the twentieth and early twenty-first century, usage of the waters of the Colorado and its tributaries, including the San Juan River and the Little Colorado River, has been governed by the 1922 Colorado River Compact, an agreement among the seven states having claims on the Colorado. The compact fully appropriated the Colorado's waters between the states, but even though the compact came into existence fourteen years after the *Winters* decision, and even though the Colorado and its tributaries flow through numerous reservation lands, including the large Navajo reservation, no water appropriations for Indian tribes were included in the Compact.

Beyond *Winters*

In fact, it would take nearly a century of litigation, including the landmark 1963 U.S. Supreme Court case *Arizona v. California,* and finally a number of negotiated water rights settlements with the tribes before a guaranteed amount of Colorado River water was made available to Indian nations. *Arizona v. California* was initiated by the state of Arizona to determine how much water the lower Colorado River Basin states (Arizona, California, and Nevada) were to receive. The federal government became involved in the case on behalf of the Indian nations of those states and as a test of the reserved-rights doctrine governing not only Indian lands but other federally owned lands as well. In practical terms, *Arizona v. California* had the result of tying the amount of Winters rights to which a tribe was entitled explicitly and directly to agriculture. Although earlier cases, such as *U.S. v. Walker River Irrigation District* (1939), had tied Indian water rights and agriculture together, *Arizona v. California* established the standard of "practicably irrigable acreage" (PIA) as the way to quantify Winters rights.

The PIA standard unleashed a number of problems. First, determining PIA proved lengthy, expensive, and controversial. It required historical, hydrological, economic, and technological studies to be conducted. Determining which lands could be irrigated practically proved highly subjective. However, the overriding problem, and one that plagued Indian water rights adjudication from the start, was that not all tribes used water for the same purposes. Some reservations are better suited for agriculture, and the cultural backgrounds of some tribes simply do not include agriculture as a significant component (despite federal efforts). Many tribes needed water for industrial purposes or, late in the twentieth century, to use in the resort developments that accompanied many reservation casinos. These needs led many tribes to seek alternative ways of securing water rights, especially after a series of congressional actions and court decisions had placed the adjudication of Winters claims in state courts.

Despite the Constitution, the Trade and Intercourse Act, and the Marshall Trilogy, which acted together to place responsibility for Indian affairs (including water rights) completely with the federal government, in 1952 Congress passed the McCarran Amendment to the Reclamation Act, which placed jurisdiction over federal water claims (including Indian Winters claims) in the state courts. In the Supreme Court's 1976 decision in *Colorado River Water Conservation District v. United States* (424 U.S. 800), purview over Indian water rights was placed explicitly in the state courts. The courts of many western states had a long history of antipathy toward Indian claims and did not feel as constrained by treaty provisions as federal courts, which is to say they felt little constraint at all.

The end result of over seventy years of litigation and contention was that Indian nations were left with an unwieldy system that refused to implement the extensive water rights they had been awarded as a result of the *Winters* decision. Tribes had extensive "paper" water rights but very little "wet" water on the reservations. This led, eventually, to a movement beginning in the 1980s to negotiate water rights settlements with the federal government and non-Indian landowners outside of the state courts. Beginning in the 1980s, the federal government began to try to convince tribes and other non-Indian westerners that negotiated streamwide adjudications and federal- (or state-) approved settlements were the best hope for getting "wet" water. Although negotiated settlements required the abandonment of Winters rights, they had more certain potential and the greatest non-Indian support for the upholding of a portion of Indian water rights. Perhaps the most important characteristic of Indian water settlements is that they provide benefits for non-Indians, ensuring more general approval than

typically meets projects solely meant to benefit tribes. Non-Indians can achieve a reasonable degree of certainty that their established water uses can continue. This certainty can be especially important to urban regions neighboring the reservations. In some cases, non-Indians have been able to obtain federal funding for projects that otherwise would have been politically impossible by "wrapping their projects in an Indian blanket"; that is, working within the context of Indian water rights settlements.

Nevertheless, as each individual settlement has demonstrated, negotiated settlements provide the states, tribes, federal government, and private water users a way to come to common solutions to problems once thought solvable only through litigation. Water exchanges, effluent exchanges, leasebacks, and water bank provisions are only a few examples of these approaches. States benefit by protecting their non-Indian citizens' future supplies of water. The federal government benefits by being able to fulfill its trust obligation to tribes. Tribes benefit by turning "paper" water, only potentially accessible through successful litigation achieved over decades, into "wet" water, which often can be used to promote economic development and self-sufficiency. Most importantly, tribes, governments, and private citizens have a chance to avoid costly, lengthy, and divisive litigation, although the negotiation process itself has proven lengthy and often even more expensive than litigation (McCool 2002).

—Steven L. Danver

See also: *American Indian Water Settlements;* Arizona v. California *(1963); Colorado River Compact of 1922;* Winters v. United States *(1908)*

BIBLIOGRAPHY

Burton, Lloyd. "American Indian Water Rights in the Future of the Southwest." In *Water and the Future of the Southwest,* edited by Zachary A. Smith, 153–76. Albuquerque: University of New Mexico Press, 1989.

DuMars, Charles T., Marilyn O'Leary, and Albert E. Utton. *Pueblo Indian Water Rights: Struggle for a Precious Resource.* Tucson: University of Arizona, 1984.

Getches, David H. "Indigenous Rights and Interests in Water under United States Law." Paper presented at the International Water Law and Indigenous Rights Seminar, Wageningen, Netherlands, March 2002.

Hare, Jon C. *Indian Water Rights: An Analysis of Current and Pending Indian Water Rights Settlements.* Washington, DC: Bureau of Indian Affairs, 1996.

Hundley, Norris C., Jr. "The Dark and Bloody Ground of Indian Water Rights: Confusion Elevated to Principle." In *Economic Development in American Indian Reservations,* Development Series

No. 1, edited by Roxanne Dunbar Ortiz. Albuquerque: University of New Mexico, 1979. Originally published in *Western Historical Quarterly* 9 (1978): 455–82.

Hundley, Norris C., Jr. "The *Winters* Decision and Indian Water Rights: A Mystery Reexamined." *Western Historical Quarterly* 13 (1982): 17–42.

Massie, Michael. "The Cultural Roots of Indian Water Rights." *Annals of Wyoming* 59, no. 1 (1987): 15–28.

McCool, Daniel. *Command of the Waters: Iron Triangles, Federal Water Development, and Indian Water.* Tucson: University of Arizona Press, 1987.

McCool, Daniel. "Indian Water Settlements: Negotiating Tribal Claims to Water." *Water Resources Update* 107 (Spring 1997): 28–32.

McCool, Daniel. *Native Waters: Contemporary Indian Water Settlements and the Second Treaty Era.* Tucson: University of Arizona Press, 2002.

McCool, Daniel. "*Winters* Comes Home to Roost." In *Fluid Arguments: Five Centuries of Western Water Conflict,* edited by Char Miller, 120–38. Tucson: University of Arizona Press, 2001.

Newell, Alan S. "First in Time: Tribal Reserved Water Rights and General Adjudications in New Mexico." In *Fluid Arguments: Five Centuries of Western Water Conflict,* edited by Char Miller, 95–119. Tucson: University of Arizona Press, 2001.

Pisani, Donald J. "Irrigation, Water Rights, and the Betrayal of Indian Allotment." *Environmental Review* 10, no. 3 (1986): 157–76.

Pisani, Donald J. *To Reclaim a Divided West: Water, Law, and Public Policy, 1848–1902.* Albuquerque: University of New Mexico Press, 1992.

Shurts, John. *Indian Reserved Water Rights: The Winters Doctrine in Its Social and Legal Context, 1880s–1930s.* Norman: University of Oklahoma Press, 2000.

Wilkinson, Charles F. *American Indians, Time, and the Law: Native Societies in a Modern Constitutional Democracy.* New Haven, CT: Yale University Press, 1987.

Wilkinson, Charles F. *Crossing the Next Meridian: Land, Water, and the Future of the American West.* Washington, DC: Island Press, 1992.

Worster, Donald. *Rivers of Empire: Water, Aridity, and the Growth of the American West.* New York: Oxford University Press, 1985.

American Indian Water Settlements

The results of litigation for Indian water rights in state courts can vary, but the process is always very expensive and all too often takes decades to conclude. Even where the rights seem plain, the capriciousness of the court system means that tribes have had to enter into lengthy and expensive litigation with no guarantee of success. The burdens that litigation places on the tribes as well as on the federal, state, and private parties to the lawsuits have persuaded all parties to consider negotiation as an alternative to litigation. With litigation appearing less and less promising to the tribes, and with the Reagan-era cutbacks even to "pork barrel" programs "under the Indian blanket," the federal government

began in the 1980s to encourage the negotiation of Indian water rights settlements. Ever since, the federal government has promoted negotiated settlements as the best way in which all parties can resolve their water claims. Concluded and implemented at both state and federal levels, these settlements have in many cases ended decades of litigation and carry with them the promise of delivering real, "wet" water to the tribes.

Since the onset of negotiated settlements in the early 1980s, twenty-one federally approved negotiated settlements of Indian water rights had been concluded as of 2008, with numerous others at various stages of tribal, state, and federal approval. Though culturally and geographically diverse, most of the tribes that have entered into settlements are in the American West. They include the Blackfeet, Chippewa Creek of the Rocky Boy Reservation, Crow, Gila River Indian Community, Hidastsa and Acara Tribes of the Fort Bertold Reservation, Kickapoo, Klamath, Lummi Nation, Mandan, Navajo, Nez Perce, Taos Pueblo, Tohono O'Odham, Utes, Warm Springs Tribe, Yurok, and Zuni. Settlement negotiations usually begin after a tribe or the United States has already become involved in a case involving water rights claimed by a state and other non-Indian water users. The negotiations necessary to achieve a water settlement involve alternative dispute resolution, which allows for all the interested parties to participate. This type of resolution is most effective when the parties disagree over issues of fact in technical data; therefore, they sometimes rely on court decisions to decide basic legal questions such as the priority date of the reservation. Rather than seeking final stream adjudications in the courts, the parties use the court-determined data to achieve a solution that will satisfy some of the desires of all sides rather than all of the desires of one side. Tribal water needs are addressed without completely eliminating non-Indian water uses, although neither side is usually able to achieve all of its goals (McCool 2002).

In a land of limited water such as the West, this means that the tribes probably will not receive their full share of water as determined by the rights bestowed by *Winters v. United States* (1908). But in return, they often get money that enables them to construct facilities or projects to put the water they are allocated to use. Such federal funding has not only allowed tribes to secure water rights but has also delivered water, which the tribes have put to beneficial use. At the same time, non-Indians gain the assurance that they will be able to continue using water without the constant threat of a tribal assertion of Winters rights. Also, similar to the "Indian blanket" method, federal or state funding is often guaranteed for projects that benefit non-Indian water claimants. Because funding is usually guaranteed in the settlement package, these agreements, in the federal context, must be approved and monies appropriated by Congress. Thus, these settlements almost always require federal and, sometimes, state legislation.

Characteristics of Legal Settlements

Every settlement is unique because the legal, geographic, and economic situations of tribes vary, as do the political factors involved. The ability of a tribe and its neighbors to achieve a settlement and the receptiveness of Congress to settlements depend on a multitude of factors. However, a review of Indian water rights settlements illustrates several characteristics common to many of them.

First, with the establishment of federal development trust funds, often along with matching state funds, the costs of the settlement are shared, and the resulting mechanisms can ensure delivery of water to both Indians and non-Indians. Sometimes such federal funds, when allocated to a tribe, can be used for the development of water resources as well as for the general economic development of the tribe. Furthermore, if the tribe is not using all of the water on its reservation, a settlement can allow it to lease water for use by non-Indians off the reservation, providing income that can help build the tribe's economic infrastructure while allowing non-Indian users access to water. Most settlement packages allow tribes to market their water, but nearly all restrict these transfers more than the transfer of non-Indian water rights is restricted. Often, state governments are enthusiastic about settlements because the settlements sometimes require that water use by Indians under the settlement be subject to state water law, at least when the water is used off the reservation. Where two or more states enter into a compact allocating the use of a river that is the source of water used to satisfy tribal water rights claims, the Indian water rights settlement agreement and accompanying legislation usually provide that the compact, or the "law of the river," will govern water use. These compacts usually limit the water that Indians can market outside of their own reservations' boundaries.

Another popular aspect included in many of the settlements is a provision for implementing environmental values. At first glance, this would seem to appeal to the tribes' sensibilities while being antithetical to the reclamation values endemic to earlier water-development projects.

However, the fact that the implementation of settlements often necessitates major construction has meant that Indian water development sometimes runs at cross-purposes to environmental laws. This has sometimes caused tribes to oppose the agendas of environmental groups. On the other hand, tribes sometimes have worked closely with environmental groups to protect tribal lands and other sacred locations (McCool 1997).

Perhaps the most important characteristic of Indian water settlements is that they provide benefits for non-Indians, ensuring more ready general approval than projects that solely benefit tribes. Non-Indians can achieve a reasonable degree of certainty that their established water uses can continue. This certainty can be especially important to urban regions neighboring the reservations. In some cases, non-Indians have been able to obtain federal funding for projects that otherwise would have been politically impossible by "wrapping their projects in an Indian blanket"; that is, working within the context of Indian water rights settlements.

Nevertheless, as each individual settlement has demonstrated, negotiated settlements provide the states, tribes, federal government, and private water users a way to arrive at common solutions to problems once thought solvable only through litigation. Solutions include water exchanges, effluent exchanges, leasebacks, and water bank provisions, among many others. States benefit by protecting their non-Indian citizens' future supplies of water. The federal government benefits by being able to fulfill its trust obligation to tribes. Tribes benefit by turning "paper" water, which could become accessible only after decades of litigation (and only if that litigation were successful), into "wet" water, which tribes often use to promote economic development and self-sufficiency. Most importantly, tribes, governments, and private citizens have a chance to avoid costly, lengthy, and divisive litigation, although the negotiation process itself has proven lengthy and often even more expensive than litigation (McCool 2002).

Since the 1980s, the federal government has been trying to convince tribes and other non-Indian westerners that negotiated streamwide adjudications and federal- (or state-) approved settlements are the best hope for getting "wet" water. Although negotiated settlements require abandonment of Winters rights, they have more certain potential and the greatest non-Indian support for the upholding of a portion of Indian water.

—Steven L. Danver

See also: *American Indian Water Rights;* Winters v. United States *(1908)*

BIBLIOGRAPHY

Colby, Bonnie G. "Tribal Water Settlements in Arizona." In *Arizona's Water Future: Challenges and Opportunities* (report of the 85th Arizona Town Hall, Grand Canyon, AZ, October–November 2004), 115–24. Tucson: University of Arizona, 2004. Available at http://ag.arizona.edu/azwater/publications/townhall/townhall.html.

McCool, Daniel. "Indian Water Settlements: Negotiating Tribal Claims to Water." *Water Resources Update* 107 (Spring 1997): 28–32.

McCool, Daniel. *Native Waters: Contemporary Indian Water Settlements and the Second Treaty Era.* Tucson: University of Arizona Press, 2002.

McGuire, Thomas R. "Indian Water Rights Settlements: A Case Study in the Rhetoric of Implementation." *American Indian Culture and Research Journal* 15, no. 2 (1991): 139–69.

Aquaculture

Aquaculture is defined as the science, art, and business of breeding and raising saltwater and freshwater organisms such as finfish, mollusks, crustaceans, and aquatic plants. The farm products are typically used for a variety of purposes, including providing food, nutritional supplements, animal feed, industrial products including biofuel and fiber, recreation, aquatic pets, and protection for endangered species. Carp, trout, catfish, tilapia, shrimp, mussels, lobsters, oysters, watercress, water chestnuts, and kelp are well-known farm-raised species. There are a variety of terms related to aquaculture, including aquafarming (a synonym for aquaculture), mariculture (aquaculture in an oceanic environment), algaculture (the production of kelp, seaweed, and other algae), and aquaponics (integration of aquaculture and hydroponics, where the latter is defined as the production of plants in a soilless medium). Despite aquaculture's tremendous potential, there is concern over its environmental impacts.

Aquaculture involves cultivating aquatic populations under controlled or semicontrolled conditions, as contrasted with commercial fishing, which involves the harvesting of wild fish. The basic centerpieces of an aquaculture system can include ponds or raceways, cages or net pens, and recirculating systems. The most economically important form of aquaculture is fish farming, which accounts for an ever increasing share of the world's fisheries production. Formerly a business for small farms, it is now being aggressively pursued by large agribusiness.

A rapidly growing global human population has resulted in increased demand for high-protein aquatic food products.

Unfortunately, there is catch stagnation in wild fisheries and an overexploitation of many popular food species, including bluefin tuna, Chilean sea bass, Atlantic cod, and several varieties of salmon. The combination of catch stagnation and the growing demand for high-quality protein provides a healthy economic climate for modern aquafarmers. Over the long term, aquaculture continues to offer the best alternative to continued depletion of the earth's natural fishery. As a result, aquaculture is growing substantially faster than all other animal food-producing sectors.

During the late twentieth and early twenty-first centuries, aquaculture has expanded, intensified, and made great technological advances. Its potential for enhancing and stabilizing local food supplies, easing the burdens of poverty, and improving rural living conditions has been recognized by international organizations such as the Food and Agriculture Organization (FAO) of the United Nations. And aquaculture is not restricted to food production. Sports anglers rely on fish hatcheries to supplement wild stock, bait organisms are grown for both sport and commercial purposes, and the cultivation of ornamental fish and plants is an important industry in some parts of the world. Aquaculture is also important for protecting endangered species, and the commercial cultivation of algae may be a significant factor in expanding the biofuel industry. While the above applications are expansive, aquaculture faces its own serious concerns, particularly with regard to sustainability, which must be dealt with responsibly and soon. For example, the industry must proceed in a more environmentally conscious manner.

History of Aquaculture

Aquaculture has a long history. Aquaculture existed in China in 500 BCE where water was trapped after river flooding subsided, leaving fish, mainly carp, impounded in natural depressions. The Japanese cultivated seaweed, and the Greeks and Romans constructed ponds for fish and shellfish cultures. Hawaiians constructed oceanic enclosures.

In central Europe, early Christian monasteries adopted Roman aquaculture practices. These technologies spread in Europe during the Middle Ages throughout areas where fish were previously scarce. Improvements in transportation during the nineteenth century made fish easily available and less expensive, even in inland areas, making aquaculture less important as a food source. Since 1980, with the worldwide demand for animal protein expanding, the practice of aquaculture has again begun to expand. By the early twenty-first century, it had become as significant a source of fish as wild fisheries.

In 2010, Valentin Abe, an aquaculture specialist from the Ivory Coast who was educated at Auburn University, Alabama, was named one of *Time* magazine's "100 Most Influential People in the World." His work raising fish in Haiti is credited with putting people to work and raising incomes in that devastated country. His entire aquaculture operation is powered with solar energy.

About 430 (97 percent) of the species cultured as of 2007 were domesticated during the last century. Domestication typically requires about ten years of research into how to keep the fish healthy, breed them in captivity, and ensure that they do not carry diseases harmful to humans. Domesticated aquatic species involve fewer risks to humans than land animals, which have historically taken a large toll on human lives through diseases such as smallpox, diphtheria, and mad-cow disease. No human pathogens of comparable virulence have emerged from marine species.

Modern Aquaculture

The worldwide practice of aquaculture runs the gamut from fairly low-technology methods to highly intensive systems. At one extreme, basic aquaculture is little more than a simple stock impoundment, using natural bodies of water and making few if any alterations to the environment. These "flow-through" operations typically use large quantities of high-quality water. But while they require limited management skill, a low initial investment, and low long-term operating costs, they also result in low yields per unit volume. At the other extreme, intensive aquaculture raises plants and animals in systems such as tanks and raceways, where the environmental parameters are carefully measured and controlled and dependence on the natural environment is minimized. Such systems require intensive management and usually involve substantial initial investment and high operating costs, but they result in much higher yields per unit volume.

With demand for aquaculture products exploding and water resources becoming increasingly restricted, many aquafarmers are turning to real-time monitoring and control technologies to grow aquatic plants and fish more rapidly and at higher densities. Additionally, the development of water-recycling technologies has made it possible to construct and operate fish farms in locations where water and land resources were previously inadequate.

When fish are grown at higher densities, dissolved oxygen (DO) and other water quality parameters become limiting factors. Furthermore, in large and intensive aquaculture operations, tighter operating parameters mean less room for error. Therefore, continuous water quality monitoring, and even automation, becomes a necessity. Automated systems can provide real-time control of oxygenators and aerators, as well as feeders, pumps, heaters, chillers, and other devices. Continuous monitoring and control of water quality parameters has two basic benefits. First, fish are grown at high densities while minimizing demands on water, energy, and labor. Second, environmental stress, the main cause of fish disease and mortality, is reduced.

In recent years, the application of biotechnology to aquaculture has sparked a "blue revolution," a counterpart to the "green revolution" in farming. The use of fish hatcheries to supply farms and enhance wild stocks has become commonplace, and the world is now in the second stage of the revolution with the use of genetic engineering—including splicing genes from one fish strain or species into another—to produce desired characteristics. Salmon have been genetically modified for faster growth, and this effort is highly controversial.

Ecological Impact of Aquaculture

Aquaculture can be more environmentally damaging than exploiting wild fisheries. Concerns include waste handling, side effects of antibiotics, competition between farmed animals and wild animals, and using smaller fish to feed more marketable carnivorous fish. However, research and commercial feed improvements have lessened some of these concerns.

Fish waste is organic and composed of nutrients necessary in all components of the aquatic food chain. Mariculture produces much higher than normal fish waste concentrations. The waste collects on the lake or ocean bottom, damaging or eliminating bottom-dwelling life. Waste can also decrease DO levels in the water column, putting further pressure on wild animals. Salmon farms are often sited in pristine coastal ecosystems, which they then pollute. A farm with 100,000 salmon discharges more fecal waste than a human community with a population of 30,000. This waste, which often contains antibiotics and pesticides, is discharged untreated directly into the surrounding aquatic environment. In Chile's fjords, salmon farms have created anoxic conditions, deadening the water, and have led to the spread of infectious salmon anemia. The solution for the salmon-farming companies has been simply to move elsewhere.

Aquaculture is becoming a significant threat to coastal ecosystems through the loss of important habitat. About 20 percent of the world's mangrove forests have been destroyed since 1980, partly due to shrimp farming. This disruption has been characterized as the marine equivalent of "slash-and-burn" farming. Over the years, hundreds of thousands of acres of Indonesian mangroves have been converted into shrimp farms. Most of these farms are abandoned within a decade because of toxic buildup and nutrient loss.

Fish can also escape from inland ponds and coastal pens, where they can interbreed with their wild counterparts, diluting wild genetic stocks. Even worse, escaped fish can become invasive, outcompeting native species.

There are also issues concerning genetic research. Getting the most value out of genetic resources means addressing the considerable ethical, environmental, and legal issues associated with genetic modification, the management of wild genetic diversity, and the collection and use of genetic resources. Bringing policies for the management of aquatic biodiversity and of the aquaculture industry up to contemporary standards is an enormous challenge, which advances in biotechnology will only magnify.

A number of methods are available to minimize the environmental impacts of aquaculture, including encouraging all aquafarmers to stay within the bounds of sustainable production levels (given their technical expertise, resources, and location). Additionally, moderate stock densities, use of high-quality feeds, aeration, settling ponds, constructed wetlands, minimal use of organic and inorganic fertilizers, government-mandated monitoring programs, and industrywide self-regulation are all important options for a sustainable aquaculture industry in the modern era.

Aquaponics

One promising extension of aquaculture is aquaponics, an integration that links recirculating aquaculture with hydroponic vegetable, flower, and herb production. The waste from a water-based biological system serves as nutrients for a land-based biological system. Aquatic animal fish waste accumulates in water as a by-product of keeping animals in a closed system or tank. This effluent-rich water, which becomes toxic to the animals, is high in nutrients required by plants. The plants take up nutrients, reducing or eliminating the water's toxicity for the aquatic animals. The now cleaner water is returned to the aquatic animal environment, and the cycle continues.

In theory, aquaponic systems do not discharge water. The systems rely on the relationship between the aquatic animals and the plants to maintain the environment. Water is only added to replace water loss due to absorption by plants, evaporation into the air, or the removal of biomass from the system. Aquaponic systems vary in size from smallish indoor units to large commercial systems. They can use either freshwater or saltwater, depending on the type of aquatic animal and vegetation. Recent advances by researchers and growers have turned aquaponics into a working model of sustainable food production.

The technology associated with aquaponics is complex. It requires the ability to manage simultaneously the production and marketing of two different types of food products. But it can be done. At the northern outskirts of Milwaukee, Wisconsin, Growing Power Inc. has fourteen greenhouses arrayed on two acres of land. Will Allen, founder of Growing Power, designed, built, and operates an aquaponic system that can be replicated for as little as $3,000. Water from tilapia and perch tanks flows into a gravel bed, where the waste breaks down to produce nitrogen that plants can use. The gravel bed supports a crop of watercress, which further filters the water. The nutrient-rich water is then pumped into overhead beds to feed crops of tomatoes and salad greens.

Future Prospects

With wild stocks declining due to overfishing and pollution, aquaculture will have a more significant role to play in meeting future demand for fresh fish, biofuels, etc. Developments in research continue to lead to improvements in aquaculture production systems, resulting in increased production efficiency, higher product quality for consumers, and a more sustainable industry. There are, however, serious environmental and ethical issues that must be addressed in a timely manner if the aquaculture industry is to survive. Aquaponics offers an important permutation for researchers, farmers, and aquaculturists.

—Roger D. Hansen

See also: *Commercial Fishing; Nonindigenous Aquatic Nuisance Prevention and Control Act of 1990; Poverty and Water*

BIBLIOGRAPHY

Burnell, Gavin, and Geoff Allen, eds. *New Technologies in Aquaculture: Improving Production Efficiency, Quality and Environmental Management.* Woodhead Food Series No. 178. Cambridge, UK: Woodhead, 2009.

Diver, Steve (updated by Lee Rinehart). "Aquaponics: Integration of Hydroponics and Aquaculture." 2006; revised 2010. http://attra .ncat.org/attra-pub/PDF/aquaponic.pdf.

FAO (Food and Agriculture Organization of the United Nations) Fisheries Department. *State of World Aquaculture* (FAO Technical Paper No. 500). Rome: FAO Fisheries Department, 2006. Available at ftp://ftp.fao.org/docrep/fao/009/a0874e/a0874e00.pdf.

Selock, Dan. *Aquaculture in the World: An Introduction to the Industry.* Rural Enterprise and Alternative Development Initiative (READI) Report No. 5. Carbondale: Southern Illinois University–Carbondale, 2001. Available at http://www.teleamerica.net/reference/ Science/AquaCulture.pdf.

Aquifers

For most of human history, people have known that by digging wells deep enough in the ground, a water supply could be obtained, even some distance from rivers, lakes, and ponds. Homes, villages, farms, and some early industries have relied on well water. Only in the past two centuries have geologists identified the system of aquifers that stores water in rock formations and clay soils, which wells tap into. The supply of water in these aquifers is finite but, in part, renewable. Water flows through aquifers in a dynamic equilibrium of discharge and recharge. In some regions, human activity is depleting aquifers more rapidly than natural cycles are replacing the water being withdrawn. Confined aquifers lie under layers of impermeable rocks or clay. When a confined aquifer is tapped to supply water, the supply is not quickly replenished and can eventually be exhausted. Unconfined aquifers closer to the surface are connected to the hydrological cycle of waters seeping from snow melt, rainfall, canals, streams, and reservoirs. Aquifers can also be degraded by accumulation of hydrocarbons—naturally or as a by-product of human industry. Some aquifers naturally contain both hydrocarbon reservoirs and water.

Observation of flow in artesian groundwater dates to the mid-1800s. In 1885, T. C. Chamberlin identified the geological features of layers that yield a water supply. These include a layer of porous material between two watertight layers above and below, an exposed edge of the porous strata to receive water from rainfall, and some incline in the layers holding the water so that water enters at a higher level and discharges at a lower level. In 1896, N. H. Darton provided an early description of a regional aquifer system in his study of "the great artesian basin of the eastern portion of South Dakota and North Dakota."

Aquifers naturally receive water from rainfall and seepage into the ground, while naturally discharging water into streams and lakes. Leakage out of the aquifer can occur hundreds of miles from the area where water flows in. Most aquifers slope; confined aquifers have potential energy with sufficient pressure to drive water through a borehole to the land surface, provided that water enters the aquifer from a higher elevation than the wellhead. Potentiometric surface maps are increasingly being used to record where this potential energy exists.

National Ground Water Association

Founded in 1948 as the National Water Well Association, the National Ground Water Association (NGWA) is a nonprofit, international professional organization with more than 13,000 members drawn from all facets of the groundwater industry. It endeavors to educate its members, government officials, and the general public on a myriad of issues related to groundwater, such as aquifer protection, the safety of well water, and geothermal energy. The NGWA sponsors numerous professional development opportunities for members, including conferences, workshops, and certification programs. Technical information is shared through three publications, namely *Ground Water*, *Ground Water Monitoring & Remediation*, and *Water Well Journal*. The organization's services to the public include the management of two specialized Web sites. Wellowner.org is intended for the dissemination of information related to the maintenance of water well systems, with a special emphasis on providing information on how to test the quality and safety of well water. Ground Water Adventurers is aimed at children. It is intended to educate them on the uses of groundwater and the need to protect this finite resource for future generations.

—John R. Burch Jr.

See also: *Wells*

BIBLIOGRAPHY

Chapelle, Francis. *The Hidden Sea: Ground Water, Springs, and Wells.* Tucson, AZ: Geoscience Press, 2007.

National Ground Water Association. http://www.ngwa.org.

National Ground Water Association. "Ground Water Adventurers." http://www.ground wateradventurers.org.

Wellowner.org. http://www.wellowner.org.

Mapping and Classification of Aquifers

Twenty-five regional aquifer systems have been identified and mapped since 1978 by the Regional Aquifer-System Analysis (RASA) Program of the U.S. Geological Survey (USGS). These include the Northern Atlantic Coastal Plain, Southeastern Coastal Plain, Snake River, Central, Gulf Coastal, Great Basin, and Northeast glacial aquifers, as well as aquifers in the northern Great Plains, High Plains, Central Valley–California, northern Midwest, and Southwest alluvial basins and the Floridan Aquifer. Each of these regional aquifers is made up of a variety of smaller aquifer systems, which lie at various depths and in different rock, clay, or gravel formations. Large areas of the High Plains Aquifer lie at depths of less than 200 feet, but in areas near the Oklahoma Panhandle, much of central Nebraska, and a small part of southern South Dakota, water lies in formations 400 to 1,000 feet deep. Distinct freshwater aquifers underlie islands in the Caribbean and Hawaii, Michigan, the Appalachian valleys, and the northern Rocky Mountains, among other areas. Using RASA findings, the USGS has assembled the first detailed maps offering nationwide graphic data on all regional aquifers into the *Ground Water Atlas of the United States.*

Geologists also classify aquifers by the age and type of rock in which water is found. Upper and Lower Cretaceous rocks contain aquifers in nearly all regions, with Cretaceous shale making up most of the Great Plains confining system. Madison Limestone, also called Mississippian, contains aquifers in the Atlantic coastal plain, much of the Midwest, and the northern Great Plains. Carbonate rocks such as limestone contain a large portion of the aquifers worldwide. Sandstone and other sedimentary rock layers of Cambrian and Tertiary origin contain aquifers in the upper Colorado and San Juan River basin and in parts of the Midwest and Great Plains. As the different ages of the rock formations suggest, in any region, there may be up to ten layers of aquifers at various depths, which may or may not flow into each other. Both hydrogeologists and speleologists have contributed to mapping aquifers—the former by means of drilling and dye tracing, the latter through physical exploration of caves.

Freshwater Aquifer Use

About 83 billion gallons per day of the freshwater used in the United States in 2000 came from groundwater, according to USGS estimates. This represents about 20 percent of total U.S. freshwater use and includes 16 billion gallons a day for public water supplies and 56.9 billion gallons for irrigation. Use of groundwater for agricultural, industrial, and urban-residential development has many effects on aquifers, on surface water, and on the land itself. These include changes in water levels, changes in recharge and discharge (water flowing into and out of the aquifers), land subsidence (which can be either elastic or long-term and nearly irreversible), sinkhole collapse, and saltwater intrusion into what had been a reliable freshwater supply.

When human development causes discharge from an aquifer to increase, natural recharge may also increase to compensate, depending on the water sources feeding the aquifer. A notable exception is the High Plains (Ogallala) Aquifer System, where saturation of water in the rock layers under Texas and western Kansas has declined by 25 percent. In west Texas and eastern New Mexico, withdrawal of water between 1960 and 1980 exceeded natural recharge by a factor of 30. In the Central Valley of California, extensive use of pumped water from the aquifer system has markedly changed the flow of water but has resulted in a new equilibrium. Instead of being recharged by streams flowing out of the mountains, groundwater flow is recharged by surface water imported for irrigation, which flows to areas where groundwater is withdrawn for irrigation. Natural discharge of groundwater into lakes and streams has sharply decreased, while recharge to the aquifer system has increased nearly six times, mostly from irrigation return flow.

Diversion of surface water for irrigation can actually raise the level of groundwater. In the eastern Snake River Plain, where the river passes through southern Idaho, intensive agriculture and irrigation had in 1980 produced an 80 percent increase in water flow through the aquifer system as compared to the earlier natural flow. Over 60 percent of the recharge is now percolation of excess water from irrigated surface land.

Aquifers in Law and Politics

Aquifers are seldom the primary focus of specific legislation, but they have been mentioned and considered at least since the Safe Drinking Water Act of 1974 (Pub. L. 93-523, 88 Stat. 1660). Section 1424(e) of the Act (42 U.S.C. 300f, 300h) provides that if an aquifer is designated as the sole or principal source of drinking water for an area, no federal financial assistance may be committed to any project that might contaminate the aquifer through a recharge zone "so as to create a significant hazard to public health." Designation of sole-source aquifers is handled by the Environmental Protection Agency (EPA), which as of March 2009 had designated seventy-seven sole-source aquifers. Designation can be on the EPA administrator's initiative or in response to a petition. The 1974 Act was amended and updated in 1977, 1979, 1980, 1986, 1988, and 1996. The Safe Drinking Water Act Amendments of 1986 (Pub. L. 99-339, 110 Stat. 1613) mandated federal monitoring and regulation of state enforcement programs under the original Act (Section 1426, 42 U.S.C. 300h-5) and established a new federally funded sole-source aquifer demonstration program to protect aquifers designated as a sole source of drinking water (Section 1427, 42 U.S.C. 300h-6).

The Clean Water Act of 1972 (Pub. L. 92-500, 86 Stat. 816-905, 33 U.S.C. Sec. 1251–1376) might have had a significant impact on aquifer water quality, since Section 208 (33 U.S.C. 1288) directed development of plans to control non–point source pollution, that is, pollution from large land areas such as runoff from agricultural land and paved urban areas. However, Section 208 has largely produced detailed state plans that were never funded and, therefore, have never been implemented. Plans prepared under Section 208 are cross-referenced in the 1986 drinking water act amendments as one criterion for demonstration projects.

Since 1976, there have been at least ten water resources development acts, largely codified in 42 U.S.C. Chapter 19B, Section 1962. Laws enacted in subsequent years have amended and updated provisions from previous acts. The Water Resources Development Act of 1986 (Pub. L. 99-662, 100 Stat. 4168) directed the U.S. Geological Survey to monitor the levels of the High Plains (Ogallala) Aquifer and report annually to Congress (Title III). USGS's response was the High Plains Water-Level Monitoring Study (HPWLMS). Reporting was reduced to every two years by the Federal Reports Elimination and Sunset Act of 1995 (Pub. L. 104-66, 109 Stat. 734).

In 2006, Congress adopted and the president signed the United States–Mexico Transboundary Aquifer Assessment Act (Pub. L. 109-448, 120 Stat. 3328–3332), which authorized the study of aquifers underlying the states of Texas, New Mexico, and Arizona and the neighboring Mexican states. Four transboundary aquifers have been designated as priorities for study: the Hueco Bolson and Mesilla Basin Aquifers in the greater El Paso/Ciudad Juárez region and the Santa Cruz and San Pedro Aquifers underlying the Arizona-Sonora border. Fifty million dollars was appropriated for ten years to fund the Transboundary Aquifer Assessment Program (TAAP).

Federal legislation includes a growing number of provisions to protect and study local aquifers, often at the initiative of local congressional representatives. The Water Resources Development Act of 2007 (Pub. L. 110-114, 121 Stat. 1041) includes two provisions for local aquifers. Section 4093 directs the secretary of the Army (acting through the U.S. Army Corps of Engineers) to conduct a feasibility study for a project supplying water to Grand County and the city of Moab, Utah, that will examine current and future demands on the Spanish Valley Aquifer. In the same Act, Section 6001 authorizes $42.5 million to carry out a project to protect the Hillsboro and Okeechobee Aquifers in Florida, previously authorized by Section 101(s)(16) of the Water Resources Development Act of 1999 (113 Stat. 276). The Acts are referenced in 33 U.S.C. 2201.

One of the few congressional acts solely concerned with a specific local aquifer, the Wichita Project Equus Beds Division Authorization Act of 2005 (Pub. L. 109-299, 120 Stat. 1473), authorized the Secretary of the Interior to assist in funding and implementing a plan for the local water supply of Wichita, Kansas. The Equus Beds Aquifer Recharge, Storage and Recovery (ASR) plan proposed to move water from the Little Arkansas River into the Equus Beds Aquifer, used by the city for municipal and industrial water. The complex plan for "restoration and storage of the aquifer" required careful provisions to take river water into a series of infiltration wells only when it exceeded certain flow levels. The mean base flow of the river is 20 cubic feet per second. Surface diversion is authorized only when flow exceeds that amount, and operation of infiltration wells is authorized only when river flow is at least double that amount. Congress authorized an appropriation for 25 percent of the total cost of the project, or $30 million, whichever is less, indexed to January 2003 prices and adjusted for fluctuations in engineering cost indexes applicable to the construction required.

More comprehensively, the Omnibus Public Land Management Act of 2009 (Pub. L. 111-11, 123 Stat. 991), directs for the first time a "systematic groundwater monitoring program for each major aquifer system located in the United States" (Section 9507[b]). While mapping of aquifers has been mandated and funded since 1978, through the RASA project, the 2009 enactment directed continuous monitoring. This reflected growing recognition over the past thirty to forty years that aquifers are both essential to human life and activity and can be degraded if not properly managed. Demand for water has exceeded the level where aquifers can be considered an open and inexhaustible resource.

Development of a body of law for preservation and management of aquifers has largely broken away from the traditional dichotomies of "liberal" and "conservative." Although President Ronald Reagan found many of the 1986 Safe Drinking Water Act Amendments to be "significant and unwarranted intrusions into local and state land-use control and water-use decisions," the principal sponsor of the Equus Beds authorization in 2005 was Senator Pat Roberts, a conservative Kansas Republican. The most devastating impact of drawing down an aquifer faster than water is replaced has occurred in western Texas, eastern New Mexico, Kansas, and Oklahoma, where irrigation for agriculture has been sharply curtailed by wells drying up or producing saline water. The 2009 Land Management Act was passed with the support of 38 Republicans joining 247 Democrats in the House of Representatives, while 77 senators voted to enact the bill, including Republicans from Tennessee, Wyoming, Utah, Idaho, Indiana, Kansas, Alabama, and Mississippi, among other states.

—Charles Rosenberg

See also: *Government Water Decision Making; Groundwater Recharge and Water Reuse; Wells*

BIBLIOGRAPHY

Calabrese, Edward J., Charles E. Gilbert, and Harris Pastides, eds. *Safe Drinking Water Act: Amendments, Regulations and Standards.* Chelsea, MI: Lewis, 1989.

Canter, Larry W., and Robert C. Knox. *Ground Water Pollution Control.* Chelsea, MI: Lewis, 1985.

Deutsch, William J. *Groundwater Geochemistry: Fundamentals and Applications to Contamination.* Boca Raton, FL: CRC Press, 1997.

Layzer, Judith A. *Natural Experiments: Ecosystem-Based Management and the Environment.* Cambridge: Massachusetts Institute of Technology, 2008.

Lerner, David, and N. R. G. Walton, eds. *Contaminated Land and Groundwater: Future Directions.* London: Geological Society, 1998.

Robins, N. S., ed. *Groundwater Pollution, Aquifer Recharge, and Vulnerability.* Geology Society Special Publication No. 130. Bath, UK: Geological Society Publishing House, 1998.

Sun, Ren Jen, and Richard H. Johnston. *Regional Aquifer-System Analysis Program of the U.S. Geological Survey, 1978–1992.* U.S. Geological Survey Circular 1099. Washington, DC: U.S. Government Printing Office, 1994.

Suthersan, Suthan S., and Fred C. Payne. *In Situ Remediation Engineering.* Boca Raton, FL: CRC Press, 2005.

Climate Change

The potential for human industry to induce warmer temperatures worldwide was first identified in the 1890s by Swedish chemist Svante Arrhenius, who estimated that doubling the concentration of carbon dioxide in the air would raise global temperatures by an average of 5°C (8°F). Carbon dioxide absorbs and retains thermal radiation from the surface of the planet, keeping the atmosphere warmer than if solar radiation absorbed on the surface naturally radiated back into space. In addition to carbon dioxide, gases with this property include methane, nitrous oxide, halocarbons, ozone, and water vapor. Arrhenius was initially more concerned that global warming might be necessary to avert a new "Little Ice Age" such as Europe experienced between 1420–1850, a conclusion advanced later by the Marshall Institute in 1989. British scientist G. S. Callendar documented a 10 percent increase in atmospheric carbon dioxide from 1900 to 1935, closely matching the amount of fuel burned during the same period. Adding new data on absorption and emission of radiation by trace gases, he concluded in a 1939 article in *Meteorological Magazine* that "as man is now changing the composition of the atmosphere at a rate which must be very exceptional on the geological time scale," the principal result of increased carbon dioxide in the atmosphere would be "a gradual increase in the mean temperature of the colder regions of the earth."

Climate change is one of the most contentious issues in science and in government. Questions and data are complex and comprehensive, so there is room for plausible doubt about any conclusion. The economic and social implications require so many changes in current practice and habits that there is great political reluctance to accept the conclusions of most geologists, ecologists, biologists, meteorologists, and chemists. There are considerable data to support the theory that rising carbon dioxide levels have created a rapid, unnatural increase in global temperatures, with mostly negative implications for rainfall, drought, ocean levels, a variety of freshwater sources (such as glacier melt into rivers), and weather. A minority of respectable scientific argument contends that this body of theory and its conclusions are wrong—although some freely admit that the climate may in fact be warming for other reasons. Political debate entertains an argument based on no science at all, that the entire notion is a hoax.

The Long-Term Geological Record

Geologists, and related disciplines, have concluded that the 4 billion year history of the earth has seen considerable fluctuation in planetary temperatures and climate. Establishing the degree of fluctuation, duration, and causes rests in part on proxy data—that is, inferring a probable fact from a known fact, similar to the use of circumstantial evidence in court. Geological evidence suggests that the earth has experienced greenhouse periods of much warmer temperatures than terrestrial life experiences now, as well as icehouse periods with much colder temperatures. These conditions alternated at intervals of 140 to 170 million years. Within the fairly recent Quaternary Period, there have been six or seven periods of advancing polar ice caps. Measured by evidence of periods when oaks and other deciduous trees grew and survived in Europe, these "ice ages" are estimated to have run in cycles of 700,000 to 800,000 years. The most recent of these ice ages ended about 15,000 years ago (Drake 2000).

Recorded human history lies within an "interglacial" period, with retreating polar ice caps and warming temperatures. Geological evidence and recorded history both show that climates have fluctuated within this geologically brief era. Between 5000 and 3000 BCE, average global temperature is estimated to have been 1.0°C–3.0°C (1.8°F–5.4°F) warmer than today. Based in part on study of tree rings from different parts of the world, scientists have determined that cooling began around 3500 BC, with a much cooler and drier period from 3000 to 1000 BC. Civilizations in the Indus Valley, Mesopotamia, and Egypt all arose during this cooler period. The best-known recent fluctuations are the Medieval Warm Period from 800 to 1200 CE, first identified by British meteorologist Hubert Lamb, and the subsequent Little Ice Age from 1420 to 1850 CE.

The Modern Warming Trend

One of the key sets of data pointing to rapid human-caused warming is a graph of northern hemisphere temperatures over the past 600 years, as reconstructed by climatologists Michael Mann, Raymond Bradley, and Malcolm Hughes (1999). While it shows continuous variation within a range of 0.8 degrees or so, it also shows almost straight-line warming of 0.6 degrees above the previous range starting in the mid-nineteenth century, a period of rapidly expanding industrial production. Five other sets of data point to a similar twentieth-century upward trend (Fagan 2008). Observations taken by Charles David Keeling of the Scripps Institute of Oceanography from towers at the Mauna Loa observatory in Hawaii from 1958 to 2003 show that during this period, atmospheric carbon dioxide increased from 316 parts per million (ppm) to 376 ppm (DiMento 2007). In contrast, atmospheric carbon dioxide before the Industrial Revolution is estimated as having been less than 285 ppm. Looking forward, from the 2007 level of 385 ppm, levels are likely to rise to between 600 and 1,000 ppm by 2100.

The impact of warmer temperatures on oceans, lakes, rivers, and water sources has been well documented. In Glacier National Park, eighteen glaciers have entirely melted away since 1966. From 1950 to 1997, snowpack in Oregon, western Washington, and northern California shrank 50 to 75 percent, which has already resulted in water rationing in some drier years. Most of the freshwater in the region depends on melting snowpack throughout the spring and summer. At the same time, flooding may increase in fall and winter, as precipitation not stored in the form of snow runs off immediately into vulnerable lower elevations. By the middle of the twenty-first century, average snowpack in the Colorado River basin is projected to decrease by 30 percent. Glaciers in the Sierra Nevada have shrunk from 31 to 78 percent in the past century, matched by an upward migration of the tree line to a level not matched in 7,000 years. Increased drought is likely, particularly in the southwestern states and in the Great Plains and Midwestern Farm Belt. Researchers at the National Oceanic and Atmospheric Administration believe that drought in the Midwest in the early twenty-first century was due in part to a 1°C rise in water temperatures in the western Pacific, reducing precipitation from the eastern Pacific across North America.

Temperatures are rising fastest in the Arctic and Antarctic regions. The Columbia Glacier in Prince William Sound, Alaska, has retreated eight miles in sixteen years. Greenland is covered by an ice sheet up to three kilometers thick, and in the past ten years, the rate of loss to melting has more than doubled from 90 kilometers annually to 220. If the Greenland ice sheet is eliminated, sea levels could rise as much as seven meters (twenty-three feet) by 2100, flooding many coastal urban areas. Even without that catastrophic event, storm surges will be an increasing threat to coastal cities. In the Southeast, higher water levels will make hurricanes much more devastating, while warmer waters may increase the intensity of hurricanes. Although it is not possible to connect the fury of Hurricane Katrina in 2005 directly to global warming, temperatures in the Gulf of Mexico were at least 1°C warmer than normal at that time. It is well established that hurricanes pick up wind speed when moving over warm ocean water. Even duck hunters are worried that a drying up of breeding grounds in the north-central states, and flooding of wet-lands along the coasts from even a 3.5-inch rise in ocean levels, could reduce duck populations by up to 39 percent by the 2030s.

Global Political Response

Political framework to evaluate climate change and measures to ameliorate it can be traced at least back to 1988, when the Intergovernmental Panel on Climate Change (IPCC) was convened by the World Meteorological Organization and the United Nations Environmental Program. IPCC's Fourth Assessment in 2007 predicted an increase in global average surface temperature by 2100 of between 1.8°C and 4.0°C (3.24°F–7.2°F). The United Nations Framework Convention on Climate Change (UNFCCC) in 1992 set a goal of returning to 1990 levels of carbon dioxide emissions into the atmosphere by 2000. This goal was never backed up by specific measures. A series of UNFCCC intergovern-mental meetings began in 1995 with the First Conference of Parties in Berlin, followed by a Second Conference in Geneva in 1996. The Third Conference in Kyoto in 1997 was the first to agree on targets to reduce emission of six greenhouse gases, but at the end of the Fourth Conference in Buenos Aires in 1998, most decisions on how to reach those targets remained open.

A conference was held in December 2009 in Copenhagen to develop a new treaty replacing the one adopted in Kyoto. Opponents of specific measures urged that economic growth required increased energy consumption and that the necessary energy for growth could not be produced or har-nessed within the reduced emission levels proposed. Ultimately, no official treaty came out of the conference. During the first decade of the twenty-first century, industri-alized nations such as the United States, the Russian Federation, and Japan resisted commitment to specific mea-sures, as did developing nations such as Brazil, India, and China. The Kyoto Protocol was ratified by 184 parties of the UNFCCC; in 2008, the United States was the only developed nation that had not ratified the treaty.

Climate Change in American Law

In 2007, acting on a petition from the state of Massachusetts, joined by California, Connecticut, Illinois, Maine, New Jersey, New Mexico, New York, Oregon, Rhode Island, Vermont, Washington, the District of Columbia, American Samoa, New York City, Baltimore, and thirteen conservation and public interest organizations, the U.S. Supreme Court affirmed that the U.S. Environmental Protection Agency (EPA) had the statutory authority to consider regulating greenhouse gases causing global warming. The 5-4 decision in *Massachusetts v. EPA,* 549 U.S. 497, did not require the EPA to find that greenhouse gases contribute to climate change. However, the Court did find that the EPA's decision not to consider the question was arbitrary and capricious, directing that the EPA "must ground its reasons for action or inaction" in the language of the Clean Air Act, Section 202(a)(1) as amended (42 U.S.C. 7521[a][1]).

The change in administration from George W. Bush to Barack Obama in January 2009 shifted executive branch priorities toward regulation of greenhouse gases. On March 24, 2009, the EPA proposed a finding that carbon dioxide and five other greenhouse gases endanger human health and the environment, which would mandate regulation under the Clean Air Act. On April 10, 2009, the EPA proposed mandatory reporting requirements for emission of carbon dioxide and other greenhouse gases, which would affect approximately 13,000 emissions sources from industries such as pulp and paper mills, ethanol production, aluminum, food processing, landfills, waste water treatment, coal, and petrochemicals. President Obama's energy and climate advi-sor, Carol Browner, said the administration would prefer a comprehensive cap-and-trade bill from Congress.

The primary bill to create a cap-and-trade system to reduce carbon emissions, the American Clean Energy and Security Act of 2009, was introduced as H.R. 2454 by Rep. Henry Waxman (D-CA), and was passed by the House of Representatives on a 219–212 vote on June 26, 2009. As this volume goes to press, the bill had not been voted on in the Senate. The bill would establish annual limits for the emission of carbon and most other greenhouse gases and, separately, for hydrofluorocarbons. Allowances for permit-ted levels of emission would in part be auctioned off by the federal government and in part distributed free of charge. Permit holders keeping their own emissions under the allowed level would be able to sell their unused allowances. The legislation also provided for tax credits or rebates to low-income families to offset the impact of higher energy prices, and it authorized funding for research, loans for clean energy projects, and other appropriations. Estimates from the Congressional Budget Office indicated that the bill would reduce federal budget deficits by $24 billion for the period 2010–2019, increasing revenues by $846 billion and spending by $821 billion. Previous legislation to cap greenhouse gas emissions, such as the Clean Power Act of 2002 introduced by Senator James Jeffords (I-VT), with twenty-two cosponsors from both parties, have not passed into law.

In the wake of the EPA moving to comply with the *Massachusetts v. EPA* decision, Rep. Marsha Blackburn (R-TN) introduced H.R. 391, which would provide by statute that "the term 'air pollutants' shall not include carbon dioxide, water vapor, methane, nitrous oxide, hydrofluorocarbons, perfluorocarbons, or sulfur hexaflouride." To be even more definite, the bill would establish that "nothing in the Clean Air Act shall be treated as authorizing or requiring the regulation of climate change or global warming," explicitly removing from the agency any statutory authority in this area. On the opposite side of the question, Rep. Fortney Stark (D-CA) introduced H.R. 594, the Save our Climate Act of 2009, to impose a tax on fuel based on tons of carbon content with the intention of reducing use of fossil fuels. Stark's bill would amend Chapter 38 of the Internal Revenue Code of 1986, which is related to environmental taxes.

Some states have previously attempted to regulate greenhouse gases without waiting for federal action. Massachusetts created its own cap-and-trade system in 2001, requiring a 10 percent reduction in carbon dioxide emissions from 1997–1999 levels. New Hampshire's Clean Power Act of 2002 established caps for emissions of carbon dioxide, sulfur dioxide, and oxides of nitrogen. Maine and Rhode Island have also developed state plans to address climate change, while the West Coast Governor's Global Warming Initiative, developed in November 2004, sets a series of policies to reduce greenhouse gas emissions in California, Oregon, and Washington. An increasing number of political bodies have recognized that while the earth's climate has gone though much warmer and colder periods than today, human culture, politics, and economics depend heavily on the temperature range of the past few thousand years. Increased production of carbon dioxide threatens to push global temperature into ranges unknown in previous human history.

—Charles Rosenberg

See also: *Acid Rain*

BIBLIOGRAPHY

Callendar, G. S. "The Artificial Production of Carbon Dioxide and Its Influence on Temperature." *Quarterly Journal of the Royal Meteorological Society* 64 (1938): 223–40. Available at http://wiki.nsdl.org/index.php/PALE:ClassicArticles/GlobalWarming/Article6/.

Callendar, G. S. "The Composition of the Atmosphere through the Ages." *Meteorological Magazine* 74 (1939): 33–39.
DiMento, Joseph F., and Pamela Doughman, eds. *Climate Change: What It Means for Us, Our Children, and Our Grandchildren.* Cambridge: Massachusetts Institute of Technology, 2007.
Drake, Frances. *Global Warming: The Science of Climate Change.* New York: Oxford University Press, 2000.
Fagan, Brian. *The Great Warming: Climate Change and the Rise and Fall of Civilizations.* New York: Bloomsbury Press, 2008.
Fleming, James Rodger. *Historical Perspectives on Climate Change.* New York: Oxford University Press, 1998.
Horner, Christopher C. *The Politically Incorrect Guide to Global Warming and Environmentalism.* Lanham, MD: Regnery, 2007.
Lamb, H. H. *Climate, History and the Modern World.* 2nd ed. London: Routledge, 1995.
Mann, Michael E., Raymond S. Bradley, and Malcolm K. Hughes. "Northern Hemisphere Temperatures During the Past Millenium: Inferences, Uncertainties, and Limitations," *Geophysical Research Letters* 26, no. 6 (1999). Available at http://www.ncdc.noaa.gov/paleo/pubs/millennium-camera.pdf.
Philander, S. George. *Is the Temperature Rising?* Princeton, NJ: Princeton University Press, 2000.

Coal Ash Ponds

The burning of coal creates coal ash. Utility companies commonly store this ash in impoundment ponds. Designs vary, depending on geographical conditions, regulation by state and federal governments, and type of ash—fly ash, bottom ash, boiler slag, or some combination. The pond is dug and dammed or diked to hold the ash in water until it settles to the bottom as sludge or slurry, while the relatively clean water is released under control to a nearby stream, lake, or water system. An ash pond is labeled by the type of ash it stores—"fly ash pond" or "bottom ash pond," for instance. Large ash ponds are known as impoundments or reservoirs.

In 2000, the U.S. Environmental Protection Agency (EPA) reported that 43 states had about 600 ash sites, ponds, and landfills. Unlined and clay-lined ash ponds and landfills in the United States may number twice what the EPA indicates, and the harm they can cause may last a century or longer. The EPA reports that peak pollution may occur between 78 and 105 years after initial operation.

Coal ash volume each year is 129 million tons, making it the second largest waste stream in the country, second only to municipal waste. It is enough to fill a million railroad coal cars yearly. Kentucky and Indiana lead the nation in production of coal ash, and both have several ash ponds. Power plants add almost 100 million tons of waste into impoundments and landfills each year.

The states have primary regulatory responsibility for coal ash.

High-Hazard Ponds

As of 2009, there were forty-four EPA-identified high-hazard coal ash piles in the United States. Their location was secret because, the EPA said, of the risk of terrorism. Senators Barbara Boxer (D-CA) and John Yarmuth (D-KY) demanded that the EPA reveal the locations. Yarmuth expressed skepticism that the EPA's terrorism risk excuse was sufficient; his district had two ash ponds, one of which was state defined as high risk for environmental problems. In June 2009, the EPA said it was acting on a recommendation by the U.S. Army Corps of Engineers, which manages the national inventory of dams. The Corps denied it had recommended secrecy and indicated that it instead wanted judicious revelation of one site at a time rather than of the entire list. Senator Boxer noted that the EPA was notifying first responders and local officials and was sending teams to the high-hazard sites to see if any posed an imminent danger.

Neither Indiana nor Kentucky had heard from the federal government about whether they had any dangerous sites, but by state standards, Kentucky had four high-hazard ash ponds and six moderate-risk ponds. The classifications were based on impact of failure rather than likelihood. Kentucky's standard for high-hazard status meant that a site had to have the potential to inflict death or serious damage in the event of failure.

The EPA says that living close to a disposal site increases cancer risk, with residents near coal ash ponds having as high as a 1 in 50 chance of getting cancer from arsenic-containing water. By comparison, the national cancer rate is 1 in over 200. Other cancer-causing elements include lead, selenium, and boron. As well as increasing the risk of cancer, coal ash sites increase the incidence of damage to vital organs and the central nervous system.

Since the 1980s, the EPA has been considering labeling coal ash as hazardous, but it has not done so. The hazardous designation would mean imposing strict controls on handling, transport, and dumping. Double-lined disposal sites and monitoring of groundwater would be mandatory at coal ash disposal sites. The Bevill Amendment of 1980 exempted coal ash from hazardous waste rules and required that the EPA study the health and environmental impacts of coal ash disposal before making a designation. The EPA reported to Congress in 1988 and 1989 that damage was not high enough to warrant overturning the Bevill Amendment.

In 2000, the EPA wanted to establish tighter coal ash regulations but backed off when utilities, coal companies, and the Clinton administration objected. The same year, environmental groups documented almost sixty cases of contamination caused by leaching. This led to a debate within the EPA between those who wanted to continue to designate coal ash sites nonhazardous, and thus let states continue to regulate them for the most part, and those who wanted tighter standards. By March, the hazardous designators were on the verge of winning. The EPA Office of Solid Waste (now the Office of Resource Conservation and Recovery) drafted a determination that the waste was hazardous, and EPA administrator Carol Browner sent it to the Office of Management and Budget for review. Energy industry pressure was intense, but the driving force in the decision was cost. The EPA said the cost would be around $1 billion per year, and the industry countered that it was higher. Edison Electric Institute estimated that a cleanup after a hazardous designation would cost the industry upward of $5 billion. One estimate was $13 billion per year. The EPA backed off, promising to issue nonhazardous guidelines for states that wanted disposal rules. After backing off, the EPA failed to issue even the less stringent standards.

The disposal of coal ash was debated during the Clinton administration, but the debate faded during the Bush administration. In 2007, an EPA analysis found that exposure to coal ash significantly increased the risk of cancer, but the EPA still did not act. Even some of those within the EPA who wanted the nonhazardous designation were becoming frustrated at the lack of any action at all.

The EPA data was first published in 2007, but it contained data that were mostly the same as those in a 2002 report unreleased by Bush officials. The 2002 report indicated that within a matter of decades, ash ponds were expected to leak boron into surface waters at concentrations 2,000 times the safe level for aquatic life and leak selenium and arsenic at 10 times the safe level. Over a single decade, according to the 2007 EPA report, sixty-seven towns in twenty-six states had suffered groundwater contamination from coal ash dumps. For instance, Anne Arundel County, Maryland, had residential well water that contained arsenic, cadmium, and thallium. The cause was polluted water leaching from a sand and gravel pit that had been the site of ash

Coal Ash Spill into the Emory River, Tennessee

On December 22, 2008, a dike burst at the Tennessee Valley Authority's Kingston Fossil Plant in Roane County, Tennessee, releasing more than 1 billion gallons of toxic coal fly ash into the Emory and Clinch Rivers. The slurry also fouled approximately 300 acres of land. It was the largest fly ash slurry spill in U.S. history.

The fly ash was a by-product of the burning of coal to generate steam power at the plant. Among the toxins identified in the ash were arsenic, cadmium, lead, manganese, and mercury. Despite the numerous dead fish in the vicinity of the spill, the Tennessee Valley Authority claimed that the water in the area was safe for human consumption.

The Tennessee Valley Authority has come under heavy criticism for its handling of a disaster that impacted two of the Tennessee River's tributaries. There is now a concerted effort in Congress to pass legislation that sets standards for the impoundment of coal fly ash.

—John R. Burch Jr.

See also: *South; Tennessee Valley Authority*

BIBLIOGRAPHY

Tennessee Valley Authority. "Kingston Recovery." http://www.tva.gov/kingston/index.htm.

storage since the mid-1990s. The polluter paid a $1 million fine in 2007.

Coal Ash Spills

Coal ash safety arose as a concern after 5.4 million cubic yards of Tennessee Valley Authority (TVA) ash spilled from a ruptured dike at Kingston, Tennessee, forty miles from Knoxville. The gray muck covered several hundred acres, including homes and properties, and poured into two sloughs that fed the Emory River, a tributary of the Clinch River that feeds the Tennessee River. Cleanup cost was estimated near $1 billion. Environmentalists noted that clean air regulations meant that the amount of toxic material on the ground had increased. Also, Kingston is surrounded by subdivisions, so its ash piles grew because the site could not expand. The site was not overflowing, though.

Initially, the residents displaced by the Kingston flood had no official word of the dangers of the sludge, as the TVA sought to minimize the risk. The TVA's position was that most of the sludge was inert and nontoxic. However, coal ash in Appalachia contains selenium, arsenic, lead, and other heavy metals that cause neurological problems and cancer. The TVA position didn't match the 2007 EPA report, which said that fly ash is carcinogenic and has heavy

metal concentrations higher than the coal itself. That report, in turn, matched a 2006 National Research Council report, which indicated that coal ash contains toxic metals in sufficient amounts to cause environmental and public health concerns, including risk to human health and ecosystems, should contaminants reach surface or drinking water. The TVA did promise to remove 2 million tons of ash waste and restore the area.

The EPA hired a contractor to measure contaminants in the soil, and all contaminants were within residential guidelines, which are much stricter than industrial guidelines, and 10 to 100 times below the EPA hazardous waste standard. Arsenic was the exception in that it exceeded the residential standard, but it was still below the industrial standard. Local officials recommended boiling water, but environmentalists went door-to-door advising that boiling the water wouldn't make the water safe.

The initial assessment was that 300 million gallons of water and sludge had escaped, constituting the worst spill in U.S. history. Comparable spills are a 1967 spill that released 130 million gallons into the Clinch River in Virginia and a 2005 spill in Northampton County, Pennsylvania, that put 100 million gallons into the Delaware River. Environmentalists want ash in lined landfills, and the EPA agreed in a 2006 report. Above-ground embankments are risky and inappropriate for permanent storage.

Regulating Coal Ash Disposal

The collapse of the Kingston coal ash pond demonstrated how weak the regulation of coal ash disposal actually is. On January 14, 2009, Rep. Nick Rahall (D-WV) introduced a bill, the Coal Ash Reclamation and Environmental Safety Act of 2009 (H.R. 493), requiring federal standards for the construction of coal ash impoundments. The proposed law would establish federal standards for design, engineering, and performance. The goal was to head off another Kingston pond incident. As a model, the bill used the standard for management of coal slurry set by the Surface Mining Control and Reclamation Act of 1977 (SMCRA). Regarding construction of disposal sites, it would apply SMCRA standards for embankment, stability, geology of the site, and potential for subsidence of subsurface strata. Plans would be reviewed by an engineer experienced in impoundment construction, with reviews during and after construction. States without their own standards would have to develop them immediately.

Rahall and Rep. Tom Bevill (D-AL) in 1980 amended the Solid Waste Disposal Act of 1980 to require the EPA to figure out how to regulate coal ash, but as of 2009, the EPA had not yet established standards for storage and use and had not yet designated coal ash as hazardous. Rahall in 2006 requested that the National Academy of Sciences study the need for regulation, and in 2007 the Subcommittee on Energy and Mineral Resources held hearings on regulation as well.

Some environmentalists, including the Environmental Integrity Project, contend that even as nonhazardous waste, the ash contains toxic elements, and they complain of lack of sufficient regulation. The industry maintains its position that the hazardous waste designation is inappropriate and counters that even though national or uniform state regulation is not in place, standards are still enforced.

State standards vary. Some states do little, while others are stringent. Some require discharge permits, and others require monitoring of water. Many lack regulations regarding maintenance of ponds. Illinois requires pond maintenance and sends inspectors to ponds and landfills to make sure that all is in order. However, the state has no regulations regarding monitoring of groundwater near coal ash pits and instead uses case-by-case criteria.

Some companies have environmental protection programs. Southern Company, an electric utility, has plants in Alabama, Florida, Georgia, and Mississippi, and it complies with the standards of the four states and collects its ash in accordance with air-quality rules. In addition, company personnel check the properties every other week, and dam safety engineers inspect the ponds at least every other year. Southern uses 30 to 35 percent of its coal-burning wastes in concrete, road construction, and other beneficial uses. Southern acknowledges the presence of arsenic, mercury, and lead in its ash but claims that they are not present in sufficient concentrations to warrant designation as hazardous. Southern Company works with state officials to ensure that its sites meet their environmental standards, in part to fend off further state regulation.

The Obama administration promised early action. In January 2009, the director of the EPA's Office of Resource Conservation and Recovery promised quick action on coal ash regulations. During her confirmation hearings to head the EPA, Lisa P. Jackson promised an immediate inventory of hazardous ponds. On March 11, 2009, the EPA announced that it would develop regulations for managing coal plant waste. It advised electric utilities that they had to provide details about the structural integrity of the up to 300 coal ash ponds in the United States, and that EPA inspectors would visit the sites. In 2010, the EPA put forward proposed regulations for public comment.

While environmentalists were watching the EPA, the Department of Interior's Office of Surface Mining, Reclamation, and Enforcement proposed to set national standards for mine filling, that is, the disposal of coal ash in active or abandoned mines. Environmentalist groups were alarmed at a proposal to make mines repositories for non-mine wastes, specifically coal ash, because they saw it as a potential hazard to groundwater.

—John H. Barnhill

See also: *Aquaculture; Government Water Decision Making; Heavy Metals in Water; Inter-Basin Water Transfer; South; Tennessee Valley Authority*

BIBLIOGRAPHY

Bruggers, James S. "EPA Secrecy on Coal-Ash List Worries Lawmakers. Some of 44 'High Hazard' Sites Might Be in Kentucky, Indiana." *Courier-Journal.com* (Louisville, KY), June 13, 2009. Reprinted at http://indianalawblog.com/archives/2009/06/environment_epa_24.html.

Dewan, Shaila. "Coal Ash Spill Revives Issue of Its Hazards." *New York Times,* December 24, 2008. Available at http://www.nytimes.com/2008/12/25/us/25sludge.html.

Espeland, Kristin. "EPA Will Regulate, Inspect Coal Ash Ponds." *WFPL News* (Louisville, KY), March 11, 2009. Available at http://www.wfpl.org/CMS/?p=3963/.

Lombardi, Kristen. "Coal Ash Debate Now Moves to Minefilling." *PaperTrail* (blog of The Center for Public Integrity). Posted February 19, 2009; last modified September 14, 2010. Available at http://www.publicintegrity.org/blog/entry/1169/.

Lombardi, Kristen. "The Hidden History: Federal Regulation Was Considered, but Fell Victim to a Bureaucratic Debate." *PaperTrail* (blog of The Center for Public Integrity). Posted January 7, 2009; last modified September 14, 2010. Available at http://www.publicintegrity.org/blog/entry/1107/.

Neville, Angela. "Best Management Practices for Coal Ash Ponds." *Power,* March 1, 2009. Available at http://www.powermag.com/coal/Best-Management-Practices-for-Coal-Ash-Ponds_1762.html.

University of Kentucky Center for Applied Energy Research. *Glossary,* s.v. "Ash Impoundment Pond." Available at http://www.caer.uky.edu/kyasheducation/glossary.shtml.

Ward, Ken, Jr. "Secret EPA Study: Big Cancer Risks from Coal-Ash Ponds." *Coal Tattoo* (blog of the *Charleston (WV) Gazette*). Posted May 27, 2009. Available at http://blogs.wvgazette.com/coaltattoo/2009/05/07/secret-epa-study-big-cancer-risks-from-coal-ash-ponds/.

Commercial Fishing

Commercial fishing has been an important trade activity on the North American continent for many centuries. Prior to the arrival of European explorers, commercial fishing activity was one element of the extensive trade networks among Native American groups. For example, in the precontact Pacific Northwest, various Native American tribes living in the Columbia River basin were well-known for their trade in salmon, which they caught using nets and traps. The most prominent such fisheries include Kettle Falls, on the Columbia River in present-day Washington State, and Celilo Falls, also on the Columbia River, in present-day Oregon. Archeological evidence suggests that these and other nearby fisheries were active sites of fishing activity as long as 10,000 years ago, although it is unclear when commercial fishing began in this region.

Early History

Commercial fishing activity was common among many of the precontact Native American groups living along the coasts, lakes, and waterways of the North American continent. While some, like the tribes of the Pacific Northwest, relied on nets and traps, others utilized canoes, harpoons, trawls, and fishhooks. Fishing weirs were also popular and effective fishing tools for groups located along rivers. These latticed structures allowed water to pass through but trapped fish as they traveled downstream.

Over the course of the late fifteenth to nineteenth centuries, however, commercial fishing among Native Americans would be greatly impacted by the arrival of European explorers and the gradual colonization of the continent. As Native American lifestyles were drastically altered by the introduction of European diseases, which decimated populations, and as European and then American settlers displaced Native American groups from their homelands, fishing activity and trade networks experienced significant disruptions. While some Native American groups have retained a tradition of commercial fishing into the present, these activities have been altered substantially in scope and practice. Native American attempts to retain traditional commercial fishing practices have been most successful in Alaska, where the state's relatively large Native population has been able to negotiate fishing treaties with the federal government.

While the arrival of European explorers led to the decline of Native American commercial fishing in North America, it also led to the establishment of new commercial fishing activity in the United States. Since the fifth and sixth centuries, European fishing vessels had sailed to the waters of Greenland and Iceland to fish for cod. As international conflicts arose in the early fifteenth century regarding the rights to these fishing grounds, a number of European nations began expanding into the waters off present-day Newfoundland and New England. Basque fishermen and expeditions from the British Isles began landing on the shores of North America prior to Columbus's arrival in the Americas in 1492, but, as they wished to keep their fishing grounds secret, they did not publicize their landfalls.

In the fifteenth and early sixteenth centuries, permanent fishing communities based on cod and whaling began to be established in coastal New England. The most significant of these were the Massachusetts settlements of Marblehead, Gloucester, New Bedford, and Nantucket. By the late seventeenth century, colonization of the region had begun to produce local markets for fish, and these communities expanded their operations to include trade in shad, salmon, and lobster. The sugar-producing markets of the West Indies were also important trading partners. Beginning around 1800, however, some of New England's freshwater fish populations began to collapse as a result of overfishing and environmental encroachments by farmers, cities, and manufacturers. Farther south, smaller fisheries also contributed to the growing American commercial fishing industry. Oysters and crabs were abundant in the bays and rivers of the mid-Atlantic coastline, and industries quickly arose to harvest and sell these resources. Similarly, commercial fishing in the Gulf of Mexico supplied markets with shrimp and other local fish and shellfish.

Significant changes in American life in the early and mid-nineteenth century would dramatically alter the fishing industries of the United States. One of the most dramatic of these changes was the opening of the trans-Mississippi frontier and the settlement of the American West. With the westward migration of American settlers came the establishment of inland freshwater fisheries on the Great Lakes, along the Mississippi and Illinois Rivers, and on the edges of various other lakes and waterways. These fisheries flourished in the trade of whitefish, pike, sturgeon, and catfish until habitat destruction and overfishing led to their decline in the late nineteenth and early twentieth centuries. As settlers reached the coasts of Alaska, salmon fisheries were founded, and commercial fishing fleets were launched to hunt whales and fur seals.

Technological Changes and Innovations

Technological change also made a massive impact on commercial fishing practices of the early nineteenth century.

This era in American history was characterized by a wave of tremendous industrial development that dramatically transformed manufacturing, often through the introduction of new tools and technologies. Many of these new inventions were adopted or adapted by the commercial fishing industry and led to many notable changes in the practice of commercial fishing in the United States and worldwide.

In the early 1800s, for example, inventors developed practical steam engines for boats. Over the course of the first two decades of the nineteenth century, sails were gradually replaced by steam power. Steam-powered winches were also developed, which enabled fisheries and fishing vessels to increase the size and weight of fishing gear significantly. Instead of relatively simple fishing lines bearing only a few hooks each, commercial fishermen began using longlines, which not only covered a greater distance than earlier fishing lines but were also capable of bearing hundreds, even thousands, of hooks. Fishing nets, traps, and pots also increased in size, especially after the process of net making became mechanized and synthetic fibers, developed in the early twentieth century, made fishing nets stronger, more durable, and less susceptible to decay in maritime environments. The size and weight of fishing gear would increase again in the early to mid-twentieth century, as internal combustion engines gradually replaced steam-powered machinery.

In addition to changing the way in which commercial fisheries caught fish, nineteenth-century innovations changed the ways in which the industry prepared and marketed its products. Following the invention of canning in 1810, there was a dramatic increase in the demand for commercial fishing, as canning allowed both fisheries and consumers to keep fish edible for months without the need for drying. As a result, canned fish could be sold not just to local markets but also to more distant buyers. Prior to this development, most fisheries had little incentive to catch more fish than could be sold to neighboring markets at any given time. This expansion of demand was further enabled by the concurrent growth of American railroads, which facilitated the shipment of canned fish to markets across the United States. By the late nineteenth and early twentieth centuries, the commercial fishing industry had expanded markets even further through the adoption of new freezing and filleting machines, as well as refrigerated shipping.

Technological innovations continued to assist the growth of the American commercial fishing industry through the mid-twentieth century. Fishing boats adapted livewells, which allowed live fish to be kept on board. Newly remodeled versions of a variety of nets and fishing lines resulted in a dramatic increase in fishing yields. In the 1940s, many of the early to mid-twentieth century's innovations were combined to produce the large factory trawler, a fishing vessel that was capable of remaining at sea for months and that had the ability to process seafood on board. Locating fish also became easier in the 1950s after commercial fishing fleets adopted sonar, a technology initially designed for military use.

These expansions in productivity would have repercussions, however. Continued high market demand, growing populations, and increased capacity due to technological innovations encouraged American commercial fisheries to catch and sell increasingly vast amounts of seafood throughout the twentieth century. In the Northwest and New England, entire local economies developed based on a reliance on local commercial fishing industries. However, as in early nineteenth-century New England and the late nineteenth-century Great Lakes region, these large-scale, intensive commercial fishing practices would have severe environmental repercussions.

Decline in Fish Populations and Environmental Impacts

In 2006, marine biologists published the results of a four-year study in the journal *Science*. This study announced that, as a result of overfishing and environmental pollutions, one-third of global fish populations were operating at a level that biologists refer to as population collapse, or population rates of less than 10 percent of their maximum levels. This report added that species-specific population declines have left gaps in the food chains of marine ecosystems, leading to dramatic population changes not just for popular food fish but throughout a wide spectrum of marine life. The report concluded that without significant changes to global commercial fishing practices, wild-caught seafood could become unavailable within the next fifty years.

Reversing this trend has proven difficult. While decreasing yields as a result of environmental decline and overfishing have had a devastating economic impact on many local commercial fishing industries, the international nature of the world's oceans and the profits to be made from commercial fishing have made many industry leaders reluctant to make dramatic reductions in their operations voluntarily. Many nations have attempted to offer solutions, however. In 1983, following an example first set by Iceland, the United Nations established the Law of the Sea, an agreement that established environmental guidelines and gave all participating countries exclusive rights to the waters extending 200 miles from their shores.

While the United States participated in and recognized this agreement, it has so far refused to become party to the treaty. In general, large-scale commercial fisheries in America have supported government resistance to this treaty. Not only would this and other similar treaties limit the practices of these industries, but they would have the effect of significantly restricting the economic viability of the large, expensive fleets of fishing vessels in which many of these industries have already invested. New restrictions that have been imposed by federal and international agreements have resulted in many fisheries being forced to replace these costly vessels with smaller, less efficient ships.

Given federal and business resistance to international or national restrictions on fishing, most attempts to curb overfishing in the United States have been scientific solutions, rather than federal or state legislation. One proposed solution to the combined problems of overfishing and high demand for seafood is aquaculture, often popularly known as fish-farming. Despite aquaculture's ancient and global roots, many varieties of aquaculture experienced a worldwide decline in popularity in the nineteenth century, as the technological improvements adopted by commercial fisheries made aquaculture a less efficient and less cost-effective method of obtaining fish and other aquatic products. However, as maritime commercial fisheries began confronting population collapses and environmental restriction laws, aquaculture once again became an attractive option. While critics of aquaculture have voiced concerns regarding the ethical treatment of fish and the potential for environmental pollution, aquaculture is now more popular than ever. However, while hatcheries and fishways have had some success, particularly in the production of salmon, pollution and practical difficulties have kept fish-farming from becoming a viable alternative.

—Skylar Harris

See also: *Aquaculture; Fish and Wildlife Service, United States; Great Lakes Fisheries Policy; National Marine Fisheries Service*

BIBLIOGRAPHY

Anderson, Lee G. *Fisheries Economics: Collected Essays.* Vol. 1. Burlington, VT: Ashgate, 2002.

Bogue, Margaret Beattie. *Fishing the Great Lakes: An Environmental History, 1783–1933.* Madison: University of Wisconsin Press, 2000.

Clover, Charles. *The End of the Line: How Overfishing Is Changing the World and What We Eat.* London: Ebury Press, 2004.

Pauly, Daniel, and Jay L. Maclean. *In a Perfect Ocean: The State of Fisheries and Ecosystems in the North Atlantic Ocean.* Washington, DC: Island Press, 2003.

Taylor, Joseph E. *Making Salmon: An Environmental History of the Northwest Fisheries Crisis.* Seattle: University of Washington Press, 1999.

Conservation Movement

Early generations of American colonists and citizens displayed only fitful interest in natural resource conservation. Most of them saw the land on which they lived as a source of unlimited natural wealth, and they saw no reason to husband the timber, water, soil, and wildlife resources that surrounded them. During the mid- and late nineteenth century, however, a growing number of prescient observers of the fast-growing, fast-industrializing United States expressed grave concerns about the young nation's feverish rate of resource consumption. By the dawn of the Progressive Era, campaigns for environmental sustainability were also being supplemented—and in some cases eclipsed altogether—by calls for wilderness and wildlife preservation. To leading acolytes of wilderness preservation like Sierra Club founder John Muir, the aesthetic and spiritual value of wild forests and untamed rivers were of incalculable value. America's conservation movement garnered new levels of public acceptance and political clout during the 1950s and 1960s, and by the 1970s environmental groups had become universally recognized as influential players in American policy making. But the preservationist agenda of the modern conservationist movement is fiercely opposed by a wide range of formidable constituencies, including private property advocates and business interests who assail state and federal environmental regulations as burdensome and contrary to America's capitalist principles.

Early Conservation Efforts

Models of environmental stewardship based on concepts of sustainable resource consumption—or outright wilderness preservation—were virtually absent from public discourse in colonial America. Tillable land, timber, water, fish, and game could all be found in great abundance wherever European settlers pushed into the interior of the New World, so talk of "conserving" these resources seemed wholly unnecessary. This state of affairs remained unchanged during the post-Revolutionary era as well, in part because of the continued perception of resource inexhaustibility, but also because governmental authority on the frontier—where much of the land, water, and resource exploitation was taking place—was exceptionally weak.

Yet even though a "Manifest Destiny" mind-set prevailed in the White House and Congress, to say nothing of the timber camps, coal mines, and rail yards of America's coalescing territorial empire, the first stirrings of a conservation ethic came to life in the mid-nineteenth century as well. The men who publicly advocated greater restraint in the nation's consumption of its natural resources were a disparate group, motivated to speak out by different concerns. Romantic painters, poets, and writers such as Thomas Cole, Albert Bierstadt, Ralph Waldo Emerson, Henry David Thoreau, George Perkins Marsh, and John Burroughs produced works that celebrated unspoiled nature and urged Americans to be more responsible stewards of wilderness. Simultaneously, a smattering of influential sportsmen, government officials, and scientists pursued more practical lines of argument for conservation. They asserted that the nation was harvesting its wildlife and exploiting and "improving" its lands and waters at an unsustainable pace that, if left unchecked, threatened the long-term security and vitality of the country.

These warnings set the stage for the first great era of wilderness conservation in the United States—an era that was unleashed with the 1901 ascension of Theodore Roosevelt to the Oval Office after the assassination of William McKinley. Roosevelt was a larger-than-life figure from the outset, renowned for his colorful personal history as a scion of wealth, western rancher, Spanish-American War hero, and reform-minded New York City police commissioner. But when he took over the reins at the White House, Americans discovered that his progressive political sensibilities extended to conservation as well.

During his two terms in office, Roosevelt dramatically reshaped federal resource- management policies, implementing sweeping new measures to protect wilderness and curb unsustainable commodification of the nation's forests and other natural resources. As Roosevelt later wrote in his autobiography (1913), he viewed these steps as both a moral imperative and a necessity of national security: "The idea that our natural resources were inexhaustible still obtained, and there was as yet no real knowledge of their extent and condition. The relation of the conservation of natural resources to the problems of National welfare and National efficiency had not yet dawned on the public mind." These same convictions were shared by Gifford Pinchot, Roosevelt's chief forester and the man most responsible for advancing the president's campaign to wrest control of the nation's environmental riches from profit-hungry corporate interests.

By the time Roosevelt left office in 1909, he had given federal protection to some 230 million acres of national land, established the national wildlife refuge system, quintupled the size of the national forest system, and laid the groundwork for the creation of a national park system. In addition, he had signed laws like the 1902 National Reclamation Act, which ushered in the modern era of federal water and land management based on long-term sustainability rather than exploitation and short-term profit.

Within a few years of Roosevelt's departure from the White House, however, the "Roosevelt Conservationists" he had created confronted a crisis that had lasting repercussions for the movement. A proposal to dam the Hetch Hetchy Valley within Yosemite National Park in order to provide water to San Francisco residents revealed deep philosophical divisions between dedicated wilderness preservationists like Sierra Club founder John Muir and "wise use" advocates like Pinchot. The latter believed that rivers, forests, and other natural resources should be harnessed and used in a sustainable manner—not simply cordoned off from development for aesthetic reasons. By the time the Hetch Hetchy Dam was finally authorized in 1913, the schism between Muir and his preservationist allies and Pinchot's camp of self-described pragmatists, who favored sustainable, multiple-use resource management, had widened into a gaping chasm. This philosophical divide would hamper the conservation movement for decades to come, and it has never been entirely bridged.

Gains and Setbacks in the Conservation Cause

During the 1920s and 1930s, American conservationists continued to lobby tirelessly for new laws and regulations that would protect endangered wildlife and preserve wilderness, rivers, forests, mountains, and valleys from exploitation and development. The absolute number of these activists remained relatively small, but many of them exerted considerable influence over public opinion and policy making at the state and federal levels by virtue of their public stations as affluent sportsmen, newspaper editors, writers, and agency administrators. They also found key institutional allies in federal departments such as the National Park Service, which prospered by framing itself as a more preservation-oriented environmental steward than the U.S. Forest Service. The latter remained firmly allegiant to the multiple-use management ethos championed by Pinchot back in the early 1900s.

The New Deal era brought both opportunities and setbacks to conservationists. On the one hand, President

Izaak Walton League

The Izaak Walton League of America is a nonprofit organization comprised of approximately 270 chapters located throughout the United States. Boasting a membership of more than 40,000, the organization endeavors to restore watersheds, eradicate pollution in all forms, protect wildlife habitats, and educate outdoor enthusiasts to follow an ethical code to protect the environment. Their advocacy and educational agendas are advanced through the quarterly publication of their magazine, entitled *Outdoor America,* and the distribution of *Conservation Currents,* a bimonthly e-newsletter.

The organization was founded in 1922 in Chicago, Illinois, by a group of Midwestern sportsmen. They named their new conservation group after Izaak Walton, a seventeenth-century Englishman who had authored *The Compleat Angler.* Led by Will H. Dilg, the League pursued an activist agenda, which included fighting the draining of marshes and river bottoms. During the mid-1920s, the organization became a model for other conservation groups as it established an office with full-time employees to lobby politicians in Washington, D.C. It also demonstrated the benefits of coalition building, as its lobbying was aided by other groups such as the General Federation of Women's Clubs.

—John R. Burch Jr.

See also: *Ecosystem Management; Wetlands*

BIBLIOGRAPHY

Shabecoff, Philip. *A Fierce Green Fire: The American Environmental Movement.* Washington, DC: Island Press, 2003.

Walton, Izaak, and Charles Cotton. *The Compleat Angler: With an Introduction by John Buchan and an Appendix Containing a Modernized Text of the Arte of Angling.* 8th Buchan ed. New York: Oxford University Press, 1974.

Franklin D. Roosevelt and his fellow New Dealers invested heavily in new programs to restore long-abused rivers, forests, and prairies to ecological health, and famous national parks including Grand Teton, Great Smoky Mountain, Olympic, and Shenandoah were created by transferring national forest holdings into the national park system. Public support for these wilderness restoration and preservation programs was strong, for Americans saw the Dust Bowl and a series of ravaging flood events in the late 1920s and 1930s as clear evidence that federal authorities had a legitimate role to play in protecting environmental resources. This recognition of worsening environmental conditions also helped bring about the creation and rapid growth of important new conservation organizations like the Izaak Walton League (founded in 1922), the Wilderness Society (1935), and the National Wildlife Federation (1936).

But New Deal policies also inaugurated a four-decade-long campaign of dam building and other federal water development projects, which permanently transformed the landscapes of the American West. Conservationists never spoke with a unified voice against these re-engineering efforts, in large measure because water was simply so integral to the daily life and economic prosperity of communities in the arid West. Years later, however, proposals to demolish these massive multipurpose dams would become a major rallying cry of conservationists across the country.

World War II and the postwar economic boom brought heavy new pressures on the nation's environmental resources, and for a time the conservation movement's reminders about limits and sustainability were drowned out by the consumerist clamor of the 1950s. The increased pace of exploitation of land, mineral, and water resources for the development of new highways, shopping centers, and subdivisions greatly alarmed observers like wildlife biologist Aldo Leopold. His famous 1949 essay collection, *A Sand County Almanac,* urged Americans toward a new land ethic that paid greater respect to the sanctity and fragility of local and regional ecosystems.

Golden Age of Conservation

Leopold's words went largely unheeded at first. But a profound shift in American attitudes and policies toward wilderness conservation took place in the 1950s and 1960s. This was an unlikely evolution in some respects, for most Americans were still reveling in the rising tide of consumption-fueled middle-class affluence. But increased affluence also brought a surge of interest in outdoor recreation and tourism—the quality of which was directly predicated on the existence of unspoiled natural areas. In addition, reports from scientists about the deteriorating quality of the nation's water and air increased public anxiety about environmental issues. These factors made ordinary Americans receptive to the concerns being voiced by conservationists.

These shifting attitudes became evident in an epic struggle over Echo Park, a remote canyon in Utah's Dinosaur National Monument. In the 1950s, five states within the Colorado River basin joined with the politically powerful Bureau of Reclamation to press for construction of a multipurpose dam in Echo Park. But a coalition of conservation groups, including the Sierra Club, the Audubon Society, and the Wilderness Society, defeated the proposal by executing a public relations campaign that generated widespread public opposition to the scheme. The Echo Park triumph showed wilderness conservationists that enlisting public support for its causes was vital, and it further illustrated—somewhat to their surprise—that they actually had the capacity to influence the country's natural resource policies in a major way.

Armed with fresh confidence and growing legions of supporters, the conservation movement registered a series of momentous legislative victories in the 1960s and 1970s. Sweeping wilderness and wildlife protection laws such as the Wilderness Act (1964), the Wild and Scenic Rivers Act (1968), and the Endangered Species Act (1973) were passed during this period, as were landmark environmental protection laws like the Clean Air Act and Clean Water Act. All of these laws were hailed by wilderness conservationists, but the passage of the Wilderness Act was cause for particular celebration. This law, which the leadership of the Wilderness Society and other conservation groups had crafted and pushed for the better part of a decade, established a federal wilderness system to protect millions of acres of undeveloped public land in America's national parks and forest reserves.

The political winds shifted dramatically for conservationists in the 1980s. The Reagan administration pursued policies of business deregulation, states' rights, and property rights that often put it at odds with environmental organizations in general and the conservation movement in particular. By necessity, conservation organizations found themselves focusing much of their energy and resources on preserving the gains of the 1960s and 1970s instead of on new conservation initiatives. This dynamic remained largely in place in the 1990s and early 2000s, a period in which orientations towards wilderness and wildlife-conservation policies and proposals became increasingly divided along partisan lines. This partisanship, characterized by general Democratic Party support for conservation laws and widespread—though not universal—Republican Party opposition to such measures, has made it increasingly difficult for the conservation movement to advance its agenda in Washington.

—Kevin Hillstrom

See also: *Ecosystem Management; Government Water Decision Making; Hetch Hetchy Dam; National Parks and Water; Roosevelt, Franklin D.; Roosevelt, Theodore*

BIBLIOGRAPHY

Gottlieb, Robert. *Forcing the Spring: The Transformation of the American Environmental Movement.* Washington, DC: Island Press, 1993.

Hays, Samuel P. *Beauty, Health, and Permanence: Environmental Politics in the United States, 1955–1985.* New York: Cambridge University Press, 1987.

Lewis, Michael, ed. *American Wilderness: A New History.* New York: Oxford University Press, 2007.

Palmer, Tim. *Endangered Rivers and the Conservation Movement.* 2nd ed. Lanham, MD: Rowman and Littlefield, 2004.

Reiger, John F. *American Sportsmen and the Origins of Conservation.* 3rd ed. Corvallis: Oregon State University Press, 2001.

Roosevelt, Theodore. *Theodore Roosevelt: An Autobiography.* New York: Macmillan, 1913.

Dam Building

The purpose of building dams has been essentially for the impounding of water from rivers or underground streams to prevent flooding, collect water for irrigation, or, in more recent years, generate hydroelectricity. All these reasons are

John S. Eastwood

John Samuel Eastwood designed and constructed the Hume Lake Dam between 1908 and 1909. It was the first reinforced concrete multiple-arch dam ever constructed.

Eastwood was born in Minnesota in 1857. He was educated as a civil engineer at the University of Minnesota during the 1870s. In 1895, he served as the chief engineer for the San Joaquin Electric Company as it constructed one of the first hydroelectric power plants in California. While working on dam projects, Eastwood determined that there were more efficient and cheaper ways to construct dams. He became an advocate of reinforced multiple-arch dam designs, which minimized the use of concrete. His designs were mocked, as critics argued that his dams would not be strong enough to impound water. He proved his critics wrong with the construction of the Hume Lake Dam.

Eastwood continuously improved upon his multiple-arch designs over the course of his career. In total, he constructed seventeen dams. He died on August 10, 1924.

—John R. Burch Jr.

BIBLIOGRAPHY

Jackson, Donald C. *Building the Ultimate Dam: John S. Eastwood and the Control of Water in the West.* Lawrence: University Press of Kansas, 1995.

Workers on the Boulder Dam (now Hoover Dam) in January 1934. An average of 3,500 laborers worked on the dam daily.
Library of Congress

noncontroversial, especially since the development of hydro-power. The result of building dams in the United States has been the opening up of much more land for agriculture and housing and the establishment of cities in locations that otherwise would have been impossible, as well as the generation of clean electricity long before there arose any major concern about greenhouse gases, global warming, and climate change. Most dams built in the United States have operated safely and have not broken. Moreover, dams in the United States were not attacked in the same way as German dams were by the British Royal Air Force "Dam Busters" during Operation Chastise, flooding land with water from the Ruhr and Eder Rivers.

However, with the construction of a great many dams in the United States, much controversy has arisen on economic, environmental, and political grounds. To some extent, the initial focus of complaints was the sheer cost of these projects, many of which ended up taking much longer than expected and costing much more than originally anticipated or budgeted for. In addition, the dramatic changes in landscape that have resulted from dam construction have been controversial. When a dam is built and starts impounding water, it forms a large reservoir or lake, inundating land where people have been living, forcing whole townships to relocate (an expensive undertaking), and in some cases devastating local Native American communities who are also forced to move or lose their tribal land. There is also a worry that dams have led to environmental problems, often heavily affecting the flora and fauna connected with the river—especially the fish—and the adjoining environment. Another argument against dams is that access to water has allowed for profligate water use in cities that would be otherwise unviable; Phoenix, Arizona, is often highlighted in this regard. On the other hand, the construction of dams has created vast lakes, which have been used by aquacultural-ists for fish breeding and by recreational users for angling, boating, and other water sports.

The cost of building dams and of dealing with other problems such as purchasing land, relocating people, and changing the local landscape was initially not as controversial as had been expected. This was partly because dam construction was seen as an effective way of providing employment for many people—the most obvious such project being Boulder Dam (now the Hoover Dam) from 1931 to 1936. This dam and many of the projects under the aegis of the Tennessee Valley Authority (TVA) were initiated specifically to provide employment during the Great Depression as part of Franklin D. Roosevelt's New Deal. Also, much contemporary press coverage was given to the cheap electricity that was generated by dams, which provided power for new factories that could be constructed near the dams' hydroelectric plants, thus further reducing unemployment.

Much of the initial opposition to the TVA did not stem from the cost of the projects, but rather from the fact that the agency cut across states' rights and affected private utility companies. Rep. Joseph Martin Jr. (R-MA), for example, said he felt that the TVA had been "patterned closely after one of the Soviet [Union's] dreams," high-lighting the increase of state control that resulted from the projects. However, some of the major problems with the TVA were internal organizational disputes that were primarily political and did not affect public acceptance of the dam-construction projects.

Impact of Dam Building on Native Americans

It is undeniable that dams have seriously affected a number of Native American communities. With the building of the Shasta Dam in California from 1938 to 1945, the Winnemem Wintu Nation lost nine-tenths of its land along the Sacramento River, including burial sites, prayer rocks, and other places of important cultural and historical significance. Construction went ahead in spite of protests

John L. Savage

John Lucian Savage was born in Cookesville, Wisconsin, on December 25, 1879. He was educated at the University of Wisconsin. While at college, he spent his summers working for the Geological Survey of Wisconsin and the U.S. Geological Survey. After graduating with a BS in civil engineering in 1903, he accepted a job as an engineering aide with the U.S. Reclamation Service. He worked with the Reclamation Service until 1908, when he joined a private firm, but he returned to the Reclamation Service in 1916. He was promoted in 1924 to chief designing engineer for the renamed Bureau of Reclamation's civil, electrical, and mechanical engineering design department. His responsibilities included the designing of irrigation systems, canals, and dams in eleven states. Among the dams he designed were the Hoover, Grand Coulee, Parker, and Shasta Dams. The construction of these dams depended on unique methods developed by Savage to pour and cure concrete. His innovations became the standards in large dam construction projects around the world. He retired from the Bureau of Reclamation in 1945. Savage died in Englewood, Colorado, on December 28, 1967.

—John R. Burch Jr.

See also: *Bureau of Reclamation; Grand Coulee Dam; Hoover Dam; Shasta Dam*

BIBLIOGRAPHY

Billington, David P., and Donald C. Jackson. *Big Dams of the New Deal Era: A Confluence of Engineering and Politics.* Norman: University of Oklahoma Press, 2006.

and environmental concerns. The Dalles Dam, which went into operation in 1957, destroyed tribal fishing lands along the Columbia River in Oregon, dramatically changing the lifestyles of many Native Americans who had previously made a living from fishing. Perhaps the most well-known case was the Kinzua Dam in northern Pennsylvania. The Seneca Nation showed that it had title to the land, which had been guaranteed to them by George Washington himself and stipulated in the Pickering Treaty of 1794. Protests were successful in delaying construction for decades after the dam's authorization in 1936. However, in spite of this plus support for the Seneca from many politicians (including John F. Kennedy who, after being elected president, went back on his promises), work on the dam began in 1960 and was completed in 1965. Not all Native Americans lost their battles over dams, however. Protests by the Yavapai Nation lead to the cancellation of plans to build the Orme Dam in central Arizona. Native Americans demonstrations against dams also received strong support from the press, especially major newspapers on the east coast.

Many Native American townships had to be relocated entirely after dams were constructed. Some tribes, such as the Allatoona in Georgia, were already seeing a gradual exodus of population before the dams were constructed. The memory of the Allatoonas' presence is preserved in the name of the Allatoona Dam, just as the flooded township of Fontana was the namesake of the Fontana Dam in North Carolina. Dingmans Ferry and Bushkill, both in the state of Pennsylvania, and Pahaquarry in neighboring New Jersey were also lost with the Tocks Island Dam.

Environmental Impact of Dams

The environmental problems created by dams came to the forefront of the debate starting in the 1960s, when environmental impact studies became more precise and detailed. The John Day Dam and the nearby Dalles Dam, both on the Columbia River in Oregon, led to the deaths of large numbers of fish that had been impounded by the dams and were thus unable to travel upstream to their spawning grounds. In the case of the Chinook salmon, not only did their numbers decline, but also an excess of nitrogen was found in the blood of those that continued to live near the John Day Dam. These concerns are now being addressed by measures introduced for the improvement of conditions for aquatic life around many dam projects. For example, in the Delaware River Basin, in 1981 only 6,392 fish were caught. However, after water quality was improved, by 1987 there were 56,000 fish caught, and by 1995 some 500,000 shad were swimming in the Delaware River. Also, environmentalists stopped the Tocks Island Dam Project from going ahead in the Delaware River; after being proposed in 1965, it was officially deauthorized in 2002. Native Americans have pointed to the effects on the natural environment as a major factor in their opposition to dam building.

Supporters of dam building point to the generation of clean energy—although the importance of this was not understood when many dams were built. Certainly the generation of hydropower was cheap—in purely financial terms—and now the United States gets 7.2 percent of its electricity from hydropower (and 70.8 percent and 19.8 percent from fossil fuels and nuclear power, respectively), according to 2004 figures. Although not a high a percentage, it does represent a large amount of power—in 2004, a total of 288 billion kilowatt-hours, almost exactly one-half the total electricity production of Canada (which generates 61 percent of its electricity from hydropower).

Supporters of dam building laud the recreational facilities that it promotes. Some dams themselves are tourist sites; the most popular of these is the Hoover Dam in Nevada. At many dams, the lakes around the dams are used as spawning grounds for fish, which attract many recreational anglers and their families. Others enjoy water sports, boating, or camping around the lakes—activities popular with family groups and youth organizations such as the Boy Scouts. The popularity of dams for recreational use depends largely on their location. For instance, the Allatoona Dam near Atlanta, Georgia has 662 campsites around the lake and earns $1 million each year from fees (in addition to $3.5 million from hydropower).

Starting in the 1980s, the environmental movement became concerned with the profligacy that has resulted from cheap electricity and easy access to water. Some argue that cheap electricity may create businesses that are otherwise unviable and may lead to the location of factories a long way from population and distribution centers. If electricity were to go up in price, or access to cheap electricity were to end for any other reason, many of these enterprises would become unsustainable.

In addition, much water has been used for short-term projects or has been wasted on city or private amenities that use water in an unsustainable manner. Critics of heavy water use tend to focus on Phoenix, Arizona, where there are many examples of such profligacy, one being the world's highest shooting fountain at Fountain Hills in the city's outer suburbs.

Yet another area of conflict that has arisen from dam building is disputes between states. One focus of such conflict is the right to use water from the Colorado River. States have argued over this frequently, even though water usage rights from the Colorado are officially split among Utah, Nevada, Arizona, and California, as well as Mexico. Efforts to manage such conflicts elsewhere have included the establishment of the Delaware River Basin Commission. Before the establishment of the commission, administration of the Delaware River had been controlled by four states, forty-three state agencies, fourteen interstate agencies, and nineteen federal agencies.

—Justin Corfield

See also: *Allatoona Dam; Dam Removal and River Restoration; Fontana Dam; Kinzua Dam; Orme Dam; Shasta Dam; Tocks Island Dam*

BIBLIOGRAPHY

Albert, Richard C. *Damming the Delaware: The Rise and Fall of Tocks Island Dam*. University Park: Pennsylvania State University Press, 1987.

Bilharz, Joy A. *The Allegany Senecas and Kinzua Dam: Forced Relocation through Two Generations*. Lincoln: University of Nebraska Press, 1998.

Lilienthal, David E. *TVA: Democracy on the March*. New York: Harper & Brothers, 1944.

Morgan, Arthur E. *Dams and Other Disasters: A Century of the Army Corps of Engineers in Civil Works*. Boston: P. Sargent, 1971.

Pearce, Fred. *When the Rivers Run Dry: What Happens When Our Water Runs Out?* London: Eden Project Books, 2006.

Rocca, Al M. *The Shasta Dam Boomtowns: Community Building in the New Deal Era*. Redding, CA: Redding Museum of Art & History, 1993.

Scarpino, Philip V. *Great River: An Environmental History of the Upper Mississippi, 1890–1950*. Columbia: University of Missouri Press, 1985.

Smith, Norman. *A History of Dams*. London: Peter Davies, 1971.

Smith, Roland. "The Politics of Flood Control: 1936–1960." *Pennsylvania History* 44, no. 1 (1977): 3–24.

Taylor, Stephen Wallace. *The New South's New Frontier: A Social History of Economic Development in Southwestern North Carolina*. Gainesville: University Press of Florida, 2001.

Dam Removal and River Restoration

For most of this country's history, dams have been regarded as symbols of progress and civilization. Wildness, whether in rivers or landscapes, was something to be conquered. This belief led to the construction of dams on virtually every river in the United States. There are more than 79,000 dams over 25 feet in height (U.S. Army Corps of Engineers 2009). An additional 2.5 million smaller dams are scattered throughout the nation (National Research Council 1992). About 600,000 miles of rivers and streams have been impacted by dams in the United States ("Hydro Facts" 2009).

The rise of environmentalism in the 1960s increased awareness of the losses and liabilities that accompanied dam construction. People began to realize that dams, while bestowing some benefits, sometimes created even greater losses. Dams greatly diminished anadromous fish runs (fish that spawn in freshwater but mature in saltwater), impacted water quality, endangered some species of plants and animals, flooded pristine canyons, and diminished opportunities for some forms of recreation. Comprehensive analyses of relative costs and benefits of dams revealed that a small portion of dams clearly did more damage than they were worth. This led to calls for the removal of some dams.

The river advocacy group American Rivers estimates over 700 dams have been removed in the United States, including 58 in 2009 (American Rivers 2009). The first dam removal to garner national attention occurred in Maine when the Edwards Dam on the Kennebec River was removed in 1999. The dam was removed against the wishes of its owner, by order of the Federal Energy Regulatory Commission, due to its impairment of endangered species habitat (Didisheim 2002).

Removal Projects

The removal of Edwards Dam set in motion a movement led by a powerful coalition in Maine of fishing organizations, Native American tribes, environmental organizations, and some business owners to remove dozens of additional dams (Natural Resources Council of Maine 2009). One of

Photograph of the Embrey Dam in Fredericksburg, Virginia, as part of it was destroyed to restore the Rappahannock's status as a "free-flowing" river.
U.S. Fish and Wildlife Service

Kelly Barnes Dam Failure

The Kelly Barnes Dam was located on Toccoa Creek, north of Toccoa, Georgia. After days of rain, the dam collapsed on November 6, 1977. The resulting flood killed thirty-nine people.

The structure was originally a rock crib dam that was completed in 1899 to impound water for a hydroelectric plant. In 1937, the Toccoa Bible Institute built an earthen dam over the original dam to generate hydroelectric power for the institution. Following the conclusion of World War II, the earthen dam was raised approximately forty-two feet above the rock foundation. By 1957, the dam was no longer needed for the generation of power. The reservoir was then utilized as a recreational resource until the dam collapsed.

The dam's failure was blamed on a number of factors related to its various stages of construction. A major problem was that leaks had eroded significant portions of the earthen fill. The earthen fill was further undermined by the metal pipes that were inserted into the dam when it was first covered by soil. They had corroded, which led to the slide that initiated the dam collapse. The disaster brought attention to the need to monitor old dams that had fallen into disrepair because they had outlived their original purpose.

—John R. Burch Jr.

See also: *Dam Building; Dam Safety and Security Act of 2002*

BIBLIOGRAPHY

Crisp, Robert L., Jr., William E. Fox, Robert C. Robison, and Vernon B. Sauer. "The 1977 Toccoa Flood: Report of Failure of Kelly Barnes Dam Flood and Findings." U.S. Geological Survey Georgia Water Science Center, 1977. Available at http://ga.water.usgs.gov/publications/ToccoaFIBReport/index.html.

Saunders, C. L., and Vernon B. Sauer. "The 1977 Toccoa Flood: Kelly Barnes Dam Flood of November 6, 1977, near Toccoa, Georgia" (U.S. Geological Survey Hydrologic Investigations Atlas HA-613). U.S. Geological Survey Georgia Water Science Center, 1977. Available at http://ga.water.usgs.gov/publications/atlas/ha-613/index.html.

the most significant efforts was a multiparty settlement in 2004 to restore much of the Penobscot River, including the projected removal of Veazie and Great Works Dams. This settlement may well become a template for negotiating complex, multiparty, multidam river restoration projects (Penobscot River Restoration Trust n.d.). Other dams have been removed on the Sebasticook, the Presumpscott, and other Maine rivers, with a total of twenty dams removed and another ten slated for possible removal (Maine Department of Environmental Protection 2010).

Another significant dam removal project is the Matilija Dam on the Ventura River in California. This 198-foot high concrete-arch dam was completed by the U. S. Army Corps of Engineers in 1948. Almost immediately, the reservoir began filling with sediment, rendering the dam useless. Even the owners of the dam, the local water district, agreed that the dam should be removed, but such an effort is not without controversy (Matilija Dam Ecosystem Restoration Project 2010). Stakeholders disagreed as to the proper removal method, what to do with the estimated 6 million cubic yards of sediment trapped behind the dam, and how to allocate a revised water-use regime to benefit endangered steelhead trout while preserving local agriculture. The dam has been notched several times, beginning the process of allowing a restored flow of water, and it will be completely removed in 2014. The removal of Matilija Dam is important because of the engineering challenge of deconstructing such a large dam and disposing of the enormous sediment load, both of which must be accomplished without damage to downstream communities and a downstream reservoir.

Another large dam-removal and restoration project is occurring on the Elwha River on Washington State's Olympic Peninsula. The Elwha River rises in the Olympic Mountains and flows north for forty-five miles to the Strait of Juan de Fuca. The Lower Elwha Klallam tribe has lived in that river valley since time immemorial, sustaining itself from abundant runs of salmon and steelhead trout. But in 1912, a local sawmill built the 110-foot-high Elwha Dam on the river as a source of hydropower. The dam completely blocked fish passage, so all ten anadromous fish runs were destroyed. In 1927, the 210-foot-tall Glines Canyon Dam was built farther upstream in a narrow mountain canyon. This concrete-arch dam was also built to generate electricity and without fish passage. When Olympic National Park was created in 1938, Glines Canyon Dam was within its boundaries.

The construction of these two dams was resisted by the Lower Elwha Klallam people, but to no effect. However, with the advent of the dam-removal era, the Lower Elwha Klallam people began leading an effort to remove both dams and restore anadromous fish runs to the Elwha River. Environmental groups, fishing organizations, and the National Park Service joined in the effort to remove the dams. The removal proposal was controversial; the town of Port Angeles, the sawmill, people who boated on the reservoirs, and the local chamber of commerce initially opposed it. But eventually the town, the chamber, and most local residents began to realize that an intact river with viable fish populations was worth far more than a small amount of hydropower. After years of negotiation, the Elwha River Ecosystem and Fisheries Restoration Act of 1992 (Pub. L. 102-495) became law, providing for the federal purchase and eventual removal of the two dams. Actual removal of the dams is scheduled to begin in 2011.

Controversial Klamath River Dam Removals

A much more controversial situation developed over proposals to remove four privately owned hydropower dams on the lower Klamath River. The Klamath follows a circuitous route that begins along the Oregon-California border, then heads north until it curves south again and enters Agency Lake and Upper Klamath Lake, which abuts the town of Klamath Falls and is the source of water for a large irrigation project built by the Bureau of Reclamation. Below the lake, the river leaves Oregon and flows southwest to the northern California coast, picking up the Trinity River along the way.

The upper river is heavily used by the Bureau's irrigation project, which provides water for 225,000 acres of cropland and then pumps the low-quality overflow water uphill back into the river. It is also home to the Klamath tribes and provides habitat for two endangered species of suckerfish, which were a traditional source of food for the tribes. The upper river basin is also home to six national wildlife refuges (U.S. Department of the Interior 2008). The lower river is used for hydropower generation from PacifiCorp's four dams. Before the dams were built, the lower river also produced the third-largest salmon runs on the west coast. Three tribes, the Yurok, Hoopa, and Karuk, lived for centuries off the river's bounty—until fish passage was blocked by the lowest dam, the Iron Gate Dam.

The Klamath River has generated every conceivable type of conflict that can be found in water policy. It pits anglers

Teton Dam Failure

The Teton Dam, approximately 305 feet tall and 3,000 feet wide, was built in Idaho across the Teton River Canyon to contain water from the flood-prone Teton River. On June 5, 1976, the dam ruptured. The resulting flood killed eleven people and damaged 110,000 acres of farmland. In total, the flood caused more than $1 billion in damages.

The dam was authorized for construction in 1964. During preconstruction planning, geologists were concerned about the suitability of the site since the canyon was comprised of rhyolite, a porous rock. Rather than abandoning the site, the U.S. Bureau of Reclamation opted to force grout into known cracks and holes when construction commenced in 1972. The agency began filling the dam's reservoir in 1975. The dam failed soon thereafter.

The dam was never reconstructed and served as an example, especially to the U.S. Bureau of Reclamation, of the need for careful site selection before dam construction even commenced.

—John R. Burch Jr.

BIBLIOGRAPHY

McDonald, Dylan J. *The Teton Dam Disaster.* Charleston, SC: Arcadia, 2006.
U.S. Department of the Interior Teton Dam Review Group. *Failure of Teton Dam: A Report of Findings.* Washington, DC: U.S. Government Printing Office, 1977. Available at http://openlibrary.org/books/OL23664245M/Failure_of_Teton_Dam/.

against farmers, upstream users against downstream users, and Indian tribes against non-Indians. There are multiple endangered species involved, water quality and quantity problems, and energy issues. There are conflicts among federal agencies, between states and the federal government, and between tribal and local governments. A very controversial drought-induced water shutoff in 2001 took water from irrigators to protect dwindling endangered salmon and steelhead runs. The following year a massive fish die-off occurred.

Despite this Pandora's box of water conflicts, most of the stakeholders signed a settlement in 2009 that resolves at least some of the issues and will remove the four dams on the lower river—*if* certain conditions are met ("Proposed Klamath River Basin" 2008; Jenkins 2008). The Klamath River clearly illustrates the high stakes involved in removing dams that affect the lives and livelihood of many people.

These case studies illustrate the range and diversity of dam removal efforts. Most removals involve small dams that have clearly outlived their usefulness. But some spark contentious political battles that often become heated and emotional, with all stakeholders investing heavily in influencing the outcome. Currently there are proposals to remove four dams on the lower Snake River, a proposal to abandon at least some of the locks and dams built by the Corps of Engineers, and a proposal to drain Lake Powell behind Glen Canyon Dam (Bonneville Power Administration 2005; Save Our Wild Salmon n.d.; Corps Reform Network n.d. ; Glen Canyon Institute n.d.). At this time, there is insufficient political support for these more radical proposals, but they clearly indicate that the days of simply assuming dams are good for society are long over.

Water Resource Allocation

Much of the conflict over dam removal derives from the larger issue of misallocation of water resources. Much of our water infrastructure was built for a society that was primarily rural. Rivers were used to irrigate crops and float barges that took the products to market. But the American economy, and our social values, have changed dramatically since the days when most of our rivers were dammed. Today, there is a significant demand for clean, healthy, intact rivers for moving-water recreation, tourism, scenic value, fish and wildlife habitat (especially for endangered species), urban water consumption, and urban amenity value. As a result, much of our water infrastructure does not meet current demands, leading to a political effort to change water management policy and renew, restore, and protect some stretches of rivers. Removing dams is just one component in a complex and multifaceted effort to restore and maintain healthy rivers. It is often the most controversial method of meeting current demands, but in some cases it is absolutely essential if a river is to meet the future needs of the nation. Dams, like water itself, will always be the focus of intense effort and controversy.

—Daniel McCool

See also: *American Indian Water Rights; Aquaculture; Government Water Decision Making; National Parks and Water; Recreational Water Rights; Urbanization*

BIBLIOGRAPHY

American Rivers. "58 Dams to be Removed in 2009." November 27, 2009. http://www.americanrivers.org/newsroom/press-releases/2009/58-dams-to-be-removed-in-2009-11-09.html.

Bonneville Power Administration. "Dam Breaching and the Lower Snake River Dams." 2005. http://www.efw.bpa.gov/Integrated FWP/DamBreachingFacts.pdf.

Corps Reform Network. http://www.corpsreform.org/.

Didisheim, Pete. *Toward a New Balance in the 21st Century: A Citizen's Guide to Dams, Hydropower, and River Restoration in Maine.* Augusta: Natural Resource Council of Maine, 2002.

Glen Canyon Institute. http://www.glencanyon.org/.

Graber, Brian, Crystal Yap, and Sara Johnson. *Small Dam Removal: A Review of Potential Economic Benefits.* Arlington, VA: Trout Unlimited, 2001.

"Hydro Facts." *Southwest Hydrology* 8, no. 5 (2009): 12. Available at http://www.swhydro.arizona.edu/archive/V8_N5/dept-hydro-facts.pdf.

Jenkins, Matt. "Peace on the Klamath." *High Country News,* June 25, 2008. Available at http://www.hcn.org/issues/373/17763/.

Lowry, William R. *Dam Politics: Restoring America's Rivers.* Washington, DC: Georgetown University Press, 2003.

Maine Department of Environmental Protection. "Dam Removals in Maine: Status as of January 1, 2010." http://www.maine.gov/dep/blwq/docstand/dams/non_hydro/dam_removals.pdf.

Matilija Dam Ecosystem Restoration Project. http://www.matilij-adam.org/.

McCully, Patrick. *Silenced Rivers: The Ecology and Politics of Large Dams.* London: ZED Books, 1996.

National Park Service. "Olympic National Park: Dam Removal—Overview." http://www.nps.gov/olym/naturescience/dam-removal-overview.htm.

National Research Council. *Restoration of Aquatic Ecosystems: Science, Technology, and Public Policy.* Washington, DC: National Academy Press, 1992.

Natural Resources Council of Maine. "Edwards Dam Gone Ten Years Today." *Insider* (blog), July 1, 2009. http://nrcm.typepad.com/nrcminsider/2009/07/edwards-dam-gone-10-years-today.html.

Penobscot River Restoration Trust. "The Project: Details." http://www.penobscotriver.org/content/4029/Details/.

"Proposed Klamath River Basin Restoration Agreement for the Sustainability of Public and Trust Resources and Affected Communities: Draft 11." Portland, OR: Ed Sheets Consulting, January 15, 2008. Available at http://www.edsheets.com/Klamath/ProposedAgreement.pdf.

Save Our Wild Salmon. "Why Remove the 4 Lower Snake River Dams?" http://www.wildsalmon.org/index.php?option=com_content&view=article&id=91&Itemid=63.

U.S. Army Corps of Engineers. "National Inventory of Dams, 2009." http://geo.usace.army.mil/pgis/f?p=397:1:1929981113380102.

U.S. Department of the Interior, Bureau of Reclamation. *The Klamath Project.* 2008. Video, 25:28; text script also available. Available at http://www.usbr.gov/mp/kbao/multimedia/Klamath_project/.

Deforestation

Deforestation is the process by which forest cover is lost and the land is converted to other uses. It is accomplished usually through logging or the burning of trees in a forested area. Humans then use the cleared land for agriculture or human settlement. Tree removal, without sufficient replanting, often results in damage to wildlife habitat, and deforested areas often decline into wasteland or desert.

Deforestation impacts the water cycle. Trees extract groundwater, which otherwise would remain unaccessed, through their roots and release it into the atmosphere. When

This 1915 photograph illustrates the result of a clear-cutting operation in a redwood forest near Crescent City, California. Such forestry methods can lead to significant problems with soil erosion.

R. Craig Jr./Corbis

a significant portion of a forest is cut down without replacement, trees no longer generate water evaporation, resulting in a drier climate. This in turn lowers the water content of the soil, thus reducing soil cohesion and causing erosion, flooding, and mudslides. Subsoil aquifers are depleted and often polluted. Drier conditions lead to the drying out of remaining vegetation, which often leads to wildfires.

Although deforestation is considered a more serious issue in the underdeveloped world—particularly with the loss of rain forest in Southeast Asia and South America—the threat of deforestation in connection with watershed management has had a growing impact on environmental politics in the United States.

Before the arrival of the Europeans, approximately half of what is now the United States was covered by virgin forest (Williams 2006, 367–68). Between 1620 (when European settlement in North America began to accelerate) and 1920, the land was cleared, mainly for agriculture, at a rate that matched population growth. After 1920, the amount of forest land increased as the use of land for agriculture declined,

despite steady population growth. The rate of reversion to forest of abandoned farmland reached a peak of 762 million acres by 1963. But forested area began to decrease again starting in 1963, and has been doing so ever since.

Early Efforts to Protect Forests

Worry over the consequences of forest loss and its connection to water quality and quantity has been a continuing feature of American politics. Beginning in the late nineteenth century, conservationists began to express concern that the United States was facing a "timber famine." Timber supplies and land had always seemed obtainable by the opening of new areas for settlement, but as settlement moved into the far West and the Pacific Northwest—the sites of the last virgin timber stands—warnings from conservationists intensified. In addition, western states were increasingly occupied with preserving forested watersheds in order to integrate irrigation, domestic water consumption, and hydroelectric power.

John Muir

During his lifetime, John Muir was regarded as the foremost proponent of wilderness values. He is now viewed as the founder of the modern environmental movement.

Born in Scotland on April 21, 1838, Muir and his family immigrated to the United States in 1849. He studied geology and botany at the University of Wisconsin at Madison. Muir supplemented his formal education by hiking more than 1,000 miles in Canada and the United States. In 1868 Muir traveled to California, where he explored the Sierra Nevada mountain range. He was particularly entranced by the Yosemite Valley, where he lived for six years, and worked to ensure that its natural beauty would be preserved for future generations. His efforts resulted in the establishment of Yosemite National Park in 1890.

Muir cofounded the Sierra Club in 1892, serving as its president until he died. His lobbying of President Grover Cleveland between 1896 and 1897 led to the establishment of thirteen national forests. His friendship with President Theodore Roosevelt resulted in the creation of additional national forests and parks. Muir died on December 24, 1914.

—John R. Burch Jr.

See also: *Hetch Hetchy Dam*

BIBLIOGRAPHY

Fox, Stephen R. *John Muir and His Legacy: The American Conservation Movement.* New York: Little, Brown & Company, 1990.
Righter, Robert W. *The Battle Over Hetch Hetchy: America's Most Controversial Dam and the Birth of Modern Environmentalism.* New York: Oxford University Press, 2005.
Worster, Donald. *A Passion for Nature: The Life of John Muir.* New York: Oxford University Press, 2008.

The initial political steps to ensure forest preservation were taken in 1877 with the creation of the Division of Forestry in the U.S. Department of Agriculture. Conservation gained momentum when Congress passed the Forest Reserve Act of 1891, which authorized the president to set aside land from the public domain. The Forest Management Act of 1897 provided an administrative mechanism for the new national forests and allowed the creation of further reserves to improve and protect the forests, assist water flow, and provide a continuing timber supply. In these two landmark Acts and a number of other laws passed in the first two decades of the twentieth century, the primary consideration was the forest-streamflow relationship—the preservation of lakes and rivers for navigation, flood control, and irrigation and the maintenance of a supply of clean drinking water.

The forest-streamflow argument gained further strength with the passage of the Newlands Act and the creation of the Reclamation Service in 1902. The prevention of deforestation and the replacement of lost timberlands with new growth came to be viewed as vital for flood control and irrigation. Conservationists linked the disastrous Ohio River floods of 1907 to logging in the watersheds of the Allegheny and Monongahela Rivers. Their arguments were instrumental in the passage of the Weeks Act of 1911, which authorized the purchase of lands for national forests in the eastern United States.

The most forceful spokesperson for the forest-streamflow thesis and for forest conservation was Gifford Pinchot. Appointed head of the Division of Forestry in 1898, Pinchot understood the public's unease over the dwindling forest lands and timber supply, along with their frustrations over the government's inability to manage forest lands and protect water resources. Pinchot gained a strong ally in Theodore Roosevelt, who ascended to the presidency after President McKinley's assassination in 1901 and became a strong supporter of conservation policies.

Pinchot's alarmism and high-handed management style also gained him many enemies, including some members of Congress who resented his close relationship with Roosevelt and rival federal bureaucrats jealous of his political success. Moreover, the theories of Pinchot and other supporters of the forest-streamflow link were being challenged by a number of studies from the U.S. Army Corps of Engineers, which argued that forests did not prevent floods and that their main benefit was to protect against soil erosion.

The forest-streamflow controversy thus triggered a number of studies of forest-water relations in the United States. Most of these dealt with the issues of flood control and the environmental consequences of changes in land use. In 1915, the Forest Service established a research branch. By the end of the 1920s, the branch had twelve regional experimental stations. Three of them began watershed study programs during the 1930s. Despite the studies begun under these programs, the forest-waterflow controversy continued in muted form for many years. By the late 1920s, the Forest

Service had backed away from its traditional position on the importance of forests in flood control and instead emphasized their role in the prevention of soil erosion.

During the 1930s, political trends, particularly President Franklin D. Roosevelt's administration's emphasis on conservation, led scientists, engineers, and conservationists to undertake definitive empirical studies of forest cover impact on flood control and erosion. Their concerns were reflected in Congress's passage of the Omnibus Flood Control Act of 1936. This legislation made the Department of Agriculture responsible for the conduct of flood control surveys on watersheds generally, the Forest Service responsible for monitoring the condition of forest watersheds, and the Soil Conservation Service responsible for monitoring agricultural watersheds. The Act required a detailed survey report and cost-benefit study before any plan for improving land for conservation purposes could be authorized.

During the 1930s and 1940s, studies growing out of congressional mandates emphasized the impact of logging and clear-cutting on streamflow and erosion. Most found that road building and skidding logs in forested areas could cause erosion if the roads were not properly positioned. Studies undertaken in the western United States revealed that logging could cause permanent damage to streams in geologically unstable areas. Environmentalists also raised concerns that logging could increase water pollution through the accelerated flushing of soil nutrients into streams. The loss of these nutrients could also inhibit the growth of new forest. These studies also presented ominous new evidence suggesting that logging combined with land use change—the clearing of forests for agricultural use or urban and industrial development—had very different consequences than cutting trees and allowing forests to regrow and that it threatened to cause permanent environmental damage.

Effects of Deforestation on Water Quality

The re-emergence of the connection between forests and water quality as a concern in the 1960s and early 1970s was linked to increased concerns over water pollution. Earlier legislation in the post–World War II period had addressed specific (or point sources) of pollution such as drainpipe discharge. Beginning in the early 1960s, scientists and policy makers took a closer look at non–point sources of water pollution—sources more difficult to identify that were closely linked to the permanent loss of forest cover and the conversion of the land to other uses, including road building, road use, housing developments, agriculture, and parking lots.

Environmentalist concerns over the connection between the loss of forest land and its impact on water quality and water supply found expression in the Clean Water Act of 1972. This legislation directly addressed non–point sources of water pollution and directed the states to look more closely at forest practices. Several states enacted legislation to regulate private forestry and changes in land use. Many states have worked cooperatively with the forest industry, private landowners, and agriculture to develop and implement measures to minimize water pollution arising from the way forests are managed.

The connection between deforestation and water quality and quantity has continued to be a major issue in the western United States. The cycle created by the harvesting of timber; the destruction of forests through strip-mining in Wyoming, Montana, and Minnesota; an unusually long drought; and the drying out of the surviving vegetation was manifest in the disastrous wildfire seasons of 2000 and 2002. In Colorado, which contains the headwaters of the Colorado, Platte, Arkansas, and Rio Grande Rivers, large wildfires threatened water quantity and quality because scorched forestland cannot retain and release water after storms, thus compounding the effects of drought, erosion, and increasing human demand on diminishing water supplies.

Surface mining has emerged as a threat to forest cover and the supply of clean water. The demand for coal, combined with a desire to gain a competitive advantage over the large strip-mining fields in the western United States, has led to the widespread practice in Appalachia of blasting forested mountaintops, as opposed to conducting traditional underground mining, to extract the coal deposits, thus minimizing costs. Although cheaper and more efficient, mountaintop removal mining raises major environmental and political issues.

A major controversy erupted in West Virginia between local landowners and Massey Energy, one of the largest and most aggressive of the coal companies. Between 1985 and 2001, Massey and other companies, with the acquiescence of the Army Corps of Engineers and other federal agencies, blasted ridgetop forests to mine large coal deposits. The practice has left miles of ridgetops, amounting to 3.4 percent of the total area of southeastern West Virginia, Tennessee, Kentucky, and Virginia, bare of tree cover.

In 2001, local landowners and environmentalists, concerned over the threat that mountaintop removal mining posed to public health and water quality, began legal action to stop mountaintop mining. They accused Massey and the other companies of complete disregard for the health of the local population and the ecological consequences of their actions. These groups warned that the loss of forest cover would further soil erosion and lead to the polluting of streams from silt, soil erosion, mudslides, and coal waste, threatening the water supply as well as causing a loss of fishing and recreation spots. If the practice continues, more than 1.4 million acres of ridgetop forests could be destroyed by the time all of the coal is mined.

Local citizens, with the backing of the Ohio Valley Environmental Coalition (OVEC), filed a class action lawsuit accusing Massey Energy of violating the Clean Water Act. This legal action, along with a civil complaint brought (some would say belatedly) by the Environmental Protection Agency for violations of the Clean Water Act in May 2007, has slowed mountaintop removal mining but not stopped it.

Government Intervention

Although deforestation issues have become more important in the eastern United States, the greatest concerns about the permanent loss of forestland continue to be about the pine ecosystems of the Mountain West. Studies by the Forest Service and the Bureau of Land Management have shown local shifts away from fire- and drought-resistant pine tree and mixed conifer stands and toward stands of small trees and other vegetation. This new cover dries out more easily and is more vulnerable to wildfires. The recent disastrous wildfire seasons in California and the Mountain West states may be attributable to the prevalence of this vegetation. However, efforts by the federal government and Congress to address these issues through more comprehensive regulations and legislation have become bogged down amid resistance from logging and mining interests, jurisdictional rivalries among the concerned federal agencies, and states' rights and property rights issues.

Forest management, the prevention of deforestation, and the link between forest cover and the supply of clean and plentiful water will continue to be central issues in U.S. environmental policy. In the early twenty-first century, officials in the federal and state policy-making agencies and elected legislators face competing claims: population growth with attending housing and commercial development requirements; demands by environmental groups to protect biological diversity; and the need for water for agriculture, industry, and residential communities.

The trend in the last three presidential administrations (George H. W. Bush, Bill Clinton, and George W. Bush) has been toward policies that minimize government intervention in favor of logging, mining, and commercial agriculture interests. The administration of George W. Bush, in particular, moved toward allowing more road building in forested areas and imposing fewer restrictions on energy companies that practice surface and mountaintop removal mining.

The course of the Barack Obama administration remains unclear, although President Obama's emphasis on the development of renewable energy resources, along with the decline in demand for lumber, is cause for optimism among environmental groups. Growing efforts to end commercial logging in old-growth forests and federally owned timberlands have intensified due to increased public concern about global warming, species loss, and the water supply. Proposed legislation, particularly the Pacific Northwest Forest Legacy Act, has the potential to alter radically the trends of the last ten years and reemphasize forest restoration and the protection of virgin forests. A growing segment of public opinion is thinking of forests as more than merely sources of timber and minerals.

—Walter F. Bell

See also: *Army Corps of Engineers, United States; Bureau of Reclamation; Clean Water Act of 1972; Conservation Movement; Desertification; Drought; Endangered Species Act (1973); Environmental Protection Agency, United States; Erosion; National Parks and Water; Pinchot, Gifford; Population Trends and Water Demand; Roosevelt, Franklin D.; Roosevelt, Theodore; Urbanization*

BIBLIOGRAPHY

Cody, Betsy A., and Pervaze A. Sheikh. "Western Water Resource Issues." CRS Report for Congress, 109th Congress (RL33565). Washington, DC: Library of Congress, Congressional Research Service, October 18, 2006. Available at http://www.nationalaglawcenter.org/assets/crs/RL33565.pdf.

Gardner, Hallie. "Cut Down." *E—The Environmental Magazine* 20, no. 2 (2009): 14–19.

Gorte, Ross W. "Forest Ecosystem Health: An Overview." CRS Report for Congress, 107th Congress (RS20822). Washington, DC: Library of Congress, Congressional Research Service, February 21, 2001. Available at http://www.nationalaglawcenter.org/assets/crs/RS20822.pdf.

MacDonald, Christine. "Forest Watch." *E—The Environmental Magazine* 20, no. 2 (2009): 30–32.

Sample, V. Alaric, and Anthony S. Chang. *Forest Conservation Policy: A Reference Handbook.* Santa Barbara, CA: ABC-CLIO, 2004.

Sarz, Richard S. "Watershed Management." In *Encyclopedia of American Forest and Conservation History,* edited by Richard C. Davis. Vol. 2. New York: MacMillan, 1983.

Shnayerson, Michael. *Coal River: How a Few Brave Americans Took on a Powerful Company—and the Federal Government—to Save the Land They Loved.* New York: Farrar, Straus, and Giroux, 2008.

Turner, Tom. *Roadless Rules: The Struggle for the Last Wild Forests.* Washington, DC: Island Press, 2009.

Williams, Michael. *Deforesting the Earth: From Prehistory to Global Crisis.* Abridged ed. Chicago: University of Chicago Press, 2006.

Desertification

Desertification is a process whereby productive land becomes nonproductive desert. It sometimes results from changes in climate, but it can also result from human activities such as overgrazing, overuse of ground water, and diversion of river water for human and industrial purposes.

Deserts are naturally occurring phenomena that grow and shrink regardless of human activity. Core deserts are surrounded by large expanses of sand stabilized by vegetation. Some deserts are clearly defined, ending abruptly as they reach mountains or other landforms that block them from less arid environments. In other cases, deserts have fringe areas that gradually transition to a more humid environment. The transition zones tend to be extremely delicate, with hollows containing vegetation that absorbs the heat and allows land to be cooler, particularly after rainfall. Human activity is possible in these areas, but only with a high likelihood that it will degrade the ecosystem.

Desertification in the United States is mostly a western problem. Arid, semi-arid, and dry subhumid areas with low rainfall are present in seventeen western states, particularly east of the Rockies in the Great Plains and in the areas between major western mountain ranges. There are also desert areas in Louisiana, Mississippi, Arkansas, and Minnesota.

The causes of desertification include overgrazing, the cultivation of marginal lands, use of sparse vegetation for fuel, poor irrigation that leads to salinization, and, more than anything else, excess human population. Replacement of nomadic patterns with sedentary ones near water supplies decreases the vegetation that protects the land from hot or strong winds. Livestock pound the soil to finer material and reduce percolation, thereby promoting erosion. Drought by itself does not promote desertification. It exacerbates a condition brought about by overexploitation of marginal land by too many people. When well managed, marginal lands can survive drought and recover with the return of rain.

Desertification harms wild species as well as domestic ones, and it promotes soil erosion by both wind and water. The water that is lost could otherwise enter the soil and nourish plants. As drought conditions continue, even long-lived plants die. Loss of plant cover reduces nutrients, further decreasing plant cover. Flooding becomes more frequent and severe because the soil no longer absorbs water. Desertification reinforces itself in a never-ending cycle of deterioration.

About a third of the world's land surface is arid or semi-arid and thus susceptible to desertification. Satellite images taken years apart show the changes in a desert and help to document the impact of animals and people on the desert fringes. If global warming alters the climate as projected, desert areas will grow by 17 percent, further enlarging the area susceptible to desertification. Desertification takes an additional 12 million hectares each year even without global warming.

Drylands are areas where agriculture or stock grazing is practiced without irrigation. In the early 1980s, 61 percent of the world's productive drylands were moderately to severely desertified. In 2009, degradation put almost a billion people in 100 countries at risk. A third of the world's people live in dryland ecosystems, which cover half of the earth's land surface. Dryland zones, particularly rural ones, have higher proportions of poor people because land degradation reduces productivity, makes living more precarious, and makes access to resources more difficult. The people who live in these areas are among the earth's poorest and among the most vulnerable. Drylands naturally are short of water, limiting their viability as providers of human needs. Between 10 and 20 percent of the world's drylands are already degraded, and desertification is ongoing.

Combatting Desertification

Most attempts to curtail desertification involve controlling the movement of soil and sand. Measures to fixate the soil include developing shelterbelts, wood lots, and windbreaks of trees and bushes. Vegetation helps to halt erosion and evaporation. Petroleum and nano-clay sprayed over the affected areas can help, but this method is feasible only in areas where it is cheap. Both materials coat seedlings to weigh them down, reducing the chance of their blowing away. In addition, they help prevent moisture loss. Boulders also help to slow wind-caused shifting, as do sand fences. Straw grids of up to a meter in area also slow wind speeds, thereby holding trees and shrubs in place until they take root. Vegetation near the base third of a dune on the windward side will hold the dune in place, and trees are effective on dune tops. Oases and farmlands in windy regions need tree fences or grass belts as windbreaks.

Sand-control measures do nothing to address other problems, however, such as the lack of water. Other efforts to combat desertification include bringing in water through pipes from distant locales or hyperfertilizing and fixating the soil. Additionally, rainwater may be harvested and runoff from nearby highlands can be used for irrigation.

Researchers are also promoting the use of crop rotation and sand-fixing plants to protect land from degradation. Some soils such as clay become too tight when dry, so tillage is necessary before planting. Planting helps enrich the soil. Legumes fix nitrogen from the air into the soil. Other solutions include the use of organic materials for construction and the stacking of stones to collect dew and reduce moisture loss during the day.

Generally, desertification develops because of poor land management in areas of low rainfall—that is, below 23.62 inches (600 mm). One such example is the Sahel, the semiarid area south of the Sahara Desert, which migrated 100 km (nearly 60 miles) southward between 1950 and 1975. Early degradation in the arid U.S. West came about primarily because of unregulated livestock grazing from the mid-1880s until the 1930s. The result was major damage to forests and rangelands, the loss of natural vegetation, and an increase in soil erosion.

Government Efforts to Prevent Desertification

Early attempts to stop desertification in limited contexts included the passage of the Forest Reserve Act of 1891 and the establishment of the U.S. Forest Service in 1905. The U.S. Grazing Service, established by the Taylor Grazing Act of 1934, has the mission of stopping overgrazing and soil deterioration on public lands. The Bureau of Land Management is the primary manager of federal rangelands in the West. In combination, these efforts promote the effective management of commodity use, including livestock and timber. They have not stopped desertification, however, which was not even recognized as a national priority until the Great Drought of the 1930s resulted in the Dust Bowl.

The Dust Bowl resulted in a large human migration from the southern Great Plains to California. At its height, almost two-thirds of the nation was in severe drought. The Soil Erosion Service debuted in 1933 to assist landholders in implementing improved agricultural and soil practices. The Farm Service Agency's predecessor debuted in the 1930s too, with the goal of agricultural conservation through better land maintenance practices on private lands. Since the 1980s, improvements in crop and range management have been ongoing, and degraded lands have diminished. Still, drought and questionable land management practices remain alive in the West.

Western rangelands endure periodic droughts, making them vulnerable to fire and land degradation. Private individuals, companies, or states own 61 percent of the land vulnerable to desertification. It is these very lands that produce most of the West's agricultural output. Irrigation is the key to allowing agriculture to thrive and also to fending off desertification in the region. Federal and state government officials work with farmers and ranchers to control soil loss and maximize water efficiency.

Federal policy is to maintain sustainability, but "sustainability" can mean different things to the different federal agencies active in land use/management. Various federal agencies have constituencies that expect the land to provide renewable energy, clean water, viable ecosystems and habitats, recreation, and economic development. Federal anti-drought policy is to be proactive and cooperative with all other players. The same cooperative approach is taken in regards to land reclamation. For example, the Department of the Interior's Water 2025 effort seeks to develop partnerships to preserve the environment and economy while using water wisely.

Although there is no single monitoring system, the Sustainable Rangelands Roundtable brings together fifty different entities to establish common criteria and indicators for rangeland evaluation. There are also diverse programs for monitoring, measuring, and reporting the threat of desertification throughout state and federal government agencies. The Heinz Center tracks and periodically reports on ecosystems, and its 2002 report, *The State of the Nation's Ecosystems: Measuring the Lands, Waters, and Living Resources of the United States,* was the first full inventory of said assets. This report, created with input from nearly 150 experts, was updated in 2008.

—John H. Barnhill

See also: *Agriculture; Climate Change; Erosion; Population Trends and Water Demand; Soil Salinization*

BIBLIOGRAPHY

GreenFacts. "Scientific Facts on Desertification." Data from 2005, summarized 2006. http://www.greenfacts.org/en/desertification/.

Heinz Center. *The State of the Nation's Ecosystems 2008*. Washington, DC: Island Press, 2008.

Sustainable Rangelands Roundtable. http://sustainablerangelands.warnercnr.colostate.edu/.

United Nations Convention to Combat Desertification. *National Report on Efforts to Mitigate Desertification in the Western United States*. 2006. http://www.unccd.int/cop/reports/otheraffected/national/2006/united_states_of_america-eng.pdf.

United Nations Environment Programme. "Turning the Land Degradation Tide on World Desertification Day." June 17, 2009. http://www.unep.org/Documents.Multilingual/Default.asp?DocumentID=589&ArticleID=6219.

Detergents

One of the problems that has been affecting the quality of water in the United States—and indeed in all industrialized countries around the world—has been the heavy use of detergents in homes and in industry. Many of these detergents have leached into the environment, affecting water both for plants and animals, as well as making it necessary to treat much water more heavily for reuse for human consumption and, sometimes, even for use for agricultural or horticultural purposes.

Essentially, the problems with detergents depend on the type of detergent being used and how it is disposed of—as well as the nature of the environment in which the detergent or other contaminant is disposed of. At the basic level are household soaps and shampoos. These are invariably washed down a drain. As they are designed for regular use by humans, the chemicals they contain are not nearly as toxic as those of many other detergents used in industry, although there is increasing concern about the quantity of soaps and shampoos being disposed of in urban areas. There is also a major concern about "bubble bath," which is also washed down the drain after use.

The Origins of Soap

Traditionally, many early detergents were made naturally. The Celts made soap from goat's tallow or wood ashes, according to Roman writers such as Pliny the Elder (CE 23–79). The Greco-Roman physician Galen of Pergamum (CE 129–c. 216) helped revolutionize the nature of medicine by insisting on the washing of hands and wounds during medical procedures, and he highlighted the need for cleanliness for medical rather than aesthetic reasons. This gradually led to particular places, such as Bristol in the west of England, becoming major centers for soap manufacture

in medieval Europe. By early modern times, the German chemist Justus von Liebig (1803–1873) famously declared that he felt that the amount of soap used by people in a country provided an accurate measure of that nation's wealth and degree of "civilization."

For the early pioneer families in North America, the work of making soap belonged to young women. They trickled clean water through an old barrel of wood ash to leach out the potash. Salt was then added, and this mixture was boiled in a kettle with bacon rinds and other fats from kitchen waste. This was then made into little cakes of soap. These initial soaps and detergents had no more adverse effect on the environment than the other residues of the pioneer lifestyle. Because of the work involved in making them, they were also used sparingly.

The manufacture of soaps was initially a handicraft, but the Leblanc process, devised by Nicolas Leblanc (c.1742–1806) for making soda ash from brine, changed that. This in turn was improved by the French chemist Michel Eugène Chevreul (1786–1889), who was able to provide scientific reasons behind the process of saponification (the conversion of fat into soap). Mass-manufactured soaps and detergents became progressively more effective but also more toxic to the environment. The work of Leblanc and Chevreul coincided with an increase in population in the United States, increased urbanization, and rising affluence, all of which combined to increase demand for mass manufacture of soaps. The end of the nineteenth century and start of the twentieth saw the first problems arising from the mass use of detergents in cities.

Environmental Issues

The problems that arose were not initially from household soaps but rather from industrial detergents. One example was the antifouling formula used to clean the undersides of ships, which removed barnacles and slowed down their reappearance. This substance was extremely toxic, but initially there were no environmental concerns as it was heavily diluted in the ocean. Also, some detergents were based on alcohol, and washing soda was mass manufactured for cleaning clothes and, later, for use in washing machines and dishwashers. These used a variety of chemicals, some of which were more harmful to the environment than others. Certain industrial cleaners and detergents, including those used in hospitals, are extremely toxic. In addition to causing problems where they were used, soaps also posed dangers to wildlife where they were manufactured.

The American biologist Rachel Carson (1907–1964), in her groundbreaking book *Silent Spring* (1962), wrote that experts in water pollution throughout the United States had become concerned that "detergents are now a troublesome and practically universal contaminant of public water supplies." This was because where water was often in most demand—in urban areas—detergents were being used at a much higher rate than in regions with lower population densities. Carson pointed out that some of these detergents are carcinogenic: "but in an indirect way they may promote cancer by acting on the lining of the digestive tract." This in turn changes human body tissues, which makes it easier for them to absorb dangerous chemicals, thus aggravating the effect of those chemicals.

To illustrate her point, Rachel Carson highlighted a study conducted in 1961 by the Environmental Cancer Section of the National Cancer Institute, working alongside the Fish and Wildlife Service. This showed that there had been an epidemic of liver cancer in rainbow trout in many hatcheries around the United States. Cancer rates had risen in fish of privately operated as well as federal and state hatcheries, and the increase was pervasive across the United States. The study showed that nearly all trout by the age of three had developed cancers. This, Carson argued, was highly revealing, and the problem was undoubtedly generalizable to other types of fish and animals. Humans might suffer effects by eating these animals or drinking the contaminated water that causes the problems in the animals.

In spite of Rachel Carson's *Silent Spring,* not until the 1970s did state governments throughout the United States began to take serious note of the dangers that detergents posed for groundwater supplies. Groundwater flows are much slower than those of surface water, and as a result, once pollutants have leeched down to underground water supplies, they are often not "flushed out" for long periods. Thus, the chemicals build up. Groundwater in some parts of the United States now has to be treated before it can be used for human consumption. That said, except near industrial plants, contamination of groundwater supplies is more often caused by runoff from agricultural fertilizers than from detergents, but detergents and soaps do exacerbate the problem.

Starting in the 1990s, many communities voiced rising concern about levels of water use, especially in arid parts of the United States such as Texas, Arizona, New Mexico, and southern California. To reduce overall freshwater usage, people started using gray water, for example by watering their lawns with wastewater from their own homes. It is easy to pipe water from washing machines and other household appliances, but because of the detergents used in dishwashers, sinks, and bathtubs, these are not used for the production of gray water. In spite of these limitations, the use of gray water has been important in reducing water consumption. Moreover, many soap and detergent manufacturers now make products that claim to be "friendly" to the environment.

—Justin Corfield

See also: *Wastewater Treatment*

BIBLIOGRAPHY
Carson, Rachel. *Silent Spring.* London: Hamish Hamilton, 1962.
Davidsohn, A., and B. M. Milwidsky. *Synthetic Detergents.* 7th ed. Harlow, UK: Longman, 1987.
Davidsohn, J., E. J. Better, and A. Davidsohn. *Soap Manufacture.* 2 vols. New York: Interscience, 1953.
Kane, J. G. *Soaps: Their Chemistry and Technology.* Hyderabad: Indian Central Oilseeds Committee, 1959.
Lloyd, J. W., G. M. Williams, S. S. D. Fister, R. P. Ashley, and A. R. Lawrence. "Urban and Industrial Groundwater Pollution." In *Applied Groundwater Hydrology,* edited by R. A. Downing and W. B. Wilkinson, 134–48. Oxford, England: Clarendon Press, 1991.
Niven, William W., Jr., ed. *Industrial Detergency.* New York: Reinhold, 1955.
Tames, Richard. *Life with the Pioneers.* London: Reader's Digest, 1996.

Dredging

Dredging—excavation that takes place partly or wholly underwater—has taken place around the world since ancient times. Sometimes dredging has been done to change waterways—especially to make it easier for ships to negotiate the shallow parts of harbors. As ships started having deeper draughts, this became more important to enable the continued use of old harbors. Also, some harbors forced ships to use a constricted route as protection against attack from enemy navies. Such routes were inefficient for commercial shipping, however. Dredging has also been done to take sediment—sand, gravel, and stones—from the waterbed for its own sake. Sometimes minerals could be extracted from the soil and sediment in river beds, as during gold rushes. Dredging is also used to make levees and earthen banks to protect populations from floods.

Dredging can dramatically change the nature of waterways and the local environment, and these changes are often controversial. The initial act of dredging releases sediment into the water column. This can cause sedimentation elsewhere or, in many cases, can lead to toxins being taken up the food chain and to temporary or even permanent damage to ecosystems, especially very delicate ones. On the other hand, the damage that results from dredging often has more to do with the subsequent use of the waterway, such as for human habitation, which further changes the environment.

Dredging in the United States

The first dredging in North America was undoubtedly for fishing, as nets were used to dredge the bottoms of sea beds to gather oysters, crabs, and other sea life. It is quite clear that some Native American tribes lived off seafood. However, these peoples were small in number, so the effects they had on the marine ecosystem were negligible.

In 1804, the Delaware flour mill owner Oliver Evans (1755–1819) invented an amphibious steam dredger, which was also the first steam-powered road vehicle in the United States. Inspired by reading about the British inventor James Watt (1736–1819) and his harnessing of steam power, Evans had wanted to make use of steam power in the United States. Many of his early inventions failed, often because of a lack of capital investment but also due to design problems. Evans named his dredge the "Orukter Amphibole," and he transported it, under its own power, to the nearby Schuylkill River. It proved to be relatively effective, and over time its dredging operations allowed coal barge traffic on the river to increase. Plans were made to use it to dredge the dockyards in Philadelphia, but the dredge sat on the dock at Philadelphia for several years before it was sold for scrap. Basic details about the machine are known, but no image of it survives.

By the time of Evans's invention, dredging had been used to improve harbors, and the technique was used to establish firm foundations for bridges and many docks. Dredging was also used in canal construction, especially when streams had to be widened or deepened or an existing canal had to be enlarged. Examples include the Chesapeake and Ohio (C&O) Canal and many of its extensions, as well as other canals throughout the United States. Some dredging occurred for military reasons during the American Civil War. For example, when Gen. Ulysses S. Grant attacked the city of Vicksburg, Mississippi, gunboats under the command of Adm. David Dixon Porter (1813–1891) had to make their way down previously inaccessible parts of the Mississippi River to bombard the city. Grant also ordered the building of canals to try to divert the river's waters. The environmental damage in the Vicksburg area was significant, but more from the artillery barrages from both sides than from the dredging or canal construction.

Environmental Impacts

The most environmentally devastating dredging in early U.S. history was associated with the search for minerals, particularly gold. In the 1849 California Gold Rush, although many gold nuggets were found on land, many more were discovered in riverbeds. The initial Gold Rush was focused on a number of rivers in the region where gold had been found—the American, the Feather, the Merced, the Stanislaus, the Tuolumne, and the Yuba—as well as the many streams that flowed into them. These rivers were all extensively dredged. The flora and fauna were destroyed either by the dredging itself, by the dumping of the sediment, by the later use of cyanide in an industrial process for getting the gold, and by waste left behind by the miners. These problems were faced by other ecosystems where gold rushes took place, such as in South Dakota in the 1870s and in Alaska in the 1890s.

Seabed mining for minerals has caused problems in the coastal United States. Outside the territorial sea boundaries of the United States, seabed dredging and other exploration is regulated by the Law of the Sea Convention and organized through the International Seabed Authority based in Kingston, Jamaica. However, dredging is uncommon here because it tends to be effective only in shallow waters.

With an increase in the amount of shipping and the size of ships starting in the late nineteenth century, it has been necessary to enlarge most U.S. ports, particularly those on the Atlantic coastline. Dredging has been used to create more specific shipping channels. Much of this dredging was done with what was known as a "bucket dredger." A wheel or chain with a number of large buckets attached was rotated, each bucket removing sediment, which was then transferred elsewhere. The bucket dredger was used for seabed mining as well as for enlarging shipping channels. It has since been replaced by various forms of suction dredging.

Operating like enormous vacuum cleaners, suction dredges disrupt the sediment by blowing low-pressure water or using a cutter. They then suck up the sediment using a centrifugal pump, a cutter-suction dredging device, or an auger with a rotating Archimedes screw. The water is returned to the sea or river, while the sediment is deposited elsewhere. Suction dredging requires enormous power, often provided by a hydraulic system. It can result in the release of toxic substances, including heavy metals, into the water column. The turbidity also can affect aquatic life, all but destroying the ecosystem. Further environmental damage is often caused when the sediment is dumped somewhere else, either on land or, more often, elsewhere underwater. Because of this, the U.S. Clean Water Act of 1972 requires that the discharge of any dredged or filled materials into the "waters of the United States" (which includes wetlands) cannot take place unless the U.S. Army Corps of Engineers has authorized it.

Dredging is used for land reclamation and for flood and erosion control and for "beach nourishment." Beach nourishment involves dredging up sand, which can then be used to replace sand on beaches that have been eroded by storms, waves, or human activity. Such dredging has helped to maintain many of the popular tourist beaches in the United States. Dredging sand and gravel from freshwater sources has been useful for the making of concrete. While these uses are often popular politically, they cause obvious environmental problems.

There are also some noncontroversial reasons for dredging. For example, police or other law enforcement authorities may use dredging to search for dead bodies or to recover objects such as weapons discarded into rivers or lakes. This generally does as little damage as possible to the environment because the dredging must be done in such a way as to reduce any potential damage to either the body or the object. Similarly, a number of dredging methods are used in underwater archaeological work, and this dredging is usually conducted for a limited time and within a small area. Dredges are also used to remove chemicals or rubbish from a marine area.

—Justin Corfield

See also: *Clean Water Act of 1972; Levees*

BIBLIOGRAPHY

Bathe, Greville, and Dorothy Bathe. *Oliver Evans: A Chronicle of Early American Engineering.* Philadelphia: Historical Society of Pennsylvania, 1935.

Hammond, Rolt. *Modern Dredging Practice.* London: Muller, 1969.

Herbich, John B. *Coastal and Deep Ocean Dredging.* Houston: Gulf, 1975.

Johnson, William Weber. *The Forty-Niners.* Alexandria, VA: Time-Life Books, 1980.

Muir Wood, A. M., and C. A. Fleming. *Coastal Hydraulics.* 2nd ed. New York: Wiley, 1981.

Rudolph, Wolfgang. *Harbor and Town: A Maritime Cultural History.* Leipzig, German Democratic Republic: Edition Leipzig, 1980.

Turner, Thomas M. *Fundamentals of Hydraulic Dredging.* Centreville, MD: Cornell Maritime Press, 1984.

Drought

Drought is a common and long-standing issue in water politics in the United States and elsewhere. Though the concept of drought is a familiar one, it has no one simple definition. Generally, scientists define drought as a period in which precipitation (such as rain or snowfall) is significantly lower than average for a given area. This means that no one standard can apply to the different climates across the United States. For example, precipitation levels that might indicate a drought in humid Louisiana could be considered above average in dry Arizona. Although a lack of precipitation is the most obvious indicator of drought, other indicators can include vegetation conditions, agricultural productivity, soil moisture, water levels in reservoirs and stream flows, and even economic impacts. Droughts can last from a few weeks to several decades.

Measuring Drought

Experts utilize a variety of methods to measure drought. The U.S. Drought Monitor uses a five-part scale that ranges from D0 to D4. D0 demarcates conditions that are "abnormally dry" but not yet severe enough to be drought; D1 indicates a 1-in-5-year level of dryness; D2 a 1-in-19-year event; D3 a 1-in-20-year event, and D4 a 1-in-50-year event.

Throughout U.S. history, policy makers and experts have utilized a variety of different indices to measure drought. Three prominent measurement methods, discussed here, are the "percent of normal" index, the Palmer Drought Severity Index, and the Standardized Precipitation Index. The so-called "percent of normal" index divides actual precipitation by the average. This is the oldest method available for measuring drought and was utilized by federal and state governments in the early twentieth century. As Richard R. Heim Jr. points out, in the first decade of the twentieth century, the U.S. Weather Bureau defined drought as any period of twenty-one or more days with rainfall at 30 percent or less of normal. Other definitions of drought used by governments and other entities in the early twentieth century included a period of fifteen consecutive days with no rain, annual precipitation that was less than 75 percent of normal, monthly precipitation below 60 percent of normal, or any amount of rainfall less than 85 percent of normal. Though this is the easiest index for the general public to understand, it also can be misleading in that there are variety of ways to determine what "normal" means. "Normal" differs for various regions and seasons, and a drought that affects agriculture may differ from a meteorological drought.

A variety of drought indices were developed in the twentieth century to remedy these issues. For example, the Munger Index, developed in 1916, measures forest fire risk. The Marcovitch Index, developed in 1930, includes both temperature and precipitation in its evaluation of drought conditions. The professionalization of meteorology led to more sophisticated understandings of interconnectivity of various components of the water cycle, leading scientists to begin to incorporate soil moisture into their analyses of drought. As one study concluded in 1955, "Drought does not begin when rain ceases but rather only when plant roots can no longer obtain moisture in needed amounts" (Heim 2002).

The Palmer Drought Severity Index (the Palmer or PDSI), devised by W. C. Palmer in 1965, incorporated these new understandings. This index is an algorithm that measures soil moisture. Today, government agencies continue to rely on the Palmer to determine when relief programs should be implemented.

A newer drought measurement, the Standardized Precipitation Index (SPI), was developed in the 1990s. It differs from the Palmer index in that it reflects a more recent understanding of the ways in which precipitation affects groundwater, reservoir storage, soil moisture, snowpack, and stream flow. It also can be applied to a variety of time scales. These advantages have led some planners in western states and the federal government to utilize the SPI instead of or in addition to the Palmer. Government and planning agencies sometimes use other methods of measuring and forecasting drought as well.

Drought in Precontact and Colonial North America

Droughts are recurring phenomena. However, humans in North American history have repeatedly created agricultural, social, and economic structures around the assumption that relatively wet conditions will be long lasting. When precipitation drops significantly below average, disruption can result. A famous pre-Columbian example of the devastating consequences of drought in North America is that of the so-called Anasazi, or ancestral Puebloans. As Colin Calloway writes, the Anasazi "experienced cycles of boom and bust," like other pioneers of the American West. The "boom," during which the famous settlements at Chaco Canyon reached their peak, occurred approximately 900–100 CE. Starting around 1130, however, drought struck. Small outlying communities were abandoned as the Anasazi consolidated into smaller numbers of larger communities, including Mesa Verde. By 1300, Chaco Canyon, Mesa Verde, and the other Anasazi settlements of the Four Corners were abandoned. The people there eventually moved southwest and founded sedentary communities called pueblos, some of which have been continuously inhabited to this day. Scholars disagree as to the exact causes of these abandonments and migrations, but drought and climate change seem to have been key factors (Calloway 2003).

Tree ring data demonstrate that severe drought also may have been a factor in the failure and near-failure of English colonies on the eastern seaboard. Colonists of the so-called "lost colony," Roanoke, disappeared during the 3 driest years out of the 800 for which data are available. Meanwhile, the establishment of Jamestown—and its so-called "starving time"—occurred during the driest 7 years out of a 770-year period (Stahle et al. 1998). These droughts may have played roles in the failure of early English attempts at agriculture and the reluctance or inability of neighboring Native groups to share their crops with the English.

Drought in U.S. History

Social as well as environmental factors shape the severity of a drought's consequences. The more people who live in a drought-plagued region, and the more those people rely upon water-intensive ways of life, the more severe the consequences of a drought. Euro-American settlement of the American West brought farmers who were accustomed to wetter climates into a more arid region. As settlement increased in the last half of the nineteenth century, so too did vulnerability to drought. The so-called Civil War drought, combined with increasing Native and Euro-American usage of the Great Plains, helped contribute to the massive destruction of bison populations (Seager and Herweijer 2007).

As Euro-Americans continued to move to the Great Plains following the Civil War, they became increasingly vulnerable to droughts like that of the 1870s, which also contributed to an increased number of locust swarms.

The 1880s, however, saw higher than average precipitation in the Plains, enabling many Euro-American farmers and boosters to convince themselves of the popular adage that "rain follows the plow," that cultivation of land somehow encouraged precipitation (Seager and Herweijer 2007).

Another drought in the 1890s was even more socially severe than the previous two because so many more families now relied on agriculture in the Plains. This drought, and resultant agricultural failures, contributed to an economic depression that affected the entire United States. The drought, with the depression, helped convince many that federal regulation and management of western water resources was necessary, leading to the 1902 Reclamation Act (Seager and Herweijer 2007).

Perhaps the most famous drought in U.S. history is the one that helped produce the so-called "Dust Bowl" in the southern Great Plains. American farmers and policy makers had assumed that the wetter than average climactic conditions of the first two decades of the twentieth century would continue. In fact, it was during this period that many federal-level policy decisions, such as the Colorado River Compact, were made. As was the case in the 1890s, the 1930s drought coincided with a severe economic depression. Donald Worster argues that the Dust Bowl disaster was more the result of human actions than climactic conditions; it was "the inevitable outcome of a culture that deliberately, self-consciously, set itself that task of dominating and exploiting the land for all it was worth" (Worster 2004, 4). As more and more Americans moved onto the Plains in the late nineteenth and early twentieth centuries, they replaced native grasses with staple crops, particularly wheat, that were much more vulnerable to drought. When drought came to the region in the 1930s, about one-third of the region "lay naked, ungrassed, and vulnerable to the winds" (Worster 2004, 94).

The Dust Bowl is thus an example of humans increasing their vulnerability to drought through social, agricultural, and economic choices. The federal government responded to the disaster by implementing policies that encouraged farmers to allow some fields to revert to native grassland and through the implementation of soil conservation districts. However, drought can only be dealt with, not prevented. A mere two decades later, Great Plains residents again experienced a drought and resultant sandstorms, the so-called "filthy fiftys." This drought helped spur increased use of new technologies, such as deep-well pumps and center-pivot sprinklers, to pump groundwater, especially from the massive Ogallala aquifer (Opie 1993).

New Ways of Conceptualizing Drought

Droughts continue to occur—they are naturally recurring phenomena, as the droughts that affected the Great Plains in 1988, the Southwest beginning in the late 1990s, and the Southeast beginning in 2005 attest. Recent understanding of drought stresses that, for planning purposes, drought should be considered a normal part of the weather cycle. Just as the Dust Bowl disaster demonstrates that drought can be exacerbated by human activity, so too can human activity help mitigate drought's effects.

—Denise Holladay Damico

See also: *Colorado River Compact of 1922; Erosion; Population Trends and Water Demand; Reclamation Act of 1902*

BIBLIOGRAPHY

Calloway, Colin. *One Vast Winter Count: The Native American West before Lewis and Clark.* Lincoln: University of Nebraska Press, 2003.

Heim, Richard R, Jr. "A Review of Twentieth Century Drought Indices Used in the United States." *Bulletin of the American Meteorological Society* 83 (2002): 1149–65.

National Drought Mitigation Center, University of Nebraska–Lincoln. "Planning for Drought: Why Plan for Drought?" 2006. http://www.drought.unl.edu/plan/whyplan.htm.

National Drought Mitigation Center, University of Nebraska–Lincoln. "U.S. Drought Monitor." Updated weekly. http://www.drought.unl.edu/dm/monitor.html.

National Oceanic and Atmospheric Association Paleoclimatology Program. "North American Drought: A Paleo Perspective." November 12, 2003. http://www.ncdc.noaa.gov/paleo/drought/drght_home.html.

Opie, John. *Ogallala: Water for a Dry Land.* Lincoln: University of Nebraska Press, 1993.

Seager, Richard, and Celine Herweijer. "Causes and Consequences of Nineteenth Century Droughts in North America." Lamont-Doherty Earthy Observatory of Columbia University, 2007. http://www.ldeo.columbia.edu/res/div/ocp/drought/nineteenth.shtml.

Stahle, David W., Malcolm K. Cleaveland, Dennis B. Blanton, Matthew D. Therrell, and David A. Gay. "The Lost Colony and Jamestown Droughts." *Science* 280 (1998): 564–67.

Worster, Donald. *Dust Bowl: The Southern Plains in the 1930s.* Rev. ed. New York: Oxford University Press, 2004.

Worster, Donald. *Rivers of Empire: Water, Aridity, and the Growth of the American West.* New York: Oxford University Press, 1985.

Ecosystem Management

A common expression used to describe the politics of water is "Whiskey's for drinking, water's for fighting." That phrase captures the history of water adjudication in the United States and the common perception that water will always be a point of contention, especially in the western United

States. This contentiousness extends to relationships among the federal government and state, county, city, and tribal governments. The history of tribal efforts to obtain water supplies, whether through litigation of Winters and other claims, cooperation with federal water projects, or negotiated settlements with the federal government, has demonstrated that each strategy carries with it significant risk in that they all depend on the federal government to bring justice to the tribes in this vital area. Charges that the federal government shirks its trust responsibility date back centuries, and the "second treaty era," as political scientist Daniel McCool has called it, has been no different (McCool 2002). Non-Indian development interests, in cooperation with the Bureau of Reclamation (BOR), have become a part of the "iron triangle" of reclamation development in which outcomes are shaped by the relationships among Congress, federal agencies, and nongovernmental interest groups. Indian tribes have therefore had a more difficult time asserting political power in recent years, both because of the ineffectiveness of the Bureau of Indian Affairs (BIA) and because the BIA exists within a Department of the Interior that is at odds with itself and its responsibility to the tribes (McCool 1987).

Nature Conservancy

The Nature Conservancy is a nonprofit organization that was incorporated in 1951 in Washington, D.C. It is dedicated to preserving ecosystems of all types through public ownership in the form of parks and wildlife refuges. It is the largest environmental organization in the world.

In 1946, the Ecologist's Union split from the Ecological Society of America. The organization renamed itself the Nature Conservancy in 1950. Its first land acquisition was a sixty-acre tract of land along the Mianus River on the border of New York and Connecticut in 1955. By 1965, the organization had grown large enough to require the services of a full-time, paid president. Beginning in 1980, it expanded outside of the United States through its International Conservation Program.

The Nature Conservancy has more than 1 million members in thirty countries. The organization is credited with the preservation of approximately 120 million acres of land and more than 5,000 miles of rivers around the world.

—John R. Burch Jr.

BIBLIOGRAPHY

Birchard, Bill. *Nature's Keepers: The Remarkable Story of How the Nature Conservancy Became the Largest Environmental Organization in the World.* San Francisco: Jossey-Bass, 2005.

Grove, Noel, and Stephen J. Krasemann. *Preserving Eden: The Nature Conservancy.* New York: H. N. Abrams, 1992.

The Nature Conservancy. http://www.nature.org/.

Ecosystem Management Models

Given the ineffectiveness and contentiousness of the past model, logic necessitates the construction of a new paradigm that will guarantee the rights of all stakeholders, allow for future development of water resources, and, as both Indian and non-Indian water use depend on the future viability of the environment, ensure ecological preservation for the foreseeable future. During the late twentieth and early twenty-first centuries, the proponents of a new model called "ecosystem management" made many claims about the possibilities of cooperative management and ecological preservation. The fact that ecosystem management proposes to have policies shaped by local needs, balancing the interests of many different constituencies, may attract many parties to this alternative scheme of power sharing, but questions remain about how feasible such an arrangement can be in practice.

During the social upheaval of the 1960s that helped spawn the modern environmental movement, the era of large-scale development began to hit a few snags. By 1970, the National Environmental Policy Act required environmental impact statements before any federal project could be implemented. The varying federal bureaucracies had survived politically by diffusing the costs of their projects and concentrating the distribution of benefits. This practice ensured the support of powerful allies, such as Rep. Wayne Aspinall (D-CO), who would shepherd projects that benefited his constituents through Congress. Of course, the development of environmental resources by this means had unintended effects on the landscape. The damming of rivers resulted in the increased salination of the water, making parts of the West unusable for agriculture. Further, in many cases, the growing urbanization of the West meant that water that was intended to irrigate western fields flowed into western cities instead.

The building of dams had, perhaps, the most dramatic effects of any man-made structures on the ecosystems of the

Center for Watershed Protection

The Center for Watershed Protection is a nonprofit organization that was founded in 1992 by Thomas Schueler in Ellicott City, Maryland. The organization works to protect watersheds located throughout the United States through educational endeavors and pioneering research in the field of watershed science. The research is usually not theoretical in nature but is instead intended to find innovative solutions to problems plaguing a particular watershed. This recognition that each watershed is unique also helps shape the organization's educational endeavors. The center works to educate local individuals and organizations to care for their local watershed, since they will be the ones most impacted by the state of their water supply. The center's methodology has proven very effective in the field and has greatly influenced the manner in which the federal government, through the Environmental Protection Agency, addresses issues impacting streams, rivers, lakes, and the country's other assorted wetlands.

—John R. Burch Jr.

See also: Environmental Protection Agency, United States

BIBLIOGRAPHY

Center for Watershed Protection. http://www.cwp.org/.
Randolph, John. Environmental Land Use Planning and Management. Washington, DC: Island Press, 2003.
Schueler, Thomas R., and Heather K. Holland, eds. The Practice of Watershed Protection: Techniques for Protecting Our Nation's Streams, Lakes, Rivers, and Estuaries. Ellicott City, MD: Center for Watershed Protection, 2000.

region. Species that relied on free-flowing rivers, such as many types of salmon, were made extinct. Weather patterns and the ecological makeup of entire regions were changed. Combined with the fact that prior policy had been largely based on political logrolling, and thus had ignored the interests of many groups, including Indians, the environmental harm caused by federal policies led to a call for a new paradigm for determining environmental policy, especially in the West. Natural resource scholars Hannah J. Cortner and Margaret A. Moote (1999) have argued that management of the environment by government, based on a politics of expertise, became necessary when the consequences of untrammeled business activity on a large scale required that collective rather than individual action be taken. However, untrammeled government development, based on a politics of interest, has also led to calls for change.

The father of the idea of ecosystem management, Aldo Leopold, stated that those who oppose government regulation have often been those guilty of bad stewardship. The idea of ecosystem management gained currency during the late twentieth century as a result of changing societal values, growing scientific knowledge, professional experience, and learning. The ultimate purpose of ecosystem management is sustainability of the environment itself, not sustainability of the products it can produce. Ecosystem management embodies four themes: that its goals are socially defined, that it advocates a holistic science, that it requires adaptable institutions, and that it involves collaborative decision making. In an environment where Indian water rights, combined with waters already used for non-Indian development and waters needed for endangered species preservation, threaten to overtax the already maxed-out western watershed, ecosystem management is necessary for the survival of all of the West's diverse populations.

The ecosystem management model assumes that a comprehensive, coordinated ecosystem approach is the wisest way to manage and conserve resources because cooperative action is essential to avoid conflicts between claimants of resources and to ensure access to and future use of resources. This approach has often led to resistance from varying interest groups and sovereignties (including Indian tribes) because of their interest in preserving rights and, often, in using natural resources to their fullest potential. When resources cross over jurisdictional lines, as they often do, political groups have been reluctant to relinquish either sovereignty or jurisdiction. When resources are shared by multiple users, each user may seek to maximize returns on the resource to the exclusion of others, as seen in the prior appropriation model of water management. Therefore, conservation and management have been dealt with on an ad hoc or as-needed basis.

Government Approaches

During the last decades of the twentieth century, many government officials began to favor a more holistic approach, adopting the concepts expressed in models of biodiversity and ecosystem management and incorporating them into laws and treaties. Some courts also started to apply this comprehensive approach and created, in essence, a legal presumption for ecosystem management. Within the United States, this principle requires that federal and state regulatory agencies apply ecosystem management to existing statutes and regulatory policies. Environmental and fisheries statutes provide broad discretion to regulators and policy makers, but that discretion must be exercised consistently with the model. Although implementation is not universal or complete, the model has largely been accepted by many American environmental policy makers, particularly those dealing with forests and fisheries, as the preferred model because it makes scientific, political, and legal sense.

Ecosystem management values decentralized decision making and adaptive management. This means that management of a western ecosystem must cut across political boundaries, such as state lines and reservation borders, as well as across ownership boundaries. Thus, a number of paradoxes inherent in ecosystem management need to be solved before it can effectively be implemented. Ecosystem management requires large-scale management, which means managing areas under separate sovereignties, including Indian tribes. Also, a paradox is involved in management for both use and preservation that has been present from the beginning of the twentieth century. Because ecosystem management values both preservation and use, and theoretically involves decision making by groups that may not agree on where the best balance between preservation and use lies, conflict seems inevitable. Ecosystem management seeks to involve federal agencies, state agencies, Indian tribes, private landowners, environmental interest groups, and commodity interest groups in the decision-making process. In the process, it may require considerable social and political changes, such as the dismantling of old systems and even agencies.

The basis for understanding the impetus behind ecosystem management is that human interactions affect natural environments. Such interactions may involve conflict, cooperation, or coordination, and they can affect natural environments whether they take place within the natural environment or some distance from it. The actions of players involved in conflict, cooperation, or coordination help define the values of natural environments and the appropriateness of behaviors within or toward the natural environment. Such conflicts often include private citizens, companies, communities, Indian tribes and reservations, and government entities. All of these groups must work together if ecosystem management is to function. Over the past ten to twenty years, Congress and the executive branch have established national policies for managing ecosystems or the components of ecosystems, but communities have played a vital role in developing behavioral regularities for using and protecting the resources in their particular ecosystems.

One reason the federal government has had a problem implementing ecosystem management is that it insists on the implementation of national standards without enough concern for community standards. Locally based decision making is an indispensable part of ecosystem management. If the federal government is truly going to become a partner in managing ecosystems, its various agencies must serve as coordinators who encourage cooperation among the parties involved rather than merely as the implementers of policy. Only in this way can government agencies establish a basis for effective, meaningful communication with their constituents for resource use and protection. When national standards are made to harmonize with community standards, the problems of government management can be avoided, which should encourage the cooperation necessary for the implementation of long-term solutions to ecosystem-wide problems.

Unlike past models of environmental management, many of the questions ecosystem management raises cannot be answered by scientific expertise alone; they require examinations of the philosophical and ethical systems of stakeholders as well. Federal resource agencies, such as the BOR, have traditionally limited public input by limiting public access to information about possible outcomes. Ecosystem management requires communities to become more educated about their localities. Many current policies (what Charles Wilkinson [1992] has termed the "lords of yesterday") such as the Hardrock Mining Law, the free and minimally regulated grazing of livestock on public lands, the encouragement of logging as the dominant use of the national forests, the building of dams that cripple salmon runs, and the management of water supplies in the West by prior appropriation schemes, are too production oriented and need to be done away with for ecosystem management to be implemented.

Even though government bodies take steps to encourage cooperation with local governments and citizen groups, some Indian communities, understandably fearful of losing any degree of their sovereignty over their natural resources, may choose not to cooperate. Consequently, it may be necessary for the government to provide incentives, such as technical and financial assistance. Further, in light of local concerns about unfunded federal mandates, incentives to participate in ecosystem management schemes take on increased importance. As with most federal programs, however, the government has imposed environmental policy on Indian tribes with very little room for tribal autonomy. As it affects Indian tribes, ecosystem management is problematic because of its inherent need for a lack of complete sovereignty. Ecosystem management implicitly requires that all of the interests in the region give up some of their control and administrative power (in other words, sovereignty). Decision making has to be shared in order to be effective. However, the limited sovereignty tribes wield is something that they have fought hard over many years to maintain. Ecosystem management's emphasis on shared decision making almost certainly would cause some Indians to question whether its implementation would mean a diminution of that sovereignty. Ecosystem management also means the implementation of some ideas that may not fit perfectly within some Indian cultural systems. It requires compromise by all parties concerned to create an agreement that places preservation above all other goals.

An ecosystem management approach differs even from prior "environmentally friendly" approaches, such as the Endangered Species Act, in that it is a method for sustaining entire environmental systems rather than preserving individual aspects of environmental systems. Further, rather than relying on environmental science alone, it includes ecological, economic, and social aspects of management. Despite ecosystem management's emphasis on orienting the entire regional environment toward sustainability, however, it has been implemented in a largely piecemeal way, with different federal bodies in charge of different parts of the ecosystem. For example, the Bureau of Land Management, the U.S. Forest Service, the National Park Service, the BOR, and the BIA implement separate programs. As a result, whereas ecosystem management has been emphasized in some areas of environmental management, rarely has it been implemented over entire ecosystem regions. This is especially true in the case of river basin systems, where Indian nations, federal bureaucracies, state governments, non-Indian citizens' groups, environmental groups, pro-development groups, and private companies all have a vested interest.

Such an ecosystem-wide scheme that requires all of the interested parties to participate can be fragile, as the resistance of one party can doom all efforts to failure. In its assessment of the BIA's ecosystem management programs on Indian reservations, the Congressional Research Service asserted that "there are no other places in the United States

where the development, use, and protection of natural resources is so fundamental to the identity, culture, and livelihood of the people who reside within them" (Morrissey, Zinn, and Corn 1994). But even though the principles embodied in ecosystem management are harmonious with many Indian belief systems, the needs for sovereignty and prosperity in modern America have made the implementation of ecosystem management on reservations problematic.

—Steven L. Danver

See also: *Aspinall, Wayne N.; Bureau of Indian Affairs; Bureau of Reclamation; National Environmental Policy Act of 1969; Winters v. United States (1908)*

BIBLIOGRAPHY

Cortner, Hannah J., and Margaret A. Moote. *The Politics of Ecosystem Management.* Washington, DC: Island Press, 1999.

McCool, Daniel. *Command of the Waters: Iron Triangles, Federal Water Development, and Indian Water.* Tucson: University of Arizona Press, 1987.

McCool, Daniel. *Native Waters: Contemporary Indian Water Settlements and the Second Treaty Era.* Tucson: University of Arizona Press, 2002.

Morrissey, Wayne A., Jeffrey A. Zinn, and M. Lynne Corn. "Ecosystem Management: Federal Agency Activities." CRS Report for Congress, 103rd Congress (94-339 ENR). Washington, DC: Library of Congress, Congressional Research Service, 1994. http://ncseonline.org/nle/crsreports/biodiversity/biodv-4.cfm.

Wilkinson, Charles F. *Beyond the Next Meridian: Land, Water, and the Future of the West.* Washington, DC: Island Press, 1992.

William C. Kenney Foundation. *Water in the West. Summary of Findings: Issues, Trends and Perceptions.* Sausalito, CA: William C. Kenney Watershed Protection Foundation, 2001.

Environmental Justice

See *Poverty and Water*

Environmental Law

See *Evolution of Environmental Law; Water Law*

Erosion

Erosion is the process of weathering whereby sediment, rock, and soil from a natural environment are, over time, moved and deposited elsewhere by water, ice, or wind. It is also the system by which rock can be transformed into sediment or sand. This process has been happening as a natural process since the beginning of Earth, but it has been increased dramatically by humans both because of their land use and their treatment of, or more correctly, mistreatment of, habitats.

Erosion and Human Activity

Many peoples since ancient times have noticed the "weathering" of their environment. The term *erosion* was first used to describe a mouth ulcer, but by the late eighteenth century it had taken on its modern usage. Although much erosion in the United States is caused by gravity and by wind, certainly one of the most problematic causes of erosion is human activity. This is particularly true where humans have transformed a landscape. One example, common around the world, is when deforestation occurs. Human destruction

The harmful effects of erosion can be seen here on a farm in Iowa. During heavy rains, topsoil, fertilizer, and pollutants are washed away.
Lynn Betts/Natural Resources Conservation Service

of forests, which can be exacerbated by forest fires and other environmental events, often leads to landslides after periods of strong rainfall. Human activity has also led to soil erosion due to wind, and this—combined with low or no rainfall— was certainly a major cause of the 1930s Dust Bowl. Some economists have highlighted the Dust Bowl as significantly exacerbating the Great Depression of the 1930s. On the other hand, natural erosion has formed interesting and beautiful rock formations, such as the wind-eroded alcove near Moab, Utah.

Since the 1930s, when lack of rainfall as well as poor farming practices brought on the Dust Bowl, the significant loss of topsoil has been seen to be a major problem facing U.S. agriculture and, hence, the U.S. economy and society. This has led to moves to conserve soil. The initial emphasis was on voluntary participation in abandoning erosive tillage systems. The Soil Bank Program (Title I of the Agricultural Act of 1956, Pub. L. 84-540) was authorized with the aim of increasing the level of agricultural production. The program was terminated two years later, but the U.S. government has continued to embark on programs to prevent further soil erosion.

For example, the practice of contouring—plowing, planting, cultivating, and harvesting according to elevation contours—has expanded. This has been particularly important in areas that have higher rainfall intensity because of the increased risk of gullying. Another system that has helped prevent land erosion has been strip cropping, in which strips of land are planted with different crops placed either along the land's contour or in such a way that they reduce the impact of the prevailing wind direction—a system further helped by regular windbreaks.

Another way to prevent topsoil erosion due to wind is to plant more crops, and this has been done by diverting water from rivers to agricultural land, including marginal agricultural land. Accomplishing these massive irrigation projects has involved the construction of large numbers of dams and irrigation systems, which have run into political problems over their location, the areas flooded, and the amount of water used, as well as the obvious financial cost in their construction. For example, irrigation—both for agriculture and horticulture—in semi-arid areas such as Phoenix, Arizona, has led to conflict with other states over the use of so much water to help conserve land that some argue should not have been used for agricultural production or for horticulture in the first place.

The Conservation Title of the Food Security Act of 1985 was a formal attempt to help prevent soil erosion. It represented a major move in U.S. government thinking from encouraging voluntary adoption to imposing legal restrictions to prevent farmers from despoiling land. The Act contained what were soon known as the "Sodbuster Provisions."

These were designed to prevent highly erodible land from being used for crop production—although any land that had been cultivated on at least one occasion between 1981 and 1985 was exempt. To enforce the Sodbuster Provisions, the Act stipulated that any land operator who violated them was not allowed to gain any benefits from price-support programs, loans from the Farmers Home Administration, storage loans from the Commodity Credit Corporation, payments from the Conservation Reserve Program, government-sponsored crop insurance, or payments under any other programs of the U.S. Department of Agriculture.

The Act also included what became known as "Swampbuster Provisions." These were designed specifically to preserve existing wetlands from being drained for conversion into agricultural land. The regulations in the Act meant that no land operators who converted wetlands would gain access to the farm benefits offered by the U.S. Department of Agriculture.

Natural Erosion

In other parts of the United States, especially on the Atlantic coast, a major problem is erosion from seawater. Strong winds have battered parts of New England, especially Maine and Massachusetts. Cape Cod has been subjected to heavy erosion, as has Nantucket Island. Indeed the Sankaty Head Light, a lighthouse constructed on Nantucket Island in 1850, had to be moved in October 2007 because the bluff on which it stood was quickly eroding.

Another form of erosion is known as gully erosion. This occurs when water flows over an area for a long period of time and gradually erodes the surface. For example, the Colorado River has cut into its high plateau, revealing on the "walls" of the canyon evidence of the different geological strata. Geologists, climatologists, and other scientists have studied this window to the past to learn about this region's development. The Grand Canyon has long been a spectacular tourist site, and similar river erosion can be seen in other parts of the United States, such as Hells Canyon on the border between Idaho and Oregon, Walnut Canyon in Arizona, and the Valley of Ten Thousand Smokes in Alaska.

There are also submarine forms of erosion. For example, the Monterey Canyon off the Pacific coast is comparable in size to the Grand Canyon. Other well-known submarine canyons formed through erosion are the Bering Canyon and the Pribilof Canyon off the coast of Alaska, the Astoria Canyon off the coast of Oregon, the Hudson Canyon near New York, and the Scripps Canyon off La Jolla, California.

Scientific studies of all of these have been used to work out the climatic conditions of the past and to predict climate change in the future.

In Alaska, there has also been ice erosion caused by avalanches, and erosion in some parts of the United States has been caused by volcanic lava, mud, or pyroclastic flows. These latter forms of erosion do not affect much agricultural land in the United States.

Since the 1990s, concern has grown that global warming is affecting the environment so significantly that arid areas may increase and present-day wetlands might start to suffer from water shortages. Rivers may shrink and even dry up entirely. Overuse of water by humans will combine with global warming to have a greater impact on the environment than would either individually. Regardless of the reason, the drying of the soil will make some areas more susceptible to wind erosion, affecting the long-term productivity of many major agricultural regions of the United States.

—Justin Corfield

See also: *Agriculture; Drought; Midwest*

BIBLIOGRAPHY

Boardman, J., I. D. L. Foster, and J. A. Dearing, eds. *Soil Erosion on Agricultural Land.* Chichester, UK: John Wiley & Sons, 1990.

Fangmeier, Delmar D., William J. Elliot, Stephen R. Workman, Rodney L. Huffman, and Glenn O. Schwab. *Soil and Water Conservation Engineering.* Clifton Park, NY: Thomson Delmar Learning, 2006.

Heimlich, R. E. "Soil Erosion on New Cropland: A Sodbusting Perspective." *Journal of Soil and Water Conservation* 40, no. 4 (1985): 322–26.

Larson, W. E., F. J. Pierce, and R. H. Dowdy. "The Threat of Soil Erosion to Long-Term Crop Production." *Science* 219 (1983): 458–65.

Lovejoy, S. B., and T. L. Napier, eds. *Conserving Soil: Insights from Socioeconomic Research.* Ankeny, IA: Soil Conservation Society of America Press, 1986.

O'Reilly, Sean, James O'Reilly, and Larry Habegger. *Grand Canyon: True Stories of Life Below the Rim.* San Francisco: Travellers' Tales, 1999.

Eutrophication

Eutrophication is the enrichment of water bodies with nutrients such as nitrogen and phosphorus that stimulate plant growth. The term derives from two Greek words, *eu,* meaning "good," and *trophic,* which refers to nutrition or nourishment. Nutrients are essential for primary and secondary productivity (i.e., food chains and webs) in all ecosystems. Limited supplies of nutrients curtail that productivity and thus the ability of organisms to reproduce. The elements nitrogen and phosphorus, found in compounds such as nitrates and phosphates, are continuously cycled among their various reservoirs on or near the earth's surface. Nitrogen is found primarily in rocks and soils, organisms, and the atmosphere; phosphorus resides mostly in rocks/soils and organisms. Such cycles are called biogeochemical cycles because biological and geological reservoirs and processes are involved. The action of nutrients and their exchanges are fundamental processes in ecosystems; nitrogen is essential for the production of proteins and amino acids, for example, while phosphorus is necessary for the synthesis of DNA and RNA and is involved in energy transfers.

In aquatic ecosystems, which comprise plants, notably algae, and animals in rivers/streams, lakes, marshes, groundwater, coral reefs, and estuarine/coastal environments, nutrient availability is determined by two sets of factors. One set of factors is natural. This consists of the nutrient content of catchment rocks and soils from which water enters aquatic environments; natural enrichment or impoverishment may occur when drainage systems cut through rocks of differing mineral content. Natural enrichment may also occur in the oceans, where upwelling brings nutrient-rich waters to the surface. Finally, nitrogen may be exchanged with the atmosphere.

The second set of factors consists of human-induced enhancement processes that distort natural biogeochemical flows. In the case of nitrogen and phosphorus, distortions occur due to fertilizers, animal waste, sewage effluent, soil erosion, and atmospheric sources. Distortions from atmospheric sources involve nitrates and nitrites, components of acid rain produced by fossil fuel combustion. This form of eutrophication, known as cultural eutrophication, is a predominant cause of water pollution.

Overall, eutrophication causes loss of biodiversity, oxygen depletion, and a decline in water quality, which, in extreme circumstances, has implications for human health. Eutrophication is a major problem worldwide, but it is especially significant in the developed world, most notably in Europe and North America. In the United States, eutrophication is a problem around most of the coastline, but especially in the Gulf of Mexico and in more than two-thirds of its estuaries. Such impairment of water bodies has serious ecological repercussions, seen in plant and animal extinctions, and economic repercussions insofar as fisheries,

tourism and recreation, and adjacent property prices may be adversely affected and drinking water compromised.

Early Research

The term *eutrophic* was first used by Carl Albert Weber (1856–1931), a German botanist, in 1907 to describe the conditions influencing the plant community in the early stages of raised bog formation. However, two European scientists, Einar Christian Leonard Naumann (1891–1934) from Sweden and August Friedrich Thienemann (1882–1960) from Germany, recognized the importance of lake water chemistry as a determinant of algal/plant communities. Between 1918 and 1930, they subsequently compiled a classification scheme for lakes based on this in combination with primary production. Their scheme introduced the term *eutrophic* to lake studies. It comprises oligotrophic (low production), mesotrophic (moderate production), eutrophic (high production), and dystrophic (low production with high humic content) waters. Both scientists also recognized the need for water management and conservation and were responsible for the development of limnology, which brings together biologists, chemists, geologists, and engineers to tackle eutrophication problems. Subsequently, modifications and expansions of the Naumann-Thienemann scheme have been made and its limitations realized.

The production of artificial nitrogen fertilizers significantly increased interest in and need for eutrophication research. This began in the late 1800s, made possible by the work of German chemists Fritz Haber (1868–1934) and Carl Bosch (1874–1940). They devised the means of combining the inert element nitrogen with hydrogen to produce ammonia on an industrial scale, enabling the vast reservoir of nitrogen in the atmosphere to be tapped as a means of producing nitrogen fertilizers.

Detection and Monitoring

Much effort has been invested in devising ways to determine degrees of eutrophication qualitatively and quantitatively and in implementing monitoring programs. Indices based on chemical and biological characteristics have been devised to reflect the components and processes of eutrophication. The U.S. Environmental Protection Agency (EPA), for example, has initiated a National Nutrient Strategy, which uses total nitrogen (TN) and total phosphorus (TP) concentrations in lakes/reservoirs and rivers/streams. These data are compiled from the EPA Legacy and

Storage and Retreival (STORET) system, the U.S. Geological Survey National Stream Quality Accounting Network (NASQAN), and the National Water Quality Assessment (NAWQA). Collected at regular intervals, the data are compared to median reference values.

Other indices involve measures of dissolved oxygen, chlorophyll, algal bloom, and the composition of diatom communities, which are primary producers and nutrient sensitive. Dissolved oxygen is of major concern because algal blooms (i.e., rapid reproduction and growth of algae stimulated by enhanced nitrogen and phosphorus inputs) cause a dense mat to form near the water's surface; this in turn inhibits oxygen exchange between the atmosphere and water. Reduced oxygen causes death in many aquatic organisms, including fish, which are an economic resource, and diminishes biodiversity. Related chlorophyll concentrations reflect algal growth, while subtle changes in the composition of lake and river diatom communities can help identify trends towards eutrophication.

Identification in the Field

Natural eutrophication has occurred throughout the geological past, but in the last 10,000 years, cultural eutrophication has occurred due to land disturbance, notably vegetation clearance for agriculture, mining, and urbanization. The resulting soil erosion and altered drainage regimes enhanced inputs of dissolved nutrients and particulate matter to water bodies. In North America, the process of cultural eutrophication was significantly accelerated with the onset of European settlement in the 1600s and, especially, in the 1800s due to mass migration from Europe and the resulting land disturbance for agriculture and settlements. However, cultural eutrophication was not formally recognized until the 1950s and 1960s. Alarms were raised in relation to the status of the Great Lakes, especially Lake Erie, and then about coastal areas such as Chesapeake Bay. Cultural eutrophication is the single most important problem today for U.S. lakes and coasts.

Lake Erie

The history of eutrophication in the Great Lakes region is well exemplified by the case of Lake Erie, which is the smallest by volume (second smallest by area) and most shallow of the five Great Lakes. By the early 1960s, algal blooms began to proliferate due to high nutrient inputs from both point sources, such as sewage treatment plants, and diffuse

sources, especially runoff from urban and agricultural sources. This situation accelerated until the mid-1970s. There were also inputs of heavy metals from industrial sources. The algae, mainly cyanobacteria or blue-green algae, are primary producers whose growth is limited, especially by phosphorus availability. When phosphorus increases in the water because of phosphate fertilizer use and/or incompletely treated sewage effluent that is rich in detergent, algal growth is stimulated. Algal blooms form on the water's surface and prohibit the exchange of oxygen between the water and the atmosphere.

Thus, Lake Erie's water became hypoxic or anoxic (characterized by local or general oxygen depletion), and many free-swimming and bottom-dwelling organisms died out. Moreover, noxious smells and rotting algal mats on beaches deterred recreational activities and fishing. This condition led to Lake Erie being named in the press the "Dead Sea of North America." It was also sufficiently serious to prompt the formation of the Experimental Lakes Area (ELA) in Canada in 1968 to examine the factors and processes involved in eutrophication. Research from the ELA has shown that the control of phosphorus is a key factor in curtailing eutrophication in most lacustrine (lake) environments. This work, coupled with legislation, has brought about major improvements in the water quality and biodiversity of Lake Erie. In 1972, the United States and Canada signed the Great Lakes Water Quality Agreement, which focused on phosphorus limitation. The cleanup was assisted by the removal of phosphorus from detergents.

Chesapeake Bay

Chesapeake Bay, bordered by Maryland and Virginia, is the largest estuary in the United States. It has a hinterland of intensively farmed cropland and only one small outlet, via an enclosed bay, which restricts water exchange with the Atlantic Ocean. Historical studies have shown that eutrophication began about 200 years ago but accelerated between the mid-1950s and mid-1980s when human population in the hinterland doubled and the use of inorganic nitrogen fertilizers tripled. Localized water quality concerns, hypoxic conditions, and public health issues were apparent in the early part of the twentieth century, but by the late 1960s, concerns were expressed about the overall eutrophication and pollution of one of the nation's significant waterways. It has been estimated that nitrogen loading increased by approximately 700 percent and phosphorus loading by 1800 percent since precolonial times.

As in the case of the Great Lakes, a program of research and nutrient reduction was instigated. This began with a five-year project funded by Congress in the late 1970s. The results highlighted nutrient overloading and led to the initiation of the Chesapeake Bay Program in 1983, which mobilized all six affected states and the District of Columbia with the objective of restoration. A new agreement was signed in 2000. The task of cleanup is enormous, and although many improvements have been achieved, much work remains. Nutrient loadings have been reduced, partly due to a soil conservation program to limit particulate matter and, hence, phosphorus inputs. Limiting nitrogen from atmospheric emissions and from nonpoint agricultural sources remain significant goals in an environment where complex interrelationships among water, sediment, nutrients, and organisms are different than those in lakes.

Eutrophication and Human Health Issues

High concentrations of nitrates in water, which mostly derive from nitrate fertilizer use, may pose a threat to human health. They can cause methemoglobinemia, or blue-baby syndrome, a condition found in infants under six months old. Nitrates are absorbed into the blood, and oxygen-carrying hemoglobin is converted to methaemoglobin. The altered molecules do not carry oxygen, needed by the brain and other organs. High nitrate levels are also tentatively linked with stomach cancer. Water companies monitor water quality in rivers and groundwater aquifers, and there are national and international limits on nitrate content to safeguard the public. In some cases, local water may need to be mixed with water from less nitrate-rich sources to comply with these standards. This increases the cost of domestic water supplies.

A further health issue, which relates to both animal and human welfare, involves the accidental contamination of water with organisms that cause problems ranging from stomach upsets to death. For example, the dinoflagellate *Pfiesteria piscicida* has been associated with fish kills in Chesapeake Bay. Animal deaths have also been associated with so-called red tides of algae in coastal regions; for example, along the Florida coast algal blooms contain *Karenia brevis,* which produces a neurotoxin. Aquatic organisms that produce symptoms of food poisoning may also be encouraged by eutrophication and can reach humans via shellfish.

Outlook

Eutrophication is a natural process, but human activities have greatly accelerated it, especially through land disturbance, fertilizer use, and sewage effluent. Although it has a long history, cultural eutrophication was only recognized in the 1960s. Mitigation programs were established in North America and Europe in the 1970s with some success. Nevertheless, eutrophication remains a major problem for rivers, lakes, and coastal regions affected by human activity.

—A. M. Mannion

See also: *Fertilizers; Phosphorous in Lakes and Rivers*

BIBLIOGRAPHY

Alexander, Richard B., and Richard A. Smith. "Trends in the Nutrient Enrichment of U.S. Rivers during the Late 20th Century and their Relation to Changes in Probable Stream Trophic Conditions." *Limnology and Oceanography* 51, no. 1 (2006): 639–54.

Conley, Daniel J., Hans W. Paerl, Robert W. Howarth, Donald F. Boesch, Sybil P. Seitzinger, Karl E. Havens, Christiane Lancelot, and Gene E. Likens. "Controlling Eutrophication: Nitrogen and Phosphorus." *Science* 323 (2009): 1014–15.

Dodds, Walter K., Wes W. Bouska, Jeffrey L. Eitzmann, Tyler J. Pilger, Kristen L. Pitts, Alyssa J. Riley, Joshua T. Schloesser, and Darren J. Thornbrugh. "Eutrophication of U.S. Freshwaters: Analysis of Potential Economic Damages." *Environmental Science and Technology* 43, no. 1 (2009): 12–19.

McGucken, W. *Lake Erie Rehabilitated: Controlling Cultural Eutrophication, 1960s–1990s.* Akron, OH: University of Akron Press, 2000.

Schindler, David W., R. E. Hecky, D. L. Findlay, M. P. Stainton, B. R. Parker, M. J. Paterson, K. G. Beaty, M. Lyng, and S. E. M. Kasian. "Eutrophication of Lakes Cannot Be Controlled by Reducing Nitrogen Input: Results of a 37-Year Whole-Ecosystem Experiment." *Proceedings of the National Academy of Sciences* 105, no. 32 (2008): 11254–58.

Smith, Val H. "Eutrophication of Freshwater and Coastal Marine Ecosystems: A Global Problem." *Environmental Science and Pollution Research* 10, no. 2 (2003): 126–39.

Everglades Restoration

The Everglades—subtropical wetlands that cover the southeastern portion of Florida—have played a key role in the local and regional environment for thousands of years. However, starting in 1877, the swampy parts of the Everglades were drained to open the land for settlement and cultivation. Following extensive flooding from two hurricanes in 1926 and 1928, land- and flood-control measures were introduced. In 1934, Congress authorized the creation of a national park to preserve some of the region, but it stipulated that no monies be dedicated to the project for at least five years. Then in 1947, President Harry S. Truman dedicated the 1.4 million acres that constitute Everglades National Park to "protect hundreds of kinds of wildlife which might otherwise soon be extinct." However, construction of canals and other flood-control measures in south Florida cut off the Everglades from its water supply, and the area became so badly damaged that a restoration project was started in the 1960s. This effort has been substantially supported by recent research on environmental damage, and a large number of restoration projects are now underway. The Everglades restoration is the most expensive (and also the most comprehensive) environmental repair project in history.

Florida's Rapid Growth

The development of Florida was dramatic during the latter nineteenth century and early twentieth century. The state's population rose from 269,493 in 1880 to 391,422 in 1890 following a sustained, though ultimately unsuccessful, attempt to drain the Everglades by Hamilton Disston. Nevertheless, the population continued to increase to 528,542 in 1900 and 752,619 in 1910. At this time, Florida governor Napoleon Bonaparte Broward urged an ambitious program of canal construction, which resulted in the creation of much new farmland.

In 1920, the state's population had reached nearly 1 million, and development continued apace. Then the Miami Hurricane of 1926 and the Okeechobee Hurricane two years later caused extensive problems. In fact, some historians and economist John Kenneth Galbraith have argued that this bursting of the speculation bubble in Florida land—specifically the land in the swampy Everglades area—helped cause the loss of confidence in 1928 that was a prelude to the Wall Street Crash of 1929 and the Great Depression.

In 1947, the local conservationist Marjory Stoneman Douglas, who had campaigned for the Everglades, wrote her book *The Everglades: River of Grass*. It was published in the same year that the whole Everglades area was beset by hurricanes that damaged much of the local infrastructure. State and federal authorities decided to address the problem by establishing the Southern Florida Flood Control Project (C&SF), which built levees and other flood control measures. From the 1950s until 1971, some 1,400 miles (2,300 km) of canals and levees were constructed to try to draw off water or hold it back. This very expensive effort was compared to the work by the Tennessee Valley Authority during the New Deal of Franklin D. Roosevelt. However, it had seemingly little effect on flooding in Florida. The C&SF also tried to use the land in the Everglades for agriculture by establishing the Everglades Agricultural Area (EAA), covering 450,000 acres, which was then used for growing sugar cane. The last major project of the C&SF was to build a canal that would "straighten" the Kissimmee River. This replaced a meandering river covering 90 miles (140 km) with a straight canal of only 52 miles (84 km). The land on either side was then turned over to agriculture, but not only had the original project totally disrupted existing ecosystems, the fertilizers and insecticides used in farming caused major problems for Lake Okeechobee.

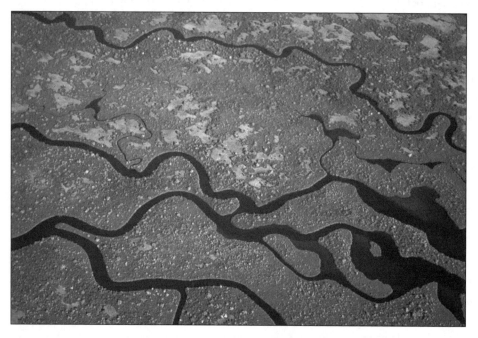

The Florida Everglades have faced increasing depletion as the population of Florida continues to grow. Efforts to preserve the Everglades have been widespread, and the area is now named a UNESCO World Heritage Site

National Park Service

Protecting the Everglades

In 1969, a plan to build a vast jetport in the Big Cypress Swamp focused attention on the Everglades and the issue of environmental protection. The increased interest in the environment found a new "hero" in Walter J. Hickel, the interior secretary whom Richard Nixon fired in November 1970 after Hickel's criticism of Nixon's Vietnam War policy. Hickel had opposed the building of the Florida jetport and had taken other positions that won support from environmentally minded people. *Time* magazine highlighted these concerns in its January 4, 1971 issue. Although it named the chancellor of West Germany, Willy Brandt, as its "Man of the Year," it also highlighted the environment as the "Issue of the Year." Exactly a year later, *National Geographic Magazine* warned of the environmental catastrophe facing the Everglades (Ward 1972). The article highlighted the impact of new housing developments and the vast amount of water that was being used for swimming pools, as well as the fact that the canals were destroying wildlife feeding grounds. And indeed, during the 1972 U.S. presidential campaign, Richard Nixon declared federal protection for the Big Cypress National Preserve, which would prevent the new jetport from being built.

After a long period of campaigning, the Everglades National Park was declared an International Biosphere Reserve by UNESCO in 1976, and three years later it was listed as a World Heritage site. In 1987, it was also listed by the Ramsar Convention on Wetlands as a "Wetland of International Importance." By this time, it was clearly recognized that the problems facing the Everglades were more complicated than simply the building of a jetport. One problem was pollution runoff from nearby industrial sites; another was fertilizer and pesticide runoff from adjoining agricultural land, especially in the north and particularly from sugar cane field in the EAA. A law in 1979 that prevented the direct dumping of chemicals into Lake Okeechobee was not effective, because chemicals were flushed into canals, which then brought water into the lake. An algal bloom covered a fifth of the lake in 1986. Elsewhere, saltwater from the Gulf of Mexico was flowing deeply into the park—especially in the winter—further endangering wildlife there. The habitat of freshwater alligators, for example, was increasingly restricted. The number of wading birds had dropped sharply, with populations in the 1970s being less than a tenth of what they had been fifty years earlier. The spread of highly flammable, water-greedy melaleuca

trees from Australia, ironically introduced to drain the wetlands, was also a problem because of the amount of water they consumed and their tendency to spread forest fires.

The main opponent of restoring the Everglades was the sugar industry, which had a powerful lobbying organization and strong supporters in the state and federal governments. Indeed, the Audubon Society was able to show that the sugar industry was responsible for donating more money to political parties and their candidates than General Motors. Agriculture poses a particular environmental problem in the Everglades. The soil in the Everglades is naturally high in phosphorous. When parts of the EAA were drained to grow sugar cane and other crops, including many types of vegetables, the soil started to oxidize. This reaction added more phosphorous to the water runoff. Sugar interests regularly tried to hamper any environmental studies of water pollution in the Everglades. In addition, the dairy industry, with 45,000 cows north of Lake Okeechobee, was estimated to generate as much raw waste each day as 980,000 people.

In the 1980s, a critically endangered Florida panther (*Puma concolor coryi*) was found dead, and tests showed that it contained levels of mercury that would be fatal to many humans. The panther was one of only a few dozen known to be in the wild. In addition, a large number of invasive species had been introduced. Besides the Australian melaleuca tree, discussed above, climbing ferns were covering the otherwise fire-resistant cypress trees, making them particularly vulnerable to the natural fires that broke out each summer. Some plants, such as the Brazilian pepper, were ornamental plants residents planted in their gardens whose seeds spread quickly via birds and the wind. The original reptiles of the Everglades had long been threatened by introduced species such as geckos, iguanas, and snakes. Perhaps the most notorious nonnative snake in the Everglades is the Burmese python (*Python molurus bivattatus*).

In 1983, Save Our Everglades was founded with a particular goal of combating large sugar cane interests, and in 1987 Congress passed the Surface Water Improvement and Management Act to clean up polluted waterways. The presence of mercury and water pollution were certainly the triggers that prompted Florida governor Lawton Chiles to introduce the Everglades Forever Bill into the state legislature in 1994. This was passed and established that the Florida Department of Environmental Protection and the South Florida Water Management District were in charge of researching water quality, controlling exotic imported species, and collecting taxes to fund these activities. Its sponsors had proposed calling it the Marjory Stoneman Douglas Act after one of the major campaigners, but she felt it did not go as far as she wanted and demanded that her name be removed.

In 1987, Florida state legislation had mandated a reduction of 40 percent in the amount of phosphorus used by sugar growers in the EAA. So far, the state has spent $2 billion in various schemes to restore the Everglades. A large amount of this was to undo the damage inflicted by previous projects. For instance, in 2000 the U.S. Army Corps of Engineers destroyed the structures that it had built along the Kissimmee River in the 1960s to "straighten" the river. It did this in the hope that the river will gradually return to its old course. In addition, a buyout plan greatly reduced the number of dairy cows. Some 35,000 acres of farmland in the EAA have been transformed back into marshland, which then serves as a buffer zone that absorbs phosphorous-containing runoff.

In July 1999, Congress agreed to a major redesign of the entire regional water management system and authorized the expenditure of $7.8 billion over the next twenty years. Many visitors still come to the Everglades National Park, but what they can do is heavily restricted. For example, anybody planning to fish needs to have a Florida state fishing license, and a permit (available free of charge from ranger stations) is required before staying overnight in the park. Campsite fires are restricted to specific areas, and if toilets are not present, all waste must be buried at least six inches deep. There are still sixteen endangered species, and five more threatened species, living in the park, which continue to be monitored.

—Justin Corfield

See also: *Levees; Wetlands*

BIBLIOGRAPHY

Alderson, Doug. *New Dawn for the Kissimmee River.* Gainesville: University Press of Florida, 2009.

Barnett, Cynthia. *Mirage: Florida and the Vanishing Water of the Eastern U.S.* Ann Arbor: University of Michigan Press, 2007.

Bransliver, Connie, and Larry W. Richardson. *Florida's Unsung Wilderness: The Swamps.* Englewood, CO: Westcliffe, 2000.

Douglas, Marjory Stoneman, and John Rothchild. *Marjory Stoneman Douglas: Voice of the River.* Englewood, FL: Pineapple Press, 1987.

Duplaix, Nicole. "South Florida Water: Paying the Price." *National Geographic* 178, no. 1 (1990): 88–113.

Galbraith, John Kenneth. *The Great Crash, 1929.* London: Hamish Hamilton, 1955.

Grunwald, Michael. *The Swamp: The Everglades, Florida, and the Politics of Paradise.* New York: Simon & Schuster, 2006.

Lodge, Thomas E. *The Everglades Handbook: Understanding the Ecosystem.* Boca Raton, FL: Taylor & Francis, 2010.

Mairson, Alan. "The Everglades: Dying for Help." *National Geographic* 185, no. 4 (1994): 2–35.

Ward, Fred. "The Imperiled Everglades." *National Geographic.* 141, no. 1 (1972): 1–27.

Evolution of Environmental Law

Environmental law in the United States was modest in scope and reach for much of the nation's history, from the colonial era right up to the early twentieth century. But the advent of the Progressive Era—and the administration of famed conservationist president Theodore Roosevelt—ushered in a more activist era of state and federal involvement in natural resource management. Since that time, the body of law governing the extraction, development, and protection of America's environmental assets has greatly expanded, and state and federal resource agencies have undergone a corresponding increase in size and authority. This evolution has been a cause for celebration among environmental organizations, but it has prompted considerable criticism from opponents, who see many modern environmental laws as unnecessarily burdensome to industry or as being unconstitutional infringements on personal freedoms.

Early Land Policy

The first environmental policies in the New World were land acquisition, distribution, and development laws and regulations. The early American colonies took varying approaches to distributing land for settlement and development. In the Chesapeake region, for example, much of the land was settled under the "headright" system, whereas the New England colonies delivered lands to organized groups of settlers (in 1681, Pennsylvania became the first colony to sell lands directly to individual buyers). These lands were obtained from Native American tribes, usually via treaties and contracts that featured terms that were extremely advantageous to the white settlers.

Most colonial land charters imposed virtually no regulations on land or water use. In addition, colonists saw their new homeland as a raw but limitless storehouse of natural wealth ripe for exploitation, and they gloried in the political, economic, and religious freedom that existed far from colonial governors or the English crown. All these factors hastened the entrenchment of an expansive concept of private property rights in the colonies that was at odds with the traditional system back in England, where the landed class owned and controlled virtually all the best land.

After the Revolutionary War, the United States embarked on a century-long path of remarkable territorial expansion. Land grants from the federal government to states, railroads, timber and mining companies, and pioneer families were an integral element of this expansion, which came to be seen as part and parcel of America's "Manifest Destiny" of continental hegemony. But this massive transfer of western lands out of the public domain and into private hands took place in extremely haphazard fashion, with little institutional control. The General Land Office, which was responsible for public domain lands in the United States from its inception in 1812 (it became part of the Department of Interior with the latter's founding in 1849), had resources to survey the land, divide it into plats, and sell it in the West—but not to guide development, monitor the environmental impact of extraction activities, or act against corporate or individual abuses of remaining public lands.

For much of this period of heady growth, which was fueled by great waves of industrialization and immigration, virtually no laws or regulations governed the exploitation or development of natural resources. Timber and oil companies, coal-mining outfits, tanneries, textile mills, foundries, sawmills, and countless other enterprises enjoyed almost complete freedom to plunder and pollute. In fact, the few federal environmental laws that *were* passed in the post–Civil War era, such as the 1872 Mining Law and the 1878 Free Timber Act, actually accelerated the liquidation of natural resources. A few conservation-oriented wildlife and fishery protection regulations were passed at the local and state levels during this era in response to dwindling harvests of commercially valuable species, but these regulations were only fitfully enforced—and they did not address the widespread habitat alteration that was responsible for much of the species loss.

This laissez-faire governing philosophy toward America's natural resources remained intact until the early 1890s, when modest but precedent-setting legislation such as the Forest Reserve Act of 1891 (which paved the way for the establishment of national forests) and the Rivers and Harbors Act of 1899 reflected a growing perception that regulatory limits had to be imposed on private exploitation of the public domain. This argument was advanced by a broad coalition of public officials, lawmakers, sportsmen, and writers who warned that the nation was heedlessly devouring its resources at an unsustainable rate.

These same conservation champions helped pass new state wildlife protection laws in the 1880s and 1890s that were stronger—and better enforced—than those of earlier vintage. These laws originated primarily in New England, then moved steadily westward through the Great Lakes and Great Plains to the Intermountain West, despite strong pockets of resistance from antiregulatory lawmakers and communities.

An even greater triumph for this coalescing community of conservation-minded Americans, though, was the Lacey Bird Law of 1900 (also known as the Lacey Act), which established federal penalties for interstate and international commerce in wild game. This law imposed major and sweeping restrictions on the market hunting practices that had destroyed or greatly reduced the populations of bison, passenger pigeon, beaver, deer, and other commercially valuable game species over the previous century. But the passage of this federal act also stood as a direct challenge to the "state ownership doctrine" that had traditionally governed land and resource policy making in the United States. Congressional passage of the Lacey Bird Law and other milestones like the Forest Reserve Act indicated that a new age of federal oversight of America's stressed natural resources was in the offing.

Resource Conservation and Sustainability

The scope of American environmental law broadened greatly during the Progressive Era, thanks in large part to the activist orientation and conservationist convictions of President Theodore Roosevelt. From 1901 to 1909, the reform-minded Roosevelt passed a stunning slate of new environmental conservation legislation into law, including the National Reclamation Act of 1902. This act dramatically expanded the federal government's role in developing and managing water and power resources—and thus economic development—in the western states and territories. He also signed the 1906 Antiquities Act, which gave Roosevelt and successor presidents the authority to preserve from commercial development "historic landmarks, historic and prehistoric structures, and other objects of historic or scientific interest" in the public domain by designating them as national monuments.

In addition, Roosevelt used his executive authority to change the institutional infrastructure that oversaw America's natural resources. During his presidency, for example, Roosevelt used the Antiquities Act to expand the national forest reserve system to 149 tracts encompassing nearly 200 million acres. But he also signed a law that transferred the responsibility for the management of this fast-expanding national forest system from the Department of the Interior to the Department of Agriculture, where U.S. Forest Service chief Gifford Pinchot introduced sustainable and science-based "wise use" regulations that became a blueprint for federal resource management for decades to follow.

Conservation policy remained a high-profile issue in the years immediately after Roosevelt's departure from the White House. The onset of World War I, though, derailed Progressive efforts to pass new wilderness conservation measures or address the urban pollution issues that had arisen as a result of industrialization and overcrowding. Funding for Progressive environmental programs was slashed, proposed new environmental laws and regulations were set aside, and logging and mining on public lands were expanded, all in service to the war effort.

After the war concluded, environmentally concerned lawmakers, officials, and activists were unable to recapture the prewar momentum they had enjoyed on conservation issues. Instead, the United States spent the so-called Roaring Twenties under the direction of business-friendly presidents and members of Congress who rejected the need for new environmental regulations. The Great Depression and the horrors of the Dust Bowl, however, led to a surge of new laws and policies that were crafted both to boost employment and restore lands and waterways that had been ravaged by decades of ecologically heedless management. The Civilian Conservation Corps, created by executive order by President Franklin D. Roosevelt on April 5, 1933, was perhaps the most momentous of these efforts, but other New Deal conservation milestones included the Taylor Grazing Act (1934), the Duck Stamp Act (1934), and the Soil Conservation and Domestic Allotment Act (1936).

These laws symbolized a steady growth in public awareness about the perils of poor environmental stewardship, but World War II and the postwar suburbanization boom placed heavy new pressure on America's natural resources. Federal lawmakers were reluctant to support any regulatory measures that might—in actuality or in perception—put the brakes on this era of startling economic prosperity and expansion. To the contrary, legislation like the Federal Aid Interstate Highway Act of 1956, the genesis of a 41,000-mile interstate highway system, further increased exploitation pressure on previously undeveloped

lands and waterways. In addition, Washington maintained its post-Progressive wariness of impinging on state and local authorities in air and water pollution control. The Water Quality Act of 1948 and the Air Pollution Control Act of 1955, for instance, provided federal grants to states for pollution control—but also included language that explicitly forbade any regulatory involvement by federal agencies.

Environmental Law in the Late Twentieth Century

The two-decade span between 1960 and 1980 is often described by historians as the golden age of American environmentalism. It was during this time that the environmental movement became a substantive and lasting fixture in the crafting and implementation of American law and public policy. But environmental groups like the Sierra Club, the Wilderness Society, the Natural Resources Defense Council, and other high-profile organizations would not have registered the level of success they enjoyed in the 1960s and 1970s without a receptive Washington.

Washington's openness to new environmental protection laws and the increased power of the environmental movement both stemmed from escalating public knowledge of—and anxiety about—deteriorating environmental conditions in wilderness areas and population centers alike. Events like the 1962 publication of Rachel Carson's *Silent Spring*, which warned of the toxic legacy of DDT and other chemical pollutants, aroused considerable public consternation, as did the 1969 chemical blaze that lit up a section of Ohio's Cuyahoga River; the 1978–1979 Love Canal scandal; and proliferating reports of species loss, declining air quality, and other environmental problems.

The tide of environmental laws generated in response to these perceived harbingers of impending ecological doom was remarkable in both depth and scope. Laws like the Wilderness Act (1964), the Land and Water Conservation Fund Act (1964), the Wild and Scenic Rivers Act (1968), the Endangered Species Act (1973), the BLM Organic Act (1976), and the Alaska National Interest Lands Conservation Act (1980) extended strong new protections to wilderness areas and threatened species of flora and fauna. Environmental health concerns, meanwhile, were the focus of landmark laws like the National Environmental Policy Act (1969), the Clean Air Act of 1970, the Clean Water Act of 1972, the Toxic Substances Control Act (1976), and the Comprehensive Environmental Response, Compensation, and Liability Act of 1980

(CERCLA), commonly known as Superfund. These and many other laws passed during the 1960s and 1970s mandated sweeping changes to the operations of existing federal agencies and created entirely new agencies and departments—including the Environmental Protection Agency—to enforce the nation's newly minted environmental and public health regulations.

Most of these 1960s- and 1970s-vintage laws remain the foundation of twenty-first-century environmental protection and regulation in the United States, albeit with assorted amendments and revisions. Efforts to pass major additional environmental laws and regulations, however, have floundered on the shoals of partisan warfare since the early 1980s. During the years of the Reagan administration, the bipartisan consensus that had existed during the presidencies of Johnson, Nixon, Ford, and Carter evaporated. The Republican Party, in part because of the influence of business interests and assorted antiregulatory, "small-government" constituencies, adopted an increasingly skeptical stance toward many proposed environmental protection laws. Some Republicans also began to frame many existing environmental regulations and laws like the Endangered Species Act as job-killing products of alarmist environmental rhetoric. Democrats, meanwhile, became—broadly speaking—even more closely allied with the environmental movement, and Democratic congressional membership has repeatedly proposed additional laws and regulations to address perceived environmental problems. But only a few of these proposals, like the Brownfields Revitalization Act of 2002, have attracted the level of bipartisan support needed to become law. As long as this partisan deadlock over the wisdom and efficacy of environmental regulation continues, prospects for new laws on the scale of a Wilderness Act or Clean Air Act appear remote.

—Kevin Hillstrom

See also: *Conservation Movement; Government Water Decision Making; Urbanization*

Sierra Club

The Sierra Club was founded by John Muir in 1892 with a mission to preserve wilderness areas in California. Today, it is one of the largest environmental organizations in the world.

The Sierra Club's initial cause was the preservation of Yosemite National Park. The organization suffered a bitter defeat in its efforts to protect Yosemite from the ravages of development during the 1920s when San Francisco won the right to dam the Hetch Hetchy Valley. Despite this setback, the organization was able to establish a number of national parks and forests throughout the western United States during the first half of the twentieth century.

The organization's primary mission began to evolve from the preservation of wilderness sites to aggressive environmental activism during the 1950s. Led by David Brower, the organization opposed dam construction projects across the United States. Beginning in the 1960s, the organization began effectively helping lawmakers craft legislation that allowed the club to pursue its agendas through the court system. The successful political strategies that the Sierra Club has pioneered since the 1960s have been extremely influential in shaping environmental activism around the world.

—John R. Burch Jr.

See also: *Echo Park Dam; Glen Canyon Dam*

BIBLIOGRAPHY

Brower, David R. *For Earth's Sake: The Life and Times of David Brower.* Salt Lake City, UT: Peregrine Smith Books, 1990.
Cohen, Michael P. *The History of the Sierra Club, 1892–1970.* San Francisco: Sierra Club Books, 1988.
Worster, Donald. *A Passion for Nature: The Life of John Muir.* New York: Oxford University Press, 2008.

BIBLIOGRAPHY

Andrews, Richard N. L. *Managing the Environment, Managing Ourselves: A History of American Environmental Policy.* New Haven, CT: Yale University Press, 1999.
Bailey, Christopher J. *Congress and Air Pollution: Environmental Policies in the United States.* Manchester, UK: Manchester University Press, 1998.
Conary, Janet S. "An Emerging Nation: The Early Presidents and the Development of Environmental Policy." In *The Environmental Presidency,* edited by Dennis L. Soden, 15–39. Albany: State University of New York Press, 1999.
Gates, Paul Wallace (with Robert W. Swenson). *History of Public Land Law Development.* Washington, DC: U.S. Public Land Law Review Commission/Government Printing Office, 1968. Reprint by Wm. W. Gaunt & Sons, 1987, available at http://content.lib.utah.edu/cdm4/document.php?CISOROOT=/wwdl-doc&CISOPTR=5226.
Payne, Daniel G. *Voices in the Wilderness: American Nature Writers and Environmental Politics.* Buffalo: State University of New York at Buffalo, 1996
Pisani, Donald J. *Water, Land and Law in the West: The Limits of Public Policy.* Lawrence: University Press of Kansas, 1996.

Fertilizers

A fertilizer can be defined as any substance that is added to soils to supply one or more essential nutrients. Many elements are vital for plant/crop growth, and any deficiency will curtail primary production (i.e., the volume of organic matter produced by photosynthesis). Some necessary elements derive from the atmosphere and water, notably carbon, hydrogen, and oxygen. All other essential nutrients derive from the soil. Those required in relatively large amounts are known as macronutrients, notably nitrogen, phosphorus, potassium, sulphur, calcium, and magnesium. Others are required in small amounts; these micronutrients are iron, molybdenum, manganese, copper, zinc, boron, and chlorine. Most soils contain all the essential nutrients but not always in sufficient quantities to optimize growth.

Fertilizers can be classified into two groups: traditional and technological or modern. Traditional fertilizers are mostly organic and include animal dung, guano (bird, seal, or bat dung), composted domestic waste, seaweed, wood/organic mulches, and lime or marl. They were widely used, often in combination with crop rotations, until the 1900s and remain significant in subsistence economies. A major turning point occurred in the early 1900s with the development of artificial nitrate fertilizers, which were produced using nitrogen from the atmosphere. This made nitrogen more accessible and encouraged a commercial and technological approach to fertilizer production at a time when it was necessary to increase food production globally to support an ever-increasing population. Associated developments included the increased mining of phosphate-rich rocks and potassium sources.

Today, three major types of commercial fertilizers are available based on the primary nutrient (i.e., nitrogen, phosphate, or potassium). Multinutrient fertilizers are also available. Fertilizers can be further classified according to formulation. For example, nitrogen may be present as ammonium nitrate or ammonium sulphate, or ammonium sulphate may be combined with lime; potassium may be present as potassium chloride or potassium sulphate. Additional considerations include the mode of application (e.g., dry granular form or liquid forms).

The commercial availability of fertilizers has made a substantial contribution to feeding the world's population and was a significant cause of increased crop productivity in the so-called "Green Revolution" of the 1950s–1970s. It was a major aspect of the industrialization of agriculture, which also embraced intensive crop and animal breeding plus chemical approaches to crop protection and animal health. However, this intensive application of nutrients has had many repercussions for environmental quality, especially in aquatic ecosystems that receive nutrient-enriched drainage. This process, known as cultural eutrophication, causes ecosystem degradation and economic losses.

History of Fertilizer Use

The nutrient enhancement of soils is as old as crop agriculture itself, approximately 12,000 years. For example, there is evidence that middens, deposits of domestic waste, were sometimes cultivated directly in prehistoric times in Europe; this practice presumably occurred because improved harvests were obtained from the organic- and nutrient-rich waste. Historically, crop rotations were developed to capitalize on the varying nutrient requirements of crops, to prevent soil-nutrient exhaustion, and to minimize pest and disease outbreaks. For example a fourfold rotation comprising wheat, turnips, barley, and clover became popular in the 1700s in England, where it contributed to the British Agricultural Revolution. The clover crop was important because it replaced fallow (a period of no cultivation to allow soil nutrient levels to recover). Also, like all leguminous plants, it has a symbiotic relationship with bacteria that have the ability to fix atmospheric nitrogen. These bacteria convert nitrogen into soluble nitrates, which disperse into the soil and are thus available to the following crop. Moreover, both turnips and clover are fodder crops; their availability meant that animal production could be increased, resulting in additional manure for the soil.

However, scientific developments in the early 1900s changed the course of agricultural history and, indeed, the broader course of history. First, the Agricultural Revolution in Europe and then the Industrial Revolution (beginning c. 1750) sparked a substantial population increase. Second, the foundations of modern scientific investigation were being emplaced and applied to agriculture due to concerns over sufficient food availability, a scenario linked with overpopulation as popularized by Rev. Thomas Robert Malthus (1766–1834). Scientifically, a significant advance was made by Fritz Haber (1868–1934) and Carl Bosch (1874–1940), both German chemists and Nobel laureates, who devised a means of combining the inert element nitrogen with hydrogen to produce ammonia on an industrial scale. This enabled the huge reservoir of nitrogen in the atmosphere to be utilized to produce the nitrogen fertilizers ammonium nitrate, ammonium sulphate, and urea. This innovation is considered to be one of the momentous developments of the twentieth century because it contributed to saving millions of lives through improved food production. Increased food security did, however, stimulate population increase, and today the global population of 6.7 billion is heavily dependent on this single energy-intensive process.

The formal recognition that phosphorus, in the form of phosphates, was an essential element for growth occurred in the early 1800s. The mining of phosphate rocks began in the 1840s in Europe and two decades later in the United States in South Carolina and Florida. In a process that started being used in Europe in the 1870s and in the United States in the 1890s, ores are treated with sulphuric acid to produce phosphoric acid, and from this, phosphate fertilizers are manufactured. Today, China, the United States, and Morocco are the major producers of phosphate rock with useful phosphorus pentoxide; together these countries generate 75 percent of world phosphate production. Essentially, phosphate mining has accelerated the cycling of phosphorus between the living and nonliving components of the earth's surface, which would otherwise occur on a geological timescale of millions of years due to sediment accumulation in ocean basins, subsequent tectonic uplift, and finally erosion.

Potassium was first recognized as an essential plant nutrient by Johann Glauder (1604–1670), a German chemist, who noted that plant growth was encouraged when saltpetre (potassium nitrate) was applied to soils. Experiments at the United Kingdom's Rothamsted research station begun in 1843 firmly established that potassium was an essential element. Today, potassium is generally applied as potash, a term given to various chemical compounds that contain potassium, including potassium oxide, potassium carbonate, potassium chlorate/chloride, and potassium sulphate. These substances occur widely on the earth's surface in sedimentary rocks, but the United States and Canada are currently the world's largest producers and exporters of potash. Some 95 percent of world production is in the form of potassium chloride, with potassium sulphate as the next most important source.

Trends in Fertilizer Use

The Food and Agriculture Organization (FAO) and the International Fertilizer Association (IFA) compile statistics on fertilizer production and use. Their data show that starting in 1960, the global consumption of fertilizers increased markedly until the mid-1980s, then declined slightly until the mid-1990s when it began to increase again. This was the case for all three major nutrients but was particularly marked for nitrogen, which showed an overall 500 percent or more increase compared with a 50 percent increase in potassium and phosphorus. Globally, the greatest increase in fertilizer consumption was in Asia, especially in China. The overall trend was mirrored in the United States, as shown in the following table.

Fertilizer Trends in the United States, 1960–2007

Year	Nitrogen	Phosphate	Potash	Total
1960	2,738.0	2,572.5	2,153.3	7,463.8
1970	7,459.0	4,573.8	4,035.5	16,068.3
1980	11,406.7	5,431.5	6,245.1	23,083.3
1990	11,076.0	4,344.7	5,202.8	20,623.5
2000	12,333.8	4,313.8	4,971.6	21,619.2
2007	13,194.4	4,571.7	5,133.3	22,899.4

Source: Based on data from the U.S. Department of Agriculture Economic Research Service, 2009.

Note: Data are in thousands of nutrient tons.

The FAO projects that world fertilizer production will increase by about 3 percent annually between 2007–08 and 2011–12 and that the United States will continue to import nitrogen fertilizers and export potash. As nonrenewable resources, world reserves of potash are extensive, but those of phosphate are declining in quantity and quality and may be sufficient for only 50–100 more years; phosphate availability may thus compromise world food supplies. In the United States, phosphate stocks are also declining, but for the near future production will match consumption. At least 50 percent of the nitrogen fertilizer used in the United States comes from Trinidad, Russia, and Middle Eastern countries, mainly because of the lower prices of natural gas, a source of hydrogen for ammonia production and a source of energy for fertilizer production, in these countries. This trend is likely to continue, possibly leaving the food supply of the United States vulnerable and making nitrogen conservation measures imperative for both environmental and economic reasons.

Impacts of Fertilizer Use

The most significant impact of fertilizer use has been the increase in world food supplies, the improved nutrition of many people, and the support of a huge increase in global population from 3.04 billion in 1960 to 6.71 billion in 2008.

The indirect ramifications of this are manifold, not least being huge carbon and ecological footprints. A further impact is the carbon footprint directly associated with fertilizer production, especially nitrogen fertilizer, and its mining and transport. Pollution also occurs due to mining, and the release of nitrous gases into the atmosphere from nitrate fertilizers is a significant component of global warming. In addition, problems may occur because of seepage of nitrate-rich water from agricultural land through underlying porous rocks into aquifers. If these water sources are exploited, their high nitrate concentrations, which are linked with health problems such as "blue-baby" syndrome and possibly gastric cancers, may be above World Health Organization guidelines and require dilution with water from elsewhere at a financial cost.

Fertilizers have also caused major alterations in natural ecosystems, especially those in aquatic environments in the developed world where fertilizer use is most intense. Lakes, rivers, estuaries, and coasts affected by runoff from fertilized agricultural land may undergo a process of cultural eutrophication (i.e., nutrient enrichment that affects food chains and webs). The availability of nitrogen and phosphorus in soluble form limits the growth of primary producers (i.e., algae and plants). Augmentation by fertilizer that is not utilized in the field and seeps or floods into aquatic environments has a rapid impact as algal/plant growth is stimulated. Algae in particular respond quickly to enhanced nutrient availability, and their accelerated growth can lead to the formation of dense algal mats at the water surface. This restricts the exchange of oxygen between the water and the atmosphere so that the water becomes anaerobic, resulting in biodiversity loss, notably the death of invertebrates, insects, and fish. In coastal areas, algal blooms sometimes form "red tides." Noxious smells, loss of habitat, and potential health hazards result in economic losses, notably as recreational activities such as water sports and fishing decline. These problems can be reversed if fertilizer is applied with care, a practice essential to reducing fossil fuel use and conserving phosphates.

Fertilizers are either traditional or industrial substances. The latter dominate fertilizer use today, especially nitrogen, phosphorus, and potassium fertilizers. Nitrogen fertilizers are produced using nitrogen from the atmosphere, while phosphorus and potassium fertilizers are mined. On a positive front, the intense use of fertilizers in the last fifty years has resulted in huge increases in food production and has underpinned a doubling of population. On a negative front, this has broadened and deepened the ecological and carbon footprints of humanity and impaired many aquatic ecosystems. Future food security depends on thin threads: photosynthesis, which utilizes less than 1 percent of solar energy; energy-intensive nitrogen fertilizers; and diminishing phosphate deposits.

—A. M. Mannion

See also: *Agriculture; Phosphorous in Lakes and Rivers*

BIBLIOGRAPHY

Cordell, D., J. O. Drangert, J. O., and S. White. "The Story of Phosphorus: Global Food Security and Food for Thought." *Global Environmental Change* 19 (2009): 292–305.

Elsworth, L. R., and W. O. Paley. *Fertilizers: Properties, Applications, and Effects.* Hauppauge, NY: Nova Science, 2008.

Erisman, J. W., M. A. Sutton, J. Galloway, Z. Kilmont, and W. Winiwarter. "How a Century of Ammonia Synthesis Changed the World." *Geoscience* 1 (2008): 636–39,

Galloway, J. N., A. R. Townsend, J. W. Erisman. M. Bekunda, Z. Cai, J. R. Freney, L. A. Martinelli, S. P. Seitzinger, and M. A. Sutton. "Transformation of the Nitrogen Cycle: Recent Trends, Questions, and Potential Solutions." *Science* 320 (2008): 889–92.

Roberts, T. L. "The Role of Fertilizer in Growing the World's Food." *Better Crops* 93, no.2 (2009): 1215.

U.S. Department of Agriculture Economic Research Service "Fertilizer Consumption and Use—By Year: Table 1. U.S. Consumption of Nitrogen, Phosphate, and Potash, 1960–2008." Updated annually. http://www.ers.usda.gov/Data/FertilizerUse/.

Fish Farming

See *Aquaculture*

Fishing

See *Commercial Fishing*

Global Warming

See *Climate Change*

Government Water Decision Making

The absence of an obvious structure for water decision making in the United States has been a perennial source of complaint and discussion. Unlike with many natural resources, where the jurisdiction over a resource resides primarily in a single federal agency, a variety of federal agencies are responsible for some aspect of water. Further, water resources management is almost always governed by a separate agency from that responsible for water quality management. State governments have primary jurisdiction over water allocation and often have independent or delegated authority for pollution programs. Tribal governments have authority over their water resources and can administer delegated federal programs.

Federal Agencies and Water Policy

The primary federal agencies with responsibility for water are the Environmental Protection Agency (EPA), the Department of the Interior (DOI), and the U.S. Army Corps of Engineers (the Corps). The EPA administers water pollution programs, including the Clean Water Act and the Safe Drinking Water Act, and it regulates certain activities in wetlands in conjunction with the Corps. It is also responsible for ocean- and estuary-related programs.

The Department of the Interior has a major role with respect to water in the United States. The U.S. Geological Survey (USGS), the Bureau of Reclamation (BOR), the Fish and Wildlife Service (USFW), and the Bureau of Indian Affairs (BIA) exercise control over water resources. The BOR is active in the seventeen western states, where it is responsible for storage and irrigation projects, as well as a host of other programs. USGS, established in 1879 to conduct land surveys, is the scientific agency of the DOI. Its staff is drawn from different scientific disciplines, and it is the leading source of information concerning U.S. water resources. USFW has a broad mission of protection of fish, wildlife, and plants and administers the Endangered Species Act. BIA is involved with tribal water rights and water-related infrastructure.

The Corps is a venerable institution, tracing its origins to the Continental Congress. Its engineering capabilities have been applied across the nation in the maintenance of waterways, flood control, recreation, water supply, hydropower infrastructure, and environmental restoration.

The Department of Agriculture should be included among major federal water agencies. This department houses the U.S. Forest Service. Forest Service lands often contain the watersheds for urban areas, which, in addition to protecting water supplies, are highly valued recreational areas. The Natural Resources Conservation Service is the successor to the Soil and Water Conservation Service and manages programs to improve watersheds on private lands.

Agricultural policies are a critical determinant of water policies, because in the western United States, approximately 85 percent of all water that is withdrawn is consumed by irrigated agriculture.

This brief sketch suggests a substantial federal role in water and one in which conflicts among agency missions are a real possibility. The Corps's approaches to flooding, for example, historically resulted in the destruction of wetlands and other riparian habitat. While the Corps has made a greater commitment to environmental protection, it is still occasionally at odds with the EPA. The nation's commitment to the protection of endangered species is tested by actions of more development-oriented agencies. Thus, USFW may be at odds with BIA or the Corps over new projects or operations. Another sort of competition is bureaucratic. Marc Reisner, in his classic *Cadillac Desert* (1986), described the ongoing competition between BOR and the Corps for new projects. The absence of a cohesive federal water policy is perhaps most apparent in the lack of agreement over the role of the federal government in water project funding. There is no consensus within Congress about what sorts of projects should receive federal funding. Federal funding appears in various types of legislation, including the Water Resources Development Act. Projects are not reviewed by other federal agencies, and occasional controversies arise over the cost-benefit analyses for these projects.

Attempts to consolidate agencies or transfer responsibilities run into formidable political obstacles. Federal water agencies have corresponding allies in congressional committees. The fragmentation in the executive branch is mirrored in Congress, where jurisdiction over water is divided among different committees.

State and Tribal Agencies

Water resource allocation is the responsibility of the states (and of tribal governments, in some instances). Each state differs in how water rights are administered, but in general, state administrators determine if an applicant has a water right, seniority of rights, and when a right can be transferred. Special districts, such as irrigation districts, may have jurisdiction over water rights among irrigators in the district. Municipal water districts are responsible for providing water to customers; this may involve construction and maintenance of delivery systems, water treatment, and procurement of water rights.

Water quality regulation typically is administered by state agencies, normally under delegated authority from the federal EPA. The framework for pollution control is established by the federal Clean Water Act, under which states and tribes establish standards for their waters and EPA establishes discharge limitations for types of industries. Point-source discharges must have a permit from EPA or from a state with delegated authority. Within-states water quality regulation usually is conducted by a different agency than that which is responsible for water allocation and management. The physical characteristics of water are not so easily divided, but very few states integrate the management of quality and quantity in a single agency.

Native American communities have unique governance authorities. Indian nations are sovereign nations with authority over reservation lands. Tribal water rights come from several sources, including treaty rights to fishing and "Winters" rights (in *Winters v. United States* [1908], the Supreme Court held that tribes have federal reserved water rights based on the water necessary for the reservation). The extent of these rights must be quantified, either through adjudications, litigation, or settlements. Settlements may provide funding for water projects to increase water availability to non-Indian communities as well as for tribes.

Through control of tribal land, tribes can affect water quality on tribal lands. Additionally, tribes can apply for "tribes as states" status under the Clean Water Act and protect the quality of water in rivers and streams that flow through tribal lands.

The poverty associated with many reservations can be seen in the lack of water infrastructure. BIA and Congress are key in determining whether funding will be procured for these purposes.

Overlapping Jurisdictions

Governance issues take on a different color when water rights among states are in play. On rivers, compacts may establish the rights among states. Compacts are negotiated among the states and the federal government and ratified by Congress. As issues arise over compliance with compacts or interpretation of them, litigation may be brought before the Supreme Court.

Some river basins encompass the United States and Canada or the United States and Mexico. Treaties between these nations may govern water rights. For example, the Great Lakes are the common interest of both U.S. states and Canadian provinces. The Great Lakes Charter allows for cooperation in regulating diversions from these lakes. The Delaware River Basin Commission

is another such model: it includes four states and a federal representative.

Compacts, treaties, and court decrees often were established under physical and social conditions that are entirely different from those of the present. For example, the treaty that governs rights between the United States and Mexico on the Rio Grande was signed when Juarez, the Mexican border city, had a population of only 20,000 people. The city has grown to 1.5 million people, but rights under the treaty are unchanged. The time at which a compact is negotiated also is important: the Colorado River Compact was negotiated when annual flows were much higher than they are on average over time. Population and variability increases may bear on the fairness of these instruments, and a changing climate will as well. Projections of changes in precipitation in the Colorado River Basin, for example, make it very difficult to imagine how the demands of each state will be met under future conditions.

Governance issues come into play in specific settings, of course, and there are a number of characteristic examples where federal, state, tribal, and municipal officials are involved in water management decision making, often with multiple voices for each level of government. Nongovernmental organizations and water beneficiaries often are participants in decision-making processes. If decisions are contrary to the interests of affected persons, those parties can bring administrative or judicial appeals. And legislative bodies can change the underlying parameters if an aggrieved entity can bring the matter to Congress or the state legislature.

The Columbia River Basin is a good illustration of the multiple entities involved in water decision making. The Basin encompasses different states, tribes with treaty rights to fish, and the United States and Canada. Its waters are used by endangered species, hydropower facilities operated by Bonneville Power, barges transporting grain, recreation seekers, and large urban centers. Each of the governmental entities has legitimate claims to jurisdiction over water management, which the Congress acknowledged in creating the Northwest Power Planning Council. There is no consensus over whether this management structure is a success, but it does give a formal structure for different entities to share perspectives and reach agreement. By one measure, the recovery of endangered species, management efforts have not been successful. Litigation and legislative attention remain focused on the Basin.

Other illustrations of multiple authorities are provided by basins where the presence of endangered species has forced water managers to work together. The perceived threat is that USFW will override water rights if the parties themselves fail to reach agreement on a means of providing water to species. Thus, in California, disputes over a host of water issues resulted in the CALFED Bay-Delta Program, in which state, federal, and other interests have attempted to address complex water management questions in a collaborative process.

The governance of water often is described as "fragmented," "dysfunctional," "Byzantine," and generally broken in some fundamental way. Why has this clumsy and seemingly inefficient structure persisted? There are several possible answers. One is that the current structure serves the status quo, which has little reason to change and decades of political capital upon which to call. Another is that the seeming confusion creates a system of checks and balances: no single entity or mission has the ability to move unilaterally, and thus more interests are represented in agency action. Although most commentators criticize governance structures, some believe that divided governance actually brings about better decisions.

Even if governance is murky, water management continues to address changing societal needs, sometimes in the face of what would appear to be insurmountable odds. The Colorado River provides a recent illustration of this. Persistent water shortages threatened the ability of states to carry out their Compact obligations. The affected states devised a plan to allocate water in times of shortage, thereby avoiding federal decision making in times of drought.

Water governance will remain a topic of interest to everyone who is involved in water in some fashion—that is, all of us. The complex structures and their relationships favor those with expertise and disenfranchise newcomers to the system. As water grows in importance across the nation, there will be more pressure to make the system more transparent.

—Denise Fort

See also: *Bureau of Reclamation; Great Lakes Charter (1985); Solid Waste Agency of Northern Cook County v. United States Army Corps of Engineers et al. (2001)*

BIBLIOGRAPHY
Cody, Betsy A., and Nicole T. Carter. "35 Years of Water Policy: The 1973 National Water Commission and Present Challenges." CRS Report for Congress, 111th Congress (R40573). Washington, DC: Library of Congress, Congressional Research Service, May 11, 2009. http://www.policyarchive.org/handle/10207/bitstreams/18517.pdf.

Reisner, Marc. *Cadillac Desert: The American West and Its Disappearing Water.* New York: Viking, 1986.
Tarlock, A. Dan. *Law of Water Rights and Resources.* Deerfield, IL: Clark Boardman Callaghan, 2009.
Western Water Policy Review Advisory Commission. *Water in the West.* Alexandria, VA: National Technical Information Service, 1996.

Groundwater Recharge and Water Reuse

Water scarcity is a fact of life in a world with a burgeoning population. Water reuse is a tool to address water scarcity. While it may seem like a novel technology, it is practiced worldwide. The deliberate reuse of water requires attention to the risks that may be presented by contaminants, to questions of the legal right to control water, and to the perspectives of communities about the source and cost of water. To begin this discussion, it is helpful to define some of the different practices that are employed to reuse water.

Water Reuse Practices

Water reuse is the deliberate treatment and storage of wastewater for later reuse. Water that is intended for reuse may be stored in surface reservoirs or in groundwater. Much of the water that we consume for industry or agriculture or as drinking water may have been "used" before, in the sense that rivers often contain discharges from sewage treatment plants and a groundwater source may have been replenished by discharges from human activities. The Colorado River is a water source for millions of people and contains water that has been used, treated, discharged to the river, withdrawn for use, treated, discharged, and so on. In that sense, water recycling is nothing new, but doing so without the intermediary of discharge to a river is what raises interest. Thus, this discussion concerns waters that have deliberately been reused, rather than the far more widespread situation in which waters are reused through withdrawals from rivers and replenished groundwater.

The primary focus of this discussion is the indirect potable reuse of water. This refers to the use of water for human consumption after the water has been treated, stored in groundwater, withdrawn, treated, and often blended with other water sources. It is called "indirect" because it is not served directly from the wastewater treatment facility but rather is stored in some fashion. This technology is being utilized now in a number of U.S. states, including most notably Florida, California, and Texas.

Direct potable reuse, the reuse of reclaimed wastewater for human consumption without storage in surface or groundwater, is the frontier in water reuse. Only one large-scale facility in the world currently utilizes direct reuse; located in Windhoek, Namibia, it serves 250,000 people. Direct reuse raises concerns having to do with public perception and with the assurance of a safe drinking water supply. As treatment technologies improve, water managers may become more comfortable with direct reuse. The public reaction to direct reuse will play a role in whether it is used in a specific community.

The primary driving force behind water reuse is the obvious one of meeting the needs of a growing population. In the Los Angeles area, for example, water from wastewater treatment plants that was previously discharged to the ocean now can be treated and reused, reducing the need to procure additional water supplies. Water from a sewage treatment plant, rather than an undesirable waste, has become a highly valuable, reliable water supply. Indeed, because of the high degree of treatment that recycling projects give to this water, it has been branded the "New Blue Water." In Israel, it is projected that reclaimed municipal wastewater will comprise 46 percent of all irrigation water by the year 2020.

Groundwater storage of remediated wastewater often is a preferable alternative to surface storage (reservoirs) for water managers. One reason is that detention in groundwater may provide additional treatment, either through infiltration or through blending with other waters. A second reason is that public acceptance of recycled water that has been stored for some period of time, perhaps especially when the storage is out of sight, is greater. Also, groundwater aquifers are less expensive to acquire than land for surface storage. In fact, there is no cost to the utilization of the aquifer, and the activity occurring on the land surface can proceed without interference. Regulatory standards may affect the relative cost of these alternatives, depending on whether a surface or groundwater discharge would face higher treatment standards.

Groundwater recharge and water reuse is costly in terms of treating the source water, recharging the aquifer, and recovering and distributing the water. The energy requirements also are noteworthy. Which alternative is appropriate for a region depends on the other alternatives available to it.

Issues Affecting Groundwater Recharge and Reuse

Some very interesting legal and institutional questions are associated with groundwater recharge and reuse. If a state

has a law specifically addressing recharge and reuse, the legal landscape is considerably simplified, but not all states have such laws. Water rights are a critical issue: a project proponent must have a right to use wastewater as compared, for example, to a downstream water user. And the project proponent must have clear rights vis-à-vis other entities that may be withdrawing from the aquifer, including specificity with respect to priority of the right to withdraw. In general, a municipality that treats wastewater will have a right to recycle that water, subject to the important caveat that a downstream water rights holder cannot be impaired by the reuse project.

Water quality issues also play an important role in determining if recharge projects are feasible. For a municipality with a wastewater stream, one factor will be the standards that must be applied to discharge. As discharges to surface waters have become more stringently regulated under the Clean Water Act, water reuse becomes a more feasible option because the additional level of treatment for reuse may not be especially costly. If water is recharged through discharge to a surface reservoir (for infiltration to groundwater or direct withdrawal), the applicable standards may include a permit under the federal Clean Water Act (a NPDES permit) and perhaps additional regulations imposed by state or substate entities. In many states, groundwater regulations will apply to the discharge.

Another means of recycling water is the injection of water. The federal Underground Injection Control Program regulates these activities as "Class Five" wells. The program may be administered by the U.S. Environmental Protection Agency (EPA) or delegated to a state agency. Again, state or substate agencies may apply additional or stricter requirements.

Water that is served to utility customers is regulated under the federal Safe Drinking Water Act or a delegated state's program. Federal law provides minimal standards for that water, which states may strengthen. The nonpotable use of reclaimed water is not regulated by federal law, but federal guidelines have been promulgated. States can and do modify these guidelines. As the use of reclaimed water for agricultural products grows, there may be more demand for uniform federal standards.

Lack of Uniform Policies

The water quality controls for recharge and reuse are not consistent across the country. Federal involvement in groundwater quality comes from a hodgepodge of programs that were not designed with the issue of water reuse in mind. State regulation varies from state to state, demonstrating a lack of comfort with the technology or differing judgments about acceptable risk. The lack of a clear policy directive across water programs means that remediation may be too stringent or too lax for the risk involved. If stringent groundwater regulation causes it to be cheaper to discharge wastewater to a lagoon or surface water body, the water quality risk may simply be transferred to another group of consumers. In general, water quality standards for surface water discharges are not based on the concept of indirect potable reuse, although that is a likely outcome for much of the water discharged to rivers.

The question of what level of government should regulate water recycling is a knotty one. At present, the EPA plays a leading role in developing drinking water standards and a secondary role in affecting surface water discharges (because states set water quality standards) and in controlling the uses made of recycled water. It does not regulate groundwater quality when recharge occurs through infiltration, but it does when injection wells are used.

There are strong arguments that the EPA should provide the scientific expertise that states need to utilize water recycling, because the federal government has more access to research funding than does an individual state. If the EPA were to regulate more by rule, rather than guidance, firms in the water industry and interested nongovernmental organizations would experience economies of scale by participating in rule making. On the other hand, the role of states as "laboratories" is a time-honored one, and the experience gained under varying regulatory schemes may advance the approaches taken in the future.

Another institutional question is whether the federal government should provide more direct support to water recharge and reuse through providing research funding and technological assistance and developing a regulatory infrastructure. There is no obvious advocate for water reuse within the federal agencies, although several agencies are involved in some aspect of water reuse (e.g., the EPA, Department of the Interior, and Department of Agriculture). The Bureau of Reclamation also has a program (Title XVI) under which it provides funding for water reuse projects.

Finally, other nations also rely upon water recycling, some to a far greater degree than does the United States. The experience of these nations should be utilized by scientists, engineers, and policy makers more than at present, because the need to improve the management of water resources is now a widely shared necessity.

—Denise Fort

See also: *Conservation Movement; Government Water Decision Making; Urban Rivers*

BIBLIOGRAPHY

National Research Council. *Issues in Potable Reuse: The Viability of Augmenting Drinking Water Supplies with Reclaimed Water.* Washington, DC: National Academies Press, 1998.

National Research Council. *Prospects for Managed Underground Storage of Recoverable Water.* Washington, DC: National Academies Press, 2008. Available at http://www.nap.edu/openbook.php?record_id=12057.

Schempp, Adam, and Jay Austin. *Water Right Impairment in Reclamation and Reuse: How Other Western States Can Inform Washington Law.* Washington, DC: Environmental Law Institute, 2007. Available at http://www.eli.org/pdf/research/western_water/Water_Right_Impairment_in_Reclamation_and_Reuse.pdf.

Heavy Metals in Water

Heavy metals include any metal with an atomic number greater than 26, the atomic number of iron. Over fifty elements have been classified as heavy metals. The U.S. Geological Survey Trace Elements National Synthesis Project monitors groundwater for the presence of the following heavy metals: antimony, arsenic, barium, cadmium, cobalt, copper, lead, mercury, molybdenum, nickel, selenium, silver, strontium, thallium, uranium, and zinc. It also monitors for iron and other lighter metals: aluminum, beryllium, boron, chromium, lithium, manganese, and vanadium. Being environmentally accessible and toxic, these pose a risk to human and environmental health. Of the six highest-ranked hazards present in toxic waste sites, listed by the U.S. Agency for Toxic Substances and Disease Registry, four are heavy metals: lead, mercury, arsenic, and cadmium. Although some metals, including copper, zinc, nickel, and chromium, are required in trace amounts by human physiology, in larger quantities these are poisonous.

Discovery and Use of Heavy Metals

Only seven metals were known for most of recorded human history: gold, silver, mercury, copper, iron, tin, and lead. Nickel was identified in 1751 in Stockholm, Sweden, by A. F. Cronstedt. Because it resists corrosion at high temperatures, it is used in gas turbines and rocket engines, and it is used in some stainless steels, as well as metal plating, nickel-cadmium batteries, and the coin named for the metal.

Worldwide production from 2007 to 2009 was 1.4 to 1.5 million tons, which exceeded recent demand.

Cobalt compounds have been used as dyes since at least 1400 BCE, but cobalt was first identified as an element in 1735 by Swedish chemist Georg Brandt. Cobalt is used to produce superalloys for aircraft engines and carbides for cutting and wear-resistant materials and in a variety of chemical applications. Total world production in recent years has been between 60,000 and 70,000 tons.

Cadmium, found in trace quantities in zinc ores, was identified in 1817 in Germany by Friedrich Stromeyer, J. C. H. Roloff, Carl Samuel Hermann, and perhaps by several other contemporaries as well. Stromeyer gave the metal its name. Annual world production is around 20,000 tons. Until the last thirty years, the primary use of cadmium was for electroplating steel to preserve it from corrosion. Discarded steel treated with this process remains a major source of cadmium pollution of groundwater. Seventy to 80 percent of cadmium production is currently used for nickel-cadmium batteries; extracting cadmium from discarded batteries and scrap is an economically viable source of the metal. Cadmium compounds continue in use for brown, yellow, and red paint pigments.

Of the world's annual production of lead, 5.4 million tons, 60 percent is used to manufacture batteries. Lead also continues to be used in pigments, glazes, solder, plastics, cable sheathing, ammunition, and weights. Since 1923, use of lead compounds in gasoline to prevent engine knocking has distributed the metal worldwide, and it often settles into the water supply, even reaching the ice cap of northern Greenland. Although lead compounds are largely banned from auto fuels sold in North America and Europe, they remain in use in many other parts of the world.

Mercury was historically used in mining, particularly gold mining, to extract the desired metal from ore. Gold would adhere to mercury, separating from the surrounding rock, and then the amalgam could be heated, evaporating the mercury. In northern California alone, an estimated 26 million pounds of mercury were used in gold ore recovery before the practice was ended, and 3 to 8 million pounds were released into waterways of the state. Abandoned mines remain a source of further pollution. Coal-fired power plants release an estimated fifty tons of mercury into the atmosphere each year in the United States, much of which settles into surface and groundwater systems.

Impact of Metals on Human Health

The most common impact of metals upon humans is damage to the brain and kidneys. Arsenic, cadmium, and nickel have been identified as carcinogens, all affecting the lungs; arsenic also affects the skin and liver, and nickel affects the upper nasal passages. Arsenic can be present in organic compounds, which are less toxic than inorganic arsenic. Arsenobentaine, found in fish at high concentrations, is relatively harmless. In its most hazardous trivalent form, arsenic destroys the integrity of blood vessels and gastrointestinal tissues, and it has lethal effects on the heart and brain. Short of death, it induces nerve damage and gangrene by destruction of blood vessels. Arsenic contaminates water naturally as well as from industrial sources—wells in some parts of the world are contaminated by arsenic dissolved into natural aquifers.

Cadmium causes kidney failure even at relatively low concentrations by damaging tubes within each nephron. Ironically, cadmium builds up in the body because, when excreted from the bloodstream, it is reabsorbed by the kidneys. It is also associated with chronic lung disease and testicular degeneration and suspected as a cause of prostate cancer. By causing leakage of calcium into urine, cadmium weakens bone structure even at low concentrations.

Lead in concentrations as low as ten micrograms per deciliter can impair brain development in children, stunt growth, and damage hearing and can induce hypertension in adults. In larger concentrations, it interferes with vitamin D metabolism, nerve conduction, hemoglobin synthesis, and fertility; causes anemia; and can result in death.

Mercury in its pure metallic form is not hazardous to ingest because it is not absorbed into the body, but mercury fumes are quite toxic when absorbed through the lungs. Mercury induces tremor, memory loss, insomnia, and delirium; absorbed by pregnant women, it causes many birth defects, impairing motor function, language, memory, and neural transmission in the developing fetus. When present in soil or water, it is synthesized by microorganisms into methyl mercury, a compound that is retained and can become dangerously concentrated as it moves up the food chain. Many fish, such as tuna, mackerel, and swordfish, have become hazardous to eat often or in large quantities for this reason.

Monitoring and Enforcement of Heavy Metals

The presence of heavy metals in water is monitored by the National Water-Quality Assessment (NAWQA) Program of the U.S. Geological Survey (USGS). Streambed sediments are also analyzed for the presence of most of these metals, and many of them are monitored in fish and clam tissue as well. Discharges of heavy metals into waters of the United States are regulated by the Environmental Protection Agency (EPA) under the Federal Water Pollution Control Act Amendments of 1972 (Pub. L. 92-500, 86 Stat. 816, 33 U.S.C. 1251–1387), also known as the Clean Water Act, as amended in 1977, 1981, and 1987. The permitting process for metals requires use of the best available technology (BAT), a more stringent standard than the best practical control technology (BPT) limitations governing conventional bacterial and oxygen-consuming pollutants. The 1972 amendments, which fundamentally reorganized the original 1948 Federal Pollution Control Act (Pub. L. 80-845, 62 Stat. 1155), define all discharges into the nation's waters as unlawful, unless specifically authorized by a National Pollutant Discharge Elimination System (NPDES) permit, authorized by Section 402 (33 U.S.C. 1342). As of 2009, enforcement relied on monitoring and reporting and permits that established limits for amounts of heavy metals allowed in wastewater streams.

Court cases specifically concerning heavy metals in water have been rare at the federal appellate level. In *United States v. Boldt,* 929 F.2d 35 (1st Cir. 1991), the conviction of a manager at a plant using toxic metals to plate electronic circuit boards was upheld; he had permitted untreated overflow from the company's wastewater pretreatment facilities containing toxic heavy metals. Numerous enforcement actions at the federal district court level have resulted in fines, community service, and prison sentences. Commonly penalties are imposed for unreported pipes discharging pollutants into waterways in violation of permits or the burying of heavy metal wastes that leached into soils and groundwater. *L.E.A.D. Group of Berks v. Exide,* 1999 WL 124473 (E.D. Pa. 1999) was a civil suit by people living near manufacturing facilities where lead batteries were made. They maintained that the facilities engaged in the unpermitted release of toxic substances, including the toxic heavy metals antimony, cadmium, lead, iron, copper, and silver. The court ruled that plaintiffs were entitled to declaratory and injunctive relief.

In 1974, Justice William O. Douglas granted a stay pending appeal that prohibited continued work on construction of the Warm Springs Dam in northern California due in part to concern that an abandoned mercury mine would be flooded by waters impounded behind the dam (*Warm Springs Dam Task Force v. Gribble,* 417 U.S. 1301). Briefs submitted presented the novelty of Solicitor General Robert Bork, representing the government, supporting the position of the Army Corps of Engineers that construction should proceed, while other components of the government, the Council on Environmental Quality and the Environmental Protection Agency, raised serious doubts about the project. Plaintiffs relied on the National Environmental Policy Act (Pub. L. 91-190, 83 Stat. 852, 42 U.S.C. 4321–4347). The Act's Section 102 (42 U.S.C. 4332[c][2]) requires a thorough environmental impact statement. Protracted litigation turned on whether the statement filed complied with the law. In 1978, Justice William Rehnquist denied a similar stay in the same case (439 U.S. 1392). The dam was completed in 1983.

A decline in the presence of heavy metals in the water supply over the past two decades may be a factor in reduced crime rates in the United States over the same period. Roger Masters at Dartmouth College found evidence linking lead and manganese neurotoxicity to aggressive behavior and crime after reviewing data for all 3,141 U.S. counties. Counties reporting toxic releases of lead and manganese had up to four times the average crime rate. Colin Crawford, at Georgia State Law School, has developed an analysis applying the legal concept of *mens rea* (the intent necessary for an act to be criminal) to Masters's data, both as to individual culpability and culpability of polluters under the distinct penalties for negligent violations, knowing violations, and knowing endangerment under the Clean Water Act.

Industrial Uses and Sources of Effluent

Heavy metals are used in a tremendous variety of industrial processes, including batteries, leather tanning, metal cleaning, plating, wires, pigments, photographic development, paper, pesticides, wood preservation, dry cleaning, fungicides, enamel, plumbing, electronics, inks, adhesives, antifreeze, and many others. A study of New York City wastewater in 1974 estimated that each day 500 pounds of copper, 340 pounds of chromium, 1,050 pounds of nickel, 670 pounds of zinc, and 65 pounds of cadmium were washed into city sewers by the electroplating industry, a major source of heavy metal pollution (Klein 1974). Between 1974 and 1991, pretreatment of city wastewaters reduced industrial metals from 3,000 pounds to 227 pounds a day (Brosnan et al. 1994). Some heavy metals are routinely flushed from city surfaces during major rainfalls, particularly lead and zinc, which derive from motor vehicle fuels and metallic surfaces. A study in the District of Columbia concluded that between

January and October 1989, storm water runoff added approximately 200 tons of zinc, 47 tons of copper, and 11 tons of lead into the district's rivers and creeks.

Heavy metals pose a significant obstacle to disposal of dry sludge from municipal wastewater treatment plants. Coagulants and precipitants are used to remove soluble metals from water before it is returned to lakes and rivers. Lime, ferric chloride, alum, and ferric sulfate are commonly applied for this purpose. If not further treated, the precipitated metals remain in the sludge. This is an issue for composting as well as ocean disposal of sludge, which is regulated by the Marine Protection, Research and Sanctuaries Act of 1972 (Pub. L. 92-532, 86 Stat. 1052, 16 U.S.C. 1431–1447f, 33 U.S.C. 1401–1445, and 2801–2805). Title I of the Act prohibits all ocean dumping in waters under U.S. jurisdiction, unless a permit is issued by the EPA. Congress set deadlines in 1977 to end all dumping of municipal sewage or industrial waste (33 U.S.C. 1414h) A December 1981 deadline was extended in 1988 to 1991. The EPA announced in 1992 that all ocean dumping of municipal sewage sludge had ended.

Another source of heavy metals in surface waters is mountaintop removal mining, which exposes rock containing trace amounts of metals to runoff water. Open pit mines are likewise a source of dissolved metals. The Flambeau Mine in Rusk County, Wisconsin, exploited only from 1993 to 1997, left a thirty-two-acre pit backfilled with waste rock containing heavy metals. Despite a drainage system to collect polluted runoff, water flowing into the Flambeau River system was found to contain copper seven times the Wisconsin standard and manganese four times the concentration provided for by permit. The mine had yielded 181,000 tons of copper, 334,000 ounces of gold, and 3.3 million ounces of silver.

There is no dispute that heavy metals in water used for drinking, swimming, or agriculture are toxic. The common objections to pollution abatement are about how to remove them and where to put the recovered metals. Once recovered, metals can be put back into use far more easily than plastics or some organic compounds. Improving technology to recover metals in solution and in sediment and the development of sustained processes to "mine" effluent as a source of metals for further application may offer the best long-term solutions. At present, enforcement efforts have diminished concentration of metals in waterways, but they have not met the optimistic goal of reducing pollution to zero.

—Charles Rosenberg

See also: *Government Water Decision Making; Wastewater Treatment*

BIBLIOGRAPHY
Brosnan, T. M., A. J. Stubin, V. Sapienza, and Y. G. Ren. "Recent Changes in Metals Loadings to New York Harbor from New York City Water Pollution Control Plants." In *Hazardous and Industrial Wastes: Proceedings of the Twenty-Sixth Mid-Atlantic Industrial Waste Conference,* edited by C. P. Huang, 657–66. Lancaster, PA: Technomic, 1994.
Crawford, Colin. "Criminal Penalties for Creating a Toxic Environment: *Mens Rea,* Environmental Criminal Liability Standards, and the Neurotoxicity Hypothesis." *Boston College Environmental Affairs Law Review* 27 (2000): 341.
Hu, Howard. "Human Health and Heavy Metals Exposure." In *Life Support: The Environment and Human Health,* edited by Michael McCally, 65–82. Cambridge: Massachusetts Institute of Technology Press, 2002. Available at http://chge.med.harvard.edu/programs/education/secondary/hhgec/documents/mccally.pdf.
Klein, L. A., M. Lang, N. Nash, and S. L. Kirschner. "Sources of Metals in New York City Wastewater." *Journal of Water Pollution Control Federation* 46, no. 12 (1974): 2653–62.
MacGregor, Alan. "Analysis of Control Methods: Mercury and Cadmium Pollution." *Environmental Health Perspectives* 12 (1975): 137–48. Available at http://www.ncbi.nlm.nih.gov/pmc/articles/PMC1475023/pdf/envhper00496-0134.pdf.
Masters, Roger D. "Environmental Pollution and Crime." *Vermont Law Review* 22 (1997): 359–82.
Masters, Roger D., Brian Hone, and Anil Doshi. "Environmental Pollution, Neurotoxicity, and Criminal Violence." In *Environmental Toxicology: Current Developments,* edited by J. Rose, 13–48. London: Taylor & Francis, 1998. Available at http://www.vrfca.org/files/vrf/article-masters-environmental-pollution.pdf.
Nriagu, Jerome O. "A History of Global Metal Pollution." *Science,* April 12, 1996.
Ryan, Mark, ed. *The Clean Water Act Handbook.* 2nd ed. Chicago: American Bar Association of Section of Environment, Energy, and Resources, 2003.
Woodard & Curran. *Industrial Waste Treatment Handbook.* 2nd ed. Boston: Butterworth-Heinemann, 2006.

Hydroelectric Dams

See *Dam Building*

Interbasin Water Transfer

As its name implies, an interbasin water transfer is the diversion of water from one watershed basin into another. Interbasin transfers have been constructed for hydropower generation, irrigation, municipal supplies, and navigation projects. Generally, the transfer is from a basin that is believed to have a surplus to one believed to have a deficit, though this is not always true in the case of hydropower and navigation projects. Basin transfers occur on a small and large scale across the United States. The exact number of transfers depends on the degree or scale of the project. *Scale* does not refer to the size of the project but rather the degree of separation between the water basins. For example, transfers can occur between two basins that drain into the same body of saltwater but are not otherwise connected. Other transfers occur across continental divides that separate bodies of saltwater, from the Pacific to the Gulf of Mexico for example. Transfers may also involve basins that terminate in inland seas or lakes. Many municipalities in the Southeast span watersheds, creating de facto interbasin transfers.

Interbasin transfers are significant because many water development projects have used them to provide water to cities to support populations larger than would otherwise be sustainable. Interbasin transfers became controversial in the last half of the twentieth century as their environmental and social consequences have become better understood. Large-scale water transfers raise the same concerns as other large-scale development projects. Additionally, in some cases they cause concern over the transfer of aquatic species and pathogens between watersheds (Cosens 2010).

Early Transfer Projects

The oldest interbasin water transfer project in the United States involved navigation: the Erie Canal, completed in 1825, was the first project to link two U.S. water basins. The first project to cross a continental divide was the Portage Canal in Wisconsin, completed in 1856. It linked the Fox River of Wisconsin, which drains to the Great Lakes, to the Wisconsin River, a tributary of the Mississippi (Ghassemi and White 2007). Another major navigation project to cross a continental divide was the Chicago Sanitary and Shipping Canal, completed in 1900. However, navigation is a second purpose of this project; the Metropolitan Sanitary District constructed the canal to flush Chicago's sewage away from the city and Lake Michigan in response to several typhoid outbreaks in the late 1800s.

Many large water development projects were undertaken in response to the growth of cities. New York City began developing the Croton River as a water source between 1842 and 1904. Because the Croton and the waterways of the Catskill Mountains tapped during the first quarter of the twentieth century are tributary to the Hudson River, most scholars do not classify this system as an interbasin transfer. However, the development of tributaries of the Delaware River, beginning with the construction of the

eighty-five-mile Delaware Tunnel in 1936, is an interbasin transfer. New York City constructed four reservoirs, Roundabout, Neversink, Prepacton, and Cannonsville, between 1952 and 1968, which provide slightly more than 1 million acre-feet of water to the city (Howe 1971).

At the same time as the development of New York City's massive waterworks, several cities in the western United States also undertook massive developments, including several interbasin transfers. Los Angeles completed the Owens Valley Aqueduct in 1913, which transfers water from the closed Owens River basin to drainages on the Pacific Ocean. Los Angeles later participated in two additional transbasin diversions. The Colorado Aqueduct transfers water from the Colorado River to the Los Angeles and San Diego metropolitan areas, and the California State Water Project transfers water from the Feather River, a tributary of the Sacramento, to the Los Angeles Basin.

Interbasin transfers also provide significant water supplies to the San Francisco Bay Area. In 1923, San Francisco completed the O'Shaughnessy Dam (Hetch Hetchy), which currently supplies about 360,000 acre-feet a year to that city. In 1929, the East Bay Municipal Utility District completed the Pardee Dam and Mokelumne Aqueduct, which supplies Concord, Martinez, and other cities along the East Bay's southern shore (Ghassemi and White 2007).

Other western cities that receive significant municipal water supplies via transbasin diversions include Salt Lake City and Denver. Salt Lake has participated in the Bureau of Reclamation's Provo River Project and the Central Utah Project, which both divert water from the Colorado River drainage to the Great Basin. Denver receives water from several projects, including water diverted across the Continental Divide through the Moffat Tunnel.

In addition to providing municipal supplies to many cities, interbasin transfers provide water to several irrigation projects in the West. In the late 1800s, many local irrigation companies constructed small interbasin transfers. These generally involved small canals that collected water at very high elevations and crossed over continental divides. After Congress created the Reclamation Service (later Bureau of Reclamation) in 1903, the federal government began construction of twenty-four irrigation projects within five years. Several of these irrigation projects included transbasin diversions. The Strawberry Project in Utah transfers water from the Colorado River drainage to the Great Basin. The Truckee-Carson Project in Nevada transfers water between the Truckee River Basin to the Lohantan

River Basin—both terminate in inland lakes with no outlets. The Milk River Project transfers water from Saint Mary's River in Canada—which drains to the Hudson Bay—to the Milk River, a tributary of the Missouri that drains to the Gulf of Mexico.

Bureau of Reclamation Projects

During the middle third of the twentieth century, the Bureau of Reclamation constructed even larger projects, several of which also included interbasin transfers. In the Imperial Valley of California, the Bureau increased an existing transfer by constructing the All-American and Coachella canals, which together transfer 2.6 million acre-feet of Colorado River water into the Imperial Valley, a closed basin that terminates in the Salton Sea (Ghassemi and White 2007). The Bureau's Central Valley Project, begun during this same period, transfers water from the Trinity River into the Sacramento and from the Sacramento into the San Joaquin, as well as connecting the Tulare Basin and Kern River Basin—both have no natural outlets—at the south end of the San Joaquin Valley. In Colorado, the Colorado–Big Thompson Project diverts approximately 578,000 acre-feet of water per year from the Colorado River to the Big Thompson River, a tributary of the South Platte.

In 1956, as part of the Colorado River Storage Project (CRSP), Congress authorized the Bureau of Reclamation to construct two interbasin transfers. The Central Utah Project enlarged the existing Strawberry Project and increased the diversions from the Colorado River Basin to the Great Basin. Political compromises in the 1980s and early 1990s changed the primary purpose from irrigation of lands in central Utah to providing a municipal supply for Salt Lake City and the urban corridor extending to its south. Included in the same CRSP legislation was the San Juan–Chama Project, which diverts water from the San Juan (Colorado River Basin) to the Chama River (Rio Grande River Basin). Congress also authorized the Frying Pan–Arkansas Project in 1962, which diverts 80,000 acre-feet a year from the Colorado Basin to the Arkansas (Ghassemi and White 2007)

As part of the Flood Control Act of 1944, Congress authorized the Bureau of Reclamation to construct the Garrison Diversion. The Bureau planned to use this project to divert 1 million acre-feet of water per year from the Missouri River. It planned to divert significant portions of the water into the Souris and Red Rivers in the Hudson Bay drainage. The Bureau halted construction in response to legal challenges and the objections of the Canadian government, which feared the diversion could introduce invasive aquatic species and decimate the commercial fishery on Lake Winnipeg. In response, Congress reformulated the project on two separate occasions, ultimately downgrading the project in size and scope to provide municipal water supplies to Minot, North Dakota, and the communities in the Red River Valley. The Canadian government remains opposed to the project unless the water is treated completely before its transfer into the Hudson Bay drainage.

These later Bureau of Reclamation projects involved extensive development of collection, storage, and conveyance systems, including variations of long tunnels, massive canals, and powerful pumps. But not all massive reclamation projects include interbasin transfers. For example, the Bureau's Central Arizona Project does not transfer water out of the Colorado River Basin. After the Supreme Court ruled in favor of this Arizona project, western states, the Bureau of Reclamation, and the Department of the Interior recognized that the river could not meet the demands of all the projects constructed and planned for its water. As a result, government and private engineers, planners, and developers devised at least twenty different massive interstate and international plans to augment the Colorado River. For example, the Interior Department proposed the Pacific Southwest Water Plan, which contemplated diversions from the Columbia (Howe and Easter 1971). The most ambitious of these schemes was the North American Water and Power Alliance (NAWAPA) contrived by the Ralph M. Parsons Company of California. The massive project, with a price tag of $100 billion in 1964, would have diverted water from Alaska and the Rocky Mountains of Canada to the prairie provinces of Canada; the Great Lakes; twenty-two states; and the Mexican states of Sonora, Chihuahua, and Baja California. While the idea has received some support among politicians in western states, the Canadian government opposed the idea from the beginning (Ghassemi and White 2007).

With the passage of the National Environmental Protection Act and the Endangered Species Act, interbasin transfers have become more difficult to get approved and construct in the United States. In addition, existing projects continue to remain controversial as their impacts on aquatic species are now better understood. Another concern raised about existing water projects is the cost of future maintenance and rehabilitation as many older projects reach the end of their design lives. Law professor Barbara Cosens observed, "Since the design life of the project bears no relation to the design life of the community that relies on it, the end result will be either continuing public subsidy or substantial social displacement" (Cosens 2010, 24). Nonetheless, climate change may increase demand for new projects.

—Adam Eastman

See also: *Bureau of Reclamation; Flood Control Act of 1944; Government Water Decision Making; Population Trends and Water Demand*

BIBLIOGRAPHY

Cosens, Barbara. "New Era of Interbasin Water Transfers." *The Water Report,* no. 72, March 15, 2010: 21–27. Available at http://www.infrastructureusa.org/wp-content/uploads/2010/03/twr-february10.pdf.

Ghassemi, Fereidoun, and Ian White. *Inter-Basin Water Transfer: Case Studies from Australia, United States, Canada, China, and India.* New York: Cambridge University Press, 2007.

Howe, Charles W., and K. William Easter. *Interbasin Transfers of Water: Economic Issues and Impacts.* Baltimore: Johns Hopkins Press, 1971.

Levees

The system of building levees has been used since ancient times to protect areas from water inundation, floods, and tsunamis. Some levees in ancient Sumeria, ancient Egypt, and the Indus Valley were major works that clearly involved thousands of people in their construction. Similarly, levees were employed in late medieval and early modern Europe, especially in the "Low Countries" (the modern-day Netherlands), where dikes were built to drain the swamps. The English introduced this system in the Fenlands during the seventeenth century. The system essentially has not changed, although with more and more urban areas—where land is covered in concrete and the soil is therefore not able to absorb as much water—the problems that levees address have been exacerbated.

In North America, Native Americans in coastal regions used small earth levees for fish farming and aquaculture. After white settlement, some early ports had to be protected by small levees. In addition, some levees were built in parts of New England to reduce swamps with the aim of creating more farmland and reducing the incidence of malaria.

The term *levee* derives from the French verb *lever* ("to rise"). Given New Orleans's continuing efforts to recover from Hurricane Katrina, it is ironic that the word was first used with its present meaning in 1720 to describe work that was undertaken around the then-French port of Nouvelle-Orléans (New Orleans). The port had been established only three years earlier, but it was already being battered by storms and was affected by hurricanes in 1721 and 1722.

Flood Control and Levee Building

Early in the history of white settlement, there were a number of floods in New England. The Merrimack River flooded in 1740 in New Hampshire. Another major flood took place in New Hampshire and Maine in October 1785; it destroyed many homes in the settlement that became Bethel, Maine. In 1806, there was another flood in Turner, Maine, and five years later Durham, Maine, was flooded. Then in 1814, a flood destroyed most of the mills in Turner in spite of the earthen banks and levees that had been built after the previous flood. The levees were increased in size, but Turner was again inundated in 1863, causing some people to decide to leave the area. The great Northeast Flood of April 1852 caused great destruction in New Hampshire, where the city of Concord was badly damaged after the Merrimack River reached its highest level since the 1780s.

The Louisiana Purchase of 1803 resulted in the acquisition of the land around the Mississippi River and the city of New Orleans. The regular flooding of lands around the Mississippi River caused much disruption to the numerous settlements along the river. The first major urban area to be inundated was Saint Louis, which was badly flooded in 1844. At that time there were no levees to protect the city, but building levees was opposed because of the cost. In 1849, Congress passed the Swamp Act, which allowed the use of federal funds to build levees. The impetus to build levees was increased with a spring flood in New Orleans in 1849, after which high earthen banks were erected; these prevented damage from subsequent spring floods.

As new areas were settled, some new cities and towns were situated too close to rivers. From January 9 to 12, 1862, the Sacramento River flooded, creating a large inland sea. Meanwhile, the Civil War raged, and Union and Confederate engineers were constructing and destroying levees to protect places or to allow their own soldiers to attack more easily.

The most damaging flood of this period was the Mill River Flood of May 1874. Heavy rains in western Massachusetts caused the destruction of many homes and the deaths of 144 people. As a result, the Massachusetts state government built large-scale levees along rivers. Seven years later, the same measures were employed around Omaha,

Breaches in the levee system that protects New Orleans from flooding resulted in catastrophic damage and numerous deaths following Hurricane Katrina in 2005.

SSGT Jacob N. Bailey/USAF/Dept. of Defense

Nebraska, and Council Bluffs, Iowa, after those two cities were also badly damaged in floods.

Many coastal cities and towns already had large levees that protected them adequately from river and sea flooding. However, people were often unprepared for intense rainfall. In June 1903, the city of Heppner, Oregon, was devastated when after heavy rain, water swept away the levees and flooded the city, killing 220 people. In the following year, Kalamazoo and Grand Rapids, Michigan, were badly flooded; in the latter case, only one person was killed in spite of the city's being very badly damaged. Michigan was again affected by flooding in March 1908.

Dayton, Ohio, situated on flat land, had erected levees to protect it from the confluence of the Stillwater River and the Mad River, but these proved inadequate in March 1913 when the Great Dayton Flood killed 361 people. Levees at nearby Delaware, Ohio, and in the state capital, Columbus, were washed away in the same flood.

In late 1926, heavy rains in the Ohio Valley and in eastern Kansas and Oklahoma prompted more levee building along the Mississippi River as the waters rose steadily. These proved effective throughout the winter, but on March 29,

1927, they broke near Elaine, Arkansas. Then the spring rains caused the Mississippi River to continue to rise, and more than half a million people had to be evacuated. A large and effective Red Cross appeal directed by Herbert Hoover, then secretary of commerce, helped him win the presidential election the following year.

The Great Mississippi Flood led to major levee building along the river. Then during the New Deal, a number of federal levee-building projects were used to employ people. Louisiana state governor Huey Long also employed many workers to prepare levees to protect New Orleans and other cities and towns. Gradually, more and more cities came to be protected from flooding. The Flood Control Act of 1941 helped as well, although it came too late to protect Los Angeles, which was inundated in 1938 as waters washed away its levees.

Since World War II, because of many changes in federal and state laws regarding water policies, there have not been as many major floods as earlier in U.S. history. Nonetheless, floods in Kansas in July 1951, Ohio in July 1969, along the Mississippi in 1993, and in northern California on New Year's Day 1997 show that no matter how high the levees are, sometimes rains or tropical storms can overwhelm them. However, impromptu levees erected in Salt Lake City in 1983 helped save that city from flooding, as they have in so many other places.

Levees have been less effective in dealing with flooding from hurricanes, such as when Hurricane Agnes in June 1972 caused flooding in some mid-Atlantic states. Certainly the most well-known case of levee failure was in 2005, when waters surging as a result of Hurricane Katrina invaded New Orleans. The city had grown out into what had been floodplains, but the Orleans Levee District, the local flood-protection authority, and the U.S. Army Corps of Engineers felt that large levees were "prohibitively expensive." The large levees in place were not all uniformly reinforced to the same level. Those that had been made to protect the lower Ninth Ward were unable to cope, and the resulting flood killed 1,836 people and severely damaged the city.

Levee Structure, Effectiveness, and Consequences

In most cases, the nature of these levees has not changed since ancient times. They were, for the most part, earthen banks, often with grass growing on them, which is useful in holding the soil together, and often reinforced with stones, rocks, and wood. Sandbags came into use in the late eighteenth century, allowing levees to be made quickly in emergencies. Nevertheless, many argue that these should be a last resort and that it is the responsibility of the government to build permanent levees along the banks of rivers and other potential flood sites. Levees today are constructed from concrete.

Construction costs have led to political debate over whether humans should live on floodplains. In addition, sometimes severe floods still occur. For example, the flooding caused by Hurricane Katrina in 2005, in spite of the massive levees in place, resulted in the heaviest loss of life of any flood in U.S. history. Also, in 2010 the state of Rhode Island experienced its heaviest flooding ever. In

Mississippi River Levee Association

The Tri-State Levee Association, later renamed the Mississippi River Levee Association (MRLA), was founded in 1912 in Memphis, Tennessee, by agriculturalists and levee officials from a number of levee districts arrayed along the lower Mississippi River who wanted the federal government to control floodwaters on the waterway and its major tributaries. The MRLA quickly launched a lobbying campaign in Washington, D.C., to convince federal legislators that Mississippi River floods were not a local problem but calamities that impacted the entire country. Thus, according to the MRLA, it was an appropriate use of taxpayers' money for the federal government to construct the infrastructure required to control floodwaters on the Mississippi River. Critics charged that the MRLA was seeking money to benefit the economic interests of wealthy planters. The MRLA found allies in Washington, D.C., through both its robust lobbying campaign and the sympathy that arose for victims of the Mississippi River floods of 1912, 1913, and 1917. The MRLA's efforts resulted in the passage of the 1917 Flood Control Act, also known as the Ransdell-Humphreys Act, which gave the federal government the primary responsibility for financing the construction of the levees required to control Mississippi River floodwaters. With its task completed, the MRLA disbanded in 1917.

—John R. Burch Jr.

BIBLIOGRAPHY

O'Neill, Karen M. *Rivers by Design: State Power and the Origin of U.S. Flood Control.* Durham, NC: Duke University Press, 2006.
Pearcy, Matthew T. "A History of the Ransdell-Humphrey Flood Control Act of 1917." *Louisiana History: The Journal of the Louisiana Historical Association* 41, no. 2 (2000): 133–59.

May and June of that year, levees of dubious value were constructed around islands in Louisiana and Florida to protect them from the Deepwater Horizon (or BP) oil spill.

Although levees and seawalls have prevented many floods, environmentalists have long been concerned about the featureless surfaces of many of these structures. Their vertical and unnatural surfaces prevent the existence, let alone the flourishing, of the marine creatures that previously lived in tidal waters. Some environmentalists have wanted to make levees more marine-friendly, providing a hospitable environment for sea snails, arthropods, limpets, and starfish. The easiest way to do this is to embed or attach earthenware flowerpots to the smooth surfaces to create microhabitats. Like rock pools, the pots fill with new seawater when the tide is high and retain water when the tide retreats. Their incorporation into a number of seawalls and levees has increased biodiversity.

—Justin Corfield

See also: *Dam Building; Dredging; Locks*

BIBLIOGRAPHY

Barry, John M. *Rising Tide: The Great Mississippi Flood of 1927 and How It Changed America.* New York: Simon & Schuster, 1998.

Bourne, Joel K. "New Orleans." *National Geographic Magazine* 212, no. 2 (2007): 32–67.

Davis, Lee. *Encyclopedia of Natural Disasters.* London: Headline, 1993.

Longshore, David. *Encyclopedia of Hurricanes, Typhoons and Cyclones.* New York: Checkmark Books, 2000.

Petroski, Henry. "Levees and Other Raised Ground." *American Scientist* 94, no. 1 (2006): 7–11.

Locks

A lock allows boats to travel smoothly along a river or canal that traverses rugged terrain. A vessel enters a section of the waterway, and gates are closed on either side of it. The level of the water between the gates is raised or lowered to the level of the next section in the direction the boat is traveling. When the water levels are equal, the gate on that side is opened, and the vessel passes to the next section. When a dam is constructed, a lock is essential for the river to remain navigable; thus locks and dams often are constructed at the same time. Locks are also used to control the flow of water in rivers, either to help irrigation or to deal with tides.

Poe Lock, part of a series of locks that permits the movement of ships from Lake Superior to the other Great Lakes, was opened in 1896. Locks allow ships to pass between bodies of water of unequal elevation by raising or lowering the water level between the lock compartments.
Library of Congress

Early Locks and Canals

The building of canals in the United States led to the need to develop locks similar to those used in canals in Britain and elsewhere. In 1817, the New York state legislature authorized $7 million to build the Erie Canal, which was completed in 1825. As with other canals, it transformed the economy of the region where it was located, opening up much of the hinterland in Michigan, Ohio, Indiana, and Illinois. It reduced freight rates from Buffalo to New York City from $100 a ton by land to $10 a ton by barge. Tolls were collected, mainly at locks, and the canal paid for itself in nine years. The tolls continued, however, until 1882, contributing to the state's general budget. Complaints eventually persuaded state legislators to end the tolls.

A rival to the Erie Canal was the Chesapeake & Ohio Canal (C&O Canal). Work started on this canal in 1828 with the aim of providing cheap transportation from the Potomac River to Atlantic seaports. Despite its location, it was unable to compete with the Erie Canal. This canal traversed extremely hilly terrain, including a major mountain ridge, requiring seventy-four locks. The locks in the C&O Canal are all swing gates or miter gates, a design that was outlined for the first time in the Renaissance by Leonardo da Vinci. The locks were lined as protection against ships bumping into them; red sandstone from Seneca was used to line some locks, and between Harpers Ferry and Hancock, limestone was used. Lock operators lived in lockhouses. The lockhouses were quite small, even though canal management preferred to hire people with large families because several workers were needed to operate the locks.

The C&O Canal proved important militarily before and during the Civil War. Where the canal crossed the Blue Ridge—now the border between Virginia and West Virginia—five locks were needed in a relatively short distance to cope with the terrain. Next to Lock 33 is the bridge over which the militant abolitionist John Brown (1800–1859), his sons, and his supporters went into Harpers Ferry to try to stage a slave uprising in the summer of 1859. The bridge was destroyed by the Confederates two years later. Fighting also took place there in September 1862 when Confederate general A. P. Hill captured Harpers Ferry during the Maryland campaign.

Along the Welland Canal—actually within Canadian territory but important for U.S. commerce—the construction of locks allowed ships to avoid Niagara Falls. The current Welland Canal—officially the Welland Ship Canal—is the fourth one, constructed between 1913 and 1932. The locks in the Welland Canal incorporate viewing platforms for sightseers. A fifth canal is currently being planned.

A complicated engineering feat was the building of the Hiram M. Chittenden Locks at Salmon Bay, Seattle, for the Lake Washington Ship Canal in 1906. Because the canal system is heavily used, two locks were constructed so that one could be closed for maintenance without restricting the flow of traffic. These locks not only had to maintain the water level of Lake Washington, which was twenty to twenty-two feet above sea level, but also prevent the mixing of freshwater from the lakes with seawater from Puget Sound. If seawater entered the lake, it could destroy the freshwater ecosystem there. Thus, a lock was designed to incorporate a basin, which catches the heavier saltwater. Also, fish, especially the Pacific salmon, spawn in the lake. Adults must be able to swim upstream to the lake, and the fry must be able to swim downstream to the ocean. To help with this, a fish ladder was built to allow fish to bypass the lock by jumping from step to step. The first fish ladder installed had ten steps, and a new one was later constructed with twenty-one steps, as well as an underground viewing chamber so people could watch the fish migrate. The Hiram M. Chittenden Locks have demonstrated that it is possible to engineer a lock system that is adapted to aquatic life.

The Panama Canal

The ability to design and build locks was tested to the full with the construction of the Panama Canal from 1904 to 1914. The original plan by Adolphe Godin de Lépinay, Baron de Brusly, drawn up in 1879, had included locks. But when the French started the canal in 1881, they planned it through a longer, sea-level route so that locks were not necessary. However, landslides from the surrounding mountains regularly filled new excavations with mud, malaria and yellow fever killed thousands of workers, and the company suffered from mismanagement. The French effort collapsed

in 1889, and it was not until the United States started work in 1904 that the idea of locks was once again raised, although the locks were not formally added to the design until 1906. U.S. rights to the Panama Canal Zone were negotiated in 1903, and President Theodore Roosevelt appointed George Washington Goethals as chief engineer in 1907. The three sets of locks that were built were larger than those originally planned because Goethals wanted to ensure that U.S. Navy ships would be able to use the canal. The locks were constructed 110 feet wide because the largest battleship being planned at the time, the *Pennsylvania,* was 98 feet wide. The *Titanic,* the largest vessel in the world at that time—still under construction—was 94 feet wide. The lock chamber was to be 1,000 feet long. These locks are widely cited as one of the major engineering feats undertaken before World War I. They were only eclipsed in the amount of concrete used by the Hoover Dam fifteen years later.

Locks on the Mississippi River

The Upper Mississippi River has had a total of thirty locks stretching from Upper Saint Anthony Falls Lock and Dam near Minneapolis, Minnesota, to the Chain of Rocks Lock at Granite City, Illinois. Most of these locks are attached to dams that were constructed to regulate water levels as well as to generate electricity. Of the thirty locks, two have since been demolished—the Meeker Island Lock and Dam between Minneapolis and Saint Paul, Minnesota, and the Lock and Dam No. 26 at Alton, Illinois.

Lock and Dam No. 7 (the Dresbach Lock and Dam) near LaCrosse, Wisconsin, was originally constructed to cope with 750,000 tons a year of traffic. As a result, like most of the other locks on the Mississippi, it is 110 feet wide and 600 feet long. By 1962 the lock was handling 7 million tons a year. Therefore, it was necessary to embark on double locking, with half the barges going through at any one time. This process increased the time of passing through a lock from fifteen minutes to an hour or longer.

Lock and Dam No. 19 at Keokuk, Iowa, was at the time of its construction the largest lock in the world in terms of water volume, being 110 feet wide and 1,200 feet long. It was also the longest until the Chain of Rocks Lock was constructed at Granite City, Illinois.

All the locks have, in spite of controversies about their size or cost, been effective at what they were designed to do. The one outstanding exception was the locks at New Orleans,

Louisiana, which were—along with insufficient levees—unable to prevent the flooding of the city in 2005 following Hurricane Katrina. These locks were located on the Industrial Canal, which itself had flooded in 1965 during Hurricane Betsy. As Hurricane Katrina approached, they were used to allow the passage of barges bringing earth and sand for the levees. However, it was one of these barges that may have caused fatal damage to the locks.

—Justin Corfield

See also: *All-American Canal; Cape Cod Canal; Erie Canal; Gallipolis Locks and Dam; Illinois and Michigan Canal; Keokuk Dam; Mississippi River Basin*

BIBLIOGRAPHY

Buehr, Walter. *Through the Locks: Canals Today and Yesterday.* New York: Putnam, 1954.
High, Mike. *The C&O Canal Companion.* Baltimore: Johns Hopkins University Press, 1997.
Mausshardt, Sherrill, and Glen Singleton. "Mitigating Salt-Water Intrusion through Hiram M. Chittenden Locks." *Journal of Waterway, Port, Coastal and Ocean Engineering* 121, no. 4 (1995): 224–27.
McCullough, David. *The Path Between the Seas: The Creation of the Panama Canal, 1870–1914.* New York: Simon & Schuster, 1977.

Mining and Water Resources

Mining is a leading producer of toxins in the environment, whether through contamination of air, water, or soil and whether in the North, South, or West. Historically, the mining industry has been indifferent to the environmental costs of its operations. Freshwater is used in large quantities to process ore, and this water is sent away as effluent, emptying into nearby water sources. Toxins include arsenic, sulfuric acid, iron, antimony, nickel, copper, and manganese. This acid mining drainage (AMD) or acid rock drainage (ARD) sometimes reaches nearby surface water or groundwater, polluting sources that in turn damage people, structures, animals, and plants. AMD also dissolves heavy toxic metals such as mercury, lead, zinc, and copper and allows them to enter nearby waters. It can raise mercury levels in fish, kill aquatic life, and reduce fish growth and reproduction.

Other water enters the environment as seepage from tailings and inadequate rock impoundments. Because this water is polluted, often dangerously so, mining threatens the water people need to live. Methyl mercury causes nerve and brain damage as well as developmental disabilities, and it collects in fish tissue. More important, the tailings and waste require centuries of management after the mine is closed, with the degree of management depending on the type of mine, local terrain, technology used, and skill and interest of the company. AMD is expensive and difficult to clean up, and contamination can last for centuries if not millennia. AMD is the cause of some of the largest and most expensive Superfund sites.

PCBs and Other Mining-Based Pollutants

Legacies of earlier, more lax, mining practices persist. In twentieth-century mines, electrical equipment may contain polychlorinated biphenyls (PCBs), man-made chemicals that were manufactured from 1929 until they were outlawed in 1978. PCBs are carcinogenic and nonbiodegradable. In the 1960s, analytical methodology became sophisticated enough to detect environmental PCBs, and PCBs were found to be in polar bears and penguins and in fish and humans around the world. The findings led to passage of the Toxic Substances Control Act (TSCA) of 1976, which banned much PCB use and closely regulates the chemicals' disposal.

The ban on PCBs made exceptions for dielectric fluids used in transformers and capacitors. The mining industry is a major user of electricity, which in turn is a major user of these types of equipment, and much of it is still in abandoned mines. Mines include quarries, underground mines, open pits, and gravel pits. Only small gravel pits are unlikely to have electrical equipment containing PCBs. Crushing and milling facilities also use PCB-containing equipment. Mining equipment includes power shovels, draglines, substations, breaker houses, smelters, and refining facilities.

Companies will willingly remove underground equipment, including electrical equipment, only if it is cost-effective to do so. Abandonment of this equipment threatens groundwater in mining districts throughout the world. When PCBs are abandoned in mines, they eventually leak into the water table, polluting the water.

Environmental Protection Agency Region 8 includes Wyoming, Utah, South and North Dakota, Montana, and Colorado, an area with many hardrock and coal mines. Over twenty years, the EPA inspected seventy-five mines in this region and found thirty-three violations of PCB regulations. The focus was on underground mines because of the potential for leakage into groundwater. Even so, one open-pit mine in 1994 was the target of a proposed $1 million fine. The mines investigated were operating mines; EPA lacked the resources to investigate abandoned mines. As mining has become more mechanized, the volume of water and waste has increased dramatically.

In northeast Oklahoma, the Picher Mining District was a major producer of lead and zinc from the 1900s to the 1940s. Today it is one of the largest Superfund sites, with millions of cubic yards of mine tailings or chat, which includes chert, dolomite, calcite, iron, zinc, manganese, lead, cadmium oxides, and sulfides. Although some chat has been taken away for gravel, asphalt, and concrete aggregate, local residents have unusually high levels of blood lead and kidney disease. Because parts of the area will not support vegetation, a fine sediment blows with the winds. Vegetation along area streams is iron stained.

Even gravel pits can be toxic polluters. A Maine study revealed that the use of abandoned gravel pits as dumps for debris or as storage sites for vehicles and equipment was common. Experience shows that using these pits as landfills degrades water quality. Reclamation is essential.

In the Midwest, hard-rock mining, not to be confused with coal, iron ore, or gravel mining, is known as metallic sulfide mining. Sulfide mining is more harmful than even iron and taconite mining. All metallic sulfide mines pollute water if there is water to pollute. Metals extracted from sulfide ore include copper, nickel, cobalt, palladium, platinum, and gold. Sulfide ore, tailings, waste rock, and the mine walls themselves, when exposed to moisture and air, create sulfuric acid. Rain or other precipitation can cause this sulfuric acid to drain from the site in a process called AMD or ARD.

Both uranium and large quantities of water are used to generate nuclear power. An average nuclear power plant requires 20–83 percent more water than an equivalent coal-fired plant, with consumption ranging from 35 to 65 million liters per day, or 13 to 24 billion liters a year. This water heats the bays and gulfs that it empties into and may also pollute these waters with salts and heavy metals. Also, in the mining of uranium ore, millions of liters are taken from local water supplies each day, destroying or damaging the environment and adding dangerous pollutants to the aquifer. Depletion can damage streams or water tables miles from the site. Likewise, Nevada's Humboldt River supported gold mining along the Carlin Trend, losing 580 billion gallons of water between 1986 and 2001. In southern Arizona, the water table is lowering and the Santa Cruz River Basin is drying up to support copper mining.

Florida Case Study

A study in defense of exploiting water in Florida itemizes most of the benefits the mining companies claim. Lee County, Florida, established the Density Reduction Groundwater Resource on 83,000 acres in 1989 as a community development compromise between the state community affairs department and the county government. Part of the area has experienced modification from agriculture, residential development, mining, and road development, while some of it is well preserved and a third is publicly owned.

The area contains one of the few deposits of construction-quality lime rock. This material is a "finite natural resource," and the state wants a reliable supply to keep the costs of road building and construction as low as possible. Mining is a billion-dollar-a-year industry in Florida. When Lee County considered opening the asset to exploitation, it

Buffalo Creek Flood

The Buffalo Mining Company, a subsidiary of the Pittston Company, owned three dams on Buffalo Creek in Logan County, West Virginia, that were used to impound coal waste. One of the dams collapsed on February 26, 1972, and released approximately 130 million gallons of water and coal sludge. Seventeen communities on Buffalo Creek were damaged by the flooding. The victims included 125 killed and more than 1,000 injured. Approximately 4,000 of the people residing in the vicinity of Buffalo Creek were left homeless.

It was revealed during the subsequent investigation that the construction plans for the Buffalo Mining Company's dams were never submitted to the West Virginia Public Service Commission, the agency responsible for oversight of dam construction. In the wake of the disclosure, legislation at both the state and national level was passed that instituted regulation of the construction and maintenance of coal waste dams.

—John R. Burch Jr.

BIBLIOGRAPHY

Erikson, Kai T. *Everything in Its Path: Destruction of Community in the Buffalo Creek Flood.* New York: Simon & Schuster, 1976.
West Virginia Governor's Ad Hoc Commission of Inquiry. *The Buffalo Creek Flood and Disaster: Official Report from the Governor's Ad Hoc Commission of Inquiry.* Charleston, WV: The Commission, 1973. Available at http://www.wvculture.org/hiSTory/disasters/buffcreekgovreport.html.

addressed evaporation from mine lakes in regard to impact on water and wetlands, drainage and wetlands, groundwater and public water quality, and the environment and community at large. The study differentiated between temporary and permanent impacts due to changes in land use, noting that changes due to mining might correct previous changes made by farming. In that case, it could make more land available for recreational use and make the land more environmentally healthy.

According to the study, mining is beneficial in that it creates lakes to provide added water storage, helping the wetlands and aquifer during dry seasons. Rather than encouraging increased evaporation and thus lowering water levels in sensitive areas, in fact lakes will store more water. Lakes are better than the aquifer for storing water because they don't have as many rocks in a given volume. In fact, lakes provide the aquifer with water during the dry season. And lakes reduce drawdown from the aquifer from wells, again helping wetlands.

In addition, according to the study, some woods and plants cause greater water loss through evapotranspiration than do lakes. Evapotranspiration, the combination of water loss from plant transpiration and water evaporation, is between 40 and 100 percent of precipitation, the lower figure in the North and Northwest and the larger figure in the Southwest.

Addressing concerns that mine drainage damages wetlands, the study says that the mine lakes shouldn't be dug across the lay of the land but should follow the contours of the land, noting that this best practice is employed by modern mines.

The study notes the concern that mining allows easier transfer of pollutants and contaminants to the aquifer. It counters that microorganisms die off after being filtered out in the groundwater environment. The county rock mines have operated near well fields for over twenty years without any negative impact on the water supply, and communities worldwide have used rock filtration to purify their water supplies for centuries.

The final benefit is that mining uses less water than agriculture, so converting land from agricultural use to mining would make more water available for the community as it grows.

Gravel Mining

Gravel mining is less intrusive than other forms of mining. The Lamoine, Maine, Conservation Commission in 2002 asked the University of Maine to examine whether the local aquifer was suffering from sand and gravel mining. It wanted an inventory of water supplies near new and reclaimed pits, an assessment of the changes if any in water quality, assignment of risk ratings, and assessment of current regulations. The study determined that no noticeable change had taken place in the hydrology of surface or groundwater. With regard to contamination, salts and nitrate had increased, but no direct link could be established with the gravel pits. And increases in chloride were attributed to winter road salting or proximity to coastal bay waters rather than mining activities. Although some of the pits have been in operation for eighty years or more, there is little documentation or living memory of their activities. At one pit, mining was occurring below the water table, and some other negligence occurred about maintaining the required separation of mining activity from the water table.

Mitigation and Environmental Activism

Mitigation actions in Utah have included creation of a sand filtration plant by a coal company to ease the worries of the local water users' association. Another approach was for an area to stop using its wells while a mining operation was occurring; in return, the mining company compensated the district and mitigated impacts on irrigation water. An alternate source of water was diverted during the mining. And a mining company whose long walls were generating subsidence that allowed cracks and leakage into surface ponds sealed off the pond bottoms with sodium bentonite, a clay with good sealant properties, to keep livestock water free of coal-mining pollutants.

Late in the twentieth century, the mining companies became more conscientious, but environmental risks remain, including sedimentation from mine roads and roiling of water during mine construction. Even with all the emphasis on environmental safeguards, at the Buckhorn Mountain gold mine in April 2009, the Crown Resources Corporation was fined $40,000 for violations of its water discharge permit. The state of Washington found that Crown was not capturing and treating water dirtied by its underground mining before discharging it into nearby streams. The mine also generated seepage, which was detected by monitoring wells and streams. Pollutants included nitrate, sulfate, and chloride. The violations persisted over a ten-month period.

Minnesota has thousands of lakes and borders Lake Superior, one of the Great Lakes, which contain a significant share of the continent's freshwater. Minnesota also has a friendly attitude toward mining companies, but it has its share of environmentalists. Minnesota environmentalists fought PolyMet, which in 2008 sought to open a metallic sulfide mine in an area whose waters were already at risk. The state Department of Natural Resources (DNR), as in other states, had a contradictory mission—to protect and to exploit the state's resources. The DNR, which has powers over financial guarantees, mode of operation, and satisfactory closedown of a site, was headed by a political appointee. The state also had inadequate resources to protect wetlands and other natural areas. PolyMet sought to mine under untested regulations, store tailings up to 240 feet high, and alter local water supplies by digging three pits. The company also fought water discharge permit and reclamation requirements. Efforts to enact mining restriction legislation failed in 2009. Conflicts between mining and conservation continue.

—John H. Barnhill

See also: *Acid Mine Drainage; Heavy Metals in Water*

BIBLIOGRAPHY

Bench, Dan W. "PCBs, Mining, and Water Pollution." Paper presented at the Mine Design, Operations & Closure Conference, Polson, MT, April 27–May 1, 2003. Available at http://www.epa.gov/Region8/toxics/pcb/papert16polson03.pdf.

Hanson, Ronald L. "Evapotranspiration and Droughts." In *National Water Summary 1988–89: Hydrologic Events and Floods and Droughts* (USGS Water-Supply Paper 2375), compiled by R. W. Paulson, E. B. Chase, R. S. Roberts, and D. W. Moody, 99–104. Washington, DC: U.S. Geological Survey, 1991. Available at http://geochange.er.usgs.gov/sw/changes/natural/et/.

Kramer, Becky. "In Brief: Mining Company Fined for Water Pollution." *Spokesman-Review,* April 29, 2009. Available at http://www.spokesman.com/stories/2009/apr/29/mining-company-fined-for-water-pollution/.

Minnesota Department of Natural Resources. "PolyMet Mining Inc./NorthMet Project." http://www.dnr.state.mn.us/input/environmentalreview/polymet/index.html.

Missimer, Thomas M., and Robert G. Maliva. "The Impact of Mining on Water Quality and Water Quantity in the DR/GR." Summary of *Mining in Lee County Benefits & Impacts* by Missimer and Maliva. Fort Myers, FL: Missimer Groundwater Science, 2008. Available at http://www3.leegov.com/dcd/CommunityPlans/SELC_DRGR/Gilkey_MiningImpactonWaterQuality.pdf.

Peckenham, John M., and Teresa Thornton. Can Gravel Mining and Water Supply Wells Coexist? Orono: Senator George J. Mitchell Center for Environmental and Water Research, University of Maine, 2006. Available at http://www.umaine.edu/waterresearch/research/gravel_mining/gravel_mining.htm.

National Parks and Water

Described by writer and historian Wallace Stegner as "America's best idea," the U.S. National Park System is a collection of protected lands—including parks, monuments, historic sites, and military battlefields—owned by the federal government and specifically designated for the enjoyment and use of the American public. Administered by the National Park Service (itself an agency within the Interior Department), the National Park System today consists of nearly 400 individual units, of which 58 are national parks ranging in size from Alaska's 13.2 million acre Wrangell–St. Elias National Park to the 5,500-acre Hot Springs National Park in Arkansas.

Early Movements to Protect Natural Landscapes

The National Park Service was established by President Woodrow Wilson in 1916, but the history of the park system dates back to the establishment of Yellowstone Park in 1872, and even that was the end result of an idea at least forty years in the making. Early surveys of the Northwest Territory by explorers like Lewis & Clark (1804) and Zebulon Pike (1806) fostered interest in documenting the great natural wonders of the American frontier: mountains, valleys, waterfalls, and river canyons, many of them unlike any other landscapes in the world. Nearly every one of these early visitors was stunned by a beauty that was, in many instances, literally beyond description. Perhaps the earliest advocate of a national park system was landscape artist George Catlin who, during an expedition up the Missouri River in 1832, ruminated over the idea of a *"nation's Park, containing man and beast, in all the wild freshness of their nature's beauty"* (quoted in Heacox 2001, 38). Like many early adventurers, Catlin feared that America's unrelenting westward expansion and exploitation of the frontier would overwhelm and subjugate natural wonders that the vast majority of Americans had never even seen.

America's water resources were frequently employed as symbols of the need to protect public lands. In 1869, John Wesley Powell's adventure down the Colorado River highlighted the need to protect the water resources of the arid West. Powell was one of the first people to see the immeasurable value of water resources in the dry Southwest, where much of the land was simply not arable. Steeped in the nineteenth-century paradigm of Manifest Destiny, however,

National Parks Conservation Association

The National Park Association (NPA) was founded on May 19, 1919, for the purpose of promoting and protecting the country's developing national park system. The NPA changed its name in 1970 to the National Parks and Conservation Association, and then changed it again in 2000 to its present form. Since 1920, the organization has continuously advocated its positions in a periodical currently entitled *National Parks*.

Working closely with the National Park Service, the organization has endeavored throughout its existence to protect the ecosystems found within national parks from threats such as pollution and the exploitation of their natural resources. Water issues have on occasion put the National Parks Conservation Association in direct conflict with the U.S. Army Corps of Engineers and the U.S. Bureau of Reclamation. The NPA was a participant in the fight against the construction of the Echo Park Dam, which threatened the Dinosaur National Monument. The NPA was also active in opposing the Central Arizona Project, especially the construction of the Bridge Canyon and Marble Canyon dams.

—John R. Burch Jr.

See also: *Bureau of Reclamation; Central Arizona Project; Echo Park Dam; Grand Canyon Dams; Solid Waste Agency of Northern Cook County v. United States Army Corps of Engineers et al. (2001)*

BIBLIOGRAPHY

Miles, John C. *Guardians of the Parks: A History of the National Parks and Conservation Association.* Washington, DC: Taylor & Francis, 1995.
National Parks Conservation Association. http://www.npca.org/.
Pearson, Byron E. *Still the Wild River Runs: Congress, the Sierra Club, and the Fight to Save Grand Canyon.* Tucson: University of Arizona Press, 2002.

Powell was convinced that the western territories of the United States would fall under the plow, but only if incoming settlers had ready access to water. That water would be supplied, he suggested, by the seemingly inexhaustible rivers of the Rocky Mountains.

Other early proponents of a park system pointed to the aesthetic rather than the practical benefits of protecting water resources. Artists like Albert Bierstadt, Thomas Moran, and other "alumni" of the Hudson River School of painters, along with early photographers such as William Brewer and Charles Leander Weed, produced numerous works that captured the grandeur of Yosemite and Yellowstone waterfalls and other water wonders of the American West. In fact, it was while camping near the geysers and thermal pools of Yellowstone in 1870 that a small party of explorers, led by General Henry Washburn, first suggested that the Yellowstone area be protected as a public park (Heacox 2001). Within two years, Congress had passed the Yellowstone Park Act,

signed by President Ulysses S. Grant on March 1, 1872. Despite the relative speed with which Yellowstone was designated, however, it would be nearly two decades more before the next jewels were added to the National Park crown in 1890: Sequoia and Yosemite National Parks, the latter largely in response to calls for protection by John Muir's Sierra Club.

The first decade of the twentieth century saw an expansion of the park system that solidified Theodore Roosevelt's reputation as the nation's greatest conservationist president. In addition to overseeing the inclusion of three new national parks (Crater Lake, Wind Cave, and Mesa Verde), Roosevelt also used the executive powers granted to him by the passage of the 1906 Antiquities Act to protect a number of other natural areas as national monuments, including Devil's Tower in Wyoming, Chaco Canyon in New Mexico, Muir Woods in California, Grand Canyon in Arizona, and Washington State's Mount Olympus.

Controversies

Water resources in the public domain were not only a primary inspiration for a national park system; they were also a flashpoint for some of its greatest controversies. Along with its status as one of the first national parks, Yosemite gained fame as the focus of the park system's first great water conflict: the damming of the Tuolumne River in Yosemite's Hetch Hetchy Valley.

The debate surrounding the damming of the Tuolumne brought to the surface conflicting ideas about how protected lands might best be utilized. It also highlighted the paradox that underpinned the establishment of the park system in the first place: namely, the idea that lands gained protection as national parks only to the extent that those lands were deemed economically "worthless." As national park scholar Alfred Runte has explained, the "worthless lands" thesis had been a central (though unwritten) tenet of early park policy, one that preceded even the establishment of Yosemite itself, which was declared by early advocates to be too remote and too rugged to be of any commercial value. Lands of extraordinary scenic beauty were seen as rightfully belonging to all Americans, then, as long as they were believed "economically valueless from the standpoint of their natural wealth" (Runte 2010, 127). Central to this debate was the very question of what "protection" actually meant, at least on a practical level. Certainly no one questioned the idea that national park resources were to be used for the benefit of the people. What was not yet determined was whether protection meant preservation of areas in their natural, untamed state or preservation merely to the extent that the areas served present or future human needs.

In the case of Hetch Hetchy, the problem centered around the fact that the valley was relatively close to San Francisco, a rapidly growing city of nearly a half million that had been searching for reliable sources of freshwater since the early 1880s. Complicating the issue further was the San Francisco Earthquake of 1906; it not only destroyed much of the city, but the resulting fires highlighted the city's vulnerability to water shortages. City planners looked longingly at the Hetch Hetchy Valley as the most appropriate location for a large reservoir, ironically because its remote location and protected status precluded any other obstacles to its impoundment.

The conflict highlighted and polarized competing principles of conservation. On one side were utilitarian conservationists, such as U.S. Forest Service head and Roosevelt confidant Gifford Pinchot, who subscribed wholeheartedly to the idea of multiple uses. To these multiple-use progressives, the proposed Hetch Hetchy dam would provide thousands of people with drinking water, flood control, and crop irrigation, all of which would be paid for by the electricity that the dam produced. Muir's Sierra Club and other strict preservationists, conversely, felt that absolute preservation was implied for lands under national park protection.

The result of this schism was a prolonged legal battle, one that pitched seeming allies into opposing ideological camps. In 1901, San Francisco's mayor, James Phelan, petitioned Interior Secretary Ethan Hitchcock for permission to construct the dam. The preservationist-leaning Hitchcock refused the request; four years later, however, James A. Garfield, Hitchcock's replacement and a friend of Pinchot's, approved the city's application (Runte 2010). Permission to construct the dam was approved by both houses of Congress by wide margins and signed by President Wilson in 1913, and the dam was completed in 1934. Although the National Park Act of 1916 prohibited any further transgressions in the National Parks themselves, Progressive conservationists saw in the damming of Hetch Hetchy a precedent for other public water projects on government-owned land.

The "gospel of efficiency" espoused by multiple-use conservationists in the early decades of the twentieth century would continue to gain converts during succeeding decades (Hays 1959). Large-scale hydropower dams became part of the American landscape, frequently constructed on various categories of public lands. As such, it was only a matter of time before another attempt was made to construct reservoirs on lands in the National Park System. That opportunity came in the late 1940s, when the Bureau of Reclamation proposed construction of a large dam on the Green River (a tributary of the Colorado) that would inundate Dinosaur National Monument, so designated by President Wilson in 1915. Part of a large multidam water storage project, the Echo Park Dam was, ironically, desirable for its lack of desirability. California's insatiable thirst for the waters of the Colorado meant that other states were limited in their allotment of its flow. Though few of these then sparsely populated states needed their allotments at the time, the Bureau assumed that future population growth would eventually mandate the need for additional water supplies, and Echo Canyon was deemed the best potential reservoir site along the available stretch of the Green River (Nester 1997).

Preservationist fears of a Hetch Hetchy redux seemed likely when, in June of 1950, Interior Secretary Oscar Chapman approved the Bureau of Reclamation's initial plans for the Echo Park Dam. This time, however, the preservationist camp, which included standard-bearers like the Sierra Club as well as newer organizations such as the Wilderness Society, engaged in a nationwide campaign to halt the project. National magazines, including *Time, Newsweek,* and *Collier's,* published articles questioning the legitimacy of the dam, while Wallace Stegner, with the aid of the Sierra Club, edited a photo-filled volume titled *This Is Dinosaur: Echo Park Country and Its Magical River* (Nester 1997). Though the book did not sell particularly well (only 5,000 copies of the first edition were printed), copies were sent to each member of Congress, as well as to influential editorial boards at newspapers across the country. Stegner's underlying message was that the preservation of Dinosaur National Monument meant the preservation of the very idea of national parks and that "some uses use things up, and some last forever" (quoted in Fradkin 2009, 189). Sierra Club executive director David Brower also oversaw the creation of a documentary film that highlighted not only the esthetic beauty of Dinosaur National Monument but also its value as one of America's national treasures.

The battle for Echo Park came to a head in 1955, when an amendment was added that excluded Echo Park from the larger dam project. Although the amendment was rejected in committee, the final Colorado Storage Project bill submitted to Congress not only excluded Echo Park but stipulated that "no dam or reservoir constructed under the authorization of this Act shall be within any National Park or Monument" (Pub. L. 84-485, Sec. 3). The act was passed and signed into law by President Dwight Eisenhower on April 11, 1956, effectively blocking any further attempts to create water impoundment projects on lands under the jurisdiction of the National Park Service.

Since the defeat of the Echo Park Dam, no serious proposals have been put forth to dam lands within the National Park System; moreover, several laws have been added to strengthen protection for waterways under the park system umbrella. Among the most important of these was the Wild and Scenic Rivers Act, passed in 1968 and signed into law by President Lyndon Johnson. While not intended to grant the same degree of protection that national park status provides, the Act grants the Interior Department the authority to identify and protect rivers that are to "be preserved in free-flowing condition, and that they and their immediate environments shall be protected for the benefit and enjoyment of present and future generations" (Pub. L. 90-542, 16 U.S.C. 1271-87). Significantly, the Act expands the Interior Department's ability to protect waterways outside of the National Park System proper, thereby recognizing the value of preserving many watercourses that are outside of large, protected areas.

—Jeffrey B. Flagg

See also: *Adirondack Park; Echo Park Dam; Wild and Scenic Rivers Act of 1968*

BIBLIOGRAPHY

Dilsaver, Lary M., ed. *America's National Park System: The Critical Documents.* Lanham, MD: Rowman & Littlefield, 1994.

Fradkin, Philip L. *Wallace Stegner and the American West.* Berkeley: University of California Press, 2009.

Hays, Samuel P. *Conservation and the Gospel of Efficiency: The Progressive Conservation Movement, 1890–1920.* Cambridge, MA: Harvard University Press, 1959.

Heacox, Kim. *An American Idea: The Making of the National Parks.* Washington, DC: National Geographic Society, 2001.

Nester, William R. *The War for America's Natural Resources.* New York: St. Martin's Press, 1997.

Runte, Alfred. *National Parks: The American Experience.* 4th ed. Lincoln: University of Nebraska Press, 2010.

Worster, Donald, ed. *American Environmentalism: The Formative Period, 1860–1915.* New York: John Wiley & Sons, 1973.

Outdoor Recreation

Outdoor recreation can be defined as a chosen activity away from home. Pigram and Jenkins (2006), in their attempt to disentangle the meaning of *recreation* from *leisure,* believe that recreation is a direct response to leisure needs. Trying to understand outdoor recreation has led academics to draw upon a number of perspectives from different academic disciplines, including geography, economics, sociology, and law. Consequently, the provision of outdoor recreation for the general public can be a challenging concept for planners, who have to consider the issues of access and resource constraints, as well as any political dimensions.

Nearly 90 percent of the U.S. population over the age of twelve participates in some form of outdoor recreation, though since outdoor recreational activities are highly dispersed, it is difficult to obtain accurate data about frequency of participation. When asked to identify the reasons they spend their recreation time in the outdoors, Americans say that they enjoy being surrounded by nature, getting in shape, spending time with family and friends, and enjoying peace and quiet. Experiencing the outdoors for recreation is influenced by a number of factors, including demographics, access and opportunity, technological innovations, and societal acceptance. In general, the relevant demographic variables are age, gender, cultural/ethnic/racial background, disposable income, and level of education. Weather conditions may also have an impact, as do the operating budgets of the providers of outdoor recreation facilities.

The total value of the outdoors for recreation is difficult to describe and impossible to place in economic terms. There is no price on the value of a sunset or rainbow, yet certainly these natural occurrences enhance our lives.

Different Types of Recreation

Outdoor recreation can be categorized as remote natural, natural, rural, or urban. Each of these classes includes land-based activities such as viewing scenery and walking, and water-based activities like canoeing and fishing. In addition, outdoor activities can be categorized as "hard" or "soft," depending on the risk involved and skill required. Hard adventure activities include caving and rock climbing, while softer activities include biking and flat-water canoeing.

The core group of outdoor activities is seen as backpacking, canoeing, kayaking (sea and river), rock climbing, bicycling, snowboarding, and skiing. Older people tend to choose deer hunting, berry picking, and ice fishing, whereas younger individuals seek challenges through extreme sports. Interestingly, in the early 1990s, bird-watching was the fastest-growing outdoor recreation activity in the United States, leading to increased environmental awareness.

Military service and outdoor recreation are clearly related, as in activities such as hunting. Surplus equipment from World War II, such as rubber rafts and jeeps, found use in white-water rafting and off-road driving. Surplus ski equipment combined with the enthusiasm of ski troop veterans contributed to the development of the ski industry. Parachuting, skydiving, and hang gliding are also derived from military activities. Global positioning devices and night vision goggles are two military technologies that have been adapted for recreational use. Similarly, the military has adopted civilian advances in the development of light-weight camping equipment.

The Department of Defense is the fifth largest manager of lands in the United States, following the Bureau of Land Management (BLM), Forest Service (USFS), Fish and Wildlife Service (FWS), and National Park Service (NPS). The recreational use of land is not a priority for the military. Both the BLM and USFS have recreation as an explicit management purpose. Although the NPS and FWS are interested in the recreational uses of the lands they manage, they place a higher priority on resource preservation.

These differences in priorities illustrate the tensions with which outdoor recreation management must contend. In practice, the majority of the outdoor settings available to the general population are provided by state and government agencies. The data created by government agencies about land use are usually based on overnight stays. However, since day visitors usually use facilities in greater numbers than people who stay overnight, the data tends to be far from accurate. When the demand for resources climbs, it is often followed by an expansion of management. When management increases, conflicts often arise over differing viewpoints on how best to use the land for recreational purposes.

Parks

Parks were initially introduced to give city dwellers access to the outdoors, and they developed gradually. As with many cities, the earliest plans for San Francisco did not include any public parks. The only green spaces available to residents were small private gardens and urban squares. In 1870, Golden Gate Park was created. It was over 1,000 hectares in size and included roads, walkways, and green space as habitat for birds and other wildlife. Just over a century later, in 1972, the park was extended to include the Golden Gate Recreational Area, which added an additional 30,000 hectares of land and water. This area, rich in natural, cultural, and

Civilian Conservation Corps

The Civilian Conservation Corps was created on March 21, 1933, with the passage of President Franklin D. Roosevelt's first recovery and relief bill by Congress. It was a public works program designed to provide employment and vocational training for single young men through the conservation and development of the nation's natural resources.

Robert Fechner served as director, but he had to coordinate programs through several cabinet departments. The Department of Labor was responsible for the recruitment of workers. The Department of War provided officers to oversee many of the work camps. The Departments of the Interior and Agriculture were responsible for the supervision of work projects.

Over its existence, the Civilian Conservation Corps employed more than 3 million men. Each received $30 a month for his labors and was required to send at least $25 of that amount to his family. The onset of World War II ended the need for the program; thus it was terminated in 1942.

—John R. Burch Jr.

See also: *Roosevelt, Franklin D.*

BIBLIOGRAPHY
Hill, Edwin G. *In the Shadow of the Mountain: The Spirit of the CCC.* Pullman: Washington State University Press, 1990.
Maher, Neil M. *Nature's New Deal: The Civilian Conservation Corps and the Roots of the American Environmental Movement.* New York: Oxford University Press, 2008.
Salmond, John A. *The Civilian Conservation Corps, 1933–1942: A New Deal Case Study.* Durham, NC: Duke University Press, 1967.

This Union Pacific Railroad advertises Boulder Dam (now called Hoover Dam) as a destination for vacationers.
Library of Congress

developed world. However, water recreation in the form of activities like fishing and canoeing may be compatible with water supply objectives. Water quality and quantity is necessary for sport fishing. Boating requires space, both for mooring and for the movement of the boats. Watercraft with engines, which may increase pollution and erode banks with their wakes, must be managed carefully. When water quality is very good, swimming can be permitted, but the water must be continuously monitored.

The Future of Outdoor Recreation

There is uncertainty about the future of outdoor recreation given the state of the global economy. Factors to be considered are the demands of a changing population and the availability of recreational space. Because society has become increasingly heterogeneous, a number of demographic trends have to be accommodated. These include more elderly and physically disabled people, the growth of minority populations who often do not have traditions of outdoor recreation in their families, and a decline in outdoor participation by the young.

These challenges will be faced by government entities wanting to create opportunities for a diverse, multicultural population, while at the same time limiting access to some outdoor resources due to environmental concerns and pressures. Consequently, there is a strong need for planning that considers the realistic capabilities of existing resources. Some futurists suggest that there will be greater emphasis on leisure, rather than work, so an additional challenge for planners will be to create meaningful experiences for people in a manner that ensures that outdoor recreation is given the priority it deserves.

—Julia Fallon

See also: *Recreational Water Rights; Urbanization*

BIBLIOGRAPHY
Jensen, Clayne R., and Steven P. Guthrie. *Outdoor Recreation in America.* 6th ed. Champaign, IL: Human Kinetics, 2006.
Pigram, John J., and John M. Jenkins. *Outdoor Recreation Management.* 2nd ed. New York: Routledge, 2006.

historical resources, is seen as the prototype of the new urban park of the twenty-first century, but there are challenges in meeting the expectations of conservationists and recreationists regarding the design and purpose of the park. Giving voice to conflicting stakeholder positions on the management of outdoor resources has stimulated increased citizen participation in the development of policy and planning resource use. Where public sector funding has been lacking, private entities have built partnerships to accomplish their goals.

Water is recognized as an attraction for park visitors. The need for a clean and plentiful supply of water for tourists can lead to conflict with water activities enthusiasts and environmentalists. The maintenance of a clean water supply overrides recreational concerns in most places around the

Pesticides

Water pollutants include fertilizer, manure, mining and industrial waste water—and pesticides. Pesticides are chemicals, usually artificial, whose purpose is the killing of unwanted animals and plants. Although used primarily in agriculture, they are also applied to golf courses, along roadways, in forests, and in urban and suburban settings, particularly for lawn maintenance.

Pesticide use was rare before World War II because alternative control techniques were cheaper. During the war, chemical companies developed military uses for herbicides and rodenticides, but the war ended in 1945. Manufacturers found themselves after the war with stockpiles of chemical weapons and no market. In the late 1940s, the companies aggressively sold their chemicals as agricultural pesticides in a virtually unregulated market. The heyday of unregulated pesticide use lasted for a quarter of a century. The Agricultural Research Service, responsible for oversight, tended to be sympathetic to the manufacturers. Pesticides killed and seriously injured those who worked carelessly with them.

In 1993, agricultural use of herbicides and insecticides reached 660 million pounds. A decade later, U.S. use reached 1.2 to 1.6 billion pounds of pesticides each year, nearly a fourth of the 5 billion pounds used worldwide. Total U.S. sales were $9.3 billion, with over a billion in exports and nearly a billion in imports as of 2002.

Pesticides sprayed on crops and lawns can enter water sources through soil erosion and runoff. They kill aquatic life, both animal and vegetable. And they appear in drinking water, even with guidelines that bar their application near the water source. The primary law regulating pesticide pollution is the Clean Water Act (CWA) of 1972 as amended. The CWA was vital to the effort to reduce pesticide pollution and poisoning, and the Environmental Protection Agency (EPA) has used it in fighting pesticides in oyster beds, mosquito control, and aerial spraying. Enforcement has fluctuated with changes in the political climate in Washington, D.C.

EPA Oversight

In the 1980s, the EPA became more assertive in monitoring pollution from runoff. An agriculture department study in 1987 found that 20 percent of Americans were drinking well water contaminated by pesticides, with the greatest

DDT

DDT, or dichloro-diphenyl-trichloroethane, is an insecticide invented in 1939 that earned its creator, Paul H. Müller, the Nobel Prize in Physiology or Medicine in 1948. It was also responsible for numerous health problems and birth defects among humans.

DDT's use in the United States began in 1943, when the Department of Agriculture informed the military that the chemical was safe to be used on soldiers as a bug repellant. The military used the chemical extensively during World War II to kill mosquitoes laden with malaria. In August 1945, permission was granted to private manufacturers to sell DDT within the United States despite evidence that the chemical was a poison to humans. By the 1950s, scientists were warning of the chemical's dangers, including its presence in breast milk, to no avail. It wasn't until the publication of Rachel Carson's *Silent Spring* in 1962 that scientists found a voice that could communicate their startling discoveries concerning DDT to the public at large.

The public furor over Carson's allegations forced the federal government to begin researching the environmental consequences of pesticide use. This eventually led to the passage of the Insecticide, Fungicide, and Rodenticide Act of 1972.

—John R. Burch Jr.

BIBLIOGRAPHY

Lytle, Mark Hamilton. *The Gentle Subversive: Rachel Carson, Silent Spring, and the Rise of the Environmental Movement.* New York: Oxford University Press, 2007.
McWilliams, James E. *American Pests: The Losing War on Insects from Colonial Times to DDT.* New York: Columbia University Press, 2008.

contamination in the northern Corn Belt. EPA studies previously had identified at least seventeen different pesticides in thirty states. In 1988, the EPA began a national survey of drinking water contamination by agricultural pesticides. The survey included over 100 pesticides in and around 1,350 public and private drinking water wells. Nationally there were about 13 million private wells and 51,000 community wells providing drinking water. The EPA expected to uncover human health risks, and it wanted a statistically reliable measure of contamination before issuing new regulations.

In the fall of 1990, the EPA released its five-year national pesticide study. The EPA study cost $12 million and took 22 months of testing—it sampled 1,300 community and rural water wells for 127 pesticides, degradates, and nitrates. One of the pesticides was hexachlorobenzene, a fungicide originally registered in the late 1940s but off the EPA register by the time of the survey, forty years later. The pesticide could vaporize and become airborne, be absorbed into the soil, or enter water supplies through leaching or runoff. Microorganisms and sunlight also

Rachel Carson

Rachel Carson came to national prominence with the publication of *Silent Spring* in 1962. The book criticized agribusiness interests, chemical companies, and the U.S. government for their indiscriminant use of pesticides, especially DDT.

Carson was born in Springdale, Pennsylvania, on May 27, 1907. She earned an MA in Zoology from Johns Hopkins University in 1932. In 1935, she gained employment as a writer for the U.S. Bureau of Fisheries. Throughout her seventeen-year career in the federal government, she wrote and edited numerous scientific publications.

In *Silent Spring,* her professional experience was evident as she leveled serious charges against the pesticide industry and used scientific data presented in language lay readers could understand to buttress her claims. The President's Science Advisory Committee studied Carson's allegations and subsequently issued a report in 1963 supporting her conclusions. In the wake of *Silent Spring,* state and federal governmental officials were forced by the public to increase regulation of pesticides, and some chemical compounds were banned from use. Carson died on April 14, 1964, less than two years after the publication of her landmark work. She was posthumously awarded the Presidential Medal of Freedom by Jimmy Carter in 1980.

—John R. Burch Jr.

BIBLIOGRAPHY

Carson, Rachel. *Silent Spring.* Boston: Houghton Mifflin, 1962.
Lytle, Mark Hamilton. *The Gentle Subversive: Rachel Carson, Silent Spring, and the Rise of the Environmental Movement.* New York: Oxford University Press, 2007.
Murphy, Priscilla Coit. *What A Book Can Do: The Publication and Reception of Silent Spring.* Amherst: University of Massachusetts Press, 2005.

Marine biologist and author of *Silent Spring,* Rachel Carson was a major force in raising public awareness of the health and environmental dangers of pesticide use, most notably of DDT.

Alfred Eisenstaedt/Time Life Pictures/Getty Images

altered hexachlorobenzene's properties. Accidental spills and improper storage near a well were other ways the fungicide entered the water supply. The survey estimated that detectable hexachlorobenzene was in 470 community water supply wells, half of 1 percent of the national total, but the imprecision of the survey meant the number could be as low as 61 or as high as 1,630. In animals, hexachlorobenzene damaged ovaries, the skin, and the liver; reduced fetal weight; and harmed the nervous system. It was also a carcinogen in laboratory tests and probably in humans as well.

The Clean Water Fund, an environmental lobby established in 1978, took the EPA to task. The survey had tested each well only once, so it failed to detect changes over time, usage, and geology. It was a snapshot that did not capture seasonal variations. And the survey commingled samples from high- and low-likelihood wells, undercounting the severity of the contamination in high-impact areas, which in some states ranged from 30 to 60 percent of wells.

The Clean Water Fund report cited EPA calculations that at least 6 million U.S. drinking water wells had detectable nitrate levels, with 250,000 having nitrates above Safe Drinking Water Act levels. Nine of the seventeen detected pesticides were known or suspected carcinogens, three caused birth defects, and five caused reproductive difficulties. When pesticides and pesticide degradates enter the drinking water, they combine with the chlorine and other disinfectants used to kill dangerous bacteria and form by-products that are linked with birth defects and miscarriages. Six thousand city wells had measurable levels of Dacthal, a herbicide used on lawns. Over 440,000 wells (4.2 percent) had at least one pesticide, and three-fourths of those (3.2 percent) had at least two. EPA regulation of the lawn care industry was minimal.

Enforcement of Regulations

Enforcement of the Clean Water Act and other legislation was variable. The Bill Clinton administration enforced the antipollution laws more vigorously than did the George W. Bush administration. During Bush's first term, prosecutions fell 30 percent for all pollution violations and 28 percent for water pollution violations. Specifically, there were seventy-three pesticide violations in the first Clinton administration, but these declined to forty-three in Clinton's second term and to twenty-six in the first Bush administration.

In March 2006, the U.S. Geological Survey (USGS) released a ten-year survey, *Pesticides in the Nation's Streams and Ground Water, 1992–2001*. The USGS study revealed, again, that many of the pesticides used in the United States were linked to cancer, neurological disorders, birth defects, and environmental damage. Application of a billion pounds of pesticides on fields, parks, gardens, and lawns inevitably generated runoff into the waterways. Ninety-six percent of all fish and 100 percent of surface water and 33 percent of aquifers in studies of major rivers and streams had discernible levels of one or more pesticides, and drinking water supplies were also contaminated with detectable pesticides. The environmental advocacy groups Beyond Pesticides and Clean Water Action called for stronger government policy and reduced pesticide use.

In November 2006, the EPA announced that it was allowing nonpermit application of pesticides over or near bodies of water. EPA claimed the move would increase public health by allowing for more effective elimination of pests and that environmental safeguards were sufficient. However, Senator Jim Jeffords (I-VT) said that the exemption would increase toxic pollution of lakes and streams, and Beyond Pesticides contended the move violated CWA limits on the maximum allowed levels of contamination.

Environmentalists sued to stop the exemption of pesticides from the CWA's National Pollution Discharge Elimination System. The EPA specifically exempted from National Pollution Discharge Elimination System's permit requirement the application of pesticides directly to water for pest control and application to control pests near or over water. The EPA decision was based on the Federal Insecticide, Fungicide, and Rodenticide Act (FIFRA), which deals with registration and application of pesticides but does not deal with water quality or aquatic ecosystems, covered by CWA. Some environmentalists questioned whether the FIFRA precautions adequately protected the public because many of the chemicals lacked toxicity and impact assessments. Also, FIFRA does not address combinations of chemicals or toxic drift, common to aerial spraying. Deb Self, the executive director of the environmental organization Baykeeper, said that the congressional mandate to the EPA to regulate pesticide pollution was unambiguous and the Bush interpretation constituted blatant disregard of that intent. Other environmental groups joined Baykeeper in filing suit against the government: they included Californians for Alternatives to Toxics, California Sportfishing Protection Alliance, National Center for Conservation Science and Policy, Oregon Wild, and Saint John's Organic Farm.

With litigation pending, the EPA in 2007 issued a final rule (71 Fed. Reg. 68483) exempting pesticides applied in accord with FIFRA rules. The rule reversed thirty years of water protection policy. Beginning in 1977, pesticide labels had to have a notice indicating they could not be discharged into water (lake, stream, pond, or public waters) without a CWA permit. The new EPA rule allowed aerial spraying of forests above streams without the permit.

The EPA informed Congress July 2008 that the Supreme Court was making enforcement of the Clean Water Act more difficult after *Rapanos v. United States,* a 4-1-4 decision in 2006 dealing with federal protection of U.S. waters, including wetlands, under the CWA. In the nine months after *Rapanos,* the EPA stopped enforcing over 300 cases. The Bush administration's position before Congress was that *Rapanos* and the 2001 *Solid Waste Agency of Northern Cook County v. U.S. Army Corps of Engineers* decision had created ambiguity.

Pesticide discharge rules were consistent with the Bush administration's interpretation of the Clean Water Act. Bush also disregarded CWA in allowing discharge of ballast water and transbasin water transfers. Each time the Bush EPA was challenged in court, it lost. The U.S. Court of Appeals for the Sixth Circuit ruled that the CWA language was not ambiguous and did not mean what the Bush EPA said it did. Environmental and public interest groups that challenged the pesticide redefinition included the Western Environmental Law Center, Waterkeeper Alliance, National Environmental Law Center, and Pace Environmental Litigation Clinic.

In July 2008, the EPA lowered the statistical value of a human life by $1 million. Environmentalists immediately contended that the lower value was to rationalize looser rules, because required cost-benefit studies would have a lower threshold for determining that any new regulation would not be cost-effective when lives saved were weighed against implementation costs. The EPA denied the claims, contending that the new figure more accurately reflected the money that American consumers were willing to spend on protection.

In January 2009, the Sixth Circuit Court of Appeals ruled that pesticides were pollutants covered by the CWA. Agricultural interests anticipated that an appeal to the

Supreme Court would follow. Agriculturalists for a long time have sought exemption from CWA's permitting process and other pesticide regulation, preferring regulation by an agricultural agency to regulation by an environmental one. Environmentalists have drawn attention in recent years to agricultural practices, particularly regarding pesticides, by suing. One especially notable instance was the lawsuit dealing with the impact of pesticides on endangered species–listed salmon; that suit tightened agricultural rules when the Supreme Court upheld the Ninth Circuit Court of Appeals's ban on spraying in a buffer area along salmon streams.

On January 7, 2009, the Sixth Circuit Court of Appeals vacated the EPA's rule that allowed use of pesticides over or near waters without a permit and required permits for all pesticides, biological or chemical, that were used on, over, or near water. The Department of Justice chose on April 9, 2009, not to ask for a rehearing, but it did request a stay until April 9, 2011, to allow the EPA to create a permitting process. The EPA also wanted the time in order to educate applicators, including governments, farmers, foresters, and the Coast Guard. Neither the EPA nor state agriculture departments had the resources to issue the thousands of permits the decision would require.

Although the EPA chose not to seek a rehearing, several agricultural organizations contended that the court had ignored the CWA definition of a "point source" and wanted the full circuit to rehear the three-judge panel's ruling. The court had to decide whether to rehear, issue a stay, or let the decision stand, with an appeal to the Supreme Court the only other step.

—John H. Barnhill

See also: *Clean Water Act of 1972; Environmental Protection Agency, United States; Safe Drinking Water Act of 1974;* Solid Waste Agency of Northern Cook County v. United States Army Corps of Engineers et al. *(2001)*

BIBLIOGRAPHY

Daniel, Pete. *Toxic Drift: Pesticides and Health in the Post–World War II South.* Baton Rouge: Louisiana State University Press, 2007.

Eilperin, Juliet. "EPA Enforcement Is Faulted: Agency Official Cites Narrow Reading of Clean Water Act." *Washington Post,* July 8, 2008.

EPA (U.S. Environmental Protection Agency). *National Pesticide Survey: Summary Results of EPA's National Survey of Pesticides in Drinking Water Wells* (EPA Number 570990NPS5). Washington, DC: U.S. Environmental Protection Agency, 1990. Available at http://yosemite.epa.gov/water/owrccatalog.nsf/.

Flashinski, Roger. "Pesticide Applications and the Clean Water Act: Is a Permit Required?" *Wisconsin Crop Manager* (blog of the Integrated Pest and Crop Management, University of Wisconsin), April 22, 2009. http://ipcm.wisc.edu/WCMNews/tabid/53/EntryId/698/Pesticide-Applications-and-the-Clean-Water-Act-Is-a-Permit-Required.aspx.

Grace, Francie. "EPA Relaxes Rules on Pesticides; Permits No Longer Needed to Use Chemicals Near Bodies of Water." *CBS News,* November 22, 2006. http://www.cbsnews.com/stories/2006/11/22/tech/main2204941.shtml.

Meyer, Jilanne. "Environmental Protection Agency (EPA) National Pesticide Survey Results, November 1990." Report for Clean Water Fund. http://www.jillhoffmann.com/EPAPEST_SVY.pdf.

Pace, Felice. "Will Pesticide Applications Require a Clean Water Permit?" *High Country News,* February 23, 2009. Available at http://www.hcn.org/blogs/goat/will-pesticide-applications-require-a-clean-water.

Wallace, Robert B., Neal Kohatsu, Ross Brownson, Arnold J. Schecter, F. Douglas Scutchfield, and Stephanie Zaza, eds. *Maxcy-Rosenau-Last Public Health and Preventive Medicine.* 15th ed. New York: McGraw-Hill Medical, 2007.

Phosphorous in Lakes and Rivers

The element phosphorous is an essential nutrient for both plant and animal life. Because of its reactivity, in nature it is rarely found in its elemental form. In the aquatic environment, it is usually found either as the soluble inorganic phosphate ion ($PO4^{-3}$) or as atoms of phosphorous in organic molecules.

The polyatomic phosphate ion, also known as orthophosphate, is found in fertilizers, phosphoric acid, and a number of industrial chemicals. Although they are often biological in origin, polymeric polyphosphates are considered another form of inorganic phosphorous. They consist of orthophosphates with energy-rich covalent bonds linking the phosphorous and oxygen atoms. They are a strong complexing agent (i.e., they easily form compounds with other substances in solution), which makes them useful as corrosion inhibitors and detergent additives. Once released into the environment, most forms of phosphorous are eventually oxidized to orthophosphates.

In animals, phosphorus is required for the development of strong teeth and bones, protein synthesis, and the metabolism of fats and carbohydrates. Phosphorous is used in ATP (adenosine triphosphate), the body's energy-storage molecule, and in cell membranes. The recommended dietary intake of phosphorous varies with age: 100 mg/day for infants, 1,250 mg/day for children 9–18 years old, and 700 mg/day for adults. In plants, phosphorous plays a role in respiration, photosynthesis, and cell growth.

Effects of Phosphorous in Water

At the present time, the U.S. Environmental Protection Agency (EPA) does not regulate the concentration of phosphorous in drinking water. In humans, excessive exposure can alter the body's balance of calcium and phosphates. This can result in bone decalcification, increase activity of the parathyroid gland, and complicate certain kidney diseases. Because phosphorous is a critical plant macronutrient, the primary environmental effect of phosphorous is to fertilize the excessive growth of algae and other aquatic plants, leading to

Phosphates in detergents have historically been a significant source of phosphorous pollution in the United States. While a nationwide ban has never been successfully enacted, local governments have stepped in to provide their own regulations. Here, supermarket customers in Spokane, Washington, examine phosphate-free dishwasher detergents. Since 2008 Spokane county has banned the use of detergents containing phosphates.

AP Photo/Young Kwak

eutrophication of rivers and lakes. In a typical alga, there is 1 phosphorous atom for every 106 carbon atoms and 16 nitrogen atoms. Since carbon and nitrogen are usually abundant in freshwater, phosphorous is the limiting nutrient. Concentrations as low as 20 to 30 parts per billion (ppb) are sufficient to promote eutrophication. By 1978, it was recognized that the key to controlling algae growth in freshwater was to control the available phosphorous.

In oceans and estuaries, carbon and phosphorous are abundant, and nitrogen becomes the limiting nutrient. Exceptions to this rule are linked to excessive pollution from domestic wastewater or agricultural runoff. Another important exception is found on the west coast of the United States where the atmospheric deposition of nitrogen is limited.

Sources of Phosphorous

Minor sources of phosphorous in surface water include the weathering of phosphate-containing rock, atmospheric deposition, and the release of industrial or food wastes containing phosphoric acid. The major anthropogenic sources of phosphorous in freshwater are agricultural runoff, detergents, and sewage discharge. Phosphate-based

fertilizers first came into use after 1842 when English agricultural chemists discovered that treating bones with sulfuric acid created "superphosphates," or P_2O_5, a readily soluble form of phosphorous that was immediately available to plants. Eventually, apatites and other phosphate-containing rocks became the basis of most commercial fertilizer production. Phosphate fertilizers promote early root formation and growth. As plants mature, phosphorous is essential for the growth of fruiting bodies and seeds. It has also been linked to improved resistance to root disease as well as increased cold tolerance. However, the greatest limitation of phosphate fertilizers is that they can bind to soil particles and become unavailable to plants. This process is governed largely by pH and the mineral content of the soil and varies widely by geographic area. In general, the greatest amounts of available phosphorous will be found in soils in the pH range of 6 to 7. The potential for phosphorous loss is greater in lands that have been overfertilized.

For many years, it was assumed that phosphorous migration between the soil and surface waters was minimal. By 1978, however, it had been determined that 88 percent of phosphorous entering the environment came from non–point sources, including cropland, rangelands, and pastures. Since the 1980s, it has become obvious that agricultural runoff is a major source of non–point phosphorous pollution. The EPA's 2000 *National Water Quality Inventory* reported that agricultural non–point source pollution was the leading cause of water quality impairments to rivers and lakes and the second leading cause of impairments to wetlands. There are two mechanisms by which phosphorous is lost from agricultural land. Where erosion carries large quantities of soil into waterways, between 60 and 80 percent of the phosphorous in the runoff will be bound to the particles. Where surface runoff contains few or no soil particles, the runoff will contain primarily dissolved phosphorous.

Another agricultural operation identified as a major source of phosphorous is concentrated animal-feeding operations, or simply feedlots. Rainwater and melting snow running over manure piles can carry phosphorous into surface water. The Coastal Zone Act Reauthorization Amendments of 1990 (CZARA) define economically achievable control measures intended to reduce pollution of coastal waters. Among the measures states will incorporate into coastal non–point source pollution control programs are those addressing nutrient pollution from farms and animal-feeding operations. The goal is to achieve maximum pollutant reduction by employing the best available non–point source pollution control practices. By the end of the first decade of the twenty-first century, several states had implemented nutrient management plans for agricultural runoff.

Historically, the use of phosphates in detergents has been a major source of nutrient pollution. Beginning in the 1950s and 1960s, sodium phosphate was used as a "builder" in household detergents. Both polyphosphates and orthophosphates were also used as detergent additives. In 1972, the median organic phosphate concentration in detergents was 42 percent; concentrations ranged from a low of less than 1 percent to a high of 74 percent. High-phosphate detergents (41% to 50%) had about a 71 percent market share. Eutrophication from phosphates was first recognized as a serious problem during the 1960s. In 1970, the federal government released a laboratory study of the amounts of phosphate present in well-known detergents so that consumers would have a general idea of which brands might cause the most environmental harm.

In the early 1970s, an estimated 50 percent of the phosphates in domestic wastewater came from detergents. At the time, scientific opinion on the environmental damage caused by phosphate detergents was not unanimous, but several states did ban them. The 1972 U.S.-Canadian Water Quality Agreement specified that the effluent from domestic wastewater treatment plants discharging into the Great Lakes and their tributaries would be limited to 1 part per million (ppm). A federal ban on phosphate detergents was briefly considered but never enacted. Throughout the 1970s, the phosphate content of domestic wastewater gradually declined, in large part due to decreased use of phosphates in detergents. But in areas where a ban was not in effect, approximately 35 percent of the phosphorus in domestic wastewater came from phosphate-containing detergents.

By 1978, domestic wastewater from treatment plants and leaking septic tanks had been identified as another major source of phosphates in lakes and rivers. A properly functioning septic system is an efficient way to remove phosphorous. But a family of only 2.5 members with an improperly percolating septic system could release up to 1,100 mg of phosphorous annually for each square meter of leach field. In sewage treatment plants, phosphorous can be removed from water by precipitation with iron or aluminum salts or with lime. The process has the added benefit of removing many other contaminants that can contribute to a high biological oxygen demand (BOD).

Chemical Composition

In any type of water, the total phosphorous concentration is the sum of the dissolved, organic, and particulate forms. Because only the soluble orthophosphate form is capable of fertilizing aquatic plants, the total concentration does not necessarily represent the potential for algal growth. If sediment particles are present, the orthophosphate concentration may decrease as they bind the particles and settle out of the water column. In most water bodies, biologically available phosphorus is roughly equal to the orthophosphate concentration plus 0.2 times the difference between the total phosphorus and the orthophosphates. Depending on the chemical conditions, it is possible for bound orthophosphates to be released from bottom sediments and enter the water column. The rate of release increases with pH. Bacterial decay of the sedimentary detritus will alter the concentrations of organic phosphates, and this also plays a role in the release of orthophosphates.

The most common chemical method of phosphorous determination is the reaction of orthophosphates with ammonium molybdate and antimony potassium tartrate in an acid medium. The resulting antimony-phospho-molybdate complex turns blue when reduced by ascorbic acid. The intensity of the blue color is proportional to the concentration of orthophosphates. A variation of this method uses the reaction between the molybdate complex and malachite green in an acidic medium to form a green color. This reaction is often used in automated phosphate analyzers.

Ion chromatography is also widely used for the determination of orthophosphate concentration in water. The sample preparation steps determine the type of phosphorous that is measured in a chemical analysis. Passing the water sample through a 0.45-micron filter will remove all of the particulate phosphates. If the filtrate is tested without additional treatment, only the orthophosphate concentration will be determined. The result is usually reported as "dissolved reactive phosphorus." Persulfate digestion of the filtrate before analysis will convert the organic phosphorus to orthophosphate. The result is usually reported as "total dissolved phosphorus." If the filtrate is treated with sulfuric acid prior to analysis the polyphosphates will be converted to orthophosphates and the results are usually reported as "dissolved acid-hydrolyzable phosphorus."

For the determination of total phosphorus, the process of analysis is identical except that the sample is not filtered prior to analysis. In this situation, the untreated sample is tested for "total reactive phosphorus." The result for the acid-hydrolyzed sample is reported as "total acid-hydrolyzable phosphorus," and the result for the digested sample is reported as "total phosphorus." By adding and subtracting the various results, it is possible to determine parameters including "total organic phosphorus," "total suspended phosphorus," "suspended reactive phosphorus," and "suspended organic phosphorus."

—Kevin Olsen

See also: *Agriculture; Aquaculture; Fertilizers*

BIBLIOGRAPHY

Booman, Keith A., and Richard I. Sedlak. "Phosphate Detergents: A Closer Look." *Journal (Water Pollution Control Federation)* 58, no. 12 (1986): 1092–1100.

EPA (U.S. Environmental Protection Agency). *Guidance Specifying Management Measures for Sources of Nonpoint Pollution in Coastal Waters* (EPA-840-B-92-002). Washington, DC: EPA, 1993. Available at http://www.epa.gov/owow/NPS/MMGI/.

EPA (U.S. Environmental Protection Agency). *U.S. EPA Fact Sheet: Orthophosphate, Drinking Water, and Public Health.* Washington, DC: EPA, 2004.

Fisher, Lawrence H., and Tamara M. Wood. *Effect of Water-Column pH on Sediment-Phosphorus Release Rates in Upper Klamath Lake, Oregon, 2001* (Water Resources Investigations Report 03-4271). Portland, OR: U.S. Geological Survey, 2004. Available at http://pubs.usgs.gov/wri/wri034271/pdf/wri034271.pdf.

Henion, Karl E. "The Effect of Ecologically Relevant Information on Detergent Sales." *Journal of Marketing Research* 9, no. 1 (1972): 10–14.

Lee, G. Fred, Walter Rast, and R. Anne Jones. "Eutrophication of Water Bodies: Insights for an Age-Old Problem." *Environmental Science and Technology* 12, no. 8 (1978): 900–908.

Merrington, Graham, Linton Windner, Robert Parkinson, and Mark Redman. *Agricultural Pollution: Environmental Problems and Practical Solutions.* London: Spon Press, 2002.

Sharpley, Andrew. *Lesson 34: Agricultural Phosphorus Management; Protecting Production and Water Quality.* Ames, IA: MidWest Plan Service, 2006. Available at http://www.extension.org/mediawiki/files/0/05/LES_34.pdf.

Sharpley, A. N., T. Daniel, T. Sims, J. Lemunyon, R. Stevens, and R. Parry. *Agricultural Phosphorus and Eutrophication.* 2nd ed. Washington, DC: U.S. Department of Agriculture, 2003. Available at http://www.ars.usda.gov/is/np/Phos&Eutro2/phos&eutrointro2ed.htm.

Welch, E. B. (with T. Lindell). *Ecological Effects of Wastewater: Applied Limnology and Pollutant Effects.* 2nd ed. London: E & FN Spon, 1992.

Population Trends and Water Demand

In 1840, before the beginning of large-scale immigration to the West, there was a strong causal link between precipitation and population density in the United States—people lived where it rained. By 1990, this relationship had been broken (Beeson et al. 2001). People moved from wet places to dry places (e.g., from the Midwest to the Southwest) because massive projects made it possible to live somewhere dry and consume water from somewhere wet. Although some claim that water followed the people, it is more accurate to argue that people followed the water. This causal pattern is problematic because water is priced below cost, which subsidizes population growth and sprawl to unsustainable levels.

Water as a Necessary Condition for Settlement

People cannot live without water, but the presence of water does not mean that people will live nearby. Put differently, water is necessary but not sufficient for human settlement. This observation matches a stylized view of history. The earliest human settlements were next to lakes and rivers. As these settlements grew and demand for water exceeded local supplies, water was imported from elsewhere. Eventually, growth would end or slow—either because it was too expensive to bring more water or because other factors (e.g., limited land area) began to bind.

Throughout history, civilizations that depended on water for prosperity and growth (e.g., Rome, Egypt, Angkor) have overextended and crashed when water supplies fell short of demand (Diamond 2005). Is the United States on that path?

Early settlements in the eastern United States had abundant water, so cities grew in different places for different reasons. When people moved west, water scarcity played a larger role in their settlement decisions. Settlement patterns began to change when technology and political will facilitated large-scale water projects.

In 1900, the populations of San Francisco and Los Angeles counties were, respectively, 340,000 and 170,000. In 1990—after many years of importing water to Los Angeles—they were 750,000 and 8.8 million (Forstall 1995a). The case in Nevada is similarly striking: in 1900, water-rich Washoe County (where Reno is located) had a population of 6,000 while arid Clark County (where Las Vegas lies) had so few people that it was included in Lincoln County, where the population was 3,000. By 1990, Washoe had 250,000 people, but Clark had grown to 750,000 (Forstall 1995b). Today, after the growth of Las Vegas into a modern metropolis and tourist destination, not to mention the large-scale development of water resources such as the construction of Hoover Dam, over 2 million people live in Clark County.

Early water importation projects were large but simple. The Los Angeles (1913) and Hetch Hetchy (1934) aqueducts used gravity to move water hundreds of miles from the Sierra Nevada mountains to southern and northern California, respectively. Later projects pumped water between basins over greater distances. The Colorado River Aqueduct (1942) and California Aqueduct of the State Water Project (1971) brought water to southern California from the Colorado River and northern California, respectively. Recent projects to desalinate brackish water and seawater and recycle wastewater have much higher energy, environmental, and monetary costs. Although some claim that these technologies can meet demand "forever," others worry that their environmental impacts and energy consumption are unsustainable.

Urban versus Agricultural Water

To know whether the American West—and the rest of the United States—is on an unsustainable path, one needs to understand water management in the western part of the country. Over 130 years ago, Powell et al. (1879) noted that water in the arid Southwest was concentrated in rivers fed by seasonal snowmelt. Although some areas had groundwater, other areas were far from any water. The 1902 Reclamation Act sought to change this situation. It established and tasked the Bureau of Reclamation with reclaiming land for settlement and farming. (The U.S. Army Corps of Engineers—founded in 1802—did similar work.) Reclamation changed landscape and population patterns, but it also resulted in environmental costs that have grown more controversial (Reisner 1993).

Large-scale irrigated agriculture is now common throughout the Southwest, and farmers control most water rights. As urban and environmental demand has grown, the tension between "highest and best use" of available water and existing property rights has increased. Although some say that "water flows towards money" (i.e., cities), money loses power when it conflicts with traditional farming or environmental values. Others contend that the public trust doctrine justifies forcible reallocation of water from agricultural to urban or environmental uses, but this view contradicts established property rights. The bottom line is that negotiations over water are slow, contentious, and disorganized—whether they take place in bureaucracies, legislatures, courts, or markets.

Although it is clear that water's "value in use" is greater in urban than in agricultural areas, it is not clear whether urban demand per acre is greater than agricultural demand. Using 2004 data, I calculated water demand per acre for two cities in Southern California—wealthy Beverly Hills (average assessed value of $4.2 million/acre) and poor Compton (average assessed value of $0.4 million/acre). Beverly Hills uses an average of 4.4 acre-feet (af) of water per acre; Compton uses 1.5 af/acre. With agricultural water use averaging 2.5 to 5.5 af/acre, there is little evidence that water use rises when farms are paved over.

Water and Sprawl

Many antigrowth activists argue that increases in water supply lead to increases in population and sprawl. Water managers facilitate this result by "building ahead of demand." They estimate future demand based on historic growth rates and per capita water use. Then they build infrastructure and secure supplies to meet that demand. This professional norm has created financial or environmental problems in some places (Los Angeles) but continues in others (Las Vegas).

Building ahead of demand drives population increases because large water projects take five to twenty years to bring online, are designed to meet *projected* growth, and are paid for by existing customers. Because expansion creates surplus capacity, extra water is sold at the cost of delivery (existing customers cover the new system's capital costs) to new customers who buy cheap houses on land that previously had no water.

Is their assumption of constant per capita demand wrong? Lifestyle water use (for pools, power showers, lawns, etc.) and settlement in hotter areas are increasing demand, but a growing awareness of conservation is decreasing it.

Does the price of water matter? Current prices are too cheap to affect demand—averaging about $3 per unit of 748 gallons—but water managers have responded to shortages with command-and-control regulations instead of "conservation pricing." Higher prices would lower the quantity of water demanded, but politicians and water managers resist raising them to avoid "hurting the poor." This problem can be avoided by selling some water cheaply—a "human right" allocation of perhaps 75 gallons/capita/day—and then selling additional water at prices high enough to choke demand down to supply. Revenue in excess of costs could be rebated per capita.

A cycle of subsidy and growth drives urban sprawl. To some, building ahead of supply seems natural and efficient, but it is neither if one is concerned about full cost allocation, sustainability, and/or undistorted resettlement decisions.

Politics and Development

Step back a moment from the facts and mechanisms of population growth and sprawl to consider the forces that support it. On the one hand, we have citizens' demand for living in cheap and sunny places. On the other, we have politicians and real estate developers who supply this living space to increase, respectively, their power and profits. All players favor expanding water systems to previously dry areas.

Resources for the Future

Founded in 1952, Resources for the Future (RFF) is a nonprofit and politically independent think tank headquartered in Washington, D.C., that employs more than forty research specialists, most of whom hold advanced degrees. The organization's research interests fall into the areas of climate, energy, transportation, urban areas, human health, and ecology. Its employees utilize the methodologies of the social sciences, with a particular emphasis on economic analysis, for their research. The RFF endeavors to share its research with the general public, academics, policy makers, environmental groups, and business interests around the world so that each respective group of decision makers can make informed choices on issues related to the environment. Much of the research is disseminated by the organization through the Internet and RFF Press. Among its publications are numerous monographs and *Resources Magazine*, which is published quarterly.

—John R. Burch Jr.

BIBLIOGRAPHY

McGann, James G. *Think Tanks and Policy Advice in the United States: Academics, Advisors and Advocates.* New York: Routledge, 2007.
Resources for the Future. http://www.rff.org/Pages/default.aspx.

The movie *Chinatown* (1974) famously portrayed the connections among water, politics, and development in southern California, and its plot is more or less accurate. In reality, William Mulholland oversaw the construction of the Los Angeles Aqueduct from Owens Valley to Los Angeles. The city used the imported water to expand, exchanging water for political control over neighboring cities and areas. The Aqueduct went into service in 1913. In 1915, Los Angeles annexed the mainly agricultural San Fernando Valley and grew by 170 square miles. Between 1910 and 1932, Los Angeles grew from 90 to 450 square miles. Although political opposition to Los Angeles's growth slowed further expansion, a pattern of using water to increase area and population density was set.

This pattern has been repeated in many places—San Diego, Las Vegas, and Phoenix, to name a few. It is popular because it turns financial assets (money for infrastructure) into "liquid" assets ("water") and these, in turn, into political and financial assets (valuable land). The pattern has slowed, however, as financial and environmental costs have increased. In some cases, cities have been forced to stop all development. The California town of Bolinas has refused new water connections since 1971. This policy is famous mostly because it is so rare in the growth culture of the western

United States. At the other extreme is fast-growing Las Vegas, where Pat Mulroy (general manager of the Southern Nevada Water Authority) promotes growth as "inevitable." Vegas residents pay far less per month and per unit than people in other U.S. cities. They also use a lot more water—250 gallons per capita per day (Southern Nevada Water Authority 2009).

Sustainability and Climate Change

Climate change stresses water supplies by increasing the variation of precipitation. Since less reliable supplies require expensive mitigation measures (more dams, bigger reservoirs, etc.), maintaining current supplies is expensive. Some cities are reacting by spending millions of dollars on plants to desalinate brackish water or seawater and/or recycle wastewater, but these plants take years to bring online, do not slow demand growth, and use massive amounts of energy.

Can demand be reduced? The conventional wisdom is that "hardened" demand—demand that is unresponsive to price—cannot be reduced, but timid price increases and lackluster conservation campaigns ("Take a shower with a friend," or "Turn in your neighbor for overwatering") do not really put "hard" to the test. Growing public awareness of decreasing water reliability can perhaps be combined with substantial price restructuring to change expectations of "lifestyle" water use and permanently lower demand. Australia offers a useful example: demand in large Australian cities is down to about 40 gallons per capita per day—about half the amount used in conservation-minded San Francisco.

By definition, sustainable water use can continue indefinitely. With much of the Southwest—and, increasingly, other parts of the country—experiencing shortages, it seems that we have moved away from sustainable water use. A simple solution would bring demand in line with supply, but there does not appear to be very much institutional, professional, or political support for this solution. It seems, indeed, that unsustainable use may continue until crisis forces change.

A Sustainable Future?

Water has affected population and growth patterns throughout history, but growing environmental consciousness and an unstable climate are disrupting these patterns. In the past, politicians directed allocation, engineers built projects, and real estate developers made money. Can these interest groups change their professional habits and institutions and no longer build ahead of demand? Not unless intense outside pressure forces them to think differently, use economic tools, and step off an unsustainable path.

—David Zetland

See also: *Agriculture; Climate Change; Groundwater Recharge and Water Reuse; Urbanization; Urban Rivers*

BIBLIOGRAPHY

Beeson, Patricia E., David N. DeJong, and Werner Troesken. "Population Growth in U.S. Counties, 1840–1990." *Regional Science and Urban Economics* 31, no. 6 (2001): 669–99. Available at http://www.pitt.edu/~dejong/ctygrow.pdf.

Diamond, Jared. *Collapse: How Societies Choose to Fail or Succeed.* New York: Viking, 2005.

Forstall, Richard L. "California Population of Counties by Decennial Census: 1900 to 1990." Washington, DC: U.S. Bureau of the Census, 1995a. Available at http://www.census.gov/population/cencounts/ca190090.txt.

Forstall, Richard L. "Nevada Population of Counties by Decennial Census: 1900 to 1990." Washington, DC: U.S. Bureau of the Census, 1995b. Available at http://www.census.gov/population/cencounts/nv190090.txt.

Powell, John Wesley, Grove Karl Gilbert, Clarence Edward Dutton, Almon Harris Thompson, and Willis Drummond Jr. *Report on the Lands of the Arid Region of the United States with a More Detailed Account of the Lands of Utah.* Washington, DC: Government Printing Office, 1879. Available at http://www.archive.org/details/cu31924032427134/.

Reisner, Marc. *Cadillac Desert: The American West and Its Disappearing Water.* New York: Penguin Books, 1993.

Southern Nevada Water Authority. *Conservation Plan: 2009–2013.* May 2009. http://www.snwa.com/assets/pdf/cons_plan.pdf.

Zetland, David. *Conflict and Cooperation within an Organization: A Case Study of the Metropolitan Water District of Southern California.* Saarbrüken, Germany: VDM Verlag, 2009.

Poverty and Water

The link between water and poverty is found in the lack of access to safe and clean water in poor and minority areas, especially those located near waterways that carry large commercial shipping traffic and near large industrial or commercial agricultural sites. These areas experience higher than usual water and air pollution from industrial activity, higher rates of disease, and a poor quality of life largely because the areas' inhabitants have no political voice and cannot protect themselves. Both in the United States and worldwide, the willingness of government and private commercial interests to take advantage of the poor and minorities to get around restrictions imposed by legislation or treaties has triggered accusations of environmental racism and demands for environmental justice from social and environmental activists.

Awareness of the connections among clean water, quality of life, economics, and race has been slow to develop. Environmentalists in the United States have focused on broader conservation issues such as endangered species, forest preservation, and clean air and water issues. The development of the environmental justice movement began in the 1990s and has become a unifying movement that transcends race, class, gender, age, and geography.

Environmental Equality

The main challenge for environmental justice workers is determining whether the federal regulations—such as the Clean Air Act, the Clean Water Act, and the Superfund—are being applied in all areas and finding out whether they are protecting the entire public rather than just higher-income neighborhoods. Growing evidence from a number of studies suggests that neighborhoods or municipalities where the populations are predominately lower-class or composed of racial/ethnic minorities have been neglected; that violations of antipollution laws and regulations are more likely to occur in these areas; and that decisions by industrial enterprises about where to locate are informed by the prevalence of poverty, economic underdevelopment, and lax state and local regulations.

Beginning in the late 1980s and early 1990s, community activists and environmental researchers began addressing the issue of environmental equity. Equity studies began analyzing the correspondence between the distribution of toxic waste and the racial, ethnic, and/or class makeup of residential areas surrounding manufacturing facilities that are likely polluters. A number of studies have shown that exposure to toxic waste products in the water supply and the air is statistically more likely to occur in poorer areas than in upper-income and white communities and that minorities and lower-class neighborhoods are more often located near industrial facilities that generate toxic waste materials that get into drinking water and the air (Lynch et al. 2004). The evidence produced by this research clearly shows that corporations make decisions about where to locate manufacturing plants and other facilities using racial and class criteria and that state and federal environmental agencies make enforcement decisions based on those same criteria.

The reasons for these decisions become apparent when one examines the differences in the manner in which the federal and state governments enforce water and air pollution laws and the penalties assessed when those laws are violated. Reviews of cases the Environmental Protection Agency (EPA) brought into civil court between 1985 and 1991 found that the government performed poorly in protecting racially and economically underprivileged areas. The average fines were much lower for companies operating in minority and low-income locations than for those in white and high-income areas. The evidence suggests these differences are due less to factors such as the seriousness of the violations, the number of past violations, the inspection history of the facility in question, or public health issues and more to the political, social, and economic importance of the constituencies involved. When extra-legal political issues begin to outweigh the legal, health, and scientific issues, the entire process is compromised.

Empirical evidence has revealed political and social variables in enforcement at the state and local government levels. States and counties conduct fewer enforcement actions in poorer counties. Generally (with some notable exceptions), Democratic governors who have large constituencies among minority and lower-class voters tend to be more vigorous in undertaking protective measures in poorer areas than their more business-oriented Republican counterparts. To gain permission to build their facilities, corporations locating in poorer areas, and the state agencies that permit them to do so, argue that they are providing jobs and economic benefits to those areas. The promise of jobs, however, is rarely fulfilled, except for low-skilled and low-wage positions. Companies rarely hire among their neighbors for higher-paying and higher-status jobs.

These same priorities are reflected on the national level. Corporations took advantage of the more permissive atmosphere of the Reagan and Bush administrations to locate in areas where they operate without fear of punishment. The Democratic administration of President Bill Clinton proved more responsive to growing protests from local environmental justice groups. In 1994, President Clinton issued Executive Order 12898 to ensure that low-income and minority communities were not disproportionately affected by air and water pollution.

A number of cases were to test the Clinton administration's sincerity. Most prominent among them was the Shintech episode in Saint James Parish, Louisiana, on the lower Mississippi River corridor. This case provides an example of how politics, economics, race, and class have affected the moral and physical health of a poor community and how these conditions triggered a wave of environmental activism.

Industrial Waste and Citizen Activism

The lower Mississippi corridor between Baton Rouge and New Orleans is the site of one of the heaviest concentrations of industrial waste dump sites in the United States. Conditions there have deteriorated badly over the last twenty-five years as companies, drawn by lax regulations and low taxes, have located there. The area has a high unemployment rate, with close to half of its residents living below the poverty line. The Mississippi River (which is the main source of the area's drinking water except for those residents who can afford bottled water) is so polluted that the fish are no longer safe to eat, and the cancer rate is so high among the inhabitants that environmental groups began referring to it as "cancer alley."

It was in this setting that the Shintech Corporation, a Japanese-owned company that manufactures plastics, proposed to build the world's largest polyvinyl chloride plastics production facility near the town of Convent in Saint James Parish, Louisiana. The community already had six operating chemical plants and an iron mill, all of which were dumping toxic substances into the Mississippi River. For years, Convent residents had complained bitterly about the slow poisoning of their water and air, but to no avail.

The Shintech proposal was the last straw. Tired of being ignored, vocal Convent residents formed Saint James Citizens for Jobs and the Environment, which sought by legal means to stop construction of the Shintech plant. A number of environmental groups, led by Greenpeace and the Tulane University Environmental Law Clinic, stepped in to aid the Convent group. In April 1997, they filed an administrative complaint under Title V of the Clean Air Act. They demanded that the EPA object to the air permits that the state of Louisiana had granted to Shintech. In addition, the Tulane Clinic filed a complaint under the 1964 Civil Rights Act, which bars discrimination by entities receiving federal funds. The EPA launched an investigation of these complaints, but before it could announce its findings, Shintech announced that it had cancelled its plans to build a plant in Convent and decided instead to move the site twenty-five miles upriver.

The Shintech episode was one of the first times a corporate polluter had been stopped due to citizen activism, organization, and grassroots mobilization as well as the support of the Clinton administration. Ironically, it did not constitute a legal victory. Because Shintech decided to relocate, the lawsuit never went to trial. Although this case represented a victory for the environmental justice movement, such victories have been rare. The battle against Shintech highlighted the powerful links between state government and industry. This affair, along with other incidents growing out of unfettered industrial development in Louisiana and other southern states, reflects the indifference of state government and industry to the interests of its poor and minority citizens located close to vital water arteries.

Other examples point to a continuing pattern of neglect of water and air safety in poor and minority areas. Residents of Camden, New Jersey, have struggled against environmental racism for years with little to show for it. County and state officials have allowed waste facilities and heavy industry to locate in Camden's low-income minority areas with little provision for protecting the inhabitants from hazardous substances generated by these facilities.

Conditions have been particularly bad in the Waterfront South area near the Delaware River, one of the most polluted waterways in the United States. In the spring of 2002, residents learned that their drinking water supply had been contaminated for more than twenty years from sewage treatment facilities and had since become a toxic waste Superfund site. In addition to pursuing toxic tort litigation, community activists initiated a campaign to inform the public, initiate a study of the site's impact on community health, and monitor cleanup. In 2002, a proposal to dispose of radioactive wastewater by discharging it into Camden's sewage system triggered intense public opposition. The issue brought together suburban and city environmentalists. Public outrage prompted state and county officials to reconsider the plan.

These cases, while showing what organized community and environmental activism can do, also pointed up limitations in the structure of the environmental laws and weaknesses in the state and federal government agencies charged with enforcing them. The central lesson in the Convent and Camden episodes is that government agencies seldom undertake actions against violators of air and water pollution laws and the threats they pose to public health and quality of life unless pressured to do so from the communities being affected.

Presidential Action

Most important is the attitude of the current presidential administration. The political tone set by the president is key to creating an atmosphere in which community action can succeed. President Clinton's Executive Order 12898 created a setting that encouraged action by community and environmental activists. When Republican George W. Bush took office in January 2001, it soon became clear that his administration would favor business and industry. The new administration drastically reduced EPA enforcement activities. A number of rulings from Bush administration officials permitted businesses to use cost-benefit analyses to justify not taking the measures they would have needed to take under the interpretation of officials in the Clinton administration to comply with the provisions of the Clean Water Act. The EPA's Criminal Investigation Division was reduced to fewer than 200 investigators (Browner 2009). Actions to protect poor communities from industrial pollution faltered, and efforts to enforce Executive Order 12898 virtually disappeared. In March 2004, the EPA's own Office of the Inspector General issued a report blasting the agency for failing to implement Executive Order 12898; for not establishing goals, expectations, and performance standards; and for not integrating environmental justice standards into its daily activities.

Since taking office in January 2009, the Democratic administration of President Barack Obama has shown itself willing to redress the balance in favor of low-income communities threatened by water pollution. It is pushing to strengthen regulations under the Clean Water Act and for passage of the Clean Water Restoration Act of 2009, which reaffirms federal jurisdiction over all waterways and strengthens the federal government's authority to regulate pollutant discharges. How far the new administration will go in regulating industry and industrial pollution in the midst of a severe recession remains to be seen.

—Walter F. Bell

See also: *Clean Water Act of 1972; Clean Water Restoration Act of 2009*

BIBLIOGRAPHY

Bacor, A. Hunter. "Environmental Pollution Control, State Government Regulation of." In *Encyclopedia of Public Administration and Public Policy,* edited by Jack Rabin. New York: Marcel Dekker, 2003.

Browner, Carol M. "Environmental Protection Agency: Restoring Scientific Integrity, Sound Regulation, Fair Enforcement, and Transparency." In *Change for America: A Progressive Blueprint for the 44th President,* edited by Mark Green and Michelle Jolin, 360–75. New York: Basic Books, 2009.

Bullard, Robert D., ed. *The Quest for Environmental Justice: Human Rights and the Politics of Pollution.* San Francisco: Sierra Club Books, 2005.

Konisky, David M. "Inequities in Enforcement? Environmental Justice and Government Performance." *Journal of Policy Analysis and Management* 28, no. 1 (2009): 102–21.

Lynch, Michael J., Paul B. Stretesky, and Ronald G. Burns. "Slippery Business: Race, Class, and Legal Determinants of Penalties Against Petroleum Refineries." *Journal of Black Studies* 34, no. 3 (2004): 421–40.

Prior Appropriation

The water rights doctrine of prior appropriation, best summed up in the expression "First in time, first in right," was first developed when Americans began moving from the eastern states, where rainfall is plentiful, to the regions west of the 100th meridian, where rainfall is much more scarce. Essentially, prior appropriation prioritizes water users based not on geography, but on the timing of their first beneficial use of the water. The earlier the claim, the higher-priority the right. In practical terms, this meant that in years of heavy rainfall, many users might make claims on waterways and make beneficial use of the waters. But, in years when rainfall was scarce, later claimants lost all of their water so that earlier claimants' full claims could be fulfilled. As opposed to riparian rights, where all the landowners along watercourses have the right to use the water, unimpaired in quality and quantity, the prior appropriation doctrine places the idea of "beneficial use" at the center.

In the East, this was not a consideration, as enough rain fell to provide for the needs of farmers without the necessity of large waterworks. However, farmers further west needed to move, store, and otherwise manipulate water in order to get it to the places where it could be used the most productively. Given that water is scarce, those who can demonstrate first that they are putting the water to productive use are entitled to as much water as they need, and those with junior rights are entitled to whatever is left. Although eastern water law was primarily riparian in nature, conflicts between mill owners over the right to use water to power their mills resulted in some of the first applications of what would become known as the doctrine of prior appropriation (Pisani 1996). However, it would be almost unheard of before Americans began to flock to the West starting in the middle of the nineteenth century. Once there, the profit motive would lead many settlers to see water as a means to success and power and water rights as only worth the yield one could generate from them (Hundley 2001). On both social and political levels, water in the West became the key to power in the region.

Prior Appropriation in California and Colorado

Two western states have been at the forefront of defining prior appropriation: California and Colorado. In California, miners from the eastern United States brought the system of riparian rights with them when they emigrated. They soon realized, however, that a system set up for agriculture in a land of plentiful rainfall was not adequate for their new situation. During the Gold Rush, miners, who usually did not own riverfront property, needed large quantities of water in order to process the ore, and the legal structures for regulating water usage had yet to be developed. Miners and farmers developed, on an ad hoc basis, customs relating to water use, which resulted in a system that was based on priority of use but still retained some of the features of a riparian system, including water rights based on property location. Reflecting the same general principles that governed the claiming of an area for mining, the system of prior appropriation received legislative approval in California in 1851 (Hundley 2001).

Conflict between the two seemingly contradictory systems has been inevitable, and each state that has sought to follow California's lead in combining the different types of systems has come to different conclusions as to how much weight to give each type of claim when they do come into conflict. The balance between the two systems is largely based on the relative merit of claims between the appropriator's beneficial use of the water and the riparian right-holder's natural claim to and reasonable use of the watercourses that run through or on the border of the land. In California itself, the state supreme court decided in the 1886 case of *Lux v. Haggin* that where riparian rights were being put to beneficial use, they were superior to appropriative rights. To clarify matters further, if a piece of land with a waterfront is subdivided into a piece with water access and a piece with no water access, the division with no water access loses its riparian right. Later, however, voters passed a law that stated that even where water rights are riparian in nature, the water itself must be put to beneficial use, or else the riparian right can be lost to a nonriparian appropriator (Dzurik 2003). Many other western states, including Oklahoma, Oregon, Kansas, North Dakota, South Dakota, Texas, and Washington, have followed California's model of a mixed water rights system.

In Colorado, no such allowance was made for the system of riparian rights with which recent immigrants from the

East might have been familiar. The slogan "First in time, first in right," found its purest expression in that state, where prior appropriation was and is the law. Although various territorial statutes recognized some riparian rights in 1861 and 1862, by the time Colorado became a state in 1876, prior appropriation had completely surpassed riparian law in common use and became the water law of the new state. Only six years later, the case of *Coffin v. Left Hand Ditch Co.* completely did away with any remaining riparian rights in the state. Alaska, Arizona, Colorado, Idaho, Montana, Nevada, New Mexico, and Utah have all chosen the Colorado system as their sole water rights law.

In 1866, Congress approved the system of prior appropriation as a way of managing the use of water for mining, agriculture, manufacturing, and all other purposes on all public lands in the United States. In so doing, Congress not only approved the practice already in place in the West, where the vast majority of public lands are located, but also abdicated its authority over control of the waters of the West, setting up a similar system as would come to dominate the areas of mining rights and grazing rights (Hundley 2001). Water became a right that no longer had anything at all to do with owning land along a waterway. The relationship between the land and the water was replaced with the ideas of physical control of the water and putting it to beneficial use. Unlike a riparian claim, which is permanent and goes along with landownership, the appropriative model asserts that one must continually put the water to beneficial use or risk losing one's position in the water rights hierarchy to the next oldest claim.

Implementing Prior Appropriation

The four keys to the implementation of a system of prior appropriation are the ideas of intent, diversion, beneficial use, and priority dates (Hutchins 2004). The first step, demonstrating intent, means that the claimant must show that he or she intends to use the water by preparing for its diversion and beneficial use. Usually, this means, along with the posting of notice or application for a permit, the construction of whatever hydraulic works are necessary to divert the water and the construction or preparation of the site where the water will be put to use. The next step, the construction or designation of a point of diversion, usually happens with the digging of ditches, laying of pipe, or instituting other means of moving the water from the watercourse to the point of use.

The first two elements are necessary to make a prior appropriation claim. The third element, putting the water to beneficial use, is necessary both to make a claim and to maintain the claim. Employing the water that the claimant has appropriated and continuing to do so in perpetuity is the key to the entire system—and its reason for existence. In the West, water is so scarce that not putting it to beneficial use was, in the minds of settlers, a waste of a precious resource. It is beneficial use that determines the size of the water right that can be claimed, and if the beneficial use ceases, so does the right. The definition of "beneficial use" has varied widely over time and between states. Agriculture has often received a priority position in defining the term, although other industrial uses and, more recently, environmental considerations may also weigh into a determination of which uses are most beneficial.

The final, defining characteristic of a prior appropriation claim is the priority date of each claim. This is how the hierarchy of water rights claims is set and maintained. The senior appropriator, with the earliest priority date, has the right to use as much water as that claim states that the appropriator can put to beneficial use. The next senior claimant has second position, and so on down the line. If there is not enough water to fulfill all of the claims, a common occurrence in a land with cyclical droughts, junior claimants cannot fulfill their claims until all claimants who are senior to them have filled their claims. If senior appropriators wish to take their full share of the watercourse, they may place a call on the river, which would cut off water from the most junior claimants until the senior claimants' needs are satisfied.

Rules governing a prior appropriation system vary, but there are some commonalities. Senior appropriators may not make changes to their claim (in terms of how they use the water or from where the water is diverted) that harm a junior appropriator's claim without the junior claimant's approval. Many different types of users—individuals; corporations; federal, state, and local government bodies; and, importantly, Indian nations—can make competing claims, and all, in theory, have equal rights to the water. Indian nations can sometimes make Winters claims, which carry a priority date of "time immemorial," meaning that they are automatically the highest-priority claimant. Although they do not depend on land ownership, appropriative claims are usually transferrable and can be sold or traded, as long as the water right claimed by the buyer is the same as that of the prior owner and will not harm any other water claimant.

States can make laws defining the term of nonuse that constitutes abandonment of the appropriative right. Usually notice is given to the appropriator, and a fair amount of time is allowed for the appropriator to resume beneficial use before the water right is lost. However, if an appropriative water right is abandoned, the claimant loses his or her place in the hierarchy of users, dropping from the most senior to the most junior claimant.

—Steven L. Danver

See also: Lux v. Haggin *(California, 1886); Mining and Water Resources; Riparian Rights;* Winters v. United States *(1908)*

BIBLIOGRAPHY

Dzurik, Andrew A. *Water Resources Planning.* 3rd ed. Lanham, MD: Rowman & Littlefield, 2003.

Hundley, Norris, Jr. *The Great Thirst: Californians and Water—A History.* Revised ed. Berkeley: University of California Press, 2001.

Hutchins, Wells A. *Water Rights Laws in the Nineteen Western States.* Clark, NJ: Lawbook Exchange, 2004.

Pisani, Donald J. *Water, Land, and Law in the West: The Limits of Public Policy, 1850–1920.* Lawrence: University Press of Kansas, 1996.

Tarlock, A. Dan. *Law of Water Rights and Resources.* New York: C. Boardman, 1988.

Wilkinson, Charles F. *Crossing the Next Meridian: Land, Water, and the Future of the West.* Washington, DC: Island Press, 1992.

Worster, Donald. *Rivers of Empire: Water, Aridity, and the Growth of the American West.* New York: Oxford University Press, 1985.

Priority Date

See *Prior Appropriation*

Privatization of Water Services

Privatization of water services in the United States can take a variety of forms. According to the National Research Council's Committee on Water Privatization, outsourcing, the most common form, can mean that a public utility contracts with private providers for services and supplies, such as laboratory work, meter reading, chemicals, or plant operation and maintenance. Other forms of privatization include the "DBO" or contract for a private company to "design, build, and operate" water service facilities. Finally, public water utilities may be sold to private companies, though this is relatively rare in the United States.

In the nineteenth century, many water services—including the provision of water for drinking, household, and other uses, as well as sewage services—were provided by private companies. Over the course of the late nineteenth and twentieth centuries, municipalities of all sizes generally took public control of these services. In the 1990s, privatization of water services again appealed to some water consumers and local governments.

An Environmental Protection Agency (EPA) study that dealt with drinking water (not sewage systems) found that, in 2000, 49 percent of "community water systems" were publicly owned (that is, owned by towns, cities, or other local governments). The other 51 percent were privately owned—of these, 27 percent were for-profit businesses and 34 percent were nonprofit entities. The remaining 39 percent of these privately owned water systems were what the EPA calls "ancillary systems"—small systems "whose primary business is not water supply but who provide water as an integral part of their principal business," such as campgrounds for recreational vehicles. Most privately owned systems, whether they were for-profit, nonprofit, or ancillary, served smaller populations. Therefore, though the number of water systems in the United States was about evenly split between public and private ownership as of the year 2000, most water customers were served by publicly owned systems. The study found differences between publicly and privately owned water systems, such as the fact that privately owned systems' total expenditures on water treatment were only 16 percent whereas public systems' expenditures were 23 percent of their respective budgets; however, it also concluded that these differences "may be due to scale, rather than ownership, since most small systems are privately owned" (EPA 2000, Vol. I, 10).

History of Privatization of Water Services in the United States

As Americans urbanized during the nineteenth century, they needed systems to provide clean, safe water and sewage systems. Generally, the latter tended to be public and municipally organized, whereas the water supply systems were owned and run by private companies. Boston, New York, and Philadelphia are notable examples of cities that grew rapidly in the late eighteenth and early nineteenth centuries, creating a demand for waterworks, a demand that was filled by private companies. Of the eighty-three water services systems in the United States in 1850, fifty were privately owned (National Research Council 2002).

By the last decade of the nineteenth century, however, more and more cities turned to public waterworks. In 1897, for example, forty-one of the fifty largest cities in the

United States had public water systems. Cities could operate public systems at a loss and make up that loss via taxes. This enabled public systems to charge about 40 percent less than private companies. Locals often were dissatisfied not only by private companies' high rates but also by the low quality of water provided. Increased understanding that water could spread diseases like typhoid and cholera convinced citizens and city leaders that the need for clean water was a matter of public health. Meanwhile, as urbanization intensified, new laws allowed municipalities to raise funds, purchase property, and operate waterworks and other public services. City leaders and boosters promoted municipal waterworks as a way to ensure continual growth and cleanliness (Melosi 2008). By 1900, slightly more than half of the 3,000 water systems in the United States were publicly owned (National Research Council 2002).

After World War I, legislative changes exempted interest payments on municipal bonds from federal income taxes, meaning that cities could issue bonds to raise money for public works like water systems at low interest rates (National Research Council 2002). The Progressive Era emphasis on efficiency, experts, and equity also helped spur the shift away from private to public waterworks. State-level regulation of waterworks, metering of water usage, new measures of water purity, and new methods of water filtration and chlorination accompanied the shift to public water systems (Melosi 2008). From the Progressive Era through World War II, wastewater systems were developed mainly to collect and dispose of waste, while water supply services usually focused on providing water through reservoirs and other methods and treating that water (National Research Council 2002).

In the decades after the Second World War, a variety of factors combined to make the provision of water services increasingly expensive. These included social and geographical trends, along with regulatory and legal developments. The last half of the twentieth century saw a major demographic shift as Americans moved away from older, industrial cities and into the so-called Sun Belt region; this period was also marked by the explosive growth of suburbs and the so-called "urban crisis." Suburbanization necessitated the construction of new water service infrastructure, which sometimes came at the cost of maintaining older, urban infrastructure (Melosi 2008).

Meanwhile, Rachel Carson's famous exposé of the presence of chemicals in drinking water, *Silent Spring* (1962), led to the Safe Drinking Water Act (1974). This law made more sophisticated testing of drinking water purity mandatory for water supply systems. The 1972 Clean Water Act likewise required secondary treatment of all wastewater treatment plants. These developments improved water quality, but they also made both water supply and wastewater systems more expensive. Maintaining water infrastructures, some of which had originally been developed over a century previously and then added onto haphazardly, also proved more and more expensive as the twentieth century wore on. Modernizing and updating the water infrastructure in the United States today would cost billions of dollars (Arnold 2004).

As water services became more expensive to maintain, two somewhat disparate trends in public opinion made these services more expensive while simultaneously limiting the funding available to them. On the one hand, water consumers and, hence, legislators, became more vocal in their demands for high-quality and environmentally sound water systems. On the other hand, the last several decades have also been marked by increasing concern about government spending at all levels—city, state, and federal. In other words, public water services have become more expensive over the last half century, while raising water and sewage rates, or taxes, to cover the cost of providing those services has been politically unpopular (National Research Council 2002).

This combination has made privatization seem attractive to many municipalities. In addition, Internal Revenue Service tax code changes in 1997 made private waterworks more viable. The late 1990s saw Atlanta, Indianapolis, Milwaukee, and Seattle contract out water services (National Research Council 2002). Privatization was particularly predominant in Texas and Puerto Rico. Seventy U.S. cities contracted with private entities to operate and maintain water supply or wastewater systems in the years 1997 to 2000 alone (Arnold 2004).

Indianapolis, where the water utility was privately owned since 1881, condemned the utility in 2000. The city then publicly owned the utility but contracted its operations out to a different private firm. In 2003, the city of Atlanta resumed control of its water system after a four-year experiment with privatization. Citizens and local politicians were concerned about rate increases and poor service, including several "boil orders" that the private company, United Water, had to issue (Arnold 2004). One city councilor commented, "My inner conservative no longer worships at the alter [sic] of privatization as I might once have done. That is for sure" (Koller 2003). In the early 2000s, New Orleans; Elizabeth, New Jersey; and Stockton and Orange County, California, all entered prolonged public debates about whether or not their water systems should be privatized (Arnold 2004).

A Global Perspective

Water services in France have mainly been privatized, with significant government subsidization of infrastructure development, since the late nineteenth century. In Thatcher-era Great Britain, regional water authorities were privatized. World Bank and United Nations policies, in addition to the potential for profit which draws private investment, have encouraged privatization of water services in poor countries. Such programs have made significant inroads, especially in the last two decades. However they are highly controversial, as is perhaps best illustrated with the events in Cochabamba, Bolivia. In 1999, Bolivia passed a law that allowed privatization of water services. The corporation International Water raised water rates significantly, leading to protests that made news worldwide (Shiva 2002).

The Debate over Privatization

Privatization of water services, both in the United States and abroad, is controversial. Proponents argue that, in poor countries, where the availability of clean drinking water and effective sewer systems is a matter of life and death, private water systems are often the *only* water systems. Frederik Segerfeldt (writing mostly about privatization abroad) contends that the profit motive and the motivation to provide efficient services due to outside competition, combined with management expertise, also give private companies an advantage over public providers. Public companies, furthermore, are at the whim of local politics—the unpopularity of raising rates often means serious delays in infrastructure maintenance, for example (Zetland 2009).

Advocates for publicly owned and operated water services, on the other hand, argue that the privatization of water services commoditizes a natural resource that should be managed communally. The profit motive, they argue, is incompatible with the public good. Private water companies usually have contractual monopolies in municipalities; consumers do not have the choice to use an alternate water service provider. Maintaining and providing water services is a very expensive endeavor, and if a private company does not have the financial wherewithal to do so, its failure can harm consumers. For example, Enron Corporation created a private water corporation, Azurix, in 1999, which failed only months before Enron's infamous collapse (Arnold 2004).

The debate about the privatization of water continues. Advantages and disadvantages of privatization are context-specific; what works for one municipality may not work for another. The availability of clean, safe drinking water and sanitation services remains crucial at a time when more and more Americans are becoming aware of the finite nature of this precious resource.

—Denise Holladay Damico

See also: *Environmental Protection Agency, United States; Owens Valley; Safe Drinking Water Act of 1974; Sewage; Wastewater Treatment*

BIBLIOGRAPHY

Arnold, Craig Anthony. *Privatization of Public Water Services: The States' Role in Ensuring Public Accountability.* Madison, WI: State Environmental Resource Center, 2004. Reprinted in *Pepperdine Law Review* 32 (2005): 561–604. Available at http://inthepublic interest.org/sites/default/files/Privatizing%20Public%20Water_ Anthony.pdf.
EPA (U.S. Environmental Protection Agency). *Community Water System Survey 2000* (EPA-815-R-02-005A/B). 2 vols. Washington, DC: EPA, Office of Water, 2002. Available at http://water.epa.gov/aboutow/ogwdw/cwssvr.cfm.
Koller, Frank. "No Silver Bullet: Water Privatization in Atlanta, Georgia—A Cautionary Tale." *CBC Radio,* February 5, 2003. Available at http://www.cbc.ca/news/features/water/atlanta.html.
Melosi, Martin V. *The Sanitary City: Environmental Services in Urban America from Colonial Times to the Present.* Abridged ed. Pittsburgh, PA: University of Pittsburgh Press, 2008.
National Research Council, Committee on Privatization of Water Services in the United States. *Privatization of Water Services in the United States: An Assessment of Issues and Experience.* Washington, DC: National Academy Press, 2002.
Shiva, Vandana. *Water Wars: Privatization, Pollution, and Profit.* Cambridge, MA: South End Press, 2002.
Zetland, David. Review of *Water for Sale: How Business and the Market Can Resolve the World's Water Crisis,* by Frederik Segerfeldt. *H-Water, H-Net Reviews,* June 2009. Available at http://www.h-net.org/reviews/showrev.php?id=24474.

Pueblo Water Doctrine

The pueblo water doctrine derives from the Spanish colonial *Plan de Pitic* and states that a Spanish *pueblo,* or town, has the right to use all the water flowing through its borders in order to meet the present and future needs of pueblo residents. This doctrine came about through the California State Supreme Court, but it has been contested and denied in New Mexico and Texas.

Plan de Pitic and Spanish Law

While Spanish and Mexican laws discussed pueblo rights, the pueblo rights did not include exclusive rights to water. Phillip II of Spain in 1573 set out detailed ordinances concerning the founding of new towns, presidios, and missions in New Spain. These instructions included sections regulating the assignment of land and water to settlers and to the pueblo as an entire community. These laws in turn drew on the older *Las Siete Partidas* of King Alfonso X "*el Sabio.*" Their rationale was equitable distribution of resources so that in times of shortage, no community or individual bore the brunt of the lack of water. Phillip's ruling was later clarified to stipulate that when locating a new pueblo, the residents should secure water first for their pueblo and then for themselves and for later settlers.

Pitic, in modern Hermasillo State, Mexico, was established in 1783, and its founding documents served as the model for all later Spanish pueblos in the *Provincias Internas.* The *Plan de Pitic,* officially recorded in 1789, states that the *pueblo de Pitic* has the right to use water from a stream flowing through it for the benefit of its residents and can act as a corporate body in regulating maintenance, distribution, and disposal of any excess waters. It also names officers, who are to oversee distribution of irrigation waters on the lands of pueblo residents outside the pueblo itself. The pueblo, although it had priority in time over other users of the stream in question, did not have exclusive right to the waters flowing through it.

Spanish water laws, and the Mexican laws that followed, concentrated on community use of water resources and on "sharing the shortage," as the historian Malcolm Ebright puts it (Ebright 2006). Springs and wells belonged to the person who owned the land around them and could be used without limit and without special permission. However, they could not be used maliciously (deliberately drying up a neighbor's well, for example), and if people had customarily used the spring before the land was granted to an individual, the new owner could not block their access. Riparian waters for domestic use, irrigation, and stock watering were assigned to individuals and communities, but that assignment did not grant exclusive use of the water. In other words, in a drought, upstream water users had to accept less water so that downstream users would at least have water for household use or for meeting the needs of livestock. In a similar manner, seniority of right did not guarantee exclusive use of a stream, especially when there was a shortage.

The needs of the greater community overrode the needs of the individual, with the limitation that the individual could not be completely deprived of his or her allotted water. This can be called the doctrine of need: greater need can override pure priority of a water right. Spanish law, in this regard, is very different from English common law and the later American water laws.

California and the Pueblo Water Doctrine

Pueblo water doctrine in California derived from riparian rights and an incorrect interpretation of the *Plan de Pitic.*

The pueblo water doctrine in U.S. law derives from a notation made in the 1886 California case *Lux v. Haggin* (69 Cal. 255) as later confirmed by *Vernon Irrigation Co. v. Los Angeles* (106 Cal. 237) in 1895. The *Lux v. Haggin* case dealt primarily with rights of downstream riparian users of the Kern River versus the rights of an upstream irrigator who had diverted water such that the riparian users suffered losses. However, in the course of the ruling, the court noted that "each pueblo was a quasi public corporation having a right . . . to the use of the waters of the stream on which it was situated" and may even have had a prior right to those waters.

The pueblo of Los Angeles, founded in 1781, claimed use of the Los Angeles River. In the 1881 case *Feliz v. Los Angeles* (58 Cal. 73), the court agreed that the town did have rights to the stream even though it had not filed a formal appropriation. According to the ruling in *Vernon Irrigation Co. v. Los Angeles,* the city not only had exclusive rights to the water running through it but also had the right to any waters that it needed to grow (i.e., streams that would come into the city limits as the city expanded in the future). This right overrode prior appropriations made by irrigators or other river users, according to the court's understanding of the *Plan de Pitic.* The California State Supreme Court upheld this decision, and the pueblo right was later granted to San Diego as well.

The flaws in this understanding of Spanish legal intent became evident when the city of San Fernando challenged

Acequia

An acequia is a community-operated network of man-made ditches used for irrigation. They work by first diverting water from a river or stream. The water is then channeled into a canal that has branches running off to irrigate individual plots of land. Any remaining waters are funneled back into the river or stream that served as the original source. The acequia networks that once abounded throughout the Southwest began with the irrigation systems created by the region's native peoples. When the Spaniards arrived, they modified the existing system using technologies that were brought to Spain by the Moors. Today, functioning acequias can be found primarily in the states of Colorado and New Mexico.

An acequia is more than just a network of irrigation ditches; it also shapes the culture of the people who depend on it. It binds a community together through the leadership of the person elected to serve as *mayordomo.* It allows agriculturalists not only to grow the food they depend on but also the produce that they market to others. Acequias help shape the surrounding landscape, as they provide the water for flora and fauna to thrive in areas that would otherwise be arid desert.

—John R. Burch Jr.

BIBLIOGRAPHY

Crawford, Stanley. *Mayordomo: Chronicle of an Acequia in Northern New Mexico.* Albuquerque: University of New Mexico Press, 1988.

Rivera, José A. *Acequia Culture: Water, Land, and Community in the Southwest.* Albuquerque: University of New Mexico Press, 1998.

Rodríguez, Sylvia. *Acequia: Water Sharing, Sanctity, and Place.* Santa Fe, NM: School for Advanced Research Press, 2006.

Los Angeles over rights to the watershed in 1955. The California Supreme Court, in deciding *City of Los Angeles v. City of San Fernando* (14 Cal. 3rd 199) in 1975, found that the original creation of the pueblo water doctrine had been in error in that the Spanish law did not allow the pueblo to claim all waters in the watershed of the stream nor to have exclusive use of them. However, the court upheld the earlier ruling on *stare decisis* and on precedent (Tyler 1990).

New Mexico and Pueblo Rights

New Mexican court decisions until 2004 upheld the pueblo water right based on California's precedent and not on New Mexican antecedents. New Mexican courts grappled with the pueblo right throughout the twentieth century. Early attempts by the towns of Tulorosa and Santa Fe to make use of the pueblo rights doctrine were struck down. Tulorosa was founded after 1848, so the doctrine did not apply (*State v. Tulorosa Community Ditch* [1914]). A later court felt that

Santa Fe was not a land grant and so not a pueblo, declaring in its 1937 ruling that "we have found neither decision nor text suggesting that a mere colony of 'squatters' could acquire under Spanish law this extraordinary power over the waters of an entirely non-navigable stream known as 'pueblo right'" (*New Mexico Products Co. v. New Mexico Power Co.* 42 N.M. 31; quoted in Hutchins 1974).

However, in 1958 the state supreme court ruled in *Cartwright v. Public Service Co. of New Mexico* (66 NM 64) that Las Vegas was indeed a pueblo, that it had priority over other users, and thus was entitled to full use of the Gallinas River in part because there were no earlier users. The last argument proved to be in error, as the dissenting Justice Frederick pointed out at the time. Based on this reading, which drew from California precedents and not from New Mexican Spanish laws and decisions, the city of Albuquerque challenged the New Mexico state engineer when he tried to restrict the city's use of four water wells. The courts decided in 1963 that the pueblo of Albuquerque had pueblo water rights based on its descent from the Pueblo de Albuquerque y San Francisco Xavier and that these overrode the state engineer's restrictions on groundwater permits within the pueblo borders (Hutchins 1974).

The Decline of Pueblo Rights

Subsequent legal decisions in Texas and New Mexico have repudiated or greatly restricted the application of the pueblo water doctrine. The city of Laredo claimed rights to the Middle Rio Grande based on the pueblo right. In deciding *In re Contests of the City of Laredo* (1984; 675 S.W. 2d 257), the Texas court maintained that "the law of New Spain did not expressly create a municipal water right in the nature of the pueblo water right" (Tyler 1990). New Mexican interpretations of the pueblo water doctrine returned to the court in the 1990s through *State ex rel Martinez v. City of Las Vegas* (880 P. 2d 868), and the New Mexico Court of Appeals ruled on July 15, 1994, that Las Vegas was not entitled to have pueblo water rights on the Gallinas because if the *Cartwright* decision came before the state supreme court again, the court would overturn it. Indeed, on further appeal of *State ex rel Martinez* in 2004, the New Mexico State Supreme Court repudiated the pueblo water doctrine, making it highly unlikely that future municipal water claims will use the pueblo rights doctrine. In California, New Mexico, and Texas, there have been and are more reliable methods a city can use to acquire water rights, even if—like

Los Angeles, San Fernando, San Antonio, or Albuquerque—the city was once a Spanish or Mexican pueblo.

—Margaret A. Bickers

See also: Lux v. Haggin *(California, 1886)*

BIBLIOGRAPHY

343 P.2d 654 (1958). 66 N.M. 64. L. J. CARTWRIGHT et al., Plaintiffs-Appellants, v. PUBLIC SERVICE COMPANY OF NEW MEXICO, a New Mexico Corporation, Defendant-Appellee.

89 P.3d 47 (2004); 135 N.M. 375; 2004-NMSC-009; STATE of New Mexico, ex rel. Eluid L. MARTINEZ, State Engineer, Plaintiff-Respondent, v. CITY OF LAS VEGAS, Defendant-Petitioner.

Ebright, Malcolm. "Whiskey Is for Drinking, Water Is for Fighting: Water Allocation to Territorial New Mexico." *New Mexico Historical Review* 81, no. 3 (2006): 299–336.

Hutchins, Wells A. *Water Rights Laws in the 19 Western States.* Vol. 2. Washington, DC: U.S. Government Printing Office, 1974. Available at http://content.lib.utah.edu/cdm4/document.php?CISOROOT=/wwdl_books&CISOPTR=10065&REC=4.

Meyers, Michael C. *Water in the Hispanic Southwest: A Social and Legal History, 1550–1850.* Tucson: University of Arizona Press, 1984.

Tyler, Daniel. *The Mythical Pueblo Rights Doctrine: Water Administration in Hispanic New Mexico.* El Paso: Texas Western Press, 1990.

Reasonable Use Doctrine

The doctrine of reasonable use, or the "American rule," represents one of the most problematic aspects of water law. Water law's intended purpose is to determine the best use for the advancement of societal needs and values and to protect all members of the community. The court's responsibility is to maintain a level playing field for all interests in society. When the many doctrines and theologies making up riparian rights come into conflict, regulation of surface water, groundwater, and percolating water is required to mediate among various stakeholders.

The nation has deemed water to be a publicly owned commodity, so the property right is not absolute. Possession is subject to regulation. Ownership is divided among multiple interests: federal and state agencies, businesses, and individuals. Government regulation may not correspond to the needs of the community and the region. Several examples show how different geographic conditions and the availability of water control alter riparian use regulation. The 1821 New Jersey state court case *Arnold v. Mundy* is illustrative when it states that "the wisdom of that law has placed it in the hands of the sovereign power, to be held, protected, and regulated for the common use and benefit (*Arnold v. Mundy,* 6 NJL 1 [NJ, 1821]).

In adjudicating cases using the reasonable use doctrine, the courts, the umpires and referees of our legal system, must consider a multitude of factors in weighing all parties' interests. Location, benefits, damage, competing interests, and possibly social values work with the police powers of all jurisdictions to attempt to apply the law for the best interests of all. The concept of "reasonable use" stems from the legal illusion of the reasonable person. This legal standard originated for issues whose application was best served by allowing ordinary reasonable people in the community to resolve the matter, whatever the subject. In most instances, its use results in jury litigation designed to reflect the views and attitudes of community justice, the common law.

This doctrine is plagued by the jurisdiction of application, time period under consideration, and the subjectivity of the law. The term *reasonable* is sufficiently vague and subjective that its use may allow all parties the latitude of self-service to disguise objectivity and minimize communal needs. One caveat: *Reasonable use* does not include malice within its definition. Should malice and/or ulterior motives be the cause for interrupting riparian rights, the court will view the situation adversely.

Legal and Historical Precedents

The fact that the western United States is a land of cyclical drought has given the reasonable use doctrine a new currency. Some in California have noted that the state must now begin considering California's water shortage as a way of life, and as such, California's constitution allows her citizens the use of "reasonable" amounts of water. However, the many competing interests desirous of water for their respective needs or purposes call into question the effectiveness of the reasonable use doctrine (Smith 2010). Also problematic is the fact that there is really no set definition of *reasonable use*. *Black's Law Dictionary* offers no objective standards, as *reasonable* is defined as "fair, proper, just, moderate, and suitable under the circumstances" (Black et al. 1990, 1265). Unfortunately, the dictionary does not offer any aid in interpreting the meaning of the aforementioned terms. The legal option subjects litigants to either a court or jury trial; anyone involved in litigation understands the vagaries of the process. Referring to riparian rights, *Black's Law Dictionary* states, "A riparian owner may make reasonable use of *his* (emphasis added) water for either natural or artificial wants. He may not so use his rights as to affect the quality or quantity available to a lower riparian owner" (*Tucker v. Bodoian*, 376 Mass. 9078, 384 NE2d. 1195; Black et al. 1990, 1266).

History provides the precedent for the evolution of the usage theory. Concern about water grew as the United States expanded westward, from the lush forests of the east coast to the arid West. The first laws, applicable in England, had been transported to the New World. Old Bailey's adherence to the common law meant that a landowner had absolute control over his or her water sources and could alter land drainage patterns as desired. Those having problems downstream had to resolve the matter by agreement, if possible.

The old English common doctrine of the common enemy legitimatized absolute control. The landowner could alter drainage without taking into account the rights of neighbors. France, a nonprimogeniture state and an adherent to the civil law code, took a different position. Since French law allowed for the division and redivision of land parcels, the country had to deal with an increasing number of small landowners. These owners had to accept water naturally flowing from above but could not modify or increase water flow downward. The proposition was to allow the natural flow of water as it traveled to lower levels.

However, water flows from many sources, which may affect its reasonable use. Water comes to the surface unimpeded and is available to the party claiming the water (i.e., the landowner). Percolating and subterranean water moves beneath the surface without any channel and is available to a property owner. The property owner may impound the rain, snow, and floodwaters gathered this way. Surplus water is available to whoever naturally acquires it on his or her property. Surface water running underground creates problems for the ownership of that water. Whose water is it? Underground reservoirs may be created by rainfall, and natural springs may tap into artificial wells used for commercial and governmental purposes. When the underwater stream causes damage to business, government, and private interests, how can one segregate the source of the damages?

In deciding whether the reasonable use standard is applicable, there are several yardsticks to be considered. Depending upon jurisdiction, there are reasonable limitations even if they cause damage to the adjacent landowner. Consider, did a reasonable need exist for the property owner to alter the drainage to make use of his or her lands? Was the alteration done in a reasonable manner in order to minimize its impact? Was this use objectively beneficial? If it were not, the rights of the person affected would not be outweighed, and the diversion might be considered unreasonable interference with the use of the land and the natural flow of the water. These are general standards, and their application is not uniformly applied due to geography, climate, economic necessity, etc.

The reasonable use doctrine has been adopted in various forms in twenty-one states. This rule allows owners of property to make "reasonable" alterations to draining, subject to not interfering with their neighbor's water rights unnecessarily. The conundrum of reasonable use can only result in litigation due to the impossibility of moving beyond subjective standards.

Recognition and Acceptance

All fifty states are legally empowered to define and determine application of riparian rights reflecting the needs of their citizens. This often results in interstate conflict, and federal authorities may have to help resolve the issue. For example, Georgia and Tennessee dispute the use of water from the Chattanooga River. Western states have had continued conflict over the use of the Colorado River. Southern California, being highly populated and arid, defines the reasonable use theory as being reflective of the state's needs. Its courts charge that the appropriation of water is limited to the public trust doctrine, a descendant of common law, which declares most riparian rights a public trust for the population in general.

The "reasonable use" theory is not universally accepted in all states. Opposing views and different systems of rights take different forms. The appropriative theory adopted in some western states views water as private property. This doctrine differs from the riparian rights concept, which sees water as a common reserve, and resembles the reasonable use theory. The regulated riparian rights philosophy recognizes the need for public control of water and attempts to regulate this public resource.

In contrast, the absolute dominion doctrine legitimizes a landowner's withdrawal of an unlimited amount of water from whatever sources, regardless of the effect upon a landowner downstream. The correlative rights theory mitigates the dominion doctrine by allowing a landowner to remove only a "reasonable" share in proportion to the amount allocated to that landowner's use. Under this theory, defining and enforcing one's share of distribution is a complicated matter, often destined for the courthouse.

If riparian issues arise that have an interstate application, as in the case of the Colorado River, the federal authorities have the right to preempt states' authority of reasonable use for the benefit of the region or country as a whole. Early in American legal history, the commerce clause was applied to navigable waterways. Federal authority is not absolute, however. The eminent domain doctrine and the Fifth Amendment to the Constitution protect the citizen from a taking of property without cause. If the need exists for the taking of one's property, the federal government is required to pay the fair market value. A jury may determine the fair market value, and noneconomic factors may influence a jury's decision.

In *Keys v. Romley* (1966), 64 Cal 2d. 396, the court decided all landowners have a duty to behave responsibly in defense of their own interests and avoid foreseeable damage to other parties. *Gdowski v. Louis* 84 Cal. App 4, 1395 (2000) states that even if the upper and lower landowners act reasonably, the downstream landowner can collect for damages. Both these cases reinforce an expectation that property owners exercise "reasonable" conduct.

The civil law rule, which may be called the natural flow rule, contradicts the common law rule. Louisiana, whose legal system has been Americanized, still retains civil law jurisdiction descended from the French code. Her laws impose a rule of strict liability for damages caused by landowners who interrupt or alter the natural flow of water. The legal rationale suggests that the best way to solve a riparian problem is to allow the natural flow of water and accept the consequences of excessive water accumulation.

Given interstate conflicts as well as conflicts with Canada, law professors, attorneys, and judges from all fifty states have prepared a volume of the *Restatements of the Law: Property* (sec. 858), published by the American Law Institute. Its memoranda are not legally binding but are highly influential because they reflect the consensus of the American legal community. Its suggestions to resolve problems concerning water include language that "allows one to withdraw and use percolating water and or ground water unless the withdrawal unreasonably harms neighboring lands by lowering the water table or decreasing water pressure; exceeds the landowner's reasonable share of water; or reduces the level of surface lakes, harming users of the lake."

As America's population continues to grow and move further into arid regions, water uses increase. We are increasingly compelled to view water as a limited resource. Out of necessity, the federal government will eventually assume greater control over our water sources and their uses. And because of its subjectivity, the reasonable use doctrine will be one of the first casualties. The *USDA Forest Service Sourcebook of State Groundwater Laws in 2005* (Chapman et al. 2005) discusses the various theories of groundwater use and provides an analysis of each of the fifty states' perspectives on the matter of water use. The document may predict the future.

—Arthur Steinberg

See also: *Government Water Decision Making; Groundwater Recharge and Water Reuse; Population Trends and Water Demand; Water Law*

BIBLIOGRAPHY

Black, Henry Campbell, and Joseph R. Nolan. *Black's Law Dictionary*. 6th ed. St. Paul, MN: West, 1990.

Chapman, Matthew, Stephen Glasser, Jack Gipsman, and Lois Witte. *U.S.D.A. Forest Service Sourcebook of State Groundwater Laws in 2005*. Washington, DC: USDA Forest Service, 2005. Available at http://www.fs.fed.us/biology/resources/pubs/watershed/groundwater/state_gw_laws_2005.pdf.

Doremus, Holly D., and A. Dan Tarlock. *Water War in the Klamath Basin: Macho Law, Combat Biology, and Dirty Politics*. Washington, DC: Island Press, 2008.

Getches, David H. *Water Law in a Nutshell*. St. Paul, MN: West, 1997.

Glennon, Robert. *Unquenchable: America's Water Crisis and What to Do About It*. Washington, DC: Island Press, 2009.

Smith, Fiona. "Dry Times Revive 'Reasonable Use' of Water Doctrine." *San Francisco Daily Journal*, May 9, 2010. Available at http://www.kmtg.com/data/news/news.php?IDD=1181937870.

Wilkinson, Charles, F. *Crossing the Next Meridian: Land, Water, and the Future of the West*. Washington, DC: Island Press, 1992.

Recreational Water Rights

Recreational water rights manage water resources for leisure consumption. Water is fundamental for recreational purposes, serving as an attraction and as a medium for participation. The amount and condition of the water is always an issue, and with the number of demands upon this resource, conflict is inevitable. Demands range from basic needs like drinking, sanitation, and waste disposal to cooling, irrigation, landscaping, and—finally—recreation, including the creation of artificial snow for skiing. The conflicts of interest among these demands may extend beyond the water itself to points of access and ancillary services like boat ramps. There may also be difficulties with the type of water and its suitability for an activity; for example, white water is needed for rafting and waves for surfing. Pollution is another concern that may impact usage, especially with recreation involving bodily contact with the water, like swimming.

Watercourses of all types meet the needs of both active and passive recreational users. Active participation in the water can include boating (sailing, powerboating, rowing, and canoeing), fishing in its different forms, and swimming (including scuba diving, snorkeling, diving, waterskiing, and surfing). Passive activities include sitting on park benches and picnic tables to view the landscape. The impacts of these activities are wide-ranging; their exact effects depend on location and may vary from coastal waters to inland waterways. There is no doubt that with greater numbers of participants in recent years, there has been an increased strain on water resources and their management, and conflict between users has also become more common.

Regulating and Managing Recreational Water Rights

Some intervention in the management of water rights has been necessary. The aim of recreational water rights is both to protect water found in natural sources like streams, rivers, lakes, and ponds and to enhance the enjoyment of it. A balance is often required among the different stakeholders, and this is where rights need clarification. The usage of the water is assessed, as is the ownership of the land bordering the banks of a watercourse. Water rights are then conferred by government agencies and by common law at the state and federal level.

Since the nineteenth century, there have been efforts in countries like Australia, New Zealand, Canada, and the United States to create green spaces in urban environments and preserve special natural places. The origin of national and state parks dates back to this time, when the need for spaces for recreation and tourism was recognized. The natural areas and green spaces that were preserved were predominantly seen as unsuitable for agriculture and industries like mining. Later, recognition of the importance of protecting the environment led to the formation of the International Union for the Conservation of Nature (IUCN) in 1948 and its listing of ten protected area categories. These included national parks to provide recreational opportunities as well as protection of landscapes, ecosystems, and habitats. Much of the development of parks and open natural spaces around the world is owed to the American example, where a desire to protect the wilderness started early in the country's history. The emphasis in the United States has been on protecting the natural environment; the needs of recreational users have been integrated in a limited manner.

As population size grows, the demands on water increase, and the limited supply of this resource becomes more apparent. In the United States, some common-law doctrines were established to resolve competing interests. These recognize that while location is a consideration in determining who has a right to the water, three common practices are required of owners: that they should leave the flow of water as it is, that they should have reasonable use of the watercourse, or that water be appropriated to be used as efficiently and economically as possible.

The ownership of the water and the land running on either side of it may be different. For example, in Colorado, the law protects the rights of boaters to use navigable rivers and streams because the water is not private property, whereas the river banks and beds are. Colorado has seen a substantial increase in the popularity of boating, reflecting a nationwide trend.

Colorado water law acknowledges that a water right exists where there is a diversion from a natural source to benefit the population. This right was developed from earlier custom and practice and led to water being used for agricultural or domestic use. However in 1992, the first recreational water right was decided, allowing a boat chute in Fort Collins, and since then other recreational water rights have been granted. A water right allows the owner to ask for help if the water supply is short, and it offers both protection and recognition that may result in further investment. A hierarchical structure ensures that older, more senior rights take precedence, providing owners with some legal protection if their water flow changes, for example, due to a diversion.

In 2001, the Colorado state legislature made further strides in managing recreational water rights when recreational in-channel diversions (RICD) were introduced. The aim was to promote positive recreational experiences by ensuring the right amount of water was available. Since then, additional regulations have limited the number of days powered craft are able to use some watercourses. A bill passed in 2006 limits water rights in a white-water park or similar recreational water facility if the water level and flow are reduced to 90 percent of normal.

The U.S. Bureau of Land Management saw more kayakers, canoeists, and rafters on the Dolores River, Colorado, in 2008 than ever before. The reason for this increase in activity, it is suggested, is due to the Dolores Water Conservancy District and its arrangement to provide details about the water releases from the McPhee Dam. It committed to updating a Web site twice weekly, stating the forthcoming water releases after getting the information from the U.S. Bureau of Reclamation, which manages the McPhee Dam

and Reservoir. With this information, recreationists can plan ahead to use the river. Moves like this demonstrate the importance of recreation on the water. Further evidence can be found in the case of the Yampa River in Colorado, where an ongoing assessment of the river is looking equally at boating, fishing, and the maintenance of water levels for the river's ecology.

Colorado's population is projected to increase by 2.8 million by 2030. Such population growth will require careful resource management. Public water officials will face challenges as they attempt to match demand and supply, as well as attempting to accommodate any new RICDs.

—Denise Fort

See also: *Government Water Decision Making; Outdoor Recreation; Reasonable Use Doctrine*

BIBLIOGRAPHY

Glyptis, Sue. *Countryside Recreation.* Harlow, UK: Longman, 1991.
Pigram, John J., and John M. Jenkins. *Outdoor Recreation Management.* 2nd ed. New York: Routledge, 2006.

Riparian Ecosystems

Riparian ecosystems are defined and shaped by the fundamental function of rivers and smaller tributary streams: the transport of water and sediments. This function extends well beyond the channel of the stream itself, since a broad area of land drains into the stream and its tributaries. A unique mix of plant and animal life develops in the transitional zone between flowing water and dry land. The term *riparian ecosystems* also applies to the biological mix along the edges of smaller lakes and ponds. Seasonal flow of water is generally moderated by shallow aquifers, which recharge at high flows, moderating flooding, and discharge back into the stream at low flows, prolonging and enhancing the quantity of water available in the rivers. Riparian areas function best with vegetation buffers (sometimes referenced as the "kidneys" of the stream and river ecosystem), which contribute to flood control, remove contaminants, and reduce excess nitrogen.

Riparian landscapes nurture a diversity of vegetation, compared to surrounding land areas, providing enhanced niches for a greater variety of wildlife. In arid grasslands or semidesert regions, river banks may be the primary location of any sizeable concentration of trees. Often, animals find corridors connecting good habitats, passing through less hospitable terrain, by following riparian systems. These corridors can also provide routes for animal movement without crossing farmland or developed residential areas. Riparian woodland is crucial to the habitat available for fish and other aquatic animals: cool, shaded water, with good tree cover, is generally more hospitable for fish and other animal life than water flowing between bare stream banks, open to the sun. This is particularly true in arid or desert regions, such as the Southwest and the Great Plains. A healthy watershed is best achieved with 70 percent forest cover on shorelines and stream banks. Short- and long-term fluctuations in flooding—timing during the year, duration, and volume—are critical to what plant life will survive in any given flood plain. Modification of such cycles can lead to a drastic decline in productivity.

Assessment of Riparian Lands and Waterways

Federal government agencies with jurisdiction for study and restoration of riparian lands and waterways include the Environmental Protection Agency (EPA); several agencies of the Department of Agriculture, including the Natural Resources Conservation Service (NRCS), the U.S. Forest Service (USFS), and the Farm Service Agency's (FSA) Conservation Reserve Program (CRP); the U.S. Army Corps of Engineers; the Interior Department's Fish and Wildlife Service (FWS); the U.S. Geological Survey (USGS); as well as many corresponding state agencies. Draft guidelines prepared jointly by the Forest Service, Agricultural Research Service, and Natural Resources Conservation Service (all in the Department of Agriculture) and by the FWS define three zones of riparian systems. The first consists of woody vegetation that is immediately adjacent to the body of water. The second is a strip of managed forest upslope from the first. Further upslope should be an herbaceous strip, which acts as a primary filter for sediments and chemical pollutants from surrounding lands draining into the stream or lake.

There are four commonly used protocols for assessing the health of a stream and its riparian environment. The simplest is the *Stream Visual Assessment Protocol,* developed by the NRCS. Application of this protocol does not require extensive biological or hydrological training, so it can easily be used by landowners assessing their own property. A more advanced protocol is the NRCS *Water Quality Indicators Guide;* even more comprehensive is the NRCS *Stream Ecological Assessment Field Handbook.* Each state water quality agency has a more

specific and intensive bioassessment protocol adapted to the specific climate, topology, and history of the state. Other stream classification methods in common use are generally referred to by the names of their authors, including Rosgen; Montgomery and Buffington; Grant and Swanson; Beschta and Robison; and Grant, Swanson, and Wolman.

General stream assessments must consider the *ecoregion* in which the stream is located, as well as the drainage area and the gradient of the slope draining into the stream. This method takes into consideration the climate, geology, vegetation, soil, history of land use, wildlife, and hydrology in which the stream exists. The EPA has defined fifteen ecoregions for the North American continent; these are subdivided into fifty-two more detailed Level II ecoregions. (Exact definitions and boundaries of ecoregions remain a matter of study and discussion among many government agencies and among biologists and geologists generally.) A third level subdivides these into 104 ecoregions, 84 of which lie within the United States. States may be even further subdivided; for example, Texas contains fifty-six Level IV ecoregions, such as High Plains, Central Great Plains, Cross Timbers, Chihuahuan Deserts, Blackland Prairies, and Gulf Coastal Plain. Precisely what plant and animal life will thrive along a river varies with the climate and surrounding landscape.

An important feature of any riparian system is a balance of stream power, sediment load, and channel roughness. If a larger volume of water is flowing at greater speed through a stream, it will erode the banks, the stream bed, or both. This can be balanced by greater channel complexity: more bends, fallen trees, roots extending into the water, rocky channels, and pools to divert the water, slow it down, and break up any single powerful current. Increased volume of sediments deposited in the stream bed renders a habitat nearly useless for fish and invertebrates and blocks many sources of nutrition. Sediment also makes the stream shallower and may widen the channel or cause more frequent overflow of the stream banks. Both woody and herbaceous plants along the banks of any stream are essential to control sediment load. Land denuded of grasses, shrubs, and trees is easily eroded, while the absence of riparian plants allows runoff to be dumped directly into river channels. Both stability of a stream and diversity of life in the adjacent ecosystem benefit from structural complexity. Many human uses of streams require the opposite: deep channels facilitate shipping, and channelization to remove loops and bends reduces the number of bridges needed and makes adjacent land more accessible for agriculture, industry, and residential development.

Protection, Restoration, and the Law

One of the more important government programs that aids restoration of riparian habitat is the Partners for Fish and Wildlife Program, focused on the 60 to 70 percent of fish and wildlife habitat located on private land. When the program was provided with expanded funding and recognition by the Partners for Fish and Wildlife Act in 2006 (Pub. L. 109-294, 120 Stat. 1351, 16 U.S.C. 3771–74), Congress estimated that 5,560 miles of riparian habitat had been restored since 1987, as well as 677,000 acres of wetlands. The program grew out of efforts by FWS to restore wild bird habitat in the prairie potholes of the upper Midwest. The distinct partnership program began restoring wetlands and upslope riparian habitat, receiving an initial congressional appropriation of $100,000. The Estuaries and Clean Water Act of 2000 (Pub. L. 106-457, 14 Stat. 1957, 33 U.S.C. 2901) provided funding specifically for the riparian habitats at the points where rivers flow into oceans or into the Great Lakes. Funding for study and restoration of riparian habitat is also provided for in the Reclamation Wastewater and Groundwater Study and Facilities Act of 1992 (Pub. L. 102-575, 106 Stat. 4664, 43 U.S.C. 390[h] et seq.) Among the many amendments proposed in later years, some have authorized, or sought to authorize, restoration of specific riparian habitats.

Some riparian ecosystems are protected by the Wild and Scenic Rivers Act (Pub. L. 90-542, 82 Stat. 906, 16 USC 1271–87), which established the National Wild and Scenic Rivers System and prescribes the methods and standards through which additional rivers may be identified and added to the system. As of June 2009, 203 rivers or portions of rivers had been designated. In every Congress, many bills are introduced that would add additional rivers to the system, but most of these fail to pass. Generally, land within one-quarter mile of the high-water mark, on a designated river, is protected from development. With some exceptions, federal lands in the protected area are unavailable for mining leases. Dams, water conduits, reservoirs, and transmission lines are generally banned along protected portions of any river. But most riparian ecosystems line the banks of streams that are far from wild and may or may not be scenic.

Habitat and Navigable Waters

In 1975, the U.S. Army Corps of Engineers adopted a regulation (40 Fed. Reg. 31320) including "freshwater wetlands" among the "waters of the United States" protected by the Clean Water Act, part of the Federal Water Pollution Control Act Amendments of 1972 (Pub. L. 92-500, 86 Stat. 816). Under Sections 301 and 502 of the act (33 U.S.C. 1311 and 1362), any discharge of dredged or fill materials into "navigable waters"—defined as the "waters of the United States"—is forbidden unless authorized by a permit issued by the Corps of Engineers, pursuant to Section 404 of the act (33 U.S.C. 1344). The Corps did not, for the first three years after passage of the Clean Water Act, include such wetlands in the "waters of the United States."

Although filling wetlands is far from the only hazard to the health and ecological balance of riparian ecosystems, this regulation is an important regulatory tool. In *United States v. Riverside Bayview*, 474 U.S. 121 (1985), the U.S. Supreme Court upheld the authority of the Corps to regulate filling of all freshwater wetlands adjacent to navigable waters, tributaries of navigable waters, and nonnavigable intrastate waters whose use or misuse could affect interstate commerce. A freshwater wetland had been defined in 1975 as an area that is "periodically inundated" and is "normally characterized by the prevalence of vegetation that requires saturated soil conditions for growth and reproduction" (33 CFR 209.120[d][2][h], 1976). In 1977, the requirement that the land be periodically inundated to qualify as a freshwater wetland was removed, providing protection for an expanded portion of riparian lands.

The Supreme Court sustained a federal district court ruling that enjoined Bayview Homes Inc. from placing fill materials on its property near the shores of Lake Saint Clair, Michigan. The U.S. Court of Appeals for the Sixth Circuit had reversed the district court, taking the view that the Corps's authority under the Clean Water Act must be narrowly construed to avoid a taking of private property without just compensation, which would violate the Fifth Amendment. The appeals court held that the property was not within the jurisdiction of the Clean Water Act, because its semiaquatic characteristics were not the result of frequent flooding by the nearby navigable waters. Therefore, the respondent was free to fill the property without obtaining a permit. A unanimous Supreme Court reversed the circuit court, ruling in an opinion by Justice Byron R. White that "the Corps has acted reasonably in interpreting the Act to require permits for the discharge of material into wetlands adjacent to other 'waters of the United States.'"

The Corps's jurisdiction, and that of the EPA, was limited in *Solid Waste Agency of Northern Cook County v. United States Army Corps of Engineers, et al.*, 531 U.S. 159 (2001), often known as SWANCC. In a hotly debated 5–4 decision, the Court ruled that the Clean Water Act did not provide authority over isolated ponds that were not tributary to a navigable waterway. The site at issue in this case was an abandoned sand- and gravel-mining site that had evolved into permanent and seasonal ponds. The solid waste agency sought to use it for disposal of nonhazardous solid waste. A dissent by Justice John Paul Stevens asserted that Congress had plainly intended the Clean Water Act to apply to such isolated waters—but the majority ruled that it could find no such intent in the law. Waters that are generally nonnavigable, are isolated, and lie entirely within a single state are accordingly not subject to the Clean Water Act.

The definition of "waters of the United States" was thrown into further question by the Supreme Court's disposition of *Rapanos v. United States*, 547 U.S. 71 (2006). Four justices would have required that there be a surface connection between any wetlands regulated by the Clean Water Act and some navigable waterway. Two dissenting opinions would have deferred to the judgment of the Corps of Engineers, recognizing that Congress had defined waters quite broadly for purposes of the Clean Water Act. Justice Anthony M. Kennedy, whose concurring opinion therefore decided the case, asserted that the term "navigable waters" is of some importance but that more specific standards could legitimately require a permit to fill wetlands with a "significant nexus" to the ecology of a tributary to a navigable waterway. Legislation introduced in 2007–2009 under titles such as the Clean Water Restoration Act would provide more precise language on congressional intent to restore the jurisdiction stripped away in the *Cook County* and *Rapanos* decisions. Since the Supreme Court was interpreting the scope of an act of Congress, not questioning the constitutional authority of Congress to pass the Clean Water Act, new legislation could restore more expansive authority to protect waters and wetlands.

—Charles Rosenberg

See also: *Clean Water Act of 1972;* Rapanos v. United States *(2006);* Solid Waste Agency of Northern Cook County v. United States Army Corps of Engineers et al. *(2001)*

BIBLIOGRAPHY

American Water Resources Association. *Riparian Ecosystems and Buffers; Working at the Water's Edge.* Proceedings of the American Water Resources Association (AWRA) Summer Specialty Conference, Virginia Beach, VA, June 30–July 2, 2008. Redhook, NY: Curran, 2008.
Brinson, Mark M., B. L. Swift, R. C. Plantico, and J. S. Barclay. *Riparian Ecosystems: Their Ecology and Status* (FWS/OBS-81/17). Kearneysville, WV: U.S. Fish and Wildlife Service, 1981. Available at http://en.scientificcommons.org/2061100/.
Eubanks, Ellen. *Riparian Restoration.* San Dimas, CA: U.S. Department of Agriculture, 2004.
Gore, James A., ed. *The Restoration of Rivers and Streams: Theories and Experience.* Boston: Butterworth, 1985.
Kusler, Jon A., and Mary E. Kentula. *Wetland Creation and Restoration: The Status of the Science.* Washington, DC: Island Press, 1990.
Pace, Michael L., and Peter M. Groffmann. *Successes, Limitations, and Frontiers in Ecosystem Science.* New York: Springer, 1998.
Riley, Ann L. *Restoring Streams in Cities: A Guide for Planners, Policymakers, and Citizens.* Washington, DC: Island Press, 1998.

Riparian Rights

After the initial phase of colonial settlement of the area that is now the United States, when everything tended to be governed by local custom and rule, the system of riparian water rights developed as the first legal means of determining the ownership and extent of water rights in the United States. It worked well in the area east of the 100th meridian, where rainfall is sufficient to allow for intensive agriculture without the construction of large-scale irrigation works. However, the limitations of the system would come into sharp focus as Americans moved ever westward during the nineteenth and twentieth centuries.

Early Water Rights

In the eastern United States, the states have regulated the use of water by a system that came down from English law. The basis of the riparian system of water rights was the idea that those who owned land along a stream also owned a right to the use of the water in that stream. In England, this legal doctrine was created to protect the interests of the landed gentry; it was then transferred to America, where landownership was more widespread. The water right went along with the ownership of the land, and if the land was sold, the water right was sold with it. However, that idea was limited, as the right was not the right of exclusive ownership but merely of the use of the water (i.e., a usufructuary right). Further, the doctrine of "natural flow" asserted that the downstream landowners had the same right to the flow of water and that the flow could not be compromised in terms of quality or quantity by the upstream owner.

As the nation gradually industrialized during the nineteenth century, water became the power that drove American factories, and more and more claimants were seeking to use the same watercourses. For example, in the early nation's largest mill town, Lowell, Massachusetts, extensive means were undertaken to ensure that all mills had fair access to the water. Flow rates were articulated in terms of the horsepower that could be generated by the mills. As a result, riverfront property that had significant changes in elevation became more valuable to mill owners because of the large amount of horsepower that could be generated by harnessing those particular parts of the river (Cech 2010). In addition, the emphasis on industrial use caused the courts gradually to begin to use the economic benefit that might be derived by landowners as a means of determining whose claims might win out in a conflict between landowners. However, the extent to which the varying factors were weighed by the courts was a matter left to the judges in the individual cases, and no set formula was ever devised.

The doctrine of "reasonable use" replaced the idea of "natural flow," creating stipulations on riparian rights that limited this doctrine's applicability to places where rainfall was heavy enough to accommodate all landowners. Of course, this created a system where court adjudication was often necessary to determine what actually constituted reasonable use in a particular place at a particular time. As a result, this system only worked well in places with average to heavy rainfall, where the utilization of water by upstream users did not have a detrimental effect on downstream users.

Tyler v. Wilkinson

The doctrine of riparian rights, along with the idea of reasonable use, gained legal backing in the 1827 Rhode Island Circuit Court decision in the case of *Tyler v. Wilkinson* (4 Mason 397, 24 F. Case 472). This oft-cited case concerned the proper, or beneficial, uses to which water rights gained through a riparian system could be put. The dispute between mill owners over their respective rights to the same river had the result of enshrining the reasonable use doctrine, with the court deciding that all riparian landowners on the same water source had equal rights to the flow of water, despite being positioned either upstream or downstream. Downstream landowners had the right to an unimpeded flow of water, but the courts, recognizing that such a rule would preclude upstream landowners from using the water, also added the reasonable use doctrine, allowing upstream users to consume a reasonable amount of water (Cech 2010). *Tyler v. Wilkinson* did not address, however, whether domestic, or "natural," uses (such as agriculture) should take precedence over "artificial" (or commercial)

uses. The preference given to agriculture grew out of the Jeffersonian ideal of the agrarian republic, in which independent, landowning farmers formed the basis of the American democracy. As this idea transfused water rights, it formed the basic assumption of almost all water rights law in the United States.

Laws in the Eastern United States

In the aftermath of *Tyler v. Wilkinson,* nearly all eastern states developed water law based on the doctrine of riparian rights. Water rights were a very simple matter, to be determined by land ownership, and as such, water rights could not (in theory) be harmed by nonuse. That is to say, a landowner who chose not to make use of the water right that accompanied the land would not lose that water right and could make complete use of it at any time of his or her choosing. Of course, as the old saying goes, possession is nine-tenths of the law, and in practical application the courts consistently favored those landowners who were already making "beneficial use" of the water over those who were not. This doctrine was taken a step further in the idea of "prescription," whereby a landowner not making use of a water right could lose that water right if another person made open use of the water for a period of twenty years. Under prescription, landowners had plenty of time to make use of the water but would lose their rights if they did not. In both the informal agreements and the court proceedings that inevitably occurred as a result of multiple riparian landowners seeking to make use of the same watercourse, the measurement of the flow of the watercourse became an essential part of determining the extent to which each landowner could make use of the water.

There were a number of limits on what landowners could do with the water that they claimed. Water claimed by riparian rights could not be used on lands other than those abutting the watercourse, so landowners could not transport water to other lands they might own to make beneficial use. Similarly, water from a riparian claim could not be stored for future use, as this would artificially diminish the amount available to other claimants. Any use of water that might be deemed to be consumptive in nature, or that diminished the stream flow available to claimants downstream, had to be adjudicated between the claimants. If a parcel of land with a riparian right were subdivided and a resulting parcel did not abut the water source, that subparcel did not have a riparian water right; instead the full right remained with the subparcel(s) abutting the watercourse. Finally, during times of water shortage, riparian claimants were expected to share the shortage equally.

A number of factors might cause a court to override the riparian claims of landowners. The Commerce Clause of the U.S. Constitution gives the federal government the preeminent right to control the navigable waters of the nation. Sometimes this right comes into conflict with the riparian rights of landowners, and in such cases the federal claim is supreme. Also, the Fifth Amendment to the Constitution gives federal, state, and local governments the right to claim land (and the water rights attached to it) through the exercise of eminent domain. However, the eminent domain clause of the Fifth Amendment requires the government making the claim to pay the landowner fair market value for the land, which could increase substantially depending on the extent of water being claimed.

Westward Movement and Water Law

As the riparian rights doctrine moved west, alterations had to be made. Some states that had originally adopted riparian systems found them untenable in a land where rainfall was scarce and seasonal. California and Oklahoma, for example, passed laws during the twentieth century that transferred all unclaimed riparian rights into that state's new system of prior appropriation. Some of these states have blended riparian and prior appropriation systems by converting riparian rights into prior appropriation rights, giving those rights the superior priority date (meaning that they would have the first right over all later water claimants). However, such a transition into a hybrid system means that the landowner must start to make beneficial use of the water right or risk losing it to another claimant. Most western states have gone through this process, and as a result, true riparian water rights systems remain only in eastern states, where rainfall is plentiful and watercourses flow year-round.

—Steven L. Danver

See also: *Reasonable Use Doctrine*

BIBLIOGRAPHY

Cech, Thomas V. *Principles of Water Resources: History, Development, Management, and Policy.* 3rd ed. Hoboken, NJ: John Wiley & Sons, 2010.
Freyfogle, Eric T. "Water Rights and the Common Wealth." *Environmental Law* 26, no. 1 (1996): 27–51.
Scott, Anthony, and Georgina Coustalin. "The Evolution of Water Rights." *Natural Resources Journal* 35, no.4 (1995): 821–979. Available at http://lawlibrary.unm.edu/nrj/35/4/05_scott_evolution.pdf.

Sherk, George William. *Dividing the Waters: The Resolution of Interstate Water Conflicts in the United States.* Cambridge, MA: Kluwer Law International, 2000.
Wilkinson, Charles F. *Crossing the Next Meridian: Land, Water, and the Future of the West.* Washington, DC: Island Press, 1992.

River Transportation

Rivers are vital for their water supply as well as the access they provide for transportation. Early records reveal that rivers have been used for transportation since the earliest times and have been seen as natural corridors through the landscape. In the United States, the history of the nation has been shaped by the economic development that transport on rivers like the Ohio in the Midwest allowed. In most cases, natural rivers have been artificially improved to include landing stages and specially constructed locks to deal with differences in water levels, bypassing waterfalls and rapids. The path of a natural river may also be shortened to speed the route. Navigation depends on the natural river flow and climatic conditions. The viability of the river for transport is based on its width and depth, which determine the size of the boats that can use it.

Water transport is not as fast as other methods, so rivers are more suitable for the transportation of goods that do not perish easily and for supplies that are not required urgently. The type of cargo transported this way includes commodities like coal, petroleum, grain, timber, chemicals, iron, and steel. Rivers that have inland ports and docks where goods can be transferred to road transport are ideal. In America, the wide rivers link inland areas to the sea, allowing ocean transport to originate by river.

Early River Transportation

The earliest forms of river transport in America were dugout canoes, skin boats, or simple rafts. Native Americans had established many trading routes long before the Europeans arrived, though accounts of their journeys are limited. In 1673, Jacques Jolliet and Louis Marquette journeyed by canoe (in this case five men in two bark canoes) into sections of the Mississippi known only to Native Americans. Their mission was religious, and they followed the rivers to gain access to different groups of people. Zebulon Pike (1779–1813) travelled the Arkansas River, developing the Sante Fe trail; in 1822, this became an east-west highway, transporting the goods of trappers and hunters. Pike had previously been a negotiator with the Sioux and had experience with exploring by river. He had travelled in the Minnesota area, which is replete with rivers, streams, and lakes that are all potentially available for transportation. As happened on many such trading routes, the means of transport evolved from human-powered boat to steamboat and then was superseded by the railroad in 1868.

First the fur trade and then commercial lumbering ensured that the Missouri River was in constant use when passable. The importance of trade was such that by 1700, different types of sailing vessels were being introduced into the Missouri area, for example, sloops, feluccas, and mackinacs. Poling on flatboats was also common until the eighteenth century, and explorers like Zebulon Pike mixed and matched different types of vessels to go to a particular destination according to the navigability of the watercourses.

Regular passengers were usually carried across rivers on sailing craft and barges, almost always accompanying cargo. Often these boats were drawn by horses that were driven along the shore on towing paths. Sometimes a rope was attached on either shore and crew or passengers pulled the boat by hand along the rope to get across. Often crossing the river depended on the weather; the freezing of rivers affected movement up- and downstream and across the water.

There were no large fleets. Transport was mainly negotiated in individual agreements with merchants who owned their own boats and people like millers who had their own barges. In the late nineteenth century, the Minnesota lumbering industry used a variety of rowing vessels to transfer trees or logs to mills. Bateaux, sacking boats, and barges were used, and log drives could be accompanied by wanigans (small chests) or wanigan rafts, which allowed room for bunks and catering. Whether boats were towed or not depended on the speed and depth of the water and other features of the river affecting navigability. Steam power could be used with newer vessels like alligators, slough hogs, or towboats.

Carrying goods by river was generally cheaper than transporting them by road, even when tolls were charged on river traffic. Inland waterway traffic continued to increase throughout the nineteenth century, but railway tonnages also increased and challenged commercial activity on rural waterways. Sometimes railroads linked with steam-packet services on rivers like the Missouri. Generally, by the late nineteenth century, road transport had taken over all the transport of freight, and only the larger waterways could be competitive because they could accommodate larger vessels, offering more speed and efficiency.

Innovations and Current Uses

New forms of river transportation allowed the experience of river travel to be not only practical but also a leisure experience in the natural world. Steamboat services on lakes as early as 1826 offered an escape from the heat of the summer and the enjoyment of the health benefits of fresh air and water. Excursions and pleasure boating became increasingly popular, and some became annual events. In the latter part of the nineteenth century, showboats and circus boats pushed by steamers made for a festive experience. Demand for outdoor leisure led to increased water activity, including fishing trips and boating; boats were powered by oar, motor, and sail, and some were houseboats.

River transportation continues to play a significant role in the world today. One example is the Mississippi River. The second longest river in the United States, the Mississippi travels over 2,300 miles from its source in Minnesota to the Gulf of Mexico near New Orleans, Louisiana. The Mississippi almost bisects the country from north to south, beginning as a small stream and then becoming almost a mile wide in some locations. Cities alongside include Minneapolis/Saint Paul, Minnesota; Saint Louis, Missouri; Memphis, Tennessee; and Baton Rouge and New Orleans, Louisiana. More than 12 million people live on or near the river, and millions more rely upon it for their water supply. In addition, over 90 million tonnes of cargo are transported along the river each year, including grain, coal, iron, and steel. The Mississippi is a vital transportation corridor and source of water for agriculture and human consumption. A series of locks and dams in the northern stretch make it possible for commercial barge traffic and recreational boaters to pass, while the wider sections further south are easily navigable.

Many of the regions through which the Mississippi flows are the poorest in the United States, so to try to improve their standard of living, several tourism and recreation corridors have been designated. The river has a rich history. Native Americans relied on the Mississippi for their survival. The river was often seen as a dividing line when the settlers were moving across America; it was a frontier of sorts. The river was used to transport slaves from the South to the North and was vital to transportation during the American Civil War. The history of the South really unfolded around the accessibility that the river created. Writings of authors like Mark Twain helped maintain a romantic image of the paddle wheeler, and such steamboats are still in use today south of Iowa. Several cruise lines travel the Mississippi; tourists can take dinner cruises between cities, for example, and the riverboat cruise companies manage to marry nostalgia with general interest information in their tours. Tourists can see historic towns from a different vantage point from the river. To encourage interest of this type, there have been attempts to improve waterfront development in cities like Saint Louis.

River transportation continues to be part of local infrastructure. For example, waterbuses are used for local transportation in places like Fort Lauderdale, Florida. Ferries provide vital communication links across rivers, bays, and channels; these vessels range from flat-bottomed, manually propelled punts to large, diesel-powered floating bridges capable of accommodating heavy vehicles. These craft can replace the building of bridges in places where bridge construction is unfeasible.

Recreation and Conservation

The joy of travelling along the river was a part of life for the privileged in the time of Charles Dickens (1812–1870), and he recorded this in his *American Notes*. Thomas Cook (1808–1892) was able to create floating grand hotels to meet all the needs and wants of his customers. The same level of amenities is available in river cruising today; indeed, river cruising has become one of the fastest-growing areas of cruising interest for U.S. vacationers, who can choose routes as varied as the Hudson River or the Columbia River Gorge. River cruising now allows passengers the opportunity to expand their education or indulge a hobby. As one travels down the Columbia, for example, one may stop for wine tastings at vineyards. Different types of vessels have been developed, and rivers may now be enjoyed from motor boats and cabin cruisers.

Increasing pressure on beautiful river landscapes has meant that some of them have been given protected status. For example, the National Wild and Scenic Rivers System was a major effort by the federal government to protect natural areas. However, this system does not afford the same level of protection as designated wilderness areas. Stewardship of the environment needs to be balanced with fishing, transportation, and agriculture as well as tourism and recreational interests.

—Julia Fallon

See also: *American Indian Water Settlements; Locks; Midwest*

BIBLIOGRAPHY

Faulks, Rex William. *Principles of Transport.* 4th ed. London: McGraw Hill, 1990.
Hall, Wes, Douglas Birk, and Sam Newell. "History of Inland Water Transportation in Minnesota." http://www.mnhs.org/places/nationalregister/shipwrecks/mpdf/inship.html.

National Rivers and Harbors Congress

Rivers and harbors legislation was notorious for its use by members of the U.S. Congress to send pork-barrel projects home to their districts. Founded in 1901, the National Rivers and Harbors Congress (NRHC) was ostensibly formed to combat the problem by independently identifying and supporting river navigation improvement projects that served the public interest. From the very beginning, its independence was a façade, as its early proponents included Theodore E. Burton (R-OH), chair of the House of Representatives Rivers and Harbors Committee, and Senator Joseph E. Ransdell (D-LA). Many of the NRHC's leaders were members of Congress or other federal officials. Its congressional supporters granted the NRHC the unprecedented ability to work directly with congressional committees and the Army Corps of Engineers on water-related issues and projects. This collaboration resulted in the rapid growth of river navigation improvement projects around the country.

The NRHC was closely aligned with the Army Corps of Engineers throughout its history. The organization helped lobby for the Corps to be allowed to expand its purview to flood-control projects. The assistance was reciprocated to the extent that the NRHC often saw the Corps's plans before they were even shared with congressional committees. By the 1960s, the organization's influence waned significantly. The members of Congress who had utilized the organization as cover for their pork-barrel projects had found other ways to funnel money to their districts. By that point, the organization could not even help its long-term ally, the Army Corps of Engineers, as the NRHC had no influence whatsoever with the environmental groups that were altering the way the Corps conducted its work.

—John R. Burch Jr.

See also: *Army Corps of Engineers, United States*

BIBLIOGRAPHY

O'Neill, Karen M. *Rivers by Design: State Power and the Origins of U.S. Flood Control.* Durham, NC: Duke University Press, 2006.

Marquette, Jacques. *The Mississippi Voyage of Jolliet and Marquette, 1673* Madison: Wisconsin Historical Society, 2003. Available at http://content.wisconsinhistory.org/cdm4/document.php?CISOROOT=/aj&CISOPTR=3134&REC=1.

Paget-Tomlinson, E. W. *The Illustrated History of Canal and River Navigations.* Sheffield, UK: Sheffield Academic Press, 1993.

Palmer, Tim. *The Wild and Scenic Rivers of America.* Washington, DC: Island Press, 1993.

Prideaux, Bruce, and Malcolm Cooper, eds. *River Tourism.* Wallingford, UK: CABI, 2009.

Rule of Capture

Capture as a defining term may be a misnomer in its application to riparian rights. Public land law dealing with natural resources has spawned the term in order to describe and justify acquisition of resources, in many cases by the wealthy and powerful. Its use to rationalize control by oil, gas, lumber, and railroad interests is glazed by national security and the need to protect the public domain. Depending on the federal administration, regulations and control for the national benefit have been lax or have attempted to preserve our resources for the future. Historian Vernon Parrington describes the quest for resources as the "great barbecue," referring to the 3,500 public land laws adopted by Congress from 1785 through 1880 that continue to exert a questionable influence on our natural resources.

Legal Origins

This rule has its origins in the ancient arid world. Along the Tigris and Euphrates, the Nile, and the Tiber, ancient peoples recognized the need to develop rules to govern conduct. Marcus Claudius Marcellus, a Roman historian and jurist, is credited with establishing the rule to prevent the kind of societal conflict that occurred in the American West. Other sources for the use of the term *capture* refer to pirates capturing someone.

The English agrarians functioned differently than their French counterparts. The former, believed in primogeniture—the eldest son received all—while the French divided their estates according to the number of sons. Thus, the two societies dealt with water differently. In 1843, Parliament established the "English rule," whereby the owner of land had exclusive rights to the percolating groundwater under the property. The rationale was that the landowner exercised the same dominion over the water as the land. In *Acton v. Blundell* (1843), the Lord Chancellor of the Exchequer's Chamber said, "The case was not to be governed by the law which applies to rivers and flow streams, but that it falls within that principle, which gives the landowner, the owner of the soil, all that lies beneath his surface; that the land immediately below is his property, whether it is solid rock, or porous ground, or venous earth, or part soil, part water; that the person who owns the surface may dig therein, and apply all that is there found to his own purposes at his free will and pleasure" (12 Mees. & W. 324, 354, 152 Eng. Rep. 1223, 1235 [Ex. Ch. 1843]).

Legal interpretation of the law during early American history still followed the English common law, a system straitjacketed by tradition. American legal antecedents evolved during the colonial period and as people migrated west, where the topography, climate, agriculture, industrial development, and law were different from those in England. Law school professors favoring the rule of capture have relied on *Pierson v. Post,* 3 Caines 175, 2 Am Dec 264 (New York), 1805. This case established capture as a tool to justify possession of sub rosa mineral wealth. The parties argued over the possession of a fox; hence, the case is called the "famous fox" case. The case asked, is pursuance of something tantamount to ownership, or does one have to have the object in one's possession and under one's control? Intention was determined to be not as important as possession.

Much of the water throughout the United States has been appropriated. Increasing population and diminishing resources will eventually greatly intensify the stakes when public and private interests conflict. Government will serve as the mediator through such agencies as the Environmental Protection Agency, unless elected office holders reduce its authority, as during the previous Bush administrations.

Use in the United States

Universally, the following uses compete for water: ground, surface, domestic, commercial, public supply, irrigation, industrial, livestock, mining, electric production, hydroelectricity, and wastewater treatment. Control over water sources is gradually becoming more contentious. Texas, with its growing population and accompanying needs, will face increasing litigation, just as happens in other arid parts of the world.

The Texas Supreme Court declared the "English Rule" law in 1904. In *Houston and Texas Central Railway v. East,* the court declared that capturing a neighbor's groundwater does not allow for legal action if the capture injures the neighbor. The decision went further, saying that any owner of soil may divert percolating water, consume it, or cut it off with impunity. In 1954, Texas asserted that ownership of land meant ownership of the water. A Texas court decision stated, "Ownership of underground water comes with ownership of the surface; it is part of the soil" (Drummond et al. 2004). In 1983 the Texas Supreme Court declared capture "a corollary to absolute ownership of the groundwater" (*City of Sherman v. Public Utility Commission*). Subterranean assets are strongly defended legally through leases reserving the assets to parties named owner; these are sometimes referred to as ground leases reserving ownership for another. The same principle applies to petroleum products.

The absolute right of capture, which encourages development, is restricted by the amorphous legal fictions of restrictions limited by reasonable use, need, and conduct without malice. The operative standard is "beneficial use." The courts are often required to interpret this term in practice. Also, often no standard regulation is in place to control overproduction/use of the various aquifer systems. Thus, landowners might attempt to protect their water rights by digging wells deeper in the absence of any objective standards.

The law of capture, also known as "the law of the biggest pump," does not only apply to water but also to oil and natural gas development and usage. When water, oil, or natural gas are withdrawn from the earth, a vacuum is created, shifting the subterranean materials; what may have been under one owner's property now is below that of another. As a result, one could eventually be removing material that had originally been under another's property. Through hydraulic fracturing, a mixture of sand and water can be pumped underground at high pressures to fracture the earth, causing a substance to migrate from under one property to another. Again, legalities apply: motive, benefit, usage, etc. Once liquids or gases are pumped to the surface, there is no indicator of origin; thus, pumping them to the surface is not evidence of ownership.

Homeowners capturing rainwater may be breaking the law without realizing it. While one homeowner's individual conduct may not affect anyone else, the amount taken collectively could influence the general welfare. Colorado, for example, has a 150-year water allocation plan, and its Department of Natural Resources contends that private appropriation will stress the future plans for the area. Technically, this is an unforeseen use of the doctrine of prior appropriation, known as the "Colorado doctrine" of water law. This doctrine does not argue about the ownership of land but instead states that the highest and best use of water is for the benefit of the community. Under this doctrine, the state exercises prior acquisition but permits its citizenry use, depending upon an assortment of factors. The definition of beneficial use of water has broadened, so using water to remove environmental dust, make snow, etc. may fall within the purview of government.

A different approach is the correlative doctrine. The water rights of a landowner are limited to a common source of groundwater such as an aquifer. The landowner may draw a reasonable share based on the amount of his or her land. The absolute dominion doctrine, on the other hand, gives the water rights below to the landowner, including any aquifer, without any liability.

Texas Groundwater Rights

Texas law provides exceptions to the absolute ownership of groundwater rights: trespass by an adjacent landowner who takes water by drilling down or slant drilling so as to cross property boundaries, malicious conduct as the reason for taking another's water, waste of artesian well water by allowing it to run off one's land or to percolate back into the water table, the presence of contaminated water in a well, pollution of groundwater, and land subsidence and surface injury resulting from negligent pumping from adjoining lands.

Given these injunctions, Texas has refused to adopt the reasonable use rule and has instead adopted the common enemy rule, which allows any landowner to take measures to protect his or her property regardless of consequences to other landowners. The rule states, "Drainage water is regarded as an enemy common to all landowners." Another water rule, the natural flow rule, recognizes that each landowner is entitled to rely upon the continuation of the (natural) water flow. If a landowner were to increase runoffs and cause damages, that landowner is liable for the damages.

Marketable water permits come into play with agriculture, whereby a community can agree or not agree to water conservation and irrigation procedures. Allowing market forces to control the environmental needs of the community resembles cap-and-trade in the use of fossil waste.

Water Rights in Other States

An examination of section 858 of *Restatements of Torts* about groundwater locations provides a description and definition of the rule of capture and other legal philosophies involved in the competition for our diminishing water sources. The absolute ownership theory, closest to English common law doctrine, applies to water regulation in eight states: Connecticut, Georgia, Indiana, Louisiana, Maine, Massachusetts, Rhode Island, and Texas.

Reasonable use theory is applicable in sixteen states and, because of its arbitrary standard, tends to inspire litigation: Alabama, Florida, Illinois, Kentucky, Maryland, Missouri, Nebraska, Pennsylvania, South Carolina, Tennessee, Virginia, and West Virginia. While these states place ownership in the landowner, four additional states—Arizona, Mississippi, New York, and North Carolina—grant ownership of the groundwater to the state.

Prior appropriation is geographically centered. Twelve states—Alaska, Colorado, Idaho, Kansas, Montana, Nevada, New Mexico, North Dakota, Oregon, Utah, Washington, and Wyoming—claim governmental ownership: New Jersey and South Dakota grant ownership to the landowner.

The correlative rights doctrine applies in five states, all of which grant the landowner the right of control. They are Delaware, Hawaii, Iowa, Minnesota, and Vermont.

The beneficial purpose rule grants three heavily industrial states ownership: they are Michigan, Ohio, and Wisconsin.

A combination of the reasonable use and correlative rights theories are used in four states. Two of these, New Hampshire and Oklahoma, adopted state control. California and Arkansas give ownership to the landowner.

—Arthur Steinberg

See also: *Prior Appropriation; Reasonable Use Doctrine; Riparian Rights; Water Law*

BIBLIOGRAPHY

Albright, Steven J. "Water, Water Everywhere . . . Now What to Do with It: An Assessment of Water Management Strategies for East Texas." Applied Research Projects, Texas State University (Paper 181). San Marcos: Texas State University, 2006. Available at http://ecommons.txstate.edu/arp/181/.

De Villiers, Marq. *Water: The Fate of Our Most Precious Resource.* Boston: Houghton Mifflin, 2000.

Drummond, Dylan O., Lynn Ray Sherman, and Edmond R. McCarthy Jr. "The Rule of Capture in Texas—Still So Misunderstood after All These Years." *Texas Tech Law Review* 37, no. 1 (2004): 1–26.

Lueck, Dean. "The Rule of First Possession and the Design of the Law." *Journal of Law and Economics* 38, no. 2 (1995): 393–436.

Rasband, James R. "When Can Courts Compel Federal Agencies to Act to Protect the Public Lands?" *Preview of United States Supreme Court Cases* (2003–2004): 348–55.

Rasband, James R., and Megan E. Garrett. "A New Era in Public Land Policy? The Shift Toward Reacquisition of Land and Natural Resources." *Rocky Mountain Mineral Law Institute* 53 (2007). Available at http://papers.ssrn.com/sol3/papers.cfm?abstract_id=1003809.

Ward, Diane Raines. *Water Wars: Drought, Flood, Folly, and the Politics of Thirst.* New York: Riverhead Books, 2002.

Salinity

Salinity is the saltiness or dissolved salt content (usually measured as total dissolved solids or TDS) of a water body; it can also refer to the salt content of soil. All water naturally contains dissolved solids as a result of weathering and dissolution of minerals in soils and geologic formations. Major ions, such as bicarbonate, calcium, chloride, magnesium, potassium, silica, sodium, and sulfate, constitute most of the dissolved solids in water and are indicators of salinity.

The world's various water supplies are currently being threatened by an influx of salts originating from human, industrial, and natural processes. Although low levels of salt are critical to the survival of all plant and animal life by contributing to healthy cell functioning, all life forms have limits to their salt tolerance. In plants, too much salt stunts growth and limits crop yields. In humans, salt regulates metabolism, but excess amounts raise blood pressure. The detrimental effects of salt accumulation are wide-ranging and critical.

Farmers must have quality water to grow their crops. Industry (including power plants) must have low-saline water for manufacturing and power generation. Residential water users will seek alternative and more expensive drinking water supplies when high saline levels start to affect potability, taste, and smell. Salinity's economic impact in the United States is substantial.

The Bureau of Reclamation has created an economic model to evaluate the impacts of salt in water that focuses on quantifiable damages. For example, crop production is reduced when salinity levels are elevated. Household water appliances may clog or corrode sooner, thereby having shorter life spans. Municipal water treatment costs increase as salinity levels rise. As an example, the Colorado River water is used to irrigate 4.4 million acres and serve water to 33 million people. The Bureau of Reclamation's model indicates that quantifiable damages from salt loads at the start of the twenty-first century were approximately $376 million a year. Other impacts from salinity are known to occur but difficult to quantify. These include contamination of groundwater from high-salinity surface water and the costs of having to grow more salt-tolerant, lower-valued crops. Unquantifiable damages such as these are also substantial.

Agriculture

The practice of irrigation involves the unintended addition of waterborne salts to the soil. Additionally, many arid-zone soils contain natural reserves of salts, which are also mobilized by irrigation. Underlying groundwater can further contribute salts to the root zone through capillary action. Unfortunately, plant roots typically extract water from the soil while leaving most of the salts behind, thus causing them to accumulate.

The problem is not new. From its earliest development in the Fertile Crescent (present-day Iraq) some 6,000 years ago, irrigated agriculture has resulted in land and water degradation that has threatened sustainability. The artificial application of water to the land has resulted in the twin phenomena of waterlogging and salination. The same processes that eventually terrorized ancient hydraulic civilizations, including those of the Tigris/Euphrates, Indus, Gila, and other river valleys, continue to plague irrigation districts today. Indeed, the problem extends far beyond the confines of the irrigated land themselves, as it affects adjacent lands and water resources, thus having a major negative impact on downstream water users.

As modern agricultural research developed in the late nineteenth century, soil salinity, drainage, and return flows were among the first topics examined. Early studies showed that plants take up only a small amount of the salts in the water. Therefore, leaching these accumulated salts—applying extra water to move them out of the root zone—is necessary for salinity control and the maintenance of agricultural productivity. This leaching, however, unless managed, increases the salinity in return flows to rivers.

Guidelines and standards for reclamation of saline soils and management to control salinity evolved from this basic information, contributing to the successful development of large irrigation projects. Saline soils were reclaimed with amendments, tillage, land leveling, and high-quality irrigation water. By the mid-twentieth century, the acreage under irrigation had stabilized, and soil salinity was perceived as a problem that had been successfully dealt with.

Recently, however, looming water scarcity has called into question the long-term viability of many of these large irrigation projects. Irrigated acreage is declining due to competition for water, with mandated conservation being imposed to address environmental issues or drought and urban water agencies buying up irrigation water. Irrigated agriculture cannot compete economically with the urban sector in a competitively priced water market. Use of desalinated water is currently not a viable option for agriculture due to its high costs. Regulations on the discharge of drainage water as surface water are increasing and have, in many instances, resulted in rising water tables, reduced leaching capability, and subsequent soil salination.

Looking beyond high-quality water resources, numerous other water supplies can be used to sustain irrigated agriculture, primarily treated municipal wastewater, brackish groundwater, and agricultural drainage water. These water supplies can be productively managed but require application of improved salinity management technologies, development of new crop varieties, and treatment processes that consider the needs of users. Using brackish waters for irrigation is not without drawbacks and added costs, but these appear minor compared to the alternatives. Clearly, this approach requires that soil salinity, as well as the concentration of various other constituents often associated with these waters, be monitored. For example, brackish and drainage waters may contain trace elements such as boron, selenium, and molybdenum, which can impair crop production or adversely impact wildlife. One method of reducing the salinity in water is to dilute it with water from a less saline source. For example, when salinity levels get too high in the lower Sevier River (central Utah), water is pumped from shallow wells into the river. This dilution has obvious costs, which must be compared to the economic loss associated with using water with high levels of salinity.

Municipalities

To manage salt levels in its municipal and industrial water, California blends Colorado River water with less saline State Water Project water from the Sacramento–San Joaquin Delta. However, as environmental and urban demands reduce exports of freshwater from the north, salinity levels in southern California are rising. A former executive director of the California Water Board has stated that "salinity in southern California is probably the biggest water problem that isn't being adequately addressed" (cited by Atwater in Black 2008, 16).

Once the salt is in the water, one of the most effective forms of salt removal is the use of desalination facilities, which typically use reverse osmosis (RO). Desalination can remove salts from groundwater, reclaimed water, and seawater. Groundwater desalination has a high priority in southern California because it is the least costly alternative and because of the large number of groundwater systems in the region. Many of the aquifers have significant salt contamination resulting from historic use of imported Colorado River water and from flood and other low-efficiency irrigation practices.

Since the start of the twenty-first century, seawater desalination has gained acceptance as a viable technology for enhancing municipal water supplies. The first large-scale municipal desalination facility in the United States recently came online in Tampa Bay, Florida. California's twelve planned desalination facilities are projected to supply over 8 percent of the state's total water demand by 2020.

The impacts of salinity are not alleviated once salts are removed from water supplies in desalination facilities. The brines that are discharged from facilities are sent to wastewater treatment plants, which often receive brine loads from industrial plants as well. Salt loads to the sewer system are further increased by the growing use of home water softeners. Cost impacts of the combined brine discharges on top of the regular municipal wastewater load can be significant; they include loss of hydraulic capacity of sewerage systems, infrastructure degradation from corrosion, loss of reclaimed water due to high salt loads, lowering of the value of and ability to reuse biosolids, and mineral salt pollutants that adversely affect downstream reuse of the watershed supplies.

Colorado River Example

Salinity control efforts on the Colorado River are moving ahead. Despite no previous record of salinity control efforts—much less salinity control successes—on a major river system in United States, Congress took an important step in 1974 by passing the Colorado River Basin Salinity Control Act (SCA), which required cost-effective salinity control on the river. The Act addressed both water quality commitments that had been made to Mexico and requirements within the United States, principally in southern California.

The lead federal agency to implement SCA was the Department of the Interior, mainly its Bureau of Reclamation. The Department of Agriculture was to also play a role, and eventually six other federal agencies became involved. Issues with Mexico were addressed by the State Department through the International Boundary and Water Commission. The states, seeking to focus their involvement, created their own organization, the Colorado River Basin Salinity Control Forum, with each of the seven states invited to appoint up to three members.

In the first decade following passage of the SCA, the principal effort was to investigate the problem and evaluate the alternatives. Significant and cost-effective salinity control solutions involved improving agricultural water delivery systems by either upgrading conveyance systems, such as canals, or making changes to on-field irrigation, such as converting from flood irrigation to sprinklers. This approach—reducing human-caused loading by return flows—has been the main thrust of the program. But an important additional activity is being carried out by the Bureau of Reclamation in the Paradox Valley of Colorado, where the deep-sourced saturated brines that were flowing into the Dolores River have now been cut off by shallow collection wells and injected into deep limestone formations.

Future

As low-cost, real-time environmental monitoring and control systems become more sophisticated, they hold great potential for salinity management. Today, water delivery systems are being monitored and controlled from the watershed to the farm. They are being optimized for water delivery given the constraints of water rights and environmental commitments. The future will bring water quality parameters like salinity into the picture.

Another technology that promises great hope for salinity management is low-cost remote sensing. Utah State University and other institutions are developing unmanned aerial vehicles (UAVs) that are equipped with inexpensive remote-sensing equipment. The combination of low-cost environmental monitoring and remote sensing will permit the development of near-real-time maps of salinity and associated variables.

The commonly utilized sensor for monitoring salinity is an electrical conductivity (EC) probe, which is inserted directly into the water or soil. EC is used as a low-cost surrogate for TDS measurements. The newer EC sensors are inexpensive, opening up the possibility for extensive monitoring of water quality conditions. They can be added easily to existing real-time environmental monitoring and/or supervisory control and data acquisition (SCADA) systems. In development are sensors that monitor specific ions; these can be used for a variety of purposes, including the identification of sources of salinity.

Once a problem is diagnosed, real-time control technologies can be used to alleviate the problem in a timely manner. For example, for site-specific management at the farm-field scale, especially when combined with management-oriented computer modeling tools, salinity conditions can be ameliorated. Rather than leaching a field with a uniform application of water, it may be possible to leach different regions with variable quantities of water, thereby reducing total water requirements or amendments. Such practices will likely require modification of irrigation systems.

Salinity management is one of the major environmental concerns of our times, and it will continue to be a concern into the foreseeable future. In many areas, water quality conditions are deteriorating, and there is a need for timely action. Salinity can be controlled both through the development and construction of new technologies and through the application of better management practices.

—Roger D. Hansen

See also: *Bureau of Reclamation; Colorado River Basin*

BIBLIOGRAPHY

Black, Mary, ed. "Too Much Salt." Special issue, *Southwest Hydrology* 7, no. 2 (2008). Available at http://www.swhydro.arizona.edu/archive/V7_N2/SWHVol7Issue2.pdf.

Postel, Sandra. *Pillar of Sand: Can the Irrigation Miracle Last?* New York: W. W. Norton, 1999.

Worster, Donald. *Rivers of Empire: Water, Aridity, and the Growth of the American West.* New York: Oxford University Press, 1985.

Selenium

Selenium is a nonmetal with the chemical element atomic number 34 and an atomic mass of 78.96; it is represented by the symbol *Se*. Element 34 is red in powder form, black in vitreous form, and metallic gray in crystalline form. It is stable in both air and water. The chemistry of selenium is similar to that of sulfur, but it is a much rarer element, rarely occurring in nature in its elemental state. It is a micronutrient required by fish, birds, and mammals, including humans, to maintain good health. Plants uptake selenium and make it available to foraging animals, but no nutritional requirement has been found in plants for the element. It

is toxic to animals in large doses. For example, at Kesterson National Wildlife Refuge, California, thousands of fish and water birds were poisoned by selenium from agricultural irrigation drainage water.

Selenium occurs naturally in a number of inorganic forms, including selenite and selenate. In soils, selenium most often occurs in soluble forms such as selenate (analogous to sulfate), which are leached into rivers very easily by runoff. Natural sources of selenium include certain selenium-rich soils and selenium that has been bioconcentrated by certain toxic plants such as locoweed. Anthropogenic sources include coal burning, mining and smelting of sulfide ores, and processing copper ores.

The glass industry consumes approximately one-third of the selenium used each year. It is used to remove the color from the glass used to make bottles. It is also used in specialized sheet glass for windows where it reduces the amount of heat that enters a building from sunlight.

Selenium is known as a photovoltaic substance. This means that it converts light energy directly into electricity. It also displays photoconductive action, in which electrical conductivity increases as more and more light shines on the selenium. These features make selenium useful for photocells. Small photocells are used to power such instruments as handheld calculators; large photocells are used to convert sunlight into electrical energy, which can then be stored in batteries.

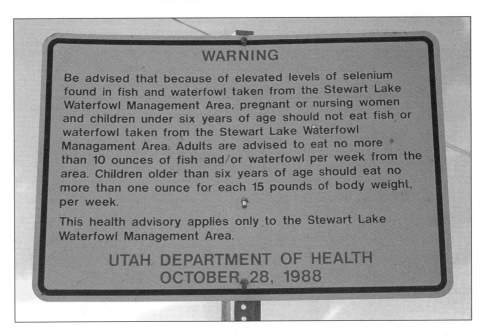

This sign warns fishers of the elevated selenium levels found in fish in Utah. Selenium is a naturally occurring element that is highly toxic in large doses.

U.S. Fish and Wildlife Service

Selenium is also used to make a variety of chemicals and pigments, antidandruff shampoos, steel alloys, human dietary supplements, and rubber production. Demand for selenium may increase in the future due to the possibility of using the element to replace lead in plumbing brass and other lead alloys.

Historical Background

In 1817, Swedish scientist Jons Jacob Berzelius discovered selenium when he found an impurity while studying the sulfuric acid produced in a local factory. It was subsequently named after the Greek word *selene,* meaning moon. This is a reference to the silvery-gray color of metallic selenium. Rarely have ores containing high concentrations of selenium been found.

As it turns out, selenium was important in the construction of the periodic table. German chemist Johann Wolfgang Dobereiner (1780–1849), whose initial work focused on finding precise ways to weigh elements, first studied strontium. As he fine-tuned his figures on strontium, he noted something unusual: its weight fell halfway between the weights of calcium and barium. Moreover, when he looked into the chemistry of strontium, it reacted like calcium and barium. Strontium was somehow a blend of two elements, one lighter and one heavier.

Dobereiner began to weigh other elements more precisely, scouting for other "triads." Sulfur, selenium, and tellurium and other triads soon came to his attention. Convinced that this was not a coincidence, he began to place these elements into groups that look similar to the columns in today's periodic table. Dmitri Mendeleev, who constructed the first periodic table fifty years later, started with Dobereiner's pillars.

Toxicity to Animals

While element 34 is an essential trace nutrient in all animals, including humans, selenium is toxic in large doses. Ranchers know this well. If not watched carefully, cattle will root out a prairie plant of the pea family know as locoweed, some varieties of which absorb selenium from the soil. Cattle that ingest locoweed begin to stumble and develop fever, sores, and anorexia. Yet they enjoy the buzz. Some imaginative historians even blame General Custer's defeat on his horses' consuming locoweed before the battle. But after decades of ranchers cursing element 34, many biochemists now believe that other chemicals in locoweed contribute just as much to the craziness and intoxication.

In high concentrations, selenium does definitely act as an environmental contaminate. Selenium poisoning of water systems can result from agricultural return flow as it passes through wetlands. This process leaches natural soluble selenium compounds (such as selenates) into the water, and the element is then concentrated in wetlands by evaporation. High selenium levels produced in this fashion have been found to cause certain congenital disorders in wetland birds.

The most well-known case of selenium poisoning in an aquatic ecosystem was at Kesterson National Wildlife Refuge in the San Joaquin Valley, California. In 1982, the U.S. Fish and Wildlife Service discovered dying waterfowl and waterfowl with birth defects and reproductive failures. Widespread fish mortality and deformities in ducks, grebes, and coots occurred in wetlands fed by agricultural drainage. The deformities most frequently observed in birds were defects of the eye, foot or leg, beak, brain, and abdomen. Investigations from 1982 to 1985 determined that the cause of the problems was a high level of selenium in the irrigation drainage water discharged into the reservoir. A congressional hearing; several television programs, including a report on a popular news magazine show; more than 100 newspaper and magazine articles; and numerous other inquiries focused on the contaminant issues. Kesterson Reservoir was closed and buried-in-place in 1988. Current water management efforts include drainage recycling, storage in groundwater aquifers, mitigated evaporation ponds, and discharge to the San Joaquin River.

Other sources of pollution include waste materials from certain mining, agricultural, petrochemical, and industrial manufacturing operations. In Belews Lake, North Carolina, nineteen species of fish were eliminated from the lake due to a high selenium concentration in the wastewater discharged from a coal-fired power plant.

Substantial physiological changes may occur in fish with high tissue concentrations of selenium. Affected fish may experience swelling of the gill lamellae. This in turn impedes oxygen diffusion across the gills and blood flow within the gills. Respiratory capacity is further reduced due to selenium binding to hemoglobin. Other problems include degeneration of liver tissue, swelling around the heart, damaged egg follicles in ovaries, cataracts, and accumulation of fluid in the body cavity and head. Selenium often causes a malformed fish fetus, which may have problems feeding or respirating; distortion of the fins or spine is also common. Adult fish may appear healthy despite their inability to produce viable offspring.

Widespread media attention and congressional interest during the mid-1980s concerning the potential for similar toxic impacts from irrigation return flow, especially in the western United States, prompted the Department of the Interior (DOI) to open an investigation. Scientists in the U.S. Geological Survey contributed considerable data and analysis on the scope of the selenium contamination associated with salinized farmlands and on the hydrological and biogeochemical processes resulting in selenium bioaccumulation. These data were important to resolving selenium toxicity problems associated with irrigated agriculture in the arid West.

In late 1985, the DOI developed a program to investigate the extent and magnitude of the problem. A management strategy was developed, committing the DOI to conduct a program that would identify and address irrigation-induced water quality and contamination problems related to its water projects in the West. No specific congressional action was taken, and the secretary of the interior approved the initiation of the National Irrigation Water Quality Program (NIWQP).

The DOI was initially selected to manage the NIWQP with an advisory group of coordinators representing the Bureau of Reclamation, Bureau of Indian Affairs, U.S. Geological Survey, and U.S. Fish and Wildlife Service. Management of the NIWQP was transferred from the DOI to the Bureau of Reclamation in fiscal year 1999. Due to significant funding reductions in fiscal year 2005, the majority of the program's activities were suspended.

Initially, twenty locations in thirteen states were identified that warranted reconnaissance investigations. This number was pared to nine in 1986, and eventually four sites were identified as having problems sufficient to warrant further investigation: Stillwater Wildlife Management Area, Nevada; Salton Sea area, California; Middle Green River Basin area, Utah; and Kendrick Project area, Wyoming.

Impacts on Humans

This list of trace elements that the human body requires is intriguing. Our cells require regular microdoses of these elements, or they start to malfunction. On this list are chromium, cobalt, copper, manganese, molybdenum, nickel, and selenium, among others. These are all substances we usually think of as the opposite of biological substances, and they are not widely discussed in the context of maintaining a balanced diet. But a diet that lacks any of them will leave a person sick or disabled, if not dead.

Selenium nutrient deficiency in humans is relatively rare in healthy, well-nourished individuals. It can, however, occur in patients with severely compromised intestinal function, those undergoing total parenteral nutrition, and in advanced-aged seniors. Alternatively, people dependent on food grown from selenium-deficient soil are also at risk.

A chronic lack of this element can cause heart cells and cartilage to die, as well as disrupt the thyroid gland. The level of selenium in the blood of AIDS patients is very strongly linked to the likelihood of death. Doctors haven't sorted out yet whether low selenium levels contribute directly to AIDS deaths or merely correlate with them, but our bodies use selenium as an antioxidant and a lack of antioxidants puts stress on cells. Given that immune cells in AIDS patients are already stressed, the lack of selenium might cause death.

Historically, China has suffered from both selenium deficiency and selenium toxicity. Keshan disease, due to selenium deficiency, was first discovered in 1935 in Keshan County (thus the name of the disease) in northeastern China. The primary myopathy is an enlarged heart. Keshan disease differs from cardiomyopathy in that it occurs primarily in children and multiparous women. Severe Keshan disease does not respond to selenium supplements, but mild cases do. Incidents of selenium toxicity have been correlated with the use of coal that contains selenium.

—Roger D. Hansen

See also: *Bureau of Reclamation; Fish and Wildlife Service, United States; Kesterson Reservoir; Salinity; United States Geological Survey*

BIBLIOGRAPHY

Harris, Tom. *Death in the Marsh*. Washington, DC: Island Press, 1991.

Kean, Sam. *The Disappearing Spoon: And Other True Tales of Madness, Love, and the History of the World from the Periodic Table of Elements*. New York: Little, Brown, 2010.

U.S. Geological Survey. "Selenium Contamination Associated with Irrigated Agriculture in the Western United States." Last modified May 12, 2005. http://menlocampus.wr.usgs.gov/50years/accomplishments/agriculture.html.

Whanger, P. D. "China, A Country with Both Selenium Deficiency and Toxicity: Some Thoughts and Impressions." *Journal of Nutrition* 119, no. 9 (1989): 1236–39. Available at http://jn.nutrition.org/content/119/9/1236.full.pdf.

Sewage

Sewage is broadly defined as any refuse matter conveyed in sewers, which are the artificial channels or conduits designed to carry off and ultimately discharge wastewater and the refuse from houses and towns. While most people associate sewage with human wastes, feces and urine make up a comparatively small proportion of sewage. Domestic kitchen water and bath water make up the bulk of it. Industrial, commercial, and medical facilities can discharge a wide range of chemicals and chemical products into sewer lines. Street drainage into sewer lines can introduce grit and stones along with miscellaneous solid wastes.

Human and chemical wastes, however, pose the greatest danger to health and the environment. A gram of feces can contain up to 10 million viruses, 1 million bacteria, 1,000 parasite cysts, and 100 worm eggs. At the start of the twenty-first century, poor sanitation, poor hygiene, and unsafe water accounts for 10 percent of all human diseases worldwide, and 90 percent of diarrhea is caused by food or water contaminated by feces.

A Need for Sanitation Improvements

It had long been known that pure water was essential for good health, but until the pioneering epidemiological work of Dr. John Snow of London (1813–1858), the connection was never methodically explored. During outbreaks of cholera in 1854 and 1857, Snow mapped the incidence of disease and traced it back to drinking water contaminated by sewage. The first edition of his groundbreaking *On the Mode of the Communication of Cholera* was published in 1849, and an expanded edition came out in 1855. Throughout the mid-nineteenth century, a growing body of evidence linked human disease to sewage contamination, although it was far from clear if the underlying cause was microscopic organisms or poisonous chemicals released from putrefying wastes. Not until the work of Louis Pasteur (1822–1895) would the role played by pathogenic bacteria begin to be widely understood.

In nineteenth century London, one in two children died at an early age, but once toilets, sewers, and basic hygienic practices such as hand washing became common, childhood mortality dropped to one in five. The first sections of London's sewers were built between 1858 and 1866. These discharged directly into surface waters, as did most of the early sewers throughout the industrialized world.

Early objections to this practice of sewage discharge into rivers and the oceans centered on the loss of plant nutrients, which ideally would have been returned to the farmlands. During the first half of the 1800s, agricultural scientists increasingly understood the nutritional needs of plants, and many regarded human wastes, food scraps, and other organic matter as rich sources of nitrogen and phosphorous.

Attempts to recycle human wastes from urban centers were hampered by several factors. Among these were the high water content of human feces, which increased transportation costs, and long composting times, which made this practice ill suited to the demands of increasingly mechanized agriculture. Not until the end of the nineteenth century and early twentieth century was the contamination of shellfish and swimming beaches by sewage discharge recognized as a source of human disease

At the start of the twenty-first century, an estimated 90 percent of the world's sewage ends up untreated in rivers, lakes, and oceans, and much of this comes from regions that have a sewage treatment infrastructure.

Sewage Treatment

Natural water bodies have a limited capacity to absorb and purify sewage discharges. Typical domestic sewage contains high levels of nutrients, especially nitrogen and phosphorous, which are utilized by growing plants. Protozoa consume pathogenic bacteria, while bacterial decomposers break down the organic matter. This capacity is limited, however, by the composition of the aquatic plants, the length of the growing season, and the available dissolved oxygen. Eutrophication is the principle environmental effect of releasing untreated sewage into surface waters. It occurs when excess nutrients fertilize the rapid growth of aquatic plants. Once the plants die, bacteria begin to decompose them and, in the process, use large amounts of dissolved oxygen. Loss of dissolved oxygen causes fish and other animals to suffocate. Without additional oxygen to continue the work of decomposition, organic matter continues to accumulate.

In industrialized countries, sewage treatment is primarily by one of two methods, septic systems and centralized treatment plants. Septic systems are used in areas where land is abundant and the cost of laying sewer lines is high. A basic septic system consists of two parts, a tank in which solids settle out from the liquid stream and a leaching field where the remaining liquids are allowed to percolate into the soil.

When sewage is collected at a centralized processing plant, the sewer lines can be constructed either as a sanitary sewer system or a combined sewer system. Sanitary sewer systems isolate the pipes that carry wastes to treatment plants (sanitary sewers) from those carrying rainwater and snowmelt off roadways and directly into rivers, lakes, or the ocean (storm sewers). Combined sewer systems use one system of pipes for both purposes. Engineers install storm tanks at various points along this type of system and emergency reservoirs at the central treatment plant. Although combined systems can hold some excess rainfall or snowmelt, large flows can overwhelm them. When this happens, the untreated sewage is released into the environment through a combined sewer overflow (CSO). The U.S. Environmental Protection Agency has estimated that as of 2002, 880 publicly owned treatment works (POTWs) receive flows from combined sewer systems. Overflows cause the discharge of 1.2 trillion gallons of storm water and untreated sewage each year.

The typical flow into sewage treatment plants is primarily liquid with only 1 to 2 percent of particulates, colloids, and dissolved compounds. The incoming flow is also rich in dissolved nutrients. Urine makes up only 5 percent of the flow but accounts for 80 percent of the nitrogen and 45 percent of the phosphorous. The amount of organic material in the sewage flow is measured by its biological oxygen demand (BOD). BOD is defined as the amount of oxygen removed from the water by bacteria as it decomposes the organic matter. BOD is typically assessed by measuring the rate at which oxygen disappears from a sealed bottle containing a sample after five days in darkness at 20°C (71.6°F). Typical BOD for untreated sewage is 600 mg oxygen per liter over five days, while unpolluted river water has a BOD of less than 5 mg oxygen per liter over five days.

Sewage treatment is divided into three stages: primary, secondary, and tertiary. Primary treatment is the removal of solids through a system of screens, settling tanks, or other physical methods that remove sand, grit, and larger solids. Up to 50 percent of the suspended solids may be removed during primary treatment. Water entering primary treatment is typically grayish brown and turbid and has a BOD of approximately 600 mg of oxygen per liter per five days. During the time that the sewage is held in settling tanks, the BOD of the water is reduced by 30 to 40 percent, and there is also a decrease in pathogens, bacteria, and viruses. From this point onward, the solids and supernatant liquid are processed separately.

The liquids then receive secondary treatment, the principle of which is that bacteria consume the remaining waste materials prior to discharge. This takes place in aeration tanks, lagoons, or trickling filters. Trickling filters are circular beds of rock fragments that are home to bacteria-grazing protozoa and consumers of organic matter. At this stage, the BOD of the supernatant water is typically reduced to 60 mg of oxygen per liter per five days, and the water is rich in phosphates, ammonia, and nitrate. The BOD is further reduced in a second settling process. The solids from this process are usually combined with those from the first sedimentation tank. They are dewatered by filtering, centrifuging, or pressing or by lying on a drying bed. The supernatant water then goes through one or more forms of tertiary treatment, which can include disinfection by chlorination, ultraviolet light, or ozone. The water may also be "polished" by filtration or percolation through activated carbon. Tertiary treatment may also include the removal of nutrients from the water, necessary to prevent the discharged water from causing eutrophication. Nutrient removal is usually accomplished by bacteria or aquatic plants.

Prevention of chemical discharges to sanitary sewers is the preferred method of ensuring that metals, synthetic compounds, and organic solvents will not reach the environment through sewage outfalls. Most treatment plants have permitting requirements limiting the amounts of these materials they can accept or discharge. Large industrial plants often have on-site sewage treatment facilities. In recent years, there has been growing concern that pharmaceutical and personal care products are not being removed from sewage effluent at treatment plants. What adverse effects these materials may have on the environment is a subject of active investigation.

In 1972, the Clean Water Act required publically owned treatment works (POTW) to adopt secondary treatment. By 1996, only 176 out of the 14,000 POTWs did not meet standards for secondary treatment. According to the Congressional Budget Office, in the period from 1972 to 1996, the amount of BOD arriving at treatment facilities increased an average of 25 percent, but the amount of BOD released from POTWs decreased by 40 percent.

Federal grants for the construction of POTWs first became available in 1956 and matched from 30 to 50 percent of construction costs. After passage of the Clean Water Act, the federal government provided up to 75 percent of the construction costs for POTWs. Federal spending on treatment works rose tenfold during the 1970s and peaked at $9.1 billion in 1980. Amendments to the Clean Water Act in 1981 reduced the federal matching share to 55 percent for facilities built after 1984. In 1987, legislation was enacted that would phase out the federal financing and replace it with a system of grants to capitalize state revolving funds. Although federal contributions were supposed to cease after

1994, it was necessary to continue appropriations, including $1.35 billion in 2002 alone.

The solid materials removed during the treatment process are referred to as sludge or biosolids. In coastal areas, these were frequently dumped into the ocean until the Ocean Dumping Ban Act of 1989 prohibited this practice. At the time, 7 million dry tons of sludge were produced in the United States each year. The sewage treatment industry was given four years to find alternate disposal strategies.

The four alternatives for sludge disposal are landfill, incineration, conversion to methane by bacterial action in large digesters, and land application. Disposal is complicated because effective removal of impurities from the liquids is essentially a process of transferring contamination to the sludge. Use of sewage sludge as fertilizer has been limited by the presence of industrial and household chemicals, pathogens, and minor pollutants such as pharmaceutical products. Several European nations no longer allow biosolids applications on farm fields, and the national farmers' associations in France, Germany, and Sweden have opposed this practice.

Future strategies for dealing with sewage focus largely on reducing the amount of water necessary to carry the wastes to treatment plants or even eliminating water flows altogether. Toilets using low-flush volumes are already in widespread use. "Gray water," which only contains waste flows from kitchens and baths, can be diverted into separate tanks and held until needed for irrigation or to flush toilets. In this system, only water containing feces and urine would be sent to treatment plants. Incinerating toilets are common in places where installing water pipes and sewer lines is impractical. This technology, as well as rapid composting, is being considered for arid regions.

—Kevin Olsen

See also: *Clean Water Act of 1972; Eutrophication*

BIBLIOGRAPHY

Daley, Robert. *The World Beneath the City.* Philadelphia: Lippincott, 1959.

Melosi, Martin V. *The Sanitary City: Urban Infrastructure in America from Colonial Times to the Present.* Baltimore: Johns Hopkins University Press, 2000.

Nemerow, Nelson L., Franklin J. Agardy, Patrick Sullivan, and Joseph A. Salvato. *Environmental Engineering: Water, Wastewater, Soil, and Groundwater Treatment and Remediation.* 6th ed. Hoboken, NJ: John Wiley & Sons, 2009.

Rosenkrantz, Barbara Gutmann, ed. *Sewering the Cities.* New York: Arno Press, 1977.

Tarr, Joel A. *The Search for the Ultimate Sink: Urban Pollution in Historical Perspective.* Akron, OH: University of Akron Press, 1996.

Soil Erosion

See *Erosion*

Soil Salinization

It has long been recognized that soil salinization reduces the productivity of soil. In the ancient world, the Greek historian Herodotus (c. 484–c. 425 BCE) wrote of salt eroding parts of the pyramids of Egypt. The Romans are said to have plowed the remains of the sacked city of Carthage with salt to prevent it ever being rebuilt—although modern scholars believe this story to be apocryphal, as salt cost too much in Roman times for such an extravagant action. Others have suggested that the Romans might, instead, have used seawater. Overall the U.S. Department of Agriculture estimates that 10 million hectares of arable land is being lost each year to salinity.

Soil Salinization in the United States

Although the salt air along the Atlantic coast of places such as Maine has been responsible for corrosion, it has not presented much of a problem for the coastal soil, which is still fairly fertile. Soil salinization is most common in arid lands where the water table is close to the surface. As with the Dead Sea in the Middle East, the salinization of the area around the Great Salt Lake in Utah has been a natural process—but in both cases the problem has been considerably exacerbated by human involvement. Agriculture has used water with high salinity for irrigation, and the clearing of trees and other aspects of development have aggravated the problem.

Soil salinization is most noticeable in places such as Colorado, where the soil around the basin of the Colorado River has become encrusted with salts. The process is accelerating as more and more water from the Colorado River is used for irrigation or human consumption. Irrigation with high-salinity water causes a decline in plant growth and crop yields. Although this has affected all types of plants, it is especially noticeable in vineyards in the San Joaquin Valley in southern California and other places connected with the wine industry.

It is estimated that as much as 9 million tons of salt per year flows down the Colorado River system annually. It is deposited along the way, as none of the river's water now reaches the ocean. The effect has been devastating in places such as the Paradox Valley in Colorado and well downstream in Welltown Mohawk in Arizona. It has been calculated that salt in the headwaters of the Colorado River is at a concentration of 50 milligrams per liter, but when the water reaches the last dam in the river, close to Las Vegas, the salt concentration is more than 700 milligrams per liter. Economists estimate that losses from salinization are as much as $330 million a year.

In some places in the Colorado River Basin, because of the amount of water available, salinity has not been a problem. This is especially true of places such as Phoenix, Arizona, where it has been deemed that water is still palatable in spite of increased levels of salts, and in Tucson, Arizona, which has been able to make use of groundwater that is mixed with water from the river.

Solutions

For the most part, the cost of building desalinization plants is too great for these projects to be deemed feasible. Following the Colorado River Basin Salinity Control Act of 1974, in 1975 certain strategies were drawn up as a part of the Colorado River Basin Salinity Control Forum in Arizona. Mexican authorities had been complaining about the high salinity levels of the Colorado River, which were affecting Mexican agriculture. In response, the U.S. government constructed a large desalination plant at a cost of $300 million near Yuma, Arizona, close to the U.S.-Mexico border. It aimed to reduce the salt from the Wellton Mohawk Irrigation District in Arizona. Agreements between the U.S. and Mexican governments stipulate that Mexico receive two cubic kilometers of usable water each year.

—Justin Corfield

See also: *Great Salt Lake; Southwest*

BIBLIOGRAPHY

Blaylock, Alan D. "Soil Salinity, Salt Tolerance, and Growth Potential of Horticultural and Landscape Plants" (B-988). Laramie: University of Wyoming, 1994. Available at http://ces.uwyo.edu/pubs/Wy988.pdf.

Frenkel, Haim, and Avraham Meiri, eds. *Soil Salinity: Two Decades of Research in Irrigated Agriculture.* New York: Van Nostrand Reinhold, 1985.

Haygarth, P. M., and S. C. Jarvis, eds. *Agriculture, Hydrology, and Water Quality.* Wallingford, UK: CABI, 2002.

Kovda, Victor Abramovich. *Land Aridization and Drought Control.* Boulder, CO: Westview Press, 1980.

Lilley, John. *Dryland Salinity in Alberta.* Edmonton: Environment Council of Alberta, 1982.

Metternicht, Graciela, and J. Alfred Zinck, eds. *Remote Sensing of Soil Salinization: Impact on Land Management.* Boca Raton, FL: CRC Press, 2009.

Pearce, Fred. *When the Rivers Run Dry: What Happens When Our Water Runs Out?* London: Eden Project, 2006.

Umali, Dina L. *Irrigation-Induced Salinity: A Growing Problem for Development and the Environment.* Washington, DC: World Bank, 1993.

Transportation

See *River Transportation*

Urban Rivers

Urban rivers are centerpieces of the cities that have developed alongside, creating a lifeline between regions and countries and contributing significantly to communication and people's livelihoods. Many American cities have rivers running through them. When members of City-Data.com were invited to vote for their favorite river city, Pittsburgh, Pennsylvania, and Saint Louis, Missouri, tied for number one. In each city, the river dominates the downtown area, and sweeping bridges provide dramatic vistas for visitors. The rivers supported industries in the past; for example, the Allegheny and Monongahela Rivers supported the steel industry in Pittsburgh. In Saint Louis, the port remains the third largest in the United States for tonnage and is used to transport bulk commodities like grain, coal, and salt as well as chemical and petroleum products.

The longest American river, the Missouri, flows along the borders of seven states down to Kansas City, Missouri; then it joins the Mississippi River at Saint Louis. The Mississippi travels through New Orleans, Louisiana, into the sea. The Missouri River's journey of 4,000 kilometers takes it from the high Rockies to the lowlands of the South. Its rich history includes providing access for fur trappers and homesteaders. Trails into the American West started on this river; for example, both the Pony Express and the first transcontinental railroad used ferries across the Missouri. The vital link the river provided led to the growth of Kansas City (with the Hannibal Bridge), and paddle wheelers took people and cargo upriver and led to the development of the Dakotas and Montana. The river has a significant impact upon the population of Kansas City today, as its confluence with the Kansas River influences the climate and the likelihood of tornados and flooding. In 1992, voters approved riverboat casino gaming, which has raised substantial funds for the city.

Historically, many cities like Kansas City have developed directly as a result of a river because of the access and communication such a watercourse brings. The river forms a significant part of the historical and modern landscape of these cities.

The Savannah River is rated as the fourth most toxic by Environment America. The Savannah River formed part of the basic infrastructure of Savannah and Augusta, Georgia, which have both been state capitals. This tidal river had a sandy bottom that caused many steamboat accidents in the nineteenth century, so the New Savannah Bluff Lock and Dam was built in 1937 to help shipping to Augusta. Between 1946 and 1985, the U.S. Army Corps of Engineers built three dams for hydroelectricity, flood control, and navigation. These dams and their reservoirs now combine to form over 120 miles of lakes and have erased the original shape and form of the river forever. River dredging operations to support the Port of Savannah are changing the ecological balance of the estuary's marshland. In the 1950s, the river was home to the Savannah River Plant, which made nuclear weapons materials.

Each urban river has a character of its own. In many cities, rivers and streams are converted into concrete channels to divert potential flood waters. Urban rivers have been altered by using hydraulic engineering methods, including concrete lining, diversion of the natural water path, change of channel to prevent flooding, straightening, installation of weirs that prevent fish passage, change in flow through inter-basin transfer pipes, deepening and widening, filling, sediment extraction, water extraction, excess sediment deposits, weed invasion, and increase of hard-surface runoff. These changes can be very damaging to a river's ecosystem. Dams, for example, are now understood to damage a river's ecosystem because they slow the current, leading to deposition of silt and destroying habitats. Also, raising the water level results in erosion and curtails the natural cleansing action at work in a free-flowing river. In addition, water temperatures in American rivers are rising, negatively impacting aquatic flora and fauna.

River Changes

In addition to being subject to human alterations, rivers are subject to natural agents of change. Flooding can have a dramatic effect, expanding channels and eroding beds and banks. Drought reduces water levels and flow. Finally, fire destroys vegetation and leaves large amounts of sediment and ash behind. Additionally, weather may have an impact on rivers; for example, wind storms affect the movement of the water and wave patterns.

Average city dwellers may not give much thought to their body waste. The reality is that in American cities, this waste goes through a series of treatments before being flushed into a river. Later, this river water will provide drinking water. Awareness has improved about water quality. As early as 1975, a suggestion was made that more people suffered from cancer in cities taking drinking water from the Mississippi River.

Riparian vegetation contributes to the geomorphic condition of urban rivers and streams. Vegetation may be removed from the banks, beds, and floodplains of rivers and streams to accommodate building there. Urban growth has led to more riverside development, and the resulting absence of vegetation has affected habitat, shade, windbreak, and visual aesthetics as well as water quality.

Urban rivers experience strong human pressures, but they also provide urban dwellers with social benefits, and the ecological structure of the river corridor offers spaces for residents to enjoy beauty and wildlife. A balance between the natural and the built environment is now seen as an important target for urban planning of the future. Moreover, rivers offer an opportunity to introduce nature into urban areas. Water is generally recognized as being of fundamental importance for all species, and the presence of water is of special relevance to people because it creates aesthetically pleasing and relaxing environments. During periods of high summer temperatures and little rainfall, for example, the presence of water provides comfort to city residents.

River Protection and Restoration

In recent decades, urban regeneration programs have sought to provide better urban environments and to improve cities' images. Water has been a significant factor in these improvements, so rivers and their corridors have been on the receiving end of considerable interventions. These interventions have taken several forms, depending on the relative position of the river in the city. For example, whether the river is central or peripheral alters the amount of space available near the river and the relationship of the river with the city and its residents. Some rivers have had green spaces created along their shores, and others have seen the construction of artificial river banks and dams to ensure the constant presence of water.

In the past decade or so, there has been a positive move worldwide toward restoring and conserving rivers rather than manipulating and controlling them. The benefits of this trend are many, including improving air quality, moderating surrounding temperatures, and preserving ecosystems. Restoration is complex, however, needing to take into account existing land use, the danger of flooding, and the impact of human activity on water quality and the ecology of the river. Many stakeholders must be considered in terms of both the physical and social aspects of any development. Thus, in some cases, rivers are being restored (i.e., returned to their pristine original state), whereas in others they are being rehabilitated or improved (i.e., returned to working order). In most urban situations, the latter objective is practicable.

Many river protection programs in the United States have not included urban rivers, but where there have been urban waterfront projects, these have been very successful in regenerating areas like that surrounding the Boise River in the capital of Idaho. On the Illinois River, modeling was used to evaluate erosion, sedimentation, and ecology, and the river bed was stabilized. After this work had taken place, fish reinhabited this section. In many cases where water quality has been poor, increasing efficiency in sewage treatments is helping to restore the aquatic environment.

In urban environments, intervention for flood control and water quality maintenance are deemed the only way to live with rivers, but increasingly rivers and streams and their associated spaces are seen as significant to quality of life. The postindustrial urban environment affords opportunities for river restoration, and the cessation of industry in some places has allowed urban streams to reconnect with larger watercourses, reviving ecological habitats.

Fluvial cities have been the focus of a research project entitled RiProCity, which developed these indicators to understand sustainability in urban river rehabilitation programs:

Citizen satisfaction with the local riverfront
River contribution to local bioclimatic change
Ecological quality of the river corridor
Flood risk
Sustainable land use
Mobility and river accessibility
Availability of local public spaces and services
Governance and sustainable management
    (Adapted from Moore and Outhet 2008.)

Greater urban populations mean greater interest in river restoration. Municipal schemes must consider the many stakeholder interests, and a multidisciplinary planning approach is required. Managing rivers in the urban environment requires careful monitoring, evaluation, and management. The European research project Urban River Basin Enhancement Methods (URBEM) may be a useful guide as it concentrates on the sustainability of the urban river and its environment. Careful analysis is made of planning and intervention; rehabilitation techniques; environmental, social, and economic impacts; attractiveness; local community involvement; and performance evaluation.

—Julia Fallon

See also: *Army Corps of Engineers, United States; Dam Building; Dam Removal and River Restoration; Erosion; River Transportation; Waterborne Diseases in Drinking Water*

BIBLIOGRAPHY

Dutzik, Tony, Piper Crowell, and John Rumpler. *Wasting Our Waterways: Toxic Industrial Pollution and the Unfulfilled Promise of the Clean Water Act*. Washington, DC: Environment America Research & Policy Center, 2009. Available at http://cdn.publicinterestnetwork.org/assets/b818d52cb8d5ba4c6530431f800bfb66/Wasting-Our-Waterways-vAM.pdf.

Jormola, J., chairperson. "Chapter 12, Session 9: Urban Rivers." In *IVth ECRR International Conference on River Restoration 2008* (Venice, Italy, June 2008), edited by B. Gumiero, M. Rinaldi, and B. Fokkens, 887–948. Available at http://www.ecrr.org/archive/conf08/proceedings.htm.

Moore, J., and D. Outhet. "River Restoration in Sydney, Australia." Paper presented at the 4th ECRR Conference on River Restoration, Venice, Italy, June 2008. Available at http://www.ecrr.org/archive/conf08/pdf/proceed15.pdf.

Palmer, Tim. *The Wild and Scenic Rivers of America*. Washington, DC: Island Press, 1993.

Thomas, Bill. *American Rivers*. New York: Norton, 1978.

Urbanization

Over half of the planet's 6.7 billion people lived in cities as of December 2008. Two-thirds of these lacked safe and clean water and sanitation. Basic sanitation and health require between 20 and 40 liters (4.4 and 8.8 gallons) of freshwater per person per day. Bathing and cooking increase the daily need to between 27 and 200 liters (6 and 44 gallons). One recommended standard is 50 liters (11 gallons) per person per day for all four uses; this level was beyond the reach of 55 countries, and 1 billion people, in 1990. Another expert says that the minimum for an acceptable living standard is 100 liters (22 gallons) per person, excluding agricultural and industrial uses. Urbanization means greater use—in 1900, the average American household use was 10 cubic meters (10,000 liters or 2,200 gallons) a year. Modern households use twenty times that amount.

Urbanization creates water-related problems for developers. A well-known example is the city of Las Vegas, Nevada. Las Vegas is a desert city whose rapid expansion has threatened to outpace its water resources several times.

Carol M. Highsmith's America, Library of Congress, Prints and Photographs Division

Percentages don't show the range of consumption, which is higher in developed countries than in developing ones. Africans use 47 liters of water (10.34 gallons) per day for personal use, Asians use 85 liters (18.7 gallons), while use in the United Kingdom is 334 liters (73.5 gallons) per day and in the United States is 578 liters (127.16 gallons) per day.

Developing world cities contend with 60 million new urbanites each year. Rapid urbanization increases demand and conflicts over who has clean water and who does not. Mismanagement and inadequate systems often mean inequitable allocation and shortages. Even cities with adequate access to clean water may lack the infrastructure to move water to new populations. This is the case in much of Latin America, where the population of many cities quadrupled between 1950 and 1980, and in Africa, which experienced sevenfold urban growth over the same period.

Agricultural Uses

Agriculture is increasingly dependent on irrigation, taking water away from cities. Worldwide, agriculture uses 69 percent of annual water consumption, industry takes 23 percent, and domestic use takes 8 percent. In Africa, agriculture takes 88 percent, with 7 percent for domestic and 5 percent for industrial use. Asia has comparable figures with 86 percent for agriculture, 8 percent for industry, and 6 percent for domestic use. Europe by contrast uses 54 percent of water for industry, with agriculture taking 33 percent and domestic use 13 percent.

Ninety percent of Indian water use is for agriculture, with 7 percent for industry and 3 percent for domestic needs. Japan uses the majority of its freshwater for rice irrigation, and Spain and Portugal still use a majority of their water for irrigation. California irrigates 2.6 million acres. In that state, 81 percent of water goes to agriculture; in Idaho, the figure is 98 percent.

In the 1990s, population in the eleven western U.S. states grew by 20 percent, compared to a national rate of 13.2 percent. The West is the fastest growing region, with changing agricultural and urban uses of water as well as requirements for species protection and recreation. Irrigated agriculture, mining, and commercial and residential development all demand more water. Residents also expect water recreation opportunities and safeguards for the environment, including wildlife. The West could define itself by limiting development to a level sustainable within constraints of a limited water supply. Instead, it is driven by development, and the pressure is intense to find water to cover growth. In 2000, urban and suburban development covered 18.4 million acres of the 325 million acres not under water, too steep, or public. Urban development covered 5.6 percent of the buildable land and less than 3 percent of all land.

Agriculture uses 90 percent of Nevada's water, while Las Vegas casinos and hotels produce 70 percent of Nevada's gross domestic product. The city receives an average of 4 inches of rain annually. Without water, the city's economy would falter, and the whole state would follow. Las Vegas is the most water-consuming city per capita in the United States. Its 360 gallons a day per person is over three times Oakland's 110 gallons and significantly higher than Los Angeles's 211 gallons. Recycling is practiced. For example, the Treasure Island Casino has a water recycling plant that cleans 100,000 gallons of room and restaurant water a day and uses it for outdoor landscaping. Although efforts to conserve have included encouraging gravel lawns and desert vegetation such as cactus, the city spends $19 per person on conservation but $103 per person on development of new sources. Officials claim that the casinos and hotels use only 3 percent of the city's consumption despite such attractions as a replica of a Venetian canal and a lake large enough for personal watercraft use.

Water scarcity often goes hand in hand with concerns over water security—having enough. Cities such as Las Vegas and Denver have accommodated rapid growth by offering farmers and ranchers more money than they can expect from raising stock or crops. Even with the cities taking more water, the amount of irrigated land has not diminished, and in some western states it has increased.

Urban Needs

Cities tend to use high-tech solutions rather than simple ones. Physical control of the resource rather than more sophisticated rules and procedures is the norm. Community-based solutions are set aside in favor of large-scale, privately run, technologically driven measures. Las Vegas shares a problem common to other cities: increasing numbers of the poor live in slums with no connection to the water system. Alternative water supplies take the form of small, private operations, as in Bogotá, Colombia, and elsewhere, which use water trucks or neighborhood standpipes for delivery.

The first major project under the 1902 Reclamation Act was the damming of the Salt River to provide a water supply for Phoenix, Arizona, the second-driest large city in the United States.

Development of water systems since has entailed storing water at high elevations or along major rivers for use in low-lying farm and urban areas to compensate for annual rainfall of only 10–20 inches. This has allowed development of areas that naturally would be uninhabitable. The traditional public responsibility for allocating water is increasingly becoming a private one.

The reach of cities for water can be extensive—and controversial. Denver's water comes from across the Continental Divide, and Las Vegas is planning for doubled water usage by 2030 by using its Colorado River allotment, building a reservoir in Colorado, buying Arizona's share of multistate compact water, and sucking water from northern agricultural counties. There is no plan to slow growth. The South Nevada Water Authority's (SNWA) plan to take water from the northeastern area of the state is creating friction between the city and rural residents who need the water themselves—for their livelihoods, not their canals. The Colorado River is also a shared source, with Nevada authorized only a relatively small percentage compared to neighboring states. In 2003, the SNWA agreed to take part of Arizona's allocation, and in 2008, it was in negotiations to build a desalinization plant on the Pacific and trade that water for some of California's Colorado River water. The SNWA also planned to build a $2 billion pipeline to suck water from Utah and points in between. Ranchers and farmers in the region were understandably upset at the idea of tying all the aquifers in northern Nevada together because a change in one region would impact the entirety. Environmentalists worried about the integrity of the Great Basin National Park, and Native Americans were concerned about having any water at all. The Goshute depended for drinking water entirely on springs fed by the aquifer in the Great Basin.

SNWA water is cheap, discouraging conservation. Average Las Vegas household consumption of 17,000 gallons a month in the summer costs $36.64 (2 cents per 10 gallons), while winter average use of 11,000 costs $21. Environmentalists want higher rates to promote conservation, but the SNWA rejects that idea. Water is the fuel for growth, and growth is the driver of Las Vegas.

Development generally means leveling the land, altering the topography of the watershed. It also means construction sites without ground cover. Uncovered soils may erode in heavy rains, and dirt and pesticides may wash into the water supply. Turbidity in the water can affect aquatic flora and fauna, force increased expensive water treatment, and deteriorate the water's attractiveness for recreation. Sedimentation can affect not only rivers and streams but also drainage ditches, intakes for city water, and reservoirs. Control of sedimentation involves the planting of vegetation to reduce erosion from unstable soils. It also may entail creation of sedimentation ponds and silt fences.

Urbanization alters the way water is retained. In rural areas with forests and pastures, rainfall enters the soil and collects as groundwater, which slowly returns to the surface through springs and seeps. Absorption, also known as infiltration, helps to reduce flooding, which reduces erosion. Cities mean concrete and blacktop for roads and parking lots and foundations for buildings. These areas become impervious to water, and rainfall has to be collected by storm sewers, which route the water into streams naturally prepared for seep and spring water. The impervious areas also contribute garbage and contaminants to the water flow. And roads and parking lots create heated runoff that can alter the temperature of local streams and kill fish due to thermal shock. To reduce flooding and contaminants, cities may build storage ponds to collect sediment and restrict water flow.

Urbanization adds to the volume of nitrates and phosphorous in the soil—and the water. Sewage and fertilizer are major contributors of nitrates. Not all wastewater treatment plants remove nitrogen. Excess nitrogen promotes the growth of aquatic plants and algae; these can clog water intakes as well as reducing light and oxygen, decreasing animal and plant diversity in affected waters. Nitrate-heavy drinking water is harmful to infants and livestock. Phosphorus from fertilizer, sewage, and industrial effluent can reduce oxygen in waters. Erosion of phosphorus-rich soil such as farmland or suburban lawns is a major polluter of water supplies, but phosphorus can exist even in groundwater and enter the supply through ordinary processes. As wastewater and sewage volumes increase, cities and towns have to expand and upgrade their water treatment facilities. Insufficiently treated or untreated water can become a problem because it carries disease-causing protozoa, viruses, and bacteria. When systems overflow, these pathogens can enter the streams and lakes.

Urbanization not only generates decreased infiltration and increased runoff flow from impervious surfaces (including roofs), but it also increases the severity and frequency of flooding. At the same time, it makes drought more of a problem during dry periods due to lower water tables. Storm water moves through urban areas at greater velocities and in larger volumes than in rural areas. There are fewer buffer zones and filters of the kind that reduce chemical pollution in rural areas. Downstream vegetation and wildlife in floodplains, estuaries, and the like are adversely affected by water scarcity. Low flow forces more intense treatment of wastewater discharges. Land development also increases erosion, with a construction site generating 10,000 times the erosion of undeveloped land. Urban sedimentation is generally more hazardous than natural sediment because it includes atmospheric chemicals as well as surface particles from wearing tires, decomposing roads, spills, and vehicle exhaust.

City growth means more houses, roads, commerce, shops—more concrete and lawn care and less grass and open area, more people and fewer deer and cows. Urban storm water runoff contains food waste, trash, air pollutants, wash water, oil and antifreeze, herbicides and pesticides from commercial and residential properties, de-icers, toxic metals, and many other spilled chemicals. Other pollutants are the now-banned chlordane, used for termite control, and now-banned PCBs, used as lubricants and in hydraulic oil and electrical transformers. The first hour of storm water runoff is commonly more polluted than the city's untreated sewage.

Urbanization alters the landscape, and it also affects regional water supplies in terms of both quantity and quality. It also puts pressure on existing water systems—treatment and distribution—to provide fair allocation of safe water. City water is piped to the house at an exceedingly small cost, making wells, standpipes, and water wagons obsolete. Convenience increases consumption. Increased consumption creates shortage and competition for a finite resource.

—John H. Barnhill

See also: *Agriculture; Ecosystem Management; Groundwater Recharge and Water Reuse; Population Trends and Water Demand*

BIBLIOGRAPHY

Alabama Cooperative Extension System. "Urbanization and How It Affects Water Quality." Last modified August 30, 2001. http://www.aces.edu/waterquality/articles/0121001/0121001.pdf.

Andrews, Richard N. L. *Managing the Environment, Managing Ourselves: A History of American Environmental Policy.* 2nd ed. New Haven, CT: Yale University Press, 2006.

Barrios, Anna. "Urbanization and Water Quality" (CAE Working Paper Series WP00-1). DeKalb, IL: American Farmland Trust's Center for Agriculture in the Environment, 2000. Available at http://www.farmlandinfo.org/documents/28573/wp00-1.pdf.

Hinrichsen, Don, Bryant Robey, and Ushma D. Upadhyay. "How Water Is Used." Population Reports 26, no. 1 (1998). Available at http://www.infoforhealth.org/pr/m14/m14chap2_2.shtml.

Society for International Development. "Urbanization and Water" (SID Briefing Paper No. 1). Rome, Italy: Society for International Development, 2008. http://www.sidint.net/docs/Urbanisation%20 and%20water.pdf.

Travis, William R. *The Geography of Water and Development in the American West* (Working Paper EB2003-0004). Boulder: University of Colorado at Boulder, Research Program on Environment and Behavior, Institute of Behavioral Science, 2003. Available at http://www.colorado.edu/IBS/pubs/eb/eb2003-0004.pdf.

U.S. Geological Survey. "The Effects of Urbanization on Water Quality." http://ga.water.usgs.gov/edu/urbanquality.html.

Valley Fill Litigation

In mountaintop removal mining, entire seams of coal that lie in horizontal layers in Appalachia's mountains are mined by blasting away and removing all material above them. Because explosives pulverize sedimentary rock, there is always a greater volume of material after mining than can be returned to the mine site. This excess material is referred to as spoil or overburden. The cheapest way to dispose of the spoil in the steep terrain of Appalachia is to fill the nearest hollow or valley, creating valley fills. Headwater streams, which begin in these hollows and valleys, are buried by the valley fills. In 2005, a joint study by the Environmental Protection Agency (EPA), the U.S. Army Corps of Engineers (Corps), the Office of Surface Mining (OSM), and other agencies revealed that 1,200 miles of Appalachian streams had been directly affected by valley fills, with 724 miles of streams completely buried between 1985 and 2001 (EPA 2005).

This type of large-scale surface mining began in Appalachia in the late 1970s. However, it was not until the mid-1990s, when demand for Appalachia's low-sulfur coal increased and large-scale machinery became more available, that the practice became common. Outside of the region, mountaintop removal was largely unknown until a feature article appeared in *U.S. News & World Report* in 1997 (Loeb 1997). Loeb reported that 15 to 20 percent of the mountains in southern and central West Virginia were being leveled by massive mountaintop removal operations.

Litigation over the environmental effects of mountaintop removal, and valley fills in particular, began soon after Loeb's article. Two environmental statutes govern valley fills, the Surface Mining Control and Reclamation Act of 1977 (SMCRA) and the Clean Water Act (CWA). Almost all of the litigation has been filed in federal court in the Southern District of West Virginia and appealed to the U.S. Court of Appeals for the Fourth Circuit. In addition, cases are currently pending in Kentucky, which, if appealed, would go to the Sixth Circuit, and in Virginia, which is in the Fourth Circuit. Two attorneys, Jim Hecker of Public Justice and Joe Lovett of the Appalachian Center for the Economy & the Environment, have represented the plaintiffs in the litigation.

Surface Mining Control and Reclamation Act

SMCRA establishes minimum federal standards to protect society and the environment from the harmful effects of coal mining. Under SMCRA, a state can submit its own regulatory program to OSM for approval. OSM can approve a state's program if it is at least as stringent as the federal program. After a state's program is approved, it becomes operative. However, OSM retains oversight to ensure the state adequately enforces the law.

SMCRA's stream buffer zone rule prohibits surface-mining activity that disturbs land within 100 feet of a perennial or intermittent stream unless the regulatory authority grants the mine operation a variance. In order to give a variance, the agency must find that the mining activity will not cause or contribute to a water quality violation and will not adversely affect the water quantity or quality or other environmental resources of the stream. Without such a variance, valley fills cannot be constructed.

Surface Mining Control and Reclamation Act Litigation

The first challenge to mountaintop removal mining, *Bragg v. Robertson,* involved West Virginia's enforcement of the stream buffer zone rule. In July 1998, plaintiffs brought suit against the West Virginia agency that administers the state's SMCRA program, arguing that the state engaged in a pattern and practice of approving stream buffer zone variances without finding that the fills would not adversely affect the water quantity or quality or the environmental resources of the stream. The plaintiffs also argued more broadly that the stream buffer zone rule could never allow variances for activities that bury substantial portions of streams.

The district court agreed and found that the stream buffer zone rule specifically protects streams from being filled with waste and that variances could not be granted for valley fills. With regard to the required findings that such fills would not adversely impact water quality or quantity or the stream's environmental values, the court stated that fills destroy streams and no impact "is more adverse than obliteration." The court noted, "If there is any life that cannot acclimate to life deep in a rubble pile, it is eliminated" (*Bragg* 72 F.Supp. 2d at 661).

On appeal, the Fourth Circuit ordered that the case against West Virginia be dismissed because the U.S. Constitution's Eleventh Amendment barred the plaintiffs from bringing their claim against the state in federal court. The court found that when a state's SMCRA program is accepted by OSM, SMCRA becomes a state law, and the federal court could not compel West Virginia to comply with its own law.

Clean Water Act

The Clean Water Act has two primary permitting programs designed to protect the integrity of the nation's waters. The EPA oversees most permitting through its power under Section 402 of the Act to permit discharges of pollutants into waters of the United States. The Corps also has authority under the Act. Under Section 404, the Corps has the narrow authority to permit the discharge of dredged or fill material into the nation's waters. That authority stems from the agency's historic authority over dam and water construction projects under the Rivers and Harbors Act.

The Corps cannot issue a permit for the discharge of dredge or fill that would cause or contribute to a significant degradation of the water. In determining whether significant degradation would occur, the Corps is required to assess the individual and cumulative impacts of the project on both the structure and function of the aquatic ecosystem. The Corps can permit a project that would otherwise cause significant degradation if it finds that the degradation would be sufficiently offset by compensatory mitigation measures undertaken by the applicant. In assessing the adequacy of any mitigation, the Corps must evaluate the structural and functional values that would be lost and compare them to the structural and functional values gained from mitigation.

The Corps maintains two types of permitting schemes for the discharge of dredged or fill materials. An applicant must either file for an individual permit under Section 404(a) or notify the Corps of its intent to conduct an activity that is covered under an existing general permit under Section 404(e). Individual permits require the Corps to perform an individualized assessment of the project, determine whether the impacts are significant enough to require

a full environmental impact statement (EIS), engage the public through a prescribed notice and comment proceeding, and issue a record of decision explaining why it chose to approve or deny the project.

General permits work very differently. Section 404(e) of the Clean Water Act allows the Corps to issue general permits that apply to specified types of projects that have only minimal individual and cumulative adverse effects. Under the general permitting scheme, the Corps solicits public comment and determines whether an EIS is necessary when the general permit is issued, not when a particular applicant asks the Corps to be covered under the permit. The Corps first issued a general permit for all filling associated with mining activities in 1982. The permit is referred to as Nationwide Permit 21 (NWP 21) and has been reissued six times, most recently in 2007. To be covered under NWP 21, an operator must send the Corps a preconstruction notification, along with a mitigation plan that has been approved by the appropriate SMCRA authority. The Corps then determines if the proposed mine falls within NWP 21 and provides the operator with written confirmation of its determination.

Clean Water Act Litigation: Individual Permits

Environmental plaintiffs have brought two challenges to the Corps's issuance of individual permits for filling streams in the Southern District of West Virginia. In the first, *Kentuckians for the Commonwealth v. Rivenburgh,* plaintiffs argued that the Corps lacked the authority to permit twenty-seven valley fills that would bury 6.3 miles of stream because its regulations specifically defined *fill* to exclude waste. In 2002, after all arguments were heard but before the district court ruled, the Corps changed its definition of *fill* to include specifically overburden from mining. Regardless of the rule change, the district court held that the Corps's issuance of permits was invalid because valley fills constituted waste, the disposal of which could not be permitted under Section 404. In January 2003, the Fourth Circuit overruled the district court and found that because *fill* was not defined by Congress in the Clean Water Act, the Corps's interpretation that spoil was fill was valid.

In *Ohio Valley Environmental Coalition (OVEC) v. Aracoma Coal,* environmental plaintiffs again challenged the Corps's issuance of individual permits for twenty-three valley fills that would impact thirteen miles of stream. In issuing the permits, the Corps had determined that because the companies had agreed to mitigate the damage by restoring or creating stream lengths elsewhere, the fills would not cause or contribute to a significant degradation of the waterways. The district court found that the Corps did not meet the Clean Water Act requirements because it failed to assess the ecological function of the headwaters that were to be destroyed. Without an adequate functional assessment, the court found that the Corps's determination that the compensatory mitigation was sufficient to offset lost values was invalid. The court ruled that the Corps had violated the Clean Water Act in issuing the permits.

On appeal, the Fourth Circuit again sided with the Corps, finding that its analysis of the likely impacts, while not containing any analysis of stream functions, was good enough because the Corps had used its best professional judgment. The court also found that the companies' plans to restore or create streams elsewhere to mitigate the complete loss of headwater streams was good enough, despite the lack of any scientific evidence showing that the creation of streams was feasible. The court found that the Clean Water Act did not require the Corps to differentiate some headwater streams from others.

Clean Water Act Litigation: Nationwide Permits

In 2003 and 2005, plaintiffs brought challenges to the Corps's use of NWP 21 in the Southern District of West Virginia and the Eastern District of Kentucky, respectively. The Kentucky court has not yet ruled on the merits, even though briefing was completed in 2008. In the first decision in the West Virginia case, *OVEC v. Bulen,* the district court found that the Corps's procedure for issuing the NWP violated the Clean Water Act. The district court held that the Corps issued NWP 21 without first finding that all activities to be covered would cause only minimal adverse environmental effects and without proper notice and public comment opportunities, as the Act requires. The Corps instead issued NWP 21 and created new, statutorily unauthorized procedures under which the required determination would be made after the NWP was issued and without public participation. The Fourth Circuit reversed, however, finding that the Corps could rely on postissuance procedures to ensure its preissuance minimal impact determination, even though the public has no right to participate in those postissuance procedures.

However, the Fourth Circuit's opinion in *OVEC v. Bulen* specifically left open the issue of whether the Corps's minimal impact determination when issuing NWP 21 was reasonable and supported by the administrative record. That issue was decided in the plaintiff's favor by the federal district court in *OVEC v. Hurst.* In March 2009, the West Virginia court ruled that because the Corps's minimal impact finding relied on the success of the mitigation required, and because the Corps had failed to provide any evidence that the mitigation would be successful or enforced, the Corps's decision that the mitigation was sufficient to offset any significant impacts was arbitrary and capricious. The ruling stopped permitting under NWP 21 in the Southern District of West Virginia.

On July 15, 2009, the Corps issued a notice proposing to suspend the use of NWP 21 to authorize valley fills and require individual permitting for those fills.

—Mary Varson Cromer

See also: *Army Corps of Engineers, United States; Clean Water Act of 1972*

BIBLIOGRAPHY

Bragg v. Robertson, 72 F.Supp.2d 642 (S.D.W.Va., 1999), *vacated by* 248 F.3d 275 (4th Cir. 2001).

EPA (U.S. Environmental Protection Agency). *Mountaintop Mining/ Valley Fills in Appalachia Final Programmatic Environmental Impact Statement* (EPA 9-03-R-05002). Philadelphia: EPA, 2005. Available at http://www.epa.gov/region03/mtntop/pdf/mtm-vf_fpeis_full-document.pdf.

Federal Water Pollution Control Act (Clean Water Act), U.S.C. 33, secs. 1251–1387 (1972).

Kentuckians for the Commonwealth v. Rivenburgh, 204 F. Supp. 2d 927 (S.D.W.Va. 2002), *vacated by* 317 F.3d 425 (4th Cir. 2003).

Loeb, Penny. "Shear Madness." *U.S. News & World Report,* August 3, 1997. Available at http://www.usnews.com/usnews/culture/articles/970811/archive_007620.htm.

Ohio Valley Environmental Coalition v. Aracoma Coal Co., 479 F. Supp. 2d 607 (S.D.W.Va. 2007), *reversed by* 556 F.3d 177 (4th Cir. 2009).

Ohio Valley Environmental Coalition v. Bulen, 410 F. Supp. 2d 450 (S.D. W.Va. 2004), *vacated in part by* 429 F.3d 493 (4th Cir. 2005).

Ohio Valley Environmental Coalition v. Hurst, 604 F.Supp.2d 860 (S.D.W.Va. 2009).

Surface Mining Control and Reclamation Act, U.S.C. 30, secs. 1201–1328 (1977).

U.S. Department of the Army, Corps of Engineers. Proposed Suspension and Modification of Nationwide Permit 21, 74 Fed. Reg. 34,311 (July 15, 2009).

Wastewater Treatment

A major environmental problem throughout the United States, as well as in all other developed countries, is the treatment of both domestic and industrial wastewater. Treatment involves the removal of a large range of contaminants from wastewater and household sewage in order to return the water to the environment or make it ready to be pumped back to houses and factories. Treatment also means removing pollutants and contaminants from industrial waste. The contaminants vary considerably and may be physical, chemical, or biological. Although some can be removed easily, a complicated series of procedures is required to eliminate most so that water can be reused.

Because of the increasing demand for water, especially in industrial areas and large cities, most major industrialized countries have a system for recycling water, and the United States is no exception. The reliance that countries place on recycling depends on their consumption levels and local precipitation levels. For example, a study of countries in the Organisation for Economic Co-operation and Development (OECD) in 1983 showed that the percentage of the population served by a wastewater treatment plant ranged from 100 percent in Sweden, to 30 percent in Japan, to only 2 percent in Greece.

While distillation is the easiest and most effective system for treating water, and does not involve a chemical reaction, the costs involved are very large. Except in rare circumstances, it is not cost-effective to use distillation to generate drinking water for humans or animals (except in the case of prepared or bottled drinks), water for human or animal bathing or washing, or water for most industrial or agricultural purposes. However, industrial vacuum distillation columns can be used when large quantities of water are required.

Early Treatments

Historically, water containing urine, fecal matter, and discarded food was "treated" more by locating the sewage works in better sites than through any major effort to deal with the wastewater itself. This approach did not prevent outbreaks of cholera in 1849. Some 4,500 people died in St. Louis, Missouri, and then 3,000 died in New Orleans, Louisiana, as the cholera was spread by untreated waste along the Mississippi River. This outbreak is believed to have resulted in the death of former president James Polk four months after the end of his term in office. This outbreak was carried by humans as well as waterways, and many people in California and other parts of the West died. Five years later, another outbreak in Chicago saw the deaths of 3,500, and an outbreak in London at the same time was clearly linked to contaminated water. These epidemics led to attempts to improve supplies of drinking water in North America, but another 50,000 died in outbreaks from 1866 until 1873, and between 1883 until 1887 another outbreak claimed 50,000 people in the Americas. In order to combat these outbreaks, civic authorities throughout the United States—and indeed the world—started systematic wastewater treatment programs.

The disposal of dead bodies was also cause for concern. In Britain until the nineteenth century, the majority of people were buried around their places of worship in churchyards, often in the center of villages or towns. The use of churchyards continued even in cities such as London. This practice was briefly followed in North America. However in the United States, urban areas started to have large municipal and public (and often nondenominational) cemeteries that were located outside major population areas—a practice that was later followed in cities in Britain as well. The increasing use of cremation has, to a large extent, ameliorated the problem of body disposal in many U.S. cities.

Industrial and Agricultural Waste

The Industrial Revolution changed the nature of waste being produced. Many early mills in North America were situated alongside rivers, allowing for effluent and waste products to be dumped into these rivers. As industry and the population grew, it became necessary to treat the wastewater produced by industrial plants in order to reduce toxicity and to prevent disease, as well as to provide water for human consumption and for agriculture or horticulture.

Since the start of the Industrial Revolution, there have been major problems with industrial waste. For example, the water used to cool machinery is often contaminated with toxic substances. In the iron and steel industry, water is not only a coolant but is also used as a lubricant, and oils and metallic solids commonly end up in the water. This is exacerbated when the metals (iron, steel, tin, copper, and chrome) have been plated, painted, or galvanized, because these processes often lead to sulfuric acid and hydrochloric acid ending up in the water. For many years such waste was discharged into the water supply—usually rivers—without any treatment.

Increased use of fertilizers, herbicides, and pesticides in both agriculture and horticulture poses problems as well. These substances have had a major effect on the water supply and again increase the need for the treatment of the water. The system of removing chemicals from agricultural waste involves collecting water in large settling tanks where an aerobic granular reactor removes nitrogen and phosphorus quite easily.

Waste Treatments

An increase in the variety of contaminants has meant that the method of treating industrial wastewater is now not dissimilar to that used in areas where mining or quarrying takes place, although in these places, slurry formed from rock particles has also been washed into rivers and into groundwater. To treat the wastewater from industry and from mining, the wastewater is put through a number of processes that gradually remove all contaminants. The first involves filtration to remove the larger particles. Then a process called sedimentation uses an aerobic granular reactor. However, neither of these processes removes very fine solids, or solids that have the same or similar density as water particles. Removing these requires ultrafiltration, whereby colloids come out of suspension, or flocculation, in which alum salts and polyelectrolytes are used. Sedimentation is usually followed by ion exchange whereby natural or synthetic resins can effectively remove calcium, carbonate, and magnesium ions and replace them with hydrogen and hydroxyl ions. As new chemicals are discovered, scientists work on different filtration techniques and develop new solvents.

This process is now fairly straightforward, but because of the size of urban areas and industrial plants, there are often civic planning concerns about the size of wastewater treatment plant needed. The location of the water beds and public worry about possible and actual odors have led to some protests over wastewater treatment plant locations. A 2010 protest that received national attention, and is typical of many, happened in Edgewood, Indiana, where the town was planning to build its own wastewater treatment works. Edgewood wanted to reduce its dependence on the city of Anderson, which was starting to charge more for water treatment to offset rising costs. In Salt Lake City, civic authorities have addressed public concerns by locating the landfill and wastewater treatment facilities next to each other and instituting an active program to recapture methane, which, in turn, is used to generate electricity.

In 2007, an oil refinery in Indiana received a permit to discharge higher levels of pollutants into Lake Michigan, leading to massive protests and petitions in Chicago. The U.S. House of Representatives voted in July 2007, by 387 to 26, to urge Indiana to reconsider the issuing of the permit.

This was to no avail, and the refinery continued operations. Following the 2010 Deepwater Horizon oil spill in the Gulf of Mexico, there were renewed calls in Indiana to change the method of treating wastewater and reduce the amount of wastewater permitted to be discharged in the first place. The oil refinery in Indiana was operated by BP, and it had often been cited for environmental violations.

In recent years there have also been problems with nanowaste—waste generated by work on nanotechnology. Because of the small size of this waste, it is not noticeable to the naked eye. As a result, it has often been overlooked, but it may seep into the water system and exacerbate existing problems.

—Justin Corfield

See also: *Detergents; Sewage*

BIBLIOGRAPHY

Azad, Hardam Singh. *Industrial Wastewater Management Handbook.* New York: McGraw-Hill, 1976.
Batterman, Stuart, Joseph Eisenberg, Rebecca Hardin, Margaret E. Kruk, Marcia Carmen Lemos, Anna M. Michalak, Bhramar Mukherjee, et al. "Sustainable Control of Water-Related Infectious Diseases: A Review and Proposal for Interdisciplinary Health-Based Systems Research." *Environmental Health Perspectives* 117, no. 7 (2009): 1023–32. Available at http://ehp03.niehs.nih.gov/article/info%3Adoi%2F10.1289%2Fehp.0800423.
Brennan-Calanan, Renee M., and Mark A. Gallo. "Bacterial Air Pollution at a Wastewater Treatment Plant." *Bios* 79, no. 4 (2008): 150–59.
Hammer, Mark J., and Mark J. Hammer Jr. *Water and Wastewater Technology.* 6th ed. Englewood Cliffs, NJ: Prentice Hall, 2008.
Kessler, Rebecca. "Water Treatment: Sweeteners Persist in Waterways." *Environmental Health Perspectives* 117, no. 10 (2009): A438. Available at http://www.ncbi.nlm.nih.gov/pmc/articles/PMC2897219/.
Roberts, David C., Christopher D. Clark, William M. Park, and Burton C. English. "A Spatial Assessment of Possible Water Quality Trading Markets in Tennessee." *Review of Agricultural Economics* 30, no. 4 (2008): 711–28.
Rosenberg, Charles C. *The Cholera Years: The United States in 1832, 1849, and 1866.* Chicago: University of Chicago Press, 1962.
Sander, Libby. "Chicagoans Protest as Indiana Lets a Refinery Add to Lake Pollution." *New York Times,* July 31, 2007. Available at http://www.nytimes.com/2007/07/31/us/31refinery.html.
Schmidt, Charles W. "The Yuck Factor: When Disgust Meets Discovery." *Environmental Health Perspectives* 116, no. 12 (2008): A524–27. Available at http://ehp03.niehs.nih.gov/article/info%3Adoi%2F10.1289%2Fehp.116-a524.
Tchobanoglous, George, Franklin L. Burton, H. David Stensel, and Metcalf & Eddy Inc. *Wastewater Engineering: Treatment and Reuse.* New York: McGraw-Hill, 2003.
Vrooman, Morrell, Jr. "Designing Wastewater Treatment Plants for Safety." *Journal of the Water Pollution Control Federation* 41, no. 3, part 1 (1969): 474–81.

Water Law

American water law consists of a complex amalgamation of case law, statutes, and regulations at both the state and federal level. This complexity is in part due to the physical nature of water: rainfall, aquifers, rivers, oceans, and the hydrologic cycle proceed apace with little regard to human-made boundaries. The geographic, social, and economic diversity of the United States, past and present, has also contributed to the development of a wide array of theories, laws, and regulatory bodies. While water rights can be privately owned, American water law also acknowledges the public nature of this precious resource. The notion that access to water is a public right stretches back to Roman and English common law traditions. After the American Revolution, water law developed differently in different states and regions. Along with the Industrial Revolution came an increasing demand to allow for private ownership of water rights. Three major systems characterize U.S. water law today: riparian, prior appropriation, and hybrid. The law continues to evolve, shaping and reflecting the balance between federal and state control over water adjudication, improved understanding of the interconnectivity of ground-water and surface water, and increased awareness of eco-logical concerns and the recreational value of water.

Water as a Public Resource

Roman doctrine articulated principles about the public nature of water. The sea was a community resource, open to all for uses such as navigation and fishing (Sax 2004). Similarly, English common law provided for the public the right to navigate and make other uses of waterways (Getches 1997). Under modern-day American water law, bodies of water that are navigable have certain protections to ensure that they remain available for public use. Private owners cannot obstruct navigability of waters that flow through their property. If a body of water was "navigable in fact" at the time that a state entered the union, that body is subject to federal regulation. States, on the other hand, use different definitions of navigability to help determine whether or not the public has the right to access certain rivers. Courts have also ruled that the public can cross private property in order to access water and beaches (Johnson 2008).

Legal Systems for Water Allocation

The different states follow three different legal systems to allocate distribution of flowing water. Twenty-nine eastern states use riparian rights. Prior appropriation has been adopted by nine western states. Ten states employ a hybrid system that combines prior appropriation and riparian rights. Hawaii and Louisiana utilize unique laws due to their respective colonial histories.

Under the riparian doctrine, water rights inhere in land ownership. One who owns land along a waterway is a ripar-ian (Worster 1985). The riparian doctrine has its roots in Roman, French, and English tradition. Under Roman law, running water, like oceans, could not be owned. Under French and English law, rights to water were usufruct—that is to say, one had the right to *use* water but not to *own* it (Getches 1997; Sax 2004). In the decades following the American Revolution, various state courts developed the riparian doctrine in response to social and geographic reali-ties. Most uses of water were agricultural, and the earliest states were located east of the 100th meridian where flow-ing water and rainfall were abundant. Early cases emphasized the importance of maintaining the natural flow of a stream (Getches 1997).

The Industrial Revolution changed how Americans used rivers and streams. Mills, for example, began to rely upon water power and diverted more and more waters from rivers and streams. Nineteenth-century case law reflected this change in two ways: by altering the criteria for riparian use of waterways from preserving natural flow to allowing for "reasonable use" of a stream and through the introduction of an alternate system of water allocation, prior appropriation.

A crucial articulation of the reasonable use doctrine came from the 1827 decision in the case of *Tyler v. Wilkinson*. In this case, a downstream mill owner took an upstream mill owner to court for diverting water from a river to the extent that it harmed the downstream owner's ability to power his mill. The court held that all riparians had equal rights to the water and that, in theory, the upstream user could not diminish the river's natural flow. The court also recognized that the "natural flow" doctrine was impracticable for pow-ering mills, which stored up a reservoir and then released the water in order to gain a greater flow—and therefore greater power. Therefore, the judge held that an upstream user could make "reasonable use" of the water (Getches 1997; Bureau of Land Management n.d.).

Today, this reasonable use doctrine continues to predom-inate in riparian water law. "Reasonable use" has been defined differently over the course of the past 200 years. In the nineteenth century, judges tended to apply the definition in ways that helped ensure the growth of industry. Today, decision makers implement this and other criteria, such as protecting ecosystems and recreational capacities (Worster 1985; Getches 1997).

In all states, even those governed by prior appropriation and hybrid systems, riparian owners have special rights to use the surface of waters that pass through or adjoin their property. Riparian owners must also, however, allow for the public to use the surface of navigable waters (Getches 1997).

Unlike the riparian system, wherein water rights are attached to land ownership, the prior appropriation system bases water rights on usage (Getches 1997). Whoever made first use of a given body of water has the superior claim to the water right. Prior appropriation, like the reasonable use doctrine, developed as the United States industrialized. Whereas "reasonable use" allowed for the accumulation and storage of water on the part of riparian landowners, prior appropriation allowed for even nonriparians to own water rights, provided they made "beneficial use" of the water.

Despite the traditional view that prior appropriation was a response to western aridity, historians have come to a consensus that it actually originated in the industrializing East as judges tried to support the rights of mill owners to dam streams (Worster 1985; Pisani 1987). Regardless, prior appropriation soon became the system for allocating water in the American West, whereas riparian water regimes continue to characterize eastern water law.

Mining and agriculture were vanguard industries in the Euro-American settlement of the West. Miners originally plied their trade upon lands that were in the public domain, controlled by the federal government. Hydraulic mining required large quantities of water. Early miners applied the same rule to water that they used for claims on gold and other minerals—"first in time, first in right." The 1882 Colorado case *Coffin v. Left Hand Ditch* signaled the official adoption of prior appropriation in western states; in this case the Colorado Supreme Court declared that the doctrine was an "imperative necessity" (Sax 2004). Over time, this system helped encourage those individuals or corporations who could afford to do so to buy up water rights. Prior appropriation thus contributed to the commodification of water (Worster 1985; Pisani 1987). Because establishing who first made use of a given waterway is so important to gaining or acquiring water rights, Spanish and Mexican precedents remain key to adjudication in the American Southwest.

Three west coast states and six states that straddle the 100th meridian, as well as Mississippi, use the hybrid system of water allocation. This system is also sometimes referred to as the "California doctrine" because it was developed earliest and most fully in California, particularly in the cases *Irwin v. Phillips* (1855) and *Lux v. Haggin* (1886). In most hybrid states, some riparian rights were already established when the state adopted prior appropriation (Getches 1997). In general, riparian rights converted to appropriative rights, even if the "beneficial use" criterion was not met until later (Bureau of Land Management n.d.).

The Federal Government and Water Law

Though much water law is determined at the state level, there are instances in which the federal government plays a role in allocating water. There are many enduring conflicts between two or more different states over, for example, a river that flows between them. The Supreme Court has jurisdiction in these disputes and has decided that such conflicts should be adjudicated using "equitable apportionment." Today, a variety of interstate compacts govern water apportionment. Some interstate compacts include the federal government as a party (Johnson 2008). In addition, the federal government has entered into water treaties with Canada and Mexico. These treaties preempt state laws (Getches 1997).

The federal government plays a role in water allocation in several other ways. In the first half of the twentieth century, the construction of large water projects, like dams for hydroelectric power, began the involvement of the Bureau of Reclamation and other federal agencies in water law. Today, the federal government plays a regulatory role through mechanisms such as the Clean Water Act, the protection of wetlands and waterways, and the Endangered Species Act (Getches 1997; Johnson 2008).

The federal government also participates in water allocation via the reserved rights doctrine, which applies to Native American reservations and some other federal lands. The reserved rights doctrine is also known as the Winters Doctrine because of its roots in the *Winters v. United States* case. In this 1908 decision, the Supreme Court ruled that a Native American reservation had a prior water right dating to the establishment of the reservation, whether or not the people living on the reservation had been using the water as of that date. The Winters Doctrine involves the federal government in water allocation decisions within states, if that decision pertains to Native American reservations. The doctrine also applies to other kinds of federal lands, such as parks, wildlife refuges, national forests, or military bases (Getches 1997).

Recent Trends in Water Law

Until the twentieth century, the origins and workings of groundwater remained mysterious. As articulated in the 1843 English case *Acton v. Blundell,* the "rule of capture" allowed property owners to pump an unlimited amount of water, even if so doing would harm adjoining landowners (Bureau of Land Management n.d.). As technologies for pumping groundwater improved in the twentieth century, courts devised a variety of methods of regulating it. Today, various states apply different methods of regulating groundwater usage. Furthermore, judges and policy makers are adapting groundwater law to account for modern understandings of the interconnectivity of groundwater, surface water, and precipitation (Getches 1997).

Urbanization also produced a huge, and ongoing, demand for municipal water in the West and East in the twentieth century. Conflicts between agricultural water users and cities are one common manifestation of this demand, as are debates over the meaning and reality of the so-called pueblo rights doctrine. Two other important trends in water law in the last decades have been increased concern on the part of courts, regulatory agencies, and lawmakers for protecting ecological values and maintaining water flow for recreational purposes (Getches 1997; Sax 2004). These concerns exemplify the ways in which social, economic, and geographic conditions shape the law.

Water law has reflected the sometimes conflicting values imbued in American history and society. Public access to water is deeply ingrained in American water law; so too is the impetus to enable private development of natural resources like water. Ensuing industrial growth has historically been protected and promoted by judges and lawmakers; now, many seek to use the law to protect the environment from the consequences of that growth. Water law is complex because it must be to account for this diversity of values, as well as the many different ways in which Americans rely upon this precious resource.

—Denise Holladay Damico

See also: *Bureau of Reclamation; Clean Water Act of 1972; Endangered Species Act (1973); Government Water Decision Making;* Irwin v. Phillips *(California, 1855);* Lux v. Haggin *(California, 1886); Pueblo Water Doctrine; Reasonable Use Doctrine;* Winters v. United States *(1908)*

BIBLIOGRAPHY

Bureau of Land Management, National Science and Technology Center. "Western States Water Laws." http://www.blm.gov/nstc/WaterLaws/abstract1.html.

Getches, David H. *Water Law in a Nutshell.* St. Paul, MN: West, 1997.

Johnson, John S. *United States Water Law: An Introduction.* Boca Raton, FL: CRC, 2008.

Pisani, Donald J. "Enterprise and Equity: A Critique of Western Water Law in the Nineteenth Century." *Western Historical Quarterly* 18, no. 1 (1987): 15–37.

Sax, Joseph L. "The History of Water Law in the United States." *Water Resources Center Archives (WRCA) News* 11, no. 1 (2004): 1, 5–7. Available at http://www.lib.berkeley.edu/WRCA/pdfs/news111.pdf.

Worster, Donald. *Rivers of Empire: Water, Aridity, and the Growth of the American West.* New York: Oxford University Press, 1985.

Water Treatment

See *Wastewater Treatment*

Waterborne Diseases in Drinking Water

Waterborne disease is chemical poisoning or infection by pathogenic microorganisms such as viruses, bacteria, protozoans, and helminths (parasitic worms) transmitted by drinking or otherwise coming in contact with contaminated water.

Types of Waterborne Disease

The table on page 193 illustrates several of the key waterborne diseases that are of concern in the United States and throughout the world with their symptoms and the microbial agents that cause them.

Transmission

Transmission of these diseases is frequently through drinking water contaminated with human or animal feces or through food prepared with contaminated water. Other routes of infection include food, soil, and person-to-person contact.

Contamination of drinking water from water systems that rely on surface water, such as lakes and rivers, can occur when human or animal waste is swept into the system. The overflow of sewage systems or breaks in lines can exacerbate the problem. According to the United Nations Children's Fund (UNICEF) and the World Health Organization (WHO), an estimated 2.5 billion people lack access to improved sanitation facilities. In addition, approximately 1 billion people could not obtain safe drinking water (White Johansson and Wardlaw 2009). Prevention of waterborne

Select Waterborne Diseases

Disease	Microbial Agent	General Symptoms
Campylobacteriosis	Bacterium (*Campylobacter jejuni*)	Fever, abdominal pain, diarrhea
Typhoid fever	Bacterium (*Salmonella typhi*)	Fever, headache, constipation, appetite loss, nausea, diarrhea, vomiting, appearance of an abdominal rash
Shigellosis	Bacterium (*Shigella* species)	Fever, diarrhea, bloody stool
Cholera	Bacterium (*Vibrio cholerae*)	Watery diarrhea, vomiting, occasional muscle cramps
Cryptosporidiosis	Protozoan (*Cryptosporidium parvum*)	Diarrhea, abdominal discomfort
Amebiasis	Protozoan (*Entamoeba histolytica*)	Abdominal discomfort, fatigue, diarrhea, flatulence, weight loss
Giardiasis	Protozoan (*Giardia lamblia*)	Diarrhea, abdominal discomfort
Hepatitis	Virus (hepatitis A)	Fever, chills, abdominal discomfort, jaundice, dark urine, diarrhea
Viral Gastroenteritis	Viruses (Norwalk, rotavirus, and other types)	Fever, headache, gastrointestinal discomfort, vomiting, diarrhea
Guinea-worm disease (Dracunculiasis)	Helminth (*Dracunculus medinensis*) a nematode worm	Edema, a blister, and eventually an ulcer, fever, nausea, vomiting

Source: Adapted from EPA (U.S. Environmental Protection Agency). *Preventing Waterborne Disease: A Focus on EPA's Research* (EPA/640/K-93/001). Cincinnati, OH: EPA, 1993. Available at http://www.epa.gov/microbes/h2odis.pdf.

disease relies upon providing clean drinking water from sanitary water systems, maintaining sanitary sewage facilities, and educating populations on how to improve hygiene.

Incidence

In developing countries, four-fifths of all of illness is caused by waterborne diseases, with diarrhea being the leading cause of childhood death. Each year, an estimated 2.5 billion cases of diarrhea occur among children under five years of age, and estimates suggest that overall incidence has remained relatively stable over the past two decades. Still, the actual incidence of waterborne disease is difficult, if not impossible, to establish for several reasons. Diseases may be asymptomatic, or they may go unreported or undiagnosed. Reporting requirements differ from jurisdiction to jurisdiction and cross-nationally. In general, waterborne disease is underreported in both developed and developing nations. In 1997, Mohanty suggested that in Hyderabad, India, hospital incidence data underreported community incidence of waterborne disease by a factor of approximately 200.

Although underreporting occurs in both developed and developing nations, it is a more serious problem in poorer nations. Here fewer persons seek medical attention due to its cost and unavailability. Overworked and underpaid physicians and other health care personnel may need to

choose between spending time on the surveillance of infectious diseases and on the treatment of patients. Therefore, observed differences between developing and developed nations in reported rates of waterborne disease are likely to be understated.

Global Burden

The World Health Organization calculates the global burden of disease (GBD) using the disability-adjusted life year (DALY). This time-based measure combines years of life lost due to premature mortality and years of life lost due to time lived in states of less than full health. Waterborne disease contributes significantly to GBD.

One of the common symptoms of many waterborne diseases is diarrhea, which involves the passage of loose or watery stools three or more times daily or more frequently than normal. Although estimating diarrhea's incidence is difficult, the World Health Organization (2010) reports that it is the second leading cause of death and malnutrition for children less than five years old, killing 1.5 million children a year. Children under five years of age are more likely to die of diarrhea than adults and older children. There are 2 billion total cases annually, and the disease accounts for 4 percent of deaths worldwide and 5 percent of disability caused by health loss. In Southeast Asia and Africa, it accounts for 8.5 percent and 7.7 percent of all deaths, respectively.

In 2010, WHO reported that 87 percent of cholera cases in the year 2000 had occurred in Africa, where there were 140,000 estimated cases with 5,000 deaths. Cholera is caused by a bacterium known as *Vibrio cholera,* which is transmitted by consuming food or drinking water that has been contaminated by human feces. As noted in the WHO report, profuse diarrhea and subsequent dehydration can cause death in up to 50 percent of severe cases. With treatment, however, death occurs in less than 1 percent of cases.

The economic burden of waterborne disease is apparent in the case of Dracunculiasis (Guinea worm disease). Located exclusively in the developing world, the disease is rarely fatal, but researchers estimate that in Nigeria, infected people lose 100 days of work per year and that infected children are absent from school for 25 percent of the year (Cairncross, Muller, and Zagaria 2002). The disease is transmitted by drinking contaminated water containing the cyclops flea. This flea ingests the Guinea worm larva, and when the flea is digested in the human stomach, the larva is released and penetrates the gut wall. After about a year, the worm emerges, and the cycle begins to repeat (World Health Organization 2010). Although the World Health Organization noted in 2010 that there were over 50 million cases in the 1950s, by 1999 the number of cases had dropped to an estimated 96,000, all located in thirteen African nations. Of those cases, 63,000 were located in the Sudan, involved at the time in a civil war. Provision of sanitary water supplies brings about the virtual eradication of Dracunculiasis in rural areas.

Recent Success

Success in the alleviation of Dracunculiasis underscores an important point about waterborne disease generally: the reduction or even elimination of many of these diseases is quite possible with a commitment to improving sanitation and providing clean water. Poverty is certainly a factor here, but the success with Guinea worm disease is an indication that poverty is not an absolute barrier. An important ingredient of success is a public policy that recognizes and deals with the problem of waterborne disease.

In dealing with the prevention of diarrhea, researchers report other simple, inexpensive, and effective methods of prevention. In 2004, Luby et al. reported the results of a study of involving the effect of hand washing on the incidence of diarrheal disease. They found that when households in squatter settlements in Karachi, Pakistan, were given soap and regular encouragement to engage in hand washing, children had a 53 percent lower incidence of diarrhea.

Although prevention of waterborne diseases is crucial, much of the success in dealing with these diseases comes through reducing the mortality rate through treatment. Perhaps the most dramatic success in dealing with the mortality of waterborne disease occurred in the latter half of the last century with the introduction of oral rehydration therapy (ORT), or the replacement of fluids and electrolytes in the treatment of dehydration due to diarrhea. Early efforts to deal with dehydration associated with diarrhea in cholera patients began in the 1830s, according to Phillips (1967), but the use of intravenous solutions did not begin for over 100 years. Oral solutions developed during the 1940s eventually led to a substantial decrease in fatality rates (King et al. 2003). During the early 1970s, researchers tested oral electrolyte solutions on refugees from Bangladesh. The successful results hastened the development of the first World Health Organization's (WHO) guidelines for ORT and the production of standard packets of oral rehydration salts. Now ORT is the primary treatment for acute gastroenteritis (King et al. 2003). With the introduction of ORT, consisting of glucose, sodium, and clean water, the mortality of children less than five years of age had dropped from 5 million to 1.5 million in 2004 (White Johansson and Wardlaw 2009).

Oral rehydration therapy works by reducing the excessive excretion of nutrients and water due to the damage diarrhea does to the intestines. When an oral rehydration salt solution reaches the small intestines, the sodium and glucose in the solution are cotransported across the intestinal lining. The increased sodium in the intestines promotes the absorption of water into the body. The discovery that glucose receptors in the intestines permit this cotransport of sodium and glucose had been hailed by some as potentially one of the most important medical advances of the twentieth century (White Johansson and Wardlaw 2009). In spite of the proven effectiveness of ORT, as of 2009 it is still available to only 39 percent of children under five years of age. UNICEF and WHO are spearheading an effort to expand its use.

Although waterborne disease takes a disproportionate toll in developing nations, it does not leave developed nations untouched. In the spring of 1933 in Milwaukee, Wisconsin, there was an outbreak of cryptosporidiosis. Kramer and other researchers (1996) used a random telephone survey to gather data on the outbreak and estimated that 403,000 residents exhibited symptoms of the disease. The median duration of the illness was nine days with twelve watery stools a day, fever, abdominal cramps, and vomiting. Existing sanitation methods were not sufficient to protect against this protozoan-based disease.

Some writers suggest that in the future, waterborne disease now concentrated in developing nations will spread to more developed areas as projected global warming results in widespread flooding and higher surface water temperatures. The result could be particularly severe in the 950 cities throughout the United States that that utilize combined sewer systems. Combined systems carry storm water and sewage in the same pipes. During heavy rains, the systems often cannot handle the volume, which results in raw sewage being dumped into lakes or waterways, including those that supply drinking water.

—Meigan M. Fields and Jerry Murtagh

See also: *Climate Change; Poverty and Water*

BIBLIOGRAPHY

Cairncross, Sandy, Ralph Muller, and Nevio Zagaria. "Dracunculiasis (Guinea Worm Disease) and the Eradication Initiative." *Clinical Microbiology Reviews* 15, no. 2 (2002): 223–46. Available at http://cmr.asm.org/content/vol15/issue2/index.dtl.

EPA (U.S. Environmental Protection Agency). *Preventing Waterborne Disease: A Focus on EPA's Research* (EPA/640/K-93/001). Cincinnati, OH: EPA, 1993. Available at http://www.epa.gov/microbes/h2odis.pdf.

Ford, Timothy Edgcumbe. "Microbiological Safety of Drinking Water: United States and Global Perspectives." *Environmental Health Perspectives* 107, no. S1 (1999): 191–206. Available at http://ehp.niehs.nih.gov/members/1999/Suppl-1/191-206ford/ford-full.html.

King, Caleb K., Roger Glass, Joseph S. Bresee, and Christopher Duggan. "Managing Acute Gastroenteritis among Children: Oral Rehydration, Maintenance, and Nutritional Therapy." *Morbidity and Mortality Weekly Report* 52, no. RR16 (2003): 1–16. Available at http://www.cdc.gov/mmwr/preview/mmwrhtml/rr5216a1.htm.

Kramer, Michael H., Barbara L. Herwaldt, Gunther F. Craun, Rebecca L. Calderon, and Dennis D. Juranek. "Surveillance for Waterborne-Disease Outbreaks—United States, 1993–1994." *Morbidity and Mortality Weekly Report* 45, SS-1 (1996): 1–33. Available at http://www.cdc.gov/mmwr/preview/mmwrhtml/00040818.htm.

Luby, Stephen P., Mubina Agboatwalla, Daniel R. Feikin, John Painter, Ward Billhimer, Arshad Altaf, and Robert M. Hoekstra. "Effect of Handwashing on Child Health: A Randomised Controlled Trial." *The Lancet* 366, no. 9481 (2005): 225–33. Available at http://www.aku.edu/CHS/pdf/SoapHealth_ARI_Lancet_Man.pdf.

Lydersen, Kari. "Risk of Disease Rises with Water Temperatures." *Washington Post*, October 20, 2008. Available at http://www.washingtonpost.com/wp-dyn/content/story/2008/10/19/ST2008101901645.html.

Mohanty, Jatish Chandra. "Environmental Health Risk Analysis of Drinking Water and Lead in Hyderabad City, India." PhD diss., Harvard University, 1997.

Phillips, Robert A. "Twenty Years of Cholera Research." *Journal of the American Medical Association* 202, no. 7 (1967): 610–14.

White Johansson, Emily, and Tessa Wardlaw, eds. *Diarrhoea: Why Children Are Still Dying and What Can Be Done.* Geneva, Switzerland: United Nations Children's Fund/World Health Organization, 2009. Available at http://7pointplan.org/diarrhoea-why-children-are-still-dying-and-what-can-be-done.pdf.

World Health Organization. "Water Sanitation and Health: Water-Related Disease." 2010. http://www.who.int/water_sanitation_health/diseases/.

Wells

Wells allow access to freshwater that is underground. Wells that occur naturally are known as artesian wells. The construction of wells is particularly important in areas where access to freshwater is, or might be, restricted. This is certainly the case in arid areas such as in the southwestern United States. However, a well is also crucial in areas where access to rivers and streams—the usual sources of freshwater—might be restricted for a period of time. This might occur in places where the rivers or streams often dry up or when people are seeking refuge in a fortified area that has been constructed on a hill, where a siege might cut off the supply of water.

Historical Background

The need for access to significant quantities of freshwater—for drinking and irrigation and other uses—has led people to settle near rivers or natural springs since ancient times. In addition, many ancient peoples dug wells to ensure a ready supply of freshwater.

Early well construction in North America mostly sought freshwater that was not far from the surface. However, the Ancestral Pueblo people in a settlement at Mesa Verde relied on a system of ducts and basins that channeled water, rather than having to rely on digging wells into the ground.

Early British settlers in North America did not dig many wells. In Britain, each village had at least one well and often more. Over time, traditions and mysticism had grown up around some of these—they were imbued with special powers, often to cure diseases—in a way that revolted many Protestants. Certainly these mystical associations were abhorred by the Puritans settlers. Wells did form an early part of public works programs in early North American settlements, and forts had wells. For the most part, however, early settlers relied more on ponds and streams. Certainly many maps of Boston dating from the 1770s show ponds rather than wells. At Mount Vernon, George Washington was able to rely on water from a nearby stream. By contrast, at Monticello, Thomas Jefferson's home regularly had insufficient water, as the original well was unable to provide enough for the running of the household; cisterns were built to store rainwater.

A number of places take their name from natural springs such as Wells, Nevada—originally Humboldt Wells—and Desert Hot Springs and Bubbling Wells, both in California. At Palm Springs, California, archaeologists have unearthed evidence of 400 to 500 years of habitation, undoubtedly because of the spring there. That water source led the Spanish to refer to the area as Agua Caliente.

As settlement in North America spread out from New England and the Atlantic coast, where freshwater from rivers, streams, and lakes was plentiful, it became necessary to start building wells in the new townships. Joseph Smith of Kirtland, Ohio, was one of many water diviners hired to ensure that wells were built at the best possible location. His son, Joseph Smith Jr., was involved in digging many wells; he later went on to found the Church of Jesus Christ of Latter-day Saints. Samuel Clemens (using the pseudonym Mark Twain) writes of many people digging wells, mainly in marginal agricultural areas; in literature, digging a well may encapsulate the concept of hard work.

Wells were always a necessity in the Southwest and West. For example, at the Alamo, in Texas, there were two wells located within the compound. One was directly behind the main gate, and the other was just to the north of the church. During the late 1870s and the 1880s, the opening up of the semiarid grasslands of Colorado, Wyoming, and the Dakotas led to many farmers digging wells in an often desperate search for water. Howard Ruede in central Kansas initially had to journey for a quarter of a mile to bring water from a stream, and his surviving letters tell of his joy at finding water at the bottom of his newly constructed well.

In Nebraska, where there were also shortages of water, some farms managed to install expensive windmill towers whereby the wind would generate the power to pump up water from far underground. And in Texas, the township of Ozana was built around a well that had been drilled by E. M. Powell, an early land surveyor; the main street was later named Waterworks Drive. The Court House Well at Jackson, California, dates from 1851 and is fifty-two feet deep. And Tyson's Well in La Paz County, Arizona, provided water for travelers passing through the township of Quartzsite. The Leal Well at Fremont, California, is 100 feet deep; it takes its name from Silviera Leal who paid for its construction on his ranch in 1925.

There are now a number of famous wells in the United States—the most well-known is perhaps Big Well in Greensburg, Kansas. Constructed in 1887 at a cost of $45,000, it initially provided water for the work on the Santa Fe and Rock Island railroads. It is now one of the largest wells in the world at 32 feet in diameter and 109 feet deep. It is believed that only Saint Patrick's Well in Orvieto, Italy, is larger. In 1972, Big Well was designated a National Museum and listed on the National Register of Historic Places (as "Greenburg Well"), and in the following year the American Water Works Association declared it an American Water Landmark. For many years, the deepest well in the United States was that built by Nobourn Thomas in 1829 in Fulton, Indiana. He discovered the water was very salty, and the well water was bottled and sold for its perceived medicinal properties.

Another famous well was built by William De La Grange in 1894 in Selma, California, where he used steam power to pump up to 350 gallons of water per minute onto his ranch at times of greatest need. And in California, the Fairhaven Pump House helped provide drinking water for people, while water from the nearby Kern River was used for irrigation.

The famous Old City Well in Camilla, Georgia, was constructed in 1880. It was not only a good location for unlimited quantities of freshwater but also became a major gathering point for locals until the installation of a water system. It was restored in 1963 as a tourist site. Also in the South, the Perine Well in Alabama was originally constructed to serve as a source of freshwater for a factory that was never built; it was then used to provide vast amounts of water for E. M. Perine, a wealthy business owner who later became the first person to install air-conditioning in any home in Alabama.

Evolution of Wells

Digging a hole by hand has been replaced by using a machine, often similar to an Archimedes screw, to dig the well. Water once raised by a bucket on a chain is now lifted by a hand pump such as the shallow lift suction hand pump; by working the handle bar, one causes water to flow out a tap.

As people farmed more marginal areas with less underground water, new strategies were developed. One of these was the design of an angled bore-hole. The more acute the angle, the longer the level of intersection of the borehole with the fracture zone, through which water was found—but also the greater possibility of missing the fracture zone. Today, environmental groups complain that water users rely far too heavily on this bore water for agriculture in very arid areas or for industry, such as semiconductor manufacturing in Albuquerque, New Mexico. By contrast, others point to the fact that the use of bore water means that there is not so much reliance on trucked water, water piped over long distances, or desalination works. Desalination uses much energy and generates large quantities of greenhouse gases. The technology used in boring water wells was also used in the search for oil. One such oil well is Discovery Well, which was built in 1899 by Roe Elwood and Frank Wisemen in Bakersfield, California.

—Justin Corfield

See also: *Agriculture; Waterborne Diseases in Drinking Water*

BIBLIOGRAPHY

Arnon, I. *Agriculture in Dry Lands: Principles and Practices.* Amsterdam, Netherlands: Elsevier, 1992.

Clark, Lewis. *The Field Guide to Water Wells and Boreholes.* Chichester, UK: John Wiley & Sons, 1988.

Misstear, Bruce, David Banks, and Lewis Clark. *Water Wells and Boreholes.* Chichester, UK: John Wiley & Sons, 2006.

Sterrett, Robert J., ed. *Groundwater and Wells.* 3rd ed. New Brighton, MN: Johnson Screens, 2007.

Walton, William C. *Groundwater Resource Evaluation.* New York: McGraw-Hill, 1970.

Wetlands

Wetlands are transitional areas between land and water that experience seasonal or permanent inundation and/or saturation at or near the surface that supports hydrophilic vegetation and hydric soils. A range of wetland types, influenced by local geomorphology, are found along the

The wetlands in the Bon Secour National Wildlife Refuge, seen here, were preserved by an act of Congress in 1980. They are home to more than 370 species of birds, as well as several endangered animal species.
National Fish and Wildlife Service

continental United States (e.g., coastal fringing marshes). They provide critical services for the environment and humans, including flood control, recreational and economic opportunities, water treatment, and habitat for many species. Until the period of environmental enlightenment in the 1970s, wetlands were viewed unfavorably in the United States, resulting in the destruction of much acreage to facilitate agricultural and land development. Over half of wetlands acreage (approximately 215 million acres) in the lower 48 states was lost from the 1780s to the 1980s (Dahl 1990; National Research Council [NRC] 1992). Today much acreage has been and continues to be lost to rising sea levels.

Other historic and present anthropogenic impacts on wetlands ecosystems include dam construction; diking, river channelizing, and stabilizing water levels to manage flooding, thus reducing sediment and nutrient delivery to the wetland; introduction of exotic species; removal of biota; increased nutrient loading from upland point and nonpoint sources; and contamination with toxic hazardous waste. Historically, U.S. federal policies, such as the Swamp Land Acts of 1849, 1850, and 1860 whose main purpose was land reclamation for agriculture (Reitze 1974, cited in NRC

National Wildlife Federation

The National Wildlife Federation, then known as the General Wildlife Federation, was founded in February 1935. Its founders included cartoonist Jay Norwood Darling and Ferdinand A. Silcox, who served as the chief forester of the United States. The organization's initial task was to lobby the U.S. Congress to pass legislation creating a national tax on ammunition to fund the creation and management of wildlife refuges. The effort led to the passage of the Federal Aid in Wildlife Restoration Act in 1937, also known as the Pittman-Robertson Act, which taxed sporting goods and ammunition at a rate of 11 percent in order to fund state fish and game commissions nationwide.

The federation is dedicated to the preservation of natural resources. It advocates for the establishment of wildlife areas that are managed using scientific methodologies. As one of the largest environmental groups in the world, the National Wildlife Federation invests heavily in educational endeavors designed to promote the preservation of natural resources around the world. It publishes *National Wildlife* for adult readers and four publications for children, *Ranger Rick, Your Big Backyard, Wild Animal Baby,* and *Ranger Rick's Just for Fun.*

—John R. Burch Jr.

See also: *Conservation Movement*

BIBLIOGRAPHY
National Wildlife Federation. http://www.nwf.org/.
Shaiko, Ronald G. *Voices and Echoes for the Environment: Public Interest Representation in the 1990s and Beyond.* New York: Columbia University Press, 1999.

1992), supported wetlands destruction and degradation. Support for these policies continued until the 1970s. Today, policies like the Clean Water Act (1972), the Water Bank Act (1970), and federal incentive programs protect and conserve wetlands. In 1988, the United States initiated a policy that development should result in no net overall loss of wetlands. To offset unavoidable losses from development, other wetlands should be created or restored (NRC 1992).

Restoration Science and Projects

Realizing the anthropogenic impacts and their cumulative effect at both local and regional levels on these ecosystems, the discipline of restoration science emerged. It quickly broadened in theory and practice to consider restoration at both individual and landscape levels. *Restoration* is actions taken and the processes involved to return a degraded site to a near resemblance of its original condition. Cumulative impact assessment has been scientifically

controversial. For example, in the evaluation of proposed development activities, the permit review process places more emphasis on impact at individual sites than at the landscape level (Gosselink, Lee, and Muir 1990, cited in NRC 1992). The NRC and other scientific bodies acknowledge the controversial nature of aquatic restoration, including of wetlands. Some of the main issues are the ad hoc nature of restoration projects, the fact that ecosystems' complexity often precludes the smooth restoration trajectories implied by some models, differing evaluation criteria as to the overall success of restoration project, inadequately stated goals for restored functional values, and lack of long-term monitoring. A central question is "Can wetlands actually be restored?" This is especially vexing when restoration is carried out in response to mitigation policies and it is in the developers' interest that completed projects are deemed successful (NRC 1992). It is recommended that a range of specific criteria be used in determining success. Progress should be assessed against natural, nondegraded reference wetlands, which will provide critical data for setting reasonable restoration goals. Nature's processes must also be allowed enough time to recoup a reasonable percentage of loss structure and function.

An example of a wetland restoration project with a landscape perspective is the Public Service Electric & Gas Company (PSEG) and the New Jersey–Delaware Estuary Enhancement Program (EEP). This estuary, one of the largest on the U.S. east coast, covers 194,000 hectares. In 1990, in response to a draft permit requirement by the New Jersey Department of Environmental Protection to install two cooling towers to eliminate impacts on aquatic fauna, PSEG proposed a wetland restoration mitigation program. Implemented in 1994, this was intended to compensate for losses to fish and invertebrates, as well as their eggs and larvae, due to power plant operations. The program was based on the premise that the salt marshes, being connected to the estuary, were valuable for the production of affected species and would mitigate losses due to the plant, thus avoiding costly retrofitting. To facilitate this, proper planning, ecological engineering, self-design principles, and adaptive management were used to restore 4,550 hectares of salt marsh, including three degraded "salt hay" farm sites totaling 1,780 hectares along the shore (in Dennis Township, Maurice River Township, and Commercial Township; see map). The salt hay farms had been diked for flood control, and connecting tidal creeks, which drained and flushed the salt marshes, had also been filled. Normal tidal hydrology was affected, reducing sediment accretion, and keeping out all but the highest tides resulted in the replacement of salt-tolerant vegetation (*Spartina alterniflora*) by less salt-tolerant plants (*Spartina patens* and *Distichlis spicata*). It also allowed the exotic *Phragmites australis* to invade. Dike breaching on the abandoned farms resulted in the ponding of water and drowning of desired grasses on the sites and in the adjoining forested area.

The EEP's major goal was restoration of normal tidal circulation, thus facilitating recolonization of desirable vegetation (to 76 percent) while reducing *Phragmites* domination to no more than 4 percent and ponded water to no more than 20 percent, thereby obtaining a functional system. Restoration time was estimated at fifteen to twenty years, based on historical data from abandoned farms along the bay where dikes had been breached by storms (Weinstein et al. 1997; Teal and Weinstein 2002). The expected vegetation cover was also used as an indicator of functional equivalency and satisfactory compliance with the permitting requirements (Hinkle and Mitsch 2005). To ensure success, adjacent, relatively undisturbed reference wetlands were selected as a basis for comparison to the restoration sites; the sites were compared using historical data, mapping technology, and ground surveys. This was a collaborative effort by experts from science, policy, and management committees. The planning and design process (1994–1996) incorporated hydrodynamic modeling, the choice of suitable restoration sites that facilitated natural revegetation by propagates, suitable elevation, an adequate supply of sediment to keep pace with sea level rise, and partially engineered channels to facilitate drainage of tidal waters. In determining the land acreage needed for restoration and productivity, a simplified aggregated food chain model was used to calculate species productivity across similar trophic levels. Annual mapping analysis since 1995 of the actual and reference sites supplied baseline information as to the status of vegetation cover change and its progress thereafter.

The project is a reported success. By 1998, after a two-year construction phase during which the major channels

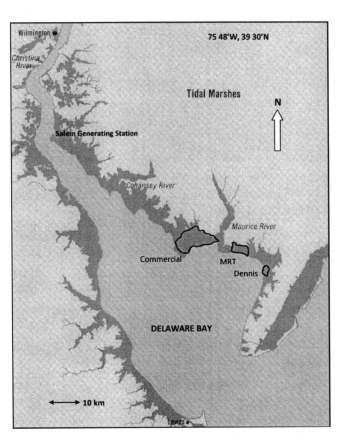

This map shows the location of the diked salt hay farms and the Salem generating station. New Jersey is on the right, Delaware is on the left.

Source: John M. Teal and Michael P. Weinstein, "Ecological Engineering, Design, and Construction Considerations for Marsh Restorations in Delaware Bay USA," *Ecological Engineering* 8, no. 5 (2002). © 2002 Elsevier. Used with permission.

were re-created, smaller channels evolved naturally, and the normal tidal regime of the land was restored. *Spartina* and other desirable vegetation species accounted for approximately 79 percent coverage, while *P. australis* was almost extirpated on the Dennis Township site. In 2004, desirable vegetation coverage was approximately 87 percent, surpassing the final restoration goal of 76 percent; for *P. australis*, coverage was 1.7 percent. On the Commercial Township site, ponded water and *P. australis* accounted for 89 percent of the site in 1996, and drowned vegetation was a significant problem. Alteration of the drainage pattern in 2000 (Teal and Weishar 2005; Hinkle and Mitsch 2005) resulted in reduction of ponded water to 8 percent by 2003. *S. alterniflora* coverage increased from 24 to 36 percent between 2001 and 2003. *P. australis* diminished to cover only about 3 percent of the site (Hinkle and Mitsch 2005).

Concerning the Maurice Township site, nonvegetated marsh plain and ponded water dominated in 1996, accounting for 77 percent of the acreage (Hinkle and Mitsch 2005).

In 1996, *S. alterniflora* was 11.3 percent and increased to 72 percent in 2003 (PSEG 2003). Restoration coverage goal for this site was 66 percent because shore birds and wading birds use portions without plant cover as habitat.

In restoration activities at four other degraded marsh sites previously dominated by *Phragmites,* restoration has successfully reduced this reed to negligible levels. Aquatic productivity and habitats have been restored and enhanced in the estuary. Monitoring programs continue as necessary.

Potential Impacts of Sea Level Rise

Wetlands worldwide are threatened by rising sea levels. They often cannot migrate inland because of preexisting human development. Consequently, extant marshes are being "drowned," eroded by wave action and sediment loss. Conversion of wetlands to open-water habitat means a dramatic change in function. Freshwater wetlands can also be lost to salt water intrusion; Louisiana's and Florida's cypress swamps are especially vulnerable.

The sea level is expected to rise (approximately 1 m to 1.5 m) along most coastlines, including along most of the United States, as a result of global warming (Hoffman, Keyes, and Titus 1983, cited in Titus, Henderson, and Teal 1984). It is projected that the contiguous United States could lose 65 percent of its coastal marshes to current sea level rise by 2100 (Park et al. 1989, cited in NRC 1992) and the future scenario is dire with little expectation for new tidal wetlands development in the next century (Cahoon et al. 2009). It is estimated that many acres of tidal marshes in Louisiana will be lost to a three-foot rise in sea level and that no new marshes will be created inland. In addition, they are becoming open water at a rate of forty square miles a year (Titus, Henderson, and Teal 1984). Experts believe that tidal freshwater marshes, located upstream in and along rivers, are less likely to be affected than their saline counterparts because of higher sediment and organic matter accretion rates. An example is the tidal freshwater marshes of the Delaware River Estuary (Craft 2007; Cahoon et al. 2009).

Some wetlands have been lost along the U.S. mid-Atlantic due to sea level rise. Mid-Atlantic estimates vary widely because of local geomorphic settings (e.g., estuarine embayment) and slope of the upland area relative to tidal marshes. These factors also influence sediment entrapment rates and peat formation, which causes vertical accretion of wetlands. Although most mid-Atlantic tidal wetlands currently are keeping pace with an approximate rate of sea level rise of about two millimeters (mm) a year (i.e., they have not become inundated or converted to open waters), large areas of the Delaware and Chesapeake Bays are able to keep pace only under optimal conditions facilitating natural processes. Some areas are now subtidal habitat and require human intervention for restoration and maintenance (Cahoon et al. 2009). It is unknown whether vertical accretion processes will keep pace with projected accelerated rates of sea level rise (about 3–4 mm annually).

Anthropogenic drivers also influence sea level rise and its effects. In Louisiana, anthropogenic alteration of the Mississippi River delta's geology and its supply of sediments is facilitating the loss of marshes and barrier islands. Development can and does restrict wetlands' natural adjustment to rising sea levels by barring wetland migration inland. If landward migration of coastal wetlands is hindered, many varieties of biota dependent on these ecosystems and their habitats will be lost.

Today's technology is capable of reducing the loss of wetlands but not without commitment of relevant resources (Titus, Henderson, and Teal 1984) and feasible environmental management policies for sustainable development. For example, some states have policies facilitating wetlands' landward migration to offset sea level rise. For effective policies to be developed, relevant data gaps must be addressed. Cahoon et al. (2009) note that a better understanding is needed regarding factors influencing vertical accretion rates such as nutrient supply, types of sediments available, and changing land use patterns. Existing numerical models must be more predictive at landscape levels and applicable in different wetlands settings. Finally, application of scientific principles and clearly defined goals determined success in the Delaware project. Working in harmony with nature's complex processes (ecological engineering) can protect, restore, and foster sustainable functional wetlands and their ecosystems.

—Shevon J. Letang

See also: *Climate Change*

BIBLIOGRAPHY

Cahoon, Donald R., Denise J. Reed, Alexander S. Kolker, Mark M. Brinson, et al. "Coastal Wetland Sustainability." In *Coastal Sensitivity to Sea-Level Rise: A Focus on the Mid-Atlantic Region,* edited by James G. Titus, 57–72. Washington, DC: U.S. Climate Change Science Program, 2009. Available at http://www.climatescience.gov/Library/sap/sap4-1/final-report/sap4-1-final-report-all.pdf.
Craft, C. "Freshwater Input Structures Soil Properties, Vertical Accretion, and Nutrient Accumulation of Georgia and U.S. Tidal Marshes." *Limnology and Oceanography* 52, no. 3 (2007): 1220–30.

Available at http://www.aslo.org/lo/toc/vol_52/issue_3/1220 .pdf.

Dahl, Thomas E. *Wetlands: Losses in the United States, 1780's to 1980's.* Washington, DC: U.S. Department of the Interior, Fish and Wildlife Service, 1990. Available at http://www.fws.gov/wetlands/_ documents/gSandT/NationalReports/WetlandsLossesUS1780s to1980s.pdf.

Hinkle, Raymond L., and William J. Mitsch. "Salt Marsh Vegetation Recovery at Salt Hay Farm Wetland Restoration Sites on Delaware Bay." *Ecological Engineering* 25, no. 3 (2005): 240–51.

(NRC) National Research Council. *Restoration of Aquatic Ecosystems: Science, Technology, and Public Policy.* Washington, DC: National Academy Press, 1992. Available at http://www.nap.edu/openbook .php?isbn=0309045347.

(PSEG) Public Service Electric and Gas Company. *2002 Site Status Report, Maurice River Township Salt Hay Farm.* Newark, NJ: PSEG, 2003.

Teal, John M., and Michael P. Weinstein, "Ecological Engineering, Design, and Construction Considerations for Marsh Restorations in Delaware Bay, USA." *Ecological Engineering* 18, no. 5 (2002): 607–18. Available at http://www.ci.uri.edu/ciip/FallClass/ Docs_2005/TealWeinstein_2002.pdf.

Teal, John M., and L. L. Weishar. "Ecological Engineering, Adaptive Management, and Restoration Management in Delaware Bay Salt Marsh Restoration." *Ecological Engineering* 25, no. 3 (2005): 304–14.

Titus, James G., Timothy R. Henderson, and John M. Teal. "Sea Level Rise and Wetlands Loss in the United States." *National Wetlands Newsletter* 6, no. 4 (1984).

Weinstein, Michael P., John H. Balletto, John M. Teal, and David F. Ludwig. "Success Criteria and Adaptive Management for a Large-Scale Wetland Restoration Project." *Wetlands Ecology and Management* 4, no. 2 (1997): 111–27. Available at http://www .montclair.edu/profilepages/media/1992/user/Restoration_ Success_Criteria1997.pdf.

Part III Law and Government

Arizona v. California (1963)

In 1952, Arizona filed suit against California and seven of its public utilities over the use of the Colorado River and its waters. Over the course of the case, Nevada, New Mexico, Utah, and the federal government were added as parties to the lawsuit. The U.S. Supreme Court was charged with determining how much water from the Colorado River and its tributaries legally belonged to each respective state. The Court referred the case to a special master in order to collect evidence, evaluate legal precedents, and make recommendations to the justices. After eleven years, Arizona emerged triumphant, as the waters of the Colorado River were apportioned under the Boulder Canyon Project Act. The annual allocations affected the first 7,500,000 acre-feet of water on the main stream of the Colorado River. Arizona was awarded 2,800,000 acre-feet, and Nevada received 300,000. Although California received an allocation of 4,400,000 acre-feet, the justices set a statutory limit on how much water California could obtain in future years. The Secretary of the Interior was charged with ensuring that all parties honored the agreements. The Secretary of Interior's duties include ensuring equitable apportionment, even in years that the Colorado River's water supply is low.

Role of the Federal Government in Water Disputes

The role of the federal government in water disputes in the Colorado River Basin had been growing gradually since the late eighteenth century. In 1894, the Carey Act authorized the Secretary of the Interior to donate lands to arid states, provided those properties were improved and irrigated. The Reclamation Act of 1902 created a funding mechanism that allowed the Secretary of the Interior and the Reclamation Service to construct reservoirs in many of those same states. Not surprisingly, the availability of federal monies for water

projects led to intense competition among the respective states for water projects that would serve the needs of their states' populaces.

On November 24, 1922, the Colorado River Commission issued the Colorado River Compact. Chaired by Herbert Hoover, the commission attempted to settle interstate conflict over the waters of the Colorado River by making allocations to each state and setting priorities that would be used to settle future issues. Although California, Colorado, Nevada, New Mexico, Utah, and Wyoming all ratified the agreement, Arizona refused.

State Conflict

The Boulder Canyon Act of 1928 set the stage for the next conflict between Arizona and California. The act resulted in the construction of the Hoover Dam and brought hydroelectric power to California. Using the Colorado River's waters, California was able to provide much-needed water to Los Angeles and transformed the Imperial Valley into an agricultural mecca. This growth came at Arizona's

---

Mark Wilmer

Mark Wilmer crafted the successful legal strategy that secured access to the waters of the Colorado River for Arizona in the landmark 1963 U.S. Supreme Court case *Arizona v. California*. The legal victory helped ensure the development of the Central Arizona Project.

Wilmer was born in East Troy, Wisconsin, on July 18, 1903. He earned his law degree from the Georgetown College of Law in 1929 and moved to Arizona. Over several decades, his law firm became one of the most prominent in the state. In 1957, Wilmer was charged with reversing Arizona's flagging fortunes in *Arizona v. California*.

Arizona v. California, argued from 1952 to 1963, remains the longest-running case in the history of the Supreme Court. Due to Wilmer's legal argument, Congress was empowered to apportion and regulate water from the Colorado River to the states of California, Arizona, and Nevada. Wilmer died on December 8, 1994.

—John R. Burch Jr.

See also: *Boulder Canyon Project Act (1928); Central Arizona Project; Hayden, Carl T.*

BIBLIOGRAPHY

August, Jack L., Jr. *Dividing Western Waters: Mark Wilmer and Arizona v. California.* Fort Worth: Texas Christian University Press, 2007.

Hundley, Norris J. *Water and the West: The Colorado River Compact and the Politics of Water in the American West.* 2nd ed. Berkeley: University of California Press, 2009.

expense, so that state took the case to the Supreme Court, arguing that the Boulder Canyon Act of 1928 was unconstitutional. In 1931, the Supreme Court rejected Arizona's argument. Three years later, Arizona argued before the Court that the Colorado River Compact guaranteed the state 1 million acre-feet of water from the Colorado River, but that argument was also rejected because Arizona had steadfastly refused to ratify the agreement. Arizona came before the Court a third time in 1936, but by then it was obvious the justices had lost their patience. They noted that Arizona would have a difficult time ever proving harm because millions of acre-feet of water flowed down the Colorado River each year unused. They also chastised Arizona's lawyers for never having made the United States a party to the suit, which was a major jurisdictional mistake. Arizona subsequently ratified the Colorado River Compact of 1922 in 1944.

Senator Carl Hayden (D-AZ) turned to the federal government to address Arizona's water needs in the same manner that the Boulder Canyon Act had impacted California's. He managed to get the Senate to approve the Central Arizona Project every year that he proposed it, beginning in 1947. The legislation never got beyond the Senate, however, because California's delegation in the House of Representatives repeatedly blocked it, claiming that not enough water was available. Unable to advance its cause in the halls of Congress, Arizona responded with *Arizona v. California*. Arizona's ultimate victory in the Supreme Court in 1963 (373 U.S. 546) paved the way for the passage of the Colorado River Basin Project Act of 1968, which included the Central Arizona Project.

In addition to asserting definitively federal supervision of the waters of the Colorado River, *Arizona v. California* also clarified the legal interpretation of the 1908 U.S. Supreme Court case *Winters v. United States,* reaffirming that American Indian water rights on reservations implicitly predated non-Indian use and that they could not be arbitrarily taken away under abandonment statutes for non-use. This Supreme Court decision went a long way toward determining current federal policy toward Indian water rights. As Charles F. Wilkinson argued, the decision let "time work triply in the tribes' favor—in stark juxtaposition to the prior appropriation system, which locks in water rights at the time of their original use" (Wilkinson 1987, 71). The court finally confirmed the assertion in *Winters* of the existence of a reserved water right for Indian tribes, a right that was completely outside of and at least

equal to any other state systems of allocation. With this opinion, the Supreme Court confirmed the idea of reserved rights that lies at the heart of the Winters doctrine. In the cases of reservations created by executive order or act of Congress, the Indian water claims were given a priority date of when the reservation was created, thus superseding the great majority of non-Indian water claims.

—John R. Burch Jr.

See also: *American Indian Water Rights; American Indian Water Settlements; Bureau of Reclamation; Boulder Canyon Project Act (1928); Carey Act of 1894; Central Arizona Project; Colorado River Compact of 1922; Hayden, Carl T.; Reclamation Act of 1902;* Winters v. United States *(1908)*

BIBLIOGRAPHY

"*Arizona v. California et al.* No. 8, Original; Supreme Court of the United States 373 U.S. 546; 83 s. Ct. 1468; 10 L. Ed. 2d 542; 1963 US Lexis 2418." LexisNexis Academic. http://www.lexisnexis.com.

August, Jack L., Jr. *Vision in the Desert: Carl Hayden and Hydropolitics in the American Southwest.* Fort Worth: Texas Christian University Press, 1999.

Burton, Lloyd. *American Indian Water Rights and the Limits of Law.* Lawrence: University Press of Kansas, 1991.

Fradkin, Philip. *A River No More: The Colorado River and the West.* Rev. ed. Berkeley: University of California Press, 1996.

Hundley, Norris, Jr. *The Great Thirst: Californians and Water: A History.* Rev. ed. Berkeley: University of California Press, 2001.

McCool, Daniel. *Command of the Waters: Iron Triangles, Federal Water Development, and Indian Water.* Berkeley: University of California Press, 1987.

McCool, Daniel. *Native Waters: Contemporary Indian Water Settlements and the Second Treaty Era.* Tucson: University of Arizona Press, 2002.

Wilkinson, Charles F. *American Indians, Time, and the Law: Native Societies in a Modern Constitutional Democracy.* New Haven, CT: Yale University Press, 1987.

Worster, Donald. *Rivers of Empire: Water, Aridity, and the Growth of the American West.* New York: Pantheon Books, 1985.

Army Corps of Engineers, United States

The Army Corps of Engineers is a federal agency of the U.S. government and a command under the U.S. Army responsible for civil works projects, construction of military facilities, and assisting during natural disasters. The Corps was founded in 1775 and continues today, serving missions in both military and civilian roles throughout the United States and the world. The headquarters for the Corps is in Washington, D.C., and the organization has directors to oversee both military programs and civil works. Today's Corps is organized into eight geographic divisions, which are then divided into districts; these divisions include Northwestern, Great Lakes and Ohio, North Atlantic, South Atlantic, Mississippi Valley, Southwestern, South Pacific, and the Pacific Ocean.

Early History

The Army Corps of Engineers can trace its history back to the Revolutionary War in 1775. However, the current version of the Corps dates to 1802, when President Thomas Jefferson authorized its establishment. Initially the Corps was headquartered in New York at the U.S. Military Academy at West Point, where a school of engineering was established for training Army officers. The academy fell under the oversight of the chief engineer, who served as inspector of West Point until 1866, when the position of superintendant was opened to soldiers from all branches of the Army.

During the Corps's early years, it oversaw river works projects, beginning with the construction of fortifications in New Orleans following the War of 1812. In 1816, the Corps was charged with the responsibility to survey and construct the National Road from Cumberland, Maryland, to Vandalia, Illinois, a project that included building a macadamized road and bridges. During the same period, the topographical engineers reporting to the Corps surveyed and mapped the western United States under the General Survey Act of 1824. In 1863, the Corps of Engineers merged with the Corps of Topographical Engineers, which led to the added responsibility for the construction of lighthouses, coastal fortifications, and navigational routes. The engineers also worked to dredge major waterways of snags and debris, allowing for safe water navigation as mandated by federal laws passed in 1824. During the Civil War, Union soldiers in the Corps were responsible for the construction of bridges, roads, and forts.

From its beginning, the Corps has been called upon to address flood control problems. Since the 1800s, it has worked on flood control projects on the Mississippi River and its tributaries. These responsibilities expanded under the Mississippi River and Tributaries Flood Control Project in 1928 and the Flood Control Act of 1936, adding the entire country to the Corps's flood control mission. In connection with this legislation, the Corps oversees construction of dams and locks, river dredging, and the inspection of levees. Federal mandates authorize the Corps to build flood protection systems in cities like New Orleans, Louisiana. This is one of the controversial missions of the Corps because,

while flood damage can be minimized, it cannot be totally prevented. The protection of persons living in coastal areas susceptible to hurricanes and other storm damage also falls under the aegis of the Corps. Today the Corps owns and operates over 600 dams and more than 250 navigation lock chambers at over 200 sites, operates and maintains 12,000 miles of commercial inland navigation channels, and maintains over 900 harbors.

In addition to flood control, the Corps also operates outdoor recreation areas. Many of these lakes, beaches, and other areas are open to the public, seeing over 300 million visitors each year and employing thousands of workers. The Corps also oversees the operation of seventy-five hydroelectric power plants producing 3 percent of the nation's electric power. Water supplies for 115 cities in the United States come from water held in Corps-built reservoirs.

Expansion

The mission of the Corps expanded to include military construction on December 1, 1941. During World War II, the Corps built military installations, both in the United States and overseas, in support of the U.S. Army and Air Force. Engineers with the Corps also designed and constructed the facilities needed for the Manhattan Project.

By the 1960s, the Corps added environmental preservation and restoration to its many responsibilities. The Corps's mission in this area is twofold since it falls under military and civil programs. Military programs oversee cleanup on former military installations, including the removal of hazardous waste, radioactive waste, and ordinance. Civil programs work to ensure that all Corps projects, facilities, and lands meet environmental standards and comply with federal regulations. For example, the Corps restores wetlands so endangered native species can survive; to date over 38,000 acres of wetlands have been restored under Corps initiatives.

Today the Corps of Engineers remains at the forefront of homeland security, providing support for military missions at home and abroad while maintaining the national infrastructure and protecting the environment.

—Theresa Hefner-Babb

See also: *Flood Control Act of 1928*

BIBLIOGRAPHY

Jones, Vincent C. *Manhattan, the Army and the Atomic Bomb.* Washington, DC: Center of Military History, U.S. Army, 1985.

Merritt, Raymond H. *The Corps, the Environment, and the Upper Mississippi River Basin*. Washington, DC: Historical Division, Office of Administrative Services, Office of the Chief of Engineers, 1984.

Thompson, Erwin N., and Daniel Van Zyle. *Pacific Ocean Engineers: History of the U.S. Army Corps of Engineers in the Pacific, 1905–1980*. Washington, DC: U.S. Government Printing Office, 1985.

U.S. Army Corps of Engineers. *The U.S. Army Corps of Engineers: A History*. Alexandria, VA: Headquarters, U.S. Army Corps of Engineers, Office of History, 2008.

Aspinall, Wayne N.

Wayne Aspinall (1896–1983) served in the U.S. House of Representatives (D-CO) from 1949 until 1973. He was heavily involved in water issues, particularly the construction of dams in Colorado and nearby states, earning the ire of many conservationists.

Personal and Political Life

Wayne Norviel Aspinall was born on April 3, 1896, in Middleburg, Ohio, the son of Mack Aspinall and Jessie Edna (née Norviel). When he was eight, his family moved to Palisade, Colorado, and he attended the University of Denver. With the United States entering World War I, Aspinall joined the Air Service of the Signal Corps; after his discharge, he returned to the university to complete his degree. He then worked as a teacher before returning to school to complete a law degree. In 1930, he was elected to the Colorado State House of Representatives, and he was speaker from 1937 to 1938. He was then elected to the Colorado State Senate, where he served until 1948. During World War II, he was a captain. In 1948, Aspinall decided to run for the U.S. House of Representatives as part of a plan to be elected governor eventually. However, he was to remain in the House of Representatives for the next twenty-four years.

It was in the House of Representatives that Aspinall found his passion, arguing for the building of more dams and for the construction of water reclamation projects. His family had traditionally been Republicans, but in 1912, the young Aspinall had become disillusioned by the failure of President William Taft in his attempt to win a second term. He then became a Democrat, but his rural background meant that he generally held conservative social views. However, his main concern was the provision of water to the farmers whom he represented in Congress—he himself ran a peach orchard.

Water Projects

One of Aspinall's first major moves was to support the Colorado River Storage Act of 1956. He and some of his allies sponsored the bill, which was to allow the damming of the Upper Basin of the Colorado River. This was controversial as it included the building of Echo Park Dam, which would flood part of the Dinosaur National Monument. Environmentalists campaigned against this, and at the height of the protest in 1954, the Department of the Interior is said to have received 20,000 items of mail, which ran against the project 80 to 1. Aspinall wanted the entire bill to be passed but realized that the strength of the opposition meant that he would have to amend his plans. In the end, he settled for a plan that did not include the Echo Park Dam and made a number of other compromises. In March 1956, the bill passed the House of Representatives 256 to 136, and it was signed into law by President Dwight D. Eisenhower.

Another irrigation scheme that Aspinall championed was the Frying Pan Arkansas Project. The aim was to divert water from the Frying Pan and the Roaring Fork Rivers in Colorado into the Arkansas River to transfer water to the drier parts of Colorado. Aspinall pointed out that the Colorado–Big Thompson Project in 1937 had opened up large areas of agricultural land in northeast Colorado, and this project would do the same for the western slope of the state. However, this project was not authorized by Congress for construction until 1962, by which time it was controversial in Colorado among many people who were worried about its cost. Soon afterwards Aspinall had to compromise on the Wilderness Bill, first introduced in 1961. Aspinall's opposition to the bill gained him much notoriety in environmental circles—Aspinall had wanted to limit the 55 million acres of protected wilderness to only 9.1 million acres. Finally he supported the bill, and the National Wildlife Federation named Aspinall "Conservationist of the Year, 1964" for his eventual help in getting the Wilderness Act of 1964 passed.

During the late 1960s, Aspinall became heavily involved in supporting the Colorado River Basin Project, which involved the construction of dams to generate energy for townships on the Lower Basin of the Colorado River. The scheme, centering on the Central Arizona Project, involved diverting some river water, meaning that part of the Grand Canyon National Monument would be flooded as well as a section of the Grand Canyon National Park. Aspinall urged local communities to accept the idea, not because the water was needed for irrigation but because the revenue earned from the electricity would help them. However, Aspinall would only support the project if five reclamation projects were undertaken in Colorado to benefit his constituents. Senator Carl Hayden (D-AZ) was critical of the linkage of Aspinall's support to these other irrigation schemes, and some enmity arose between the two politicians as a result. A media campaign against Aspinall included an advertisement by the Sierra Club that mocked his arguments with the rhetorical question: "Should we flood the Sistine Chapel so tourists can get nearer the ceiling?" The bill was finally passed in 1968 as the Colorado River Basin Act, but not before Aspinall had been forced to compromise and drop the plans for the Grand Canyon dams. His five irrigation projects in Colorado were included in the final legislation.

The liberal movement sweeping through the Democratic Party swept him aside. A challenge from Richard Perchlik in 1970 was unsuccessful, but Alan Merson defeated him in the 1972 party primary. Merson lost to a Republican in November. In 1976, Aspinall supported Republican Gerald Ford's presidential election bid and resumed his law practice. He died on October 9, 1983.

—Justin Corfield

See also: *Bureau of Reclamation; Colorado River Storage Project Act of 1956; Dam Building; Lower Colorado River Basin Project Bill (1965)*

BIBLIOGRAPHY

Schulte, Steven C. *Wayne Aspinall and the Shaping of the American West.* Boulder: University Press of Colorado, 2002.

Sturgeon, Stephen Craig. *The Politics of Western Water: The Congressional Career of Wayne Aspinall.* Tucson: University of Arizona Press, 2002.

Babbitt, Bruce

Bruce Edward Babbitt (1938–) served in the Clinton administration from 1993 to 2001 as the forty-seventh secretary of the interior. An environmental lawyer, Babbitt opposed the government-subsidized industries that had long shaped the development of the American West. He aimed to shift the Interior Department from a focus on profiting from the land to protecting the land.

Babbitt was born on June 27, 1938, in Los Angeles, California, into a prominent Arizona ranching family and is a third generation westerner. He grew up in Flagstaff, Arizona, in the shadow of the Grand Canyon. The Babbitts had been among the original settlers in Flagstaff in 1886,

arriving just as the frontier began to close. The family purchased an enormous amount of ranch property during the Great Depression and still retains a 500,000-acre spread (two-thirds the size of Rhode Island). In essence, Babbitt is one of the elite westerners that he opposed as head of the Department of the Interior.

Babbitt earned a BS in geology from the University of Notre Dame in 1962 and an MS in geophysics later that same year from the University of Newcastle in England. He had intended to go into the mining industry but became intrigued by the prospect of social involvement. Babbitt received a law degree from Harvard University and passed the Arizona Bar in 1965. After volunteering for VISTA and as a civil rights marcher in the South, Babbitt took a job in 1967 as an attorney in Phoenix. He then took his interest in the environment into the policy-making realm.

Making his first foray into elective politics, Babbitt, a Democrat, won office in 1974 as attorney general of Arizona. He served in that position until 1978, when he became governor of Arizona. He remained in that office until 1987. In the wake of a near nuclear disaster in Pennsylvania, he also acted from 1979 to 1980 as a member of the President's Commission on the Accident at Three Mile Island. Babbitt then chaired the Nuclear Safety Oversight Committee as well as the National Groundwater Policy Forum. As governor, Babbitt focused on environmental and resource management concerns. He backed the Arizona Groundwater Management Act of 1980, which remains the most comprehensive water regulatory system in the United States. Babbitt also created the Arizona Department of Water Resources and the Arizona Department of Environmental Quality. He is additionally credited with a major expansion of his state's park system.

Appointed secretary of the interior in 1993, Babbitt became one of the very few men in this post who has served two full terms. A longtime critic of the department, Babbitt broke with earlier Interior chiefs by seeking to keep the federal government out of the dam-building business and objecting to the commercialization of the National Park System. He is credited with establishing a forest plan for the Pacific Northwest, helping to restore the Florida Everglades, aiding in the passage of the California Desert Protection Act, and promoting legislation to enhance the National Wildlife Refuge system. Quite possibly the only interior secretary to be a certified firefighter, Babbitt used his knowledge of fires to create a new federal wildfire policy that emphasized the role of fire in the maintenance and restoration of natural ecosystems. Donning a yellow fireproof shirt and taking up a shovel, he occasionally joined in fighting wildfires. Babbitt pioneered the use of habitat conservation plans under the Endangered Species Act and worked with Clinton to establish new national monuments, including the Grand Staircase Escalante National Monument in Utah. Babbitt also returned wolves to Yellowstone National Park, largely because of the critical role that the animals play in the ecosystem as well as their significance to American cultural heritage.

Babbitt's tenure in Interior proved controversial. Western senators accused him of conducting a war on the West with his efforts to reform environmental law. In his defense, Babbitt pointed out that most westerners did not ranch or mine. He envisioned a "New West" that emphasized good stewardship of the land and publicly disparaged the "Lords of Yesterday." Perhaps not surprisingly, Babbitt was charged with trying to control how westerners used their land and water. In particular, he ran afoul of both environmentalists and ranchers who disagreed with his management of 500 million acres of public lands. Babbitt tried to raise significantly the grazing fees paid by ranchers who run livestock over public lands but had to settle for a minor hike. The episode infuriated environmentalists who had hoped to overturn grazing policies instituted during the previous three Republican presidential administrations. He also backed a significant reduction of logging on federal lands because the practice of clear-cutting had resulted in soil and debris clogging rivers with sediment. This plan ran into significant opposition in Congress, which ultimately weakened it substantially.

Babbitt had limited impact as Interior Secretary. He never managed to effect as much change as he hoped because of the opposition of powerful western legislators. Some of his environmental initiatives were overturned during the subsequent presidency of George W. Bush. Upon leaving government office, Babbitt served as the president of the World Wildlife Fund and joined the board of directors of the Lincoln Institute of Land Policy. Babbitt, who idolizes fellow conservationist Theodore Roosevelt, has written several works relating to the art and beauty of the American West. His recent publications have focused on environmental policy. In 2005, Babbitt published *Cities in the Wilderness*. The book describes his land use philosophy and lays out a framework for a national land use plan.

—Caryn Neumann

See also: *Everglades Restoration; Pacific Northwest Electric Power Planning and Conservation Act (1980); Roosevelt, Theodore*

BIBLIOGRAPHY

Babbitt, Bruce E. *Cities in the Wilderness: A New Vision of Land Use in America*. Washington, DC: Island Press, 2005.

Dombeck, Michael P., Christopher A. Wood, and Jack E. Williams, eds. *From Conquest to Conservation: Our Public Lands Legacy*. Washington, DC: Island Press, 2003.

Boulder Canyon Project Act (1928)

The Boulder Canyon Project Act was enacted by the U.S. Congress in 1928 to allow for the construction of the Boulder Dam, later renamed the Hoover Dam. Although the building of the dam remains heavily identified with the Great Depression, and it did provide work for many people during the Depression, its origins go back long before then, and indeed the work was authorized and started before the Wall Street crash of 1929.

President Herbert Hoover had negotiated much of the framework of the project six years earlier when he had been secretary of commerce. Although the project offered obvious benefits in terms of flood control, irrigation, and hydropower, there had long been problems among the seven states involved—Arizona, California, Colorado, Nevada, New Mexico, Utah, and Wyoming—over the equitable distribution of water and power. Members of Congress from the affected states lobbied vigorously, all eager that their constituencies should benefit from this massive infrastructure project. In particular Senator Key Pittman (D-NV) and Senator Tasker Oddie (R-NV) argued that their state should get more than the 18 percent allotment of power that was being proposed; they wanted Nevada to get a third of the power generated. In addition, Arizona made a large claim for water. Under the terms of the Boulder Canyon Project Act, work on the project would go ahead once the act was ratified by six of the seven states. In 1924, a compact had been drawn up to which the seven states had already agreed, in principle, subject to final ratification by their state legislatures.

As president, Herbert Hoover continued to make the Boulder Canyon Project Act a priority, and he and its supporters steered it through Congress. The legislation authorized the expenditure of $165 million, and some representatives from eastern states balked at the cost.

Nonetheless, Congress did pass it. The United States was enjoying a period of prosperity, and most people expected the boom to continue. The ambitious dam proposal embodied the "can do" attitude of the United States, shown fourteen years earlier in the completion of the Panama Canal. The dam was to be taller than a sixty-story building and consume more concrete than that needed to make a highway from New York to San Francisco. It would also be bigger than the Great Pyramid in Egypt.

Colorado, Nevada, New Mexico, Utah, and Wyoming agreed to the Act, and it was hoped that California would also do so readily. On June 25, 1929, Herbert Hoover signed a proclamation that put into effect the compact once it was ratified by six of the affected states. He said that he hoped the dispute between Arizona and California might be resolved and that the two states "may compose their mutual problems which have hitherto prevented Arizona from joining the compact." Hoover stated that the compact was, in his view, the "most important action ever taken in that fashion under the Constitution . . . [and] with Arizona in, the whole basin will have settled their major question of water rights for all time" (Hoover 1929).

California agreed to the Boulder Canyon Project Act, but Arizona still held out. Indeed, the state appealed to the U.S. Supreme Court and denounced the criticism of their claims by Secretary of the Interior Ray Lyman Wilbur. Arizona's claim was based on the project's effect on the navigability of the Colorado River. However, in May 1931, the Supreme Court refused to invalidate the Act by a unanimous decision in the case *Arizona v. California* (283 U.S. 423). Its ruling accepted the Colorado River Compact's (1922) language that "Inasmuch as the Colorado River has ceased to be navigable for commerce and the reservation of its waters for navigation would seriously limit the development of its Basin, the use of its waters for purposes of navigation shall be subservient to the uses of such waters for domestic, agricultural, and power purposes" (IV[a]). Justice Louis Brandeis, who rejected the arguments of Arizona, stated the ruling, and the project was started. In spite of this decision, Arizona still tried to get the Colorado River Compact and the terms of the Boulder Canyon Project Act changed. However, representatives of the other six states met and rejected Arizona's proposals.

—Justin Corfield

See also: Arizona v. California *(1963); Hoover Dam*

BIBLIOGRAPHY

Aldridge, Rebecca. *The Hoover Dam.* New York: Chelsea House, 2009.

"Colorado River Compact, 1922." http://www.usbr.gov/lc/region/pao/pdfiles/crcompct.pdf.

Gates, William H. *Hoover Dam, Including the Story of the Turbulent Colorado River.* Los Angeles: Wetzel, 1932.

Hoover, Herbert. "Statement on Signing a Proclamation on the Colorado River Compact and the Boulder Canyon Project." June 25, 1929. Available at John T. Woolley and Gerhard Peters, *The American Presidency Project,* http://www.presidency.ucsb.edu/ws/index.php?pid=21842.

"Hoover Proclaims Boulder Dam Pact." *New York Times,* June 26, 1929.

Pearce, Fred. *When the Rivers Run Dry: What Happens When Our Water Runs Out?* London: Eden Project, 2006.

Stevens, Joseph E. *Hoover Dam: An American Adventure.* Norman: University of Oklahoma Press, 1988.

Boundary Waters Treaty (1909)

The 1909 Boundary Waters Treaty (BWT) between the United States and Britain (Canada) governs the uses and quality of surface waters that flow over the boundaries along the U.S.-Canada border.

> For the purpose of this treaty boundary waters are defined as the waters from main shore to main shore of the lakes and rivers and connecting waterways, or the portions thereof, along which the international boundary between the United States and the Dominion of Canada passes, including all bays, arms, and inlets thereof, but not including tributary waters which in their natural channels would flow into such lakes, rivers, and waterways, or waters flowing from such lakes, rivers, and waterways, or the waters of rivers flowing across the boundary.

Thus, the treaty ranges from Maine and the Maritimes to the U.S.-Canada border in Alaska.

Treaty Origins

The agreement was negotiated by U.S. Secretary of State Elihu Root and Sir George Gibbons of Canada. British Ambassador to the United States James Bryce provided the official connection between the parties, as Canada did not yet have full control over its foreign policy. One can imagine the treaty as being part of an extended diplomatic period where the United States and Britain resolved a number of outstanding disputes between the two countries, something both Root and Bryce were keen to achieve (Dorsey 1998). The countries also created a standing international commission (Article VII), the International Joint Commission (IJC), to help prevent future conflicts. The IJC, formed in 1910, consists of three Americans and three Canadians, appointed by their respective governments.

Treaty Provisions

The parties were particularly concerned that competing interests in water for power, agriculture, and industry would prompt conflict. Moreover, the U.S. Corps of Engineers, among others on both sides of the border, was alarmed that navigation on the Great Lakes might be impaired if parties on either side began to divert waters from the Great Lakes, as Chicago had done with the Chicago River in 1900. This concern was addressed in Article I of the Treaty. It provides that the Great Lakes may be navigated freely by citizens of both nations and that any laws, regulations, or duties levied must be applied equally to Canadian and U.S. users. It also extends this rule to the internal U.S. waters of Lake Michigan and to connecting canals that existed or would exist.

While Article II preserves the right of either side to divert waters and grandfathered in existing diversions, diversions may not injure the other party. Article III requires the two parties to get IJC approval for any diversions of water for power or other purposes that would alter the natural level of the Great Lakes. Data on the levels exist from roughly 1860, information the IJC uses to this day. Article IV provides that the IJC must approve dams and other projects that would obstruct the rivers in such a way as to alter the levels of the Great Lakes. The effect of these provisions is that firms and public power entities who seek to change their diversion levels must get the IJC's review and permission. Not often does an international organization have this authority over private or quasi-private actors in nations.

Article IV, in a single line, forbids transboundary pollution that negatively affects the health, well-being, and economy of the other party. This rule has led to a number of U.S.-Canada references to the IJC. It has also been cited as a reason for the 1972/1978 Great Lakes Water Quality Agreement (GLWQA) and the 1987 Protocol to the GLWQA.

Article V addresses diversions on the Niagara River, but it has largely been superseded by the 1950 Niagara River Treaty. Article VI treats the St. Mary and Milk Rivers of Montana, Alberta, and Saskatchewan as a single river for power and irrigation purposes. It divides the water between the two and specifies times of the year when the parties may take water out prior to the actual division based on the flow. The IJC's operations under this article often intersect with the planning of irrigation boards.

Article VIII sets out general decision rules for use by the IJC. The treaty is possibly unique in the world in its stated hierarchy of uses for the waters it covers. First priority goes to water for drinking and sanitation. Second is for navigation. Industrial and agricultural uses get the lowest priority. In order to meet its duties regarding water levels, it may require compensatory or other works be built first. The IJC can create local boards to manage local conflicting uses (e.g., for the Lake of the Woods) or for irrigation as on the St. Mary's, Milk, and Souris Rivers. The agreement permits either party to submit a reference to the IJC for study and recommendations (Article IX). Actual practice in the last century is for both the Canadian and American governments to submit references with the same wordings to their respective sections. There is also a general arbitration clause in the Treaty (Article X), which has never been used even though one of the stated rationales in the Treaty's preamble is to "settle all questions which are now pending." Were the arbitration clause ever to be used, it would allow Canada and the United States to submit *any* issue of mutual concern to the IJC for arbitration.

As originally conceived by Root and Gibbons, the IJC was to be a more robust form of an international arbitration court than the one found in The Hague Arbitration rules of 1906. The aims and requirements of the Boundary Waters Treaty, however, have led to an IJC that relies on scientific and engineering expertise rather than law. Such expertise allows it to solve the thornier aspects of local competing uses rather than taking them to a distant tribunal for resolution.

—Mary Durfee

See also: *Great Lakes; International Joint Commission (United States and Canada)*

BIBLIOGRAPHY

Dorsey, Kurkpatrick. *The Dawn of Conservation Diplomacy: U.S.-Canadian Wildlife Protection Treaties in the Progressive Era.* Seattle: University of Washington Press, 1998.

Gibbons, Alan O. "Sir George Gibbons and the Boundary Waters Treaty of 1909." *Canadian Historical Review* 34, no. 2 (1953): 124–38.

International Joint Commission. http://www.ijc.org.

Munton, Don. "Great Lakes Water Quality: A Study in Environmental Politics and Diplomacy." In *Resources and the Environment: Policy Perspectives for Canada,* edited by O. P. Dwivedi. Toronto, ON: McClelland and Stewart, 1980.

Nossal, Kim R. "Institutionalization and the Pacific Settlement of Interstate Conflict: The Case of Canada and the International Joint Commission." *Journal of Canadian Studies* 18 (Winter 1983–84): 75–87.

Spencer, Robert Allan, John J. Kirton, and Kim Richard Nossal, eds. *The International Joint Commission Seventy Years On.* Toronto, ON: Centre for International Studies, University of Toronto, 1981.

Willoughby, William R. "The International Joint Commission's Role in Maintaining Stable Water Levels." *Inland Seas* 28, no. 2 (1972): 109–118.

Brazos River Authority

The Brazos River cuts a swath right through the middle of Texas, from its origins near the Texas–New Mexico border to where it empties into the Gulf of Mexico just south of Houston. It is the longest river in Texas, and its watershed covers approximately 42,000 square miles, approximately one-sixth of the land in the state. As such, the Brazos was a natural target for reclamation efforts in the early decades of the twentieth century. Today, the Brazos produces some 6.75 billion gallons of water for the cities and farms of Texas.

Efforts to develop the river as a resource began during the reclamation era, with the establishment of the Brazos River Impoundment Association in 1902. A second group, the Brazos River and Valley Improvement Association, was founded in 1915. But it would not be until the late 1920s that necessary government money would allow for the taming of the Brazos. Beginning in 1923, the State of Texas funded a study of all of the rivers in the state in order to find where both the incidence of flooding and the potential for development indicated that state money could help to reclaim a watershed. The Brazos, which had flooded as recently as 1921, was a natural choice. To that end, in 1929 the Texas state legislature created the Brazos River Conservation and Reclamation District, which later, during the 1950s, was renamed the Brazos River Authority (BRA).

Goodbye to a River

Goodbye to a River documents a three-week canoe trip that was taken by John Graves and his dachshund during the fall of 1957 on the Brazos River in Texas. It was a personal journey for the author, as he was saying farewell to a stretch of river that he loved but was being permanently altered by the construction of several hydroelectric dams. Although much of the narrative focuses on Graves's relationship with the river, he also wrote about how the Brazos River impacted first the lives and cultures of Native peoples, such as the Comanches and Kiowas, and later Euro-American settlers. While Graves was personally enraged by the decision to construct the dams, he did not write the monograph as an effort to thwart their construction. He instead accepted the inevitability that the dams would usher in ecological changes that would shape how the Brazos impacted future generations of Texans.

—John R. Burch Jr.

BIBLIOGRAPHY

Busby, Mark, and Terrell Dixon, eds. *John Graves, Writer.* Austin: University of Texas Press, 2007.

Graves, John. *Goodbye to a River: A Narrative.* New York: Knopf, 1960.

Graves, John. *John Graves and the Making of "Goodbye to a River": Selected Letters, 1957–1960,* edited by David S. Hamrick. Houston, TX: Taylor Wilson, 2000.

The establishment of what would become the BRA placed the responsibility for the development and control of water resources of a major watershed in the hands of a public agency. The agency is responsible to the Texas state legislature and is charged with maximizing the use of the Brazos River's waters for the good of the entire state. Initially, the BRA was tasked with the construction of thirteen dams on the Brazos and its tributaries, though it would never come close to completing that many works. Its first construction project, a hydroelectric dam that created the Possum Kingdom Reservoir, was completed in 1941 just northwest of Fort Worth. As with many other projects of this era, the federal government had a hand in funding the construction through a sizable grant from the Works Progress Administration. Since then, three additional reservoirs have been created by BRA dam projects: Lake Granbury, just southwest of Fort Worth (completed in 1969); Lake Limestone, east of Waco (completed in 1978); and Lake Alan Henry, southeast of Lubbock (completed in 1994). The BRA has also cooperated with the Army Corps of Engineers through the years in its flood abatement efforts. This cooperation has resulted in an additional nine dam/reservoir projects in the Brazos

River watershed. The BRA administers these projects along with the Corps. These joint projects are Whitney (completed in 1951), Belton (completed in 1954), Proctor (completed in 1963), Waco (completed in 1965), Somerville (completed in 1967), Stillhouse Hollow (completed in 1968), Georgetown (completed in 1980), Granger (completed in 1980), and Aquilla (completed in 1983).

Concerns and Goals

One of the main concerns of the BRA is ensuring water quality and controlling salination of the river. However, to many, the environmental issues facing the Brazos River Basin are much more serious. Beginning in the early 1990s, the BRA began to work with the Texas Natural Resource Conservation Commission, the U.S. Soil Conservation Service, and the Lower Colorado River Authority to improve the quality of water in the Brazos. As with most watersheds that have been heavily dammed, the natural cycles of river flow and occasional flooding have been interrupted. The use of Brazos River water and the flood control effects of the dams have had consequences not only on aquatic life but also on the wetlands that are a part of the watershed.

Also, the stated goals of reclamation, facilitating urban development and providing a water supply to agriculture, have implications as well, as industrial pollution and the buildup of silt have a detrimental impact on water quality. Development in suburban Houston has eaten into Brazos River wetlands with the construction of residential and commercial areas. If the BRA is going to create a sustainable future for the Brazos River Basin, it is going to have to continue dealing with all of these issues, and it must expand the range of groups it works with to include both organizations that specialize in environmental restoration and local community groups. Only in this way can it forge a truly cooperative effort that can create a plan to keep the river basin a vital and feasible resource into the future.

—Steven L. Danver

See also: *Army Corps of Engineers, United States*

BIBLIOGRAPHY

Brazos River Authority. http://www.brazos.org.
Hendrickson, Kenneth E., Jr. *The Waters of the Brazos: A History of the Brazos River Authority, 1929–1979.* Waco, TX: Texian Press, 1981.
Texas State Historical Association. "Brazos River Authority." http://www.tshaonline.org/handbook/online/articles/BB/mwb1.html.
The Nature Conservancy. "Columbia Bottomlands/Brazos River Project: Conservation in the 'Cradle of Texas.'" http://www.nature.org/wherewework/northamerica/states/texas/preserves/art26883.html.

Bureau of Indian Affairs

The Bureau of Indian Affairs (BIA) was created as an element of the Department of War in 1834. Its purposes were to assist, subjugate, and if necessary exterminate Indians. In 1849, the BIA moved to the Department of the Interior (DOI), where it oversaw the end of treaty making in 1871, the allotment of Indian lands late in the century, and the sale of "excess" lands. Reform came with the Meriam Report of 1924, the Indian New Deal, and a rebirth that collapsed with Termination in 1953. By the 1970s, assimilation and termination gave way to self-determination. Through the twists and turns of Indian policy, the BIA remained the primary administrator of Indian affairs. The BIA is the federal entity responsible for fulfilling the government's trust obligations to Native Americans, including the guaranteeing of rights, such as water rights, that belong to the tribes.

Water Rights

Indian reservations are mostly in the West, where water is scarce and the rule (from the doctrine of prior appropriation) is "First in time, first in right." Unlike in the East, where riparian rights give water to the owner of the land abutting the water source, when western water is short, those with the oldest right take all they need, and the next senior repeats the process until all water is gone. Indian appropriative water rights have three sources. Aboriginal rights rest on occupancy from time immemorial. New Mexico Pueblo rights derive from Spanish land grants and the Treaty of Guadalupe Hidalgo. Most modern Indian water rights result from *Winters v. United States* (1908), which effectively placed the BIA in an adversarial relationship with the Bureau of Reclamation by giving Indians rights that Reclamation was honoring for whites. In *Winters*, the non-Indians diverted water after establishment of the reservation but before the Indians used the water themselves. The court ruled that reserved water rights were implied in the creation of the reservation. Over half a century later in 1963, *Arizona v. California* affirmed that creation of a reservation implied the right to necessary water, but it also established that the Indian right was based not on the reservation's population but on its practicable irrigable acreage.

One part of the BIA's mission is to oversee the rights given by Indian treaties. However, Indian treaties do not give water rights but merely recognize them. When the tribes agreed to cede lands to the United States in return for reservations, Indians reserved all rights not expressly given up. Among the reserved rights is that to sufficient water to make the reservations viable, including maintenance of wildlife, livestock, and farms. These rights, according to some courts, pass to non-Indians who purchase Indian allotments. The federal government recognizes these rights but restricts non-Indian users in order to ensure primary benefit to the tribes. Some tribes may lease water to nontribal users with congressional permission. This provision is controversial because junior users have long used Indian water for free.

Negotiations and Litigation

The *Winters* decision itself generated hundreds of cases and many victories, but often tribes won the right to the water but not the resources to develop it, which the BIA was supposed to provide. Meanwhile, another agency within the DOI, the Bureau of Reclamation (BOR) was helping non-Indians develop Indian-claimed water. Upstream users continued diverting water that historically had flowed onto Indian lands. Starting in the late 1970s, negotiation became preferable to litigation. The DOI fielded thirty-two negotiating teams, and it produced many agreements, making it attractive to Indians. But too often the settlement was interpreted differently by the parties or agreements failed to identify specific funds or a water source. In the Reagan/Bush era and the post-1994 Clinton years, water development funds came out of other Indian programs. Both the BIA and its parent, the DOI, also ran into problems with a cost-cutting Office of Management and Budget. At one time or another, the BIA has been the target of criticism from all sides, with charges of incompetence and corruption from the courts, Congress, and the president. Nineteenth-century BIA field employees were often allied with Anglo Americans against Indian interests. Between 1834 and 1996, there were over 1,000 investigations, reports, commissions, and calls for reform of the BIA. In the current era, reform and abolition calls are ongoing. Although under attack from many sides, still the BIA perseveres.

Congress guarantees and reserves water for reservations and subordinates junior claimants. Nonuse does not alienate Indian reserved water rights. The tribes have, over the past two decades, become increasingly active in quantifying and using their rights under federal and tribal law. As tribal governments attempt to counter state and individual claims, issues arise over what constitutes irrigable acreage and whether states can regulate non-Indians on reservations. Indian tribes have jurisdiction over the water uses of their members and activities on the reservation. The BIA water program has the goals of obtaining water rights for Indians, securing congressional ratification of the rights, and helping the tribes to manage their resources in support of their trust lands. The rights recognized by the federal government often conflict with state water rights laws. Recourse for Indians denied water under state law is to the courts, and at least fifty suits were under way at any given time in the 1990s.

However, since the onset of the water rights settlement era during the 1980s and 1990s, tribes and states are increasingly choosing negotiation over extremely costly litigation. In the field, the BIA Water Rights Negotiation/Litigation Program funds documentation and surveys to determine water supplies, potential irrigable acreage, ownership of and owner priority for water, sources of water, diversion points and methods, and fish and wildlife needs for water. The program can also fund materials that speed state and federal adjudications and negotiations. The BIA does help tribes litigate but more often works to settle claims without legal action. One way to resolve disputes is through the Indian Water Rights Commission, whose mandate is to give back to tribes water that the federal government has taken away. The Water Management, Planning, and Pre-Development Program funds research and studies on wise use of tribal resources once they are decreed, adjudicated, or otherwise made available. The BIA often works with other government components to establish water inventories, quality measures, and other data. The Bureau also funds reservation water use plans, surveys, drought management, and other plans and measures. Sometimes the BIA also helps tribes to implement their settlements. The agency serves as a hands-on manager for some irrigation projects and systems to the point of allocating water and billing users. The Indian Dams Safety Act of 1994 requires BIA maintenance of fifty-three Indian-land dams for safety, flood control, irrigation, fish and wildlife habitats, recreation, and drinking and industrial uses.

A Questionable Relationship

However, the BIA relationship with Native Americans has been inconsistent, especially as it concerns water rights and development. When the Kickapoo tribe sued in 2006 to get the State of Kansas and the U.S. Natural Resources Conservation Service to build a reservoir, the outside agency assisting was not the Bureau of Indian Affairs (BIA) but the private Native American Rights Fund (NARF). During the fourteen years that the Fort Berthold Reservation in North Dakota sought to establish its own water standard, the BIA was absent. When the Oglala Sioux needed help enforcing conservation measures on the reservation, NARF, rather than the BIA, was there to help. And when the Snake River Nez Perce came to a water agreement with Utah after sixteen years, the BIA was absent.

Calls for abolition of the BIA draw defenders, including tribes and Indian leaders. While critics contend that the BIA is manipulating the tribes, the counterargument is that it is better to deal with a known quantity than to take chances on a new and untried agency. The BIA might be weak, but it does hire many Indian people in positions of significant responsibility. So it appears that the BIA will remain the sole federal government agency committed to the federal trust responsibility to manage Indian lands and money.

—John H. Barnhill

See also: Arizona v. California *(1963); Bureau of Reclamation; Environmental Protection Agency, United States;* Winters v. United States *(1908)*

BIBLIOGRAPHY

Burton, Lloyd. *American Indian Water Rights and the Limits of Law.* Lawrence: University Press of Kansas, 1991.

McCarthy, Robert. "The Bureau of Indian Affairs and the Federal Trust Obligation to American Indians." *BYU Journal of Public Law* 19, no. 1 (2004): 1–160. Available at http://www.law2.byu.edu/jpl/papers/v19n1_Robert_McCarthy.pdf.

McCool, Daniel. *Native Waters: Contemporary Indian Water Settlements and the Second Treaty Era.* Tucson: University of Arizona Press, 2002.

Native American Rights Fund. "Snake River Basin Adjudication, Nez Perce Tribe Water Rights." http://www.narf.org/cases/nezperce.html.

Williams, Susan M. "Overview of Indian Water Rights." 2001. http://www.citizensleague.org/what/committees/study/water/resources/Overview%20of%20Indian%20Water%20Rights.pdf.

Bureau of Reclamation

The U.S. Bureau of Reclamation (BOR) was founded as the U.S. Reclamation Service on July 17, 1902, with the passage of the Reclamation Act of 1902. Initially organized under the auspices of the U.S. Geological Survey (USGS), the Reclamation Service was charged with developing irrigation and reservoir projects that would make arid land suitable for agriculture. In 1907, it was separated from the USGS and made an independent bureau within the Department of the Interior. Renamed the BOR in 1923, its primary focus then changed to the construction of large, multipurpose dams, which both impounded large amounts of water and created hydroelectric power. Today, the Bureau supplies water to 31 million individuals residing in Arizona, California, Colorado, Idaho, Kansas, Montana, Nebraska, Nevada, New Mexico, North Dakota, Oklahoma, Oregon, South Dakota, Texas, Utah, Washington, and Wyoming. It is also the second-largest hydroelectric power provider in the West. Its fifty-eight power plants provide electricity to 3.5 million households.

Early Projects

When the Reclamation Service was created, its projects were supposed to be initially financed through the Reclamation Fund from revenues derived from the sale of federal lands in western states. The fund was intended to be replenished through profits made from the sale of water to farmers. Although not specifically stated in the Reclamation Act of 1902, the monies made from the sale of land within a specific state had to be spent within that state. This proved controversial because Texas did not contain any federal lands and thus did not receive any reclamation projects. The U.S. Congress passed legislation in 1906 to provide a funding mechanism for Texans to benefit from the Reclamation Service.

The first two decades of the Reclamation Service's existence were fraught with many embarrassing blunders. Many of the problems were the fault of the engineers whom the Service employed. They tended to be educated in the East and did not know much about agriculture. Despite their lack of practical knowledge, they tended to refuse to listen to advice from farmers in the West. Thus, many projects cost much more than the farmers could ever realistically repay. Other lands were overirrigated and therefore required expensive drainage systems. Poor judgment led to irrigation projects on lands that were not suitable to irrigation. The biggest problems were the result of land speculation, where a small group of wealthy, corrupt individuals enriched themselves at the expense of poor agriculturalists. Although there were notable successes, far more money was expended from the Reclamation Fund than was ever taken in. By the 1920s, the newly dubbed BOR began to receive significant amounts of federal funding for its work.

Changing Roles

The passage of the Boulder Canyon Project Act in the 1920s marked a change in the role of the BOR. Its mandate to irrigate small farms throughout the West was replaced with a mission to construct multipurpose dams designed both to generate hydroelectric power and control the waters of entire river systems. This new mission generated conflicts with the U.S. Army Corps of Engineers, which was engaged in the same type of work and thus correctly viewed the BOR as a competitor for federal dollars.

From the 1930s to the early 1960s, the BOR, and to a lesser extent the Corps, transformed the western landscape. Among the BOR's achievements were the construction of Boulder/Hoover Dam, Flaming Gorge Dam, Grand Coulee Dam, and Glen Canyon Dam. By the 1960s, the BOR's influence was at its peak. Under the leadership of BOR director Floyd Dominy, backed by U.S. Senator Carl Hayden (D-AZ), the Bureau was able to launch expensive projects that had questionable benefits for the public at large. By the early 1970s, its political influence waned as large-scale water projects fell into disfavor. The environmental movement, which had been gaining influence throughout the 1960s, was further empowered by the passage in 1970 of the National Environmental Policy Act. The act's requirement that environmental impact statements be conducted before any construction took place made it very difficult for the BOR to continue its large-scale projects. The political clout of the BOR had declined so rapidly in less than a decade that President Jimmy Carter proposed eliminating a number of its projects from the 1977 federal budget.

During the 1980s, the BOR declared victory with a claim that the West had been officially reclaimed, thereby suggesting that its initial mission had been completed successfully. This conveniently allowed the agency to refocus not only on managing small-scale water development projects throughout its seventeen-state service area but also on providing low-cost electricity and water to the general populace.

—John R. Burch Jr.

American Water Resources Association

The American Water Resources Association (AWRA) is a nonprofit professional organization that serves educators, researchers, and managers working on issues related to water resources. It fosters the professional development of its membership by sponsoring conferences that allow participants to share their research and gain feedback from peers. With a multidisciplinary membership, the AWRA also allows for the development of professional networks with colleagues from outside one's area of specialty. The research created by the AWRA's members is disseminated through the publication of conference proceedings; podcasts; and three periodicals, *Water Resources Impact, AWRA Connections,* and flagship publication *Journal of the American Water Resources Association* (JAWRA). JAWRA was first published in 1965 as the *Water Resources Bulletin.*

—John R. Burch Jr.

BIBLIOGRAPHY

American Water Resources Association. http://www.awra.org.
Riley, J. Paul, and Jerry R. Rogers. "The American Water Resources Association: Past, Present, and Future." 2004. http://www.awra.org/about/history.pdf.

See also: *Dominy, Floyd E.; Glen Canyon Dam; Hayden, Carl T.; Hoover Dam; Intermountain West; National Environmental Policy Act of 1969; Pacific Coast; Reclamation Act of 1902*

BIBLIOGRAPHY

Billington, David P., and Donald C. Jackson. *Big Dams of the New Deal Era: A Confluence of Engineering and Politics.* Norman: University of Oklahoma Press, 2006.
Clarke, Jeanne Nienaber, and Daniel C. McCool. *Staking Out the Terrain: Power and Performance Among Natural Resource Agencies.* 2nd ed. Albany: State University of New York Press, 1996.
O'Neill, Karen M. *Rivers by Design: State Power and the Origins of U.S. Flood Control.* Durham, NC: Duke University Press, 2006.
Pisani, Donald J. *Water and American Government: The Reclamation Bureau, National Water Policy, and the West, 1902–1935.* Berkeley: University of California Press, 2002.
Pisani, Donald J. *Water, Land, and Law in the West: The Limits of Public Policy, 1850–1920.* Lawrence: University Press of Kansas, 1996.
Reisner, Marc. *Cadillac Desert: The American West and Its Disappearing Water.* New York: Viking, 1986.
Rowley, William D. *The Bureau of Reclamation: Origins and Growth to 1945.* Washington, DC: U.S. Government Printing Office, 2006.

California–Nevada Interstate Water Compact (1971)

The California–Nevada Interstate Compact was intended to regulate the waters of the Truckee, Carson, and Walker Rivers as well as the water from Lake Tahoe. After thirteen years of negotiations, the compact was signed on July 25, 1968. The California legislature ratified the agreement on September 19, 1970, and Nevada ratified the agreement the following year on March 5, 1971. The compact is particularly interesting because, although California and Nevada entered into the agreement and abided by its requirements, the compact was never ratified by the U.S. Congress and was therefore never legally binding. Because the U.S. Department of the Interior believed that the compact would deny the Paiute Tribe water rights to Pyramid Lake, located on the Truckee River in Nevada, it opposed ratification. Congress never voted on the compact. The water distribution within the Truckee, Carson, and Walker Rivers was finally resolved with the Truckee River Operation Agreement, California and Nevada, which implemented most of the original California-Nevada Interstate Compact.

Establishing a Compact

During the early 1900s, California and Nevada had occasional conflicts over the water of the Truckee River. In 1935, California and Nevada entered into the Truckee River Agreement to resolve their disputes over the division of water from the river. Economic development occurring around Lake Tahoe in the 1940s created additional demands on the water of the rivers, which caused conflict over water resources to re-emerge between California and Nevada, and the states began to move toward an interstate compact to regulate their shared water resources.

In 1955, both states formed committees to negotiate an interstate compact. President Eisenhower signed a bill that authorized the negotiation of a compact between the states. California appointed five representatives to the commission from the river basin region of eastern California and two representatives from the state government. Nevada appointed seven representatives to its commission, six of who represented users of the water resources and one who represented the state government. The two commissions divided the negotiations into four areas: the Carson River, the Truckee River, the Walker River, and Lake Tahoe. The negotiations focused primarily on surplus water that did not have pre-existing claims from any current users. It took a number of years to collect enough data to determine the amount of water subject to negotiations. The negotiations lasted thirteen years before the two states reached an agreement.

Dissatisfaction from Congress and Subsequent Legislation

Upon California and Nevada's approval of the compact, the states sent the compact to Congress for ratification. The negotiation of the compact had begun under the Eisenhower administration fifteen years prior to the compact's arrival in Congress, and views on water rights had evolved in the Department of the Interior (DOI) over this time. The DOI believed that the compact violated the agreement between the U.S. government and the Paiute tribe that had created the tribe's reservation in Nevada. The reservation encompassed Pyramid Lake, which was part of the Truckee River Basin, and provided fishing for the tribe. The DOI argued that the creation of the reservation guaranteed the Paiute tribe's rights to the waters of Pyramid Lake, although this was not explicitly in the agreement that created the reservation.

In *United States v. Nevada and California* (1973), the federal government attempted to nullify the compact before Congress could ratify it. The federal government argued that the compact entered into by California and Nevada divided water that the federal government had allocated in 1859 when Congress created the Paiute Reservation. It also argued that the compact violated the decision in *United States v. Orr Water Ditch Co.* (1944 and revisited in 2010), which settled a dispute over the Derby Dam on the Truckee River between the United States and Nevada. The U.S. Supreme Court ruled that the DOI did not have legal grounds to block the compact because it was currently before Congress. The opposition from the DOI and the legal battle resulted in a number of members of Congress opposing the compact. Most importantly, both senators from California opposed the compact. Because of the rise of opposition, Congress never acted upon the compact, leaving it in legal limbo.

In 1990, Congress passed the Fallon Paiute Shoshone Indian Tribes Water Rights Settlement Act of 1990. The act allocated $65 million to the Paiute tribe to redevelop its fishery at Pyramid Lake, which had been severely impacted by the diversion of the Truckee River; of this, $25 million was designated a fishing fund and $40 million was designated an economic development fund. Within the Fallon Paiute Shoshone Indians Tribes Water Rights Settlement Act was the Truckee-Carson-Pyramid Lake Settlement Act, which instructed the DOI to negotiate a distribution of the water originally covered by the California-Nevada Interstate

Compact. With the settlement of the water rights of the Paiute Tribe, one of the key roadblocks to ratification of the original compact was removed. In 1995, the Nevada legislature passed a joint resolution urging Congress to ratify the compact. Congress once again did not take action, however, instead deciding to leave the negotiations to the DOI.

In 2008, the DOI reached an agreement to regulate the shared waters between California and Nevada with the Truckee River Operating Agreement, California and Nevada (TROA). The TROA provides for the allocation of water resources between California and Nevada and charges the federal government with the responsibility of managing the allocation through the release of water from the federal reservoirs located on the Truckee River. The TROA also adds provisions for protecting endangered species within the river basin that were not addressed in the California-Nevada Interstate Compact but are necessary because of the Endangered Species Act. With the successful negotiation of the TROA, the California-Nevada Interstate Compact became obsolete. Both states had complied with it for over thirty years, but it was never ratified by Congress and therefore was never legally binding.

—Adam M. Sowards

See also: *American Indian Water Rights; Truckee-Carson Project; Truckee-Carson-Pyramid Lake Water Rights Settlement Act of 1990*

BIBLIOGRAPHY

McCool, Daniel. "Indian Water Settlements: The Prerequisites of Successful Negotiation." *Policy Studies Journal* 21, no. 2 (1993): 227–42.

Pisani, Donald J. "The Strange Death of the California-Nevada Compact: A Study in Interstate Water Negotiations." *The Pacific Historical Review* 47, no. 4 (1978): 637–58.

Taylor, Willie R. "Truckee River Operating Agreement, California and Nevada." *Federal Register* 73, no. 17 (2008): 4614–15. Available at http://frwebgate.access.gpo.gov/cgi-bin/getpage.cgi?position=all&page=4614&dbname=2008_register.

"Truckee River Operating Agreement." 2008. http://www.usbr.gov/mp/troa/final/troa_final_09-08_full.pdf.

California v. United States (1978)

The case of *California v. United States*, 438 U.S. 645 (1978), came to the U.S. Supreme Court during the construction of the New Melones Dam on the Stanislaus River in California. The Flood Control Act of 1944 originally authorized the construction of the New Melones Dam. Initially, the project was to be built and operated by the U.S. Army Corps of Engineers. Subsequently, in the Flood Control Act of 1962, Congress extended the project and provided that the Bureau of Reclamation under the Secretary of the Interior would be responsible for its operation.

During the course of construction, opponents to the project complained of the impact of the new dam on white river rapids and on the archeological resources and limestone caves adjacent to the river. Some of the opposition hinged on the amount of water contained in the reservoir. It was principally this last concern that set up the conditions for the case.

The case itself involved a dispute between the U.S. Bureau of Reclamation and the Water Resources Control Board of California. The Secretary of the Interior sought state permits to impound 2.4 million acre-feet of unappropriated water with the construction of the New Melones Dam. The Water Resources Board granted the permits after determining that there was sufficient unappropriated water but attached a list of twenty-five conditions. The most significant condition limited the amount of water that the Bureau could impound until it submitted an appropriate plan for the use of the water.

The Bureau of Reclamation sought relief in federal district court. It noted that Section 8 of the 1902 Water Reclamation Act said that the Secretary of the Interior must not interfere with the laws of the state governing water use and must act in conformity with the state law. Nevertheless, it claimed that Section 8 of the 1902 Reclamation Act required the Bureau to observe the form and not the substance of the law. The Bureau agreed that the act required it to seek permits but argued that the Water Resources Control Board must grant the permits without conditions as long as there was sufficient unappropriated water.

The State of California relied heavily on Section 8 of the 1902 Reclamation Act, claiming that it permitted the Water Resources Control Board to place any conditions it wanted on the permits. The district court ruled in favor of the Bureau of Reclamation, holding that the United States must apply to the state for a permit but only as a matter of comity and that the state must issue the permit as long as there was sufficient unappropriated water. The federal Court of Appeals upheld the finding of the federal District Court in part, but it argued that application for the permits was not a matter of comity but rather of law.

In a six-to-three decision, with Justices White, Brennan, and Marshall joining in dissent, the U.S. Supreme Court held that Section 8 of the 1902 Water Reclamation Act permits a state to impose any condition on the use, distribution, appropriation, or control of water, thus reversing the decision of the Court of Appeals.

Justice Rehnquist wrote the decision for the Court, arguing that the legislative history of the 1902 Act supported the finding of the Court, as did the history of federal and state relations within the field of water law. The only limit on a state's authority to impose such conditions arises if the conditions interfere or conflict with a clear congressional directive. The Court also disavowed any dicta in the cases of *Ivanhoe Irrigation District v. Mc Cracken* (357 U.S. 275), *City of Fresno v. California* (372 U.S. 627), and *Arizona v. California* (373 U.S. 546) that might have suggested a contrary conclusion.

The Supreme Court noted that the Court of Appeals had ruled that California could not place conditions on permits granted to the Bureau of Reclamation. Since this precluded the appeals court from reaching the issue of whether or not the conditions imposed by the Water Resources Control Board were in conflict with congressional directives, the case was remanded for further consideration in line with the present ruling.

In his dissenting opinion, Justice White stated that the Court's decision represented an entirely new construction of Section 8 of the 1902 Reclamation Act. After briefly reviewing several cases, he suggested that all of them are contrary to the Court's decision. The earlier cases viewed Section 8 as limited to the acquisition and not the distribution of water, according to White.

In spite of the litigation, the Army Corps of Engineers completed the New Melones Dam project in 1979, and the dam is currently under the management of the Bureau of Reclamation. The project's reservoir has a capacity for 2.4 million acre-feet of water. According to the Bureau, it provides for flood control, irrigation and municipal water supplies, peak use period hydroelectric production, recreation, and fish and wildlife enhancement.

—Jerry Murtagh

See also: *Army Corps of Engineers, United States; Bureau of Reclamation; Flood Control Act of 1944*

BIBLIOGRAPHY

Brickson, Betty, and Water Education Foundation. *Layperson's Guide to the Central Valley Project.* Sacramento, CA: Water Education Foundation, 1994.

Seglund, Wanda, ed. *Layperson's Guide to New Melones Dam.* Sacramento, CA: Western Water Education Foundation, 1982.

U.S. Department of the Interior, Bureau of Reclamation. "Central Valley Project." http://www.usbr.gov/projects/Project.jsp?proj_Name=Central Valley Project&pageType=ProjectPage.

Carabell v. U.S. Army Corps of Engineers (2006)

Rapanos v. United States (04-1034) and *Carabell v. United States Army Corps of Engineers* (04-1384) come to the U.S. Supreme Court as consolidated cases on a writ of certiorari to the Sixth District Court of Appeals. The cases involve disputes between the Army Corps of Engineers (Corps) and two Michigan land developers over the application of the Clean Water Act to their efforts to fill in wetlands that do not abut navigable waterways. The Corps took the position that the Clean Water Act authorized it to regulate wetlands that were not in close proximity to navigable waters but connected to them hydrologically. The lower courts upheld the position of the Corps. The Supreme Court vacated the judgment and remanded.

The Cases

Rapanos, claiming that his property was just a cornfield with ditches, proceeded to fill it in with sand in spite of an order to cease and desist. The government subsequently brought civil and criminal charges against him. The district court found Rapanos guilty of violating Section 301 of the Clean Water Act. The court in the criminal trial found him guilty, but the judge refused to sentence him and instead fined him $185,000 and placed him on probation for three years (Brief of New York State 2006).

Carabell sought a permit from the Michigan Department of Environmental Quality (DEQ) to fill in 15.96 acres of wetland. He claimed that there was no connection between the wetlands and any body of water because a fabricated berm separated them from the Sutherland-Oemig drain. The Corps denied his request on the grounds that the wetlands had a "significant nexus" to navigable waterways (Brief of the Corps 2006).

In Rapanos's case, the Sixth Circuit Court affirmed the ruling of the district court, noting that although the wetlands did not abut navigable waterways since they were at least eleven miles from the Kawkawlin River, they nevertheless had a significant nexus with the river through surface water that connected to tributaries that wound their way to the Kawkawlin River.

The Sixth Circuit noted in Carabell's case that the wetland is adjacent to a ditch, which connects to the Sutherland-Oemig drain. Water from the drain flows into the Auvase Creek, which in turn flows into Lake Clair, part of the Great

Lakes drainage system and a regulated navigable water of the United States. Subsequently, it affirmed the district court's decision in favor of the plaintiff (*Army Corps of Engineers* 2000).

These two cases were of interest to the U.S. Supreme Court, perhaps for several reasons, but in part because two previous cases had raised an unanswered question about the Corps's authority over wetlands. In the case of *United States v. Riverside Bayview Homes* (1985), the Supreme Court had upheld the authority of the Corps over wetlands adjacent to navigable waters. However, in *Solid Waste Agency v. U.S. Army Corps of Engineers* (2001), the Court held that the Corps had gone too far in its effort to extend the reach of its authority over wetlands. The Corps had sought to apply its 1986 Migratory Bird Rule, which treated isolated waters as within its jurisdiction if migratory birds depended upon the waters.

The Supreme Court's Decision

A divided Supreme Court failed to answer directly the question posed by the two cases: that is, whether wetlands with only a hydrological connection to navigable waterways fall under the purview of the Clean Water Act. Justice Scalia, joined by Chief Justice Roberts and Justices Thomas and Alito, wrote the plurality opinion for the Court. Justice Kennedy wrote a concurring opinion to form the majority. Justice Stevens filed a dissenting opinion, joined by Justices Souter, Ginsburg, and Breyer, and Justice Breyer filed his own dissent (*Rapanos* 2006).

In the plurality decision, Justice Scalia noted that the 1954 *Webster's New International Dictionary* defined waters as relatively permanent standing or flowing bodies of water. He concluded that the term *waters* used in the Clean Water Act statute could only refer to permanent streams, rivers, lakes, and other such bodies of water. Scalia held that the Act did not give jurisdiction over wetlands with only a hydrological connection to navigable waters through ordinary dry channels where water sometimes flows, since such channels did not constitute "waters of the U.S." The plurality decision held that the Clean Water Act conferred jurisdiction only over wetlands with a permanent surface water connection to navigable waterways. The Court vacated the judgment of the Court of Appeals and remanded it for further consideration based on the Supreme Court's decision (*Rapanos* 2006).

Justice Kennedy, the fifth vote to form a majority, noted that the Clean Water Act seeks to maintain the "chemical, physical, and biological" integrity of navigable waters by restricting dumping and the filling in waters of the United States. Based on this observation, he reasoned that the Clean Water Act intended jurisdiction over wetlands that have a "significant nexus" to navigable waters. He argued that a "significant nexus" exists if the wetlands connect in such a way as to affect significantly the chemical, physical, and biological integrity of covered waters. If the effect is ephemeral or only speculative, a "significant nexus" does not exist. Agreeing with the plurality that the facts made it unclear as to whether or not such a nexus existed, he agreed to vacate the judgment and remand (*Rapanos* 2006).

Justice Stevens's dissent applied a two-step rule that had been introduced in *Chevron U.S.A. v. Natural Resources Defense Council* (1984), providing that when a statute is found to be ambiguous and an agency's interpretation of the statute is reasonable, the Court should defer to the agency. Stevens also noted that *Riverside* was controlling since that case, unanimously decided, held the Clean Water Act to "cover all traditionally navigable waters; tributaries of these waters; and wetlands adjacent to traditionally navigable waters or their tributaries" (*Rapanos* 2006).

—Jerry Murtagh

See also: *Army Corps of Engineers, United States; Clean Water Act of 1972; Wetlands*

BIBLIOGRAPHY

Army Corps of Engineers, U.S. v. Rapanos, 235 F.3d 236, 259–60 (6th Cir. 2000).

Brief for New York State et al., *Rapanos v. United States* (04-1034) and *Carabell v. United States Army Corps* (04-1384) (2006).

Brief of Army Corps of Engineers et al., *Rapanos v. United States* (04-1034) and *Carabell v. United States Army Corps of Engineers* (04-1384) (2006).

Chevron U.S.A., Inc. v. Natural Resources Defense Council, Inc., 467 U.S. 837, 842–45 (1984).

Li, Ya-Wei, and Euwyn Poon, "*Rapanos v. United States* (04-1034); *Carabell v. United States Army Corps of Engineers* (04-1384): Oral argument: February 21, 2006." *LII Bulletin* (Cornell University Law School). http://topics.law.cornell.edu/supct/cert/04-1034.

McDonald, Matthew A. "*Rapanos v. United States and Carabell v. United States Army Corps of Engineers*." *Harvard Environmental Law Review* 31, no. 1 (2007): 321–332. Available at http://www.law.harvard.edu/students/orgs/elr/vol31_1/macdonald.pdf.

Rapanos, 235 F.3d 236, 259–60 (6th Cir. 2000).

Rapanos v. United States, 126 S. Ct. 2208, 2209 (2006).

Solid Waste Agency v. U.S. Army Corps of Engineers (SWANCC), 531 U.S. 159 (2001).

United States v. Riverside Bayview Homes, 474 U.S. 121 (1985).

Carey Act of 1894

U.S. Senator Joseph M. Carey (R–WY) created the Carey Act in 1894 to unify control over land and water so that private companies could use large blocks of public land as collateral for their investments in irrigation projects. The Carey Act provided that each state that contained desert land, as defined by the Desert Land Act, could select up to 1 million acres of federal land for reclamation. The state would not own the land but would merely serve as a trustee for the settlers. The state could either construct hydraulic works on its own or negotiate contracts with private companies. These companies had to submit their plans for reclamation to the Secretary of the Interior. Once a private firm received its money, all additional proceeds from the sale of lands would go to the state. Construction and settlement of all projects had to be completed within ten years of the passage of the Carey Act. No person could acquire more than 160 acres, with none of land to be leased, and at least 20 of the 160 acres had to be cultivated by settlers.

Origins of the Carey Act

Carey, a rancher and developer, realized the need for the legislation when he participated in the largest irrigation scheme in Wyoming but, after building 100 miles of canals in the mid-1880s, proved unable to secure title to the public lands served by the ditches. His bill aimed to serve the needs of states, such as Wyoming, Montana, and Idaho, whose largest streams carried much unclaimed water. The Carey Act avoided the issue of leasing grazing lands, probably because of controversy over earlier such proposals. It also answered critics of California's Wright Act by providing for state control over land prices and the distribution of water. In essence, the Carey Act served as a compromise bill that struck a balance among unconditional cession, autonomous state reclamation programs, private reclamation efforts under strong state supervision, and a centralized federal program. The legislation blocked speculators from monopolizing land, and since the state guaranteed the price of water rights, it protected settlers from confiscatory rates. To those legislators who opposed federal reclamation, the Carey Act did not commit the nation to spend any money. Instead, the law transferred costs of identifying potential reclamation projects to the states.

The Carey Act in Practice

Buffalo Bill Cody, the showman responsible for creating the popular image of the West in his Wild West Show, headed one of the first companies to take advantage of the Carey Act. Cody sought to focus on cooperation and interdependence rather than the individualism and autonomy traditionally associated with the West. He saw irrigation as a way of building stronger communities. He also hoped to bring people from crowded cities to help them enjoy the wide open spaces of the West. Cody chose land at the foot of the Shoshone Mountains, about thirty-five miles from Yellowstone National Park. The area had an ideal gradient for irrigation ditches as well as rich soil. By the time that Cody's company completed nine miles of ditches in Wyoming, the federal government had made the first transfer of land under the Carey Act in March 1896. However, Cody's Shoshone Land and Irrigation Company spent $80,000 on fifteen miles of ditches but could only attract about a dozen farmers who wanted only 400 acres of land. The company sold its water rights for $10 an acre, but it cost the firm $22 an acre to provide the water. As a result, the company nearly went bankrupt, and Cody had to dip into his savings to keep it afloat. Work on the irrigation ditches stopped in 1897. Following passage of the Newlands Act in 1902, Cody sold much of his land to the federal government.

The Shoshone Land and Irrigation Company's experience was fairly typical of the Carey Act companies. Most of the firms that tried to take advantage of the legislation quickly ran out of money, and the expected flood of new settlers never materialized. Many of the farmers who attempted to make use of the land lacked enough capital to carry them through the lean years before their farms would become productive. Additionally, as with the land chosen by Cody's company, much of the reclaimed land proved to be too far from rail lines and major markets to enable farmers to sell crops easily. Speculators managed to take advantage of the Carey Act, since the Interior Department's review process took months and the surveying of potential reclamation land could not be kept secret. The Populists, briefly politically powerful in the West in the 1890s, also objected to the Carey Act on the grounds that it aided monopolies. Sheep ranchers voiced opposition to the law on the same grounds. They opposed any public land being ceded to the state on the grounds that the land wound up in the hands of a few wealthy individuals and corporations at the expense of wool growers and the state itself. Sheep growers favored the open range, something destroyed by land cessions, because shepherds could simply move animals to fresh pasture once they had stripped vegetation from one tract of government land.

By 1900, the numbers of sheep in states like Wyoming had grown considerably since the institution of the Carey Act.

In 1895, Secretary of the Interior Hoke Smith proclaimed in his annual report that the Carey Act had failed. Smith, a Georgian with little interest in irrigation, clearly did not give the new law much of a chance. The opposition within Interior, combined with the other challenges, effectively crippled the legislation. By 1902, 669,476 acres had been set aside for irrigation projects in four of the ten states covered by the Act, but only about 12,000 acres had been reclaimed throughout the West.

—Caryn Neumann

See also: *Reclamation Act of 1902*

BIBLIOGRAPHY

Pisani, Donald J. *To Reclaim a Divided West: Water, Law, and Public Policy, 1848–1902.* Albuquerque: University of New Mexico Press, 1992.

Worster, Donald. *Rivers of Empire: Water, Aridity, and the Growth of the American West.* New York: Oxford University Press, 1992.

Carpenter, Delphus E.

Delphus Carpenter (1877–1951) of Colorado sought to protect the water rights of western states from both a federal government that sought to centralize control over the nation's resources and the water-grabbing state of California. Carpenter played the leading role in creating the Colorado River Compact of 1922 and in negotiating thirteen of the sixteen water allocation agreements approved between 1922 and 1971.

Delphus "Delph" Emory Carpenter was born in Greeley, Colorado, on May 13, 1877, as the second son of Iowa-born parents who had established a home in the cooperative agricultural venture of Union Colony on the Cache la Poude River. His status as a son of pioneers gave Carpenter a sense of obligation to Colorado as well as strong pride in his agricultural roots. It also gave him a lifelong interest in irrigation. Carpenter understood the importance of western rivers to the growth of the West. He believed that successful economic development required a sound system for irrigating agriculture, and he wanted the power over the water to be reserved to the states.

The challenges faced by farmers who needed to obtain water from irrigation ditches influenced Carpenter to pursue a career in water law. His father, observing the arrival of increasing numbers of immigrants from the East, had urged Carpenter to conceive of some plan to minimize conflict in Colorado over water. Accordingly, Carpenter earned a law degree from the University of Denver in 1899 while serving as an apprentice to Denver attorneys and continuing to help on the family farm. He developed a reputation as an exceptionally hard worker. Carpenter set up his own law office in Greeley and began to focus on a political career. He married Dot Hogarty in 1901, and the couple would eventually produce one son and three daughters.

Early Political Career

In 1908, the Republican Carpenter became the first native-born Coloradan to be elected to the state senate. After four years as a state senator, Carpenter received an appointment to serve as Colorado's interstate streams commissioner. Believing that no greater duty existed than public service, Carpenter eagerly accepted the position. It would become his life's work and lead Coloradans to remember him as the state's greatest benefactor.

At the beginning of the twentieth century, major threats to the security of western water rights emerged in the form of federal irrigation projects and the federal government's assertion of control over surplus water in western streams, especially interstate ones. The irrigation projects that began after passage of the Reclamation Act of 1902 increased pressure on the West's limited supply of surface water. Colorado's position at the headwaters of the Rio Grande, Arkansas, and Colorado Rivers made it into an important player in the West. Like other western states, Colorado feared that rapid population growth in southern California would permit that state to grab a large share of the Colorado River. Colorado also did not want the federal government to control its future.

Colorado River Compact

Carpenter joined most other small ranchers and farmers in the West in his opposition to conservation. He feared an expanding centralized government, thereby placing him in opposition to the Progressive national mood. Progressives wanted to ensure multipurpose development of the nation's rivers through commissions with broad powers to authorize and construct projects. Carpenter, with his small-farm upbringing, discomfort with eastern intellectuals, and distrust of urban populations, strongly rejected a greater federal presence in the West. Carpenter realized that states could preserve better control of their water supply by negotiating compacts that would prevent costly litigation. If such agreements were created prior to the construction of dams, reservoirs, and irrigation projects, economic development could take place with full knowledge of the amount of water available. Carpenter applied the U.S. Constitution's Compact Clause to interstate streams to forge a compromise between states' rights advocates and government officials that enabled western development to occur with minimal conflict. Under the Compact Clause, states were allowed to negotiate treaties among themselves with congressional permission. While states had used treaties to settle fishing rights and boundary disputes, no states had yet used treaties to settle interstate stream conflicts.

Both the U.S. Congress and the U.S. Supreme Court approved the Colorado River Compact, Carpenter's greatest legacy. The compact among Utah, Wyoming, Colorado, New Mexico, Arizona, Nevada, and California, signed on November 24, 1922, divided the river water equally between the upper and lower river basins. The compromise diminished the fears of the four Upper Basin states that they would not have sufficient water for growth, while also allowing California to continue its growth and permitting the federal government to construct Hoover Dam. However, the negotiators miscalculated the river flow at 20 million acre-feet instead of the correct 13 million acre-feet. The error has made it difficult to adhere to the agreement.

In 1933, newly elected Democratic governor Edwin C. Johnson removed Carpenter from his position as Colorado interstate streams commissioner. Carpenter, who had always disdained partisan politics to concentrate on goals that had the potential to improve the world in which he lived, was shocked by the move. He was so emotionally connected to his position that he had trouble vacating his office and offered to work at a reduced salary. However, long plagued by Parkinson's disease, Carpenter no longer had the physical ability to continue, and in 1934, Carpenter became bedridden. With his wife's assistance, Carpenter continued to correspond about matters pertaining to water rights for decades. He died on February 27, 1951.

—Caryn Neumann

See also: *Colorado River Compact of 1922; Reclamation Act of 1902*

BIBLIOGRAPHY

Hundley, Norris. *Water and the West: The Colorado River Compact and the Politics of Water in the American West.* Berkeley: University of California Press, 1975.

Tyler, Daniel. *Silver Fox of the Rockies: Delphus E. Carpenter and Western Water Compacts.* Norman: University of Oklahoma Press, 2003.

Cary v. Daniels (Massachusetts, 1844)

The rise of water-powered industries in the American Northeast during the first half of the nineteenth century was a major source of increasing conflict and litigation regarding water rights. *Cary v. Daniels* was a legally significant case of this time because it set a precedent that encouraged courts to consider the industrial use of water as a special use distinct from agricultural and other traditional uses.

Origins of the Case

The case arose as a result of a conflict between two mill owners, William Cary and Albert Daniels, whose mills relied on water power from the Charles River in Medway, Massachusetts. The mills were located about a quarter of a mile apart on the Charles River. Both mills commonly operated by periodically opening a gate in a dam that was situated between the two properties. Opening this gate prevented water from backing up and becoming slow or stagnant at the mill upstream, a sawmill. Until 1833, these mills were commonly owned by a coalition of tenants, which included Cary and Daniels. In 1833, the common owners sold their properties to a James Wilson. In 1837, Cary purchased the upstream sawmill. In 1838, Daniels purchased the downstream mill.

When the dam downstream from the upper mill was washed away in a flood, Daniels constructed a new, larger dam closer to the downstream mill. This newly constructed dam blocked more water than had the previous dam, causing the water level behind the dam to rise. This slowed the speed of the water flow upstream at Cary's dam considerably, causing the river to deliver significantly less power to Cary's sawmill. Additionally, the location of the new dam prevented Cary from easily traveling to the dam to open the gate and increase water flow to restore power, as had been the practice in earlier years.

In response, Cary filed a lawsuit against Daniels. Cary alleged that Daniels's new dam constituted an improper interference with the river that had negatively impacted Cary's use of his own mill and that Daniels was preventing Cary from accessing the new dam to open the gate, as had been the practice when both mills were under common ownership. Following a trial by jury, Cary was awarded a total of $400 for both complaints. Daniels challenged this verdict, at which point the case was taken to the Supreme

Judicial Court of Massachusetts in 1844 to determine if the judgment should be entered upon the verdict.

Before the Court

The case was heard by Chief Justice Lemuel Shaw, who, like other jurists of his time, relied upon English common law to make decisions regarding property rights, including riparian rights. These common-law principles held that all landowners whose property fell along a body of water had a right to a reasonable use of the water in its natural condition, giving all riparian property holders relatively equal access rights and none of them the right to use the water in such a way as to affect the other landowners negatively.

However, this principle of reasonable use proved a poor fit considering the emerging uses of water in the mid-nineteenth century, as it necessarily limited the heavy consumption of water that newly developing water-power industries necessitated. Shaw's decision aimed to update this principle to accommodate the new uses of water presented by water-power technologies. It was Shaw's opinion that manufactories and other industries that relied upon water power were of such significance to the American economy and public that their use of water constituted a special use that transcended traditional boundaries of reasonable use.

This new principle still held that each industry owner was entitled to reasonable use, but it redefined this use to consider both the needs and desires of the community and the ongoing development of hydraulic technologies. Under this new definition of reasonable use, a landowner operating a water-powered mill could not entirely obstruct the flow of water, but the landowner could consume far more water than landowners up- and downstream, as long as that landowner could claim that this use was justified by the greater service to the community that the industry provided.

Perhaps most importantly for William H. Cary and Albert Daniels, however, Shaw's decision also placed a greater emphasis on prior appropriation than earlier legal decisions had done. Given the new uses for water by water-powered industries, and the amount of water they needed, Shaw observed, it would frequently be the case that demands for water would outstrip the capabilities of a given body of water. In these cases, he ruled, the landowner who had begun appropriating water prior to the establishment of other industries along the river had the greater right of access. This right was maintained even if it negatively affected other industry owners up- or downstream, provided that this earliest owner was

making a reasonable effort to take advantage of water-power technologies that could alleviate the other landowners' complaints and was not intentionally interfering with the water access of others to create a monopoly.

Therefore, since Daniels had taken ownership of his mill after Cary had established his use of the Charles River, and prior use of the river during the period when both were cotenants had established a practice of use for Cary to expect upon taking ownership, Daniels had erred in constructing a dam that was larger than the one that had been in place earlier and that negatively affected Cary's use of the Charles River. However, while this portion of the jury's verdict was upheld, the court overturned the jury's decision on Cary's second complaint, ruling that, once the two properties were under separate ownership, Cary no longer had the right to enter the downstream property to open the gate on the downstream mill's dam.

For later court cases, *Cary v. Daniels* set an important precedent in a rapidly industrializing nation. Whereas earlier courts had upheld the principle of reasonable use in order to encourage regular distribution of riparian rights, with little respect to the purpose behind the use, later courts relied upon *Cary v. Daniels* to give special consideration to the industrial usage of water. This decision eroded the tradition of ensuring equal distribution of water rights among landowners, but it significantly encouraged and enabled the growth of water-powered industries and the continued industrialization of America.

—Skylar Harris

See also: *Dam Building*

BIBLIOGRAPHY

Cumbler, John T. *Reasonable Use: The People, the Environment, and the State, New England, 1790–1930*. New York: Oxford University Press, 2001.
Hall, Kermit L., Paul Finkelman, and James W. Ely Jr. *American Legal History: Cases and Materials*. 3rd ed. New York: Oxford University Press, 2005.
Lauer, T. E. "The Common Law Background of the Riparian Doctrine." *Missouri Law Review* 28 (1963): 60–107.

Clean Water Act of 1972

The Clean Water Act, formally known as the Federal Water Pollution Control Act Amendments of 1972, aimed to restore and preserve the nation's waterways. The legislation, which reflected an increasing interest in the environment by

Edmund Muskie was an American politician who served as governor of Maine, as a U.S. senator, and later as secretary of state under President Carter. As a senator, he introduced the Clean Water Act of 1972.

Gene Forte/Consolidated News Pictures/Getty Images

the public, marked a shift in federal responsibilities from distributing water to protecting it.

From the founding of the nation to the twentieth century, the federal government had defined protection of the waterways as ensuring a means of waterborne transportation. In the twentieth century, the government began to focus on ensuring an adequate water supply for agricultural and personal consumption. With the Water Quality Act of 1948, Congress addressed the quality of the water supply for the first time. However, the legislation proved extremely inadequate. The focus on state efforts to establish individual water quality standards led to a patchwork of regulations that failed to consider water as a resource that moved. The regulations did not control the discharge of pollutants at the source, thereby permitting contaminated water to spread around the country.

Poor River Quality and Legislation Opposition

By 1970, America's waterways were dumps. The oil- and chemical-laden Cuyahoga River in Cleveland, Ohio, had caught fire on several occasions. Major rivers, such as the Androscoggin and the Kennebunk Rivers in Maine, were stinking open sewers. One wag even described the Connecticut River as the prettiest sewer in America. Many beaches were closed to the public, while fish had vanished from many waterways. The Chesapeake Bay and the Great Lakes had ceased to be productive fisheries. The situation had become a crisis. John Blatnik of Minnesota, the prime mover behind the Clean Water Act in the House of Representatives, warned in 1972 that if Congress did not take immediate action, despite the cost, then it would undoubtedly face the task of paying later when perhaps no amount of money would be sufficient to repair the damage. Edmund Muskie of Maine, who designed the law and spearheaded it through the Senate, believed that the American public demanded fishable and swimmable rivers. Supporters of the legislation in both houses of Congress wanted to stop the use of any river, lake, stream, or ocean as a waste treatment system.

Despite the apparent need for the Clean Water Act, opponents of the legislation were numerous. Opposition to the legislation came in response to the specific pollution control requirements as well as the time schedules imposed upon industry. (The schedules to ensure fishable and swimmable water throughout the nation by 1983 and to eliminate the discharge of pollutants by 1985 were ultimately not met. By 1992, 30 percent of waterways failed to meet designated water quality standards.) Opponents also worried about the federal financial commitment. However, strong public interest in protecting the environment prompted Congress to approve the bill.

Legislation Components

The Clean Water Act set three broad goals: the biological integrity of receiving waters, the maximum use of available technology, and the ultimate goal of zero discharge. It established a national system that required individual permits for discharges of pollutants into U.S. waters. It created pollution control standards based on the best available technology for major industrial categories. The legislation established a floor for the protection of water quality and wetlands but allowed states to administer their own programs after they had obtained approval from the Environmental Protection

Agency. States were free to create stricter standards than the federal example. The legislation focused on surface waters, with groundwater falling under the 1974 Safe Drinking Water Act.

The 1977 amendment to the Clean Water Act established three categories of pollutants: toxic, conventional, and nonconventional. Toxic pollutants are various chemicals, including those on an initial list of 129 substances. In *Train v. Colorado PIRG* in 1976, the U.S. Supreme Court defined toxic pollutants as those that would indirectly or directly cause death, disease, behavior abnormalities, cancer, genetic mutations, physiological malfunctions, or physical deformities. Conventional pollutants include suspended solids and fecal coliform bacteria. Nonconventional pollutants include ammonia, chlorine, and iron.

The Clean Water Act is widely acclaimed as one of the most significant pieces of environmental legislation passed by Congress. The waterways are far cleaner than they were in 1972. Fish have returned to waters that had appeared to be dead. Lake Erie and the Potomac River, two notoriously polluted waterways, have been restored to health. The total population served by central sewers and secondary treatment or better has jumped dramatically since 1972. Federal construction grants built about 4,000 sewer systems and 2,000 treatment plants between 1972 and 1988. By 1988, less than 1 percent of the urban population routinely generated and discharged untreated wastes. Industrial facilities that release pollutants have reduced their pollutant loads by 90 percent.

The legislation has been faulted, however, for being too narrow. The Clean Water Act does not address cross-media pollution prevention,

Cuyahoga River Fire

The Cuyahoga River, which passes through Cleveland, Ohio, before emptying into Lake Erie, was notorious during the 1960s for its pollution. Among the pollutants were industrial waste, oil, chemicals, raw sewage, and garbage. The river's state was such that a Federal Water Pollution Control Administration employee observed that "the Lower Cuyahoga has no visible life, not even low forms such as leeches and sludge worms that usually thrive on waste" ("Environment" 1969).

On June 22, 1969, the Cuyahoga River erupted in flames that extended more than twenty feet into the air. While the fire lasted only about twenty minutes, it consumed two railroad bridges and filled downtown Cleveland with noxious smoke. The media attention that followed severely damaged Cleveland's reputation across the United States, as the city became infamous for its polluted waterway.

The fire proved a boon to the environmental movement, which seized upon the event to highlight the need for clean water and sustainable development. It proved to be such an effective symbol that it was credited with helping pass the Clean Water Act of 1972.

—John R. Burch Jr.

BIBLIOGRAPHY

"Environment: The Cities; The Price of Optimism." *Time*, August 1, 1969. Available at http://www.time.com/time/magazine/article/0,9171,901182-1,00.html.

The Cuyahoga River flows through industrial Cleveland into Lake Erie. The river, for years polluted with industrial waste, caught fire in 1969 and became a symbol of environmental degradation. The photo above was taken a year before the fire.

Alfred Eisenstaedt/Time & Life Pictures/Getty Images

American Water Works Association

The American Water Works Association (AWWA) is a nonprofit, international professional organization with more than 60,000 members. The group's membership is drawn from all facets of the water industry. It was founded in St. Louis, Missouri, on March 29, 1881, by twenty-two individuals representing water utilities based in Illinois, Indiana, Iowa, Kansas, Kentucky, and Tennessee. Its members were not only interested in the supply of water but also wanted to ensure that it was safe to drink. The typhoid epidemic that began in the 1890s enabled the organization both to demonstrate the expertise of its members on water issues and to become active in the legislative arena. A member of the AWWA discovered that the filtration of water drastically reduced the number of deaths associated with the disease. In response, government officials began acting on the recommendations made by the AWWA. Soon thereafter, the AWWA began working to establish standards for its members to adopt in their local areas. Since the first standards were developed in early 1908, the organization has become recognized as the standard setting organization in the water industry worldwide.

—John R. Burch Jr.

BIBLIOGRAPHY

American Water Works Association. http://www.awwa.org.
McTigue, Nancy E., and James M. Symons, eds. The Water Dictionary: A Comprehensive Reference of Water Terminology. Denver, CO: American Water Works Association, 2009.

Clean Water Restoration Act of 1966

The Clean Water Restoration Act of 1966 (CWRA) was one of several amendments to the Federal Water Pollution Control Act of 1948 (FWPCA). The CWRA defined "navigable waters of the United States . . . [as] all portions of the sea within the territorial jurisdiction of the United States, and all inland waters navigable in fact." The CWRA made several modifications to the 1948 FWPCA.

The legislation transferred responsibility for administration to the Secretary of the Interior with the rationale that it would "consolidate in one agency all of the water-related activities of the United States government," including conservation use and pollution control, "and facilitate the administration's proposal for a Clean Rivers Program" (Andreen 2003). It also authorized the Secretary of Interior, in cooperation with the Secretary of Agriculture and the Water Resources Council, to conduct a comprehensive study of the effects of pollution, including sedimentation, in the estuaries and estuarine zones of the United States on fish and wildlife, sport and commercial fishing, recreation, water supply and power, and other specified uses. Procedures for abating domestic pollution that damages the health or welfare of citizens in a foreign country were also outlined. In addition, the amendments prohibited individuals, except as permitted by regulations issued by the Secretary of Interior, from discharging oil into the navigable waters of the United States.

The bill increased grants for waste treatment facilities and for agencies responsible for water pollution control. It also provided support for research and training. Although President Lyndon Johnson only requested $50 million for the first year of the program, Congress authorized $450 million for 1968, $700 million for 1969, $1 billion for 1970, and $1.25 billion for 1971. The actual appropriations for 1968 and 1969 amounted to $200 million (Andreen 2003).

with the result that efforts to protect rivers, lakes, and estuaries have occasionally led to facilities and treatment systems that pollute groundwater supplies. Urban and agricultural runoff is responsible for a large portion of water pollution, but the legislation did not consider these types of contaminants. Combined storm water and sewage overflows remain problematic, as does the need to expand focus from the chemical quality of water to include the ecological integrity of entire aquatic systems. An end to pollution discharges is not always enough to restore the fish and wildlife in a lake or river ecosystem.

—Caryn Neumann

See also: *Clean Water Restoration Act of 1966; Clean Water Restoration Act of 2009; Water Quality Act of 1987*

BIBLIOGRAPHY

Moore, Emmett Burris. *An Introduction to the Management and Regulation of Hazardous Waste.* Columbus, OH: Battelle Press, 2000.
U.S. Congress, Senate Committee on Environment and Public Works. *The Twentieth Anniversary of the Clean Water Act: Hearing Before the Committee on Environment and Public Works, United States Senate, One Hundred Second Congress, Second Session, September 22, 1992.* Washington, DC: U.S. Government Printing Office, 1992.

In addition to the increased funding, the bill removed any ceilings on the dollar amount that a locality could receive in federal aid for individual projects. The federal contribution to project costs could be 30 percent. This could be raised to 40 percent if the state participated; thus the federal program would pay 40 percent, the state 30 percent, and local municipalities 30 percent. In addition, the new act granted federal assistance for financing basic planning concepts developed in the abatement of pollution. The projects were to be financed for no longer than three years at 50 percent of the total cost (Greiner 1968).

The CWRA also amended the 1924 Oil Pollution Control Act, extending coverage to inland as well as coastal waters. It transferred administrative control from the Army Corps of Engineers to the Federal Water Pollution Control Administration. The Act also increased penalties to a maximum of $10,000 and authorized the government to remove spilled oil from the water or shorelines and then sue the responsible parties for the cost of cleanup (Greiner 1968).

As the 1960s came to a close, there was a perception that existing enforcement procedures were too time consuming. There was also a continuing concern that water pollution standards suffered from difficulties in "linking a particular discharger to violations of stream quality standards" (Copeland 1999). These concerns and the increasing public interest in environmental issues paved the way for the FWPCA of 1972, which effectively replaced the 1948 FWPCA and its subsequent amendments.

—Jerry Murtagh

See also: *Army Corps of Engineers, United States; Water Pollution Control Act (1948)*

BIBLIOGRAPHY

Andreen, William L. "The Evolution of Water Pollution Control in the United States—State, Local, and Federal Efforts, 1789–1972: Part II." *Stanford Environmental Law Journal* 22 (2003): 215–94. Available at http://papers.ssrn.com/sol3/papers.cfm?abstract_id=554122.

Copeland, Claudia. "Clean Water Act: A Summary of the Law." January 20, 1999. http://ncseonline.org/NLE/CRSreports/water/h2o-32.cfm.

Graham, Fred. "One Pollution Act Hinders Another: Water Law Curbs Actions on Ocean Oil Pollution." *New York Times,* April 16, 1967.

Greiner, Fred J. "Dairy Industry and Environmental Waste." *Journal of Dairy Science* 51, no. 7 (1968): 1151–53. Available at http://download.journals.elsevierhealth.com/pdfs/journals/0022-0302/PIIS0022030268871450.pdf.

Johnson, Lyndon B. "Special Message to the Congress Proposing Measures to Preserve America's Natural Heritage." February 23, 1966. Available at John T. Woolley and Gerhard Peters, *The American Presidency Project,* http://www.presidency.ucsb.edu/ws/index.php?pid=28097.

Mangone, Gerald. *United States Admiralty Law.* The Hague, Netherlands: Kluwer Law International, 1997.

Clean Water Action

Clean Water Action (CWA) was founded in 1972 by David Zwick. It has approximately 1.2 million members who are engaged in both environmental research and grassroots organizing. The CWA's political advocacy work is enhanced by its effective educational campaigns targeting the general populace.

The origins of the CWA can be traced to *Water Wasteland: Ralph Nader's Study Group Report on Water Pollution,* by David Zwick and Marcy Benstock, which was published in 1971. Published while events such as the fire on the Cuyahoga River were still fresh in the minds of many people, the study laid out why the protection of water resources was critical to the future of the United States. In its first year of existence, the CWA helped write portions of the Clean Water Act of 1972. It has subsequently worked not only to help shape legislation, such as the establishment of the Hazardous Response Trust Fund, but has been vigilant in opposing efforts by legislators to weaken environmental protections. Its current efforts include getting legislation passed to regulate coal ash ponds and working to ensure that the U.S. Congress passes the Clean Water Restoration Act of 2009.

—John R. Burch Jr.

See also: *Clean Water Act of 1972; Coal Ash Ponds; Hazardous Substances Response Trust Fund (Superfund)*

BIBLIOGRAPHY

Clean Water Action. http://www.cleanwateraction.org.

Zwick, David, Marcy Benstock, and Ralph Nader. *Water Wasteland: Ralph Nader's Study Group Report on Water Pollution.* New York: Grossman, 1971.

Clean Water Restoration Act of 2009

The Clean Water Restoration Act of 2009, also known as the Clean Water Protection Act, was introduced in 2008 in the 110th Congress both to address jurisdictional issues raised by recent U.S. Supreme Court decisions and address executive measures introduced during the George W. Bush administration. This legislation seeks to clarify the authority of federal government agencies, particularly the Environmental Protection Agency (EPA) and the U.S. Army Corps of Engineers, to protect wetlands that are not adjacent to navigable waters.

Supreme Court Intervenes in Wetland Regulation

For the past thirty-five years, the Clean Water Act of 1972 has given the federal government the power to protect U.S. waterways from industrial and agricultural pollution, to ensure public health, and to protect the natural environment. During the administration of President George W. Bush, however, the political climate shifted against environmental regulation by the federal government. All three branches of the national government turned decisively to the right. Republicans controlled Congress until 2006. The Supreme Court witnessed the appointment of new conservative justices, and it undermined federal authority to regulate wetlands through two cases, *Solid Waste Agency of Northern Cook County (SWANCC) v. U.S. Army Corps of Engineers* (2001) and *Rapanos v. U.S. Army Corps of Engineers* (2006). President Bush himself was openly hostile to environmental regulation and appointed agency heads and cabinet members who shared his views.

In the *SWANCC* case, a majority of the justices held that nonnavigable inland waterways are not protected by the 1972 Clean Water Act solely because they could serve as habitat for migratory birds. In *Rapanos,* a rare three-way vote (4-1-4) resulted in the determination that federal jurisdiction would have to be decided case by case, based on whether or not the wetlands in question had a "significant nexus" to traditional navigable waters. A wetland met this test if it significantly affected the chemical, biological, or physical quality of navigable waters.

Both decisions generated considerable controversy surrounding both the authority of the federal government and its environmental consequences. Property rights advocates praised *Rapanos* for limiting federal wetlands controls, but the decision roused concerns among conservationists and legal scholars, who worried that it would accelerate ongoing losses of wetlands.

Although the split decision in *Rapanos* left the door open to corrective action from Congress, it had a negative affect on federal pursuit of pollution cases involving wetlands. An EPA internal memo of March 2008 found that, between July 2006 and March 2008, the agency failed to pursue 304 cases of Clean Water Act violations because of "jurisdictional uncertainty" growing out of Supreme Court rulings and that 500 more had been adversely affected by those decisions (Bronski 2009).

New Legislation

The policy vacuum left by *Rapanos* led members of Congress concerned with wetlands conservation to rectify the effects of the Court's rulings. In 2008, Senator Russell Feingold (D-WI) and Representative James Oberstar (D-MN) introduced the Clean Water Protection Act, which aimed to use congressional power to re-establish the original authority and intent of the Clean Water Act. The measure soon bogged down in committee and never made it to the floor of either the House of Representatives or the Senate. Senator Feingold reintroduced the measure in April 2009 as the Clean Water Restoration Act.

The bill's critics, led by private property advocates, developers, and commercial agriculturalists, argue that Congress never intended the Clean Water Act to apply to nonnavigable waters and that the new act is a gross expansion of CWA's original authority from navigable to all waters. The bill's supporters, a coalition of more that 300 organizations, point out that passage would restore the original act's intent, not expand it. They assert that the 1972 act explicitly defined *navigable waters* as "waters of the United States" and that the *navigable waters* term is outdated. The new bill restores the authority as it was originally intended by removing the *navigable* term and inserting a specific list of covered waters.

With the Obama administration in power and Democrats controlling Congress, expectations were high that Congress would pass the Clean Water Restoration Act of 2009. Clean water was a central plank in the Democratic Party platform in the 2008 election campaign. Furthermore, President Obama appointed pro-conservation figures to key environmental posts. Colorado Democrat Ken Salazar, the new Secretary of the Interior, received a 100 percent rating from the League of Conservation Voters while in the Senate. Lisa Jackson, appointed to head the Environmental Protection Agency, earned a reputation as a tough regulator while head of the New Jersey Department of Environmental Protection. Environmentalists view President Obama as environmentally friendly and able to understand the link between environmental and economic health. How far the legislation goes, however, will depend on the ability of its supporters to mobilize popular support in the face of a severe recession and a determined opposition.

—Walter F. Bell

See also: *Army Corps of Engineers, United States; Clean Water Act of 1972; Environmental Protection Agency, United States; Rapanos v. United States (2006); Solid Waste Agency of Northern Cook County v. United States Army Corps of Engineers et al. (2001); Wetlands*

BIBLIOGRAPHY

Bronski, Peter. "Muddy Waters: The Push for Better Clean Water Protection." *E: The Environmental Magazine* 20, no. 2 (2009): 34–35. Available at http://www.emagazine.com/view/?4574.

Sponberg, Adrienne Froelich. "Supreme Court Ruling Leaves Future of Clean Water Act Murky." *Bioscience* 56, no. 12 (2006): 966. Available at http://caliber.ucpress.net/toc/bisi/56/12.

Weeks, Jennifer. "Protecting Wetlands: Is the Government Doing Enough?" *CQ Researcher* 18, no. 34 (2008): 793–816.

Clinton, DeWitt

DeWitt Clinton (1769–1828) was born on March 2, 1769, in Little Britain, New York. After completing his early education at Rev. John Moffat's grammar school, Clinton attended Kingston Academy for two years and then Columbia College, where he received an AB in 1786. After graduation, he studied law with Samuel Jones Jr. and gained admittance to the bar in 1790. Clinton never practiced law but instead used his legal training in both politics and in conducting land transactions in western New York. Politics attracted Clinton while he was a law student because his uncle, George Clinton, was serving as governor of New York. Upon passing the bar, young Clinton became private secretary to the governor and secretary to both the Board of Regents and the Board of Fortification. These appointments allowed Clinton to bypass the usual process of serving in an apprentice-type position in the party prior to holding a political appointment. This lack of experience would hamper his political career in future years.

Political Life

In 1795, Clinton's uncle chose not to run again, and Democratic-Republican Clinton lost his government appointments. He opted to return to Columbia to study natural science but returned to political office in 1797 when he was elected to the state assembly. In 1798, he won

Portrait of DeWitt Clinton (1769–1828), a New York politician who served in many offices during his lifetime. It was largely due to his efforts that the Erie Canal was built, a feat that revolutionized westward transportation in the nineteenth century.
Library of Congress

election to the state senate. His political clout increased in 1801 when he was appointed to the governor's Council of Appointment. Then in 1802, he was selected to fill the U.S. Senate seat abandoned by John Armstrong. Clinton resigned from the Senate to become the mayor of New York City, a position he held from 1803 to 1815 with only two breaks in service. As mayor, Clinton worked to improve a variety of services in the city, such as sanitation, education, and health services; he also oversaw the construction of fortifications in the city. In 1810, he was appointed to the Canal Commission, which was charged to explore the design and construction of a canal from the Hudson River to the Great Lakes.

By 1812, Clinton was viewed as presidential material by both the Federalists and the antiwar faction of the Democratic-Republicans in New York. The United States was fighting the British in the War of 1812, and New Englanders believed Clinton could end the war. Clinton lost to James Madison by an electoral vote of 128–89, receiving support from all of the New England states except Vermont. Due to his affiliation with the Federalists during the election, Clinton lost his support base in the New York assembly and senate, which cost him the 1814 election. In 1815, Clinton was again without an elected office, having lost both his position as lieutenant governor and mayor. However, he retained his position on the Canal Commission.

Clinton and the Erie Canal

Clinton took charge of the canals project, which had been languishing since 1792 due to funding problems, politics, and continuous debate about the route. He advocated the construction of two canals from the Hudson River to the Great Lakes. The canals would provide economic and military advantages for the country because internal trade could be conducted between the northeast and the western states and territories. The canals could also be used to supply the military in the west in a more efficient manner. After the War of 1812 ended, the country turned to internal markets for its manufactured goods, and the canals would provide the needed routes. Clinton's plan was adopted by the state legislature on April 15, 1817, and the groundbreaking took place on July 4 of the same year in Rome, New York.

In 1816, Clinton had been elected governor of New York, and he was re-elected by a narrow margin in 1820 against political opposition led by Martin Van Buren, the political leader of the Tammany Hall faction. He chose not to run for re-election in 1822. Clinton retained his position as president of the Canal Commission after leaving office until April 1824, when members of the Albany Regency political faction, led by James Tallmadge, removed him from office, a move that was not sanctioned by the party's leader Martin Van Buren. His removal was questioned by many because Clinton had never taken a salary in his fourteen years of service, he was synonymous with the canal, and the Regency faction could not benefit politically from the removal. The reaction across New York was so strong that Clinton was elected governor under the People's Party banner by a large margin of 17,000 votes in 1824.

The canals were completed in 1825, and celebrations were held on October 26. The finished Erie Canal reached 362 miles from Buffalo to Lake Erie; the Champlain Canal reached 71 miles from the Hudson River to Lake Champlain. The canals were engineering marvels. The Erie Canal was a trench 40 feet wide and 4 feet deep with 83 locks and an 802-foot-long aqueduct across the Genesee River.

After the successful completion of the Erie Canal, Clinton was re-elected to the governor's office in 1826. He did not complete that term, dying suddenly on February 11, 1828, in Albany, New York. The state voted to provide for his family after his death. Clinton's legacy is forever linked with the Erie Canal, or "Clinton's Big Ditch." Without his constant support, the canal would never have been completed because of the political and economic complications of the times. Clinton also left a lasting mark on New York public education and the sciences and had a hand in the establishment of numerous cultural and civic organizations.

—Theresa Hefner-Babb

See also: *Erie Canal*

BIBLIOGRAPHY

Chalmers, Harvey, II. *The Birth of the Erie Canal.* New York: Bookman Associates, 1960.

Cornog, Evan. *The Birth of Empire: DeWitt Clinton and the American Experience, 1769–1828* New York: Oxford University Press, 1998.

De Bear Bobbé, Dorothie. *De Witt Clinton.* New York: Minton, Balch, 1933.

Koeppel, Gerard T. *Bond of Union: Building the Erie Canal and the American Empire.* Cambridge, MA: Da Capo Press, 2009.

Shaw, Ronald E. *Erie Water West: A History of the Erie Canal, 1792–1854.* Lexington: University of Kentucky Press, 1966.

Colorado Doctrine of Water Rights

The "Colorado Doctrine" was the genesis of the implementation of the water system of prior appropriation, which quickly spread throughout most other western states as the alternative to the riparian water allocation system that American settlers had brought with them from the eastern United States. Although some states have adopted models of water appropriation that combine prior appropriation with other types of water rights, such as riparian rights or pueblo rights, the Colorado Doctrine remains the purest form of prior appropriation and is in use in Alaska, Arizona, Colorado, Idaho, Montana, Nevada, New Mexico, Utah, and Wyoming.

Even before Colorado became a state, its territorial supreme court recognized the inapplicability of the riparian doctrine that was almost universal before the 1860s. In its 1872 decision in the case of *Yunker v. Nichols,* the court found that water could be diverted from a stream and conveyed to a location where it could be put to more beneficial use. In its 1876 state constitution, Colorado instituted the first statewide prior appropriation system. This was deemed necessary because if riparian water rights holders used all of the water to which they would be entitled under a riparian rights system, in a semiarid state like Colorado, there would be little water left for anyone else. This was of particular concern for the mining industry, which had already gone through its first boom period and had settled into a large-scale corporate mining operation, requiring large amounts of water, at the time of Colorado statehood. When water is scarce, the courts and later the constitutional convention decided, water is best put to use in places where it can be of the greatest benefit, which may not be along the courses of waterways. Consequently, in Colorado and other states following this doctrine, ownership of land along a waterway carries with it no inherent water right, as it does in a riparian system.

In 1882, the Colorado Doctrine was tested in the courts with the case of *Coffin v. Left Hand Ditch Co.* (6 Colo. 443). The case revolved around a dispute between one group of landowners along the South St. Vrain River near Longmont, Colorado, and another group of landowners not far away along what was known as Left Hand Creek. A ditch had been dug in 1860 to transport water to lands along the dry Left Hand Creek, but the owners of these lands had made an appropriation water rights claim to the waters of the South St. Vrain. Coffin was one of a number of farmers who owned land along the South St. Vrain but were alarmed to find that the river had dried up entirely thanks to the diversion through the ditch to Left Hand Creek. After a couple of almost-violent confrontations where guns were present, the case went to court. Essentially, Coffin and his farmer friends were making a riparian claim (as their land was on the South St. Vrain), and the Left Hand Ditch parties were making a claim of appropriation, having filed a claim and put the water to beneficial use. The court upheld the state constitution, in that it rejected the riparian claim in favor of the appropriative claim, and the Colorado Doctrine became permanently enshrined in state law.

In most cases, the Colorado Doctrine holds that the water user who files an appropriative claim can file the claim for as much land as they can irrigate at the time of the claim's filing. This became law in Colorado Territory in 1859, when a miner named David Wall filed a claim to irrigate two acres of land devoted to vegetables. However, the law states that any further expansion of irrigated land for which a claimant might seek water would have to be subject to a new claim. As that new claim would be more recent than the original claim, the new claim would have junior

rights to the old claim, as well as any other claims made on that watercourse in the interim (Cech 2010).

Another part of the Colorado Doctrine that has influenced water rights law throughout the West is the preference it gives to agricultural uses of water over industrial or any other type of water use. This was enshrined in section 6 of the Colorado constitution and upheld in the 1891 case of *Strickler v. City of Colorado Springs* (16 Colo. 61, 26 P. 313). Over the next sixty years, Colorado courts expanded the rights of prior appropriation to include water from wells and water drawn for domestic purposes.

—Steven L. Danver

See also: *Prior Appropriation; Riparian Rights; Water Law*

BIBLIOGRAPHY

Cech, Thomas V. *Principles of Water Resources: History, Development, Management, and Policy.* 3rd ed. Hoboken, NJ: John Wiley & Sons, 2010.

Corbridge, James N., and Theresa A. Rice, eds. *Vranesh's Colorado Water Law.* Rev. ed. Niwot: University Press of Colorado, 2000.

Corbridge, James N., Theresa A. Rice, and Stuart Corbridge, eds. *Vranesh's Colorado Water Law: 2003 Supplement, Including Cases and Materials Through 2003.* Boulder: University Press of Colorado, 2004.

Dunbar, Robert G. *Forging New Rights in Western Waters.* Lincoln: University of Nebraska Press, 1983.

Dzurik, Andrew A. *Water Resources Planning.* 3rd ed. Lanham, MD: Rowman & Littlefield, 2003.

Johnson, Kirk. "It's Now Legal to Catch a Raindrop in Colorado." *New York Times,* June 28, 2009. Available at http://www.nytimes.com/2009/06/29/us/29rain.html.

Colorado River Basin Act of 1968

The Colorado River Basin Act was the last major piece of legislation dividing up the waters of the Colorado River. The major provision of the bill—approval of the Central Arizona Project aqueduct—would be the last major diversion of the river and would ensure that Arizona would receive its designated 2.8 million acre-feet (maf) of water each year, provided there was enough water in the river to fill everyone's needs.

In the years after the 1922 Colorado River Compact, the seven basin states charted their own courses toward claiming and diverting their share of water. Since the Compact only divided the water between the upper and lower river basins, most of the arguments that ensued involved dividing shares among individual states. Afraid that the southern basin states would soon divert much more than their fair share of Colorado River water, the upper basin states came to an agreement in 1948. The two major contending states of the southern basin—Arizona and California—dragged on their arguments over shares of the river through the 1940s and through a Supreme Court case from 1952 to the final settlement in 1964. The major point of contention was California's claim that Arizona did not need the full 2.8 maf from the Colorado River because of water from the Salt and Gila Rivers. California claimed that it needed the Arizona allotment of water and had long been using much more than its 4.4 maf allotment.

Legislation Takes Shape

When the Supreme Court finally ruled in Arizona's favor, long-laid plans for a Central Arizona Project (CAP) canal became possible. Arizona needed funding for the aqueduct project to begin, and this need became the primary impetus for the 1968 bill. At first, Senator Carl Hayden (D-AZ) drafted a bill entitled the "Lower Colorado River Basin Project Bill" in 1965. However, Representative Wayne Aspinall (D-CO) was in control of the House Interior Committee and delayed hearings on the bill. He was afraid that CAP would take away Colorado's undeveloped water allowance. He therefore inserted several Colorado water projects, forcing Arizona and others to support his plans in order to obtain CAP approval.

While Arizona appeared to be the largest beneficiary of the bill, authorization of CAP was not an unclouded victory. In order to gain California's support, the bill dictated that in times of drought, Arizona's CAP would bear the brunt of any cutbacks. Other basin states received project approval and funding in the bill. Colorado received five small projects, Utah two, and New Mexico one. Nevada was addressing its water needs in a separate bill, and Wyoming wasn't asking for anything. In the end, Arizona's project was the costly and controversial piece, but Aspinall's other small projects helped create at least the illusion of a larger, regional plan to garner the necessary approval in Congress.

Another interesting provision of the bill almost seems like a formality: a restatement of the treaty obligation to Mexico signed in 1944 that promised to deliver 1.5 maf of Colorado River water to Mexico each year. A closer look at that section reveals an interesting twist to the larger story of the Colorado River. Not only does the section reaffirm this treaty commitment, but it also states that meeting this obligation would be a "national responsibility," not just a regional one. While some saw this provision in the bill as an unfair shifting of responsibility from the Basin states to the nation, it slipped through without a major challenge.

Strained Resources

Western lawmakers understood that the Colorado River was overallocated. Studies in the years following the 1922 Compact clearly demonstrated that this bill and subsequent ones divided up more water than was actually available. Most now believed that for everyone to receive the water shares promised them, the Colorado River would have to be augmented. Not only Arizona's CAP would be tapped to meet needs, but major augmentation of the river might be needed just to meet treaty obligations with Mexico. However, Senator Henry Jackson (D-WA) chaired the Senate Interior Committee, which would need to approve the 1968 bill, and he adamantly refused to support any augmentation plans from the Columbia River. Therefore, the bill specifically placed a ten-year moratorium on river augmentation plans that would draw water from the Columbia River or any other natural rivers.

Because of these two conflicting sections of the bill—one making national funding for Colorado River augmentation possible and one banning such augmentation from other rivers—an unexpected outcome of the bill's passage was experiments with "weather modification." Mostly, these experiments involved cloud seeding with silver iodide to encourage rainfall. Between 1970 and 1975, the federal government subsidized these projects along the San Juan mountain ranges. The environmental outcomes of these experiments are unknown, but most scientists eventually agreed that there was little or no evidence that cloud seeding actually worked.

Nearly seventeen years after the passage of the Colorado River Basin Project Act, Arizona opened a major section of its CAP aqueduct and began taking its share of Colorado River water for the first time. California continued to develop alternative water supplies and managed to reduce its own use of Colorado River water to the 4.4 maf it was allotted. Subsequent laws have addressed other issues, such as salinity and drought management. Recent efforts have focused on reducing the human impact on water quality and river wildlife and finding a balance between recreational and municipal uses.

—April Summitt

See also: *Aspinall, Wayne N.; Central Arizona Project; Colorado River Basin; Lower Colorado River Basin Project Bill (1965)*

BIBLIOGRAPHY

August, Jack L., Jr., *Vision in the Desert: Carl Hayden and Hydropolitics in the American Southwest.* Fort Worth: Texas Christian University Press, 1999.

Schulte, Steven C. *Wayne Aspinall and the Shaping of the American West.* Boulder: University Press of Colorado, 2002.

Sturgeon, Stephen C. *The Politics of Western Water: The Congressional Career of Wayne Aspinall.* Tucson: University of Arizona Press, 2002.

Colorado River Compact of 1922

The 1922 Colorado River Compact is generally considered the foundation of the so-called "Law of the River" governing the use of water on the Colorado River in the United States. The Compact, as it is usually known, established the framework for allocating the river's water among the seven U.S. states that share the Colorado River Basin. It does so by dividing the Basin into two parts: the Upper Basin, which includes a small part of Arizona and the four states of Colorado, New Mexico, Utah, and Wyoming; and the Lower Basin, comprised of most of Arizona and California and Nevada. Under the Compact's terms, 7.5 million acre feet (maf) of water is allocated to each basin. Allocation of Colorado River water within each basin was left for later resolution.

Protecting the Upper Basin

The Compact emerged from Basin state concerns in the early twentieth century that rapid growth of irrigated agriculture in the Lower Basin states, particularly California, would adversely affect the water claims of the Upper Basin states. After the federal Reclamation Act was passed in 1902, ambitious plans were advanced to dam the Colorado River, harnessing its water and taming its seasonal floods. Such projects alarmed Upper Basin interests. The U.S. Bureau of Reclamation's approval in 1919 of a project

George H. Maxwell

George Hebard Maxwell was born June 3, 1860. He began his professional career as a lawyer but eventually also became a lobbyist and journalist. He devoted most of his professional efforts to water-related issues. Believing that most of the wealthy individuals and corporations moving westward were interested in monopolizing water for their economic benefit, Maxwell became an advocate for giving the federal government control of water in order to protect the welfare of the general citizenry.

In 1897, Maxwell helped form the National Irrigation Association, ostensibly to educate the public about the benefits of irrigation. Maxwell used the organization to lobby the federal government on water issues. His periodical, *Maxwell's Talisman,* built political support among the general public. Maxwell's lobbying resulted in his coauthoring the Newland-Hansbrough Bill, also known as the National Reclamation Act of 1902. He was also instrumental in the establishment of the nation's flood control policy through his work on the Newlands River Reclamation Amendment to the Rivers and Harbors Bill of 1917.

Until his death on December 1, 1946, Maxwell continued his advocacy on behalf of the federal government's efforts to control water in the West. Many of these projects, especially those involving the Colorado River, also benefitted his adopted state of Arizona. His achievements resulted in his being honored in 1941 as the "Father of Reclamation" by the National Reclamation Association.

—John R. Burch Jr.

See also: *Bureau of Reclamation*

BIBLIOGRAPHY

Pisani, Donald J. *Water and American Government: The Reclamation Bureau, National Water Policy, and the West, 1902–1935.* Berkeley: University of California Press, 2002.

Strom, Claire. *Profiting from the Plains: The Great Northern Railway and Corporate Development of the American West.* Seattle: University of Washington Press, 2003.

advanced by the Imperial Irrigation District (IID) to build a conveyance canal on the U.S. side of the border that would end the district's dependence on the existing Alamo Canal, which ran through Mexico, amplified these concerns. This project, dubbed the All-American Canal, would enable the IID to use a larger share of Colorado River water, potentially augmenting California's claims to the Colorado if the rule of prior appropriation practiced in western states were to be applied. A U.S. Supreme Court decision delivered in June 1922, *Wyoming v. Colorado,* supported the application of prior appropriation doctrine in cases that concerned the Colorado River, lending urgency to the situation.

The Upper Basin's response was led by Colorado's state water commissioner, Delph Carpenter, a brilliant attorney dubbed the "Silver Fox" by his colleagues. In May 1921, anticipating an adverse Supreme Court decision, Carpenter proposed that the seven Basin states meet and forge a compact to divide the Colorado's waters equitably. The states' legislatures agreed, and the federal government, which had a voice by virtue of the fact the river was deemed navigable, agreed to send an emissary.

A Meeting of the Basin States

The meeting convened at Bishop's Lodge near Santa Fe, New Mexico, in November 1922. Its delegates, collectively assembled as the Colorado River Commission, immediately clashed over how to divide the water among the seven states. With delegates deadlocked and adamant in defending their states' interests, the federal delegate, Secretary of Commerce Herbert Hoover, advanced the idea of sidestepping allocations to individual states and simply dividing the river geographically and quantitatively between the Upper and Lower Basin states. The delegates unanimously agreed. Hoover proposed and the delegates agreed to set the boundary between the upper and lower river basin at Lee's Ferry, Arizona, and to allocate 7.5 maf of water annually to each basin, with the lower basin having claim to an additional 1 million maf if sufficient surplus were available. Having been admonished by Secretary of State Charles Evans Hughes not to neglect Mexico's claim to the river, Hoover persuaded his colleagues to recognize a potential future allocation of water to Mexico, the burden of which would come, first, from any surplus flow on the Colorado River and, second, if surplus were insufficient, in equal shares from the upper and lower basin.

The delegates also agreed to a set of priorities for the use of Colorado River water. Article IV of the Compact stipulates these priorities as domestic uses, agricultural uses, and hydropower generation. Navigation, the foundation of the federal government's interest in the river, was listed after hydropower with the formal recognition that "the Colorado River has ceased to be navigable for commerce and the reservation of its waters for navigation would seriously limit the development of its Basin" (Art. IV[a]).

The Compact

Signed on November 24, 1922, the Compact provided the basis for the subsequent allocation of water within the Upper and Lower divisions of the Basin. Using the Compact's allocation of 7.5 maf of water annually to each basin, the 1928 Boulder Canyon Project distributed 51.7 percent of Upper Basin water to Colorado, 23 percent to Utah, 14 percent to Wyoming, 11.25 percent to New Mexico, and 0.7 percent to Arizona. Of the Lower Basin's allocation, California received 58.7 percent, Arizona 37.3 percent, and Nevada 4 percent. In 1944, the U.S.-Mexico Water Treaty allocated 1.5 maf annually to Mexico, this U.S. obligation to be satisfied as provided in the Compact.

Large dams and extensive irrigation works would soon follow these allocations. Yet the Compact inadvertently gave rise to many of today's disputes over the waters of the Colorado River by overallocating the Basin's water. Its assignment of 15 maf plus an expected surplus of at least 1 million acre-feet was based on the assumption that the Colorado River produced as much as 18 maf annually. That has since proved wrong. Actual runoff averages around 15 maf annually, complicating the satisfaction of legal claims on the river, including Mexico's treaty entitlement. Contemporary worry about climate change adds to the region's water uncertainty.

Recent Law of the River developments reflect these concerns. In 2001, the U.S. Department of the Interior implemented an agreement with the Basin states that would, over a period of fifteen years, ratchet down California's overreliance on the river's surplus flows. In 2007, Interior announced another agreement establishing rules for conserving water in the Lower Basin to cope with prolonged drought but did not address the U.S. obligation to Mexico. Yet despite its shortcomings, the Compact was farsighted. It resolved the most contentious disputes over Colorado River water allocation and set the cornerstone for basinwide development.

—Stephen P. Mumme

See also: *Boulder Canyon Project Act (1928); Colorado River Basin; United States–Mexico Water Treaty (1944)*

BIBLIOGRAPHY

"Colorado River Compact, 1922." http://wwa.colorado.edu/colo rado_river/docs/CO%20River%20Compact.pdf.

Hundley, Norris, Jr. *Water and the West: The Colorado River Compact and the Politics of Water in the American West.* 2nd ed. Berkeley: University of California Press, 2009.

Reisner, Marc. *Cadillac Desert: The American West and Its Disappearing Water.* Rev. ed. New York: Penguin, 1993.

Worster, Donald. *Rivers of Empire: Water, Aridity, and the Growth of the American West.* New York: Oxford University Press, 1992.

Colorado River Storage Project Act of 1956

In the Colorado River Storage Project Act of 1956 (CRSP), the U.S. Congress authorized the construction of major dams and water development projects in Utah, Wyoming, Colorado, and New Mexico. The legislation allowed these states to develop significant portions of their allotments under the Colorado River Compact of 1922. CRSP also served as a catalyst for the Upper Colorado River Compact of 1948 and set additional precedents for water law. Considerable controversy surrounded the passage of the legislation and has continued over different aspects of its associated projects.

For several decades prior to the passage of CRSP, the upstream states sought federal aid to construct projects and to protect their water rights. Their fears that they would lose their water rights to California and Arizona if they did not construct projects led to the adoption of the Colorado River Compact of 1922. Later, the Upper Basin successfully lobbied during debate over the Boulder Canyon Project Act for a portion of the dam's power revenues to be used to fund investigations for new projects in the Upper Basin. The Boulder Canyon Adjustment Act of 1939 provided additional funds for this purpose. The results of these investigations led to the formation of the CRSP.

Bureau of Reclamation officials felt that before the project could be authorized, the Upper Basin states needed to make a formal division of their share of the river under the 1922 compact. The four states began negotiations in 1946, reaching an agreement in 1948 that apportioned the 7.5 million acre-feet allotted to the states on a percentage basis (Colorado 51.75%, New Mexico 11.25%, Utah 23%, and Wyoming 14%), while allotting that portion of Arizona that lay within the Upper Basin 50,000 acre-feet.

Congressional Action

In 1950, the Bureau of Reclamation presented its plan for the CRSP to Congress. Because the Bureau of Reclamation's engineers determined irrigators could not repay project costs within fifty years at an affordable rate, Upper Colorado Regional Director Eugene O. Larson proposed adopting the formula of the Flood Control Act of 1944. Under the so-called Pick-Sloan Plan, hydropower revenues generated at large storage dams would help repay a portion of the associated irrigation projects. Additionally, the large reservoirs behind the dams would provide holdover storage to meet the obligations to the Lower Basin states under the Colorado River Compact, as well as provide flood control and recreation benefits. The legislation also set a precedent by terming the costs of recreation and flood control benefits "nonreimbursable." Because the public at large, rather than irrigators and power users, received the benefit of these features, the U.S. Treasury repaid the associated costs.

Congress failed to act on the 1950 proposal, so Senator Arthur V. Watkins (R-UT) reintroduced CRSP in 1953 with the endorsement of the newly elected Eisenhower administration. However, the legislation met with stiff opposition over the project's costs and over the proposed storage dam at Echo Park, located within the boundaries of Dinosaur National Park. Debate over the project stretched over several sessions of Congress. The turning point came in 1955 when Representative Wayne Aspinall (D-CO), chair of the House Interior Committee, removed the Echo Park Dam from the House version of CRSP. Aspinall had supported the dam, but he felt that passage of the entire CRSP package was more important than including the dam at Echo Park. In exchange for dropping plans for a dam within the National Park System, conservationists, led by the Sierra Club's David Brower, agreed not to oppose the new legislation, which would build the dam at the alternate site of Glen Canyon.

Glen Canyon Unit was the key to the CRSP, providing nearly two-thirds of the storage capacity and three-fourths of the power generation. The CRSP also authorized construction of three additional storage units: the Flaming Gorge, Curecanti, and Navajo units. Construction on the Flaming Gorge, Navajo, and Glen Canyon dams began within a year, and the dams and their associated power plants were completed by 1964. Construction on the Curecanti Unit, renamed the Aspinall unit in 1980, began in 1962. This unit consists of three stair-step reservoirs behind the Blue Mesa, Morrow Point, and Crystal dams. The final feature, the Crystal Power Plant, entered operation in 1978.

The CRSP also authorized construction of eleven participating projects spread among Colorado, New Mexico, Utah, and Wyoming. Congressional action added an additional eleven projects in 1962, 1964, and 1968. The bulk of these projects has been completed; however, portions of the Central Utah and Animas–La Plata projects are unfinished, and five additional projects have been deemed infeasible and cancelled.

The Bureau of Reclamation operates and maintains the storage units of the CRSP. Power generated by the project is marketed and distributed by the federal Western Area Power Administration (WAPA). In an effort to protect their interests in the CRSP, a majority of the public utilities that receive project power under the preferential terms of the legislation organized the Colorado River Energy Distributors Association (CREDA) in 1978.

Criticisms of the Project

While project proponents highlight the irrigation, power generation, flood control, and recreation benefits of the CRSP, the project has been attacked on many fronts over its life. Fiscal conservatives, environmentalists, and others have criticized the use of subsidized water by participating projects to grow low-value crops, which contribute to the increasing salinity levels of the Colorado River. Several of these projects, including Central Utah and Animas–La Plata have neglected to resolve Native American water right claims. These criticisms landed several of the CRSP participating projects on President Jimmy Carter's so-called "hit list." Additionally, opponents have attacked CRSP dams for their role in threatening several fish species native to the Colorado River system. Perhaps the most controversial component of CRSP remains the Glen Canyon Dam, which has impacted native fish and degraded environmental conditions in the Grand Canyon. While measures taken since the completion of an environmental impact statement in 1996 have reduced some of these impacts, power generation at the dam has been severely reduced, and the ecological problems remain unresolved. Similar measures, with similar results, have been implemented at the Flaming Gorge and Aspinall units.

—Adam Eastman

See also: *Animas–La Plata Project; Aspinall, Wayne N.; Boulder Canyon Project Act (1928); Colorado River Basin Act of 1968; Colorado River Compact of 1922; Echo Park Dam; Flaming Gorge; Flood Control Act of 1944; Glen Canyon Dam; Intermountain West*

BIBLIOGRAPHY

Harvey, Mark W. T. *A Symbol of Wilderness: Echo Park and the American Conservation Movement.* Seattle: University of Washington Press, 2000.

Sturgeon, Stephen C. *The Politics of Western Water: The Congressional Career of Wayne Aspinall.* Tucson: University of Arizona Press, 2002.

Terrell, John Upton. *War for the Colorado River.* Glendale, CA: Arthur H. Clark, 1965.

U.S. Department of the Interior, Bureau of Reclamation. *The Colorado River: A Natural Menace Becomes a National Resource.* Washington, DC: U.S. Government Printing Office, 1946.

Colorado River Water Conservation District v. United States (1976)

This U.S Supreme Court case involved a question of the effect of the McCarran Amendment on the jurisdiction of federal district courts over water rights suits brought by the United States. In effect, the McCarran Amendment permits suits over water rights against the U.S. government to be handled in state courts. This brings into high relief the question of the ability of elected state judges to balance fairly the interests of states, private parties, and Indian tribes.

The McCarran Amendment

The U.S. Code (28 U.S.C. 1345) provides federal district courts with original jurisdiction over "all civil actions, suits, or proceedings commenced by the United States, or by any agency or officer," except as otherwise provided by an act of Congress. The McCarran Amendment (codified in 43 U.S.C. 666) provides that those bringing suits over water rights can sue the United States in state court. Furthermore, for the purpose of such suits, the United States waives its sovereign immunity and must abide by the decisions of state courts with the same rights of appeal as any other party.

In the *Colorado River* case, the United States filed suit in federal district court in Colorado, pursuant to 28 U.S.C. 1345, against 1,000 citizens of that state seeking a declaration of their rights to reserved water rights on certain federal lands, parks, and Indian reservations. Shortly after the United States filed suit, one of the defendants filed suit in state court seeking to adjudicate the same rights. This party contended that the McCarran Amendment gave the state court exclusive jurisdiction over cases involving water rights. The state court dismissed the case on abstention grounds and did not reach the question of exclusive jurisdiction.

Subsequent to the dismissal in district court, the Court of Appeals for the Tenth Circuit reversed the decision of the federal district court on grounds that the abstention doctrine did not apply and the district court had jurisdiction under 28 U.S.C. 1345.

Decision by the Supreme Court

The U.S. Supreme Court granted certiorari in the case. Justice Brennan delivered the opinion of the Court, arguing that (a) the McCarran Amendment did not divest the federal district court of jurisdiction under 28 U.S.C. 1345, (b) the

Amendment gives the state court concurrent jurisdiction over cases involving water rights, and (c) the federal district court erred in dismissing on the grounds of abstention. He noted that the dismissal could "not be supported under that doctrine in any of its forms" but added that there are principles other than the abstention doctrine that deal with the issue of contemporaneous jurisdiction (*Colorado River* 1976). Justice Brennan noted that these principles stem from concerns for "wise judicial administration, giving regard to conservation of judicial resources and comprehensive disposition of litigation" (*Kerotest Mfg. Co. v. C-O-Two Fire Equipment Co.,* 342 U.S. 180, 342 U.S. 183, 1952).

In the present case, Justice Brennan noted, the most important consideration counseling against contemporaneous exercise of concurrent jurisdiction was the legislative purpose of the McCarran Amendment: "the clear federal policy evinced by that legislation is the avoidance of piecemeal adjudication of water rights in a river system." He added that since Colorado has a comprehensive system of water administration, the avoidance of piecemeal adjudication could be served by dismissal of the federal court proceeding.

The Court noted other considerations counseling against concurrent jurisdiction. In particular, Justice Brennan noted (a) the absence of any district court involvement other than filing of the complaint, (b) the extensive involvement of state water rights with 1,000 defendants, (c) the inconvenience of requiring some defendants to travel 300 miles to the district court in Denver, and (d) the existing participation by the United States in Divisions 4, 5, and 6. Based on these observations, the Court reversed the decision of the Court of Appeals.

In addition to the considerations outlined in *Colorado River,* the Court added two more criteria in the case of *Moses H. Cone Hospital v. Mercury Construction Corp.* (460 U.S. 1 1983). Noting that the Court should not apply the criteria established in *Colorado River* in a mechanical fashion, it added that the Court should also consider which forum's substantive law governs the merits of the litigation and whether or not the state proceedings will protect the rights of the parties.

Effects of the Ruling

Two years after the decision, Robert Abrams, writing in the *Stanford Law Review,* suggested that an immediate consequence of the *Colorado River* decision was "virtually [to] assure adjudication of all [water] claims in state courts, which will have strong incentives to discriminate against federal claims in favor of state and private uses" (Abrams 1978, 1111). He added that this process would hamper the development of federal lands, interfere with congressional policies, and in particular create problems for Indian tribes in the adjudication of reserved water rights.

Concerns about Indian reserved water rights stem from the fact that most western states use the prior appropriation doctrine for allocating water rights. The prior appropriation doctrine provides water rights to those who first divert water to their own beneficial use. Unlike reserved water rights, retained regardless of use, holders of prior appropriation rights can abandon or lose them if they cease to put the water to beneficial use. Others critics have joined Abrams in recent years, expressing concerns about the ability of elected state judges to balance fairly the interests of states, private interests, and particularly the reserved water rights of Indian tribes (Blumm, Becker, and Smith 2006).

In their 2006 review of the impact of the McCarran Amendment and the *Colorado River* decision on Indian reserved water rights claims, Michael Blumm, David Becker, and Joshua Smith lend credence to Abrams's concerns. After an analysis of five state court decisions and one federal district court decision during what they refer to as the McCarran Amendment era, they conclude that "no tribe among the six studied here was able to improve streamflows substantially through successful litigation of its reserved water rights" (1201).

On the other hand, Alexander Wood, in an extensive review of the *Colorado River* decision, notes that federal courts have continued to exercise their jurisdiction "when distinct federal questions and claims are involved, federal proceedings were more mature than concurrent state proceedings, or an alternative federal statutory provision mandated federal judicial review" (Wood 2008, 273).

—Jerry A. Murtagh

See also: *Colorado River Compact Act of 1922; Colorado River Basin Act of 1968; Colorado River Storage Project Act of 1956*

BIBLIOGRAPHY

Abrams, Robert H. "Reserved Water Rights, Indian Rights, and the Narrowing Scope of Federal Jurisdiction: The Colorado River Decision." *Stanford Law Review* 30, no. 6 (1978): 1111–48.

Blumm, Michael C., David H. Becker, and Joshua D. Smith, "The Mirage of Indian Reserved Water Rights and Western Stream Flow Restoration in the McCarran Amendment Era: A Promise Unfulfilled." *Environmental Law* 36 (2006): 1156–203. Available at http://papers.ssrn.com/sol3/papers.cfm?abstract_id=922865.

Colorado River Water Conservation District v. U.S., 424 U.S. 800 (1976).

Shurts, John. *Indian Reserved Water Rights: The Winters Doctrine in Its Social and Legal Context, 1880s–1930s.* Norman: University of Oklahoma Press, 2000.

Wood, Alexander. "Watering Down Federal Court Jurisdiction: What Role Do Federal Courts Play in Deciding Water Rights?" *Journal of Environmental Law and Litigation* 23, no. 1 (2008): 241–74. Available at http://www.law.uoregon.edu/org/jell/docs/231/23_241.pdf.

Colville Confederated Tribe v. Walton (Washington, 1978)

The case arose from a dispute between the Colville Confederated Tribes and Boyd Walton concerning the use of groundwater in the basin in the state of Washington. The Colville Tribes brought suit in federal district court seeking an injunction against Walton's use of surface and groundwater in the No Name Creek basin. The State of Washington intervened, claiming authority to grant permits for water use on reservation lands, and the court consolidated the case with a suit brought by the United States against Walton.

The Colville Confederated Tribes

At the close of the Civil War, settlers began to encroach on lands owned by the Colville Confederated Tribes. At the time, the Colvilles had no treaty with the United States and no reservation. The farmer in charge at Fort Colville expressed concerns that violence could erupt if the United States did not establish a reservation to protect Indian rights. President Grant, acting on a request from the Commissioner of Indian Affairs, issued an executive order creating the Colville reservation in July 1872. Twenty years later, the United States took the northern half of the reservation, approximately 1.5 million acres, from the tribes and opened it for settlement.

In 1948, Walton purchased three allotments from an Indian owner who, at the time, was irrigating thirty-two acres of land by diverting water from No Name Creek, which lies entirely within the Colville Tribes' reservation. The Indian owner was not a member of the Colville Confederated Tribes. Walton obtained a permit from the state to irrigate sixty-five acres of land by diverting one cubic foot of water per second from No Name Creek. At the time of the action, Walton was irrigating 104 acres of land and using additional water for stock and domestic purposes.

The district court noted that trout and salmon were traditional foods for the Colvilles and that fishing also had religious significance for the tribes. Construction of dams on the Columbia River had destroyed the salmon runs on which they relied. Consequently, the tribes introduced Lahonton trout into Omak Lake. These trout thrive in saline waters but require freshwater for spawning. The tribes prepared the lower reaches of No Name Creek for spawning, but Walton's irrigation during the summer months depleted the water necessary for the task.

The court also found that 1,000 acre-feet of water were available in No Name Creek during an average year. Of this 1,000 acre-feet, the court found that the Colville Tribes had a reserved right to 666.4 acre-feet per year. The remaining 333.6 acre-feet of water per year were not subject to the Colvilles' reserved water rights, according to the ruling, and an additional 237.6 acre-feet of reserved water was not currently used. The court held that this water was available for appropriation subject to the Colvilles's superior right and that Walton had a right to irrigate the thirty-two acres of land with water appropriated by prior use at the time of his purchase.

The court refused to allocate water for the Colvilles's propagation of trout, even though it held that the tribes were "potentially entitled" to the use of such water. This refusal was based on a finding that the federal government provided the tribe with fingerlings (young fish). The court also ruled that the state could regulate water not reserved for the tribes' use. The Colville Tribes and the state appealed parts of the district court ruling.

In 1985, the federal appeals court reversed and remanded the decision of the district court after two previous considerations of the case in 1980 and 1981. The appeals court held that Walton had a right to sufficient water to irrigate the thirty-two acres of land under irrigation at time of the original purchase. It noted that there had been no variation in this acreage for a quarter century during which the original non-Indian owners, the Whams, had farmed the land. Based on this observation, it could find no reason to believe that the intent of the owners was to increase the amount of land under irrigation over time. The district court had reduced the water available to the tribes from 666.6 acre-feet per year to 428.8 acre-feet per year due to the fact that the tribes were not using their entire reserved water share. The appeals court held that such a reduction of reserved water rights due to nonuse was impermissible and that the court should have allotted the full 666.6 acre-feet.

With respect to the Omak Lake fishery, the court cited its opinion in Walton II, saying the tribe had a reserved right "to sufficient water to permit natural spawning of the trout . . . and the Indian allottees have a right to share in the reserved water, based on the irrigable acreage owned, without any reduction for non-use." Based on this observation, the appeals court found that the tribes had a share of 350 acre-feet of reserved water rather than the 187.2 acre-feet allocated by the trial court.

The appeals court addressed the state's claim that it could regulate water use on the reservation in 1981, noting that tribal or federal control of water rights on the reservation would not impact state water rights. The 1985 court did not disturb this finding. After over a decade and a half of litigation, the case could be considered a victory for the Colville Confederated Tribes.

—Jerry Murtagh

See also: *American Indian Water Rights;* United States v. Powers *(1939);* Winters v. United States *(1908)*

BIBLIOGRAPHY

Bakken, Gordon Morris, ed. *Law in the Western United States.* Tulsa: University of Oklahoma Press, 2000.
Colville Confederated Tribes v. Boyd Walton Jr., et ux, et al., 752 F.2d 397 (9th Cir. 1985).
Colville Confederated Tribes v. Walton, 460 F.Supp. 1320 (E.D. Wash. 1978) (Walton I).
Colville Confederated Tribes v. Walton United States, 647 F.2d 42 (9th Cir. 1981) (Walton II).

Confederated Tribes of the Umatilla Reservation v. Alexander (1977)

The case involves a dispute between the Confederated Tribes of the Umatilla Indian Reservation (CTUIR) and the Army Corp of Engineers concerning the construction of the Catherine Creek Dam in Oregon. The CTUIR sought a declaratory judgment against the construction and operation of the dam, arguing that it would have a significant negative impact on the tribe's reserved fishing rights.

The Umatilla took the position that their 1855 treaty with the United States provided them with reserved fishing rights and that those rights would be abrogated by construction and operation of a dam that would inundate their traditional fishing stations as well as limit the availability of a variety of fish. The 1855 treaty provided for reserved hunting, fishing, gathering, and farming rights and reads in part:

"the exclusive right of taking fish in the streams running through and bordering said reservation is hereby secured to said Indians, and at all other usual and accustomed stations in common with citizens of the United States, and of erecting suitable buildings for curing the same; the privilege of hunting, gathering roots and berries and pasturing their stock on unclaimed lands in common with citizens, is also secured to them" (Kappler 1904, 694–98)

Oregon District Court Judge Belloni ruled in favor of the Umatilla, noting that several traditional fishing stations would be inundated by the reservoir created by the construction and operation of the proposed dam. Belloni did not accept the argument of the U.S. Army Corps of Engineers that planned mitigating measures, such as trapping chinook salmon and hauling them above the dam, would adequately compensate the Umatilla for their loss. In spite of such measures, Belloni found that the dam would prevent all wild fish from swimming upstream and the steelhead trout run would be eliminated entirely at all stations upstream from the dam. The result was the destruction of the treaty right to fish at all usual and accustomed stations within the reservoir.

Judge Belloni noted that Congress had originally authorized the dam in 1965 and that the Corps of Engineers did not discover a conflict between the planned construction and the fishing rights of the Umatilla until 1971. This precluded the possibility that Congress intended to abrogate the fishing rights of the Umatilla. Against this background, Belloni held that reserved fishing rights could not be abrogated by a federal agency absent a clear congressional intention to abrogate, that no such intention had been shown, and that the construction and operation of the dam would constitute an unauthorized taking of the reserved fishing rights of the Umatilla.

—Jerry Murtagh

See also: *American Indian Water Rights; Army Corps of Engineers, United States*

BIBLIOGRAPHY

Bernholz, Charles D., and Robert Weiner Jr. "The Palmer and Stevens 'Usual and Accustomed Places' Treaties in the Opinions of the Courts." *Government Information Quarterly* 25 (2008): 778–79. Available at http://digitalcommons.unl.edu/cgi/viewcontent.cgi?article=1179&context=libraryscience.
Confederated Tribes of the Umatilla Indian Reservation v. Alexander, 440 F. Supp. 553 (D. Ore. 1977).
Goodman, Edward. "Protecting Habitat for Off-Reservation Tribal Hunting and Fishing Rights: Tribal Co-Management as a Reserved

Right." *Environmental Law* 30, no. 2 (2000): 279–362. Available at http://findarticles.com/p/articles/mi_hb3153/is_2_30/ai_n28790788/.

Kappler, C. J. *Indian Affairs: Laws and Treaties.* Vol. 2: *Treaties.* Washington, DC: U.S. Government Printing Office, 1904.

Dam Safety and Security Act of 2002

Dams control floods and promote recreation, economic development, and safe drinking water. But the benefits come with risks if the dams are managed or maintained improperly. Some of the largest disasters in U.S. history have been dam collapses. The Johnstown flood of 1889 caused 2,209 deaths after the South Fork Dam failed. In 1928, the St. Francis Dam just north of Los Angeles collapsed, killing 420. Between 1940 and 1960, 35,000 dams were built. By 2009, there were over 80,000 dams of more than 10 feet in height in the National Inventory of Dams (NID). The NID listed 11,811 high-hazard dams and 13,407 significant-hazard dams.

The first dam safety regulation came early in the twentieth century, with California's program in the 1920s being among the first. The federal dams built by the Army Corps of Engineers and Bureau of Reclamation early in the century established safety standards, and states slowly developed their own programs. However, unlike most infrastructure, many dams are privately owned. The federal government owns only 4.7 percent of the 80,000 registered dams, while 58 percent are owned privately, 16 to 20 percent belong to local governments, and 4 percent are owned by states. Federal regulation of dams involves the departments of Agriculture, Defense, Energy, Interior, Labor, and State (International Boundary and Water Commission); the Federal Energy Regulatory Commission; the Nuclear Regulatory Commission; and the Tennessee Valley Authority. The Federal Emergency Management Agency (FEMA) administers the national program through the Interagency Committee on Dam Safety.

Not until dams failed in significant numbers in the 1970s was interest high enough for a national program and some state programs to be enacted. During that decade, there were failures at Buffalo Creek Dam in West Virginia, Canyon Lake Dam in South Dakota, Teton Dam in Idaho, Kelly Barnes Dam in Georgia, and Laurel Run Dam in Pennsylvania. All told, some 450 lives were lost and over $1.5 billion in damage incurred. The 1996 National Dam Safety Program (NDSP) Act was the first effort to improve dam safety. Reauthorized in 2002 and 2006, it remained underfunded, with states limited to improvement programs (technical assistance, training, research) and unable to conduct actual repairs.

Provisions of the Law

The 2002 Dam Safety and Security Act (Pub. L. 107-310) committed the federal government to better support states in making their safety programs stronger, increasing technical training and research, and developing the NID. The coalition that lobbied for passage included the Association of State Dam Safety Officials, the U.S. Society on Dams, and the American Society of Civil Engineers, as well as federal agencies such as FEMA, the Corps of Engineers, the Department of the Interior, and the Federal Energy Regulatory Commission. Sponsored by Representative Bill Shuster (R-PA), the Act modified the National Dam Safety Program Act (NDSA) of 1996 to replace a patchwork of federal and state programs with a unified set of federal guidelines for dam safety. The bill reauthorized the NDSA and continued to support research, technology transfer, cooperation, and training. Grant assistance continued to the state safety programs that regulated 95 percent of the 80,000 dams in the United States. The legislation also required the head of FEMA to prepare a strategic plan and assist in developing state-level programs, and it continued the requirement for data systems, public policy, research, and training of state staff and inspectors. It was funded through fiscal year 2006.

The Dam Safety and Security Act also added dam security as a goal, asked states to require owners to improve dam security, added limits on the authority of the Interagency Committee on Dam Safety (ICODS) to exchange information at the federal level, better defined the federal relationship with the states, and called for a stronger commitment to national dam programs to safeguard life and property. It also added research on information technology to collect and report on safety data, conduct vulnerability assessments, and safeguard sensitive information. The extension of the program for another four years increased funding to $8.6 million a year through 2006. Research funding rose from $1 million to $1.5 million a year. Training rose from $0.4 million to $0.6 million. FEMA was authorized an average of $9.96 million for fiscal years 2007–2011 for research, training, and database management.

Ongoing Concerns

The American Society of Civil Engineers (ASCE) lauded the renewal of the Dam Safety and Security Act for maintaining and preserving the safety of dams, particularly in light of heightened awareness of security risks after September 11, 2001. When ASCE called for renewal of the 2002 act as it was about to expire in September 2006, it asked for adequate funding for all federal agencies, including the departments of Interior and Defense. ASCE also asked for stronger state legislation, modeled on the FEMA Model State Dam Safety Program, to cover nonfederal dams in a comparable manner as those covered by the NDSA of 1996. The National Dam Safety Program at this time was under the Department of Homeland Security.

In 2005, an ASCE report noted that there were still 3,500 unsafe dams, despite federal and state corrective efforts. The safety program remained underfunded. Aside from the customary concerns over deterioration, there were concerns for security, as federal law enforcement and intelligence agencies had defined dams as possible terrorism targets. The 20,000 nonfederal dams were particularly vulnerable because they were not covered by the federal assessment and security improvement programs.

A 2000 study by the Association of State Dam Safety Officials indicates that $30 billion is needed to remove obsolete dams and bring the others into compliance. Of all U.S. dams, 95 percent are or should be regulated at the state level. Thus, federal assistance to the states remains necessary. A different study estimates the cost of repairing nonfederal dams at $36.2 billion and the repair of federal dams at $10.1 billion. Another 2,038 dams, built under the Natural Resource Conservation Service partnership with local communities from 1948 on, require $200 million in repairs; 74 percent of these were built before 1970.

Aside from being underfunded, state programs are variable in scope and enforcement powers. In addition, only a third of nonfederal high hazard dams have an emergency action plan in case of catastrophic failure.

—John H. Barnhill

See also: *Dam Building; Dam Removal and River Restoration; National Dam Safety Program Act of 1996*

BIBLIOGRAPHY

(ASCE) American Society of Civil Engineers. "Policy Statement 280—Responsibility for Dam Safety." July 25, 2009. http://www.asce.org/Content.aspx?id=8346.

(ASCE) American Society of Civil Engineers. "President Bush Signs National Dam Safety and Security Act into Law." *Water and Wastes Digest,* December 9, 2002. Available at http://www.wwdmag.com/President-Bush-Signs-National-Dam-Safety-and-Security-Act-into-Law-NewsPiece3950.

Juch, Martha F. "Dam Safety in the Balance: Juggling Regulations, Ownership, Economics and Public Interests in Texas." *Texas Civil Engineer* 78, no. 3 (2008): 15–17. Available at http://www.labond.com/Dams/Documents/tce78-3_Su08p10-17.pdf.

Lane, Nic. *CRS Report for Congress: Aging Infrastructure; Dam Safety.* Washington, DC: Congressional Research Service, March 25, 2008. Available at http://www.fas.org/sgp/crs/homesec/RL33108.pdf.

Davis, Arthur Powell

The director of the U.S. Bureau of Reclamation from 1914 until the position was abolished in 1923, Arthur P. Davis (1861–1933) was a hydraulic and irrigation engineer. Involved in work on a number of dams, he was also the eponym of the Davis Dam in Colorado and became known as the "father of the Boulder Dam."

Early Life

Born February 9, 1861, on the family farm near Decatur, Illinois, the son of John Davis and Martha Ann (née Powell), Arthur Powell Davis was a nephew of both the naturalist

Arthur Powell Davis (1861–1933) was a civil engineer and an expert on large water-based infrastructure with the U.S. Bureau of Reclamation as well as international agencies. He is best known as the father of the Boulder (Hoover) Dam and for his surveying work on the Panama Canal.
Library of Congress

John Wesley Powell and the educationalist William Bramwell Powell. Arthur Davis's paternal grandfather, Joseph Davis, from Kentucky, had served in the Black Hawk War, and his paternal grandfather, Joseph Powell, was a Methodist minister who had left England for North America in 1830.

In 1872, the Davis family moved from Decatur to Junction City, Kansas, and Arthur Davis went to the local high school and then Kansas State Normal School, Emporia. He then started helping his father, who had taken over the *Junction City Tribune,* before going to Washington, D.C., where he studied at Columbian College (now George Washington University), gaining a Bachelor of Science degree in 1888.

At the age of twenty-one, Davis started work with the U.S. Geological Survey as an assistant topographer. Two years later, he was appointed as a topographer to the Rocky Mountain Division, and then he joined the Irrigation Survey. In the Southwest Section of the U.S. Geological Survey, he was involved in studying rainfall and flood control and was in charge of stream measurements; he worked in Arizona, New Mexico, and California. His first published reports were *River Heights for 1896* and *Irrigation Near Phoenix, Arizona.* He then worked on the surveying of the eventual Panama Canal and the other proposed route through Nicaragua from 1898 until 1901, and this served as the basis of his article in the *U.S. Geological Survey,* "Hydrography of the American Isthmus." He was also the author of sections of the *Report of the Nicaragua Canal Commission 1897–1899,* and *Elevation and Stadia Tables.*

Two years later, Davis was appointed supervising engineer. In 1907, he was appointed president of the American Academy of Arts and Sciences, and in 1908, he became chief engineer in the U.S. Reclamation Service. Davis then went to Puerto Rico, where he worked on an irrigation project, and he accompanied President Taft to Panama to examine the possibilities of building the Panama Canal. In 1909, he served as a consulting engineer for the Panama Canal.

Government Work

In 1914, Davis went to China under the auspices of the American National Red Cross with Major General William Sibert and Daniel W. Mead. There they made a survey of the Huai River and reconnoitered the Honan, Anhwei, and Kiangsu provinces. Back in the United States, Davis was involved in planning for a number of dams. The first two were the Shoshone Dam in northwestern Wyoming, which was the highest dam in the world when it was completed, and the even taller Arrowrock Dam near Boise, Idaho. Davis then worked on the Elephant Butte Dam on the Rio Grande River in New Mexico before turning to the construction of two tunnels, the four-mile Strawberry Tunnel and the six-mile Gunnison Tunnel, built between 1905 and 1909 in Colorado. These dams and tunnels were described in Davis's next book, *Irrigation Works Constructed by the United States Government.* Davis also wrote, with Herbert M. Wilson, *Irrigation Engineering.* In 1920, with the Kincaid Act, Davis had to report on how to stop the lower Colorado River from flooding California's Imperial Valley. The next projects that Davis worked on were the Roosevelt Dam on the Salt River in Arizona and the Boulder Dam on the Colorado River. The latter was completed in 1936, after Davis had died.

In June 1923, Hubert Work, the secretary of the interior, decided to change the nature of the Reclamation Service and abolished the position of director. This was essentially the firing of Davis, and some engineers protested. Davis then served as a technical advisor for the United States and as an arbitrator on the British-American Pecuniary Claims Arbitration and then accepted the position of chief engineer and general manager of the East Bay Municipal Utility District in California, an area that included the eastern part of the San Francisco Bay, including Oakland and Berkeley. There Davis was involved in the planning and construction of a large reservoir on the Mokelunne River, as well as aqueducts and tunnels.

Davis had been to Turkestan in Russian Central Asia in 1911, and in 1930 Davis was appointed chief consulting engineer for irrigation in Turkestan and Transcaucasia, now part of the Soviet Union. He worked there for two years, returning to the United States in September 1931. An article about his work in Central Asia, in which he supervised the building of a large hydroelectric system for the Soviet government, appeared in *Civil Engineering* in January 1932. He was then appointed to the position of consulting engineer with the Bureau of Reclamation and continued work on the Boulder Dam project. In February 1933, Davis underwent an operation that was unsuccessful, and he died on August 7, 1933.

—Justin Corfield

See also: *Bureau of Reclamation*

BIBLIOGRAPHY

New York Times. "A. P. Davis Is Dead: Eminent Engineer." August 8, 1933: 17.

Who Was Who in America. Vol. 1: *1897–1942*. Chicago: Marquis, 1943.

Woodward, Sherman M. "Arthur Powell Davis." In *Dictionary of American Biography: Supplement 1,* 224–226. New York: Charles Scribner's Sons, 1944.

DeConcini, Dennis W.

A U.S. senator from Arizona from 1977 until 1995, Dennis DeConcini (1937–) was involved in sponsoring a critical amendment to the Panama Canal Treaty (1977) that allowed the control of the canal to return to Panama. He also served on the Energy and Water Development Subcommittee of the Senate.

Early Life and Career

Born on May 8, 1937, in Tucson, Arizona, Dennis Webster DeConcini was the son of Evo Anton DeConcini (1901–1986), who was from Ironmountain, Michigan, and Ora (née Webster). He served as Arizona's attorney general from 1948 to 1949 and was a justice on the Arizona Supreme Court. Educated at the University of Arizona, he graduated with a bachelor's degree in 1959 and gained a law degree four years later, after which he started practicing as an attorney. Despite being somewhat shy, in 1965 he was appointed to the staff of the governor of Arizona, Samuel Pearson Goddard Jr., where he served until the end of Goddard's term in 1967 as legal counsel and administrative assistant. It was Goddard who did much to get governors of nearby states to support the Colorado River Basin Project and, in particular, the Central Arizona Project. As a result, many farmers in Arizona managed to get a reliable water supply, which provided the basis for rapid population and economic growth.

Senate Work

From 1973 to 1976, DeConcini was the Pima County attorney, and he founded the law firm DeConcini, Yetwin and Lacy where he remains a partner. In 1976, he ran as a Democrat for a U.S. Senate seat and won. He served in the Senate until January 1995, where he played an important role in forging the Panama Canal Treaty of 1977. President Jimmy Carter wanted to return sovereignty over and control of the Panama Canal to Panama by the year 2000, in return for a guarantee of the neutrality of the canal and access for U.S. ships. The agreement was controversial. DeConcini was able to broker a consensus by which the United States was able "to take such steps as each [the U.S. and Panamanian governments] deems necessary, in accordance with its constitutional processes, including the use of military force in the Republic of Panama, to reopen the Canal or restore the operations of the Canal, as the case may be" ("Panama Canal Treaty of 1977," "Treaty Concerning the Permanent Neutrality and Operation of the Panama Canal," Conditions [1]). Known as the DeConcini Reservation, this language helped some of the opponents of the treaty support it, although it offended many Panamanians. President Carter and the Panamanian Chief of Government Omar Torrijos signed the Panama Canal Treaty and Neutrality Treaty on September 7, 1977. It was the DeConcini Reservation that President George H. W. Bush invoked when he sent soldiers into Panama in 1989.

During the 1980s, DeConcini was once more involved in the Central Arizona Project. Its aim was to provide more irrigation water to the Phoenix and Tucson regions of Arizona by diverting waters from the Colorado River. The Welton-Mohawk Irrigation District was established, and the Yuma Desalination Plant was built. DeConcini also sponsored legislation to allow federal funding of the Headgate Rock Dam's hydroelectric plant, a solar energy plant at Red Rock, and another solar energy plant at the Sky Harbor International Airport in Phoenix.

During his eighteen years in the U.S. Senate, Dennis DeConcini was involved in many other important deliberations, being chair of the Intelligence Committee from 1993 until 1995 and a member of the Judiciary Committee. He also served on the Senate Subcommittee on Defense, Energy, and Water Development. Reviewing DeConcini's Senate career, the *Wall Street Journal* reported that he had passed more legislation than any other senator with the exception of Henry "Scoop" Jackson from Washington state (cited in University of Arizona Library n.d., "Biographical Note").

DeConcini garnered notoriety for his involvement in the 1980s' savings and loan crisis, becoming known as a member of the "Keating Five." He left the Senate on January 3, 1995, resuming his legal practice in Tucson. His papers have been deposited in the University of Arizona Library's special collections.

—Justin Corfield

See also: *Army Corps of Engineers, United States; Central Arizona Project; Colorado River Basin Act of 1968; Lower Colorado River Basin Project Bill (1965)*

BIBLIOGRAPHY

Cavini, Vittorio. *A True Story: The DeConcini Family History.* Translated by Loretta Reich. Tucson, AZ: Hats Off Books, 2006.

DeConcini, Dennis, and Jack L. August Jr. *Senator Dennis DeConcini: From the Center of the Aisle.* Tucson: University of Arizona Press, 2006.

"Panama Canal Treaty of 1977." http://www.cfr.org/publication/ 12637/panama_canal_treaty_of_1977.html.

University of Arizona Library Special Collections. "Dennis DeConcini Papers: 1944–2003." http://speccoll.library.arizona.edu/applications/ deconcini/uams399_m1.html.

Delaware River Basin Compact (1961)

The Delaware River Basin Compact involves the states of Pennsylvania, New Jersey, and Delaware. This compact, signed in 1961, addresses river pollution as well as flood management, wildlife management, and water allocation as it relates to protecting the freshwater river from salinization at the river's delta. The compact created a commission charged with managing the river basin in terms of the above concerns.

The Delaware River Basin Compact was created to address the growing usage of the basin's surface water. The Delaware River provides drinking water for Philadelphia and a portion of metropolitan New York City. After the turn of the twentieth century, industrial uses and population growth began to strain the basin's water quality. In the 1940s, the U.S. Wildlife Service considered the river so polluted and lacking in oxygen that aquatic life could not survive in its water. River quality began to improve in the 1950s as water authorities throughout the basin began to improve sewage treatment.

Because of the demands on the river by two large metropolitan areas, local governments in and near the basin desired a way to manage it across municipal and state lines. The Delaware River Basin Compact created an oversight commission to manage many issues involving water quality, water quantity, and water allocation.

In the late 1950s and early 1960s, New York City began looking beyond the Hudson River for water sources. Three reservoirs were built in the Upper Delaware River Basin to supply water to the city of New York. This required an inter-basin transfer of water because New York City was not located within the Delaware River Basin. The city of Philadelphia was also very interested in the Delaware River because of its size and its proximity to Delaware Bay. During times of drought, the salinity of the Delaware River near Philadelphia would increase because of upstream intrusion from the bay. A minimum flow rate was established to prevent saltwater intrusion into the lower river.

The compact was not just consented to by Congress, as was typical with previous river basin compacts; it included the federal government as a full signatory member. In 1961, the nation's first federal interstate compact was signed into law. While the compact bound all parties for 100 years, the federal government could withdraw at any time. Membership in the commission included a representative from each state signatory and the federal government. The commission's budget was also funded by each state that was party to the agreement and the federal government.

The Delaware River Basin Commission's work is becoming more diverse as it takes on more complex issues of water quantity and water quality. Its activities often extend into land management to control water quality and quantity before water reaches the river. As a result, the commission is involved in supporting efforts of local governments in managing water resources.

The Delaware River Basin covers approximately 13,539 square miles with a majority of the basin (50.3%) within Pennsylvania's borders. The river's basin lies also within Delaware, New Jersey, and New York's borders. Its headwaters are in New York's Catskill Mountains. The river empties into the Delaware Bay of the Atlantic Ocean. The Delaware is the longest undammed river east of the Mississippi, extending 330 miles from the confluence of its east and west branches at Hancock, New York, to the ocean. The river is fed by 216 tributaries, the largest being the Schuylkill and Lehigh rivers in Pennsylvania.

The 782 square mile Delaware Bay lies roughly half in New Jersey and half in Delaware. The watershed drains only four-tenths of 1 percent of the total continental U.S. land area. Approximately 15 million people rely on the waters of the Delaware River Basin for drinking and industrial use. These users include about 7 million people in New York City and northern New Jersey who live outside the Basin. New York City gets roughly half its water from three large reservoirs located on tributaries to the Delaware. The Delaware River Port Complex (including docking facilities in Pennsylvania, New Jersey, and Delaware) is the largest freshwater port in the world.

According to testimony submitted to a U.S. House of Representatives subcommittee in 2005, the port complex generates $19 billion in annual economic activity.

The Delaware River Basin Compact was created to address issues of water quality and quantity. Because rivers do not follow state boundaries, a basinwide governing authority was needed to manage these concerns. The Delaware River Basin Compact created that authority in the Delaware River Basin Commission. Over time, the commission has evolved to manage not only water surface issues but also issues of soil and land within the Basin. This changing focus in mission reflects the dynamic and complex issues of water quality and quantity.

—James Newman

See also: *Delaware River Basin; Fish and Wildlife Service, United States; Population Trends and Water Demand; Safe Dinking Water Act of 1974*

BIBLIOGRAPHY

Albert, Richard C. "The Historical Context of Water Quality Management for the Delaware Estuary." *Estuaries and Coasts* 11, no. 2 (1998): 99–107.

Zimmerman, Joseph Francis. *Interstate Relations: The Neglected Dimension of Federalism.* Westport, CT: Praeger, 1996.

Department of the Interior v. Klamath Water Users Protective Association (2001)

The Supreme Court's 2001 decision in the case of *Department of the Interior v. Klamath Water Users Protective Association* is unique in that it centers on whether communications between a federal agency and an American Indian nation are exempt from the provisions of the Freedom of Information Act (FOIA). The numerous interpretations of the Act and its provisions have confused the legal community. This case centered on the privacy of documents passing between the American Indian nations of the Klamath River Basin and the federal government.

The Klamath Water Users Protective Association (KWUPA), a nonprofit agency, consists of users of water in the Klamath River Basin in the American northwest through a federal reclamation project. Most of KWUPA's members are public corporations that receive water from the project, including the Klamath Indian nations. The Bureau of Reclamation (BOR), a part of the Department of the Interior (DOI), regulates water usage in the Klamath River Basin. Another part of the DOI, the Bureau of Indian Affairs (BIA), in consulting with the Klamath Tribes had corresponded about how the water rights in the Klamath Basin were to be allocated. An international conflict had ensued when different tribes made demands on the water levels, one group opting to maintain high water levels to protect the fisheries on the Klamath River and the others demanding a release of water for the benefit of downriver fisheries. Were the latter to occur, a reduction of water levels and the resulting shortages might cause economic injury in dry years.

The BOR had exempted a number of documents that it had exchanged with the Klamath Tribes under an exemption in the FOIA when the KWUPA had sought access to the documents. With no resolution yet, in 1995 the DOI instigated a program to prepare for a long-term operation of the project. Its intentions were to find a middle ground for the competing interests. Specialists conducted meetings. However, the meetings amplified the disagreements between those seeking irrigation and those fearing that the water allotment would be cut. The DOI signed an agreement with the Klamath Tribes to consult and cooperate in fulfilling its trust obligations. Additional claims were made by the DOI to determine water rights for all tribes in the Klamath River Basin.

KWUPA requested information under the FOIA in order to learn what materials were being used to prepare and complete the project's operational plan. The DOI did not fully honor the request, releasing only a portion of the necessary information. Eventually, the DOI provided additional documentation, and finally only seven documents had not been made available. This material was deemed important enough to cause the association to institute proceedings under the FOIA. The government, at the behest of the BOR, argued that the parties were in "trust" and thus the communications were intragovernmental communications, exempted from the provisions of the FOIA. The government's position caused a conflict of interest between the two DOI entities, the BOR and the BIA.

Judicial Intervention

The tribes had sought the release of documents held by the DOI, who denied the release of the seven documents, as decided by the trial court. The district court granted the DOI summary judgment, arguing that since the documents were not considered inter- or intra-agency materials, they "played a role in the agencies' deliberations with regard to current water adjudication/or the anticipated plan of operation." The Supreme Court agreed, justifying its decision by arguing that the Klamath Basin nations were not in litigation with the government but merely in consultation and thus they retained sovereignty due to a trust relationship for decision-making purposes. But although the DOI initially prevailed in its exemption request, the Ninth District Court of Appeals ruled the tribe's "direct interest" in the "agency's water-allocation decision making disqualified them from protection as a threshold matter." The appellate court accepted the interagency exemption requested by the tribes.

Standards for Determination

On appeal, the Supreme Court ruled the seven documents had to be released and deemed they should be available to all parties involved. The Court based its decision on a number of factors. First, the records under debate could not be denied given the trust relationship and the conflict of interests. The existence of "competitive self-interest" required the parties to have all the available materials to defend their positions, especially in a situation where the parties were not dealing at arm's length. Second, the "outside consultant" language of the exemption permitted the introduction of outside sources and expertise. The brief provided many examples of the breadth of evidentiary support available to make a determination. The Court referred to the: "functional test" within the exemption. Third, prior consultation with certain individuals, such as the president or members of Congress, might cloud the issue. The Court, therefore, determined it must not interpret the exception in any way that could injure the power of the litigants to present their case. This might affect the "threshold test." Fourth, the possibly dispositive nature of the issue at hand meant that questions could arise about the protection of any settlement-related records under the umbrella of privilege. This amounted to a nondisclosure agreement preventing all issues and facts from becoming public. Finally, the potential impact on the exemption might make it necessary to seek new legislation regarding its enforcement.

In the final analysis, the Supreme Court affirmed the reversal, holding that the documents were not exempt from disclosure under an exemption of the FOIA. The Court declared that communications between the Klamath Tribes and the BOR were not "intra-agency or inter-agency" communications, because the tribes retained limited sovereignty and thus did not qualify as agencies of the federal government.

—Arthur Steinberg, PhD, JD

See also: *American Indian Water Rights;* Winters v. United States *(1908)*

BIBLIOGRAPHY

Colby, Bonnie G., John E. Thorson, and Sarah Britton. *Negotiating Tribal Water Rights.* Tucson: University of Arizona Press, 2005.
Prosser, Tony. *The Regulatory Enterprise: Government, Regulation, and Legitimacy.* New York: Oxford University Press, 2010.

Dominy, Floyd E.

Floyd E. Dominy (1909–2010) was doubtless the most colorful commissioner in the history of the U.S. Bureau of Reclamation (BOR). He was an important subject in two popular and influential books focusing on water in the

Floyd Dominy (1909–2010) joined the Bureau of Reclamation in 1946. He would rise through the ranks, becoming its most prominent and powerful commissioner in 1959. His most notable action as commissioner was the damming of the Colorado River at Glen Canyon, creating Lake Powell.

Bureau of Reclamation

western United States: Marc Reisner's *Cadillac Desert* and John McPhee's *Encounters with the Archdruid*. Dominy joined the BOR in 1946 as a land settlement specialist and eventually moved on to supervise the Allocations and Repayment Branch, Division of Irrigation, from 1950 to 1957. Dominy served as assistant commissioner from 1957 to 1958 and associate commissioner from 1958 to 1959, before being elevated to the position of commissioner in 1959. Notable accomplishments during his term as commissioner included completion of the Glen Canyon, Flaming Gorge, and Navajo dams as part of the Colorado River Storage Project. Dominy also played a major role in the authorization and construction of several other federal water development projects.

Dominy was born on a subsistence farm in Adams County, Nebraska, and attended the University of Wyoming, majoring in agricultural economics. He graduated in 1933, during the depths of the Great Depression, and after a brief period of teaching school, he became a county agricultural extension agent in Wyoming. Dominy's hardscrabble early years in Nebraska and Wyoming left him skeptical about the future of the small subsistence farm, and he showed scant interest either in the family farm or in maintaining the 160-acre limitation on cheap water. Dominy understood that the water policy had been a subsistence program when the BOR was established in 1902, but by the time he was commissioner in the 1960s, the western United States had changed dramatically.

Dominy argued that the Colorado River needed to be tamed; the cycle of flood and drought should be managed. Others doubted that continuing intensive development of the West was a wise thing to do; they thought that some parts of the region should be left wild—that settlement should be discouraged rather than invited. But Dominy was convinced that nature could be manipulated to make life less difficult for human beings. Glen Canyon Dam and Lake Powell are an expansive example of his vision.

As part of a unique compromise, the Sierra Club dropped its objections to the construction of Glen Canyon Dam on the Utah/Arizona border. David Brower, then the Sierra Club's executive director, eventually came to consider this decision his biggest environmental mistake. Brower, the environmental activist, was the perfect foil for Dominy, the determined dam builder.

During the 1960s, Dominy was extremely effective in getting Bureau of Reclamation projects funded. He was successful not just because western politicians were effective at getting monies allocated to projects that would benefit their states but also because Dominy used a wide variety of potent arguments. Federal reclamation projects, Dominy argued, produced many of the nation's vegetables and fruits, particularly during the winter when crops could be grown only in the Southwest. He enjoyed pointing out that the ten most-visited BOR-constructed reservoirs attracted more vacationers and tourists per year than the ten most heavily visited national parks, thereby taking pressure off the National Park Service. Dominy also testified that irrigating land increased its value, along with the value of the crops. This improved the tax base and the quality of schools and other public amenities.

Dominy genuinely believed that the dams and canals built by the Bureau of Reclamation had improved the living standards of the region's rural and urban residents. Many historians have argued that the economic growth came at too high a cost to the environment and that Native Americans and other groups did not share in the wealth produced by the projects. But Dominy never wavered in his vision of a developed West.

When he retired from the BOR, Dominy was the longest serving commissioner in its history, having served from 1959 to 1969 under Presidents Eisenhower, Kennedy, Johnson, and Nixon. Following retirement, Dominy established residence in the Northern Shenandoah Valley in western Virginia and devoted his considerable energies to the Angus cattle business. Dominy died in 2010 at the age of 100. According to then commissioner Michael Connor, "Reclamation has a long history of 'larger than life' Commissioners and Floyd was certainly at the top of that list" (U.S. Bureau of Reclamation 2010).

—Roger D. Hansen

See also: *Bureau of Reclamation; Colorado River Basin; Glen Canyon Dam*

BIBLIOGRAPHY

McPhee, John. *Encounters with the Archdruid.* Farrar, Straus, and Giroux, 1981.

Pisani, Donald J. "A Tale of Two Commissioners: Frederick H. Newell and Floyd Dominy." In *The Bureau of Reclamation: History Essays from the Centennial Symposium.* Vol. 2, edited by Brit Allen Storey, 637–50. Denver, CO: Bureau of Reclamation, U.S. Department of the Interior, 2008. Available at http://www.usbr.gov/history/Symposium_2008/Historical_Essays.pdf.

Reisner, Marc. *Cadillac Desert: The American West and Its Disappearing Water.* Rev. ed. New York: Penguin, 1993.

U.S. Bureau of Reclamation. "Reclamation Remembers the Life of Floyd Dominy." April 23, 2010. http://www.usbr.gov/newsroom/newsrelease/detail.cfm?RecordID=32289

Douglas, William O.

Associate Justice William O. Douglas (1898–1980) was the longest-serving justice of the U.S. Supreme Court in history, holding his position from 1939 to 1975. An outspoken liberal, Douglas authored several important decisions and, outside of the courtroom, invested considerable energy in promoting various causes. His roots in the Pacific Northwest and the outdoors led him to conservation causes and brought personal insights to decisions related to water law and politics.

Early Life

Born in Maine, Minnesota, in 1898, Douglas moved as a young boy first to Estrella, California, and then to rural Washington State. He eventually settled in Yakima, Washington, after his father died in 1904. As a young child, he fell ill and remained relatively weak throughout his youth. To strengthen himself, Douglas began hiking in the nearby foothills and later in the Cascade Mountains. A driven and talented student, he graduated high school as a valedictorian and earned a scholarship to Whitman College. Later, he started Columbia Law School in 1922; after graduating, he taught there for some years before moving to Yale Law School. His expertise on bankruptcy and corporate reorganization brought him national attention, and he served on and later chaired the Securities and Exchange Commission in the mid-1930s. A loyal New Dealer, Douglas was rewarded with an appointment to the Supreme Court in 1939.

Connections to Water

Douglas connected to water in personal, political, and legal ways. In many books and articles for popular audiences from the 1950s through the 1970s, the justice explored his own experiences with western American waters. Douglas told stories of fishing in mountain lakes, canoeing on rivers, and hiking along the ocean. In these settings and more, from Washington to Maine to Texas, he forged a close relationship with the natural world and its waters. He valued the solitude he found there and believed such sanctuaries should be protected from commercial exploitation and ecological despoliation so that future generations of Americans would have access to healthy environments in which to rest and recreate.

Besides identifying with and writing about natural watercourses, Douglas worked politically to protect water, especially from pollution. In *A Wilderness Bill of Rights* (1965) and other books and magazine articles, for instance, the justice described numerous water-related problems, including fouling by industrial pollution and the dumping of raw sewage into rivers from the Potomac in Washington, D.C., to the Willamette in Oregon. Concerned about deteriorating conditions, Douglas spoke to and wrote for popular audiences so that they would understand such environmental problems and demand changes from their political leaders and resource managers. He believed that individuals ought to be protected from pollution and have access to unspoiled nature (Sowards 2009).

Court Decisions

Douglas wrote several Supreme Court decisions, including some dissents, that offered important legal ideas regarding water and related law and revealed his perspectives on natural resources. His perspectives were not always predictable. In dissents in *Arizona v. California* (1963) and *Federal Power Commission v. Oregon* (1955) and the majority opinion in *United States v. District Court In and For the County of Eagle* (1971), Douglas favored the states', rather than the federal, government and courts. Despite the fact that most often western state law promoted river development, these opinions found Douglas on the side of environmental protection. For example, he did not favor the proposed Pelton Dam in *FPC v. Oregon* (Wilkinson 1990).

Scholars have singled out Douglas's opinion in *Udall v. Federal Power Commission* (1967) for specific significance related to water (Sowards 2009; Wilkinson 1990). A private utility applied to the Federal Power Commission (FPC) to build a hydroelectric dam on the Snake River on the Idaho-Oregon border in 1960 at a place called High Mountain Sheep. Soon thereafter, the federal government proposed its own dam to offer public power. The FPC gave the license to the private utility, but the U.S. government appealed. Writing for a 6–2 majority, Douglas dispensed with the private versus public power debate to focus on broader interests. Citing recreational interests and threats to anadromous fish, Douglas questioned whether any dam should be built, an unusual position at the time. Although the decision remanded the issue to the FPC, Douglas effectively quashed the dam in the name of public interest. The opinion also used the word *ecology* for the first time in Supreme Court history, and it was the first opinion to reject an FPC decision, marking the beginning of increasingly assertive federal courts that monitored administrative decisions with greater scrutiny (Sowards 2009).

Besides his well-known championing of civil liberties, civil rights, privacy, and democracy, Justice Douglas stood as arguably the most prominent public figure interested in conservation in his era (Sowards 2009). His dozens of books for the public and his four decades of public service made him a well-known figure, although he often took controversial stands in such areas as free speech and foreign policy. His personal life, too, was controversial, as he married four times and did not shy from political activism. On the Court, Douglas set records for term of service and wrote the most majority opinions, concurring opinions, and dissenting opinions of any other justice.

In 1974, Douglas suffered a stroke, and he resigned at the end of 1975. On January 19, 1980, Douglas died in Washington, D.C. The William O. Douglas Wilderness Area in Washington's Cascade Mountains honors his activism on behalf of nature. Similarly, the Chesapeake and Ohio Canal National Historical Site is dedicated to him. Douglas's work on and off the Court brought attention to a range of issues and promoted strong protective measures for environmental protection, not least for water resources.

—Adam M. Sowards

See also: Arizona v. California *(1963); Evolution of Environmental Law; Udall v.* Federal Power Commission *(1967); Water Law*

BIBLIOGRAPHY

Douglas, William O. *A Wilderness Bill of Rights.* Boston: Little, Brown, 1965.

Sowards, Adam M. *The Environmental Justice: William O. Douglas and American Conservation.* Corvallis: Oregon State University Press, 2009.

Wilkinson, Charles F. "Justice Douglas and the Public Lands." In *"He Shall Not Pass This Way Again": The Legacy of Justice William O. Douglas,* edited by Stephen L. Wasby, 233–48. Pittsburgh: University of Pittsburgh Press, 1990.

Electric Consumers Protection Act of 1986

Enacted on October 16, 1986, the Electric Consumers Protection Act (ECPA) amended the Federal Power Acts of 1920 and 1935. The new law increased the enforcement powers of the Federal Energy Regulatory Commission (FERC) by giving equal and fair consideration to non-power-generating entities such as recreation, fish, wildlife, and the surrounding environment. The new law was designed to provide the FERC with greater licensing powers involving the construction of new hydroelectric power plants. Higher licensing fees were attached to new power plant applications as a way of protecting land, water use, and water quality. Federal and state fish and wildlife agencies were also required to advise the regulatory commission of any new regulations they adopted. The FERC had to mandate studies to determine the benefits of building new power plants on the nation's waterways in order to make sure that such plants would not have detrimental effects on the water systems and their surrounding habitat.

Early Legislation

The Commerce Clause of the U.S. Constitution, as stated in Article 1, section 8, remains the most powerful source of Congress's right to enact legislation governing social and economic matters within the United States. As early as 1824, in *Gibbons v. Ogden,* Chief Justice John Marshall ruled in favor of the expansion of federal regulatory power involving the protection of the nation's navigable waterways. Subsequent Supreme Court decisions throughout the nineteenth century also reinforced the federal government's authority with respect to protecting and regulating all navigable water systems in order that they remain free and open to commerce.

In the late nineteenth and early twentieth centuries, Congress enacted a series of laws governing the use of the country's navigable rivers and harbors. The settlement of the West, industrial expansion, and rapid urbanization placed additional burdens on the nation's water systems. In 1890, the Rivers and Harbors Act expressly forbade building any object not authorized by Congress that would interfere with "navigable capacity." In 1920, as urban America's increasing demand for electricity necessitated building more power plants, the Federal Water Power Act empowered Congress with the authority to regulate the use of navigable rivers for the generation of hydroelectric power. In particular, construction of electric power plants on rivers and waterways had not been addressed by the Rivers and Harbors Act. The protection of the federal interest in navigability had been limited in scope. The new law was the first general piece of congressional legislation supported by environmentalists, and it established a total plan for national regulation and comprehensive development of the country's water resources.

Specifically, the 1920 act established a Federal Power Commission (now the Federal Energy Regulatory Commission) with full authority to license the construction and operation of hydroelectric projects on the nation's navigable waterways. Requirements were set in place to protect national forests, Native American lands, and the "navigable capacity" of the nation's waterways. In addition, plans for any construction project had to meet the approval of the U.S. Army Corps of Engineers. In 1935, the Act was amended with the establishment of an independent regulatory agency composed of five members appointed by the president and confirmed by the U.S. Senate to ensure that electric rates were reasonable and fair to consumers. It also stipulated that any new hydroelectric projects must assist in developing waterways for the benefit of interstate or foreign commerce, as well as for recreational purposes.

The impetus for even greater protection of the nation's waterways began in the 1960s and 1970s, sparked by the publication of Rachael Carson's *Silent Spring* and promoted by the enactment of a national annual Earth Day. The push for nuclear power plants, met by considerable opposition from groups such as the Clamshell Alliance in New England and the Abalone Alliance in California, also caused the federal government to adopt stricter legislation for protecting the country's waterways. On October 16, 1986, Congress enacted Public Law 99-495, also known as the Electric Consumers Protection Act. This law expanded the Federal Power Commission's authority to protect the recreational uses of the nation's rivers, its fish and wildlife, and other environmental conditions. Among the new considerations taken into account were energy conservation and protection of and mitigation of damage to fish and wildlife, especially their spawning grounds and habitats. The new law further augmented the Public Utility Regulatory Policies Act of 1978, which sought to promote conservation of electric energy through more efficient use of nonutility generators and qualified cogenerators.

Focus and Significance of the Act

The primary focus of the 1986 act was to improve electric efficiency along with preserving the environmental quality of the nation's navigable waterways. Section 10A of the Act required that applicants engaged in the generation or sale of electric power must include plans for performance capabilities that encouraged or assisted customers in conserving electricity costs. It also spelled out those recommendations developed by federal and state agencies regarding flood control, navigation,

irrigation, and preservation of Native American lands. Section 4 specified licensing procedures covering the applicant's operating and load characteristics (i.e., kilowatts) and how such power would be used for the applicant's own industrial facility and related operations, including anticipated impact on those communities slated to be served. Section 8 defined regulations governing the construction of new dams and diversion projects. Such hydroelectric projects could not be built on any portion of a natural waterway included in a state or national wild and scenic river system—that is, one possessing unique natural, recreational, cultural, or scenic qualities. This section also determined the amount of energy government dams and other structures owned by the United States could produce and charge in any one year. Lastly, section 12 stipulated the civil penalties for violating the law. Any generating company found in violation of the law after receiving a notice and opportunity for a public hearing would be subject to a fine not to exceed $10,000 for each day that such violation or failure or refusal to comply persists.

The significance of the 1986 Electric Consumers Protection Act is that it was the first major amendment to the hydroelectric licensing provisions of the 1935 act. The Federal Power Act of 1935 was amended in four major ways. First, the importance of environmental consideration in the licensing process for hydroelectric applicants was substantially increased, and the role of federal and state fish and wildlife agencies was expanded. Second, benefits for hydroelectric projects at new dams and diversions were eliminated unless those projects were in line with the new, stringent environmental conditions. Third, municipal considerations on relicensing power plants were abolished. Previously, restrictions had been eased in order to produce more electricity for industrial and customer demand. Finally, the commission's enforcement powers were expanded greatly with the addition of financial penalties, which could be assessed on violators of the law. The new law went a long way toward protecting fish, wildlife, water quality, and recreational uses of the nation's waterways.

—Chuck Howlett

See also: *Army Corps of Engineers, United States; Federal Energy Regulatory Commission; Federal Power Commission; Fish and Wildlife Service, United States*

BIBLIOGRAPHY

Clowes, Brian W., ed. *Waterpower '87: Proceedings of the International Conference on Hydropower, Portland, Oregon, August 19–21, 1987.* 3 vols. New York: American Society of Civil Engineers, 1988.

Coggins, George Cameron, Charles F. Wilkinson, and John D. Leshy. *Federal Public Land and Resources Law*. 4th ed. New York: Foundation Press, 2001.

Electric Consumers Protection Act of 1986. Public Law 99-495, 100th Cong. Stat 1243.

Federal Energy Regulatory Commission. "Hydropower." http://www.ferc.gov/industries/hydropower.asp.

Federal Energy Regulatory Commission. *Hydropower: The Use and Regulation of a Renewable Resource*. Washington, DC: Government Printing Office, 1987.

Findley, Roger W., and Daniel A. Farber. *Environmental Law in a Nutshell*. 7th ed. St. Paul, MN: Thomson/West, 2008.

Glicksman, Robert L., and George Cameron Coggins. *Modern Public Land Law in a Nutshell*. 3rd ed. St. Paul, MN: Thomson/West, 2006.

Ellender, Allen J.

A politician from Louisiana, Allen Ellender (1890–1972) was speaker of the Louisiana House of Representatives from 1932 until 1936 and, from 1937 until his death thirty-five years later, represented Louisiana in the U.S. Senate. A strong supporter of sugar cane interests, Ellender was twice chair of the Senate Committee on Agriculture. In water regulation, he became well known for his 1971 amendment to weaken the Clean Water Act of 1972 by trying to remove many of the provisions for dealing with dredged soil and make it easier to dump this soil for disposal or use in land reclamation.

Allen Ellender (1890–1972) was a long-serving Democratic senator from Louisiana. He is well known for amendments he added to the Clean Water Act of 1972.

Library of Congress

Early Life and Work

Allen Joseph Ellender was born on September 24, 1890, in Montegut, Louisiana, the son of Wallace Richard Ellender and Victoria (née Javaux). He studied at St. Aloysius College in New Orleans and then at Tulane University, where he graduated in 1913. Ellender was admitted to the Louisiana Bar and worked as a city attorney in Houma, Louisiana, from 1913 to 1915 and as a district attorney in Terrebonne Parish from 1915 to 1916. A delegate to the Constitutional Convention of Louisiana in 1921, he was a member of the Louisiana State House of Representatives from 1924 until 1936, being floor leader from 1928 until 1932 and speaker from 1932 until 1936.

Senate Career

Ellender joined the U.S. Senate in 1937 and remained a senator until his death. A Democrat with impeccable credentials, he took the Senate seat that had been held briefly by Oscar Kelly Allen Sr., who died soon after taking up the seat. Prior to that, it had been held by Huey Long, the "Kingfish," who had been assassinated in September 1935 just before he was expected to announce his bid for the U.S. presidency. During his thirty-five years in the U.S. Senate, Ellender was not without controversy. When many Democrats from Southern states supported Strom Thurmond in his presidential bid in 1948, Ellender remained loyal to Harry S. Truman. It was move he never regretted, although Senator Joe McCarthy (R-WI) was later to accuse Ellender of being "soft on communism."

In 1960, Ellender managed to fend off a challenge from Republican George W. Reese Jr., and he ensured that Louisiana supported the election of John F. Kennedy. After he won the Democratic nomination for the Senate in 1966, the Republicans did not even nominate a candidate to stand against him. In 1971, Ellender was recipient of the Watchdog of the Treasury Award and was also named Man of the Year in the *Society of Agriculture: The Progressive Farmer Magazine*.

In 1971, Ellender introduced an amendment to Senate Bill 2770 (later known as the Clean Water Act). In doing this, Ellender clearly defied the urgings of Senator Edmund Muskie (D-ME), who had introduced the bill. Muskie did not want to include a separate program that allowed discharges of dredged material but rather to treat that material the same as all other polluting discharges. This would ensure tighter regulation over all possible contaminants. Ellender's amendment, however, gave responsibility for monitoring discharges of "dredged materials" specifically to the U.S. Army Corps of Engineers. Environmentalists felt this arrangement would dilute the Clean Water Act.

Muskie had to counter with a substitute amendment that allowed the Environmental Protection Administration to deny a permit if the "dredged materials" would adversely affect the supply of municipal water, flora or fauna, breeding areas for these, or places that were used for recreation. The issue of "fill material" that was used to convert wetlands and other areas for development was not covered in the bill, which was passed by the Senate on November 2, 1971.

Ellender died in Houma, Louisiana, on July 27, 1972. The Allen J. Ellender Memorial Library at Nicholls State University in Thibodaux, Louisiana, was named after him.

—Justin Corfield

See also: *Agriculture; Army Corps of Engineers, United States; Clean Water Act of 1972; Dredging*

BIBLIOGRAPHY

Dean, Virgil W. *An Opportunity Lost: The Truman Administration and the Farm Policy Debate.* Columbia: University of Missouri Press, 2006.

Ellis, William B. "The EPA Veto and Related Matters." In *Wetlands Law and Policy: Understanding Section 404,* edited by Kim Diana Connolly, Stephen M. Johnson, and Douglas R. Williams, 283–304. Chicago: Section of Environment, Energy and Resources, American Bar Association, 2005.

Finley, Keith M. *Delaying the Dream: Southern Senators and the Fight against Civil Rights, 1938–1965.* Baton Rouge: Louisiana State University Press, 2008.

Kerr, Robert S. *Land, Wood, and Water.* New York: Fleet, 1960.

Ruppenthal, Karl Maxwell. *Issues in Transportation Economics.* Columbus, OH: Charles E. Merrill Books, 1965.

Elwha River Ecosystem and Fisheries Restoration Act (1992)

During the last year of President George H. W. Bush's administration, he signed the Elwha River Ecosystem and Fisheries Restoration Act calling for restoration of the river and the almost destroyed salmon and steelhead runs, including the removal of two aging dams if necessary. This legislation, passed in 1992, was a high-water mark for the American environmental movement and seemingly indicated a new commitment to environmental restoration in America.

Salmon Loss

The Elwha River is located on the northern shore of the Olympic Peninsula of Washington State. The river is approximately 40 miles long and includes roughly 280 miles of tributary streams and river in its watershed. With most of the river's watershed contained within the Olympic National Park, the river and its riparian habitat is very healthy and has been for several decades. But there are no salmon upstream of the Elwha Dam, which was originally built in 1913 by the Olympic Power Company. The construction of this dam to provide hydroelectricity for the town of Port Angeles, located six miles east of the dam, and for industrial development on the northern Olympic Peninsula immediately began the destruction of one of the great salmon and steelhead runs of the Pacific Northwest. The river had hosted approximately 400,000 fish a year, including all five types of Pacific salmon and three species of steelhead trout. Moreover, the river was famous for its large chinook or king salmon, some of which reached over 100 pounds.

Washington State Fish Commissioner Leslie Darwin, a progressive conservationist who had been critical of the fishing industry in Washington state as a journalist, immediately fought to protect the fish runs on the Elwha River, threatening to remove the dam if necessary. He lost that fight and, in a compromise, forced the dam owners to pay for a fish hatchery that was so unsuccessful, it was shut down within a few years of its construction.

While the river's salmon runs declined precipitously over the following decades, members of the Elwha Klallam Tribe, who live in a reservation on the river's banks, and local conservationists and environmentalists demanded greater efforts to protect and restore fisheries in the river. The creation and passage of the Elwha River Restoration Act was the result of a remarkable process of activism and consensus building in the Elwha River region and Washington state. The Lower Elwha Klallam Indian Tribe had first challenged the existence of the Elwha and Glines Canyon dams by filing to block federal relicensing of the dams in 1976. This opened the way for a flurry of activism as area activists and environmental groups, including Friends of the Earth, the Sierra Club, and the Audubon Society, gained intervener status in the effort to block relicensing of the dams. The Elwha Klallam Tribe and environmentalist group efforts to stop relicensing of the dams and force the Federal Energy Regulatory Commission (FERC) to consider the dams' environmental impacts blossomed into a local and regional environmental movement to remove the dams and restore the once remarkable salmon and steelhead runs.

Dam Removal

As they gained greater political support, particularly from Representative Al Swift (D-WA), the activists arrived at what they called "the creative solution." This involved convincing the Bonneville Power Administration to guarantee to provide the power lost from removal of the dams at the cost that Daishowa Paper Manufacturing was paying at that time to get power from the two dams. Also, measures were instituted to reduce wasteful power practices and thereby reduce costs. The central goal in this strategy was to avoid a federal judgment that might result in shutting down the pulp mill, the loss of hundreds of jobs, and bitterness among the local population. The appeal of the creative solution is revealed when one notes the supporters of dam removal: the owners of the dams, the owners of the mill receiving power from the dams, the Port Angeles Chamber of Commerce, and, of course, the environmental groups, the Elwha Klallam, the Department of Interior, and the National Park Service among others. Remarkably, almost total consensus was achieved prior to the creation of the restoration legislation.

Although the legislation was passed with such strong support, resistance to the dam removal efforts immediately arose. Ironically, the key source of this dissent was one of the original supporters, Senator Slade Gorton (R-WA). Never a friend of environmental or Indian interests, he had reluctantly supported the bill. With the Republican takeover of Congress in 1994, Gorton switched his position and openly declared his opposition to dam removal. Gorton was key to the future of the Elwha River because of his seniority in the Washington state congressional delegation and his position on the Senate Appropriations Committee, which controls government spending. Without his backing, dam removal and river restoration would be impossible. Moreover, when environmental groups begin pressing for removal of larger dams, like the four on the Lower Snake River in Washington state, Senator Slade Gorton tied funding for Elwha River and fisheries restoration to guarantees that no major dams would be removed from either the Snake or Columbia Rivers. Finally, President George W. Bush's administration was not interested in dam removal, so river restoration was slowed for the eight years following the Clinton administration.

The dams are now scheduled to be removed in 2012. A natural recovery approach will be employed, requiring removal of portions of the dams and allowing steady erosion of the mountains of sediment stuck behind the dams through rainfall, snowmelt, and river flow. Wild populations of salmon will be allowed to repopulate the river along with careful use of hatchery stocks in order to rebuild populations that exist more quickly than nature could manage alone or to put in place populations that are currently extinct on the river. The restoration of the Elwha River holds much promise both for providing a model of ecological restoration and for providing answers to scientific questions as the process unfolds over the next several decades.

—Jeff Crane

See also: *Dam Removal and River Restoration; Lower Snake River Compensation Plan; Riparian Ecosystems*

BIBLIOGRAPHY

Grossman, Elizabeth. *Watershed: The Undamming of America.* New York: Counterpoint, 2002.

Lowry, William Robert. *Dam Politics: Restoring America's Rivers.* Washington, DC: Georgetown University Press, 2003.

Trosper, Ronald L. *Resilience, Reciprocity, and Ecological Economics: Northwest Coast Sustainability.* New York: Routledge, 2009.

Endangered Species Act (1973)

The Endangered Species Act of 1973 (ESA) is the federal tool for conserving threatened and endangered plants and animals, as well as their habitats. Under the ESA, the Department of the Interior identifies and lists endangered species, prohibits their taking (hunting, killing, harassment, or capture) as well as the sale and transport of the animals, sets aside conservation funds to enable the purchase the land and water of ecosystems where endangered species live, allows state-federal cooperative agreements with federal financial assistance, and provides for establishment of penalties as well as rewards. President Richard Nixon signed the ESA into law on December 28, 1973, replacing the 1969 Endangered Species Conservation Act. Previously, the only other law that specifically mandated an ecosystem approach to conservation and management of natural resources was the Marine Mammal Protection Act of 1972, which banned the taking of marine mammals and established a moratorium on their sale, export, and import.

National Audubon Society

The National Audubon Society is a nonprofit organization comprised of independent chapters that are dedicated to the preservation and restoration of natural ecosystems, especially those supporting bird populations. The organization maintains community-based centers and nature sanctuaries that are used to educate individuals about nature. Its advocacy and educational missions are supported through publications such as the Peterson's Wildlife Guides series and *Audubon Magazine.*

In 1886, George Grinnel used *Field and Stream* magazine to call for the organization of conservation clubs around the country. He proposed that the clubs be called Audubon Societies, in honor of John James Audubon, a naturalist and artist. His efforts to create a national organization ended in 1888 due to a lack of money and inability to create an organizational structure. Individual chapters continued to function, however, and eventually organized themselves and created a funding mechanism for a central treasury. The funds were used to launch *Bird Lore* in 1899, which was renamed *Audubon Magazine* in 1941. The National Association of Audubon Societies was incorporated in 1905.

Throughout its existence, the organization has promoted the study and protection of birds. During the latter half of the twentieth century, it joined with other conservation groups in advocating for the protection of all animals and habitats. Its efforts helped in the passage of legislation such as the Clean Water Act of 1972 and the Endangered Species Act. Its joint activities with other organizations led to a lack of focus for the organization. In response, the National Audubon Society recommitted its efforts to the study and protection of birds.

—John R. Burch Jr.

See also: *Clean Water Act of 1972*

BIBLIOGRAPHY

Graham, Frank, Jr., and Carl W. Buchheister. *The Audubon Ark: A History of the National Audubon Society.* New York: Knopf, 1990.
National Audubon Society. http://www.audubon.org.
Orr, Oliver H., Jr. *Saving American Birds: T. Gilbert Pearson and the Founding of the Audubon Movement.* Gainesville: University Press of Florida, 1992.

Amendments and Provisions

The ESA has been amended a number of times since it was first passed. Amendments added coverage for sea otters, elephants, scrimshaw, and other wildlife and wildlife products. Amendments have provided exceptions for emergencies and national security. Economic impact studies became mandatory in 1978. Grayrocks Reservoir in Wyoming and Tellico Dam in Tennessee got expedited consideration for specific projects under 1980 changes. In 1988, the Department of the Interior and Department of Agriculture got equal authority to restrict imports and exports of plants, and municipal corporations came under the law. With amendments in 1996, the ESA covered fisheries as well. The ESA committed the United States to the Convention on International Trade in Endangered Species of Wild Fauna and Flora, which the United States had just signed on March 3, 1973, and the Convention on Nature Protection and Wildlife Preservation in the Western Hemisphere, which it had signed on October 12, 1940.

Under the ESA, federal agencies must work with the Fish and Wildlife Service (FWS) or the National Oceanic and Atmospheric Administration (NOAA) Fisheries Service to ensure that proposed activities will not put any listed species or habitat at risk. The "taking" of listed species is also prohibited, as are import, export, and commerce in listed species. FWS manages land and freshwater species, and NOAA is responsible for marine and anadromous species (the latter live in the sea but breed in freshwater). As of February 20, 2008, FWS listed 1,574 endangered species, including 599 plants, and 351 threatened species, including 148 plants. NOAA cited 1,930 endangered or threatened species as of May 26, 2009, with 1,355 located entirely or in part in the United States and its territorial waters.

Controversies

Controversy about the ESA has arisen frequently, as its rules often hamper unfettered access to water. Both business and urban development in many ways depend on a steady supply of water. Over the course of the twentieth century, this need led to the reclamation movement, which has dammed most of the large rivers of the nation. Migratory fish lost their migration routes; shallow-water feeding grounds disappeared. However, since the signing of the ESA, new dams have become more difficult to construct because of the wildlife studies necessary to comply with the ESA. Further, the ESA has been used in attempts to reverse some of the damage that has been done by reclamation projects.

Efforts to restore habitats for endangered species have not solely been at the behest of the federal government. For example, by the mid-1990s, 90 percent of the water for the 2.6 million people in the San Diego area came from the Colorado River and the Sacramento–San Joaquin Delta. The water industry and the environment were in conflict. When demand neared the capacity of the two sources, area communities began reclaiming sewage water for golf courses and drinking water. Local politicians sought to overturn water restriction laws, including the Delta Act, the Endangered Species Act, the Clean Water Act, and the Safe Drinking Water Act. Urban legislators and the water district claimed that the Central Valley agriculturalists were taking 80 percent of the state's water, while farmers backed a proposed state veto of city projects when water ran short. And the delta had environmental issues—the large-scale diversion of water had brought the delta smelt and chinook salmon near extinction, and the Sacramento splittail minnow was close behind.

Further north, for several years the farmers and environmentalists had been fighting over how to allocate the Klamath River's waters. Irrigators and salmon alike contend with ever larger diversions for Silicon Valley and California agribusiness. The Klamath tributary, the Trinity, is colder and better for salmon, but it is dammed and diverted to California's Central Valley over 400 miles away. An irrigation district larger than Rhode Island claims 1.15 million acre-feet of Trinity/Klamath water, twice what Oregon farmers use. From the semiarid desert, irrigation water enters the San Joaquin River burdened with selenium and pesticides. Klamath River suckerfish and coho salmon are near extinction, with coho down 90 percent since 1950. In 2002, low water levels contributed to the spread of a gill rot disease that killed approximately 35,000 salmon. Conservationists blamed the episode on decisions by the Bush administration. However, the head of the Bureau of Reclamation denied the relevance of his decision to divert water from the river to southern Oregon irrigators.

In April 2009, farmers, farm workers, and local officials in California's Central Valley protested reductions in water. The valley was enduring its third year of drought, the economy was tanking, and the federal government cut the valley's allocation of water. Many of the farmers had let their fields lie fallow during the drought. Protesters wanted a new canal to divert water from the Sacramento River to the Central Valley. They also wanted an easing of the environmental protection of delta smelt, whose ecosystem was the Sacramento–San Joaquin Delta, a critical waterway for transport of water from the wetter north. The state estimated that the drought would cause job loss for 23,700 workers and cost $477 million in farm income.

Protecting endangered species is expensive and not always popular. When water ecosystems are destroyed, so are plants and animals, and wildlife and people are without a water supply, and pollutants exacerbate the global atmosphere's crisis.

—John H. Barnhill

See also: *Central Valley Project; Clean Water Act of 1972; Safe Drinking Water Act of 1974; Tellico Dam*

BIBLIOGRAPHY

Curtis, Jeff, and Bob Davison. "The Endangered Species Act: Thirty Years on the Ark." *Open Spaces* 5, no. 3 (2003): 8–19. Available at http://www.open-spaces.com/article-v5n3-davison.php.

Czech, Brian, and Paul R. Krausman. *The Endangered Species Act: History, Conservation, Biology, and Public Policy*. Baltimore: Johns Hopkins University Press, 2001.

Layzer, Judith A. *Natural Experiments: Ecosystem-Based Management and the Environment*. Cambridge, MA: MIT Press, 2008.

Energy Security Act (1980)

The Energy Security Act of 1980 is a general term used to describe seven major acts passed by the U.S. Congress: the U.S. Synthetic Fuels Corporation Act, the Biomass Energy and Alcohol Fuels Act, the Renewable Energy Resources Act, the Solar Energy and Energy Conservation Act, the Solar Energy and Energy Conservation Bank Act, the Geothermal Energy Act, and the Ocean Thermal Energy Conversion Act. These were all signed into law by President Jimmy Carter on June 30, 1980, who had supported most of the bills. Prior to that, the final versions were approved by a House-Senate conference committee on June 16, passing the Senate 78–12 on June 19 and the House 317–93 on June 26. The purpose of the bills was to conserve energy at a time of rising fuel costs. The legislation came at the height of a record-breaking heat wave in the Southwest, with Texas alone attributing seventy-eight deaths to the heat.

Impetus for Legislation

The impetus for the Energy Security Act can be traced back to the sharp oil price increases of 1973–1974, which caused economic hardship in the United States and many other countries. President Gerald Ford tried unsuccessfully to persuade Congress to take some action in 1975 and again in 1976. In 1979, another dramatic rise in the price of oil once again created an energy crisis in the United States and internationally, promoting inflation and economic crisis.

Jimmy Carter's administration worried not only about the rise in price of oil but also about the possibility that the supply of oil could be seriously disrupted. The United States and Iran, a major oil producer, were involved in a long-running standoff over American hostages held in the U.S. embassy in Teheran. In addition, the Iran-Iraq War threatened to upset the equilibrium of the entire Middle East. President Carter wanted to ensure energy security for the United States. He emphasized the search for and use of synthetic fuels and renewable energy resources, in particular hydropower.

Push for Energy Reduction

On July 10, 1979, President Carter signed a proclamation to limit air-conditioning in offices to temperatures no lower than 78°F (25.5°C) and heating water in commercial buildings to no more than 105°F (40.5°C). The temperatures were determined by the Energy Department, which had calculated that some 5 million office buildings throughout the United States were responsible for a quarter of all the power used in the entire country. Then on July 15, 1979, Carter issued a statement that would lead to the Energy Security Act of 1980. It foresaw the establishment of a government-sponsored energy security corporation that would have a congressional charter and would plan directly for reducing U.S. dependence on imported fuels, especially oil from the Middle East. On June 26, 1979, the first provisions, authorizing a price support system for synthetic fuels, were passed in the House of Representatives 368–25.

A renewed interest in hydropower meant that existing power stations might be enlarged and new ones constructed. Many environmentalists had been arguing for years that hydropower represented the major renewable source of power in the United States and that more resources should have been put into this sector. Pollution from the use of gasoline and in the transportation of oil from the Middle East and elsewhere to the United States caused environmental impacts. Higher oil prices had motivated the private sector to conduct more offshore oil and gas exploration, with the attendant environmental risks, and to consider constructing more nuclear power plants, which require large amounts of water to operate and create radioactive waste.

Although most of the public and the press were captivated by the idea of developing more synthetic fuels, the scientific community focused on developing geothermal power and oceanic thermal energy. In mid-May 1980, the Massachusetts Institute of Technology published a report titled *Coal—Bridge to the Future,* which argued that coal could satisfy half to two-thirds of U.S. energy needs for the next twenty years (from 1980 until 2000). However, to achieve that goal, worldwide coal production would have to increase threefold.

—Justin Corfield

See also: *Conservation Movement; Southwest*

BIBLIOGRAPHY

Ahrari, Mohammed E. "A Paradigm of 'Crisis' Decision Making: The Case of Synfuels Policy." *British Journal of Political Science* 17, no. 1 (1987): 71–91.

Ahrari, Mohammed E. "Congress, Public Opinion, and Synfuels Policy." *Political Science Quarterly* 102, no. 4 (1987–1988): 589–606.

"The Geopolitics of Oil." *Science* 210, no. 4476 (1980): 1324–27.

Environmental Protection Agency, United States

In the 1960s, Rachel Carson's emotional descriptions of environmental despoliation in *Silent Spring* catalyzed the environmental movement. By 1969, the Nixon administration could not ignore environmentalism, even as it dealt with a recession and the Vietnam War. President Nixon's first acts brought accusations of tokenism, so Nixon was prepared when Senator Gaylord Nelson's (D-WI) National Environmental Policy Act (NEPA) arrived at the White House. On New Year's Day 1970, Nixon signed the NEPA and symbolically made the 1970s the decade of environmentalism. The year 1970 brought the first Earth Day and a report calling for an independent Environmental Protection Agency (EPA) to consolidate environmental functions, including establishment and enforcement of standards, research, assistance to other levels of government, and advice to the president.

EPA Functions and Enforcement Powers

The EPA absorbed functions, including the Department of the Interior's Federal Water Quality Administration, originally a public health activity. The EPA began operation on December 2, 1970, and on December 11, 1970, EPA director William Ruckelshaus gave the mayors of Cleveland, Detroit, and Atlanta six months to bring their cities into compliance with clean water standards. EPA also dealt with sewage spills and marine toilet standards early on. The EPA is responsible for enforcing clean water legislation, including the Clean Water Act of 1972 (CWA), the Safe Drinking Water Act of 1974 (SDWA), the 1977 and 1995 amendments to the CWA, and the 1986 and 1996 amendments to the SDWA.

The level of EPA enforcement has varied depending on which political party is in power. With bipartisan congressional support and pressure from environmentalist groups united as the so-called Group of Ten, the EPA grew rapidly in the 1970s, from a $455 million budget its first year to a 1981 budget of $1.35 billion. The mood shifted under Ronald Reagan's pro-business, antiregulation administration. EPA head Anne Burford opposed enforcement of environmental regulations, and the EPA budget shrank by a third and its staff by a fifth between 1980 and 1983. Reagan backed off under environmentalist pressure in the mid-1980s, replacing Burford and signing the Resource Conservation and Recovery Act Amendments of 1984, the Safe Drinking Water Act Amendments of 1986, and the Superfund Amendments and Reauthorization Act of 1986.

The environmental movement splintered in the 1980s, with grassroots opposition centering on local environmental threats and larger organizations focusing on international issues. Environmental legislation foundered due to a stalemate in Congress, and funding remained inadequate. Even so, the EPA reported in 2000 that 70 percent of major rivers, streams, and lakes were clean enough for fishing, twice the 1970 percentage. Nevertheless, 62 million Americans in 2000 lived with air or water below federal standard.

During the George W. Bush administration, the opinions of EPA career officials sometimes were overturned or ignored. Political appointees rejected reports of excess lead in the air, carbon dioxide in the atmosphere, and arsenic in water. When environmental activity occurred, it was usually at the state or local level; the EPA was slow to intervene. Coal companies controlled West Virginia. When the energy crunch led to demands for looser environmental regulations, decades of environmental abuse led environmentalists to fight for tighter enforcement instead. For four years environmentalists sued. Repeatedly, the West Virginia state supreme court overturned rulings that Massey Energy, the state's third-largest coal company, had polluted rivers, violated land use permits, and endangered the health of West

Virginians. Finally, the EPA sued Massey, citing over 4,500 instances of pollution with heavy metals, acid drainage, and slurry—all violations of the Clean Water Act of 1972. Massey paid $20 million, the largest civil suit payout in EPA history, and set aside $10 million for future mitigation while agreeing to rework waste storage sites and set aside riverfront land for conservation.

Enforcement Actions

The EPA has sometimes refused to take the consumer's side. In May 2008, the EPA indicated that it was unlikely to eliminate perchlorate from drinking water. Perchlorate is a toxic ingredient of rocket fuel that causes thyroid problems and developmental harm, particularly in fetuses. It is found at more than 395 sites in 35 states. An EPA spokesperson told the Senate that the agency was aware of the prevalence of the substance and the health risks it posed but was awaiting results of a study of how much perchlorate came from water and how much from foods eaten. The 2005 EPA standard of 24.5 parts per billion was, according to critics that included the EPA's own Children's Health Protection Advisory Committee, not protective. EPA inaction led states to set their own standards—California in 2007 established 6 parts per billion, and Massachusetts had a standard of 2 parts per billion.

On a local scale, one can look at New Berlin, Wisconsin, which has naturally occurring radium in its well water. Radium in drinking water has been linked to cancer. While seeking water from elsewhere, the city's water utility claimed that the radium level was harmless. The city had years before agreed to meet the 1976 EPA standard but now contended that the standard was never finalized and that New Berlin's 5.4 picocuries per liter met the 1997 Safe Drinking Water Act's 5.0 picocuries standard. The city contended that commercial water softener can virtually eliminate radium but the city would have to spend nearly a million dollars to apply this solution.

Again on a national level, environmentalists complained that the EPA was not enforcing the Clean Water Act's anti-dumping provisions sufficiently, particularly after the Bush administration in 2002 exempted mountaintop removal mining rubble, which it reclassified as fill material suitable for dumping into streams. Supporters of this interpretation claim that the fill is the same material that goes into highways, but critics note that it's full of toxic selenium. Mountaintop removal generates millions of tons of fill. Efforts to improve are under way. The 2009 Clean Water

Protection Act had over 115 sponsors, twice the number for the version that failed in 2007. Like other proposed laws since the 2002 ruling, it sought to reverse the decision that defined toxic waste as fill. Proponents sought this legislation to counter a Fourth Circuit Court ruling that had reduced the requirements for environmental impact studies for mountaintop removal mining. In early 2009, the U.S. Army Corps of Engineers was flooded with applications for new removals.

In January 2009, Barack Obama chose Lisa P. Jackson as head of the EPA. At her confirmation hearing, she promised to "restore scientific and legal integrity" after years of political and industry interference.

—John H. Barnhill

See also: *Clean Water Act of 1972; Hazardous Substances Response Trust Fund (Superfund); National Environmental Policy Act of 1969; Safe Drinking Water Act of 1974*

BIBLIOGRAPHY

Broder, John M. "E.P.A. Pick Vows to Put Science First." *New York Times,* January 14, 2009. Available at http://www.nytimes.com/2009/01/15/us/politics/15webjackson.html.

Collin, Robert W. *The Environmental Protection Agency: Cleaning Up America's Act.* Westport, CT: Greenwood, 2006.

Hays, Samuel P. *A History of Environmental Politics since 1945.* Pittsburgh, PA: University of Pittsburgh Press, 2000.

Lewis, Jack. "The Birth of EPA." November 1985. http://www.epa.gov/history/topics/epa/15c.htm.

Environmental Quality Improvement Act (1970)

The Environmental Quality Improvement Act of 1970 amended the National Environmental Policy Act of 1969 and introduced new provisions, including assigning additional responsibilities to the Council on Environmental Quality, the head of which, appointed by the U.S. president, had cabinet status.

Council on Environmental Quality

The National Environmental Policy Act (NEPA) was the first official action of President Richard Nixon on January 1, 1970. The Act stated that "it is the continuing policy of the Federal Government . . . to create and maintain conditions under which man and nature can exist in productive harmony" (Sect. 101). Much of the initiative for the original bill came from Senator Henry M. Martin (D-WA), who had

long wanted a Council of Environmental Quality. Nixon announced the membership of the body on January 29, 1970, with the chairman being Russell E. Train, the undersecretary of the Department of the Interior and a former president of the Conservation Foundation. The other members were Robert Cain, the conservation and resource reporter for the newspaper *Christian Science Monitor,* a former White House press correspondent for the U.S. Information Agency, and the Pulitzer Prize winner in 1969 for his writings on national parks; and Gordon J. F. MacDonald, the vice chancellor for research and graduate affairs at the University of California.

The initial duties assigned to the Council were (1) to study the condition of the nation's environment, (2) to develop new environmental programs and policies, (3) to coordinate the various federal environmental programs, (4) to see that all activities of the federal government took into account any environmental considerations, and (5) to present annual reports on environmental problems. An Office of Environmental Affairs was created within the Department of State. Its first director was Christian A. Herter Jr., a former vice president of Mobil Oil Corporation and son of Christian A. Herter Sr., who had been secretary of state under President Dwight D. Eisenhower. In addition to his role as director, Herter Jr. was also given the title of special assistant to the secretary of state for environmental affairs.

Need for Revisions to the 1969 Act

However, it was soon apparent that changes were needed in the National Environmental Policy Act of 1969. Nixon wanted to push the measures further, and on February 10, 1970, he transmitted to Congress a thirty-seven point plan for the national environment, which included dealing, either by administrative action or executive order, with (1) water pollution management, (2) air pollution control, (3) solid waste management, (4) the improvement of parklands and public recreation facilities, and (5) "organizing for action." In his 1971 State of the Union address, Nixon stated that he would "propose programs to make better use of our land, to encourage a balanced national growth—growth that will revitalize our rural heartland and enhance the quality of life in America. And not only to meet today's needs but to anticipate those of tomorrow, I will put forward the most extensive program ever proposed by a President of the United States to expand the Nation's parks, recreation areas, open spaces in a way that truly brings parks to the people where the people are. For only if we leave a legacy of parks will the next generation have parks to enjoy" (Nixon 1971).

In terms of water pollution management, Nixon felt that the Environmental Quality Improvement Act of 1970 would put the Environmental Protection Agency in a far better position than before. The Act provided staff support for the Council on Environmental Quality, enabling this office to monitor environmental issues much more closely, in particular the dumping of rubbish in oceans. The Act laid the basis for the Marine Protection, Research, and Sanctuaries Act of 1972.

—Justin Corfield

See also: *National Environmental Policy Act of 1969; National Parks and Water; Outdoor Recreation*

BIBLIOGRAPHY

Friedman, Leon, and William F. Levantrosser. *Richard M. Nixon: Politician, President, Administrator.* New York: Greenwood Press, 1991.
"National Environmental Policy Act (NEPA)." http://www.epa.gov/compliance/nepa/.
Nixon, Richard M. "Annual Message to the Congress on the State of the Union." January 22, 1971. Available at John T. Woolley and Gerhard Peters, *The American Presidency Project,* http://www.presidency.ucsb.edu/ws/index.php?pid=3110.
Weiner, Edward. *Urban Transportation Planning in the United States: An Historical Overview.* Westport, CT: Praeger, 1999.
Weiner, Edward. *Urban Transportation Planning in the United States: History, Policy and Practice.* New York: Springer, 2008.

Estuary Restoration Act of 2000

Enacted into law in November 2000, the Estuary Restoration Act of 2000 mandated an estuary habitat restoration strategy to be developed by November 1, 2001, with a goal of restoring 1 million acres of estuary habitat by 2010. Projects and methods for reaching this goal include restoring salt marsh vegetation, installing fish ladders to reclaim native fish runs, replanting sea grasses, building and seeding oyster reefs, and restoring tidal flows to land that has been drained or impounded by dikes. In urban areas, some industrialized rural areas, and estuaries where chemical pollutants have been deposited from upstream or by ocean currents, removing chemical contamination is essential.

Legislative Process

Originally introduced in the House as H.R. 1775, the Act was effusively praised in floor debate. Stating that "estuaries

are places where freshwater meets the open sea, creating some of the most diverse and productive habitat in the country," Rep. Sherwood Boehlert (R–NY) noted that 75 percent of the commercial fish and shellfish catch in the United States comes from estuaries, more than 70 percent of Americans visit coastal areas every year, and that more than 110 million Americans live in coastal regions that rely on estuaries for water supply. Among the estuaries mentioned by various representatives were Chesapeake Bay, Galveston Bay, San Francisco Bay, the Central Mississippi Flyway, and many areas of the Great Lakes.

In the Senate, the Act was ultimately incorporated into Title I of S. 835, entitled the Clean Waters and Clean Bays Act of 2000. A total of thirty states, as well as the District of Columbia, the commonwealths of Puerto Rico and the Northern Mariana Islands, the U.S. Virgin Islands, American Samoa, and Guam, were ultimately eligible for estuary habitat restoration plans. The law that was finally sent to President Clinton for signature, the Estuaries and Clean Waters Act of 2000, was recorded as Public Law 106-457, 114 Stat. 1957 and 1958, with the Estuary Restoration Act codified at 33 U.S.C. 2901–909.

Administration

Provisions of the law were entrusted to the Secretary of the Army (overseeing the U.S. Army Corps of Engineers), an ex officio member of the Estuary Habitat Restoration Council created by the Act. This council also included the administrator of the Environmental Protection Agency, and undersecretaries or service directors from the departments of Commerce, Interior, Agriculture, and any other federal agency the president might designate. Congress anticipated, but did not require, that the director of the Fish and Wildlife Service would be the Interior Department designee, and the undersecretary for Oceans and Atmosphere would represent the Commerce Department.

Estuary habitat and restoration projects were to be considered and selected by the council. The law authorized the federal government to share up to 65 percent of the cost of approved projects, or as much as 85 percent for pilot programs testing innovative technology. Appropriations were authorized in the amounts of $40 million for fiscal year 2001, $50 million for 2002 and 2003, $60 million for 2004, and $75 million for 2005. Other provisions authorized $1.5 million each year from 2001 to 2007 for monitoring data on restoration projects; $4 million for each of fiscal years 2002,

2003, 2004, and 2005 to carry out a long-term estuary assessment project; and $30 million for each fiscal year from 2008 through 2012 for technical assistance to estuary habitat restoration projects.

A draft of the Estuary Habitat Restoration Strategy mandated by the Act was published in the *Federal Register* on May 3, 2002; after public comment and additional revision, the final strategy was published in December of the same year. In late 2010, the council initiated a process for revising and updating that strategy. The Gulf of Maine, Long Island Sound, the Albemarle and Pamlico Sounds, Narragansett Bay, the Hudson-Raritan Estuary, Puget Sound, and Tampa Bay were among the estuaries targeted, in addition to those specifically highlighted in congressional debate.

Estuary Ecosystems and Restoration

Estuaries have been clinically defined as partially enclosed bodies of coastal water, open to the ocean but diluted by freshwater from watersheds flowing into the sea. (The Estuary Restoration Act also covers Great Lakes estuaries, which are entirely freshwater.) Estuaries not only teem with diverse animal and plant populations, they also attract dense concentrations of human settlement and industry. Large rivers emptying into oceans are attractive transportation corridors, support fisheries harvests, and attract industrial and urban development. Landscapes with convenient access to water are attractive for recreational use.

The natural transition from land to water is often disrupted by concrete and stone structures for erosion control, which interrupt many biological connections. Changes in the amount of water delivered to coastal lands; shifts in the seasonal timing of water flows; increased sediment; decreases or overwhelming increases in various nutrients; and changes in water circulation, temperature, and salinity all disrupt complex patterns of life.

Specialists in stream and watershed restoration recommend at least five years, sometimes decades, of monitoring estuary restoration projects. From this perspective, the success of the 2000 Act cannot be fully evaluated until at least 2015, probably later. Physical restoration merely begins a long period of spontaneous interaction among ocean and river currents, plant growth, and returning animal populations, which cannot be neatly predicted. Ecological health of estuaries is often evaluated by monitoring anadromous fish runs, particularly salmon, which live their adult lives in the ocean but breed in freshwater. The presence of such fish not only reflects a healthy food chain and diminished concentration of toxic chemicals, but migration transfers nutrients and organic matter from the ocean to freshwater systems that other organisms rely on.

In 2004, the National Oceanic and Atmospheric Administration (NOAA) launched the National Estuaries Restoration Inventory. According to this database, by late 2010, a total of 1,785 restoration projects had been completed, 202 were being implemented, and 113 were in the planning stages. A total of 196,820 acres had been restored as close as possible to their natural state, including wetland, upland, submerged, and riverine habitats. Upland habitats include beaches and dunes, as well as maritime forests and rocky shorelines. Riverine refers to both instream habitats and riparian zones adjacent to river banks. NOAA lists 2,102 projects, but the total area restored is a little less than one-fifth of the million acres envisioned when the law was adopted.

A team from NOAA, developing methods for monitoring restoration of estuary habitats, pioneered consideration of social and economic impact for local communities impacted by restoration projects. Community uses of the restored area and the esthetic, economic, and cultural impacts of restoration were all recommended for inclusion in the monitoring process, not only to increase public support but to cultivate understanding of the long-term benefits.

—Charles Rosenberg

See also: *Aquaculture; Commercial Fishing; Dredging; Salinity; Wetlands*

BIBLIOGRAPHY

Brown, Kandi, and William L. Hall (with Marjorie Snook and Kathleen Garvin), eds. *Sustainable Land Development and Restoration: Decision Consequence Analysis.* Boston: Elsevier/Butterworth-Heinemann, 2010.

Cunningham, Storm. *The Restoration Economy: The Greatest New Growth Frontier.* San Francisco: Berrett-Koehler, 2002.

National Estuaries Restoration Inventory. https://neri.noaa.gov/neri/.

Rice, Casimir A., W. Gregory Hood, Lucinda M. Tear, Charles A. Simenstad, Gregory D. Williams, Lyndal L. Johnson, Blake E. Feist, and Philip Roni. "Monitoring Rehabilitation in Temperate North American Estuaries." In *Monitoring Stream and Watershed Restoration,* edited by Philip Roni, 167–207, Bethesda, MD: American Fisheries Society, 2005.

Thayer, Gordon W., and Center for Sponsored Coastal Ocean Research (U.S.). *Science-Based Restoration Monitoring of Coastal Habitats.* Silver Spring, MD: U.S. Dept. of Commerce, National Oceanic and Atmospheric Administration, 2003.

Federal Energy Regulatory Commission

The Federal Energy Regulatory Commission (FERC), headquartered in Washington, D.C., is a U.S. federal agency established in 1977 that has jurisdiction over interstate electricity sales and nonfederal hydropower projects. Its official mission statement is that it "regulates and oversees energy industries in the economic, environmental, and safety interests of the American public." This means that it is involved in regulating "the transmission and sale of natural gas for resale in interstate commerce," "the transmission of oil by pipeline in interstate commerce," and "the transmission and wholesale sales of electricity in interstate commerce." The Commission is also involved in licensing and inspecting privately owned, municipal, and state hydroelectric projects; approving the "siting and abandonment of interstate natural gas facilities," including pipelines and storage facilities; ensuring the safe operation and reliability of proposed and operating liquefied natural gas terminals; ensuring the reliability of high-voltage interstate transmission systems; monitoring and investigating energy markets; overseeing environmental issues that relate to natural gas and hydroelectric projects and other "major electricity policy initiatives"; and administering the "accounting and financial reporting regulations and conduct of regulated companies" (FERC 2010).

Prior to its formation, the responsibilities of FERC were performed by the Federal Power Commission (FPC), which had been established in 1930 to exercise oversight of and coordinate federal hydropower development by members of the U.S. Cabinet. In 1977, Charles B. Curtis was appointed to run the FPC, and on October 1, 1977, this agency was transformed into the FERC.

Charles B. Curtis was a political independent. He served under Jimmy Carter but on December 3, 1980, he submitted his resignation, effective January 1, and stated that he believed that Georgina Sheldon, a Republican, should take over. Curtis later went on to become a deputy secretary at the Department of Energy. Sheldon was acting chair for two months, but in March 1981, Charles M. Butler III (1943–) was appointed as the new head. From Midland, Texas, he had served in the Army and then trained as a lawyer, becoming chief legislative assistant to U.S. Senator John Tower (R–TX).

The next chair, Raymond J. O'Connor, held the position from 1983 until 1986. He had been the executive vice president and director of Prudential-Bache Securities. Under his leadership, it was revealed that the commission had received 5,000 applications in the previous five years, and of the 900 projects it had licensed, some 600 were already operating.

Anthony G. Sousa was briefly chair in 1986 and then was succeeded by Martha O. Hesse (1942–), the first woman to hold this position. From Hattiesburg, Mississippi, and with an MBA from the University of Chicago, she had been assistant secretary for management and administration at the Department of Energy. Keen on changing the role of the FERC, Hesse wanted to become more actively involved than before. Although much of her work dealt with natural gas, she did fast-track a number of hydropower generation programs. She remained in office until 1989, when she was replaced by Martin L. Allday; Hesse became an executive at a natural gas company.

Allday (1926–) was a lawyer who had been born in El Dorado, Arkansas, and became an examiner in the oil and gas division of the Railroad for the Commonwealth of Texas. He then practiced in Texas with the Superior Oil Company and later in private practice. A close friend of President George H. W. Bush, he remained FERC chair until 1993, when he was replaced by Elizabeth Anne Moler (1949–). A lawyer from Salt Lake City, Utah, she had worked for the U.S. Senate Commission on Energy and Natural Resources from 1976 to 1977 and had been deputy secretary at the Department of Energy from 1997 until 1998 (and acting secretary in 1998). In 1997, James J. Hocker was appointed chair of the FERC, remaining in that role for the next four years. Curtis L. Hebert Jr. was chair for some months during 2001. Then he was replaced by Patrick H. Wood III. Joseph T. Kelliher was appointed in 2005 and was replaced by Jon Wellinghoff, the current incumbent, in early 2009. Wellinghoff had been a member of FERC since 2006, and before that he was an attorney in private practice focusing on renewable energy, energy efficiency, and distributed generation.

—Justin Corfield

See also: *Federal Power Commission*

BIBLIOGRAPHY

(FERC) Federal Energy Regulatory Commission. "About FERC." http://www.ferc.gov/for-citizens/about-ferc.asp.

Hershey, Robert D., Jr. "Tower Aide Getting Energy Job." *New York Times,* March 31, 1981.

Hershey, Robert D., Jr. "U.S. Energy Official Joining First Chicago." *New York Times,* October 17, 1989. Available at http://www.nytimes.com/1989/10/17/business/business-people-us-energy-official-joining-first-chicago.html.

Kilbourn, Peter T. "Washington Watch." *New York Times,* October 13, 1986.

Schmidt, William E. "Hydroelectric Dams Generate Debate." *New York Times,* December 11, 1984.

Federal Land Policy and Management Act (1976)

The Federal Land Policy and Management Act (FLPMA) became Public Law 94-579, also known as An Act to Establish Public Land Policy; to Establish Guidelines for its Administration; to Provide for the Management, Protection, Development, and Enhancement of the Public Lands; and for Other Purposes. This law, signed on October 21, 1976, by President Gerald Ford, is the organic act revising the duties of the Bureau of Land Management (BLM) under the Department of the Interior as created under the Reorganization Plan Number 3 of 1946.

Origins of the Act

The origins of the FLPMA began in 1971 when the first legislation was proposed by the Nixon administration. The initial purpose of this law was to replace a number of outdated and duplicative laws and consolidate them into one piece of legislation under a single federal agency. By the time it reached the White House in 1976, the law had modified the mission of the BLM and had addressed a variety of regulations and authorities for related interests. Several versions of legislation originated in the House of Representatives and Senate between 1971 and 1974. The final version was a combination of S.507 passed by the 94th Congress and H.R. 13777 negotiated in a joint conference committee in August 1974. After several meetings the conference report came to vote in both the House and Senate, which approved the legislation on September 30 and October 1, 1974, respectively.

Act Provisions

The current law has seven major sections or titles. Title I establishes policy and definitions. Title II focuses on land use planning and land acquisition and disposition. It establishes guidelines for inventorying all public lands, including their resources and recreational and scenic value. The secretary of the interior also was authorized to conduct boundary studies and to develop, maintain, and revise existing land use plans for all public lands, national forests, and tribal lands. Title II also provides guidelines for the sale, withdrawal, acquisition, and exchange of public lands held by the federal government. Title III focuses on the administration of the Bureau of Land Management, re-establishing the agency's purpose and the responsibilities of its director and other authorized personnel. The director may establish service charges and other payments and capital funds, authorize studies, make agreements and contracts for surveys, and establish councils representing the general public.

Title IV establishes guidelines for range management. Regulations in this section discuss grazing fees, grazing leases and permits, and establishment of grazing advisory boards. This section also covers the management of certain horses and burros. Title V provides legal guidance regarding rights-of-way on public lands. The BLM is authorized to grant rights-of-way for water systems and distribution; the transport of liquids, gases, and solid materials; systems to create electric energy and forms of communication; and roads and other means of land transport, particularly in national forests; and any other facilities deemed necessary for the public. Additional sections of Title V discuss right-of-way corridors, general provisions, terms and conditions, and suspension or termination of rights-of-way. Further discussion of rights-of-way for federal agencies, conveyance of lands, existing rights-of-way, and the effect of this section on other laws completes Title V.

Title VI of the FLPMA discusses designated management areas. It details how the California Desert Conservation Area and King Range will be studied in depth and be under the joint management of the Department of Defense and Department of Agriculture. This section also calls for the review of all lands identified in the inventory required by section 201(a) of the Act within fifteen years of the passage of the law. In later years, Congress added the Yaquina Head Outstanding Natural Area (1980), Fossil Forest Research Natural Area (1983), and lands in Alaska (1980) under this section for review, mapping, and monitoring of the withdrawal of minerals. Each section indicates specific guidelines for reporting.

Title VII of the FLPMA focuses on the law's effect on existing rights, repeal of existing laws, and severability. The law indicates that it does not change contracts and agreements made prior to its passage, thus grandfathering in existing agreements between persons and the government. The law also repeals laws relating to homesteading and small tracts, disposal, withdrawal, administration of public lands, and rights-of-way.

In passing this comprehensive legislation, Congress made major modifications to the administration of public lands and repealed legislation dating back to the mid- to late 1800s. Major influences on this legislation included increasing environmental awareness, the multiple policies and practices in place prior to the passage of the law, and an increase in the number of groups that sought to use public lands. The impact of the FLPMA law has been far-reaching and largely positive. Focus has shifted to how public lands and natural resources are used and restored. Additionally, increased access to educational materials, studies, and maps of public lands makes the public a more informed citizenry. The growth of population in western states, where many of these public lands are located, increases the importance of properly allocating these lands and their resources. This legislation provided both guidance and challenges for the Bureau of Land Management and continues to do so today.

—Theresa Hefner-Babb

See also: *Recreational Water Rights; Water Law*

BIBLIOGRAPHY

Foss, Phillip O., ed. *Federal Lands Policy.* New York: Greenwood Press, 1987.

Miller, Richard O. "FLPMA: A Decade of Management Under the BLM Organic Act." *Policy Studies Journal* 14, no. 2 (1985): 265–73.

Schwartz, Eleanor R. "A Capsule Examination of the Legislative History of the Federal Land Policy and Management Act (FLPMA) of 1976." *Arizona Law Review* 21 (1979): 285. Available at http://www.blm.gov/pgdata/etc/medialib/blm/ca/pdf/news/pdfs.Par.13664.File.dat/FLPMA_CapsuleHistory.pdf.

U.S. Department of the Interior, Bureau of Land Management and Office of the Solicitor, eds. *The Federal Land Policy and Management Act, As Amended.* Washington, DC: U.S. Department of the Interior, Bureau of Land Management Office of Public Affairs, 2001. Available at http://www.blm.gov/flpma/FLPMA.pdf.

Federal Power Commission

This body was organized on June 23, 1930, as an independent commission of the U.S. government, with its five members nominated by the president and confirmed by the Senate. Its task, as outlined in the Federal Water Power Act of 1920, was to provide for the licensing of hydroelectric projects that were built on land or on navigable water that was owned by the federal government.

Early Leaders

Prior to the establishment of the Federal Power Commission (FPC), the tasks delegated to it were essentially performed by Newton Diehl Baker (1871–1937), who had served as mayor of Cleveland and then as U.S. secretary of war from 1916 until 1921. Bringing a firmness of leadership to the Federal Power Commission, Baker, a lawyer by training, soon became more interested in the League of Nations and was appointed to the Permanent Court of Arbitration.

In December 1930, George Otis Smith (1871–1944) was appointed chair of the FPC. George Smith had first thought of becoming a journalist but instead had turned to geology, completing his doctorate at Johns Hopkins University and then joining the U.S. Geological Survey (USGS). In 1907, Smith had become director of the USGS, and he saw his role as balancing the interests of the private sector and government agencies rather than siding with the latter, as many had hoped. When Herbert Hoover appointed him chair of the FPC, Smith wanted to regulate private power companies, but supporters of public power felt he was an enemy of their plans. As a result, in November 1933, President Roosevelt apparently "suggested" that Smith resign. In retirement, Smith allied himself with private power concerns, and indeed when he died eight years later, he was in Augusta, Maine, to attend a board meeting of the Central Maine Power Company.

Roosevelt replaced Smith with Frank Ramsay McNinch (1873–1950), a lawyer from North Carolina who had been a member of that state's house of representatives and then mayor of Charlotte. Appointed as a member of the FPC when it was created in 1930 (his nomination being opposed by Democrats at the time), his time as its chair from 1934 until 1937 coincided with the Tennessee Valley Authority and other major infrastructure projects of the New Deal. The Federal Power Act of 1935 extended his jurisdiction to cover the interstate transmission and sale of electric energy and other related areas. In 1935, McNinch represented the United States at the Executive Council of the World Power Conference at The Hague, the Netherlands. Two years later, McNinch was appointed to chair the Federal Communications Commission, and in 1939, Clyde Leroy Seavey (1874–1943), the FPC's vice chair, was appointed as his replacement. Seavey had been one of Roosevelt's early appointments as a member of the FPC—he was an accountant and auditor who had been born in Illinois but had spent much of his career up to that time in California. He helped implement some elements of the Flood Control Act of 1938. However, Seavey was not in the position for long, with the appointment of Leland Olds (1890–1960) on June 8, 1939.

A former journalist and economist from Rochester, New York, Olds had spent six years as secretary of that state's power authority. He wanted to continue the FPC's focus on supporting the concept of "public interest" with increased regulation of the private power companies. However, Olds also believed in market competition and free enterprise, arguing that regulation was needed to ensure that the public received the best possible result from the free market. With the United States entering World War II, Olds was able to reduce the public focus on the controversies over ownership and concentrate on power generation with bipartisan support. This enabled the extension of electricity to many formerly neglected rural areas and kept prices low. These two moves resulted in increased use of electricity, which in turn incentivized the promotion of federally funded hydropower schemes. In 1944, Olds was reappointed for another five years, but when it came to the renewal of his position in 1949 by Harry S. Truman, the confirmation hearings saw attacks on Olds by Senator Lyndon B. Johnson (D-TX) and the unearthing of Olds's radical writings of the 1920s.

Basil Maxwell Manly (1886–1950) took over from 1944 to 1945. He was a progressive liberal, an economist, and a longtime public official. Appointed to the FPC in 1933 and made vice chair in December of that year, he had helped with the passage of the Public Utility Act of 1935 and had a particular interest in natural gas as a source of energy in preference to hydropower. Indeed, when he left the FPC, he became vice president of the Southern Natural Gas Company. He then handed the chair back to Olds, who continued until 1947, when he failed to get his appointment confirmed by the Senate; the vote was 53–15 against him.

Later Leadership

The next chair, Nelson Lee Smith (1899–1984), was from Baltimore, Maryland. Smith was an economist with a doctorate from the University of Michigan. An author of several books and journal articles on public utilities, he remained in charge until 1950. His successor, Monrad C. Wallgren (1891–1961), then became chair for two years, resigning in 1951. Following Wallgren, Thomas Chalmers Buchanan (1895–1958) was briefly chair. From Beaver, Pennsylvania, he had been secretary for the Department of Forest and Waters for the Conservation Department for the Commonwealth of Pennsylvania. He served until 1952,

when the Senate Commerce Committee voted 9–4 against his reappointment in spite of President Truman's support.

The next chair, Jerome K. Kuykendall (1907–1987), held the position from 1953 until 1961. A lawyer from Washington state, he had been chair of the Washington State Public Service Commission prior to his nomination by President Dwight D. Eisenhower. He immediately took a proactive stance with the FPC in October 1953, allowing the state of Washington to intervene in the case *National Hell's Canyon Association, Inc. v. Federal Power Commission* over the construction of the Hell's Canyon High Dam in spite of the costs involved. The case was ultimately settled by the U.S. Supreme Court in 1957, with the Idaho Power Company being allowed to construct three dams in the vicinity of Hell's Canyon on the Snake River.

After John F. Kennedy was elected in 1960, the new president was keen to replace Kuykendall with his own nominee, Joseph Charles Swidler. Kuykendall was allowed to remain until the end of his tenure in June 1952, but he agreed to hand over the department to Swidler. Swidler (1907–1997), a lawyer born in Chicago, Illinois, had been a member of the legal department of the Tennessee Valley Authority and at the time of his appointment was living in Nashville, Tennessee, where he worked as a consultant to a utility management company. He was chair from 1961 until 1966, and he was also a member of the Water Resources Council from 1964 until 1965. He is best remembered for reducing the price of electricity, allowing the public to benefit financially on the construction of dams in the 1940s, 1950s, and early 1960s. Swidler retired from the FPC to run his legal practice and was replaced by Lee C. White.

Lee C. White (1923–) was born in Omaha, Nebraska, and had trained as an electrical engineer before turning to the law. He had worked for John F. Kennedy when the latter was a U.S. senator and then president, and he had been President Lyndon Johnson's special counsel. He continued to be involved in disputes over power production, the construction of or enlargement of dams and hydropower plants, and the increasing cost of generating power. The next chair, appointed in 1969, was John Nicholas Nassikas (1917–1998), a lawyer from Manchester, New Hampshire. Nassikas faced problems over granting licenses to hydroelectric projects, but his real problems were with oil price increases and the effect this had on power prices. He was best known for his deregulation of the natural gas industry, as he believed that the utility industry could not build power plants fast enough to keep up with demand. Nassikas also faced problems when it was revealed that some members of the FPC held shares in power companies, a potential conflict of interest. When Nassikas left in 1975, he was replaced by Richard L. Dunham. Dunham was in turn replaced two years later by Charles B. Curtis. On October 1, 1977, the FPC was replaced by the Federal Energy Regulatory Commission.

—Justin Corfield

See also: *Federal Energy Regulatory Commission; Tennessee Valley Authority; Water Power Act of 1920*

BIBLIOGRAPHY

Baum, Robert D. *The Federal Power Commission and State Utility Regulation*. Washington, DC: American Council on Public Affairs, 1942.

Brooks, Karl Boyd. *Public Power, Private Dams: The Hell's Canyon High Dam Controversy*. Seattle: University of Washington Press, 2006.

Funigiello, Philip J. *Toward a National Power Policy: The New Deal and the Electric Utility Industry, 1933–1941*. Pittsburgh, PA: University of Pittsburgh Press, 1973.

Harris, Joseph P. "The Senatorial Rejection of Leland Olds: A Case Study." *American Political Science Review* 45, no. 3 (1951): 674–92.

McCraw, Thomas K. *TVA and the Power Fight, 1933–1939*. Philadelphia: Lippincott, 1971.

Swidler, Joseph C. *Power and the Public Interest: The Memoirs of Joseph C. Swidler*. Edited by A. Scott Henderson. Knoxville: University of Tennessee Press, 2002.

Salmon and Steelhead Trout

The wild salmonid population in North America has been in decline for much of the last century. The causes are many, including overfishing, water pollution, and the construction of dams that prevent the fish from reaching their spawning grounds. The passage of the Endangered Species Act forced government entities to find ways to bolster salmonid populations. All efforts have proven ineffective.

One strategy was to use fisheries to raise salmonids that would then be used to stock waterways. This allowed officials to augment fish populations without having to pass legislation protecting wild salmonids. The fisheries program has succeeded in introducing salmonid species into waterways where they are not native, thereby injecting an invasive species into those ecosystems.

Overfishing is a problem that extends outside of the United States. International agreements have been negotiated with other countries to regulate the fishing industry. One notable example is the Pacific Salmon Treaty, which was signed by the United States and Canada in 1985.

Dams that interfere with the movements of salmonids between the ocean and rivers have been particularly harmful. Attempted solutions have included the construction of fish ladders and the use of barges to get the fish past the dams. The inability to address the problem has led conservationists to call for the removal of dams in order to save salmonids from extinction.

—John R. Burch Jr.

BIBLIOGRAPHY

Cone, Joseph, and Sandy Ridlington, eds. *The Northwest Salmon Crisis: A Documentary History*. Corvallis: Oregon State University Press, 1996.

Shepard, Michael Perry, and A. W. Argue. *The 1985 Pacific Salmon Treaty: Sharing Conservation Burdens and Benefits*. Vancouver: UBC Press, 2005.

Taylor, Joseph E., III. *Making Salmon: An Environmental History of the Northwest Fisheries Crisis*. Seattle: University of Washington Press, 1999.

Fish and Wildlife Coordination Act (1934)

The Fish and Wildlife Coordination Act (FWCA) was enacted on March 10, 1934, when Franklin D. Roosevelt was president. It was intended to protect fish and wildlife when they were threatened by federal action in connection with water projects. Its enactment took place during the New Deal, when a large number of federally funded construction projects were undertaken to provide employment. It allowed the U.S. Fish and Wildlife Service to evaluate the impact on fish and wildlife that construction of proposed water resource projects, such as dams and locks, would have.

The FCWA provided the legal authority for the Department of Agriculture and the Department of Commerce to assist both federal and state agencies in increasing or maintaining levels of fish, birds, and mammals and the aquatic and land vegetation that the animals depend on for their food. This became increasingly important as more and more dams created lakes. It also authorized the study of the effects of pollution, including domestic sewage, on fish and wildlife.

The aim of the FCWA was to ensure that water resource development projects did not have a detrimental effect on fish or wildlife and that their impact on flora and fauna would be given as much consideration as other factors. The Act allowed the Department of the Interior—at that time headed by Harold L. Ickes—to provide assistance to federal, state, and private agencies and organizations to help with "developing, protecting, rearing and stocking all species of wildlife, resources thereof, and their habitat." This legislation was a public recognition that some water projects had detrimental effects on fish and wildlife. Therefore, the Act acknowledged that these projects had to be planned more carefully and that the impact on the environment—on all types of wild animals and fish—had to be studied and taken into account prior to the start of any construction work.

With a vast increase in the number of federally funded dams and other projects during the 1930s and the early 1940s, Harold Ickes supported many conservation projects. He was authorized, under the Act, to provide assistance to and cooperate with federal and state authorities, as well as public and private organizations, to conserve wildlife. At the same time, he was to allow public access to areas for fishing and for hunting, wherever possible. These two mandates led to a considerable enlargement of the Fish and Wildlife Service. This in turn did much to expand publically accessible recreational fishing facilities throughout the United States.

The FCWA was amended in 1946 to stipulate that any federal agency that sought to control or modify a body of water consult with the U.S. Fish and Wildlife Service and relevant state fish and wildlife agencies, but projects connected with the Tennessee Valley Authority were specifically excluded from the law's provision. Further amendments enacted in 1958 authorized the Secretary of Interior to provide public fishing areas and accept donations of land and funds. Subsequently, the Fish and Wildlife Service became an important model for environmental protection authorities in other countries. The role of Fish and Wildlife Service employees was brought to the public's attention through the Birdwatcher's Mystery series of books by Christine Goff, which tell the story of fictional U.S. Fish and Wildlife special agent Angela Dimato as she solves crimes that involve environmental problems, often the illegal pollution of rivers.

—Justin Corfield

See also: *Fish and Wildlife Service, United States; Ickes, Harold; Roosevelt, Franklin D.*

BIBLIOGRAPHY

Daniel, Clarence, and Robert Lamaire. "Evaluating Effects of Water Resource Developments on Wildlife Habitat." *Wildlife Society Bulletin* 2, no. 3 (1974): 114–18.

Jacobs, Mark L. "Harold Ickes: Progressive Administrator." PhD thesis, University of Maine, 1973.

Lear, Linda J. *Harold L. Ickes: The Aggressive Progressive, 1874–1933.* New York: Garland, 1981.

Lear, Linda J. *Rachel Carson: Witness for Nature.* New York: Henry Holt, 1997.

McKenna, Michael G., and Bill Lynott. "Taking the Offense in Wildlife Management." *Wildlife Society Bulletin* 12, no. 1 (1984): 79–81.

Fish and Wildlife Service, United States

The U.S. Fish and Wildlife Service was established within the Department of the Interior in 1940. Its primary mission is to conserve, protect, and enhance fish, wildlife, plants, and their habitats for the ongoing benefit of Americans. As part of this aim, the Fish and Wildlife Service oversees the U.S. National Wildlife Refuge System, operates the country's national fish hatcheries, and administers the 1973 Endangered Species Act. It also manages fish and wildlife for sport and protection. Thus, it has wide-ranging and often complicated and contradictory responsibilities.

Early Structures

The contemporary shape of the Fish and Wildlife Services traces back to 1871, when Congress created the U.S. Commission of Fish and Fisheries to study and protect the dwindling supply of food fish in the United States. In 1903, Congress incorporated the U.S. Fish Commission into the Bureau of Fisheries in the Department of Commerce and Labor, giving the new agency duties both to conserve fish and promote fisheries as a commercial resource. The Bureau remained largely the same until 1940, when President Franklin Roosevelt merged it with the Bureau of Biological Survey and placed the new U.S. Fish and Wildlife Service in the Department of the Interior. With the addition of the Biological Survey, the Service transformed into a more diverse organization, expanding its concerns beyond a singular focus on fish to protect a range of wildlife and habitats (Clarke and McCool 1996).

Operating the National Fish Hatchery System is the oldest conservation activity assigned to the Fish and Wildlife Service. Established concurrently with the U.S. Commission of Fish and Fisheries in 1871, the national hatcheries arose out of federal concerns over declining fish resources. The Service initially managed hatcheries to enhance the nation's food supply, then expanded its use of hatcheries to restore native fish populations and meet recreational fishing needs.

The agency operates more than seventy hatcheries and provides an important piece of the conservation puzzle in the United States. Since fish ignore boundaries and can be caught outside of the agency's jurisdiction, scholars and government officials often fail to give the Fish and Wildlife Service adequate credit for its fisheries enhancement efforts (Clarke and McCool 1996).

The Service's other primary function is to manage the National Wildlife Refuge System. President Theodore Roosevelt established Pelican Island in Florida as the nation's first refuge in 1903. The refuge system has since expanded to include more than 500 refuges across the United States, where they serve as protected habitat for fish and wildlife, particularly waterfowl. The agency historically utilizes the refuges both to preserve fish and wildlife populations and proliferate them for hunting, fishing, and other recreational uses. Reflecting those objectives, the Service has received revenues, starting in 1934, from taxes on bird-hunting licenses, known as Duck Stamps, to fund the management and acquisition of wetlands and other waterfowl habitats. To generate more funding, the Service also opened refuge lands to grazing, trapping, and other uses (Vileisis 1997). National refuges more firmly established wildlife as a public resource, helping to secure the Fish and Wildlife Service's place as a vital federal agency (Hays 2000).

Recent Responsibilities and Programs

In the 1970s, the responsibilities of the Fish and Wildlife Service expanded further with the passage of the 1973 Endangered Species Act. The Service now oversaw the protection of threatened and endangered flora and fauna, including invertebrates and plants. The agency was largely successful in managing the Act due to its previous experience with preserving critical habitat for fish and wildlife (Hays 2000; Vileisis 1997). Yet the new duties also taxed the Service's resources and contradicted its historical role as a resource promoter. The Endangered Species Act created a large administrative burden for the agency and pitted the

Service against private property advocates and industries and indigenous groups struggling for resource rights (Clarke and McCool 1996). As with past programs, the Endangered Species Act required the Service to balance a range of interests.

Aside from its major duties, the Fish and Wildlife Service engages in several smaller programs. It operates a law enforcement program, employing officers to combat habitat destruction, wildlife trafficking, and exploitation of fish and wildlife resources. It oversees the Hanford Reach National Monument in Washington and the Papahānaumokuākea Marine National Monument in Hawaii. The Service also partners and cooperates with other federal agencies. In particular, Congress made the Fish and Wildlife Service a consultant for Section 404 of the Clean Water Act, sharing administration of the nation's wetlands with the Army Corps of Engineers, Environmental Protection Agency, and

---

American Fisheries Society

Founded as the American Fish Culturalists Association in 1872, the American Fisheries Society (AFS) is a nonprofit, international professional organization dedicated to advancing the field of fisheries science. Headquartered in Bethesda, Maryland, the AFS works to improve professional development opportunities for the fisheries industry by sponsoring meetings and workshops, as well as offering certification programs. The AFS's many publications include the periodicals *Fisheries, Journal of Aquatic Animal Health, Marine and Coastal Fisheries, North American Journal of Aquaculture, North American Journal of Fisheries Management*, and *Transactions of the American Fisheries Society*.

From the organization's inception, the members of the AFS have endeavored to influence legislation impacting fish and fisheries. Among the AFS's first legislative efforts was the protection of salmon runs in the Pacific Northwest, which continues to this day. The AFS's efforts on behalf of salmon included their inclusion on the endangered species list. Although the organization's initial efforts focused on North America, its emphasis on the use of scientifically based methodologies for the development of fisheries and the preservation of aquatic ecosystems has combined with globalization to provide opportunities for the AFS to shape legislation all over the world.

—John R. Burch Jr.

See also: *Endangered Species Act (1973)*

BIBLIOGRAPHY

American Fisheries Society. http://www.fisheries.org/afs/index.html.
Cone, Joseph, and Sandy Ridlington, eds. *The Northwest Salmon Crisis: A Documentary History.* Corvallis, OR: Oregon State University Press, 1996.

To ensure that populations of fish remain stable, the U.S. Fish and Wildlife Service operates about seventy fish hatcheries where fish are raised and released into the wild.

U.S. Fish and Wildlife Service

National Marine Fisheries Service (Vileisis 1997). Such programs symbolize the Service's diverse yet rather unfocused organization and mission as a conservation and preservation agency.

The scope of the Service's mission and management activities make it both important and problematic. Scholars mention that its array of responsibilities for fish, wildlife, and habitat have allowed it to carve out a niche as a versatile federal agency taking a lead role in implementing ecosystems management. Yet that reputation, rooted in the Service's chaotic organizational history and dual mandate to conserve and promote resources, has also been a weakness. The agency typically received little funding and support and remained a secondary service organization throughout the twentieth century. Moreover, it also became the center of controversies over endangered species and declining fishing industries (Clarke and McCool 1996; Cooley 1963).

Today the Fish and Wildlife Service marches forward. It continues to administer the Endangered Species Act and manages the nation's hatcheries and wildlife refuges. It influences nearly every aspect of conservation and environmentalism in the United States, and it gained more funding and land under its jurisdiction through the Alaska National Interest Lands Conservation Act in 1980 and the more recent National Wildlife Refuge Improvement Act of 1997.

Yet it garners little public recognition compared to other federal agencies (Clarke and McCool 1996). Still, the Fish and Wildlife Service remains a harbinger of resource conservation and promotion, as well as an important federal agency.

—Daniel Karalus

See also: *Clean Water Act of 1972; Endangered Species Act (1973); Wetlands*

BIBLIOGRAPHY

Clarke, Jeanne Nienaber, and Daniel C. McCool. *Staking Out the Terrain: Power and Performance among Natural Resource Agencies.* 2nd ed. Albany: State University of New York Press, 1996.

Cooley, Richard A. *Politics and Conservation: The Decline of the Alaska Salmon.* New York: Harper and Row, 1963.

Hays, Samuel P. *A History of Environmental Politics since 1945.* Pittsburgh, PA: University of Pittsburgh Press, 2000.

Vileisis, Ann. *Discovering the Unknown Landscape: A History of America's Wetlands.* Washington, DC: Island Press, 1997.

Flood Control Act of 1928

Following a series of destructive floods throughout the United States in the late nineteenth and early twentieth centuries, the U.S. Congress passed the Flood Control Act of 1928 on May 15, 1928, in an effort to protect both people and property. The Flood Control Act of 1928 was the largest public works project ever authorized by Congress at the time. It helped make flood control a national issue. The new law also helped increase research and advances in the area of flood control.

The Need for Legislation

As manufacturing, agriculture, and trade increased in the latter half of the nineteenth century, the economy of the United States depended more and more on trade and travel. Goods and products, from textiles to food, were shipped from one end of the country to the other via railroads, steamboats, and eventually automobiles. With this economic growth came many new problems. One was frequent flooding along major river valleys. The late nineteenth century and early twentieth century saw an increase in the number of floods throughout the United States in all of the major river valleys. One key reason for these severe floods was heavy deforestation and soil erosion along many rivers. The U.S. government issued its first flood control measure in 1879, following a huge flood along the Mississippi River. Steps were also taken to combat deforestation and soil conservation. Levees were the main source of flood control at that time, and the federal government helped to finance a series of levees along the Mississippi River, hoping to contain floodwaters within the riverbed and its tributaries. Levees continued to be the primary type of flood control used for the next thirty years. However, two terrifying floods in 1912 and 1913 devastated the lower Mississippi River region and showed that levees on their own were insufficient for flood control. But not until another devastating flood hit the lower Mississippi in 1927 was action finally taken in Washington, D.C.

The 1927 flood in the lower Mississippi region was the result of high waters from throughout the Mississippi River's drainage area, which covers roughly 41 percent of the continental United States. In essence, the bulk of the nation's high waters all channeled south toward the Gulf of Mexico, bringing destruction and devastation to the states in that area. Between 250 and 500 people were killed, and 500,000 people were forced out of their homes and into refugee camps. Sixteen million acres of land were covered in floodwaters. Congress could not ignore this flood and knew that it had to take drastic action before more damage was inflicted.

After lengthy debate, the Flood Control Act of 1928 was passed. As part of the law, the U.S. Army Corps of Engineers was authorized to design and construct projects along the Mississippi River that would prevent devastating floods in the future. Out of this law, the Mississippi River Valley Project took shape, which would ultimately prevent over $100 billion in damages over the next eighty years. The goal of the Mississippi River Valley Project, as its name implied, was flood control of the Mississippi River and its alluvial valley. The head of the U.S. Army Corps of Engineers, Major General Edgar Jadwin, created a new flood control plan. Levees were still a part of Jadwin's flood control plan, but he also rerouted river water through controlled outlets and floodways throughout the Mississippi River Valley.

The Cost of Flood Control

Flood control projects came with certain stipulations, some of which prompted objections by local governments and levee districts. The biggest concern was the cost to local communities. Local states, towns, or districts had to agree to take over all maintenance of a flood control project once it was completed. Local communities also had to agree to provide, free of charge to the U.S. government, all rights of way for levee foundations and levees along the main tributary of the Mississippi River between Cape Girardeau in Missouri and Head of Passes at the Gulf of Mexico. Local entities

further had to promise that the federal government would not be held liable for any damages from future floods. Building on the Rivers and Harbors Act of 1918, the federal government was also able to buy, condemn, and receive donated lands needed for easements in flood control projects.

There was a great debate over the matter of local financial contributions. The way Congress looked at the issue, forcing local states and towns to contribute money toward flood control projects would keep costs down. In other words, towns and cities would not propose outlandishly expensive projects if they were helping to fund them. Congress also argued that flood control projects were in the special interest of individual communities and that the local population should invest in its own protection. However, in the end, it was found that local entities had already invested a significant amount of money in flood control: $292 million to be exact. And since it was already painfully clear that a destructive flood could wreak havoc far beyond a single town, city, or even state—trade and commerce could come to a complete standstill in all directions—Congress decided the federal government could cover the bulk of the costs. An emergency fund was set up as part of the law, with $5 million set aside for rescue work and repair and maintenance of any flood control project along the Mississippi River or one of its tributaries that was damaged by flooding.

The Flood Control Act of 1928 was the first law to make flood control a federal government priority. Over the next eighty years, more flood control laws were passed, expanding on the 1928 Act. Not only did the Act protect persons and property, it ensured that national commerce would not be interrupted due to natural disasters. Congress recognized the economic hazards of a large-scale flood. The law also encouraged more studies of flood prevention and prompted soil and forestation conservation acts.

—Lorri Brown

See also: *Flood Control Act of 1936; Levees*

BIBLIOGRAPHY

U.S. Army Corps of Engineers. *Laws of the United States Relating to the Improvements of Rivers and Harbors from August 11, 1790 to January 2, 1939.* 3 vols. Washington, DC: U.S. Government Printing Office, 1940.

U.S. Army Corps of Engineers. "Multipurpose Waterway Development." In *The U.S. Army Corps of Engineers: A Brief History.* http://www.usace.army.mil/History/Documents/Brief/07-development/develop.html.

U.S. Army Corps of Engineers, Mississippi Valley Division. "1928 Flood Control Act." http://www.mvd.usace.army.mil/mrc/history/AppendixE.htm.

Flood Control Act of 1936

By the 1930s, flood control had become increasingly important to the federal government. In 1928, the first major federal flood control act was made into law, targeting the Mississippi and Sacramento Rivers. However, even after the Flood Control Act of 1928 was passed, river valleys throughout the United States were still beset with floods, which were deemed a menace to the welfare of the entire nation, not just the states and communities directly affected. The Flood Control Act of 1936 was introduced by Riley J. Wilson (D-LA) and signed into law by President Franklin D. Roosevelt on June 22, 1936. President Roosevelt saw the Flood Control Act of 1936 as an opportunity to combat the effects of the Great Depression by creating jobs, as well as to protect the environment. The new law demonstrated U.S. government commitment to the protection of people and their property. It also elevated flood control to a federal concern, where previously it had been considered a state or local issue, with the exception of the Mississippi and Sacramento Rivers.

The Need for More Flood Control

The 1930s saw many new laws in the United States. Social Security, the Banking Act of 1935, and the Public Utilities Holding Company Act were passed to protect consumer interests and aid working people. Such projects as the Tennessee Valley Act (TVA) of 1933, the Soil Conservation Act of 1935, and the Rural Electrification Act were aimed at creating jobs while improving lives of rural citizens throughout the United States. The Flood Control Act of 1936 was deemed vital for the protection of the quality of life of U.S. citizens. Initially, flood control was placed under the War Department (later the Department of Defense). However, watersheds, water flow retardation, and soil erosion (a major contributor to flooding) were under the direction of the U.S. Department of Agriculture. The need for work, coupled with the destructive Great Flood of 1936 in New England, prompted more legislation.

In March 1936, a fierce storm blew across the Northeast, dumping unprecedented amounts of rain and causing rivers to swell and flood the surrounding countryside, with the most damage occurring in Pennsylvania. During the Great Flood of 1936, eighty-four people in Pennsylvania were killed and $67 million in damage was done just along the Susquehanna River. Many towns, like Johnstown, Pennsylvania, were covered in up to fourteen feet of water.

This was not the first flood in Pennsylvania history or even in Johnstown history. In 1889, Johnstown had been the scene of one of the most ferocious floods in U.S. history. The town had been covered with 10 feet of water, killing 77 people and leaving 50,000 people homeless. In cities like Pittsburgh, life came to a standstill, with neither clean drinking water nor any electricity or telephone service available.

Similar scenes had played out throughout the United States for many years, but the personal and economic devastation from the Great Flood of 1936 prompted the federal government to take control. In Pennsylvania, federally sponsored dams were constructed along the state's rivers. The largest flood control project at the time was constructed over five years at Johnstown. When it was finished in 1943, the channels of the Stony Creek and Little Conemaugh had been realigned and lined with nine-mile-long concrete side slopes. This ambitious project would have never been possible without the aid of the federal government.

Flood Control Projects

Thanks to the many flood control projects built as a result of the Flood Control Act of 1936, ambitious systems of reservoirs, levees, and dams were put in place to prevent disastrous floods from occurring. Approximately 8,000 dams, 200 locks, and more than 25,000 miles of inland and intracoastal navigation channels were built. Millions of miles of canals, pipes, and tunnels were also built for flood control. The 1936 Act stipulated that potential flood control projects had to offer more economic benefit than the cost of constructing them. And as with the Flood Control Act of 1928, local communities had to take an active interest in the construction and maintenance of all flood control projects. The 1936 law authorized approximately $310 million for flood control projects, with no more than $50 million being spent in the first year. Local communities had to meet specific requirements in order to qualify for a flood control project. They had to provide land, easements, and rights-of-way for construction, and they had to promise not to hold the federal government responsible for any damages accrued during construction. As with the Flood Control Act of 1928, local communities, states, and levee districts had to promise to maintain flood control projects after completion.

The Flood Control Act of 1936 helped to save billions of dollars in property damage and protected thousands of lives. Critics point out that flooding still occurs, even with federal flood control. In 1977, Johnstown, Pennsylvania, suffered another severe flood, which caused eighty-five deaths and

$300 million in damages. In 1993, the Mississippi River Basin flooded the Midwest, causing more than $20 billion in damage. In 2006, Hurricane Katrina broke the levees of New Orleans, causing an estimated $125 billion in damage. While flood control has come a long way since its inception at the start of the twentieth century, there is still work to be done.

Floods are a natural phenomenon. However, due to human influence, especially deforestation and soil erosion, floods have become natural disasters, costing millions of dollars in damage and taking lives. However, without the Flood Control Act of 1936 and the amendments that followed it, the scope of damage would be even greater. The 1936 Act has been amended and added onto over the years, not only as protection against flooding but also as protection for the environment.

—Lorri Brown

See also: *Flood Control Act of 1928*

BIBLIOGRAPHY

Arnold, Joseph L. *The Evolution of the 1936 Flood Control Act.* Washington, DC: U.S. Army Corps of Engineers, 1988.

U.S. Army Corps of Engineers. *Laws of the United States Relating to the Improvement of Rivers and Harbors from August 11, 1790 to January 2, 1939.* Vol. 3. Washington, DC: U.S. Government Printing Office, 1940.

U.S. Army Corps of Engineers. "Multipurpose Waterway Development." In *The U.S. Army Corps of Engineers: A Brief History.* http://www.usace.army.mil/History/Documents/Brief/07-development/develop.html.

Flood Control Act of 1944

President Franklin D. Roosevelt signed the Flood Control Act of 1944 (Pub. L. 78-534), also known as the Pick-Sloan plan, into law on December 2, 1944. The bill forced the cooperation of two competing federal agencies, the Army Corps of Engineers and the Bureau of Reclamation. It also authorized a dramatic alteration of the Missouri River by calling for the creation of a six-foot navigation channel between Sioux City, Iowa, and St. Louis, Missouri; construction of five massive flood control dams turning 800 miles of the river into reservoirs; and numerous other irrigation dams and projects on the Missouri River's tributaries.

Flood Control Studies

First in the River and Harbor Act of 1927, and again in the Flood Control Act of 1928, Congress mandated that the Army Corps of Engineers complete comprehensive flood control studies on many of the nation's rivers, including the Missouri. The Corps's investigation culminated in a massive report presented to Congress in 1933 and published in 1935 as House Document 238. The report focused on improving navigation on the Missouri and recommended the construction of the Fort Peck Dam for flood control and navigation.

The Corps's report on the Missouri River cleared the way for Roosevelt to authorize Fort Peck Dam in 1934 under the authority of the National Industrial Recovery Act. Congress agreed to the authorization of Fort Peck Dam in 1935. President Roosevelt also called for the coordinated development of river basins throughout the country, using his model for the Tennessee Valley Authority to maximize flood control, power generation, navigation, and irrigation. In 1937, Rep. Usher Burdick (R–ND) introduced legislation to create a Missouri Valley Authority, but the bill died in committee. In 1938, Congress moved forward with authorization of a hydroelectric plant at the Fort Peck Dam, stipulating that the Corps of Engineers would construct the plant but that the Bureau of Reclamation would distribute and market the power, giving preference to public utilities and rural electrification cooperatives.

As a result of this authorization, the Bureau of Reclamation began studies of the distribution and use of hydropower in the upper Missouri River Basin. With inexpensive power a possibility, the agency renewed investigations into ways to pump irrigation water from the Missouri River. The Bureau of Reclamation assigned these investigations to William Glen Sloan, who determined that the best use of the power and water would be a comprehensive development plan for the entire Missouri River.

Originally, the two agencies cooperated in their planning, spurred on by calls for a Missouri Valley Association, which would have stripped project construction and oversight from both agencies. As the scale of both the navigation and irrigation projects grew to become mutually exclusive in the minds of their respective proponents, the Corps of Engineers and the downstream states pushed for a nine-foot navigation channel from Sioux Falls to St. Louis, which would preclude the diversion of water for irrigation. The Bureau of Reclamation, on the other hand, pushed for irrigation diversions that would limit navigation to a six-foot channel. Cooperation turned into competition, which stalled development efforts.

Legislative Action

Devastating floods along the Missouri in 1943 motivated Congress to take quick action to regulate the river. Colonel Lewis Pick presented plans to Congress that favored the navigation improvements supported by the Army Corps of Engineers. The Bureau of Reclamation hastily completed Sloan's proposals for the river favoring irrigation development. Once again facing the prospect of a Missouri Basin Authority, the two agencies ultimately reached a compromise to allow the five massive flood control dams on the river and most of the irrigation projects proposed by Sloan. Thereafter, Congress authorized the Pick-Sloan plan as Section 9 of the Flood Control Act of 1944.

To the disappointment of President Roosevelt, the Act did not create a Missouri River Authority. Though he stated at the bill's signing that he still hoped Congress would do so, political divisions prevented the measure from being adopted. Instead, the Corps of Engineers would oversee construction of the flood control dams at Garrison, Oahe, Big Bend, Gavins Point, and Fort Randall, and the Bureau of Reclamation would construct projects it estimated would irrigate millions of acres. Section 9 provided blanket authorization for the list of the dams and irrigation projects in the Pick-Sloan plan. Revenues not needed to repay the costs of the main stream dams would be pooled into a basinwide fund to pay for irrigation projects too expensive for irrigators to repay themselves.

The project has not always lived up to the expectations envisioned by its planners. Drought years have caused serious conflict among irrigation, navigation, and recreational interests, which want to use the projects' waters differently. When it became apparent that hydropower revenues would not pay for all of the irrigation projects envisioned by Sloan, Congress amended the Act in 1964 to require all unbuilt irrigation projects to be reauthorized by Congress. President Carter further altered the Pick-Sloan Project when he cut the Oahe and Narrows projects and modified the Garrison Diversion as part of his "Hit List." Despite these limitations, the Flood Control Act of 1944 remains historically significant because it dramatically altered the environment of the northern Great Plains and negatively impacted several Native American tribes when reservoirs inundated significant portions of their reservations.

—Adam Eastman

See also: *Army Corps of Engineers, United States; Bureau of Reclamation; Flood Control Act of 1928; Fort Peck Dam; Garrison Dam; Missouri River Basin; Roosevelt, Franklin D.*

BIBLIOGRAPHY

Ferrell, John R. *Big Dam Era: A Legislative and Institutional History of the Pick-Sloan Missouri Basin Program.* Omaha, NE: Missouri River Division, U.S. Army Corps of Engineers, 1993.

Thorson, Jared E. *River of Promise, River of Peril: The Politics of Managing the Missouri River.* Lawrence: University Press of Kansas, 1994.

Flood Control Act of 1960

The Flood Control Act of 1960 is located under Title 2 of Public Law 86-645, known by the popular name River and Harbors Act of 1960. The legislation's official title is An Act Authorizing the Construction, Repair, and Preservation of Certain Public works on Rivers and Harbors for Navigation, Flood Control, and for Other Purposes. President Dwight D. Eisenhower signed the bill into law on July 14, 1960, updating the River and Harbors Act signed in 1930.

Prior to the passage of this act in 1960, Congress had authorized a series of flood control laws starting in 1902. These laws authorized channel and navigation improvements in various flood-prone areas in the western states of Wyoming, Oregon, Washington, and Idaho. The 1960 Act expanded the role of the U.S. Army Corps of Engineers (Corps) in flood control.

Legislative Chronology

The Flood Control Act of 1960 had its roots in S. 497, passed by the U.S. Senate in 1958 and vetoed by President Eisenhower. Rep. Clifford Davis (D-TN) introduced H.R. 7634 on June 9, 1959, in the U.S. House of Representatives, and the bill was sent to the Committee on Public Works. The bill contained routine biennial flood control appropriations and none of the projects in the Senate bill. H.R. 7634 was reported by the committee, debated, and passed by the House on July 16, 1959, with a total of $1.6 million in appropriations. From the House, the bill went to the Senate Committee on Public Works, which added projects to the existing legislation. The full Senate discussion of the committee's conference report emphasized making sure the final version of the legislation would be approved by President Eisenhower. Senators participating in the discussions included Lyndon Johnson (D-TX) and Robert S. Kerr (D-OK). The House rejected the amendments proposed by the Senate, and a joint committee was formed to arrange a compromise. The final amendments were approved by the House on July 2, and the bill passed the Senate on July 14, 1960.

The final version of H.R. 7634 became Public Law 86-645. Section 201 of the law reauthorized Public Laws 74-738 and 75-761, passed in 1936 and 1938 respectively, allowing for the continuation of channel improvements or channel rectification projects currently in place. The 1944 legislation requirements regarding plans, proposals, and reports related to navigation, flood control, and irrigation projects also applied to the 1960 law. The purpose of the legislation included addressing flooding, in response to floods in the spring of 1959; the impact of water resources on the national and state economies; and the recreational activities possible at the various project locations.

Improvement Projects

The majority of the 1960 legislation focused on improvement projects in various states. The Corps was authorized to conduct studies for each project, including drawing up the necessary plans, specifications, and writing any relevant reports. Each project listed in Section 203 of the law indicated the cost estimated by the Corps and already had a report on file. Unlike those in previous legislation, these flood control projects would occur in states located in the northeastern and southern United States, as well as the western states. The following rivers were included: Connecticut River Basin, Mississippi River Basin, Trinity River Basin, Guadalupe River Basin, Brazos River Basin, Red-Ouachita River Basin, Arkansas River Basin, Rio Grande River Basin, Missouri River Basin, Ohio River Basin, Great Lakes Basin, Mojave River Basin, Los Angeles River Basin, Great Salt Basin, Columbia River Basin, and many others. As a result, the legislation had a far-reaching impact on many communities that frequently experienced seasonal flooding.

In addition to detailing the various flood control projects authorized by Congress, the law also required the Corps to publish information on floods and flood damages. Information on flood-prone areas and ways to eliminate problems was to be made available upon request of state officials according to Section 206. The law authorized a sum not to exceed $1 million in a fiscal year for the dissemination of such reports. Additional changes to Section 206 over the years raised the amount of allotted expenditures for informational reports from the Corps from $1 million to $15 million in 2006. The law also authorized the use of public roads for all related construction and, when necessary, the building of new roads. All roads were to be repaired and returned to original or improved condition at a project's end. Section 208 also mandated flood control surveys of drainage areas of the United States and its territories.

The 1960 law received updates each time a new project was authorized by Congress. Today the Rivers and Harbors Acts and Flood Control Acts are revised and updated in omnibus legislation titled Water Resources Development Acts. Since the passage of the Flood Control Act of 1960, it has been revised with projects added and funding allotted for repairs. Along with other flood control acts, it has resulted in a number of projects to change navigational channels, construct dams, form reservoirs, and provide a source of hydroelectric power. The acts also require the routine survey of flood-prone areas and the dissemination of information to individuals and government entities alike to prevent development and limit damage and loss of life and property due to flooding.

The Flood Control Act of 1960, by way of the Rivers and Harbors Act of 1960, initially was just a routine biennial appropriations request by Congress. However, in light of the 1958 veto by Eisenhower, Congress had to provide further information, check points, and justify each project included in the bill. This legislation set the tone for further flood control acts and placed further accountability on the U.S. Army Corps of Engineers.

—Theresa Hefner-Babb

See also: *Army Corps of Engineers, United States*

BIBLIOGRAPHY

Flood Control Act of 1960, Pub. L. No. 86-645, 74 Stat. 480. http://www.fws.gov/habitatconservation/Omnibus/R&HA1960.pdf.
"Title 33: Navigation and Navigable Waters." http://www.law.cornell.edu/uscode/433/usc_sup_01_33.html.
U.S. Army Corps of Engineers, Walla Walla District. "Digital Project Notebook: Public Laws." http://www.nww.usace.army.mil/dpn/publaw.htm.

Flood Control Act of 1962

The Flood Control Act (FCA) of 1962, which amended the FCA of 1944, was Section 2 of Pub. L. 87-874, the Rivers and Harbors Act of 1962. FCAs were Section 2 of the Rivers and Harbors acts until 1974. Occasional acts to deal with flooding date to the nineteenth century, but the first act to deal exclusively with flood control was a response to flooding in the Northeast in 1917. The FCA of 1928 was in response to the Mississippi River flood of 1927, and regular flood control legislation began during the New Deal, with acts following at one- to four-year intervals until 1970. In 1974, the FCAs and Water Resource Development Acts (WRDAs) were removed from Rivers and Harbors legislation and enacted as stand-alone laws in even-numbered years. WRDAs are omnibus bills for U.S. Army Corps of Engineers projects across the United States. Section 205 of the FCA of 1962, the redefining of small flood control projects as small projects for flood control and related projects, in conjunction with the WRDAs of 1974 and 1976, authorized expenditure of $30 million annually for small flood control projects and related purposes, with a limit of $2 million per project except in major disaster areas (where the limit was $3 million).

Flood Control Projects

The 1962 Flood Control Act specified that projects must have a go-ahead from local authorities within five years and that provision should be made where possible for future hydroelectric capabilities. Like other flood control acts, the 1962 Act authorized dozens of water projects throughout the United States, contingent on funding, but its major significance is that it replaced "reservoir areas" with "water resource development projects" and gave the chief of the Corps of Engineers authority to allow local interests to construct, operate, and maintain water facilities. The contributions by local interests were in kind, and local control was required. Not until 1986 did a WRDA mandate cost sharing as actual cash contribution, but flood control acts as early as 1936 had required some sort of contribution, such as easements or other in-kind payments. As long as payment was in kind, there was less incentive to test the market viability of a project. Requiring the local sponsor to put up cash was a real test of commitment.

Projects were initiated for hurricane and other flood protection, navigation improvements, reservoirs, wildlife refuges, various studies of water quality, town sewer systems, and so on. One provision renamed an auxiliary channel in the Mississippi River system to honor retiring Rep. Will M. Whittington (D-MS). Another honored late Senator W. Kerr Scott (D-NC) by naming a dam and reservoir for him. The most expensive project was $13 million for work in Miami/Dade County, and New Orleans got $7 million in projects. Russellville, Arkansas, got a sewage outfall in the Dardanelles Dam. An add-on to an Iowa project specified local responsibilities, including a small cash payment. Replacement of two bridges destroyed by flooding in Arkansas totaled $115,000.

Older projects became larger as their purposes were redefined beyond simple flood control. The New Melones dam was authorized in 1944 to replace the old dam, which was not controlling flooding on the Lower San Joaquin and Stanislaus rivers in California. The 1962 Act expanded the project to be a multipurpose unit of the Central Valley Project. The New Melones unit was to provide, aside from flood control, improved water quality, irrigation and storage, municipal water, power, fisheries, and recreation. The new dam was 625 rather than 355 feet and had a capacity of 2.4 million acre-feet rather than 450,000 acre-feet, with 450,000 acre-feet set aside for flood control.

Challenges

Because of the lag between authorization and the onset of a project, there was ample time for opponents to challenge the broader definition of flood control. The Sierra Club sued in 1973 to void construction of a Kickapoo River dam in Wisconsin, authorized under the expanded definition of 1962. The Sierra Club contended in part that the Corps had failed to secure local participation by two downstream communities. The lower court ruled that the failure was not sufficient to terminate the project but that the Corps's failure to write an adequate environmental impact statement was. The dam was originally intended to contain the Kickapoo, known historically for its tendency to flood. The reservoir was to cover 1,780 acres, flooding a 12-mile section of the river popular with canoeists and noted for its scenic attractiveness and rare plants. Two small downstream towns were required to share costs for supplemental levees.

The plaintiffs claimed that the Kickapoo authorization in the 1962 Act had expired after five years because the Corps had failed to notify the downstream towns of their obligation and the towns had not otherwise indicated their willingness to participate. The court ruled that the canoeists and environmentalists had no standing in the matter of the levees because their interest was affected by the dam itself. Similarly, failure of the Corps to get participation agreements from the small towns to be protected by the levees was not relevant to the building of the dam, for which proper paperwork was filed.

A 1998 challenge to the Corps's definition of "water project" under the 1962 FCA failed. Clearwater County, Idaho, claimed the Dworshak Dam was, under the 1962 FCA, restricted to flood control, power generation, and recreation.

The Corps countered that fish and wildlife conservation was a legitimate function. The engineers claimed that House Document 403, which implemented the Act, authorized construction of water improvements not only for flood control, power, and recreation but also for navigation, pollution abatement, water supplies, and fish and wildlife conservation. Because fish and wildlife conservation would stimulate the area's recreational attributes and provide economic benefits to the county, it met the law's requirement to consider the economic impact of any use. The court agreed that the FCA, in the context of the Fish and Wildlife Coordination Act, required that wildlife conservation receive equal consideration with other elements in water resource development projects. The FCA of 1962 did not mandate adjustments to accommodate, but it didn't bar them either. The Corps was free to expand activities as it wished for projects listed under the FCA of 1962.

As late as 2010, projects from the 1962 Act remained unfinished. One near Alamogordo, New Mexico, was a $4.2 million construction of two diversion channels to reroute water that, in 2006, caused $7 million in flood damage in Otero County.

—John H. Barnhill

See also: *Army Corps of Engineers, United States; Flood Control Act of 1928; Flood Control Act of 1936; Flood Control Act of 1944; Flood Control Act of 1960; Mississippi River Flood of 1927*

BIBLIOGRAPHY

Heasley, Lynne. *A Thousand Pieces of Paradise: Landscape and Property in the Kickapoo Valley*. Madison: University of Wisconsin Press, 2005.

Miller, Eugene Willard, and Ruby M. Miller. *Natural Disasters: Floods; A Reference Handbook*. Santa Barbara, CA: ABC-CLIO, 2000.

Miller, Norman. *Environmental Politics: Stakeholders, Interests, and Policymaking*. 2nd ed. New York: Routledge, 2009.

Fort Peck–Montana Compact (1985)

When the Fort Peck–Montana Compact was completed in the spring of 1985, it was the largest Indian water rights

---

Red River Gorge Controversy

The Red River is a tributary of the Kentucky River that received congressional authorization to be dammed as part of the Flood Control Act of 1962. Individuals residing in Powell County, Kentucky, where the dam was going to be built greatly desired a reservoir project. The land targeted for flooding included the Red River Gorge, known for its sandstone cliffs and natural bridges.

Unbeknown to dam supporters, the Sierra Club had taken an interest in the Red River Gorge. The Sierra Club organized the Kentucky section of the organization in March 1967 in order to begin building a local grassroots movement. To bring attention to the cause nationally, it recruited Supreme Court Justice William O. Douglas to conduct a hike for the national media. Led by nationally known Kentuckians such as Harry Caudill, Wendell Berry, and Ray Harm, the local chapter of the Sierra Club quickly organized and mobilized its resources to build alliances with other organizations to save the Red River Gorge.

The Red River Gorge controversy was one of the successes of the Sierra Club in its national effort to save wilderness areas from development. Unfortunately, the Red River Gorge today is suffering severe ecological damage from the tourists who now visit its natural wonders.

—John R. Burch Jr.

See also: *Douglas, William O.*

BIBLIOGRAPHY

Burch, John R., Jr. *Owsley County, Kentucky, and the Perpetuation of Poverty.* Jefferson, NC: McFarland, 2008.

---

settlement made to that point. More than twenty years later, it is still one of the largest ever. It was also the first agreement to be negotiated between a state government and an Indian tribal government without a federal mandate.

The Fort Peck Reservation is home to several bands of the Assiniboine and Sioux tribes, who are collectively known as the Fort Peck Tribes. The tribes have a total membership of about 11,000 enrolled members, with about 6,000 living on the reservation. The lands within the reservation boundaries total more than 2 million acres. Of this, about 378,000 acres are tribally owned, and about 548,000 are owned by individual Indian families as a result of the allotment process of the late nineteenth and early twentieth centuries.

An important Supreme Court case in the early twentieth century, *Winters v. United States* (1908), affirmed the rights of Indian tribes to sufficient water for agricultural production on their reservations. The court reasoned that since Congress wanted the reservation Indians to become farmers and ranchers, there was an implied assertion of a right to water necessary for such pursuits. Although the Fort Peck reservation lands have more than 100 miles of Missouri River shoreline, below the U.S. Army Corps of Engineers's massive Fort Peck Dam, the rights of the tribes to use the water for irrigation or other development purposes was not securely protected until the Fort Peck–Montana Compact was made.

Origins and Terms of the Compact

The negotiations that led to the compact began because of concerns about a new water use law passed by the Montana legislature in 1973. This law required state permits for new water rights claims or for any changes to existing rights. Some tribal governments in Montana were concerned about the potential impact this law might have on state jurisdiction over water rights on reservation lands. In 1979, Montana created the Montana Reserved Water Rights Commission, a nine-person board that has the authority to negotiate water issues among the state, federal agencies, and tribal governments and to submit any negotiated agreements to the state legislature for final approval. Negotiations between the commission and the Assiniboine and Sioux tribes on the Fort Peck reservation were essentially completed by 1983, but the compact was not submitted to the state legislature at that point because of ongoing federal litigation that might have impacted the state's ability to enter into such an agreement. Negotiations between the tribes and the commission resumed in October 1984, and the compact was approved by the Montana legislature in the spring of 1985, winning significant majorities in both houses. The compact was also approved by the governing council of the Fort Peck Tribes.

The compact between the state and the Fort Peck tribes secures the use of over a million acre-feet per year for the reservation, roughly 300 billion gallons. The tribes can manage the water without much oversight by any state or federal agency; federal approval is needed only for marketing water to off-reservation users. In Montana, outside of reservation lands, water law provides a definition of "beneficial uses" to which all proposed water usage must conform. On the Fort Peck reservation, the tribes can authorize any use without regard to this state requirement, although water sold to off-reservation users must meet the requirements of the state law. Under the compact's terms, the tribes adopted a water code that was submitted to the Secretary of the Interior and was subsequently approved in October 1986. Approval by

the Department of the Interior was necessary because that agency holds legal title to all reservation lands. The compact provides that the tribes cannot permanently alienate or transfer any water rights. The tribe has the authority to regulate the water use of all holders of allotted lands, both Indian and non-Indian.

The Fort Peck Irrigation Project, a Bureau of Reclamation project that predates the compact, remains under federal jurisdiction. A few existing water rights of both Indian and non-Indian landowners within the reservation boundaries are not affected by the compact. A special three-person board adjudicates any disputes among the tribes, individual Indians, and non-Indian users. One member of this board is appointed by the tribes and one by the governor, and these two members in turn select the third member.

As with virtually every issue involving the use of Missouri River water, the Fort Peck–Montana Compact caused some controversy between residents of the Upper Missouri Basin and the lower basin. Residents of Nebraska, Iowa, and Missouri, where the maintenance of a river channel sufficient for commercial navigation is an important economic concern, worried that water they needed in the lower basin was being diverted for use in Montana. Congressional opposition by representatives and senators from the states in the lower basin held up final federal approval of the compact.

Administering the Water

The Fort Peck tribes received rights to more water than had any other tribes up to that point. However, the compact provided no state or federal funds to build the facilities needed to manage the water resources. In the early twenty-first century, only a small fraction of the water the tribes have a right to is being used on the reservation because of the lack of infrastructure for irrigation or other development.

To facilitate the construction of a water system on the reservation, the Fort Peck tribes have partnered with the Dry Prairie Rural Water Authority, an organization that will provide municipal, rural, and industrial water supplies for a four-county area in northeastern Montana, outside the boundaries of the reservation. A separate project, the Assiniboine and Sioux Rural Water System, will serve the reservation. Together these two projects make up one regional program known as the Fort Peck Reservation Rural Water System. When the project is completed, the tribes will lease part of their water rights to off-reservation users at no cost. President George W. Bush signed the legislation authorizing federal expenditures on this project in October 2000.

Recent proposals have been made for expanded irrigation on the Fort Peck Reservation. This would allow the production of high-value vegetable crops, which could potentially return more profits to the farmers than the small-grain crops now being produced by dry-land farming.

—Mark S. Joy

See also: *American Indian Water Rights; American Indian Water Settlements; Missouri River Basin; Winters v. United States (1908)*

BIBLIOGRAPHY

Anderson, Robert T. "Indian Water Rights and the Federal Trust Responsibility." *Natural Resources Journal* 46, no. 2 (2006): 399–437. Available at http://papers.ssrn.com/sol3/papers.cfm?abstract_id=1138864.

Lambrecht, Bill. *Big Muddy Blues: True Tales and Twisted Politics along Lewis and Clark's Missouri River.* New York: Thomas Dunne Books, 2005.

Sly, Peter W. *Reserved Water Rights Settlement Manual.* Washington, DC: Island Press, 1988.

Thorson, John E. *River of Promise, River of Peril: The Politics of Managing the Missouri River.* Lawrence: University Press of Kansas, 1994.

General Survey Act of 1824

With the General Survey Act of 1824, the U.S. Congress authorized the president to employ civil and military engineers and to order surveys. The surveys were to be conducted of land routes or waterways that were deemed important for commercial exchange, for mail delivery, or for military reasons. The Act led to significant improvements of roadways and canals, and it particularly benefitted the navigation of the Ohio and the Mississippi Rivers and, later, the Missouri River. It might be thought of as being a natural outgrowth of the general spirit of improvement that was part of the American Enlightenment. One of its most important effects was to promote and facilitate westward expansion in nineteenth-century America.

To understand the General Survey Act of 1824, one needs to see it in historical context. The 1824 Act was a natural outgrowth of late eighteenth-century and early nineteenth-century efforts to promote navigation. Of note is Albert Gallatin's report *Public Roads and Canals* (1808). Gallatin was secretary of the treasury under President Thomas Jefferson, who wanted the federal government to play a more significant role in implementing internal improvements. Gallatin's report promoted government assistance of navigation and even recommended a constitutional amendment that would permit the U.S. Army Corps of Engineers's involvement in nonmilitary improvements to that end.

President James Madison later called for a constitutional amendment similar to the one Gallatin had recommended, in part because the issue of internal improvement was seen to be intimately connected to the building of a stronger nation. Other political leaders of the time, such as Henry Clay and John Quincy Adams, shared those thoughts. John C. Calhoun aimed to tap into that same spirit with his "bonus bill" (passed by Congress in 1817), which called for 1.5 million of federal funds (the yearly dividends from the Second Bank of the United States) to be given to the states for the construction of roads and canals. But Madison, a "strict constructionist," vetoed the bill, claiming that the U.S. constitution did not authorize the federal government to be involved in nonmilitary internal improvements. However, by the late 1810s, Corps engineers were already regularly involved in federal projects. In a way, then, the General Survey Act of 1824 may be seen as government law catching up with the reality of the times.

Soon after the General Survey Act was passed, President Monroe created a Board of Engineers for Internal Improvements to administer its details. Twenty-four engineers (both civilian and military) were assigned to the board. The Board of Engineers immediately set to work on several projects, with potential canal routes getting the bulk of its attention. The Board issued a list of twenty-seven canals in order of their importance to defense and commerce. The routes topping this list were those that joined the Delaware River to the Raritan River, the James River to the Ohio River, the Connecticut River to Boston, and Lake Champlain to the Saint Lawrence River. By the end of the 1820s, the federal government had been involved in almost 100 internal improvement projects.

Despite these successes, in the 1830s several factors—including the growth of railroads and increased sectional tensions—contributed to the decline and eventual death of the General Survey Act of 1824. In 1831, the Board of Engineers was terminated, and in 1838, the General Survey Act was effectively repealed with the passage of an act that provided for the organization of the Corps of Topographical Engineers.

—Mark G. Spencer

See also: *Army Corps of Engineers, United States*

BIBLIOGRAPHY

Alperin, Lynn M. *History of the Gulf Intracoastal Waterway*. Washington, DC: U.S. Army Engineer Water Resources Support Center, Institute for Water Resources, 1983.

Goodrich, Carter. "National Planning of Internal Improvements." *Political Science Quarterly* 63, no. 1 (1948): 16–44.

Hill, Forest G. *Roads, Rails, and Waterways: The Army Engineers and Early Transportation*. Norman: University of Oklahoma Press, 1957.

Marcus, Alan I., and Howard P. Segal. *Technology in America: A Brief History*. San Diego, CA: Harcourt, Brace & Jovanovich, 1989.

Shallat, Todd. "Engineering Policy: The U.S. Army Corps of Engineers and the Historical Foundation of Power." *The Public Historian* 11 (1989): 7–27.

Great Lakes Charter (1985)

The Great Lakes Charter (GLC) is an intergovernmental agreement that was created to govern water diversions from the Great Lakes Basin. It was created under the auspices of the Council of Great Lakes Governors, which in 1983 appointed a task force to study how to protect the waters contained within the Great Lakes. The task force's recommendations resulted in the drafting of the GLC, which was signed on February 11, 1985, by the governors of Michigan, Indiana, Pennsylvania, Wisconsin, Minnesota, Ohio, New York, and Illinois and the premiers of Quebec and Ontario.

Early Proposals

The history of water diversions from the Great Lakes dates back to at least the 1800s. However, the early water diversions were not of a scale that would have seriously threatened the long-term health of any of the lakes found within the Great Lakes Basin. Beginning in the late 1950s, grandiose water diversion plans began to be developed in western states. These were intended to solve these states' chronic water shortages at the expense of water sources from throughout North America.

For example, the North American Water and Power Alliance (NAWAPA) called for the creation of a network of interconnected rivers and reservoirs that would extend from Alaska to northern Mexico. NAWAPA included a proposal to construct a Canadian–Great Lakes Waterway, which would connect the Great Lakes to the West's water network. The western states envisioned using the Great Lakes as reservoirs in which excess water from Alaska and Canada could be stored until needed. NAWAPA was never implemented, but had it been, it would have permanently flooded large areas of the states within the Great Lakes Basin and have radically altered the ecosystems of each of the lakes.

On the heels of NAWAPA's decline in the mid-1960s came a proposal from Canada to construct the Great Recycling and Northern Development Canal, which came to be known as the GRAND Canal. The planners envisioned diverting water from Lake Huron and Lake Superior to both the prairies of western Canada and the headwaters of the Colorado River. Like NAWAPA, the GRAND Canal never made it past the proposal stage.

While the NAWAPA and GRAND Canal proposals had unnerved the residents of the Great Lakes Basin, it was the 1981 proposal to construct a coal-slurry pipeline from Wyoming to the Great Lakes that spurred the negotiations that ultimately resulted in the passage of the GLC. Initially, Powder River Pipeline Inc. (PRPI) wanted to build an approximately 1,900-mile pipeline to transport coal slurry to stations in Duluth, Minnesota, and Milwaukee, Wisconsin. The problem was that water was needed to create the coal slurry, and water was not readily available in Wyoming. Thus, the company made plans to build a separate pipeline to transport water from Lake Superior to Wyoming. Although the PRPI plan was ultimately abandoned because the company could not convince the U.S. Congress to pass the eminent domain legislation it needed, the governors of the states bordering the Great Lakes were convinced that they had to do something to prevent other states from taking their water (Annin 2006).

Goals and Achievements of the Charter

In 1983, the governors of Illinois, Indiana, Michigan, Minnesota, Ohio, and Wisconsin founded the Council of Great Lakes Governors. One of the council's first priorities was to formulate a basinwide water policy. The result of approximately two years of work by the members of the council and their counterparts in other Great Lakes states and provinces was the GLC. The charter depended on public trust doctrine to declare the waters of the Great Lakes to be a public resource that was shared among the residents of the Great Lakes Basin. Since it was a shared and finite resource, any diversion of its waters that adversely affected the water levels of any of the respective lakes threatened not only the environment but also the economy and general welfare of the citizenry (Annin 2006).

The GLC's greatest achievement was that it created a framework in which the elected leaders of the states and provinces that bordered the Great Lakes could work together on issues that affected them all. They created a mechanism whereby they could share information to help make informed decisions about how to protect the Great Lakes from outside entities. The document also contained basinwide water standards, which some of the states used to pass legislation making those regulations legally binding within their territorial boundaries.

One problem with the GLC was that it was a nonbinding agreement. Although the terms of the document were not enforceable, however, the GLC did give the political leaders of the respective states and provinces a collective voice that demonstrated to any entity planning to obtain water from any of the Great Lakes that such an endeavor would face stiff opposition. Another problem was that the GLC was probably unconstitutional in the United States, since states did not have the authority to negotiate binding international agreements. Recognizing that the charter was only a stopgap measure, the governors turned to the U.S. Congress to endorse the charter's goals. In response, Congress passed the Water Resources Development Act (WRDA) in 1986. The WRDA was much more restrictive than the GLC because many environmental groups lobbied to shape the legislation. The WRDA not only prevented the Great Lakes from being raided from without but also heavily restricted intrabasin diversions. In addition, it provided each of the states the right to veto any diversion of Great Lakes water, even transfers that did not cross state boundaries. Since the WRDA is federal legislation, the vetoes are enforceable.

—John R. Burch Jr.

See also: *Great Lakes; Great Lakes Legacy Act of 2002*

BIBLIOGRAPHY

Annin, Peter. *The Great Lakes Water Wars*. Washington, DC: Island Press, 2006.

Annin, Peter. "The Great Lakes Water Wars." http://www.great lakeswaterwars.com/.

Council of Great Lakes Governors. "The Great Lakes Charter: Principles for the Management of Great Lakes Water Resources." February 11, 1985. http://www.cglg.org/projects/water/docs/GreatLakesCharter.pdf.

Heinmiller, B. Timothy. "Do Intergovernmental Institutions Matter? The Case of Water Diversion Regulation in the Great Lakes Basin." *Governance* 20, no. 4 (2007): 655–74.

Great Lakes Fisheries Policy

The Great Lake system includes about 18 percent of the world's fresh surface water. More than 3,500 species of plants and wildlife, some unique in the world, live there. Great Lakes flora and fauna are affected by Americans and Canadians who over the past two centuries have brought the region agriculture, urbanization, and industry. The $7 billion fishing industry in the Great Lakes Basin employs over 800,000 people. The aquatic communities are volatile, with rapid alterations in abundance, and the fishery experts managing the Great Lakes have come to manage the lakes as ecosystems. Ecosystems require coordination among many jurisdictions and government agencies.

A Need for Regional Policies

Because all the Great Lakes except Michigan abut both the United States and Canada, a regional policy works better than state-by-state or province-by-province policies. The first such regional agreement was the 1909 Boundary Waters Treaty, which established the International Joint Commission as a means of resolving water quality and quantity disagreements between the two nations. In 1972, the Great Lakes Water Quality Agreement was signed; it was amended in 1978 to address toxic contamination and evolved over time to encompass an ecosystem approach that recognized the interrelationships among water, land, and air. The Protocol of 1987 identified forty-three areas of concern, including environmentally degraded shoreline areas, and mandated joint national and state/provincial efforts to develop remediation plans. Additional agreements include the 1994 Ecosystem Charter for the Great Lakes–Saint Lawrence Basin, a joint air quality agreement, the 1997 Binational Toxics Strategy, and the Great Lakes Charter. Aside from binational agreements, Canada has federal water and fisheries acts; and the United States has acts dealing with coastal management, a joint agreement for the Great Lakes Basin, an act to control nonindigenous aquatic nuisances, and the Great Lakes Fishery Act of 1956.

Establishing the Commission

In 1955, both nations agreed to the Convention on Great Lakes Fisheries and established the Great Lakes Fishery Commission (GLFC). The commission develops research programs and recommends ways to maximize sustained productivity. It also has responsibility for a sea lamprey eradication program, coordinating research and recommending ways to enhance the native fish population while reducing the sea lamprey presence. The motivation for the agreement was the failure of the two nations to establish an effective joint campaign against the sea lamprey, a nonnative fish whose population expanded rapidly in the Great Lakes to the significant detriment of indigenous fish. Sea lampreys originally entered the Great Lakes early in the twentieth century through shipping canals.

The sea lamprey is an aquatic vertebrate that resembles an eel in shape and can grow to be almost a yard long. Lampreys live in both fresh- and saltwater and feed parasitically on the body fluids of fish hosts. Sea lampreys may kill up to six of seven fish they attack, and an average lamprey kills forty pounds of fish during its lifetime. They prey on all large fish, including trout, salmon, catfish, walleye, and sturgeon. Before their entry into the Great Lakes system, Canada and the United States took about 15 million pounds of lake trout from Lakes Huron and Superior each year. By the early 1960s, the catch was down to 300,000 pounds.

The GLFC works with Fisheries and Oceans Canada as well as the U.S. Army Corps of Engineers and the Fish and Wildlife Service to control lampreys. It also conducts research in conjunction with the U.S. Geological Survey and universities in the Great Lakes Basin. The lamprey population has been reduced by 90 percent in most areas. Native species can again spawn and survive, but total eradication of the sea lamprey is unlikely, so the battle against it is ongoing.

Commission Functions

The GLFC deals with two nations, two provinces, eight states, increasing numbers of Indian tribes and First Nations, as well as dozens of agencies and organizations involved in fishery management. Stakeholders include commercial users, environmentalists, and others, and all seek to influence the GLFC. Until 2002, the GLFC emphasized ecological concerns over human needs. That year, it began human dimensions research—including the role of human dimensions in decision making, legal and institutional structure for better management, and the stakeholder's role. The GFLC makes decisions by consensus, which raises concerns that the consensus choice is often the lowest common denominator. GLFC programs include restoration of lake and brook trout, lakewide fish inventories, status reports, fleet status monitoring, and overall vision and strategic statements. One major change has been a shift to focusing on optimum sustained yield (OSY) rather than maximum sustained yield, which has meant integrating an understanding of social and ecological impacts into management decisions.

By 2004, the GLFC was working to expand its knowledge of the legal and institutional components of fisheries management as well as improving stakeholder involvement for better management decisions. In March 2010, prior to the release of an Interagency Ocean Policy Task Force report, the Obama administration ended public input. Commercial and recreational fishermen at the United We Fish rally in Washington, D.C., expressed opposition to potential restrictions on fishing in oceans, coastal waters, and the Great Lakes. Opponents blamed the Obama administration for following the same anti-use agenda espoused by the Pew Environmental Group, Greenpeace, and others. The fishing organizations claimed that science-based fishery management was being thrown aside by environmentalists. Other pro-use organizations were the U.S. Recreational Fishing and Boating Coalition and the Congressional Sportsmen's Foundation. They feared a loss of a million jobs and billions of dollars out of the economy as well as millions in tax revenues.

Binational programs have reduced toxic chemicals, aided in construction of better wastewater treatment facilities, and improved management practices to control pollutants at their sources. Canada and Ontario and U.S. state and federal governments and other stakeholders use the Lake Superior Binational Program to implement the Aquatic Invasive Species Complete Prevention Plan. Another binational effort is the State of the Lakes Ecosystem Conferences. In April 2010, Canada and Ontario extended their 2007 fisheries and habitat protection agreement until 2011.

The International Joint Commission (IJC) issues biennial reports on the Great Lakes Water Quality Agreement. In 2000, the IJC indicated that efforts to guarantee clean and safe water, air, and fish were deficient. In April 2010, Lake Superior alone had eighty-eight invasive species—fish, plants, and waterborne organisms—brought in by ballast water from oceangoing vessels and other avenues. In July 2010, five states sued the federal government to close off points of entry for Asian carp, which had plagued the Mississippi River basin since the mid-1990s and were present in the Little Calumet River, which feeds Lake Michigan. Foreign species pose an ongoing threat to outcompete native fish, destroy habitat, reduce harvest, and damage commercial and recreational activity.

—John H. Barnhill

See also: *Great Lakes; Great Lakes Charter (1985); International Joint Commission (United States and Canada)*

BIBLIOGRAPHY

Dobson, Tracy, Shawn J. Riley, and Marc Gaden. "Human Dimensions of Great Lakes Fishery Management: New Research Thrust of the Great Lakes Fishery Commission." *Society and Natural Resources* 18 (2005): 487–91. Available at http://www.glfc.org/research/human dimensions.pdf.

Great Lakes Fishery Commission. "Fisheries Management." Available at http://www.glfc.org/fishmgmt/.

Taylor, William W., and C. Paola Ferreri, eds. *Great Lakes Fisheries Policy and Management: A Binational Perspective.* East Lansing: Michigan State University Press, 1999.

Great Lakes Legacy Act of 2002

The Great Lakes Legacy Act of 2002 (GLLA) authorized the administrator of the Environmental Protection Agency (EPA) to assist in the remediation of sediment contamination in the Great Lakes and to assist the research and development of new technologies for that purpose. The law is administered by the EPA's Great Lakes National Program Office (GLNPO). The GLLA became law as Title I of the Great Lakes and Lake Champlain Act of 2002 on November 12. Signed by President George W. Bush, the act became Pub. L. 107-303, 116 Stat. 2355. The Great Lakes Legacy Reauthorization Act of 2008 (Pub. L. 110-365, 122 Stat. 4021) extended the law and provided renewed funding for the programs it authorized. Both laws amended portions of 33 U.S.C. § 1268, which codified Section 118 of the Federal Water Pollution Control Act. The GLLA's research and development program is codified as 33 U.S.C. § 1271a. The law has not been the subject of significant appellate litigation.

The Great Lakes contain about 84 percent of North America's surface freshwater and about 21 percent of the world's supply. Used since the early nineteenth century for commercial transportation and fishing, the lakes and their tributary rivers have been the site of intensive industrial development and mining and have supported large urban centers, with all the forms of pollution and degradation that these uses entail. The lakes have also supported extensive recreation and tourism—uses that require clean water, healthy stocks of fish, and unspoiled scenic panoramas but that themselves can produce overcrowding, intensive land use, destruction of wildlife habitat, and increased pollution.

Sediments removed, or targeted for removal, include polychlorinated biphenyls (PCBs), polycyclic aromatic hydrocarbons (PAHs), and industrial heavy metals. The original Act authorized expenditures of $250 million over five years, from fiscal year 2004 through fiscal year 2008. However, the money actually allocated fell as low as $10 million in 2003 and was less than $25 million in 2004. The EPA's GLNPO estimates that full cleanup of all sites may require $4 billion. Despite efforts to increase funding in the 2008 reauthorization to $150 million a year, the administration of then-president George W. Bush indicated he would only sign a bill that continued federal funding at the original $50 million per year level. President Barack Obama's first proposed budget included $475 million for cleaning and restoring the lakes, as part of a ten-year, $5 billion program, but ultimate disposition by Congress is uncertain.

Prior Legislation

Prior to passage of the GLLA, and contemporary with the Act's operation, other major legislation has also addressed water pollution problems and restoration of the Great Lakes. Four of the lakes lie between the United States and Canada; the fifth, Lake Michigan, is also of joint concern since it is contiguous with Lake Huron. The Boundary Waters Treaty, signed by the United States and Great Britain in 1909, dealt primarily with water levels, but Article 4 of the treaty acknowledged water pollution as a joint concern. The Great Lakes Water Quality Agreement, signed by Prime Minister Pierre Trudeau and President Richard Nixon on April 15, 1972, expanded the mandate of the International Joint Commission (IJC) created by the 1909 treaty with the goal of cleanup and protection of all the lakes.

The Great Lakes Basin Compact of 1955, formed by legislative action in each state bordering the lakes, was not granted congressional consent until July 1968, in Pub. L. 90-419. The law provides each state with three votes in a Great Lakes Commission to coordinate policy regarding use, preservation, and water quality of the lakes. A more comprehensive compact, entered into in 2008 by the states of Illinois, Indiana, Michigan, Minnesota, New York, Ohio, Pennsylvania, and Wisconsin was approved by Congress in Pub. L. 110-342, 122 Stat. 3739. This compact regulates the use of lake waters and requires any user outside of the lakes' drainage basin to return all water to the lakes. The John Glenn Great Lakes Basin Program, Section 455 in the Water Resources Development Act of 1999 (Pub. L. 106-53, 113 Stat. 269–392) provided for a comprehensive study of all navigation improvements, environmental restoration activities, remedial action, sediment management and removal, erosion prevention, flood prevention, and other activities of the U.S. Army Corps of Engineers in the Great Lakes. It was codified as 42 U.S.C. § 1962d-21

Areas of Concern and Projects

Forty-three Areas of Concern (AOCs) have been identified under the GLLA: twenty-six located entirely within the United States, twelve in Canada, and five that are shared by both countries. Remedial Action Programs (RAPs) have been or are being developed for each of these AOCs. The EPA has assigned each AOC in the United States a RAP liaison. Expenditures under the U.S. law require a "nonfederal sponsor"—which may be a state or local government, a private industry, a consortium of either, or a public-private partnership—which will provide 35 percent of the cost of the remedial program.

The nonfederal partner must enter into an agreement to keep its expenditures for similar remediation programs in the AOC at or above the level of the previous two years. This Maintenance of Effort (MOE) requirement ensures that federal funds enable additional work, rather than simply providing a different funding source for work already in progress. The first projects completed included sites at Ashtabula, Ohio; Black Lagoon, Michigan; Hog Island, Wisconsin; Ruddiman Creek, Michigan; and Saint Marys River/Tannery Bay (Sault Ste. Marie, Michigan). Additional projects are underway at Kinnickinnic River, Wisconsin; Grand Calumet, Indiana; and Ottawa River, Ohio. The EPA reports that almost 800,000 cubic yards of contaminated sediments have been removed from rivers draining into the Great Lakes since the program was created in 2002, out of 10 to 30 million cubic yards of sediment that needs to be removed.

—Charles Rosenberg

See also: *Clean Water Act of 1972; Clean Water Restoration Act of 1966; Clean Water Restoration Act of 2009; Detergents; Dredging; Environmental Protection Agency, United States; Eutrophication; Great Lakes Charter (1985); Great Lakes Fisheries Policy; International Joint Commission (United States and Canada); Outdoor Recreation; Pesticides; Sewage; Water Pollution Control Act (1948); Wetlands*

BIBLIOGRAPHY

Annin, Peter. *The Great Lakes Water Wars*. Washington, DC: Island Press, 2006.
Bence, James R., and Lloyd C. Mohr. *The State of Lake Huron in 2004*. Ann Arbor, MI: Great Lakes Fishery Commission, 2008.
Botts, Lee, and Paul R. Muldoon. *Evolution of the Great Lakes Water Quality Agreement*. East Lansing: Michigan State University Press, 2005.
Clapp, David F., and William H. Horns. *The State of Lake Michigan in 2005*. Ann Arbor, MI: Great Lakes Fishery Commission, 2008.
Dempsey, Dave. *On the Brink: The Great Lakes in the Twenty-First Century*. East Lansing: Michigan State University Press, 2004.
Ernst-Treutel, Alexis. *The Great Lakes*. Madison: Wisconsin Legislative Reference Bureau, 2008.
Grady, Wayne. *The Great Lakes: The Natural History of a Changing Region*. Vancouver, BC: Greystone Books, 2007.
Morrison, Bruce J., and Steven R. LaPan. *The State of Lake Ontario in 2003*. Ann Arbor, MI: Great Lakes Fishery Commission, 2007.
Snitow, Alan, and Deborah Kaufman. *Thirst: Fighting the Corporate Theft of Our Water*. With Michael Fox. San Francisco: Jossey-Bass, 2007.
U.S. Congress, House Committee on Transportation and Infrastructure. *Great Lakes Legacy Reauthorization Act of 2008: Report (To Accompany HR-6460) (Including Cost Estimate of the Congressional Budget Office)*. Washington, DC: U.S. Government Printing Office, 2008.
U.S. Environmental Protection Agency, Great Lakes National Program Office. "The Great Lakes Legacy Act." http://www.epa.gov/glnpo/sediment/legacy/index.html.

Hayden, Carl T.

Carl Trumbell Hayden (1877–1972) served as a member of the U.S. House of Representatives from 1912 until 1927 and in the U.S. Senate from 1927 until 1969, becoming the first senator to serve seven terms. Hayden (D-AZ) was involved in flood control projects and the construction of dams to help with irrigation in Arizona.

Hayden was born on October 2, 1877, in Hayden's Ferry (now Tempe), Arizona, the son of Charles Trumbell Hayden and Sallie Calvert (née Davis). He attended the Normal School of Arizona at Tempe, graduating in 1896, and then attended Stanford University from 1896 to 1900. From 1902 to 1904 he was a member of the Tempe town council, and from 1904 to 1906 he was the treasurer of Maricopa County. He then served as county sheriff from 1907 until 1912. In 1912, Hayden was elected to the U.S. House of Representatives, holding the seat for the next fifteen years. In 1918, after the United States entered World War I, Hayden served as a major in the infantry, but not before he had introduced an amendment to the military manpower bill that prevented conscripts from buying their way out of military service.

Early Projects

During his first term in Congress, Hayden developed an interest in flood control, and he introduced legislation

Carl Hayden (1877–1972) served in the U.S. House of Representatives as well as the Senate, becoming the first senator to serve seven terms. He is remembered for his interest in water rights and irrigation in the American Southwest.

Library of Congress

authorizing the San Carlos Irrigation Project to build a reclamation project for the Gila River. Critics claimed that Arizona had already received more than its share of federal funds. To hide the appropriations, Congress included them in the annual Indian Appropriations Act. The diversion dam, completed in 1922, was named after Hayden and Senator Henry Fountain Ashurst (D-AZ), who had also helped get funding for the dam. Two years later, the final parts of the San Carlos Irrigation Project were funded when Senator Ralph H. Cameron (R-AZ) reintroduced the San Carlos Bill. It was passed and then signed into law by President Calvin Coolidge; the dam was named the Coolidge Dam.

Hayden focused on Colorado River water rights. Some business interests in California supported by Rep. Phil Swing (R-CA) and Senator Hiram Johnson (P/R-CA) wanted to build a water storage dam and construct the All-American Canal. These plans had been debated for many years, and western states had been arguing over the apportionment of the project's water. Arizona in particular believed that it would not get a fair allocation of water, and Hayden and others opposed the project. Hayden used a variety of parliamentary procedures to prevent the Swing-Johnson Bill from reaching the floor of the House. Hayden then decided to contest a seat for the U.S. Senate.

Senate Career

From 1927 until 1969, Carl Hayden served in the U.S. Senate for Arizona. His main focus was irrigation projects for arid lands in Arizona and elsewhere to expand the amount of farmland under cultivation. Hayden's first speech lasted nine hours, as he filibustered the Swing-Johnson Bill, still alive in the Senate. However, Hayden rarely spoke in subsequent Senate debates, earning himself the nickname of "Silent Senator." Nonetheless, he wielded enormous power in committees. As Arthur Edson of the Associated Press was to write, "He has kept his mouth shut while astutely pushing out invisible tentacles of power" (Cohen 1971).

During the late 1920s, Hayden fought against the Boulder Canyon Project because he wanted Arizona to gain more of the project's water. After near defeat in the 1932 elections and with President Franklin D. Roosevelt introducing the New Deal, the senator then decided to support the Boulder Canyon Project, and he used his political skills to get government funding for more irrigation and hydroelectric projects. These included the Central Valley Project and the Grand Coulee Dam. Then with the advent of World War II, Hayden urged more irrigation projects to increase crop yields for the war effort and to generate hydroelectricity.

By the 1950s, Hayden had become heavily involved in the Central Arizona Project. This would use water from the Colorado River to irrigate vast areas of Arizona. California challenged the project in court (*Arizona v. California*), a case that took ten years to resolve. This project was one of the major issues in Hayden's re-election campaign in 1962. California lost the court challenge, but Rep. Wayne Aspinall (D-CO) opposed the project, offering to support it only if Colorado gained far more than Hayden was offering. Not until September 30, 1968, was the Central Arizona Project given final approval. President Lyndon B. Johnson called the day "Carl Hayden Day," and Hayden responded that he considered the Central Arizona Project "the most significant accomplishment" of his career.

Retiring in 1968 after fifty-six years in Congress, Hayden wanted his aide Roy Elson to succeed him in the Senate, but Elson was defeated by Barry Goldwater (R-AZ). In retirement, Hayden went back to Tempe and started writing about Arizona pioneers, including his own family. He died on January 25, 1972, and was buried at Twin Butte Cemetery in Tempe. Both Barry Goldwater and Lyndon B. Johnson spoke at his memorial service.

Although the Central Arizona Project did open up large parts of the state to agriculture, it has been criticized for using water from the Colorado River that, arguably, could have been used more effectively in other states.

—Justin Corfield

See also: Arizona v. California *(1963); Army Corps of Engineers, United States; Boulder Canyon Project Act (1928); Central Arizona Project; Central Valley Project; Dam Building*

BIBLIOGRAPHY

August, Jack L., Jr. *Vision in the Desert: Carl Hayden and Hydropolitics in the American Southwest.* Fort Worth: Texas Christian University Press, 1999.
Cohen, J. "Carl Hayden—Man of History and Few Words." *Los Angeles Times,* April 18, 1971.
Johnson, James W. *Arizona Politicians: The Noble and the Notorious.* Tucson: University of Arizona Press, 2002.
Rice, Ross R. *Carl Hayden: Builder of the American West.* Lanham, MD: University Press of America, 1994.

Hazardous Substances Response Trust Fund (Superfund)

The Hazardous Substances Response Trust Fund was established in 1980 by the Comprehensive Environmental Response, Compensation, and Liability Act (CERCLA). It was funded through a tax on the chemical and petroleum industries that raised $1.6 billion over five years. The trust fund, more commonly known as "Superfund," is administered by the Environmental Protection Agency's (EPA) Office of Solid Waste and Emergency Response.

The EPA's Superfund cleanup process begins with the listing of contaminated sites in the Comprehensive Environmental Response, Compensation, and Liability Information System (CERCLIS). Inclusion in the CERCLIS database does not mean that a site qualifies for immediate clean-up. It just ensures that the EPA conducts

an inspection of the site. If a particular site contains contaminants or hazardous waste that poses an immediate, or short-term, threat to the environment and/or human health, then the site is placed on the National Priorities List (NPL). A determination is then made of how best to clean up the site, with actual work beginning soon thereafter. Once the site has been cleaned, the EPA begins a long-term monitoring process to ensure that the contaminants have been removed or neutralized. Only after the EPA has completed the post-cleanup testing is the site removed from the NPL. The last step in the process is to revitalize the formerly contaminated site so that it can be used once again in a productive fashion.

The impetus for the passage of CERCLA was the controversy that erupted during the 1970s over Love Canal, located near Niagara Falls, New York. Members of the community had been suffering medical ailments from living on top of a long-abandoned and forgotten toxic dump site. President Jimmy Carter declared a federal emergency on August 7, 1978, and provided federal funding to relocate many of the families that resided on the landfill. In response to the problem, the U.S. Congress crafted CERCLA to clean up similar sites located throughout the United States.

In 1984, Congress required the EPA to create regulations for the design and operation of underground storage tanks. In response, the EPA created the Underground Storage Tank program under the Superfund umbrella to prevent the release of petroleum and related hazardous substances into the environment. The program was funded in 1986 with the creation of the Leaking Underground Storage Tank Trust Fund, which derived much of its funding from an excise tax on motor fuels.

Despite the Superfund nickname, the Hazardous Substances Response Trust Fund was underfunded from the start. Democrats in the U.S. Congress had settled for minimal funding in order to pass the legislation prior to Ronald Reagan's inauguration as president. President Reagan's distaste for government regulation of industry resulted in his administration's undermining of CERCLA's goals through the active support of industrial interests when they came into conflict with the EPA. Harshly criticized across the entire political spectrum, CERCLA proved to be a great disappointment. After the expenditure of $1.6 billion over five years, only 6 of the approximately 1,800 hazardous waste sites identified by the EPA had been cleaned up.

Since CERCLA had only been authorized for five years, Congress passed the Superfund Amendment and

Reauthorization Act (SARA) in 1986. The SARA legislation added $9 billion to the trust fund, which was renamed the Hazardous Substances Superfund. It also included comprehensive revisions to the program, including a broadening of the fund's tax base to include corporations outside of the chemical and petroleum industries.

In 1990, Congress expanded the scope of the Hazardous Substances Superfund in the Oil Pollution Act to give the EPA responsibility for cleaning up oil spills. Despite the new mandate, Congress was leery of continuing the authorization for the Superfund program for another extended period of time. Through most of the 1990s and into the 2000s, Congress passed annual appropriations to keep Superfund cleanup projects active. Congress finally reauthorized and expanded the Superfund program with the passage of the Small Business Liability Relief and Brownfields Revitalization Act of 2002.

—John R. Burch Jr.

The Army Creek Landfill was once a repository for municipal and industrial waste, which contaminated the area. Recently, under the aegis of the EPA's Superfund, the landfill has been reformed into an area for wildlife.
NOAA Restoration Center Collection

See also: *Oil Pollution Act of 1990*

BIBLIOGRAPHY

Anderson, Terry Lee, ed. *Political Environmentalism: Going Behind the Green Curtain.* Stanford, CA: Hoover Institution Press, 2000.

Barnett, Harold C. *Toxic Debts and the Superfund Dilemma.* Chapel Hill: University of North Carolina Press, 1994.

Environmental Statutes. 2008 ed. 2 vols. Lanham, MD: Government Institutes, 2008.

Hird, John A. *Superfund: The Political Economy of Environmental Risk.* Baltimore: Johns Hopkins University Press, 1994.

Nakamura, Robert T., and Thomas W. Church. *Taming Regulation: Superfund and the Challenge of Regulatory Reform.* Washington, DC: Brookings Institution Press, 2003.

Small Business Liability Relief and Brownfields Revitalization Act. Pub. L. No. 107-118, 115 Stat. 2356 (2002). http://epa.gov/brownfields/laws/sblrbra.htm.

Switzer, Carole Stern, and Peter Gray. *CERCLA: Comprehensive Environmental Response, Compensation, and Liability Act (Superfund).* 2nd ed. Chicago: American Bar Association, Section of Environment, Energy and Resources, 2008.

U.S. Government Accountability Office. *Environmental Protection Agency: Major Management Challenges; Report to the Subcommittee on Interior, Environment and Related Agencies, Committee on Appropriations, House of Representatives* (GAO-09-434). Washington, DC: U.S. Government Accountability Office, 2009. Available at http://www.gao.gov/products/GAO-09-434.

Highlands Water Protection and Planning Act (2004)

New Jersey's Highlands Water Protection and Planning Act was enacted on August 10, 2004, in response to the need to adopt a regional planning approach to protect the valuable natural resources of the Highlands region in northwestern New Jersey that were being negatively impacted by population growth, construction, and suburban sprawl. The New Jersey Highlands is part of a 3.5 million acre region encompassing three states; New York, Connecticut, and New Jersey. New Jersey's portion totals 859,358 acres (Highlands Water Protection and Planning Council 2008) and includes eighty-eight municipalities in seven counties—Warren, Bergen, Passaic, Hunterdown, Morris, Somerset, and Sussex. The region has lush forests, large undeveloped lands, pristine rivers, and streams of exceptional water quality that provide drinking water to

64 percent of New Jersey. It also contains valuable historical sites.

Recommendations of a Highlands Task Force created by Governor James E. McGreevy's Executive Order No. 70 on September 19, 2003, provided the basis for the law. Recommendations targeted preservation of the natural resources and enhancement of the Highlands citizens' quality of life. The Task Force focused on an integrated, balanced approach to regional planning that sought to protect and preserve water quality, drinking water supplies, contiguous forests, and biodiversity; preserve farmland; promote historic, cultural, and recreational resources; and develop economic and redevelopment opportunities utilizing smart-growth approaches (New Jersey Legislature 2004).

Protecting the Highlands

In early 1907, the Potable Water Commission Report recognized the value of the Highlands water resources to New Jersey. In 2002, recognizing the area's water resources, extensive forested areas, biodiversity, and recreational attributes, the U.S. Forest Service designated the region as nationally significant, and it became New Jersey's first Special Resource Area. Studies conducted by the Forest Service in 1992 and 2002 revealed that the natural resources of the Highlands faced significant risk from unrestrained growth that increased water demands; threatened water systems' productivity and quality; and increased impervious surfaces, thus affecting the recharge of aquifers that provided thousands of residents with groundwater. Aquatic wildlife habitat and uplands and forests were also jeopardized by changing land use patterns that increased deforestation and forest fragmentation. Therefore, it was estimated that water treatment costs would escalate to $30 billion by 2054 (New Jersey Legislature 2004). Development had resulted in a loss of 65,000 acres of New Jersey's Highlands since 1984. Many of these natural resources are owned by private as well as public entities resulting in uncoordinated land use planning. Action was therefore necessary to protect these environmentally sensitive lands.

Impact of the Bill

The bill received mixed reactions from the public in the affected areas. Proponents like environmentalists and some municipal authorities considered it a sensible approach to regional planning. Homeowners, farmers, other municipal authorities, and builders were very critical. Builders said it made minimal allowances for new housing and would affect job creation; homeowners worried about restrictions on their ability to make additions to their homes; farmers were concerned about a government "land grab" and viability of their farms; towns were concerned about the loss of revenues from property taxes, loss of planning powers, funding mechanisms for compensating landowners for the loss of right to development, and restrictions on paving roads.

Recognizing the need for sustainable development, the bill delineates specific boundaries within the seven counties as the Highlands region, of which 415,000 acres are a core Preservation Area and the other half is a Planning Area. Preservation is achieved through strategies like land acquisition by the state, regional planning, and a Transfer of Development Rights Program. In the Planning Area, urban development is allowed under the Transfer of Development Rights Program. In "sending zones" in the Preservation Area, rights to build more residences are sent out to "receiving areas" in municipalities in the Planning Area, where building is permitted.

To accommodate the buying and selling of development rights, a Transfer of Development Rights Bank was established. To manage the bank and implement and coordinate regional planning to protect drinking water sources, a Highlands Drinking Water Protection and Regional Planning Council was established. Fifteen local citizens, county officials, and bipartisan representatives make up the Council. In the Preservation Area, the Council is to permanently prohibit development in identified zones and has some authority to review and accept or reject public and private projects meeting certain criteria. Only those applications that conform to the Regional Master Plan and the goals of the bill are considered for approval. Local zoning and master plans of municipalities located partially or completely within the Preservation Area must also conform to the Regional Plan. The Regional Master Plan was adopted on July 17, 2008. Of note, the Council's role in the Planning Area is only advisory.

Concerning the Preservation Area, the New Jersey Department of Environmental Protection's role is to develop more applicable stringent environmental rules and regulations to major nonresidential and residential projects. Municipalities are compensated for lost property tax revenues imposed by the building restrictions through a Municipal Property Tax Stabilization Board.

The full impact of this landmark bill has not yet been determined. Gottlieb (2010) notes risks for landowners in the environmentally sensitive zones. Among these is the reluctance of municipalities in the Planning Area to allow increased density and limited developers' market demand for development rights in the Preservation Area. Risk management will be important to future local government decisions and the Transfer of Development Rights Program's design. But, Gottlieb states, recent developers' market trends show positive signs on the Highlands periphery.

—Shevon J. Letang

See also: *Water Pollution Control Act (1948)*

BIBLIOGRAPHY

Gottlieb, Paul. "Summary of the New Jersey Highlands Water Protection and Planning Act." Last updated October 27, 2010. http://njaes.rutgers.edu/highlands/.

Highlands Water Protection and Planning Council. "Highlands Regional Master Plan." 2008. http://www.highlands.state.nj.us/njhighlands/master/rmp/final/highlands_rmp_112008.pdf.

New Jersey Legislature. *Committee Meeting of Senate Environment Committee Assembly Environment and Solid Waste Committee: Senate Bill No. 1 and Assembly Bill No. 2635 (The "Highlands Water Protection and Planning Act")*. Trenton, NJ: Office of Legislative Services, Public Information Office, Hearing Unit, 2004.

Ickes, Harold

Harold LeClair Ickes (1874–1952) was born on March 15, 1874, in Frankstown Township, Pennsylvania. He graduated from the University of Chicago in 1897 and worked as a journalist with various Chicago newspapers over the next few years while attending law school. During this period, he became active in reform politics, supporting Progressive candidates and initiatives. It was the beginning of a lifelong association with political movements. In 1907, he graduated with a law degree from the University of Chicago and established a successful, but irregular, law practice, which he maintained until 1933. Ickes worked on the presidential campaigns of Progressive Party candidates Theodore Roosevelt and Charles Evans Hughes. His involvement in politics was interrupted by World War I and his service overseas with the Young Men's Christian Association (YMCA), where he performed a variety of tasks for the U.S. Army. Ickes returned from the war in 1919 and returned to reform politics. He assisted with the campaigns of Hiram W. Johnson in 1920 and 1924. Although a Republican, Ickes placed his support and campaign skills behind Democrat Franklin Delano Roosevelt in the 1932 presidential election. His work won notice from the newly elected president.

Federal Positions

Ickes hoped to obtain an appointment in the new administration and lobbied Senator Hiram Johnson (P/R-CA) towards this end. The positions he desired included commissioner of Indian affairs and either first assistant secretary or secretary of the interior. After a brief meeting with Roosevelt on February 21, 1933, in New York, Ickes was offered the secretary of the interior position, an office he would hold for a record term of thirteen years. Ickes's main qualification for this position was his reputation as a competent administrator for a variety of organizations. Ickes's personal interests in conservation and the needs of the American Indian also made the Interior Department a logical choice. As secretary, his foremost goal was to restore the reputation of the position, which was still suffering from the Teapot Dome and other scandals during the Harding administration. In addition to giving Ickes a cabinet position, Roosevelt also tapped him for the directorship of the New Deal's Public Works Administration (PWA), which lasted from 1935–1939.

During his tenure as secretary of the Interior, Ickes worked to improve the reputation of the department and to broaden conservation efforts across the nation. From his youth, Ickes had an interest in conservation and nature, which was greatly expanded by his friendship with Gifford Pinchot, secretary of the interior under Theodore Roosevelt. These influences would lead him to greatly expand the National Park Service during his tenure from 8.2 million acres to over 20 million. Ickes also advocated, albeit unsuccessfully, for the relocation of the Forest Service from the Department of Agriculture to the Department of the Interior. As secretary, he strongly supported John Collier, the commissioner of Indian Affairs, and worked to change Washington's attitude toward Native Americans. In 1939, Ickes arranged for singer Marian Anderson's concert at the Lincoln Memorial when the Daughters of the American Revolution would not allow her to use Constitution Hall.

While serving as director of the Public Works Administration, Ickes oversaw the funding of a variety of public works projects. The PWA received over $6 billion over its existence, which was meted out along with various contracts for government projects. The PWA built hundreds of schools, public buildings, sewer systems, and hospitals throughout the country. Larger projects under the PWA included the Lincoln Tunnel and the Triborough Bridge in New York, Grand Coulee Dam in Washington State, and the highway between Key West and mainland Florida. Ickes also authorized contracts that increased the size of the U.S. Navy, including by building the aircraft carriers *Yorktown* and *Enterprise*. Military and civilian aviation projects were also funded during this period. Ickes worked to balance the need for infrastructure projects like dams with environmental conservation. His administrative practices did come under fire because of his tendency to examine every contract to prevent graft within his department. Ickes often had to fight for funding for his projects because the Works Progress Administration, headed by Harry Hopkins, had priority within the Roosevelt administration.

When Roosevelt died in April 1945, Ickes continued to serve in the administration of Harry S. Truman. However, when Truman opted to nominate California oil executive Edwin W. Pauley as undersecretary of the Navy, Ickes resigned in protest, thus ending the longest tenure in American history as secretary of the interior. Pauley later withdrew his nomination. Upon his resignation in February 1946, Ickes continued to remain at the forefront of politics. He returned to journalism as a frequent contributor to the *New Republic* and wrote a syndicated newspaper column entitled "Man to Man." He was vocal in his criticism of a number of notables, including General Douglas MacArthur; Senator Joseph McCarthy (R-WI); Thomas E. Dewey, governor of New York; and Richard Nixon, then a member of Congress from California. He showed support for President Harry S. Truman on most key issues but did not fail to criticize other aspects of the administration. Ickes died on February 3, 1952, in Washington, D.C., from a heart attack.

—Theresa Hefner-Babb

See also: *Bureau of Indian Affairs; Grand Coulee Dam; Pinchot, Gifford; Roosevelt, Franklin D.*

BIBLIOGRAPHY

Clarke, Jeanne Nienaber. *Roosevelt's Warrior: Harold L. Ickes and the New Deal.* Baltimore: Johns Hopkins University Press, 1996.

Daniels, Roger. "Harold Le Clair Ickes." In *Dictionary of American Biography.* Vol. 14, suppl. 5, *1951–1955.* New York: Scribner, 1977.

Ickes, Harold L. *The Autobiography of a Curmudgeon.* Chicago: Quadrangle Books, 1969.

White, Graham, and John Maze. *Harold Ickes of the New Deal: His Private Life and Public Career.* Cambridge, MA: Harvard University Press, 1985.

In re: General Adjudication of All Rights to Use Water in Big Horn River System (Wyoming, 1988 and 1992)

A debate has persisted, mostly fought in the courts, regarding whether the federal government, state government, or tribal government has final jurisdiction over water use on Indian reservations in situations where the interests of both Indians and non-Indians are concerned. This series of court decisions culminated in the Wyoming State Court's *Big Horn* decisions.

Some courts are wary of any tribal administration over non-Indians in settings where non-Indians are the majority in the specific area in question. However, in the Ninth Circuit Court's 1981 decision in *Colville Confederated Tribes v. Walton,* the court ruled that the tribe had jurisdiction over water rights originally set up as reserved rights, even after the land had passed out of Indian hands. In so doing, the court also expressly recognized important tribal interests in regulating both Indian and non-Indian water use on the reservation. The tribes argue that they have authority over water use by the non-Indian successors to the original allottees, or *Walton* rights holders, as a matter of tribal sovereignty. The non-Indian users only have access to the tribe's water through the consent of the tribe. The tribes have argued that the treaty-based water right derives from the tribes' ownership and has never been abrogated. By declining to hear the further appeal of *Walton,* the Supreme Court confirmed tribal sovereignty in cases like these.

Reservation water use and regulation by tribes, and not states, has not only been essential in protecting the interests of the tribes in their reservation water resources but has ramifications for tribal sovereignty in general. In order to be equitable, the administration of water sources that serve both Indian and non-Indian users must be cooperative.

Case Background

In 1988, the Wyoming state courts established such a cooperative system in their decision in *In re: General Adjudication of All Rights to Use Water in Big Horn River System* (753 P.2d 76, Wyoming, 1988). The state court set up a system in which the tribes govern water used by the tribe on the reservation and the state administers non-Indian on-reservation water rights. The crisis that brought about this decision began when the legislature of the state of Wyoming began to examine the allocation of its waters in 1977. That year, the threat of an implementation of Winters rights by the Eastern Shoshone and Northern Arapaho tribes of the Wind River Indian Reservation led the state to file suit to adjudicate the claims of the tribes and approximately 20,000 other water rights holders in the Bighorn River Basin. A special master was appointed to investigate the case, and four years later he reported his findings. The special master's report declared that the Indians of the area had the right to enough water to meet the original purposes of the reservation, which were multiple, as the reservation was to serve as the Indians' homeland in perpetuity. Once this determination was made, the case began its journey through the courts (McCool 2002).

The Decision and Its Implications

The Wyoming Supreme Court handed down two major decisions in the case. In the 1988 decision, known as *Big Horn I,* the court decided that the Wind River tribes did indeed have reserved water rights that preceded all other state users, but it also decided that the original purpose of the reservation was limited to agriculture and thus the amount of water reserved should be based on the "practicably irrigable acreage" (PIA) standard established in *Arizona v. California.* The PIA standard the court used was controversial, to say the least. In order to implement this standard, experts are required to examine soil characteristics, hydrology, and economics in order to determine how much reservation land can be irrigated. This places a limit on the Winters rights a tribe can assert, in that the amount of water reserved is based on how much could be used if all possible lands were, in fact, being used for irrigated agriculture, ignoring all other possible tribal water uses.

So, as with the *Powers* decision, *Big Horn I* began with the assumption that irrigated agriculture was the sole basis of Indian reserved water claims. The Supreme Court had a chance to overrule the PIA standard and its dependence on agriculture when it heard arguments in the appeal of the state's decision in 1989. Justice Sandra Day O'Connor recused herself from the decision after having come out in support of the state's position. The case resulted in a split vote that left the original decision and, consequently, the PIA standard in place (McCool 2002). In 1992, the Wyoming State Court codified this limitation on what the tribes could do with the water. This decision, known as

Big Horn II, stipulated that the tribes could not convert their water use from irrigation to in-stream flow without first conforming to the same restrictive rules as states.

The tribes had decided to use a portion of the water to augment stream flows in the reservation and restore the fishery. The tribe wanted to recover the ecosystem as well as augment opportunities for tourism and recreation. However, non-Indian water users on allocated parts of the reservation who were already using the water objected. Unfortunately for the tribe, *Big Horn II* rejected the tribes' attempts to use water for in-stream flows, as Wyoming state law did not recognize in-stream uses as "beneficial." Wyoming law stipulated that only the state owns an in-stream flow right. The net effect of the court's decision was to reinforce a reserved right for Indian tribes in the Wyoming State Court, but such a right could only be implemented for water designated for agricultural use. To use any of that water for anything other than agriculture placed it in the same category as non-Indian use: controlled by the state.

This case has been through the Wyoming State court five times and to the Supreme Court once. As such, along with many other cases, it demonstrates the interminability of litigation in the assertion of Winters rights.

—Steven L. Danver

See also: Arizona v. California *(1963);* Winters v. United States *(1908)*

BIBLIOGRAPHY

Hartman, Gary P. "The Big Horn River General Stream Adjudication." *Wyoming Lawyer* 32, no. 5 (2009). Available at http://wyomingbar.org/bar_journal/article.html?id=254&-session=wybar_user:42F944791b90d10184OYq2026A92.

McCool, Daniel. *Native Waters: Contemporary Indian Water Settlements and the Second Treaty Era.* Tucson: University of Arizona Press, 2002.

Inland Waterways Commission

In 1907, Theodore Roosevelt, buoyed by his success in launching the Panama Canal, appointed an Inland Waterways Commission. Concerns had arisen about the conservation of waterways and the need to revive river navigation. Roosevelt was clear that he wanted the waterways to be improved and controlled. He also saw waterways as a significant enough resource to be dealt with nationally; prior to this, water power had largely been managed locally. The Inland Waterways Commission recommended in 1908 that the American rivers, lakes, and canals be considered in relation to their role in water purification, power sources, flooding, and effect on the land. Congress then went on to create the National Waterways Commission to ensure this work continued under a single executive agency that would undertake developments with a multipurpose approach. With its role and function established in 1909, the National Waterways Commission produced a report in 1912 with the clear aim to promote waterborne trade.

The period leading up to the establishment of the Inland Waterways Commission had a significant influence on Roosevelt's domestic and foreign policy interests. A number of critical waterway events happened during this time. First, as governor of New York, Roosevelt appointed a commission to develop a state waterway policy. The outcome was that the declining Erie Canal would be replaced with another that would be toll-free, cope with much larger vessels, and take a similar route but link with Lake Oneida and the Mohawk River. Roosevelt had become president when the plan was approved in 1903.

The period after the Civil War had been something of a heyday for steamboats and towboats on American rivers, but they fell into decline with the advent of the railroad. For example, freight carrying on the Mississippi reached its peak in 1880 but succumbed to railroads, which could carry freight east and west and build rail to grain- and cotton-growing areas. The Civil War had prevented some planned lock enlargements, and by the time these projects resumed, trading patterns had changed.

At the end of the nineteenth century, however, Germany was looming as an international threat. The United States felt that control of any canal that had access to South America was critical and sought agreements to protect its interests there. Coincidentally, the Panama Canal opened just a few days after World War I began, and it, along with improvements to domestic rivers, led to considerable transhipments and trade.

The Illinois and Michigan Canal was opened in 1848, connecting the Great Lakes to the Mississippi River; it was largely replaced by the wider and shorter Chicago Sanitary and Ship Canal in 1900. Also, the seventy-seven–mile Illinois and Mississippi Canal, later called the Hennepin Canal, connected the Illinois River below LaSalle to Rock Island on the upper Mississippi starting in 1907. The growth of Chicago meant that further work was needed to cope with its sewage and water quality. The Ohio River had experienced an increase in traffic, and as railroad rates increased, some local businesspeople began their own transportation company. This soon failed because established railroads undercut their prices, but generally rising rail costs prompted more river activity and federal funds were used to improve river navigation. By 1907, the Ohio canalization was approved, allowing more cargo to travel the Mississippi. The Rivers and Harbors Bill of 1907 authorized an investigation into the possibility of a fourteen-foot channel from St. Louis, Missouri, to the Gulf of Mexico. By the time the Panama Canal was completed in 1914, government funding had built the south section of this channel to New Orleans, Louisiana, and the northern link to Chicago.

Unregulated railroad competition had dramatically reduced the use of waterborne shipping, and railroads were carrying freight that was better suited to water transport. Railroads and waterborne trade could complement each other, however. President Roosevelt believed that perishable foodstuffs and any expensive factory goods should travel by rail, while bulky cargo like coal and timber should be transported by water, a much cheaper option. This arrangement would increase the profits of the railroads, which in turn would reduce consumer prices, helping the nation's economy. Also, water transportation contributed significantly to the livelihoods of people in riverside towns. Roosevelt had an appreciation for the linking of different modes of transport as seen in Germany, which was believed to have an efficient economy.

Roosevelt had a personal experience on the water when he travelled by steamboat to Keokuk, Iowa, to give an address to a deep waterway convention. At that convention, he stated that there were now 12,000 miles of navigable river in the Mississippi River Valley but that these were underused for commercial trade. Roosevelt recognized the value of these natural highways for transportation; he also knew that adaptations were needed to make rivers efficient for this purpose. He felt that giving rivers sufficient width and depth to play this role in the national economy was the responsibility of the federal government. He viewed the work to date as having been piecemeal rather than strategic, but he believed that with sufficient planning, the rivers could supplement the railroads. Planning needed to encompass the combined interests of navigation, irrigation, flood prevention, and hydroelectric power development.

—Julia Fallon

See also: *Erie Canal; River Transportation; Rivers and Harbors Act of 1899*

BIBLIOGRAPHY

Hadfield, Charles. *World Canals: Inland Navigation Past and Present.* Newton Abbot, UK: David and Charles, 1986.

Pisani, Donald J. "Water Planning in the Progressive Era: The Inland Waterways Commission Reconsidered." *Journal of Policy History* 18, no. 4 (2006): 389–418.

International Boundary and Water Commission (United States and Mexico)

The International Boundary and Water Commission (IBWC), United States and Mexico, is the lead diplomatic and administrative agency managing boundary and water agreements in force between the two countries. Originally established as the International Boundary Commission in 1889, the current body is constituted under the authority of Article 2 of the landmark United States–Mexico Water Treaty, signed in 1944.

Commission Composition and Objectives

The IBWC is comprised of two national sections, each operating under the oversight of its respective foreign ministry. Reflecting the organization's mission, the headquarters of each section is located at the U.S.-Mexican border, with the U.S. section in El Paso, Texas, and the Mexican section in Ciudad Juárez, Chihuahua. Each section oversees field units located along the international boundary. Under Article 2 of the 1944 Treaty, each section of the Commission is comprised of an engineer-commissioner, two principal engineers, a secretary, and a legal advisor. The members of each national section enjoy diplomatic privileges in the territory of the other country.

The Treaty entrusts IBWC to oversee the boundary and water agreements to which both nations are party. The contemporary commission is also institutional partner and technical advisor for various binational environmental agreements, programs, and agencies adopted by the two countries. The boundary agreements in its charge include the formative Treaty of Guadalupe-Hidalgo, signed in 1848; the 1884 and 1889 Boundary Conventions; the Chamizal Convention of 1963; and the 1970 Boundary Convention. The principal water agreements are the 1906 Rio Grande Water Convention and the 1944 Water Treaty governing the allocation of treaty water on the Rio Grande and the Colorado Rivers, respectively. The Commission is authorized to interpret these agreements, and its decisions, recorded as minutes, are binding on each country once approved by their governments. As of June 2009, the IBWC had signed 314 minutes.

Accomplishments of the IBWC

Since 1944, the IBWC has earned an international reputation for technical competence and diplomatic achievement, brokering treaty-related agreements and assisting the foreign ministries in settling a number of critical disputes related to the treaty regime (Mumme and Moore 1999). Under the early leadership of U.S. commissioners Lawrence M. Lawson (1927–1954), Leland H. Hewitt (1954–1962), and Joseph F. Friedkin (1962–1986) and Mexican commissioners Rafael Hernandez MacGregor (1941–1947) and David Herrera Jordan (1947–1979), the IBWC oversaw the development of major reclamation works on the border rivers, including the Amistad, Falcon, and Anzalduas Dams on the Rio Grande River and the Morelos diversion dam on the Colorado River.

In 1961, an international dispute over the salinity of treaty water delivered to Mexico erupted when the United States began draining brackish water from a Yuma Valley irrigation district to the Colorado River. The dispute, which seriously tested the capacity of the IBWC to resolve differences arising from the 1944 Treaty, turned on conflicting national interpretations of the Treaty's Articles 3 and 10 bearing on the priority of treaty water uses and specific commitments regarding the acceptable sources of Colorado River water. With nationalistic sentiments aroused, the salinity crisis persisted for more than a decade, eventually reaching the presidential agenda in both countries. The IBWC is credited with brokering the eventual solution based on careful technical assessment of the impact of salinity on Mexican water uses and crafting an equitable solution based on salt parity of waters in the lower reach of the Colorado River (Ward 2003). These provisions are codified in the IBWC's Minute 242, signed in 1973.

The Commission has also been instrumental in crafting solutions to vexing boundary issues, most arising from the meandering of the Rio Grande River along its 1,200-mile boundary reach. The Commission notably devised a technical and diplomatic solution to a long-persisting territorial dispute at El Paso and Ciudad Juárez over the Chamizal area, a controversy dating to the 1860s that had defied all efforts to resolve the problem, including a failed arbitration in 1911. The 1963 agreement, based on partition of the disputed tract, channelization of the Rio Grande River through metropolitan El Paso and Ciudad Juárez, and compensation to aggrieved property owners, provided the political and diplomatic foundation for the negotiation of the 1970 Boundary Convention, which established procedures for the settlement of all future boundary disputes.

The IBWC also plays an important role in solving sanitation and water quality problems along the border. Pursuant to Article 3 of the 1944 Water Treaty, the IBWC operates international wastewater treatment plants along the boundary. The IBWC's Minute 261, signed in 1979, broadened its sanitation mandate to include transboundary water pollution. The IBWC partners with U.S. and Mexican environmental authorities, as well as state and local and tribal governments, in addressing sanitation and pollution problems at the international boundary. The 1983 U.S.-Mexico Border Environmental Cooperation Agreement (known as the La Paz Agreement) recognizes the IBWC as the lead agency for binational dealings on transboundary water pollution problems. Since 1994, the IBWC has also been a technical advisor to the Border Environment Cooperation Commission.

While the IBWC is known as a technically oriented agency that oversees the allocation of treaty water, manages international dams, and maintains the international boundary, it has an active diplomatic agenda. Since 2000, it has grappled with a number of difficult international water and boundary issues, including a dispute over Mexico's provision of Rio Grande River treaty water, a groundwater dispute over U.S. lining of the All-American Canal in California's Imperial Valley, conservation of the endangered Colorado River Delta, and border security impacts on the international boundary. Water's importance for a rapidly growing border population at a time of persistent drought and growing concern with the regional impact of climate change ensures an active agenda for the IBWC in the twenty-first century.

—Stephen P. Mumme

See also: *United States–Mexico Transboundary Aquifer Assessment Act of 2006; United States–Mexico Water Treaty (1944)*

BIBLIOGRAPHY

Mumme, Stephen P. "Innovation and Reform in Transboundary Resources Management: A Critical Look at the International Boundary and Water Commission, United States and Mexico." *Natural Resources Journal* 33, no. 1 (1993): 93–120. Available at http://lawlibrary.unm.edu/nrj/33/1/08_mumme_transboundary.pdf.

Mumme, Stephen P., and Scott T. Moore. "Agency Autonomy in Transboundary Resource Management: The United States Section of the International Boundary and Water Commission, United States and Mexico." *Natural Resources Journal* 30 (1990): 661–84. Available at http://lawlibrary.unm.edu/nrj/30/3/11_mumme_agency.pdf.

Mumme, Stephen P., and Scott T. Moore. "Innovation Prospects in U.S.-Mexico Border Water Management: The IBWC and the BECC in Theoretical Perspective." *Environment and Planning C: Government and Policy* 17, no. 6 (1999): 753–72.

Ward, Evan R. *Border Oasis: Water and the Political Ecology of the Colorado River Delta, 1940–1975*. Tucson: University of Arizona Press, 2003.

International Joint Commission (United States and Canada)

The International Joint Commission (IJC) was created in 1909 when the United States and Canada, the latter under the authority of the British government, entered into the Boundary Waters Treaty of 1909. The IJC was the first bilateral institution created by the United States and Canada (Holsti and Levy 1974). It consists of six members, with the president of the United States appointing three and the prime minister of Canada appointing three. Prior to Canadian independence from Great Britain, the governor of Canada appointed the Canadian members. Each nation's delegation elects a chairperson and a secretary. The national chairperson serves as the chair when the IJC meeting is in his or her country; meetings alternate between the United States and Canada. The IJC has created twenty-seven water boards, which are comprised of an equal number of representatives from both countries. The IJC is charged with managing the transboundary freshwater shared by the United States and Canada in eight river basins and the Great Lakes (Dombrowsky 2008). The treaty identifies transboundary water as any water that serves as the border between the two nations, dissects the border between the two nations, or is a tributary flowing from waterways that constitute the border of the two nations.

Formation of the IJC

The Boundary Waters Treaty of 1909 came about because of two separate disputes. The first dispute centered on the water level of Lake Erie and the flow of the Niagara River. The second dispute dealt with the distribution of water from the Saint Mary and Milk Rivers. In the Boundary Waters Treaty, the United States and Canada agreed not to divert water from Lake Erie and the Niagara River to maintain the current level of Lake Erie and evenly divide the waters of the Saint Mary and Milk Rivers. The treaty went beyond resolving these disputes and created the IJC to resolve future disputes over the allocation of freshwater resources shared by the United States and Canada. In 1925, the Lake of the Woods Treaty expanded the IJC's jurisdiction to include the Lake of the Woods, which was entirely in Canadian territory and therefore not subject to the Boundary Waters Treaty. The Great Lakes Water Quality Agreements expanded the scope of the IJC from focusing entirely on distribution of water to include pollution and water quality in the Great Lakes (Heinmiller 2007).

Powers

The International Joint Commission has a variety of powers delegated to it by the Boundary Waters Treaty (MacKay 1928). The commission has the executive power to administer the agreements in Article V over Lake Erie and the Niagara River and Article VI, which covers the Saint Mary and Milk Rivers. The IJC also has the power to adjudicate any dispute involving shared freshwater resources between the United States and Canada. Either nation can bring a dispute to the IJC for resolution.

Over time, the IJC has developed appellate jurisdiction by ruling on decisions of the various water boards that it has created. Water boards were first created because of a dispute over the development of the Saint Mary River. Both the United States and Canada sought to develop hydroelectric facilities on the river simultaneously. The IJC approved both projects; however, there was a need to coordinate their development. The United States and Canada agreed to create a water board with one engineer from each country to coordinate the projects, with the IJC being authorized to resolve deadlocks on the water board. After the IJC created the Saint Mary River Water Board, it frequently used boards to manage water development projects. For example, it created the International Saint Lawrence Board of Control to oversee the development of hydroelectric plants on the Saint Lawrence Seaway. Upon completion of the plants, the board remained in place to monitor the operations and guarantee that the project conformed to the orders of the IJC (Kenworthy 1960). The boards are typically dominated by engineers and scientists and do not tend to be very political.

Another major power of the IJC is the power to investigate. Both nations must request that the IJC investigate a water issue. The commission has typically used its investigatory power to explore the feasibility of hydroelectric development projects.

Success of the IJC

The International Joint Commission is one of the most successful international water management organizations in the world for a variety of reasons. The first is that although each nation appoints three representatives to the commission, the commissioners are expected to represent the legal requirements of the Boundary Waters Treaty rather than the commissioners' national interests. Thus, the commission makes rulings based on scientific data and expert analysis rather than political considerations.

The second reason for its success is that the organization almost always reaches consensus in its rulings. The fact that the decisions of the IJC are typically unanimous increases the political weight of the decisions and pressures the two nations to comply.

Finally, the United States and Canada typically filter issues before they submit them to the IJC. The two countries informally propose projects to one another before forwarding them to the IJC. This removes the political element from the IJC and allows the commission to focus on the legal aspects of the proposal. Of the twelve requests to divert water that the nations submitted to the IJC since 1909, all were either accepted or withdrawn because of an alternative project (Heinmiller 2007). Overall, the International Joint Commission serves as the model international organization for managing shared water resources between nations.

—Thomas E. Sowers II

See also: *Great Lakes Charter (1985); Great Lakes Legacy Act of 2002; Saint Lawrence Seaway*

BIBLIOGRAPHY

Dombrowsky, Ines. "Integration in the Management of International Waters: Economic Perspectives on a Global Policy Discourse." *Global Governance* 14, no. 4 (2008): 455–77.

Heinmiller, B. Timothy. "Do Intergovernmental Institutions Matter? The Case of Water Diversion Regulation in the Great Lake Basin." *Governance* 20, no. 4 (2007): 655–74.

Holsti, Kal J., and Thomas Allen Levy. "Bilateral Institutions and Transgovernmental Relations Between Canada and the United States." *International Organization* 28, no. 4 (1974): 875–901.

Kenworthy, William E. "Joint Development of International Waters." *The American Journal of International Law* 54, no. 3 (1960): 592–602.

MacKay, Robert A. "The International Joint Commission between the United States and Canada." *The American Journal of International Law* 22, no. 2 (1928): 292–318.

Irwin v. Phillips (California, 1855)

The 1848 discovery of gold at Sutter's Mill in California proved to be a massive stimulus for migration, drawing approximately 300,000 people to the American West. Many of these migrants arrived with the intention of establishing their own gold-mining ventures, and an informal system of local governance soon developed to regulate these early miners. Through the formation of local mining districts and committees, and without the intervention of formal legislation, rules were established and institutions were created to enforce these standards.

One important form of regulation that these early mining districts provided was the management of water, an important resource for miners. From the small-scale miner who panned for gold in local rivers to the large-scale enterprises that relied on complex constructions, miners in the mid-nineteenth century required water to help separate valuable gold from the gravel and sand surrounding it. As the local population increased, however, these early systems of local governance became increasingly unable to manage demands for resources. Such was the case in 1855, when the case of *Irwin v. Phillips* was brought to the California Supreme Court, where it was heard by Justice Solomon Heydenfeldt.

Case Background

This case became significant for its role in establishing the doctrine of prior appropriation of water as a leading principle for allocating water resources in the American West, a region where water has often been in short supply. It also played a role in establishing formal legal priorities regarding the usage of water resources in California and other western states. The case was fought between Matthew Irwin and Robert Phillips. In 1851, Irwin began diverting the south fork of Poor Man's Creek, a stream located on federal land, in order to create a canal. In addition to using this canal to mine his own claim of land, Irwin sold access to this canal to miners in Eureka, California. In 1852, Irwin had also created a dam, which he used to increase the supply of water in the canal.

Phillips, along with his partners in the mining operation Bradie and Company, began using the stream after Irwin had already established his canal and dam. Phillips and his partners found that their downstream location failed to provide them with a sufficient flow of water for their mining operation. They also found that Irwin's dam flooded part of the land they could claim for mining, which would have been available if the south fork of Poor Man's Creek had been left in its natural state. Phillips began cutting through Irwin's dam in an attempt to redivert the stream to its original course and increase the water flow at his location downstream.

Irwin took Phillips to a local mining committee court for trespassing. Although these committees traditionally supported established prior claims to waterways such as Irwin's, the case was decided in favor of Phillips, ruling that, while Irwin was diverting the waterway for primarily sale to others, Phillips intended to use it for his own purposes. In this decision, the mining committee placed a priority on the water rights of miners over the water rights of those who sought to sell access to water. Irwin appealed for a jury trial in a state court, which reversed the mining committee's decision and sided with Irwin, based on his prior appropriation of the stream. Phillips then appealed the case to the California Supreme Court.

Phillips's argument for appeal rested on the principles of English common law, which had become the basis for rulings on riparian and other rights elsewhere in the United States. According to English common law concepts of riparian rights, Irwin was violating a principle that prevented individuals from diverting a waterway from its natural course, as all persons who held property along a waterway were entitled to equal shares of the water based on reasonable use. According to this argument, Irwin's diversion of the stream infringed upon the rights of Phillips and others to their fair share of the waterway in its natural state.

In turn, Irwin argued that the distribution of resources in California mandated a new approach to water rights, one that allowed the first person who became established along a waterway to claim as much of that resource as was desired, without consideration of the needs of future settlers along that waterway. It was Irwin's contention that English common law principles of equal reasonable use were a poor fit for environmental conditions in California, which was rich in mineral reserves but lacking in water resources. While there were enough water resources in the eastern United States to support reasonable and equal use, Irwin reasoned, to enforce similar standards in California would leave all potential consumers of water resources with inadequate supplies. According to this reasoning, the best way to ensure that state waterways remained productive was to allow persons to utilize available water resources to whatever extent was needed, based upon earliest claims to the waterway, without regard to future reliance on that water source.

The Decision

Ultimately, the California Supreme Court sided with Irwin and allowed him to continue diverting the stream to furnish his mining operation. While the court acknowledged that this decision broke with English common law approaches to water rights, and with prior rulings elsewhere in the United States, the court was swayed by Irwin's argument for special consideration of environmental conditions. In doing so, the court declared that California's approach to water rights must take into consideration the conditions faced by miners, as well as others whose industry relied on water resources.

This ruling set the foundation for later courts to require future settlers to take land and waterways in the condition they were found and bar them from undermining the established rights of prior settlers, regardless of their effect on the available water supply at the time of settlement. While the ruling served to uphold traditional local mining customs in this respect, it undermined local practices of prioritizing water use for mining over other usage, such as selling access, providing support for later development of nonmining economic activity. As a broader effect, the case assisted later courts in breaking with traditional notions of riparian rights to adapt the law in accordance with regional environmental concerns, a contribution that would become increasingly important in the western United States as it became more settled and developed over the course of the later nineteenth and early twentieth centuries.

—Skylar Harris

See also: *Dam Building; Mining and Water Resources; Recreational Water Rights*

BIBLIOGRAPHY

Hall, Kermit L., William M. Wiecek, and Paul Finkelman. *American Legal History: Cases and Materials.* 2nd ed. New York: Oxford University Press, 1996.

Kanazawa, Mark T. "Efficiency in Western Water Law: The Development of the California Doctrine, 1850–1911." *Journal of Legal Studies* 27, no. 1 (1998): 159–85.

Littlefield, Douglas R. "Water Rights during the California Gold Rush: Conflicts Over Economic Points of View." *Western Historical Quarterly* 14, no. 4 (1983): 415–34.

Kansas v. Colorado (1907)

This case involved a dispute between the states of Kansas and Colorado regarding water rights to the Arkansas River. Kansas brought the suit, asking the U.S. Supreme Court to enjoin the state of Colorado and several corporations within the state from disturbing the "natural and customary flow" of the Arkansas River through Kansas and its territory. The United States intervened, claiming the right to regulate the flow of the river in the interest of reclaiming arid land.

Justice Brewer summarized the argument of the United States as claiming that "all legislative power must be vested in either the state or the National Government; no legislative powers belong to a state government other than those which affect solely the internal affairs of that State; consequently all powers which are national in their scope must be found vested in the Congress of the United States." In addressing the position of the United States, Brewer made two arguments. First he found that the U.S. government is one of the enumerated powers laid out in the constitution and that acceptance of the position taken by the United States would undermine the principle of enumerated powers. Second, he argued that the government's position would contravene the meaning of the Tenth Amendment's provision reserving to the states and to the people powers not granted to the United States nor prohibited to the states.

Brewer held that while the United States may regulate the flow of waters within territories, it cannot regulate their flow with the boundaries of a state except to improve their navigability. Since the United States did not claim a need to protect or improve the navigability of the Arkansas River, the Court dismissed its suit.

Arguments

At the time, Kansas employed the doctrine of riparian rights, which holds that each owner of land adjacent to a waterway has the right to reasonable use of the water. The right is linked to the ownership of the land, and water in short supply is typically apportioned on the basis of the frontage of the property on the waterway. The doctrine requires that the right to the use of water must be apportioned equitably among the landowners. This common law doctrine is distinguished from the doctrine of prior appropriation, which holds that the first person to divert water to beneficial use can continue to use the water as long as the beneficial use continues. Colorado, on the other hand, like most western states where water is scarce, applied the doctrine of prior appropriation.

Attorneys for Kansas argued, in part, that Kansas entered the union before Colorado, suggesting that the doctrine of prior appropriation might be applied in the case. They further argued that after considerable development in Kansas that relied on the Arkansas River, the state of Colorado began to appropriate water, resulting in immeasurable losses to the state of Kansas and its citizens.

Colorado argued that the Arkansas River is actually two rivers, the Colorado Arkansas and the Kansas Arkansas. The state based its claim on the fact the river dries up along some of its stretch in Arkansas during certain times of the year. Indicating that the Colorado Arkansas is completely within state boundaries, Colorado claimed the right to regulate the flow of the river.

Addressing the suit, the Court noted that "in a qualified sense and to a limited extent, the separate states are sovereign and independent" and that, consequently, the Court would need to sit as an international law tribunal in order to adjudicate the case.

Noting that Kansas brought the case to the Court, Justice Brewer argued that it would be appropriate to employ the riparian rights doctrine and to treat Colorado and Kansas like landowners along a waterway. In that case, the right of Kansas to an injunction would depend upon a finding that the current division of water usage between the two states was inequitable and favored Colorado.

Findings

The Court found that Colorado's use of water from the Arkansas River did affect the flow into Kansas, but it added that "the detriment to Kansas by the diminution of the flow of the water, while substantial, is not so great as to make the appropriation of the part of the water by Colorado an inequitable apportionment between the two states." Based upon this finding, the Court dismissed the case without prejudice, pointing out that the current evidence did not support a claim of inequitable distribution but that if such a condition should arise, Kansas could refile its petition. The holding in this case became the basis for the Supreme Court's doctrine of "equitable apportionment" of interstate waters.

One important outcome of this case is that Colorado must share with other states water that arises largely within the state, in particular from the rain and snow within the Colorado Rocky Mountains. As Cronin and Loevy note, Colorado took measures to avoid permitting the Court to be the final arbiter of water usage in the region by entering into compacts with other states. The compacts had provisions that required states not making beneficial use of their allocations to reduce those allocations, an agreement similar to the prior appropriation doctrine but beginning with an initial agreement concerning the allocation of water (Cronin and Loevy 1993).

The Court appeared to limit the authority of the United States severely by emphasizing that its right to regulate waterways was entirely limited to the improvement of navigation. However, only one year later, in the *Winters v. United States* (1908) decision, the Court recognized the reserved water rights of the U.S. government on Indian reservations and other federal lands and laid the framework for more extensive federal control.

—Jerry Murtagh

See also: *Prior Appropriation; Riparian Rights;* Winters v. United States *(1908)*

BIBLIOGRAPHY

Cronin, Thomas E., and Robert D. Loevy. *Colorado Politics and Government: Governing the Centennial State.* Lincoln: University of Nebraska Press, 1993.

Hughes, Charles Evans. *The Supreme Court of the United States: Its Foundation, Methods, and Achievements: An Interpretation.* New York: Columbia University Press, 1928.

Kansas v. Colorado, 206 U.S. 46 (1907).

Olson, James Stuart, Mark Baxter, Jason M. Tetzloff, and Darren Pierson, eds. *Encyclopedia of American Indian Civil Rights.* Westport, CT: Greenwood Press, 1997.

Shurts, John. *Indian Reserved Water Rights: The Winters Doctrine in its Social and Legal Context, 1880s–1930s.* Norman: University of Oklahoma Press, 2003.

Winters v. United States, 207 U.S. 564 (1908).

Lower Colorado River Basin Project Bill (1965)

Three years after Arizona won its Supreme Court case against California (*Arizona v. California,* 1963), Arizona lawmakers put forward the Lower Colorado River Basin Project Bill to authorize the construction of the Central Arizona Project (CAP) aqueduct and pumping stations. This project, long in the planning, would enable Arizona to use its share of Colorado River water for the first time and send it to the center of its desert. The bill also called for region-wide water planning and funding, river augmentation studies, and, most controversially, the building of two dams in the Grand Canyon to generate electricity to help pay for lower basin projects. Although this bill was never passed, it became the basis of the successful Colorado River Basin Project Act of 1968.

Early Attempts at Legislation

Twice before in the early 1950s, Senator Carl Hayden (D-AZ) put forward bills for the Central Arizona Project, or CAP, but they were not passed. After Arizona won its Supreme Court case against California, Hayden once again drafted a bill he thought would finally receive the support needed for passage. However, such a bill would have to pass through the House Interior Committee, chaired by Rep Wayne Aspinall (D-CO). Although Aspinall had generally been favorable to Arizona plans for CAP, he had developed concerns about how much water was actually available in the river for the implementation of the plan. There were good reasons for this concern, as many researchers had long suggested that the river was already overallocated. To address these questions, Aspinall asked Interior Secretary Stewart Udall for an assessment of Colorado River water flows and the feasibility of the plan for CAP. In 1963, just as it became clear that Arizona was going to win its court case against California, Udall replied with a comprehensive plan he called the Pacific Southwest Water Plan. Udall argued that there was plenty of water in the river for CAP and outlined a plan for building two dams that would generate enough electricity to pay for it and other projects. Although this bill was never seriously considered, it became the basis for the Lower Colorado River Basin Project Bill.

Bill Provisions

The two dams that Secretary Udall suggested should be built would be in the Grand Canyon. One would be a "tall" dam at the top of the canyon at Marble Canyon, and the other would be a short dam at the other end in Bridge Canyon. The idea to dam parts of the Grand Canyon was not a new one, and in fact, many western water planners believed at least one of the two dams would inevitably be built. They carefully argued that neither dam would inundate any part of the Grand Canyon National Park and would only increase the beauty of the region. These two dams were never designed to store water but merely to

generate hydroelectricity; some called them "cash registers" to fund other projects.

In addition to the plans for the canyon dams, Hayden's proposed bill gave an enormous gift to California that in many ways overturned Arizona's gains from the Supreme Court case. Hayden was more interested in obtaining funding and approval for CAP than anything else, so he inserted into the bill a provision that if there should be a future water shortage, the burden would fall upon CAP. Water from CAP would be used to supplement shortfalls other states might experience, especially California. Although some thought Hayden was selling Arizona out, Hayden thought it a small price to pay for passage of the bill. He was correct; this provision did help him gain California's support for the bill.

The other major portion of the bill called for vigorous examination of ways to augment the flow of the Colorado, specifically from the Columbia River. Although Aspinall delayed hearings on the bill, opposition from Senator Henry Jackson (D-WA) meant this portion of the bill would not be approved. Washington State and other northwestern states were adamantly opposed to long-discussed plans to augment the Colorado River with the Columbia. Eventually, Aspinall recommended the removal of this aspect of the bill. However, without augmentation, Aspinall remained convinced that CAP would only be possible by using water allocated to, but not yet used by, the upper basin states. He called for water flow and usage reports from each of the governors of Colorado River Basin states and held up debate on Hayden's bill for many months.

Finally, Aspinall decided on a plan that he thought would solve his problem with CAP. He continued to fear that building CAP would take water away from the upper basin, but he also knew that he needed Arizona to support some of his plans for Colorado. So he created a revised plan, dropped the word *Lower* from the bill, and put forward the Colorado River Basin Project. In the revised bill, Aspinall retained all the previous bill's provisions for CAP, and he added five Colorado water projects. He argued that these projects would now give something to everyone and would increase support in Congress. Rep. Morris Udall (D-AZ) and others argued that Aspinall was "blackmailing" Arizona with his Colorado projects. They were all, in fact, within Aspinall's district, and none had the approval or support of the Bureau of Reclamation. The Bureau did eventually create new financial studies to help Aspinall's projects pass muster in Congress because it favored a bill authorizing CAP.

The Lower Colorado River Basin Project was a new bill by the time it was seriously discussed in Congress. By 1967, vigorous opposition to any Grand Canyon dams from the Sierra Club and the general public forced Aspinall to remove any such plans from the bill. In early 1968, this change was made as well as a ban on any river augmentation plans to tap another river for ten years. The Lower Colorado River Basin Project bill started out as a plan for the lower basin but would end up as the basis for the more comprehensive 1968 Act, the last major piece of legislation diverting Colorado River water.

—April Summitt

See also: *Central Arizona Project; Colorado River Basin Act of 1968*

BIBLIOGRAPHY

August, Jack L., Jr. *Vision in the Desert: Carl Hayden and Hydropolitics in the American Southwest.* Fort Worth: Texas Christian University Press, 1999.

Schulte, Steven C. *Wayne Aspinall and the Shaping of the American West.* Boulder: University Press of Colorado, 2002.

Sturgeon, Stephen C. *The Politics of Western Water: The Congressional Career of Wayne Aspinall.* Tucson: University of Arizona Press, 2002.

Lower Snake River Compensation Plan

The Lower Snake River Compensation Plan (LSRCP) is a program, authorized as part of the Water Resource Development Act of 1976 (90 Stat. 2917, Pub. L. 94-587), to compensate for fish and wildlife losses caused by four dam projects on the lower Snake River in Washington and Idaho. The program is established and growing, as thirty-four years after its passage, the U.S. Army Corps of Engineers listed twenty-three fish hatcheries. Of these, the U.S. Fish and Wildlife Service (FWS) operates three, and nine are federally owned but operated by the states of Idaho, Oregon, and Washington in the Snake, Salmon, and Clearwater rivers watersheds. The FWS owns or operates twenty-one hatcheries throughout the Columbia River Basin; the Snake River flows into the Columbia south of Pasco, Washington.

Congressional action was in part a response to a special report submitted May 30, 1975, by Colonel Nelson P. Conover, Walla Walla District Engineer, and Colonel Edwin S. Townsley, Division Engineer, North Pacific, Army Corps of Engineers. Conover wrote that the Lower Snake River Project had been authorized by Congress on March 2, 1945, without any mention of fish or wildlife measures. The project resulted in construction of the Ice Harbor, Lower Monumental, and Little Goose dams and the Lower Granite Locks and Dam, completed between 1962 and 1978. The primary purpose was to provide for slack-water navigation of the dams; the secondary purpose was to generate electric power.

Facilities to assist fish in passing up- and downstream had been incorporated into the dams, but studies showed a decrease in fish and wildlife populations, including spring/summer chinook salmon, fall chinook, coho salmon, steelhead, rainbow trout, westslope cutthroat trout, bull trout, sturgeon, deer, waterfowl, pheasant, quail, and chukar partridge. The Fish and Wildlife Coordination Act (PL 85-624) enacted August 12, 1958, provided direction to the Corps of Engineers to recommend compensation measures, which in turn would require appropriations by Congress.

Dams, Fish, and Game

Additional dams had been built since 1958, including Hells Canyon Dam on the Snake River (completed in 1967); the nearby Oxbow Dam (1961) and Brownlee Dam (1959); and the Dworshak Dam, constructed 1969–1973 on the North Fork Clearwater River, at one time one of the most productive rivers in the Columbia River Basin for spring chinook and steelhead. Native salmon populations in the Clearwater River Basin had already been extirpated by the Lewiston Dam, built in 1927 by Island Power and Light Company near Lewiston, Idaho. The Lewiston Dam was removed in 1973 as part of the Lower Granite Project to make Lewiston an inland seaport. Coho salmon were declared extinct from the Snake River in 1986, although efforts have been made to reintroduce stocks from the lower Columbia River. Reintroduction of coho salmon into the Clearwater River was initiated by the Nez Perce Tribe in 1995.

The plan authorized by Congress initially provided for three hatcheries with facilities to trap and hold 2,290 to 3,390 adult female chinook salmon or steelhead trout, producing between 101,800 to 1.4 million pounds of smolts and returning 18,300 to 55,100 adults to each project area. Appropriations were made to the Corps of Engineers to acquire the land and build the facilities, which would be operated by the Fish and Wildlife Service (FWS) or the National Marine Fisheries Service. A separate hatchery would produce 93,000 pounds of trout annually to stock local streams.

Within a period of 10 years, 750 acres of land were to be acquired to replace some of the sport fishery lands in the project area. The land would be owned by the States of Washington and Idaho, with the costs reimbursed by the Corps of Engineers. To compensate for loss of upland game bird habitat, 400 acres of riparian land would be purchased and a perpetual easement purchased on another 8,000 acres of farmland, subject to wildlife management plans. In the canyons along the Snake River, the Corps would acquire 15,000 acres of land in perpetual easement to compensate for losses of chukar partridge habitat, with 50 small select parcels acquired throughout this land to construct bird-watering devices. An estimated 20,000 game birds would be stocked by the Washington Department of Game a year for a 20-year period.

Congress didn't actually allocate any money for the plan until 1978. By 1983, fish hatcheries had been built, or sites identified and construction begun, at McCall, Idaho; Crystal Springs near Buhl, Idaho; and Sawtooth near Stanley, Idaho, and on upper tributaries of the Clearwater River in Idaho. Also, the existing Hagerman National Fish Hatchery in Bliss, Idaho, and the Dworshak National Fish Hatchery at Ahsahka, Idaho, had been expanded.

Modification and Review

In 1986, the plan was modified by the Water Resources Development Act of 1986 (Pub. L. 99-662, 100 Stat. 4082) and retitled the Lower Snake River Fish and Wildlife Compensation Plan. Authorization in the original bill for payment to the State of Washington to maintain a game bird farm was modified to emphasize natural game bird production. By 2009, the intended 8,400 acres of game land had been acquired and nearly all of the 15,000 acres for chukar habitat. These lands are scattered among nearly fifty different sites in the plan area. Total federal expenditures as of 2006 were just over $237 million.

In the early twenty-first century, FWS review teams advocated moving from specific compensation measures for specific projects to "a holistic and integrated strategy that combines habitat, hydropower and harvest needs for conserving and managing fishery resources" (FWS 2006, iii). This will require balancing short- and long-term goals, hatchery-propagated and naturally spawning populations, and conservation and harvest, as well as investigating genetic and ecological interactions between fish from hatcheries and those hatched in the wild.

Some critics consider the entire "compensation" approach to be flawed. Fisheries biologist James Lichatowich wrote in

1999 that although LSRCP "generally makes use of the latest information and is implemented with a high degree of professionalism," it has "like the other efforts begun during the optimistic 1970s, fallen far short of its goals" (215). An ironic highlight appeared in published proceedings of a 1998 public review, which suggested that the hatcheries, built to compensate for the impact of the dams, could only restore fish population if the dams were removed. Lichatowich also points out, however, that salmon depletion is the consequence of hundreds of stresses over more than a century, including the previously unrecognized problem of diminished ocean productivity.

—Charles Rosenberg

See also: *Columbia Basin Project; Dam Building; Fish and Wildlife Service, United States; Intermountain West; Snake River Basin*

BIBLIOGRAPHY

FWS (U.S. Fish and Wildlife Service). *Columbia River Basin, Columbia Plateau Province, Deschutes River Watershed: Assessments and Recommendations, Final Report.* Portland, OR: FWS, 2006. Available at http://www.fws.gov/pacific/fisheries/hatcheryreview/Reports/warmsprings/WarmSpringsReviewFinalReport_004.pdf.

FWS (U.S. Fish and Wildlife Service). *Idaho Lower Snake River Compensation Plan, State Operated Facilities: Assessments and Recommendations, Draft Report.* Portland, OR: FWS, 2009. Available at http://www.fws.gov/Pacific/fisheries/Hatcheryreview/Reports/snakeriver/IdahoLSRCPReviewDraftReport_24Apr2009_Public.pdf.

FWS (U.S. Fish and Wildlife Service). *Oregon Lower Snake River Compensation Plan, State Operated Hatcheries: Assessments and Recommendations. Draft Report.* Portland, OR: FWS, 2009. Available at http://www.fws.gov/Pacific/fisheries/Hatcheryreview/Reports/snakeriver/OregonLSRCPReview_4December2009_DraftReport.pdf.

FWS (U.S. Fish and Wildlife Service). *Washington Lower Snake River Compensation Plan, State Operated Hatcheries: Assessments and Recommendations, Draft Report.* Portland, OR: FWS, 2009. Available at http://www.fws.gov/Pacific/fisheries/Hatcheryreview/Reports/snakeriver/WashingtonLSRCPReviewDraft%20Report_25September2009_Public.pdf.

Lichatowich, James A. *Salmon Without Rivers: A History of the Pacific Salmon Crisis.* Washington, DC: Island Press, 1999.

Peterson, Keith. *River of Life, Channel of Death: Fish and Dams on the Lower Snake.* Lewiston, ID: Confluence Press, 1995.

U.S. Army Corps of Engineers, Walla Walla District. *Special Report for Congress: Lower Snake River Fish and Wildlife Compensation Plan.* Walla Walla, WA: U.S. Army Corps of Engineers, 1983. Available at http://www.fws.gov/lsnakecomplan/Reports/LSRCPreports.html.

U.S. Army Corps of Engineers, Walla Walla District. *Special Report: Lower Snake River Fish and Wildlife Compensation Plan.* Walla Walla, WA: U.S. Army Engineer District, 1975. Available at http://www.fws.gov/lsnakecomplan/Reports/LSRCPreports.html.

Williams, Richard Nicholas, ed. *Return to the River: Restoring Salmon to the Columbia River.* Boston: Elsevier Academic Press, 2006.

Lux v. Haggin (California, 1886)

In 1886, the case of *Lux v. Haggin* became one of the most controversial legal struggles to confront the California Supreme Court since its establishment in 1849. The question that the case sought to resolve pitted proponents of riparian rights against supporters of prior appropriation, and the court sought to reconcile English common law practices with the arid conditions of the American West.

The case began when Charles Lux, Henry Miller, and other minor plaintiffs filed a suit against James Ben Ali Haggin, Lloyd Tevis, and William Carr. Lux and Miller owned the Lux-Miller Cattle Company, as well as considerable amounts of land throughout California, Oregon, and Nevada. The defendants in the case were similarly wealthy and politically well connected. Haggin and Carr had both made financial and political fortunes with the Southern Pacific Railroad Company and all were heavily invested in land, mining, and various financial ventures throughout the West.

The Dispute

The plaintiffs and defendants were in a dispute over rival claims to the Kern River, which ran through the California's Central Valley before draining into swamplands and the shallow Buena Vista Lake. Following an 1850s venture to develop these swamplands, which failed in the 1860s, Lux and Miller, along with a number of other, smaller cattle ranchers, purchased this land from the federal government. In 1872, Lux and Miller purchased 40,000 of the 90,000 acres available for sale. In 1876, Lux and Miller finalized the claims to their land and began draining the swamplands and installing the irrigation canals needed to raise livestock.

Two years before, in 1874, Haggin, Tevis, and Carr had purchased thousands of acres of land upstream from Lux and Miller's holdings. Haggin's new holdings, the largest of the three, contained a number of minor irrigation channels previously used by small farmers. Haggin planned to expand and extend these irrigation channels before subdividing his holdings. This earned him significant support from local developers, who saw it as an opportunity for economic growth and agricultural expansion. Haggin's actions incited criticism, however, when the region began to suffer from drought. Local farmers and ranchers working south of Haggin blamed the recently constructed irrigation canal for exacerbating drought conditions, arguing that it was diverting water that would have normally reached their lands, even during dry spells. Following unsuccessful negotiations, seventy-eight suits were filed against Haggin and other landholders, requesting that the full use of the Kern River be restored to landholders downstream in accordance with their legal rights.

The Trial and Decision

During the ensuing trial, Haggin et al. countered that the largest landholders, Miller and Lux, were not, in fact, riparian owners. The defendants argued that the plaintiffs' location in the swamplands lacked the banks and steady flow of water that defined a waterway; the plaintiffs were, as a result, not entitled to the rights that came with their title. More important to the case's historical and legal relevance, however, was the defendants' argument against the use of riparianism in California law. The defendants argued that riparian rights, the basis for the plaintiffs' suits, were established as common law in the water-rich regions of England and the American Northeast, but were a poor fit with California's comparatively arid environment. In the interest of the common good and the overall development of the state, they contended, water rights should be based on a doctrine of prior appropriation. According to this reasoning, as Haggin et al. had begun appropriating water before Lux and Miller, their use of the river was justified by prior appropriation.

This latter argument would make *Lux v. Haggin* especially significant for establishing California's formal doctrine for water use. In 1850, the legislature of California had voted to base water law on English common law, as had most state legislatures. This approach, known as riparian doctrine, declared that waterways were an intrinsic part of land and property that could not be legally altered and that all property holders along a waterway had a right to reasonable and equal use of that resource. However, since 1850, the actual practices of California's industries had done much to erode and challenge this decision. For example, miners frequently redirected water away from streams and rivers to supply mining claims with necessary water. Frequently, this water was diverted from federally owned lands, and the government made no effort to enforce its right to these waters.

As a result, many judges that were confronted with cases involving rival claims to water chose not to rely on the riparian principles adopted in 1850 but instead to rely on the same principles they used for land-based property disputes, which established an approach to water rights that emphasized the principle of first use or prior appropriation.

This principle held that the first to begin using a waterway was allowed to claim what usage was appropriate, regardless of the desires or interests of potential future settlers along that waterway.

Lux v. Haggin forced the California Supreme Court to choose between these two approaches to the issue of water rights. The county judge who first heard the case favored prior appropriation, arguing that Haggin's actions had addressed a natural need and had provided a benefit to the community by transforming unusable land into productive properties. The court added that California's local customs and public opinion favored a first-use approach to water rights. Miller and Lux then appealed to the state supreme court. In 1884, three members of the California Supreme Court argued that past decisions in favor of prior appropriation had nullified the 1850 ruling and agreed that common-law riparian doctrine was a poor fit with California's climate. The four-member majority, however, disagreed with both arguments, but they agreed to hold a new hearing in acknowledgment of the rising controversy surrounding the case. The new hearing resulted in no change, and in 1886, the California Supreme Court ordered a new trial.

Following this ruling, Haggin and Carr organized and funded an existing faction mobilizing public protest and political pressure, but they were unable to persuade the governor to overturn the ruling or remove the four justices who supported it. However, in recognition of this dissent, the 1887 Wright Act was adopted, which provided publicly favored irrigation districts like Haggin's with the power to employ eminent domain. The legislature also made the symbolic gesture of rescinding portions of the water code that recognized riparian rights, a move that did not change the recognition of riparian rights as being vested under the common law.

Before the new court-ordered trial could begin, *Lux v. Haggin* was settled out of court. In 1888, Miller and Haggin signed a contract that apportioned the Kern River between the plaintiffs and defendants. Both sides of the legal battle went on to continue investing in California properties. Miller, in particular, benefited from the *Lux v. Haggin* ruling, as he used the case repeatedly in the following years to sue successfully against infringements upon his claims to waterways on properties elsewhere in the state, further embedding riparian doctrine over prior appropriation rights into California law.

—Skylar Harris

See also: *Prior Appropriation; Riparian Rights; Water Law*

BIBLIOGRAPHY

Bakkin, Gordon Morris. "A Law for Water in the West." In *American Legal History: Cases and Materials,* 2nd ed., edited by Kermit Hall, William M. Wiecek, and Paul Finkelman. New York: Oxford University Press, 1996.

Charles Lux et al., Appellants, v. James B. Haggin et al. The Kern River Land and Canal Company, Respondent, 69 Cal. 255, 10 P. 674 (1886).

Freyfogle, Eric T. "*Lux v. Haggin* and the Common Law Burdens of Modern Water Law." *University of Colorado Law Review* 57 (1986): 485–525.

Hundley, Norris, Jr. *The Great Thirst: Californians and Water—A History.* Rev. ed. Berkeley: University of California Press, 2001.

Marine Protection, Research, and Sanctuaries Act of 1972

The Marine Protection, Research, and Sanctuaries Act of 1972 sought to reduce the dumping of waste at sea in line with U.S. President Richard M. Nixon's January 1971 State of the Union Address. In this address, he reiterated his support for the thirty-seven-point program that he wanted to implement in conjunction with the National Environmental Policy Act of 1969 and the Environmental Quality Improvement Act of 1970. One of the key planks of this program was to prevent further pollution of waterways. As a result, the President's Water Pollution Control Advisory Board wanted to draw up a national policy on dumping.

Impact of Dumping in New York

The impetus for the Marine Protection, Research, and Sanctuaries Act of 1972 came from New York City under Mayor John V. Lindsay, who had wanted to dump rubbish from the city into the open sea. Doing so would reduce the cost of waste disposal and prevent further deterioration in air quality from using incinerators. New York City was running out of landfill sites, with those on Staten Island expected to be full within ten or fifteen years. City authorities also noted that many other communities "don't want New York City's garbage" (Lyons 1972). The State of New Jersey was opposed to the proposed garbage dumping and lobbied for stricter controls to be imposed to prevent it. In fact, such dumping was already illegal under 1899 federal legislation, but the law had only been enforced by the U.S. Army Corps of Engineers a few times and was widely flouted.

New York City authorities wanted to dump rubbish in the Atlantic Ocean just south of Ambrose Light in Lower

New York Bay. They contended that it would have little effect on the environment. However, a report by the National Marine Fisheries Service in June 1972 showed that the health of marine life was deteriorating. The study showed a higher rate of bacteria and heavy metals in the tissues of sea creatures and even reported that fish were found with cigarette filters in their stomachs. In spite of this, Jerome Kretchmer, the environmental protection administrator for New York City, told the *New York Times* that the dumping should go ahead as long as there was no negative environmental impact. In response, New Jersey governor William T. Cahill signed a law on June 1, 1971, to restrict dumping and publically urged that all waste dumping be prohibited in any water within 100 miles of U.S. shores.

Environmental Protection Agency Control

The Marine Protection, Research, and Sanctuaries Act of 1972 transferred enforcement authority from the U.S. Army Corps of Engineers to the Environmental Protection Agency (EPA), giving the latter the power to determine in what circumstances dumping could take place. When the legislation was being debated in Congress, the Senate was adamant that the EPA should have the final say, whereas the House of Representatives wanted to leave enforcement with the Corps of Engineers. Finally, the law was approved by a voice vote in both houses and went into effect six months after its introduction on October 13, 1972. It gave the federal government the authority to prosecute anybody involved in illegal dumping and punish the guilty party with a fine of up to $50,000 for each act of dumping and up to a year's imprisonment. The Act covered an area up to twelve nautical miles off the coast. This would include the area of sea south of the Ambrose Light, where the dumping by Mayor Lindsay was to have taken place. The Act also appropriated $9.1 million through June 1974 for the administration of the legislation, and it gave the Department of Commerce the full authority to create marine sanctuaries where no dumping of any kind would be allowed. The Department of Commerce would also be able to monitor the effect of dumping in ocean areas in general.

One of the major tests of the Act was when the City of Camden in New Jersey applied to the EPA to allow it to dump sewage fifty miles from the coastline. The EPA granted the city an interim permit. The EPA also granted an interim permit to the Chevron Oil Company in Perth Amboy, New Jersey, which wanted to dump caustic waste

106 miles from shore. Other applications were soon made by Westchester County; the City of Long Beach; the Sewage Authority of Middletown, New Jersey; and the Joint Meeting of Essex and Union Counties of New Jersey.

Although much of the initial focus was on the area around New York and New Jersey, DuPont wanted to dump waste in the Gulf of Mexico 230 miles off the coast of Florida. However, the EPA told DuPont on October 3, 1974, that it had to stop as the agency was not able to establish that there would not be "unreasonable environmental degradation" (Hill 1974). Another consideration in the EPA's decision was that dumping in the Gulf would affect other countries, and Russel E. Train, the administrator of the EPA, wanted the United States to set a good example. At that time, it was also made public that DuPont was dumping, at sea, waste generated by three plants in Texas, one in New Jersey, and one in Delaware.

—Justin Corfield

See also: *Army Corps of Engineers, United States; Environmental Quality Improvement Act (1970); National Environmental Policy Act of 1969; National Marine Fisheries Service; Wastewater Treatment*

BIBLIOGRAPHY

Hill, Gladwin. "Du Pont Must End Dumping in Gulf: E.P.A. Bars Disposal of Chemicals Off Florida." *New York Times,* October 4, 1974.

Lyons, Richard D. "City Is Rebuffed on Ocean Dumping." *New York Times,* October 14, 1972.

New York Times. "Camden Is Allowed to Dump in Atlantic." April 28, 1973.

Ofiara, Douglas D., and Joseph J. Seneca. *Economic Losses from Marine Pollution: A Handbook for Assessment.* Washington, DC: Island Press, 2001.

Metropolitan Water District of Southern California

The Metropolitan Water District of Southern California (usually known as MWD or Met) is a wholesale water agency that imports water from northern California and the Colorado River via the State Water Project and Colorado River Aqueduct, respectively, for distribution to its twenty-six member agencies. Fourteen members are cities (Burbank, Los Angeles, Pasadena, etc.) that retail water to customers. Twelve members (the San Diego County Water Authority [SDCWA] plus eleven municipal water districts—confusingly called "MWDs"—such as MWD of

Orange County, West Basin MWD, etc.) sell water wholesale or retail. Met water flows to about 19 million customers of over 200 retail agencies, making Met the largest water utility in the United States by population served and volume of treated water delivery. Although few customers have heard of Met, almost everyone in the industry has, since Met is big: Met has a 5,200 square mile service area, a $2 billion budget, 2,000 staff members, and 2 million acre-feet per year of water deliveries (Met 2010).

Met's institutional structure is also interesting. The California legislature established Met as a public corporation with the power of taxation. Met is governed as a self-regulating consumer cooperative, with a thirty-seven member board of directors appointed by its member agencies. Since agencies are heterogeneous on many dimensions (service area, population, governance, local supply, staff), Met's policies emerge from compromises among conflicting interests.

Origin and Development

The Metropolitan Water District Act in 1928 directed Met to build an aqueduct from the Colorado River to California's south coast basin. In the same year, the U.S. Congress passed the Boulder Canyon Project Act, authorizing construction of Hoover Dam and other projects. These acts were related: the Colorado River Aqueduct (CRA) needed Hoover Dam power to pump water to southern California.

Met's thirteen founding members were cities, but Los Angeles dominated Met—financially, culturally, and operationally—from the start. This domination was nominally constrained by limiting the city's votes on the board to 50 percent. Member votes are in proportion to their share of total assessed land value. Los Angeles's share—over 70 percent in Met's early years—did not drop below 50 percent until 1949. Los Angeles allowed this "taxation without representation" because it was going to use Hoover power

Mono Lake Controversy

During the 1930s, the Los Angeles Department of Water and Power (LADWP) began acquiring water rights in the Mono Basin. Within a decade, the LADWP had secured the rights to water from a number of streams that fed Mono Lake, including Lee Vining, Parker, Rush, and Walker. The limitations of Los Angeles's aqueduct system prevented wholesale importation of the waters until the 1960s, when a second aqueduct was constructed to divert water from the Mono Basin. The loss of water from its tributaries resulted in a significant drop in Mono Lake's water level, resulting in severe damage to the local ecosystem. The lake's salinity quickly increased, negatively impacting the brine shrimp and fly populations that sustained migrating birds, such as California gulls.

By 1978, the National Audubon Society, Sierra Club, Friends of the Earth, California Trout, and the Mono Lake Committee had launched a number of lawsuits to protect and restore Mono Lake. In *National Audubon Society v. Superior Court*, decided on February 17, 1983, a key victory was obtained that established the concept of public trust in water legislation. The decision essentially determined that the needs of the local wildlife at Mono Lake superseded Los Angeles's water rights. The public trust concept, which required that environmental concerns be taken into account when determining water rights, was then expanded in subsequent lawsuits. The lawsuits eventually forced the LADWP to compromise with the environmental groups. It was agreed that the water level of Mono Lake would be maintained at a minimum of 6,392 feet above sea level. By the late 1990s, Mono Lake's ecosystem had begun to be visibly restored to its former glory.

—John R. Burch Jr.

BIBLIOGRAPHY

Hundley, Norris, Jr. *The Great Thirst: Californians and Water—A History.* Rev. ed. Berkeley: University of California Press, 2001.
Libecap, Gary D. *Owens Valley Revisited: A Reassessment of the West's First Great Water Transfer.* Stanford, CA: Stanford University Press, 2007.
Starr, Kevin. *Coast of Dreams: California on the Edge, 1990–2003.* New York: Alfred A. Knopf, 2004.

(under separate contracts) to drive Southern California Edison out of the city.

The CRA began deliveries in 1941, but Met's water was too expensive. Even with break-even pricing, Met's water cost a multiple of local water. Met used higher property taxes (projected 0.10 percent taxes reached 0.50 percent) to lower prices to "competitive" levels. Unfortunately, low prices did not boost demand to meet supply. So Met decided to grow.

Despite mutual misgivings, Met and SDCWA had complementary needs (too much supply and demand, respectively), and SDCWA joined in 1946. By 1949, SDCWA was buying half of Met's water. The SDCWA annexation created two precedents: it was a wholesale member, and it was outside the south coast basin. The next break came in 1950, when Pomona MWD (now Three Valleys MWD) joined Met and stretched Met's charter—"to provide water for domestic use"—to include agricultural use.

These early developments are important because they created patterns that would come to haunt Met. First was the friction between members that experienced different costs and benefits. Flaxman (1976) calculated that SDCWA paid an average price of $69 per acre-foot while Los Angeles paid an average cost of $532 per acre-foot. Second was the culture of growth and sprawl; 97 percent of Met's post-1943 increase in service area came from new members. Perhaps the beginning of the end was the 1952 Laguna Declaration in which Met promised "to provide its service area with adequate supplies of water to meet expanding and increasing needs in the years ahead"—in exchange for a continued monopoly over water imports.

This pledge was soon put to the test. In the 1963 *Arizona vs. California* decision, the Supreme Court reduced California's supply from the Colorado River to 4.4 million acre-feet. This ruling cut Met's rights from 1,212 thousand acre-feet (taf) to 550 taf. Although Met had prepared for this outcome by signing contracts for over 2 million acre-feet from the State Water Project (SWP) in 1960, its median deliveries since the SWP began operations in 1972 have been 684 taf. The main reason for lower deliveries is that the SWP was never "completed," with unbuilt dams in northern California and the 1982 defeat of the Peripheral Canal. Another reason is that SWP water costs more than CRA water.

With supply in trouble and demand hardening, shortage was on the horizon. Met asked members to cut demand by 10 percent during the 1977 drought. During the 1987–1991 drought, Met hit members with 20 percent cuts.

Soon Met faced internal squabbles among members. The chief protagonist was SDCWA, which protested the disconnect between purchases and votes. Since SDCWA lacked outside options (Met provides over 70 percent of its supply), it felt vulnerable to decisions made by other members. SDCWA has tried to reduce dependency, but most of its choices are complicated and expensive.

Today, Met is struggling to maintain supply in the face of shocks from climate change and regulatory restrictions on SWP operations, but it has mostly succeeded in finding enough water to keep a full "water portfolio." In 2009, after

three years of drought, Met was again rationing members—this time by 10 percent.

Importance of the Metropolitan Water District

Met is one of the earliest and biggest water wholesalers in the United States. It constructed the Colorado River Aqueduct and provided major support for the State Water Project. Its impact on southern California's urban development (simultaneously bringing sprawl and security) cannot be understated. As an organization, it has functioned reasonably well, but its survival has occasionally depended on its monopoly power. As a provider of water to 19 million people, Met's existence is not in doubt, but its form and operations are likely to evolve.

—David Zetland

See also: *Arizona* vs. *California (1963); Boulder Canyon Project Act (1928); Colorado River Aqueduct; Colorado River Compact of 1922; Hoover Dam*

BIBLIOGRAPHY

Flaxman, B. E. "The Price of Water: Who Pays and Who Benefits? A Policy Study of the Metropolitan Water District of Southern California." Masters thesis, Claremont Graduate School, 1976.

Met (The Metropolitan Water District of Southern California). "The Metropolitan Water District of Southern California at a Glance." http://www.mwdh2o.com/mwdh2o/pages/news/at_a_glance/mwd.pdf.

Zetland, David Jason. *Conflict and Cooperation within an Organization: A Case Study of the Metropolitan Water District of Southern California.* Saarbrueken, Germany: VDM Verlag, 2009. Available as 2008 dissertation at http://papers.ssrn.com/sol3/papers.cfm?abstract_id=1129046.

Mississippi River Commission

Established by Congress on June 28, 1879, the Mississippi River Commission (MRC) was charged with establishing and coordinating plans to prevent flooding and securing navigation of the Mississippi River and its tributaries, thus impacting 41 percent of the United States and parts of Canada. The seven-member commission consists of three civilians and four federal personnel.

Flooding Spurs Action

Following the Great Mississippi Flood of 1874, Congress not only provided aid to the victims but also created a joint commission to study the flooding problem. The commission's report recommended a levees-only policy, which eventually became the official position of the new Mississippi River Commission. Its creation, following the Compromise of 1877 that ended Reconstruction, reflected a willingness by President Rutherford B. Hayes to support Southern internal improvements.

Navigation clearly fell under interstate commerce, but the U.S. Supreme Court had invalidated spending public money for private purposes in *Loan Association v. Topeka* (1874). Debate over this issue continued into the 1930s. Meanwhile, railroads superseded river transportation, in part by getting river maintenance on tributary streams eliminated from Congress's annual Rivers and Harbors bills and by buying up and closing down steamship companies. Congress practiced micromanagement, denying the MRC the right to use bank revetments and, from 1881 to 1890, even the right to repair or construct levees unless intended for navigation purposes. Meanwhile, the MRC also struggled to make the river safer during low water periods, using dredge boats to clear away obstacles.

While navigation declined, floods increased. Major floods under the MRC's watch came in 1882, 1883, and 1884. However, the MRC, forced to operate fiscally on a year-by-year basis and with no appropriation at all in 1889, floundered.

Despite floods, the overflow lands of the Missouri boot heel, eastern Arkansas, and the Yazoo region of Mississippi lured settlers. These regions were transformed as state legislation authorized the formation of local levee and drainage districts. Following the severe floods of 1912 and 1913, Congress in 1917 passed the first Flood Control Act. Under its provisions, the MRC would supervise local groups who also were required to provide financial matches. Committed to a levees-only policy, the MRC rejected using reservoirs and, in the lower valley, began closing the outlets that Mississippi floodwaters had traditionally used, notably Cypress Creek, Bayou Lafourche, and the Atchafalaya River.

By the fall of 1926, the MRC concluded that the entire river from Rock Island, Illinois, to New Orleans, Louisiana, was at last protected. The MRC was proved wrong by the Great Flood of 1927, when there were 17 breaks in the Mississippi River levee system and 200 in levees on tributary streams. Eleven million acres went under water.

The New Deal and Beyond

Following a series of major floods, the idea of using reservoirs on tributary streams came to the fore. Proposed for decades but rejected as too expensive, dam building coincided with the New Deal's goal of restoring employment.

After 1941, the modern Mississippi River and Tributaries (MR&T) project emerged.

During the 1940s, the MRC's attention shifted to the Old River region, between Natchez and Baton Rouge, Louisiana, where the Mississippi River showed a strong inclination to move west entirely into the Atchafalaya basin. This route would cut some 180 miles off the river, thus isolating Baton Rouge and New Orleans. The MRC's response, the Old River Control Structure, was beset by troubles from the time of its construction in 1963. It nearly collapsed during the Great Flood of 1973.

After 1970, it was no longer possible to view the MR&T project as a plumbing problem alone. Recreational interests demanded to be heard, with some supporting dam construction and others opposing. The passage of the National Environmental Policy Act of 1969 gave wildlife and environmental groups standing, and these groups hastened to get on the agenda of MRC meetings. Indeed, the long-serving corps of civilian members provided extra weight to the needs of local levee boards, state governments, and private citizens. Sometimes seen as heavy-handed, the U.S. Army Corps of Engineers had to tolerate and even employ archaeologists, historians, and lawyers.

Hurricane Katrina put the Corps on the spot in New Orleans and elsewhere along its path, but the floodwaters were not those of the Mississippi, and the MRC's levees held firm. However, in the hurricane's aftermath, the National Levee Safety Program worked from the premise that complete safety was unattainable and that people living on floodplains should either leave or be forced to get expensive flood insurance. Since these parties were often assessed for levee and drainage upkeep, many residents felt that they were being discriminated against. These complaints found one major forum with the MRC.

—Michael B. Dougan

See also: *Army Corps of Engineers, United States; National Environmental Policy Act of 1969*

BIBLIOGRAPHY

Barry, John M. *Rising Tide: The Great Mississippi Flood of 1927 and How It Changed America.* New York: Simon and Schuster, 1997.
Bradley, James H. *Through Winds of Change: A History of the Memphis District, U.S. Army Corps of Engineers, 1998–2007.* Memphis, TN: U.S. Army Corps of Engineers, Memphis District, 2007.
Camillo, Charles A., and Matthew T. Pearcy. *Upon Their Shoulders: A History of the Mississippi River Commission from Its Inception through the Advent of the Modern Mississippi River and Tributaries Project.* Vicksburg, MS: Mississippi River Commission, 2004.

Clay, Floyd M. *A Century on the Mississippi: A History of the Memphis District, U.S. Army Corps of Engineers, 1876–1981.* Memphis, TN: U.S. Army Corps of Engineers, Memphis District, 1986.

Pabis, George S. "Restraining the Muddy Waters: Engineers and Mississippi River Flood Control, 1846–1881." Ph.D. diss., University of Chicago, 1996.

Reuss, Martin. *Designing the Bayous: The Control of Water in the Atchafalaya Basin, 1800–1995.* College Station: Texas A & M University Press, 2004.

Mississippi River Flood of 1927

The Mississippi River flood of 1927 was one of the most destructive and costly natural disasters in the history of the United States. In the spring and summer of 1927, the floodwaters impacted ten states: Illinois, Kentucky, Missouri, Kansas, Tennessee, Arkansas, Oklahoma, Mississippi, Louisiana, and Texas. The natural disaster killed 246 people and displaced nearly 700,000 individuals. Additionally, the flood caused nearly $400 million in economic damages. While the Mississippi River flood of 1927 devastated the Mississippi Valley, the natural disaster also had a significant political and cultural impact upon the rest of the nation during the early twentieth century.

During the summer of 1926, heavy rains began to fall on the Midwest, which caused the upper Mississippi River to swell. In April 1927, Southern communities such as Greenville, Mississippi, continued to experience record rainfall; city officials reported nearly eight inches of rain. Although the U.S. Army Corps of Engineers maintained that the levees along the Mississippi River could withstand all of the water, local residents evacuated the area and fled to Northern states. On April 21, the Pendleton and Mound Landing, Mississippi, levees collapsed, which produced widespread flooding throughout the lower Mississippi Valley. By the summer of 1927, the flood had covered millions of acres of agricultural land.

Political and Social Impacts

On April 22, 1927, President Calvin Coolidge appointed Secretary of Commerce Herbert Hoover as head of the

The catastrophic flooding of the Mississippi River in 1927 displaced hundreds of thousands of residents of the Mississippi Valley. Here, evacuees live in tents in a refugee camp in Greenville, Mississippi.

The Granger Collection, New York

flood recovery and relief effort. During the next few months, Hoover mobilized the American Red Cross, Veterans Bureau, National Guard, U.S. Public Health Service, and Rockefeller Foundation for the rescue operations. He also negotiated with the Illinois Central and the Texas Pacific Railroads to provide free transportation for the refugees and to reduce freight rates during the national crisis. Additionally, Hoover reluctantly endorsed the Mississippi River Commission's plan to dynamite the Caernarvon levee in order to direct floodwaters away from New Orleans and its inhabitants. While dynamiting the Caernarvon levee ensured the safety of New Orleans, other communities along the Mississippi River needed to be rescued from the rising water. Addressing these concerns, Hoover authorized the establishment of a recovery fleet, which consisted of 799 Navy vessels and Coast Guard ships, as well as 27 seaplanes. In the spring of 1927, rescue workers searched for survivors and carried individuals who were stranded on rooftops, levees, or Indian mounds to safety. The seaplanes also benefited the relief operations by spotting additional refugees and inspecting the levee conditions. Hoover's rescue and recovery efforts garnered him national attention, which he utilized to gain the Republican presidential nomination in 1928. Therefore, the Mississippi River flood of 1927 helped Hoover defeat Democratic candidate Alfred E. Smith to win the presidency in November 1928.

As Hoover set rehabilitation policies and organized relief efforts, the American Red Cross quickly responded to the national emergency by spending nearly $17 million and establishing 154 refugee camps, which contained Army tents and other temporary shelters. During the spring of 1927, nearly 300,000 refugees migrated to these relief camps, where they remained until the floodwaters subsided that summer.

By May, African American refugees were complaining about discriminatory behaviors and other abuses within the camps. Hoover responded to these allegations by establishing a Colored Advisory Commission, which investigated the relief camps' conditions. Under the leadership of Robert Russa Moton, the eighteen-member commission reported that various camps lacked sufficient food and drinking water. The commissioners also noted that the camps' overcrowded conditions produced diseases such as dysentery, pellagra, and typhoid fever. Upon learning of the refugees' mistreatment, Hoover instructed Moton to conceal this information from the news media because he believed that these reports would tarnish his image as a national hero, thus hindering his political aspirations. In exchange for Moton's refusal to publicize the findings, Hoover agreed to propose a land resettlement plan and antilynching legislation as well as appoint African Americans to federal positions once he was elected president.

Following the presidential election of 1928, Hoover abandoned these policies in support of other national issues. Disheartened by Hoover's failure to keep his promises, Moton and other African American leaders refused to vote for Hoover in the presidential election of 1932. Thus, Hoover's actions contributed to the shift in African American voting patterns away from the Republican Party and towards the Democratic Party by the mid-twentieth century.

As the floodwaters began to recede in the summer of 1927, racial violence erupted throughout the flooded region as white Southerners accused African Americans of stealing food and drinking water, failing to contribute to the recovery effort, and attacking local residents. These allegations led to increased hostilities between the white and African American communities, which armed themselves with guns and other weapons. For example, the National Guard held African American refugees against their will and forced them to work on nearby farmlands. In August, thousands of African Americans refused to accept these inhumane conditions and moved to the North. Therefore, the racial unrest within these Southern communities contributed to the Great Migration of African Americans to Northern cities during the mid-twentieth century.

Flood Control Legislation and Public Opinion

Despite the successful rescue and relief operations, federal officials supported the establishment of several flood control reforms to prevent future natural disasters. On May 15, 1928, President Coolidge signed the Flood Control Act of 1928, which authorized the U.S. Army Corps of Engineers to build additional reservoirs and improve existing levees along the Mississippi River and its tributaries.

The Mississippi River flood of 1927 also altered the American public's perception of the federal government's role during a national crisis. Prior to the natural disaster, Americans supported only limited federal involvement, as local volunteers performed a majority of the recovery and relief work. However, the flood's scope and destructive nature provided a solid foundation for President Franklin

D. Roosevelt's New Deal programs, and individuals turned to the federal government for relief and assistance during national emergencies.

While the Mississippi River Flood of 1927 was one of the most devastating events in U.S. history, the natural disaster also impacted American politics by propelling Herbert Hoover to the presidency and encouraging federal officials to approve flood control reforms. The national crisis also had social implications, as the flood heightened racial tensions throughout the lower Mississippi Valley, contributing to the mass northward migration of African Americans.

—Kevin Brady

See also: *Army Corps of Engineers, United States; Flood Control Act of 1928; Levees; Midwest*

BIBLIOGRAPHY

Barry, John M. *Rising Tide: The Great Mississippi Flood of 1927 and How It Changed America.* New York: Simon & Schuster, 1997.

Daniel, Pete. *Deep'n as It Come: The 1927 Mississippi River Flood.* Fayetteville: University of Arkansas Press, 1996.

Smith, Richard Norton. *An Uncommon Man: The Triumph of Herbert Hoover.* New York: Simon & Schuster, 1984.

Missouri River Navigation and Channelization Project

The Missouri River was a commercial byway as far back as the fur-trading days of the early nineteenth century. After steamboats were developed and adapted for shallower western rivers, commercial navigation on the Missouri became an important industry, from the mouth of the river at Saint Louis to Fort Benton, Montana, which was as far upriver as steamboats could travel. With the arrival of railroads, much of the river navigation on the upper Missouri gradually diminished.

Navigation Projects on the Missouri

The U.S. Army Corps of Engineers was given the authority to regulate navigation on the nation's major rivers in 1824, but the Corps had little impact on the Missouri River before the early twentieth century. In the 1870s, riverboat owners and shippers lobbied Congress for a five-foot-deep channel from Sioux City, Iowa, to the mouth of the river at Saint Louis. The government did little in response to these requests until 1912, when Congress passed the Rivers and Harbors Act. This bill authorized the Corps to begin a project to ensure the maintenance of a six-foot-deep channel for navigation from Kansas City, Missouri, to Saint Louis. By 1925, this project had been extended upstream to Sioux City, Iowa. By World War II, the Corps had spent nearly $300 million on this channelization project. Several other Rivers and Harbors Acts between 1917 and 1945 had provisions for projects to facilitate navigation on the lower Missouri River. The passage of the Flood Control Act of 1944, which incorporated the Pick-Sloan Plan for the development of the Missouri Basin, also had a significant impact on plans for navigation of the river. The Pick-Sloan Plan called for massive dams that could provide sufficient water storage to maintain a nine-foot navigation channel. The depth of the channel was increased to nine feet so that the larger barges used on the Mississippi River could also be used on the Missouri.

The Missouri River Bank Stabilization and Navigation Project, approved in 1945, was the major plan designed to facilitate navigation on the lower Missouri. From Sioux City to Saint Louis, a nine-foot-deep channel was created. Most of the channel below Kansas City was completed by 1932. From 1932 to 1940, most of the stretch from Kansas City to Sioux City was completed. A series of flood control levees was also built on both sides of the same stretch of river. This project was officially completed in 1981. The channelized portion of the river is 735 miles long. Besides providing for navigation, the stabilization of the channel and the construction of the levee system have allowed for both the agricultural and urban development of much of the floodplain land in the region. The main stem dams built on the upper Missouri and the channelization of the lower portions of the river have divided the Missouri into three sections that are roughly equal in extent—about one-third of the river is impounded behind huge dams in Montana and the Dakotas, about one-third is channelized, and about one-third remains somewhat free-flowing.

The use of the river by commercial shippers never achieved the levels predicted by the Corps of Engineers. Tonnage peaked in the late 1970s and has declined since. Currently, the bulk of what is moved on the river is relatively low-value sand and gravel, moved only short distances from where it is quarried to shore facilities, where it is processed or transferred to ground transportation.

Managing the river to provide navigation on the channelized section has led to considerable controversy in recent decades. In times of drought, there is not enough water, even with the main stem flood control reservoirs, to maintain the navigation channel consistently. Conversely, in times of severe flooding, much of the infrastructure needed to maintain the channel can be washed away.

Environmental Impact of Commercial Navigation

Environmental concerns have been increasing about the impact of the use of the Missouri River for commercial navigation. Channelization and related projects have greatly altered the riparian ecosystem of the lower Missouri valley, leading to debates as to whether the economic benefits of continued navigation are worth the environmental trade-offs involved. Channelization has eliminated sandbars that were important to many kinds of wildlife, and it has greatly diminished the diversity of habitat for fish and other aquatic species. The river's connection with oxbows, side channels, and backwater areas has been eliminated.

The historic flow regime of the river has also been altered. Before the construction of the flood control dams, the river rose in the spring with the snow melt from the Great Plains and mountains. Then, in the summer, a period of low flows followed. Today, the flood control structures can eliminate or at least tame the spring rise, and then in the summer, greater releases from the dams can maintain a higher flow.

In addition, channelization has narrowed the area within the floodplain where the river flows. Historically, the river wound back and forth over a wide area known as a "meander belt." Now behind the wing dams and other structures built to force the water into a central channel, sediment accumulates, which eventually creates new land in a process known as "accretion." With levees protecting this new land from flooding, much of what was riparian wildlife habitat is now farmable land or can be developed for residential and industrial uses. Channelization also straightened the river in many places and eliminated many bends and oxbows, shortening the river by approximately seventy-two miles.

Because of environmental concerns, the Corps of Engineers began the Missouri River Fish and Wildlife Mitigation Project in 1986 to try to restore habitat lost due to changes made to the river. Despite projects such as this, controversy and litigation have continued over the environmental impact of adapting the river for navigation.

—Mark S. Joy

See also: *Army Corps of Engineers, United States; Levees; Missouri River Basin; River Transportation*

BIBLIOGRAPHY

Lambrecht, Bill. *Big Muddy Blues: True Tales and Twisted Politics Along Lewis and Clark's Missouri River.* New York: Thomas Dunne Books, 2005.

National Research Council. *The Missouri River Ecosystem: Exploring the Prospects for Recovery.* Washington, DC: National Academy Press, 2002.

Schneiders, Robert Kelley. *Unruly River: Two Centuries of Change Along the Missouri.* Lawrence: University Press of Kansas, 1999.

Thorson, John E. *River of Promise, River of Peril: The Politics of Managing the Missouri River.* Lawrence: University Press of Kansas, 1994.

Montana Stream Access Law (1985)

The Montana Stream Access Law of 1985 is the broadest such law in the West. It provides that any stream or river with the capability of supporting recreation must be available to the public whether or not the stream or river is navigable and regardless of who owns the streamside. A "river" is anything between the river's ordinary high-water mark, the line the water draws on land by covering it long enough to make the area below the line different physically from the area above. The adjacent floodplain is not part of the river, nor are extraordinarily high water marks. Recreation includes fishing, hunting, swimming, floating, boating, water-related pleasure activities, and unavoidable or incidental uses.

Court Action on Stream Access

In the late 1970s, after harassment on the Smith and Dearborn Rivers, anglers and floaters sued landowners. While the case worked its way through the courts, the state legislature attempted in 1981 and 1983 to enact an access law. The Montana Supreme Court ruling of 1984 was broader than the unsuccessful legislation, which would have opened only the larger rivers. The court ruled that both navigable and nonnavigable rivers were open for scientific and recreational uses. In 1985, the legislature enacted the Montana Stream Access Law. At statehood, the Equal Footing Act had given Montana ownership of navigable waters up to the high-water line. Montana has forty-two such rivers and streams. Nonnavigable streams are private property, but the law requires easement for recreational users.

Prior to the law, from 1889 to 1985, owners strung barbed wire fences across streams, claiming they had to control their cattle. After 1985, property values on streams soared. On June 7, 2000, the Mountain States Legal Fund (MSLF) sued to overturn public stream access. The MSLF represented three large landowners who contended that they had lost privacy and income. Landowners warned of wildfires and damage from trespassers, reduced fish populations, and lowered profit-making opportunities for owners who charged for fishing. Advocates of open fishing countered that Montana should not create a landed gentry and private fisheries. The public paid to protect habitat and develop fisheries, and in conformity with Montana tradition, it should have access to the waterways. In 2001, the district court ruled against MSLF, the Ninth Circuit Court of Appeals dismissed the MSLF appeal, and the U.S. Supreme Court declined to hear the case.

Law Coverage

The coverage of the law is extremely broad, including virtually every stream or river on private property. Many have obstructions, and recreational users may climb above the high-water mark to maneuver around the obstructions. However, users may not cross private property to reach a stream. Passage must be across unfenced land with no keep-out signs or splashes of orange paint, but if the area is posted or painted, the user merely has to ask permission of the owner. Owners are generous with their orange markings and signs and stingy with permission. Thus, users must cross on bridges if the road does not follow the river, there is no designated fishing access site, and the river does not cross federal or state land. A bridge is an access point available to all potential users.

Controversies

In the early 1990s, Madison County landowners began building barbed wire fences attached to public bridge abutments to keep recreationists away from public streams. County commissioners outlawed the fences in 1995. The owners sued, citing unconstitutional takings. In 1997, the county rescinded the ordinance. In 2004, Madison County began issuing permits to owners to attach fences to bridges and required that sportsmen pay for construction of gates or stiles and a public recreational responsibility education program. Angry anglers pressured the commission to rescind the permits, and owners sued. The attorney general ruled in 2000 that the commissioners could force landowners to take down their paint, signs, and wire blocking county bridges to recreational users and defined where recreationists could

move across private land. In 2003, the barbed wire fences still blocked boaters and other recreational users. Madison County commissioners declined to enforce the attorney general's ruling. Even after a 2005 Montana Supreme Court ruling for the public, landowners, supported by the Mountain States Legal Foundation, continued to block public access. A 2005 bridge-access law failed in a Montana House of Representatives committee, with ten Democrats for and ten Republicans opposed.

Clarifying the Law

In 2008, the lawsuit brought by environmentalists against the county in 2004 was finally heard by the Montana Supreme Court and quickly resolved in the environmentalists' favor. In 2009, the state legislature amended the law to clarify owners' rights at bridges after the court decisions. Fences were permitted for the control of livestock or management of property, but they could not interfere with access by the road right-of-way (usually thirty feet from the center of the road). The public was not to trespass beyond the right-of-way, and for prescriptive roads (roads that the public has long used as a thoroughfare but that are not government owned or maintained), the right-of-way was the roadway only. The law established a complaint process that could culminate, if owners balked, in Fish, Wildlife, and Parks building appropriate access by rail fences, stiles, gates, rollovers, or walkovers, at either its own expense or that of a third party. There is no requirement for landowners to build gates, landowners retain the right to fence the waterway as long as there is portage access to both sides of the bridge, the owner and wildlife department (not the public) negotiate the type of access at a bridge site, most prescriptive roads are exempt, and landowners are not responsible for payment. Permitted uses do not include trapping, hunting, camping, or hiking, and operation of ATVs is barred.

There is no public access to stock ponds or private impoundments on intermittent streams or irrigation canals or drainage ditches, nor is there access to or by dry streambeds. In December 2008, the state supreme court ruled that the public had access to Mitchell Slough, a side channel of the Bitterroot River. Since the early 1990s, wealthy landowners had blocked public access to this channel and had prevailed against a lawsuit in a lower court. But in 2004, the newly elected Democratic governor reversed the previous governor's closing of the slough, and the state supreme court ruled that the lower court's decision—that the slough was so modified by humans as to be an irrigation ditch—was absurd. The ruling thwarted a potential threat, that of rich landowners "improving" waterways and then getting the conservation board to rule them no longer natural, thereby closing them to the public. Access advocates noted that the Bitterroot River and its tributaries had dams and irrigation channels, and all of Montana's rivers had been altered to some extent.

—John H. Barnhill

See also: *Outdoor Recreation; Recreational Water Rights*

BIBLIOGRAPHY

Breeding, Rob. "Stream Access Wins Decisively in Montana." *High Country News,* December 8, 2008. Available at http://www.hcn .org/wotr/stream-access-wins-decisively-in-montana.

Johnson, John W. *United States Water Law: An Introduction.* Boca Raton, FL: CRC, 2008.

Montana River Action. "The Stream Access Law: Profit at Expense of Montanans." http://www.montanariveraction.org/stream.access .html.

Mulholland, William

A hydraulic engineer, William Mulholland (1855–1935) was involved in the building of the Los Angeles (or Owens River) Aqueduct, which provided water from the Sierra Nevada to Los Angeles, ending worry about water shortages in the city.

Early Life and Career

William Mulholland was born on September 11, 1855, in Belfast, Ireland, the son of Hugh Mulholland and Ellen (née Deakers). He was educated at the Christian Brothers' College in Dublin and then served as a sailor for four years. After arriving in New York in the early 1870s, he worked on ships in the Great Lakes and then in lumber camps in Michigan before moving to Pittsburgh, Pennsylvania, where he joined an uncle who ran a dry goods business.

In 1877, Mulholland moved to California where he worked at digging artesian wells. The following year, he worked as a ditch tender (or *zanjero*) for the Los Angeles Water Company. At this time, he educated himself about civil engineering, mathematics, and hydraulics. As a result, just five years later, he was appointed superintendent of the Los Angeles Water Company. Immediately, Mulholland started overhauling the operations of the company, which at that time had only one reservoir, inadequate for a city the size of Los Angeles. Mulholland would transform the

William Mulholland (1855–1935) was the superintendent of the Los Angeles Water Company. He is best known for his role as overseer of construction for the Los Angeles Aqueduct, which provided much-needed water for the burgeoning City of Los Angeles.
The Granger Collection, New York

company into one with 3,800 miles of pipes and 65 reservoirs and tanks.

Los Angeles Aqueduct

As Los Angeles grew, Mulholland had to figure out how to bring even more water to the city. He decided to see whether it was possible to bring water from the Sierra Nevada mountain range and made the 500-mile round trip to Owens Lake in a buckboard wagon with a team of mules. After forty days of surveying, Mulholland believed that it was possible to build an aqueduct from the lake to the city and that doing so would supply enough water for more than 2 million people.

Mulholland then planned and supervised the construction of the Los Angeles Aqueduct, which was estimated to cost $24.5 million and take five years to complete. There was some opposition to this ambitious idea. Mulholland issued a series of bonds to raise money to pay for the construction and spoke about the viability of the project at public meetings throughout the city. Work started in 1909, and it was completed in 1913 at slightly under the estimated cost. When the first water arrived in Los Angeles, Mulholland remarked, "There it is—take it."

The Los Angeles Aqueduct was soon known around the world. The largest municipal aqueduct, it crossed mountains, valleys, and deserts. Furthermore, it required the construction of twenty-seven earthen dams. Large though the Los Angeles Aqueduct was, the demand for water in Los Angeles soon exceeded supply, and Mulholland started drawing up plans for an even larger water supply system that would draw from the Colorado River. The work of surveying 60,000 square miles to determine the best route was tasked to the Metropolitan Water District, which was created in 1928 to provide water for thirteen cities in California, including Los Angeles.

As work began, on March 12, 1928, the Saint Francis Dam on the San Francisquito Creek collapsed, killing more than 600 people. This was the second greatest loss of life in California's history (after the San Francisco Earthquake of 1906). Mulholland had supervised the construction of the dam, and the foundation material was found to be defective. The *Los Angeles Times* quoted him as saying, "If there is any responsibility here—it is mine alone." Forced to retire in December 1928, Mulholland then took up work as an advisor and became a consulting engineer on a number of other irrigation and water supply projects. He worked on the Engineering Board of the Water Resources and Development of the State of California, and as a consulting engineer in other parts of California and for Seattle, Washington. Mulholland's reputation, however, was overshadowed by the Saint Francis Dam disaster.

In December 1934, he suffered a cerebral hemorrhage from which he died on July 22, 1935. Survived by his wife and five children, he was buried in the Forest Lawn Memorial Park, Los Angeles.

—Justin Corfield

See also: *Los Angeles Aqueduct; Metropolitan Water District of Southern California*

BIBLIOGRAPHY

Jackson, Donald C., and Norris Hundley. "Privilege and Responsibility: William Mulholland and the St. Francis Dam Disaster." *California History* 82, no. 3 (2004): 8–47. Available at http://www.ce.jhu.edu/perspectives/handouts_unprotected/stfrancis.pdf.

New York Times. "Mulholland Dead: Famous Engineer." July 23, 1935.

Outland, Charles F. *Man-Made Disaster: The Story of St. Francis Dam, Its Place in Southern California's Water System, Its Failure, and the Tragedy of March 12 and 13, 1928 in the Santa Clara River Valley.* Glendale, CA: A. H. Clark, 1963.

Robinson, Burr A. "William Mulholland." In *Dictionary of American Biography: Supplement 1,* edited by American Council of Learned Societies, 224–226. New York: Charles Scribner's Sons, 1944.

Toner, Guy L. "San Francisquito Canyon Dam Disaster." Unpublished manuscript, 1928.

Wiley, Andrew Jackson, and California St. Francis Dam Commission. *Report of the Commission Appointed by Governor C. C. Young to Investigate the Causes Leading to the Failure of the St. Francis Dam Near Saugus, California.* Sacramento: California State Printing Office, 1928.

National Dam Safety Program Act of 1996

The National Dam Safety Program Act (NDSPA) was part of the Water Resources Development Act, signed into law October 12, 1996 (Pub.L. 104-303). Relevant laws are the Water Resources and Development Act of 1996 (Pub. L. 104-303) and the Dam Safety and Security Act of 2002 (Pub. L. 107-310), which extended the Act through 2006. The Dam Safety and Security Act of 2002 amended the program act to continue through 2006 and strengthened antiterrorist provisions. The National Dam Safety Program Act is currently reauthorized through 2011 under Pub. L. 109-460. The goal is to involve all stakeholders in increased safety of dams.

Pub. L. 109-460 requires the U.S. Army Corps of Engineers to maintain a database of all dams in the United States that includes dam safety assessments based on state or federal inspection. The Federal Emergency Management Agency (FEMA) is required to develop a strategic plan incorporating performance measures as well as goals, priorities, and target dates. The National Dam Safety Program (NDSP) grants monies to states for safety programs to cover the 79,500–80,000 U.S. dams. Training and research are also key elements.

Dam Risks

About a third of the 80,000 dams in the inventory are either "high" or "significant" hazards to property or life should they fail. Unsafe nonfederal dams in the United States, those identified by the states as such, numbered approximately 3,341 in 2004. Dams are aging and deteriorating, and when they fail, they cause millions of dollars in damage to ever-growing downstream populations. Dams and levees sometimes fail with virtually no notice. Particularly dangerous are flash floods, which can cause a dam breach within six hours and a failure two hours after the breach. Slower breaches and failures may occur days or weeks after large snow melts or debris jams. Dams alter groundwater levels, affecting wells and crops, and improperly released water can flood downstream and drown anglers and swimmers, cause erosion and channel degradation, and degrade water quality. Dam operators are liable for damages, even if their dams conform to state standards.

Reducing Dam Risks

The NDSP was designed to reduce the risks from dam failure by developing a program that included federal and non-federal stakeholders in hazard reduction efforts. Among its provisions are the following: development of technologically and economically workable procedures and programs to help guarantee that new and existing dams are safe; promotion of appropriate engineering practices in site selection and dam design; construction, operation, and maintenance; and emergency preparedness. Safety and public education are also included.

Since it became operational in 1998, the NDSP has helped reduce risk of dam failures, but it has not eliminated them. Its funding was low, given the size of the problem. Funding for the program in 2004 was $8.6 million, with $6 million for state grants, $1.5 million for research, and $0.5 million for inspectors. Administrative overhead costs $0.6 million. The Association of State Dam Safety Officials naturally wants higher funding for state grants as well as earmarks in the FEMA budget for the program.

State Regulation

Total state grants between 1998 and 2004 totaled $21.6 million; Texas, Oklahoma, and Kansas received over $1 million each, while Puerto Rico, Alaska, and Hawaii received under $165,000 each. Grants provide state-level training for dam owners and state personnel. They also buy equipment such as computers, cameras, and other technology for inspection and analysis. Before the NDSP, many owners lacked the resources to make necessary repairs. While some states funded these repairs, there was no national program for funding rehabilitation other than the Small Watershed Rehabilitation Act, which applies strictly to the 10,000 dams built by the Department of Agriculture

in the mid-twentieth century. Safety for 95 percent of dams is a state responsibility, and state commitment is variable. Although state budgets range as high as $6 million, the low is no money at all, and the average is $450,000 for an average of 1,500 dams inspected by 6 inspectors. Another consideration is that the impact of dam failure commonly crosses state lines.

The U.S. Army Corps of Engineers is responsible for the national inventory, which, as of 2004, had data from all states but Alabama. The inventory in 2004 contained about 78,000 dams owned by state and local governments, businesses, and private citizens. Other federal agencies have responsibility for oversight of dams. The Bureau of Reclamation (BOR) oversees its own power and irrigation dams such as Grand Coulee in Washington state. The Corps of Engineers oversees some power-producing dams. The Federal Energy Regulatory Commission (FERC) regulates nonfederal power-producing dams, while states normally regulate dams that produce no power and are not owned by the BOR or the Corps. FEMA is responsible for safety as coordinator of federal aid to state programs.

State levels of regulation vary widely. Washington state regulates projects not covered by the federal agencies that are over ten feet tall or have an impound of ten acre-feet. California regulates its own and FERC dams but exempts privately owned and non-power-producing dams and those smaller than ten feet or ten acre-feet. Utah has a dam safety program in the state engineer's office. The inventory sorts dams by size, use, and risk. It identifies, locates, and provides construction information as well as maintenance history for the state's dams.

Minnesota has dams for maintaining lake levels, producing power, controlling floods, and providing drinking water. Causes of dam failure have included poor design, operation, or maintenance as well as floods. Minnesota instituted its Dam Safety Program in 1978 after the initial attempt at federal legislation arising from a series of dam failures that killed scores of people in the 1970s. Minnesota's program includes rules for building and operating a dam, a database, standards for permits, inspections, and repairs (with the state paying for its own dams and assisting local governments with funding theirs). Minnesota exempts dams smaller than six feet or impounding fewer than fifteen acre-feet. In some cases, dams under twenty-five feet and impounding less than fifty acre-feet are exempt. The Minnesota database contains 900 dams. For the most part, state guidelines have continued to improve, inspections have increased, emergency plans have been developed, and permitting times have gotten faster, and coordination with emergency agencies and exercises have improved.

—John H. Barnhill

See also: *Dam Building; Dam Removal and River Restoration; Dam Safety and Security Act of 2002*

BIBLIOGRAPHY

Bumgarner, Jeffrey B. *Emergency Management: A Reference Handbook.* Santa Barbara, CA: ABC-CLIO, 2008.

Minnesota Department of Natural Resources. "Dam Safety in Minnesota." 2010. http://www.dnr.state.mn.us/waters/surface water_section/damsafety/safety.html.

Rogers, Jerry R, ed. *Great Rivers History: Proceedings and Invited Papers for the EWRI Congress and History Symposium, May 17–19, 2009, Kansas City, Missouri.* Reston, VA: American Society of Civil Engineers, 2009.

National Environmental Policy Act of 1969

During the ten years from 1959 to 1969, legislative proposals began to reflect the distinction between conservation (wise use of natural resources), antipollution efforts, and a much more comprehensive concern with human activity's relation to the entire natural biosphere. The National Environmental Policy Act (NEPA) was the product of at least ten years of congressional debate, during which Congress received and declined to pass into law the Resources and Conservation Act, introduced by Senator James E. Murray (D-MT) in 1959, and similar bills introduced in 1961 by Senator Clair Engel (D-CA) and Senator Gale McGee (D-WY), by Senator McGee in 1963, and by Senator George McGovern (D-SD) in 1965. These bills were opposed by both the Eisenhower and Kennedy administrations and by many federal agencies. The Ecological Research and Surveys Bill, introduced by Senator Gaylord Nelson (D-WI) in 1965, also did not come to a vote, but Title II of NEPA incorporated many of its provisions.

The law passed by Congress in 1969 began in the Senate as S. 1075, introduced by Senator Henry Jackson (D-WA). Reported by the Committee on Interior and Insular Affairs and placed on the Senate calendar July 9, 1969, the bill was passed the next day and sent to the House of Representatives, where similar legislation introduced by Rep. John Dingell (D-MI) had been delayed by arguments over jurisdiction between different committees. After a number of Dingell's proposals were incorporated into Jackson's bill by a House-Senate conference committee in December 1969, the final bill was approved by both houses and sent to President Richard M. Nixon, who signed it January 1, 1970. Pub. L. 91-190 was entered as 83 Stat. 852 and codified at 42 U.S.C. 4321–4347.

NEPA Policies

NEPA established a national policy to "promote efforts which will prevent or eliminate damage to the environment and biosphere and stimulate the health and welfare of man" (42 USC § 4321). To oversee this new policy, NEPA established the Council on Environmental Quality (CEQ), with three members appointed by the president, subject to confirmation by the advice and consent of the Senate. This council is generally authorized "to review and appraise the various programs and activities of the federal government in the light of the policy set forth" (42 USC § 4344) in NEPA and to recommend national environmental policies to the president.

Legal scholars are uncertain whether this statutory language, in itself, provides authority to issue regulations or guidelines for federal agencies. CEQ received explicit authority to issue guidelines from Executive Order 11,514, issued by President Nixon on March 5, 1970. In 1977, President Jimmy Carter, in Executive Order 11,991, empowered CEQ to issue regulations binding on all federal agencies. Final regulations were issued in 1978, and the U.S. Supreme Court has stated that "CEQ's interpretation of NEPA is entitled to substantial deference" by federal courts (*Andrus v. Sierra Club* 442 U.S. at 358).

Environmental impact assessments (EIA), required for all federal agency actions or projects that have a significant impact on the environment, are one of the most effectual results of NEPA. Senator Jackson observed at a hearing on S. 1075 that unless legislation imposed a procedure that "departments must comply with," the bill's "lofty declarations are nothing more than that" (*Hearings* 1969, 116). He recognized that in practice, federal agencies have considerable discretion to proceed however they wish, even in conflict with a congressional statement of policy. Because written assessments and, in a smaller number of cases, environmental impact statements (EIS), are mandatory under the Act, courts can hold agencies to strict compliance. In many areas of administrative law, including substantive provisions of environmental law, courts often defer to the discretion of each agency.

Controversies and Weakened Power

In fact, many federal agencies maintained that NEPA did not apply to them, or they complied in a very limited manner. CEQ's guidelines, first published in the *Federal Register* in 1971, were given added force by the District of Columbia Circuit Court of Appeals in the 1971 case of *Calvert Cliffs' Coordinating Committee, Inc. v. AEC*, 449 F.2d 1109. A Maryland public interest group brought a challenge to the Atomic Energy Agency's (AEC) licensing of nuclear power plants, specifically a partially constructed plant on the Chesapeake Bay. The author of the court's opinion, Judge Skelly Wright, wrote that the basic substantive policy set forth in NEPA Section 101, which mandated that federal agencies "use all practicable means and measures," left wide discretionary power to each agency. Section 102 contains "procedural" provisions "which are designed to see that all federal agencies do in fact exercise the substantive discretion given to them." Thus, the provision that each agency consider environmental factors "to the fullest extent possible" was a strict requirement "which must be rigorously enforced by the reviewing courts." It is critical to understand that this language does not provide an escape hatch for foot-dragging agencies; it does not make NEPA's procedural requirements somehow "discretionary." Congress did not intend the Act to be such a paper tiger.

On Ronald Reagan's first day in office as president in 1981, he cut half the positions for the CEQ staff, signaling that his vision of "regulatory relief" for business and industry would include considerable indifference to environmental impact. He was unable to abolish the council, however, because it was established by statute. The legislative strategy pursued in Reagan's first term, to weaken or repeal NEPA and other environmental laws, foundered on congressional

Council on Environmental Quality

The Council on Environmental Quality (CEQ), which consisted of three board members appointed by the president of the United States, was created by the National Environmental Policy Act of 1969. The CEQ's members were responsible for formulating policies designed to improve the environment. Its responsibilities included conducting studies and reporting the subsequent results to both the president and the U.S. Congress.

The creation of the CEQ was controversial from the very beginning. It was first proposed in 1967 by Senator Henry Jackson (D-WA), who wanted the office created to coordinate the many federal agencies whose responsibilities involved environmental matters. The idea was opposed by President Richard Nixon, who opted instead to create the Environmental Quality Council (EQC) as a cabinet-level post by executive order on May 29, 1969. Believing that the EQC was an ineffective organization intended to put forth the mirage that the president was interested in addressing environmental issues, members of Congress created the council they envisioned in the National Environmental Policy Act of 1969.

During the Nixon and Ford administrations, the CEQ was largely ignored. Its influence grew under President Jimmy Carter, who used its studies to shape environmental policy. The council's power quickly waned under the successive administrations of Presidents Ronald Reagan and George H. W. Bush. In 1993, President Bill Clinton replaced the CEQ with the White House Office on Environmental Policy.

—John R. Burch Jr.

BIBLIOGRAPHY

Clark, Ray, and Larry W. Canter, eds. *Environmental Policy and NEPA: Past, Present, and Future.* Boca Raton, FL: St. Lucie Press, 1997.
Glasson, John, Riki Therivel, and Andrew Chadwick. *Introduction to Environmental Impact Assessment.* 3rd ed. New York: Routledge, 2005.

and public opposition. During his second term, his messages to Congress accompanying annual CEQ reports worked to establish an environmental policy for his administration, asserting in 1988 that "the necessary relationship between freedom and opportunity," included "progress in restoring and maintaining the quality of the human environment" (Peterson 2004, 149).

President Bill Clinton also proposed eliminating the CEQ; he wanted to replace it with an environmental policy advisor to the president. The council has never returned to the influential position it held during the 1970s. The most vigorous enforcement of NEPA has been through citizen action in the courts, mostly centered on the adequacy and thoroughness of environmental impact statements and review of whether environmental factors have been considered to the fullest extent possible. Litigation has declined over the years, as environmental policy has become routinely integrated into the planning of government-funded projects.

During NEPA's first quarter century, over 26,000 environmental impact statements, and perhaps a hundred times as many environmental assessments were completed. In the spring of 1994, CEQ initiated a comprehensive study of NEPA's strengths and limitations, calling upon the original framers of NEPA, other members of Congress, representatives of government agencies and businesses, citizen groups, attorneys, Native American tribes, personnel who had drafted CEQ regulations, and representatives of state and local government to participate. The law has increased public involvement in planning and decision making by government agencies, and it has increased public access to information about agency plans. Private businesses seek more flexibility, less time-consuming processes, and a balance between costs and benefits, but many companies appreciate a consistent, predictable process for factoring environmental concerns into business planning.

—Charles Rosenberg

See also: *Army Corps of Engineers, United States; Evolution of Environmental Law; Watt, James G.*

BIBLIOGRAPHY

Andrus v. Sierra Club, 442 U.S. 347 (1979).

Bregman, Jacob I. *Environmental Impact Statements.* 2nd ed. Boca Raton, FL: CRC Press, 1999.

Buck, Susan J. *Understanding Environmental Administration and Law.* 2nd ed. Washington, DC: Island Press, 1996.

Caldwell, Lynton Keith. *The National Environmental Policy Act: An Agenda for the Future.* Bloomington: Indiana University Press, 1998.

Calvert Cliffs' Coordinating Committee, Inc. v. AEC, 449 F.2d 1109 (1971).

Hearings on S. 1075, S. 237, and S. 1752 Before the Senate Committee on Interior and Insular Affairs, 91st Cong., 1st Sess. (April 1969).

Lindstrom, Matthew J., and Zachary Alden Smith. *The National Environmental Policy Act: Judicial Misconstruction, Legislative Indifference, and Executive Neglect.* College Station: Texas A&M University Press, 2001.

NEPA ("National Environmental Policy Act"). http://ceq.hss.doe.gov/laws_and_executive_orders/the_nepa_statute.html.

Peterson, Tarla Rai, ed. *Green Talk in the White House: The Rhetorical Presidency Encounters Ecology.* College Station: Texas A&M University Press, 2004.

Warren, Louis S. *American Environmental History.* Malden, MA: Blackwell, 2007.

National Historic Preservation Act of 1966

In 1956, President Eisenhower passed the National Interstate and Defense Highway Act, which was designed to make transportation of military equipment and personnel easier throughout the country. An unintended result of this Act was the demolition of many historic properties. During the Kennedy administration in the early 1960s, the Urban Renewal Program was developed to help bring new life into cities. As with the National Interstate and Defense Highway Act, an unintended result was further destruction of historical sites.

In response to the public outcry, First Lady "Ladybird" Johnson compiled several essays regarding the value of America's historic sites into one report entitled *A Heritage So Rich.* This report spread public awareness about the value of historical sites and their destruction, and it helped prompt the National Historic Preservation Act of 1966 (Pub. L. 89-665, 16 U.S.C 470 et seq.), signed by President Lyndon B. Johnson. The general purpose of the Act was to preserve designated historic places for future generations. The Act states that "the preservation of this irreplaceable heritage is in the public interest so that its vital legacy of cultural, educational, aesthetics, inspirational, economic, and energy benefits will be maintained and enriched for future generations of Americans." It was also hoped that an increased knowledge of the nation's historic resources and the encouragement of preservation would promote economic growth, as more federal and federally funded projects were developed.

Components of the Act

The National Historic Preservation Act has four major components: an Advisory Council on Historic Preservation, a State Historic Preservation Office, the National Register of Historic Places, and the Section 106 Review Process. Section 106 can impact the development of water resources in that it requires federal agencies, such as the Bureau of Reclamation and the Army Corps of Engineers, to take the effects of their undertakings on historic sites into account. The presence of such sites can stop reclamation projects, and even when their presence does not stop construction, it can cause delays so that the sites can be fully studied and, if at all possible, preserved. The Advisory Council on Historic Preservation, which makes such decisions, is made up of twenty members from both the public and private sectors. It meets four times a year, with its main purpose being to advise the president and Congress on historic preservation issues. It also works to develop policies and guidelines concerning historic sites within the United States and its associated territories. The Advisory Council is also responsible for any conflicts that occur within the Section 106 Review Process.

The State Historic Preservation Office oversees individual statewide historic properties. There are fifty-nine State Historic Preservation Offices, one per state and the rest for designated territories and districts, such as Puerto Rico and the Virgin Islands. Other responsibilities of the State Historic Preservation Office include preparing and implementing a comprehensive statewide historic preservation plan and educating, training, and offering technical assistance to the public about historic preservation. The office maintains historical and archeological databases. It is also responsible for nominating and evaluating properties for the National Historic Register, which is the nation's official list of districts, sites, buildings, structures, and objects deemed worthy of preservation.

The National Parks Service operates the National Register of Historic Places. For a site or building to be added to the National Historic Register, it must meet certain criteria and be considered worth preserving. However, being added to the National Register of Historic Places does not automatically make a building or site immune to change or even demolition. Inclusion on the Register does make a property eligible for certain grants, loans, and tax incentives.

The Section 106 Review Process is another part of the National Historic Preservation Act that helps protect historical sites from damage or severe alteration. Section 106 requires a thorough review of any projects, either federally or privately funded, that will impact a listing on the National Register of Historic Places. According to Section 106, if a project won't have any harmful effects on a historical site, the applying agency must document it in writing. If a project will alter a historic site, then the applying agency must first work with the local State Historical Preservation Office as well as all other interested parties (home or business owners with properties nearby, for example) to ensure that the plan is reviewed and the public is allowed to comment on it. Section 106 also encourages different approaches to construction projects, but, like the National Register of Historic Places, it does not make properties or structures immune to alterations or even total destruction.

To qualify for the National Register for Historic Places, sites need to meet certain criteria, including age and integrity: Is the property old enough to be considered historic (generally at least fifty years old), and does it still look much the way it did in the past? Another aspect considered is significance: Is the property associated with events, activities, or developments that were important in the past? Was it home to someone of historical importance? Is the site known for significant architectural history, landscape history, or engineering achievements? Can the site be used to divulge historical information, as an archeological site might be able to?

Expanding the Act

There have been three major extensions of the National Historic Preservation Act since its inception in 1966. In 1976, Section 106 was extended to include archeological sites and other historic resources, not just those on the National Register of Historic Places. In 1980, Section 110 was added: it "sets out the broad historic preservation responsibilities of Federal agencies and is intended to ensure that historic preservation is fully integrated into the ongoing programs of all Federal agencies" ("Secretary of the Interior's" 1998, ¶ 1). In 1992, Native American and Native Hawaiian preservation efforts were given special preservation recognition.

The National Historic Preservation Act has increased the number of jobs in the fields of history and archeology. Currently more than 80,000 sites are listed on the National Register of Historic Places, representing approximately 1.4 million individual resources, including buildings, sites, districts, structures, and objects. The Act, which originally targeted individual buildings (which were typically converted into museums), has stretched to cover entire neighborhoods, reservations, and districts. These facts indicate that the National Historic Preservation Act has indeed been a success. Thanks to the National Historic Preservation Act, the rich heritage of the United States, including the uniqueness of different regions, has been preserved through these sites. Many tourist attractions throughout the country are rooted in local history, which might not have been saved if not for this Act.

—Lorri Brown

See also: *National Parks and Water*

BIBLIOGRAPHY

Duerksen, Christopher J., ed. *A Handbook on Historic Preservation Law.* Washington, DC: Conservation Foundation and National Center for Preservation Law, 1983.

"National Historic Preservation Act of 1966, As amended through 2000 [With annotations]." http://www.achp.gov/NHPA.pdf.

National Register of Historic Places. http://www.nps.gov/history/nr/.

"The Secretary of the Interior's Standards and Guidelines for Federal Agency Historic Preservation Programs Pursuant to the National Historic Preservation Act: Section 110 of the National Historic Preservation Act (16 U.S.C. 470)." As published in the *Federal Register* April 24, 1998. http://www.nps.gov/history/hps/fapa_110.htm.

Tunnard, Christopher. "Landmarks of Beauty." In *With Heritage So Rich: A Report of a Special Committee on Historic Preservation,* edited by Albert Rains and Laurance G. Henderson. New York: Random House, 1966.

National Marine Fisheries Service

The National Marine Fisheries Service (NMFS) was established as a division of the National Oceanic and Atmospheric Administration (NOAA). Based in Silver Spring, Maryland, it exercises stewardship over all living marine resources and their habitats between 3 nautical miles (370 km) and 200 nautical miles (about 6 km) from the U.S. coast, this being the area covered by the U.S. Exclusive Economic Zone. The NMFS mission statement notes that the service is tasked to "conserve, protect, and manage living marine resources in a way that ensures their continuation as functioning components of marine ecosystems, affords economic opportunities, and enhances the quality of life for the American public" (NOAA Fisheries Service n.d.).

One of the major roles of the NMFS, stipulated by the Magnuson-Stevens Fishery Conservation and Management Act of 1976, is to assess and predict fish stocks and ensure that fishing practices comply with all fisheries regulations and are as efficient as possible. In addition, under both the Marine Mammal Protection Act of 1972 and the Endangered Species Act of 1973, the NMFS is responsible for the recovery of protected marine species such as whales and sea turtles; however, it must do so without interfering unnecessarily with economic and recreational interests. The NMFS must also promote sustainable fisheries while preventing lost economic potential due to overfishing and environmental degradation.

Overall, the NMFS has had a large number of successes. In 1970, for example, Clyde MacKenzie, an authority on shellfish, helped to restore oysters in Long Island Sound off the coast of Connecticut. Later that year, the NMFS was involved in the testing of swordfish, which had started to show large concentrations of mercury; also showing abnormal levels of this dangerous element were Alaskan fur seals, Great Lakes salmon, and some tuna tested by the Food and Drug Administration. The mercury, entering the marine environment through industrial pollution, was thought to have been ingested by small marine organisms, which were then eaten by small fish and then by larger fish and seals. This discovery was widely publicized, and the NMFS stated that it would start testing many species of ocean fish to see how widespread the problem was. In May 1974, the NMFS dealt with fifteen Russian trawlers that cut through the fishing gear of an American lobster boat eighty-five miles south of Nantucket Island, Massachusetts.

The NMFS has also exercised stewardship over whale populations. In 2007, it issued regulations to prevent fatal fishing gear entanglements. Environmental groups had proposed such regulations for two years to protect the North Atlantic right whale, as only 350 were thought to remain. Furthermore, the shipping lanes in and out of Boston Harbor were changed starting July 1, 2007, to avoid as many collisions with right whales as possible.

—Justin Corfield

See also: *Endangered Species Act (1973)*

BIBLIOGRAPHY

Davenport, Stephen, Jr. "Comeback of the Oyster." *New York Times Magazine,* December 20, 1970.

Lichtenstein, Grace. "Fish Scares Trim Sales and Worry Fulton Dealers." *New York Times,* June 18, 1971.

Lyons, Richard D. "FDA May Impose Swordfish Curbs; Mercury in Tests Reported to Exceed Guidelines." *New York Times,* December 23, 1970.

NOAA Fisheries Service (National Oceanic and Atmospheric Administration's National Marine Fisheries Service). http://www.nmfs.noaa.gov/.

Stankus, Francis. "L.I. Biologists Puzzled by Fish Kill Mystery." *New York Times,* October 10, 1971.

New Mexico v. Aamodt (1976 and 1985)

Given the ambiguous nature of American Indian water rights in general (what water historian Norris Hundley Jr. called "confusion elevated to principle") and the even more complex nature of Pueblo Indian water rights, it is not surprising that the extent of Pueblo water claims would have to be decided in the courts. The suit was initiated by the water engineer of the State of New Mexico in 1966 as part of his effort to have the entire Rio Grande Basin allocated. The central point at issue between the state and the Pueblos in *New Mexico v. Aamodt* was whether the Pueblos were subject to state water law under the doctrine of prior appropriation, rather than the reserved rights doctrine applied to Indian tribes under the *Winters* decision.

Aamodt I

In 1969, after the original decision by the state water engineer had determined that the Pueblos were to be subject to New Mexico's prior appropriation water laws, the All Indian Pueblo Council (AIPC) began to compile legal materials for an appeal to the Tenth Circuit Court of Appeals. The Pueblos also demanded that Interior Secretary Walter Hickel meet with them and explain the government's inaction in defending their rights in *Aamodt*. In November 1972, with the *Aamodt* litigation still pending, the AIPC prepared a report called *The Right to Remain Indian: The Failure of the Federal Government to Protect Indian Land and Water Rights*. This report eloquently documented the inherent contradiction between the role of the United States as trustee for the tribes and its responsibilities in connection with water development for non-Indians. The report then went on to point out the legal responsibilities of government as trustee to provide water to the Pueblos in accordance with the guidelines set out in the *Winters* and *Arizona v. California* decisions. Central to the Pueblos' argument of governmental failure was that the federal government had been remiss in protecting Pueblo waters in the face of growing non-Indian demand as the West experienced a post–World War II population boom.

In 1976, the Tenth Circuit Court of Appeals reached an initial decision known as *Aamodt I* (537 F.2d 1102, 1976). The court reversed the decision of the U.S. District Court, which had upheld the state engineer's determination. The Pueblos argued that they had a federally reserved right to enough water to irrigate all of their irrigable lands. The court agreed, to a large extent, ruling that the Pueblos fall under state law only when they acquire lands with appurtenant pre-existing state law water rights. However, as such rights did not apply to the vast majority of Pueblo landholdings, *Aamodt I* can be rightfully seen as arguing that most Pueblo lands, and their appurtenant water rights, are outside the jurisdiction of state prior appropriation law.

The Pueblos considered *Aamodt I* to be a great victory, as they believed the appeals court decision would mean that the district court would have to rule that the Pueblos' lands did indeed possess a federally reserved right. In 1983, the Pueblos moved for a summary judgment in the *Aamodt* case. They were stunned when the judge presiding in the case, Edwin Mechem, denied their motion. Mechem declared that the issue of whether the *Winters* doctrine was applicable to the Pueblos' lands was still undecided. Because the Treaty of Guadalupe Hidalgo, which conveyed the territory of New Mexico to the United States, had guaranteed that all the land and water rights possessed by Mexican citizens (which the Pueblos were) would be honored, it was an important first step to determine what their rights were before the American period. The state argued that the Pueblos' rights were to be considered as equal to those of any other citizen. This "equal" status had important ramifications for the Pueblos in the modern context. The Pueblos' lands had been confirmed by Spanish land grant rather than by federal government order, giving their lands a different status than that of other Indian reservations.

Aamodt II

With all of this in mind, finally in 1985 the courts spoke on Pueblo water rights again in *Aamodt II* (618 F.Supp 996, 1985). Judge Mechem decided that the vast majority of the Pueblos' lands were not to be considered as being reserved by the federal government for the Pueblos and, thus, would not possess *Winters* reserved water rights. As a result, the Pueblos were not entitled to the same status as other tribes because the means by which their lands had been established was different. In a fairly original ruling in the annals of Indian natural resource law, Mechem based the bulk of the Pueblos' claims on federal law regarding the land's aboriginal title rather than on treaty rights. In essence, *Aamodt II* declared that while the Pueblos' lands were not subject to New Mexico's prior appropriation laws, neither did they possess *Winters* rights. However, the decision still was not final, as it did not determine the extent of Pueblo Indian water rights. It would take over two decades of inaction before that question would be answered.

Despite the case's interminable nature, the *Aamodt* decisions have allowed the Pueblos to determine the purpose and place of their water use, without submitting to state prior appropriation law, at least on some of their lands.

With the continuing growth of the urban West, the demands on New Mexico's water supply will never decrease. The problem is that the Pueblos, were they to be granted a large Winters or other federal water award, could conceivably claim more water than New Mexico's already apportioned share of the waters of the Colorado and Rio Grande Rivers.

The possible use of some Pueblo water rights to allow non-Indian rights access to water during droughts required negotiated agreements with the Pueblos. After six years of settlement talks ordered by the federal courts, an agreement was reached in 2006, and approved by Congress in 2010, among the four pueblos, the city of Santa Fe, and the State of New Mexico that protects existing water users and allows for future non-Indian growth. The Pueblos had to give up their Winters rights (as with most negotiated water settlements) but were guaranteed a permanent water right and, more importantly, a steady, reliable supply of water.

—Steven L. Danver

See also: Arizona v. California *(1963);* Winters v. United States *(1908)*

BIBLIOGRAPHY

All Indian Pueblo Council. *The Right to Remain Indian: The Failure of the Federal Government to Protect Indian Water Rights.* Native American Legal Materials Collection No. 1040. Albuquerque, NM: All Indian Pueblo Council, 1972.

Atencio, Steve. "First in Time First in Rights." *New Mexico's 19 Pueblo News* 1, no. 11 (1974).

Klein, Don. Memorandum to S. E. Reynolds, April 10, 1977, RE: Proposed 25 C.F.R. PART 260, 42 F.R. 14, 885, March 17, 1977. Governor Bruce King Papers, New Mexico State Records Center, Santa Fe.

Maynez, A. Patrick. "Pueblo Indian Water Rights: Who Will Get the Water? *New Mexico v. Aamodt.*" *Natural Resources Journal* 18 (1978).

Montoya, Harry B. "Aamodt Settlement a Good End to Decades of Litigation." *Santa Fe New Mexican,* October 31, 2009. Available at http://www.santafenewmexican.com/opinion/My-View-Aamodt-settlement-a-good-end-to-decades-of-litigation.

Newville, Ed. "Pueblo Indian Water Rights: Overview and Update on the Aamodt Litigation." *Natural Resources Journal* 29, no. 1 (1989): 251–78.

Rosenfelt, Daniel M. *Report on the Protection of Pueblo Indian Rights to the Use of Water in the Rio Grande Basin: A Discussion of Pending Litigation.* Albuquerque: University of New Mexico School of Law Library, 1969.

Sheridan, Mark F. *Law of the Rio Grande: Pueblo Indian Water Rights, the Federal Law Sources; A Non-Pueblo Position.* Santa Fe, NM: Holland & Hart, 2002. Available at http://www.westernwaterlaw.com/articles/nonpuebl.pdf.

Newell, Frederick H.

Frederick H. Newell (1862–1932) worked for the U.S. Geological Survey, becoming its chief engineer and then its director from 1907 until 1914. Involved in countless surveys, he helped to develop the irrigation of the western United States.

Early Life and Surveys

Frederick Haynes Newell was born on March 5, 1862, in Bradford, Pennsylvania, the son of Augustus William Newell and Anna Maria (née Haynes). Augustus was a civil engineer. Both his parents had been born in Massachusetts, and Frederick grew up in Newton, Massachusetts. His mother died when he was young, and he was brought up by his aunts. Interested in genealogy, he wrote an account of his family that appeared in the *New England Historical and Genealogical Register* in 1893. He studied at the Massachusetts Institute of Technology, where he earned a Bachelor of Science in mining engineering, before

Frederick H. Newell (1862–1932) in a photograph taken circa 1903. Newell was an engineer with the U.S. Geological Survey who worked mainly on irrigation projects.
Library of Congress

working on land surveys in Pennsylvania, Virginia, Colorado, and elsewhere for three years. On October 2, 1888, the U.S. Geological Survey hired him as an assistant hydraulic engineer. He worked under John Wesley Powell and, for the next fourteen years, was involved in carrying out surveys for projects to irrigate the arid western part of the United States. Many of his surveys were published, including *Hydrography of the Arid Regions* (1891), *Report on Agriculture by Irrigation in the Western Part of the United States* (1894), *The Public Lands of the United States and Their Water Supply* (1895), and *Irrigation in the United States* (1902 and revised in 1906).

Reclamation Work

In 1902, the Reclamation Act became law, and Newell, who had helped in the drafting of it, was made the chief engineer of the Reclamation Service, working under Charles D. Walcott. In 1903, he was made secretary of the National Geographic Society. Then in 1907, Newell was appointed director of the Reclamation Service, which soon afterward was made an independent bureau within the Department of the Interior. During this time, Newell was involved in surveying for twenty-five irrigation projects that cost a total of $100 million. These projects saw the construction of several dams, tunnels, and canals; the creation of reservoirs, and the erection of power plants and pumping stations. These provided enough water for an additional 1.5 million acres of land to be brought under cultivation.

He also conducted surveys in Hawaii, which led to his book *Hawaii, Its Natural Resources and Opportunities for Home-Making* (1909). Based on his work in Puerto Rico, he wrote a report titled *Natural Resources of Puerto Rico*. He also wrote, with D. W. Murphy, *Principles of Irrigation Engineering, Arid Lands, Water Supply, Storage Works, Dams, Canals, Water Rights and Products* (1913), *Irrigation Management: The Operation, Maintenance, and Betterment of Works for Bringing Water to Agricultural Lands* (1916), and *Water Powers of Virginia*.

Later Life

In 1914, Newell was replaced as director of the Reclamation Service by Arthur Powell Davis (nephew of John Wesley Powell and an important engineer in his own right), and Newell went on to become a consulting engineer, publishing a series of papers called *Engineering as a Career* (1916) and *Water Resources: Present and Future Uses* (1920). However, Newell was unsatisfied with this role, and the following year

he was appointed head of the Department of Civil Engineering at the University of Illinois. Then in 1918 Newell was awarded the Cullum Gold Medal by the American Geographical Society for his achievements in irrigation. In 1919, he wrote a short booklet, *Asiatic Turkey: Its Problems and Resources,* published by the university. Although he liked his role at the University of Illinois, he found life in Urbana, Illinois, awkward and isolating. In 1920, he resigned and moved to Washington, D.C., having been made president of the American Association of Engineers the previous year. Then in 1924, with A. B. McDaniel, he founded an engineering consulting firm, the Research Service, with himself as president.

Newell served on the U.S. Land Commission, the Inland Waterways Commission, the Advisory Board on Fuels and Structural Materials, and, briefly, the Illinois State Board of Examiners of Structural Materials. His last work was as editor of *Planning and Building the City of Washington* (1932).

Frederick Newell had married Effie Josephine Mackintosh in 1890, and they had two sons and two daughters; his older son predeceased him. He died on July 5, 1932, in Washington, D.C., from heart failure. His papers are held in the Library of Congress.

—Justin Corfield

See also: *Inland Waterways Commission; Reclamation Act of 1902*

BIBLIOGRAPHY

Davis, Arthur Powell. "Frederick Haynes Newell." In *Dictionary of American Biography,* Vol. 13, 456–57. New York: Charles Scribner's Sons, 1934.
Jackson, Donald C. "Engineering in the Progressive Era: A New Look at Frederick Haynes Newell and the U.S. Reclamation Service." *Technology and Culture* 34, no. 3 (1993): 539–74.
Newell, Frederick Haynes. *Irrigation in the United States.* Rev. ed. New York: T. Y. Crowell, 1906.

Newlands, Francis G.

Francis Griffin Newlands (1848–1902), a Democratic member of the U.S. House of Representatives (1893–1902) and of the Senate (1903–1917) from Nevada, was one of the "big three" of the irrigation movement during the late nineteenth and early twentieth centuries. Along with George Maxwell, the leader of the National Irrigation Association, and Frederick Newell, of the U.S. Geological Survey, Newlands crafted and then introduced into Congress the Reclamation Act (or Newlands Act) of 1902, which was signed into law by President Theodore Roosevelt

Francis G. Newlands (1848–1902) was a Democratic member of Congress from Nevada in both the House of Representatives and the Senate. He was the sponsor of the Reclamation Act of 1902, which provided federal funding for irrigation projects throughout the United States. Library of Congress

on June 17, 1902. The Reclamation Act provided federal funding for large-scale irrigation projects in the arid western United States. It authorized the Secretary of the Interior to identify locations and to construct dams and reservoirs in sixteen western states and territories: Arizona, California, Colorado, Idaho, Kansas, Montana, Nebraska, Nevada, New Mexico, North Dakota, Oklahoma, Oregon, South Dakota, Utah, Washington, and Wyoming. The Act created the Reclamation Service, which in turn hired an army of engineers to construct irrigation works. Early projects included Milk River, Montana; the Newlands Project on the Truckee River in Newlands's home state; and Salt River, Arizona. Newlands was elected to the Senate in 1903, and there he continued to promote federal reclamation, which he viewed as essential to the economic development of the western states.

Early Life

Newlands was born to Scottish immigrants on August 28, 1848, in the antebellum river town Natchez, Mississippi.

Newlands's childhood was characterized by mobility, loss, and financial insecurity. After losing their father to alcoholism, Newlands and his four siblings were raised by their mother.

Newlands, by then known as Frank to his family, entered Yale at the age of fourteen but was forced to withdraw in 1866 due to financial problems; his stepfather had died of cholera; a sister was divorced; and his eldest brother, gravely wounded during the Civil War, was enduring an ongoing convalescence (Rowley 1996). Newlands returned to what was then his family's home in Washington, D.C., and attended law school at Columbian University (later George Washington University). Upon entrance to the bar of the District of Columbia in 1869, Newlands began to attend important social and political events throughout the city, and he capitalized on his relationship with a friend of his stepfather's, Secretary of the Interior Orville H. Browning. According to his biographer, William D. Rowley, Newlands was not a part of the inner social workings of Washington, but he learned—through study and attendance of critical social events—the proper attire, habits, and conduct of an educated person from an elite family (Rowley 1996). He put this training to use when he moved to San Francisco in 1870, where he met and married Clara A. Sharon, the daughter of William Sharon, the Comstock Lode magnate and one of the wealthiest men on the Pacific Coast. After his wife and father-in-law died, Newlands relocated to Nevada, where he sought opportunity as an irrigation advocate in the wake of the bust of the Comstock Lode. Despite having to fight off criticism from Nevada residents who resented the Sharon fortune as being that of a robber baron, Newlands was elected to the House in 1893.

Political Ambitions and Reclamation Work

Water issues and irrigation became the cornerstones of Newlands's political ambitions. As early as 1889, Newlands was calling for extensive surveys of water usage and water resources and the cession of public domain land for the development of irrigation projects, a stance consistent with his view that water conservation meant use for agriculture and that unutilized water constituted wasted water. Newlands was chosen as Nevada's delegate to the first irrigation congress, held in Salt Lake City, Utah, in 1891. An additional irrigation congress, held in California in 1893, formally called for the cession of public lands to states for the purposes of irrigation development and settlement (Elliott 1987, 176). The resulting Carey Act authorized the Secretary of the Interior to cede up to 1 million acres to arid states if the states agreed to irrigate and occupy the lands. Few states could muster the financial footing to make the Carey Act work, however, and only Wyoming launched Carey Act projects during the 1890s. The most successful Carey Act projects, the Twin Falls projects of Idaho, were established during the first decade of the twentieth century (Idaho State Historical Society 2004, 7–10). The Carey Act's failures led to the push for federal funding realized in the Reclamation Act.

As a senator, Newlands's views represented the "western wing of the Progressive movement" (Rowley 2000, 102). Newlands supported irrigation as part of a Progressive reform plan that embraced efficiency and national conservation, a position consistent with that of Theodore Roosevelt. In areas of race relations, however, Newlands was an antebellum Democrat—he believed that nonwhites had no voting role in a functional democracy, a stance consistent with that of many southern and western Progressives.

Newlands was re-elected to the Senate in 1908. He continued to advance the cause of federal reclamation. As a member of the 1909 Senate Irrigation and Reclamation of Arid Lands Committee, he disagreed with fellow committee members who believed that the Reclamation Service had built too many projects too quickly. His minority report, cosigned by fellow irrigation supporter Senator William Borah (R–ID), argued that the majority of settlers on the majority of projects succeeded (Pisani 2002). Newlands also chaired the Committee on Corporations Organized in the District of Columbia and served on the Committee on Revolutionary Claims and the Committee on Interstate Commerce during his Senate career.

Newlands died on December 24, 1917, in Washington, D.C. He is buried at Oak Hill Cemetery.

—Laura Woodworth-Ney

See also: *Carey Act of 1894; Newell, Frederick H.; Reclamation Act of 1902*

BIBLIOGRAPHY
Dudley, Shelly C. "The First Five: A Brief Overview of the First Five Reclamation Projects." Available at http://www.waterhistory.org/histories/reclamation/reclamation.pdf.

Elliott, Russell R. *History of Nevada*. With the assistance of William D. Rowley. Lincoln: University of Nebraska Press, 1987.

Idaho State Historical Society. "The Carey Act in Idaho." 2004. http://www.history.idaho.gov/Carey_Act.pdf.

Linenberger, Toni Rae. *Dams, Dynamos, and Development: The Bureau of Reclamation's Power Program and Electrification of the West.* With contributions by Leah S. Glaser. Washington, DC: United States Department of the Interior, Bureau of Reclamation, 2002.

Pisani, Donald J. *Water and American Government: The Reclamation Bureau, National Water Policy, and the West, 1902–1935*. Berkeley: University of California Press, 2002.

Rowley, William D. "Francis G. Newlands, Water for the West, and Progressivism." In *The Human Tradition in the Gilded Age and Progressive Era*, edited by Ballard C. Campbell, 101–118. Wilmington, DE: SR Books, 2000.

Rowley, William D. *Reclaiming the Arid West: The Career of Francis G. Newlands*. Bloomington: Indiana University Press, 1996.

Newlands Act
See *Reclamation Act of 1902*

Nonindigenous Aquatic Nuisance Prevention and Control Act of 1990

On November 29, 1990, the U.S. Congress passed the Nonindigenous Aquatic Nuisance Prevention and Control Act of 1990 (NANPCA) to address the ecological and economic crises of infestations of nonindigenous species in the Great Lakes that threatened "the diversity or abundance of native species or the ecological stability of infested waters, or commercial, agricultural, aquacultural or recreational activities dependent on such waters" (NANPCA 1990, § 1003[1]). Congress passed NANPCA (Pub. L. 101-646) in response to evidence that nonindigenous species such as the zebra mussel (*Dreissena polymorpha*) and Eurasian ruffe fish (*Gymnocephalus cernuus*) had damaged the ecosystems and associated economies of the Great Lakes, the world's largest freshwater port system, as well as other large lakes and river systems. Congress subsequently adopted several amendments to strengthen the Act's prevention and control programs, including the National Invasive Species Act of 1996.

Invasive Species in the United States

The perchlike ruffe first found its way into Lake Superior in the early to mid-1980s from the ballast tank of an ocean-going ship in Duluth-Superior Harbor in Minnesota. It spread via recreational boats and barges throughout Lake Superior and to Thunder Bay, Ontario, to Lake Huron, and to the Saint Louis River. A single female ruffe lays 13,000–200,000 eggs each year. In addition, it is known to eat the

Zebra mussels are a species native to Eurasia. Since arriving in North America in the 1980s, they have spread from the Great Lakes region to the Mississippi River and California, causing significant ecological damage. Zebra mussels can attach to boats and move freely between bodies of water.
U.S. Fish and Wildlife Service

eggs of other fish, including the yellow perch, with which it competes for food and habitat. As a result, the ruffe threatened native species, including the yellow perch, and the food sources of other game fish in the Minnesota fisheries program.

The zebra mussel was the second nonindigenous species to raise concerns among government officials and scientists in the late 1980s; a 1981 Canadian report predicting its invasion had failed to generate public attention or regulatory action. After a biologist working for the Detroit Edison Company first noticed the zebra mussel in Lake Saint Clair, Michigan, in July 1988, scientists determined that the bivalve from the Caspian Sea had been introduced into American waters by untreated ballast water from a foreign vessel. The mussels, which can produce up to 40,000 eggs each year, spread quickly throughout the Great Lakes, into the Mississippi River and Hudson River systems, and into other bodies of water, including the headwaters of Chesapeake Bay. Its financial impact was quickly felt. Zebra mussels "colonized" boat hulls, sank navigational buoys, clogged pipes used in municipal drinking-water systems and power-plant-cooling systems, and rendered unusable a variety of smaller commercial and recreational structures. Marine ecologist James T. Carlton described the zebra mussel's presence as "one of the outstanding invasions of North

America in the past 200 years" (quoted in Raloff 1992, 56). In May 1989, shortly after zebra mussels were discovered in North America, the Canadian government established guidelines encouraging ships to exchange their ballast in the ocean rather than in the Great Lakes.

Controlling the Spread of Invasive Species

To halt the spread of invasive species, NANPCA charged federal agencies with studying the impact of ballast water exchange on native species in the Great Lakes and devising ballast management regulations and sampling procedures, and it authorized the Aquatic Nuisance Species Task Force, comprising the National Oceanographic and Atmospheric Administration, U.S. Fish and Wildlife Service, and other agencies, to develop and implement programs for monitoring, controlling, and studying invasive species. The Act also charged the U.S. Army Corps of Engineers, a member of that task force, with developing a research and development program to control zebra mussel populations in particular. In 1992, the Corps established the Zebra Mussel Research Program (ZMRP) in conjunction with federal, state, private, and academic groups. The program yielded new monitoring methods and nontoxic filter systems to prevent mussels from clogging water intakes.

NANPCA led to the U.S. government creating ballast-water control guidelines similar to Canadian guidelines; in May 1993, those guidelines became the world's first ballast-water control law, requiring rather than recommending that foreign ships bound for the Great Lakes exchange ballast water in the open ocean. This requirement was subsequently extended to ships operating in the Hudson River watershed, considered a gateway to the Great Lakes.

In 1996, Congress adopted a more comprehensive amendment to NANPCA, the National Invasive Species Act (NISA) of 1996 (Pub. L. 104-332). This amendment identified new invasive species operating in ecosystems beyond the Great Lakes, including the mitten crab (*Eriocher sinensis*) found on the Pacific Coast and the brown mussel (*Perna*

perna) found in the Gulf of Mexico, two examples of "thousands" of nonindigenous species now found in the United States. In addition, the Act noted the potential for environmental, ecological, and economic damage from "aquatic nuisance vegetation species" such as the hydrilla and water hyacinth. The Act principally highlighted, however, the threat of the zebra mussel, cataloging new bodies of water it had invaded or threatened, including the Chesapeake Bay, which received the most foreign ballast water in the country. NISA established both new ballast-water exchange requirements and education and technical assistance programs to ensure compliance with them. It also established grounds for collaborating with foreign governments, especially Mexico and Canada, and operational requirements for U.S. Department of Defense vessels to adhere to new ballast-water exchange guidelines. It further charged the NISA Task Force with securing regional cooperation via Regional Panels, starting in the American West, and authorized funding for state-level education and control programs.

Critics of NISA, such as the Union of Concerned Scientists, contend that congressional funding of its programs has been inconsistent; that it neglects other mechanisms by which invasive species enter large bodies of water, especially those beyond the Great Lakes, the focus of NANCPA and NISA; and that ballast-water exchange programs by themselves are not sufficient to counter the threat of new invasions. In addition, NISA expired in 2002. Although the federal government has not amended or extended NISA, state governments have created their own programs. California, for example, adopted the 2003 Marine Invasive Species Act and the 2006 Coastal Regulations, Coastal Ecosystems Protection Act. Senator Carl Levin (D-MI) proposed a new incarnation of NISA, the National Aquatic Invasive Species Act of 2009, which Congress has not yet adopted as of this writing.

—Paul C. Rosier

See also: *Army Corps of Engineers, United States; Fish and Wildlife Service, United States; Great Lakes*

BIBLIOGRAPHY

McLean, Mike, and Douglas A. Jensen. "Ruffe: A New Threat to Our Fisheries" (OHSU-FS-064). 2nd ed. Great Lakes Sea Grant Network, 1996. Available at http://www.ohioseagrant.osu.edu/_documents/publications/FS/FS-064%20Ruffe%20A%20new%20threat%20to%20our%20fisheries.pdf.

NANPCA (Nonindigenous Aquatic Nuisance Prevention and Control Act of 1990). 16 U.S.C. § 4701 et seq. Available at http://anstaskforce.gov/Documents/nanpca90.pdf.

Raloff, Janet. "From Tough Ruffe to Quagga: Intimidating Invaders Alter Earth's Largest Freshwater Ecosystem." *Science News* 142, no. 4 (1992): 56–58. Available at http://findarticles.com/p/articles/mi_m1200/is_n4_v142/ai_12508323/.

Union of Concerned Scientists. "The National Invasive Species Act." August 2002. http://www.ucsusa.org/assets/documents/invasive_species/nisa-1.pdf.

Oil Pollution Act of 1990

The Oil Pollution Act (OPA) of 1990 is designed to broaden the abilities of the Environmental Protection Agency to respond to oil spills and to prevent spills from occurring in the first place. It is focused on the cleanup of spills on navigable waters and shorelines. A company is not permitted to ship oil into the United States without first creating a plan to prevent spills and to deal with a spill if one occurs. Along the lines of protecting the environment from oil damage, the OPA established the Oil Spill Liability Trust Fund, which provides up to $1 billion per spill for removal costs and the restoration of natural resources.

The legislation, which received strong support from both Democrats and Republicans in Congress, was essentially an effort to learn from the mistakes that led to the disastrous 1989 *Exxon Valdez* disaster in Prince William Sound in Alaska. This spill killed vast numbers of wildlife, contaminated the soil, and destroyed the livelihood of an entire community. Its effects have lasted for a generation and are estimated to last for many more.

Provisions of the Legislation

Several provisions in the OPA are obviously designed to prevent a repeat of the *Exxon Valdez* spill. Notably, the OPA mandates a double-hull design for oil tankers. A double hull would not have prevented the *Exxon Valdez* spill, but it might have reduced the amount of oil spilled by about 60 percent. The OPA also requires the testing of anyone holding a merchant mariner's license to determine if the individual has used alcohol or dangerous drugs. The captain of the *Exxon Valdez* was too drunk to operate the tanker under his command.

The OPA contains several other noteworthy sections. Congress concluded that the best interests of the United States were served by participating in an international oil pollution agreement that would prevent oil spills and guarantee prompt compensation for damages resulting from incidents. Since much of the oil being transported in

Exxon Valdez Oil Spill

On the night of March 23–24, 1989, the single-hulled supertanker *Exxon Valdez* ran aground on Bligh Reef in Prince William Sound in the Gulf of Alaska. The accident, which was blamed on the tanker's inebriated captain Joseph Hazelwood, resulted in the second-largest oil spill in U.S. history. Eleven million gallons of crude oil fouled more than 1,500 miles of shoreline. It was estimated that the oil killed approximately 250,000 birds, 2,800 otters, and more than 300 harbor seals. The accident decimated the region's commercial fishing economy, as the oil killed numerous fish and millions of their eggs.

Although Exxon spent more than $2 billion to clean up the region, oil residue continues to be discovered. In order to prevent a similar disaster in the future, oil companies operating in Alaska pledged to phase out single-hulled oil tankers by 2015. Public outrage over the *Exxon Valdez* incident was credited with the enactment of the Oil Pollution Act of 1990.

—John R. Burch Jr.

BIBLIOGRAPHY

Exxon Valdez Oil Spill Trustee Council. *Final Environmental Impact Statement for the* Exxon Valdez *Oil Spill Restoration Plan.* Anchorage, AK: *Exxon Valdez* Oil Spill Trustee Council, 1994. Summary available at http://www.evostc.state.ak.us/Universal/Documents/Restoration/1994RestorationPlanEISSummary.pdf.

American waters crosses through Canadian waters, the OPA requires the secretary of state to work with Canada to prevent discharges of oil into the Great Lakes. The OPA also requires tugboat escorts for all large tank vessels traveling through difficult waters, such as those in the Strait of Juan de Fuca and Haro Strait, both between Washington state and Vancouver. To guarantee that tankers are being guided by competent sailors, the secretary of state evaluates the training standards of foreign countries that send oil vessels into American waters.

The OPA contains a section, titled "Prince William Sound Provisions," that established the Prince William Sound Oil Spill Recovery Institute to identify and develop the best available techniques, equipment, and materials for dealing with oil spills in the arctic and subarctic environment. The legislation expressly requires the Institute to assess the long-range effects of the *Exxon Valdez* spill on the environment, the economy, and the well-being of the people in Prince William Sound. It is not permitted to make recommendations on any matter not directly related to the *Exxon Valdez* spill, which is likely an effort by legislators to limit the environmental activism of those individuals associated with the Institute. The OPA also requires tank vessels and facilities operating as part of the Trans-Alaska Pipeline Act to preposition oil spill containment and removal equipment in Prince William Sound. It advises that such equipment should include escort vessels with skimming capability, barges to receive recovered oil, and heavy-duty sea-pumping equipment that would help protect the environment, particularly fish hatcheries. The *Exxon Valdez* spill decimated hatcheries. The OPA further created an oil spill removal organization in the sound that consists of enough trained personnel to immediately remove a discharge of 200,000 barrels of oil.

The Prince William Sound Provisions close with a section prohibiting tank vessels that have spilled more than 1 million gallons of oil into the marine environment after March 22, 1989, from operating on the navigable waters of the sound. The *Exxon Valdez* spill took place on March 24, 1989, and spilled 10.8 million gallons of oil. Exxon took legal action in 1998 against the federal government on the grounds that the OPA constituted a bill of attainder, which is a regulation unfairly directed at one company alone. In 2002, Exxon lost in a ruling by the Ninth Circuit Court of Appeals. Under these particular regulations, the OPA has blocked more than a dozen vessels from traveling through Prince William Sound.

It is impossible to determine how many oil spills have been prevented by the OPA. However, it is noteworthy that no tanker disaster on the scale of the *Exxon Valdez* has occurred since passage of the legislation. If an oil tanker did ground in the same manner, the provisions of the OPA would likely prevent the same amount of environmental destruction from taking place. The successful management of an oil spill depends on the information that responders possess about the spill's ability to impact human health, groundwater, surface water, and soil. The OPA provides responders with much of this information as well as the equipment necessary for a quick response. However, it is quite possible that not all spills, especially small ones, are reported by oil transporters for fear of legal and financial consequences.

—Caryn Neumann

See also: *Environmental Protection Agency, United States*

BIBLIOGRAPHY

Moore, Emmett B. *An Introduction to the Management and Regulation of Hazardous Waste*. Columbus, OH: Battelle Press, 2000.

U.S. Congress, House Committee on Merchant Marine and Fisheries. *Compilation of Selected Coast Guard and Marine Transportation Laws with the Oil Pollution Act of 1990*. Washington, DC: U.S. Government Printing Office, 1993.

Pacific Northwest Electric Power Planning and Conservation Act (1980)

Passed by Congress in 1980 during the final days of the Jimmy Carter administration, the Pacific Northwest Electric Power Planning and Conservation Act (Pub. L. 96-501) established the Northwest Power Planning Council (NWPPC). This council was given the responsibility of providing comprehensive energy and conservation management for the states of Montana, Idaho, Washington, and Oregon, all part of the Columbia River Basin, to reduce costs through conservation, manage resources for the region more effectively, and develop alternative energy resources. The governor of each of the four states appoints two members to the council, with leadership of the council rotating among the states. The need to balance power production and distribution against environmental impacts drove this legislation, and the Act requires that the council take steps "to protect, mitigate and enhance the fish and wildlife, including related spawning grounds and habitat, of the Columbia River and its tributaries, particularly anadromous fish which are of significant importance to the social and economic well-being of the Pacific Northwest and the Nation and which are dependent on suitable environmental conditions" (§839[6]).

Origins of the Legislation

The reasons for this legislation were multiple. Disputes over proper allocation of public power, the collapse of Columbia River salmon and steelhead runs, interest in improving energy efficiency, and concern over future energy production and use drove Congress to create the Power Planning Council. The Act required the council to determine energy demand for a twenty-year period. It also compelled the Bonneville Power Administration (BPA) to pursue conservation measures before purchasing new power outputs and to prioritize conservation and alternative energy production such as wind, thermal, and solar power. The council also had

to preserve and restore salmon populations while pursuing this complex energy-use mandate.

To a large degree, the tribulations of Columbia River salmon were the genesis for this Act. Salmon populations were in so much danger that the National Marine Fisheries Service was moving to list several Columbia River salmon as endangered in 1979. The impetus for the legislation then, was to protect salmon while preventing federal intervention in Columbia River Basin hydroelectric production. The Columbia River Basin Fish and Wildlife Program (CRBFWP) was created in 1982 to implement the environmental goals of the legislation.

Effectiveness of the Program

The effectiveness of this program was soon tested. A 1984 request by fish agencies for increased water releases to raise low river levels and speed the migration of salmon smolts to the ocean was weakened by the Northwest Power Planning Council. This revealed the fundamental tension and weakness in the agency created by the Act, as well as its lack of regulatory power. Public utilities expressed concern over the difficulty of power planning if water were to be released at different and unpredictable times based on seasonal stream conditions. The compromise was to schedule the water releases in advance, ignoring the reality of river hydrology and limiting the program's effectiveness.

The creation of this council has increased the dependence on technological solutions to fishery problems. The solutions to salmon declines have been consistently dependent on science and technology. Fish-friendly turbines, the transport of salmon smolts downstream on barges past reservoirs and turbines, reservoir drawdowns, increased tracking and research on salmon and smolt migration, and incentive programs for killing predators like the northern pikeminnow have cost billions of dollars while providing limited value. The value for the council and for the BPA is that the Act has seemed to offer solutions during the ongoing and worsening salmon crisis, thereby preventing more radical measures such as dam removal. Funds have also been directed at restoration of important salmon, steelhead, and other wildlife habitat as well as the outright purchase of important land for restoration and protection, with more than 350,000 acres having been purchased by 2003.

In 1994, Congress created the Independent Scientific Group (ISG) to study the continuing problems with Columbia and Snake River salmon. Noting the complexity of causes for continued salmon declines, the ISG proposed a return of the rivers to a condition as close to original ecosystem function as possible. This necessarily entails habitat restoration and reservoir drawdowns and could lead to dam removals. A furious debate erupted in the interior Pacific Northwest in the late 1990s over the future of the dams, salmon, and jobs in an economy consisting of logging, farming, river transportation, and aluminum smelting, which depend on hydroelectricity and the river lock system. Salmon advocates called for the removal of four dams on the Lower Snake River to achieve the stated goal of the ISG. While the dams were left intact, this debate led to the listing of some salmon as endangered and enhanced the ability of the Power Planning Council to compel changes in river use to improve salmon runs. The ongoing salmon crisis portends future calls for stronger measures, including dam removals, to protect and restore salmon, even while climate change is increasing the importance of hydroelectricity.

While the council has been limited by its lack of authority and the multiple, conflicting mandates that must be managed, it has sought to make improvements and progress where possible. The approach to fisheries and wildlife management has evolved over the last thirty years. The Power Planning Council via the CRBFWP promotes a flexible, complex program that moves beyond the simple model of technology and hatchery production to replace lost fish. For example, the hatcheries have been designed to prepare fish for a wild environment and to make their behavior more consistent with the wild salmon they will mix with in the river, reducing damage to wild salmon.

Likewise, looking forward to 2030, the Power Planning Council is seeking increased production via more efficient energy use. The regional population is expected to grow by approximately 4 million people, close to the increase of the last thirty years, and the senior citizen population is expected to double. This will necessarily increase demand for energy. In its sixth power plan (2009), the council called for greater conservation in the region, hoping to meet 58 percent of energy use growth by 2014 and increasing that to 85 percent over the next twenty years. Moreover, it seeks to meet new energy demands with alternative power sources.

—Jeff Crane

See also: *Columbia Basin Project; National Marine Fisheries Service*

BIBLIOGRAPHY

Bean, Michael J., and Melanie J. Rowland. *The Evolution of National Wildlife Law.* 3rd ed. Westport, CT: Praeger, 1997.
Feldman, David Lewis. *Water Policy for Sustainable Development.* Baltimore, MD: Johns Hopkins University Press, 2007.
Marston, Ed, ed. *Western Water Made Simple.* Washington, DC: Island Press, 1987.
National Research Council. *Upstream: Salmon and Society in the Pacific Northwest.* Washington, DC: National Academy Press, 1996.
Pacific Northwest Electric Power Planning and Conservation Act (aka Northwest Power Act), 16 U.S.C. 839 et seq. http://www.nwcouncil.org/library/poweract/default.htm.

Pacific Southwest Water Plan

In 1963, Secretary of the Interior Stewart Udall proposed the Pacific Southwest Water Plan. Anticipating the Supreme Court decision in the landmark *Arizona v. California* case, Udall recognized an urgent need for a comprehensive plan to allow orderly development to proceed. Disputes over the allotment of the Colorado River between Arizona and California after World War II had postponed the construction of the Central Arizona and other projects in the lower basin while the Supreme Court adjudicated the issue. Udall hoped the plan would solve long-standing water issues in southern California and Arizona and predicted the plan would fundamentally change the nature of western water politics.

Projects of the Plan

In April 1963, the Department of Interior distributed the draft plan to the states for review. The plan proposed the immediate construction of the Central Arizona Project, an investigation of the feasibility of augmenting the Colorado River by importing water from the Pacific Northwest, and a Pacific Southwest development fund to pay for the augmentation schemes. The proposals to augment the Colorado River from sources in northern California resulted in serious opposition. To soothe concerns, the Department of Interior dropped all reference to specific augmentation plans in the final draft.

The plan's development fund was based on the model used by the Central Valley Project, Pick-Sloan Missouri Basin Project, and Colorado River Storage Project. Hydropower revenues from the proposed Bridge and Marble Canyon dams would pay for augmentation, leading some to term them "cash register dams." The plan also proposed that a large portion of the project's cost be declared nonreimbursable to supply water to meet U.S. treaty obligations with Mexico. In addition, at the request of the states, the revised draft for the augmentation scheme included the use of power revenues to keep the price of water the same as if it had been diverted directly from the Colorado River. However, municipal and industrial water was to remain unsubsidized. The Bureau of Reclamation also deleted plans for a demonstration desalination plant in the initial phase.

The initial phase of the plan called for the construction of the Central Arizona Project, the Moapa Valley Pumping Project in Nevada, the Southern Nevada Water Supply Project, the Dixie Project in Utah, the Hooker Dam in New Mexico, and a number of American Indian irrigation projects, as well as participation in the enlargement of a portion of the California Aqueduct to facilitate the importation of water from northern California's Trinity River. Objections to the plans to divert water from northern California led to development of plans to divert water from the Columbia River in the Pacific Northwest. Reclamation had already completed advance planning on these projects, and separate legislation was pending in Congress. The total cost of the initial phase was $3.1 billion. In addition to the traditional water projects, the initial plan proposed saving 680,000 acre-feet of Colorado River water by pumping irrigation water that had seeped into the water table back out of the ground for reuse, by eradicating salt cedar—also known as tamarisk—from 42,000 acres of federal non-Indian land, and installing 141 miles of drains.

Criticism of the Plan

Objections to the plan arose on many fronts, including continued rivalry between California and Arizona, concerns of upper basin states about the overappropriation of the river, and environmentalists' concerns over proposed dams in the Grand Canyon. After the Department of the Interior dropped specific mention of importation of more northern California water, the Bureau of Reclamation unofficially began investigating importation from the Columbia River. These plans bolstered support for the plan among upper basin states but provoked the ire of residents of Oregon and Washington, including Senator Henry "Scoop" Jackson (D-WA), who held the important chairmanship of the Senate Committee on Interior and Insular Affairs.

The most pitched political battles occurred over the proposed dams at Marble and Bridge Canyons. While the Bureau of Reclamation made an effort to minimize the encroachment of Bridge Canyon's reservoir, under the Pacific Southwest Water Plan the reservoir behind the proposed 673-foot-high dam would flood a small portion of Grand Canyon National Park and all of the Grand Canyon National Monument. The Bureau of Reclamation had considered a 570-foot-high dam, but it felt the increased revenues of the higher dam were needed to keep other features affordable. Although the order creating Grand Canyon National Monument specifically allowed the construction of Bridge Canyon Dam, preservation groups fought the proposals. Motivated by the loss of Glen Canyon, David Brower of the Sierra Club would not accept any of the proposed compromises. Despite losing its nonprofit status over advertising it placed in prominent newspapers, the Sierra Club held firm.

As a result, Udall unveiled a new plan in February 1967 that addressed the Sierra Club's concerns. The new plan cut the two Grand Canyon dams and expanded the park's boundaries. In place of the dams, the plan substituted a coal-fired power plant, the Navajo Generating Station near Page, Arizona, as the power source for the pumps to lift the Colorado from Lake Havasu into the Central Arizona Project's aqueduct. The new plan also addressed the controversy over importation from the Pacific Northwest. In a move to placate the powerful Senator Jackson, the bill called for a ten-year moratorium on any diversion from the Columbia River. The new plan became the basis for the Colorado River Basin Act passed the following year.

—Adam Eastman

See also: Arizona v. California *(1963); Central Arizona Project; Colorado River Basin Act of 1968; Interbasin Water Transfer; Lower Colorado River Basin Project Bill (1965); National Parks and Water; Udall, Stewart*

BIBLIOGRAPHY

Dean, Robert. "'Dam Building Still Had Some Magic Then': Stewart Udall, the Central Arizona Project, and the Evolution of the Pacific Southwest Water Plan, 1963–1968." *Pacific Historical Review* 66, no. 1 (1997): 81–98.

Johnson, Rich. *The Central Arizona Project, 1918–1968.* Tucson: University of Arizona Press, 1977.

U.S. Department of the Interior, Bureau of Reclamation. *Pacific Southwest Water Plan: Report, January 1964.* Washington, DC: Bureau of Education, 1964.

Pick-Sloan Plan

See *Flood Control Act of 1944*

Pinchot, Gifford

Gifford Pinchot (1865–1946) served as governor of Pennsylvania from 1923 to 1927 and again from 1931 to 1935. Before that, he was the first chief of the U.S. Forest Service from 1905 to 1910. In that position, he sought to get as much use as possible from timber resources and came up with some of the terminology now applied to conservation.

Born on August 11, 1865, at Simsbury, Connecticut, Gifford Pinchot was the son of James Pinchot, who had made his fortune from timber and land speculation, and his wife Mary Jane (née Eno). Later in life, James Pinchot became concerned about the way in which he had despoiled the environment and endowed the Yale University School of Forestry in 1900, where his son would later be a professor.

Gifford Pinchot (1865–1946) was an American politician and forestry expert. He served as the first chief of the U.S. Forest Service and later as governor of Pennsylvania. He was best known for his battles with timber companies and his stance that preservation could be profitable.
Library of Congress

Forestry Work

Gifford Pinchot attended Yale University and completed postgraduate studies at the French National Forestry School. This coincided with his father also becoming active in promoting conservation. Gifford Pinchot was appointed, in 1896, to the National Forest Commission by the National Academy of Sciences. Soon after, President Grover Cleveland charged him with the development of a management plan for western forests. Two years later, Pinchot was promoted to head the Forestry Division. Then in 1900, Pinchot, with Henry S. Graves, who had been with him at Yale, moved to the Yale University School of Forestry where he was a professor from 1903 to 1936. Pinchot also founded the Society of American Foresters in 1900, which has done much to raise the profile of forestry management in the United States.

Essentially Pinchot recognized that private companies often made short-term decisions for the environment—and certainly he saw the damage that his father had done to forest environments. Up to the 1900s, the aim of the U.S. government had been to allow the private sector to exploit government landholdings. As chief of the U.S. Forest Service, Pinchot changed this policy and took back stewardship of some land that had already been turned over to private companies and individuals. Pinchot was careful to maintain an effective public relations operation to promote his programs, highlighting and even generating news stories that achieved his objectives. Because he controlled the national forest reserves, he also established a political power base, which he used to fight legislation that promoted logging. Pinchot fought many battles with timber interests and urged that forests be preserved for future generations. This, he argued, was not just for the benefits of the trees and other flora and fauna but also for the benefit of water catchments and, hence, for farmland irrigation.

By 1907, Pinchot had been so successful that his enemies in Congress introduced provisions to the Agriculture Bill to prevent any more forest reserves from being made in the western states. However, Pinchot had the support of President Theodore Roosevelt, who, just minutes before he lost his power to create more national forests, declared 16 million acres (65,000 km²) to be new national forests—these became known as the "midnight forests." Pinchot had a far harder time dealing with President Howard Taft, and he secretly and then openly attacked Taft's decisions, mainly through organized leaks of information to sympathetic journalists. In 1910, Taft fired Pinchot, who then founded the National Conservation Association, becoming its president from 1910 to 1925.

During the late 1910s, Pinchot became active in Pennsylvania state politics, and in 1920 Governor William Sproul appointed him the state's commissioner of forestry. Pinchot himself was elected governor twice, serving 1923–1927 and again 1931–1935. A Republican, Pinchot was considered for his party's nomination for the presidential election in 1924 but declined to run. During his second term as governor, which coincided with the Great Depression, he supported increasing the relief for the unemployed and the regulation of public utilities and construction. He lost three bids for the U.S. Senate and lost the gubernatorial election in 1938.

In retirement, he wrote about his life as a forester and advised President Franklin D. Roosevelt on forestry. In World War II, he developed a fishing kit for lifeboats. He died of leukemia on October 4, 1946. He was honored by the naming of Gifford Pinchot National Forest in Washington state and the Gifford Pinchot State Park in Lewisberry, Pennsylvania. The Pinchot sycamore, the largest tree in Connecticut, was also named after him.

—Justin Corfield

See also: *Conservation Movement; Deforestation; Roosevelt, Theodore*

BIBLIOGRAPHY

Balogh, Brian. "Scientific Forestry and the Roots of the Modern American State: Gifford Pinchot's Path to Progressive Reform." *Environmental History* 7, no. 2 (2002): 198–225.

McGeary, Martin Nelson. *Gifford Pinchot: Forester-Politician.* Princeton, NJ: Princeton University Press, 1960.

Miller, Char. *Gifford Pinchot and the Making of Modern Environmentalism.* Washington, DC: Shearwater, 2001.

Penick, James, Jr. "Gifford Pinchot." In *Dictionary of American Biography: Supplement 4, 1946–1950,* 663–66. New York: Charles Scribner's Sons, 1974.

Pinchot, Gifford. *The Conservation Diaries of Gifford Pinchot.* Edited by Harold K. Steen. Chicago: Island Press, 2001.

Pinchot, Gifford. *The Fight for Conservation.* New York: Doubleday, Page, 1910. Available at http://www.archive.org/details/fightfor conserva11pinc.

Pinkett, Harold T. *Gifford Pinchot: Private and Public Forester.* Urbana: University of Illinois Press, 1970.

Ponder, Stephen. "Gifford Pinchot: Press Agent for Forestry." *Journal of Forest History* 31, no. 1 (1987): 26–35.

Powell, John Wesley

A geologist and naturalist, John Wesley Powell (1834–1902) surveyed many U.S. waterways and published geological surveys. He was also an uncle of Arthur Powell Davis, who was prominent in irrigation engineering.

Early Life

John Wesley Powell was born on March 24, 1834, in Mount Morris in western New York State. His father, Joseph Powell, was a preacher in the Methodist Episcopal Church. Both his father and his mother, Mary (née Dean), came to the United States in 1830 to settle in New York City. They then lived in Jackson, Ohio, South Grove, Wisconsin, and Bonus Prairie and Wheaton, Illinois. As a result of the family moving constantly, John Wesley Powell's childhood and his education were disrupted. He did, however, study at a Methodist preparatory school and then at Wheaton College and later attended the preparatory department of Illinois College in Jacksonville.

After completing his education, John Wesley Powell planned to become a Methodist preacher, but he became interested in natural history. He took some voyages alone on the Mississippi and Ohio Rivers. In 1854, he joined the Illinois Natural History Society and spent much time wandering the countryside. Soon Powell was the secretary of the society. With the outbreak of the American Civil War, Powell was commissioned as a second lieutenant and then was promoted to captain in the artillery. He was wounded in the elbow at the Battle of Shiloh in April 1862 but recovered and was promoted to major.

Western Expeditions

In January 1865, John Wesley Powell became a professor of geology at the Illinois Normal University. Over the next

John Wesley Powell (1834–1902), a geologist, led several important expeditions to survey western rivers in the late nineteenth century. Shown above is Powell with his team during their exploration of the Colorado River.

Library of Congress

and bulletins were published starting in 1883. Beginning in 1894, a series of folio atlases were issued on a scale of four miles to the inch. These provided hydrographers and others with much more information than was previously available to the public. This information also allowed the start of a number of controversial irrigation projects, causing some animosity toward Powell.

Powell was also interested in Native Americans. As director of the Rocky Mountain Survey starting in 1877, he worked on *Contributions to North American Ethnology,* published in eight parts from 1877 to 1893. In 1879, he was appointed director of the Bureau of Ethnology under the auspices of the Smithsonian Institution.

Ill health caused Powell to end some of his projects, and one of his arms had to be amputated. John Wesley Powell died on September 23, 1902, at his family's summer house in Haven, Maine. He was survived by his wife and their daughter. The John Wesley Powell Memorial Museum was established in Page, Arizona; it has an oversized replica of the longboat used by Powell to explore the Colorado River.

—Justin Corfield

See also: *United States Geological Survey*

BIBLIOGRAPHY

Dellenbaugh, Frederick Samuel. *The Romance of the Colorado River.* New York: G. P. Putnam's Sons, 1902.

Gilbert, Grove Karl, ed. *John Wesley Powell: A Memorial to an American Explorer and Scholar.* Chicago: Open Court, 1903. Available at http://www.archive.org/details/johnwesleypowell00gilbrich.

Merrill, George P. "John Wesley Powell." In *Dictionary of American Biography,* Vol. 15, 146–48. New York: Charles Scribner's Sons, 1935.

Stegner, Wallace. *Beyond the Hundredth Meridian: John Wesley Powell and the Second Opening of the West.* Boston: Houghton Mifflin, 1954.

Stephens, Hal G., Eugene M. Shoemaker, and John Wesley Powell. *In the Footsteps of John Wesley Powell: An Album of Comparative Photographs of the Green and Colorado Rivers, 1871–72 and 1968.* Boulder, CO: Johnson Books, 1987.

Worster, Donald. *A River Running West: The Life of John Wesley Powell.* New York: Oxford University Press, 2001.

few years, he took students and other interested parties across Colorado's Rocky Mountains, protected by soldiers provided by General Ulysses Grant. On one of these visits, Powell saw the Green River and the Colorado River and considered exploring them in more detail. He did so in 1869 on an expedition financed by the Smithsonian Institution and with money granted by Congress. Embarking on boats where the Green River was crossed by the Union Pacific Railroad on May 24, 1869, the group emerged at the mouth of the Grand Canyon on August 29, having travelled nearly 900 miles. Succeeding years brought further explorations, and Powell became director of the second division of the U.S. Geological and Geographical Survey of the Territories. In 1880, he became director of the U.S. Geological Survey and served in that position until 1894.

Powell wrote of his explorations in a number of books. His first was *Explorations of the Colorado River of the West and Its Tributaries* (1875), and this was subsequently revised and enlarged as *Canyons of the Colorado* (1895). He also wrote *Report on the Lands of the Arid Region of the United States* (1878). Powell's report encouraged some people to begin the opening up of new territories. More importantly, it led to some people deciding to conduct much larger geological surveys. This led to the establishment of the U.S. Geological Survey, which soon became the largest and most well-funded body of its kind in the world. Detailed hydrographical and geological surveys took part around the country,

Public Utility Regulatory Policies Act (1978)

The initial bill, H.R. 4018, was introduced in Congress on February 24, 1977, by Rep. Thomas B. Evans Jr. (R–DE) and was entitled "A Bill to Suspend Until the Close of June 30, 1979, the Duty on Certain Doxorubicin Hydrochloride Antibiotics." The short title is the more familiar Public Utility Regulatory Policies Act of 1978 (PURPA). The legislation was not confined to H.R. 4018; other bills included S. 2114, H.R. 8444, and H.R. 4018. The final legislation was Pub. L. 95-617.

Provisions of the Bill

S. 2114 consisted of provisions to ensure that the state regulatory authorities, in combination with nonregulated utilities, would report to the Secretary of Energy. It also described other duties of the Secretary of Energy for setting standards for the energy industry.

H.R. 8444, as introduced by Thomas "Lud" Ashley (D–OH), was the National Energy Act. It set specific goals for 1985, including the reduction of annual growth of energy demand to less than 2 percent, reduction of oil imports to less than six barrels a day, reduction of gas consumption by 10 percent of 1977 levels, improvement of the efficiency of heating and cooling systems, increase of coal production by 400 million tons over 1976 levels, and use of solar energy in at least 2.5 million homes.

The portion of the legislation that H.R. 4018 deals with is broken up into six titles. Title I states that contracts made by federal agencies for selling wholesale electricity to electric utilities are bound to PURPA laws, including laws on block rates, seasonal rates, and adjustment clauses. Title I also requires energy companies to show rate-schedule information to consumers. Title II allows the Federal Energy Regulatory Commission (FERC) to set standards that require utilities to engage in transactions with qualifying cogenerators and small power producers. Title II places FERC in charge of providing exemptions to utilities under specified circumstances. Title III sets standards for retail sales of natural gas, including the shutoff of natural gas to consumers. Title IV calls for standards on small hydroelectric projects where dams already exist. In addition, Title IV prohibits loans for new dam construction and excludes dams from licensing. Title V sets standards for consideration of new crude oil transportation construction. These standards differ from other portions of the bill because they are to be set by the Secretary of the Interior instead of the Secretary of Energy.

Energy Crisis

This legislation was created in response to the energy crisis in the 1970s, specifically, concerns about electricity created by the oil embargo. PURPA was designed to do several things, including to augment electric generation, increase efficiency, and establish more equitable rates for consumers (Abel 1998).

In September of 1971, OPEC began raising oil prices in response to the Arab-Israeli war. That was followed by an OPEC embargo against the United States for siding with Israel. People panicked and formed long lines at gas stations. Consumers wrote letters to encourage politicians to take action. In 1973, the government started allocating and implementing price controls for gasoline. The following year, utilities were required to switch from natural gas to coal (Gettinger 1985).

The Carter administration accelerated the response to the energy crisis by declaring that dealing with energy issues was the "moral equivalent of war" and creating the Department of Energy in 1977 (Gettinger 1985). This acceleration led to the Fuel Use Act of 1978, which prevented natural gas from being used for new generating technology until it was repealed in 1987. Another major outcome of this time was PURPA. In 1978 and 1979, there was substantial public interest over energy issues due to consumer prices. Public interest died down in the 1980s in response to more comfortable consumer prices.

Foundations for PURPA

PURPA was not merely a product of the energy crisis. It had its foundation in the Federal Utility Act of 1935 (FUA), which can be broken down into the Federal Power Act (FPA) and the Public Utilities Holding Company Act (PUHCA). The FPA required the FERC to set fuel and efficiency rules for small power production facilities. The PUHCA was designed to protect consumers from monopolies.

Historically, PURPA was important in that it protected consumers and the environment from inefficiencies in energy production. The mandatory purchasing requirement was believed to be anticompetitive and harmful to the consumer, leading to reforms in the twenty-first century. The

Energy Policy Act of 2005 was enacted to change the criteria for mandatory purchase requirements where utilities were operating in competitive markets. The Energy Policy Act also requires the FERC to determine on a case-by-case basis which companies qualify as Qualified Facilities (QFs). In addition, FERC has decided that some of the exemptions to QFs were no longer necessary. The main concern about the new changes is that if Qualified Facilities are chosen on a case-by-case basis, the standards set by FERC will begin to erode (Hornstein 2006).

The most recent change to PURPA is the Energy Independence and Security Act of 2007, which allowed rates to be changed by any utility and created incentives for utilities to develop cost-effective energy efficiencies to promote future energy investment (Burr 2008). The PURPA legislation is just as valid now as when it was originally created. The recent reforms were responses to inefficiencies in the original legislation. It is likely that increased competition will come from the new reforms.

—Landon S. Utterback

See also: *Federal Energy Regulatory Commission; Pacific Northwest Electric Power Planning and Conservation Act (1980)*

BIBLIOGRAPHY

Abel, Amy. "CRS Report for Congress: Electricity Restructuring Backgrounds: The Public Utility Regulatory Policies Act of 1978 and the Energy Policy Act of 1992" (98-419 ENR). Washington, DC: Library of Congress, Congressional Research Service, 1998. Available at http://www.policyarchive.org/handle/10207/bitstreams/609.pdf.

Burr, Michael T. "PURPA Redirected: The Latest 'Incremental' Policy Changes Might Realign Utility Financial Initiatives." *Public Utilities Fortnightly* 146 (2008): 4–6. Available at http://www.fortnightly.com/display_pdf.cfm?id=02012008_Frontlines.pdf.

Gettinger, Steven. "Who Remembers Gasoline Lines? The Energy Crisis May Be Over, but Some in Congress Worry the Nation Is Still Unprepared." *CQ Guide to Current American Government* 43 (Spring 1985): 75.

Hornstein, Michael D., J. S. Gebhart Stoermer. "The Energy Policy Act of 2005: PURPA Reform, the Amendments and Their Implications." *Energy Law Journal* 27, no. 1 (2006): 25.

Public Utility Regulatory Policies Act of 1978, Pub. L. 95-617 (1978).

Rapanos v. United States (2006)

Rapanos v. United States, 547 U.S. 715 (2006), decided on June 19, 2006, by a 5–4 judgment of the Supreme Court, involved the destruction of wetlands by a developer. The Court narrowed the ability of the government to regulate wetland use in a decision that appears to have weakened the Clean Water Act. The decision has been faulted for its lack of clarity.

Case Background

The case began in the 1980s when Michigan developer John Rapanos and several associates planned to build homes and a shopping center on three wetlands. The Michigan Department of Environmental Quality warned Rapanos that the areas were protected wetlands under the Clean Water Act. This legislation prohibits anyone from placing fill in "navigable waters" without first obtaining a permit. Nevertheless, Rapanos filled in fifty-four acres of wetlands in Michigan's Arenac and Midland Counties without first obtaining legal permission to do so. He also ignored cease-and-desist orders from the U.S. Environmental Protection Agency.

The wetlands that Rapanos destroyed lay near ditches or man-made drains that eventually emptied into navigable waters. While Rapanos argued that the wetlands were not navigable, the federal government disagreed and brought civil proceedings against him. The district court found that the United States had jurisdiction over the wetlands because they were adjacent to federal waters. It held Rapanos liable for violating the Clean Water Act. The Sixth Circuit Court affirmed the decision, since the wetlands had hydrologic connections to navigable waters. Rapanos took his case to the Supreme Court with legal representation from the Pacific Legal Foundation, a public interest group dedicated to protecting property rights.

The Court's Decision

The Supreme Court, in a decision that legal scholars subsequently derided as "muddy," vacated the earlier decisions and sent the case back to the lower courts for further review. The Court ruled that the Sixth Circuit had applied an incorrect standard to determine whether the wetlands were covered by the Clean Water Act. Chief Justice John Roberts, Justice Antonin Scalia, Justice Clarence Thomas, Justice Antony Kennedy, and Justice Samuel Alito ruled against the government. Scalia, writing for the majority, decided that the phrase "waters of the United States" includes only relatively permanent, standing, or continuously flowing bodies of water. This definition does not include channels linking wetlands to navigable waters. Scalia argued that Congress needed to make a clear statement about wetland protection before intruding into an area of traditional state authority, such as land-use regulation, and before authorizing federal action that stretched the limits of Congress's commerce power. As Scalia phrased it, "isolated ponds" are not "waters of the United States." Only wetlands with a continuous surface connection to other waters that makes it difficult to mark a boundary line qualify as "waters of the United States." Justice Roberts, in a concurring opinion, pointed out that the Court had ruled in *Solid Waste Authority of Northern Cook County v. Army Corps of Engineers,* 531 U.S. 159 (2001), that the Corps only had limited authority to regulate. Roberts concluded that the Corps had failed in its duty to set boundaries on its authority that would serve to guide developers and had essentially ignored the earlier Court ruling.

The dissenting justices were John Paul Stevens, Steven Breyer, David Souter, and Ruth Bader Ginsburg. Stevens, in a rather harsh dissenting opinion, condemned the Court for forcing the revision of regulations that had served to protect water quality for decades. He noted that the Clean Water Act had been approved by Congress. Stevens deferred to the wisdom of the Corps in its determination that wetlands preserve the quality of America's waters by providing habitat to aquatic animals, keeping excessive sediment and toxic pollutants out of adjacent waters, and reducing downstream flooding. He found the Corps's interpretation of "waters of the United States" to be a reasonable interpretation of a statutory provision.

In the wake of the Supreme Court decision, Rapanos reached a settlement in December 2008 with government regulators. He paid a $150,000 penalty for filling in wetlands. Additionally, he agreed to construct 100 acres of wetlands and buffer areas in Arenac and Midland Counties. The agreement also called for 134 acres to be preserved in Midland County, with the State of Michigan holding a conservation easement. In essence, both Rapanos and the government lost this case.

Consequences of the Decision

Following the court decision, the enforcement of the Clean Water Act deteriorated. In 2008, U.S. Representatives Henry A. Waxman (D-CA), chair of the Oversight and Government Reform Committee, and James J. Oberstar (D-MN), chair of the Transportation and Infrastructure Committee, charged that the *Rapanos* ruling and the George W. Bush administration's enforcement of the decision had effectively narrowed the jurisdiction of the Clean Water Act. Both members of

Congress complained that Rapanos forced federal agencies to go through a time-consuming and resource-intensive process of demonstrating a significant nexus to traditional navigable waters before they could assert jurisdiction under the Clean Water Act. Documents obtained by the House committees indicated that multiple Environmental Protection Agency (EPA) field offices were unable to enforce water protection regulations as effectively as in the past. For example, the EPA's Dallas field office reported in January 2008 that at least seventy-six oil spill cases had been confirmed without any follow-up penalties or corrective actions sought due to difficulties in asserting jurisdiction in the wake of *Rapanos*. This same field office further noted that companies discontinued spill prevention and control measures based on their contention that any spills posed no threat to jurisdictional waterways. A March 4, 2008, memo from an EPA assistant administrator in charge of enforcement stated that the agency chose not to enforce as many as 300 potential Clean Water violations between July 2006 and December 2007 because of regulatory uncertainty after *Rapanos*.

—Caryn Neumann

See also: *Clean Water Act of 1972; Environmental Protection Agency, United States;* Solid Waste Agency of Northern Cook County v. United States Army Corps of Engineers et al. *(2001)*

BIBLIOGRAPHY

Braddock, Theda. *Wetlands: An Introduction to Ecology, the Law, and Permitting.* Lanham, MD: Government Institutes, 2007.

Johnson, Timothy R., and Jerry Goldman, eds. *A Good Quarrel: America's Top Legal Reporters Share Stories from Inside the Supreme Court.* Ann Arbor: University of Michigan Press, 2009.

Reclamation Act of 1902

The Reclamation Act of June 17, 1902, is often referred to as the Newlands Act in reference to the support of Representative and Senator Francis G. Newlands (D-NV), one of the central supporters of the bill in the Congress. The act was the culmination of years of agitation and political maneuvering by westerners who wanted to tap federal money and create a pool of engineering expertise for dam building and water delivery for irrigation. Leaders in the movement included William Smythe, a Nebraska journalist, and George Maxwell, a California lawyer—each of whom actively participated in organizations aimed at promoting irrigation in the West. While their motivations were fairly

Beyond the Hundredth Meridian

Beyond the Hundredth Meridian: John Wesley Powell and the Second Opening of the West, authored by Wallace Stegner, served as the definitive biography of John Wesley Powell for more than half a century. The author detailed Powell's scientific expeditions, including his explorations of the Colorado River in 1869 and 1871 through 1872, and demonstrated how those experiences shaped his vision of utilizing the federal government and scientific knowledge to develop the West and its natural resources for the good of the country at large. His efforts resulted in the creation of the U.S. Geological Survey and the Bureau of American Ethnology. Stegner portrayed Powell's accomplishments as an individual crusade that was ultimately thwarted by members of Congress and capitalists determined to shape the West for their personal benefit.

—John R. Burch Jr.

See also: *Powell, John Wesley*

BIDLIOGRAPHY

Darrah, William Culp, Ralph V. Chamberlain, and Charles Kelly, eds. *The Exploration of the Colorado River in 1869 and 1871–1872: Biographical Sketches and Original Documents of the First Powell Expedition of 1869 and the Second Powell Expedition of 1871–1872.* Salt Lake City: University of Utah Press, 2009.

Stegner, Wallace. *Beyond the Hundredth Meridian: John Wesley Powell and the Second Opening of the West.* Boston: Houghton Mifflin, 1953.

complex, their stated objective was "reclamation" of the arid lands of the West by application of water so that small farmsteads could spring up and the West could be settled and economically productive (i.e., "homemaking").

Irrigation congresses in the 1890s actively promoted federal participation in irrigation; at the same time, opposition to the movement developed, particularly in the Midwest and South. It was argued that more agricultural production was not needed and would compete with the already established farms of the country.

Early Support

The first federal steps in the movement occurred when Congress printed John Wesley Powell's *Report on the Lands of the Arid Region of the United States, with a More Detailed Account of the Lands of Utah* in 1878. Congress later authorized the "irrigation survey" by the U.S. Geological Survey (USGS) beginning in 1889. Congress closed down that survey after a few years because powerful voices in the West opposed the USGS proposal that irrigable lands be withdrawn from the public domain pending development of irrigation projects. This proposal was an attempt to prevent speculation in lands whose value would sharply increase if proved irrigable. In spite of Congress's quashing the irrigation survey, the USGS continued to study the water resources of the United States. Powell is often cited as the "father" of reclamation because of his *Arid Lands* and his leadership of the USGS during the irrigation survey. While Powell did call attention to the need for irrigation and settlement, Congress adopted a program that varied substantially from what he had proposed as a model for settlement.

Over time, supporters coalesced around Francis G. Newlands. Included in this group were Frederick Newell, a hydraulic engineer in the U.S. Geological Survey; Gifford Pinchot, a well-to-do, progressive forest advocate; and California attorney George Maxwell. While this coalition seems odd today because of the political, and some would argue inappropriate, separation of reclamation in the Department of the Interior from forestry in the Department of Agriculture, the alliance can be understood in terms of the group's recognition that a sustained, high-quality water supply was inextricably tied to forest management.

By 1900, the movement was strong enough to have the two major parties include irrigation in the West in their platforms, but legislation was stymied by opposition in Congress. However, the West had gained new power in the Senate as the "Omnibus" states (i.e., North Dakota, South Dakota, Montana, Idaho, Wyoming, and Washington) joined the Union in 1889 and 1890, and, in 1901, Senator Thomas Carter (R-MT) filibustered a rivers and harbors bill favored by eastern and southern senators after opposition had killed several irrigation proposals sponsored by westerners.

Irrigation gained a new supporter when Theodore Roosevelt became president upon the assassination of William McKinley in 1901. Roosevelt advocated an active, outdoors lifestyle and had lived in and visited the West. He understood firsthand the benefits irrigation could bring to that region. In his autobiography he wrote, "The first work I took up when I became President was the work of reclamation. Immediately after I had come to Washington . . . before going into the White House, Newell and Pinchot called upon me and laid before me their plans for National irrigation of the arid lands of the West, and for the consolidation of the forest work of the Government" (Roosevelt 1913, 409).

Act Passage

With Roosevelt's support and the newly realized power of senators from the West, the Reclamation Act passed in 1902. Its primary provisions included establishment of the Reclamation Fund, which received public land sales revenues to pay for projects; authority for the secretary of the interior to study, approve, and contract for construction of projects; repayment of construction costs by water users into the Reclamation Fund; a limit of 160 acres per landowner; the requirement that federal reclamation must recognize state water law; and provision to allow water users to operate the projects but for the federal government to retain ownership until Congress determines otherwise.

In July 1902, the secretary of the interior placed the U.S. Reclamation Service within the Division of Hydrography in the USGS. In 1907, the Reclamation Service was separated from the Geological Survey, and in 1923, the secretary changed the name to U.S. Bureau of Reclamation.

Over the years, the reclamation program expanded as Congress added municipal and industrial water, hydroelectric power, and rural culinary water supply projects to the Bureau of Reclamation's responsibilities. Currently, depending on the water year in the West, Reclamation irrigates around 10 million acres, about one-third of the irrigated acreage in the American West. While the Bureau of Reclamation operates over 180 projects, 5 projects account for about one-half of its irrigated acreage—Minidoka in Idaho, Boulder Canyon in California, Central Valley in California, Colorado–Big Thompson, and Columbia Basin in Washington state.

—Brit Allan Storey

See also: *Dam Building; Powell, John Wesley*

BIBLIOGRAPHY

Pisani, Donald J. *From the Family Farm to Agribusiness: The Irrigation Crusade in California and the West, 1850–1931.* Berkeley: University of California Press, 1984.
Pisani, Donald J. *To Reclaim a Divided West: Water, Law, and Public Policy, 1848–1902.* Albuquerque: University of New Mexico Press, 1992.
Pisani, Donald J. *Water and American Government: The Reclamation Bureau, National Water Policy, and the West, 1902–1935.* Berkeley: University of California Press, 2002.
Pisani, Donald J. *Water, Land, and Law in the West.* Lawrence: University of Kansas Press, 1996.
Roosevelt, Theodore. *Theodore Roosevelt: An Autobiography.* New York: Macmillan, 1913.
Rowley, William D. *The Bureau of Reclamation: Origins and Growth to 1945.* Vol. 1. Denver, CO: Bureau of Reclamation, 2006.
Rowley, William D. *Reclaiming the Arid West: The Career of Francis G. Newlands.* Bloomington: Indiana University Press, 1996.

Reclamation Projects Authorization and Adjustment Act of 1992

Signifying a new commitment on behalf of the federal government to the continuing development of water resources in the West, but also taking into account environmental concerns and protection, Congress passed and President George H. W. Bush, on October 30, 1992, signed the Reclamation Projects Authorization and Adjustment Act (RPAAA). The bill funded a number of water projects, but the main thrust of the bill had to do with the continuing development of and protection of fish and wildlife around California's Central Valley Project. Title 34 of the law, the Central Valley Project Improvement Act, demonstrated a basic change in priorities in water policy in California.

Although the Central Valley Project (CVP) had created one of the greatest crop-growing regions in the world, by the early 1990s, its unintended side effects were apparent. Salination had created wastelands in some sections, such as the Westlands Water District. The wildlife of the valley, teeming before Europeans arrived, had been decimated by years of agriculture and water development. The goal of the bill was to make sure that the preservation and encouragement of fish and wildlife would not impede continued water flow to farms through the CVP. Importantly, it allowed for a system of voluntary water sales and transfers. This system would accommodate future growth of the state's agricultural industry and meet the Republican president's goal of creating a more market-driven system to encourage conservation goals. However, its most groundbreaking impact was to add the preservation of fish and wildlife to the CVP's purposes. To that end, it set a goal of doubling anadromous fish runs by 2002 and set up a $50 million fund and set aside up to 800,000 acre-feet of CVP water per year to promote fish and wildlife restoration (Dunning 1993).

In addition to funding the CVP, the RPAAA funded the completion and/or refurbishing of a number of other reclamation projects throughout the western United States, including water-recycling programs in southern California, the replenishment of Mono Lake in eastern California, the Buffalo Bill Dam and Reservoir in Wyoming, the Central Utah Project, the Cedar Bluff Unit in Kansas, the Vermejo and Elephant Butte Projects in New Mexico, the Glen Canyon Dam in Arizona, the Sunnyside Valley Irrigation District in Washington, the Platoro Dam and Reservoir and the Leadville Mine Drainage Tunnel in Colorado, the Mountain Park Project in Oklahoma, and water-planning studies under the auspices of a South Dakota Preservation and Restoration Trust.

—Steven L. Danver

See also: *Reclamation Act of 1902*

BIBLIOGRAPHY

Byrnes, Patricia. "In the Wake of the 102nd Congress (Environmental Legislation)." *Wilderness,* December 22, 1992.
Dunning, Harrison C. "Confronting the Environmental Legacy of Irrigated Agriculture in the West: The Case of the Central Valley Project." *Environmental Law* 23 (1993): 943–969. Available at http://www.nationalaglawcenter.org/assets/bibarticles/dunning_irrigated.pdf.

Refuse Act of 1899

The Refuse Act, also known as section 13 of the Rivers and Harbors Act of 1899, prohibits the deposit of all refuse, except that flowing from streets and sewers in a liquid state, in navigable waters without a permit from the U.S. Army Corps of Engineers (Corps). In places without harbors, the law allows mines to deposit debris as long as the debris does not interfere with shipping. The legislation is primarily a legal, punitive tool that initially had more to do with aiding commerce and protecting public safety than guarding the environment. Violations of the law are punishable by fines of $500 to $2,500 per count.

Call for Legislation

The legislation aimed to protect ships and other watercraft from striking hidden objects. Such strikes, which could sink ships, were a notable shipping hazard and had resulted in a number of deaths over the years. Bridges, wharves, dredging, dumping, and all the activities of a developing industrial economy also served to obstruct waterways in the nineteenth century. The federal government claimed the right to assure free navigation to all. Before the Civil War, this claim had been largely theoretical. The postwar investment in civil works meant that the issue would become a practical one. New York became the first state to seek federal assistance, since its harbor straddled two states and New Yorkers did not trust their neighbors in New Jersey to protect their common property. The Port of New York was endangered by dredging, filling, dumping, and construction work. The New York legislation met indifference in Congress, but it contained virtually every basic idea contained in future laws to prevent obstruction of the waterways.

Pushed by the Corps, lawmakers took another look at a Refuse Act in the 1890s. By this time, hydraulic mining in the far West had washed tons of rubble into the rivers of California's Central Valley, provoking lawsuits by farmers. Congress still refused to treat the matter urgently. However, the New York Chamber of Commerce succeeded in having a section written into the Rivers and Harbors Act that forbade dumping into New York Harbor. An expansion of this legislation, which applied to the rest of the country, passed in 1890. Enforcement varied dramatically across the nation, with some U.S. attorneys taking vigorous action against violators and some declining to take any action. As problems with the law piled up, the Corps sought a new law. The 1899 Refuse Act was largely drafted and promoted by the Corps.

The 1899 Refuse Act proved exceptionally broad and durable. As time passed, court decisions and congressional action made the Refuse Act apply to pollution as well as shipping hazards. Liberal judicial interpretations combined with the passage of many other laws to minimize pollution, maximize recreation, protect esthetics, and preserve natural resources. *Refuse* has been interpreted by the courts to include oil and other nonsolid pollutants apart from municipal waste. The focus has been on enhancing the public interest rather than private gain. In essence, the Refuse Act is a broad grant of authority and a powerful legal tool for preventing the pollution of navigable waters.

Enforcement

However, for most of the Refuse Act's life, few paid much attention to it. Folksinger Pete Seeger noted as much in his 1973 song "Bring Back Old 1899." Over the years, the Corps issued only a few permits for the discharge of industrial wastes, leaving virtually every plant that discharged any wastewater in at least technical violation of the law. Journalists in the 1960s noted that the legislation gave the Corps the power to stop pollution and assailed the Corps for failing to do so. In its defense, the Corps noted that it had been created to prevent the obstruction of waterways and that pollution control was out of its area of expertise.

As the environment became a matter of public concern in the late 1960s, the administration of President Richard Nixon indicated that it did not intend to enforce the Refuse Act against many polluters. Attorney General John Mitchell did not believe that it would be in the interest of the government to bring a lawsuit against polluting companies when these same firms were spending significant amounts of money to reduce the pollution. Environmental groups disagreed with Mitchell's decision and sought to force enforcement of the law. In 1970, the Conservation and Natural Resources Subcommittee of the Committee on Government Operations of the House of Representatives approved of lawsuits by private individuals as a means of insuring against laxity by public officials in enforcing statutes that protect the public. The subcommittee found that the Justice Department's position was contrary to the mandate of the 1899 Act, which forbade discharges without a Corps permit. It called for the active participation of American citizens to help bring a halt to the degradation of our waters and environment.

The congressional rebuke did not spur Mitchell to action, nor did it create a spate of lawsuits. A few months later, high mercury levels were found in food fish. Finding that the Water Pollution Control Act of 1948 provided no effective effluent controls, the Justice Department turned to the Refuse Act and brought suit in July 1970 against eleven of the largest mercury dumpers. Nixon then issued a presidential order on December 23, 1970, instructing the Corps to implement a permit program under the Refuse Act.

The old legislation banned dumping but did not set rules for clean water. The Water Pollution Control Act Amendments of 1972 determine how clean the water has to be, essentially surpassing the 1899 legislation.

—Caryn Neumann

See also: *Army Corps of Engineers, United States; Rivers and Harbors Act of 1899; Water Pollution Control Act (1948)*

BIBLIOGRAPHY

Bakken, Gordon Morris, and Brenda Farrington, eds. *The American West: Environmental Problems in America's Garden of Eden.* New York: Garland, 2000.

Degler, Stanley E. *Federal Pollution Control Programs: Water, Air, and Solid Wastes.* Washington, DC: Bureau of National Affairs, 1971.

Fallows, James M. *The Water Lords.* New York: Grossman, 1971.

Rio Grande Water Convention (1906)

The Convention between the United States and Mexico Providing for the Equitable Distribution of the Waters of the Rio Grande for Irrigation Purposes, signed on May 21, 1906, was the first treaty apportioning shared waters between the United States and Mexico. It was also the first such treaty in North America, antedating the U.S.–Canada 1909 Boundary Waters Treaty. As such, its development is historically significant in defining emerging international legal obligations related to shared watercourses.

The 1906 Convention addresses the allocation of water on the upper reach of the Rio Grande River from its headwaters in Colorado as far south as Fort Quitman, Texas, where Mexico's Conchos River joins the Rio Grande. The convention is quite simple. Mexico is allocated 60,000 acre-feet of water annually, the remaining flow to be taken by the United States. In effect, the United States receives more than 90 percent of the average annual flow of the upper Rio Grande River, a volume of roughly 1 million acre-feet of water as measured at New Mexico's Otowi Gauge (Reynolds 1968). Mexico's allotment is predicated on the estimated maximum uses of Mexican settlers in the Valle de Juarez in 1906. The United States, in turn, agreed to build a storage dam upstream of Las Cruces, New Mexico, at Elephant Butte wholly at its expense. Mexico agreed to waive all damage claims and renounce any further claims on this reach of the river. The treaty also provides that in the event of an extraordinary drought or serious accident to the U.S. irrigation system upstream, the volume of water delivered to Mexico would be reduced in proportion to the reduction of deliveries to the United States.

Agreement Foundations

The agreement has its antecedents in the landmark Treaty of Guadalupe Hidalgo, signed in 1848, and the Gadsden Treaty of 1853. These treaties, which set the modern boundary between the United States and Mexico, failed to address the division of international waters between the two countries (Hundley 1966).

In 1879, Texans in El Paso pressed the State Department to approach Mexico concerning alleged illegal diversions by Mexicans in the Juarez Valley. Mexico rejected these claims. There things stood until 1888 when drought aggravated local tensions. El Paso citizens commissioned a report by

Anson Mills, a military engineer. On the strength of Mills's report, the U.S. Congress authorized the initiation of diplomatic talks with Mexico to settle the dispute (Hundley 1966). At this point, Mexico took the initiative, attributing the shortage to U.S. diversions in the Rio Bravo headwaters (Enriquez Coyro 1975). In 1895, Mexico intensified its efforts, claiming $35 million in damages and accusing the United States of failing to honor the navigation clauses of the Treaty of Guadalupe Hidalgo and the Gadsden Treaty (Hundley 1966).

The immediate result was an infamous determination in 1896 by U.S. Attorney General Judson Harmon, known worldwide as the "Harmon Doctrine." On the question of navigation, Harmon disregarded the inclusive language of the original treaties and drew upon the Boundary Convention of 1884, which limited common navigation rights to actually navigable channels. He asserted the Rio Grande was historically unnavigable at El Paso, rendering the navigation clauses inapplicable (Hundley 1966). Under this reading, any U.S. diversions upstream were unencumbered by its commitments on the international reach of the river. Harmon sharpened the point, finding that the United States had no obligation to negotiate with Mexico at all on the basis of its absolute municipal sovereignty in international law and its geographic status as upper riparian (Enriquez Coyro 1975). He did concede that the United States might consider some arrangement on the basis of comity.

The Road to an Agreement

Despite this harsh reading, the two countries continued discussions through their foreign ministries and the International Boundary Commission (IBC), established in 1889. In 1896, the IBC, its U.S. Section chaired by Mills, was asked to consider the possibility of an equitable division of water between the two countries. The IBC's final report attributed the problem of local scarcity to upstream diversions in the United States and supported Mexico's claim of wrongful deprivation. It called for construction of an international dam just upstream of El Paso to secure to each nation its "legal and equitable rights," with the impounded waters to be divided equally between the two countries (Hundley 1966).

The IBC's recommendations, unfortunately, were soon obstructed by the speculative efforts of the Rio Grande Dam and Irrigation Company, a British-American partnership of water speculators bent on construction of a dam nearly 125 miles upstream at Elephant Butte, New Mexico.

Dealing with the U.S. Interior Department instead of State, and pursuing their case through the American courts, these investors successfully opposed the El Paso dam, blocking the proposal until 1903 when their claims were struck down. By then, however, New Mexico state officials had managed to persuade the State Department that a dam at Elephant Butte was desirable, and they obtained congressional funds for the job. No consideration of Mexico's position was given. When Mexico protested, the United States denied any obligation to its downstream neighbor under international law, ignoring more than twenty years of negotiations and court decisions that, Harmon's opinion notwithstanding, assumed the contrary (Enriquez Coyro 1975). The United States nevertheless offered to reach an international agreement with Mexico. Left with few options, Mexico eventually acquiesced to U.S. pressure.

For all its controversy, the 1906 Convention enabled Rio Grande reclamation to proceed, providing a reliable, if insufficient, water supply for the Valle de Juarez in later years and securing U.S. development upstream. Mexico's experience with what it remembers today as the Disaster of 1906 later informed its diplomatic strategy in the case of the 1944 Water Treaty, an agreement that effectively laid the Harmon Doctrine to rest.

—Stephen P. Mumme

See also: *Boundary Waters Treaty (1909); International Boundary and Water Commission (United States and Mexico); United States–Mexico Water Treaty (1944)*

BIBLIOGRAPHY

Enriquez Coyro, Ernesto. *El Tratado entre Mexico y los Estados Unidos de America sobre Rio Internacionales, tomo I y tomo II.* Mexico, D.F.: Facultad de Ciencias Politicas y Sociales, Universidad Nacional Autonoma de Mexico, 1975.

Hundley, Norris, Jr. *Dividing the Waters.* Berkeley: University of California Press, 1966.

Reynolds, Steve. "The Rio Grande Compact." In *International Water Law Along the Mexican-American Border: A Symposium Held during the 44th Annual Meeting of the Southwestern and Rocky Mountain Division of the American Association for the Advancement of Science, Apr. 29-30, 1968, El Paso, Texas,* edited by Clark S. Knowlton, 48–63. El Paso: University of Texas at El Paso, 1968.

Rivers and Harbors Act of 1899

The body of law commonly known as the Rivers and Harbors Act of 1899 required that a permit be obtained from the U.S. Army Corps of Engineers (Corps), technically from the Secretary of the Army, for any obstruction or alteration of any navigable waters of the United States. Section 13 defined as an unlawful act throwing "any refuse matter of any kind or description whatever other than that flowing from the streets and sewers and passing therefrom in a liquid state, into any navigable water of the United States" (33 U.S.C. 109). The point at the close of the nineteenth century was to prevent activities that might obstruct navigation, threaten damage to harbor or river improvements, get in the way of excavation, or interfere with flood control measures. Accordingly, that portion of the law became known as the "Refuse Act." Although very different in scope and purpose, this law provides the foundation for later water pollution control legislation, including the Water Pollution Control Act of 1948 (Pub. L. 80-845, 62 Stat. 1155), the Water Pollution Control Act Amendments of 1972 (Pub. L. 92-500, 86 Stat. 816), and subsequent amendments. The 1972 legislation, often referenced as the Clean Water Act, went far beyond keeping waterways clear of refuse to "restore and maintain the chemical, physical, and biological integrity of the Nation's waters" (33 U.S.C. 1251[a]).

Reasons for Legislation

In 1899, the immediate problem motivating the law was the manner in which very tangible industrial wastes and unregulated construction of bridges and wharves were encroaching on the federal duty to ensure free navigation upon "the waters of the United States." Sawmill waste in New England choked rivers to the extent that navigation was threatened, as did waste from hydraulic mining in California. Rubble washed into California rivers by mining operations provoked lawsuits from angry farmers, which combined with local economic pressure to curtail or reopen the mines. As early as the 1850s, the New York Chamber of Commerce had identified unrestricted dredging, filling, dumping, and construction by private parties (some of them large business enterprises) as hazardous to the viability of the city's port. Efforts in the 1880s to regulate bridge building were opposed by well-funded railroad lobbies. Farmers' organizations, on the other hand, supported river improvement and protection, believing that competitive water shipping would hold down rail-shipping rates—which farmers generally considered extortionate.

Earlier legislation, passed in 1890, prohibited obstruction of navigation but proved ineffective. There were notable successes, including the arrest of a sawmill owner for dumping mill waste into the Ohio River without a permit and a case against the city of Cleveland, cited for allowing contractors

to dump dredging waste into Lake Erie. However, Attorney General Richard Olney ruled that language forbidding any dumping that tended to "impede or obstruct navigation" meant that for each offense, the government must prove a specific obstruction. Most obstruction built up over time, not from a single act of dumping.

Bill Passage

Senator William P. Frye (R-ME) secured amendments in the Commerce Committee to that year's Rivers and Harbors Bill (H.R. 11795) on February 24, 1899, primarily making appropriations for rivers, harbors, reservoirs, irrigation, and flood control. The newly inserted Rivers and Harbors Act constituted sections 9 through 20 of the omnibus appropriation bill. Frye quietly asserted that the amendments merely codified existing law—a partial truth, since they provided for more streamlined enforcement and more concise, unambiguous language. A conference committee meeting from March 1 to March 3 argued a good deal about local projects to be funded and the feasibility of a Panama Canal, but the Rivers and Harbors Act provoked no controversy, remaining in the final law recorded as 30 Stat. 1121. The Rivers and Harbors Act appears in the U.S. Code at 33 U.S.C. 401–466.

Section 10 of the Rivers and Harbors Act requires a developer or landowner building any wharf, pier, or other structure in the water to obtain a permit from the Corps. Modified by later acts that have added a great deal to U.S.C. Title 33, this section has become the primary legal foundation for protection of wetlands and regulation of landfill. Courts have accepted expansion of the original discretionary authority to approve or deny permits, primarily concerned with navigation, in light of more recent laws and policies. The Fish and Wildlife Coordination Act requires the Corps to consult with the Fish and Wildlife Service to prevent loss and damage to wildlife resources. Further, the Corps must consider the National Environmental Policy Act, which applies to all "policies, regulations, and public laws of the United States" and "all agencies of the Federal Government" (42 U.S.C. 4332[1–2]), when approving or denying a permit.

Consideration of ecological as well as navigational concerns in the permitting process was upheld in the landmark case *Zabel v. Tabb,* 430 F.2d 199 (5th Cir. 1970), where the plaintiffs asserted that denial of a landfill permit amounted to a "taking" of property without compensation in violation of the Fifth Amendment to the federal constitution. Two landowners in Florida sought a permit to dredge and fill land along the shoreline of Boca Ciega Bay (an arm of

Tampa Bay) to construct a trailer park. The district engineer for the Corps, Colonel R. H. Tabb, recommended that the permit be denied, even though the landfill would have no adverse effects upon navigation, due to harmful effect upon the fish and wildlife of the bay. The ecological hazards were highlighted by opposition from the Florida Board of Conservation, the County Health Board of Pinellas County, and the county's board of commissioners. The Fifth Circuit Court of Appeals upheld this as a proper legal consideration. The court found that there was no taking of private property because "the waters and underlying land are subject to the paramount servitude in the Federal government which the Submerged Lands Act expressly reserved as an incident of power to the Commerce Clause" (*Zabel v. Tabb* 1970, VI). In plain English, the waterways are a public resource, so a landowner denied a permit to fill them has had no private property "taken" from him or her. In 1972, the Corps was given more explicit duties by the Clean Water Act to regulate dredging and filling in the "waters of the United States," including many wetlands.

—Charles Rosenberg

See also: *Army Corps of Engineers, United States; Clean Water Act of 1972; Evolution of Environmental Law; Fish and Wildlife Coordination Act (1934); Mining and Water Resources; National Environmental Policy Act of 1969; River Transportation; Wetlands*

BIBLIOGRAPHY

Adams, David A. *Renewable Resource Policy: The Legal-Institutional Foundations.* Washington, DC: Island Press, 1993.

Ballard, Joe N. *The History of the U.S. Army Corps of Engineers.* Darby, PA: Diane, 1998.

Cowdrey, Albert E. "Pioneering Environmental Law: The Army Corps of Engineers and the Refuse Act." *Pacific Historical Review* 44, no. 3 (1975): 331–49.

Goldstein, William A. "Environmental Law—Consideration Must Be Given to Ecological Matters in Federal Agency Decision—*Zabel v. Tabb.*" *Boston College Law Review* 12, no. 4 (1971): 674–85.

Zabel v. Tabb (Alfred G. Zabel and David H. Russell, Plaintiffs—appellees, v. R. P. Tabb, Colonel, Corps of Engineers, District Engineer, Department of The Army, Jacksonville, Florida, District; Stanley R. Resor, Secretary of the Army; and United States of America, Defendants—appellants United States Court of Appeals, Fifth Circuit). 430 F.2d 199, July 16, 1970. http://cases.justia.com/us-court-of-appeals/F2/430/199/463171/.

Roosevelt, Franklin D.

Franklin Delano Roosevelt (1882–1945) was born in Hyde Park north of New York City on January 30, 1882. Roosevelt received his education at the Groton School, Harvard University, and Columbia Law School. Roosevelt did not complete his law degree at Columbia, opting instead to take the bar exam without the degree. He successfully passed the bar exam in New York and worked as a law clerk until 1910 when he was drawn to politics, which ultimately became his primary career. When offered the Democratic nomination to run for a New York Senate seat in 1910, Roosevelt accepted and was elected; he was reelected in 1912. Roosevelt received an appointment in 1913 to the position of assistant secretary of the Navy in the Wilson administration and remained there until 1920. He was selected as the vice presidential candidate for the Democratic Party in 1920 with James Cox of Ohio. The Cox-Roosevelt ticket lost to Republicans Warren G. Harding and Calvin Coolidge in a decisive election, but the election brought Roosevelt to the forefront of the Democratic Party.

Roosevelt returned to private business, working at a Wall Street firm after the election. He then fell victim to poliomyelitis in 1921, which left him paralyzed for the rest of his life. After a period of recuperation, Roosevelt returned to the public eye in 1928 as a supporter of Al Smith, the Democratic candidate for president in 1924 and 1928. Despite Smith's failure to get elected president, the state and national exposure brought Roosevelt to the governorship of New York in a narrow election in 1928 and again in 1930. In 1932, Roosevelt ran as the Democratic candidate for president and won the first of four successive elections to the office.

Conservation and Water Projects

As a politician and the owner of a tree farm in upstate New York, Roosevelt sought ways to improve conservation of the land and water. Many of these ideas became part of the New Deal programs instituted in his first two terms as president. As a New York state senator, he served as chair of the New York Commission on Forests, Fish, and Game and helped set up the Department of Conservation in New York. During his terms as governor, Roosevelt emphasized reforestation, water power protection and development, and other conservation-related projects.

After becoming president of the United States in March 1933, Roosevelt implemented a number of programs on a national scale that had worked in New York. The purpose of the programs was twofold: conservation and relief for unemployed Americans. Roosevelt's first program, proposed at the Democratic National Convention, was the Civilian Conservation Corps (CCC); this was established in March

1933 under the Emergency Conservation Work Act. The administrators of the CCC oversaw a variety of activities across the nation, including the planting of trees, road construction, and construction of recreational facilities.

The Public Works Administration (PWA), led by Harold Ickes, started in 1933 and was responsible for completing projects related to flood control, water power, and reclamation. Workers in the PWA helped to complete Boulder Dam, now Hoover Dam, on the Colorado River two years early, bringing flood control and hydroelectric power to the Colorado River basin.

The Works Progress Administration (WPA), established in 1935 and administrated by Harry Hopkins, undertook a variety of projects, including construction of roads, bridges, improvement of parks and playgrounds, and building of flood control and irrigation dams.

The Tennessee Valley Authority (TVA), established in May 1933, oversaw the construction and operation of over sixteen dams in a seven-state region along the Tennessee River in the southeastern United States. Additionally, the TVA undertook reforestation and erosion control projects in the region to aid in flood control. Roosevelt sought additional projects like the TVA for other river systems in the country, but Congress would not fund them.

Other legislation during the Roosevelt administrations continued the conservation programs of the early years. Roosevelt authorized the addition of 18 million acres to the national parks and forest systems during his presidency, adding to the legacy started under President Theodore Roosevelt. The Soil Erosion Act of 1935 stated the policy of Congress to control and prevent soil erosion; control floods; and keep reservoirs, rivers, and harbors open and free of impairment. It also created the Soil Conservation Service under the Department of Agriculture. In June 1936, Roosevelt signed the Flood Control Act, which authorized construction of flood control measures on dams and in harbors and all related water tributaries. Additional flood control projects completed by the U.S. Army Corps of Engineers during the Roosevelt administration include the Grand Coulee and Bonneville Dams on the Columbia River in Washington state.

Roosevelt left a lasting imprint on the United States in many respects. Many of his New Deal programs sought to combine work relief for the unemployed with the latest in conservation techniques. Roosevelt's environmental programs expanded the National Parks System and national forests. His conservation projects reduced erosion and

helped farmers to institute crop rotation. Major flood control legislation is a part of his legacy that continues to provide hydroelectric power, prevent floods, and provide recreational areas for all to enjoy.

Roosevelt died of a cerebral hemorrhage on April 12, 1945, in Warm Springs, Georgia. He was buried at his estate in Hyde Park, New York.

—Theresa Hefner-Babb

See also: *Army Corps of Engineers, United States; Flood Control Act of 1936; Grand Coulee Dam; Hoover Dam; Ickes, Harold; Roosevelt, Theodore; Tennessee Valley Authority*

BIBLIOGRAPHY
Burns, James MacGregor. *The Lion and the Fox.* New York: Harcourt Brace, 1956.
Jenkins, Roy. *Franklin Delano Roosevelt.* New York: Holt, 2003.
King, Judson. *The Conservation Fight: From Theodore Roosevelt to the Tennessee Valley Authority.* Washington, DC: Public Affairs Press, 1959.
Owen, A. L. Riesch. *Conservation Under FDR.* New York: Praeger, 1983.

Roosevelt, Theodore

Theodore Roosevelt (1858–1919) served as the twenty-sixth president of the United States. He did more than any other president to protect the nation's wildlife and waterways. Among his contributions were the Panama Canal, Crater Lake National Park, Grand Canyon National Monument, and the Pelican Island National Wildlife Refuge in Florida. He placed 230 million acres under federal protection and established 150 new national forests.

Early Life and Political Career

Theodore Roosevelt was born in New York City on October 27, 1858. As a child, he was asthmatic and nearsighted. His early ambition was to become a zoologist, an interest that resulted in his publishing two ornithology books while in college. He graduated from Harvard in 1880, after shifting his major from natural history to political economy. He subsequently attended Columbia Law School.

From 1882 to 1884, he served in the New York State Assembly and was elected minority leader in 1883. As a legislator, he sought to reform conditions experienced by residents of New York City tenements. During the 1880s and 1890s, he held several posts, including U.S. civil service commissioner, president of the Board of Police Commissioners (New York City), and assistant secretary of the Navy.

In this 1903 photo, President Theodore Roosevelt stands atop Glacier Point in Yosemite National Park. A noted outdoorsman, President Roosevelt was the first president to make natural conservation a national priority.

Library of Congress

Presidency and Conservation Projects

On November 8, 1898, he was elected governor of New York. Two years later, he was elected vice president of the United States alongside William McKinley. Following McKinley's assassination, Roosevelt became president. His first speech to Congress, on December 3, 1901, included strong conservationist language.

Roosevelt feared that Germany might attempt to construct a canal in Central America, so he acted first. On June 28, 1902, Roosevelt influenced Congress to pass the Isthmian Canal Act. He supported the Panamanians in their revolt against Colombia and, in November 1903, signed a treaty with Panama allowing the construction of the Panama Canal. The waterway was completed in 1914. Although Roosevelt considered his action to be an extension of the Monroe Doctrine, the new canal also promised to save ships from the dangers and time required to navigate around Cape Horn, on the southern tip of South America.

When Roosevelt assumed the presidency, there were five national parks. During his tenure as president, and in the years following, Roosevelt was responsible for the formation of over fifty wildlife refuges, eighteen national monuments, and five national parks: Crater Lake, Oregon (1902), Wind Cave, South Dakota (1903), Sullys Hill, North Dakota, (1904, became a national game preserve in 1914), Platt, Oklahoma (1906), and Mesa Verde, Colorado (1906). In 1903, Roosevelt issued an executive order that created Pelican Island in Florida as the first federal bird reservation. He established fifty-four additional wildlife refuges during his presidency. Many of the bird refuges were on islands or lakes and support waterfowl that have been since placed on the Endangered Species list, such as the brown pelican, least tern, and piping plover.

Roosevelt took advantage of the Antiquities Act of 1906, also known as the National Monuments Act, to use executive orders to create national monuments. This circumvented Congress, whose action was necessary to create national parks. During his second term, conservation became his central domestic issue. The first national monument he created was Devil's Tower in Wyoming (1906). He established the Grand Canyon in Arizona as a national monument in 1908; it gained national park status in 1919.

The Reclamation Act of 1902 authorized the Secretary of the Interior to build reservoirs in arid regions of the West. Roosevelt's administration sponsored twenty-one irrigation projects, designed to establish farms for the relief of urban congestion. Early projects included the Milk (Montana), Newlands (Nevada), and North Platte (Nebraska) Rivers. As a former president in 1911, Roosevelt dedicated the newly finished Theodore Roosevelt Dam on the Salt River near Phoenix, Arizona.

In 1905, the Transfer Act reassigned the management of forest reserves from the General Land Office within the Department of the Interior to the Bureau of Forestry in the Department of Agriculture. The agency was renamed the Forest Service, and Gifford Pinchot served as its first chief. Its principal objectives were to manage the forests for timber production, protect the grasslands from overgrazing, and provide watershed protection.

The Inland Waterways Commission, formed in 1907, sought to improve inland navigation inside the United States. In 1908, the president hosted the Governors' Conference on Conservation, which was intended to help states create their own forests and conservation programs. One of its outcomes was the creation of the National Conservation Commission and forty-one similar state commissions.

Roosevelt vetoed two bills that would have privatized hydroelectric power sites in the West. He wanted Congress to establish leasing legislation that would prevent monopolies and serve public interests. His executive orders reserved hydropower sites in sixteen states and 75 million acres of public coal lands. The subsequent controversy continued beyond his term as president and was eventually settled by both the passage of the Mineral Leasing Act of 1920 and the formation of the Federal Water Power Commission.

After leaving the presidency, Roosevelt wrote prolifically and continued his environmental efforts. In 1912, he again ran for president on the ticket of the Bull Moose Party, with conservation as the centerpiece of his platform. Although Woodrow Wilson was elected president, Roosevelt's conservation philosophy had taken root and would permeate American thought. He died on January 6, 1919, in Oyster Bay, New York, of arterial thrombosis.

—Ralph Hartsock

See also: *Bureau of Reclamation; National Parks and Water; Pinchot, Gifford; Reclamation Act of 1902; Theodore Roosevelt Dam*

BIBLIOGRAPHY

Cutright, Paul Russell. *Theodore Roosevelt: The Making of a Conservationist.* Urbana, IL: University of Chicago Press, 1985.

Lansford, Tom. *Theodore Roosevelt: A Political Life.* Hauppauge, NY: Nova Science, 2004.

Theodore Roosevelt Association. "About Theodore Roosevelt." http://www.theodoreroosevelt.org/.

Udall, Stewart L. "Men Must Act: The Roosevelts and Politics." In *The Quiet Crisis,* 126–46. New York: Holt, Rinehart and Winston, 1963.

Safe Drinking Water Act of 1974

S. 433 was introduced by Senator Warren Magnuson (D-WA) on January 18, 1973. It was entitled "An Act to Amend the Public Health Service Act to Assure that the Public is Provided with Safe Drinking Water, and for Other Purposes." It was signed by President Gerald Ford on December 16, 1974. The bill directs the administrator of the Environmental Protection Agency (EPA) to set water regulations within ninety days of enactment and to set provisions for maximum contaminant levels. The states are responsible for enforcement of the law, including the exemption of certain public water systems for financial reasons if public health is not jeopardized. Limits are placed on underground injection to protect groundwater. The administrator of the EPA is authorized to declare a water contamination emergency provided he or she notifies the state and local authorities. The administrator is also authorized to conduct research and grant appropriate monies to the states to carry

Water Fluoridation

During the 1940s, dentists in Wisconsin came to believe that water fluoridation held the promise of stemming the rampant tooth decay of the time, which usually resulted in much of the populace losing their teeth. Their theory led Grand Rapids, Michigan, to become the first city in the United States to add fluoride to its public water supply in 1945. Preliminary studies demonstrated that the fluoridated water was successful in preventing tooth decay among children, which led both the U.S. Public Health Service and the American Dental Association to endorse water fluoridation in 1950. Despite the endorsements, water fluoridation proved controversial. Many opponents claimed that fluoridation programs were violations of their individual rights, akin to communism or Nazism. Others argued that the fluoride caused health problems such as cancer, osteoporosis, Alzheimer's disease, and Down syndrome.

Water fluoridation has proven to assist significantly in the reduction of tooth decay in the areas where it has been introduced. It cannot be solely credited for the trend, as fluoride is also routinely present in toothpaste, mouthwash, and many processed foods and drinks. The presence of fluoride in so many products occasionally causes humans to be exposed to toxic levels of the substance. This threat of toxicity led the Environmental Protection Agency in 1986 to limit the fluorine level to 4 milligrams per liter of water.

—John R. Burch Jr.

See also: *Environmental Protection Agency, United States*

BIBLIOGRAPHY

Committee on Fluoride in Drinking Water, National Research Council. *Fluoride in Drinking Water: A Scientific Review of EPA's Standards.* Washington, DC: National Academies Press, 2006.

Ward, John W., and Christian Warren, eds. *Silent Victories: The History and Practice of Public Health in Twentieth-Century America.* New York: Oxford University Press, 2007

National Water Resources Association

The National Water Resources Association was founded as the National Reclamation Association on December 6, 1932. It is presently organized as a nonprofit federation of state organizations and caucuses, such as the Agri-Business Council of Arizona, Texas Water Conservation Association, and Municipal Water Supply Caucus. Although the organization is now focused on national issues, it still reflects its origins as a grassroots organization based in the western portion of the United States.

The National Reclamation Association was founded to promote the development of water resources in the West. From its founding through the 1950s, the association worked closely with state and federal elected officials to shepherd irrigation projects and dams from the authorization through construction phases. The association proved extremely efficient, as it was involved in the planning of most western water projects over its first two decades of existence.

By the 1960s, it had become evident that the organization had outlived its primary mission since large-scale water projects had fallen into disfavor. The association's membership responded by renaming itself the National Water Resources Association in 1969 and changing its focus from the West's water issues to those of the nation as a whole. Since the 1970s, the NWRA's membership has worked to support and strengthen such initiatives as the Clean Water Act, Endangered Species Act, and Safe Drinking Water Act.

—John R. Burch Jr.

See also: *Clean Water Act of 1972; Endangered Species Act (1973)*

BIBLIOGRAPHY

National Water Resources Association. http://www.nwra.org/.
National Water Resources Association Policy Development Committee. National Water Resources Association 2010 Mission Statement & Objectives, Resolutions, and Policy Statements. Arlington, VA: National Water Resources Association. Available at http://www.nwra.org/pdf/resolutions2010.pdf.

out the Act. The Act established the National Drinking Water Council of fifteen people to advise the administrator of the EPA.

The Safe Drinking Water Act was created to promote the safety of the public health, but more specifically, it was a reaction to the discovery of inadequacy in existing law. Throughout the twentieth century, laws pertaining to drinking water had been established from time to time. In 1962, the most comprehensive reforms prior to 1974 were established, which resulted in the regulation of twenty-eight substances. Due to the green revolution in the 1960s, increased attention was focused on factories and farms as sources of water pollution. This resulted in the commissioning of numerous studies of water pollution. In 1969, the Public Health Service found that only 60 percent of the water treatment systems surveyed met all of the standards. Over half of all treatment facilities had major deficiencies in water purification (EPA 2000).

The Safe Drinking Water Act in short was a result of technological advancement. The greater application of technology to farming created a situation where more chemicals were being added to the water supply. At the same time, technology could now purify water. This combination of increased pollution, increased awareness, and mechanical ability to come up with the solution led to the Safe Drinking Water Act of 1974.

The Safe Drinking Water Act has been amended several times since its original draft, first in 1986 and again in 1996. The original draft only regulated twenty-three contaminants and was weak in terms of enforcement. The EPA was given three years to set limitations on eighty-three additional contaminants. Technological benchmarks were also to be established for the filtration and disinfection of surface water. Water supply systems were to be monitored every five years for regulated contaminants. Lead and solder piping for drinking water was banned. Funds and technical water supply assistance would be provided to small water-monitoring systems that could not afford to comply with the law. Groundwater protection would be granted for recharge lands (Raloff 1986).

In 1996, there were more concerns about efficiency. A State Drinking Water Revolving Loan Fund was established to help public water systems comply with the law. Consumer confidence reports were developed, which contained information on local contaminants. In 2002, the government established the Public Health Security and Bioterrorism Preparedness Act as a response to the terrorist attacks on September 11, 2001. Title IV of that act required community water systems serving more than 3,300 people to conduct vulnerability tests and create emergency response plans.

Two current issues for the Safe Drinking Water Act include concerns about underground carbon dioxide storage and the gap between funding and spending. The Safe Drinking Water Act also now requires the EPA to compose a Contaminant Candidate List (CCL) every five years to determine and rank unregulated contaminants. CCL 1 was created in 1998, CCL 2 was created in 2003, and CCL 3 was created in 2008. As of 2008, there were ninety-three chemicals and eleven microbiological contaminants on the list. The EPA determined in July of 2008 that eleven of the contaminants would not be regulated. The EPA also decides every five years which thirty contaminants should be monitored. Contaminants that are regulated have potentially adverse side effects or are found in water supplies with high frequency. Regulation of contaminants may also occur if an opportunity to increase public safety is foreseen (Tiemann 2008).

With a growing population and an increase in the ability to pollute due to technology, the Safe Drinking Water Act at the very least provides security. It would be difficult to imagine what the water supply would be like now if the Safe Drinking Water Act had never existed. It is also comforting to know that the bill has been amended several times to strengthen its regulatory effect.

—Landon S. Utterback

See also: *Environmental Protection Agency, United States*

BIBLIOGRAPHY

EPA (U.S. Environmental Protection Agency). "The History of Drinking Water Treatment" (EPA-816-F-00-006). Washington, DC: United States Environmental Protection Agency, 2000. Available at http://www.epa.gov/ogwdw/consumer/pdf/hist.pdf.
EPA (U.S. Environmental Protection Agency). "Safe Drinking Water Act (SDWA)." http://water.epa.gov/lawsregs/rulesregs/sdwa/index.cfm.
Raloff, J. "Congress Toughens Drinking Water Rules." *Science News,* May 31, 1986.
Tiemann, Mary. *Safe Drinking Water Act (SDWA): Selected Regulatory and Legislative Issues* (CRS Report for Congress RL34201). Washington, DC: Congressional Research Service, 2008. Available at http://www.policyarchive.org/handle/10207/bitstreams/19967_Previous_Version_2008-09-10.pdf.

Schad, Theodore M.

Theodore M. Schad (1918–2005) was a civil engineer who served in U.S. federal and private agencies, including as executive director of the National Water Commission. During his long career in hydrology and water management, he was seen as an expert in the field, with his opinion actively sought by many policy formulators.

Early Life

Theodore MacNeeve Schad was born on August 25, 1918, at Baltimore, Maryland, the third child and second son of William H. Schad and Emma M. (née Scheldt). His father worked in maintenance and had been born in Maryland, the fourth son of a shoemaker; Theodore's paternal grandfather was the son of migrants from Germany. His mother was also from Maryland, both of her parents also having been born in the state. John, Theodore's older brother, became a salesperson for a natural gas company, and Theodore went to study at Johns Hopkins University, spending his summer holidays of 1937 and 1938 on rural electrification projects in southern Maryland and northern Virginia. He graduated with a degree in civil engineering in 1939 and then spent a year with the U.S. Army Corps of Engineers—essentially completing graduate work in hydrology—before he started with the Bureau of Reclamation at the Department of the Interior.

Water Policy Work

During the early 1940s, Schad was involved in project investigations in the Pacific Northwest and then joined the U.S. Army Corps of Engineers in Seattle. Initially he was in the Specifications Section, and then he worked as the reports coordinator for rivers and harbors in the Engineering Division. In 1946, he started with the Office of the Commissioner, Bureau of Reclamation, in Washington, D.C., working his way up from staff engineer to be the assistant chief of the Program Coordination Division. In 1952, he went to the United Kingdom, sailing on the *Queen Elizabeth,* to work as an engineer with Amexco in London; his wife found work there as a librarian.

Leaving the Bureau of Reclamation in 1954, he moved to the Bureau of the Budget and was staff director of the U.S. Senate Select Committee on National Water Resources from 1959 to 1961. He then worked for the Library of Congress Legislative Reference Service from 1961 to 1968. At the Library of Congress, Schad was the senior specialist on engineering and public works and regularly helped researchers locate information on water resources, which remained his special interest. Starting in 1966, he was the deputy director of the Legislative Reference Service.

In 1968, the National Water Commission was established by Congress with seven members, and Schad was its executive director from 1968 to 1973. The task of the commission was to provide independent advice to the president and Congress on water resources policy. The commission published its final report, *Water for the Future,* in June 1973, and many of its recommendations were acted upon.

Schad then became executive director of the National Academy of Sciences Commission on Natural Resources from 1973 to 1983, and he was also, from 1973 to 1977, the executive secretary of the Environmental Studies Board and from 1973 to 1976 the principal staff officer for Committees on Water Quality Policy. In 1979, he chaired the Committee on Water Resources Research. His last appointment, from 1984 to 1986, was as executive director of the National Ground Water Policy Forum.

After his retirement in 1986, he spent nearly two years as a consultant to Ronco Consulting Corporation, and in 1990 was appointed as a consultant to the Ford Foundation's Western Water Policy Project. He helped write the report *Preparing for an Uncertain Climate* in October 1993, which outlined possible scenarios for U.S. government action when facing climate change and other previously unforeseen problems. In 2000, he wrote the foreword to Peter E. Black's and Brian L. Fisher's *Conservation of Water and Related Land Resources.*

In 1950, Schad was awarded the Meritorious Service Award of the U.S. Department of the Interior, and twenty years later he was made an honorary member of the American Water Works Association. In 1978, he was given the Iben Award of the American Water Resources Association. He died on October 19, 2005, at Arlington, Virginia. His papers relating to his time as executive director of the National Water Commission are held in the Morgan Library, Colorado State University, Fort Collins.

—Justin Corfield

See also: *Army Corps of Engineers, United States; Bureau of Reclamation*

BIBLIOGRAPHY

Black, Peter E., and Brian L. Fisher. *Conservation of Water and Related Land Resources.* Boca Raton, FL: Lewis, 2001.

Reuss, Martin. *Interview with Theodore M. Schad* (EP 870-1-61). Water Resources: People and Issues. Alexandria, VA: Office of History and Institute for Water Resources, U.S. Army Corps of Engineers, 1999.

Rosen, Howard, and Marin Reuss, eds. *The Flood Control Challenge: Past, Present, and Future.* Chicago: Public Works Historical Society, 1988.

Worster, Donald. *Rivers of Empire: Water, Aridity, and the Growth of the American West.* New York: Pantheon Books, 1985.

Senate Select Committee on National Water Resources

Although it only existed from April 1959 until January 1961, the Senate Select Committee on National Water Resources had an impact on water policy in the United States that lasted far longer than the committee itself. A product of partisan politics, the Select Committee came into being as a result of President Dwight D. Eisenhower's drive to cut the federal budget by looking for proposed dam projects that might be eliminated. Driven not only by a desire to cut federal expenditures, Eisenhower viewed such projects as the Tennessee Valley Authority (and its multiple dams covering a nine-state area) as "socialism." Projects that had been proposed and even started during the New Deal faced elimination, and Eisenhower implemented a "no new starts" policy on both of the federal agencies responsible for dam building, the U.S. Army Corps of Engineers and the Bureau of Reclamation (Palmer 2004). Congress, however, ignored this provision, approving funding for many new reclamation projects. Pro-reclamation members of Congress formed the Select Committee in an effort to combat the president's policies and provide some evidence as to changes that should be implemented in the nation's reclamation efforts.

Committee Creation and Hearings

On April 20, 1959, the Senate passed S.R. 48 (which as a resolution did not need presidential approval). It called for the establishment of a temporary committee made up of two members of each of the four Senate committees that dealt with water (Agriculture and Forestry, Interior and Insular Affairs, Interstate and Foreign Commerce, and Public Works) in order to study how best to use the water resources of the nation. Senator Robert S. Kerr (D-OK), a longtime supporter of public power works and the powerful chair of the Public Works Committee, was chosen to head the Select Committee. Further, the resolution charged the Select Committee to look forward, specifically, to come up with a set of recommendations concerning the water needs of a burgeoning population, the agriculture needed to sustain it, and the industries needed to employ it through 1980.

The Select Committee, whose efforts were largely shaped by committee staff director Theodore "Ted" Schad, proceeded to hold a series of twenty-three field hearings in an attempt to gather information from all of the constituencies concerned: state officials, local government officials, and private citizens. It also commissioned a series of thirty-two studies that examined different aspects of the future water needs of the nation. All of the information gathered was then used to assemble the Select Committee's final report, presented on January 30, 1961, which was extremely influential in shaping the future water policies of the nation.

The activities of the committee were principally focused on the supply of and demand for water, especially in the western states, where the population was growing most rapidly. As a result, the committee had many staff members from western states. After all of the hearings and studies were assembled, a 100-page report was delivered to Congress, stating that there was a need for more scientific research on the future water needs of the nation and that biennial assessments of the supply-demand relationship were needed going forward (Reuss 1999). However, what resulted was not exactly what some pro-reclamation senators, who wanted the report to be a diatribe against the now outgoing Eisenhower administration, had in mind. For one thing, the stirrings of the modern environmentalist movement can be seen, in that the report recommended that some "certain streams be preserved in their free-flowing condition because their natural scenic, scientific, aesthetic, and recreational values outweigh their value for water development and control purposes now and in the future" (quoted in Palmer 2004, 159). The report's recommendations for future actions were few but weighty.

Committee Recommendations

The first recommendation was that the federal government, in cooperation with state governments, should undertake a comprehensive study of each major river basin in the United States, list the ways that the basin was being utilized, and outline the potential for further development. Secondly, and probably more importantly, the report recommended that the federal government take primary responsibility for initiating a coordinated scientific research plan on water (Reuss 1999). By the time the report was issued, the John F. Kennedy administration had taken office, and it enthusiastically accepted the recommendations. Kennedy, in his first message to Congress, advocated for the National Academy of Sciences to lead the water research effort. After Senator Kerr died in January 1963, Senator Clinton Anderson (D-NM) took up the report's recommendations, eventually resulting in the passage of the Water Resources

Research Act of 1964 and the Water Resource Planning Act of 1965.

—Steven L. Danver

See also: *Schad, Theodore M.; Water Resources Planning Act of 1965; Water Resources Research Act of 1964*

BIBLIOGRAPHY

Hamilton, Roy. "The Senate Select Committee on National Water Resources: An Ethical and Rational Criticism." *Natural Resources Journal* 2 (1962): 45–54.

Holmes, Beatrice Hort. *History of Federal Water Resources Programs and Policies 1961–70.* Washington, DC: U.S. Department of Agriculture Economics, Statistics, and Cooperative Service, 1979. Available at http://ir.library.oregonstate.edu/xmlui/bitstream/handle/1957/11437/His_Fed_Wat_Rec.pdf.

Palmer, Tim. *Endangered Rivers and the Conservation Movement.* 2nd ed. Lanham, MD: Rowman & Littlefield, 2004.

Reuss, Martin. *Interview with Theodore M. Schad (EP 870-1-61).* Water Resources: People and Issues. Alexandria, VA: Office of History and Institute for Water Resources, U.S. Army Corps of Engineers, 1999.

Schad, Theodore M. "An Analysis of the Work of the Senate Select Committee on National Water Resources, 1959–1961." *Natural Resources Journal* 2 (1962): 226–47.

Small Watershed Program, U.S. Department of Agriculture

The Small Watershed Program of the U.S. Department of Agriculture (USDA) is the product of several pieces of legislation, including the Soil Conservation Act of 1935, the Flood Control Act of 1936, the Flood Control Act of 1944, the Agricultural Appropriations Act of 1953, and the Watershed Protection and Flood Control Act of 1954. Together these acts and numerous amendments authorized the USDA to construct more than 11,000 dams on over 2,000 small watershed projects in partnership with local authorities in 48 states over the past 75 years.

Small watershed projects are based on the watershed planning idea that the integrated management of soil and water resources at the watershed scale through a combination of land treatment and the construction of small dams will reduce soil erosion and sedimentation, control flooding, and enhance agricultural productivity. The origins of this idea can be traced back to the nineteenth-century writings of such thinkers as George Perkins Marsh and John Wesley Powell and to the early twentieth-century efforts of Progressive Era conservationists to coordinate watershed planning at the federal level. With a few exceptions, such as the Weeks Act (1911), which authorized the U.S. Forest

Service to acquire eastern lands for the protection of water supplies, the watershed planning idea had little effect on public policy until the 1930s. At that time, it became influential in the thinking of President Franklin D. Roosevelt and other New Deal administrators, who saw it as central to their efforts to link environmental, economic, and social objectives in a comprehensive program for natural resource management.

Early Watershed Management Practices

The watershed-planning idea was first put into widespread practice by the Soil Erosion Service (SES) and its successor agency, the Soil Conservation Service (SCS), during the 1930s. SES was established in the Department of Interior in 1933, but after the passage of the Soil Conservation Act of 1935, it was transferred to the USDA and became SCS. Congress charged SCS with the task of addressing the endemic soil erosion then affecting many parts of the United States. To accomplish this objective, SCS established watershed demonstration projects across the country to demonstrate better land management practices to farmers such as the using hillside terraces, contour plowing, strip cropping, establishing grassed waterways, converting marginal lands into forest and pasture, and building water management structures to heal gullies and control runoff. Between 1933 and early 1944, SCS administered some 150 watershed demonstration projects in 45 states.

Many advocates of watershed planning argued that the combination of land treatment and small dams could dramatically reduce the size of floods by increasing the capacity of soils to absorb rainwater and by impounding excess runoff in upstream reservoirs. This point of view gained national prominence with the publication of *Little Waters: Their Use and Relation to the Land* by Harlow S. Person in 1936. President Franklin D. Roosevelt was a proponent of the "little waters" approach to flood control, and, due to his influence, provisions for investigating the potential for implementing a nationwide upstream flood control program were included in the Flood Control Act of 1936 (Pub. L. 74-738), which authorized the USDA to cooperate with the U.S. Army Corps of Engineers to develop plans for a comprehensive flood control program on the river systems specified in the Act. The Corps was given responsibility for developing plans for the construction of large dams on the main river channels, while the USDA was given responsibility for

conducting preliminary examinations and detailed surveys of watersheds to evaluate the feasibility of upstream flood control projects.

Between 1937 and 1944, USDA conducted 157 preliminary examinations and 51 detailed surveys to determine the potential for upstream flood control projects in the selected watersheds. The survey teams were interdisciplinary parties of soil conservationists, hydrologists, engineers, economists, appraisers, and farm management specialists. Their studies provided critical new understanding of the relationships among land use, soil erosion, and stream hydrology, and they helped to lay the groundwork for the establishment of procedures for the appraisal of flood damages, the estimation of costs and benefits for potential flood control projects, and the design of small watershed projects. The USDA ultimately recommended to Congress that flood control projects should be established on eleven of the watersheds surveyed under the Flood Control Act of 1936. Appropriations for these projects were included in the Flood Control Act of 1944 (Pub. L. 78-534). After World War II, there were some questions as to whether the USDA had the legal authority to build dams. These issues were resolved by an amendment to the Agricultural Appropriations Act of 1950 (Pub. L. 81-759) that explicitly authorized the USDA to build flood control structures.

Through the 1940s and early 1950s, support for small watershed projects grew, as they came to be seen by some as an alternative to the large dams and reservoirs planned by the Army Corps of Engineers and the Bureau of Reclamation for the Missouri and Arkansas River Valleys. In these years, a rural grassroots movement emerged to protest the construction of large dam projects, claiming that they were too costly to build and maintain, that they dispossessed farmers and inundated fertile bottomlands, and that the reservoirs they impounded would, in time, be rendered worthless by the deposition of sediment. The locus of this movement was in the prairie-plains states on the western tributaries of the Mississippi River, where many rural residents maintained a populist resentment of what they perceived to be "big government" dam programs serving downstream interests at their expense. Led by the National Informal Citizens Council on Watershed Conservation, they advocated for the creation of a permanent small watershed program. The conflict between advocates of big dams and proponents of the small watershed approach gave rise to what became known as the flood control controversy.

Government Support for Watershed Protection

The flood control controversy was brought to a head by the election of 1952. That year Dwight D. Eisenhower, a supporter of small watershed projects, became president. In the spring of 1953, Eisenhower sent a message to the Congress signaling his support for a law that would create a permanent authority for a small watershed program in the USDA. Shortly thereafter, Rep. Herman Carl Andersen (R-MN) inserted an amendment to the Agricultural Appropriations Act of 1954 (Pub. L. 83-156), which allocated $5 million that SCS used to establish fifty-eight pilot watershed projects in thirty-one states. The following year, Rep. Clifford Hope (R-KS) and Senator George D. Aiken (R-VT) sponsored bills to create a permanent small watershed program in the USDA. The resulting Watershed Protection and Flood Control Act (Pub. L. 83-566) became law in August 1954.

The Watershed Protection and Flood Control Act authorized the USDA to provide technical and financial cost-sharing assistance to landowners to construct small dams with no more than 5,000 acre-feet of capacity on watersheds no larger than 250,000 acres in size. Subsequent amendments generally granted the USDA authority to provide more generous assistance; to construct bigger projects; and to expand the number of authorized purposes for which watershed projects could be constructed to include the provision of municipal and industrial water supply, the protection of fish and wildlife habitat, and recreation. Passage of the Watershed Protection and Flood Control Act was significant because it created a permanent small watershed program in the USDA and it established SCS as an independent water resources management agency in the federal government alongside the Army Corps of Engineers and the Bureau of Reclamation.

—Samuel Stalcup

See also: *Army Corps of Engineers, United States; Bureau of Reclamation; Flood Control Act of 1936; Flood Control Act of 1944; Powell, John Wesley; Roosevelt, Franklin D.*

BIBLIOGRAPHY

Leopold, Luna B., and Thomas Maddock, Jr. *The Flood Control Controversy: Big Dams, Little Dams, and Land Management.* New York: Ronald Press, 1954.

Morgan, Robert J. *Governing Soil Conservation: Thirty Years of the New Decentralization.* Baltimore: Published for Resources for the Future by The Johns Hopkins University Press, 1965.

Peterson, Elmer. *Big Dam Foolishness: The Problem of Modern Flood Control and Water Storage.* New York: Devin-Adair, 1954.

Rosen, Howard, and Martin Reuss. *The Flood Control Challenge: Past, Present, and Future, Proceedings of a National Symposium, New Orleans, Louisiana, September 26, 1986.* Chicago: Public Works Historical Society, 1988.

Simms, D Harper. *The Soil Conservation Service.* New York: Praeger, 1970.

Soil and Water Resources Conservation Act of 1977

In the 1970s, soil conservation became a concern for constituencies other than farmers. The Soil and Water Resources Conservation Act of 1977 (RCA) became law on November 18, 1977. Amended in 1985 and 1994, the RCA mandates that the secretary of agriculture establish and maintain an ongoing program of evaluation of soil, water, and water-related resources, including fish and wildlife habitats. The Act also requires a program that helps users and owners to conserve soil and water.

Soil conservation has been an agreed-to need since the dust bowl and erosion crisis of the Great Depression. For decades, the Soil Conservation Service had provided education on safeguarding soil quality, and a typical farmer now and then sat on a state soil conservation committee or worked with the soil conservation district. Farmers became comfortable with the idea of taking care of their soil, internalizing and understanding that a return to the earlier crisis-causing practices was undesirable. Farmers had no quarrel with government programs that were consistent, focused on the matter at hand, and to a great extent voluntary.

In the 1970s, as environmentalism played a stronger role in conservation, Congress determined that demand was increasing for soil, water, and water related resources. It also saw that the sustained use of the resource base required that the government, specifically the U.S. Department of Agriculture (USDA), have in place a program that gives it the technical competence, the information, and a delivery system to provide land users assistance regarding conservation, watershed protection, flood prevention, fish and wildlife management, animal husbandry, community development, recreation, and related uses. The RCA beefed up conservation by broadening its purposes and establishing a more formal system of management. The USDA had the option, if it chose, of developing plans and technical assistance programs dealing with subsurface water, flood risk reduction, and agricultural water salinity, and the secretary had to report on these plans and assistance by 1987.

Soil and Water Programs

The secretary of agriculture had to develop a National Soil and Water Conservation Program (SWCP) and develop a National Resource Inventory that appraises soil, water, and water-related resources each five years. The Act required comprehensive surveys and reports to Congress by 1979, 1986, 1995, and 2005. The Soil Conservation Service became the National Resource Conservation Service (NRCS). The SWCP is the NRCS guide for performing its duties in the context of current and future needs of competing constituencies, including landowners and land users. The USDA continually collects information on fish and wildlife habitats, current and projected demand, laws and policies and programs at the state and federal levels, and costs and benefits of various approaches to conservation and irrigation.

The Act also mandated a national soil and water conservation program in cooperation with state and national organizations and the public by 1979 with updates in 1987, 1997, and 2007. The program would provide overall guidance for helping users and owners of private or nonfederal lands. Appraisals included quality and quantity of water and soil, state and federal laws, and cost-benefit studies of conservation methods. The first two assessments included nonfederal rangeland, and they determined if the quality was excellent, good, fair, or poor. The 1997 survey sampled 77,000 sites for type of soil, vegetation, and slope. Within fifteen years, the program included over 350,000 sites. The full appraisal of soil and water resources and the evaluation of options for reducing erosion were new, as were the ongoing reporting and upgrading requirements. The approach was popular. In the immediate aftermath of the original law, which demonstrated that conservation had a broad base of support from the national to the local level, state and local governments aggressively enacted soil conservation measures and became more responsive to broader constituencies. Many states developed the conservation programs that they have today as a response to the RCA. Also, both federal and state governments increased funding for conservation programs.

Developing the RCA

NRCS studies rely on assistance from state soil and water conservation agencies, conservation districts, and citizen groups. The National Association of Conservation Districts (NACD) provides conservation districts with national leadership and a unified voice for natural resource conservation.

In the late 1970s, the NACD and many local districts provided significant input into the development of the first RCA. Conservation districts are a good avenue for getting stakeholders on board. They involve the public and relay landowner priorities and other inputs, and the NACD ties the local inputs into a national conservation priority. The NACD and USDA worked together on the RCA and publicized the finished product. The NACD developed a ten-year series, *RCA Notes,* that kept conservation districts and other stakeholders informed as states planned and budgeted and the RCA unfolded. The first RCA was delivered in 1982; it addressed water availability and condition given consumption patterns and export trends. Alternative scenarios were developed for soil erosion, decline in the water table, urbanization, and impacts on important habitat. RCA conservation strategies were part of the 1985 Farm Bill as the Conservation Reserve Program and sodbuster, swampbuster, and conservation compliance. The second RCA built on the first and prioritized erosion and water quality as national concerns.

The Act had a termination date of December 31, 2008. The RCA was reauthorized in the Food Conservation Act of 2008. The scope of the RCA expanded to include the impacts of climate change and renewable energy, and it mandated delivery that a national appraisal documenting current status and future trends be delivered to Congress in January 2011. In addition, the National Conservation Program, due to Congress in January 2012, will provide information on current and future conservation programs, both those already in effect and those needed. The Act emphasizes the importance of stakeholder feedback and input regarding existing and new programs. Stakeholder input allows the USDA to measure the effectiveness of ongoing programs and identify new ones as conditions and needs change. When the USDA called for citizen input in 2009, it specified that it wanted to identify the most pressing natural concerns on private lands. It also sought input as to the effectiveness of current conservation (e.g., in terms of technical assistance, easements, cost sharing, land retirement, research, and local leadership). And it solicited alternative approaches (e.g., tax credits or environmental service markets).

—John H. Barnhill

See also: *Conservation Movement; Erosion*

BIBLIOGRAPHY

Libby, Lawrence W. "Policy Alternatives to Manage Supply: Conservation of Soil and Water Resources." *Increasing Understanding of Public Problems and Policies* (1981): 93–106. Available at http://ageconsearch.umn.edu/bitstream/17602/1/ar810093.pdf.

National Association of Conservation Districts."Resources Conservation Act (RCA)." Available at http://nacdnet.org/events/rca/.

U.S. National Research Council, Committee on Rangeland Classification. *Rangeland Health: New Methods to Classify, Inventory, and Monitor Rangelands.* Washington, DC: National Academies Press, 1994. Available at http://www.nap.edu/openbook.php?record_id=2212.

Solid Waste Agency of Northern Cook County v. United States Army Corps of Engineers et al. (2001)

The case of *Solid Waste Agency of Northern Cook County v. United States Army Corps of Engineers et al.* involved the question of whether or not the U.S. Army Corps of Engineers (Corps) could exercise regulatory authority over an abandoned sand and gravel pit in northern Illinois used by migratory birds. The U.S. Court of Appeals held that the Corps had such authority, but the U.S. Supreme Court reversed that ruling in a 5–4 decision.

Background of the Case

Justice Rehnquist, speaking for the Court, noted that 23 suburban Chicago cities and villages had formed a consortium, the Solid Waste Agency of Northern Cook County (SWANCC), to purchase 533 acres of land for the purpose of establishing a disposal site for baled nonhazardous waste. The property, a former mining site, consisted of sand and gravel pits abandoned since 1960. In the interim, a successional stage forest had developed with seasonal and permanent ponds of "varying size (from under one-tenth of an acre to several acres) and depth (from several inches to several feet)" (SWANCC 2001).

SWANCC contacted the Corps to determine whether it would be necessary to apply for a permit to fill in some of the permanent and seasonal ponds. Initially, the Corps had issued a decision saying that the permit would not be necessary. Subsequently, the Illinois Nature Preserves Commission informed the Corps that a number of migratory birds inhabited the site. The Corps identified 121 bird species, several of which depended on an aquatic environment for

survival, and issued a revised opinion asserting authority over the site under the migratory bird rule.

The Corps claimed that because migratory birds moved from state to state and had an impact on interstate commerce, Congress had granted the authority to protect them under the Commerce Clause of the U.S. Constitution. The Court of Appeals in hearing the case noted "that in 1996 approximately 3.1 million Americans spent $1.3 billion to hunt migratory birds (with 11 percent crossing state lines to do so) as another 17.7 million Americans observed migratory birds (with 9.5 million traveling for the purpose of observing shorebirds)" (*Solid Waste Agency* 1999).

Opinion

In delivering the 5–4 opinion, Justice Rehnquist held that the Corps had exceeded its authority under section 404(a) of the Clean Water Act by attempting to use the migratory bird rule to regulate waters in abandoned sand and gravel pits located entirely within the state of Illinois and not adjacent or hydrologically connected to any navigable waterways. Rehnquist added that Congress had never indicated a clear intent to apply section 404 to isolated intrastate waters based entirely on an effect on interstate commerce (Baumgartner 2005).

Rehnquist also indicated that when a statute can be interpreted either in a way that "pushes the limits" of congressional authority or in way that falls clearly within the limits of congressional authority, the Court will opt for the latter interpretation to avoid complicated constitutional issues. He found that Congress based its authority on its right to regulate navigable waters and that therefore the Court did not need to explore the question of whether Congress had the authority to pass the Act because of the impact of migratory birds on interstate commerce.

In reaching this decision, the Rehnquist Court distinguished the case from the *Riverside Bayview Homes* case, where the Court had held that the Corps's authority extended to wetlands that abutted navigable waterways. In that case, Rehnquist noted, there was a significant nexus between the wetlands and the navigable waterway.

The Court also rejected the Corps's contention that the failure of Congress to take action to limit the Corps's broader interpretation of the Clean Water Act indicated support for the Corps's interpretation.

Because the Court held that there was no clear congressional intent to extend the Clean Water Act to isolated nonnavigable waters, it did not reach the question of whether

Congress has the authority to regulate such waters under the Commerce Clause. The failure of the Court to reach the question of the constitutional authority to regulate isolated waterways under the Commerce Clause has meant a continuing debate in the lower courts concerning the regulation of wetlands.

In the wake of SWANCC, some writers have suggested some interesting solutions to the conflict between the national government's effort to protect the environment and the Court's efforts to impose increasingly restrictive interpretations on the powers of Congress under the Commerce Clause. Jody Freeman and Charles Kolstad (2007) suggest that Congress might leverage the authority it has over some wetlands to, in effect, regulate those over which it has no constitutional authority. In a program analogous to cap and trade, Congress could permit owners of regulated wetlands to mitigate their costs of compliance by purchasing credits from owners of nonregulated wetlands, who in turn would agree to meet certain environmental standards. Congress would need to oversee the efforts of the owners of the non-regulated wetlands in order to regulate the wetlands over which they had authority.

—Jerry Murtagh

See also: *Clean Water Act of 1972*

BIBLIOGRAPHY

Baumgartner, Mathew B. "SWANCC's Clear Statement: A Delimitation of Congress's Commerce Clause Authority to Regulate Water Pollution." *Michigan Law Review* 103 (2005): 2137–71.

Freeman, J., and C. D. Kolstad, eds. *Moving to Markets in Environmental Regulation: Lessons from Twenty Years of Experience.* New York: Oxford University Press, 2007.

Solid Waste Agency v. United States Army Corps of Engineers, 191 F.3d 845 (1999).

SWANCC (*Solid Waste Agency of Northern Cook County v. Army Corps of Engineers*), 531 U.S. 159 (2001).

United States v. Riverside Bayview Homes, Inc., 474 U.S. 121 (1985).

Spanish Water Law

Spanish colonists who settled in the greater Southwest region of North America brought with them legal and cultural values about water that had a lengthy history and application in New Spain and on the Iberian Peninsula. This body of Spanish water law was more often a product of local practices than legal codes, the result of several hundred years of application by irrigators and judges. It heavily influenced the modern water rights and laws of the territories taken over by the United States after the Mexican-American War.

Foundations

The legal antecedents of early Spanish water law drew from both the Romans and the Moors, though the latter proved to be more influential in Spain due to the technologies used and the religious importance of water in Islam. Moorish customs included ideas that everyone had basic rights to water, that pre-existing water rights always maintained priority, and that all water use should be beneficial and not wasteful. King Alfonso X codified Spanish law in 1265 in *Las Siete Partidas,* reflecting the twin heritages found in contemporary medieval Spain. *Las Siete Partidas* established general principles rather than specific regulations, but it was the only legal code in place as Spain extended its empire to the Western Hemisphere.

Rather than extend *Las Siete Partidas* to include New Spain, the crown instead governed its new lands by royal decrees (*cedulas*), ordinances, and regionally based resolutions. These brought the basic concepts of the *Partidas* to New Spain, but most were modified to meet local conditions or to accommodate institutions that had existed prior to Spanish arrival. In 1681, these many laws and regulations were drawn together in the nine-volume *Recopilación de leyes de los reynos de las Indias*. This work explicitly stated that original ownership of all land, water, and minerals in New Spain belonged to the Spanish crown, who in turn could make grants (*mercedes*) to settlers or for the protection of native inhabitants.

The *Recopilación*

The *Recopilación* and the later 1789 *Plan de Pitic*, a self-described model of how to form new Spanish communities based on the *Recopilación,* included explicit instructions on laying out new settlements. These included details on establishing an acequia system to provide water for the community and limited irrigation, complete with basic rules on its operation and regulation of water distribution. As with the *Recopilación* itself, minor local deviations adapting to local conditions resulted over time.

While the *Recopilación* offered many details about communities, it was less specific on water issues and rights for larger land grants. Early Spanish land grants did not automatically include water rights, which increasingly were treated separately because of the underlying belief that water must be regulated in the interest of all. While grants included inherent water rights for basic purposes, such as drinking, bathing, fishing, and watering of domestic livestock, these rights did not extend to greater agricultural or industrial uses such as farming, grazing, or mining. Educated colonists who sought land grants made sure to request the granting of accompanying water rights. For some specific types of grants, such as a *tierras de pan llevar* (land for growing bread, or irrigable land), it was understood that water rights were attached. The process, however, could be quite confusing and often resulted in local disputes, particularly if sedentary Indians lived nearby.

Water Rights and American Indians

The *Recopilación* made it clear that Indians had special standing. While this might appear to some as a priority or protected status, it was one based in a combination of Spanish paternalism to protect the "innocents" and economic colonialism to exploit the new lands and sometimes the natives themselves. New grants of either land or water could not be made to the detriment of local Indian interests, and it was generally understood that Indians did have priority rights "for their needs" or to "irrigate their lands." The protection and recognition of these rights was often a local balancing act (Taylor 1975).

A 1754 royal ordinance ordered officials in New Spain to simplify the process of acquiring water rights and to ensure that those rights were extended to Indians. Generally as before, it was hoped that local people could resolve their own disputes, but if necessary disputes could be resolved judicially with a *repartimiento de aguas*. If matters came to that point, the judge or official had a great deal of latitude to decide the matter, and the decisions came to have full legal status virtually equal to the *Recopilación*, so any violators could be fined or subjected to other penalties. Through these means, local customs and dispute resolutions ultimately ruled the day and became the basis for subsequent legal considerations.

Even after Mexican independence from Spain in 1821, use of these historical customs to address water disputes continued, and the system of Spanish water law was uninterrupted. Even the Treaty of Guadalupe Hidalgo in 1848 ending the Mexican-American War recognized this code through its assurance that the property rights of Mexican owners would be protected. Since water was considered a property right under Spanish and Mexican water law, it

had to be fully recognized by the United States and territorial or state governments. As former Mexican territories organized in the late nineteenth century, legal authorities began to codify these Spanish customs and regulations, such as rules for acequia associations and the principles of appropriation, priority in time, and beneficial use of water.

Thus, Spanish water law and customs became the fundamental basis of modern water law in many former areas of New Spain in the United States. This long historical heritage of Spanish water law is still drawn upon today in legal disputes about rights and priorities of different groups, including Indians and modern landowners who trace their rights back hundreds of years to original Spanish grantees. While much of this is formally codified or referred to in court cases, many practitioners in this field must have a solid understanding of the fundamentals of Spanish water law to address today's issues and concerns.

—Cameron L. Saffell

See also: *Recreational Water Rights; Southwest*

BIBLIOGRAPHY

Clark, Ira G. *Water in New Mexico: A History of Its Management and Use.* Albuquerque: University of New Mexico Press, 2002. Originally published 1987 by University of New Mexico Press.

Meyer, Michael C. *Water in the Hispanic Southwest: A Social and Legal History, 1550–1850.* Tucson: University of Arizona Press, 1984.

Rivera, José A. *Acequia Culture: Water, Land, and Community in the Southwest.* Albuquerque: University of New Mexico Press, 1998.

Taylor, William B. "Land and Water Rights in New Spain." *New Mexico Historical Review* 50, no. 3: (1975): 189–212.

State ex rel. Reynolds v. Miranda (New Mexico, 1972)

Up until 1969, little case law addressed whether an intentional diversion of water had to occur in order to establish an appropriative water right—a legally recognized right to a defined amount of water. This matter was tested that year, when New Mexico landowner Lorenzo Miranda filed an application with the State Engineer's office to change a surface diversion for irrigation from the natural flow in Abo Wash to drilled irrigation wells in the Rio Grande water basin. State Engineer Steve E. Reynolds challenged the application, contending that Miranda did not possess a legal water right. The New Mexico Supreme Court ruling in the case, *State ex rel. Reynolds v. Miranda* (1972), utilized

The Milagro Beanfield War

The Milagro Beanfield War, directed by Robert Redford, is a comedic dramatization of the politics of waters rights in northern New Mexico during the latter portion of the twentieth century. The story was built around the David versus Goliath trope, with developer Ladd Devine in the Goliath role. Through his usurpation of the water in the Milagro Valley, Devine had rendered infertile land that had once supported generations of farm families. He required the water to develop a recreation area that included golf courses. Devine was aided by the state government, which not only provided him with all the zoning permits that he required but also passed legislation that favored his interests over those of local landowners. Devine was opposed first by John Mondragon, who acquired some of Devine's water supply to irrigate his family's fields, which he used to grow pinto beans. Both the harassment of Mondragon by government officials and the success of his bean fields inspired other members of the community to oppose Devine's recreation project. Despite having all the governmental, legal, and financial support he required to complete the construction project, Devine ultimately abandoned his plans in the face of escalating community opposition. The people of Milagro Valley proved in their victory against overwhelming odds that the importance of water to fulfill the needs of the local populace outweighs the interests of capitalists.

—John R. Burch Jr.

BIBLIOGRAPHY

Longo, Peter J., and David W. Yoskowitz, eds. *Water on the Great Plains: Issues and Policies.* Lubbock: Texas Tech University Press, 2002.
Milagro Beanfield War. DVD. Directed by Robert Redford. Universal, Focus Features, 2005.
Nichols, John Treadwell. *The Milagro Beanfield War.* New York: Holt, Rinehart and Winston, 1974.

opinions from other western states to establish that a man-made diversion was necessary to create a valid appropriation claim. This decision has continuing implications in the modern application of water for conservation, ecological, and recreational purposes.

Background

Miranda believed his water rights had been claimed and completed by his predecessors prior to 1907, when New Mexico's statutory water law was first adopted. The intermittent flows through Abo Wash across Miranda's land resulted in wild grasses on which cattle grazed and that were sometimes harvested for winter use. Sometime after World War I, an arroyo naturally formed in the wash, diverting much of the flow from the grassland. Miranda claimed that this historical use constituted a perfected water rights appropriation—one for which he could change the point of diversion (Kury 1973).

The district trial court and counsel for both parties stipulated that the case would hinge on a single legal point: Are the "physical efforts of man resulting in a visible diversion of water" necessary to establish a water right in New Mexico? Miranda's counsel based their argument on several Colorado cases, including *Thomas v. Guiraud*, which suggested that diversion was irrelevant as long as water was successfully applied to beneficial use. They also cited *Town of Genoa v. Westfall*, a case that prohibited Genoa from diverting waters that were the source of Westfall's springs, in which the court had ruled in part that his using the water for his cattle and home constituted a "beneficial purpose" (Kury 1973; *Reynolds v. Miranda* 1972).

The Decision

In the state supreme court decision, Justice Montoya wrote that Miranda's contention was misplaced; the Colorado court had defined dual requirements of both actual and beneficial use in order to exclude the necessity of a man-made diversion to establish a water appropriation. The mere cutting of grasses by Miranda's predecessors, the Court suggested, did not show intent. Their failure to divert water from the arroyo after its formation was further recognition of this lack of intent.

The court instead pointed to a 1926 New Mexico case, *Harkey v. Smith*, which indicated that it was necessary both to make use of the water as well as divert it and that no appropriation could be effected without both. "The intent, diversion, and use must coincide." The court also cited the 1902 Nevada case *Walsh v. Wallace*, a similar case in which Nevada had considered whether a man-made diversion was necessary to establish a valid appropriation on lands where the owner had cut the wild grasses and grazed cattle. That court had also decided that there must be a diversion followed by both intent and actual action to apply the water to beneficial use. Based on these precedents, a unanimous court ruled against Miranda.

Controversies

Within a year, Channing Kury (1973) expressed grave concerns about the state supreme court's analysis and the implications of its ruling. Since the court said that a man-made diversion is necessary to gain a water right, then it could be reasonably concluded that if water rights are purchased, that the maintenance and use of a man-made diversion is necessary to avoid losing those rights by abandonment or forfeiture. If, for example, a conservation group bought a canyon and all the water rights to ensure a natural flow, the group could lose its rights even if the water use was beneficial in nature. While the court limited its decision to agricultural cases, Kury feared that water rights holders who watered livestock could be at risk or that the finding could be extended to nonagricultural cases. He labeled the decision as "unnecessary embellishments" of the appropriation doctrine, having undesirable effects, and called for it to be overruled.

State Engineer Reynolds (1980) suggested that Miranda made clear there could be no "instream" water right—a matter not fully appreciated until President Carter's administration, when several federal agencies sought to develop policies to protect and enhance instream flows, perhaps as Kury's example suggested. Since New Mexico's stream flows were not fully appropriated, Reynolds felt the matter was still open to some debate, but the Miranda decision meant that the federal government could not override water rights granted or administered by the states.

More recently, law professor Denise Fort (2000) reviewed New Mexico's efforts to define instream flow protections and the obstacles presented by the Miranda decision. During Reynolds's tenure as state engineer through 1991, his office adamantly opposed any legislative or legal efforts to overturn or bypass Miranda, despite great political and public pressure to do so. Relief came when state senators asked the federal attorney general for a formal opinion on whether instream flows for recreational or ecological purposes could be recognized in state law. The 1998 opinion issued by Tom Udall suggested that the matter was likely only pertinent to the transfer of water rights, as he believed that applications for new water rights were unlikely in a state where water rights appeared to be fully appropriated. It acknowledged, however, the state engineer's opinion that any instream water rights still had to be measured by mechanical devices. With those restrictions, the opinion in effect stated that instream flows could not be guaranteed through legislative means, but it did define circumstances under which water rights could be reallocated to achieve a more balanced water policy. Thus, for example, federal agencies could acquire and apply instream water rights to protect federally listed endangered species in New Mexico's rivers.

While not an outright adoption of instream water flow rights, Udall's opinion did establish the means for recognizing such rights, thus bypassing the implications of the Miranda decision. This could reshape the debates in New Mexico and other arid western states regarding man-made diversions and appropriative water rights, particularly for those that predate water laws adopted in the twentieth century.

—Cameron L. Saffell

See also: *Recreational Water Rights; Wells*

BIBLIOGRAPHY

Fort, Denise D. "Instream Flows in New Mexico." *Rivers* 7, no. 2 (2000): 155–63. Available at http://http://repository.unm.edu/handle/1928/9072.

Kury, Channing R. "Comment: The Prerequisite of a Man-Made Diversion in the Appropriation of Water Rights—*State ex. rel. Reynolds v. Miranda.*" *Natural Resources Journal* 13, no. 1 (1973): 170–75.

Reynolds, Steve E. "A Historical Perspective of Water Management in Mexico." In *A Quarter Century of Water Research: Proceedings of the Twenty-Fifth Annual New Mexico Water Conference,* 20–31. Water Resources Research Institute (WRRI) Report No. 124. Las Cruces: New Mexico Water Resources Research Institute, 1980.

Reynolds v. Miranda (State ex rel. Reynolds v. Miranda), 83 N.M. 443, 493 P.2d 409 (1972).

Superfund

See *Hazardous Substances Response Trust Fund*

Tennessee Valley Authority

The Tennessee Valley Authority (TVA) is a federally owned corporation created by Congress in 1933 as part of President Franklin Delano Roosevelt's New Deal. It is a world-renowned example of regional water and power planning and has been visited by many foreign officials, eager to use it as a model to modernize their countries. Roosevelt intended the TVA to fulfill many objectives for the Tennessee

308 Surveys

The idea for the 308 surveys was pioneered in the 1920s during the planning process for the development of projects that eventually came under the auspices of the Tennessee Valley Authority. The thoroughness of the exhaustive reports on the Cumberland and Tennessee Rivers in Tennessee proved very educational to members of Congress, who found it much easier to appropriate money for the costly water projects in the Tennessee Valley knowing that all of the possibilities for development had been explored.

In House Document 308, first introduced in the U.S. House of Representatives in 1925 and later incorporated into the Rivers and Harbors Act of 1927, members of Congress called for the creation of comprehensive general surveys of the major rivers and their tributaries scattered throughout the United States. The surveys were used to determine how best to improve waterways for the purposes of navigation, the prevention of floods, the irrigation of crops, the impoundment of water, and power generation. The resulting documents became known as "308 reports."

—John R. Burch Jr.

See also: *Army Corps of Engineers, United States*

BIBLIOGRAPHY

Johnson, Leland R. *Engineers on the Twin Rivers: A History of the Nashville District, Corps of Engineers, United States Army.* Nashville, TN: U.S. Army Engineer District—Nashville, 1978.

U.S. Army Corps of Engineers, U.S. Federal Power Commission, and U.S. Congress, House of Representatives. *House Document No. 308.* Washington, DC: U.S. Government Printing Office, 1926.

distributors who serve more than 8.8 million customers in seven states. This power comes from twenty-nine hydroelectric dams, eleven coal-fueled plants, eight combustion turbine plants, fifteen solar plants, one wind-powered site, and three nuclear power plants. The service area covers most of Tennessee and parts of Alabama, Georgia, Kentucky, Mississippi, North Carolina, and Virginia.

The TVA operates 49 dams and reservoirs and manages 293,000 acres of public land. Of these dams, 34 are specifically operated to control flooding. Approximately 50 million tons of goods are shipped annually on the Tennessee River at much lower rates than either rail or trucking transportation costs. The TVA also employs approximately 45,000 people in the region. When the TVA was created, the most important change it made in the region was that it brought electricity to people. Ultimately, it also attracted industries to the area that provided much-needed jobs.

Expansion and Controversies

Although the Tennessee Valley Authority is probably the longest-lasting legacy of Roosevelt's New Deal, it met with strong opposition when first proposed. Although some felt that private electric companies were charging too much and profiting unfairly, many others were uncomfortable with government-run public utilities. Detractors labeled the TVA as a tool of socialism and feared such government interference in the economy. Eventually, depression conditions helped Roosevelt overcome resistance in Congress.

During the 1940s, the Tennessee Valley Authority began the construction and operation of twelve hydroelectric plants to provide electricity for the manufacture of aluminum. At the same time, it continued building dams, locks, and other structures to control the flow of the Tennessee River. It also developed fertilizers, which it advertised locally by sending out agents to encourage farmers to use the new products. By the early 1940s, the TVA had set up approximately 15,000 demonstration farms along the Tennessee River to serve as teaching centers. The TVA also

River Valley, including flood control, navigation, electricity generation, and general economic development. It was the first and remains the largest regional planning agency created by the federal government.

Objectives and Responsibilities

During the Great Depression of the 1930s, President Roosevelt looked for ways to address the economic distress of particularly hard-hit areas. In fact, the Tennessee River Valley had already been very poor before the Depression, and many people in the region did not yet have electricity. The farmers along the river suffered from seasonal flooding, erosion, and undernourished soils. Part of the goal for the TVA was to create manufacturing facilities for fertilizers and to provide training for area farmers on modern agricultural techniques. In many ways, the TVA was supposed to be an agency that would completely renovate Appalachia.

The TVA's primary responsibility is the production and sale of electricity. It is the largest public power company in the United States and sells its electricity to power

Although the intention was to improve the lives of people along the river, displaced families were often worse off than they had been before.

Another major issue the TVA faced in its development years concerned environmental impact. In 1973, Congress passed an amended Endangered Species Act, and in that same year, biologists determined that TVA construction plans for Tellico Dam in east Tennessee would so severely damage the habitat for a small fish called the snail darter that the fish would likely become extinct. Lawsuits followed, and the Supreme Court ruled that construction of Tellico Dam must stop. After several more years of arguments, congressional supporters passed an amended version of the Endangered Species Act in 1979 that exempted Tellico Dam. The dam was finally completed, and the snail darter was transplanted to the Hiwassee River, where it later flourished. It was removed from the endangered species list in the 1980s.

While power generation is the primary purpose of the TVA, it has also responded to public demand for recreational facilities along the river. In the early 1990s, the TVA created a "TVA Lake Improvement Plan" to enhance water levels in ten TVA lakes during the summer. The TVA also addressed water quality concerns raised by area residents. Although the water in the Tennessee River is generally considered good, there is concern about low dissolved oxygen (DO) levels that adversely affect aquatic life. The TVA has worked to decrease DO levels in various ways and to protect habitat. While challenges remain, the TVA remains a successful agency after more than seventy-five years of existence.

—April Summitt

See also: *Fertilizers; Roosevelt, Franklin D.;* Tennessee Valley Authority v. Hill *(1978)*

BIBLIOGRAPHY

Creese, Walter L. *TVA's Public Planning: The Vision, the Reality.* Knoxville: University of Tennessee Press, 1990.

Gray, Aelred J., and David A. Johnson. *The TVA Regional Planning and Development Program: The Transformation of an Institution and Its Mission.* Aldershot, UK: Ashgate, 2004.

Hargrove, Erwin C. *Prisoners of Myth: The Leadership of the Tennessee Valley Authority, 1933–1990.* Princeton, NJ: Princeton University Press, 1994.

Miller, Barbara A., and Richard B. Reidinger. *Comprehensive River Basin Development: The Tennessee Valley Authority.* Washington, DC: The World Bank, 1998.

Whisnant, David E. *Modernizing the Mountaineer: People, Power, and Planning in Appalachia.* Knoxville: University of Tennessee Press, 1994.

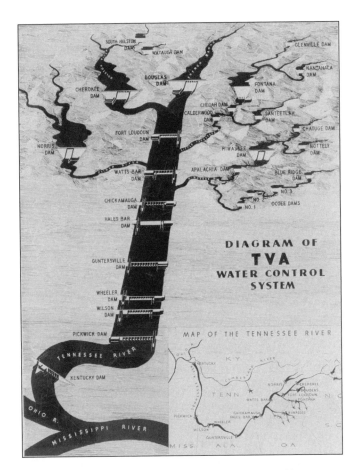

Created by a congressional act and signed into law by Franklin Roosevelt in 1933, the Tennessee Valley Authority was a multifaceted plan that included improvement of degraded agricultural land, reforestation, and, most notably, the construction of numerous hydroelectric dams. This early map shows the extent of planned damming of the Tennessee River.
Library of Congress

worked on forestry issues, including fire control, improved logging methods, and reforestation.

Through most of the 1940s and '50s, the TVA was federally funded, but in 1959, it became largely self-financing through the sale of bonds to private investors. In the 1960s, the TVA built two nuclear plants and planned to build more in the future. However, in the next decade, increased worries over the safety of nuclear power and the nation's economic troubles resulted in retrenchment rather than growth. Although conditions improved in the late 1980s, the TVA focused more on power conservation and cost reduction rather than on building new facilities.

Various other issues confronted the TVA during its decades of construction and development. One was the dislocation of people from areas flooded by TVA dams.

Appalachian Water Resources Survey

The Appalachian Water Resources Survey (AWRS) was conducted by the Office of Appalachian Studies, U.S. Army Corps of Engineers in response to the 1965 Appalachian Regional Development Act. Its purpose was to examine how the development of water resources within Appalachia could alleviate the region's persistent poverty.

The creation of the Tennessee Valley Authority established a model that many Appalachians sought to emulate. Most of the variations of the model were justified using three reasons: the dams would stop the devastating floods that regularly ravaged valleys, the building of multipurpose dams would create energy and jobs, and the lakes would create a tourism industry. The dreams of recreating the TVA throughout Appalachia remained a forlorn hope until the passage of the Appalachian Regional Development Act, which in section 206 called for an exploration of how to develop Appalachia's water resources.

Although the AWRS examined decades of development ideas from within the region, the political realities of the 1970s made it difficult to implement any of its recommendations. The Nixon administration had little interest in funding projects within Appalachia because it had been a signature cause for both John F. Kennedy and Lyndon B. Johnson. Also, the legislative successes of the environmentalist movement made the types of large-scale water projects desired by people within Appalachia impossible to fund.

—John R. Burch Jr.

See also: *Army Corps of Engineers, United States*

BIBLIOGRAPHY

Burch, John R., Jr. *Owsley County, Kentucky, and the Perpetuation of Poverty.* Jefferson, NC: McFarland, 2008.
Corps of Engineers, Cincinnati, Ohio. *Development of Water Resources in Appalachia, Main Report, Part VI.* Vol. 15, *History, Coordination, and Cooperation.* Cincinnati, OH: Ft. Belvoir Defense Technical Information Center, 1970.
Eller, Ronald D. *Uneven Ground: Appalachia Since 1945.* Lexington: University Press of Kentucky, 2008.

Tennessee Valley Authority v. Hill (1978)

Tennessee Valley Authority v. Hill, 437 U.S. 153 (1978), was the U.S. Supreme Court's first application of the Endangered Species Act (ESA) of 1973 (87 Stat. 884, 16 U.S.C. § 1531 et seq.) to a major government project. A majority of six justices ruled that the law unambiguously required the Tennessee Valley Authority (TVA) to cease construction of the Tellico Dam on the Little Tennessee River. The Court's ruling remains good law to guide application of the ESA,

but it led to substantial congressional amendment of the statute and became a springboard for sharp public debate over environmental policy. In a 2001 poll of environmental law professors to identify the ten most important cases in their field, *TVA v. Hill* received the largest number of votes.

Background

The determining fact for this ruling was the discovery of a previously unidentified fish, the snail darter (*Percina (Imostoma) tenasi*), a two-and-a-half-inch perch adapted to shallow, clear, cool rivers flowing over rocky shoals. The dam would destroy its only known habitat. Underlying the case was a long-running dispute pitting a coalition of farmers, sports enthusiasts, environmentalists, and portions of the Cherokee nation, who favored preservation of the river, against the TVA's strategy for economic development. Section 4 of the ESA authorizes the secretary of the interior to declare a species of animal or plant life endangered. Section 7 specifies that federal departments and agencies must ensure that the continued existence of endangered species is not jeopardized by destruction of critical habitat.

Tellico Dam originated in 1959 as the showcase for TVA's new mission. General Manager Aubrey Wagner observed that "if past methods for justifying and financing [dam and reservoir] projects are continued in the future, few, if any, more dams will be built in the Tennessee Valley." Projected costs for new projects exceeded the benefits of power generation, navigation, and flood control. Searching for "new and different methods we can devise for justification and financing" (Aubrey J. "Red" Wagner, quoted in Wheeler and McDonald 1986, 24), the TVA looked to land enhancement, recreation, and "general economic benefits" (Future Dams and Reservoirs Committee, quoted in Wheeler and McDonald 1986, 37).

TVA proposed to condemn three times the land needed for the reservoir, and it ultimately dispossessed over 300 family farms on some of the best agricultural bottomland in the United States. Local opposition began as early as September 1964. A study reported in the summer of 1971 that the costs of the Tellico Dam would far outweigh its benefits. When the snail darter was identified, farmer Asa McCall observed, "We've never heard of this little fish before, but if it can save our farms, our rivers and valley, I say let's try it" (quoted in Wheeler and McDonald 1986, 192). There was also local support for the dam, led by the Tri-County Development Association. Opposition initially pitted defense of private property, and skepticism about wasteful government spending, against an agency that epitomized New Deal development of an impoverished region. By the time Tellico Dam was completed, critics of strict environmental protection laws had become the project's most ardent supporters.

Completion of the dam was delayed by an injunction under the National Environmental Policy Act of 1969 (NEPA; 83 Stat. 852, 42 U.S.C. § 4321 et seq.), because the TVA had not complied with the Act's requirement for an environmental impact statement. That injunction, issued in response to *Environmental Defense Fund v. TVA,* was dissolved in late 1973, when a federal judge ruled that the TVA was in compliance with NEPA (371 F.Supp. 1004, ED Tenn. 1973). A few months earlier, the snail darter was discovered by University of Tennessee ichthyologist Dr. David A. Etnier.

The Decision

The Supreme Court's ruling was a conservative one, deferring to the plain language of a congressional statute. Although Chief Justice Warren Burger observed during oral arguments that the snail darter's discovery was "a handy handle to hold onto" for litigants who "just don't want this project" (quoted in Plater 2004, 16), he wrote the majority opinion affirming that "in our constitutional system, the commitment to the separation of powers is too fundamental for us to preempt congressional action by judicially decreeing what accords with 'common sense and the public weal'" (*TVA v. Hill*). Zygmunt J. B. Plater, attorney arguing against the dam, compared the snail darter to a canary in a coal mine, as a wide range of human concerns were inevitably tied in to defense of the darter's habitat.

Congress, having the power to amend the statute, did so repeatedly, increasing the text of section 7 from 129 words to 4,603. One amendment, in 1978, established an Endangered Species Committee empowered to grant exemptions as it balanced public interests against the value of a species. This committee soon became known as the "God Squad." Although expected to approve completion of the Tellico Dam, the committee denied an exemption.

The Court's ruling did not prevent construction of the Tellico Dam. On June 18, 1979, a rider was added in the House of Representatives to the Energy and Water Development Appropriations Act of 1980 (Pub. L. 99-69, 93 Stat. 437, 449–50) explicitly exempting the Tellico Dam from the Endangered Species Act. The controversial provision was described by Plater (2004) as a "late-night, porkbarrel rider" (6). Senator Howard Baker (R–TN) succeeded in getting the amendment approved in the Senate.

TVA v. Hill, never overturned, has been cited in over 1,000 published cases in federal and state courts. The case established that once a federal project is shown to jeopardize an endangered species, an injunction is mandatory, not discretionary. Congressional amendments to the law in 1978 emphasized constructive consultation should take place to seek reasonable alternatives so that federal agencies could perform their missions without destruction of critical habitat.

—Charles Rosenberg

See also: *Dam Building; Endangered Species Act (1973); Evolution of Environmental Law; National Environmental Policy Act of 1969; Prior Appropriation; Riparian Ecosystems; Tellico Dam; Tennessee Valley Authority*

BIBLIOGRAPHY

Bean, M. J. *The Evolution of National Wildlife Law.* 2nd ed. Urbana, IL: Praeger, 1983.

Murchison, Kenneth M. *The Snail Darter Case: TVA versus the Endangered Species Act.* Lawrence: University Press of Kansas, 2007.

Plater, Zygmunt J. B. "Endangered Species Act Lessons Over 30 Years and the Legacy of the Snail Darter, a Small Fish in a Porkbarrel." *Environmental Law* 34, no. 2 (2004): 289–308. Available at http://papers.ssrn.com/sol3/papers.cfm?abstract_id=617581.

(*TVA v. Hill*) *Tennessee Valley Authority v. Hill,* 437 U.S. 153 (1978).

Wheeler, William Bruce, and Michael J. McDonald. *TVA and the Tellico Dam, 1936–1979: A Bureaucratic Crisis in Post-Industrial America.* Knoxville: University of Tennessee Press, 1986.

Truckee-Carson-Pyramid Lake Water Rights Settlement Act of 1990

With the development of the Newlands Reclamation Project in the early twentieth century, Pyramid Lake in Nevada, sacred to the Pyramid Lake Paiutes and the source of their livelihood, fishing, became a shadow of its former self. The Truckee River that fed into the lake was diverted to a reclamation project, which was the first fruits of federal efforts to stimulate and control the development of water interests in the West. In 1902, the passage of the Reclamation Act, sponsored by Rep. Francis Newlands (D-NV), began the modern age of western water development. The first project funded by the new apparatus, devised by and named after Newlands himself, was also the first case in the new century in which Indians had to deal with a massive loss of water rights due to non-Indian water development (Wilkinson 1992).

Newlands Project

The Newlands Project was the first large-scale attempt by the federal government to subsidize irrigated agriculture in the West, creating an immense project near Fallon, Nevada. The original proposal intended to divert the waters of the Carson River in order to feed the project, but when those waters proved insufficient, reclamation officials turned their eyes toward the Truckee River. The construction of Derby Dam, thirty-five miles upstream from Pyramid Lake, resulted in the halving of the river's flow, which both lowered the level of the lake by seventy feet and permitted the buildup of silt. Insufficient flow led to the salination of the lake and the death of the Lahontan cutthroat trout, the primary source of livelihood for the area's Paiutes. In the case of *Pyramid Lake Paiute Tribe v. Morton* (1973), a federal district court ruled that the allocation of water by the Interior Department violated the government's trust responsibility toward the Indians (Fixico 1998). However, it took the cooperation of environmentalist groups, reacting in response to the highly toxic materials leached out as a by-product of Newlands irrigation, to get the diversions from the Truckee River reduced. Ironically, this has had the unfortunate side effect of concentrating the leached toxins (Wilkinson, 1992).

After fourteen years of negotiations, the California-Nevada Interstate Water Compact was signed in 1968 to allocate waters in Lake Tahoe and the Truckee, Carson, and Walker river basins. The agreement served the interests of local water-user groups in Nevada and California but infringed, once again, on water rights of the Pyramid Lake Paiutes. Finally, the compact of 1968 was amended, and the California and Nevada state legislatures approved the new version in 1971. However, Congress refused to ratify it on numerous occasions between 1971 and 1986.

Settlement

Efforts to create a federally approved settlement would not come to fruition until the Pyramid Lake Paiutes were included in the settlement. Pyramid Lake was not only a sacred site to the tribe but the home to the Pyramid Lake cui-ui and Lahontan cutthroat trout, which had been a main source of sustenance for the tribe. After a few years of negotiations among the tribe, the federal government, and the states, the Truckee-Carson-Pyramid Lake Water Rights Settlement Act was agreed upon. The settlement not only apportioned the waters of Lake Tahoe and the Truckee and Carson Rivers between California and Nevada, but it also addressed the needs of the Pyramid Lake Paiutes and Pyramid Lake itself. In a departure from most prior water settlements that included Indian tribes, water for agriculture was not a major consideration, as the Pyramid Lake Paiutes were not traditionally an agricultural people. Rather, the tribe's water rights were used to ensure that the threatened fish species were restored, that Pyramid Lake itself was replenished, and that the Lahontan Valley's wetlands were protected.

The settlement act established Stampede Reservoir for the specific purpose of propagating the endangered Pyramid Lake cui-ui and Lahontan cutthroat trout, set aside $65 million to restore the two fish species, gave $43 million to the Pyramid Lake Paiutes for the purpose of increasing their land and water rights, and ensured that the Newlands Project would be operated in a way that would not be destructive to Indian water sources, such as Pyramid Lake.

Although the fish restoration efforts have been hugely successful and Pyramid Lake is reviving, water in the region continues to be scarce due to the same factors that impact water rights throughout the Southwest. The aridity of the region and the continued pressures of increasing urban development, in this case the immense growth of Reno, mean that while the settlement has guaranteed the Pyramid Lake Paiutes a fair deal, disputes over water in the area will likely continue unabated.

—Steven L. Danver

See also: *Newlands, Francis G.; Reclamation Act of 1902*

BIBLIOGRAPHY

Fixico, Donald L. *The Invasion of Indian Country in the Twentieth Century: American Capitalism and Tribal Natural Resources.* Niwot: University Press of Colorado, 1998.

Pratt, Jeremy. *Truckee-Carson River Basin Study Final Report: Report to the Western Water Policy Review Advisory Commission.* Seattle, WA: Clearwater Consulting, 1997.

Rusco, Elmer. *A Reporter at Large: Dateline—Pyramid Lake, Nevada.* Reno: University of Nevada Press, 1999.

Seney, Donald B. "The Changing Political Fortunes of the Truckee Carson Irrigation District." *Agricultural History* 76, no. 2 (2002): 220–31.

Wilkinson, Charles F. *Crossing the Next Meridian: Land, Water, and the Future of the West.* Washington, DC: Island Press, 1992.

Stewart Udall (1920–2010) was an American politician and staunch conservationist, most notable for serving as secretary of the interior under Presidents Kennedy and Johnson. Under his tenure, the Wilderness Act of 1964 was passed, preserving millions of acres of wilderness. Here, Udall testifies before the Senate Subcommittee on Air and Water Pollution in 1967, warning of the need for legislation to avoid oil spills.

AP Photo/Harvey Georges

Udall, Stewart

Stewart Udall (1920–2010) served as the secretary of the interior for two administrations, those of presidents John F. Kennedy and Lyndon B. Johnson. He was responsible for the Land and Water Conservation Fund, the Wild and Scenic Rivers Act, the Endangered Species Preservation Act, and the Wilderness Act. During his tenure, the National Park Service added four national parks, six national monuments, eight national seashores, twenty historic sites, and fifty-six wildlife refuges.

Early Life and Congressional Service

Stewart Lee Udall was born on January 31, 1920, in Saint Johns, Arizona. His grandfather, David King Udall, founded the town in 1880; his father, Levi Stewart Udall, became a state justice. Stewart Udall grew up in a Mormon family; attended Eastern Arizona Junior College in Thatcher, Arizona; and served during World War II as a gunner in the U.S. Army Air Force. He later completed a Bachelor of Laws at the University of Arizona in 1948 and practiced law for six years in Tucson with his brother, Morris Udall. He was elected to the U.S. House of Representatives in 1954 and served his entire tenure there on the Committee of Interior and Insular Affairs (1955–1960). On the basis of his utilitarian philosophy, he voted for the dams in Glen Canyon and Flaming Gorge. A strong environmentalist, Udall influenced the formation of the Great Swamp National Wildlife Refuge in New Jersey in 1960; this became the first area designated as wilderness by the Department of the Interior in 1968.

Secretary of the Interior

In 1961, John F. Kennedy nominated Udall to become secretary of the interior, a post he held until 1969. He was responsible for several legislative acts that affected water resources: the Wilderness Act (1964), the Endangered Species Preservation Act (1966), the Colorado River Basin Project Act of 1968 (Pub. L. 90-537; 82 Stat. 885), and the Wild and Scenic Rivers Act (1968).

The Wetlands Preservation Bill, enacted as the Wetlands Loan Act (1961, Pub. L. 87-383), enabled the government to acquire marshlands needed to replenish migratory waterfowl populations. Udall was instrumental in the passage of the Land and Water Conservation Fund Act (1964; Pub. L. 88-578), a grant assistance program designed to encourage federal or state agencies to acquire land for preservation of resources and provide outdoor recreation. It provided funds to acquire lands for national parks (North Cascades, Redwood), recreation areas (Flaming Gorge), and national seashores (Padre Islands, Cape

North American Water and Power Alliance

The North American Water and Power Alliance (NAWAPA), a continent-wide water development project, was first envisioned in the 1950s by Donald McCord Baker. The plan called for creating a network of interconnected rivers and reservoirs that extended from the Yukon River in Alaska to northern Mexico. A connection from the new waterway to the Great Lakes was also proposed through the creation of the Canadian–Great Lakes Waterway. It was believed that the project, which would have impacted thirty-three states in the United States, seven provinces in Canada, and portions of northern Mexico, held the promise to make available approximately 36 trillion gallons of water.

Baker's idea was championed by the Ralph M. Parson Company, and its earliest proponents included Stewart Udall, the Bureau of Reclamation, and the U.S. Army Corps of Engineers. Supporters of the plan claimed that NAWAPA would address the water needs of the western portion of the United States. Over the course of the 1960s, the plan began to fall into disfavor as opponents drew attention to its environmental costs. Rivers, such as the Fraser and Columbia that salmon needed to spawn, would have been drastically altered. The water levels of each of the Great Lakes would have increased substantially as the lakes were used for storage. Millions of acres of land across North America would have been inundated. The potential consequences for the environment proved too much for the project's supporters to overcome.

In truth, NAWAPA's supporters were primarily from the western United States. Canadians generally viewed the plan with disdain, noting that they bore a substantial portion of the environmental costs with comparably few benefits. Despite NAWAPA's apparent demise during the 1970s, the idea continues to reappear periodically.

—John R. Burch Jr.

See also: *Army Corps of Engineers, United States; Bureau of Reclamation*

BIBLIOGRAPHY

McCool, Daniel. *Command of the Waters: Iron Triangles, Federal Water Development, and Indian Waters.* Tucson: University of Arizona Press, 1994.

Reisner, Marc. *Cadillac Desert: The American West and Its Disappearing Water.* New York: Viking, 1986.

Monument and Park. After taking a raft trip in 1967 on the Colorado River, Udall changed his mind. On July 31, 1968, Congress also prohibited construction of dams on the Colorado River between the Hoover and Glen Canyon Dams.

During his service as secretary of the interior, Udall advocated for and influenced Congress to form four national parks. Canyonlands (Utah, 1964) lies at the confluence of the Colorado and Green Rivers in Utah, upstream from the Glen Canyon National Recreation Area. Once a marine habitat and now desert, it was subject to uranium mining in the 1950s. While Floyd Dominy, commissioner of the Bureau of Reclamation, saw a future dam at this confluence, Udall envisioned the national park. Guadalupe Mountains (Texas, 1966), though arid today and situated 3,600 to 8,749 feet above sea level, stands as a fossil reef of an ancient tropical ocean. Redwood trees require large amounts of precipitation, and Redwood National and State Park (California, 1968) is involved in watershed restoration. The marbled murrelets, waterfowl that reside in the park, are on the California endangered species list and the federal threatened species list. North Cascades (Washington, 1968), near the Skagit River and Ross Dam, has cascading waterfalls and several glaciers.

Other Work

Udall authored several books during and after his public service. Primary among them is *The Quiet Crisis* (1963). This history of conservation and environmentalism in the United States emphasizes two strands of thought: first, to manage resources such as timber, fish, game, grazing land, and minerals for the use of future generations; second, to preserve forests, wilderness areas, parklands, and watersheds for recreational use or aesthetics. Udall demonstrates these needs by reviewing the history of natural resource usage from pre-Columbian America to the impact of American naturalists, such as John Wesley Powell, Frederick Law Olmstead, and John Muir. He also describes how politicians

Lookout). Grants to states have averaged $100 million dollars per year, and over 10,000 projects have allowed states to acquire such lands as the Allagash Wilderness Waterway (Maine) and Elephant Butte Lake State Park (New Mexico) and plan for future projects, such as the Palmetto Island State Park (Louisiana).

During the early part of his tenure as secretary of the interior, Udall favored provisions of the Pacific Southwest Water Plan that allowed construction of dams at Bridge (Hualapai) and Marble Canyons in Arizona; the resulting water would have occupied parts of Grand Canyon National such as Thomas Jefferson, Theodore Roosevelt, and Gifford Pinchot acted decisively in favor of the environment. He addresses future concerns about the exploitation of natural resources, even noting that gold mining depleted river banks. His *America's Natural Treasures: National Nature Monuments and Seashores* (1971) describes thirty-eight national monuments, nine national wildlife refuges, and over twenty national seashores and scenic rivers. After his service in the cabinet, Udall moved to New Mexico. Starting in 1978, as a private attorney, he sought court action to aid victims of nuclear weapons testing. His efforts came to fruition in 1990 when President George H. W. Bush signed a compensation bill.

As secretary of the interior, Udall added more land to the national park system, including national seashores, than any other administration. And the environmental movement saw a growth previously unmatched. Momentum created during Udall's tenure at the Department of the Interior made it possible to create the Environmental Protection Agency early in the Nixon administration. Stewart Udall passed away at his home in Santa Fe, New Mexico, on March 20, 2010.

—Ralph Hartsock

See also: *Colorado River Basin Act of 1968; Dominy, Floyd E.; Endangered Species Act (1973); Wetlands; Wild and Scenic Rivers Act of 1968; Wilderness Act of 1964*

BIBLIOGRAPHY

de Steiguer, J. Edward. "Stewart L. Udall and the Quiet Crisis." In *The Origins of Modern Environmental Thought,* 53–65. Tucson: University of Arizona Press, 2006.

Nash, Roderick. *Wilderness and the American Mind.* 4th ed. New Haven, CT: Yale Nota Bene, 2001.

Peterson, Ross. "Sharing America: The Environmental Legacy of Stewart Udall." In *Dreams, Myths, and Reality: Utah and the American West,* edited by William Thomas Allison and Susan J. Matt, 223–239. Salt Lake City, UT: Signature Books, 2008.

Udall, Stewart. *The Quiet Crisis.* New York: Holt, Rinehart and Winston, 1963.

Udall v. Federal Power Commission (1967)

In 1967, the U.S. Supreme Court handed down its decision in *Udall v. Federal Power Commission* (1967). This 6–2 decision written by Justice William O. Douglas prevented a dam from being built on the Snake River, but it also signaled a shift in environmental law with far-reaching consequences.

Case Origins

Beginning in the 1930s, large-scale federal hydroelectric dam projects spread throughout the nation, with many concentrated in the Pacific Northwest. As this development increased, private power companies attempted to compete with federal projects by constructing and operating their own hydroelectric dams. Whether public or private, potential hydroelectric projects required licensing approval from the Federal Power Commission (FPC). Many of these dam projects ultimately spelled doom for streams' fish runs, and anglers, fisheries biologists, American Indians, and conservationists increasingly opposed building these projects (Brooks 2006). *Udall v. FPC* fit within this ferment.

The deepest gorge in the United States, Hells Canyon on the Idaho-Oregon border, offered engineers an ideal dam site. In the 1950s, the federal government proposed a high dam in the canyon, but a private power company, Idaho Power Company, opposed that plan. Instead, Idaho Power hoped to place four low dams on the river. The political interests involved in this debate were complicated. Ultimately, though, Idaho Power prevailed, representing a rejection of New Deal public power planning and the triumph of Snake River management for agricultural purposes in the upper Snake basin (Brooks 2006). But Idaho Power's triumph was incomplete.

Idaho Power succeeded in building three dams: Brownlee Dam, Oxbow Dam, and Hells Canyon Dam. The fourth dam, proposed for a site known as High Mountain Sheep, caused the controversy that headed to the Supreme Court. The federal government, through Secretary of Interior Stewart Udall, intervened with a counterproposal for a public power dam. After multiple hearings, the FPC granted the private dam its license. Udall protested in part because he wanted to slow the construction until issues related to the effect of the dam on anadromous fisheries could be remedied. The appeal led to rehearings with the FPC and eventually entered the federal court system and went to the U.S. Supreme Court (Brooks 2006; Sowards 2009).

The Decision

William O. Douglas, appropriately the Court's only member from the Northwest, wrote the majority opinion. Most observers saw the critical question in this case as whether the dam would be operated as a public or a private one. Rather than simply weighing in on that question, the Court asked the FPC to reconsider "whether any dam should be constructed" (*Udall v. FPC*). Citing several laws that required recreation or fish and wildlife considerations, including the Federal Power Act (1920), Fish and Wildlife Coordination Act (1958), and the Anadromous Fish Act (1965), the Court emphasized a larger set of concerns than had the FPC. In the opinion, Douglas questioned whether the region required the additional power the dam at High Mountain Sheep would produce. He also pointed out that the "ecology of a river is different from the ecology of a reservoir built behind a dam" (*Udall v. FPC* 1967). This first use of *ecology* in Supreme Court history reflected the changing times and priorities being used to decide cases bearing on water-related and other environmental issues.

After questioning the propriety and necessity of the High Mountain Sheep dam on these various grounds, the Court pursued another line of reasoning that was even more significant. This position focused on the so-called public interest. In the era, it was commonly presumed that hydroelectric power development was in the public interest. Yet environmental values were changing at the time of *Udall,* and the Court reflected this shift. Pointing out that the FPC had failed to consider the dam's public interest in a broad enough capacity, Douglas wrote, "The need to destroy the river as a waterway, the desirability of its demise, the choices available to satisfy future demands for energy—these are all relevant to a decision . . . but they were largely untouched by the Commission" (*Udall v. FPC* 1967). By so reasoning, Douglas, for the Court, urged a complete reassessment of dam building, arguing that free-flowing rivers, salmon, and other wildlife all constituted important public interests worthy of consideration (Sowards 2009). Although technically the Court's decision remanded the case to the FPC to review the issue in light of the Court's reasoning, the decision practically ended the pursuit of building a dam at High Mountain Sheep. It was the first time the Court had rejected an FPC licensing agreement since the FPC had been granted the power to license dams with the Water Power Act of 1920.

The legal developments that culminated in *Udall v. FPC* were important. *Udall* announced a broadening of the public interest. Gradually, federal courts had been allowing new arguments into the courts and new petitioners. One result was opinions like this one, which saw arguments that pursued environmental ends against economic aims. Also, *Udall* represented a change in administrative law, a process that had been underway for decades. This change marked a rise in judicial review of administrative decisions. That is, courts deferred less to federal agencies, such as the FPC, and they demanded more exacting reviews of proposed projects from natural resource management and agencies (Brooks 2006). Surprisingly, conservationists won this battle, getting more than they expected (Sowards 2009). For these reasons, *Udall v. Federal Power Commission* became a critical postwar decision for environmental and water law and presaged the growing importance of environmental litigation and the growing role of federal courts in settling environmental disputes.

—Adam M. Sowards

See also: *Douglas, William O.; Evolution of Environmental Law; Fish and Wildlife Coordination Act (1934); Hells Canyon Dam; Snake River Basin; Udall, Stewart; Water Law; Water Power Act of 1920*

BIBLIOGRAPHY

Brooks, Karl Boyd. *Public Power, Private Dams: The Hell's Canyon High Dam Controversy.* Seattle: University of Washington Press, 2006.
Sowards, Adam M. *The Environmental Justice: William O. Douglas and American Conservation.* Corvallis: Oregon State University, 2009.
Udall v. FPC (*Udall v. Federal Power Commission*), 387 U.S. 428 (1967).

United States Army Corps of Engineers

See *Army Corps of Engineers, United States*

United States Environmental Protection Agency

See *Environmental Protection Agency, United States*

United States et al. v. State of Washington et al. (1979)

One of the leading cases in a complex pattern of litigation concerning treaty rights of Native American nations historically residing in what are now the states of Washington and Oregon, *United States et al. v. State of Washington et al.* dealt with Indians' "right of taking fish at usual and accustomed grounds and stations." The controversy was ultimately resolved by the U.S. Supreme Court in a decision commonly cited as *Washington v. Washington State Commercial Passenger Fishing Vessel Association* (77-983, 443 U.S. 658,

1979). The controversy traces back to a ruling in 1974 by George H. Boldt, federal district judge in the western district of Washington state, that the state had violated fishing rights reserved by treaty to the Native American tribes (*United States v. Washington,* 384 F. Supp. 312, 405-08; W. D. Wash. 1974). Five years earlier, Judge Robert C. Belloni had similarly ruled that the Oregon's state government had imposed invalid restrictions on Native American fishing rights (*Sohappy v. Smith,* 302 F. Supp. 899; D. Or. 1969).

The Cases

The cases that ultimately were accepted for review by the Supreme Court included state appeals from Judge Boldt's attempts to enforce his original ruling and petitions from the United States, as trustee for the Makah Tribe, Lower Elwha Band of Clallam Tribe, Port Gambleband of Clallam Tribe, Suquamish Tribe, Lummi Tribe, Nooksack Tribe, and Swinomish Indian Tribal Community, for review of decisions by the Supreme Court of Washington, which rejected federal jurisdiction, setting aside Judge Boldt's interpretation of the treaties. The Supreme Court vacated and remanded both decisions by the state supreme court of Washington, *Puget Sound Gillnetters Assn. v. Moos,* 88 Wash.2d 677, 565 P.2d 1151 (1977), and *Fishing Vessel Assn. v. Tollefson,* 89 Wash.2d 276, 571 P.2d 1373 (1977), as well as *Puget Sound Gillnetters Assn. et al. v. United States District Court for the Western District of Washington* (78-139). Disposition of *Washington v. United States* (78-119) affirmed a decision by the U.S. Court of Appeals for the Ninth Circuit, 573 F.2d 1118, which sustained the treaty rights at issue.

All of these cases were rooted in a series of six treaties signed by the governor of Washington Territory, Isaac Stevens, in 1854–1855. In exchange for $207,500, the signatory tribes ceded millions of acres of land to the United States, reserving their right to fish at their "usual and accustomed grounds and stations . . . in common with all citizens of the Territory" (Treaty of Point No Point 1859, Art. 4). The controversy was not a new one in 1979; the Supreme Court observed that it had already issued six decisions interpreting fishing rights under the same set of treaties. As almost every court to hear the controversy observed, when the treaties were signed in 1854 and 1855, the supply of fish was thought to be inexhaustible. None of the parties foresaw that this resource would become scarce. Development of a commercial fishing industry at the close of the nineteenth century and subsequent conservation measures to prevent overfishing, together with discriminatory state regulation, had crowded the original inhabitants out of a great part of the traditional use of their usual and accustomed fishing places.

The Decision

The Supreme Court emphasized that a treaty between the United States and a Native American tribe is, like any treaty, a contract between two sovereign nations. As the tribes signing the treaties had not been at war with the United States, the Court deemed it reasonable to assume that they negotiated as equals. They were not granted special consideration to fishing rights but simply reserved rights they already possessed, while giving up large areas of land. The ruling rejected the argument that upon statehood, the terms of such treaties could be abrogated or revised by state law, and it found that treaty rights belonged to the tribes who signed the treaties, as quasi-sovereign entities, not to individual Native Americans as individuals.

Judge Boldt had ruled that Native American tribes who signed the treaty held rights to approximately half of the anadromous fish runs in the territories they had. The Court, relying on previous Supreme Court rulings, rejected the argument that the treaty language merely guaranteed individual Indians access to usual and accustomed fishing sites and an "equal opportunity" to try to catch fish.

For the most part, Judge Boldt's original finding that the tribes concerned were entitled to a defined share of the total fish runs, not merely to an opportunity to put fishing nets into the water, was sustained. The Supreme Court accepted the lower court ruling that Native Americans were entitled to "a 45% to 50% share of the harvestable fish that will at some point pass through recognized tribal fishing grounds" (*U.S. v. Washington* 1979). This was designated as a maximum share, recognizing both the equal right of "all citizens of the territory" and the necessity to limit the total number of fish caught so that the species did not become extinct. That maximum was to be reduced as feasible such that the tribes that signed the treaties would have "so much as, but no more than, is necessary to provide the Indians with a livelihood—that is to say, a moderate living."

Congress responded to the growing friction between descendants of non-Native immigrants, who had become accustomed to practice large-scale commercial fishing and sport fishing, and Native Americans newly confirmed in their right to a share of the fish runs. The Salmon and Steelhead Conservation and Enhancement Act, December 22, 1980, codified as 16 U.S.C. § 3301, provided funds for buying out the boats and equipment of nontreaty fishers, who had too much capacity for their remaining share of the supply, while establishing cooperative programs involving the United States, the states of Washington and Oregon, and the treaty tribes. The latter programs were to promote economic well-being, coordinate research, and manage habitat while improving the quality and opportunity for recreational fishing. This case, as well as the line of cases closely related to it, remains essential authority for state and federal regulation of fishing and fish runs in Washington and Oregon. Both the states and the tribes concerned have adopted parallel regulations, which remain closely supervised by federal courts.

—Charles Rosenberg

See also: *American Indian Water Rights; Commercial Fishing; Endangered Species Act (1973); National Marine Fisheries Service*

BIBLIOGRAPHY

Belsky, Martin H. "Indian Fishing Rights: A Lost Opportunity for Ecosystem Management." *Journal of Land Use and Environmental Law* 12, no. 1 (1996): 45–62. Available at http://www.law.fsu.edu/journals/landuse/Vol121/Belsky.pdf.

Cohen, Fay. *Treaties on Trial: The Continuing Controversy over Northwest Indian Fishing Rights.* Seattle: University of Washington Press, 1986.

Miller, Bruce. "The Press, the Bold Decision, and Indian-White Relations." *American Indian Culture and Research Journal* 17, no. 2 (1993): 75–97.

Taylor, Joseph. *Making Salmon: An Environmental History of the Northwest Fisheries Crisis.* Seattle: University of Washington Press, 1999.

Treaty of Point No Point, Washington Territory–S'Klallam–Chimakum–Skokomish, April 29, 1859. http://www.historylink.org/index.cfm?DisplayPage=output.cfm&File_Id=5637.

U.S. v. Washington (United States et al. v. State of Washington et al.). 443 U.S. 638 (1979). http://ftp.resource.org/courts.gov/c/US/443/443.US.658.77-983.78-139.78-119.html.

United States Fish and Wildlife Service

See *Fish and Wildlife Service, United States*

United States Geological Survey

The U.S. Geological Survey (USGS) is an agency established in 1879 under the U.S. Department of the Interior. The agency specializes in research related to biology, geography, geology, geospatial information, and water.

Origins

The USGS has its origins in a variety of federal agencies. Coastal mapping was done in the nation's early years by the Department of the Treasury and later by the Navy. A number of states conducted their own geological surveys in the 1820s and 1830s in order to learn more about their mineral and agricultural resources. The Corps of Topographical Engineers was established in 1838 with the commission to map the West. Four additional surveys were commissioned prior to the establishment of the USGS, including the Geological Exploration of the Fortieth Parallel directed by Clarence King in 1867, Dr. F.V. Hayden's Geological Survey of the Territories administered by the Department of the Interior, the Smithsonian and Interior exploration of the Colorado River led by John Wesley Powell, and finally the Geographical Surveys West of the 100th Meridian led by George Wheeler. The pursuit of these surveys made it apparent that surveying efforts needed to be consolidated in the interest of both time and accuracy. The National Academy of Sciences recommended, in a bill signed by President Henry Harrison on March 3, 1879, that the USGS be established under the Department of the Interior.

Expanding Responsibilities

The scope of the USGS has grown since its founding in 1879. Under Clarence King, the first director (1879–1881), the survey studied mining districts. John Wesley Powell (1881–1894) broadened the survey to include topographic mapping, as well as stratigraphic and paleontologic studies. Powell also oversaw hydrographic and topographic surveys to determine streamflow in the arid regions of the United States. Powell was succeeded by Charles Walcott in 1893. Walcott sought to improve the quality of topographic maps and to resume conducting mining geology investigations. The success of the USGS resulted in the creation of a Division of Mining and Mineral Resources in 1900. As appropriations increased, the survey expanded its investigations to include studies of streams, underground water, and water utilization. By the turn of the century, the scope of USGS work grew to include mapping and a wide variety of geological, hydrographic, and forest investigations. In 1905, the USGS started mapping coal deposits in the West and conducting fuel studies on coals and lignites to see how they might be used by industry. George Smith served as director from 1907 to 1931, when the USGS began to undertake surveys for land classification, river development programs, and coal mine accident investigations.

During World War I, the USGS explored for petroleum resources and war-related minerals. During the conflict, many of the agency's topographic personnel served in the Army Corps of Engineers. When the USGS reached its fiftieth year in 1929, nearly 44 percent of the nation had been mapped. In addition, streamflow had been measured at over 2,200 locations. In 1931, Walter Mendenhall took over as director and remained in the position until 1943. When Franklin D. Roosevelt became president in 1933, USGS services were needed to help with the Tennessee Valley Authority (TVA) and other public works projects. The survey conducted aerial photography to create the maps needed for the TVA project and conducted studies on rainfall and runoff and how they impact flood control. In 1940, the USGS helped the military by creating maps of strategic areas and continued its support throughout the war years.

Mendenhall was succeeded by William E. Wrather (1943–1956), who sought to complete the topographic mapping of the country and continue the search for mineral resources. As the survey approached its seventy-fifth year, new methods of surveying were developed that increased the speed and accuracy of mapping. In 1956, Thomas B. Nolan took over as director and increased the agency's emphasis on geology. The agency also expanded investigations to include the photogeologic mapping of the moon, astronaut training, and marine studies to locate mineral resources in the seas.

After 1965, the agency continued to grow under the directorships of William Pecora (1965–1971), Vincent McKelvey (1971–1978), Henry Menard (1978–1981), Dallas Lynn Peck (1981–1993), Gordon P. Eaton (1994–1997), Charles G. Groat (1998–2005), and Mark Myers (2006–2009). In 1970, the USGS published the first edition of the *National Atlas of the United States*, which contained over 700 maps. In the agency's second century, it took on new challenges, including the disposal and release of hazardous waste, groundwater contamination, problems related to aquifers on

the High Plains, and the prediction of natural disasters like earthquakes and volcanic eruptions.

The USGS remains at the forefront of geological research during the twenty-first century. The agency continues to meet its original mission of classifying public lands and examining the geologic structure and mineral resources of the nation. Over time, the USGS has expanded its output via technological advances that aid in the creation of maps and field-related research. Discoveries made by this agency aid other federal agencies and researchers throughout the world. The future of the agency will be affected by changes in scientific research and technology and challenges posed by our changing climate and environment.

—Theresa Hefner-Babb

See also: *Aquifers; Army Corps of Engineers, United States; Powell, John Wesley*

BIBLIOGRAPHY

Manning, Thomas G. *Government in Science: The U.S. Geological Survey, 1867–1894.* Louisville: University of Kentucky Press, 1967.

Rabbitt, Mary C. *A Brief History of the U.S. Geological Survey.* Washington, DC: Government Printing Office, 1979.

Rabbitt, Mary C. *The United States Geological Survey, 1879–1989.* Washington, DC: Government Printing Office, 1989.

National Institutes for Water Resources

The National Institutes for Water Resources (NIWR) are fifty-four Water Research Institutes and Centers that were created as a state and federal partnership by the Water Resources Research Act of 1984. Each of the fifty states has one institute, usually located at the institution designated in 1862 as a land-grant university. Additional institutes are located in the District of Columbia, Guam, Puerto Rico, and the U.S. Virgin Islands. Each institute is charged with conducting research on water issues related to its respective state or territory. In addition, each institute is assigned to one of eight regional groupings. This structure is intended to facilitate research that addresses problems beyond an individual state's borders. Since each institute is intended to focus only on state and regional water issues, the U.S. Geological Survey (USGS) works with the NIWR to coordinate the overall focus of the research programs. The major benefit of this arrangement is that it allows for scientists employed by the USGS to work with their counterparts at public universities and research institutes to address the present and future water needs of the U.S. populace.

—John R. Burch Jr.

BIBLIOGRAPHY

National Institutes for Water Resources. http://snr.unl.edu/niwr/.

United States v. Cappaert (1974)

United States v. Cappaert arose as a dispute concerning the reservation of water rights at Devils Hole, Nevada. President Truman designated this site as a national monument in 1952 because of its "scenic, scientific, and educational interest." Devils Hole is a remnant of the prehistoric Death Valley Lake System formed during the Pleistocene epoch. It consists of a water-filled striated limestone cavern over 500 feet deep cut into the side of a hill. The cavern, formed in part by fault action, contains a unique species of pupfish (*Cyprinodon diabolis*) that has been isolated for 10,000 to 20,000 years (National Park Service n.d.).

According to the National Park Service, the pupfish "feed and spawn exclusively on a shallow rock shelf near the surface, feeding on the algae and diatoms found there" (National Park Service n.d., "Devils Hole Pupfish"). A fall in the water level can expose the rock shelf and limit the fish's activities. In 1968, the Cappaerts, owners of a large farm located two-and-a-half miles from Devils Hole, began pumping groundwater from a basin or aquifer that also feeds Devils Hole. The National Park Service monitors the level of water in Devils Hole by means of a copper washer installed on the side of the cavern in 1962. Prior to the Cappaerts' pumping, the water level had stayed relatively stable at 1.2 feet below the marker. By 1972, it was 3.93 feet below the marker; it can be no more than 3.0 feet below for the pupfish to feed and spawn.

The Case

In 1970, the Cappaerts applied to the state engineer for permits to change the use of water from several of their wells. The National Park Service filed a protest with the state engineer, who held a hearing in December of 1970. An attorney from the National Park Service presented evidence that the United States was conducting a study to determine if the underground water supplying the Cappaerts' wells was hydrologically connected to Devils Hole. The Park Service asked that the state engineer postpone the Cappaerts' petition or deny it until the United States completed the study. The engineer declined to postpone his decision and issued the permits.

In 1971 in federal district court, the United States sought to enjoin the Cappaerts from pumping water from certain wells, claiming that the United States had a reserved water right to sufficient water to accomplish the purposes of maintaining Devils Hole. In 1974, the district court permanently enjoined the Cappaerts from pumping water from the specified well, holding that in reserving land for the Devils Hole spring, the United States reserved appurtenant, unappropriated waters necessary for accomplishing the purpose of the reservation. The court also held that one purpose of the reservation was the preservation of the Devils Hole pool and the pupfish within it.

The Cappaerts appealed the decision of the district court. The appeals court affirmed the decision of the district court. It held that the implied reservation of water doctrine applied to groundwater as well as surface water. It further held that the Cappaerts and their successors had held no water rights in 1952, that the state and the United States had concurrent jurisdiction to resolve the dispute, and that the administrative hearings for the Cappaerts' permit did not bar the United States from pursuing its case in federal court. In 1976, the U.S. Supreme Court granted certiorari to consider the scope of the implied doctrine regarding reservation of water rights." The Court noted that no previous Supreme Court case had involved the application of the implied-reservation-of-water-rights doctrine to groundwater. It found that the surface water in Devils Hole pool and the groundwater on the Cappaerts' land was hydrologically connected, and it held that "the United States can protect its water from subsequent diversion, whether the diversion is of surface or ground water" (*Cappaert v. United States* 1976). The Court noted further that the 1952 McCarran Amendment (43 U.S.C. § 666), which allows the United States to be joined to a water rights lawsuit as a defendant, repeals federal jurisdiction over water rights but only waives the sovereign immunity of the United States if it is joined in state court as a party.

The Decision

In addition to its other findings, the Court in Cappaert noted that "the implied-reservation-of-water-rights doctrine, however, reserves only that amount of water necessary to fulfill the purpose of the reservation, no more" (*Cappaert v. United States* 1976). This observation, based in part on the Court's decision in *Arizona v. California,* raises serious concerns on the part of Indian tribal water users.

Sylvia Liu notes that two cases, *Cappaert v. United States* and *United States v. New Mexico,* are primarily relied on by state water users when arguing for courts to consider the impact on non-Indian water users of quantifying Indian water rights (Liu 1995). In Cappaert, the Court tailored its decision to the minimal needs of Devils Hole. This approach,

Liu suggests, moves away from the Winters Doctrine, in which the Court inferred congressional intent to reserve enough water to allow the tribes to develop fully on the basis of a reservation of tribal land (Liu 1995). She argues that an approach that defers to non-Indian water users would repeat historical inequities (Liu 1995).

According to the U.S. Fish & Wildlife Service, the population of pupfish has never exceeded 553. In the 1990s, for unexplained reasons, the population began to decline until in the fall of 2006, only thirty-eight pupfish remained. The National Park Service began a program to prevent the extinction of the pupfish in 2006, in part by developing an artificial food supply. By April of 2009 the estimated number of Pupfish reached seventy (U.S. Fish & Wildlife Service n.d.).

—Jerry Murtagh

See also: Arizona v. California *(1963); Groundwater Recharge and Water Reuse;* Winters v. United States *(1908)*

BIBLIOGRAPHY

American Antiquities Preservation Act, 34 Stat. 225, 16 U.S.C. § 431.
Cappaert v. United States, 426 U.S. 128 (1976).
Liu, Sylvia F. "American Indian Reserved Water Rights: The Federal Obligation to Protect Tribal Water Resources and Tribal Autonomy." Environmental Law 25, no. 2 (1995): 425–62.
National Park Service. "Death Valley: Devils Hole." http://www.nps.gov/deva/naturescience/devils-hole.htm.
U.S. Fish & Wildlife Service, Nevada Fish & Wildlife Office. "Devils Hole Pupfish." http://www.fws.gov/Nevada/protected_species/fish/species/dhp/dhp.html.
United States v. Cappaert, 375 F. Supp. 456 (D. Nev. 1974).

United States v. Powers (1939)

This case involves, in part, a reaffirmation of the Winters Doctrine from the *Winters v. United States* (1908) Supreme Court case, which held that when the United States created Indian reservations, it also reserved water rights sufficient to meet its purpose in establishing the reservations. It moves beyond the Winters Doctrine, however, in holding that when there are allotments of tribal land to individual Indians, those Indians have reserved water rights derived from those of the tribe.

Origins

The case began in 1934 in federal district court with the United States seeking a bill to enjoin certain members of the Crow Indian Tribe from diverting waters from Lodge Grass Creek and Little Bighorn River in Montana. The district court dismissed the bill, and the federal appeals court affirmed the judgment of the lower court. The U.S. Supreme Court granted certiorari and, in its decision, also affirmed the decision of the lower court.

The United States supported its request for an injunction with four main points. First, prior to 1885, the Department of the Interior had initiated irrigation projects diverting water from Lodge Grass Creek and Little Bighorn River. These projects eventually were capable of irrigating 20,000 acres of land. Second, the first allotments to the predecessors of the respondents did not occur until 1901. Third, because Congress had given the secretary of the interior control of reservation waters, projects begun under his authority "prior to allotments of respondents' lands sufficed to dedicate and reserve sufficient water for full utilization of these projects. . . . Rights acquired by the allottees were taken subject to this reservation." And finally, the drought occurring between 1931 and 1934 made it impossible to irrigate the 8,000 acres of land previously under cultivation without assistance from the irrigation projects (*United States v. Powers* 1939).

On their part, the respondents claimed that the establishment of the Crow Indian Reservation, pursuant to an 1868 treaty with the United States, resulted in reserved water rights sufficient to meet the needs of the reservation (*Winters v. United States,* 207 U.S. 564). They further contended that when allotments of land were made to Indian tribal members, "some portion of tribal waters essential for cultivation passed to the owners" (*United States v. Powers* 1939).

The Decision

In rendering the decision, Justice James Clark McReynolds noted that the Treaty of May 7, 1868, between the United States and the Crow Indians provided for the United States to survey land on the Crow Reservation and divide the land into equal parcels to be farmed by individual Indians. He found that the treaty implied the reservation of sufficient water to meet the agricultural needs of the individual plots. McReynolds further found that the "allottees and their grantees" acquired a reserved water right to water necessary for cultivation. Furthermore, no subsequent legislation denied allottees the use of waters necessary for cultivation. Based upon these observations, the Court affirmed the decision of the court of appeals denying the request for a permanent injunction.

In 2005, Nathan Brooks noted that the case of *United States v. Powers* was the only allottee water rights case to come before the Court and that it left some important issues unresolved. The ruling by the Court held that allottees were entitled to "some portion" of the reserved water rights available to the reservation, but it stopped short of any discussion of the proportion of reserved water rights available to the allottees, saying in the opinion, "We do not consider the extent or precise nature of respondents' rights in the waters. The present proceeding is not properly framed to that end" (*United States v. Powers* 1939).

In a later case, the Court sought to resolve this issue. In *Colville Confederated Tribes v. Walton* (1981), the Court held that "the extent of an Indian allottee's right is based on the number of irrigable acres he owns. If the allottee owns 10% of the irrigable acreage in the watershed, he is entitled to 10% of the water reserved for irrigation." The question left open is how allottee water rights can be quantified if tribal reserved water rights are based on land used for nonagricultural purposes.

—Jerry Murtagh

See also: *American Indian Water Rights;* Winters v. United States *(1908)*

BIBLIOGRAPHY

Brook, N. "Indian Reserved Water Rights: An Overview" (RL32198). Congressional Research Service. January 24, 2005. https://www.policyarchive.org/bitstream/handle/10207/1917/RL32198_20050124.pdf.

Colville Confederated Tribes v. Walton, 647 F.2d (9th Cir. 1981).

United States v. Powers, 305 U.S. 527 (1939).

Water for Indian Allotments: The San Xavier Reservation Allottees' Struggle for Water 1975–2007. http://www.ilwg.org/documents/12.Water%20For%20Indian%20Allotments.pdf.

United States–Mexico Transboundary Aquifer Assessment Act of 2006

The United States–Mexico Transboundary Aquifer Assessment Act of 2006 (TAAA; Pub. L. 109-448) authorizes the U.S. Secretary of the Interior to study the hydrogeological nature and map and model a set of priority transboundary aquifers in cooperation with U.S. border states and Mexico. The TAAA is intended to address the lack of information on groundwater basins straddling the 1,956-mile boundary with Mexico.

Over eighteen groundwater basins are found along or across the international boundary. While some of these aquifers have been previously studied by the U.S. Geological Survey, Mexico's National Water Commission, the International Boundary and Water Commission, and other university and private sector hydrologists, most are inadequately studied and poorly understood despite the general aridity and scarcity of water in the border region.

Groundwater Needs and Concerns

Many border communities, ranches, and farms have long relied on groundwater as either a primary or secondary source of freshwater. The adjacent cities of El Paso, Texas, and Cuidad Juarez, Chihuahua, for example, rely heavily on the groundwater of the Hueco and Mesilla Bolsons for their municipal needs. Studies by the Texas Water Development Board projected depletion of the freshwater of the Hueco Bolson by 2030. Further attention to the exhaustion of local groundwater came from a binational assessment in 1998 coordinated by the International Boundary and Water Commission (IBWC). These concerns contributed to El Paso Water Utilities's decision to build a desalinization plant in order to make better use of remaining brackish waters in the Hueco Bolson. Other transboundary groundwater basins are found along the Rio Grande, San Pedro, and Santa Cruz Rivers crossing the Arizona-Sonora boundary; in the lower Colorado River zone; and in the coastal hills and along the Tijuana River on the California–Baja California boundary.

Binational concern with transboundary groundwater dates back to the negotiations for the 1944 Water Treaty. In those negotiations, the issue was laid aside as complicating talks on other issues, in good measure owing to a lack of hydrological knowledge of groundwater resources along the Colorado and Rio Grande Rivers (Enriquez Coyro 1976). Later, as Mexican pumping increased during the Salinity Crisis (1961–1973), the two countries noted the need for a comprehensive groundwater agreement in the International Boundary Water Commission's 1973 agreement settling the salinity problem (Mumme 2000). There has since been relatively little binational cooperation or progress towards reaching agreement on how to manage this shared resource cooperatively and sustainably.

Functions of the Transboundary Aquifer Assessment Act

The Transboundary Aquifer Assessment Act was intended to address the lack of binational consensus regarding the source and availability of border water supplies by establishing a scientific program to comprehensively assess priority transboundary aquifers. A *transboundary aquifer* is an aquifer that underlies the boundary of a participating state and Mexico. The TAAA designates the Hueco Bolson and Mesilla aquifers along and near the Rio Grande, San Pedro, and Santa Cruz Rivers as the priority transboundary aquifers and, in a rare departure for U.S. domestic water legislation, specifically names Mexico as a stakeholder and affected party under terms of the Act. Additional aquifers underlying the Texas and New Mexico boundary with Mexico may be subsequently named by the U.S. secretary of the interior. No reference is made to aquifers in the lower Colorado River region or the Pacific coast, and it may be assumed that these aquifers are excluded from the application of the statute.

The secretary of the interior is instructed to work with appropriate Mexican federal agencies and other organizations to form partnerships and receive information deemed helpful in implementing the program. The secretary is also to coordinate with U.S. border states, tribal governments, and other entities that may be monitoring or assessing groundwater reservoirs in the priority transboundary aquifers. The legislation is careful to affirm that it may not be construed to delay or affect the execution or operation of any works related to the waters located in the territory of the United States and governed by the 1944 Water Treaty. The assessment program is to be undertaken over a span of ten years, terminating in 2016, with $50 million authorized to be appropriated for its implementation. In its initial phase, the secretary of the interior is to work with state water resource agencies and institutes and other relevant partners to develop study plans, timelines, and cost estimates for the study of each of the designated priority transboundary aquifers.

In congressional testimony, Dr. P. Patrick Leahy of the U.S. Geological Survey stated that "allocation of groundwater in the border region is poorly regulated because little is known about its availability, sustainability, and quality; about how groundwater interacts with surface water bodies; and about the susceptibility of ground water to contamination" (Leahy 2006). He expressed the need for broad collaboration in transboundary aquifer assessment, including binational efforts to advance international understanding of North American watersheds. The TAAA will address the need for more complete and better data systems necessary to enhance scientific understanding of causal mechanisms affecting the dynamics of transboundary aquifers. Framed thusly, the TAAA is a promising first step toward a process that may eventually lead towards cooperative sustainable management of shared groundwater along the U.S. boundary with Mexico.

—Stephen P. Mumme

See also: *United States–Mexico Water Treaty (1944)*

BIBLIOGRAPHY

Enriquez Coyro, Ernesto. *El Tratado entre Mexico y los Estados Unidos de America sobre Rios Internacionales.* Mexico, D.F.: Universidad Nacional Autonoma de Mexico, 1976.

International Boundary and Water Commission. *Transboundary Aquifers and Binational Ground Water Database for the City of El Paso/Ciudad Juarez Area.* El Paso, TX: International Boundary and Water Commission, 1998. Available at http://www.ibwc.gov/Water_Data/binational_waters.htm.

Leahy, P. Patrick. *United States–Mexico Transboundary Aquifer Assessment Act: Hearings on S. 214/H.R. 469, Before the House Committee on Resources, Subcommittee on Water and Power,* 104th Congress (May 10, 2006) (statement of Dr. P. Patrick Leahy, acting director, U.S. Geological Survey, U.S. Department of the Interior). Available at http://www.usgs.gov/aboutusgs/news_events/testimony.asp.

Mumme, Stephen P. "Minute 242 and Beyond: Challenges and Opportunities for Managing Transboundary Groundwater on the Mexico-U.S. Border." *Natural Resources Journal* 40, no. 2 (2000): 341–78. Available at http://lawlibrary.unm.edu/nrj/40/2/08_mumme_242.pdf.

United States–Mexico Water Treaty (1944)

The United States–Mexico Treaty Regarding Utilization of Waters of the Colorado and the Tijuana Rivers and of the Rio Grande (hereafter the 1944 Water Treaty or Treaty) is indisputably the most important binational agreement between the two countries in the matter of managing their shared water resources and resolving disputes related to the use of these waters. Signed February 3, 1944, and ratified by the Mexican Senate in September 1944 and the U.S. Senate in April 1945, the Treaty sets the parameters of the two nations' water endowments on the major boundary rivers. It thus determines to an extraordinary degree the potential and limits of national development in the arid lands that define the border between the two countries. By authorizing hydraulic infrastructure for economic development and flood control, it provided the degree of water security in matters of supply and management that enabled both countries to proceed with reclamation projects vital to the national governments and basin states on both sides of the boundary.

Treaty Provisions

The Treaty is in many respects two treaties in one, one dealing with the Rio Grande and the other with the Colorado River. The Treaty also addresses problems of international sanitation and the management of the treaty itself and other boundary and water treaties to which the two nations are party. Its leading provisions are found in Articles 2, 3, 4, 10, and 21. Articles 2 and 21, respectively, establish and define the authority and duties of the International Boundary and Water Commission, United States and Mexico (IBWC), an international body designed to administer and interpret the Treaty and other boundary and water treaties between the two countries. Article 3 stipulates the priority of uses of treaty waters and entrusts the IBWC with arriving at solutions to international sanitation problems at the boundary. Article 4 allocates the waters of the middle and lower sections of the Rio Grande River and, with other articles, provides for its development. Article 10, in turn, allocates the water of the Colorado River and, with other articles, provides for its development.

In the case of the Rio Grande River, where Mexico receives 60,000 acre-feet of water on the upper Rio Grande under provisions of the 1906 U.S.-Mexico Water Treaty, the Treaty stipulates that Mexico will provide the United States with an annual average of 350,000 acre-feet of water. On the Colorado River, as stipulated in Article 10, Mexico is guaranteed 1.5 million acre-feet of water annually, except under circumstances of an extraordinary drought, the determination of which is likewise unspecified.

Controversies

Since ratification, the Treaty has been praised as one of the world's premier examples of peaceful management of international rivers. The two countries have generally been able to reach agreement on the controversies that have surfaced. The document has not been without controversy, however, and contains certain ambiguities and omissions that are sources of contention.

The problem of water quality was the first difficulty to surface, provoking a decade-long dispute. The source of the problem was a phrase in Article 11 dealing with the Colorado River, which required Mexico to accept waters "whatever their origin." This passage appeared to conflict with language in Article 3, which stipulated domestic-municipal and agricultural uses as the Treaty's top water priorities. Under the terms of IBWC Minute 242, signed in 1973, the United States accepted an obligation to provide Mexico with water whose salinity was roughly equivalent to that found at Imperial Dam on the lower Colorado River. While the agreement was specific to the Colorado River, it is widely seen to extend the Treaty's application to the quality of international waters. In 1979, this interpretation was strengthened by the IBWC's Minute 261, which draws on the authority of Article 3 to authorize the IBWC to address transboundary water pollution problems along the international boundary. Under this authority, the IBWC has been instrumental or otherwise partnered with domestic environmental agencies in developing protocols to assess water quality and safeguard public health on the Rio Grande, San Pedro, Santa Cruz, Colorado, New, and Tijuana Rivers.

Other problems have arisen in the areas of drought management, groundwater, and ecological uses of treaty water. Drought problems were anticipated by the Treaty's drafters and signatories (Hundley 1966). The Treaty established two regimes for drought management. The first, applicable to the Colorado River and also found in the 1906 Water Treaty on the upper Rio Grande, provided for proportional reduction in water supply in the event of extraordinary drought. This provision has never been tested, but it has gained binational attention as prolonged drought has reduced water flows on the Colorado. The complicating issue is whether severe drought in part of the basin upstream justifies proportional reductions to Mexico or whether any reduction requires a general drought. The Treaty is silent in this respect.

The second regime applies to the section of the Rio Grande from the Rio Conchos to the Gulf of Mexico (CSIS, ITAM, and UT 2003). Under the Treaty's Article 4, which requires Mexico to provide the United States with 350,000 acre-feet of water annually averaged over a five-year cycle, in the event of extraordinary drought the United States may agree to roll over any Mexican arrears to the next five-year cycle, though Mexico remains obligated to meet its arrears and comply with its regular obligation in the new five-year cycle. The treaty provides that when at least two of the international dams are filled to capacity, then Mexico's debt is erased, triggering a new five-year accounting cycle. Unfortunately, the implementation of these provisions is complicated by the general ambiguity attaching to the term *extraordinary drought.*

The Treaty's application to the management of transboundary groundwater resources is also a source of controversy. Minute 242 refers to groundwater in its solution to the Colorado River salinity problem, but the two countries have not seen fit to apportion their shared groundwater formally, complicating water management in the border area. Some critics argue that the Treaty is also deficient in providing for the ecological uses of shared water resources; such critics point to vulnerable marshlands and habitat now threatened by the overappropriation of water resources on the rivers.

—Stephen P. Mumme

See also: *International Boundary and Water Commission (United States and Mexico); Rio Grande Water Convention (1906)*

BIBLIOGRAPHY

CSIS, ITAM, and UT (Center for Strategic and International Studies, Instituto Tecnológico Autónomo de México, and University of Texas at Austin). *U.S.-Mexico Transboundary Water Management: The Case of the Rio Grande/Rio Bravo; Recommendations for Policymakers for the Medium and Long Term.* Washington, DC: CSIS, 2003. Available at http://csis.org/files/media/csis/pubs/binational_council.pdf.

Hundley, Norris. *Dividing the Waters.* Berkeley: University of California Press, 1966.

Mumme, Stephen P. "Minute 242 and Beyond: Challenges and Opportunities for Managing Transboundary Groundwater on the Mexico-U.S. Border." *Natural Resources Journal* 40, no. 2 (2000): 341–78. Available at http://lawlibrary.unm.edu/nrj/40/2/08_mumme_242.pdf.

Mumme, Stephen P. "Revising the 1944 Water Treaty: Reflections on the Rio Grande Drought Crises and Other Matters." *Journal of the Southwest* 45, no. 4 (2003): 649–70.

Wallace, Henry A.

Henry Agard Wallace (1888–1965) was editor of *Wallace's Farmer* and served as secretary of agriculture and vice president of the United States during the administration of Franklin D. Roosevelt. During the Truman presidency, he served as secretary of commerce from March 1945 to September 1946. His pioneering efforts in breeding hybrid corn, devising the first corn-hog ratio charts, and encouraging soil and water conservation during the Great Depression arose from his lifelong commitment to the agrarian way of life in America.

Early Life

Wallace was born on a farm on October 7, 1888, near the small town of Orient, Iowa. After attending public schools, he went to Iowa State College (now university), graduating in 1910. He then worked for his family's magazine, *Wallace's Farmer,* based in Des Moines. His father, Henry Cantwell Wallace, was the managing editor.

While working for the family magazine, young Henry distinguished himself in the area of agricultural development. He was interested in plant genetics and achieved fame for developing high-yielding strains of hybrid corn, which he introduced in 1913. Two years later, he devised the first corn-hog ratio charts, revealing the statistical probability of trends in the market place. His accomplishments won him the reputation of being an expert in farm economics.

After his father's death in 1924, Wallace took full control of the family magazine, through which he later launched a bitter attack on the Hoover administration's opposition to any price-fixing legislation. In 1928, having abandoned family ties to the Republican Party, Wallace supported the Democratic candidate, Al Smith of New York, for president. Four years later, after Columbia University economist Rexford G. Tugwell introduced him into the inner circle of Franklin D. Roosevelt, he found himself occupying the same cabinet post as his late father, who had served as secretary of agriculture from 1921 to 1924.

New Deal Policies

Wallace immediately became an important representative of early New Deal reform measures. Overproduction in the agricultural and industrial sectors was a cause of the Great Depression. In response to the economic crisis, Wallace strongly promoted the Agricultural Adjustment Act of 1933. The Act instituted price benefits to farmers in return for acreage and production controls on the major staple crops of tobacco, hogs, cotton, and wheat. Wallace called for adjusting farm prices and production, as well as seeking a balance between agriculture and the rest of the country's economy. In 1933, at the height of the Great Depression, almost a quarter of the nation's population still lived on farms, and matters pertaining to farming remained of high political and economic importance. Wallace wanted to restore the farmers' position in the national economy in a rebirth of Jeffersonian agrarian idealism.

Tied to his concern for agricultural overproduction was the matter of water and soil conservation. In a series of radio speeches and publications, Wallace promoted greater public awareness of developing scientific methods of soil building or avoiding soil depletion. He noted that many of the nation's streams were suffering from pollution, pastures and hillsides had been plowed indiscriminately, erosion by water had destroyed more than 50 million acres of land, and, in the High Plains region, wind erosion had nearly ruined 4 million acres and remained a threat to nearly another 60 million acres. Such soil erosion had disastrous effects on the farming community and the nation's water supply.

Wallace conveyed his views on the political economy of the New Deal in his 1934 book, *New Frontiers*. This was his manifesto in support of measures addressing subsistence farming, rural poverty, land-use planning, water and soil conservation, and erosion control. He argued that better management of the headways of America's great rivers had to be undertaken. The erection of new dams, reservoirs, and levees needed careful monitoring. Most importantly, he pointed out that the plowing of millions of acres of pasture and the drainage of the land had become such an obsession that rivers were being straightened, lake levels and water tables had dropped, and underground water reserves had declined so much that it was almost impossible to obtain well water in numerous farm areas during dry seasons. Faced with such realities, Wallace observed, American legislators must promote social and economic balance.

Vice Presidential Career

Seeking these "new frontiers" defined Wallace's role as secretary of agriculture from 1933 to 1940, when he was selected to run as vice president in Roosevelt's third term. During this period, he stood behind legislation like the Soil Conservation and Domestic Allotment Act of 1936 (Pub. L. 74-46). This Act created the Soil Conservation Service, which provided technical aid and support to farmers in 41 states to prevent soil erosion and remedy soil wastage in 141 damaged watershed areas. The establishment of the Soil Conservation Service, in particular, demonstrated that a coordinated program of soil and water conservation was economically effective and that a majority of farmers and ranchers were willing to take the lead in conservation plans. It represented one of Wallace's most important measures.

Wallace also assisted the Resettlement Administration's efforts in 1935 and 1936 to readjust the use of land suffering from soil depletion and to help families locate suitable land for resettlement. The creation of the Tennessee Valley Authority, designed to control erosion and reduce bad land practices in the entire watershed of the Tennessee River, which flowed through seven southern states, was another dimension of Wallace's reform crusade for the wiser use and protection of the nation's natural resources, especially rivers, lakes, and streams.

Wallace's political side was more complex than most people would care to consider. In 1948, he campaigned as

the Progressive Party's candidate for president on the platform of endorsing Soviet-American cooperation and promoting civil rights. His election defeat ended his political career but re-energized his interest in agricultural experimentation, which he conducted on his farm in South Salem, New York. He remained devoted to the soil and lived out the rest of his life as the intellectual embodiment of agrarian idealism. He died in nearby Danbury, Connecticut, on November 18, 1965.

—Chuck Howlett

See also: *Roosevelt, Franklin D.; Tennessee Valley Authority*

BIBLIOGRAPHY

Blum, John Morton, ed. *The Price of Vision: The Diary of Henry A. Wallace, 1942–1946*. Boston: Houghton Mifflin, 1973.

Culver, John C., and John Hyde. *American Dreamer: The Life and Times of Henry A. Wallace*. New York: W. W. Norton, 2000.

Ekirch, Arthur A., Jr. *Man and Nature in America*. Lincoln: University of Nebraska Press, 1973.

Kennedy, David M. *Freedom from Fear: The American People in Depression and War, 1929–1945*. New York: Oxford University Press, 1999.

Maze, John, and Graham White. *Henry A. Wallace: His Search for a New World Order*. Chapel Hill: University of North Carolina Press, 1995.

Schapsmeier, Frederick H. *Henry A. Wallace of Iowa: The Agrarian Years, 1910–1940*. Ames: Iowa State University Press, 1968.

Wallace, Henry A. *New Frontiers*. New York: Reynal & Hitchcock, 1934.

Wallace, Henry A. *Whose Constitution?* New York: Reynal & Hitchcock, 1936.

Water Pollution Control Act (1948)

The Federal Water Pollution Control Act (FWPCA; 33 U.S.C. 26) is a federal law that regulates the pollution of surface water in the United States. Originally enacted on June 30, 1948, the FWPCA was passed by the 80th U.S. Congress as Pub. L. 80-845. It was the first congressional effort to control water pollution, and it set the standard for future legislation by placing primary responsibility for water quality with state authorities. The FWPCA directed the Public Health Service to provide technical assistance to state authorities responsible for setting water quality standards. State and municipal pollution control and water treatment programs would be developed in consultation with the surgeon general. The Public Works Administration was charged with assisting states and municipalities in the construction and renovation of water treatment facilities in order to prevent the discharge of pollutants into interstate waterways. The combined goal of these provisions was to improve the sanitary conditions of surface waters in order to provide healthy water for public consumption, recreation, and the propagation of aquatic wildlife.

Amendments and Revisions

Since its enactment, the FWPCA has been amended and revised multiple times, most significantly by the 1972 Clean Water Act (CWA; Pub. L. 92-500) and the 1987 Water Quality Act (Pub. L. 100-4). Though the titles of these Acts are occasionally used interchangeably in common parlance, they are distinct laws that often reflect substantially different approaches to the prevention and abatement of surface water pollution. The original FWPCA and each of its amendments are officially incorporated in 33 U.S.C. 26, but its current language reflects only the provisions passed with the CWA and subsequent amendments, as these served to replace, rewrite, and reorganize extensively all substantive provisions set forth in the original 1948 FWPCA.

Prior Legislation

Prior to the passage of the FWPCA, a number of minor laws addressed water pollution. The 1890 Rivers and Harbors Appropriations Act included measures to protect interstate trade by preventing the dumping of obstructive waste into navigable rivers. However, the Act was amended in 1899 to exempt liquid refuse entering waterways from streets and sewers. The 1912 Public Health Service Act attempted to address concerns over clean water resources by authorizing the federal government to investigate sources of waterborne disease and pollution and to provide technical advice to state and municipal authorities. However, enforcement mechanisms were limited. Numerous other bills were introduced before Congress in the years leading up to enactment of the FWPCA, but most stalled or failed from a lack of support or budgetary concerns. In the meantime, waterways continued to be a principal site for municipal waste and sewage disposal. By the end of World War II, these practices, compounded by industrial growth and increasing urbanization, had contributed to the often dire state of the nation's waterways. Concerns about water safety and public health bolstered support for federal legislation, but many lawmakers were hesitant to expand federal authority over state water rights. The FWPCA was the outcome of a legislative compromise that allowed for federal protection of water quality, while restricting authority to interstate water bodies.

Weaknesses and Further Amendments

While compromise allowed for passage of the FWPCA, the law was so weakened that there was little prospect for it to have a significant or lasting impact on the improvement of national water quality. The Act neither prohibited pollution nor set national water quality standards. Instead, federal agencies were assigned research and advisory roles, and enforcement mechanisms were handed over to unfunded state agencies, which were often pressured to ensure favorable regulatory environments for state industries. Federal intervention was permitted only when pollution from one state threatened the health or welfare of people in another state and then only with the permission of the offending state. While the FWPCA authorized millions of dollars for a grant program that would support the construction and renovation of municipal water and sewage treatment facilities, no funds were appropriated. Due to these limitations, few enforcement measures were ever taken, and investment in pollution abatement measures varied greatly among states.

In the decades following passage of the FWPCA, multiple amendments were introduced that attempted to remedy the weaknesses inherent in the original Act. The 1956 Water Pollution Control Act provided funds for the wastewater facility construction program and stipulated that facilities comply with state pollution control plans approved by the surgeon general. A 1961 FWPCA amendment extended the Act and provided additional funding for construction grants. The 1965 Water Quality Act established the Federal Water Pollution Control Administration, an agency that required states to determine and enforce water quality standards. The last major FWPCA amendment was the 1970 Water Quality Improvement Act, which reaffirmed state rights to set water quality standards but stipulated that federal authorities should approve such standards.

By that time, however, there was significant public support for complete revision of national water quality legislation. Frustration with the FWPCA, growth of the U.S. environmental movement, a widely publicized fire on the Cuyahoga River in 1969, and establishment of the Environmental Protection Agency (EPA) in 1970 combined with pressure to renew or expand environmental protection laws before the 1972 United Nations Conference on the

Human Environment. The CWA, while officially an amendment to the FWPCA, represented a complete revision of the law and introduced entirely different approaches to ensuring water quality and controlling water pollution in the United States. The CWA significantly expanded the authority of the federal government, granting the EPA rights to establish national water quality standards and enforce regulations related to municipal and industrial waste. While the FWPCA is no longer active, and by most accounts was not a successful attempt to control water pollution, its implementation did help to raise national support for more comprehensive federal legislation and for approaches to wastewater treatment that consider both public health and general water quality.

—Sya Buryn Kedzior

See also: *Clean Water Act of 1972; Environmental Protection Agency, United States; Wastewater Treatment; Water Quality Act of 1987*

BIBLIOGRAPHY

Committee on Restoration of Aquatic Ecosystems—Science, Technology, and Public Policy; Water Science and Technology Board; Commission on Geosciences, Environment, and Resources; and National Research Council. *Restoration of Aquatic Ecosystems: Science, Technology, and Public Policy*. Washington, DC: National Academy Press, 1992. Available at http://www.nap.edu/catalog.php?record_id=1807.

Silyok, V. A. *Environmental Laws: Summaries of Statutes Administered by the Environmental Protection Agency*. New York: Nova Science, 2001.

Stoddard, Andrew, John B. Harcum, Jonathan T. Simpson, James R. Pagenkopf, Robert K. Bastian. *Municipal Wastewater Treatment: Evaluating Improvements in National Water Quality*. New York: John Wiley and Sons, 2002.

Water Power Act of 1920

The Water Power Act of 1920 (41 Stat. 1063, 16 U.S.C. 791 et seq., Pub. L. 66-280) was the first attempt by Congress to establish a comprehensive policy toward and uniform regulation of hydroelectric power development on navigable waters and any other waters located within the public domain. The Act created the Federal Power Commission (FPC), with the secretaries of war, the interior, and agriculture being designated ex officio as the commissioners. The FPC was delegated jurisdiction over "all projects involving the construction, operation, and maintenance of dams, water conduits, reservoirs, power houses, transmission lines" affecting "navigable waters of the United States, . . . other waters of the United States over which Congress has jurisdiction

under its authority to regulate commerce, . . . [and] public lands or reservations" (Federal Power Commission 1921, 5). Regulations issued in 1921 included a requirement that license applicants provide evidence of compliance with all state laws concerning the beds and banks of rivers and authorization to engage in the business of developing and transmitting electrical power.

Legislative Provisions

The long-standing question of how to allocate a finite number of sites with natural hydropower potential was resolved by delegating responsibility for decisions about individual projects to an independent agency. The legislation was intended to provide a consistent set of clear and commonly understood rules for the exercise of the discretion authorized by statute. Congress directed that the FPC should review all plans for hydroelectric projects, whether initiated by private companies or by the federal government, and that it should license power plants as well as transmission lines on navigable streams and public lands. The statute contemplated fifty-year leases, after which the FPC would audit the operator's financial records and allow any federal, state, or municipal agency to take over the plant upon payment of the initial investment, with deduction for depreciation. (In practice, licenses are often, but not always, renewed for the same operator after written proposals and public hearings.) However, the statute reserved to the states control, appropriation, and distribution of water used in irrigation or for municipal or other purposes.

Passage of the Water Power Act, June 10, 1920, terminated a two-decade debate between private power companies, who were willing to accept federal regulation but opposed any government fees imposed on licenses to generate power. Gifford Pinchot, president of the National Conservation Association and the first Forest Service chief (under President Theodore Roosevelt), led the demand that any legislation include authorization of a water power fee for private use of a common resource. Generally, the House of Representatives agreed, while the Senate was more receptive to the power companies. This stalemate prevented significant hydropower projects on navigable waters from 1913 until 1920, when the act that Congress finally passed, and President Woodrow Wilson signed, provided for minimal fees, generating little federal revenue.

The final form of the law also disappointed those who had argued for a comprehensive program integrating power generation, flood control, irrigation, and other uses of water resources, which had been briefly legislated in section 18 of the 1917 Rivers and Harbors Act. Representative and then Senator Francis G. Newlands (D–NV) had forcefully advocated for such a multiuse approach until his death in 1919, as did California water law specialist George H. Maxwell, organizer of the National Irrigation Association. For a time they had advanced a comprehensive approach by cooperating with Representative and later Senator Joseph E. Ransdell (D–LA) and Rep. Benjamin G. Humphreys II (D–MS), who were primarily interested in flood control along the Mississippi River. Congress moved back toward more coordinated hydropower development in 1928 when it authorized the Boulder Canyon Project, designated for the purposes of irrigation, flood control, and electricity production.

Disorganization and Weaknesses

The FPC was assigned at least forty-five distinct jobs, but the statute provided little definition of its powers and allocated few resources. As a result, administration and enforcement were disorganized and often nonexistent. On paper, at least three-quarters of the potential supply of hydroelectric power in the United States was within FPC jurisdiction. Only 10 percent of this estimated capacity had already been developed prior to adoption of the Act. Passed at the conclusion of the nominally progressive Wilson administration, the law was not a priority for the Republican administrations of Warren Harding and Calvin Coolidge. Between 1921 and 1927, the FPC budget was cut by two thirds, while the comptroller of the treasury ruled that nothing in the law authorized the FPC to hire its own staff. It had to borrow staff from the departments of the three cabinet secretaries sitting on the commission.

Not until 1928 did Congress explicitly allocate funds for the FPC to hire its own permanent staff. In 1930, the commission of ex officio cabinet officers was replaced with a five-member bipartisan commission, appointed by the president with the advice and consent of the senate, serving for five-year terms. The law provides that no more than three members of the commission may be from the same political party. Significant amendments expanding or revising the FPC's mandate include the Federal Power Act of 1935, the Natural Gas Act of 1938, amendments in 1940 to the Natural Gas Act, the National Energy Act of 1978, and the Energy Policies Act of 1992. In 1977, the FPC was reorganized as the Federal Energy Regulatory Commission (FERC).

One of the many weaknesses that emerged in the regulatory system set forth by the Act is the potential for Congress to legislate licensing for individual projects or set site-specific requirements that favor or disfavor particular applicants or operators. A recent example is the Mohawk River Hydroelectric Power Licensing Act of 2006, introduced that year as S. 2070 by Senator Charles Schumer (D–NY). The bill would have opened the door to a competing application that had been filed thirteen years after the statutory deadline. Trade and conservation organizations, from the National Hydropower Association to American Rivers, objected that creating case-by-case exceptions to a consistent set of rules, especially for the benefit of a single utility, would destroy the integrity of the entire process. In the end, the existing licensee, Erie Boulevard Hydropower, was granted a new forty-year license in 2007, although the license remained in litigation for several more years.

—Charles Rosenberg

See also: *Conservation Movement; Dam Building; Electric Consumers Protection Act of 1986; Federal Energy Regulatory Commission; Federal Power Commission; Pinchot, Gifford; Public Utility Regulatory Policies Act (1978)*

BIBLIOGRAPHY

Dzurik, Andrew Albert. *Water Resources Planning.* Lanham, MD: Rowman & Littlefield, 2002.

Federal Power Commission. *Federal Power Commission: Rules and Regulations as Amended by Order No. 11 of June 6, 1921, Governing the Administration of the Federal Water Power Act.* 1st rev. issue. Washington, DC: 1921.

Hays, Samuel P. *Conservation and the Gospel of Efficiency: The Progressive Conservation Movement, 1890–1920.* Pittsburgh, PA: University of Pittsburgh Press, 1999.

Hughes, Thomas Parke. *Networks of Power: Electrification in Western Society, 1880–1930.* Baltimore: Johns Hopkins University Press, 1983.

Pisani, Donald J. *Water and American Government: The Reclamation Bureau, National Water Policy, and the West, 1902–1935.* Berkeley: University of California Press, 2002.

Water Quality Act of 1987

The Water Quality Act of 1987 was the second major amendment to the Clean Water Act of 1972 (Federal Water Pollution Control Amendments of 1972). The first major amendment was the Clean Water Act of 1977. Laws concerning water pollution had been enacted as early as 1912; the major ones were the Federal Water Pollution Control Act of 1948 and the Water Quality Act of 1965. However, the Water Quality Act of 1987 signaled a shift in government policy to enforcement of far broader water quality objectives.

Clean Water Act of 1972

The purpose of the Clean Water Act and its amendments was to reduce the level of pollution in waterways in the United States, specifically by eliminating the release into water of high amounts of toxic materials and ensuring that surface waters met all health standards for human sport and recreation. The 1972 law massively increased and standardized pollution regulations, but as loopholes were found and as technology advanced so that new levels of toxicity could be measured, the regulations had to be modified.

One of the major sources of pollution that neither the 1972 Act nor its 1977 amendment addressed was storm water runoff. Both agricultural storm water discharges and irrigation return flows were specifically exempted from permit requirements. Research was conducted to minimize the economic impact of regulating these sources of pollution.

1987 Legislation

The focus of the Water Quality Act of 1987 was on regulating storm water runoff from industrial sources and municipal storm drains. In addition, it imposed stricter regulations on storm water runoff from other sources that had not been covered in the 1972 Act and its 1977 amendment. It had been politically expedient to omit these areas in order to get the original Act through Congress. However, during the 1970s and the early 1980s, research into storm water runoff showed that it was affecting water quality throughout the country. The U.S. Environmental Protection Agency (EPA) conducted the Nationwide Urban Runoff Program (NURP), which highlighted and documented the extent of pollution from runoff from municipal storm drains. Increasing levels of pollution were linked to increasing urbanization and suburbanization, as well as the use of some storm drains for litter and illegal dumping of industrial chemicals and other pollutants.

The environmental movement urged the government to respond to the problem of storm water runoff. When the Water Quality Act of 1987 was first introduced, it passed the House by a vote of 408 to 0 and passed the Senate by 96 to 0. However, President Ronald Reagan vetoed it by refusing to sign it into law after Congress had adjourned. His claim was that the cost of the legislation—$18 billion in grants and loans over eight years—was far too expensive. He countered with a $6 billion proposal. Senator Robert Dole (R-KS) reintroduced the bill in January 1987 with broad bipartisan support; it had 160 cosponsors in the House and 75 cosponsors in the Senate, and a presidential veto could be easily overturned. The legislation passed both houses and was signed into law.

The Water Quality Act required that individuals and companies responsible for industrial and municipal storm water runoffs separate their storm sewer systems and obtain National Pollutant Discharge Elimination System (NPDES) permits, though it was still possible to obtain exemptions. The EPA was increasingly involved in regulation of all pollution in storm water runoff. However, the EPA also handed over much of the responsibility for enforcement to the states, which were allowed a certain degree of flexibility to deal with local cases as they arose.

In March 2009, bills were introduced in Congress to update the legislation, specifically to redefine the nature of "fill material" and prevent pollution from "slag heaps" and other mining waste. Some would also like to amend the Water Quality Act to ensure its inclusion of wetlands; their status under the law has been ambiguous, depending on courts' definitions of "navigable waters."

—Justin Corfield

See also: *Clean Water Act of 1972; Environmental Protection Agency, United States;* Rapanos v. United States *(2006)*

BIBLIOGRAPHY

Hegewald, Mario. "Setting the Water Quality Agenda: 1988 and Beyond." *Journal of the Water Pollution Control Federation* 60, no. 5 (1988): 588–93.
Kehoe, Terence. *Cleaning Up the Great Lakes: From Cooperation to Confrontation.* De Kalb: Northern Illinois University Press, 1997.
Korpics, J. Joseph. "Regulation of Storm Water Point Source Discharges." *Journal of the Water Pollution Control Federation* 60, no. 1 (1988): 50–56.
Porter, J. Winston. "Waste Management: A Look to the Future." *Journal of the Water Pollution Control Federation* 61, no. 5 (1989): 600–604.
Shabecoff, Philip. "Clean Water Bill Back in Congress." *New York Times,* January 7, 1987.

Water Resources Development Act of 1986

The Water Resources Development Act of 1986 (WRDA) reorganized how local and federal agencies carried out water projects across the United States. Motivated by costly and chaotic water development projects across the country, Congress passed the Act to ease the federal budget, generate greater water development efficiency, and extend federal funds to a greater number of water projects. The WRDA sanctioned new water development, imposed environmental regulations on water projects, and instituted cost-sharing mandates, requiring local and state agencies to contribute to water development funding and increasing their decision-making power. One of the first cost-sharing measures undertaken by Congress, the Act impacted how water development occurred, as well as how federal and nonfederal agencies operated, well into the future.

Preceding Legislation

Before 1986, Congress had addressed water development with other pieces of legislation. Numerous Flood Control Acts and River and Harbor Acts from 1938 to 1972 focused on curtailing flood damage and enhancing navigation. The Acts authorized the U.S. Army Corps of Engineers (Corps) to administer water projects with federal funds. The Water Resources Development Act of 1974 consolidated funding and authorization for flood control, navigation, and other projects for the Corps into one bill, creating the first omnibus water bill. Each of these bills added more water projects and expanded the federal budget for water development. By the late 1970s and early 1980s, the Carter and Reagan administrations sought to limit what they viewed as haphazard water spending. The Carter administration failed to garner adequate support to restrict water development with a navigation fuel tax, but the Reagan administration's alliance with environmental groups and focus on decentralizing costs helped lead to the passage of the WRDA (Hays 1987).

Conditions of the Act

The passage of the WRDA also resulted from a rather cunning political strategy. It combined several water development and planning reforms with authorizations for numerous water projects and an increase in funding for the Corps. To see those projects come to fruition, legislators had to accept reform, and the Act breezed through the 99th Congress in 1986. The WRDA authorized hundreds of new port development, inland navigation, flood control, and stream bank and shoreline erosion projects, but it also deauthorized older, unfunded projects. The Act changed the business end of water projects the most. It mandated cost sharing, limited cost overruns, set ceilings on construction spending, and constrained the inflation of benefits in cost-benefit analyses (Clarke and McCool 1996). Moreover, it created new programs and offices that allowed the Corps to administer and financially support its projects with less federal funding and involvement.

Cost sharing, the centerpiece of the WRDA, had the greatest impact on water projects and agencies. It required nonfederal project sponsors, namely state and local governments, to provide anywhere from 25 to 100 percent of project costs up front. As a result, local agencies assumed a greater role in planning and decision making and became more cost-conscious (National Research Council 1999). They began to select projects based on local support and the market economy, eliminating many projects deemed unnecessary or too pork laden (Reuss 1991). Despite initial resistance to the cost-sharing requirement, the Corps eventually embraced its access to nonfederal funding sources as vital to its success and longevity, particularly when federal dollars were scarce (Clarke and McCool 1996). Yet nonfederal and federal groups often endured tense relationships because of cost sharing, as making cash commitments to water projects could exacerbate local impatience with the slow planning process of the Corps (National Research Council 1999). Thus, the cost-sharing reform in the Act changed the business and political climate for both federal and nonfederal agencies.

The WRDA also forced the Corps and other agencies to put greater emphasis on the environmental impacts of water development. It required fish and wildlife mitigation work to occur simultaneously with water project construction, and it established an Environmental Mitigation Fund to implement fish and wildlife mitigation efforts related to water projects. In addition, the WRDA gave the Corps the authority to modify existing water projects to improve the environment. Watershed restoration of the Kissimmee River in Florida and restoration of anadromous fish runs in the Columbia River Basin in the Northwest, as well as other attempts to remedy past environmental damage, were largely the product of provisions in the Act (Clarke and McCool 1996). Due to the WRDA, federal and nonfederal groups not only had to be more aware of economic factors but also had to be more environmentally conscious.

Subsequent Legislation

After 1986, Congress passed seven more Water Resources Development Acts, most recently in 2007, imposing further reforms and authorizing more water projects. The most notable amendments to the WRDA included adding further cost-sharing measures and placing increased emphasis on environmental protection. The Water Resources Development Act of 1988 extended cost-sharing mandates to more water projects, including those not constructed by the Corps. In 2000, Congress further amended the WRDA to require greater public input and reflect a better understanding of ecological restoration. In all, legislation after the WRDA continued to emphasize Americans' greater environmental concerns and kept distributing cost and planning burdens to nonfederal agencies.

Scholars point out that both lawmakers and agency leaders in the 1980s called the Water Resources Development Planning Act historic and revolutionary (Clarke and McCool 1996). The Act's cost-sharing provisions alone made it historically significant, as local agencies for the first time gained a strong voice in federal affairs. The WRDA also spread management, planning, and accountability across multiple levels of government, putting water development costs more squarely on project users and beneficiaries (Reuss 1991). The Act ultimately impacted government, business, nature, and the market, enhancing the efficiency of a range of U.S. water projects while regulating them more closely and reflecting the growing economic and environmental awareness of the latter part of the twentieth century.

—Daniel Karalus

See also: *Army Corps of Engineers, United States; Water Resources Development Act of 1996; Water Resources Development Act of 2007*

BIBLIOGRAPHY

Clarke, Jeanne Nienaber, and Daniel C. McCool. *Staking Out the Terrain: Power and Performance among Natural Resource Agencies,* 2nd ed. Albany: State University of New York Press, 1996.
Hays, Samuel P. *Beauty, Health, and Permanence: Environmental Politics in the United States, 1955–1985.* New York: Cambridge University Press, 1987.
National Research Council. *New Directions in Water Resources Planning for the U.S. Army Corps of Engineers.* Washington, DC: National Academy Press, 1999.
Reuss, Martin. *Reshaping National Water Politics: The Emergence of the Water Resources Development Act of 1986.* Fort Belvoir, VA: Institute for Water Resources, U.S. Army Corps of Engineers, 1991.

Water Resources Development Act of 1996

The Water Resources Development Act of 1996, enacted by the U.S. Congress on October 12, was the seventh Water Resources Development Act. It was to be administered by the U.S. Army Corps of Engineers (Corps). Its aim was to balance the use of water resources among the states, draw up plans for water development projects, and manage conservation projects. It also sought to streamline existing laws, alter funding levels, and address specific problems associated with specific projects.

Amending the Water Resources Development Act of 1986, the 1996 law changed the earlier Act's cost-sharing provisions in relation to dredged material disposal areas. It also acknowledged the potential for sediment decontamination as a result of technological advances since the Water Resources Development Act of 1992. It terminated the technical advisory committee for monitoring reservoirs established under the Water Resources Development Act of 1990. The Act also included amendments to a large number of other Acts, including the Rivers and Harbors Act of 1946, Rivers and Harbors Act of 1958, Flood Control Act of 1969, and Flood Control Act of 1970.

Provisions of the Legislation

The Water Resources Development Act of 1996 authorized the development of specified water resources. It also envisioned the use of conservation measures to ease navigational problems, achieve flood control, preserve the environment, restore land that had been damaged, protect the coastline from soil erosion, and generate hydropower. The Act also empowered the Corps to address issues related to navigation, bluff stabilization, flood control, the reduction of storm damage, shoreline and stream bank protection, and hurricane damage prevention measures and safety improvements in eight states: Alaska, California, Delaware, Florida, Indiana, Louisiana, Maryland, and New Jersey. The Corps was directed to carry out projects to prevent flooding in California, Illinois, Louisiana, Michigan, Missouri, Montana, New York, and Oregon. It was also tasked with bank stabilization in Indiana, Pennsylvania, and Tennessee; habitat and environmental restoration projects in California, Oregon, and Utah; and sediment removal in Minnesota.

The cost-sharing provisions of the Water Resources Development Act of 1986 were revived, and that law's scope was expanded to included dredged material disposal facilities. The nonfederal share of costs for nonstructural and other flood projects was raised from 25 percent to 35 percent. In addition, nonfederal stakeholders had to agree to participate in projects involving floodplain management and flood insurance programs by preparing plans and developing guidelines to reduce flood damage. The 1996 Act also added terms not included in the Water Resources Development Act of 1990 in regard to the removal of dredged material and the disposal of contaminated sediment, with guidelines for the protection and restoration of aquatic ecosystems.

The Water Resources Development Act of 1996 supported a number of existing projects with alterations. These projects involved flood control, navigation, the control of beach erosion, and the restoration of stream banks. Funds were also allocated for wetlands research in five states, and direct aid was granted to Louisiana for its Mississippi River Delta Region project aimed at reducing flood damage.

Some specific projects outlined in the Act included the allocation of extra funds to repair damage to the New York State Canal System and to protect shoreline in New York. Funding was also included for flood control measures in Montana, Pennsylvania, Rhode Island, Tennessee, Virginia, Washington, and West Virginia.

—Justin Corfield

See also: *Army Corps of Engineers, United States; Water Resources Development Act of 1986; Water Resources Development Act of 2007*

BIBLIOGRAPHY

Lapping, Mark B., and Owen J. Furuseth, eds. *Big Places, Big Plans.* Burlington, VT: Ashgate, 2004.

Rogers, Peter. *America's Water: Federal Roles and Responsibilities.* Cambridge, MA: MIT Press, 1996.

Water Resources Development Act of 2007

The Water Resources Development Act of 2007, passed by the U.S. Congress on November 8 over a veto by President George W. Bush, was the tenth Water Resources Development Act. In addition to reauthorizing the Water Resources Development Act, it also authorized flood control, navigation, and environmental projects by the United States Army Corps of Engineers (Corps).

During George W. Bush's administration, there had been a lack of support for water conservation measures and other environmental programs. Thus, a number of members of Congress joined forces to try to get the Water Resources Development Act of 2007 passed. The initial Bill (H.R. 1485) was sponsored by Rep. Jim Oberstar (D-MN), who had long been concerned with environmental issues.

Legislation Projects

The bill sponsored by Oberstar authorized the secretary of the Army to develop a number of projects that would improve water resources in rivers and harbors around the United States. One of the largest projects in the bill addressed navigation and ecosystem improvements along 854 miles of the Illinois waterway system, from the confluence of the Mississippi and Ohio Rivers to the Saint Anthony Falls lock on the Mississippi in Minneapolis, Minnesota. It budgeted $1.8 billion for the installation of mooring facilities at various existing locks and the construction of new locks.

The Act also earmarked funds for restoration of the Florida Everglades. Federal and state governments were each to pay $682.5 million of the $1.4 billion cost. The improvements promised to improve the flow of water in the Everglades. In addition, $187.7 million in federal funds, with the state government providing matching funds, was authorized for restoration work on the Picayune Strand in south Florida. Both federal and state authorities then contributed $40 million for various other improvements. The project called for the construction of bridges along the Tamiami Trail between Tampa and Miami, Florida, which was becoming an important tourist site.

The other major project in the Bill was the launch of the Coastal Louisiana Ecosystem Protection and Restoration Task Force. Its purpose was "to protect, repair, restore and maintain" the ecosystems in the Louisiana coastal zone, which had been badly affected by Hurricane Katrina in 2005.

The bill easily passed the House of Representatives by 394 to 25. However, it quickly ran into problems in the Senate. The Senate Committee on Environment and Public Works drew up a substitute bill that addressed some of the concerns committee members had highlighted in the initial bill. One had to do with the printing of the bill. The disclosure table was in small type and formatted as an image, making it unsearchable by computer. The other problem was far more serious. The Congressional Budget Office realized that, according to its calculations, the Senate bill cost $31.5 billion, whereas the bill in the House of Representatives would have cost only $13.2 billion.

The Senate ultimately drafted an identical bill to the one that had been passed in the House. This passed the Senate by 89 votes to 7. The bill in the Senate was then amended with an extra $15 billion allocated to Gulf Coast projects to protect New Orleans and the surrounding area from hurricanes. In addition, there were significant changes in the amounts allocated to be spent in succeeding years. Finally, the Senate version of the bill limited the number of projects that the Corps could undertake to forty.

Bush's Unsuccessful Veto

President George W. Bush vetoed the bill on November 2, 2007, citing what he viewed as the legislation's lack of fiscal responsibility and a concern that it made false promises of funds to local communities that Congress would not keep. In response, Democratic members of Congress, joined by many Republicans, sought to have the veto overridden. Rep. Charles Boustany Jr. (R-LA) opined that if the Water Resources Development Act were not passed, the Gulf coastline would disappear. Senate majority leader Harry Reid (D-NV) described the veto as "irresponsible" and the threat of further vetoes "reckless." On the other hand, a group known as Taxpayers for Common Sense, established in 1995, opposed the bill, regarding many of the projects as being "pork barreling."

The House of Representatives voted by 361 to 54 to override the presidential veto on November 6, 2007. The next day, the Senate voted 79 to 14 to override the veto. It was the first override of a veto during the Bush presidency.

—Justin Corfield

See also: *Army Corps of Engineers, United States; Water Resources Development Act of 1986; Water Resources Development Act of 1996; Water Resources Planning Act of 1965*

BIBLIOGRAPHY

Abrams, Jim. "House Votes to Override Water Bill Veto." *Washington Post,* November 7, 2007. Available at http://www.washingtonpost.com/wp-dyn/content/article/2007/11/06/AR2007110601753.html.
Lowry, William R. *Repairing Paradise: The Restoration of Nature in America's National Parks.* Washington, DC: Brookings Institution Press, 2009.
Smiley, Tavis, and Stephanie Robinson. *Accountable: Making America as Good as Its Promise.* New York: Atria Books, 2009.
Weisman, Jonathan. "On Water Bill, House Votes to Override Bush Veto for First Time." *Washington Post,* November 7, 2007. Available at http://www.washingtonpost.com/wp-dyn/content/article/2007/11/06/AR2007110602317.html.

Water Resources Planning Act of 1965

Along with the Water Resources Research Act of 1964, the Water Resources Planning Act of 1965 was the U.S.

Congress's attempt to implement the 1961 recommendations of the Senate Select Committee on National Water Resources. Concerns about properly utilizing the nation's water resources so as not to stymie the growth of western cities, agriculture, and industry ran alongside increasing awareness of and concern about water pollution. Both of these sometimes competing agendas could be seen in the Water Resources Planning Act (WRPA). Also, the WRPA demonstrated the Lyndon B. Johnson administration's belief that national planning efforts needed to be made in concert with local and state planning in order to make adequate use of resources, like water, in which the entire nation has an interest.

The WRPA set up funds to establish fifty commissions to study American river basins on an individual basis; it authorized a matching fund of $6 million (to be matched by the states) and a federal grant fund of $5 million per year. It also gave the respective commissions priorities for the data they collected and asked them to produce reports that would detail the different priorities for each basin and set an agenda for future utilization, construction of water projects, and environmental goals (Sea Grant Program 1972). Importantly, it established the term *river basin* as an ecological unit, foreshadowing the emphasis on ecosystem management that would come about twenty years later. However, the WRPA, because of political concerns, did not take this emphasis on river basins to its logical conclusion, ending the extent of each commission's authority at state lines. Further, the National Water Commission, which was created to oversee the state commissions, could not consider the viability of interbasin water transfers, because doing so would have required basinwide, interstate agencies, which would naturally infringe on the rights of the states to control their waters (Newson 2009).

However, the WRPA did signify a stride forward in the recognition of the impact human development has on watercourses and river basins. First, it allowed for a flexible planning regime that took into account the views of the federal government, state and local governments, and even individual water users. It recognized, for the first time, the competing priorities of agriculture, urbanization, industrialization, and recreation and the strain that they were placing on the nation's waterways (Brooks 2002).

Despite the WRPA's recognition of the environment as a concern when creating national and state water plans, the scientists who gave testimony during the formulation of plans were relegated to discussing specific issues that usually remained unaddressed. Larger ecological issues were often ignored because of the economic and political ramifications of their solutions. Public debates over the recommendations in state after state were politically polarized, with pro-development interests squaring off against environmentalists and states' rights supporters arguing with those who saw a larger, federal management as the only solution to cross-border, ecosystem-wide problems.

Regardless of its shortcomings, the WRPA represented the first stirrings of a massive shift in focus in formulating water policy. Taking place in the same era as the publication of Rachel Carson's influential book *Silent Spring* (1962), when environmental awareness was first coming to the public's attention, the WRPA was one of the first expressions of that awareness in terms of federal policy. Whereas development and reclamation were once the sole goals of federal policy, environmental protection began to become a growing concern, and this concern would lead to later legislation, such as the Wilderness Act (1964), the National Environmental Protection Act (1969), and the Endangered Species Act (1973).

—Steven L. Danver

See also: *Ecosystem Management; Endangered Species Act (1973); National Environmental Policy Act of 1969*

BIBLIOGRAPHY

Brooks, Richard Oliver, Ross Jones, and Ross A. Virginia. *Law and Ecology: The Rise of the Ecosystem Regime.* Burlington, VT: Ashgate, 2002.

Carson, Rachel. *Silent Spring.* Boston: Houghton Mifflin, 1962.

Newson, Malcolm. *Land, Water, and Development: Sustainable Management of River Basin Systems.* 3rd ed. New York: Routledge, 2009.

Sea Grant Program. *The Evolving Role of the Federal Government in the Management of Lake Michigan.* Ann Arbor: William L. Jackson School of Natural Resources, The University of Michigan, 1972.

Water Resources Council

The Water Resources Planning Act of 1965 was passed to centralize the development of national water policy and to coordinate the activities of the federal agencies and departments involved in managing water resources across the United States. Title I of the Act created the Water Resources Council (WRC). Its membership was officially comprised of the secretaries of the departments of Agriculture, Commerce, Energy, Housing and Urban Development, Interior, and Transportation, although much of the work was conducted by subordinates. The Environmental Protection Agency was added to the council in 1970.

In 1973, the WRC issued its *Principles and Standards for Planning Water and Related Land Resources.* The document proved controversial, as critics charged it favored environmental concerns over economic development. That view was shared by President Ronald Reagan, who had the WRC set new guidelines in 1983 with the issuance of *Economic and Environmental Principles and Guidelines for Water and Related Land Resources Implementation Studies.* Reagan's administration subsequently abolished the council.

—John R. Burch Jr.

See also: *Environmental Protection Agency, United States*

BIBLIOGRAPHY

Committee to Assess the U.S. Army Corps of Engineers Water Resources Project Planning Procedures, National Research Council. *New Directions in Water Resources Planning for the U.S. Army Corps of Engineers.* Washington, DC: National Academies Press, 1999.

Thompson, Stephen Andrew. *Water Use, Management, and Planning in the United States.* New York: Academic Press, 1998.

Water Resources Council. *Economic and Environmental Principles and Guidelines for Water and Related Land Resources Implementation Studies.* Washington, DC: U.S. Water Resources Council, Department of the Interior, 1983.

Water Resources Council. *Principles and Standards for Planning Water and Related Land Resources.* Washington, DC: U.S. Government Printing Office, 1973.

Water Resources Research Act of 1964

Coming on the heels of the work of the Senate Select Committee on National Water Resources, which had issued its report in 1961, Congress passed the Water Resources Research Act of 1964 (WRRA). This legislation was a first step in implementing the Select Committee's recommendations for heightened academic study of the nation's water resources in order to create a sustainable future for all of the nation, but particularly for the western states, where water was increasingly scarce and people were increasingly moving. The Select Committee had called for increased research by the federal government, state governments, and local governments, and the WRRA placed the responsibility for that research squarely in the hands of academic water researchers nationwide.

The WRRA sought to use the state land-grant universities to attack the problem of the future of the nation's water resources. The land-grant universities were created by the Morrill Act of 1862, and the Hatch Act of 1887 pioneered the strategy later used by the WRRA. The Hatch Act was the federal government's way of putting the best minds in the nation to work in order to improve American farmers' yields. To that end, the Hatch Act established Agricultural Experiment Stations at each of the land-grant state universities. Similarly, the WRRA established a water resources research institute and technology center in each of the nation's fifty-four land-grant universities. Each of the states would receive $75,000 in 1965, $87,500 during each of the following two years, and $100,000 annually thereafter to fund its water research institute (Clark 1987). The WRRA also established a $1 million appropriation to be used at the discretion of the secretary of the interior to fund studies of water-related issues by institutions other than the water research institutes. The Committee on Water Resources Research was tasked with coordinating the various water research efforts (Holmes 1979).

The water research institute program, under the auspices of the U.S. Geological Survey, had a number of goals. First, it set out to fund research on water problems that would expand the understanding of the factors involved. Second, it endeavored to encourage science students to enter water resource fields. Third, it was intended to train a new cadre of water engineers. Fourth, it set out to connect the scientific study of water resources with the work of managers of water infrastructure and the interests of the general public whom it impacted. The studies were to encompass a host of water-related issues: scientific, engineering, legal, social, economic, and ecological (Clark 1987).

After the state water research institutes' first ten years of existence, the Congressional Research Service (CRS) assessed their effectiveness and concluded that, despite rather meager funding, they had conducted effective studies that had played important roles in determining water policy on the local, state, and federal levels. Further, even though the funding for the institutes had subsided, they had created many permanent institutions for the ongoing study of water-related topics. However, the CRS also concluded that without increased funding, the institutes would face the

possibility of closing or curtailing their activities. In response, Congress approved increased funding levels during the late 1970s and early 1980s (National Research Council 2004). A larger effort was made in 1984 with congressional passage of the Water Resources Research Act of 1984, which reauthorized the program. With expanded funding came an expanded mission: now the water resource institutes are tasked not only with evaluating future water needs and issues but also with assessing their effect on agriculture and the environment. Various acts have reauthorized this program on an almost annual basis, and it remains the largest government effort to shape water policy today.

—Steven L. Danver

See also: *Senate Select Committee on National Water Resources; Water Resources Planning Act of 1965*

BIBLIOGRAPHY

Clark, Ira G. *Water in New Mexico: A History of Its Management and Use.* Albuquerque: University of New Mexico Press, 1987.

Holmes, Beatrice Hort. *History of Federal Water Resources Programs and Policies, 1961–1970.* Washington, DC: Government Printing Office, 1979.

Milazzo, Paul Charles. *Unlikely Environmentalists: Congress and Clean Water, 1945–1972.* Lawrence: University Press of Kansas, 2006.

National Research Council, Committee on Assessment of Water Resources Research. *Confronting the Nation's Water Problems: The Role of Research.* Washington, DC: National Academies Press, 2004.

Watt, James G.

James G. Watt (1938–) is an attorney who served as President Ronald Reagan's first secretary of the interior. His implementation of Reagan's agenda of decreasing environmental restrictions on businesses gained him many critics, and his inability to communicate his vision effectively led to his downfall. Although Watt was simply carrying out Reagan's wishes, he became the scapegoat for frustrated environmental interest groups, who demanded his resignation in 1983.

Early Life and Environmental Philosophy

James Gaius Watt was born on January 31, 1938, in Lusk, Wyoming, and was raised on a farm. He did very well in school and after high school attended the University of Wyoming, where he earned a BA in 1960 and a law degree in 1962. After graduation, he left home for Washington, D.C., where he worked for Senator Milward L. Simpson (R-WY). His other notable jobs before serving as Reagan's secretary of the interior included working as a legal advisor for the U.S. Chamber of Commerce and the Federal Power Commission.

In the late 1970s, Watt and Reagan publicly supported the "Sagebrush Rebellion." The Sagebrush Rebels wanted states to take over federally owned land within their borders and utilize it for their own benefit. The Rebels reveled in the newly elected Reagan administration, their new ally. While the Rebels rejoiced, however, environmentalists believed that federally protected western lands in twelve states were in danger of being destroyed.

Watt and Reagan were like-minded when it came to environmental issues. Neither man considered himself a conservationist. Instead, both believed that nature was there to be used for the benefit of people. Both men held to the notion that, although many people supported environmental causes, most people set a higher priority on jobs and economic growth. They accused environmentalists of being elitists who cared more about trees and animals than human life and progress. They refused to set any limits, even environmental, on the nation's future. They ignored warnings of environmental doom because they believed that, if people were allowed to be free, American innovation would solve any problems that would arise.

Secretary of the Interior

By the time Watt became secretary of the interior, he had earned a reputation for putting business interests above environmental concerns. He reinforced this image during his first year in office, when he sat down for an interview with the *National Journal*. During the interview, he explained that he had sued for the use of wilderness land in the 1970s because the Carter administration had refused to lease it (Mosher 1981). More importantly, during the interview, he expressed his faith in giving the marketplace free rein in matters concerning the environment. Watt's views gave his environmental critics cause for concern, but his actions made them furious. Claiming to have God on his side, Watt allowed new oil drilling off the Pacific Ocean coast. He deregulated the mining industry. He allowed formerly protected wilderness lands to be used for commercial interests, such as timbering and grazing, and for private expansion and development. He also increased the cost of admission to national parks.

Ironically, although both Watt and Reagan had strikingly similar environmental philosophies, many critics regarded Reagan, a former actor, as naïve, but they held Watt responsible for the administration's policies. Also, in contrast, Reagan possessed the gift of political rhetoric, while Watt was lacking in that department. To make matters worse, Watt made no attempts to appease his critics. Instead, he continued to erode public confidence by making blunt and off-color comments, which offended environmental and minority groups. Watt's rhetorical failure—his inability to communicate his vision effectively—eventually went too far. A variety of important interest groups and constituencies threw their full weight against the administration, and soon administration leaders began pushing for Watt's resignation. Although Watt had some staunch supporters, including the president, he had managed to offend too many people to be allowed to keep his post. Interestingly, William Patrick, who replaced Watt, followed the same general environmental policies, but Patrick's policies failed to generate anything resembling Watt's firestorm.

Later Life

After his resignation, Watt went back to his law practice and devoted two years to penning a book. However, instead of chronicling his rise and fall as secretary of the interior, Watt wrote about his fundamentalist Christian, conservative views on a variety of topics, including the environment. Watt believed that everything could be explained in very simple, black-and-white, two-sided terms. Namely, environmentalists liked liberals, but they hated conservatives. In fact, Watt claimed that some of President Jimmy Carter's environmental policies were much worse than Reagan's policies, but that during the Carter years, environmentalists were silent because they supported the president's overall liberal agenda (Watt and Wead 1985).

According to several reviewers, Watt's book was neither well balanced nor well written, which may explain, in part, why it was not well received by the public. Also, many historians disagreed with Watt's assessment, and they pointed to the Reagan administration's abuses of 1970s environmental restrictions. Consequently, Watt's legacy remains marred by critical histories that detail business practices of dumping, using pesticides, generating toxic waste, and countless other abuses of the environment that occurred during his watch.

—Rolando Avila

See also: *Mining and Water Resources*

BIBLIOGRAPHY

Cawley, R. M., and W. Chaloupka. "James Watt and the Environmentalists: A Clash of Ideologies." *Policy Studies Journal* 14 (1985): 244–54.

Goldzwig, S. "James Watt's Subversion of Values: An Analysis of Rhetorical Failure." *Southern Speech Communication Journal* 50 (1985): 305–326.

Lash, Jonathon. *A Season of Spoils: The Reagan Administration's Attack on the Environment.* New York: Pantheon Books, 1984.

Mosher, L. "Reagan and the GOP Are Riding the Sagebrush Rebellion—But for How Long?" *National Journal* 13 (1981): 476–81.

Watt, James G., and Doug Wead. *The Courage of a Conservative.* New York: Simon & Schuster, 1985.

Western Water Policy Review Advisory Commission

The Western Water Policy Review Advisory Commission (hereinafter the Commission) was established by an act of Congress. By law, its membership consisted of sixteen members, drawn from relevant congressional committees, cabinet officials, and citizens from across the western United States. President George H. W. Bush made appointments to the Commission, but President Clinton replaced most with his own appointees and named the chair.

Foundations

The Commission was the brainchild of Senator Mark Hatfield (R-OR), who had a reputation for independence and a deep familiarity with western resource issues. His perspective was shaped by the Columbia River Basin, where an abundance of state, federal, tribal, environmental, irrigation, and other organizations have a role in managing the waters of the basin. The Commission was charged by Congress with assessing the region's water needs and the condition of its waters and, most importantly, with addressing dysfunctions in how the federal government managed water. The Commission held meetings across the western United States, heard testimony from concerned citizens and officials, and had reports prepared by experts in water issues. The Commission's report, *Water in the West,* was issued in 1998 and can be found in federal depository libraries and online.

Role of the Federal Government

The federal role in western water was due for review. If one dates the establishment of a strong federal presence in western water to 1902, the time of the passage of the Reclamation Act, it is evident that ensuing social and political change has transformed the West in ways unimaginable at the turn of the previous century. Although the federal role was integral to the establishment of irrigation in the West, and to intensive settlement, agriculture now is a small part of the West's economy. States have far more capacity to plan and finance water infrastructure, and a continuing federal presence can be a source of irritation to state officials. At the same time, the federal presence may be supported by tribal officials, environmentalists, and others who benefit from multiple authorities.

The Report and Recommendations

The Commission's report provided an overview of how water is used in the West and of the demographic and economic changes occurring in the region. The many challenges facing water managers in the West were described, with an emphasis on achieving sustainability. Water is managed by different agencies of the federal, state, and tribal governments, each with differing mandates, and these mandates were assessed.

The primary author of the Commission's report was A. Daniel Tarlock, with Commission members reviewing each chapter of the report as it was being written in open meetings. The Congressional Research Service provided a report on "House and Senate Committee Jurisdiction and Executive Branch Responsibility over Water Resources." The Commission also solicited reports from well-known experts on aquatic ecosystems; Columbia Basin water law; federal budgeting for water projects; climate change; water use; drought management; Indian water rights; demographic, economic, and value change; watershed management; alternative dispute resolution; the states' perspectives; water quality; western hydropower; western law use; and the position of the Upper Basin states. Additionally six river basins were summarized by leading experts: the Columbia, the Colorado, the Platte, the Sacramento–San Joaquin, the Truckee–Carson, and the Rio Grande.

The policy recommendations of the Commission had two major themes. The first was that the federal government's water policies should be based on sustainability: "Sustainable water use seeks to achieve a balance between the capability of a system to meet social needs and its biological capacity" (Western Water Policy Review Advisory Commission 1998, xiv). In the hundreds of pages of federal laws relating to water, there is almost no mention of this concept, but the Commission found that the convergence of a growing population, increased water use, and deteriorating ecosystems necessitated making sustainability a guiding principle. If this concept were adopted, it would be necessary to make water decisions that included ecosystem values and that considered the long-term maintenance of "environmental, social, economic, and cultural values" (Western Water Policy Review Advisory Commission 1998, xiv).

The second theme was that of reordering governance around river basins rather than the political borders on which most institutions are based. Federal agencies would be empowered to act at a basin level and would be required to collaborate with other federal agencies, as well as other governmental entities. Daniel McCool has dubbed the federal-state relationship that now reigns as an "iron triangle" in which federal agency heads, key members of Congress, and the appropriate state water agency pursue water projects with little local input. The integration of agencies at the basin level would allow "more public participation, more democracy in the management of a basin's rivers" (Western Water Policy Review Advisory Commission 1998, xvii).

Since the release of the Commission's report, climate change has moved to the center of research and discussion about water resources in the West. Many of the tensions over federal and state roles are heightened by climate change. Species protection is one of them: How can aquatic species, already threatened with extinction, survive in altered climate regimes? Likewise, runoff from snowpack is expected to decline greatly with warmer winters, leaving less for downstream irrigators. Should the federal government engage in a new round of building reservoirs for western irrigators, or is irrigation of arid lands becoming too expensive to continue into the twenty-first century? And where will the water for increased energy development in the West come from? These questions will keep alive the discussion about the mission of federal water policy and how the federal government relates to states, tribes, and citizens.

Calls for national reviews of water policy continue to grow. The report of the Western Water Commission is part of a tradition of such reports, addressing both water and federal public lands. These reports rarely result in direct action by federal agencies or the Congress, but they are part of larger conversations that mark changing beliefs about public policies. The ongoing desire to rationalize national water policy reflects the indispensable nature of water and its multiple values.

—Denise Fort

See also: *Columbia Basin Project; Drought; Reclamation Act of 1902; Truckee-Carson Project*

BIBLIOGRAPHY

Benson, Reed D. "Recommendations for an Environmentally Sound Federal Policy on Western Water." *Stanford Environmental Law Journal* 17 (1998): 247–70.

McCool, Daniel C. *Command of the Waters: Iron Triangles, Federal Water Development, and Indian Water.* Tucson: University of Arizona Press, 1987.

Neuman, Janet C. "Federal Water Policy: An Idea Whose Time Will (Finally) Come." *Virginia Environmental Law Journal* 20 (2001): 107–118.

Western Water Policy Review Advisory Commission. *Water in the West: Challenge for the Next Century.* Albuquerque: University of New Mexico, 1998. Available at http://preventionweb.net/go/1785.

Wild and Scenic Rivers Act of 1968

The National Wild and Scenic Rivers Act of 1968 was a landmark piece of legislation that embodied a gradual but relentless shift in public attitudes about the intrinsic value of wild, free-flowing rivers and other unimproved natural areas. For much of America's history, waterways had been enthusiastically converted into "working rivers"—resources outfitted with dams, reservoirs, and other alterations for the purposes of commercial navigation, irrigation, and electric power generation. In the 1960s, however, rising public concern about the nation's diminished storehouses of wilderness land prompted a reassessment of federal river policies, and in 1968, Congress responded with the National Wild and Scenic Rivers Act (Pub. L. 90-542; 16 U.S.C. 1271–87). This measure, signed into law by President Lyndon B. Johnson on October 2, 1968, formally established a federal system to keep American rivers with outstanding natural, cultural, and recreational values in a free-flowing condition for the enjoyment of present and future generations.

Background

As with many other wilderness protection laws passed by Congress in the 1960s, the drive to provide federal protection to the nation's remaining free-flowing rivers had actually begun in the 1950s. At that time, a small group of wilderness conservationists, including John and Frank Craighead, Paul Bruce Dowling, Joseph Penfold, and Sigurd Olson, had begun lobbying lawmakers and drumming up public support for new wild river protections. These efforts paid visible dividends in 1965, when the Water Resources Planning Act created a Federal Water Resources Council to coordinate national water resource

The Noatak River, in northwest Alaska, is designated as a Wild and Scenic River. Signed into law in 1968, the National Wild and Scenic Rivers Act allowed for the designation and protection of rivers of environmental, cultural, or recreational significance. By 2008, more than 160 rivers had been added to the list.
U.S. Fish and Wildlife Service

development and preservation issues. But it was not until the Wild and Scenic Rivers Act was passed and signed that policy mechanisms were put in place to safeguard permanently "certain selected rivers of the Nation which, with their immediate environments, possess outstandingly remarkable scenic, recreational, geologic, fish and wildlife, historic, cultural, or other similar values . . . in free-flowing condition" (Wild and Scenic Rivers Act of 1968, § 1[b]).

Impact of the Act

The Wild and Scenic Rivers Act had a particularly intense impact at the U.S. Army Corps of Engineers and the Bureau of Reclamation, two federal agencies that had spent much of the previous four decades erecting multipurpose dams and other federally funded water development projects on the nation's waterways. Ever since the New Deal, these agencies had been closely allied with key congressional leaders and pro-development industries in the dam-building

cause, and their massive public works had been integral to the economic development of the nation in general and the West in particular. The Wild and Scenic Rivers Act, however, served notice that the halcyon days of unquestioned support for Corps and Bureau dam-building programs were at an end in Washington, D.C., and that outdoor recreation and wilderness conservation had emerged as important and enduring considerations in federal water management policy making. Indeed, Johnson characterized the federal Wild and Scenic Rivers System, created by the Act, as a belated but essential reversal of policy away from the dam-building ethos that had long held sway in America.

Under the provisions of the Wild and Scenic Rivers Act, rivers may be designated for inclusion in the Wild and Scenic Rivers System by Congress or the secretary of the interior. Rivers are eligible for protection if they and the lands surrounding them possess outstanding scenery, wilderness, fish and wildlife habitat, recreation possibilities, or cultural and historic value. Sections of waterways and river tributaries are eligible for inclusion in the system, as are entire rivers of a free-flowing character. Rivers entered into the system may be managed by federal or state authorities, and language in the protection program still allows for various recreational and agricultural practices, residential development, and other uses, depending on the classification of the river in question. In addition, inclusion of a river in the Wild and Scenic Rivers System does not affect existing water rights or the existing jurisdiction of states and the federal government over waters as determined by established principles of law. However, the language of the Act explicitly prohibits the Federal Energy Regulatory Commission (FERC) from granting a permit for water projects "on or directly affecting" rivers designated as wild and scenic. In addition, the Act prohibits federal licensing of any development activity that is incompatible with protection of designated rivers and their corridors.

Classifications

Wild and Scenic Rivers are classified under one of three different categories: "wild," "scenic," or "recreational." Wild river areas are rivers (or sections of rivers) that are undammed, unimpounded, and generally inaccessible by motor vehicle, with undeveloped shorelines and pristine watersheds. These are true wilderness rivers, and *wild* is the most frequently employed designation in the system. Scenic river areas are rivers or sections of rivers that are free of impoundments and have mostly undeveloped shorelines or watersheds but that are more readily accessible by road. Finally, recreational river areas are waterways that have a history of active development (such as past impoundments or diversions) and are easily accessible by road or railway but that still house natural and recreational qualities that make them worthy of protection.

By 2008, the Wild and Scenic River System had expanded from its original 12 rivers to include more than 11,400 protected waterway miles on 166 rivers in 38 states

---

American Rivers

American Rivers is a nonprofit conservation organization with approximately 65,000 members working to protect rivers across the United States. The organization was founded in 1973 to enforce the provisions of the Wild and Scenic Rivers Act of 1968. Its members have been active in protecting not only the Wild and Scenic Rivers Act but also complementary pieces of environmental legislation such as the Clean Water Act of 1972 from efforts to weaken or abolish them. American Rivers is best known for the publication of *America's Most Endangered Rivers,* an annual list of ten rivers in desperate need of public attention and resources. It has proven an effective tool because it not only identifies the problems faced by the respective waterways but also identifies all the key stakeholders and prescribes a course of action that can be realistically implemented. One course of action at which American Rivers members have proven particularly adept in recent years has been the restoration of rivers to their optimal free-flowing form through dam removal.

—John R. Burch Jr.

See also: *Army Corps of Engineers, United States; Clean Water Act of 1972; Dam Removal and River Restoration*

BIBLIOGRAPHY

American Rivers. http://www.americanrivers.org/.
Rosenberg, Kenneth A. *Wilderness Preservation: A Reference Handbook.* Santa Barbara, CA: ABC-CLIO, 1994.

---

and Puerto Rico. More than 5,385 of these river miles are designated as wild, while the rest are classified as either scenic (2,531 miles) or recreational (3,519 miles). The river miles protected under the Act account for a little more than one-quarter of 1 percent of the nation's total river mileage. On March 30, 2009, President Barack Obama made one of the largest additions to the federal Wild and Scenic River System since the early 1990s when he signed the Omnibus Public Lands Management Act of 2009 into law. This legislation included an amendment designating 316 miles of river in southwestern Idaho's Owyhee-Bruneau Canyonlands for inclusion in the Wild and Scenic River System.

—Kevin Hillstrom

See also: *Army Corps of Engineers, United States; Bureau of Reclamation; Water Resources Planning Act of 1965*

BIBLIOGRAPHY

Coyle, Kevin J. *American Rivers Guide to Wild and Scenic River Designation: A Primer on National River Conservation.* Washington, DC: American Rivers, 1988.
Lowry, William R. *Dam Politics: Restoring America's Rivers.* Washington, DC: Georgetown University Press, 2003.

The Wilderness Society

The Wilderness Society is a nonprofit organization headquartered in Washington, D.C. It endeavors to protect wilderness areas through collaborations with other environmental groups and educational endeavors, rooted in science, for individual citizens, landholders, conservation groups, and politicians at all levels of government. Its efforts have resulted in the acquisition of approximately 110 million acres for the National Wilderness Preservation System.

The organization, founded in 1935, included among its founders Benton MacKaye, Robert Sterling Yard, Robert Marshall, and Aldo Leopold. They were guided by a "land ethic" philosophy espoused by Leopold. They intended for their group to lead the effort to save the vanishing wilderness areas of the United States. Their foresight was confirmed in 1964, when the Wilderness Act was signed into law by President Lyndon Baines Johnson. The legislation had been authored by Howard Zahniser, who had served as the Wilderness Society's executive secretary.

In addition to working towards getting more land designated as protected wilderness areas, the society continues to help push legislation through the political process in Washington, D.C. The Wilderness Society has contributed to the passage of basically every bill that impacts the environment since its founding, including the Wild and Scenic Rivers Act, the National Forest Management Act, the National Wildlife Refuge Improvement Act, and the California Desert Protection Act of 1994.

—John R. Burch Jr.

See also: *Wilderness Act of 1964*

BIBLIOGRAPHY

Harvey, Mark W. T. *A Symbol of Wilderness: Echo Park and the American Conservation Movement.* Seattle: University of Washington Press, 2000.
Harvey, Mark W. T. *Wilderness Forever: Howard Zahniser and the Path to the Wilderness Act.* Seattle: University of Washington Press, 2005.
The Wilderness Society. http://www.wilderness.org/.

McPhee, John. *Encounters with the Archdruid.* New York: Farrar, Straus and Giroux, 1971.
Palmer, Tim. *Endangered Rivers and the Conservation Movement.* Rev. ed. Lanham, MD: Rowman and Littlefield, 2004.
Palmer, Tim. *The Wild and Scenic Rivers of America.* Washington, DC: Island Press, 1993.
Wild and Scenic Rivers Act of 1968, Pub. L. No. 90-542, 16 U.S.C. §1271–87 (1968). http://www.rivers.gov/publications/wsr-act.pdf.

Wilderness Act of 1964

The Wilderness Act of 1964 established the first federally recognized legal definition of *wilderness* and created the National Wilderness Preservation System (NWPS). This legislation, signed into law on September 3, 1964, by President Lyndon B. Johnson, initially protected approximately 9.1 million acres of land and installed mechanisms for the management of those lands. The Act also allowed for future expansion by granting Congress the authority to add other lands through legislation.

Wilderness Protection

Protecting wilderness through federal legislation may have began in part with the creation of the first National Parks and National Forests during the late nineteenth century, but federal designation did not protect specified lands from the incursion of roads or structures, dams, or reservoirs or from extractive industries such as lumbering or mining. The idea of protecting certain publicly held lands as "wilderness" dates only to the 1920s, when a regional office of the U.S. Forest Service (USFS) independently designated over 500,000 acres of Gila National Forest as "wilderness." This action encouraged the USFS to consider a nationwide wilderness system, which came to fruition in 1929 with the Forest Service's "L-20" regulations. The L-20 regulations set apart certain National Forest lands as "primitive areas." The management concept governing the "primitive areas" was that these lands should not be developed or used for human purposes. However, nothing stopped the USFS from backing away from the original intention of establishing "primitive areas," and no legal framework existed to protect these lands from extractive uses or development.

The L-20 regulations were replaced in 1939 by the "U" regulations. The U regulations provided stricter oversight than the L-20 regulations for the protection of primitive areas, but the new regulations did not apply immediately. In fact, the regulations required that the USFS first review and reclassify all of its primitive area holdings, totaling approximately 14 million acres as of 1939, to determine which ones should be protected under the U system. The authority to reclassify these lands was granted to the secretary of agriculture. The reclassification process would take decades and, in 1964, remain unfinished. This lengthy process galvanized conservation organizations against the USFS and its new regulations.

Drafting the Wilderness Act

The vulnerability of National Park and National Monument lands also became apparent in 1950 when the federal government proposed to build Echo Park Dam on the Green River in Dinosaur National Monument. Conservation organizations such as the Wilderness Society fought passionately against the Echo Park proposal. Serving as executive secretary of the Wilderness Society at this time was Howard Zahniser. When Congress passed the Colorado River Storage Project Act in 1956, the removal of the Echo Park Dam proposal from this legislation signaled a landmark victory for conservationists. The struggle over Echo Park led Howard Zahniser of the Wilderness Society to the belief that if wilderness were to be protected, such protection would have to be put into law by Congress rather than be left to the discretion of the federal agencies overseeing public lands.

During the spring and summer of 1956, Zahniser wrote a first draft of what would be the Wilderness Act. The original bill was written to prohibit logging, grazing, mining, road construction, and motorized vehicle traffic, among other nonconforming uses, in the 14 million acres of National Forest wilderness, wild, and primitive areas. The bill had little support in 1956, especially within the USFS and National Park Service, both of whom opposed the bill. In the eight years that followed, Congress debated various versions of the Wilderness Act. Resistance to these proposed bills was most aggressive and incessant from those interests seeking to profit from mining, ranching, and water development.

Congressional Debates

When the Wilderness Act was first proposed to Congress in 1956, state water agencies in the West strongly opposed the bill. Senator Thomas Kuchel (R-CA) was a particularly

Howard Zahniser

Howard Clinton Zahniser served the Wilderness Society as executive secretary, beginning in 1945, and became its executive director in 1962. He forged a partnership with David Brower of the Sierra Club that proved instrumental in saving the Dinosaur National Monument from being flooded by the construction of the Echo Park Dam. His greatest legacy was the passage of the Wilderness Act.

Zahniser was born on February 25, 1906. He received his undergraduate degree from Greenville College in Illinois in 1928. In 1931, he began employment in the Department of Agriculture's Bureau of Biological Survey. From 1942 to 1945, he worked in the Bureau of Plant Industry, Soils and Agricultural Engineering for the Department of Agriculture. Disillusionment with the federal government led to him join the Wilderness Society's professional staff.

While working for the Wilderness Society, he helped David Brower create coalitions of environmental groups to advance an activist agenda. From 1956 to 1964, he crafted and shepherded various versions of the Wilderness Act through the U.S. Congress. As the Wilderness Act was on the verge of passage, Zahniser suffered a heart attack. He died on May 5, 1964, four months before President Lyndon B. Johnson signed the Wilderness Act of 1964 into law.

—John R. Burch Jr.

See also: Echo Park Dam

BIBLIOGRAPHY

Harvey, Mark W. T. A Symbol of Wilderness: Echo Park and the American Conservation Movement. Seattle: University of Washington Press, 2000.
Harvey, Mark W. T. Wilderness Forever: Howard Zahniser and the Path to the Wilderness Act. Seattle: University of Washington Press, 2005.

vocal opponent of the original Wilderness Act, and it was Kuchel's influence that eventually forced Zahniser in 1958 to add a clause granting presidential authority to permit reservoirs in wilderness areas. Facing mounting opposition from state water agencies, in 1959 Zahniser added yet another clause to the bill, stating that the Act did not exempt the federal government from following state water laws. Even with this new language, opposition to the bill continued. In August 1959, western senators introduced an amendment to the bill granting Congress sole authority to add new wilderness lands to the system, thereby giving themselves considerable authority to block any future expansion of the wilderness system if they so chose. In September 1961, Senator Clinton Anderson (D-NM) pushed the bill, with all its new amendments, through the Senate where it passed 78–8. However, the bill failed in the House as Rep. Wayne Aspinall (D-CO) tied up the bill, thereby delaying a House vote until the congressional session expired. During 1962 and 1963, Aspinall was the Wilderness Act's greatest foe. For Aspinall, the most important criterion for acceptance of the bill was that it must grant Congress sole authority to designate new wilderness lands. Aspinall's influence on the final language of the Wilderness Act should not be understated.

In July 1964, the House followed the Senate's lead and finally passed the Wilderness Act 374–1. The Act was a compromise at best, but it was held as a watershed event in the history of American environmentalism. Since the passage of the Act, Congress has exercised its authority to designate new wilderness areas time and time again. In so doing, Congress has added over 100 million acres of wilderness to the NWPS. As of May 2009, the NWPS comprised 756 wilderness areas within 44 states, a total of nearly 109.5 million acres. Perhaps the most lasting influence of the Wilderness Act is its language. The bill's definition of wilderness as "an area where the earth and its community of life are untrammeled by man, where man himself is a visitor who does not remain" (Wilderness Act 1964, § 2[c]) has inspired both politicians and ordinary citizens worldwide to reimagine their relationship with nature.

—Gregory Rosenthal

See also: *Aspinall, Wayne N.; Echo Park Dam*

BIBLIOGRAPHY

Harvey, Mark. *Wilderness Forever: Howard Zahniser and the Path to the Wilderness Act.* Seattle: University of Washington Press, 2005.

Nash, Roderick Frazier. *Wilderness and the American Mind.* 4th ed. New Haven, CT: Yale University Press, 2001.

Scott, Doug. *The Enduring Wilderness: Protecting Our National Heritage through the Wilderness Act.* Golden, CO: Fulcrum, 2004.

Wilderness Act of 1964, Pub. L. No. 88-577, 16 U.S.C. § 1131–36. http://www.wilderness.net/index.cfm?fuse=NWPS&sec=legisAct.

Wilderness Institute at the University of Montana, the Arthur Carhart National Wilderness Training Center, and the Aldo Leopold Wilderness Research Institute. "Wilderness.net." http://www.wilderness.net.

Winters v. United States (1908)

Winters v. United States was argued before the U.S. Supreme Court on October 24, 1907, and was formally decided on January 6, 1908. It is the landmark case that established how the federal government would view American Indian water rights in the western United States, giving American Indian tribes the potential right to make vast claims on the scarce waters of the West.

Prior to the *Winters* decision, many western states determined water ownership based on when landholders had appropriated their water rights. The individual with the earliest claim could use the water as he or she saw fit as long as the water was used beneficially. *Winters v. United States* created an implied reserved right to the water required by Native American groups on reservations that prioritized them over other landholders. The status change was justified through the federal treaty process. At the time the respective tribes negotiated the creation of their reservations, they made land concessions in exchange for lands that were to be permanently reserved for their use. In the *Winters* decision, the Supreme Court ruled that when the tribes agreed to this trade-off, they retained all rights not specified in the treaty. Ownership of reservation lands retained all of the rights of landowners, including water rights, and in the context of the doctrine of prior appropriation, *Winters* gave the tribes the earliest possible priority date of "time immemorial," making their water claims, in theory, superior to any non-Indian claims. However, despite the codification of this idea in what became known as the "Winters Doctrine" in 1908, western states would continue to ignore the precedent for more than a half century.

Origins

The case had its origins before the establishment of Montana. In 1874, the federal government reserved significant portions of what would become Montana for the use of a number of Native American groups, including the Gros Ventre, Blackfeet, and Crow. Within the decade, U.S. citizens began clamoring for the land occupied by the native groups. The federal government subsequently made a number of new treaties that included additional land cessions by the Indian peoples. One of these treaties, negotiated in 1888, created the Fort Belknap Native Reservation for the Gros Ventre and the Assiniboine. The Indian tribes got a much smaller reservation, while large amounts of land were returned to the federal government and subsequently redistributed to the general public.

The Milk River formed the northern boundary of the reservation. Beginning in 1889, its waters were used to irrigate the reservation's land, which was necessary for both raising crops and pasturing animal herds. As the reservation's agricultural processes grew, so did its need for water. By 1898, the reservation was irrigating approximately 30,000 acres of land.

Through the Homestead and Desert Land Acts, a number of other interests emerged that also had designs on the waters of the Milk River. Henry Winters, the Matheson Ditch Company, and Cook's Irrigation Company all began posting the necessary signage upriver of the Fort Belknap Reservation to become official settlers and make the necessary claims to own the waters of the Milk River for their purposes. After the required posting period, the respective entrepreneurs began constructing dams, reservoirs, and ditches in order to impound the river's waters. Winters's Empire Cattle Company quickly bought out the other companies, thereby acquiring their rights to the Milk River. Winters and his business associates believed that their water claims predated that of the Indians who resided in the relatively new Fort Belknap Native Reservation.

The United States sued Henry Winters, John W. Acker, Chris Cruse, Agnes Downs, and the Empire Cattle Company in order to stop their water diversions. The federal government won in both the district court and the appeals court. Winters appealed to the U.S. Supreme Court. In an 8–1 decision, Winters's appeal was denied. In truth, the case was not decided on its merits but on a technicality. Since it was determined that the American Indian groups of the Fort Belknap Indian Reservation had an implied water right, the justices never had to judge the merits of the arguments made by Winters and the other members of the Empire Cattle Company. This oversight allowed western states to ignore the implications of *Winters v. United States* for decades, since they could argue that it was a very narrow decision impacting one reservation. The true ramifications of *Winters v. United States* would not be unquestionably revealed until the conclusion of *Arizona v. California* in 1963.

—John R. Burch Jr.

See also: *American Indian Water Rights; American Indian Water Settlements; Arizona v. California (1963)*

MNI Sose Intertribal Water Rights Coalition

The MNI Sose Intertribal Water Rights Coalition is a nonprofit corporation founded in 1993 by twenty-eight sovereign Indian nations whose homelands are located in the Missouri River Basin. The coalition's members work together to address issues related to Native American water rights, especially as they relate to the Winters Doctrine. The organization has also endeavored to ensure that its members receive equitable benefits from the Flood Control Act of 1944, such as access to low-cost hydroelectric power generated by the Missouri River. The coalition has strengthened its respective member tribes through educational endeavors and access to technical assistance. The organization also facilitates communication among members through its computer network.

In addition to promoting partnerships among member nations, the coalition also works to forge relationships with environmental groups, stakeholders that rely on the Missouri River for water and or hydroelectric power, and government agencies at all levels. These relationships, such as the one established with the Environmental Protection Agency, are intended to ensure that the respective Native American nations play an active role in helping to make decisions that impact their homelands. They also allow for member nations to gain the administrative and technical knowledge they require to manage their own water resources.

—John R. Burch Jr.

See also: *American Indian Water Rights; Environmental Protection Agency, United States; Flood Control Act of 1944; Missouri River Basin; Winters v. United States (1908)*

BIBLIOGRAPHY
Bad Moccasin, Richard. "MNI Sose Intertribal Water Rights Coalition." In *Encyclopedia of the Great Plains*, edited by David J. Wishart, 856. Lincoln: University of Nebraska Press, 2004.
Environmental Protection Agency, Region 7. "The MNI Sose Intertribal Water Rights." http://www.epa.gov/region7/citizens/care/mnisose.htm.

BIBLIOGRAPHY
Burton, Lloyd. *American Indian Water Rights and the Limits of Law.* Lawrence: University Press of Kansas, 1991.
Fowler, Loretta. *Shared Symbols, Contested Meanings: Gros Ventre Culture and History, 1778–1984.* Ithaca, NY: Cornell University Press, 1987.
McCool, Daniel. *Command of the Waters: Iron Triangles, Federal Water Development, and Indian Water.* Berkeley: University of California Press, 1987.
Pisani, Donald J. *Water, Land, and Law in the West: The Limits of Public Policy, 1850–1920.* Lawrence: University Press of Kansas, 1996.
Shurts, John. *Indian Reserved Water Rights: The Winters Doctrine in Its Social and Legal Context, 1880s–1930s.* Norman: University of Oklahoma Press, 2000.
"*Winters v. The United States.* No. 158. Supreme Court of the United States 207 U.S. 564; 28 S. Ct. 207, 52 L. Ed. 340; 1908 U.S. Lexis 1415." LexisNexis Academic. http://www.lexisnexis.com/.

Part IV Places and Projects

402

Adirondack Park

The Adirondack Park in northern New York is the largest contiguous protected area in the lower 48 states, a park containing more than 2,800 lakes and ponds, 1,200 miles of rivers, and an estimated 30,000 miles of brooks and streams. Established in 1892, the Adirondack Park is older than every National Park except Yellowstone (1872) and Yosemite (1890) and, at roughly 6 million acres, is almost three times the size of Yellowstone. Frequently overlooked in the American park system due to its status as a state, rather than a national park, the Adirondack Park is nevertheless one of the most important land-use experiments in American history, a unique mixture of public and private lands that contains nearly 90 percent of the designated wilderness east of the Mississippi River, interspersed around and between the private holdings of nearly 150,000 permanent and 200,000 seasonal residents.

Establishment of the Adirondack Park was driven by a variety of factors, including forest health and outdoor recreation, but it was the abundance of freshwater that inspired New York citizens to push for protection of the region beginning in the 1860s. New York led the nation in timber production in 1850, when more than a billion board-feet of Adirondack timber were shipped to mills via the region's extensive river system (Harris 2008), leading to anxiety among downstate business interests that denuded watersheds might compromise flows on Adirondack waterways, including the Hudson River and Erie Canal. Fire from cinders spewed by the locomotives that eventually cut into the heart of the region added to the worries of early advocates of forest protection. These dual concerns led the legislature to establish a Forest Preserve in 1885 and, seven years later, a formal park boundary (later referred to as the "Blue Line"). Then, in 1894, the state-owned lands within the Park were declared "forever wild" via the addition of Article VII, Section 7 to the New York State Constitution, making the Adirondack Forest Preserve the most strongly protected land in the nation.

Despite the protection afforded Forest Preserve lands, numerous proposals were put forth to construct large-scale hydroelectric dams in Adirondack Park. Although a small amount (up to 3%) of Forest Preserve land had been set aside for reservoirs through the passage of the Burd Amendment in 1913, these reservoirs were intended primarily for municipal water supply and stream-flow regulation rather than for power generation (Graham 1984).

What's more, the patchwork nature of public-private land ownership essentially created a de facto barrier to the construction of large dams, which required the flooding of large contiguous areas. Still, the Machold Storage Law (1915) established river-regulating districts throughout the state, and eventually two large impoundments were constructed inside the Blue Line: the Stillwater Reservoir in 1922 and the Sacandaga Reservoir in 1930. However, both of these projects were built for flood control primarily, with power generation included as a secondary benefit.

Regardless of the obstacles to large-scale dam building in the Park, proponents were encouraged by former New York governor and now President Franklin Roosevelt's establishment of the Tennessee Valley Authority (TVA) in 1933. The TVA, a New Deal organization formed specifically for the purpose of harnessing the rivers of the Tennessee Valley, was seen by many as a model of social engineering, an organization "clothed with the power of government but possessed of the flexibility and initiative of a private enterprise" (Roosevelt, quoted in TVA n.d., ¶ 1). The most significant Adirondack proposals were put forward by the Black River Regulating District for dams on the Moose River, near Panther and Higley Mountains. First proposed in the 1920s, the proposals gained traction during the Depression and began to move forward in the early 1940s.

The legal, political, and public relations battle that ensued came to be known as the "Black River War," pitting utilitarian conservationists against strict preservation advocates. The latter group was headed by a tireless Forest Preserve devotee named Paul Schaefer, a home builder from Schenectady. Although aligned against powerful, moneyed interests from all over New York State, Schaefer's grassroots organization, Friends of the Forest Preserve, proved adept at garnering and mobilizing public support for the protectionist stance. Using techniques such as mail campaigns and documentary filmmaking, it not only defeated the dam proposals (via the Ostrander Amendment in 1953) but ushered in a new national perspective about the costs of large-scale dam building, one that would set the benefits of flood control, improved navigation, and clean power against the costs of increased siltation, damage to fisheries, and destruction of lowland forests.

—Jeffrey B. Flagg

See also: *Erie Canal; Roosevelt, Franklin D.; Tennessee Valley Authority*

BIBLIOGRAPHY

Graham, Frank, Jr. *The Adirondack Park: A Political History*. Special research by Ada Graham. Syracuse, NY: Syracuse University Press, 1984. Originally published 1978 by Knopf.

Harris, Philip J. *Adirondack: Lumber Capital of the World*. Frederick, MD: PublishAmerica, 2008.

TVA (Tennessee Valley Authority). "TVA: From the New Deal to a New Century." http://www.tva.gov/abouttva/history.htm.

All-American Canal

The All-American Canal, believed to be the largest irrigation canal in the world, is situated along the hot and arid divide between the United States and Mexico. This irrigation canal stretches for eighty-two miles (132 km), conveying 26,155 cubic feet of water per second from the Colorado River to the Imperial Valley in California. There is no other source of drinking water for the nine cities it serves and no alternative form of irrigation for the fourth most productive agricultural region in the United States, comprising 500,000 acres.

The All-American Canal, finished in 1942, is the world's largest irrigation canal. Located near the U.S.-Mexico border, it is said to be the nation's most dangerous body of water, with several people drowning in it each year.

Bureau of Reclamation, Lower Colorado Region

At the time of the 1919 All-American Canal survey report, the situation of the lower Colorado River was both unique and complex due to the physical characteristics of the river and the delta cone; the international boundary line; and human modifications to the river, its delta, and channels. It was argued that had the character of the Colorado River been better known, it would never have been made part of the boundary between the United States and Mexico.

The river had a history of flooding and changing the direction of its flow. For example, Native Americans confirmed that the Colorado River had once emptied into the Salton Basin, forming an inland sea (now called the Salton Sea). The river's temperamental nature required the increasingly burdensome and complicated maintenance of barriers, then the task of the Imperial Navigation District. Sediment buildup also prevented navigation. However, the livelihood and survival of many depended on the river's regular flow.

Work began on surveying the area around the Laguna Dam to divert water into the Imperial Valley at the end of the nineteenth century. These surveys followed the right bank of the Colorado River and stayed near the international boundary line between the United States and Mexico. In 1916–1917, the Imperial-Laguna Water Company made surveys for an All-American Canal that ran parallel with the international boundary.

The preliminary plans formed at the beginning of the twentieth century highlight the engineering and other challenges that the proposed canal posed. At this time, more land was being brought under cultivation, and more water was needed. The Imperial Irrigation District, which was responsible for the delivery of water, struggled with water losses and capacity constraints. Blowing sand that filled the canal was another difficulty, but the planting of grass and shrubs on ridges on either side overcame it.

The current 82 miles of All-American Canal, featuring a total drop of 175 feet, a width varying from 150 to 700 feet, and a depth varying from 7 to 50 feet, were completed in 1942. The canal was built by the Bureau of Reclamation, which owns the canal, but the Imperial Irrigation District manages its operation. Water is diverted to a number of large and small branches. From east to west, the main four branches are the Coachella Canal, East Highline Canal, Central Canal, and Westside Main Canal. These four branches as well as the wider network of canals mean a much reduced amount of water finally drains into the Westside Main Canal.

While crop yields have increased due to irrigation, there are problems with drainage and salinity. Desilting basins are needed so that sediment does not fill the canal. Also, the lack of a lining leads to considerable seepage, so the All-American Canal Lining Project is building a new concrete-lined stretch.

There are now eight hydroelectric power plants along the canal. They are relatively small, and their electricity generation depends on water delivery needs. Storage reservoirs were envisioned in 1919 to improve water supply provision throughout the entire basin of the river, and today the Imperial Irrigation District has regulating reservoirs for water storage. The Senator Wash Reservoir also functions as an off-stream regulating reservoir for the canal.

The All-American Canal is a vital means of supplying water to California's Imperial Valley, and it plays a role in managing the Colorado River.

—Julia Fallon

See also: *Bureau of Reclamation; Colorado River Basin*

BIBLIOGRAPHY

Hundley, Norris, Jr. *The Great Thirst: Californians and Water—A History*. Rev. ed. Berkeley: University of California Press, 2001.

Mead, Elwood, W. W. Schlecht, C. E. Grunsky, and Porter J. Preston. *The All-American Canal: Report of the All-American Canal Board*. Washington, DC: Government Printing Office, 1920.

Starr, Kevin. *Golden Dreams: California in an Age of Abundance, 1950–1963*. New York: Oxford University Press, 2009.

Waterman, Jonathan. *Running Dry: A Journey From Source to Sea Down the Colorado River*. Washington, DC: National Geographic, 2010.

Allatoona Dam

When Allatoona Dam was constructed in 1949 on the Etowah River in Georgia, north of Atlanta, it created Lake Allatoona and flooded the former gold-mining settlement of the same name. The population of the township had fallen considerably after the Civil War, and the remaining inhabitants were relocated when the dam was built. The dam was named after Allatoona Creek.

The building of Allatoona Dam was authorized by the Flood Control Acts of 1941 and of 1946 to hold back some of the water from the Etowah River before it merged with the Ostanaula River and then with the Coosa River at the township of Rome. The dam reduced the flooding of agricultural land in nearby areas and created a dependable water supply. It also generated hydropower for cotton mills, livestock farms, and houses in the region. Another benefit was the recreational lake it created.

The U.S. Army Corps of Engineers started building the dam in April 1946 under the direction of resident engineer Charles A. Jackson. Jackson had worked on the construction of the Conchas Dam in New Mexico and the John Martin Dam in Colorado. The Allatoona Dam is a gravity-type structure with a gate that controls the spillway that rises 190 feet above the river bed. Made from 500,000 cubic yards of concrete, the dam was designed with four outlet conduits. The cost of construction, including the relocation of the local population, the purchase and clearing of the land, and other costs, came to $31.5 million.

Initially the dam worked well, and after the power plant started operation on January 31, 1950, the energy generated served the local cotton industry. Two of the three turbines at the start of the project generated 50,000 horsepower each. The original plan was for Lake Allatoona to have a shoreline of 260 miles, cover an area of 20,300 acres, and have maximum water storage of 389,000 acre-feet. At its peak, Lake Allatoona reached 861.19 feet in depth. However, during the 1980s, there was a severe drought, which reached its peak in 1986. This considerably reduced the amount of water in Lake Allatoona. The area exposed by the lower water level revealed many tree stumps, old roads, and even the foundations of farm buildings. Local children soon began to play in the exposed areas.

In 2006, it was estimated that the building of the Allatoona Dam had saved $80 million in flood prevention, and the hydroelectric power it generated earned the federal treasury $3.5 million each year. In addition, about $1 million in fees were collected from campers—the Corps of Engineers operated 662 campsites at the lake—and other recreational users. It was also noted that 281 people had drowned in the lake over the same 56-year period, many while fishing or sailing. Lake Allatoona was reported to be the most frequently visited lake in Georgia because of its fishing facilities; it is especially popular with people from Atlanta, who have easy access to the lake.

—Justin Corfield

See also: *Army Corps of Engineers, United States*

BIBLIOGRAPHY

Popham, John N. "Big Dam in Georgia Nears Completion." *New York Times*, October 2, 1949.

Animas–La Plata Project

The Animas–La Plata Project (A-LP) has the dubious distinction of being the last and one of the most expensive and controversial large water projects ever to be undertaken by the Bureau of Reclamation. Congress originally authorized A-LP to benefit farmers growing low-value crops in the La Plata River Basin in southwest Colorado and northwest New Mexico. Escalating costs and environmental problems attracted many critics of A-LP, and for over three decades the project sat as varying interests debated its future. The project continued to be considered and was eventually reauthorized in 2000 primarily because in the 1980s, national and local politicians, water users, and federal agencies reengineered A-LP as an Indian water project that would satisfy Ute tribes' long-standing claim to water development on their reservations. Since 2000, Reclamation has constructed a pumping plant on the Animas River, a conduit, and a storage reservoir at Ridges Basin. A-LP will not be fully functional, however, until nonfederal government cost-sharing partners put up the money to construct distribution lines to the Ute Indian reservations the project is intended to serve.

The Animas and La Plata Rivers are two south-flowing tributaries of the San Juan River. The larger of the two rivers, Animas River, rises in the San Miguel and Needle Mountains and flows in a southerly direction through a deep and narrow canyon for most of its course before opening up into a broad valley about fifteen miles north of Durango, Colorado. To the west of Animas River over a divide is the La Plata River, which also runs in a southerly direction from the San Juan Mountains. For years, white landowners in the La Plata River Basin have irrigated and dry-farmed on a small scale. The idea behind A-LP was to divert water from the more voluminous Animas River over the divide to the La Plata River Basin where the land was more suitable for agriculture.

The Bureau of Reclamation contemplated a diversion project on the Animas River from 1904 to 1906 but concluded that the rough character of the land made any diversion plan impracticable. Private irrigation interests subsequently considered similar water projects, but, again, nothing came of these proposals. Reclamation returned to the idea in a 1924 report, then studied the idea more thoroughly beginning in 1938. In 1954, it issued a report contemplating irrigation delivery to 66,020 acres in Colorado and 20,600 acres in New Mexico. But it was no simple project, either technically or politically. The complexity of the project derived from the water rights and supply issues across two water basins and two states and its large price tag.

As the projects were moved from the drawing board to the halls of Congress, A-LP underwent a substantial facelift. Developed in 1962 as an irrigation project, at the behest of the Bureau of the Budget (the predecessor of today's Office of Management and Budget), it shed a large chunk of irrigated acreage and reallocated the water to municipal and industrial purposes. A-LP also became tied up in larger debates over development in the Colorado River Basin, especially the Central Arizona Project (CAP). Rep. Wayne Aspinall (D-CO) decided to slip A-LP and other upper basin water projects into the Colorado River Basin Project Act, which was authorized on September 30, 1968 (Pub. L. 84-485).

Despite the provision in the Act that A-LP would be built concurrently with CAP, little progress was made on A-LP. The project was still saddled with economic and environmental problems. Consequently, opposition to the project had begun to coalesce. Moreover, the federal government had become weary of funding large-scale projects. The Reagan administration cut funding for water projects and required local communities and interests to participate in cost-sharing initiatives. In 1985, Rep. Mike Strang (R-CO) successfully inserted A-LP start-up funding in the supplemental fiscal year appropriations, contingent on water users reaching a cost-sharing agreement. State and local interests reached an agreement in 1986. In negotiations over cost sharing, it had been decided that the project should be the cornerstone of the Ute Indian water rights settlement.

The question of Indian water rights derives from the moment Congress carved out reservations for Indian tribes. Prior appropriation governed water law in the West, but in general, Native tribes lacked the means to develop water within their borders. Indians won a major victory in 1908 when the Supreme Court ruled in *Winters v. United States* that water rights on reservations would be maintained. Since the decision, tribes have turned to the courts to claim water that, in many cases, has already been diverted and used upstream of the reservation. Realizing that resolving the issue out of court would be preferable, various water interests and the Ute Mountain Ute and Southern Ute tribes began to hammer out a settlement that provided for the full resolution of Indian water rights claims through construction of A-LP. Congress passed the Colorado Ute Indian Water Rights Settlement Act in 1988.

Beneath the surface of these agreements lay discontent. Some tribal members objected to the settlement. The project was also extremely unpopular among environmentalists, who fought the project on economic and environmental grounds. Critics of the dam won a major victory when in 1991, the Fish and Wildlife Service issued a final opinion that the full water project would affect the Colorado pike-minnow, an endangered species. In subsequent years, an alternative plan was drafted, which was referred to as A-LP "lite." This plan would still implement the Indian water rights settlement but would irrigate much less acreage. Still controversial, the Colorado Ute Settlement Act Amendments of 2000 were enacted by Congress. Construction on the scaled-down project—Ridges Basin Dam and Reservoir, Durango Pumping Plant, Ridges Basin Inlet conduit—began shortly after authorization. Eventually, a pipeline extending to the Navajo Nation at Shiprock, New Mexico, will need to be constructed so that water from the project will actually be made available to user groups it is intended to serve.

—Jedediah Rogers

See also: *American Indian Water Rights; Bureau of Reclamation; Winters v. United States (1908)*

BIBLIOGRAPHY

Animas–La Plata Project Collection (M 092). Center of Southwest Studies, Fort Lewis College, Durango, CO.

Ingram, Helen M. *Water Politics: Continuity and Change.* Albuquerque: University of New Mexico Press, 1990.

U.S. Bureau of Reclamation. *Definite Plan Report: Animas–La Plata Project, Colorado–New Mexico.* Denver, CO: U.S. Bureau of Reclamation, 1979.

Wayne N. Aspinall Papers (M008). Department of Special Collections and Archives, Penrose Library, University of Denver.

Arkansas River Basin

The Arkansas River rises from mountain runoff near Leadville, Colorado, and ends by entering the Mississippi River after traversing some 1,460 miles. The sixth-longest American river drains almost 195,000 square miles, an area ranging from the Rocky Mountains to almost all of north Arkansas.

The river consists of distinct components. A mountain stream from its source near Leadville to Canon City, Colorado, it is noted for mountain scenery, notably Royal Gorge, and is used by white-water enthusiasts and fly fishers. The second phase of the river is that of a meandering Great Plains stream. Beginning in the 1870s, the river's waters began to be used for irrigation. Salinity eventually affected not only the fields but also the nearby parts of the High Plains aquifer. In the 1950s, farmers turned to groundwater wells. Consumptive pumping lowered the surface water, further reducing the stream flow. Excessive consumption of water from the High Plains aquifer resulted in the Arkansas River becoming a sinking stream from the Colorado state line to Dodge City, Kansas.

Water quality does not improve since the river picks up salt from underlying bedrock in the Arkansas River Lowlands and the Wellington-McPherson Lowlands. Hence, the Arkansas River in Kansas currently presents problems of freshwater saline contamination, lowered groundwater tables, and high nitrate concentrations. Additional saline elements can be found in Oklahoma.

Oklahoma's Kaw Dam, completed in 1976, was the first of the dams on the Arkansas River. Erected for flood control, it also generates electricity. Keystone Dam was completed in 1964 for flood control, with a generating plant being added in 1968. Several regionally important streams enter the Arkansas River in Oklahoma, notably the Salt Fork, Neosho (Grand), and Illinois. The lower Verdigris is utilized as the Arkansas River's head of navigation at Catoosa. The Webbers Falls Lock and Dam cover the former site of a rock escarpment that once posed a major obstacle to navigation. Other Oklahoma components of the McClellan-Kerr Arkansas River Navigation System include the Robert S. Kerr Lock and Dam, the Chouteau, and the W. D. Mayo. Because the Arkansas River in Oklahoma has long been a rich source of high-quality sand and other valuable features, litigation over the issue of federal takings of tribal rights has reached the U.S. Supreme Court repeatedly (*Choctaw Nation v. Oklahoma* [1970] and *U.S. v. Cherokee Nation* [1987]). A claims settlement act passed by Congress in 2002 eventually compensated the Cherokee, Choctaw, and Chickasaw nations $40 million for past damages and for dry riverbeds and affirmed the tribes' custody of active river channels.

The Arkansas River in Arkansas is entirely a part of the McClellan-Kerr Navigation System, except for a short section where the system utilizes the former White River cut-off as a canal. Thirteen locks and dams make up the system. Flood control has remained one justification for the construction of the McClellan-Kerr Arkansas Navigation System, which was completed in 1971. The series of dams effectively removed sediment from the river, thus creating numerous recreational opportunities.

—Michael B. Dougan

See also: *American Indian Water Rights; McClellan-Kerr Waterway*

BIBLIOGRAPHY

Bolton, S. Charles. *25 Years Later: A History of the McClellan-Kerr Arkansas River Navigation System in Arkansas.* Little Rock, AR: U.S. Army Corps of Engineers, Little Rock District, 1995.

Clay, Floyd M. *A History of the Little Rock District, U.S. Army Corps of Engineers, 1881–1979.* Washington, DC: U.S. Government Printing Office, 1979.

Davis, Clyde Brion. *The Arkansas.* New York: Farrar & Rinehart, 1940.

Mapes, Ruth B. *The Arkansas Waterway: People, Places, Events in the Valley, 1817–1971.* Little Rock, AR.: University Press, 1972.

Staub, Frank J. *The Upper Arkansas River: Rapids, History, and Nature, Mile by Mile; From Granite to the Pueblo Reservation.* With contributions by Peter Anderson. Golden, CO: Fulcrum, 1988.

Auburn Dam

Auburn Dam, like Glen Canyon Dam, is among the most controversial federal water projects. When Congress authorized the Auburn-Folsom South Unit of California's Central Valley Project in 1965, the Bureau of Reclamation designed the dam on the American River as a star in its pantheon of large dams. The government eventually spent over $300 million on foundation work, a diversion tunnel, studies testing seismic conditions, cost-benefit analyses, and dam design, but none of this ultimately led to project completion. Conceived originally as a multipurpose project primarily catering to irrigation and water interests in central California, the dam became a local and even national battleground for nearly half a century. At issue were the project's cost feasibility, dam safety, water rights, and environmental concerns.

The American River, a Sacramento River tributary, is located about midway between the northern and southern extremes of the Central Valley in Sacramento, San Joaquin, Placer, and El Dorado Counties. Auburn lies at the western edge of this landscape in the foothills where the low and high countries converge. The dam at Auburn had been designed to link the two regions—to store water from the mountains and to capture flood runoff before it devastated the populous land below.

Flooding

Since the establishment of Sacramento and towns like Auburn in the Sierra foothills during the 1849 Gold Rush,

flooding has been a perennial concern. People built levies to keep the streams and rivers in their beds. Folsom Dam, built by the U.S. Army Corps of Engineers, and the proposed Auburn Dam were among those structures designed to tame the erratic river. The endgame was not merely flood control, however. Large dams on the American River reflected the Progressive Era notion that the state's water resources ought to be controlled and utilized to the last drop to create an agricultural empire in the Central Valley. The problem was water allocation—the possibility of diverting water from the well-watered northern part of the state to the drier yet fertile valleys in the south where farms and towns could be established. In 1933, the state legislature passed the Central Valley Project Act to authorize a massive water scheme to be funded primarily by state bonds; in 1937, Congress reauthorized the project to be constructed under provisions of federal reclamation laws for river regulation, navigation, flood control, irrigation, and power.

Federal engineers originally designed Auburn Dam as a 700-foot-high earth-fill dam. Fearing the low quality of earth-fill materials and difficulty in securing them, they changed the design to a thin double-curvature-arch dam, which would have been the longest such span in the world. For over a decade, work crews constructed a long, steel-truss bridge over a portion of the planned reservoir, built the diversion tunnel, and prepared the foundation for the arch dam.

Controversies

Environmental groups opposed the dam on grounds that it adversely affected the canyon and river. They filed suit, attempting to delay construction pending a review of the environmental impact report. That environmentalists called into question the basis of a dam at Auburn at a time when the antidam movement had begun to generate momentum should come as no surprise. However, two events entirely unrelated to environmental opposition derailed the construction of Auburn Dam. The first was a 5.7-magnitude earthquake on August 1, 1975, that struck Oroville, California, about forty-five miles from Auburn. A second nonlocalized event probably did as much to change the trajectory of Auburn Dam as the earthquake at Oroville—the catastrophic collapse of the Bureau of Reclamation's new earthen dam on the Teton River in southeastern Idaho on June 5, 1976. Both events gave rise to safety concerns of a dam at Auburn. If the dam were to collapse, a wall of water would wash out Folsom Dam and imperil the lives and property of people along the American River, including in Sacramento.

In 1977, President Jimmy Carter listed Auburn Dam among those water projects he planned to cut or modify. The Bureau and the state of California initiated major seismic and geologic reviews of the dam site to determine the location of fault lines and the type of structure best suited for the area. In 1980, Carter's interior secretary, Cecil Andrus, responded to the studies and announced that a safe dam could be built if issues of water rights and costs versus benefits could be worked out.

If the major issue at Auburn prior to 1980 was dam safety, after 1980 it was economics and flood control. The price tag of the dam jumped as the Bureau of Reclamation proposed construction of a large concrete dam. During the Reagan era, attempts were made to convince local water organizations and municipalities to share the costs of constructing the multipurpose dam. Politicians like Reps. Norman Shumway (R-CA) and John Doolittle (R-CA) introduced legislation for further studies and reauthorization of a multipurpose dam, but the cost of recommitting federal dollars always seemed more than Congress would appropriate. After a violent flood nearly toppled Folsom Dam in 1986, some proposed a smaller, less expensive flood control structure. In the meantime, environmental groups consistently pointed out that any dam on the American River would be destructive to the environment, and they urged politicians to find other means, like higher levies, to control floods. In December 2008, the state of California revoked the federal water rights to Auburn Dam, essentially killing the project, although the dam has never been officially decommissioned.

Few public works projects have seen as much drama over such a long period as Auburn Dam. It was not simply that one issue doomed the project; rather, interested parties haggled over many points for half a century. For all camps, the fate of the lower American River transcended the immediate issue of a dam and became a veritable symbol of systemic conflicts over resource allocation, development, and scarcity in the United States.

—Jedediah Rogers

See also: *Bureau of Reclamation; Central Valley Project; Echo Park Dam; Glen Canyon Dam*

BIBLIOGRAPHY

Arthur, Harold G. Interviews by Brit Allan Story, Bureau of Reclamation, 1994 and 1995, Denver, CO. Transcript, National Archives and Records Administration, College Park, MD.

Johnson, Stephen, Robert Dawson, and Gerald Haslam. *The Great Central Valley: California's Heartland.* Berkeley: University of California Press, 1992.

Reisner, Marc. *Cadillac Desert: The American West and Its Disappearing Water.* New York: Viking, 1986.

Bonneville Dam

Bonneville Dam blocks the Columbia River approximately forty miles upstream from Portland, Oregon. Nearly 1,500 feet long, more than 130 feet wide, and almost 200 feet high, the dam includes 2 powerhouses, and today the 20 turbines produce more than a million kilowatts of hydroelectric power. The associated reservoir, Lake Bonneville, stretches nearly fifty miles upstream.

Bonneville Dam crosses the Columbia River almost 150 miles from the river's mouth. The dam impounds water at

The Bonneville Dam was completed in 1937 as one of the water reclamation projects begun under President Roosevelt's New Deal. The Dam spans the Columbia River in Bonneville, Oregon.
Library of Congress

Henry Kaiser

Henry John Kaiser was born on May 9, 1882, in Canajoharie, New York, to parents who were poor German immigrants. He dropped out of school at age 13 and began working in a dry-goods store. Soon thereafter, he also took a job as a photographer's apprentice. He bought the photography business when he was 22. It was the first of many businesses he would own over his distinguished career. He proved particularly adept at securing financing and government contracts for his businesses, especially during Franklin D. Roosevelt's administration.

Kaiser was a key participant in many water-related projects, especially during the New Deal era. He helped lead the companies that constructed the Hoover, Bonneville, Grand Coulee, and Parker Dams. Although none of his companies won the bid to construct the Shasta Dam, he still provided the sand and gravel required for the project. His companies also helped build piers for the Oakland to San Francisco Bay Bridge, the levees on the Mississippi River, and a thirty mile long aqueduct to supply water to New York City.

Regardless of what industry he was involved in, his companies were usually very successful. He was a unique industrialist, in that he was admired by both the management staffs of his companies and his union employees. In 1965, the American Federation of Labor–Congress of Industrial Organizations recognized him as the first industrialist to receive its award for distinguished service to organized labor. He lived the last years of his life in Hawaii, where he died on August 24, 1967.

—John R. Burch Jr.

See also: *Grand Coulee Dam; Hoover Dam; Roosevelt, Franklin D.; Shasta Dam*

BIBLIOGRAPHY

Foster, Mark S. *Henry J. Kaiser: Builder in the Modern American West.* Austin: University of Texas Press, 1989.

Heiner, Albert P. *Henry J. Kaiser, American Empire Builder: An Insider's View.* New York: Peter Lang, 1989.

The U.S. Army Corps of Engineers issued its famous "308 Report," written by Major John Butler, during President Herbert Hoover's administration. This report outlined the Corps's ambitions for the Columbia River system, including ten main-stem dams to coordinate an entire river system to achieve flood control, better navigation, and hydroelectricity production. In the early 1930s, President Franklin D. Roosevelt's New Deal programs developed plans for public works projects and coordinated regional economic development. In 1933, the Public Works Administration began construction on Bonneville Dam.

Bonneville Dam's construction brought to light two important issues. The first concerned power generation. Public power advocates wanted the federal government to distribute the hydroelectric power generated by the dam cheaply to regional residents and industry. Private power partisans favored a limited role for the federal government. The 1937 Bonneville Power Act, which created the Bonneville Power Administration (BPA) to manage the power grid, amounted to a compromise. It prioritized public power but did not establish as large and as powerful a federal entity as private power advocates feared. The BPA built regional transmission lines and marketed the power from Bonneville Dam. The dam generated so much power that it needed to attract residents and industry to use it. Soon after the power became available, World War II created great demand for industry, such as the region's many aircraft and shipbuilding plants. Demand increased throughout the second half of the century, and a second powerhouse was completed in 1982.

The second issue, which has become only more important as time has passed, was fish. Dams kept anadromous fish, including salmon and steelhead, from swimming upstream to spawn, thereby completing their biological imperative of returning to their natal streams to reproduce. The "308 Report" called for fish passage at each of the projected dams. Engineers spent $7 million installing fish

the site of the Cascade Rapids, a longtime American Indian fishing site. Before the dam, the river at Cascade Rapids was home to abundant fish, including salmon, steelhead, and white sturgeon. Even pinnipeds like sea lions and seals swam this far upriver. For centuries, the river's life helped sustain Native peoples.

When Euro-Americans arrived in the Pacific Northwest, the human relationship with the river at Cascade Rapids changed. Commercial interests wanted to improve the navigation of the river. The Cascade Locks and Canal, finished in 1896, allowed steamboats to bypass the rapids. Eventually, however, those locks and canals were insufficient for the industrial dreams of regional boosters.

ladders and elevator-like lifts at Bonneville, along with diversions to help keep young salmon from going over or through the dam. This one dam and its passage facilities might not have irreversibly harmed anadromous runs, but the steady accumulation of more dams in the Columbia-Snake river system from the 1940s to the 1960s, some of which did not have fish passage systems, decimated the fish populations and harmed their continued viability. By 1992, tribal and conservation interests succeeded in getting Snake River chinook and sockeye salmon listed under the Endangered Species Act. Fish recovery remains a multibillion dollar industry with marginal results. Meanwhile, the submersion of Cascade Rapids, along with other Native fisheries, has meant that Native groups remain displaced from the fishing culture that helped them thrive for centuries.

Bonneville Dam symbolizes the great hopes engineers and bureaucrats placed in the power of technology to transform nature into valuable goods for society. As the first major federal dam on the Columbia River, Bonneville can be seen as the starting point of the evolution of the river system into what historian Richard White called an "organic machine" (1995). The power generated at Bonneville Dam spread throughout the region, supporting industry and electrifying much of the Northwest at some of the nation's lowest prices. These great achievements, however, have been offset by the tragic decline of salmon and the displacement of those who rely on salmon for their economic livelihoods and cultural continuation. In this way, Bonneville Dam represents a central dilemma of modern life: how to balance human needs and natural requirements. In 1987, Bonneville Lock and Dam was designated a National Historic Landmark.

—Adam M. Sowards

See also: *Dam Building; Endangered Species Act (1973); Grand Coulee Dam; Locks; Pacific Coast; River Transportation*

BIBLIOGRAPHY

Blumm, Michael C. "The Northwest's Hydroelectric Heritage." In *Northwest Lands, Northwest Peoples: Readings in Environmental History,* edited by Dale D. Goble and Paul W. Hirt, 264–94. Seattle: University of Washington Press, 1999.

Dietrich, William. *Northwest Passage: The Great Columbia River.* New York: Simon & Schuster, 1995.

U.S. Army Corps of Engineers, Portland District. "Bonneville Lock & Dam." http://www.nwp.usace.army.mil/locations/bonneville .asp.

White, Richard. *The Organic Machine: The Remaking of the Columbia River.* New York: Hill and Wang, 1995.

Boulder Dam

See *Hoover Dam*

California Aqueduct

The 444-mile California Aqueduct (formally the "Governor Edmund G. Brown California Aqueduct") transports water for the California State Water Project (SWP), which is operated by the California Department of Water Resources (DWR). The aqueduct moves water from northern California to urban users, primarily, and also to some farms in the southern half of the state.

Beginning with reservoirs on upper tributaries of the Feather River at Lake Davis, Frenchman Lake, and Antelope Lake, SWP water reaches Oroville Dam in the foothills. Oroville forms the largest SWP reservoir. From there, water moves down the natural channel of the Feather River, then enters the Sacramento River. At the Sacramento–San Joaquin Delta, the Central Valley's two major river arteries, the Sacramento and San Joaquin Rivers, merge before entering San Francisco Bay and the Pacific Ocean. At that point, some water is diverted into the North Bay Aqueduct towards Napa and Solano Counties. Much of the water in the delta is pulled southward by powerful pumps at the Harvey O. Banks Delta Pumping Plant, where the California Aqueduct starts.

A few miles to the south, a South Bay aqueduct shunts some water toward Alameda and Santa Clara Counties. In the primary conduit, water continues down the west side of the San Joaquin Valley. Cars traveling Interstate 5 parallel the aqueduct route and cross over it several times. Sixty-three miles south of the delta, some water may be shunted by pumps "off-stream" up to the San Luis Reservoir, jointly operated by the DWR and the federal Central Valley Project (the federal Delta-Mendota Canal also parallels the aqueduct in this northern section). Further south, a Coastal Branch directs water toward cities in San Luis Obispo and Santa Barbara counties. The balance of aqueduct water encounters the Tehachapi Mountains at the south end of the San Joaquin Valley. Here, the A. D. Edmonston Pumping Plant lifts water 1,926 feet into tunnels through the mountains. Lifting each acre-foot demands 3,000 kilowatt-hours of electricity. The SWP is California's largest energy consumer, and this pumping station burns more energy than any other single user or facility in the state.

Peripheral Canal

The Peripheral Canal was an artificial waterway that was proposed for construction in California as part of California S.B. 200, which was signed by Governor Edmund "Jerry" Brown on July 18, 1980. It was to be a 42-mile-long waterway that was 400 feet wide and 30 feet deep that would divert more than 7 million acre-feet of "surplus" water from the Sacramento River in Northern California to the San Joaquin Valley in the southern portion of the state. A major supporter of the proposal was the Metropolitan Water District of Southern California, which was responsible for the water supply of cities such as San Diego and Los Angeles. Opponents of the canal in Northern California charged there was no excess water in the Sacramento River because as recently as 1975 to 1977, the region has been parched by a severe drought. Environmentalists also cautioned that diverting the waters would alter the fragile ecosystem of the marshy delta in the vicinity of San Francisco Bay. Environmental groups, such as the Sierra Club, joined with opponents of the canal to collect enough signatures to put the fate of the Peripheral Canal in the hands of the voters. Voters rejected Proposition 9 in 1982, thereby rejecting construction of the waterway.

Southern Californians have not given up hope of addressing their water problems at the expense of their northern neighbors. Governor Arnold Schwarzenegger hoped to rekindle construction of the Peripheral Canal by using California's economic difficulties during 2009 to exert pressure on California's legislators to support the endeavor.

—John R. Burch Jr.

BIBLIOGRAPHY

Hundley, Norris, Jr. *The Great Thirst: Californians and Water; A History.* Rev. ed. Berkeley: University of California Press, 2001.

been violating the California Endangered Species Act by not protecting threatened and endangered fish species from the impact of its pumping operations, a judge ordered that pumps serving the California Aqueduct be operated at a reduced volume during the months when smelt mass nearest the pumps. In 2008 and 2009, the salmon fishing seasons were canceled due to low numbers in the fall run of chinook (*Oncorynchus tshawytscha*). In 2010, the State Water Resources Control Board adopted flow criteria for the delta that indicated that, to protect and restore the ecosystem, less water needs to be exported and more allowed to flow out to the ocean.

To complete the SWP, a peripheral canal had been envisioned to move water around the edge of the delta, keeping it separated from tidal saltwater before entering the aqueduct. In 1982, the legislature approved an $11.6 billion construction project. But, in a referendum vote in the June 1982 election, 63 percent of the electorate voted against the canal.

In 2010, an $11.14 billion bond was approved by the legislature for the November ballot. Planning for another peripheral canal was included, along with new dams and water conservation measures. Peripheral canal options included a dual-conveyance system for water movement flexibility or an alternative tunnel passing underneath the delta. Concerns that a canal would facilitate even more diversions made the proposals controversial. The state's budget problems also made it a poor time to ask voters to approve new debt. Facing negative polls, the water bond was pulled from the 2010 election with a promise that it would be back in 2012.

—David Carle

See also: *Central Valley Project; Endangered Species Act (1973); Los Angeles Aqueduct*

BIBLIOGRAPHY

deBuys, William Eno. *Salt Dreams: Land and Water in Low-Down California.* Photographs by Joan Myers. Albuquerque: University of New Mexico Press, 2001.

Below the Tehachapis, the West Branch of the aqueduct brings water to the Pyramid and Castaic reservoirs in north Los Angeles County. An East Branch flows by the Mojave Desert city of Palmdale, sending water to Silverwood Lake, in the San Bernardino Mountains and Lake Perris, a reservoir in Riverside County.

Twenty-nine agencies hold contracts for SWP water. Their purchases cover the SWP's major operating costs and slowly chip away at repayment of the $1.75 billion bond that was approved by voters in 1960 to fund the construction of project facilities.

From 1990 to 1999, the average amount of water diverted from the Sacramento–San Joaquin delta was 4.6 million acre-feet. From 2000 to 2007, the average increased to 6 million acre-feet. A collapse in the delta ecosystem coincided with those increased water diversions, though water pollution and competition from invasive species were contributing causes. In 2007, after ruling that DWR had

Green, Dorothy. *Managing Water: Avoiding Crisis in California.* Berkeley: University of California Press, 2007.
Hundley, Norris, Jr. *The Great Thirst: Californians and Water; A History.* Rev. ed. Berkeley: University of California Press, 2001.
Reisner, Marc. *Cadillac Desert: The American West and Its Disappearing Water.* Rev. ed. New York: Penguin, 1993.

Cape Cod Canal

The lockless Cape Cod Canal is approximately 32 feet deep, 500 feet wide, and 17.5 miles in length. It connects Buzzard Bay with Cape Cod Bay, thereby shortening the travel distance over water between New York City and Boston by roughly 75 miles. Its construction made Cape Cod an island.

Since at least the seventeenth century, humans have sought an alternative to sailing around Cape Cod. Known for its dangerous currents, fog, ice, and hazardous shoals, Cape Cod has been a graveyard for many ships and their crews. In 1697, politicians in Massachusetts called for the construction of a canal in order to save the lives of sailors and protect shipborne cargo. Like many other canal proposals to follow through the centuries, it never made it to the construction phase. The primary reason that proposals languished was that proponents emphasized the need to save the lives of sailors. To individuals with access to the monies required for construction, the canal's economic benefits had to outweigh its cost, and in their eyes, most proposals failed this test.

By the late eighteenth century, a new reason for the canal came to the fore. Military officials had determined that a canal would prove useful during war. Construction commenced during March 1884, but the project was abandoned after approximately 7,000 feet of earth had been dug up. One of the obstacles to digging the canal was the presence of large boulders along the route, which had been deposited by glaciers at the end of the Ice Age.

During June 1909, August Belmont Jr.'s Boston, Cape Cod, and New York Canal Company began construction of the Cape Cod Canal using plans drafted by William Barclay Parsons, who served as the project's chief engineer. Over the first two years, workers succeeded in constructing a railroad bridge and two highway bridges over the canal's future channel. Work on the waterway did not progress as quickly due to the need to dynamite many glacial boulders. The canal, which had a depth of fifteen feet, opened to one-way traffic on July 29, 1914. Although opened to great fanfare, the waterway's shortcomings were already evident. It was too shallow for many of the ships that investors had hoped would supply the tolls required for them to make a profit. The canal was soon deepened to twenty-five feet, which increased traffic. Unfortunately for the Boston, Cape Cod, and New York Canal Company, the tolls collected never offset its expenses adequately.

The U.S. government assumed control of the Cape Cod Canal in 1918 after a coal barge was sunk by a German U-boat off the coast of Massachusetts. Ten years later, the federal government transferred responsibility for the Cape Cod Canal to the U.S. Army Corps of Engineers (Corps), which continues to maintain the waterway to this day.

Under the auspices of the Corps during the 1930s, a number of improvements were made to the Cape Cod Canal. The railroad and highway bridges that spanned the waterway were replaced, using workers from the Public Works Administration, with more aesthetically pleasing designs. The new railroad bridge, which features representations of lighthouses on either end, is a vertical lift bridge; at

The Cape Cod Canal, completed in 1914, cut travel distance between Boston and New York by about 75 miles. Its completion made Cape Cod an island. In this 1914 picture, Cape Cod Canal Construction Company president, August Belmont, opens the gates to let water through during the construction of the Canal.
Library of Congress

the time of construction, its lift span was the longest in the world. The canal was widened to 500 feet, making it the world's widest artificial waterway at the time, and deepened to 32 feet. This expansion allowed the canal to open to two-way traffic.

Since attaining its present size during the 1930s, the Cape Cod Canal has been used extensively to ship commercial cargo, and it is also heavily used by pleasure boaters. It forms a portion of the Atlantic Intracoastal Waterway, which extends from Boston, Massachusetts, to Key West, Florida.

—John R. Burch Jr.

See also: *Army Corps of Engineers, United States; Intracoastal Waterway*

BIBLIOGRAPHY

Conway, J. North. *The Cape Cod Canal: Breaking Through the Bared and Bended Arm.* Charleston, SC: History Press, 2008.
Farson, Robert H. *The Cape Cod Canal.* Middletown, CT: Wesleyan University Press, 1977.
Morris, Gloria. *Modern Marvels: Cape Cod Canal.* DVD. New York: History Channel, 2005.
U.S. Army Corps of Engineers. "Cape Cod Canal." http://www.nae .usace.army.mil/recreati/ccc/ccchome.htm.

Carlsbad Irrigation Project

Settlement of the American West has long been linked to the availability of water. In eastern New Mexico, early irrigation focused on the Pecos River. Extensive private ventures in the area, for all their ambitious intent, eventually met failure. Like many irrigation projects across the West, the Carlsbad Project was resurrected by the U.S. Reclamation Service (USRS). As one of the earliest and extensive USRS projects, Carlsbad offers an example of mixed nineteenth- and twentieth-century technology, and many of its structures are listed as historic landmarks.

The Carlsbad Project is located along the Pecos River in the Chihuahuan Desert of southeastern New Mexico near Carlsbad. The project's water supply derives from the Pecos River Basin's 16,990 square miles and from diversion of the Black River fifteen miles southeast of Carlsbad.

Early Promotion

Most late nineteenth-century history of the Trans-Pecos reflects ranching interests, with ranchers first appropriating water rights for cattle and sheep along small tributaries of the Pecos. Investigators for John Wesley Powell's U.S. Geological Survey suggested that with the proper irrigation tools in place, the region would become a prime growing area.

Early promoters of Pecos country irrigation included Pat Garrett. Garrett established an 1,800-acre farm near Roswell in the mid-1880s and met New Yorker Charles Bishop Eddy, a Colorado rancher who had established a cattle operation on the Pecos River near Seven Rivers in 1881. Intrigued by Garrett's vision of capturing waters from the Hondo River, Eddy began promoting irrigation in the Pecos Valley while accumulating vast tracts of land and water rights. As in many parts of the West, land acquisitions along the Pecos resulted from manipulation of the Desert Land Acts of 1877 and 1886.

In 1888, Garrett and Eddy enlisted the support of Robert Weems Tansill, a Chicago cigar manufacturer, and Charles W. Greene, a newspaper publisher and promoter. Settlers began arriving as early as 1888, and the town of Eddy (later renamed Carlsbad) was officially founded in 1889.

The most important player to emerge in the unfolding history of private irrigation in the lower Pecos Valley was James J. Hagerman, who assumed control of irrigation and transportation enterprises in the 1890s. He incorporated the Pecos Valley Railroad Company and constructed a rail line from Eddy (Carlsbad) to Pecos, Texas, in 1891 to improve access to markets. Hagerman attempted to provide greater coordination of valley development with the incorporation of the Pecos Valley Company in 1893.

Flooding and Financial Constraints

In August 1893, seasonal flooding washed out Avalon Dam, two bridges, and a wooden flume across the Pecos. Concurrently, the collapse of silver prices precipitating the Panic of 1893 dried up Hagerman's primary source of capital, which was his substantial interest in Colorado silver mines. Hagerman invested what he could into rebuilding Avalon Dam, constructing rail lines to Roswell, and building a second dam and reservoir to meet the needs of a burgeoning canal system.

Promotional efforts by the New Mexico Bureau of Immigration proclaiming the Pecos a veritable "fruit belt" had little to do with actual experience. Vineyards and orchards succumbed to dust storms, root disease, and an erratic water supply. Further experimentation with a variety of crops in the region met with limited success.

The precarious financial condition of the irrigation company forced it into receivership in 1898, placing the company's plant and operation under the authority of the Pecos Irrigation Company on August 17, 1900. Under receivership, company fortunes improved temporarily, with construction of a rail line to Amarillo, Texas, and the introduction of cotton. By 1902, however, following engineering reports, it was painfully obvious to company directors Francis Tracy and Robert Tansill that massive improvements were necessary to make the system viable for the long term.

Luring USRS chief Frederick H. Newell to Carlsbad, Robert Tansill discussed the possibility of a bailout under provisions of the Reclamation Act of 1902. Tansill died in December of 1902, and Tracy became the standard-bearer of the company. For decades he advocated federal assistance for the lower Pecos, while at the same time criticizing competing USRS projects and water users impacting Pecos Irrigation interests.

Following another devastating flood in October 1904, the Pecos Water Users Association, led by Tracy, launched a massive advocacy campaign to convince the USRS to purchase and rehabilitate the entire irrigation system. On November 28, 1905, the secretary of the interior approved rehabilitation of the project to prevent its cultivated land from returning to wasteland. The Pecos Irrigation and Improvement Company accepted $150,000 for the remains of the dilapidated irrigation system. Another $450,000 was allocated for its restoration.

Since the early days of the project, the federal government has played a large role on the Pecos, lining canals with concrete, improving existing structures, and building two additional dams at Fort Sumner and Brantley. The Carlsbad Project has been plagued by a number of problems over the years: canal and dam leakage; high water salinity; the predominance of water-robbing phreatophytes in the form of tamarisks, or salt cedars; contention between the Water Users' Association and the federal government; and conflicts among water users within New Mexico, as well as between those in New Mexico and those in Texas. A water compact between the two states in 1925 lingered without approval until a new agreement became law in 1949. Since that time, competition over Pecos River water and litigation over water rights have continued in earnest.

—Stephen Bogener

See also: *Bureau of Reclamation; Newell, Frederick H.*

BIBLIOGRAPHY

Bogener, Stephen. "Carlsbad Project." 1993, last updated April 24, 2009. http://www.usbr.gov/projects/.

Bogener, Stephen. *Ditches Across the Desert: Irrigation in the Lower Pecos Valley.* Lubbock: Texas Tech University Press, 2003.

Clark, Ira G. *Water in New Mexico: A History of its Management and Use.* Albuquerque: University of New Mexico Press, 1987.

Keleher, William Aloysius. *The Fabulous Frontier: Twelve New Mexico Items.* Santa Fe, NM: Rydal Press, 1945.

Lingle, Robert T., and Dee Linford. *The Pecos River Commission of New Mexico and Texas: A Report on a Decade of Progress, 1950–1960.* Carlsbad, NM: Rydal Press, 1961.

Sheridan, Thomas E. *The Bitter River: A Brief Historical Survey of the Middle Pecos River Basin.* Boulder, CO: Western Interstate Commission for Higher Education, 1975.

Central Arizona Project

The Central Arizona Project (CAP) is a 336-mile system of aqueducts, tunnels, and canals that distributes over 1.5 million acre-feet of water annually from the Colorado River at Lake Havasu to the counties of Maricopa, Pinal, and Pima, which include the metropolitan areas of Phoenix and Tucson, Arizona. The CAP serves a population of over 5 million people, most of whom live in alluvial basins, the result of faulting and volcanism.

Much of the area served by the CAP is arid or semiarid. In spite of this, beans, squash, and cotton are grown, mostly on land that is irrigated. The area served by the CAP is largely below 2,000 feet above sea level: the water begins at Lake Havasu, about 600 feet above sea level, traverses Phoenix at 1,090 feet, and ends near Tucson at 2,389 feet. Mountains are near both cities, with Mount Lemmon northeast of Tucson towering over 9,000 feet above sea level. Canals cross the Agua Fria, Salt, and Gila Rivers.

CAP diverts water resources from the Colorado River Basin, a semiarid region. Much of the area that CAP traverses experiences temperatures in excess of 100 degrees Fahrenheit, with more than a hundred days a year above that mark. On average, only twelve days exhibit measurable precipitation. Large areas are covered with limestone and sandstone, originally deposited in the Paleozoic or Mesozoic eras. The Sonoran Desert covers much of southwestern Arizona. Flora consists of small, leaved trees (palo verde), cactus (saguaro, barrel, prickly pear, hedgehog), desert ironwood, cholla, and grasses. Statewide, a disproportionate number of threatened or endangered species reside in Arizona, including the Sonora tiger salamander, masked bobwhite, desert pupfish, and ocelot.

Culturally, the Colorado River served as the watershed for Anasazi, Hohokam, Hopi, and other Native American groups for thousands of years preceding European exploration. After colonization by Spanish and Mexicans, most of Arizona became part of the United States in 1848, with the Gadsden Purchase added in 1853. By the late nineteenth century, Pima Indians irrigated along the Gila River to raise crops within the border of their reservation. Further settlement by whites allowed farmers to raise cattle and sheep and to grow alfalfa, dates, and barley. Phoenix and Tucson boomed during the 1940s due to military activity and reclamation projects.

Although the Central Arizona Project was authorized in 1968, its history extends well before that date. From 1918 onward, several people and organizations worked toward a project that could distribute water to the communities of Phoenix, Tucson, and Yuma. The Colorado River Basin includes parts of Arizona, California, Nevada, New Mexico, Wyoming, Colorado, and Utah. In 1922, the Colorado River Compact was organized to divide the waters of the basin equally among the users, with each share being about 7.5 million acre-feet per year. The lower basin comprised Arizona, California, and Nevada. In 1946, the Central Arizona Project Association organized to lobby Congress for authorization of a canal and dams. Court litigation, primarily in the landmark case of *Arizona v. California* (1963), delayed the project for over twenty years. On September 30, 1968, President Lyndon Johnson signed the Colorado River Basin Project Act of 1968 (Pub. L. 90-537; 82 Stat. 885), which had been sponsored by Senators Carl Hayden (D-AZ) and Paul Fannin (R-AZ), authorizing construction. Actual construction, by the Bureau of Reclamation, began at Lake Havasu in1973 and concluded in 1993 near Tucson. It cost $4 billion.

The Central Arizona Project provides water to agricultural lands in the counties of Maricopa, Pinal, and Pima; municipal water supplies for Phoenix and Tucson; and power generation, outdoor recreation, wildlife conservation, and sediment control. With regard to power, construction on the Navajo Generating Station started in April 1970, and the third unit became operational in April 1976. Located near Page, Arizona, in the northernmost reaches of the state, this coal-powered station supplies energy to the Central Arizona Project, as well as other customers in the region.

Since the development of dams and diversions, such as CAP, along much of its length, the Colorado River has become drier and saltier. Less than 1 percent of the river's water makes it all the way to the river mouth in the Gulf of California. Environmentalists have criticized CAP because 50 percent of the water in the system is lost through evaporation.

—Ralph Hartsock

See also: *Colorado River Basin; Hayden, Carl T.*

BIBLIOGRAPHY

Arizona State University Libraries. "Colorado River Central Arizona Project Collection." http://digital.lib.asu.edu/.
Central Arizona Project. http://www.cap-az.com/.
Johnson, Rich. *The Central Arizona Project, 1918–1968.* Tucson: University of Arizona Press, 1977.
U.S. Bureau of Reclamation. *Central Arizona Project.* Washington, DC: Department of the Interior, Bureau of Reclamation, 1995.

Central Utah Project

The Central Utah Project (CUP) is the largest Bureau of Reclamation project in Utah. Congress authorized it in 1956 as a participating project in the Colorado River Storage Project. To manage its size, the Bureau of Reclamation divided the CUP into six parts, termed *units*. The CUP is important not just because of its size but because its legal and legislative history mirrors the historical changes within the Bureau of Reclamation.

The initial authorization included the Bonneville, Jensen, Upalco, and Vernal units. After the project's authorization, the Bureau of Reclamation altered the CUP's plans several times. The Bureau completed construction of the Jensen and Vernal Units in Uintah County, Utah. These units each feature a reservoir and associated irrigation canals and municipal water pipelines. The Upalco and the Uintah Unit—authorized by the Colorado River Basin Act of 1968—were not constructed due to geologic problems at the proposed dam sites. The Central Utah Water Conservancy District constructed a replacement project for the Uintah and Upalco Units in 2008 by enlarging the existing Big Sand Wash Reservoir in Duchesne County and coordinating management between existing water users.

The Bonneville Unit is the largest and most complex unit of the CUP. Related reservoirs and water supply works are spread across Utah. In the Uinta Basin, the Starvation Reservoir stores water from the Strawberry and Duchesne River for irrigation and municipal use. The thirty-six-mile Strawberry collection system, a series of pipelines, long tunnels, and two regulating reservoirs, collects water from tributaries of the Duchesne River and diverts the flow to the Strawberry Reservoir. The project enlarged the capacity of the existing Strawberry Reservoir by four times with the construction of the Soldier Creek Dam six miles downstream from the original reservoir.

The water stored in the Strawberry Reservoir, located in the Colorado River drainage, is diverted into the Bonneville drainage via a series of tunnels and pipelines for agricultural and municipal use in central Utah. Additional municipal water for northern Utah and Salt Lake counties is stored in the Jordanelle Reservoir on the Provo River above Heber City. Rights to the water needed to fill the reservoir are secured through a paper exchange. Downstream water users receive their water from Strawberry Reservoir, which is released into Utah Lake, allowing the Provo River water to be held upstream for diversion.

The project has always enjoyed strong support in Utah, especially among state politicians and water developers who saw it as the only way for Utah to utilize fully the state's share of the Colorado River granted under the 1922 Colorado River Compact. The importance of the project to the state provided the incentive for Utah to push for the Upper Colorado Basin Compact of 1948 and the Colorado River Storage Project. The CUP's supporters originally planned for additional direct diversion from the Green River via either pumping from behind the proposed Echo Park Dam inside Dinosaur National Monument or, alternatively, diverting water through a long gravity tunnel from Flaming Gorge Reservoir. These plans constituted the "ultimate phase," or the Ute Indian Unit, of the Central Utah Project. The Colorado River Basin Act of 1968 authorized feasibility studies for this unit. Subsequent investigation and political uncertainty over the best use of the water led the Bureau in 1980 to recommend ceasing further investigation.

As a result of these changes, which affected a water rights agreement with the Northern Ute Tribe, and due to increased construction costs, the project needed reauthorization legislation to continue construction. After considerable debate and compromise, Congress passed the Central Utah Project Completion Act (CUPCA) in 1992. The legislation included financial compensation to the Uintah and Ouray Ute Tribes for lost water rights. The legislation also transferred oversight of the remaining construction of the project from the Bureau of Reclamation to the local project sponsor, the Central Utah Water Conservancy District. The transfer of construction oversight by Congress helped signal the end of the Bureau of Reclamation's mission of building water development projects.

CUPCA also addressed long-standing environmental controversies regarding minimum stream flows, environmental mitigation of project features, and provisions for water conservation. These concerns surfaced during the formulation of environmental impact statements; a 1974 lawsuit, *Sierra Club v. Stamm*, which claimed a deficiency in the environmental impact statements; and in a review undertaken by the Department of the Interior as President Carter pursued his controversial "hit list" of projects he viewed as pork-barrel spending.

As a result of CUPCA, two counties voted to pull out of the CUP, resulting in the elimination of a significant portion of planned irrigation development in central Utah. Additional environmental objections resulted in a final reformulation that has converted the last block of agricultural water to a municipal supply. As a result, the CUP now primarily supplies municipal water.

—Adam Eastman

See also: *Colorado River Basin Act of 1968; Colorado River Storage Project Act of 1956; Echo Park Dam; Interbasin Water Transfer; Intermountain West; National Parks and Water; Strawberry Valley Project*

BIBLIOGRAPHY

Eastman, Adam. "From Cadillac to Chevy: Environmental Concern, Compromise, and the Central Utah Project Completion Act." In *Utah in the Twentieth Century,* edited by Brian Q. Cannon and Jessie L. Embry, 343–84. Logan: Utah State University Press, 2009.

Central Valley Project

The Central Valley Project (CVP) is the Bureau of Reclamation's largest, encompassing thirty-five counties in California's Central Valley, an area about 500 miles long and 60 to 100 miles wide. It provides water to three-quarters of the irrigated land in California and one-sixth of the irrigated land in the United States, and it includes some of the country's largest dams. The Central Valley Project consists of nine interrelated divisions that link the Sacramento and San Joaquin Rivers, import water from the Trinity River in the Klamath River Basin, and interact with the California State Water Project.

In the Sacramento River basin, Shasta Dam provides flood control and water storage. Additional water is diverted into the Sacramento from the Trinity River and is regulated

The Keswick Dam regulates water that is diverted from the Sacramento River into the Trinity River. The dam was built as part of the Central Valley Project, which provides water to most of the croplands in California.

Library of Congress

Resources. The William R. Gianelli Pumping-Generating Plant pumps surplus water from the Delta-Mendota Canal and the California Aqueduct into San Luis Reservoir, the largest off-stream storage reservoir in the United States. When water flow through the Delta Division becomes too low, water is released from San Luis into the Delta-Mendota Canal and the California Aqueduct. The San Felipe Division diverts water from San Luis Reservoir into lands west of the Coastal Mountain Range, south of San Francisco Bay (Stene 1994/2009).

The Central Valley Project's history is as complex and complicated as the project itself. The project originated in the California State Water Plan in the early 1930s. The cost of the project led to calls for federal involvement and construction. The project became a turf war by the Keswick Reservoir. Folsom Dam and Reservoir on the American River provide flood control on the American and Sacramento Rivers and supply irrigation water via the Folsom South Canal. The project provides irrigation water in the San Joaquin basin through the coordinated operation of the Friant and Delta divisions. Except for flood control and irrigation releases to downstream users, Friant Dam, twenty-five miles northeast of Fresno, impounds or diverts the entire flow of the San Joaquin River. Irrigation water is diverted at the dam either south into the Friant-Kern Canal or north through the Madera Canal.

The Delta Division links the Sacramento and San Joaquin Rivers. Water is transported from the Sacramento River to the San Joaquin River delta area via the Delta Cross Channel Canal. The Tracy Pumping Plant lifts water from the delta 197 feet into the Delta-Mendota Canal to provide water to the San Luis Unit and to replace water diverted at Friant Dam. Also in the delta is the Contra Costa Pumping Plant, which lifts water into the Contra Costa Canal for irrigation and municipal use.

The San Luis Unit is a joint venture between the Bureau of Reclamation and the California Department of Water between the U.S. Army Corps of Engineers and the Bureau of Reclamation. The Corps built several of the CVP's dams, including Folsom and New Melones Dam on the Stanislaus River, as flood control projects. As a result, at various times controversy brewed over the applicability of the 160-acre limitation in the Reclamation Act of 1902. The issue was especially acute in the Central Valley because of the dominance of large growers (Hundley 1992). Even though two-thirds of California farms consisted of fewer than 100 acres, 80 percent of the farmland existed in holdings of over 1,000 acres (Stene 1994/2009). A water contract with the Westlands Water District resulted in a lawsuit and action by the Carter administration to enforce acreage limitation. After years of debate, Congress attempted a compromise solution in the Reclamation Reform Act of 1982. This legislation increased the limitation to 960 acres and eliminated the residency requirement for farmers.

The project has also been controversial because of social justice and environmental issues. Significant controversy arose from a large bird kill at the CVP's Kesterson Reservoir as a result of excessive selenium in agricultural runoff. Also, a 1975 earthquake within fifty miles of the dam site led seismologists to question whether the weight of the water to be impounded within the dam's reservoir could potentially cause enough geologic stress on a local fault zone to trigger an earthquake. In 1992, Congress passed the Central Valley Project Improvement Act to address concerns over irrigation subsidies and environmental restoration of Central Valley fisheries.

—Adam Eastman

See also: *Army Corps of Engineers, United States; Auburn Dam; Bureau of Reclamation; Friant Dam; Kesterson Reservoir; Selenium; Shasta Dam; Westlands Water District*

BIBLIOGRAPHY

Hundley, Norris, Jr. *The Great Thirst: Californians and Water, 1770s–1990s.* Berkeley: University of California Press, 1992.
Stene, Eric A. "Central Valley Project." 1994, last updated August 31, 2009. http://www.usbr.gov/projects.

Colorado–Big Thompson Project

The Colorado–Big Thompson is one of the largest and most complex projects constructed by the Bureau of Reclamation. It is the largest of thirty-seven transmountain diversion projects in Colorado. The project provides supplemental irrigation water to approximately 720,000 acres in the South Platte River Basin. The project also supplies municipal and industrial water to a dozen communities; produces 690 million kilowatt-hours of electricity marketed to customers in Colorado, Wyoming, and Nebraska; and provides recreation benefits.

The project spans 250 miles east-to-west from the high plains of eastern Colorado to the western slopes of the Rocky Mountains, while the service area stretches 65 miles north-to-south from near the Wyoming border to the city of Boulder. The project uses more than 100 major structures to transfer up to 310,000 acre-feet of water a year from the Colorado River to the Big Thompson River and deliver the project's benefits. These two watersheds are bridged by the 13.1-mile Alva B. Adams Tunnel, which runs 3,800 feet beneath the Continental Divide and beneath Rocky Mountain National Park. Snowmelt from the western slope is gathered, stored, and regulated by four reservoirs and is pumped up to Grand Lake and the west portal of the tunnel. From the east portal, numerous structures store, regulate, and divert the water to end users. An elevation change of 2,800 feet between the east

portal and the foothills is used to generate hydropower. The project's pumps use 70 million kilowatt-hours of electricity, while the balance is sold to defray project construction costs.

Different interests studied proposals to make a transbasin water diversion in the area of Grand Lake, beginning with an appropriation from the Colorado state legislature in 1889 to study a diversion using canals. In 1904, the Reclamation Service completed a study proposing a twelve-mile tunnel from Grand Lake to the east slope. Economic and political realities led the government to choose smaller projects spread across the West rather than a few massive projects on the scale of the Grand Lake proposal. However, local interests kept the idea afloat until the Great Depression and drought of the 1930s justified renewed studies.

Local water users ran into two major obstacles as they pushed their Grand Lake Project. First, water users downstream on the Colorado feared the massive diversion scheme would impair their water rights. Second, preservationists feared the project would damage Rocky Mountain National Park, created in 1915. After years of debate, Congress authorized the project on June 24, 1937. At the behest of Rep. Edward Taylor (D-CO), interests from both drainages agreed to add the 152,000 acre-feet Green Mountain Reservoir, 13 miles southeast of the town of Kremmling, to compensate western slope interests. Reclamation agreed to abstain from construction within the park boundaries by running a diversion tunnel underneath the park. World War II slowed work on the massive project, which the Bureau of Reclamation completed in stages. It completed the last major west-slope structure, the Granby Pumping Plant, in 1951. The project began full delivery of water in 1957. Later, the Northern Colorado Water Conservancy District undertook expansion of the project by constructing the Windy Gap Project amid significant environmental controversy.

The Colorado–Big Thompson Project stands out from other reclamation projects because of its size and complexity. Further, the project differed from earlier reclamation projects for three reasons. First, it was not a traditional reclamation project in that it provided supplemental water to existing farmlands rather than opening new land to agriculture. Second, water users claimed project water would not drastically increase the value of their properties and persuaded Congress to exempt the project from the 160-acre-per-person limitation of the 1902 Reclamation Act. Finally, almost 50 percent of repayment costs would be liquidated by hydroelectric generation.

—Adam Eastman

See also: *Carpenter, Delphus E.; Colorado River Basin; Colorado River Compact of 1922; Interbasin Water Transfer; National Parks and Water; Roosevelt, Franklin D.; United States–Mexico Water Treaty (1944)*

BIBLIOGRAPHY

Autobee, Robert. "Colorado-Big Thompson Project." 1996, last updated June 26, 2008. http://www.usbr.gov/projects/.

Tyler, Daniel. *The Last Water Hole in the West: The Colorado–Big Thompson Project and the Northern Colorado Water Conservancy District.* Niwot: University Press of Colorado, 1992.

Colorado River Aqueduct

The Colorado River Aqueduct (CRA) conveys water from the Colorado River (at Lake Havasu/Parker Dam on the California/Arizona border) to Lake Mathews, which is near Riverside, California. Starting at an elevation of about 450 feet, water is pumped through 5 plants (a total lift of 1,617 feet) over 242 miles of dry, uneven terrain to a final elevation of about 1,350 feet. The CRA has 92 miles of tunnels, 63 miles of lined canals, 55 miles of covered canals, and 29 miles of inverted siphons. It has a rated capacity of 1,800 cubic feet per second (cfs), which means that it can move 1.3 million acre-feet of water per year. After entering service in 1941, the CRA played a critical role in southern California's post–World War II growth. Today, the CRA supplies 20 to 25 percent of the 4 million acre-feet of water used in urban southern California each year. (An acre-foot of water will cover one acre one foot deep; it's approximately 326,000 gallons or 1.23 megaliters of water.)

The CRA was built by the Metropolitan Water District of Southern California (MWD) between 1933 and 1941. MWD was formed in 1928 to build and operate an aqueduct that would bring water to a "parched" southern California. Although MWD promised that the CRA would relieve "imminent" water shortages, increase property taxes only slightly, create jobs, and "perfect" MWD's rights on the Colorado River, three of these claims were false. There was no shortage of water in the region as a whole, property taxes rose steeply, and MWD's water rights were cut from 1,212 thousand acre-feet (taf) to 550 taf in the 1963 *Arizona v. California* decision. The CRA did employ 10,000 workers—about 1.2 percent of all workers in the region. Nonetheless,

voters believed MWD and approved the $220 million bond—the largest in the region's history—in September 1931. The CRA actually cost $190 million.

CRA pumps use hydroelectric power that travels over 237 miles of transmission lines from Hoover Dam. The Department of the Interior awarded 36 percent of the fifty-year contracts for Hoover power to MWD in April 1930—before MWD had the money to build the project that would use the power. Today, MWD has contracts for 28.5 percent of Hoover Dam's 2,080-megawatt capacity. These contracts are sufficient to pump 800 taf of water; MWD needs to buy power on the "open market" to cover the next 500 taf. Depending on volume and energy prices, it costs MWD $70–$100 per acre-foot to move water through the CRA. In comparison, MWD pays $135–$294 per acre-foot for water it buys from the State Water Project.

The CRA is significant in several ways. Like the 1913 Los Angeles Aqueduct (LAA, 485 cfs capacity) and the 1934 Hetch Hetchy Aqueduct (HHA, 465 cfs capacity), it brings water to urban areas. Unlike these gravity-flow aqueducts, it uses pumps to move water. Further, the CRA was put into operation without any firm customers. The LAA was built for existing municipal and industrial users, and HHA was built for municipal and industrial users in the San Francisco Bay Area.

The CRA's "supply without demand" character emerged from conflicting needs. Although Los Angeles had plenty of water from the LAA, it ran the LAA at full capacity to generate power. The city used its "surplus" water as a reward to neighboring areas that agreed to annex to the city. Between 1910 and 1932, Los Angeles grew from 90 to 450 square miles. Robert Townsend's 1974 film *Chinatown* portrayed the manipulation of water shortages by land developers using imported water in a fictionalized plot that mixed the histories of the LAA and CRA. Los Angeles wanted the CRA and put up the money to study the idea and form MWD only because the CRA made Hoover Dam—and its generating capacity—more likely. Neighboring cities (e.g., Pasadena and Burbank) wanted a water supply that was not controlled by Los Angeles. They made a deal: Los Angeles would provide money; the other twelve founding members of MWD would provide political support in the state capitol and Washington, D.C. Los Angeles got 19 percent of the contracts for Hoover power in 1930 and gets 15.4 percent today.

The trouble began when the per unit cost of CRA water turned out to be roughly three to five times the cost of local water. At breakeven prices, demand was weak: MWD projected sales of 400 cfs but only sold 20 cfs in 1942. MWD's solution—subsidized prices and expansion—eventually created demand but also established a precedent of cheap water and sprawling urbanization that continued into the 1980s.

On a positive note, nobody claims that the CRA harms the environment—unlike the LAA or HHA. That's because everyone assumes that the Colorado River will be diverted. Colorado overallocation originates with a badly designed Colorado River Compact.

For current residents of southern California, the CRA is a valuable source of water for their increasingly drought-prone region. Unfortunately, they may not understand that the CRA probably increased demand more than supply. Put differently, the CRA's development made today's shortages *more* likely.

—David Zetland

See also: Arizona v. California *(1963); Boulder Canyon Project Act (1928); Colorado River Compact of 1922; Hoover Dam*

BIBLIOGRAPHY

San Diego County Water Authority. *Annual Report.* San Diego, CA: San Diego County Water Authority, 1946.

Zetland, David. *Conflict and Cooperation within an Organization: A Case Study of the Metropolitan Water District of Southern California.* Saarbruecken, Ger.: VDM Verlag, 2009.

Colorado River Basin

The Colorado River Basin is the watershed straddling the Colorado River. The Colorado River serves seven western states within the United States (Colorado, Wyoming, Utah, New Mexico, Nevada, Arizona, and California) as well as the Mexican states of Baja California and Sonora; the latter comprise just 2 percent of the total watershed. Though small compared to many larger North American rivers, the Colorado River is a vital water source for the basin's inhabitants and its fauna and flora, making it one of the most intensively utilized rivers in the world today.

From headwaters in the Rocky Mountains, the Colorado runs 1,450 miles to empty into the Gulf of California. It is served by a watershed of 246,000 square miles.

Along its course, the river is joined by numerous tributaries, including the Green, Yampa, Gunnison, Dolores, San Juan, Little Colorado, Virgin, and Gila Rivers and numerous lesser streams. Its average annual flow of 15 million acre-feet (maf) is just 3 percent of the flow of the Mississippi River, but its location in the arid Southwest has historically amplified its economic and social importance.

The Colorado River traverses diverse geographic zones in its descent. Its headwaters are across the Southwest from Utah and Wyoming through Colorado to the Gila Range in New Mexico and Arizona and reaching as far south as Sonora in Mexico. Mountain peaks in the central Rockies rise above 14,000 feet. At midbasin, the Colorado River cuts spectacularly through the sandstone buttes and mesas of Colorado, Utah, and Arizona, where it carves the landscapes of the Grand Canyon, Canyonlands, Arches, Bryce, and Zion National Parks and numerous other parks. Below Arizona's Mogollon Rim, the basin drops sharply to the Sonoran Desert where scant precipitation and extreme temperatures prevail.

Harnessing the river's waters has been central to regional development. The Colorado River supports many of the region's most productive agricultural areas and its largest cities (Las Vegas, Nevada; Phoenix, Arizona), including cities

Water Education Foundation

The Water Education Foundation is a nonprofit organization based in Sacramento, California. Founded in 1977, its primary mission is to foster an impartial understanding of all aspects of water issues and to assist in the resolution of water resource problems in California and other western states. The foundation creates easy-to-understand educational materials that it targets towards three distinct audiences: government officials who make water policy; advocacy groups, businesses, and officials in urban population centers that are involved in addressing the respective water needs of their primary constituencies; and the general populace. Information intended for lay citizens is often distributed through media outlets, such as newspapers and periodicals. The organization also disseminates data through its Web site, research reports, videos, and other publications. Its best-known publications are the bimonthly periodical *Western Waters*, which began publication in 1977, and the biannual report entitled *River Report*, which focuses on the Colorado River Basin.

—John R. Burch Jr.

BIBLIOGRAPHY

Llamas, Ramón, and Emilio Custodio, eds. *Intensive Use of Groundwater: Challenges and Opportunities.* Lisse, Neth.: A. A. Balkema, 2002.

Water Education Foundation. http://www.watereducation.org/.

served by out-of-basin diversions such as Los Angeles and San Diego in California; Denver, Colorado; and Mexicali and Tijuana in Baja California, Mexico. The river serves 25 million people, irrigates 3 million acres, hosts 22 major storage dams (all in the United States), and generates 11.5 million kilowatt-hours of electricity. In addition to its core municipal, industrial, agricultural, and hydropower uses, its many reservoirs supply recreational opportunities for local populations and tourists.

Controversies over the Colorado River's water abound. The river is one of the most heavily litigated waterways in the United States and the most intensively administered. Settlement of these disputes led to interstate and international agreements that as a body comprise the "Law of the River." Major elements of this river law include the 1902 U.S. Reclamation Act, the 1922 Colorado River Compact, the 1928 Boulder Canyon Act, California's Seven Party Agreement, the 1944 Mexican Water Treaty, the U.S. Supreme Court's 1964 decree in *Arizona v. California,* the Colorado River Basin Project Act of 1968, and the Colorado River Basin Salinity Control Act of 1974—nearly fifty separate international, federal, and interstate statutes comprise this still evolving body of law.

Overallocation of water entitlements contributes to the difficulties that U.S. basin states have encountered in managing the river's water. The 1922 Colorado River Compact famously allocated 7.5 maf of water annually to both the Upper Basin and the Lower Basin states, its authors believing the river produced as much as 18 maf of water a year. Actual runoff averages around 15 maf. In 1944, the Mexican Water Treaty allocated 1.5 maf of water annually to Mexico, further reducing the volume of water available to U.S. stakeholders.

The discrepancy between hydrological reality and legal entitlement continues to vex the basin's water managers. Adding to legal uncertainty are unresolved claims by U.S. Indian tribes. Yet another persistent issue is how to ration water among stakeholders in times of drought to comply with the 1944 United States–Mexico Water Treaty. Ecological needs in the Colorado Delta remain unmet. Climate change may further complicate existing allocations. Such pressures ensure that water conservation will shape the basin's future.

—Stephen P. Mumme

See also: Arizona v. California *(1963); Colorado River Compact of 1922; United States–Mexico Water Treaty (1944)*

BIBLIOGRAPHY

Fradkin, Philip L. *A River No More: The Colorado River and the West.* New York: Alfred A. Knopf, 1981.

Pontius, Dale. *Colorado River Basin Study: Final Report; Report to the Western Policy Review Advisory Commission.* With SWCA Inc. Environmental Consultants. Tucson, AZ: 1997. Available at http://wwa.colorado.edu/colorado_river/docs/pontius%20colorado.pdf.

Columbia Basin Project

The largest single reclamation project in the United States, the Columbia Basin Project covers a region of more than 2.5 million acres. Centered in central Washington State, the project's dams and canals serve as vital infrastructure to deliver water to farms throughout the project area. The Columbia Basin Project developed over time and may still be growing; its importance in transforming the economy and environment of the interior Pacific Northwest is difficult to overestimate.

The Columbia Basin is an extensive, arid landscape that drains into the Columbia River. The Columbia River courses through the region and had historically provided prodigious runs of anadromous fish for Native inhabitants, whose two greatest fishing spots were Celilo Falls and Kettle Falls (both now beneath reservoir waters). The basin, also called the Columbia Plateau, is characterized by low rainfall but rich soil with native plant communities of bunchgrasses and sagebrush.

In the early twentieth century, farmers and regional boosters found the Columbia Basin a place needing irrigation, although damming the Columbia River seemed a challenging engineering task since the river was wide and could run 500 feet down in canyons. The Bureau of Reclamation, state commissions, and private developers scouted the region, imagining the basin filled with small family farms producing food and creating vibrant communities. Competing plans for irrigating the basin emerged: one to tap the Pend Oreille River and funnel the water through a gravity-fed canal, another to dam the much larger Columbia and pump water into a coulee to await distribution through canals. Each project had its own regional boosters. After a long campaign, the pumping plan at Grand Coulee finally was authorized in 1933 when President Franklin D. Roosevelt included it in the Public Works Administration as part of his New Deal approach to ameliorating the economic effects of the Great Depression.

The plans for the Columbia Basin Project were myriad, matching the diverse needs of the time and place.

A primary motivation was the president's desire to put unemployed Americans to work; more than 12,000 workers were employed, a maximum of 7,400 at any given time, and a total of 56 million manhours per put into the dam alone. Of more durable importance were other missions. Since its beginning in 1902, the Bureau of Reclamation, which administers the project, had promised to construct reclamation projects that would promote small farms in arid western landscapes by building dams and canals and providing water at subsidized rates. Such projects helped promote agricultural development in rural areas, and federal engineers planned to irrigate more than a million acres with the Columbia Basin Project. Many dams in reclamation projects were multipurpose, providing hydroelectricity and flood control functions as well as irrigation water. Grand Coulee Dam and the supporting Columbia Basin Project's complex of reservoirs, canals, and other dams are good examples.

Grand Coulee Dam, the cornerstone of the project, opened in 1942. Although the dam immediately provided much-needed hydroelectric power, the irrigation system took another decade to become operational. In May 1952, water from Lake Roosevelt, Grand Coulee Dam's enormous reservoir, pumped into the adjacent Banks Lake and then into the canal system, carrying water throughout central Washington to irrigate new farms' fields. The Columbia Basin Project continued expanding throughout the postwar decades, including more dams and canals to serve expanding farmland.

The results have been impressive. Farmers, veterans, and others flocked to the Columbia Basin to take up these lands. While the numbers have fluctuated over half a century, more than 10,000 people have lived on more than 2,000 project farms. Meanwhile, average farm size has gradually increased from approximately 100 acres in the mid-1950s to more than 260 acres today. Roughly 2.5 million acre-feet of water are annually delivered to Columbia Basin farmers, who use it to grow fruits and grains along with some specialty crops (Northwest Power and Conservation Council n.d.). Although planners anticipated the project would serve more than a million acres, today between 600,000 and 700,000 acres are irrigated. The economic benefits from this additional agricultural productivity amount to more than $500 million annually. The recreational and flood control benefits derived from the project's reservoirs and dams add another $70 million each year, while the power provided generates close to $1 billion dollars.

Despite these real benefits, the Columbia Basin Project has not been an unmitigated success. The growing average farm size reflects national changes in agricultural economics and the evolution (or failure) of the initial Bureau of Reclamation vision of supporting small, family farms. Arguably the largest problem with the Columbia Basin Project has concerned anadromous fish populations. Grand Coulee Dam ended salmon and steelhead runs up the river past that point. The multiple dams and canals, along with agricultural practices, also transformed landscapes in ways that degraded anadromous fish habitat and promoted invasive fish species. For Native peoples who maintained fishing rights and whose relationship with salmon was sacred, this sacrifice in the name of economic growth and progress remains a grievous violation.

Still, the Columbia Basin Project transformed the Columbia Plateau in ways most promoters and much of the public imagined. For some, though, it remains incomplete. Occasionally, politicians or farmers encourage reinvestment in the project to put the remaining 300,000 acres under irrigation. It remains to be seen whether these plans will develop, but the agricultural reclamation dream still animates many who hope to maximize resource use for economic gain.

—Adam M. Sowards

See also: *Bureau of Reclamation; Dam Building; Grand Coulee Dam; Pacific Coast; Roosevelt, Franklin D.*

BIBLIOGRAPHY

Northwest Power and Conservation Council. "Columbia River History: Columbia Basin Project." http://www.nwcouncil.org/history/ColumbiaBasinProject.asp.

Pitzer, Paul C. *Grand Coulee: Harnessing a Dream.* Pullman: Washington State University Press, 1994.

Simonds, William Joe. "Columbia Basin Project." Bureau of Reclamation History Program. Denver, CO: 1998. Available at http://www.usbr.gov/projects/.

Dalles Dam

Dalles Dam crosses the Columbia River adjacent to the community of The Dalles, Oregon, about eighty-five miles east of Portland. Completed in 1957 by the U.S. Army Corps of Engineers, Dalles Dam is 260 feet high and nearly 9,000 feet long. Its hydroelectric capacity is roughly 1,800 megawatts. The dam's reservoir, Lake Celilo, backs up twenty-three miles to the next dam on the Columbia River, the John Day Dam. Although one of many dams built in the mid-twentieth century on the Columbia River, Dalles Dam was possibly the most controversial because it inundated a historic Native American fishery at Celilo Falls.

Celilo Falls were just less than 200 miles from the mouth of the Columbia River. There, multiple ice age floods slammed through the Cascade Mountains, leaving in their wake a complex of falls, islands, and other obstructions about fifteen miles long with Celilo being the most prominent. Native traditions hold that Coyote destroyed a rock dam built by sisters who hoarded fish behind it. When Coyote released salmon, indigenous communities enjoyed access to arguably the region's greatest fishery. Archeological evidence indicates that humans have been fishing at the falls for more than 10,000 years. A significant basis of northwestern Native culture was the salmon fishery in the mid-Columbia River, where tribal members gathered annually to harvest millions of pounds of salmon and to build strong cultural bonds among various groups. So important was this indigenous fishery that when territorial governor Isaac Stevens entered into treaties with tribes, Native leaders ensured their people would have continued access to "usual and accustomed" fishing grounds at Celilo Falls and elsewhere. Since first contact between Indians and non-Indians in the region, this stretch of river has been a contested place; both Indian and non-Indian anglers have sought access to its rich salmon resources, and recreational and commercial anglers have vied for space on the river.

As part of larger regional developments, the federal government long imagined a dam at The Dalles. In the early twentieth century, the U.S. Army Corps of Engineers, the Bonneville Power Administration, and the Bureau of Reclamation, along with other state and private organizations, remade the Columbia River Basin through dozens of dams that provided hydroelectric power, flood control, irrigation, and other economic benefits. Congress finally approved the Dalles Dam in 1950, and construction began two years later. Many local and regional residents expected a big economic payoff with industrial development fed by the cheap hydroelectric power generated at the dam; The Dalles anticipated an industrial renaissance.

Not consulted, or downright ignored, Native Americans objected to these developments, as did some non-Native commercial fishers. The Dalles Dam would inundate Celilo Falls and the Native community of Celilo Village just upstream from the dam site, ruining this fishery and damaging residents' economic livelihoods and cultural continuity.

The Bureau of Indian Affairs (BIA) initially opposed the dam and worked to obstruct it, and the U.S. Fish and Wildlife Service (USFWS) also worried about the negative impact the Dalles Dam would impose on the anadromous fishery. However, a policy shift in the BIA and the comparative lack of power of the UWFWS in the federal bureaucracy meant that what was widely perceived to be progress would proceed. Although the dam did promote economic growth, the benefits proved to be far less than boosters had promised.

The federal government compensated for the lost fishery in two ways. First, it supported efforts to restore fish runs. Hatcheries were established to produce more salmon through artificial propagation. Recovering salmon and steelhead runs through such means has become a billion-dollar business but has yielded disappointing results, as some runs still have reached endangered or threatened status. Second, the U.S. Army Corps of Engineers negotiated settlements with Indians who claimed a treaty right to Celilo Falls and nearby areas. These tribes included the Yakama, Warm Springs, Umatilla, Nez Perce, and some unaffiliated American Indians. Collectively, the negotiations were complicated by inter- and intra-Indian politics, not to mention federal agencies' self-interest. In the end, the federal government relocated Celilo Village and paid Indians what collectively amounted to several million dollars. However, this one-time payment was arguably inequitable compensation for what had been a renewable resource; the equivalent of one year's income was exchanged for the effective end of a lifeway thousands of years old.

The Dalles Dam remains a powerful symbol today, generating power for industry and offering flood control, while the great indigenous fishing sites lay buried beneath Lake Celilo's placid waters.

—Adam M. Sowards

See also: *Army Corps of Engineers, United States; Bureau of Indian Affairs; Dam Building; Fish and Wildlife Service, United States; John Day Dam; Pacific Coast*

BIBLIOGRAPHY

Barber, Katrine. *Death of Celilo Falls.* Seattle: Center for the Study of the Pacific Northwest/University of Washington Press, 2005.

Northwest Power and Conservation Council. "Columbia River History: Celilo Falls." http://www.nwcouncil.org/history/CeliloFalls.asp.

U.S. Army Corps of Engineers, Portland District. "Recreation at your Corps Lakes." http://www.nwp.usace.army.mil/locations/home.asp.

Delaware River Basin

The Delaware River Basin includes parts of Delaware, Pennsylvania, New Jersey, and New York. It is regulated by the Delaware River Basin Commission, whose stated purpose is to ensure fair usage of water by all the states concerned through "collective and balanced control." The commission was created when the four states reached a compact signed into law on October 27, 1961. Decisions of the commission affect an area extending from the Delaware River's headwaters near Hancock, New York, to the mouth of the Delaware Bay.

Two concerns were paramount with regard to the river. One was equitable sharing of water. The other was pollution. During World War II, the water was found to be deficient in the oxygen required by fish and other aquatic life. Other concerns included flood mitigation and the provision of recreational activities such as boating and fishing. Prior to the establishment of the commission, forty-three state agencies, fourteen interstate agencies, and nineteen federal agencies had jurisdiction over various parts of the waterway.

The membership of the commission consists of the four state governors from Delaware, New Jersey, New York, and Pennsylvania, as well as a federal representative who is appointed by the president of the United States. All the members are allowed to appoint two alternate members who can attend meetings when they cannot do so themselves. The current federal representative is Brigadier General Peter A. "Duke" DeLuca of the North Atlantic Division of the U.S. Corps of Engineers.

In 1962, the commission approved the first Comprehensive Plan, which included the controversial Tocks Island Dam. After years of conflict with environmental groups, the dam was deauthorized in 1992. At the second annual meeting in 1963, plans were developed to establish a hydroelectric power project. Two years later, the water supply was declared to be in a state of emergency. The commission established a water pollution abatement campaign in 1968, the first of its kind, which set water quality standards. The Beltzville Reservoir on the Lehigh River vastly improved water quality, which helped rebuild the fish stock, at a cost of $23 million.

The work of the commission has gradually paid off. In 1981, the only commercial fishery on the nontidal Delaware River had its largest catch since 1896—6,392 shad. This was evidence that water quality had improved. Just six years later, improvements in water quality led to 56,000 Delaware River shad being landed in just nine weeks. By 1995, it was estimated that some 500,000 shad were swimming in the Delaware River. These successes have enabled the commission to extend its jurisdiction over other nearby areas.

—Justin Corfield

See also: *Army Corps of Engineers, United States; Tocks Island Dam*

BIBLIOGRAPHY

Albert, Richard C. *Damming the Delaware: The Rise and Fall of Tocks Island Dam.* University Park: Pennsylvania State University Press, 1987.

Delaware River Basin Commission. http://www.state.nj.us/drbc/.

Menzies, Elizabeth G. C. *Before the Waters: The Upper Delaware Valley.* New Brunswick, NJ: Rutgers University Press, 1966.

Echo Park Dam

Echo Park Dam was proposed in the 1940s to be built in Dinosaur National Monument near the confluence of the Green River and Yampa River just east of the Utah-Colorado border. The proposal mobilized the conservation movement, which by 1956 had successfully blocked the dam. The controversy surrounding Echo Park Dam was a watershed event in post–World War II environmental politics.

Dinosaur National Monument straddles the Utah-Colorado border just south of Wyoming. In this dry, rocky landscape, President Woodrow Wilson designated a tiny monument in 1915 to protect dinosaur fossils found there, and President Franklin D. Roosevelt significantly expanded it in 1938. Dinosaur National Monument became a popular spot for outdoor recreation. The monument, administered by the National Park Service (NPS), contained the spectacular gorges of the Green and Yampa river valleys. Engineers coveted the steep canyons as perfect dam sites, while postwar outdoor enthusiasts found the beauty and isolation of the region ideal for wilderness recreation.

In the late 1940s, the Bureau of Reclamation proposed a dam within the monument's boundaries at a site called Echo Park. The dam was part of the proposed billion-dollar Colorado River Storage Project (CRSP), which would include ten dams in the basin to fuel economic growth throughout the Intermountain West. Irrigation, hydroelectric power, and flood control were to be the principal benefits of CRSP, and these benefits were welcome to a region aspiring to significant economic growth, especially the

David Brower

David Brower was named the Sierra Club's first executive director in 1952, a post he held until 1969. Under his leadership, the Sierra Club was transformed into a national organization committed to environmental activism.

Brower was born on July 1, 1912, in Berkeley, California. As a young man, he developed a love of the wilderness through mountain climbing. He joined the Sierra Club in 1933 and was named to its board of directors in 1941. After becoming the organization's executive director, he led the successful battle to save the Dinosaur National Monument. Although other victories followed, Brower's abrasive and confrontational style offended both friends and enemies. He resigned the executive directorship of the Sierra Club in 1969 when it became obvious that the board of directors planned to fire him. Brower returned to the Sierra Club's board of directors in 1982, only to resign in May 2000 as a protest against the organization's passivism in the face of environmental challenges around the world.

His uncompromising devotion to environmental causes resulted in his nomination for the Nobel Peace Prize on three different occasions. He died on November 5, 2000.

—John R. Burch Jr.

See also: *Glen Canyon Dam*

BIBLIOGRAPHY

Brower, David Ross. *For Earth's Sake: The Life and Times of David Brower.* Salt Lake City, UT: Peregrine Smith Books, 1990.

Cohen, Michael P. *The History of the Sierra Club, 1892–1970.* San Francisco: Sierra Club Books, 1988.

upper Colorado River Basin states. The Bureau believed Echo Park to be a superior dam site because it anticipated low evaporation from the reservoir. At this time throughout the American West, the Bureau of Reclamation enjoyed substantial power to promote economic growth, significant support from western policy makers and the public, and a strong reputation for expertise and competence. Given this context, it is somewhat surprising the agency's proposal faced any opposition; however, the center of public opinion was shifting.

Besides witnessing the rise of economic development, the postwar era saw a rise in outdoor recreation, such as hiking and river rafting. The National Park Service became a powerful federal booster for such activities, but the greatest power rested with increasing numbers of conservationists and their organizations. Members of the NPS administration and, even more importantly, the Sierra Club and the Wilderness Society rose up in arms to defend Dinosaur National Monument from the Bureau's plans. Led by the Sierra Club's David Brower and the Wilderness Society's Howard Zahniser, conservationists in the early 1950s mobilized in two primary ways and succeeded in making Echo Park the central front in the burgeoning wilderness movement. First, they built a grassroots movement. Concerned citizens and activists wrote articles for the national press, publicizing the importance of the issue and what would be lost if a dam were built within the national park system. Their coup de grâce was *This Is Dinosaur* (1955), a book edited by Wallace Stegner designed to publicize Echo Park with beautiful pictures and prose. The publisher, Alfred Knopf, donated a copy to each member of Congress.

The second tactic, which built on growing public support, found conservationists directly engaging Congress and other federal employees. Members of the grassroots movement flooded their representatives with letters. Critics of the dam pressured the Bureau to search for alternative dam sites. More dramatically, in congressional hearings, Brower challenged technical details of Reclamation's plans, specifically the evaporation rate from the proposed reservoir, and helped dismantle the Bureau's undisputed expertise. After years of political wrangling, wilderness advocates succeeded; by 1956, a new CRSP bill passed Congress without the Echo Park Dam as part of the proposal.

The Echo Park campaign had multiple impacts. Conservationists pledged not to protest the new CRSP with the Echo Park Dam removed. However, the new plans included a high dam at Glen Canyon on the Utah-Arizona border, a dam that became the most controversial dam in the West. Brower and others deeply regretted this compromise. Still, historians recognize the movement as a galvanizing event for conservationists and as the beginning of modern environmentalism. The attention these activists garnered helped keep future plans for dam development within the national park system from succeeding. Echo Park remains, in the words of historian Mark Harvey, "a symbol of wilderness" (2000).

—Adam M. Sowards

See also: *Colorado River Basin; Colorado River Storage Project Act of 1956; Conservation Movement; Glen Canyon Dam; National Parks and Water*

BIBLIOGRAPHY

Harvey, Mark W. T. *A Symbol of Wilderness: Echo Park and the American Conservation Movement.* Seattle: University of Washington Press, 2000. Originally published 1994 by University of New Mexico Press.

Nash, Roderick. *Wilderness and the American Mind.* 3rd ed. New Haven, CT: Yale University Press, 1982.

Rothman, Hal K. *The Greening of a Nation? Environmentalism in the United States since 1945.* Edited by Gerald Nash and Richard W. Etulian. Fort Worth, TX: Harcourt Brace, 1998.

Edwards Aquifer

The Edwards Aquifer, which covers about 3,500 square miles within Texas, is the major source of freshwater for the San Antonio and Austin areas. The aquifer is actually honeycombed, water-bearing, limestone rock that is between 300 to 700 feet thick. It is a fault-zone aquifer; water seeps through broken limestone to refill the water supply. The San Antonio segment of the aquifer, which extends in a 160-mile, arch-shaped curve from Brackettville to Kyle, is between five and forty miles wide at the surface. This segment contains most of the artesian wells and provides most of the water used for agricultural purposes. The Barton Springs segment, not as heavily used, extends from Kyle to Austin. The Edwards Aquifer feeds the Comal and San Marcos Springs, which contribute to the Blanco and Guadalupe Rivers.

The Edwards Aquifer consists of the contributing zone, the recharge zone, and the artesian zone. The 5,400-square-mile Edwards Plateau, also known as the Texas Hill Country, contains the contributing zone, also known as the drainage or catchment area. The land, which is 1,000 to 2,300 feet above sea level, collects water from rainfall, with the water running off into streams that flow over limestone or seeping into the water table. The water proceeds to the recharge zone, a 1,250-square-mile area where fractured limestone allows large amounts of water to flow into the aquifer. The Edwards Aquifer water typically moves from southwest to northeast.

As recharge water moves downward due to gravity, the resulting pressure forces some water upward into artesian wells and springs. Some springs, notably the San Antonio and San Pedro Springs, are usually dry because of the high amounts of water pulled out of the aquifer for human purposes. These springs only flow when water levels are very high. The Comal and San Marcos Springs usually flow year-round.

The Edwards Aquifer is critical to the well-being of the Texas environment. Freshwater input from the Guadalupe River is essential to its coastal estuary, where shrimp and many species of commercially valuable fish hatch. The aquifer also provides water for four species on the federal endangered species list: the fountain darter, two kinds of salamander, and a type of wild rice. The geology of the Edwards Aquifer makes it unusually susceptible to pollution. Nitrate contamination of the aquifer has significantly increased over the decades, apparently because the fertilizers used on Texas farms leach very quickly into the aquifer.

Historically, crop irrigation has represented the single largest area of water consumption in Texas. For decades, farmers in central Texas have been pumping water from the Edwards Aquifer to irrigate their fields. At the same time, the cities of San Antonio and Austin have been tapping the underground reservoir to support population growth. The many demands on the Edwards Aquifer pose concerns. As more water is pumped out of the aquifer, the water level drops, decreasing the flow out of the San Marcos and Comal Springs. If the springs go dry, the rare species they support will not survive there. When the aquifer drops to 619 feet above sea level, the water flow at Comal Springs comes to a halt. In 1990, 1.3 million central Texas farmers and residents drew half a billion gallons of water from the Edwards Aquifer each day. As the populations of Austin and San Antonio have increased, more water has been pulled from the aquifer. Additionally, climate change may alter the amount of water flowing underground to recharge the aquifer. Texas is already experiencing intensifying drought conditions.

The people who are dependent on the Edwards Aquifer have taken steps to protect their water supply, but competing demands have made agreement difficult to achieve. To safeguard their drinking water, both Austin and San Antonio have been purchasing open space that lies over the aquifer with the aim of reducing the amount of water pulled out for farm use. The Edwards Aquifer Authority was formed in the early 1990s to regulate pumping and to maintain water quality. In 2007, it established a pumping cap of 572,000 acre-feet, but it has struggled to establish water quality standards. Parochialism and the inability to see the Edwards Aquifer as part of a holistic environment have complicated efforts to protect the water supply.

—Caryn Neumann

See also: *Aquifers; Fertilizers*

BIBLIOGRAPHY

Maclay, Robert W. *Geology and Hydrology of the Edwards Aquifer in the San Antonio Area, Texas.* Austin, TX: U.S. Geological Survey, 1995.
Miller, Char, ed. *On the Border: An Environmental History of San Antonio.* Pittsburgh, PA: University of Pittsburgh Press, 2001.

Elephant Butte Reservoir

Formed by the Elephant Butte Dam on the Rio Grande, the Elephant Butte Reservoir is 125 miles north of El Paso, Texas, in south-central New Mexico. The reservoir covers 57 square miles and has a storage capacity of about 2.1 million acre-feet of water, which is used to provide irrigation for over 150,000 acres and year-round power generation for area residents.

The construction of a reservoir on the Rio Grande was the subject of much debate prior to the completion of the dam in 1916. The issues included interstate and international water appropriations among New Mexico Territory, Texas, Mexico, and Colorado; domestic agricultural conflicts among farmers in the vicinity of Ciudad Juarez, Chihuahua; El Paso, Texas; and the Mesilla Valley of New Mexico; the natural cycles of water flows, floods, and droughts; and, in the end, debates over private versus federal funding for the project. Many of these difficulties had to be addressed before the project could move forward.

A Senate Select Committee on Irrigation and Reclamation visited the region in 1889 to assess the situation at about the same time the state of Texas requested that Congress pass legislation to define the rights and privileges of western citizens regarding the use of interstate streams. Locally, residents of El Paso complained that their cross-border neighbors in Juarez were building a dam in violation of an 1884 U.S.-Mexico agreement that prohibited both countries from installing structures that could alter the course of the Rio Grande and thus the international boundary. In response, the International Boundary Commission (IBC) was established and given jurisdiction over water issues. The IBC was not in place, however, until 1894.

In the meantime, tensions rose over various plans to build a reservoir on the American side. A proposal from El Paso in 1888 would have placed a dam about three miles north of that city, creating a lake fifteen miles long and seven miles wide. While the proposal gained support in Juarez and within the Texas congressional delegation, southern New Mexicans reacted unfavorably because the site would not serve their irrigation needs and would flood much fertile land in southern Mesilla Valley (Clark 1987).

The debate reached a fever pitch by 1895 after a severe water shortage the preceding year and the announcement that a private company had filed papers in New Mexico Territory for the purpose of constructing a dam near Elephant Butte. Residents in both El Paso and Juarez voiced concerns that such a dam would take away water from a potential international dam, contribute to water shortages downstream, and violate several international treaties.

Within a couple of years, several rival companies were pursuing a New Mexico dam, and the Rio Grande Dam & Irrigation Company (RGD&IC) emerged as the leader. The RGD&IC had secured numerous rights-of-way for laterals, canals, and a diversion dam in the Mesilla Valley, thus not only setting up a strong potential network but gaining the support of local farmers. Diplomats on both sides of the border tried to negotiate a mutually agreeable solution for all.

The situation changed radically with the passage of the Reclamation Act in 1902. A Reclamation Service engineer suggested that the new agency develop a larger, shallow reservoir behind a higher dam a short distance below the RGD&IC site that could impound enough water to irrigate all the farmlands of southern New Mexico and the El Paso–Juarez Valleys, as well as address concerns about high evaporation rates, silt content, and flooding. It took several years to work out the legal details, but the essence of this compromise proposal moved forward. In 1910, the secretary of the interior directed the Reclamation Service to complete the Rio Grande Project as quickly as possible. The agency finished the first downstream diversion dam in 1908 and the Elephant Butte Dam and Reservoir in 1916 (Clark 1987).

Water from the Elephant Butte Reservoir is allocated to three entities: Elephant Butte Irrigation District (southern New Mexico), El Paso County Water Improvement District No. 1, and Mexican users in the Juarez Valley. The American associations organized during the Rio Grande Project not only provide water to farmers but also collect fees to pay for the project. Caballo Dam was built in the late 1930s downstream of Elephant Butte Dam to provide a secondary storage reservoir and to replace capacity in the original reservoir lost due to river siltation.

Today the Elephant Butte Reservoir continues to function much as it was originally designed a century ago. A state park established in the 1920s and developed with improvements by the Civilian Conservation Corps in the 1930s provides recreational activities at the reservoir. The reservoir and irrigation system it supports are forecast to be operational for many more decades, though increasing urbanization and competing water interests may change its function from agriculture to other uses.

—Cameron L. Saffell

See also: *International Boundary and Water Commission (United States and Mexico); Rio Grande River Basin*

BIBLIOGRAPHY

Clark, Ira G. *Water in New Mexico: A History of Its Management and Use.* Albuquerque: University of New Mexico Press, 1987.
Elephant Butte Irrigation District. *General Data and Information.* Las Cruces, NM: Elephant Butte Irrigation District, 1998.
Lester, Paul A. "History of the Elephant Butte Irrigation District." MA thesis, New Mexico State University, 1977.

Erie Canal

Built between 1817 and 1825, the Erie Canal opened a water transportation route from the Hudson River at Troy, New York, just north of Albany, to Lake Erie at Buffalo. When completed, the canal was 363 miles long and 40 feet wide at the top of the channel, and it had a minimum depth of 4 feet of water. It carried boats 61 feet long and 7 feet wide with a draft of 3.5 feet and a capacity of 10 to 11 tons. Between 1905 and 1918, the canal was enlarged to an average width of 125 feet and 12 foot minimum depth, abandoning much of the original channel while making use of rivers bypassed by the earlier construction. At this time, it was also incorporated into the New York Barge Canal System. The new system accommodated barges 300 feet long and 43.5 feet wide with capacity of up to 3,600 tons. The 83 original locks, 90 feet long and 15 feet wide, were replaced with 35 locks that were 328 feet long and 45 feet wide. On the Lockport-Niagara Escarpment, two flights of five locks each, built 1823–1825, were replaced with two power-operated locks.

The total rise running east to west is 566 feet. Rising 420 foot from tidewater level on the Hudson, through a series of locks in the Mohawk Valley, the canal descends to 366 feet above sea level east of Syracuse, then goes upward another 200 feet to Lake Erie. The Mohawk River valley runs over rapids and waterfalls through a steep gorge approaching Albany, so the canal crosses the river on an aqueduct, following shelves cut in the stone sides of the mountains. Another major feature is the crossing of the Irondequoit Valley, 4,950 feet from rim to rim, on three natural ridges joined by two stone and earth embankments 76 feet above the valley floor. The Rochester Aqueduct, 802 feet long, crosses the Genesee River on 11 stone arches.

DeWitt Clinton, as mayor of New York City and then governor of New York, provided the political will that committed the state to build the Erie Canal. Thomas Jefferson, a political ally of Clinton, thought federal underwriting of the canal a "little short of madness" in 1809. The initial cost of construction was $7 million. Previously, shipping a ton of freight from Lake Erie to the Hudson cost $100 and took two weeks by the primitive roads available in the early nineteenth century. When freight was shipped by barge on the

A barge travels along the Erie Canal in this watercolor from the late 1820s. At the time of the canal's completion in 1825, the Erie Canal was by far the longest canal in the world. An engineering marvel, it opened up the country west of the Appalachians to trade and commerce.
The Granger Collection, New York

canal, the cost was reduced to $10 a ton, taking only three and one-half days.

Like many early nineteenth-century canal projects, construction relied heavily on the labor of at least 3,000 Irish immigrants, about half settling permanently in the area. Governor Clinton also released minor offenders from prisons and jails on condition that they work on the canal at regular rates of pay. Typical remuneration was $12 per month in addition to board and crude housing at the work sites. An important asset was the discovery by Assistant Engineer Canvass White of a limestone deposit right in the path of the canal that was suitable for making hydraulic cement, previously manufactured only in Europe. Over half a million bushels were mined and processed for the canal's locks.

Commercial use of the canal reached its peak in the 1890s. By the early 1960s, the canal ceased to be of significant commercial use. In 1992, in order to redevelop the canals for recreation and tourism, responsibility for the entire state system was transferred from the state's Department of Transportation to the New York State Thruway Authority. In 1995, a Canal Recreationway Commission prepared a plan that led to increased use by pleasure boats and recreational anglers and the conversion of mule towpaths to bicycle routes.

—Charles Rosenberg

See also: *Clinton, DeWitt; Interbasin Water Transfer; Locks; Outdoor Recreation; River Transportation; Saint Lawrence Seaway*

BIBLIOGRAPHY

Condon, George E. *Stars in the Water: The Story of the Erie Canal.* Garden City, NY: Doubleday, 1974.

Shaw, Ronald E. *Erie Water West: A History of the Erie Canal, 1792–1854.* Lexington: University Press of Kentucky, 1966.

Sheriff, Carol. *The Artificial River: The Erie Canal and the Paradox of Progress, 1817–1862.* New York: Hill and Wang, 1996.

Svejda, George J. *Irish Immigrant Participation in the Construction of the Erie Canal.* Washington, DC: Division of History, U.S. Office of Archeology and Historic Preservation, 1969. Available at http://www.nps.gov/history/history/online_books/ohio/labor.pdf.

Flaming Gorge

Flaming Gorge, a canyon in northeastern Utah, is the site of a concrete dam along the Green River. This dam created a large reservoir and a National Recreation Area of the same name. The reservoir's crest elevation is 6,047 feet above sea level, and it has a storage capacity of 3,788,900 acre-feet of water. Construction lasted from 1958 to 1964. Its crest lies 502 feet above the bedrock, making this the third largest dam in the Colorado Basin behind Hoover and Glen Canyon Dams.

During the Proterozoic eon, the Flaming Gorge area was near the coast of a massive continent, near sea level. Much of the region's bedrock was formed during various uplifts of the Uinta Mountains; the oldest bedrock dates from the Proterozoic. Colorful rock formations of red, orange, green, and gray were formed later, during the Triassic and Jurassic periods, and a large number of dinosaur fossils have been found in the area. Well-preserved fish fossils have been found in an area that was a lake during the Eocene epoch 40 to 50 million years ago.

The terrain around Flaming Gorge is mountainous and semiarid. Flora include alpine species and shrubs. Animals resident in the area include moose, elk, mule deer, and pronghorn antelope as well as mustangs (wild horses), cougars, and black bears. Smaller mammals—bobcats, badgers, squirrels, and chipmunks—are plentiful. Bald eagles, hawks, owls, heron, jays, and ravens inhabit the region

Native Americans occupied this area about 400 CE. They grew crops such as squash, beans, and corn. By the tenth century, they lived in permanent houses and traded with Native groups from the Plains. By the fourteenth century, due perhaps to climate change, the Native population had left the region. By the nineteenth century, several Ute tribes occupied an area from western Utah to central Colorado, including the Four Corners area.

John Wesley Powell explored the Uinta Mountains region in 1872 and visited the gorge. He observed how the sandstone's reddish color reacted with the sunlight and named the canyon Flaming Gorge. Powell was intrigued by the Moenkopi and Chinle formations, which date from the Triassic period.

The Flaming Gorge Dam is upstream from the point originally planned for the highly controversial Echo Park Dam, which would have been inside Dinosaur National Monument. In 1956, conservationists succeeded in stopping the Echo Park Dam from being built. The Flaming Gorge Dam is near Dutch John, Utah, and downstream from Flaming Gorge, Horseshoe Canyon, Red Canyon, and Beehive Point, all of which are currently underwater. The dam was dedicated on August 17, 1964, by First Lady Claudia "Lady Bird" Johnson.

During the early 1980s, the Bureau of Reclamation evaluated the dam for possible detrimental effects upon four endangered fish species: the Colorado pikeminnow, humpback chub, razorback sucker, and bonytail. As a result, in 1987, the Bureau instituted the Upper Colorado River Endangered Fish Recovery Program, and in 2000 it issued flow and temperature recommendations for fish living downstream from the dam. These actions were intended to restore riparian ecosystems in two areas below the dam, Canyonlands National Park and Dinosaur National Monument. In 2008, the Bureau of Land Management ceased to allow energy providers to lease certain lands that border national parks and monuments in Utah, including those near Flaming Gorge.

The Flaming Gorge National Recreation Area, established in 1968, covers 207,363 acres and has a shoreline of 375 miles. The reservoir extends ninety-one miles north to a point near the town of Green River, Wyoming. The recreation area and its facilities are operated by the U.S. Forest Service as a part of the Ashley National Forest. The reservoir is home to a number of fish species, including German brown trout, kokanee salmon, and channel catfish. The dam includes a power plant that generates 500,000 megawatts annually. Below the dam, the Green River is known for its rainbow trout and white-water rapids that allow rafting.

—Ralph Hartsock

See also: *Echo Park Dam; Powell, John Wesley*

BIBLIOGRAPHY

National Park Service. *A Survey of the Recreational Resources of the Colorado River Basin.* Washington, DC: U.S. Department of the Interior, National Park Service, 1950. Available at http://www.nps.gov/history/history/online_books/colorado/index.htm.

Sprinkel, Douglas A. "Geology of Flaming Gorge National Recreational Area, Utah-Wyoming." In *Geology of Utah's Parks and Monuments: Millennium Field Conference,* edited by Douglas A. Sprinkel, Thomas C. Chidsey Jr., and Paul Bradley Anderson, 277–99. Salt Lake City: Utah Geological Association, 2000.

U.S. Geological Survey. "Green River, Flaming Gorge, and Red Canyon: Historic Photographs of Powell Survey Second Expedition, 1871–2." Available at http://3dparks.wr.usgs.gov/.

Fontana Dam

Fontana Dam is located on the Little Tennessee River in Swain and Graham Counties, North Carolina. When it opened in 1944, it was the fourth largest dam in the world and the biggest dam in the United States east of the Rocky Mountains. It remains the tallest dam in the eastern United States. It was constructed with a budget of $29 million and has been hailed as one of the great marvels of construction in that part of the United States.

The dam took its name from the lumber and copper-mining town of Fontana, which was flooded by the dam's creation of Fontana Lake. The villages of Bushnell, Forney, and Judson were also flooded. Before construction of the dam, engineers made and tested a number of scale models at the Tennessee Valley Authority (TVA) hydraulic laboratory at Norris, Tennessee. The TVA sought to provide electrical power to the region, especially Maryville, Tennessee, and Bryson City, North Carolina, with a single large dam.

Although there was much local support for the project, construction work was delayed by a deadlock over construction costs between the federal government and the Aluminum Company of America (ALCOA), each blaming the other for intransigence. ALCOA had started investigating a source of cheap power around 1910. In 1913, ALCOA purchased the Tallassee Power Company (Tapoco) and began pushing for a dam to be constructed to generate power. On August 14, 1941, the TVA and ALCOA signed an agreement that gave the TVA possession of the Fontana Dam upon its construction and all the electrical output of Tapoco. In return, ALCOA would get access to the power it required for twenty years.

Work on the dam started on January 1, 1942, during World War II. The dam was completed after just over two and one-half years and formally opened on November 7, 1944. It is 480 feet tall and 2,365 feet long. The project manager, F. C. Schlemmer, was one of the first six men hired by the TVA when it was established. He briefly left the TVA for a better-paid position in a private company, but he soon returned to the government agency because he was so attached to working on the Fontana Dam.

Fontana Lake, which was created by the dam, gets its water from the Little Tennessee River. Gradually the lake became a site of recreation for many Americans, and by the late 1970s, the wild trout streams that flowed into the lake were attracting anglers from across North Carolina and beyond.

—Justin Corfield

See also: *Tennessee Valley Authority*

BIBLIOGRAPHY

Collier, Christopher Percy. "What Time Do They Turn the River On?" *New York Times,* October 20, 2006.

Durisch, Lawrence L. "The TVA Program and the War Effort." *Journal of Politics* 8, no. 4 (1946): 531–37.

Gunther, John. *Inside USA.* London: Hamish Hamilton, 1947.
Taylor, Stephen Wallace. *The New South's New Frontier: A Social History of Economic Development in Southwestern North Carolina.* Gainesville: University Press of Florida, 2001.

Fort Peck Dam

The first flood control dam to be constructed on the Missouri River, Fort Peck Dam was built between 1933 and 1940. It is located in northeastern Montana, approximately seventeen miles from the town of Glasgow. Besides providing flood control, the dam was also intended to generate hydroelectric power and to provide water storage that would enable the maintenance of a navigable river channel on the lower Missouri River. Because of the commercial interests involved with river navigation, the project was authorized as part of President Franklin D. Roosevelt's National Industrial Recovery Act in 1933. Construction of the dam began within ten days of the signing of the authorization. President Roosevelt visited the site and made a speech there on August 6, 1934.

When it was built, Fort Peck Dam was the largest dam in the world and was considered an engineering marvel. While it no longer holds that distinction, it is still the largest dam of its particular type—a hydraulic, earth-filled dam. The dam is 250 feet high and more than 4 miles long. It is 4,900 feet wide at its base and 50 feet wide at the top, and it contains more than 125 million cubic feet of fill material. The inaugural issue of *Life* magazine in November 1936 had a photograph of the Fort Peck dam by Margaret Bourke-White on its cover; this photograph was also later used on a U.S. postage stamp. Fort Peck Lake, created by the dam, is the fifth largest man-made lake in the United States, stretching over 130 miles upstream from the dam. The lake has 1,600 miles of shoreline and can store 18.9 million acre-feet of water. The entire lake lies within the Charles M. Russell National Wildlife Refuge.

Building the dam caused a massive influx of workers into a remote rural area. More than 10,000 workers were involved at the height of construction in 1936. Eighteen boomtowns grew up around the project to serve the needs of these workers, bringing another 30,000 to 40,000 people into the region. Boats needed for the construction project were built in a shipyard constructed at the work site. Four large dredges were built to dredge the river bottom, and other boats were constructed to pump the slurry that went into the dam. Much of the riprap for the dam came from a quarry at Snake

Butte, thirty miles away. A railroad line was built to bring the stone from the quarry to the construction site.

The closure of the dam across the Missouri River occurred on June 24, 1937, although finishing work on the dam continued until 1940. A massive slide of the fill materials on September 22, 1938, set back construction temporarily. Over 5 million cubic yards of fill material slid off the dam structure and back into the river. More than thirty workers were carried away by the sliding fill material. While most were rescued, eight men lost their lives in the disaster. After investigations into the cause of the slide, modifications were made to the design of the dam, including widening the base and lessening the angle of the slope of the dam face.

The first hydroelectric powerhouse at Fort Peck was begun in 1941, and it produced its first electricity in July 1943. A second powerhouse was built in 1961. The water that powers these generators runs through four diversion tunnels, each twenty-four feet in diameter and more than a mile long. Today, the Fort Peck power plants produce about 1 billion kilowatt-hours of electricity per year. Most of this power is sold to several rural electric cooperatives in the region.

The Fort Peck Dam was built before the Pick–Sloan Plan was adopted for the development of the Missouri River basin. When that plan was approved, however, Fort Peck was incorporated into it, and enlargements and improvements were planned for the reservoir. The multiple purposes that the Fort Peck Dam and other upper Missouri River reservoirs were intended to fulfill has led to continuing political debates over which of these purposes should have priority. For example, in drought years, residents and politicians from the upper Missouri region question the use of water from their region to maintain barge navigation hundreds of miles away on the lower Missouri River. In general, in all of the upper Missouri basin reservoirs, irrigation has come to have a lower priority than flood control and maintaining river navigation in the lower basin.

—Mark S. Joy

See also: *Dam Building; Missouri River Basin*

BIBLIOGRAPHY

Lonnquist, Lois. *Fifty Cents an Hour: The Builders and Boomtowns of the Fort Peck Dam.* 2nd ed. Helena, MT: MtSky Press, 2006.
Thorson, John E. *River of Promise, River of Peril: The Politics of Managing the Missouri River.* Lawrence: University Press of Kansas, 1994.
U.S. Army Corps of Engineers. "Fort Peck Dam & Lake Homepage." http://www.nwo.usace.army.mil/html/Lake_Proj/fortpeck/welcome.html.

Friant Dam

This concrete gravity dam is located on the upper part of the San Joaquin River about fifteen miles north of Fresno, California. It was built between 1937 and 1942 to help with the irrigation of farmland in the San Joaquin Valley through the Madera and Friant-Kern Canals, part of the massive Central Valley Project. Crops in this area included citrus fruits, grapes, plums, nectarines, and cotton, all of which require a great deal of water. The dam was also intended to help with flood control. The lake that the dam created, Lake Millerton, is maintained by the Bureau of Reclamation and hosts a fish hatchery and provides recreational opportunities. The construction of the dam was closely tied to the work on the nearby Shasta Dam.

Although not the primary goal of constructing the dam, a 25-megawatt power plant was built nearby to generate hydroelectricity for the Friant Power Authority and two smaller power plants. The Madera Canal, which takes water north, was completed in June 1944, and the Friant-Kern Canal, which takes water south, was completed several years later. The latter allowed the irrigation system to be expanded from the Friant Dam to the Kern River, 157 miles away. Together, these canals provided large amounts of water to the San Joaquin Valley.

Opponents of the Friant Dam included farmers of land in the San Joaquin Valley that was often irrigated when the original water systems flooded. When the Friant Dam removed the danger of flooding, it also deprived some of these farmers of water, leading to litigation, particularly in the case *Miller & Lux, Inc. v. Madera Irrigation District* (Superior Court, Fresno County, No. 25729, 1933).

The lakes created by construction of the Friant Dam and the Shasta Dam were quickly developed for recreational use. Many tourists today use Lake Millerton for camping, fishing, swimming, and water-skiing.

—Justin Corfield

See also: *Bureau of Reclamation; Central Valley Project; Shasta Dam*

BIBLIOGRAPHY

Eiselen, Elizabeth. "The Central Valley Project: 1947." *Economic Geography* 23, no. 1 (1947): 22–31.
Goodall, Merrill. "Land and Power Administration of the Central Valley Project." *Journal of Land & Public Utility Economics* 18, no. 3 (1942): 299–311.
Maass, Arthur A. "Administering the CVP." *California Law Review* 38, no. 4 (1950): 666–95.
Ostrom, Vincent. "State Administration of Natural Resources in the West." *American Political Science Review* 47, no. 2 (1953): 478–93.
Simpich, Frederick. "More Water for California's Great Central Valley." *National Geographic Magazine* 90, no. 5 (1946).
Treadwell, Edward F. "Developing a New Philosophy of Water Rights." *California Law Review* 38, no. 4 (1950): 572–87.

Fryingpan-Arkansas Project

The Fryingpan-Arkansas Project, or Fry-Ark as it is popularly known, is a complex water project built by the Bureau of Reclamation to deliver water from the snowy slopes west of the Continental Divide in Colorado to agricultural interests in the Arkansas River Valley and cities along Colorado's Front Range. The diversion of water from the western slope across mountain passes was a complicated undertaking of enormous size and scope: it required six storage dams; seventeen diversion dams and structures; hundreds of miles of combined canals, conduits, tunnels, and transmission lines; and two power plants, switchyards, and substations.

On the western slope of the Continental Divide are the headwaters of countless rivers and streams that flow into the Colorado River. The two rivers directly involved in this project are the Roaring Fork River, which flows northwesterly through the town of Aspen and into the Colorado River, and the Fryingpan River, which runs east-west into Roaring Fork River. On the other side of the Continental Divide, the Arkansas River originates in the Sawatch and Sangre de Cristo Ranges, flows south, and descends 6,600 feet for 150 miles before proceeding east through south-central and southeastern Colorado. Sometimes, by the time the river reaches Kansas, most of the water has been used in Colorado. Any remaining water eventually trickles into the Mississippi River—making a total journey of 1,459 miles. The Arkansas River is small compared to eastern rivers and does not consistently provide the flow necessary to irrigate parched fields.

Diverting Water

Transmountain diversion projects have long been a source of bitter dispute in Colorado, and residents on the western slope have resented the Front Range for its insatiable demand for water. But those on the east side probably have good reason to lust after the water—not only because higher concentrations of people in the cities require it but also because Colorado does not use its full share of water from the Colorado River Basin. Early on, diversion efforts were a target of local and private enterprise. The cities of

Denver and Colorado Springs undertook the Blue River project; Denver also built Dillon Reservoir, the Moffat Tunnel, the Vasquez Tunnel, and others for the purpose of conveying water from western Colorado to the state's capital. Private companies financed the Otero Canal, Clear Creek Reservoir, and Busk-Ivanhoe Tunnel. The first transmountain diversion project on the Arkansas was the Twin Lakes System, operated since 1935 by the Colorado Canal and later expanded as part of Fry-Ark.

The overappropriation of water from the Arkansas had long been a major concern, and in the 1920s, local farmers and irrigation promoters began to envision a large-scale transmountain diversion project to remedy the problem. They justified the developments not just for irrigation but to meet power, municipal water, and other associated needs, such as flood control. The dream of supplementing the Arkansas River with water from the western slope took shape as the Gunnison-Arkansas Project proposed diverting 800,000 acre-feet of water per year from the Gunnison River to the eastern slope. In 1947, the Bureau of Reclamation decided the original plan was too big, too costly, and too controversial. Even the smaller Fryingpan-Arkansas Project's design to divert 69,200 acre-feet from the upper Roaring Fork River Basin and channel it across the Continental Divide came under fire from opponents, who believed water on the western slope ought to be kept where it originated to support future growth.

The Project

The Southeastern Colorado Water Conservancy District, formed in 1958, assumed the responsibility of repaying a portion of the reimbursable costs of the project, exclusive of Ruedi Dam and Reservoir. At a formal ceremony on January 13, 1965, Colorado members of Congress and Secretary of the Interior Stewart L. Udall met to sign the contract under which the water conservancy district would repay $60 million of the total construction costs. The district, which holds the water rights for the Fryingpan-Arkansas River, began the fifty-year repayment schedule in 1982. It also assumed the job of distributing water to users on the Eastern Slope.

The Fryingpan-Arkansas Project is interesting in that it was authorized and constructed during a period of both ambitious federal involvement in water projects and mounting distrust of and opposition to expensive, complicated water projects. Fry-Ark took a lengthy ten years for authorization. Were it not for the firm yet cautious support of powerful Colorado Representative and chair of the House Interior and Insular Affairs Committee Wayne Aspinall, the water project might never have seen the light of day.

Construction was also lengthy, as the beneficiaries waited another two decades before the entire project became operational. Probably about a dozen contracted work projects, large and small, kept crews busy between 1964 and the early 1980s. Construction proceeded intermittently, beginning at the higher elevations on the western slope; continuing on the collection system connecting the two sides; and capping off with the dams, reservoirs, and power plants on the eastern slope. Some features of the original plan were modified or abandoned. Some were simply infeasible or unnecessary, like the Otero Canal and Power Plant and Clear Creek Dam (the canal and dam were eventually constructed, but not by the Bureau of Reclamation). Pueblo Dam was one of seven recently constructed earth-fill dams earmarked for operative changes following the collapse of Teton Dam in June 1976. Reclamation also relocated sections of the Fountain Valley Conduit, which transports water for municipal and industrial uses.

Farmers use a sizable portion of project water, but the vast majority of it goes to urban and metropolitan areas, and the proportion of irrigation to municipal/industrial use continues to decrease. Approximately 60,000 acres of irrigated cropland have been dried up so that municipal and industrial users can have access to water. Along with the development and growth of the Front Range come water-related challenges, and it is never certain how best to allocate water and where to tap into new water resources. The matter of water supply has concerned elected officials and other interested parties, and from time to time these groups come together to discuss the transfer of water within the state of Colorado.

—Jedediah Rogers

See also: *Aspinall, Wayne N.; Udall, Stewart*

BIBLIOGRAPHY

Milenski, Frank. *Water: The Answer to a Desert's Prayer.* Edited by Beatrice Spade. Boone, CO: Trails, 1990.

U.S. Department of the Interior, Bureau of Reclamation. *Annual Project History, Fryingpan-Arkansas Project.* Vols. 1–19, 1963–1981 (Accession No. 8NN-115-90-039). Records of the Bureau of Reclamation, Record Group 115. National Archives and Records Administration—Rocky Mountain Region, Denver, CO.

U.S. Department of the Interior. *Water and Power Resources Service Project Data, 1981.* Denver, CO: U.S. Government Printing Office, 1981. Available at http://www.archive.org/details/waterpowerresour00unit/.

Gallipolis Locks and Dam

Located in Ohio and West Virginia, 40 miles northeast of Huntington, West Virginia, the Gallipolis Locks and Dam control the water in the Ohio River. They take their name from the town of Gallipolis, Ohio.

In 1790, French migrants were encouraged to settle in this location, and plans were drawn up by Etienne Hallet, who had fled the French Revolution the previous year. This project was also supported by the naturalist Antoine Francois Saudrain de Vigni. Although the French settlement was never realized in this form, the town of Gallipolis was founded around this time.

In the mid-twentieth century, plans were drawn up for building a dam on that part of the Ohio River. A dam would provide hydropower, which would be useful in the region. However, ships needed to navigate the Ohio River, so a series of locks had to be built as well. The initial project started construction in the 1930s, and the dam and locks were completed by October 1937. At its completion, the dam was the largest roller dam in the world and cost $10.4 million. Its eight concrete pillars, each 135 feet high, were spaced at 125 feet intervals across the river.

The initial construction was largely uncontroversial. However, pressure arose to change the locks and dam and to enlarge the entire project. Starting in the late 1960s, there was concern about how much enlargement would cost. Senator Robert Byrd (D-WV) was an important force in moving funding through Congress, especially as money had to be allocated for the construction of the Bonneville Lock and Dam in Oregon and Washington at the same time. The cost of the new project was estimated in 1987 to be $127.6 million. Guy F. Atkinson Construction Co. Operating Unit headed the project, which would further control the river, develop responsible water planning, and provide hydropower. The final cost was $217.6 million. After it was completed, tests on fish and other aquatic life showed no significant changes, except that there seemed to be fewer shorthead redhorse, black buffalo, and quillback.

—Justin Corfield

See also: *Bonneville Dam; Locks*

BIBLIOGRAPHY

Clay, R. Berle, and Charles M. Niquette. "Middle Woodland Mortuary Ritual in the Gallipolis Locks and Dam Vicinity, Mason County, West Virginia." *West Virginia Archaeologist* 44, no. 1–2 (1992): 1–25.

Johannesen, Eric. *A Cleveland Legacy: The Architecture of Walker and Weeks.* Kent, OH: Kent State University Press, 1999.

Kemp, Emory Leland. *The Great Kanawha Navigation.* Pittsburgh, PA: University of Pittsburgh Press, 2000.

Simon, Thomas P., ed. *Assessing the Sustainability and Biological Integrity of Water Resources Using Fish Communities.* Boca Raton, FL: CRC Press, 1999.

Tolchin, Martin. "Congress: Hitching a Ride on Capitol Hill." *New York Times,* May 2, 1984.

Garrison Dam

Located on the Missouri River approximately seventy-five miles upstream from Bismarck, North Dakota, Garrison Dam was built between 1947 and 1960 as part of the Pick-Sloan Plan, authorized by Congress in the Flood Control Act of 1944. The dam, one of the largest rolled-earth dams in the world, is 12,000 feet long, 210 feet high, 2,600 feet wide at the base, and 60 feet wide at the top. It contains more than 70 million cubic feet of earth fill and more than 1.5 million cubic feet of concrete. The dam forms Lake Sakakawea, named for the Shoshone Indian woman (sometimes called Sacajawea) who accompanied the Lewis and Clark expedition from the Mandan villages on the Missouri River west into Montana. Lake Sakakawea is one of the largest man-made lakes in the United States, extending upstream about 178 miles to Williston, North Dakota. The lake is six miles wide at its widest point and averages two to three miles wide. The maximum depth is 180 feet at the face of the dam. When the lake is at its normal operating level, it covers 368,000 acres and has 1,300 miles of shoreline. The lake can store nearly 23 million acre-feet of water.

After damaging floods in the lower Missouri River basin in 1942 and 1943, Colonel Lewis A. Pick of the U.S. Army Corps of Engineers began working on a massive plan for several dams on the main stem of the Missouri and perhaps more than a hundred smaller dams on its tributaries. The Corps's plans were concerned primarily with flood control and maintaining significant water for navigation on the lower Missouri. W. G. Sloan, a Bureau of Reclamation engineer, was working on similar plans, but his focused on providing water for irrigation and hydroelectric power generation. President Franklin D. Roosevelt wanted to create a Missouri Valley Authority, patterned after the Tennessee Valley Authority, to oversee all development in the Missouri basin. Neither the Bureau of Reclamation nor the Corps wanted another federal agency involved, so they compromised and created the Pick-Sloan Plan for the Missouri

River basin, which Congress incorporated into the Flood Control Act of 1944.

Construction of the dam and the associated electrical power plant brought hundreds of workers into this rural area, with a peak employment of 2,300 in the fall of 1952. The dam across the river was closed in April 1953. In January 1956, the first three hydroelectric generators were installed. Today, there are five generators with a total capacity of 515,000 kilowatt-hours. Depending on water levels and demand for electricity, the Garrison plant produces between 1.8 and 2.6 billion kilowatt-hours of electricity per year. Seven major transmission lines carry this power to various substations. Production and marketing of this power is overseen by the Western Area Power Administration.

In 1957, the Bureau of Reclamation announced plans for the Garrison Diversion Unit, a massive project designed to bring water from the Missouri River to east-central North Dakota for municipal water supplies, industrial use, and irrigation. The plan called for an elaborate system of pumping stations, 8 reservoirs, and over 6,700 miles of canals. Planners envisioned irrigating about 1 million acres of land. The project was estimated to cost over $500 million, in 1956 dollars, and would take several decades to complete. Over time, the Garrison Diversion project has proven highly controversial and has faced much criticism over its costs, its environmental impact, and whether the proposed irrigation is desirable. Congress and several presidential administrations have scaled back the plan in various ways, and only a fraction of what was originally planned has been built.

Building the Garrison Dam had a profound and largely negative impact on the Three Affiliated Tribes (now known as the Mandan-Hidatsa-Arikara Nation) living on the Fort Berthold reservation in North Dakota. More than 156,000 acres of their reservation, including the best agricultural lands in the river bottoms, were covered by Lake Sakakawea. Eighty percent of the reservation population—more than 300 families—had to be relocated. The lake disrupted the way people lived, worked, and traveled through the region. Unemployment, which was virtually unknown on the reservation before the lake was built, rose significantly afterwards. The Mandan-Hidatsa-Arikara Nation initially received $12.6 million from the government in exchange for the land taken and to pay for relocating schools, community facilities, cemeteries, and monuments. In 1992, Title XXXV of Public law 102-575 authorized more than $209 million in additional compensation to the Mandan-Hidatsa-Arikara Nation for their losses from the Garrison Project.

—Mark S. Joy

See also: *Dam Building; Flood Control Act of 1944; Missouri River Basin*

BIBLIOGRAPHY

Lawson, Michael L. *Dammed Indians: The Pick-Sloan Plan and the Missouri River Sioux, 1944–1980.* Norman: University of Oklahoma Press, 1982.

Robinson, Elwyn B. *History of North Dakota.* Fargo: Institute for Regional Studies, North Dakota State University, 1995. Originally published 1966 by University of Nebraska Press.

U.S. Army Corps of Engineers. "Garrison Dam." http://www.nwo .usace.army.mil/html/Lake_Proj/garrison/dam.html.

Glen Canyon Dam

Glen Canyon, located in northern Arizona, is the site of a concrete dam across the Colorado River prior to its entry into the Grand Canyon. The dam's crest elevation is 3,715 feet above sea level, and it has a storage capacity of 27 million acre-feet of water. It creates Lake Powell, which extends into Utah. Construction lasted from 1957 to 1964. This project has stirred controversy since it was planned in the 1950s.

Glen Canyon Dam is fed by the Colorado River and two tributaries, the Green River and the San Juan River. Both tributaries flow into the Colorado River inside Utah. Several natural formations are found on the periphery of the Glen Canyon Recreation Area, the result of the dam: Rainbow Bridge, Natural Bridges, and Grand Staircase–Escalante National Monuments and Arches and Canyonlands National Parks. The dam was built where the lower Colorado River Basin meets the upper at Lee's Ferry, Arizona.

Bedrock of the Colorado plateau was deposited from the late Carboniferous period (300 million years ago) to the late Cretaceous period (85 million years ago). Prominent surface configurations are the Triassic period Chinle formation, Jurassic period Wingate Sandstone, and the subsequent Tertiary-Quaternary uplifts. Aridity in the southern reaches of the Great Basin Desert allows small shrubs and cacti (sagebrush, Mormon tea, greasewood, narrow-leaf yucca, prickly pear cactus) and low-lying grasses (big sacaton, needlegrass) to flourish.

Since about 600 CE, early Native Americans of this region have resided in the canyons of the San Juan River. From 900 to 1300, the Anasazi built adobe structures and masonry cliff dwellings and raised maize, squash, and beans in the area. They lived concurrently with the Fremont people until their exit from the region in the late thirteenth century. Tree ring data indicate a drought began around 1276 and lasted into the following century. In subsequent centuries, Diné (Navajo), Paiutes, and Southern Utes settled the land. In 1776, Silvestre Vélez de Escalante and Francisco Atanasio Domínguez explored the region in search of a route from Santa Fe, New Mexico, to California. Following the U.S. acquisition of the region from Mexico after the Mexican-American War (1846–1848), geologist John Wesley Powell explored the region in 1869 and 1871–1872. In the late 1870s, in what became known as "San Juan country," Mormon settlers farmed in the canyon and along the San Juan River.

Congress authorized the Glen Canyon Dam as part of the Colorado River Storage Project on April 11, 1956. From his office in Washington, D.C., President Dwight D. Eisenhower initiated the first explosion on October 15, 1956, by sending a telegraph signal to the canyon. To transport material over the river, a new bridge, 1,271 feet long and 700 feet above the river, was completed in 1959, shortening the previous supply route's distance from 200 miles to under one-quarter mile. The Bureau of Reclamation erected a camp in northern Arizona; it was named the Community Page in honor of the commissioner John C. Page.

The Glen Canyon National Recreation Area, established in 1972, encompasses 266 square miles of water. Lake Powell, named after the explorer John Wesley Powell, reaches far into southeastern Utah. Over 4 million tourists visit this lake each year. Today, Lake Powell is better suited to support largemouth bass, black crappie, bluegill, and striped bass than its native species. Glen Canyon Dam is obligated to release 8.23 million acre-feet of water per year, but in the late 1990s, river inflow was less.

Environmentalists have long attempted to halt construction of dams in the Colorado plateau. In 1956, conservationists succeeded in stopping the Echo Park Dam from being built inside Dinosaur National Monument, but they possibly lost Glen Canyon in that process. The Colorado River Basin Project included stipulations that no national

The Glen Canyon Dam was completed in 1964. It is the second-largest dam on the Colorado River. With its completion, Lake Powell was created. Its construction and continued existence has been a source of controversy since its inception.

Bureau of Reclamation, Lower Colorado Region

parks or monuments could be flooded by waters from a dam. Today several organizations are requesting the decommissioning of Glen Canyon Dam, among them Living Rivers/Colorado Riverkeeper headquartered in Moab, Utah, and the Glen Canyon Institute in Salt Lake City, Utah. Chief among their concerns is that Lake Powell loses nearly 1 million acre-feet of water, or 8 percent of the flow, due to evaporation in its desert environment and to its porous sandstone banks.

—Ralph Hartsock

See also: *Echo Park Dam; Flaming Gorge; Powell, John Wesley*

Lake Powell

Lake Powell was created by the damming of the Colorado River in Glen Canyon by the Glen Canyon Dam. Most of the lake is located in Utah, although it does extend into Arizona. When its 186 miles of territory is filled to capacity, it is the second largest man-made reservoir in the United States. Named after John Wesley Powell, the lake is the centerpiece of the National Park Service's Glen Canyon National Recreation Area.

Glen Canyon's natural beauty rivaled that of the Grand Canyon, but it was little known when Glen Canyon Dam was approved for construction. Conservationists discovered its grandeur and the artifacts of more than a millennia of Native American habitation after they were too late to save. Glen Canyon began to disappear in 1963 as Lake Powell began to fill.

During the early years of the twenty-first century, an extended drought led to much of Glen Canyon re-emerging as Lake Powell evaporated. The beauty of the exposed geological features led many conservationists to call for the decommissioning of Glen Canyon Dam and the permanent draining of the lake. Due to the water needs of so many downriver communities, such as Phoenix, Arizona, and Las Vegas, Nevada, it is doubtful that state or federal authorities would ever heed those calls.

—John R. Burch Jr.

See also: Colorado River Basin; Powell, John Wesley

BIBLIOGRAPHY

Farmer, Jared. Glen Canyon Dammed: Inventing Lake Powell and the Canyon Country. Tucson: University of Arizona Press, 1999.
Powell, James Lawrence. Dead Pool: Lake Powell, Global Warming, and the Future of Water in the West. Berkeley: University of California Press, 2008.

BIBLIOGRAPHY

Anderson, Paul B., Thomas C. Chidsey Jr., Douglas A. Sprinkel, and Grant C. Willis. "Geology of Glen Canyon National Recreation Area, Utah-Arizona." In Geology of Utah's Parks and Monuments: Millennium Field Conference, edited by Douglas A. Sprinkel, Thomas C. Chidsey Jr., and Paul B. Anderson, 301–35. Salt Lake City: Utah Geological Association, 2000.
Farmer, Jared. Glen Canyon Dammed: Inventing Lake Powell and the Canyon Country. Tucson: University of Arizona Press, 1999.
Martin, Russell. A Story That Stands Like a Dam: Glen Canyon and the Struggle for the Soul of the West. Salt Lake City: University of Utah Press, 1999.
Miller, Scott K. "Undamming Glen Canyon: Lunacy, Rationality, or Prophecy?" Stanford Environmental Law Journal 19, no. 1 (2000): 121–207. Available at http://livingrivers.org/pdfs/ScottMiller Report.pdf.

Grand Canyon Dams

The Grand Canyon, one of the greatest natural sites in the United States, was carved by the Colorado River. The river's flow used to vary during the year from a half million gallons per day in the fall up to 100 million gallons a day in the spring following the snowmelt. A desire to regulate the river's flow led to the construction of the Glen Canyon Dam from 1960 to 1963 at the northeastern end of the Grand Canyon. The river's flow is now 3 to 7 million gallons per day. The dam was opposed by the Sierra Club, Friends of the Earth, and many other environmental groups. Although the dam affects the flow of water through the Grand Canyon, it is seventeen miles outside the boundary of the Grand Canyon National Park.

Construction of the dam was opposed by a variety of stakeholders. Initially the Bureau of Reclamation argued that the dam would have to be built on Navajo sandstone, which is porous and crumbles easily, resulting in major engineering problems. New plans put two dams at nearby Dinosaur National Monument, which stirred public protest. The Bureau of Reclamation relented in 1956 and did not build a dam within the national monument.

Many people argued that the 710-foot-high Glen Canyon Dam was costly and unnecessary—"a monumental example of the harm that can be done when bureaucrats are seized with a compulsion for concrete," as Robert Wallace wrote so elegantly. However, the major objection was to its creation of Lake Powell, which flooded an area that John Wesley Powell had acclaimed as one of the most beautiful in the United States. In return, the dam promised cheaper hydropower for Las Vegas, Nevada, and Phoenix and Tucson, Arizona.

In addition to flooding the region, the dam has had adverse environmental impacts on the river itself. Silt is trapped on the upstream side of the Glen Canyon Dam, and much of it settles in Lake Powell. It is estimated that the dam prevents 85 percent of the sediment from flowing downriver, leading to the extinction, or near extinction, of some native fish such as the squawfish, the razorback sucker, the humpback chub, and the bony-tail chub. On the other hand, nonnative fish introduced for recreational fishing, such as the rainbow trout and carp, have thrived. Evening out the river's annual flow has also meant that downriver beaches are no longer cleaned by floodwater. In addition, more hikers use the area, sometimes leaving behind rubbish and human waste.

One of the arguments in favor of building the dam was that it would bring more tourists to the region. In 1967, 2,100 people were involved in white-water rafting on the Colorado River. This had increased to 15,000 by 1973. Tourism authorities claimed that this rise was due to the river being "tamed" by the Glen Canyon Dam. In 2001, the area had 3.5 million visitors who enjoyed the water with canoes, motor boats, jet skis, and even houseboats.

—Justin Corfield

See also: *Bureau of Reclamation; Colorado River Basin; Glen Canyon Dam; National Parks and Water; Powell, John Wesley*

BIBLIOGRAPHY

Dolnick, Edward. *Down the Great Unknown: The Conquest of the Grand Canyon.* London: HarperCollins, 2003.

Jennings, Jesse D. *Glen Canyon: An Archaeological Summary.* Salt Lake City: University of Utah Press, 1998.

Martin, Russell. *A Story That Stands Like a Dam: Glen Canyon and the Struggle for the Soul of the West.* New York: Henry Holt, 1989.

Powell, James Lawrence. *Dead Pool: Lake Powell, Global Warming, and the Future of Water in the West.* Berkeley: University of California Press, 2008.

Wehr, Kevin. *America's Fight over Water: The Environmental and Political Effects of Large-Scale Water Systems.* London: Routledge, 2004.

Construction of the Grand Coulee Dam provided thousands of men with work during the Great Depression. When completed, the Dam was the largest concrete structure in the world.
Library of Congress

Grand Coulee Dam

The largest concrete structure on earth when built, Grand Coulee Dam is a testament to Americans' twentieth-century commitment to monumental engineering projects and the desire to put nature to work. This dam in eastern Washington State's arid channeled scablands was completed in 1942. Statistics reveal the Grand Coulee Dam's massive dimensions: 5,223 feet long, 550 feet high, 12 million cubic feet of concrete. Its hydroelectric power turbines generate 6,809 megawatts. Its reservoir, Franklin D. Roosevelt Lake, backs up 150 miles, covering 82,300 acres with a total capacity just shy of 9.4 million acre-feet.

Ancient floods scoured this landscape, removing practically all the soil and life forms in their path. Because dozens of these floods over 1,500 years stripped the land, much of the Columbia Plateau was comparatively barren of ecological relationships. The ancient riverbed Grand Coulee lay in this area, known as the channeled scablands. Close by these rock-strewn hills and plateaus were

rich soils on which crops could be raised if water were provided.

By the turn of the twentieth century, regional boosters and government planners saw the inland Northwest as untapped resources awaiting human engineering to put them to use. A Wenatchee, Washington, newspaper editor, Rufus Woods, along with allies, led the public campaign to dam the Columbia River and irrigate the lands that many thought to be underdeveloped. The dam would provide security for existing plateau farmers and attract new farmers. Because of engineering challenges, financial costs, and political calculations, however, construction did not begin, despite significant campaigning in the 1920s.

However, by the 1930s, with the Great Depression causing significant unemployment, President Franklin D. Roosevelt saw a dam at Grand Coulee as an ideal way to promote agricultural development in the inland Northwest

Bonneville Power Administration

The Bonneville Power Administration (BPA) is a federal agency operating under the auspices of the U.S. Department of Energy. Headquartered in Portland, Oregon, the BPA is responsible for the distribution of electricity generated by federal dams located on the Columbia River, as well as power generated by nonfederal facilities such as wind farms and a nuclear power plant. The electricity is sold by the BPA at cost to private electrical power companies serving the Pacific Northwest region.

During the 1930s, President Franklin D. Roosevelt and politicians from the Pacific Northwest envisioned the creation of the Columbia Valley Authority (CVA), which they modeled after the Tennessee Valley Authority. The key components of the proposed CVA, namely the Bonneville and Grand Coulee Dams, both were completed while the CVA languished in the U.S. Congress. Unable to obtain legislation creating the CVA and needing to distribute hydroelectric power from the new dam, President Roosevelt opted to compromise by signing the Bonneville Power Act on August 20, 1937, which created the BPA. By the 1940s, the BPA was in conflict with the Bureau of Reclamation and a number of private electrical companies over the pricing of electricity generated on the Columbia River. Ultimately, the BPA model triumphed, resulting in the Pacific Northwest having some of the cheapest electricity rates in the United States today.

—John R. Burch Jr.

See also: *Bonneville Dam; Roosevelt, Franklin D.; Tennessee Valley Authority*

BIBLIOGRAPHY

Billington, David P., and Donald C. Jackson. *Big Dams of the New Deal Era: A Confluence of Engineering and Politics.* Norman: University of Oklahoma Press, 2006.
Bonneville Power Administration. http://www.bpa.gov/.
Brooks, Karl Boyd. *Public Power, Private Dams: The Hells Canyon High Dam Controversy.* Seattle: University of Washington Press, 2006.

and alleviate unemployment. Approved as part of the Public Works Administration in 1933, Grand Coulee Dam was built between 1933 and 1942. Its construction employed over 12,000 workers who put in 56 million man-hours. The primary purpose of the dam, the linchpin of the Columbia Basin Project, was irrigation. However, construction finished just after the United States entered World War II, and the hydroelectric power the dam generated became its principal benefit. Managed along with Bonneville Dam through the Bonneville Power Administration, Grand Coulee Dam furnished the power necessary to fuel wartime manufacturing, especially the nuclear research being done at Hanford, Washington. This power represented a critical component of the American war effort. A decade later, irrigation, the original top priority, finally became functional.

Grand Coulee Dam has produced significant economic, cultural, and environmental impacts. Power capacity expanded further in the 1970s, supporting further economic growth. Flood control value has also been important. The benefits from the dam and associated projects amount to more than $1.5 billion annually. The most significant ecological impact of the dam has been a radical change to anadromous fisheries. The dam blocked more than a 1,000 miles of salmon spawning streams, destroying a central natural heritage of the region. Grand Coulee Dam and Lake Roosevelt created new habitat, but it has promoted exotic, not indigenous, species. This extreme environmental change contributed to tragic cultural consequences, because Plateau Indians had made salmon central to their culture and economy for centuries. The transformed habitat forced American Indians to relocate and adapt central elements of their culture, a change that has been difficult. For most non-Indians, though, the dam and its associated projects represented monumentalism, an achievement to and testament of human progress. Grand Coulee Dam is also a tourist destination, and Lake Roosevelt attracts recreational visitors who boat, fish, and camp in and along the reservoir. As the largest dam in the Columbia River System, Grand Coulee Dam is the key to a multipurpose system designed to produce maximum benefit for humans from a natural system.

—Adam M. Sowards

See also: *Bonneville Dam; Bureau of Reclamation; Endangered Species Act (1973); Pacific Coast; Roosevelt, Franklin D.*

BIBLIOGRAPHY

Pitzer, Paul C. *Grand Coulee: Harnessing a Dream.* Pullman: Washington State University Press, 1994.
U.S. Department of the Interior, Bureau of Reclamation. "Grand Coulee Dam Statistics and Facts." Revised May 2010. http://www.usbr.gov/pn/grandcoulee/pubs/factsheet.pdf.
White, Richard. *The Organic Machine: The Remaking of the Columbia River.* New York: Hill and Wang, 1995.

Great Lakes

The Great Lakes are five lakes along the border of Canada and the United States: Lake Superior, Lake Michigan, Lake Huron, Lake Erie, and Lake Ontario. Together these lakes comprise approximately 94,000 square miles of water.

The largest of the Great Lakes is Lake Superior. In fact, Lake Superior is the largest body of freshwater on earth. It is approximately 355 miles long and 160 miles across at its widest point. All around Lake Superior hills rise up, some as high as 1,000 feet. Along the southern shore is gray and red sandstone. Other minerals found around Lake Superior include iron, copper, shale, and limestone.

Lake Michigan is the second largest of the Great Lakes. It is the only one of the lakes that is entirely within the borders of the United States. Lake Michigan stretches 320 miles in length and is about 70 miles in width. It has an area of 22,400 square miles and is 868 feet deep. Lake Michigan has three main harbors—Chicago; Milwaukee, Wisconsin; and Grand Haven, Michigan. It has been a bustling site of commerce since the earliest frontier settlements.

The third and fourth largest of the Great Lakes are Lake Huron and Lake Erie, respectively. Lake Huron is approximately 190 miles wide and 250 miles long and covers about 21,000 square miles. Along Lake Huron are forests of pine, cedar, and spruce. There are several islands within Lake Huron, including the Duck Islands, Cockburn Island, and Drummond Island. Lake Erie is located the furthest south of all the Great Lakes. It separates Canada to the north from the states of New York, Pennsylvania, Ohio, and Michigan. Lake Erie stretches 246 miles in length and ranges from 30 to 60 miles across. It covers roughly 10,000 square miles. Unlike the other Great Lakes, Lake Erie is very shallow, only 200 feet deep. For this reason, navigation on the lake is challenging. Lake Erie is home to a special kind of laminated clay, aptly named Erie Clay, left over from passing glaciers millions of years ago.

The smallest of the Great Lakes is Lake Ontario. Located between New York and Canada, Lake Ontario is 180 miles long from east to west and roughly 35 miles wide, covering 6,300 square miles. Around Lake Ontario are broad plains to the north and high ridge of land to the south. The lake is fed by the Niagara River, as well as by the Oswego and Black Rivers. Lake Ontario is connected to Lake Erie by the Welland Canal, which was first built in 1824.

The first settlers of the Great Lakes region were Native Americans, including the Chippewa, Fox, Huron, Iroquois, Ottawa, Potawatomi, and Sioux. Jesuit missionaries and explorers arrived during the seventeenth century, the most famous being Samuel Champlain. European settlers began to arrive in earnest in the late eighteenth and early nineteenth centuries. Immigrants from Europe arrived looking for good farming land; thus, agriculture became the mainstay of the Great Lakes economy. However, upon the completion of the Erie Canal, which connected Lake Erie with the Hudson River in 1825, the Great Lakes region became a crossroads of trade and manufacturing.

Prior to the construction of the Erie Canal, easterners and, later on, immigrants who wished to travel to the Old Northwest (present-day Wisconsin, Illinois, and Minnesota) had to travel several weeks over rough roads. The canal cut travel time by a third and freight-shipping costs in half. The success of the Erie Canal spurred canal building in rivers all around the Great Lakes. Almost overnight, towns and cities sprang up, filled with houses, shops, and factories. This prompted even more immigrants to leave the east coast for unsettled lands in the West. Trading flowed both east and west through the Great Lakes region. Settlers came from both the eastern United States and Europe to the newly accessible lands surrounding the Great Lakes and beyond. Steam boats, railroad lines, and telegraphs would build upon the economic success of the Erie Canal.

Throughout the nineteenth and twentieth centuries, manufacturing was the hub of economic activity in the Great Lakes region, although it become less significant over the years. Tourism and recreational boating and fishing are now popular in the Great Lakes. The Great Lakes also supply drinking water to the millions of people. These lakes have always played a vital role in the culture and economy of the region. From the times of Native American settlements through today, the Great Lakes have shaped the lives of the people who lived along its shores.

—Lorri Brown

See also: *Erie Canal; Great Lakes Charter (1985); Great Lakes Fisheries Policy*

BIBLIOGRAPHY

Annin, Peter. *The Great Lakes Water Wars*. Washington, DC: Island Press, 2009.

Caldwell, Lynton Keith. *Perspectives on Ecosystem Management for the Great Lakes: A Reader*. SUNY Series in Environmental Public Policy. Albany: State University of New York Press, 1988.

Great Lakes Science Center. http://www.glsc.usgs.gov/.

Taylor, William W., and C. Paola Ferreri. *Great Lakes Fisheries Policy and Management: A Binational Perspective*. Canadian Series. East Lansing: Michigan State University Press, 1999.

Great Salt Lake

The Great Salt Lake, located northwest of Salt Lake City, Utah, is a landlocked lake with an average depth of about 20 feet and 10,000 miles of shoreline. At about seventy-five miles long and thirty-five miles wide, it is the largest body of water west of the Mississippi River and the largest saltwater lake in the Western Hemisphere. The salinity of the water averages about 12 percent, making it much saltier than the ocean. While the water is unsuitable for consumption, the lake is a popular recreational spot for sailing, kayaking, and bird watching. No fish can survive the lake's salinity. There are two Utah state parks on the lake: Antelope Island and Great Salt Lake State Park.

The name, Great Salt Lake, seems to have resulted from casual references to the water as a salt lake. When trapper James Clyman and several companions became the first white men to circle the lake in 1826, they were awed by its size. Other explorers had thought that the lake was part of the Pacific Ocean.

The Great Salt Lake is a remnant of ancient Lake Bonneville, which covered 20,000 square miles and much of present-day Utah, Idaho, and Nevada about 10,000 to 30,000 years ago. About 145 miles wide and 345 miles long, the lake went through three major levels. The first level, Bonneville, gave the lake a depth of more than 1,000 feet. When the waters reached the top of Red Rock Pass in northern Cache Valley, the lake overflowed into the Snake River, a tributary of the Columbia River. As the pass was worn down by the massive overflow, the lake dropped about 375 feet. At the Provo level, the longest of the three periods, the lake stabilized. Subsequent climate changes increased evaporation, and the lake shrank to its third level, the Stansbury. After a period of rising and falling, the lake declined to its present fluctuating level. As the freshwater evaporated, minerals that had been widely dispersed became concentrated. Lacking natural outlets, the lake concentrated mineral deposits, reaching its present salty state. Heavy spring runoffs dilute the salt content. At present, a railroad dam has cut off the northern half of the lake, making it especially salty with a salinity averaging from 20 to 25 percent.

The salinity of the water limits aquatic life. Although dead fish are seen at times, these are carried in, already dead, by streams. Millions of brine shrimp thrive in the lake and supply a flourishing fish food industry. Brine flies often blacken the white sand beaches as they bask in the sun, but they do not bite humans.

The number of minerals in Great Salt Lake has sparked the development of a mineral extraction industry. Several companies extract salt using solar evaporation. Water is pumped into ponds, where it is evaporated by the sun, and the process is repeated to build up a salt layer. The salt is then scooped up, processed, and sold. A few firms extract magnesium and other metallic chemicals. Elements suspended in the water include sulfate, magnesium, potassium, calcium, and traces of chlorine.

Another major industry that is dependent upon the lake is tourism. When the first Mormons arrived in the area in 1847, they recounted that a person could float like a cork on the water. With the arrival of the Utah Central Railroad in 1870, the first lake resort opened. In 1893, the famous Saltair resort opened, and several competitors followed. However, the fickle nature of the water played havoc with tourism and killed off all the resorts except Saltair, which is now operated as part of the Great Salt Lake State Park. The shallow nature of Great Salt Lake means that winds can quickly whip up treacherous waves. The lake is also prone to shrinking and rising.

When the lake reached a record low in 1963 of 4,191 feet above sea level, some of the lake's ten major islands became peninsulas. In 1983, when the lake reached a historic high, its waters flooded houses, farmland, and a nearby freeway. Huge pumps were constructed to deposit excess water into Utah's west desert. The pumps were shut down in 1989. Water management remains an issue, albeit one that has attracted little public attention.

—Caryn Neumann

See also: *National Parks and Water; Outdoor Recreation*

BIBLIOGRAPHY

Czerny, Peter G. *The Great Salt Lake*. Provo, UT: Brigham Young University Press, 1976.

Morgan, Dale L. *The Great Salt Lake*. Salt Lake City: University of Utah Press, 2002.

Topping, Gary, ed. *Great Salt Lake: An Anthology*. Logan: Utah State University Press, 2002.

Hells Canyon Dam

There are two Hells Canyon dams, one that was built and one that was not; their stories are entwined. The existing Hells Canyon Dam blocks the Snake River where the river forms the border between Oregon and Idaho. At mile 247 of the Snake River, the concrete dam is 330 feet tall, impounds 188,000 acre-feet of water in the Hells Canyon

Reservoir, and has a power capacity of around 400 mega-watts. It was completed in 1967. The proposed dam that never was built would have been nearby, but it would have been much higher at nearly 750 feet and would have stored 3.5 million acre-feet of water.

North America's deepest gorge, Hells Canyon, averages about 1 mile deep, is 10 miles wide, and is more than 70 miles long. Mountains, 8,000 feet in elevation, surround the isolated canyon. Historically, hundreds of thousands of anad-ramous fish—chinook, coho, and sockeye salmon along with steelhead trout—forced their way upstream through Hells Canyon to spawn in tributaries and mountain lakes through-out the inland Northwest. Indigenous populations harvested these fish, along with plant foods and game throughout the region. Euro-Americans and some Asian immigrants arrived in the nineteenth century to homestead and mine, displac-ing native populations. Mostly, the canyon remained isolated from human populations and economies. Today, 652,488 acres lie within the Hells Canyon National Recreation Area (HCNRA), 215,000 acres are designated wilderness, and three rivers (Snake, Imnaha, and Rapid) are designated Wild and Scenic Rivers.

In the 1940s and 1950s, the federal government looked to Hells Canyon as a site for a huge public hydroelectric dam, Hells Canyon High Dam. This proposed high dam stemmed from New Deal–era economic planning and pub-lic power desires, along with engineers' and planners' desires to add the Snake River Basin to the power grid begun in the Columbia River Valley. They believed cheap public power would help transform the Snake Basin much as it was doing to the Columbia Basin, adding significant industrial, commercial, and residential capacity. The Hells Canyon High Dam would also expand irrigation projects in south-ern Idaho.

However, public dams faced stiff opposition by a consor-tium of private power companies who also coveted Hells Canyon for a complex of smaller dams. Tiring of federal intervention and fearing the lower basin dams would jeop-ardize water availability and rights for upper basin irrigators, Idahoans largely opposed the federal proposal. With sup-portive politicians in national office in the 1950s, these combined forces enjoyed support in slowing the public power project. Idaho Power Company led the opposing campaign by developing an alternative three-dam Hells Canyon complex. These low, run-of-the-river dams would generate hydroelectric power but offer less grandiose trans-formations than the High Dam plans.

Meantime, concerns over anadromous fish attracted attention. As the larger Columbia Basin developed its hydro-electric power and irrigation projects, anadromous fish paid the ultimate cost. Grand Coulee Dam blocked all upstream migration on the Columbia River; Hells Canyon High Dam would do the same for the Snake River. The alternative Hell Canyon Complex, including Brownlee, Oxbow, and Hells Canyon dams, would not do much better. Although origi-nally conceived with fish passage capacity, the Hells Canyon Complex was not constructed with such facilities. Funds were set aside to study the fish passage problem, but invest-ments in research could not solve the problem. From the 1950s during initial licensing hearings, and more recently in the 2000s for relicensing hearings with the Federal Power Commission (later the Federal Energy Regulatory Commission), concerns over the dams' impact on anadro-mous fish remained the most prominent issue.

The dams' effects on fish runs have been negative, but much of the damage to these fish populations comes from habitat changes throughout the basin and the many dams downstream. With several Pacific salmon on the endangered or threatened species list, debates over the public interest of dams and their hydroelectric power benefits versus the pub-lic interest of river recreation and fish remain ongoing and seemingly intractable. In this regard, Hells Canyon Dam offers an exemplary history of the challenging balancing act western rivers have been asked to achieve in providing hydroelectric power, irrigation water, and fish habitat.

—Adam M. Sowards

See also: *Dam Building; Endangered Species Act (1973); Federal Power Commission; Snake River Basin*

BIBLIOGRAPHY

Brooks, Karl Boyd. *Public Power, Private Dams: The Hells Canyon High Dam Controversy.* Seattle: University of Washington Press, 2006.

Northwest Power and Conservation Council. "Columbia River History: Hells Canyon Dam." http://www.nwcouncil.org/history/HellsCanyon.asp.

Hetch Hetchy Dam

Hetch Hetchy Dam, officially known today as O'Shaughnessy Dam, ranks as one of the most fabled and controversial dams ever built in the United States. When construction of the 312-foot-high curved gravity dam was completed on California's Tuolomne River in 1923, a 12.5-kilometer-long reservoir with a storage capacity of 117 billion gallons had

Tuolumne River Trust

The Tuolumne River Trust was formed in 1981 in California to fight a planned hydroelectric project that would have constructed two dams on the Tuolumne River and one on the Clavey River, a tributary of the Tuolumne. The river's defenders had legislative tools available to them that were not in existence at the time the Tuolumne River had been dammed in the Hetch Hetchy Valley. Intense lobbying by the trust resulted in eighty-three miles of the Tuolumne River being designated a National Wild and Scenic River in 1984, thus making it off-limits to dam builders. In 1995, the organization stopped the damming of the Clavey River.

The trust faces many challenges in protecting the Tuolumne River, because the river is not only a wildlife habitat but also a source of water and electricity for farmers in California's Central Valley and for cities such as San Francisco. The organization is presently working to preserve the habitat of the river's chinook salmon population, which is extremely endangered.

—John R. Burch Jr.

See also: *Wild and Scenic Rivers Act of 1968*

BIBLIOGRAPHY

Palmer, Tim. *The Sierra Nevada: A Mountain Journey.* Washington, DC: Island Press, 1988.
Tuolumne River Trust. http://www.tuolumne.org/.

men were determined to end the nation's profligate overconsumption of its natural resources, but they still viewed America's timber, mineral, and water resources as essential fuel for economic growth. To so-called "Roosevelt conservationists," the Hetch Hetchy Dam proposal was perfectly congruent with the ascendant progressive vision of sustainable, multiple-use resource management.

Sierra Club founder John Muir and other advocates of wilderness preservation mounted a spirited campaign to derail the dam plan. Using books, newspaper editorials, public lectures, and private meetings with members of Congress, Muir and his allies publicized the natural beauty of the Hetch Hetchy Valley, pointed to other water development alternatives available to San Francisco Bay officials and residents, and warned that no national park would be safe from commercial development if a dam was permitted in Yosemite.

Ultimately, however, proponents of the dam scheme in Sacramento and Washington, D.C., weathered the complaints raised by the Sierra Club and other detractors and secured congressional approval for the dam. Congressional hearings convened in 1909 to consider the issue were key to this effort. The hearings featured influential testimony from Pinchot and Garfield, who enjoyed formidable reputations as "sensible" conservationists. Both officials defended the "sustainable use" underpinnings of the Hetch Hetchy proposal and characterized opponents of the dam as earnest but misguided. Their testimony, combined with lingering public sympathy for San Francisco residents in the wake of the 1906 earthquake, reassured many waffling members of Congress that a vote for the dam was both legitimate and politically safe.

Wilderness preservationists managed to delay approval of the dam for another few years. In 1913, however, Congress passed the Raker Act, which authorized the damming of Hetch Hetchy Valley in Yosemite National Park. President Woodrow Wilson signed the legislation on December 19, 1913, and construction began the following year. The dam was completed in 1923, when it was named O'Shaughnessy Dam in honor of Michael M. O'Shaughnesssy, the chief engineer for the project.

been carved into the Sierra Nevada Mountains. This reservoir became (and remains) a leading source of water and electricity for San Francisco and Oakland, whose city founders had been at the forefront of the effort to build the dam. But the location of the Hetch Hetchy Dam—within the boundaries of Yosemite National Park—also drew a firestorm of criticism from America's fledgling wilderness preservation movement. In fact, the Progressive Era battle over Hetch Hetchy exposed deep schisms between the utilitarian and preservationist wings of the Theodore Roosevelt–era conservation movement.

The idea of diverting Tuolumne River water to the San Francisco Bay Area via aquaduct was first broached in the early 1880s, but the notion did not build any real momentum until 1901, when San Francisco mayor James Phelan filed for water rights in the Hetch Hetchy Valley. Policy makers and business leaders wrangled indecisively over the proposal until 1908, when President Theodore Roosevelt's interior secretary, James Garfield, granted San Francisco the right to develop the water resources of the valley. Philosophically, this decision was fully in keeping with the natural resource development sentiments of Roosevelt and Gifford Pinchot, his famous national forest chief. These

Hydroelectric power generation from the facility began two years later.

Hetch Hetchy Dam has been in operation ever since, and it currently provides water to an estimated 2.4 million Californians in San Francisco, San Mateo, and Alameda Counties, as well as communities in the San Joaquin Valley. But the project remains a sore subject in many quarters. Proposals to remove the dam and restore the Hetch Hetchy Valley to its pre-dam condition continue to be floated by the Sierra Club and other environmental groups, and the Raker Act's numerous regulations and provisions have made administration of the facility a challenge for various stakeholders in the San Francisco Bay Area. More recently, critics have charged that the privately owned Pacific Gas and Electric (PG&E), which sells the hydroelectric energy generated at the dam to San Francisco residents, is operating in violation of the Raker Act, which stipulated that Hetch Hetchy power be sold directly to citizens through a municipal power agency at the cheapest possible rates.

—Kevin Hillstrom

See also: *Pinchot, Gifford; Roosevelt, Theodore*

BIBLIOGRAPHY

Righter, Robert W. *The Battle Over Hetch Hetchy: America's Most Controversial Dam and the Birth of Modern Environmentalism*. New York: Oxford University Press, 2005.

Simpson, John W. *Dam! Water, Power, Politics, and Preservation in Hetch Hetchy and Yosemite National Park*. New York: Pantheon Books, 2005.

U.S. Congress, House Committee on Public Lands. *San Francisco and the Hetch Hetchy Reservoir: Hearings Held Before the Committee on the Public Lands of the House of Representatives, January 9 and 12, 1909, on H.J. Res. 223*. Washington, DC: U.S. Government Printing Office, 1909.

Hoover Dam

Hoover Dam is situated in Black Canyon on the Colorado River about thirty miles southeast of Las Vegas, Nevada, on the Arizona-Nevada border. The dam, completed in 1935, reaches 726.4 feet from bedrock to the roadway, is 660 feet wide at the base and 45 feet wide at the top, spans a distance of 1,244 feet between the canyon walls, and weighs 6,600,000 tons.

Hoover Dam is located in an area of the southwestern United States where temperatures during the summer can reach 125 degrees and control of the water supply is crucial to prevent spring floods and summer droughts. The dam's foundation and abutments are made of andesite breccias, a rock of volcanic origin. The dam itself is a concrete arch gravity type constructed of concrete, steel, and metal pipe.

The dam forms the Lake Mead Reservoir, the largest man-made lake at 247 square miles, reaching 110 miles up the Colorado River and 35 miles up the Virgin River. The lake can hold 25,876,000 acre-feet of water (1 acre-foot equals 325,851 gallons). The dam can release 96,000 cubic feet of water per second from the lake. The reservoir provides both water and recreation for the surrounding area.

Prior to the dam's construction, the Colorado River would flood during the spring rains and dry up during summer droughts. Major floods on the river between 1905 and 1907 caused the U.S. Bureau of Reclamation to be consulted for a solution. While water rights for the states of Wyoming, Colorado, Utah, New Mexico, California, Nevada, and Arizona were being negotiated, the Bureau and the U.S. Geological Survey turned their attention to determining where to locate the dam. Surveyors evaluated over

Construction on the Hoover Dam (then known as Boulder Dam) began in 1931 and was completed in March 1936. The dam, situated on the Colorado River near the Arizona-Nevada border, provides electricity to Arizona, California, and Nevada as well as other benefits to the Colorado River region.
Library of Congress

Elwood Mead

Elwood Mead served as the U.S. commissioner of reclamation from 1924 to 1936. In that capacity he directed the Boulder/Hoover Dam project, which served as the capstone to his distinguished career.

Mead was born on January 16, 1858. He received a BS degree from Purdue University in 1882. A year later, he received a graduate degree in civil engineering from Iowa Agricultural College. When Wyoming attained statehood in 1890, he wrote the portion of the state's constitution that addressed water use and developed the legal codes and government infrastructure necessary to implement his directives. Known as the "Wyoming System," it served as a model for other states and for countries such as Australia. From 1907 to 1915, he served as chair of the state rivers and water supply commission in Victoria, Australia. He returned from Australia to teach as the University of California at Berkeley until 1924, when he assumed his post at the Bureau of Reclamation.

Mead died on January 26, 1936. The Hoover Dam's reservoir was named Lake Mead in his honor.

—John R. Burch Jr.

See also: *Boulder Canyon Project Act (1928); Bureau of Reclamation*

BIBLIOGRAPHY

Kluger, James R. *Turning on Water with a Shovel: The Career of Elwood Mead.* Albuquerque: University of New Mexico Press, 1992.
Pisani, Donald J. *Water and American Government: The Reclamation Bureau, National Water Policy, and the West, 1902–1935.* Berkeley: University of California Press, 2002.

seventy sites along the river and selected two in the lower basin, Boulder Canyon and Black Canyon. In February 1922, the Fall-Davis report recommended that a high dam be constructed at Boulder Canyon. This was followed in 1924 by the Weymouth report, which indicated the feasibility of building a dam at Boulder or Black Canyon. Black Canyon was selected because of the bedrock depth and geologic structure and the fact that the dam would not have to be as high.

President Calvin Coolidge signed the Boulder Canyon Project Act on December 21, 1928. The act included five measures: approval of the Colorado River Compact; a provision that if the pact were not unanimous among the seven states, it would become a six-state pact; a provision that if California were included, that state would have to limit its water usage; authorization of construction of the dam under the Colorado River Dam fund and of the transfer of $165 million to the fund; authorization of the All-American Canal system and $165 million for construction of the project. In September 1930, it was announced that the dam would be called "Hoover Dam" in honor of the current president, Herbert Hoover, but this would not become official until Congress passed additional legislation in April 1947.

According to the dam construction legislation, the purpose of the dam was threefold. First, the dam would provide for river regulation, better navigation, and flood control. Secondly, the dam would form a reservoir to provide water storage for irrigation and domestic use plus the assurance of the agreed water rights. Finally, the dam would provide hydroelectric power for the region.

Construction on the dam project began in November 1931 with the excavation of tunnels to divert the river. Actual dam construction began on June 6, 1933, with the first bucket of concrete, and the project was completed on March 1, 1936. President Franklin D. Roosevelt dedicated the dam on September 30, 1935. The final structure includes four tunnels used to divert the river during construction, upper and lower cofferdams, the dam, power plant, spillways, valve houses, and intake towers. In 1995, a new visitor center and parking structure opened to the public.

The construction of Hoover Dam has benefitted the Colorado River region in many ways. Flood control measures prevent the loss of lives and property, and expensive sediment removal is no longer necessary. Irrigation provides water to the lower basin states and Mexico on a regular basis, and water is available to the Southwest for domestic, industrial, and municipal use. The Lake Meade reservoir provides a national recreational area for use by the public, and fish and wildlife conservation programs protect the animals in the region. Hoover Dam also provides pollution-free hydroelectric power for Arizona, California, and Nevada.

—Theresa Hefner-Babb

See also: *Bureau of Reclamation; Roosevelt, Franklin D.*

BIBLIOGRAPHY

Dunar, Andrew J., and Dennis McBride. *Building Hoover Dam: An Oral History of the Great Depression*. Twayne's Oral History Series No. 11. New York: Twayne, 1993.

U.S. Department of the Interior, Bureau of Reclamation. *Hoover Dam*. Washington, DC: U.S. Government Printing Office, 1985.

U.S. Department of the Interior, Bureau of Reclamation, Lower Colorado Region. *Hoover Dam*. Boulder City, NV: U.S. Department of the Interior, Bureau of Reclamation, Lower Colorado Region, 2006.

Illinois and Michigan Canal

The Illinois and Michigan Canal opened in 1848. Ninety-six miles long, it connected Lake Michigan to the Illinois towns of Peru and LaSalle on the Illinois River, one of the Mississippi River's tributaries. It contributed to the late nineteenth-century development of Chicago, which was laid out as a canal town, and to the growth of northern Illinois. At that time, it was 60 feet wide at water level but narrowed to 36 feet at its bottom. Its depth was six feet. There were four feeders into the canal and five aqueducts. Originally there were seventeen locks, but these eventually were reduced to fifteen. The lock lift ranges from 3.5 to 12.5 feet.

The Illinois and Michigan Canal Commission was formed in 1828. Challenges quickly arose to complicate construction of the waterway. Among these were lack of equipment, flooding, irritating insects, and lack of labor, resulting in the canal costing $6.5 million and taking twelve years to build. Irish immigrants did much of the work. These workers often had to blast through dolomite or cut through solid rock. The project engineer was William Gooding, who completed his task in 1848.

Between the terminuses of LaSalle and Chicago, the canal passed through a number of prominent towns. The communities all saw significant population growth during the time of the canal's construction. Population grew tenfold between the 1830s and 1850s, concentrated mainly in Chicago but extended along the waterway.

The Illinois and Michigan Canal allowed commodities shipped along the Mississippi River to be brought from the south into Chicago, then across the Great Lakes to the Erie Canal, and then out to the eastern seaboard. Access to ready transportation allowed Chicago to develop as a manufacturing center. The canal was busy, but traffic could be limited by the seasonally low water in the Illinois River. After its construction, the canal began charging tolls for use. The highest amount of tolls was collected in 1865, when $302,000 was received. By 1871, enough revenue was generated that the canal started paying for itself. Originally built as a towpath canal, where freight-bearing barges were pulled by mules and horses, it was eventually superseded by railroads.

The history of the Illinois and Michigan Canal is inextricably linked with that of Chicago. As the city's population increased, the need to rid the city of polluted water became more acute. Arranging suitable disposal of garbage and sewage resulted in the building of the Chicago Sanitary and Ship Canal and the development of the Illinois Waterway, still in use today. Some money was spent on restoration of the Illinois and Michigan Canal during World War I for defense purposes, particularly on the stretch between Joliet and LaSalle, but then the canal went into decline, closing to navigation in 1933. The canal's demise was due to a combination of competition from railroads and the need for alternative water supplies.

As part of President Franklin D. Roosevelt's New Deal, the Civilian Conservation Corps started restoring portions of the Illinois and Michigan Canal during the New Deal era. The canal was designated the first U.S. National Heritage Corridor in 1984 by Congress. Portions of the old canal are still open; they are used for canoeing and boating and offer a wide range of natural and man-made attractions. The Canal Corridor Association claims that the Illinois and Michigan Canal is one of America's best-kept secrets because without it, the state of Illinois and the city of Chicago would not be what they are today.

—Julia Fallon

See also: *Illinois Waterway; Roosevelt, Franklin D.*

BIBLIOGRAPHY

Hadfield, Charles. *World Canals: Inland Navigation Past and Present*. New York: Facts on File, 1986.

Lamb, John. "I & M Canal (A Corridor in Time)." http://www.lewisu.edu/imcanal/welcome.htm.

Ranney, Edward, and Emily Harris. *Prairie Passage: The Illinois and Michigan Canal Corridor*. Urbana: University of Illinois Press/Canal Corridor Association, 1998.

Illinois Waterway

The Illinois Waterway connects Lake Michigan at the mouth of the Chicago River with the Mississippi River at Grafton, Illinois. It follows the Chicago Sanitary and Ship

Canal, the lower Des Plaines River, and the Illinois River while passing through the cities of Chicago, Peoria, and Joliet. Completed in 1933 by the U.S. Army Corps of Engineers, the 336-mile waterway consists of eight navigation dams and locks with the result that a "stairway of water" drops 163 feet from Lake Michigan to the Mississippi River.

The waterway has its roots in the fur trade of the seventeenth and eighteenth centuries. The French who traded manufactured items with Native Americans for pelts, mostly beaver, used the Illinois River as a commercial route. Fur trader Louis Joliet (1645–1700), who explored the Mississippi River, suggested that a water route linking the Great Lakes to the Gulf of Mexico via the Illinois and Mississippi Rivers would speed up the process of shipping beaver pelts from the New World to Europe. By the 1830s, grain farmers dominated the economy of the Illinois River Valley, and they faced the same difficulties as the fur traders in getting their products to market. The transportation problem prompted the construction of the Illinois and Michigan Canal, which was completed in 1848. The canal, with fifteen locks, ran from Chicago to LaSalle, Illinois. It helped speed the growth of Chicago as well as such canal towns as Joliet and Peoria. Soon surpassed by the railroad, the canal closed in 1933.

Canals, such as the Illinois and Michigan, were too narrow for large barges that carried grain, coal, and petroleum products. The wider Illinois Waterway replaced the canal. The state of Illinois started the waterway in 1920; by 1929, the state had only finished two-thirds of the waterway but had spent 80 percent of the money designated to complete the project. At that point, the federal government took over construction with the aim of helping to speed the growth of commercial waterway traffic. Reflecting the mind-set of the era, the U.S. Army Corps of Engineers paid no attention to environmental concerns. The waterway was seen as a commodity, not something that had any value beyond commercial concerns.

On the Illinois Waterway, eight dams hold back water to form eight pools that are similar to long, narrow lakes. These dams raise the water level enough to accommodate large barges which require nine feet of water in which to operate. Several dams on the river used tainter gates, which work in a seesaw fashion to control the amount of water withheld to maintain the nine-foot depth. Special wicket dams at Peoria and LaGrange are used during normal and low water levels. During high water, the wickets are lowered to the river bottom and towboats can bypass the locks, simply passing over the lowered wickets. When the water levels return to normal, the tows must again use the locks.

A lock is essentially a water elevator. Based on the principle that water always seeks a lower level, water is raised and lowered using underground tunnels and filling/emptying valves. No pumping is required in the process. For a towboat going downstream, the lock is first filled by opening the filling valve. The emptying valve and the upper and lower gates are closed, so the level of the chamber rises to the upstream level. The upper gate opens and the tow moves in. To lower the towboat, the gates are closed behind it, the filling valve is closed, and the emptying valve is opened. The pressure of the higher water in the lock drains to the downstream level in minutes. The lower gates are then opened and the towboat moves out on the lower water level. For a towboat going upstream, the process is reversed.

The Illinois Waterway has become a tourist site. Visitors can see the locks and dams as well as take a recreational boating trip on the river. At Starved Rock Lock, near Utica, Illinois, visitors can sees exhibits related to the transportation history of the Illinois Waterway as well as the present-day workings of the navigation system.

—Caryn Neumann

See also: *Army Corps of Engineers, United States; Illinois and Michigan Canal*

BIBLIOGRAPHY

Hay, Jerry M. *Illinois Waterway Guidebook*. Floyds Knobs, IN: Indiana Waterways, 2009.
National Academy of Sciences, and National Research Council. *Inland Navigation System Planning: The Upper Mississippi River–Illinois Waterway*. Washington, DC: National Academy Press, 2001.

Intracoastal Waterway

The Intracoastal Waterway stretches approximately 3,500 miles along the Atlantic and Gulf coasts, providing a navigable route free of the hazards associated with the open sea. The Atlantic Intracoastal Waterway begins at Boston and runs 2,500 miles via canals and bays to the official start at Norfolk, Virginia, and terminates at Key West, Florida. The Gulf Intracoastal Waterway extends approximately 1,050 miles from Carrabelle, Florida, to Brownsville, Texas. Parts of the waterway are natural, including inlets, rivers, bays, and sounds, while other parts are man-made canals. The waterway is part of the so-called Great Loop that provides circumnavigation of the eastern half of North America.

In 1808, Treasury Secretary Albert Gallatin introduced the idea of a canal connecting Boston to Brownsville. In 1824, Congress authorized surveys of a cross-Florida canal. Then Congress turned its attention elsewhere until the mid-1870s, when it authorized a survey for a connected system from Donaldsonville, Louisiana, to the mouth of the Rio Grande at the Texas-Mexico border. Advocates saw the Gulf Intracoastal Canal as part of an 18,000-mile transportation system from the Great Lakes through the Mississippi and tributaries and along the western Gulf coast. However, railroads refused to transship goods that came by canal. When the discovery of oil at Spindletop, Texas, created a demand for transportation, interest revived. The Rivers and Harbors Act of 1905 authorized another survey. Also in 1905, Congress appropriated money for completing the Gulf canal from New Orleans, Louisiana, to Brownsville, and by 1949 it was built.

The Intracoastal Waterway is a man-made waterway that facilitates water transportation on the East Coast. It starts in Boston, Massachusetts, with a series of canals and bays until Norfolk, Virginia, where the official water route begins and extends to Key West, Florida.
Tony Santana/U.S. Army Corps of Engineers

In Florida, Saint Augustine boosters did the first dredging. New Englanders brought capital to the speculative exercise. Local Florida chambers and associations such as the Atlantic Deeper Waterways Association pressed at the turn of the century for a public waterway. The final contribution came from the U.S. Army Corps of Engineers, which did all the surveys and in 1929 took over the project to convert a toll canal into an integral part of the Atlantic Intracoastal Waterway.

In the 1950s, promoters wanted to extend the waterway south along the Gulf coast to Tampico and Veracruz, Mexico, and to cut a 160-mile canal across Florida to connect the Gulf with the Atlantic Inland Waterway. Congress approved the canal but did not appropriate the estimated $87 to $108 million it would cost. Environmentalists blocked the shortcut canal, and in 1971, they convinced President Richard M. Nixon to stop a segment of the Florida Intracoastal Waterway that potentially could harm the freshwater aquifer. Environmentalists also blocked a section from east of Carrabelle to Tampa Bay, Florida, in 1983 by demanding a study of the waterway's potential impact on mangrove beds, marsh grasses, and a unique ecosystem.

The Gulf canal links to ten deep-draft ports (twenty-five feet or deeper) and twenty-six shallow-draft channels. The canal connects the Gulf coast to a system of 28,000 miles of waterways across the United States, made New Orleans the second-largest seaport in the United States, made Houston a coastal city, and took forty years to finish.

Commercial users pay a fuel tax for maintenance and improvement of the toll-free waterway. Around 1920, the Corps of Engineers began keeping records of barge tonnage. During World War II, the Gulf waterway allowed ships to carry 90 million tons of supplies without worrying about German U-boats. In 1956, 41 million tons of freight were carried over 7 billion ton miles. Between 1968 and 1984, the waterway moved 65 million tons of goods a year, and in 2002, it moved 63.39 short tons of cargo worth $25 billion in 99,000 trips. The waterway has provided employment for 145,000 people, including a fishing fleet that in 1985 brought in 100 million pounds of shrimp, fish, oysters and crabs. Production from the fleet in 1999 was 25.7 million pounds worth $32.6 million wholesale.

The North American Free Trade Agreement (NAFTA) revived dreams of the Mexican Intracoastal Waterway, but it stalled when Texas governor George W. Bush expressed environmental concerns in 1997. Linking the upper and lower Laguna Madre by the waterway in 1949 had altered that waterway's salinity. Over a period of forty years, the changed salinity, unceasing dredging, and agricultural runoff destroyed 30 percent of the Laguna Madre's sea grass beds and altered the ecosystem accordingly.

The waterway's barges carry petroleum and petroleum products, manufactured goods, building materials, and food-stuffs. The waterway is also popular with recreational boaters, including snowbirds from the East Coast. In the 1990s, the maintenance budget of the Corps of Engineers shrank, and the Corps had to prioritize maintenance dredging based on tonnage. By law, the waterway is to be at least twelve feet deep, but inadequate funding means that shoaling or shallow water of seven to nine feet occurs in various places. By 2007, this was a serious concern for recreational boaters on the Atlantic Intracoastal Waterway.

—John H. Barnhill

See also: *Army Corps of Engineers, United States; Rivers and Harbors Act of 1899; Salinity*

BIBLIOGRAPHY

Crawford, William G. *Florida's Big Dig: The Atlantic Intracoastal Waterway from Jacksonville to Miami, 1881 to 1935.* Cocoa: Florida Historical Society Press, 2006.

Leatherwood, Art. "Gulf Intracoastal Waterway." In *The Handbook of Texas Online.* http://www.tshaonline.org/handbook/online/articles/rrg04.

Time. "Business: The Intracoastal Waterway." October 1, 1956. Available at http://www.time.com/time/magazine/article/0,9171,862435,00.html.

Young, Claiborne S. "Changing Times on the Atlantic Intracoastal Waterway." *Marinalife* (Fall 2008): 41–45. Available at http://www.marinalife.com/magazine/Fall08-Intracoastal%20Waterway.pdf.

John Day Dam

John Day Dam is located on the Columbia River and primarily benefits the states of Oregon and Washington. Construction began in 1958, and the dam was completed in 1971 at a cost of $511 million. It currently has a power generation capacity of 2.48 million kilowatts.

The call for the construction of the John Day Dam dates back to May 1954, when Secretary of the Interior Douglas McKay proposed building yet another dam between the Dalles and McNary Dams. The issue soon became political as Republicans in Oregon urged President Dwight D. Eisenhower to push through the project to help Washington and Oregon generate hydropower for the Pacific Northwest.

It was finally decided that the John Day Dam should be located twenty-eight miles east of The Dalles, Oregon, and slightly south of the mouth of the John Day River. A scale model was built in the hydraulic laboratory of the U.S. Army Corps of Engineers, but construction did not start until The Dalles Dam was built.

By this time, disagreement had arisen over whether the hydropower generated by the John Day Dam would be controlled by a private company or a government entity. The Eisenhower administration eventually settled for a "partnership policy," sharing the proceeds with the Pacific Gas and Electric Company and the Washington Power Company. In return, the two companies had to raise almost 90 percent of the $310 million—the original estimated cost for the dam. The power utilities were offered the power generated from the dam equal to the cost of their financial input. Their investment was expected to repay itself in about fifty years. Eisenhower outlined the plan in his first State of the Union address in 1953. Some people criticized the Eisenhower administration for the role that the two private power companies would have in controlling the output of the power plants attached to the dams. Democrats saw the project as an example of Republicans handing over public assets to the private sector without adequate financial compensation or oversight.

The other major debate over the John Day Dam was the sheer length of time it took to be constructed. The federal government poured money into the project to pay for both cost overruns and the inability of the two power utility companies to provide their share of the funding. By 1961, the government had spent $418 million. In 1968, at a cost of $448 million, the first hydroelectric power from the dam was generated.

The new lake resulting from the dam was called Umatilla after a Native American group in Oregon. The lake forced three towns to be relocated: Arlington and Boardman in Oregon and Roosevelt in Washington.

From an environmental point of view, the John Day Dam and other nearby dams have depleted several species of fish, who have been unable to swim upstream to spawn. Indeed one survey showed that the number of fish—especially chinook salmon—in the part of the river near the dam had declined from 200,000 fish in the 1950s to only 72,000 in 1966. Many died just downriver of the John Day Dam, some from an excess of nitrogen in the blood.

In 1971, the dam was finally completed, and the power generated has been of considerable help to the agricultural sector, as well as to the nearest major town, Goldendale, 20 miles north of the dam.

—Justin Corfield

See also: *Columbia Basin Project*

BIBLIOGRAPHY

Baxter, R. M. "Environmental Effects of Dams and Impoundments." *Annual Review of Ecology and Systematics* 8 (1977): 255–83. Available at http://home.comcast.net/~naprocopio/readings/Baxter_1977 .pdf.

Davies, Lawrence E. "Pacific Northwest Is Watching Construction of John Day Dam." *New York Times,* October 15, 1961.

Due, John F. "The Effects of Railroad Abandonment on Agricultural Areas: A Case Study." *Illinois Agricultural Economics* 15, no. 2 (1975): 14–22.

Joyce, Stephanie. "Is It Worth a Dam?" *Environmental Health Perspectives* 105, no. 10 (1997): 1050–55. Available at http://www.ncbi.nlm .nih.gov/pmc/articles/PMC1470397/pdf/envhper00323-0032- color.pdf.

New York Times. "Utility Men Hail Eisenhower Stand." June 15, 1955.

Kaiparowits Power Project

The proposed Kaiparowits Power Project focused concern on the overappropriation of the Colorado River and the development of energy resources of the Colorado Plateau. It also became the focus of environmental controversy and a motivation behind new environmental regulation in the 1970s.

Following the completion of Glen Canyon Dam, Arizona Resource Company (ARC), a partnership of Arizona Public Service, Southern California Edison, and San Diego Gas and Electric Company, proposed constructing the largest coal-fired power plant in the United States about fifty miles north of the dam. The utilities sought to take advantage of the abundant coal beds of the Kaiparowits Plateau in southwestern Utah and the water stored in Lake Powell. Initial plans anticipated burning up to 30,000 tons of coal per day, trucked from three nearby deep-shaft mines, to produce up to 3,500 megawatts of electricity per year.

Utah governor Calvin Rampton and other Utah politicians of both political parties strongly supported the proposal. However, some officials objected to the use of a significant portion of the state's limited allocation of the Colorado River to generate power for out-of-state users at the cost of other planned developments. Debate intensified on January 15, 1964, when ARC filed an application with the Utah State Engineer's office for the right to withdraw 200,000 acre-feet per year from Lake Powell. The U.S. Bureau of Reclamation formally objected to the application because ARC had not signed a contract to purchase water from the agency and because the filing conflicted with plans for the Central Utah Project (CUP). At a hearing in December, ARC reduced its request to 102,000 acre-feet.

To resolve the conflict, representatives of the Utah Water and Power Board and the Central Utah Water Conservancy District (CUWCD) negotiated an agreement with ARC during the early months of 1965. Anticipating that the predicted life span of the power plant and the construction schedule for the ultimate phase of the CUP would overlap by only a few years, the utilities agreed to subordinate their water rights to the CUP after 2010. They also agreed to recognize the water rights of the Ute Tribe to smooth ongoing negotiations between the tribe and the Bureau of Reclamation and CUWCD so as to allow construction of the CUP's Bonneville Unit to proceed. The state engineer approved the application on September 3, 1965.

The Department of the Interior remained skeptical of the plan. After several meetings arranged by Governor Rampton, Secretary of the Interior Stewart Udall endorsed the project in September 1968. A year later, on October 2, 1969, ARC executed a contract with the United States to purchase water from Lake Powell at a cost of $7 per acre-foot. The utilities and the government also signed two additional agreements that day to coordinate the operation of the Navajo Generating Station—a coal-fired power plant near Page, Arizona, which Congress had authorized in the Colorado River Basin Act of 1968—and the government's hydroelectric plants on the Colorado.

During the 1970s, environmental concerns grew over the air pollution generated by the plant and its proximity to several national parks. These concerns had clout because Congress had to approve the right-of-way for the pump station on Lake Powell and a portion of the water line between the reservoir and the plant, both of which were within the boundaries of the Glen Canyon National Recreation Area. Further, after passage of the National Environmental Policy Act, environmental groups compelled the Department of the Interior to conduct an environmental impact statement for the proposed plant. As delays, costs, and opposition to the project mounted, the utilities ultimately acquiesced to the pressure and canceled the project in April 1976. Later plans by the Dutch firm Andalex Resources to develop coal mines on the Kaiparowits Plateau came to an end when President Bill Clinton created the

Grand Staircase–Escalante National Monument in September 1996.

—Adam Eastman

See also: *Central Arizona Project; Central Utah Project; Colorado River Basin Act of 1968; Glen Canyon Dam; Udall, Stewart*

BIBLIOGRAPHY

Sproul, David Kent. "Environmentalism and the Kaiparowits Power Project, 1964–1976." *Utah Historical Quarterly* 70, no. 4 (2002): 356–71. Available at http://utah.ptfs.com/awweb/main.jsp?flag=browse&smd=1&awdid=1.

U.S. Bureau of Land Management. *Final Environmental Impact Statement: Proposed Kaiparowits Project.* Washington, DC: Department of the Interior, 1976.

Wilkinson, Charles. *Fire on the Plateau: Conflict and Endurance in the American Southwest.* Washington, DC: Island Press/Shearwater Books, 1999.

Keokuk Dam

The Keokuk Dam, on the upper Mississippi River near the town of Keokuk, Iowa, led to the formation of Pool 19 (Lake Cooper), which destroyed the Des Moines Rapids. The rapids had long prevented traffic from heading north on the Mississippi River. The opening up of this portion of the Mississippi River to traffic helped trade but led to many local environmental problems.

Prior to the construction of the Keokuk Dam, there had been a smaller dam at the same site. Local business interests felt that a much larger dam would help trade. A Boston management firm was brought in to organize the financing. Constructions began on the dam in 1910 and continued until 1913. The dam was designed by Colonel Hugh L. Cooper, who had designed other dams and hydroelectric installations in the United States and overseas. He had been involved in the Muscle Shoals project in Alabama, and, in 1926, he went to the Soviet Union where he helped design hydroelectric projects on the Dnieper River. Cooper was assisted by Royal D. Edsell, a New York civil engineer, who later would become president of the Keokuk and Hamilton Bridge Company.

The moveable section of the Keokuk Dam had 119 separate rectangular sliding gates to control water flow. It was second in length to the Aswan (Low) Dam on the Nile in Egypt. The lake formed by the Keokuk Dam, named Lake Cooper, had a shoreline of 240 miles. The dam's power generation was under the oversight of Stone & Webster, based in Boston; the fact that the controlling firm was not local led to some political problems.

Although the dam did solve a number of issues, it also caused environmental problems. For example, the accumulation of silt led to a decline in the diversity of plant life, fish, and mussels. The decreased number of mussels caused major problems for the pearl-button industry in Iowa. Also, sewage from Minneapolis–Saint Paul, Minnesota, backed up behind the dam, gradually took a toll on flora and fauna. Runoff of fertilizers from agricultural land also caused problems. By 1967, aerial photography showed that the vast majority of diving ducks spent their time in only 28 percent of the lake. This demonstrated that the environmental problems had become localized. By this time, the Izaak Walton League of America had adopted the Keokuk Dam as one of its causes.

A new main lock for the dam was constructed between 1952 and 1957. It was 1,200 feet long and 110 feet wide, making it capable of handling a number of barges at the same time, and was similar to the locks employed on the Panama Canal.

—Justin Corfield

See also: *Agriculture; Mississippi River Basin*

BIBLIOGRAPHY

Praeger, W. E. "The Birds of the Des Moines Rapids." *The Auk* 42, no. 4 (1925): 563–77.

Scarpino, Philip V. *Great River: An Environmental History of the Upper Mississippi, 1890–1950.* Columbia: University of Missouri Press, 1985.

Thompson, Douglas. "Feeding Ecology of Diving Ducks on Keokuk Pool, Mississippi River." *Journal of Wildlife Management* 37, no. 3 (1973): 367–81.

Kesterson Reservoir

Kesterson Reservoir was the site of unprecedented selenium poisoning of wildlife during the early 1980s. Located in Merced County in the San Joaquin Valley, the southern half of California's 400-mile-long Central Valley, the 1,280-acre Kesterson Reservoir was part of the 5,900-acre Kesterson National Wildlife Refuge (NWR). Kesterson and a dozen other national wildlife refuges, along with numerous state wildlife areas, were created in the Central Valley during the twentieth century in an attempt to restore a small part of the valley's wetlands, which are estimated to have occupied 4 million acres at the time of California statehood in 1850 and which provide important wintering habitat for the migratory waterfowl of the Pacific Flyway. The deaths and deformities of waterfowl and other wetland birds at Kesterson Reservoir, caused by extremely high levels of selenium in the agricultural drainage that supplied the reservoir, focused national attention on the need for a clean water supply for the nation's wetlands.

Selenium, a naturally occurring element that is a nutrient in small doses but a toxin at higher concentrations, was leached by irrigation water from the soils of 42,000 acres of the 600,000-acre Westlands Water District (WWD), collected in on-farm underground drains, and deposited in Kesterson Reservoir via the San Luis Drain. The drain was a feature of the U.S. Bureau of Reclamation's San Luis Unit of the Central Valley Project, which was constructed during the 1960s to supply water to the WWD. The Bureau originally planned the San Luis Drain to extend nearly 200 miles northward through the San Joaquin Valley to the Sacramento–San Joaquin Delta, but political opposition to the discharge of contaminated agricultural wastewater in the delta halted construction. Ultimately, the Bureau completed only eighty-five miles of the San Luis Drain from the WWD to Kesterson Reservoir, which became a terminal reservoir.

The Bureau acquired the Kesterson NWR site, which was composed of grassland and seasonally flooded marshes, in 1968 with the intention of operating the refuge in conjunction with the San Luis Drain project. In 1970, the Bureau and the U.S. Fish and Wildlife Service signed a cooperative agreement for the management of the refuge. In planning for Kesterson, both the Bureau and the Service ignored warnings about the dangers that selenium posed to wildlife. In the late 1970s, highly seleniferous subsurface drainage water from the WWD began entering the twelve interconnected ponds of Kesterson Reservoir. By 1981, the flow into the reservoir consisted almost entirely of subsurface drainage; problems quickly arose. In 1982, Gary Zahm, manager of the San Luis NWR Complex, of which the Kesterson NWR was a part, reported declining conditions for fish and wildlife at Kesterson, and on June 7, 1983, Fish and Wildlife Service biologists Harry Ohlendorf and Felix Smith discovered the first of hundreds of horribly deformed dead and dying embryos and chicks at the reservoir. Black-necked stilts, American avocets, and several duck species were affected. The Bureau of Reclamation attempted to downplay the significance of the selenium threat to wildlife. However, in 1984, U.S. Geological Survey scientists found that selenium concentrations in irrigation wastewater entering the San Luis Drain from the WWD ranged from 140 to 1,400 micrograms per liter (µg/L), as compared to concentrations in typical uncontaminated freshwater of 0.2–0.4 µg/L.

The amassing of unquestionable scientific evidence, combined with intense media pressure and petitions by neighboring landowners, culminated in the February 1985 California State Water Resources Control Board order for the Bureau of Reclamation to solve the selenium problem at Kesterson. The subsurface drains from the WWD were plugged in 1986, but for the next several years, the Board rejected the Bureau's cleanup plans as inadequate. Finally, in July 1988, the Board ordered the Bureau to fill in the Kesterson ponds, thereby converting Kesterson Reservoir from an aquatic to a terrestrial habitat and immobilizing the selenium present at the site. By the early 1990s, selenium concentrations had stabilized at elevated, but nontoxic, levels. In 1996, the Kesterson NWR, with the exception of the 1,280 acres of former reservoir ponds, was renamed the Kesterson Unit of the San Luis NWR.

The ecological disaster at Kesterson prompted an investigation of irrigation projects and drainage facilities constructed or managed by the Bureau of Reclamation at twenty-six project areas in fourteen of the seventeen western states. This investigation, the National Irrigation Water Quality Program (NIWQP), found deformities from selenium toxicosis at five sites, three of which were as seriously poisoned as Kesterson. However, because irrigation return flows are characterized as non–point source pollution, they are not subject to strict regulation under the federal Clean Water Act, and little has been done in the aftermath of Kesterson to remediate this problem. In 2005, the NIWQP was defunded and most of its programs suspended.

—Philip Garone

See also: *Bureau of Reclamation; Clean Water Act of 1972; Wetlands*

BIBLIOGRAPHY

Garone, Philip. *The Fall and Rise of the Wetlands of California's Great Central Valley.* Berkeley: University of California Press, 2011.

Lemly, A. Dennis, Susan E. Finger, and Marcia K. Nelson. "Sources and Impacts of Irrigation Drainwater Contaminants in Arid Wetlands." *Environmental Toxicology and Chemistry* 12, no. 12 (1993): 2265–79.

Presser, Theresa S., and Ivan Barnes. "Selenium Concentrations in Waters Tributary to and in the Vicinity of Kesterson National Wildlife Refuge, Fresno and Merced Counties, California." U.S. Geological Survey Water Resources Investigations Report 84-4122. Menlo Park, CA: U.S. Geological Survey, 1984. Available at http://wwwrcamnl.wr.usgs.gov/Selenium/Library_articles/PresserWRIR84_4122.pdf.

Kinzua Dam

Located in the Allegheny National Forest in Pennsylvania, the Kinzua Dam is six miles east of the township of Warren. The dam was authorized by the Flood Control Act of 1936, and those of 1938 and 1941, with the aim of reducing flooding. Public meetings were held in Jamestown, New York, in 1946 over the dam, and the Allegheny Senecas protested the decision to build the dam. They would have to be relocated because their reservation in New York would be flooded by the dam's reservoir. Work was delayed due to protests not only from the Seneca but also from the residents of the town of Corydon, located at the confluence of the Allegheny River and Willow Creek. Corydon would have to be evacuated because of the dam, and the Boy Scouts of America would lose nearby Camp Olmsted.

After protests from Cornelius V. Seneca, president of the Seneca Nation, in 1957, New York governor W. Averell Harriman urged that the U.S. Army Corps of Engineers (Corps) reconsider its plans. There were about 1,000 Senecas. They had been given their reservation lands by the Pickering Treaty of 1794, and George Washington had assured their nation that the treaty would be honored. The Seneca also argued that the cost of the Kinzua Dam would be much more than building a few smaller dams at the headwaters of the Allegheny River but provide no greater benefits.

On January 21, 1957, the U.S. Court of Appeals refused to overturn a decision by a lower court that had allowed the Corps to start a detailed survey in preparation for construction. Congress authorized $1 million to start work on the dam and appointed the New York City engineering firm of Tippetts, Abbett, McCarthy and Stratton to evaluate the project. However, the Seneca continued to battle in the courts. The Corps claimed that the Seneca would lose 9,014 acres but would be left with 21,455 acres. The Seneca countered that 12,236 acres of the remaining land were on hillsides, and 9,219 acres had been leased to non-Indians under acts of Congress in 1875 and 1891. Therefore, the dam would leave them with fewer than 2,000 usable acres.

Construction started on October 22, 1960, with Secretary of the Army Wilber N. Brucker and Pennsylvania governor David L. Lawrence each scooping up a symbolic spade of earth. By this time, the cost of the project was estimated to be $114 million. Supporters of the dam were anxious to get work underway before the upcoming presidential election, as presidential candidate John F. Kennedy had promised that the Senecas would not have to be moved if he were elected. President Kennedy failed to fulfill this promise after he was elected, however, and the Seneca went to court again, arguing that the government had broken a treaty that had guaranteed that they would have perpetual ownership of the land.

The Kinzua Dam was eventually completed and opened in 1965. It is 179 feet high and 1,897 feet long. The Allegheny Reservoir created as a result is now Pennsylvania's deepest lake.

—Justin Corfield

See also: *Army Corps of Engineers, United States*

BIBLIOGRAPHY

Bilharz, Joy A. *The Allegany Senecas and Kinzua Dam: Forced Relocation through Two Generations.* Lincoln: University of Nebraska Press, 1998.

Hauptman, Laurence M. "General John S. Bragdon, the Office of Public Works Planning, and the Decision to Build Pennsylvania's Kinzua Dam." *Pennsylvania History* 53, no. 3 (1986): 181–200. Available at http://dpubs.libraries.psu.edu/DPubS?Service=UI&version=1.0&verb=Display&handle=psu.ph.

Morgan, Arthur E. *Dams and Other Disasters: A Century of the Army Corps of Engineers in Civil Works.* Boston: P. Sargent, 1971.

Rosier, Paul C. "Dam Building and Treaty Breaking: The Kinzua Dam Controversy, 1936–1958." *Pennsylvania Magazine of History and Biography* 119, no. 4 (1995): 345–68.

Smith, Roland M. "The Politics of Pittsburgh Flood Control: 1936–1960." *Pennsylvania History* 44, no. 1 (1977): 3–24.

Weber, Michael P. *Don't Call Me Boss: David L. Lawrence, Pittsburgh's Renaissance Mayor.* Pittsburgh, PA: University of Pittsburgh Press, 1988.

Klamath Irrigation Project

The Klamath Irrigation Project is divided between Oregon (62%) and California (38%). Currently, water from the project irrigates 210,000 acres of farmland in the region, namely hay, alfalfa, barley, oats, wheat, and pasture. In the twentieth century, the project transformed wetlands and rangelands into productive cropland and facilitated the region's economic and demographic growth. Despite these benefits, the project has been criticized for its impact on wildlife, especially anadromous fish and migratory waterfowl.

The Klamath Basin and the project area extend over a diverse landscape. The project begins in an arid landscape east of the Oregon Cascade Range, dotted with many lakes and some rivers. Nearly 200,000 acres of natural wetlands existed before agricultural reclamation drained the landscape. This vast waterscape provided critical habitat for migratory birds. The river basin meanders through the forested mountains and on to the Pacific Ocean in northern California. The Native Americans who lived in the area had a highly developed fishing-hunting-gathering economy. As elsewhere, disease and warfare had reduced Native populations. The Modoc War in 1872–1873 resulted in the remaining indigenous populations being settled on reservations and facilitated Euro-American settlement of the region. Although nonindigenous miners had arrived in the area in the 1850s, agricultural settlement did not begin until after the war. By the 1880s, farmers began irrigating fields and orchards. To increase the scale of reclamation projects, the farmers desired public assistance.

The Reclamation Act of 1902 furnished the policy mechanism to facilitate public involvement. The legislation supported federal investment in reclamation projects, headed by the Reclamation Service (later Bureau of Reclamation). Planning began in 1903, and, after settling water rights issues with a private canal company, the federal government in 1905 approved the Klamath Irrigation Project. The project enjoyed virtually unanimous approval from local farmers, who would benefit from an infusion of funds into marginal private projects and development of more extensive engineering works. Construction began in 1906 and eventually included several canals (e.g., Main, East, South) and diversion dams (e.g., Clear Lake, Lost River, Gerber). Throughout the twentieth century, engineers built up the project, and farmers benefitted from the water.

The Klamath Irrigation Project radically altered the Klamath Basin's ecological relationships. The hydraulic engineering involved fundamentally replumbed the basin's drainages. Upper Klamath Lake is the main storage reservoir for the project, and there is a limited capacity to store water beyond a year. Consequently, irrigation diversions lowered the lake level and reduced wetland environments dramatically and dangerously for those species that require such ecosystems, such as migrating waterfowl and fish. Beginning in the 1930s and continuing throughout the twentieth century, environmental legislation attempted to mitigate the impacts of reclamation; however, economic priorities have tended to overrule the interests of fish and fowl.

The National Environmental Policy Act (1969), Endangered Species Act (1973), and other legislation gave greater voice to ecological interests, because these measures required government agencies to assess the environmental costs of their projects and to protect species from endangerment and extinction. In 1988, the Lost River sucker and the shortnose sucker were listed as endangered species, and in 1997, the coho salmon was listed as a threatened species, setting the stage for social and economic conflict. Compounding the issue were the water rights of American Indian tribes, primarily the Klamath in the Upper Basin and the Yurok in the Lower Basin. Legal doctrines reserved water rights and the right to fish for tribal peoples, but history and power structures have combined to make it difficult for Native peoples to exercise those rights.

A crisis point was reached in the late 1990s and early 2000s when a drought descended on the region. Scarce water had to be allocated to serve multiple needs, including Indian water rights, endangered species protection, waterfowl habitat, and irrigation. Low water levels caused an estimated 33,000 dead salmon to wash up on stream banks one year. Twice in 2002, the Bureau of Reclamation shut off water delivery to more than 1,400 farmers. Farmers illegally forced open headgates, and threats of violence toward federal managers and local tribes were all too frequent. Debates over science and law continue to plague this project and the basin.

The Klamath Irrigation Project illustrates a common challenge in arid landscapes: for too long too many have taken too much from too little. Competing uses among human communities and economies, along with competing needs for fish and wildlife, combined with competing legal requirements, have made the Klamath Basin and its reclamation project one of the most difficult, complex environmental issues in the American West.

—Adam M. Sowards

See also: *American Indian Water Rights; Bureau of Reclamation; Dam Building; Drought; Endangered Species Act (1973); Pacific Coast; Water Law; Wetlands*

BIBLIOGRAPHY

Doremus, Holly D., and A. Dan Tarlock. *Water War in the Klamath Basin: Macho Law, Combat Biology, and Dirty Politics*. Washington, DC: Island Press, 2008.

Robbins, William G. *Landscapes of Conflict: The Oregon Story, 1940–2000*. Seattle: University of Washington Press, 2004.

U.S. Bureau of Reclamation. "Klamath Project." http://www.usbr.gov/projects/.

Lake Lanier

Lake Lanier, officially Lake Sidney Lanier as designated by the U.S. Army Corps of Engineers, is a man-made reservoir along the Chattahoochee River about forty miles north of Atlanta, Georgia. The reservoir, created by Buford Dam, has provided drinking water for the metropolitan area of Atlanta since the 1950s. Today, Lake Lanier provides drinking water for over 3 million people. Lake Lanier has roughly 690 miles of shoreline and approximately 38,000 acres of surface water. The deepest part of the lake is located on the north side of Buford Dam in the original river channel at an elevation of 911 feet above sea level. When the lake is at its full level, it is 160 feet deep.

The area surrounding the lake is some of the most expensive real estate in Georgia. Undeveloped lots of a fraction of an acre sell for over $1 million. The area provides recreation to thousands of tourists each year who engage in fishing and boating. Many of the visitors reside in the greater Atlanta area.

The lake is located in a region that is known for its high humidity and has annual rainfall of about sixty inches. The landscape around the lake is green and lush and includes forests and farmland. Underneath the lake is a piedmont, absent of underground aquifers.

Shortly after World War II, civic leaders and then-mayor William Hartsfield realized the Chattahoochee River would not be able to continue to meet the water needs of Atlanta and its surrounding area, whose population was growing rapidly. Civic leaders, led by Hartsfield, pushed for a reservoir to be created north of the city along the Chattahoochee River. This goal was realized when construction for Buford Dam began in 1950. The dam began generating electrical power in 1957. By 1959, the reservoir created by the dam along the Chattahoochee River, Lake Lanier, was full. Buford Dam is managed by the Corps of Engineers, which controls the amount of water released through the dam. The Corps of Engineers also manages all other reservoirs and dams along the Chattahoochee River.

In addition to wanting a large freshwater reservoir, local inhabitants wanted to mitigate the threat of seasonal flooding. Buford Dam was built to protect downstream areas from the seasonal water flow and has allowed the land to become more attractive for commercial and residential development. After the threat of flooding was largely eliminating, suburban areas north of Atlanta began to develop quickly.

One challenge faced by those who manage Lake Lanier's water levels is the water flow of the Chattahoochee River as it feeds Lake Lanier. The Chattahoochee River does not provide a strong water flow into the lake. The lake was created upriver from Atlanta because it is the source of freshwater for the city. Unlike other major population centers, Atlanta is located closer to the origins of the river and its tributaries instead of being located near its mouth. When unusually high demands are made downstream or when precipitation is lower than normal, the lake is not replenished as necessary.

Over the past fifty years, the metropolitan area of Atlanta has experienced rapid growth. Initially, Lake Lanier and the Chattahoochee River were able to sustain that growth. However, by the 1990s, Atlanta was straining the capacity of Lake Lanier and the Chattahoochee River, especially during drought years. Lake Lanier has experienced historically low water levels in recent decades. Not only did the metropolitan area's rapid growth increase the amount of water being used, but the amount of pollution flowing into the lake and river also increased.

The state of Georgia became entangled with Alabama and Florida in legal battles over water levels along many lakes and rivers in the Apalachicola-Chattahoochee-Flint River Basin and neighboring Alabama-Coosa-Tallapoosa River Basin. Because of its importance in supplying freshwater to the Atlanta area, Lake Lanier is at the center of these legal battles. The primary issues are the purpose of the reservoir and who determines its water level. As development in the Atlanta area grows, so does its demand for water. The future of Lake Lanier as a reliable freshwater source for Atlanta and its surrounding areas, provider of electricity, and a recreation destination depend on conservation by downstream users.

—James Newman

See also: *Army Corps of Engineers, United States; Outdoor Recreation*

BIBLIOGRAPHY

Jordan, Jeffrey L., and Aaron T. Wolf. *Interstate Water Allocation in Alabama, Florida, and Georgia: New Issues, New Methods, New Models.* Gainesville: University Press of Florida, 2006.
U.S. Army Corps of Engineers, Mobile District. "Apalachicola-Chattahoochee-Flint River." http://water.sam.usace.army.mil/acf frame.htm.
U.S. Army Corps of Engineers, Mobile District. "Lake Sidney Lanier." http://lanier.sam.usace.army.mil/.

Lake Powell

See *Glen Canyon Dam*

Land Between the Lakes National Recreation Area

Land Between the Lakes (LBL) is a federal recreation area between the Tennessee and Cumberland Rivers on the border between Tennessee and Kentucky about ninety miles north of Nashville. The narrow and low area has been known as Between the Rivers since the 1830s or 1840s.

LBL is the largest inland peninsula in the United States as well as the second-largest contiguous block of forest east of the Mississippi. Established in 1964, it is a peninsula of 170,000 acres between Kentucky Lake, created by the Tennessee Valley Authority (TVA) in 1944, and Barkley Lake, created by the U.S. Army Corps of Engineers (Corps) in 1965. The last dam downstream on the Tennessee River was at Gilbertsville, Kentucky. It formed Kentucky Lake and forced the removal of the population that had lived there. The Corps dammed the Cumberland River to create Barkley Lake. The two lakes were at the same elevation, and the Corps connected them with a lock-free canal, thereby reducing the shipping distance to the Gulf of Mexico from the Cumberland Valley. The impoundment of the Tennessee and Cumberland Rivers to create Lake Barkley and Kentucky Lake created an inland peninsula, which President John F. Kennedy designated in 1963 as a national recreation area. Downstream from the lakes, the two rivers diverge again. Initially the TVA was administrator of the park. The TVA wanted an experimental site for its multiple-use approach to recreation.

On the Tennessee side of the LBL are several historic sites. The Civil War–era Fort Henry is a living history museum. On Trace Road, which runs the length of the park, are the ruins of the Great Western Iron Furnace (at one time, the area had seventeen functioning iron furnaces). Areas are set aside for hunting, and there is a youth camp. The Kentucky side includes the Woodlands Nature Center, which educates the public about the environment, wildlife, geography, botany, and geology. There are also a planetarium and a youth camp. The park also has stables, gift shops, campgrounds, 300 miles of trails, and a large herd of buffalo, added in the 1970s. Osprey and bald eagles returned to the park in the 1980s, elk in 1996, and in 1991 UNESCO designated the park a world biosphere reserve.

The creation of Land Between the Lakes required acquisition of 103,000 acres and relocation of about 2,700 people from 900 families in four communities in Kentucky and four in Tennessee. Some were happy to get a new start and left peacefully, but others were extremely unhappy, objecting vehemently to their forced relocation and the destruction of their communities. Towns evacuated by force included Tharpe and Model, Tennessee, and Golden Pond, Kentucky. Area residents were particularly resentful of losing their homelands not to a lake but to a park. The poor and poorly educated felt victimized by their government. A few even picked up their shotguns, prepared to defend their homes from condemnation, but only a few shot-out tires ensued.

To make the deal palatable, promises were made that tourism and recreation from the area would improve the local economy. The promised benefits did not fully materialize. The TVA endured budget cuts in the late 1980s and 1990s that reduced public and outdoor programs at the park. Some were ready for the park to close or for its administration to be transferred to state or local governments. The TVA wanted to rid itself of non-core functions in preparation for electricity generation deregulation in the 1990s, and the Land Between the Lakes Protection Act of 1998 allowed it to do so, giving administration of the area to the U.S. Forest Service. Critics regarded the transfer as a violation of the original mandate of the TVA. People who had lived in the condemned area and their descendants lobbied for return of most of the land to their ownership because it was no longer being used for the purpose that had justified its condemnation. They were unsuccessful, however.

LBL is a demonstration of how an area with limited resources could become an economic asset. It remains the only such demonstration site and is the basis for a $600 million tourism industry. About 2 million people a year visit the park. They come from all fifty states and thirty foreign countries.

—John H. Barnhill

See also: *Outdoor Recreation; Tennessee Valley Authority*

BIBLIOGRAPHY

Henry, Joseph. Milton. *The Land Between the Rivers.* Dallas, TX: Taylor, 1970.
Van West, Carroll. "Land Between the Lakes National Recreation Area." In *Tennessee Encyclopedia of History and Culture,* edited by

Carroll Van West. Nashville: Tennessee Historical Society/Rutledge Hill Press, 1998. Available at http://tennesseeencyclopedia.net/imagegallery.php?EntryID=L005.

Wallace, Betty Joe. *Between the Rivers: History of the Land Between the Lakes*. Clarksville, TN: Austin Peay State University, Center for Field Biology, Department of History and Philosophy, 1992.

Los Angeles Aqueduct

The Los Angeles Aqueduct delivers water from the Owens Valley and the Mono Lake Basin in the eastern Sierra to the city of Los Angeles. Completed in 1913, the 233-mile aqueduct became the first major long-distance water delivery project in California.

In 1900, the city of Los Angeles had a population of only 102,000 people, yet it was growing fast and local water supplies were going to limit future growth. Former Los Angeles mayor Fred Eaton convinced city water engineer William Mulholland that an aqueduct project from the Owens Valley was feasible. Eaton began quietly acquiring water rights. The plan was announced publicly in 1905, and city voters approved bonds to fund land purchases. In 1907, another bond passed to pay for construction. William Mulholland engineered a route that used tunnels and siphons so that the water flowed by gravity the entire distance. On November 5, 1913, after only six years for construction, the aqueduct

The Los Angeles Aqueduct was completed in 1913 and carried water over 230 miles to satisfy the needs of the growing city. "Deadman's Syphon," pictured above, illustrates some of the topographical challenges of delivering water over a great distance.
Library of Congress

reached San Fernando. In a ceremony attended by 43,000 people, the water gates were opened, and William Mulholland's brief historic speech was delivered: "There it is—take it!"

The city of Los Angeles acquired Owens Valley water rights by, ultimately, purchasing 300,000 acres in the valley over the objections of local farmers and townsfolk. Those protests turned violent, at times, and included dynamiting of the aqueduct. The city responded by sending armed guards to patrol the aqueduct route. The federal government cooperated with the city's goals by withdrawing public land in the Owens Valley from new settlement and authorizing the right-of-way where the aqueduct crossed public land.

Today Los Angeles owns 98 percent of the privately held lands in the Owens Valley. Final land purchases required another bond issue, approved by voters in 1930 at the height of the Great Depression, to fund land acquisition up to the north end of the Owens Valley. The same bond also funded an extension of the aqueduct 100 miles further north.

The Mono Basin extension to the aqueduct would handle all of the water from four creeks—Lee Vining, Parker, Walker, and Rush Creeks—which had supplied most of the annual supply entering Mono Lake. The new project took seven years to complete and required the boring of an eleven-mile tunnel beneath the volcanic Mono Craters, plus diversions and conduits from the creeks and a dam to form Grant Lake. Another new reservoir south of the Mono Basin, in Long Valley—the headwaters region of the Owens River—was named Crowley Lake and became the largest storage reservoir in the system.

A second barrel of the Los Angeles Aqueduct was completed in 1970, doubling its capacity southward from the lower Owens Valley. The ability to export more water accelerated the project's environmental impacts on Mono Lake and the Owens Valley. The Los Angeles Aqueduct transports about 400,000 acre-feet each year—enough for the domestic use of 3 million people (today the city has a population of 4.5 million, made possible with additional water from the Colorado River and the California State Water Project).

Court orders have forced Los Angeles to return some water to the eastern Sierra. By 1982, after forty years of stream diversions from Mono Lake, that inland sea had lost half its volume and doubled in salinity. The unique lake ecosystem, with brine shrimp and flies that fed over a million birds, was in danger of collapse. Islands where California gulls (*Larus californicus*) nested had been connected to shore by lowered water levels, giving access to coyotes. Dust was blowing off the exposed lakebed, causing particulate air quality standards to be exceeded.

Lawsuits brought by the Mono Lake Committee, National Audubon Society, and CalTrout produced a series of court rulings that found the water diversions had damaged environmental and aesthetic values held in trust for the public. Completely drying up streams was also a violation of the state's fish and game code. In 1994, the state Water Resources Control Board amended the city's water licenses to reduce diversions, requiring that Mono Lake be filled high enough to protect the lake ecosystem and control the dust and requiring restoration of fisheries in the tributary streams. Los Angeles's water exports were reduced by about two-thirds (the city had been taking about 110,000 acre-feet per year). The aqueduct still takes water from the Mono Basin because the court required balancing of the needs of the city with those of the environment.

By the 1920s, diversion of the Owens River had caused Owens Lake, at the south end of the Owens Valley, to dry up. Alkaline dust blown off the exposed lakebed exceeded air quality standards for fine particulates and threatened public health. The courts have also ordered Los Angeles to apply water and other dust-control measures to solve that problem.

—David Carle

See also: *Mulholland, William; Owens Valley*

BIBLIOGRAPHY

deBuys, William Eno. *Salt Dreams: Land and Water in Low-Down California.* Photographs by Joan Myers. Albuquerque: University of New Mexico Press, 1999.
Green, Dorothy. *Managing Water: Avoiding Crisis in California.* Berkeley: University of California Press, 2007.
Hundley, Norris, Jr. *The Great Thirst: Californians and Water; A History.* Rev. ed. Berkeley: University of California Press, 2001.
Reisner, Marc. *Cadillac Desert: The American West and Its Disappearing Water.* Rev. ed. New York: Penguin Books, 1993.

Los Angeles River

The Los Angeles River once flowed but, in the second decade of the twenty-first century, is a river in name only.

Chinatown

The film *Chinatown*, written by Robert Towne and directed by Roman Polanski, is loosely based on William Mulholland and his work on behalf of Los Angeles to acquire the waters from the Owens Valley. Towne and Polanski used Vietnam War era distrust of public officials to suggest that Los Angeles's acquisition of the water was the result of a conspiracy between a water regulator and real estate developers. That particular conspiracy theory had found favor within the Owens Valley for decades before the movie was made, but it was not supported by the voluminous documentation resulting from the litigation that had occurred during the years of the water fight between Los Angeles and the Owens Valley. Although the Oscar-winning movie is a work of fiction, many viewers continue to believe that it is an accurate depiction of a seminal moment in California's Water Wars.

—John R. Burch Jr.

See also: *Mulholland, William; Owens Valley*

BIBLIOGRAPHY

Chinatown, DVD. Directed by Roman Polanski. Hollywood, CA: Paramount, 2007.
Erie, Steven P. *Beyond Chinatown: The Metropolitan Water District, Growth, and the Environment in Southern California.* With the assistance of Harold Brackman. Stanford, CA: Stanford University Press, 2006.
Mulholland, Catherine. *William Mulholland and the Rise of Los Angeles.* Berkeley: University of California Press, 2000.

The concrete bed and banks stretch fifty-one miles from the suburbs of the San Fernando Valley to the Pacific Ocean. Little water flows in the river's wide channel for most of the year, and nearly all that does is treated sewage and oily street runoff. The river is probably best known today as a place where Hollywood movie studios film high-speed car chases.

Prior to the establishment of the city of Los Angeles, the river looked much like any other. It meandered through a forest of willow, sycamore, and elderberry. Its overflow filled vast marshlands, which were home to waterfowl and small animals. Steelhead trout spawned in the river. When the first Europeans passed through present-day Los Angeles in the eighteenth century, they counted more than two dozen Native American villages alongside the banks of the river. As an important source of water and one of the few streams in the area that flowed year-round, the river largely determined the location of Los Angeles. For more than a century, the river provided drinking water as well as the irrigation water that helped make southern California into the most important agricultural region in the West.

Los Angeles possessed exclusive legal rights to the river's water, helping to guarantee its emergence as the dominant city in the region. As Los Angeles grew, however, the demand for water became so great that the river's entire surface flow had to be diverted for domestic use. The flood-plain forest that had spread along its banks was cleared for cultivation and its trees cut for fuel. The marshlands were replaced with roads, factories, and houses. Eventually, much of the river's underground flow was also pumped to the surface to meet the rapidly expanding water needs of the city. The river became dry most of the year.

The river was unpredictable and prone to flooding. A catastrophic flood in 1914 prompted government officials to create a comprehensive regional flood control system. In 1915, the Los Angeles County Board of Engineers began conducting topographical surveys of flood-prone areas and interviewing long-term residents to gain a better understanding of past floods. A second catastrophic flood in 1934 spurred efforts to control the river. The only environmental concern considered by the Los Angeles County Flood Control District in the 1930s was whether stream channels should be left open or covered completely like sewers. Residents also had little concern for the natural character of the river. Beginning in 1935, massive flood control reservoirs were constructed on the lowlands to regulate peak stream flows. The river itself was straightened, deepened, and widened, and its new channel was lined with concrete to provide floodwaters with the quickest route to the sea.

Toward the end of the twentieth century, the Los Angeles River became the subject of revitalization attempts by local citizens. Mayor Tom Bradley, upon his reelection in 1989, pledged to make the river one of the priorities of his administration. In January 1990, he created the Los Angeles River Task Force. The task force called for the removal of the river's concrete channel in some places and increased public access to the river. In 1990, the Natural History Museum of Los Angeles obtained a grant from the state Department of Fish and Game to survey the existing plant and animal life along the river. In 1991, the Los Angeles County Board of Supervisors directed the county Department of Public Works to develop a Los Angeles River master plan. In that same year, Friends of the Los Angeles River and LA Beautiful sponsored a conference on the future of the river. Meanwhile, the U.S. Army Corps of Engineers announced its intention to build concrete walls two to eight feet high atop levees along the last twelve miles of the river to increase flood protection. Not surprisingly, massive opposition quickly arose to this plan. Environmentalists claimed that the project would further degrade the river, increase urban

blight, reduce property values, and waste water while providing only short-term flood protection. In the end, in 1997, the needs of flood control won out over the long-term interest in improving the river. The challenge that continues to face environmentalists is how to make people care about a river that looks so little like one.

—Caryn Neumann

See also: *Army Corps of Engineers, United States; Urban Rivers*

BIBLIOGRAPHY

Gumprecht, Blake. *The Los Angeles River: Its Life, Death, and Possible Rebirth.* Baltimore: Johns Hopkins University Press, 1999.

Mansfield Dam

The Mansfield Dam, originally named the Marshall Ford Dam, was built between 1937 and 1941 on the Colorado River in Texas. It created Lake Travis, named after William Travis, one of the heroes of the Texan Army in the Texan War for Independence. Construction involved both the Lower Colorado River Authority and the Bureau of Reclamation. When the dam was completed, its name was changed to Mansfield Dam, in honor of Joseph Jefferson Mansfield (1861–1947), a member of the U.S. House of Representatives for Texas from 1917 until his death.

Plans had been developed during the 1930s to "tame" the Colorado River as it flowed through Texas. These plans had the support of the former state senator Alvin J. Wirtz and James "Buck" Buchanan, the chair of the U.S. House Appropriations Committee and eponym of the Buchanan Dam. The resulting dam is 278 feet high, 7,089 feet long, and 213 feet thick at the base. Along the top of the dam is a two-lane highway, but this is now only used for service vehicles; normal traffic uses a four-lane bridge on the downstream side of the dam. The dam, which was the fifth largest in the world at the time of its construction, is still operated by the Lower Colorado River Authority.

The team that constructed the dam was led by brothers Herman Brown and George R. Brown. The cost of construction was partly financed through the New Deal, but the Browns had to borrow heavily to build it, and construction ran into problems from the start as the government did not own all the land on which the dam was being built. However, an aspiring Texan politician, Lyndon B. Johnson, managed to push through a new plan that raised the height of the dam at a cost of $27 million, and he obtained $5 million in extra subsidies that ensured that the Brown brothers finished with a $1 million profit. The Browns's company went on to become one of the biggest construction companies in twentieth-century America; it was eventually acquired by Halliburton.

Located near Austin, the capital of Texas, the Mansfield Dam quickly became the center of what became known as "Texas's Little TVA," so called after the Tennessee Valley Authority (TVA). During massive flooding on June 30, 1940, the dam was credited with holding back much of the water, preventing the situation from becoming far worse than it was. The Mansfield Dam also proved useful during the flood of May 26, 1957, when major thunderstorms caused 2,100 people to flee the Dallas–Fort Worth area. Three gates on the dam were closed to prevent flooding between Austin and the Gulf of Mexico. The dam has continued to help control floods in the region.

—Justin Corfield

See also: *Bureau of Reclamation*

BIBLIOGRAPHY

Adams, John A., Jr. *Damming the Colorado: The Rise of the Lower Colorado River Authority, 1933–1939*. College Station: Texas A&M University Press, 1990.

Pratt, Joseph A., and Christopher James Castaneda. *Builders: Herman and George R. Brown*. College Station: Texas A&M University Press, 1999.

McClellan-Kerr Waterway

The McClellan-Kerr Arkansas River Navigation System, named after two of its major sponsors, John Little McClellan and Robert S. Kerr, U.S. senators from Arkansas and Oklahoma respectively, runs 443 miles from Catoosa, Oklahoma, on the Verdigris River near Tulsa, to the Mississippi River. A minimum nine-foot-deep navigation channel was achieved by constructing seventeen locks and dams (an eighteenth was added in 2004). In addition, three upstream reservoirs, Oologah, Keystone, and Eufala, were built to ensure a stable water supply.

The 1,460-mile-long Arkansas River historically had failed to support consistent navigation. A cartoon drawn by Arkansas editor William Minor Quesenbury in the 1850s showed a keelboat stranded on a sandbar while cattle waded the river. Flooding was also a problem. The Flood of 1927 sent a wall of water (estimated at between eight and ten feet) down from Fort Smith that destroyed levees and washed

away the Baring Cross Railroad Bridge in Little Rock, prompting river promoters to organize the Arkansas River Flood Control Association and seek federal money.

Fort Smith *Southwest-Times Record* editor Clarence F. Byrns championed navigation. Despite an initial finding that a navigation project was too expensive, Congress in 1936 created a Southwest Division of the Corps of Engineers and charged it with flood control on the Arkansas and other area river basins. In 1946, the Arkansas Basin Development Association got Congress to authorize construction of the Arkansas-Verdigris Waterway. Item by item, funding started in 1948, but it was stopped by the outbreak of the Korean War.

One technical problem, that the Arkansas River carried some 100 million tons of silt annually, was solved by University of California at Berkeley professor Hans Albert Einstein's system of using narrower channels to increase water speed so that the river could clean itself. Hence, three upriver dams were no longer required. In 1955, work resumed on the Oologah Reservoir and began on the Keystone and Eufala projects and the locks and dams in Arkansas.

The $1.2 billion project had many opponents. President Dwight D. Eisenhower thought the project too expensive, while a *Life* magazine article in 1963 called it "the most outrageous pork-barrel project in the United States." After the waterway was completed in 1971, no great transportation boom resulted. In the first year, it carried 4,294,048 tons of freight; in 1987, the tonnage rose to only 7,915,037. Nine million tons were needed to justify the project. In 2006, the system carried a record 14.0 million tons; in 2008 the figure fell to 11.3 million tons. Sand and rock, agricultural commodities, and other heavy items predominate; shipping down the system greatly outweighs upstream deliveries.

On the lower Mississippi River, thirty-barge shipments are not uncommon. However, on the McClellan-Kerr Navigation System, the original 600-by-110-feet locks could only hold eight barges. Negotiating the locks required barges to be lashed together in a square three sideways and three deep, with the tow boat filling the missing space. The addition of tow haulage equipment allowed a "double cut," with the machinery pulling through the first nine barges and the towboat then bringing through the other six.

Flood control was an important motivation for building this project. The Flood of 1990 caused problems in the operation of the locks. On April 22, 1990, the *Greenville*, towing eight barges, was pushed out of its alignment when entering Lock and Dam 4 by an "outdraft," an alteration from normal current direction caused by excessive water flow. The towboat hit the rock revetment and then the guide wall leading into the lock. The physical contact ("allision") caused the barge unit to break up, resulting in the sinking of one barge and damage to several others. The Arkansas River Company sued the United States, claiming that the U.S. Army Corps of Engineers had a duty to correct navigational hazards, while the Corps sued the company for negligence in damaging the lock and dam. The U.S. District Court held that the Flood Control Act of 1928 immunized the government from any damages caused by river floodwaters or by the operation of a flood control project and held that the company was liable for the damages to the dam. Legally at least, flood control and not navigation alone had legal standing. According to Corps estimates, the flood control inherent in the system prevented more than $1.3 billion in losses between 1974 and 1987.

The series of dams also promoted sport fishing and other recreational activities. Hydroelectric power, more than 1 billion kilowatt-hours of electricity annually, comes from six dams. Riverfront development, especially in Little Rock, Arkansas, includes the 4,226-foot-long Big Dam Bridge over the Murray Lock and Dam.

Water quality has long been a problem. The diversion of headwaters into agriculture, the decline in the water table, and the presence of salt in Oklahoma all impact water quality. The aging of the system became evident in 2009 when almost half of the Corps's $137 million stimulus money was used to fund a few of the most urgent repairs to the system.

—Michael B. Dougan

See also: *Arkansas River Basin; Army Corps of Engineers, United States; Dam Building; Levees; Locks*

BIBLIOGRAPHY

Arkansas River Company v. United States of America, 947 F. Supp. 941 (1996).

Bolton, S. Charles. *25 Years Later: A History of the McClellan-Kerr Arkansas River Navigation System in Arkansas.* Little Rock, AR: U.S. Army Corps of Engineers, Little Rock District, 1995.

Goss, Kay C. "McClellan-Kerr Arkansas River Navigation System." In *The Encyclopedia of Arkansas History & Culture.* http://www.encyclopediaofarkansas.net/.

Wheeler, Keith, Henry Sudyam, Norman Ritter, Bill Wise, and Howard Sochurek. "Now—See the Innards of a Fat Pig." *Life,* August 16, 1963.

Mississippi River Basin

The Mississippi River is the longest river in the United States and the fifth longest in the entire world. The Mississippi River Basin covers thirty-two states and two Canadian provinces. Approximately 18 million people rely on the Mississippi River Basin for their water supply. Both historically and today the Mississippi plays an integral part in the nation's commerce, providing transportation, industrial power, and recreational opportunities.

The Mississippi River flows 2,333 miles from Lake Itasca, near the border of Minnesota and Canada, to the Gulf of Mexico. The drainage basin of the Mississippi River is the second largest in the world, covering 1.83 million square miles. The river's twelve major tributaries include the Missouri, Ohio, and Tennessee Rivers; in total 30,700 miles of streams empty into the basin along with 3,000 reservoirs. Shaped like a funnel, the Mississippi River is wider at the top, narrowing sharply before emptying itself through its delta in Louisiana. The Mississippi River Basin is the main site of navigable inland waterways in the United States, helping to form a system 12,350 miles long.

Because of its size, the upper Mississippi River Basin is considered a nationally significant ecosystem, as well as a nationally significant navigation system. In 1924, Congress established the Upper Mississippi River Wildlife and Fish Refuge, covering 195,000 acres. Today three national refugees along the upper Mississippi River total 285,000 acres.

The lower part of the Mississippi River Basin is comprised of a 600-mile long alluvial plain. Its width varies from 25 miles to 125 miles. This plain, which covers 35,000 square miles, would be perpetually covered in water during flood seasons if not for man-made flood control measures.

As early as 1879, it was apparent that improvements would be needed along the Mississippi and its tributaries if the basin were to be used for economic purposes. The Mississippi River Commission was established, becoming the nation's earliest organized effort at flood control. Channels were dug along the river and levees were put in place to help control flooding. However, flooding continued along the Mississippi River Basin, so a series of additional flood control measures was put in place. In 1914, fifty-two levee drainage districts were established between Rock Island, Illinois, and Cape Girardeau in Missouri. In 1927, a devastating flood along the Mississippi River prompted Congress to pass the Flood Control Act of 1928, bringing flood control to a national level. The Mississippi River and Tributaries project was established, providing a plan for the construction of levees, channel improvements, and drainage of the river. In 1936, more flood control measures were put in place. Most recently, in 1954, flood controls were undertaken to prevent the capture of the Mississippi River by the Atchafalaya River in south-central Louisiana.

Today the Mississippi River Basin is still vital to the U.S. economy. Heavy commercial traffic along the river transports grains, coal, petroleum products, sand, salt, and building materials. Of the Mississippi River Basin, 60 percent is cropland and pasture; the area provides fertile ground for soybeans and corn. Close to $2 million is generated from commercial fishing along the river, while a remarkable $1 billion is generated from recreation in the upper basin region. The Mississippi River Basin also provides energy for twenty-nine power plants along the upper portion of the river. Seven billion gallons of water from the river's surface are used every day as cooling water for energy production.

If left uncontrolled, the Mississippi River and its tributaries would be a huge liability, as seen in the great flood of 1993, which caused $12 billion in damage. However, thanks to comprehensive flood control and environmental precautions, the river basin is instead a strong asset.

—Lorri Brown

See also: *Army Corps of Engineers, United States; Flood Control Act of 1928; Flood Control Act of 1936*

BIBLIOGRAPHY

Arnold, Joseph L. *The Evolution of the 1936 Flood Control Act.* Washington, DC: Office of History, U.S. Army Corps of Engineers, 1988.
Mississippi Valley Division, U.S. Army Corps of Engineers. "Appendix E: 1928 Flood Control Act." http://www.mvd.usace.army.mil/mrc/history/AppendixE.htm.
Theiling, Charles H. "Habitat Rehabilitation on the Upper Mississippi River." *Regulated Rivers: Research & Management* 11, no. 2 (1995): 227–38.

Missouri River Basin

The Missouri River is the longest waterway in the United States, flowing 2,473 miles from western Montana before joining the Mississippi River near Saint Louis, Missouri. The

Mississippi River Fish Kills of 1963–1964

In November 1963, large numbers of dead fish appeared on the lower portion of the Mississippi River and its tributaries, including the Atchafalaya River in Louisiana. Louisiana's Office of Water Pollution Control determined that the fish did not die of natural causes. Thus it notified the Public Health Service (PHS). After ruling out parasites and diseases as the culprits, scientists from the PHS determined that the fish had been killed by the pesticide endrin, which was used extensively on tobacco crops. The determination that endrin was to blame unleashed a political firestorm while fish continued to die.

Politically, the fish kills could not have come at a worse time for pesticide companies, such as Velsicol. Those companies had been claiming that Rachel Carson's *Silent Spring* was wrong about the environmental dangers of pesticides. The fish kills provided vivid images to support Carson's contentions. Velsicol was ultimately identified as the source of much of the endrin present in the Mississippi River through its waste-treatment plant in Memphis, Tennessee. Another source of endrin was the many farms located within the Mississippi River's watershed. The U.S. Department of Agriculture had desperately attempted to show that farms were not the source of the endrin in order to prevent the U.S. Congress from either heavily restricting the use of the pesticide or banning its use entirely. Unfortunately, interest in regulating the use of endrin did not yield immediate results, as the chemical was responsible for the deaths of many pelicans in Louisiana in 1975. The pelicans most likely got the endrin through the fish that they ate. Endrin was not banned until 1984.

—John R. Burch Jr.

See also: *Pesticides*

BIBLIOGRAPHY

Daniel, Pete. *Toxic Drift: Pesticides and Health in the Post–World War II South.* Baton Rouge: Louisiana State University Press, 2007.
Lytle, Mark H. *The Gentle Subversive: Rachel Carson,* Silent Spring, *and the Rise of the Environmental Movement.* New York: Oxford University Press, 2007.

Missouri River Basin, the area drained by the river, covers 513,000 square miles, roughly one-sixth of the land of the continental United States. It includes all or parts of ten states and encompasses a region of great diversity, from a lush, humid area in the lower basin to the barren, semi-arid plains of the upper basin.

The federal government has never formulated a single, comprehensive plan for the management and development of water resources in the Missouri Basin. Instead, a variety of plans have attempted to balance the interests of several federal agencies, ten state governments, twenty-five Indian tribes, and scores of municipalities throughout the region. Numerous multipurpose projects have been constructed in the basin, but debates continue about which purposes should take priority.

The U.S. Army Corps of Engineers was given authority to regulate navigation on the nation's major rivers in 1824, but it did relatively little on the Missouri before the early twentieth century. In 1912, the Corps began a project to ensure the maintenance of a six-foot-deep channel for navigation from Kansas City to the mouth of the river near Saint Louis. By 1925, this project had been extended upstream to Sioux City, Iowa. By World War II, the Corps had spent nearly $300 million on this channelization project.

The most comprehensive program for the Missouri Basin is the Pick-Sloan Plan, which Congress incorporated into the Flood Control Act of 1944. Based on previous congressional directives, the Corps of Engineers and the Bureau of Reclamation had both prepared flood control plans for the basin. The Corps's plan, produced by Colonel Lewis A. Pick, focused on flood control, navigation, and hydroelectric power generation. The Bureau of Reclamation's plan was prepared by W. G. Sloan, one of its regional engineers. Sloan's plan emphasized irrigation, reclamation, and some power production.

President Franklin D. Roosevelt wanted to create a Missouri Valley Authority, similar to the Tennessee Valley Authority, to provide overall management for the development of the Missouri Basin. Congress considered this proposal several times, but both the Corps of Engineers and the Bureau of Reclamation opposed this concept, not wishing to see another federal entity created to manage Missouri Basin water issues. Hoping to forestall the creation of a Missouri Valley Authority, the two agencies harmonized their plans, and in November 1944 they presented the results as the Pick-Sloan Plan, which Congress incorporated into the Flood Control Act of 1944.

Under the Pick-Sloan Plan, the Corps of Engineers constructed five major dams on the main stem of the Missouri. A sixth dam, Fort Peck Dam in northeastern Montana, was already in place but was incorporated into the overall plan for the basin. The other main stem dams were Garrison Dam, in North Dakota, and Oahe Dam, Big Bend Dam, Fort Randall Dam, and Gavins Point Dam, all in South Dakota. In addition to these Corps of Engineers projects, the Bureau of Reclamation built Canyon Ferry Dam near Helena, Montana. Besides these main steam dams, twenty-two dams were built on tributary rivers. Together, these reservoirs have a total storage capacity of more than 70 million acre-feet of water. A nine-foot-deep navigation channel was also created for hundreds of miles on the lower portions of the Missouri, and a system of levees was put in place downstream from Sioux City, Iowa. Forty-one hydroelectric power plants, with a combined capacity of 2.8 million kilowatts, were installed on main stem and tributary dams.

The Pick-Sloan Plan has provided clearly evident benefits through flood control, electrical power production, and river navigation. But the plan was controversial from the very beginning because of its massive scope and disputes over which of the various uses of Missouri River water should take precedence. Many critics have also questioned the overall environmental impact of the massive changes made to the river system. In addition, some have noted that the major dams have had a disproportionately negative impact on Native American communities, which have lost hundreds of thousands of acres of reservation lands to the reservoirs in the upper basin but have seen little economic benefit in return. Congress has tried to address many of these issues in subsequent legislation, and there has been almost continual litigation in the federal courts between various parties and their interests in the resources of the Missouri Basin. Technology and engineering have largely tamed the Missouri River, but doing so has raised numerous environmental, legal, and political issues that seem to portend continuing controversy.

—Mark S. Joy

See also: *Army Corps of Engineers, United States; Bureau of Reclamation; Dam Building; Flood Control Act of 1944; Fort Peck Dam; Garrison Dam; Missouri River Navigation and Channelization Project; River Transportation*

BIBLIOGRAPHY

Lawson, Michael L. *Dammed Indians: The Pick-Sloan Plan and the Missouri River Sioux, 1944–1980.* Norman: University of Oklahoma Press, 1994.

Ridgeway, Marian E. *The Missouri Basin's Pick-Sloan Plan: A Case Study in Congressional Policy Determination.* Urbana: University of Illinois Press, 1955.

Thorson, John E. *River of Promise, River of Peril: The Politics of Managing the Missouri River.* Lawrence: University Press of Kansas, 1994.

Navajo Indian Irrigation Project

First proposed in the 1930s and finally authorized by the U.S. Congress in 1962, the Navajo Indian Irrigation Project (NIIP), which was to have been an Indian companion project to the non-Indian San Juan–Chama Project, has constantly suffered from a lack of prioritization within federal agencies and a lack of funding from Congress, and it has never been fully implemented.

The NIIP promised to either directly or indirectly employ over one-quarter of the Navajo population and to decrease the tribe's dependency both on the traditional Navajo economic activity of sheep herding and, more importantly, on federal welfare funds. But it did not take long for the Navajos to find out that there is a great difference between gaining congressional approval for the construction of a project and obtaining congressional appropriations to fund actual construction. Although the Navajos were now legally entitled to the project, obtaining funding took longer than many court cases for water rights. The original completion date of 1979 was pushed back repeatedly. The Navajo Nation government, which was potentially entitled to huge water claims on the San Juan and Little Colorado Rivers thanks to the Winters Doctrine, did all it could to spur action. However, when Congress was faced with competing funding requests for the San Juan–Chama Project (to be built by the much more powerful Bureau of Reclamation and completed ahead of schedule in 1972), the non-Indian water project won out. During that same period, the NIIP received only 41 percent of its requested appropriations.

Appropriations for the NIIP finally began to increase during the first half of the 1970s, thanks to activist tribal chair Peter MacDonald. The Navajo Agricultural Products Industry (NAPI), a tribal-owned corporation, was established to guide the development of the NIIP and to plan for its use. The roles of the NAPI were to include the supervision of the operation of the NIIP, the construction of everything necessary for its operation within the guidelines set by the Navajo Tribal Council, the formulation of a long-range for the development of the NIIP, and the establishment of a program to promote the tribe's goal of developing an agribusiness to attract possible investors and customers. Also during the 1970s, the Navajo government established the Navajo Water Commission, an organization charged with the daunting task of protecting Navajo water rights in the federal and state realms.

In April 1976, six years after the entire project was to be complete, the first block of the NIIP opened up. It contained approximately 9,300 acres, just shy of 8.5 percent of the total irrigated lands promised to the tribe. NAPI established farm schools on the newly irrigated lands to train Navajos how to take full advantage of the water. Although few in number, graduates of the farm schools stood ready to put their knowledge into practice. NAPI anticipated fulfilling its mission and developing into a large, corporate agribusiness for the employment of many Navajos and for the benefit of the entire tribe. NAPI argued that the completion of Block One was the culmination of a dream, but it was painfully aware that the problem of inadequate funds still stymied the fulfillment of the project's potential. The larger problem NAPI had to face was how to turn a project that was decades behind schedule into a profitable agribusiness before tribal members grew completely disheartened with the endeavor.

Within its first decade of operation on the NIIP irrigated lands, NAPI would prove as disappointing as the entire process up to that point had already been. By the early 1980s, NAPI was facing possible bankruptcy due to countless problems in the appropriation of federal money to fund project construction, the logistics of bringing the project online, and some poor decisions regarding operational matters. The Navajo Nation was in poor financial shape as well and in no position to fund many important tribal programs, much less bail out NAPI. To keep NAPI functioning, in 1984 the Navajo Nation was forced to accept a proposal from the Bureau of Indian Affairs (BIA) for a $25 million, interest-free loan. It was clear that the NIIP had not been a panacea for the tribe's water rights problems in the San Juan Basin. It was also clear that the only way to solve the problem permanently was through an agreement on the long-term use of the San Juan's waters. By this time, a general stream adjudication for the San Juan Basin had been in the court system for ten years but had made very little progress. Because of the vastness of the Navajo lands within the basin, federal and state officials have assumed that the Navajos would use the waters solely for agriculture.

By 1999, the NIIP had fallen over twenty years behind schedule and could irrigate just over 60 percent of the planned 110,000 acres. However, the Navajo Nation still could potentially assert huge Winters claims to the San Juan River, which could threaten the certainty of continued water supplies to non-Indian users and the area's large cities. That realization brought negotiators back to the table, resulting finally in the Navajo Nation Water Rights settlement, which concluded negotiations in 2005 and was approved by Congress in 2009. With the settlement, Navajos have concrete rights to the water. If the

NIIP is ever fully implemented, it will be able to make use of it.

—Steven L. Danver

See also: *Bureau of Indian Affairs; Bureau of Reclamation; Winters v. United States (1908)*

BIBLIOGRAPHY

Bureau of Indian Affairs, Branch of Land Use Planning. "Comprehensive Plan for Navajo Indian Irrigation Project." March 1972. Native American Studies Library, University of New Mexico, Albuquerque.

Glaser, Leah. *The Navajo Indian Irrigation Project*. Denver, CO: U.S. Bureau of Reclamation History Program, 1998.

Iverson, Peter. *Diné: A History of the Navajos*. Photographs by Monty Roessel. Albuquerque: University of New Mexico Press, 2002.

Lawson, Michael L. "The Navajo Indian Irrigation Project: Muddied Past, Clouded Future." *Indian Historian* 9, no. 1 (1976): 19–29.

Ogallala Aquifer

A groundwater aquifer that underlies 174,000 square miles of the High Plains, the Ogallala Aquifer is beneath Nebraska, western Kansas, and northwest Texas, as well as smaller portions of Oklahoma, New Mexico, Colorado, Wyoming, and South Dakota. The aquifer is believed to hold more than 3 billion acre-feet of water in layers of water-saturated gravel beds 150 to 300 feet thick starting between 50 and over 250 feet below the surface.

The Ogallala Aquifer is nonrenewable. Its original source was so-called fossil water—water held in underground aquifers for thousands or even millions of years—that drained between 10,000 and 25,000 years ago from glaciers in the Rocky Mountains. Today groundwater replacement occurs from surface percolation at the rate of two-tenths to one inch of water per year. In the meantime, users (mostly irrigation farmers) are pumping up to several feet of water out of the aquifer annually.

Early settlers and geologists first suggested that the Ogallala groundwater was contained in cavernous lakes or flowed through underground rivers. In reality, it slowly trickles southeastward through sandy gravel beds at a rate of two to three feet a day. The nonrenewability of the aquifer is a significant concern because farmers use its water to irrigate up to 7 million acres of farmlands for grain and cotton production.

The first regular users of the Ogallala Aquifer were railroads, which erected windmills to power wells as they crossed the region. As farmers moved into the area, they too began setting up windmill pumps for home and garden use rather than for large-scale farming. With the emergence of mechanical pumping, an alternative to the windmill emerged. Powered by a steam engine, the centrifugal pump could deliver a great deal of water, but it had to be placed in a hand-dug pit close to the water level. This meant that much of the Ogallala Aquifer—in those areas where water was more than a couple of dozen feet below the surface—was still inaccessible. As gas engines became more commonplace, underground pumping became more feasible and economical.

The drought years of the Dust Bowl pointed to the need for irrigation water for farming. The Great Depression, however, meant that most producers could not afford pump irrigation systems until after World War II. During the drought cycle of the early 1950s, pumping of the Ogallala Aquifer quickly expanded. In a ten-year period ending in 1957, the number of irrigation wells in the Texas portion of the aquifer increased by a factor of ten; similar increases occurred in other Ogallala states. Rather than using irrigation as a water source of last resort, farmers came to use it as a dependable water source for expanding production. Particularly in dry years, farmers pumped heavily with little concern about the ongoing depletion of the Ogallala Aquifer.

The belief that the Ogallala Aquifer was an everlasting resource unraveled by the 1950s. The first warnings were sounded by hydrologists as early as 1938, but farmers had to see water levels drop more than a foot per year during the late 1940s and 1950s to recognize that their long-held beliefs were wrong. Groups organized to conserve the aquifer. The High Plains Underground Water Conservation District (HPUWCD) on the Texas south plains was the first (1952), followed by similar districts in Oklahoma (1972) and Kansas (mid-1970s). Based on sound agricultural economic management and the democratic participation of landowners, the districts established programs to minimize water use and increase efficiency, for example, by using a center-pivot irrigation system instead of open canals to transport water to the fields. These programs evolved into long-term conservation strategies to stretch the longevity of the Ogallala Aquifer. Today, in some areas of the Great Plains during wet years, depletions from groundwater usage have been reduced to almost zero. Future conservation programs may reverse the historical trend of depletion.

Prognoses of the future of the Ogallala Aquifer vary widely. As historian John Opie (2000) states, at worst the Ogallala water will become inaccessible in the next twenty years, causing the region to revert to a deserted wasteland. At best, he says, progressive thinking can reassess the Ogallala and the High Plains agriculture that is dependent upon it to create a model for sustainable development. Sustainability, then, is the key. If good water can continue to be available and be economical, then settlement and farming will be maintained. Once the Ogallala Aquifer is depleted, however, the patterns of land use and community that emerged in the twentieth century will themselves disappear.

—Cameron L. Saffell

See also: *Aquifers*

BIBLIOGRAPHY

Green, Donald E. *Land of the Underground Rain: Irrigation on the Texas High Plains, 1910–1970.* Austin: University of Texas Press, 1973.

Kromm, David E., and Stephen E. White, eds. *Groundwater Exploitation in the High Plains.* Lawrence: University Press of Kansas, 1992.

Opie, John. *Ogallala: Water for a Dry Land.* 2nd ed. Our Sustainable Future series, Vol. 13. Lincoln: University of Nebraska Press, 2000.

Ohio River Basin

The Ohio River Basin covers 163,000 square miles in the states of Illinois, Indiana, Kentucky, Maryland, New York, North Carolina, Ohio, Pennsylvania, Tennessee, Virginia, and West Virginia. More than twenty-five metropolitan areas are part of this region. The primary river in the basin, the Ohio River, is formed by the confluence of the Allegheny and Monongahela Rivers at Pittsburgh, Pennsylvania. Major downstream tributaries join the Ohio as it flows 981 miles in a southwesterly direction to join the Mississippi River at Cairo, Illinois. Of the six Mississippi natural tributary drainage patterns, the Ohio supplies the largest volume of flow.

The land in the Ohio Basin is divided into three parts, which correspond to the major physiographic provinces in the region. The Appalachian Plateau in the eastern basin is characterized by rugged topography. The permeable sand and gravel deposits in the valleys of the drainage system provide moderate groundwater supplies. The area has extensive forest cover, poor quality soils, narrow valleys, steep stream gradients, flash floods during the rainy season, and low stream flows during dry seasons. The Central Lowlands in the northwestern third of the basin is the result of several glaciations. They left soil deposits that are now some of the richest agricultural lands in the basin. The land is flat to slightly rolling, and the drainage pattern has been significantly altered from the original prior to glaciation. In some

instances, buried preglacial streams provide extensive groundwater resources. The Interior Low Plateau in the southwestern third of the basin is dominated by the limestone rock that covers most of this region. This rock has resulted in rolling terrain, forming the Lexington Plains and Bluegrass Regions where farming predominates. Areas of local rugged relief are forested with thin soils. Groundwater has the variability typical of that in limestone areas.

There are four basic sources of pollution in the Ohio Basin: runoff from agricultural and forested land, mining runoff from both abandoned and active mines, runoff from urban areas, and stream bank erosion. By the time the environmental movement rose in the 1960s, the Ohio River Basin contained more than 60 percent of the bituminous coal reserves in the United States. Slightly less than half of the land in the basin was in agricultural use, but the basin was also heavily populated, with the population expected to explode in the coming decades. The Water Resources Planning Act of 1965 created the Ohio River Basin Commission in 1971 to develop a regional water and land resources plan. The primary purpose of the plan was to identify the best means of preserving the basin while developing the region's renewable resources. The commission consisted of representatives from the eleven states, nine federal agencies (Agriculture; Army; Commerce; Energy; Health, Education, and Welfare; Housing and Urban Development; Interior; Transportation; and the Environmental Protection Agency), and one interstate compact (Ohio River Valley Water Sanitation Commission) that were responsible for parts of the basin. The commission recommended an environmental study of the basin, coordinated flood plain management across state borders, and made an effort to determine the proper amount of water that should remain in streams to meet the needs of fish and wildlife.

The Ohio River region contains some of the nation's most suitable coal-operated power plant sites, since coalfields are within easy reach. Just after the Arab oil embargo of 1973–1974, Congress ordered the Environmental Protection Agency (EPA) to assess the potential environmental, social, and economic impacts of a concentration of power plants in the Ohio River Basin. The EPA found a high concentration of water pollutants, with nineteen of the twenty-four largest streams in the area violating at least three of the twenty pollutant standards of the era. The EPA concluded that the power plants would have little impact on water quality since the water was already so heavily polluted through other sources.

While the water quality improved in the next years as a result of various legislative efforts, significant concerns about the future of the Ohio River Basin remained. In October 2009 and February 2010, seventy-three agencies and organizations covering state, local, and federal governments; nonprofit organizations; industry; and academia voluntarily convened to discuss their collective interest in the future of water resources in the Ohio River Basin. The groups formed the Ohio River Basin Collaboration Initiative to recommend strategies and coordinate actions to achieve sustainable economic growth, protect the environment, and ensure public safety.

—Caryn Neumann

See also: *Environmental Protection Agency, United States; Water Resources Planning Act of 1965*

BIBLIOGRAPHY

Ohio River Basin Commission. *Ohio Main Stem: Water and Related Land Resources Study Report and Environmental Impact Statement.* Cincinnati: Ohio River Basin Commission, 1978.

Ohio River Basin Commission. *The Ohio River Basin: The Regional Water and Land Resources Plan and Environmental, Economic, and Social Impact Statements.* Cincinnati: Ohio River Basin Commission, 1979.

Orme Dam

In the early 1970s, plans emerged to build a dam in central Arizona where the Verde and Salt Rivers converge. The concept of building a dam there had been discussed since the 1940s, and it had the support of Senator Barry Goldwater (R-AZ). It also had the full backing of the U.S. Bureau of Reclamation. The dam was intended to regulate the flows of both the rivers. Its construction would flood 24,000 acres. The impounded water could be used for irrigation and hydropower generation. It also offered other benefits, including fishing and boating on the lake.

However, the project was controversial from the start. The lake would cover some of the Fort McDowell Indian Reservation, where the Yavapai people lived. There were 425 people in that Native American nation. State authorities offered to build them homes and provide cash benefits to compensate them for having their property flooded. Because the dam would transform the lives of the Yavapai, the Indians put the issue to a vote. In spite of being offered $40 million, 61 percent of the Yavapai rejected the deal. This was, after all, the land where their ancestors were buried and where they

had lived for a century after ending their nomadic lifestyle, Other Native American tribes offered their support.

The "Old Guard" within the Bureau of Reclamation, who had great faith in engineering nature, saw going ahead with the project as an article of faith. The positive results in terms of water regulation and the ability to irrigate nearby fields was unarguable. The Yavapai would be compensated, and they would be able to find other similar land elsewhere. However, a "New Guard" within the Bureau urged further consultation before work went ahead. Due to the National Environmental Policy Act of 1969, the issue was heavily contested within the Bureau. The New Guard supported the Yavapai, arguing that without its traditional land, the tribe would cease to exist as a Native American nation; its people would lose both their cultural ties and their identity.

The Yavapai started petitioning the federal government. They also held a meeting at the Phoenix Civic Center, where thousands of people came to support them. Soon afterwards, one hundred Yavapai completed a three-day march to publicize their cause. The issue soon got the attention of environmental campaigners elsewhere in the United States. In the end, the protests and legal challenges led to federal authorities withdrawing plans for the dam.

—Justin Corfield

See also: *Bureau of Reclamation; National Environmental Policy Act of 1969*

BIBLIOGRAPHY

Braatz, Timothy. *Surviving Conquest: A History of the Yavapai Peoples.* Lincoln: University of Nebraska Press, 2003.

Carter, Luther J. "Grand Canyon: Colorado Dams Debated." *Science* 152, no. 3729 (1966): 1600–1605.

Coffeen, William R. "The Effects of the Central Arizona Project on the Fort McDowell Indian Community." *Ethnohistory* 19, no. 4 (1972): 345–77.

Espeland, Wendy Nelson. "Bureaucrats and Indians in a Contemporary Colonial Encounter." *Law & Social Inquiry* 26, no. 2 (2001): 403–33. Available at http://www.swanet.org/twitter/encounter.pdf.

Espeland, Wendy Nelson. *The Struggle for Water: Politics, Rationality, and Identity in the American Southwest.* Chicago: University of Chicago Press, 1998.

Owens Valley

The Owens Valley in southeastern California is ninety miles long and about twenty miles wide, a trough bounded by the Sierra Nevada Mountains to the west and the White and Inyo Mountain ranges to the east. Topographic extremes are its most striking visual aspect: Mount Whitney, at 14,494 feet the tallest peak in the lower forty-eight states, lies directly east of Lone Pine, which is only 3,800 feet above sea level.

Because the valley is east of the Sierra crest, it is in the rain shadow of the mountains, and valley floor vegetation is dominated by Great Basin desert scrub. The town of Independence, in the middle of the valley, averages only five inches of rainfall each year. Snowmelt from the steep eastern face of the Sierra Nevada runs off and is carried by the Owens River the length of the valley to a terminus in Owens Lake. That lake was, until the early years of the twentieth century, a shallow inland sea, fifteen miles long and ten miles wide, that attracted millions of migratory birds.

The Paiute Indians of the Owens Valley had developed a system of ditches to water crops. Later settlers further diverted the Owens River into an extensive irrigation system that, by 1920, served 50,000 acres of pastureland and 25,000 acres of cropland. But, after 1913, the city of Los Angeles began buying farms to acquire water rights, starting in the south near the intake of the Los Angeles Aqueduct. The imperialistic pressure exerted on unwilling rural landowners became an unattractive part of western water history.

In the 1930s, Los Angeles extended its aqueduct into the Mono Lake Basin and finished purchasing most of the land in the Owens Valley. Today the distant city owns 98 percent of the privately held Owens Valley land. Though the desires of its original settlers were thwarted, much of the land remains accessible to the public for outdoor recreation. The eastern Sierra is today a playground for city dwellers who treasure its undeveloped open space.

Los Angeles supplements its Owens River surface supply by pumping Owens Valley groundwater into its aqueduct. The impacts of lowered water tables on springs and seeps, marshland, shrubs and trees, and wildlife were argued in long-running court cases and negotiations among Inyo County, environmental groups, and Los Angeles. In the modern valley, dry uplands are no longer punctuated to the same extent by wet streams and corridors of riparian vegetation. Groundwater pumps can extinguish such desert ecosystems, especially when the threat is exacerbated by other disturbances like grazing and off-road vehicle use.

In 1970, Los Angeles completed a second barrel of the aqueduct, doubling its capacity. The city announced that it intended to increase groundwater pumping in the valley, decrease irrigation on its lands there, and export more water from the Mono Lake Basin. But in 1970, the California Environmental Quality Act had been passed, requiring the preparation of environmental impact reports (EIRs). Inyo County successfully sued the Los Angeles Department of Water and Power (LADWP) to force the agency to file an EIR. The EIRs prepared by Los Angeles in 1976 and in 1979 were both rejected by the courts as inadequate. In the years that followed, a series of settlements was proposed but found wanting, as Inyo County, Los Angeles, and environmental groups negotiated. Deadlines for a final, acceptable EIR were repeatedly pushed back.

In December 2006, finally, the Lower Owens River Project restored flowing water to the lower sixty-two miles of the river. A judge had become exasperated with Los Angeles delaying implementation of the rewatering plan and forced action by fining LADWP $5,000 a day. Just before the restored river flows reach the Owens Lake bed, the water is pumped back into the aqueduct, so that water losses for Los Angeles are minimized. Riparian vegetation, wildlife, and people—on foot and kayaks—followed the water and returned to the river channel.

Meanwhile, water levels in Owens Lake, which once covered more than 100 square miles, had plummeted after the Owens River was diverted into the Los Angeles Aqueduct. It passed the "Dead Sea" effect of increased salinity to rapidly become that oxymoron: a dry lake. Dust blowing off the alkaline lake bed began to violate the air quality standard for fine particulates and damage the health of people in the region. Los Angeles has been required to install dust control measures on thirty square miles of lakebed. Native salt grass is grown with a drip-watering system on some of that acreage. The remaining twenty-seven square miles are treated with ponded water.

—David Carle

See also: *Los Angeles Aqueduct; Salinity*

BIBLIOGRAPHY

deBuys, William Eno. *Salt Dreams: Land and Water in Low-Down California.* Photographs by Joan Myers. Albuquerque: University of New Mexico Press, 1999.

Green, Dorothy. *Managing Water: Avoiding Crisis in California.* Berkeley: University of California Press, 2007.

Hundley, Norris, Jr. *The Great Thirst: Californians and Water; A History.* Rev. ed. Berkeley: University of California Press, 2001.

Reisner, Marc. *Cadillac Desert: The American West and Its Disappearing Water.* Rev. ed. New York: Penguin Books, 1993.

Pecos River Basin

The Pecos River of the nineteenth century, unlike its faint twenty-first century shadow, was a formidable watercourse, stretching 925 miles from the Sangre de Cristo Mountains northeast of Santa Fe to its eventual merger with the Rio Grande at present-day Lake Amistad in Texas. For most of its path, the Pecos River parallels the Rio Grande, flowing in an east-southeast direction from its source 13,000 feet above sea level, where numerous creeks and heavy snows contribute to its volume. The river drains some 44,000 square miles of land.

For forty miles, the Pecos rushes clear and cold through mountainous terrain frequented for years by the Cicuye (Pecos) and Picuris Indians and, later, by the religious Penitentes, members of a lay fraternity of Catholic men, who painfully trudged to the high country bearing crosses and suffering other hardships during Holy Week each year. From mountain headwaters, the river travels through desert or semidesert regions where ephemeral tributaries generate highly variable water flows each year. Besides tributary contributions, the river receives significant inflow from underlying aquifers when it reaches southeastern New Mexico.

The river's topography changes dramatically from alpine forests and meadows along its upper reaches to scrubland from Fort Sumner to near Carlsbad, Arizona. The topography changes yet again as the river nears Texas, reflecting the flora and fauna of the Chihuahuan Desert, and, in the lower reaches of the river, deep canyons appear. Principal cities along the river in New Mexico are Las Vegas, Santa Rosa, Fort Sumner, Roswell, Artesia, and Carlsbad; in Texas, the main city on the river is Pecos.

History

Long before Francisco Vázquez de Coronado crossed eastern New Mexico in 1541, and cattle ranchers discovered the rich grasslands along the Pecos three centuries later, descendants of the Anasazi had settled on the Rio Grande and as far east as the Pecos. Coronado counted three villages during his unsuccessful bid to find gold in the Southwest.

Coronado was followed by Antonio de Espejo in 1583, who called the river Río de las Vacas, or River of Cows, because of the number of buffalo nearby. Gaspar Castaño de Sosa followed the Pecos northward, calling it Río Salado because of its salty taste, a characteristic lamented by countless cattle ranchers, including Charles Goodnight in the 1860s. According to Adolph Bandelier, *Pecos* first appears in Juan de Oñate's chronicles in reference to the Indian pueblo of Cicuye, now known as the Pecos Pueblo. Mexicans and Mexican Americans long called the river Río Puerco (the Dirty River, or River of Pigs). The earliest Spanish

settlement was founded in 1636 at San Miguel del Bado in the upper Pecos valley.

Following the Mexican American War, Randolph Marcy and J. H. Simpson in 1849 explored and surveyed a route between Fort Smith and Santa Fe where the government wished to establish a wagon road. Non-Indian Mexican American settlers along the Rio Bonito worked in part to provide food for the military, which established Fort Stanton in 1855 to help defend against Mescalero Apache raids in central New Mexico. Anglo settlers soon moved to a small settlement near Fort Stanton called "La Placita" by its Mexican settlers, which the newcomers renamed Lincoln; it was the seat of Lincoln County by 1869.

Most late nineteenth-century history of the Trans-Pecos reflects ranching interests, with cattle ranchers establishing water rights along small Pecos tributaries. Investigators for John Wesley Powell's U.S. Geological Survey in 1878 suggested that the region could become a prime growing area. Beginning in the 1880s, the lower Pecos Valley in New Mexico saw an ambitious scheme to use Pecos waters to irrigate a million acres of land. The project eventually included extensive dam, canal, and lateral systems and was backed by far-flung investors. The Reclamation Service resurrected the project at the turn of the century after floods destroyed vital components of the irrigation network and private corporate interests had entered bankruptcy.

The primary use of both surface and groundwater along the Pecos today is agricultural irrigation. Two irrigation districts at Carlsbad and Fort Sumner irrigate up to 25,000 and 7,000 acres, respectively. The Carlsbad Project operates four reservoirs on the Pecos River with a combined storage capacity of 176,500 acre-feet. The Pecos Valley Artesian Conservancy District (PVACD) irrigates 120,000 acres almost exclusively, with groundwater pumped from aquifers in the Roswell Artesian Basin, which lies west of the Pecos River. Groundwater extraction over the last sixty years has caused a significant reduction in the volume of the Pecos River.

Role of the Federal Government

Since the early days of the Carlsbad Project, the federal government has played a large role on the Pecos, improving existing structures and building dams at Fort Sumner and Brantley. The Carlsbad Project has been plagued by canal and dam leakage, high water salinity, the predominance of water-robbing phreatophytes, and contention between the Water Users' Association and the federal government.

Conflicts between water users in New Mexico and those in Texas have escalated as demand for water has increased. An interstate water compact in 1949 has had little effect on the states' claims over water or ensuing litigation.

—Stephen Bogener

See also: *Carlsbad Irrigation Project; United States Geological Survey*

BIBLIOGRAPHY

Bogener, Stephen. *Ditches Across the Desert: Irrigation in the Lower Pecos Valley.* Lubbock: Texas Tech University Press, 2003.

Clark, Ira G. *Water in New Mexico: A History of Its Management and Use.* Albuquerque: University of New Mexico Press, 1987.

Keleher, William Aloysius. *The Fabulous Frontier: Twelve New Mexico Items.* Santa Fe, NM: Rydal Press, 1945.

Lingle, Robert T., and Dee Linford. *The Pecos River Commission of New Mexico and Texas: A Report on a Decade of Progress, 1950–1960.* Carlsbad, NM: Rydal Press, 1961.

New Mexico Office of the State Engineer. http://www.ose.state.nm.us/isc_pecos_carlsbad_project.html.

Sheridan, Thomas E. *The Bitter River: A Brief Historical Survey of the Middle Pecos River Basin.* Boulder, CO: Western Interstate Commission for Higher Education, 1975.

Platte River Basin

The Platte River Basin is in the Great Plains and covers Colorado, Wyoming, and Nebraska. The river, named for the French word for "flat," has two major branches, the North Platte and South Platte Rivers. The rivers rise in the Rocky Mountains and join in western Nebraska just to the west of the 100th meridian. The basin has a drainage area of 86,000 square miles and is largely fed by spring snowmelt in the Rocky Mountains. Precipitation on the Great Plains contributes additional water to the channels.

The Platte River Basin began to undergo major changes in about 1860 as the water resources of the region began to be developed. These water uses have continued to increase with growth in population and land development. Most of the land in the Platte River Basin is used for agriculture, and irrigation of farmland is the major water use in the basin. Surface water is stored in reservoirs and diverted from channels to canals for irrigation, for municipal use, and for power generation. Groundwater is developed extensively in the basin. All these factors have changed the paths of the river channels by affecting the distribution and timing of stream flows and the transport of sediments. Expanding woodlands and narrowing river channels have altered the riverine environment. These changes have harmed wildlife, as the basin contains important habitat for migratory and breeding birds. The North American Central Flyway is within a portion of the Platte River corridor. Three birds (whooping crane, piping plover, interior least tern) and one fish (pallid sturgeon) that are listed under the Endangered Species Act live and breed in the basin.

The protection of federally listed species has been in tension with water management in the Platte River Basin since about 1980. Dam construction, new diversions, and federal relicensing of power projects have come into conflict with the needs of endangered and threatened species. These conflicts were sharpened by ongoing litigation among the basin states over division of the waters of the North Platte River, which is not governed by an interstate compact.

In 1997, in an effort to resolve disputes over the welfare of these listed species, the basin states and the federal government established a governance committee. Environmental and water-use interests also joined the group. The committee was charged with developing and implementing a recovery program for the endangered and threatened species. Progress proved more slowly than expected, however. Meanwhile, implementation of the Endangered Species Act in the basin became increasingly controversial as the U.S. Fish and Wildlife Service issued a series of jeopardy opinions, finding that any new depletions of the Platte River would have to be compensated by mitigation measures. A lawsuit forced the designation of critical habitat for the local population of the piping plover. Members of the committee began to question the science supporting the current management of the basin's listed species and sought an outside review of the science before the recovery program was made final. In 2003, the Department of the Interior obtained an independent evaluation of the species by the National Research Council. These researchers, who included biologists, engineers, farmers, and geographers, concluded that the current Platte habitat conditions would eventually result in the extinction of the endangered species.

The National Research Council identified several other problems that remain of concern. It noted that there is no systemwide, integrated operation plan or data-collection plan for the Platte River Basin. The U.S. Geological Survey had warned about the absence of reliable data in 1983, but the warning went unheeded. The result of a lack of data is that natural and engineered variations in flows in one part of the basin have unknown effects on other parts of the basin, especially with respect to reservoir storage, groundwater storage, and river flows. There is no larger regional context for research in and management of the basin, so decision making occurs without regard to habitats outside of the basin. Water quality data is also not integrated into habitat suitability guidelines. The National Research Council concluded that future climatic changes, such as global warming, may exacerbate conflicts between wildlife habitat availability and human use.

—Caryn Neumann

See also: *Endangered Species Act (1973); Fish and Wildlife Service, United States; United States Geological Survey*

BIBLIOGRAPHY

Eschner, Thomas R., Richard F. Hadley, Kevin D. Crowley, J. E. Kircher, and M. R. Karlinger. *Hydrologic and Geomorphic Studies of the Platte River Basin.* U.S. Geological Survey Professional Paper 1277. Washington, DC: U.S. Government Printing Office, 1983.
National Research Council. *Endangered and Threatened Species of the Platte River.* Washington, DC: National Academies Press, 2005.

Rio Grande River Basin

Stretching from the mountains of Colorado southward to the Gulf of Mexico, the Rio Grande is the fifth largest river in the United States and twentieth largest river in the world. Its river basin encompasses over 300,000 square miles, including parts of Colorado, New Mexico, Texas, and four Mexican States. Despite its impressive length and breadth, the Rio Grande is not a navigable river and in many places is often completely dry. The Rio Grande serves as a boundary between the United States and Mexico, where it is known as the *Rio Bravo del Norte* (The Brave River of the North).

The Rio Grande begins deep in the forests and mountains of Colorado at Canby Mountain, within the San Juan Mountain Range. Roughly half of the Rio Grande River Basin is arid or semi-arid in climate, keeping the river flow significantly lower than that of other major waterways in the United States, such as the Mississippi or Missouri Rivers. Much of the Rio Grande is situated at significantly high elevations. It starts in Colorado at 12,000 feet above sea level. Along its route toward the Gulf of Mexico, the Rio Grande carved gorges and valleys throughout Colorado, New Mexico, and Mexico, including the San Luis Valley in Colorado and the Rio Grande Gorge in New Mexico. The southern two-thirds of the river make up the political border between the state of Texas and four Mexican states—Chihuahua, Coahuila, Nuevo Leon, and Tomaulipas.

Several types of vegetation grow in the river basin of the Rio Grande. From the north, the river begins amid forests of spruce, fir, and aspen. The river travels south and southeast through more mountains, hills, tablelands, depressions steppes, and desert. A large part of the Rio Grande River Basin is made up of savanna grasslands, which are used for cattle grazing. Periodically along the river basin are rich farmlands, made arable by irrigation from the river. At its southern tip, the Rio Grande turns into a sandy delta. Twelve tributaries empty into the Rio Grande. The principle tributaries include the Pecos, Devils, Chama, and Puerco Rivers in the United States and the Conchos, Salado, and San Juan Rivers in Mexico. While the Pecos River has the largest drainage basin (over 44,000 square miles), the Conchos River in Mexico contributes twice as much water to the Rio Grande than any of the other tributaries.

The earliest inhabitants of the Rio Grande River Basin were the Pueblo and Navajo tribes, who referred to the river as Big River and Great Waters. In 1519, Hernán Cortés arrived in Mexico, bringing with him Spanish dominion that would last until the nineteenth century. The Rio Grande marked the northernmost boundary of the Spanish colonies in Mexico and eventually served as a boundary between Mexico and the Republic of Texas and, later, Mexico and the United States.

Many modifications have been made to the Rio Grande over the past century. Several dams have been built along its banks, including Cochiti Dam, Amistad Dam, Elephant Butte Dam, and Caballo Dam. Technological advances have not come without significant price. Drainage dwindles significantly along the Rio Grande from southern New Mexico and upper Texas, mainly due to irrigation. Below Presidio, Mexico, the Rio Conchos restores the water flow before it empties into the Gulf of Mexico. Because of drought and overuse of the river's waters, critics have dubbed the near-barren stretch of river bed from El Paso, Texas, through Ojinaga, Chihuahua, as the "Forgotten River." More recently, various organizations have recognized the Rio Grande as an important facet of American history and culture. In 1997, the United States designated the Rio Grande as an American Heritage River. Two parts of the river have been designated as National Wild and Scenic River systems—one in New Mexico and one in Big Bend National Park, Texas.

Despite its shallow waters, the Rio Grande River Basin continues to play a vital role in the development of both the United States and Mexico. In the face of drought and overuse, civic groups throughout the Southwest have taken steps toward protecting the river basin so that it may continue to shape the fortunes of both countries.

—Lorri Brown

See also: *Elephant Butte Reservoir; Wild and Scenic Rivers Act of 1968*

BIBLIOGRAPHY

Barraclough, Geoffrey. *HarperCollins Atlas of World History*. 2nd rev. ed. Ann Arbor, MI: Borders Press/HarperCollins, 2001.

Benke, Arthur C., and Colbert E. Cushing. *Rivers of North America*. San Diego, CA: Elsevier Academic Press, 2005.

Goode, Paul J., Edward Bowman Espenshade, John C. Hudson, and Joel L. Morrison, eds. *Goode's World Atlas: 19th Edition*. Chicago: Rand McNally, 1995.

Saint Lawrence Seaway

The Saint Lawrence Seaway is a joint United States–Canada route creating an inland waterway from Lakes Superior and Michigan, eastward through Lakes Huron, Erie, and Ontario, into the Saint Lawrence River, up to Montreal, and beyond to Sept-Îles and the Gulf of Saint Lawrence on the Atlantic Ocean. The seaway is composed of a mixed system of canals, channels, and locks. It has a total length of 3,774 kilometers and can accommodate vessels up to 225.5 meters long and 23.8 meters wide, with a draft of up to 8.2 meters. It is a vital component of North American infrastructure, and over the last fifty years, the total traffic passing along its length has included approximately 2.5 billion tons of commercial cargo with an estimated value of $375 billion.

The development of this waterway system started in the late eighteenth century. It began with channels added to the Saint Lawrence River and continued steadily into the early part of the twentieth century. The need to expand the waterway then became more acute after World War II due to Ontario's desire for more electrical power. As a result, the Wiley-Dondero Act was passed in 1954 to create a partnership between the United States and Canada to complete the waterway. Each country created a seaway authority to oversee construction, and the new seaway opened in 1959.

The Saint Lawrence Seaway was a major engineering feat. Some new canals were constructed to replace the old fourteen-foot channels, and other channels were built to cope with the differing water levels of various stretches of river. The new waterway included seven locks of the same width and depth as the Welland Canal, which connects Lake Ontario and Lake Erie. Power plants and dams were constructed along the waterway to generate electricity. Linking up the separate sections of the seaway involved moving towns and villages along with rail and road infrastructure. The result was a seaway with a total of twenty locks.

The cost of the Saint Lawrence Seaway for both the United States and Canada was in the hundreds of millions of dollars, though some of the expense was recouped in tolls or power sales. Its benefits have been significant. For example, it has allowed Canada to become an exporter rather than an importer of iron ore. The cargo transported on the seaway includes agricultural products, iron ore, coal, and cement.

Technological advances have improved the transit of freight and the quality of the seaway over time. Modifications to the size of locks and the introduction of much larger vessels have reduced the number of transits required on the Welland Canal and the Great Lakes. Arrester cables carried on vertically rising booms now assist in the lifting required at the locks, and the addition of lock gates has improved security. However, some of the locks are not wide enough and some of the waterways are not deep enough to accommodate the largest ocean-going vessels. Therefore, there are limits to how far some ships can travel along the seaway. Unfortunately, the projected cost of the dramatic alterations needed to accommodate the largest ships is currently deemed prohibitive.

More than 2,000 pleasure craft use the Saint Lawrence Seaway during the shipping season. Clear restrictions exist on the weight and length of pleasure craft that may use a system designed for large cargo ships, but specially designated areas and support systems are in place to make cruising the waterway possible.

—Julia Fallon

See also: *Army Corps of Engineers, United States; Great Lakes*

BIBLIOGRAPHY

Becker, William H. *From the Atlantic to the Great Lakes: A History of the U.S. Army Corps of Engineers and the St. Lawrence Seaway*. Honolulu, HI: University Press of the Pacific, 2004.

Hadfield, Charles. *World Canals: Inland Navigation Past and Present*. New York: Facts on File, 1986.

Parham, Claire Puccia. *The St. Lawrence Seaway and Power Project: An Oral History of the Greatest Construction Show on Earth*. Syracuse, NY: Syracuse University Press, 2009.

Sinacer, Souad, and David Edwards-May. *North American Waterways: Map and Index*. Seyssinet, France: Euromapping, 2005.

Salton Sea

Located in southern California's Colorado Desert, on the border of Imperial and Riverside Counties, the Salton Sea is the largest inland body of water in California at approximately thirty-five miles long, fifteen miles wide, and twenty-nine feet deep on average. The sea is the result of a rather catastrophic mistake, as early Imperial Valley developers attempted to tap the unpredictable Colorado River to irrigate the desert. The Salton Sea raises important questions concerning the interplay between people and the environment.

Today's Salton Sea is not the first body of water to fill the basin referred to as the Salton Sink. As the unruly Colorado River changed its course over time, occasionally it would flow into the Sink, creating a temporary lake that would eventually evaporate completely under the desert sun. These previous incarnations of the sea are collectively referred to as Lake Cahuilla, after a local Native American group.

The current Salton Sea came into existence at the turn of the twentieth century. Dr. Oliver Wozencraft was the first American to tout the agricultural possibilities of today's Imperial Valley region; however, his plan languished when the federal government failed to support it. In 1896, the California Development Company formed under the leadership of Charles R. Rockwood with the goal of bringing water to the Colorado Desert. Agreeing with Wozencraft's earlier assessment, Rockwood decided that what is now the Imperial Valley would be an ideal farming area, if it only had water. To secure that water, Rockwood and his associates, including engineer George Chaffey, decided to harness the Colorado River through a series of dikes and canals. They completed the main canal in 1902, but by 1904 silt had blocked it. Farmers in the valley began to protest, fearing the loss of their crops, so Rockwood decided to make a cut in the canal to allow the water to flow. In 1905, a year of heavy runoff from storms and snow, the cut widened and broke completely, releasing the full flow of the Colorado River to gush into the dry, low Salton Sink and creating an inland sea in place of the desert. Water poured into the Sink for two years before the Southern Pacific Railroad finally managed to close the cut and redirect the river back to its original bed.

During the 1950s, sport fish were successfully introduced into the Salton Sea, and by the 1960s, the area hosted a boom in tourism. Promoters advertised the Salton Sea as the next Mediterranean Riviera, an ideal vacation spot for residents of southern California's growing urban areas. People came to fish, boat, water-ski, and take advantage of all the recreational activities the sea had to offer. Yet the boom proved short-lived. Flooding along the shore and increasing environmental problems drove tourists away by the late 1970s.

The Salton Sea provided an important stop for migrating birds on the Pacific Flyway, so although the tourists left, the birds kept coming. With the destruction of the majority of California's inland wetlands and disruption of the Colorado River Delta habitat in Mexico, birds became dependent on this new site for food, rest, and nesting opportunities. The sea offered an essential habitat for water birds such as pelicans and grebes.

Today, with the Colorado River highly regulated, agricultural runoff feeds the sea, keeping it from evaporating like its predecessors. Unfortunately, this water is high in salinity and laced with fertilizers, pesticides, and other agricultural chemicals. As the sea's water continues to evaporate, the salt and chemicals are left behind in higher and higher concentrations. These conditions lead to algae blooms and spiking bacterial levels, which cause massive fish die-offs and sickens the birds. Furthermore, as the growing city of San Diego purchases increasing amounts of water from Imperial Valley farmers to serve its domestic needs, the water that would become Imperial runoff and make its way to the Salton Sea is now watering San Diego's thirsty lawns.

The Salton Sea is currently unsustainable. The water is already saltier than the ocean, and its salinity is increasing at a rate of approximately 1 percent a year. With this steady rise in salinity, elevated levels of selenium—a naturally occurring element that becomes toxic in high concentrations—and reoccurring bacterial blooms, some sort of intervention will need to take place to ensure the viability of the habitat for fish and birds. Multiple proposals exist to stabilize the water level and salinity of the sea, but decision makers have yet to settle on a course of action.

—Eliza L. Martin

See also: *Colorado River Basin; Outdoor Recreation; Salinity*

BIBLIOGRAPHY

deBuys, William Eno. *Salt Dreams: Land and Water in Low-Down California.* Photographs by Joan Myers. Albuquerque: University of New Mexico Press, 1999.

Metzler, Chris, and Jeff Springer. *Plagues and Pleasures on the Salton Sea.* DVD. New York: Docurama/New Video Group, 2007.

Stringfellow, Kim. *Greetings from the Salton Sea: Folly and Intervention in the Southern California Landscape, 1905–2005.* Santa Fe, NM: Center for American Places, 2005.

Shasta Dam

Shasta Dam, which impounds the Sacramento River, is located near Shasta Lake City, California. It became the central element of the Central Valley Project, which provides water for irrigation to the San Joaquin Valley. The aim was to meet increasing demand for water, as agricultural practices had shifted from cattle ranching to raising wheat and then to intensive agriculture. Although average rainfall was generally enough for farming, rainfall fluctuated widely, and there were many years when farmers did not have enough rain. In other years, there were often floods.

The Shasta Dam is a curved gravity concrete dam and is 3,460 feet long and 602 feet high. At its base, it is 543 feet wide. Construction of the dam started in 1938, and it was completed in 1945. Its initial costs were estimated at $35.9 mil-

Construction of the Shasta Dam started in 1938 and ended in 1945. The dam is one of the most important structures of the Central Valley Project, and the Shasta Reservoir created by the dam remains the largest in California.
Library of Congress

lion, and it accounted for nearly half the total of the engineering contract letters in the July 1938 issue of the *Engineering News Record*. The cost eventually rose to $100.7 million. The dam was billed as being the second-largest structure in the world upon its completion. It contained 5.61 million cubic yards of concrete, making it larger than the Great Pyramid in Egypt but only half as big as the Grand Coulee Dam.

The Winnemem Wintu, Native Americans who had lived in the area for generations, objected to the dam, whose lake flooded their burial grounds. The 125 tribal members were heavily affected by the alteration to the landscape. Construction required the relocation of 180 burial sites to Shasta Lake City. In addition, 90 percent of the Winnemem Wintu lands were lost. Although the remains were reburied, the Winnemem Wintu were never compensated for their land. They remained under threat after the dam was completed, because they stood to lose another twenty-six village sites, along with burial grounds and prayer rocks, if the water level rose even another six feet. One of the threatened sites was where the victims of the Kaibai Creek massacre had been buried in 1854. These men, women, and children had

been killed by white settlers, and their descendants hoped that their bones might lie in peace.

The dam also significantly impacted wildlife and the environment. People deployed houseboats on the lake, and these increased the level of pollution. The California wild trout, in particular, lost two of their habitats in the Upper Sacramento River and the McCloud River, both of which were inundated.

Shasta Dam has provided farmers with a dependable supply of water, and it has generated some hydroelectric power. The dam has also meant that the Sacramento–San Joaquin Delta is now free from ocean saltwater, and this has helped increase the number of chinook salmon, especially since the construction of a spawning and rearing facility.

—Justin Corfield

See also: *Agriculture; Central Valley Project; Grand Coulee Dam*

BIBLIOGRAPHY

Angel, Arthur D. "Who Will Pay for the Central Valley Project of California?" *Journal of Land & Public Utility Economics* 22, no. 3 (1946): 266–72.

Frank T. Crowe

Francis Trenholm Crowe is best known for the construction of the Hoover Dam from 1931 to 1936. He also supervised the construction of the Shasta Dam for Pacific Constructors Inc. from 1938 to 1945.

Crowe was born on October 12, 1882. He received a BS in civil engineering in 1905 from the University of Maine. He built his first dam in 1910 while employed by the U.S. Reclamation Service. In 1913, he completed the Arrowrock Dam in Idaho, which was the highest dam in the world at the time. He left federal employment in 1925 and built dams for private firms for the rest of his career.

Crowe constructed nineteen dams during his distinguished career. His achievements resulted in the American Society of Civil Engineers awarding him an honorary membership in 1943. He died on February 26, 1946.

—John R. Burch Jr.

See also: *Bureau of Reclamation; Central Valley Project; Hoover Dam*

BIBLIOGRAPHY

Billington, David P., and Donald C. Jackson. *Big Dams of the New Deal Era: A Confluence of Engineering and Politics.* Norman: University of Oklahoma Press, 2006.
Dunar, Andrew J., and Dennis McBride. *Building Hoover Dam: An Oral History of the Great Depression.* Twayne's Oral History Series No. 11. New York: Twayne, 1993.
Stevens, Joseph E. *Hoover Dam: An American Adventure.* Norman: University of Oklahoma Press, 1988.

Meigs, Peveril, III. "Water Planning in the Great Central Valley, California." *Geographical Review* 29, no. 2 (1939): 252–73.
Rocca, Al M. *America's Master Dam Builder: The Engineering Genius of Frank T. Crowe.* Lanham, MD: University Press of America, 2001.
Rocca, Al M. *The Shasta Dam Boomtowns: Community Building in the New Deal Era.* Redding, CA: Redding Museum of Art & History, 1993.
Simpich, Frederick. "More Water for California's Great Central Valley." *National Geographic Magazine* 90, no. 5 (1946): 645–64.

Snake River Basin

The Snake River Basin remains one of the most rugged and isolated drainages in North America. Its serpentine river—the largest tributary of the Columbia River—travels 1,056 miles from Yellowstone National Park in present-day Wyoming to its linkage with the Columbia River in present-day Washington State. Along the way, the Snake River drops from 9,840 feet above sea level to just 340 feet at its confluence with the Columbia. It travels through both Yellowstone and Grand Teton National Parks; flows through the Rocky Mountain foothills; meanders through southern Idaho's broad desert plain; creates a waterfall spectacle at Shoshone Falls; and cuts through Hell's Canyon, which at 8,000 feet is the deepest gorge in North America. The Snake drains a basin of approximately 109,000 square miles, or an area about 450 miles in length and width, and courses through parts of Wyoming, Idaho, Oregon, and Washington on its way to meet the Columbia River.

Geological fireworks have defined the basin's topography. When the massive Bonneville Lake burst through its banks about 15,000 years ago, it sent 350 feet of water rushing through the Snake's channels at 70 miles per hour. The flood scoured canyon walls and scattered house-sized boulders throughout the Snake River Plain. Along the plain's northern border, volcanic activity between 15,000 and 2,000 years ago created the 60-mile-wide Craters of the Moon lava field, where basalt lava deposits reach depths of more than 10,000 feet. Present-day visitors to the National Craters of the Moon Monument encounter miles of cinder cones, lava tubes, and diverse lava flows that deterred earlier generations of settlement.

The Native tribal groups of the Snake River Basin relied heavily on the river for subsistence and built their villages along it. The Palouse, Clearwater, and Salmon Rivers, all tributaries of the middle Snake, defined the aboriginal territory of the Nez Perce. The Shoshone-Bannock peoples inhabited the arid Snake River Plain, including the Boise River drainage area. The basin's rugged terrain forced the Shoshone-Bannock to rely on complex food storage methods, such as meat preservation in underground caves, and forced them to undertake long-distance migrations in search of bison herds. The Snake River Basin houses two Indian reservations: the Nez Perce Reservation near Lapwai, Idaho, and the 544,000-acre Fort Hall (Shoshone-Bannock) reservation in southeastern Idaho created by the 1868 Fort Bridger Treaty.

Oregon Trail travelers passing through the basin in present-day southern Idaho noted the desert conditions of the Snake River Plain in their diaries. Lack of rainfall—under seven inches in some high plateau and desert areas—inhibited non-Indian settlement until the Carey Act (1894) and the Newlands Reclamation Act (1902) provided support for state and federal irrigation projects (Idaho State Historical Society n.d.). The Twin Falls South Side project—under the direction of Ira B. Perrine's Twin Falls Land and Water Company—opened in 1904 and became one of the most successful Carey Act irrigation projects in the United States. The Reclamation Service's Minidoka and Boise projects brought additional settlement to the Snake River Plain during the early twentieth century. Irrigated agriculture and related industries fueled population growth in the Snake River Basin during the twentieth century, and in 1990, the U.S. Geological Survey (USGS) estimated that 391,000 people were living in the Upper Snake River Basin.

Today the Snake River Basin encompasses the urban centers of Jackson Hole, Wyoming; Idaho Falls, Pocatello, Twin Falls, Boise, Meridian, and Nampa/Caldwell, Idaho; and Kennewick/Pasco, Washington. Between Jackson Lake Reservoir in Wyoming and the King Hill irrigation project in Idaho, 13.2 million acre-feet of Snake River water is diverted to irrigate more than 2.3 million acres of sugar beets, potatoes, corn, grains, dry beans, alfalfa, and various seed crops. Snake River aquaculture (i.e., fish farms) accounts for 75 percent of the nation's rainbow trout production. Tourism associated with reservoirs, camping, and fishing has emerged as an important economic driver for the region, while controversy has raged over recovery efforts for endangered Snake River salmon and steelhead fish populations.

Water rights disputes within much of the Snake River Basin have been resolved through a lengthy court process begun in 1987, which resulted from the 1984 Swan Falls Agreement between the State of Idaho and the Idaho Power Company. As of 2008, the adjudication process had cost water users and Idaho taxpayers more than $80 million and resolved more than 133,000 water rights claims.

—Laura Woodworth-Ney

See also: *American Indian Water Rights; Aquaculture; Carey Act of 1894; Lower Snake River Compensation Plan; Newlands, Francis G.*

BIBLIOGRAPHY

Idaho State Historical Society. "Snake River Basin." Idaho State Historical Society Reference Series No. 294. http://www.history.idaho.gov/Reference%20Series/0294.pdf.
Palmer, Tim. *The Snake River: Window to the West.* Washington, DC: Island Press, 1991.
United States Geological Survey (USGS)/Water Resources of Idaho. "National Water-Quality Assessment Program: Upper Snake River Basin." Last modified April 22, 2009. http://id.water.usgs.gov/nawqa/factsheets/LOW.165.html.
University of Idaho. "Extension in Twin Falls County: Aquaculture." http://www.uidaho.edu/extension/twinfalls/aquaculture.
Walker, Deward E. *Indians of Idaho.* Moscow: University Press of Idaho, 2006.

St. John's Bayou/New Madrid Floodway Project

The St. John's Bayou Project, also known as the New Madrid Floodway Project, was authorized by the U.S. Congress in 1954 to try to protect low-lying land in Missouri from flooding from the Mississippi River. During floods in the region four years earlier, 12,000 people had to be evacuated. The project involved closing a 1,500-foot gap in the Mississippi River levee in southeastern Missouri.

Prior to the start of construction, there had been flooding in New Madrid County and in nearby Mississippi County about every three years; flooding had occurred sixteen times between 1957 and 2002. In 2002, 77,400 acres were inundated, which resulted in the loss of crops, as well as damage to houses, cars, roads, and other property and infrastructure. The recurrent floods led the U.S. Army Corps of Engineers (Corps) to draw up plans for the floodway. Environmental concerns were soon raised. The U.S. Fish and Wildlife Service raised objections that the construction of the floodway would be damaging to fish and wildlife in the river. The U.S. Department of Agriculture wanted the project, which would prevent the flooding of farmland. Rep. Jo Ann Emerson (R-MO) spoke about flood damage to crops on a regular basis, urging that construction proceed.

The Corps, on July 20, 2005, announced that it would not build the New Madrid Floodway, citing legal challenges from environmental groups and the strict requirements of the Clean Water Act. The Corps anticipated that the project would be defeated in the courts, mainly over prospective damage to the city of East Prairie, Missouri, which the New Madrid Floodway would not protect. In order to protect East Prairie, the Corps would need to put a levee along the St. James Ditch at a cost of an additional $11 million and greater environmental impact.

One year of construction work had been completed—with an estimated cost of $107 million—when it was halted by order of the U.S. District Court for the District of Columbia on September 19, 2007. In his decision in the case *Environmental Defense et al. v. U.S. Army Corps of*

Engineers et al., Judge James Robertson stated that the Corps had "improperly manipulated" its modeling of wildlife habitats to ensure that the project would comply with the Clean Water Act and the National Environmental Policy Act, which it otherwise would not. At issue was the fact that the New Madrid Floodway might damage or destroy up to 80,000 acres of floodplains and wetlands. Judge Robertson ordered that the work already completed, estimated to cost $7 million, be undone. Environmentalists welcomed this decision. Members of the Missouri Coalition for the Environment and other groups argued that the money to be spent would result in no real benefit and that the floodway would not solve the flooding problem. However, local farmers were critical of the decision, arguing that some of the environmentalist protestors were themselves unaffected by the flooding and, hence, should not have had such a major voice in the decision-making process.

—Justin Corfield

See also: *Agriculture; Army Corps of Engineers, United States; Clean Water Act of 1972; Fish and Wildlife Service, United States; Mississippi River Basin; National Environmental Policy Act of 1969*

BIBLIOGRAPHY

Landers, Jay. "Judge Halts Corps's Flood Control Project in Missouri." *Civil Engineering* 77, no. 12 (2007): 28, 30–32.

Missouri Coalition for the Environment. "St. Johns Bayou/New Madrid Floodway Project." http://www.moenviron.org/water qualitystjohn.asp.

New York Times. "Missourians Quit Flood-Peril Area." January 18, 1950.

Taylor, Betsy. "Construction Ordered Stopped on New Madrid Floodway." *Southeast Missourian,* September 18, 2007. Available at http://www.semissourian.com/story/1277906.html.

U.S. Army Corps of Engineers, Memphis District. "St. Johns Bayou and New Madrid Floodway." http://www.mvm.usace.army.mil/StJohns/overview/default.asp.

Strawberry Valley Project

The Strawberry Valley Project is the first water project constructed by the Reclamation Bureau in the state of Utah. The project diverts water from the Strawberry River—a tributary of the Duchesne River—to farms in southern Utah County. The project is significant as it was among the first to apply hydropower revenues towards repayment. It is also significant because it primarily provided water to existing farms; only thirty-five new farms were opened on the public domain.

The Strawberry Valley is a broad alpine valley that lies at an elevation of about 7,500 feet near the ridge separating the Colorado River and drainage of the Great Salt Lake, also called the Bonneville Basin. Prior to construction of the project, local ranchers used the valley to graze sheep and cattle. It had been included within the original boundaries of the Uintah and Ouray Ute Reservation. The withdrawal of reservation lands to serve as a reservoir site occurred in connection with the allotment of the reservation, which the Ute's protested to little effect.

Ranchers from the southern Utah County community of Spanish Fork were the first to conceive of the idea of a storage reservoir in the valley and a diversion tunnel. Subsequent investigation by the state engineer in 1902 led to a petition that the project be taken up by the newly created Reclamation Service.

Construction on the project began at the West Portal of the Strawberry Tunnel in 1906. Crews continued excavation of the 3.8-mile tunnel from both sides of the mountain and completed work on June 20, 1912. Construction of the Strawberry Dam began in 1908, and the project engineer closed the sluice gates in July 1912. The final work on the dam and the first water diverted through the tunnel occurred in September 1913. The first distribution canal was completed in early 1916, and the Strawberry Water Users' Association (SWUA) took over operation and maintenance at that time. Congress modified the original repayment terms under the Fact Finders Act of 1924, and the government and the SWUA entered into a new fifty-year repayment contract in 1926. The SWUA completed repayment of project costs in 1974, using hydropower revenues and recreation and grazing fees collected at the Strawberry Reservoir to subsidize the repayment.

The project provided approximately 60,000 acre-feet of water per year for irrigation in southern Utah County around the towns of Mapleton, Spanish Fork, and Payson. The region became well-known for its production of sugar beets, fruits, and vegetables.

After taking control of project operation and maintenance, the SWUA constructed additional distribution canals and two power plants. During the severe drought of the 1930s, the SWUA dug a ditch to divert additional water to the reservoir from Current Creek. The Bureau of Reclamation subsequently studied enlarging the project. The enlargement plans became the basis for the Central Utah Project (CUP). The CUP's Bonneville Unit imports additional water from ten streams that are tributary to the Strawberry or Duchesne Rivers and that drain the south slope of the Uinta Mountains of eastern Utah. This water is stored in an enlarged Strawberry Reservoir. The Soldier Creek Dam is located six miles downstream from the original reservoir and raised the height of the reservoir forty-five feet. The resulting reservoir capacity of 1.1 million acre-feet is more than quadruple the original capacity.

Following the construction of the Soldier Creek Dam the original Strawberry Dam was breached in 1984. Because the CUP increased the amount of water diverted, a new tunnel was needed. The new Syar and Sixth Water Tunnels and a connecting pipeline deliver water through the divide. SWUA water is now mixed with CUP water, and the original Strawberry Diversion Tunnel has been kept as a backup in case maintenance needs or an emergency shuts down the new diversion works.

—Adam Eastman

See also: *Central Utah Project; Drought; Interbasin Water Transfer; Intermountain West; Reclamation Act of 1902*

BIBLIOGRAPHY

Alexander, Thomas G. "An Investment in Progress: Utah's First Federal Reclamation Project, the Strawberry Valley Project." *Utah Historical Quarterly* 39, no. 3 (1971): 286–304. Available at http://publications.utah.gov/search/quarterly.html.

MacKay, Kathryn L. "The Strawberry Valley Reclamation Project and the Opening of the Uintah Indian Reservation." *Utah Historical Quarterly* 50, no. 1 (1982): 68–89. Available at http://publications.utah.gov/search/quarterly.html.

Tellico Dam

The Tellico Dam was constructed by the Tennessee Valley Authority (TVA). It is located near Knoxville, Tennessee, on the Little Tennessee River north of the main stem of the Tennessee River. It was one of the last dams built during the era when hundreds of dams were built throughout the United States.

Construction of the dam was clouded with considerable controversy. Plans for the dam were drawn up in the early 1960s, when wider environmental concerns were arising in America and around the world about the effect of dams on the landscape. Opposition to the dam also came from many landowners, who saw dams as a threat to their property, and their influential advocate in Washington, Senator Allen J. Ellender (D-LA). Nevertheless, the TVA was anxious to develop a series of multipurpose projects on the Tennessee River, and it approved the dam in 1963.

Construction of the dam went forward and was nearing completion in the early 1970s when another delay occurred, resulting from an environmental study showing that the snail darter (*Percina tanasi*), a small and then-endangered fish, was living in the river and would be adversely affected by the dam. The Endangered Species Committee met and was asked to issue a waiver under the Endangered Species Act, but it decided unanimously against doing so. A lawsuit under the Endangered Species Act resulted, and an injunction was issued to prevent completion of the dam. The TVA then appealed the ruling. The subsequent case, *Tennessee Valley Authority v. Hill,* was ultimately argued before the U.S. Supreme Court. The justices upheld the decision of the lower court by a vote of 6–3, affirming the injunction. They stated that they could neither defer to agencies nor independently determine whether saving the snail darter was more important than the projected economic benefits of building the dam. As a result, the Supreme Court felt that it did not have the authority to evaluate the validity of the TVA's cost-benefit analysis. The Court further ruled that the Endangered Species Act specifically stated that listed species were not to be harmed, whereas the dam would in fact eradicate an endangered species.

Charles Schulze, chairman of the President's Council of Economic Advisers, wanted the project to go ahead, since by the time of the Supreme Court ruling it was nearly complete. However, the justices had left a loophole in their opinion, noting that the U.S. Congress had the power to make exceptions to the Act. This is what finally allowed the dam to be completed, as Congress, urged on by Senator Howard Baker (R-TN), exempted the Tellico Dam from the Endangered Species Act. In 1979, the gates of the dam were closed, and Tellico Lake started to form. The new lake soon became popular, resulting in a real estate boom on the land overlooking it. Plots that had been worth $500 per acre were soon changing hands for several hundred thousand dollars per acre. As for the snail darter, it survived after being relocated to a different river, and its conservation status has since been upgraded from "endangered" to "threatened."

—Justin Corfield

See also: *Tennessee Valley Authority;* Tennessee Valley Authority v. Hill *(1978)*

BIBLIOGRAPHY

Ballal, S. K. "Tellico Dam Furor Involves More Than Snail Darter." *BioScience* 27, no. 9 (1977): 586.

Christy, E. Jennifer. "Congress Hooks Snail Darter." *BioScience* 27, no. 5 (1977): 320.

Murchison, Kenneth M. *The Snail Darter Case: TVA versus the Endangered Species Act.* Lawrence: University Press of Kansas, 2007.

Plater, Zygmunt J. B. "Tiny Fish/Big Battle." *Tennessee Bar Journal* 44, no. 4 (2008). Available at http://www.tba.org/Journal_Current/200804/TBJ-200804-coverStory.html.

Wheeler, William Bruce, and Michael J. McDonald. *TVA and the Tellico Dam, 1936–1979: A Bureaucratic Crisis in Post-Industrial America.* Knoxville: University of Tennessee Press, 1986.

Tennessee-Tombigbee Waterway

The Tennessee-Tombigbee Waterway is the largest navigation project ever built by the U.S. Army Corps of Engineers. It is essentially a navigational shortcut between the Tennessee River and the Tombigbee River, allowing vessels to travel south to the Gulf of Mexico. Passing through parts of Alabama and Mississippi, it consists of 232 miles of canal and straightened river with 10 locks and dams. It begins at the Pickwick Lake of the Tennessee River in the north and extends south to Demopolis, Alabama. The project required the excavation of more than 300 million cubic yards of earth—more than the Panama Canal and one and a half times what was required to build the Suez Canal. Construction started in 1972 and was completed in 1985.

As early as the 1760s, French settlers in the region recommended construction of a canal to connect the two rivers. In the early nineteenth century, both Tennessee and Alabama also explored the concept. President Ulysses S. Grant authorized an engineering investigation of the waterway in 1874–1875. Although engineers reported that the project was feasible, it was not financially practical. The Corps of Engineers continued to explore the possible waterway into the twentieth century, finally obtaining congressional approval in 1946.

Not everyone was supportive of the planned waterway. Some members of Congress thought that it was an unnecessary expenditure of federal dollars. Thus, although Congress had approved the project, it was not funded until 1968. Southern members of Congress expected the project to create much-needed jobs, especially for minorities. In 1971, Richard Nixon funded the Tennessee-Tombigbee project. He hoped this action would help win over southern voters for his re-election. Construction began in December 1972.

Throughout the next decade, the project faced the challenges of two lawsuits and a president who wanted to end federal funding for large water projects. The first lawsuit was filed in 1971; the Environmental Defense Fund used the new National Environmental Protection Act (NEPA) to argue that the Corps of Engineers had not done a thorough review of the environmental impact as required by this law.

In another lawsuit in 1976, the Environmental Defense Fund again argued that the Corps was not conducting appropriate impact reviews or mitigating any such impact.

Although litigation dragged on for years, the Corps of Engineers won both cases and continued construction. President Jimmy Carter tried to terminate funding for the waterway but reversed his position when he discovered the widespread public support of the project in the South. In spite of presidential support and ongoing congressional funding, many regarded the project as an enormous and costly boondoggle with very little oversight or accountability. Over the years, the Corps of Engineers would make efforts to comply with NEPA and calm the concerns of environmentalists. It hired archeology teams to conduct excavations, but very few other types of historical surveys were conducted. While some historians protested, archeologists generally supported the project because it brought them hard-to-find funding and excavating opportunities in regions previously untouched.

When the waterway was finally completed in 1985, it had cost approximately $2 billion, and its construction had provided only a very small number of jobs to poor minorities. Although the construction phase had not provided the financial benefits Alabama and Mississippi had hoped for, many believed the waterway would now prove its worth to shipping. However, as the years went by, very few shippers actually used the Tennessee-Tombigbee Waterway. The Mississippi River was much wider and better for the navigation of barge-tows, which often pushed as many as forty-five barges at once. Barge tows on the Tennessee-Tombigbee could only maneuver up to eight barges. Although a severe drought in 1988 forced some shippers to use the waterway instead of the Mississippi River, the largest group of users was and remains recreational boaters.

In many ways, the Tennessee-Tombigbee Waterway serves as a perfect case study for the conflict between a growing environmentalist movement and the politics of public projects. It also reveals the difficulty of conducting an accurate cost-benefit analysis for large projects in an ever-changing economic environment. Still, the waterway stands as a tribute to the engineering acumen of the modern age and the ability to control and direct water to suit human needs and desires.

—April Summitt

See also: *Army Corps of Engineers, United States; National Environmental Policy Act of 1969*

BIBLIOGRAPHY

Donahue, John M., and Barbara Rose Johnston, eds. *Water, Culture, and Power: Local Struggles in a Global Context.* Washington, DC: Island Press, 1998.

Stine, Jeffrey K. *Mixing the Waters: Environment, Politics, and the Building of the Tennessee-Tombigbee Waterway.* Akron, OH: University of Akron Press, 1993.

Stine, Jeffrey K. "The Tennessee-Tombigbee Waterway and the Evolution of Cultural Resources Management." *Public Historian* 14, no. 2 (1992): 6–30.

Theodore Roosevelt Dam

Once among the world's tallest masonry structures, Roosevelt Dam is named after President Theodore Roosevelt. Instrumental in approval of the Newlands-Hansbrough Bill, also known as the Federal Reclamation Act of 1902, Roosevelt dedicated the dam in March 1911. The dam, located seventy-six miles northeast of Phoenix, Arizona, at the confluence of the Tonto and Salt Rivers, was among the first approved and constructed after the Reclamation Act was passed. Unique, as well as eye-appealing, construction used cyclopean rubble-masonry in the gravity arch dam and incorporated Greco-Roman style architecture.

By 1900, the American population was migrating west, and President Roosevelt was convinced that the key element to initiating growth and development was the reclamation of the mostly desert lands in the region. This could be accomplished by constructing irrigation systems for the storage, diversion, and development of natural water resources. The Reclamation Act paved the way for the Salt River Project, which included construction of the dam. John O'Rourke and Company of Galveston, Texas, was awarded the contract for the dam's construction. O'Rourke employed a diverse group of workers from Mexico, China, and Spain, as well as African Americans, Italian Americans, and American Indians.

Begun in 1903, the original dam was constructed as a reservoir for the Salt River Project and for flood control in the Salt River Valley. Devastating floods hampered construction in 1905, pushing back completion to 1911 and raising the original price tag of $3 million to $10 million. The dam, one of five original projects authorized by the federal government, was the first to be completed in spite of delays. In 1906, Congress authorized the Reclamation Service to produce and sell hydroelectric power at the Salt River Project. The dam had a hydroelectric generating capacity of 36,000 kilowatts. The Reclamation Service viewed the Roosevelt Dam as an example of success and a showpiece for the agency. The dam is considered the primary factor in the settlement of central Arizona. The irrigation made possible by the reservoir has turned the desert around Phoenix into productive farmland.

At the time of completion, the dam rose to a height of 280 feet and was 723 feet long. In 1911, its engineers boasted that the dam was wide enough for two Ford Model Ts to pass abreast while crossing it. Originally known as "Salt River Dam #1," the dam and reservoir were not officially named after Theodore Roosevelt until 1959.

In 1986, after several previous modifications, a ten-year renovation began at a cost of $430 million, over forty times the original budget of the structure. The ambitious project included resurfacing the entire dam with concrete and

Originally named "Salt River Dam 1," the Theodore Roosevelt Dam in Arizona was one of the first dams to be built after the passage of the Reclamation Act of 1902.

Library of Congress

raising its height to 357 feet, thereby increasing the storage capacity by 20 percent. The surface area of 22-mile-long Roosevelt Lake increased to almost 20,000 acres, creating a shoreline of 128 miles.

The renovation project was completed in 1996. It included construction of the Roosevelt Lake Bridge, which was designed to accommodate today's traffic, and upgrades to the hydroelectric power plant. The American Consulting Engineers Council designated the bridge one of the top twelve bridges in the nation, citing its overall design, size, eye appeal, and design challenge as factors in the selection. Renovations at Roosevelt Dam used 444,000 cubic yards of concrete and 6.7 million pounds of reinforcing steel. The lake was filled to 100 percent capacity in February of 2009.

As part of the 1986 renovation, many new recreational facilities were also funded. These included 1,515 individual campsites, 80 picnic sites, group campgrounds, boat launch areas, and fish-cleaning stations. A marina, sheriff's aid station, and numerous upgrades to access roads were also included.

—Randy Taylor

See also: *Bureau of Reclamation*

BIBLIOGRAPHY

Davis, Arthur P. "Reclamation of Arid West by Federal Government." *Annals of the American Academy of Political and Social Science: American Waterways,* 31, no. 1 (1908): 203–18.

Davis, Arthur P. *Water Storage on Salt River, Arizona.* U.S. Geological Survey Water Supply and Irrigation Paper No. 73. Washington, DC: U.S. Government Printing Office, 1903.

Hansen, Brett. "History Lesson: Conquering the Arizona Desert; The Theodore Roosevelt Dam." *Civil Engineering* 78, no. 8 (2008): 44–45.

Kendrick, Gregory D. "The Historic American Engineering Record and Reinterpreting the History of the West." *Public Historian* 15, no. 2 (1993): 81–86

Smith, Karen L. *The Magnificent Experiment: Building the Salt River Reclamation Project, 1890–1917.* Tucson: University of Arizona Press, 1986.

Zarbin, Earl A. *Roosevelt Dam: A History to 1911.* Phoenix, AZ: Salt River Project, 1984.

Tocks Island Dam

The Tocks Island Dam Project was first formulated after a 1955 flood on Tocks Island in the Delaware Water Gap between Pennsylvania and New Jersey. The project's aim was to provide freshwater to the cities of New York and Philadelphia and to generate hydroelectric power. It rapidly became one of the more controversial projects of the U.S. Army Corps of Engineers (Corps), which had the task of implementing the project. Its shelving resulted in the Delaware remaining the last major undammed river in the United States.

The August 1955 flood, which threatened Trenton, New Jersey—resulted in roughly 100 deaths (73 were reported on August 19 alone) and damage to property in the Delaware River basin estimated in the billions of dollars. As a result, local authorities decided to draw up a proposal for flood control and urged the U.S. Congress to build a dam. The dam was intended to regulate water, reduce flooding, and generate hydroelectric power, while the lake the dam would create—to be called the Tocks Island National Recreation Area—would provide recreation facilities. The project also promised to create a new supply of freshwater for Philadelphia and New York; a drought in the region accentuated this need in the early 1960s.

The dam was officially authorized in 1962, when Congress allocated $192.4 million for the project as part of the Flood Control Act of 1962. This led to forced sales of land to the U.S. government. Many people objected to the price the government offered, while others did not want to move since their families had lived in the area for several generations. In addition, three townships were scheduled to be lost: Dingmans Ferry and Bushkill in Pennsylvania and Pahaquarry in New Jersey.

Local protests against the Tocks Island Dam Project led to the formation of the Delaware Valley Conservation Association, led by Nancy Shukaitis and Ruth Jones. They gained the support of William O. Douglas, an associate justice on the U.S. Supreme Court. Douglas visited the region around Sunfish Pond with his wife in 1967, and the two were soon strong supporters of the group "Save Sunfish Pond." In 1975, the Delaware River Basin Commission voted three to one against the dam. This led to the Scenic and Wild Rivers Act of 1978, and that in turn led to the creation of the Middle Delaware Scenic and Recreational River. Any realistic hope of constructing the dam was now gone.

Other factors also contributed to the project's failure. The cost, estimated to be about $65 million, was deemed prohibitive. In addition, it was found that the geology of the region would not support a dam of the type planned, causing Secretary of the Interior Stewart L. Udall to switch from being one of the dam's major supporters to being a leading opponent. The whole project was reviewed in 1992 and rejected, with the proviso that it would be examined again ten years later. In 2002, the project was finally deauthorized, and today the land is maintained by the National Park Service as the Delaware Water Gap National Recreation Area.

—Justin Corfield

See also: *Army Corps of Engineers, United States; Douglas, William O.; Udall, Stewart; Wild and Scenic Rivers Act of 1968*

BIBLIOGRAPHY

Albert, Richard C. *Damming the Delaware: The Rise and Fall of the Tocks Island Dam*. University Park: Pennsylvania State University Press, 1987.

Feiveson, Harold A., Frank W. Sinden, and Robert H. Socolow, eds. *Boundaries of Analysis: An Inquiry into the Tocks Island Dam Controversy*. Cambridge, MA: American Academy of Arts and Sciences/Ballinger, 1976.

Kraft, Herbert C. *The Miller Field Site, Warren County, N.J.: A Study in Prehistoric Archaeology. Part One: The Archaic and Transitional Stages*. South Orange, NJ: Seton Hall University Press, 1970.

Menzies, Elizabeth G. C. *Before the Waters: The Upper Delaware Valley*. New Brunswick, NJ: Rutgers University Press, 1966.

Snyder, Frank E., and Brian H. Guss. *The District: A History of the Philadelphia District, U.S. Army Corps of Engineers, 1866–1971*. Philadelphia: U.S. Army Engineer District, 1974.

Truckee-Carson Project

The Truckee-Carson Project, later renamed the Newlands Project, was one of the first projects constructed by the U.S. Reclamation Service. The secretary of the interior authorized the project, along with four others, on March 14, 1903. The original plan proposed the reclamation of over 300,000 acres of land in western Nevada around the community of Fallon. Congress officially renamed the project in March 1919 to honor Senator Francis G. Newlands (D-NV), who was the sponsor of the Reclamation Act of 1902 and the Truckee-Carson Project.

The project operates by diverting water from the Truckee River into the Carson River and by regulating the flows of both rivers from upstream reservoirs. The principal feature of the project is the Derby Diversion Dam on the Truckee River and the thirty-two-mile-long Truckee Canal. Derby Diversion Dam is an earthfill embankment structure 31 feet high and 1,300 feet long with a concrete control structure. The Truckee Canal was constructed at the same time as the dam. The canal's route includes three tunnels ranging in length from 309 feet to 1,521 feet. Control gates along the canal permit irrigation of adjacent lands. On June 17, 1905,

the second anniversary of the Reclamation Act, Senator Francis G. Newlands led the official dedication ceremonies of the Derby Diversion Dam and Truckee Canal.

Water is delivered to farmers in the Lahontan Valley through two canals originating at the Carson River Diversion Dam, located five miles downstream from the terminus of the Truckee Canal. The nine-mile-long "T" Canal serves lands on the north side of the river, while the twenty-seven-mile-long "V" Canal serves lands on the south side. The first water deliveries to project settlers began in February 1906.

To ensure an adequate supply of water in the late summer when the natural river flows are at their lowest, the Reclamation Service planned to supplement the river using Lake Tahoe. However, local water users and property holders protested. The Reclamation Service began preliminary work on the Lake Tahoe Dam in 1905, only to be stopped by a court order. An agreement reached in 1913 resolved the protracted legal battle, and the government completed the dam at Lake Tahoe that year. The small dam at the lake's natural outlet controls the top 6 feet of the lake, creating an effective storage capacity of 730,000 acre-feet.

In December 1910, after several years of water shortages and the inability of the government to gain control of the waters of Lake Tahoe, the secretary of the interior approved plans for Lahontan Dam on the Carson River. Construction of the dam and power plant began in February 1911 and was completed in early 1915.

Serious water shortages and drainage problems plagued the project in its early years. As a result, the project never came close to the envisioned size of 300,000 acres. While the total land irrigated by project waters varies from year to year, the project serves a maximum of 73,000 acres. To solve the serious drainage problem, project farmers formed the Truckee-Carson Irrigation District on November 16, 1917, and entered into a repayment contract with the government for the construction of a drainage system. Construction on the system began in 1921. Contractors completed the initial 230 miles of drains in 1928, which effectively mitigated the problem.

The construction of Lahontan Reservoir and Lake Tahoe Dam partially solved the project's chronic water shortages. However, controversy over the project's water rights in Lake Tahoe and the water rights of the Pyramid Lake Paiute remained unresolved for decades. Project diversions from the Truckee River at Derby Dam had dramatically lowered the level of Pyramid Lake, altering its chemistry and threatening both the fish and the Paiutes who relied upon the lake. A combination of legislative and judicial wrangling from the late 1960s to the early 1990s led to the California-Nevada Interstate Water Compact and the Truckee-Carson-Pyramid Lake Water Rights Settlement Act of 1990, which have helped to resolve most of the controversies surrounding the project. However, efforts to fulfill the provisions of these settlements remain contentious, as project water users oppose mitigation actions that diminish their water supplies.

—Adam Eastman

See also: *American Indian Water Rights; American Indian Water Settlements; Bureau of Reclamation; California-Nevada Interstate Water Compact (1971); Reclamation Act of 1902; Truckee-Carson-Pyramid Lake Water Rights Settlement Act of 1990*

BIBLIOGRAPHY

Pisani, Donald J. *Water and American Government: The Reclamation Bureau, National Water Policy, and the West, 1902–1935.* Berkeley: University of California Press, 2002.
Simonds, William Joe. "Newlands Project." 1996, last updated July 22, 2008. http://www.usbr.gov/projects/Project.jsp?proj_Name=Newlands+Project.

Public Works Administration

The Federal Emergency Administration of Public Works was created by Title II of the National Industrial Recovery Act of 1933. Later known as the Public Works Administration, it was intended to create jobs through large-scale public works projects like hospitals, bridges, railroads, schools, and multipurpose dams. Among the dams constructed with its monies was the Tygart Dam in West Virginia.

Secretary of the Interior Harold Ickes directed the Public Works Administration from 1933 to 1939. Over the course of the agency's existence, it spent more than $6 billion on infrastructure improvements across the United States. Despite the number of projects completed under its aegis, the Public Works Administration did not impact chronic unemployment in a significant manner. It was abolished in 1941 as the country shifted its economic and industrial focus at the onset of World War II.

—John R. Burch Jr.

See also: *Ickes, Harold; Roosevelt, Franklin D.*

BIBLIOGRAPHY

Phillips, Sarah T. *This Land, This Nation: Conservation, Rural America, and the New Deal.* New York: Cambridge University Press, 2007.
Smith, Jason Scott. *Building New Deal Liberalism: The Political Economy of Public Works, 1933–1956.* New York: Cambridge University Press, 2006.

Tygart Dam

The Tygart Dam is located on the Tygart Valley River (or Tygart River) in east-central West Virginia, close to the town of Grafton. The U.S. Army Corps of Engineers began construction on the dam in 1938 with the main goal of controlling the frequent floods on the Monongahela River that had been damaging crops and threatening homesteads. Another goal was to reduce the crest of the Ohio River when it flooded. The lake created by the dam was to be kept low, which would allow it to cope with floods as well. The dam was constructed solely for navigation and flood control, with no hydropower plant constructed.

The initial cost estimate for the dam was $11.8 million, of which $1.4 million was designated solely for the purpose of rerouting a nearby railroad line. The estimated time to complete the dam was 29 months, and 2,200 people would be employed in its construction. The project was authorized on January 11, 1934, during the Great Depression when there was a need to get as many people working as quickly as possible. Therefore, the federal government eagerly agreed to cover the entire cost of the project.

When completed, the dam was 1,921 feet long and 230 feet high, and its base was 207 feet thick. The dam created a large reservoir—Lake Tygart—covering 3,440 acres with a 32-mile shoreline. The new lake inundated land from Grafton to the township of Moatsville to the south, and it soon became a popular tourist attraction for swimmers, anglers, and hikers.

The dam has served its purpose in regulating the flow of the river. A gauge in the town of Dailey, upstream of the dam, has shown that the annual mean flow of the river for the ninety years since 1915 has been 358 cubic feet per second, with the lowest flow (zero) recorded during several periods in 1930 and 1953. The highest flow, recorded on May 17, 1996, was 19,900 cubic feet per second.

—Justin Corfield

See also: *Army Corps of Engineers, United States*

BIBLIOGRAPHY

Billington, David P., and Donald C. Jackson. *Big Dams of the New Deal Era: A Confluence of Engineering and Politics.* Norman: University of Oklahoma Press, 2006.

Ford, Darlene, Taylor County Historical and Genealogical Society, Marvin Gelhausen, Wayne McDevitt, Rick Reese, and Peggy Robinson. *Taylor County.* Charleston, SC: Arcadia, 2000.

Hamilton, Carolyn Fortney. *West Virginia's Lower Tygart Valley River: People and Places.* Colfax, WV: TVR Press, 2004.

Parker, Arthur. *The Monongahela: River of Dreams, River of Sweat.* University Park: Pennsylvania State University Press, 1999.

Wahiawā Dam and Reservoir

The Wahiawā Dam and Reservoir are located in the town of Wahiawā on the central plateau of the island of Oʻahu in Hawaiʻi, about twenty miles northwest of the city of Honolulu. The reservoir, popularly known as Lake Wilson, is the largest freshwater impound in the Hawaiian Islands with a capacity of 2.5 billion gallons, total area of 260 acres, and average depth of 26 feet. The dam is an earth and rockfill structure with a crest length of 460 feet and crest height of 98.5 feet above the original streambed. The dam stands at the confluence of the north and south branches of the Kaukonahua Stream and forms the reservoir in a total of seven miles of the stream branches' gulches. The two arms of Lake Wilson encompass the town of Wahiawā and have become a feature of the town landscape.

Kaukonahua Stream traditionally supported a Native Hawaiian community based on the cultivation of wetland taro, with a population estimated as high as 5,000. As with other communities across Hawaiʻi, however, this traditional agricultural system was supplanted by the sugar industry, which amassed land and water to support large-scale, water-intensive plantations. Wahiawā Dam and Reservoir were constructed from 1905 to 1906 relatively inexpensively for $300,000 by the former Waialua Sugar Company, a subsidiary of Castle & Cooke/Dole Foods, as a part of the larger irrigation system for its sugar plantation in the Waialua and Haleʻiwa regions of Oʻahu's north shore.

Wahiawā Reservoir collects water from 17 square miles of watershed lands on the western side of the Koʻolau Range. In addition to stream water, it receives groundwater through a twelve-mile network of ditches and tunnels. The reservoir then connects to an irrigation system that includes thirty miles of ditches, tunnels, and siphons.

Historically, Wahiawā Reservoir supplied an average of 30 million gallons a day (mgd) of the total 90 mgd of surface and groundwater used by Waialua Sugar on 12,000-plus acres of sugar cane. After Waialua Sugar closed in 1996, water use for irrigation declined significantly; more recently, the reservoir has supplied an average of 10 mgd to smaller diversified farms on about 6,400 acres.

Over the years, the reservoir has developed other uses besides irrigation. The state of Hawaiʻi has stocked and managed it as a public fishing area since 1957, and it remains the largest freshwater sport fishery in the state. The reservoir has also been used since the 1920s for sewage effluent disposal from Honolulu's municipal Wahiawā Wastewater Treatment Plant. The plant currently discharges about 2 mgd of secondarily treated (R–2) effluent into the reservoir.

The decline of the sugar industry in Hawaiʻi has raised questions about the future of former plantation irrigation infrastructure, including Wahiawā Dam and Reservoir. Various challenges confront the ongoing management and use of the reservoir. The reservoir has had recurring problems with impaired water quality, odors, sewage spills, and fish kills, and a well-publicized outbreak in 2002 of the invasive plant *Salvinia molesta* required an extensive public eradication effort. Major concerns also surround the safety of the aging dam to the downstream north shore communities. Against this backdrop of uncertainty over future uses and liabilities, proposals have surfaced for the state of Hawaiʻi potentially to acquire Wahiawā Dam and Reservoir.

—Isaac Moriwake

See also: *Waiāhole Ditch*

BIBLIOGRAPHY

Ernest K. Hirata & Associates. "Dam Safety Inspection: Wahiawa Dam, Oahu, Hawaiʻi." Honolulu: Hawaii Division of Water and Land Development, 1995.

Haile, Alemayehu. "A Historical Review and Reconstruction of the Water Rights and Water Leasing Situation of Wahiawa Reservoir and Its Tributaries." MS diss., University of Hawaii at Mānoa, 1976.

Southichack, Mana K. *Wahiawa Irrigation System Economic Impact Study.* Honolulu: Hawaii Department of Agriculture, 2008. Available at http://hawaii.gov/hdoa/adc/adc-reports/WIS/.

Wilcox, Carol. *Sugar Water: Hawaii's Plantation Ditches.* Honolulu: University of Hawaii Press, 1996.

Waiāhole Ditch

The Waiāhole Ditch is an irrigation system on the island of Oʻahu in Hawaiʻi that collects water from the wetter, windward (eastern) side of the island and delivers it to the island's dry central plain. Oahu Sugar Company historically used the system to help irrigate its 13,000-acre sugar plantation, but since the plantation closed in 1995, the system has carried greatly reduced flows for diversified agricultural operations on former plantation lands. After Oahu Sugar's closure, the Waiāhole Ditch became the focus of a major legal and political battle over the future use of the water. The result was the first-ever restoration of stream flows in Hawai'i and the landmark 2000 decision of the Hawai'i Supreme Court on the public trust doctrine and instream flows along the lines of the famous Mono Lake case in California.

The Waiāhole Ditch extends about twenty-five miles in length. The system collects dike-impounded groundwater contained in mountain lava rock, as well as some surface water, from the Ko'olau Range. Beginning in the back of Kahana Valley in windward O'ahu at an elevation of 790 feet, the system diverts about 2 million gallons a day (mgd) from the Kahana Stream. It then traverses the windward side of the Ko'olaus, passes under the Ko'olau crest, and emerges on the leeward side, collecting groundwater along the way. A series of ditches, flumes, and siphons transports the water to the fields in the central plain (Wilcox 1996).

Oahu Sugar, established in 1897, conceived the Waiāhole Ditch in 1905 to supplement its groundwater wells. After several years of studies, construction of the system began in 1913 and concluded in 1916. Although the initial plan was to collect surface water from windward streams, the project encountered dike-impounded groundwater during construction. These flows diminished and stabilized over time. Several additional development tunnels were excavated laterally from the main system between 1925 and 1935, one of which was extended in 1964. The original construction cost $2.3 million and mobilized up to 900 or more Asian immigrant laborers. It is considered one of the most notable water engineering accomplishments in Hawai'i because of the challenges of tunneling through the Ko'olaus while contending with the released groundwater. Historically, the Waiāhole Ditch delivered about 28 mgd of Oahu Sugar's total use of 140 mgd.

The Waiāhole Ditch's construction caused direct reductions in the flow of several windward streams, which derive their perennial flow from groundwater, including Waiāhole, Waianu, Waikāne, and Kahana Streams. Dramatic reductions in flow affected not only the streams and Kāneohe Bay, the largest estuary system in Hawai'i, but also the Native Hawaiian communities who relied on these waters for their subsistence culture based on farming wetland taro and fishing.

In 1993, Oahu Sugar announced its closure, and legal action commenced before the state Water Commission over the Waiāhole Ditch's water diversions. Windward community groups sought to restore flows to windward streams, but a powerful array of former plantation landowners, corporate farmers, and government officials, including the state governor and attorney general, advocated for continued leeward diversions. In 1994, a complaint against the dumping of water in leeward gulches led to an interim settlement under which unused water was returned to windward streams. After extensive proceedings, the commission issued its final decision in 1997, roughly following the interim restoration and returning about half of the water to windward streams.

Appeals followed, and the Hawai'i Supreme Court issued its decision in 2000, reversing the commission's determination in favor of further instream use protection. The court's decision strongly affirmed the public trust doctrine, maintaining that the state has the authority to revisit prior diversions and the duty to protect public trust instream uses where feasible. The court adopted the Mono Lake precedent. However, the court developed it further in holding that the public trust doctrine established a presumption in favor of public trust purposes and placed the burden on off-stream diverters to justify their uses. The Waiāhole Ditch case is regarded, along with Mono Lake case, as among the most significant cases on the public trust doctrine.

The state of Hawai'i has operated the Waiāhole Ditch since acquiring it in 1999. While the ditch continues to supply irrigation for agriculture on a reduced land area, which is gradually giving way to development in the postplantation era, it is increasingly known for the historic legal case that bears its name.

—Isaac Moriwake

See also: *Wahiawā Dam and Reservoir*

BIBLIOGRAPHY

In re Waiāhole Ditch Combined Contested Case Hr'g, 94 Haw. 97, 9 P.3d 409 (2000).

Sproat, D. Kapua'ala, and Isaac H. Moriwake. "Ke Kalo Pa'a O Waiāhole: Use of the Public Trust as a Tool for Environmental Advocacy." In *Creative Common Law Strategies for Protecting the Environment,* edited by Clifford Rechtschaffen and Denise Antolini, 247–84. Washington, DC: Environmental Law Institute, 2007.

Wilcox, Carol. *Sugar Water: Hawaii's Plantation Ditches.* Honolulu: University of Hawai'i Press, 1996.

Westlands Water District

Settlers in the southwestern Central Valley of California were handicapped by a lack of surface water, and well technology didn't develop sufficiently for them to use groundwater for larger-scale irrigation until about 1915. As a result of groundwater development, in 1922 settlers irrigated some 33,000 acres. A surge in irrigated acreage began about 1936 and continued through World War II. As a result, by the mid-1940s, farm size in the area generally ranged from 1,000 to 5,000 acres.

Secretary of the Interior Harold Ickes and President Franklin Delano Roosevelt authorized construction of some parts of the Bureau of Reclamation's Central Valley Project in 1935. Then, hoping to build upon the Central Valley Project, in 1942 the Westside Landowners Association began to develop a water project. In 1952, the Westlands Water District legally organized, eight years before the federal government authorized the San Luis Unit of the Central Valley Project in 1960. The Westlands Water District took over the activities of the Westside Landowners Association. The San Luis Unit is a joint project, jointly operated, of the federal Bureau of Reclamation and California's State Water Project.

The Bureau of Reclamation and the district signed a water supply contract in 1963. Reclamation initiated construction that same year and completed most initial construction in the 1960s. The Westplains Water Storage District, generally lying west of Westlands and the current route of the San Luis Canal, organized in 1962 and included over 200,000 acres of land. Its inability to obtain water from the State Water Project encouraged it to look to Reclamation for water supply, and Reclamation supported a merger of the Westplains and Westland districts. This merger occurred in 1965. The Westlands Water District, which now includes about 600,000 acres of the richest agricultural land in the world, lies on the southwest side of the Central Valley, beginning several miles south of Los Banos and extending to about Kettleman City and California State Route 41. The Bureau of Reclamation provides water to the district through the San Luis Canal. The area contains many large holdings, which triggered controversy over the 160-acre limitation imposed on landowners in the Reclamation Act in 1902. As a result of lawsuits by landholding activists, Congress passed the Reclamation Reform Act (RRA) in 1982, which recognized both current political realities and the evolution of farming since passage of the Reclamation Act in 1902. In the RRA, Congress increased the acreage limitation sixfold to 960 acres.

Cadillac Desert

Cadillac Desert, written by Marc Reisner, posits that the control of water has driven the development of the western United States. Initially, most water projects were small in scale and intended to serve the needs of the general populace. Reisner argues that beginning in the 1930s, greed, vanity, arrogance, foolish ideas, and competition between states and federal agencies began driving the development of large-scale water projects. The monograph's narrative primarily focuses on the dam-building era that began in the 1930s, which transformed much of the West from useless desert to sprawling population centers. During that era's half century, most of the West's rivers were dammed or diverted for agricultural use. In particular, Reisner details the politics of how the Colorado River's waters were distributed to the states of Arizona, California, Colorado, New Mexico, Nevada, Utah, and Wyoming through the Colorado River Compact. Although water fueled the West's development, Reisner concludes with the pessimistic view that water also threatens the region's future as the supply of water dwindles and existing water delivery systems deteriorate. He offers possible solutions to the West's water problems in a book he coauthored with Sarah F. Bates entitled *Overtapped Oasis.* In 1997, *Cadillac Desert* was adapted as a four-part award-winning PBS documentary.

—John R. Burch Jr.

See also: *Colorado River Compact*

BIBLIOGRAPHY

Cadillac Desert: Water and the Transformation of Nature. VHS. Directed by Jon Else and Linda Harrar. Alexandria, VA: Columbia Tri Star Television/PBS Home Video, 1997.

Reisner, Marc. *Cadillac Desert: The American West and Its Disappearing Water.* New York: Viking, 1986.

Reisner, Marc, and Sarah F. Bates. *Overtapped Oasis: Reform or Revolution for Western Water.* Washington, DC: Island Press, 1990.

The original authorization of the San Luis Unit directed the Bureau of Reclamation to provide drainage for the district, and at one point, Reclamation estimated that drainage would carry 100 train carloads of salt a day out of the area. While working on the drainage issue, Reclamation partnered with the Fish and Wildlife Service to use drain water to develop the Kesterson National Wildlife Refuge. High concentrations of selenium in the drain water, however, resulted in the death and deformity of birds in the refuge. The refuge was closed, and standing water was eliminated in the refuge. Irrigators had to conserve water and develop techniques to prevent drainage from occurring. To date, large expenditures of energy and money have gone into the drainage problem and several alternative approaches have been developed, but no drainage project has been completed due to environmental concerns. Without drainage, some lands have become alkaline and gone out of production, while others are threatened with high levels of saline groundwater. Reclamation has purchased some alkaline lands to remove them permanently from production.

Cropping patterns in the district have evolved from predominately annual row and sown crops to a higher percentage of perennial crops (e.g., fruit and nuts as well as vineyards), which are seriously compromised during droughts. Some sixty major crops are produced in the district; they include fruits, nuts, vegetables, grains, and forage. In 2008, producers worked almonds, cotton, pistachios (21,113 acres), safflower, tomatoes (86,011 acres), and wheat on more than 20,000 acres each, while they tended alfalfa, barley, cantaloupes, garlic, onions, sorghum, grapes, and lettuce on more than 10,000 acres each.

—Brit Allan Storey

See also: *Bureau of Reclamation; Central Valley Project; Ickes, Harold*

BIBLIOGRAPHY

Green, Dorothy. *Managing Water: Avoiding Crisis in California.* Berkeley: University of California Press, 2007.

Hundley, Norris, Jr. *The Great Thirst: Californians and Water; A History.* Rev. ed. Berkeley: University of California Press, 2001.

Reisner, Marc. *Cadillac Desert: The American West and Its Disappearing Water.* Rev. ed. New York: Penguin Books, 1993.

Westlands Water District. http://www.westlandswater.org/.

Wilson Dam

Wilson Dam is located near the town of Florence, Alabama, in the Shoals Area on the Tennessee River. One of the main natural features of the Tennessee River in this area is a thirty-seven-mile stretch of craggy rapids known as Muscle Shoals. Early histories of the European settlement of Alabama include a number of accounts of boat pilots trying to navigate this treacherous stretch of river. One of the main reasons for constructing a dam there was to make the river more navigable. Another was to supply hydropower for the munitions factories that were built in the area during World War I. Authorization for the dam's construction was included in the National Defense Act of 1916, and construction began in 1918 with the U.S. Army Corps of Engineers in charge. It was originally going to be called the Muscle Shoals Dam but was renamed in honor of President Woodrow Wilson. The dam was finished in 1927 at a cost of $47 million.

The main controversy over construction came about when a large piece of concrete crashed down on twenty men who were working on the dam. Officials were unable to move the concrete, so they left the bodies buried at the bottom of the dam. A memorial marker dedicated to the men was constructed later on the lookout to the Wilson Lock. Wilson Dam also turned out to be the most expensive of all the dams constructed during the twentieth century relative to power generated. As Anne O'Hare McCormick (1930) wrote in the *New York Times,* "It is the greatest mass of masonry so far piled up by man. In the five years since its completion it has worked the least of any power plant of proportionate size, cost and capacity."

The dam was officially opened in August 1927 and was placed under the control of the Tennessee Valley Authority (TVA) when the TVA was formed in 1933. It is now one of nine TVA dams on the Tennessee River. The dam has a neoclassical design and was declared a National Historic Landmark in 1966. It is 137 feet high and 4,541 feet wide, with a hydropower station at one end. The main lock is 110 feet high and 600 feet long with a maximum lift of 100 feet, making it the lock with the highest single lift east of the Rocky Mountains. An auxiliary lock has two chambers that operate in tandem, each 60 feet deep by 300 feet long. In 2006–2007, an average of 3,700 vessels passed through the locks annually. The construction of the dam led to the formation of Lake Wilson, which covers 15,500 acres and has a capacity of 53,600 acre-feet.

The Wilson Dam has long been a popular tourist site, and the area includes a campground and boating facilities. On the north side of the river near the dam, the 300-foot Renaissance Tower on Hightower Place has a restaurant on the top floor and is open to the public in the morning and afternoon. On the second level of the tower is an aquarium featuring the local fish, and on the grounds is the Hall Memorial Native Plant Garden. Another site popular with tourists is on the south bank of the river, in the Muscle Shoals Reservation.

—Justin Corfield

See also: *Army Corps of Engineers, United States; Tennessee Valley Authority*

BIBLIOGRAPHY

Billington, David P., and Donald C. Jackson. *Big Dams of the New Deal Era: A Confluence of Engineering and Politics.* Norman: University of Oklahoma Press, 2006.

Jackson, Donald C. *Great American Bridges and Dams.* New York: Wiley, 1988.

McCormick, Anne O'Hare. "The Great Dam of Controversy." *New York Times,* April 20, 1930.

Wolf Creek Dam

The Wolf Creek Dam is a multipurpose dam on the Cumberland River near Jamestown, Kentucky. The dam produces hydroelectricity, regulates water levels to reduce the flooding of nearby farmland, and releases water to ensure consistent navigability of the lower Cumberland River. It also created Lake Cumberland, which is used for recreation. The Flood Control Act of 1938 and the River Harbor Act of 1946 helped pave the way for Wolf Creek Dam. However, delayed by the departure of construction workers and others to fight in World War II, it was not completed until 1950.

Largely built on an earthen embankment, the dam itself is made from concrete. Problems have arisen with the karsted bedrock foundation that forms the base of both the dam and Lake Cumberland. It has caused some seepage, which has gradually become worse. This problem was discovered in 1968, and subsequent investigations by local officials led to additional grouting of the dam's foundation and the placement of sinkholes designed to reduce pressure on the dam. These efforts met with some temporary success, but in 1975, the much more complicated solution of building a new wall was undertaken.

The work on the wall was completed in 1979 and it was thought that this had solved the problem, but in the early 2000s seepage was noticed again, a result of the formation of solution channels in the rock. Channel formation has been exacerbated by the fact that some of the limestone in

the bedrock has been dissolving due to the presence of a weak carbonic acid formed by rain and snowmelt containing dissolved carbon dioxide. Coincidental problems with lower lake levels increased pressure on dam management to deal with the problem of lost water. Furthermore, in January 2007, the U.S. Army Corps of Engineers (Corps) designated the dam as having a "high risk" of failure. This has led to another effort to regrout the dam, and the work is expected to be completed in 2014 at a cost of $309 million.

One survey by the Corps showed that if the dam had failed, the resulting flood would have caused as many as 100 deaths and destroyed $3 billion in buildings, infrastructure, and agriculture. *Popular Mechanics* also claimed that the failure of the dam would be one of the five worst disasters that could happen in the United States. To address these concerns, a siren warning system was built in nearby counties in October 2007.

—Justin Corfield

See also: *Army Corps of Engineers, United States*

BIBLIOGRAPHY

Edelmann, Alex T. "Kentucky Accepts T.V.A. Power." *Journal of Land and Public Utility Economics* 18, no. 4 (1942): 481–84.

Novotny, Vladimir, and Peter A. Krenkel. "Simplified Mathematical Model of Temperature Changes in Rivers." *Journal of the Water Pollution Control Federation* 45, no. 2 (1973): 240–48.

Troxler, Robert W., and Edward L. Thackston. "Predicting the Rate of Warming of Rivers Below Hydroelectric Installations." *Journal of the Water Pollution Control Federation* 49, no. 8 (1977): 1902–12.

Wright Patman Dam

The Wright Patman Dam is made from concrete and filled with earth. It is located on the Sulphur River in northeast Texas, and water impounded by the dam created the Wright Patman Lake. Prior to the building of the dam, regular flooding with attendant crop losses had occurred on nearby farmland whenever the Sulphur and Red Rivers overflowed their banks.

Originally called the Texarkana Dam and Lake Texarkana, the dam and lake are located near the city of Texarkana, which straddles the Texas-Arkansas border. Famous as the birthplace of the 1992 presidential candidate Ross Perot, it is also where conservationist and author James Theodore Richmond (1890–1975) spent the latter part of his life. During the 1940s, an influx of settlers created increased land use pressure in the region, resulting in more marginal land being put under cultivation. Likewise, new farms and residences created an increased demand for power. The construction of the dam was authorized as part of the Flood Control Act of 1946, and work began in 1948. Its design and construction were the responsibility of the New Orleans District of the U.S. Army Corps of Engineers (Corps). Water began to be routed through the dam's control gates in 1953, and the construction process continued until 1956.

Wright Patman Lake is large enough to contain about three square kilometers of flood water. The nine parks around the lake are maintained by the Corps. In 1973, responsibility for the maintenance of the dam and lake were transferred to the Fort Worth District of the Corps, and the project was renamed in honor of Rep. Wright Patman (D-TX), who had been a member of the U.S. House of Representatives since 1929. Patman continued to represent Texas in the House until his death in 1976.

—Justin Corfield

See also: *Army Corps of Engineers, United States*

BIBLIOGRAPHY

Servos, Mark R, Kelly R. Munkittrick, John H. Carey, and Glen J. Van der Kraak, eds. *Environmental Fate and Effects of Pulp and Paper Mill Effluents.* Delray Beach, FL: St. Lucie Press, 1996.

United States Congress, House Committee on Appropriations. "Energy and Water Development Appropriations Bill, 2004: Report (to accompany H.R. 2754)." Washington, DC: US Government Printing Office, 2003. Available at http://frwebgate .access.gpo.gov/cgi-bin/getdoc.cgi?dbname=108_cong_reports& docid=f:hr212.108.pdf.

Yakima Irrigation Project

The Yakima irrigation project occupies 175 miles of land along both sides of the Yakima River in Yakima Valley in south-central Washington State. The valley is tucked into the arm of the Columbia River; its eastern and southern borders are formed by the river's arc, and its western and broken northern boundaries are formed by the Cascade Range. The valley is part of the Columbia River's massive drainage basin. At 220 miles long, the Yakima begins at Snoqualmie Pass, east of Seattle, and drops more than 2,500 feet in elevation on its way to Richland, where it meets the Columbia River. The Columbia pours more water into the Pacific Ocean than any other river in North and South America.

The topography of the Columbia River drainage was defined by relentless volcanic activity. Between 17 and 6 million years ago, waves of lava flows poured onto the drainage basin, eventually reaching depths of 6,000 feet. Over thousands of years of successive flows, the lava gradually settled into a slightly depressed plain known as the Columbian Plateau. More recently, about 1 million years ago, the Columbian Plain witnessed an enormous flood when glacial Lake Missoula burst through its ice dams. Over a period of 2,500 years, this cycle of ice and flood stripped away soils and carved deep canyons. At Wallula Gap, on the Columbia River, 200 cubic miles of water jammed up against an opening that could handle only 40 cubic miles per day. Behind the gap, water pooled in the Yakima and other drainage basins to create temporary Lake Lewis.

The Yakima Valley rests along what was once a freeway for millions of salmon and other fish species. The ancient peoples of the Columbia Plateau and their descendants, the fourteen tribes and bands of the Confederated Tribes of the Yakama Nation, relied on salmon for food and ritual. The groups spent their time on the river during the fish runs, while in the winter they lived along tributaries in tule-mat structures. During the salmon run, men would spear or net the fish while women cleaned and dried or barbecued the meat. Because of the quality and quantity of the prized chinook salmon, the central Columbia became a center of Native American trade, commerce, and cultural interaction. The Lewis and Clark Expedition (1804–1806) benefited from its trade contact with these Columbia River groups.

In 1855, the social/political climate of the Yakima area changed dramatically when Kamiakin, then the chief of the Yakama tribe, rejected the terms of a reservation treaty negotiated by Isaac I. Stevens, territorial governor of Washington, and forged an alliance of tribal leaders to protect tribal lands from non-Indian settlement. The resulting conflict, known by non-Indians as the Yakima War, did not end until the tribal groups were defeated on the battlefield in 1858. Today, the Federated Tribes of the Yakama Nation occupy the Yakama Nation Reservation, which in 2000 comprised about 5,661 square kilometers and had a recorded population of 31,799 people.

The Yakima Valley began to attract non-Indian agricultural settlement during the 1860s, but with an average annual rainfall of only 7.5 inches, irrigation was a necessity. The Yakama leader Kamiakin may have become the basin's first irrigator when he constructed a quarter-mile-long trench from a creek to his garden. In 1889, Walter

N. Granger founded the Yakima Land and Canal Company, which established the Sunnyside Irrigation Project, the first commercial irrigation project in the region. Federally aided irrigation came with the establishment of the Reclamation Service's Yakima Project, authorized in December 1905. Initial Reclamation Service efforts included construction of the Sunnyside Diversion Dam (1907) and the expansion of the Sunnyside Canal (1907–1911). The project now irrigates approximately 464,000 acres and includes five diversion dams, six reservoir lakes, and two hydroelectric power plants (Bureau of Reclamation 1993). About 97 percent of the total surface water withdrawals in Yakima and Kittitas Counties are for irrigation (Kent 2004).

The project's main crops include apples, grapes, hops, mint, and pears. The Yakima Valley is the nation's top producer of Concords and Niagaras, both varieties of juice grapes. Washington State produces nearly one-half of all Concord and 40 percent of Niagara grapes grown in the United States. The Yakima Valley is also known for its wine production. Vintners planted the first Syrah grapes in Washington State in the Yakima Valley in 1986.

—Laura Woodworth-Ney

See also: *Columbia Basin Project*

BIBLIOGRAPHY

Bureau of Reclamation History Program. "Yakima Project." 1993. http://www.usbr.gov/projects/Project.jsp?proj_Name=Yakima+Project.

Courtney, Ross. "The Yakima Valley's Other Grape Harvest." *Yakima Herald-Republic,* October 23, 2008. Available at http://www.yakimaherald.com/stories/2008/10/23/the-yakima-valley-s-other-grape-harvest.

Kent, Christopher A. "Water Resource Planning in the Yakima River Basin: Development vs. Sustainability." *Yearbook of the Association of Pacific Coast Geographers* 66 (2004): 27–60.

U.S. Geological Survey, Cascades Volcano Observatory, Vancouver, WA. "Columbia Plateau, Columbia River Basin, Columbia River Flood Basalts." http://vulcan.wr.usgs.gov/Volcanoes/ColumbiaPlateau/summary_columbia_plateau.html.

Utley, Robert Marshall, and Wilcomb E. Washburn. *Indian Wars.* Boston: Houghton Mifflin, 2002.

Index

Page numbers in bold type indicate principal treatment of topics. Page numbers followed by p denote photographs or other illustration.

A

Aamodt I (New Mexico v. Aamodt (1976)), 323
Aamodt II (New Mexico v. Aamodt (1985)), 323–324
Abandoned Mine Land Initiative, 45
Abandoned Mine Reclamation Act of 1990, 12
Abandoned Mine Reclamation Fund, 44
Abandonment and prior appropriation, 151
Abe, Valentin, 58
Aboriginal water rights. *See* American Indian water rights
Absolute dominion doctrine vs. reasonable use doctrine, 158
Acid mine drainage (AMD), **43–45**
  auger mining, 44
  coal mining, 43–44
  Iron Mountain Mine, 43p
  iron sulfide, 43
  legislative initiatives, 44–45
  mining influences, 43–44
  mountaintop removal, 44
  pyrite, 43–44
  strip-mining, 43–44
  treatment, 45
  water resources and, 128
  yellow boy, 43
Acid rain, **45–48**
  cap and trade, 47–48
  current policy, 47–48
  defined, 45
  effects and reduction efforts, 46–47
  historical background, 47–48
  Industrial Revolution, 46
  Mt. Mitchell State Park, 46p
  nitrogen oxides, 45–46, 48
  sulfur dioxide, 45–48
  tree damage by, 46p
Acid Rain Program, 46
Acreage limitation under Reclamation Act of 1902, 418, 487
ACSI (Appalachian Clean Streams Initiative), 45
Acton v. Blundell (1843), 168, 192
Adirondack Forest Preserve, 403
Adirondack Park, **403–404**
Advisory Council on Historic Preservation, 320–321
African Americans and Mississippi River flood of 1927, 311–312
AFS (American Fisheries Society), 271
Agricultural Adjustment Act of 1933, 379
Agricultural Appropriations Act of 1950, 354–355
Agriculture, **48–51**
  Clean Water Act and, 50
  CVP and, 50

Everglades restoration and, 104–105
irrigation, 49–50, 144
land, water, and reclamation, 49–50
new users and new conflicts, 50
salinity, 171
transportation and obstructions, 48–49
urbanization, 182–183
wetlands, 48–50
Agriculture Department, U.S. (USDA)
  watershed protection, 355
  Wetlands Reserve Program, 14
Air Pollution Control Act of 1955, 108
Alaska National Interest Lands Conservation Act of 1980, 272
All-American Canal, **404–405**, 404p, 446
All-American Canal Lining Project, 405
Allatoona Dam, **405**
Allegany Senecas, 16
Allocation of water resources
  dam removal and river restoration, 82
  Intermountain West, 3–5
  jurisdiction and, 113–115
  legal systems for, 190–191
  Rio Grande Water Convention, 343
  state jurisdiction, 113
A-LP (Animas–La Plata Project), 406–407
AMD. *See* Acid mine drainage
American Clean Energy and Security Act of 2009 (proposed), 65
American Fisheries Society (AFS), 271
American Indian water rights, **51–55**. *See also specific tribes*
  beyond *Winters*, 53–54
  BIA and, 216–217
  Colorado River Compact and, 53
  early treaties and rulings, 51–52
  ecosystem management and, 95
  federal takings claims, 407
  Hopi Indians, 51p
  Interior Department and, 5
  in Intermountain West, 3–5
  irrigation, 52
  Marshall Trilogy, 51–52, 54
  practicably irrigable acreage, 53
  prior appropriation, 4
  reserved rights doctrine, 3–5, 39, 53
  river transportation, 166
  settlements. *See* American Indian water settlements
  Shasta Dam impact on, 77
  sovereignty rights over, 4
  Spanish water law and, 359
  trust relationship, 51–52
  Winters case. *See Winters v. United States*

American Indian water settlements, **55–57**
  benefits to non-Indians, 56
  BIA and, 217
  environmental values, 56
  federal funding for projects, 55–56
  legal settlements, characteristics of, 56
American Recovery and Reinvestment Act of 2009 (ARRA), 33
American Revolution, effect of, 16
American Rivers (advocacy group), 79, 395
American rule. *See* Reasonable use doctrine
American Society of Civil Engineers (ASCE), 244
American Water Resources Association (AWRA), 219
American Water Works Association (AWWA), 230
Anadromous fish, 370, 443
Anadromous Fish Act of 1965, 370
Anasazi
  drought and, 93
  Pecos River Basin and, 470
Animas–La Plata Project (A-LP), **406–407**
Antiquities Act of 1906, 107, 132, 348
Appalachian Clean Streams Initiative (ACSI), 45
Appalachian Water Resources Survey (AWRS), 364
Aquaculture, **57–60**
  aquaponics, 59
  defined, 57
  dissolved oxygen, 58
  ecological impact of, 58–59
  future prospects, 59
  genetic modification, 58–59
  history of, 57–58
  modern aquaculture, 58
Aquaponics, 59
Aquatic nuisance prevention, 13–14, 327–329
Aquatic Nuisance Species Task Force, 328
Aquifers, **60–63**. *See also specific aquifers*
  CWA, 62
  deforestation and, 83
  freshwater aquifer use, 61
  in law and politics, 61–63
  mapping and classification of, 61
  Midwest, 8–9
  NGWA, 60
  rainfall and, 60
  RASA Program, 61
  Safe Drinking Water Act of 1974, 61–62
  sole-source designation, 62
  studies, 62
Arizona v. California (1963), **207–208**
  BIA and, 216
  Boulder Canyon Project Act, 207, 213